THE MANAGEMENT AND CONTROL OF QUALITY

THIRD EDITION

JAMES R. EVANS
UNIVERSITY OF CINCINNATI

WILLIAM M. LINDSAY
NORTHERN KENTUCKY UNIVERSITY

WEST PUBLISHING COMPANY
MINNEAPOLIS/ST. PAUL   NEW YORK   LOS ANGELES   SAN FRANCISCO

■ Production Credits

Copyediting: Cheryl Wilms

Text Design: Roslyn Stendahl, Dapper Design

Composition: Parkwood Composition

Indexing: Terry Casey

TO OUR FAMILIES

WEST'S COMMITMENT TO THE ENVIRONMENT

In 1906, West Publishing Company began recycling materials left over from the production of books. This began a tradition of efficient and responsible use of resources. Today, up to 95 percent of our legal books are printed on recycled, acid-free stock. West also recycles nearly 22 million pounds of scrap paper annually—the equivalent of 181,717 trees. Since the 1960s, West has devised ways to capture and recycle waste inks, solvents, oils, and vapors created in the printing process. We also recycle plastics of all kinds, wood, glass, corrugated cardboard, and batteries, and have eliminated the use of styrofoam book packaging. We at West are proud of the longevity and the scope of our commitment to our environment.

Production, Prepress, Printing and Binding by West Publishing Company.

 TEXT IS PRINTED ON 10% POST CONSUMER RECYCLED PAPER

Printed with **Printwise**
Environmentally Advanced Water Washable Ink

COPYRIGHT ©1989, 1993   By WEST PUBLISHING COMPANY
COPYRIGHT ©1996   By WEST PUBLISHING COMPANY
610 Opperman Drive
P.O. Box 64526
St. Paul, MN 55164-0526

Printed in the United States of America

03 02 01 00 99 98 97 96   8 7 6 5 4 3 2 1

Library of Congress Cataloging-in-Publication Data

Evans, James R. (James Robert), 1950–
    The management and control of quality / James R. Evans, William M.
Lindsay.
        p.   cm.
    Includes bibliographical references and index.
    ISBN 0-314-06215-7 (Hard)
    1. Production management—Quality control—Statistical methods.
 2. Quality assurance.   I. Lindsay, William M.   II. Title.
  TS156.E93 1996
 658.5'62—dc20   95-21956
                                                                  CIP

■ CONTENTS IN BRIEF

■ CONTENTS

Management Issues in Quality 101   PART 2

PART 3   Technical Issues in Quality 565

■ PREFACE

Once again, we are amazed by the changes that have occurred in the quality profession over the past three years. We have witnessed widespread interest in quality among business educators—both in teaching and practicing the basic principles of total quality—and remarkable growth in the number of courses in which quality principles are taught. To meet this growing interest, we designed this edition to maintain a comprehensive and up-to-date focus on the principles and practices of total quality.

We substantially reorganized, and in most cases, rewrote the first 13 chapters of this book. Drawing upon the experiences of the first author as a Baldrige Examiner, these chapters are heavily influenced by the framework and essential content of the Malcolm Baldrige National Quality Award criteria. Many of the cases added in this edition come from training materials used in the Malcolm Baldrige National Quality Award program. We believe the principles of total quality as reflected in the Baldrige Award provide the best overall synthesis of the concept of quality.

The highlights of this edition include

■ Essentially new chapters on customer focus, leadership and strategic planning, quality measurement and information management, process management and continuous improvement, organizing and implementing TQM, and quality management evaluation and assessment.

■ Substantial revisions of the introductory chapter, quality management philosophies, principles of total quality management, human resource management, employee involvement, and product and process design chapters.

■ An updated version of all other chapters to ensure complete and timely coverage, including many new Quality in Practice cases.

■ "Quality Profiles" of Baldrige-winning and other leading companies that provide basic background about the company and results achieved from their quality efforts. These companies are cited extensively throughout Parts 1 and 2 as we describe leading quality management practices.

The following specific topics include new or expanded coverage:

■ Total quality and competitive advantage
■ Service system quality
■ Deming's System of Profound Knowledge
■ Deming's red bead and funnel experiments
■ Foundations of total quality management
■ TQM and traditional management practices
■ Understanding customer needs and measuring customer satisfaction
■ Strategy formulation and deployment
■ Seven management and planning tools
■ Measurement and information management
■ Process management
■ Poka-yoke for services

- Empowerment
- HRM practices for quality
- Personal quality
- Self-managed teams
- Planning for implementation
- Sustaining the quality organization
- Malcolm Baldrige National Quality Award
- European and Canadian Quality Awards
- ISO 9000 and QS 9000
- Six sigma quality
- Commercial SPC software
- *c*- and *u*-charts

End-of-chapter material has been revised to include four distinct categories:

1. *Review Questions:* designed to help students check their understanding of the major concepts presented in the chapter.

2. *Discussion Questions:* open-ended or experiential in nature, designed to help students expand their thinking or tie practical experiences to abstract concepts.

3. *Problems:* designed to help students develop and practice skills.

4. *Cases:* nearly all of which are new, designed to help students apply the knowledge they have gained to unstructured or more-comprehensive situations. The number of cases has been greatly increased from the second edition. Most of them are drawn from real, published or personal experiences, or highly realistic situations.

OVERVIEW OF THIS BOOK

In this book, quality management is viewed as composed of two related systems—the management system and the technical system. The management system is concerned with planning to meet customers' needs, organizing resources, managing for continuous improvement, and facilitating employee involvement. Chapter 1 provides an introduction to the concepts and definitions of quality. The remainder of Part 1 continues the introduction to quality management by comparing and contrasting the production of goods and services in Chapter 2 and the various quality management philosophies in Chapter 3.

Part 2, Chapters 4 through 13, focuses on total quality management and methods by which it can be implemented in the management systems of organizations. Chapter 4 introduces the principles of TQM and contrasts them with traditional management practices. The major goal of a quality system is customer satisfaction. Chapter 5 discusses customer focus and describes methods of achieving and measuring customer satisfaction. Top management must provide the leadership necessary for setting the tone and carrying out the requirements of an ongoing, dynamic quality policy. Chapter 6 deals with the critical roles of leadership and strategic planning in a quality system. To meet customer needs, quality must be integrated in the product design process; this is the subject of Chapter 7. Good management requires good data. Chapter 8 discusses the measurement and management of quality-related information.

All significant work is performed by processes. A process consists of the policies, procedures, steps, technology, and personnel needed for carrying out a segment of operations within an organization. Most processes cross organizational boundaries within an operating unit and require coordination across those boundaries. Total quality management takes a process view and strives to improve these processes and their coordination. This is the topic of Chapter 9.

Human resource management is a key component of total quality, because quality is the responsibility of everyone in the organization, from the operators on the production floor to the chief executive officer. People such as machine operators, assembly-line workers, ticket agents, nurses, and waitresses are typically the individuals who build quality into products and services most directly. First-line supervisors must provide motivating climates for those employees, direct them in proper procedures, work together with them to locate problems, and assist in eliminating sources of error. Middle management must plan, coordinate, execute, and monitor the established quality policy. These issues are the subject of Chapter 10. Structures for employee involvement and team approaches to decision making, quality improvement, and problem solving are properly seen as extensions of human resources management; they are discussed in Chapter 11.

In Chapter 12 these concepts are integrated by examining some frameworks for assessing TQM activities, primarily those of the Malcolm Baldrige National Quality Award and ISO 9000 quality standards. How to organize the quality effort in order to ensure that quality-related initiatives will succeed in an organization is the subject of Chapter 13.

Part 3, Chapters 14 through 17, is devoted to the technical system of quality management. Chapter 14 discusses the subject of quality control down in the trenches of manufacturing and service organizations. The appendix to Chapter 14 provides a review of important probability distributions used in quality assurance. Chapters 15 and 16 examine the methods of statistical process control. The planning and design of processes for producing goods and services of high reliability are described in Chapter 17. Part 3 clarifies the inherent interactions between the structure of the management system and the technical system in organizations that produce quality goods and services.

At the end of each chapter of the book, approximately two "Quality in Practice" case studies are presented that describe applications of quality concepts in manufacturing and service organizations. These cases reinforce the chapter concepts by showing how they have been implemented successfully.

Quality is an exciting and rapidly changing field. The quality revolution has moved from manufacturing into services, governmental operations, and educational institutions—and indeed, into the minds of consumers. Career opportunities for bright individuals with a strong quality focus in business and engineering are endless. In fact, most businesses now expect the people they interview for entry-level positions to understand the principles of total quality. As you embark on the study of this discipline, keep in mind its broad range of applications in your life.

SOFTWARE SUPPLEMENTS

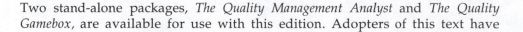

Two stand-alone packages, *The Quality Management Analyst* and *The Quality Gamebox*, are available for use with this edition. Adopters of this text have permission to copy and distribute the software and *The Quality Management Analyst* manual to their students during the terms in which the book is used. *The Quality Management Analyst* includes modules for

- Statistical analysis
- Probability computations
- Linear regression and scatter diagrams
- Process capability analysis
- Reliability computations
- Control charts
- Acceptance sampling
- Pareto analysis.

In addition, *The Quality Management Analyst SPC Simulation* is included in the package to allow instructors to generate data sets for control chart analysis having specified characteristics. This feature is very useful for classroom illustrations and student projects.

The Quality Gamebox is a collection of simulations for teaching concepts of variability. This software was developed and graciously provided by PQ Systems, Inc.

INSTRUCTOR'S SUPPORT MATERIAL

In addition to the software supplements mentioned above, the following support materials are available.

- The *Instructor's Manual* contains answers to end-of-chapter exercises as well as the latest available version of the Baldrige Award criteria and examiner training case. This case and supplementary material is useful for MBA classes.

- A new *Test Manual* has been prepared by Al Guiffrida, Daemen College.

- A set of Transparency Masters is available both as hard copy and on a disk that can be used with Microsoft PowerPoint.

POSSIBLE COURSE OUTLINES

Because the material is comprehensive, it cannot be covered fully in one semester or quarter. The book is designed to be flexible in meeting instructor needs. We have used the book in both technically oriented undergraduate courses in operations management and in managerially oriented MBA electives. We believe that undergraduate majors in industrial or operations management are best served by developing hands-on knowledge that they will be able to use in their entry-level jobs. Thus, a typical course for these students should probably be slanted toward the technical material found in Part III along with foundations from Part I and a brief overview of selected topics in Part II. For MBAs, coverage of most of the first 13 chapters is more appropriate.

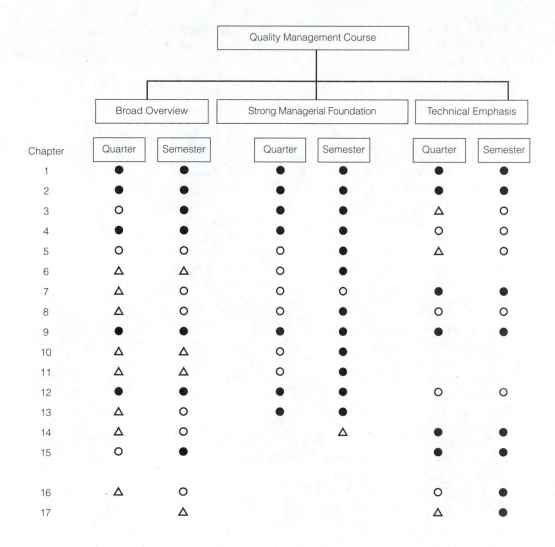

Chapter	Broad Overview		Strong Managerial Foundation		Technical Emphasis	
	Quarter	Semester	Quarter	Semester	Quarter	Semester
1	●	●	●	●	●	●
2	●	●	●	●	●	●
3	○	●	●	●	△	○
4	●	●	●	●	○	○
5	○	○	○	●	△	○
6	△	△	○	●		
7	△	○	○	○	●	●
8	△	○	○	●	○	○
9	●	●	●	●	●	●
10	△	△	○	●		
11	△	△	○	●		
12	●	●	●	●	○	○
13	△	○	●	●		
14	△	○		△	●	●
15	○	●			●	●
16	△	○			○	●
17		△			△	●

● Cover most of chapter in depth, using one or more cases.

○ Include selected sections, possibly a case.

△ Highlight key issues, basic concepts, and terminology.

The above tree diagram and matrix diagram (yes, we really do try to use quality tools!) show suggested coverage for a broad range of courses based on the authors' experiences.

ACKNOWLEDGMENTS

We are extremely grateful to the following reviewers and colleagues who have provided excellent feedback and suggestions during the development of this and previous editions. They include:

Everett Adam, Jr.
Suraj Alexander
Sant Arora
Ronald G. Benson
Roger W. Berger
F. Dean Booth
Dan Bullard
Wallace Carlson
Jaya Chandra
Sohail Chaudry
William Collins
Maling Ebrahimpour
Astrid L. H. Eckstein
Scott Edgett
Barbara Flynn
James Gilbert
Karen Gritzmacher
Russell Heikes

George Heinrich
William H. Hendrix
Jeffrey Heyl
Larry W. Jacobs
Ross Johnson
Frank Kaminsky
Richard Legault
David Lewis
John S. Loucks, IV
Joseph Nachlas
R. Natarajan
Behrooz Parkideh
Kathryn Plum
Brooke Saladin
Harold J. Schramm
Karyll N. Shaw
Charles B. Shrader

It would be impossible to name all of the quality professionals, students, colleagues, editors, and family members who have contributed to this book by sharing their information, criticism, guidance, and support. Suffice it to say that we owe a great debt to dozens of people who have influenced this project. Special thanks go to our first editor, Richard Fenton, and to Mary Schiller, Esther Craig, and Amy Hanson from West Publishing Company for all their encouragement and hard work.

We continue to do our best to improve this book in our quest for quality. We welcome any and all comments and suggestions.

James R. Evans (EVANS@UC.EDU)
William M. Lindsay (LINDSAY@NKU.EDU)

The Quality System

Ever heard of Globe Metallurgical? It's a small company, employing 210 people at plants in Beverly, Ohio, and Selma, Alabama. In the late 1980s the company was producing about 100,000 tons of ferroalloys and silicon metal for more than 300 customers. Several years earlier, however, with the decline of the automobile and steel industries in the early 1980s, and a glut of low-priced imported material from Brazil, Argentina, and Canada, Globe was losing millions of dollars annually. In 1985 only two of the five furnaces at Beverly were operating, and more than a third of the work force had been laid off. Furthermore, 44 customer complaints resulted in the return of 49,000 pounds of product that year. The company was in serious trouble.

By 1987, however, customer complaints had decreased by 91 percent, to just 4, and no product was returned. Globe's employee accident rate had decreased while the industry average had increased. Absenteeism dropped; in 1987 one plant reported only 4 days of absenteeism for its 135 employees. Annual sales were projected to increase by 30 percent during 1988. How did Globe do it? With a simple strategy: they aimed their sights at becoming the lowest-cost, highest-quality producer in the world. Just about every professional in the quality field knows about Globe by now. In 1988, it was one of the first recipients of the United States' premier quality award, the Malcolm Baldrige National Quality Award. On June 8, 1987, the year that Globe began to reap the benefits of its strategy, *Business Week* introduced a special report with this statement:

> Quality. Remember it? American manufacturing has slumped a long way from the glory days of the 1950s and '60s when "Made in the U.S.A." proudly stood for the best that industry could turn out. . . . While the Japanese were developing remarkably higher standards for a whole host of products, from consumer electronics to cars and machine tools, many U.S. managers were smugly dozing at the switch. Now, aside from aerospace and agriculture, there are few markets left where the U.S. carries its own weight in international trade. For American industry, the message is simple: Get better or get beat.[1]

Globe Metallurgical is one of only a handful of companies that proactively focused on quality improvement during the 1980s. Unfortunately, many others did not, as evidenced by the statements in *Business Week.* During the 1970s—when

1. "The Push for Quality," *Business Week,* 8 June, 1987, 131.

the quality of many products manufactured in Japan and other countries surpassed that of U.S. products—and into the 1980s, the United States received a rude awakening as the nation's manufacturers lost significant market share to its global competitors. The publicity surrounding the quality of Japanese manufacturers, in particular, and its impact on U.S. companies' competitiveness made quality a subject of vital national importance. Quality has captured the attention of consumers, industrialists, and government officials alike.

Quality in this country—and the world—has come a very long way since 1980. By the mid 1990s Motorola had reinvented itself into a high-tech company and was selling more cellular telephones in Japan than Japanese manufacturers. Xerox had reversed a declining sales trend and gained back a sizable market share from its Japanese competitors, regaining its status as the world market leader in technology and customer service. U.S. automobile manufacturers had narrowed the quality gap with Japanese competitors; by 1993 the Ford Taurus had overtaken the Honda Accord as the top-selling car in America. Quality is a major focus of the health care industry, and the Clinton administration has viewed quality as a principal strategy for "reinventing government." Since 1989, U.S. corporate leaders have hosted deans of business and engineering schools at an annual Total Quality Forum in attempting to improve the teaching and practice of quality in higher education.

Companies around the world have placed quality high on their agendas. For example, KLM Royal Dutch Airlines initiated a quality program in the late 1980s in which every employee attends a quality awareness course. Each department draws up an annual quality improvement plan that becomes part of the overall business plan. Switzerland-based Ciba-Geigy, Ltd., initiated quality improvement efforts in its factories, including those in Mexico and Argentina. South Korean firms are investing billions of dollars to improve quality and competitiveness,[2] and China is learning about quality from U.S. consultants such as Earl Conway, retired Corporate Director of Quality for Procter & Gamble.

The quest for quality continues. A special issue of *Business Week* in October 1991 stated that "[the quest for quality is] a global revolution affecting every facet of business. . . . For the 1990s and far beyond, quality must remain the priority for business."[3] Sadly, however, much remains to be done. A 1993 survey conducted by the Quality Research Institute, a Princeton, New Jersey–based partnership of Philip Crosby Associates and the Gallup Organization, found that 84 percent of Americans believe that U.S. business management is more concerned with profits than with delivering quality goods and services to consumers. Of the workers responding to the survey, 86 percent said they would feel more committed to achieving their company's financial goals if their business managers were more concerned with delivering quality to the consumer.[4] As a member of the emerging generation of business leaders, you have an opportunity and a responsibility to improve the quality of your company and society.

Part 1 introduces the basic concepts of quality. Chapter 1 discusses the history, definition, and importance of quality in manufacturing and service organizations. Chapter 2 examines the characteristics of quality in manufacturing and service organizations. Chapter 3 introduces the management philosophies that are guiding the quality revolution. These topics provide the foundation for the quality principles and practices that are the subject of the remainder of the book.

2. Louis Kraar, "Korea Goes for Quality," *Fortune,* 18 April, 1994, 153–159.
3. "The Quality Imperative," *Business Week,* 25 October, 1991, 7.
4. "Survey: Four of Five Americans Believe Bottom Line Takes Precedence over Quality," *APICS: The Performance Advantage,* April 1993, 17.

Introduction to Quality

Despite what many believe, quality is not a new concept in modern business. In October 1887, William Cooper Procter, grandson of the founder of Procter & Gamble (see Quality Profile), told his employees, "The first job we have is to turn out quality merchandise that consumers will buy and keep on buying. If we produce it efficiently and economically, we will earn a profit, in which you will share." Mr. Procter's statement addresses three issues critical to managers of manufacturing and service organizations: productivity, cost, and quality. Productivity (the measure of efficiency defined as the amount of output achieved per unit of input), the cost of operations, and the quality of the goods and services that create customer satisfaction all contribute to profitability. Of these three determinants of profitability—productivity, cost, and quality—the most significant factor in determining the long-run success or failure of any organization is quality. Good quality of goods and services can provide an organization with a competitive edge. Good quality reduces costs due to returns, rework, and scrap. Good quality increases productivity, profits, and other measures of success. Most importantly, good quality generates satisfied customers, who reward the organization with continued patronage and favorable word-of-mouth advertising. Quality has even become a focal point for industry–union cooperation. In working with Chrysler Corporation to improve quality, a UAW vice president succinctly stated the importance of quality: "No quality, no sales. No sales, no profit. No profit, no jobs."

In this chapter we examine the concept of quality. We discuss the history and importance of quality in business and some ways in which it is defined.

THE HISTORY AND IMPORTANCE OF QUALITY

In a broad sense, **quality assurance** refers to any action directed toward providing consumers with products (goods and services) of appropriate quality. Quality assurance, usually associated with some form of measurement and inspection activity, has been an important aspect of production operations throughout history.[1] Egyptian wall paintings from around 1450 B.C. show evidence of measurement and inspection. Stones for the pyramids were cut so precisely that even today it is impossible to put a knife blade between the blocks. The Egyptians' success was due to the consistent use of well-developed methods and procedures and precise measuring devices. The Egyptians also entertained the idea of interchangeable bows and arrows. Since variation in materials, craftspeople, and tools existed, some method of quality control was necessary.

Historical Background

During the Middle Ages in Europe, the skilled craftsperson served both as manufacturer and inspector. Since the "manufacturer" dealt directly with the customer, considerable pride in workmanship existed. Craft guilds, consisting of masters, journeymen, and apprentices, emerged to ensure that craftspeople were adequately trained. Quality assurance was informal; every effort was made to ensure that quality was built into the final product by the people who produced it. These themes, which were lost with the advent of the industrial revolution, are important foundations of modern quality assurance efforts.

During the middle of the eighteenth century, a French gunsmith, Honore Le Blanc, developed a system for manufacturing muskets to a standard pattern using interchangeable parts. Thomas Jefferson brought the idea to America, and in 1798 the new U.S. government awarded Eli Whitney a contract to supply 10,000 muskets to the government in two years. The use of interchangeable parts necessitated careful control of quality. Whereas a customized product built by a craftsperson can be tweaked and hammered to fit and work correctly, random matching of mating parts provides no such assurance. The parts must be produced according to a carefully designed standard. Whitney designed special machine tools and trained unskilled workers to make parts to a fixed design that were measured and compared to a model. Whitney underestimated the effect of variation in production processes, however, (an obstacle that continues to plague American managers to this day). Because of the resulting problems, Whitney needed more than 10 years to complete the project. Nonetheless, the value of the concept of interchangeable parts was recognized, and it eventually led to the industrial revolution, making quality assurance a critical component of the production process.

The Early 20th Century

In the early 1900s, the work of Frederick W. Taylor, the Father of Scientific Management, led to a new philosophy of production. Taylor's philosophy was to separate the planning function from the execution function. Managers and engineers were given the task of planning; supervisors and workers, the task of execution. This approach worked well at the turn of the century, when workers lacked the education needed for doing planning. By segmenting a job into specific work tasks and focusing on increasing efficiency, quality assurance fell into the hands of inspectors. Manufacturers were able ship good-quality products, but at great costs. Defects were produced, but removed by inspection. Plants employed hundreds, even thousands, of inspectors. Inspection was thus the primary means of quality control during the first half of the twentieth century.

Eventually, production organizations created separate quality departments. This artificial separation of responsibility for quality assurance from production workers led to indifference regarding quality among workers and their managers. Many upper managers concluded that quality was the responsibility of the quality department and turned their attention to output quantity and efficiency. Because they had delegated so much responsibility for quality to others, upper managers gained little knowledge about quality, and when the quality crisis hit, they were ill-prepared to deal with it.

Ironically, one of the leaders of the industrial revolution, Henry Ford, Sr., developed many of the fundamentals of what we now call "total quality management" in the early 1900s. This was discovered when Ford executives visited

Japan in 1982 to study Japanese management practices. As the story goes, one Japanese executive referred repeatedly to "the book," which the Ford people learned was a Japanese translation of *My Life and Work,* written by Henry Ford and Samuel Crowther in 1926 (New York: Garden City Publishing Co.). "The book" had become Japan's industrial bible, and Ford Motor Company had strayed from its principles over the years. The Ford executives had to go to a used book store to find a copy when they returned to the United States.

The Bell System was the leader in the early modern history of industrial quality assurance.[2] It created an inspection department in its Western Electric Company in the early 1900s to support the Bell operating companies. Although the Bell System achieved its noteworthy quality through massive inspection efforts, the importance of quality in providing telephone service across the nation led it to research and develop new approaches. In the 1920s, employees of Western Electric's inspection department were transferred to Bell Telephone Laboratories. The duties of this group included the development of new theories and methods of inspection for improving and maintaining quality. The early pioneers of quality assurance—Walter Shewhart, Harold Dodge, George Edwards, and others including W. Edwards Deming—were members of this group. It was here that the term **quality assurance** was coined. These pioneers developed many useful techniques for improving quality and solving quality problems. Thus, quality became a technical discipline of its own.

The Western Electric group, led by Walter Shewhart, ushered in the era of **quality control.** Quality control goes beyond simply preventing defects in manufactured goods or errors in service operations by inspection; it is focused on eliminating the problems that *cause* defects. Shewhart is credited with developing control charts, which became a popular means of identifying quality problems in production processes and ensuring consistency of output. Others in the group developed many other useful statistical techniques and approaches.

During World War II, the U.S. military began using statistical sampling procedures and imposing stringent standards on suppliers. The War Production Board offered free training courses in statistical methods that had been developed within the Bell System. The impact on wartime production was minimal, but the effort developed quality specialists, who began to use and extend these tools within their organizations. Thus, statistical quality control became widely known and gradually adopted throughout manufacturing industries. Sampling tables labeled *MIL-STD,* for *military standard,* were developed and are still widely used today. The discipline's first professional journal, *Industrial Quality Control,* was first published in 1944, and professional societies—notably the American Society for Quality Control—were founded soon after.

■ Post-World War II

After the war, during the late 1940s and early 1950s, the shortage of civilian goods in the United States made production a top priority, and the push to produce large quantities of goods led to a decline in quality. During this time, two U.S. consultants, Drs. Joseph Juran and W. Edwards Deming, introduced statistical quality control techniques to the Japanese to aid them in their rebuilding efforts. A significant part of their work focused on the *management* of quality, rather than on purely technical issues. Managing quality transcended preventing defects and led to the notion that all business processes could be improved continually, resulting not only in better quality, but improved productivity. The Japanese integrated quality into their management practices and developed a culture of continuous improvement (sometimes referred to by the Japanese term *kaizen*, pronounced ki - zen). In the United States, quality remained the province of the specialist for some time.

Improvements in Japanese quality were slow and steady; some 20 years passed before the quality of Japanese products exceeded that of Western manufacturers. By the 1970s, primarily due to the higher quality levels of their products, Japanese companies made significant penetration into Western markets. One of the more startling facts was reported in 1980 by Hewlett-Packard. In testing 300,000 16K RAM chips from three U.S. and three Japanese manufacturers, Hewlett-Packard found that the Japanese chips had an incoming failure rate of zero failures per 1,000 compared to rates of 11 and 19 for the U.S. chips. After 1,000 hours of use, the failure rate of the U.S. chips was up to 27 times higher. In a few short years, the Japanese had penetrated a major market that had been dominated by American companies. The automobile industry is another, more publicized, example. The June 8, 1987, *Business Week* special report on quality noted that the number of problems reported per one hundred 1987 domestic models in the first 60 to 90 days of ownership averaged between 162 and 180. Comparable figures for Japanese and German automobiles were 129 and 152, respectively. The U.S. steel, consumer electronics, and even banking industries also were victims of global competition. U.S. business recognized the crisis.

■ The U.S. "Quality Revolution"

The decade of the 1980s was a period of remarkable change and growing awareness of quality by consumers, industry, and government. During the 1950s and 1960s, when "made in Japan" was associated with inferior products, U.S. consumers purchased domestic goods and accepted their quality without question. During the 1970s, however, increased global competition and the appearance of higher-quality foreign products on the market led U.S. consumers to consider their purchasing decisions more carefully. They began to notice differences in quality between Japanese- and U.S.-made products and they began to expect and demand high quality and reliability in goods and services at a fair price. Consumers began to expect products to function properly and not to break or fail under reasonable use, and courts of law supported them. Extensive product recalls mandated by the Consumer Product Safety Commission in the early 1980s and the *Challenger* space shuttle disaster in 1986 increased awareness of the importance of quality. Consequently, consumers are more apt now than ever before to compare, evaluate, and choose products critically for total value—quality, price, and serviceability. Magazines such as *Consumer Reports* and newspaper reviews make this task much easier.

Obviously, the more technologically complex a product, the more likely something will go wrong with it. Government safety regulations, product recalls, and the rapid increase in product-liability judgments have changed society's attitude from "let the buyer beware" to "let the producer beware." Businesses have seen that increased attentiveness to quality is vital to their survival. Xerox discovered that its Japanese competitors were selling small copiers for what it cost Xerox to make them. A Westinghouse vice president of corporate productivity and quality summed up the situation by quoting Samuel Johnson's eighteenth-century remark: "Nothing concentrates a man's mind so wonderfully as the prospect of being hanged in the morning." The goal of total quality excellence is now recognized as a key to worldwide competitiveness and is being promoted throughout industry.[3] Most major U.S. companies have instituted extensive quality improvement campaigns, and the very concept of quality has taken on the new meaning of satisfying customers.

One of the most influential individuals in the quality revolution was W. Edwards Deming. In 1980, NBC televised a special program entitled "If Japan Can . . . Why Can't We?" The widely viewed program revealed Deming's key role in the development of Japanese quality, and his name was soon a household word among corporate executives. Although Deming had helped to transform Japanese industry three decades earlier, it was only then that he was asked to help U.S. companies. From 1980 until his death in 1993, his leadership and expertise helped many U.S. companies—such as Ford Motor Company, General Motors, and Procter & Gamble—to revolutionize their approach to quality.

As business and industry began to focus on quality, the government recognized that quality is critical to the nation's economic health. In 1984, the U.S. government designated October as National Quality Month. In 1985, NASA announced an Excellence Award for Quality and Productivity. In 1987, the Malcolm Baldrige National Quality Award, a statement of national intent to provide quality leadership, was established by an act of Congress. The Baldrige Award has become the most influential instrument for creating quality awareness among U.S. business. In 1988, President Reagan established the Federal Quality Prototype Award and the President's Award for governmental agencies. Many states have developed, or are in the process of developing, award programs for recognizing quality achievements in business and in education.

The late 1980s and early 1990s was a time of unprecedented growth and interest in quality, fueled in part by publicity surrounding the winners of the Malcolm Baldrige National Quality Award. In the automobile industry, for example, the efforts of Chrysler, General Motors, and Ford at retooling their manufacturing operations, developing new designs, and devising new promotional campaigns have all been focused on quality. Traditional manufacturing approaches to quality control have been recognized as inadequate and replaced by improved managerial tools and techniques. These efforts have shown tangible results. By 1991, the number of problems reported per 100 domestic cars in the first 60 to 90 days of ownership had dropped from the 1987 average of about 170 to 136. Nevertheless, Japanese manufacturers had reduced their average from 129 to 105 during that period and held seven of the top ten spots in the J. D. Power and Associates Survey. The gaps continue to narrow, however, and U.S. firms have now regained much of their global competitiveness.

By 1989, Florida Power and Light was the first non-Japanese company to be awarded Japan's coveted Deming Prize for quality; AT&T Power Systems (see Quality Profile) was the second in 1994. By the mid 1990s thousands of professional books had been written, and quality-related consulting and training had blossomed into an industry. Companies began to share their knowledge and experience. Each October, industry leaders celebrate National Quality Month with a nationwide satellite telecast.

Until the 1980s, most U.S. companies focused on maintaining quality levels by using inspection and control, rather than on improving quality through management practices. In the 1980s, most companies altered their approach to quality control in reaction to a global competitive crisis. Today, quality management and control is recognized as the foundation of business competitiveness and is proactively integrated with all business practices. Executives at Xerox (see Quality Profile) designed a program called "Crisis of Opportunity," to help the company to discover and act on opportunities to improve quality when things are going well, rather than waiting for a crisis to occur.

QUALITY PROFILE

AT&T Power Systems

AT&T Power Systems, based in Mesquite, Texas, employs 2400 people and makes electrical power systems for telecommunications equipment. Although the company won Japan's Deming Prize in 1994, it set out in 1990 to improve its business, not to win an award. Their objective was to improve quality without building extensive bureaucracy—a problem that had arisen at Florida Power and Light.

In early 1992, AT&T Power Systems worked with the Union of Japanese Scientists and Engineers (JUSE) consultants to implement total quality management processes. In mid 1993, they invited JUSE experts back to assess their quality systems. The consultants provided extensive feedback and indicated that the firm's performance could make it a contender for the Deming Prize. In pursuing the award, the company submitted a 400-page application and subjected its managers to four days of questioning by Japanese examiners. All managers were called upon to describe their responsibilities in three minutes and to answer detailed questions, backed up by documentation, for the rest of an hour. (The Deming Prize is discussed in more detail in Chapter 12.) Since beginning its push for quality, the company has increased its customer base sixfold and cut its inventories in half. It relies on more than 250 employee teams to identify and implement improvements.

SOURCES: "Bags Deming, Baldrige on Same Day," and "Deming Legacy Gives Firms Quality Challenge," Copyright *USA Today,* 19 October, 1994, 1B, 2B. Reprinted with permission.

■ Future Challenges

Not every company has developed an obsession with quality, however, and the implications for competitiveness are startling. A study by Ernst & Young and the American Quality Foundation published in 1991 found that 55 percent of U.S. firms were using quality information to evaluate their performance at least monthly, but that 70 percent of Japanese firms were.[4] Eighteen percent of U.S. businesses were doing this less than once a year; the comparable figure in Japan was 2 percent, and in Germany it was 9 percent. Financial and sales reviews tend to occur much more frequently than do quality reviews in the United States.

The quality movement has resulted in many successes, but also in many failures. Most of the successes and failures have been due to managerial attitudes and commitment to quality. All of the rhetoric about quality has led some people to criticize its value and impact. Skeptics will continue to sound off, but the principles of quality will remain. As Edwin L. Artzt, former CEO of Procter & Gamble and chairman of the 1992 National Quality Month campaign stated, "Quality has been, and will remain, the key management imperative. Leaders of the best companies profoundly believe in, and promote, the core values of customer-focused quality."

DEFINING QUALITY

Quality can be a confusing concept, partly because people view quality relative to differing criteria based on their individual roles in the production–marketing chain. In addition, the meaning of *quality* has evolved as the quality profession has grown and matured. Neither consultants nor business professionals agree on a universal definition. Thus, it is important to understand the various perspectives from which quality is viewed in order to fully appreciate its role throughout the parts of a business organization.[5]

Xerox Corporation Business Products and Systems

Xerox Business Products and Systems (BP&S), headquartered in Stamford, Connecticut, employs more than 50,000 people at 83 U.S. locations. It manufactures more than 250 types of document-processing equipment and generates more than half of the corporation's domestic revenues. Copiers and other duplicating equipment account for nearly 70 percent of BP&S revenues. The company attempts to define quality through the eyes of the customer. By analyzing a wide variety of data gathered by exhaustive collection efforts including monthly surveys of about 40,000 equipment owners, the company identifies important customer requirements. This information is used to develop concrete business plans with measurable targets for achieving the quality improvements necessary for meeting customers' needs. Xerox measures its performance in approximately 240 key areas of product, service, and business performance relative to world leaders, regardless of industry. In the five years of continuous improvement culminating in the firm's winning the Malcolm Baldrige National Quality Award in 1989, defects per 100 machines were decreased by 78 percent, unscheduled maintenance was decreased by 40 percent, and service response time was improved by 27 percent. These successes seem to affirm the Xerox Quality Policy statement that "Quality is the basic business principle at Xerox."

SOURCE: Malcolm Baldrige National Quality Award *Profiles of Winners*, National Institute of Standards and Technology, Department of Commerce.

■ Judgmental Criteria

One common notion of quality, often used by consumers, is that it is synonymous with superiority or excellence. In fact, *Webster's New World Dictionary* (Second College Edition) defines quality as "that which makes something what it is; characteristic element; basic nature, kind; the degree of excellence of a thing; excellence, superiority." This view is referred to as the *transcendent* (*transcend*, "to rise above or extend notably beyond ordinary limits") definition of quality. In this sense, quality is "both absolute and universally recognizable, a mark of uncompromising standards and high achievement."[6] As such, it cannot be defined precisely (you just know it when you see it). It is often loosely related to a comparison of features and characteristics of products and promulgated by marketing efforts aimed at developing quality as an image variable in the minds of consumers. Common examples of products attributed with this image are Rolex watches and Mercedes-Benz and Cadillac automobiles.

Excellence is abstract and subjective, however, and standards of excellence may vary considerably among managers and consumers. Hence, the transcedent definition is of little practical value to managers. It does not provide a means by which quality can be measured or assessed as a basis for decision making.

■ Product-Based Criteria

Another definition of quality is that it is a function of a specific, measurable variable and that differences in the quality reflect differences in quantity of some product attribute, such as in the number of stitches per inch on a shirt or in the number of cylinders in an engine. As a result, quality is often mistakenly assumed to be related to price: the higher the price, the higher the quality. However, a product—a term used in this book to refer to either a manufactured good or a service—need not be expensive to be considered a quality product by consumers. Both a Timex and a Rolex provide the time, for example. Likewise, many inexpensive restaurants provide "quality" food and service. One of the problems with this definition is that it does not depend on some external standard or reference; thus, the assessment of product attributes may vary considerably among individuals.

User-Based Criteria

A third definition of quality is based on the presumption that quality is determined by what a customer wants. Individuals have different wants and needs and, hence, different quality standards. This leads to a user-based definition: quality is defined as "fitness for intended use," or how well the product performs its intended function. Both a Cadillac and a Jeep Cherokee are fit for use, for example, but they serve different needs and different groups of customers. If you want a highway touring vehicle with luxury amenities, then a Cadillac may better satisfy your needs. If you want a vehicle for camping, fishing, or skiing trips, a Jeep might provide higher quality.

Nissan's experience provides an example of applying the fitness-for-use concept.[7] Nissan tested the U.S. market for Datsun in 1960. Although the car was economical to drive, U.S. drivers found it to be slow, hard to drive, low-powered, and not very comfortable. In essence, it lacked most of the qualities that North American drivers expected. The U.S. representative, Mr. Katayama, kept asking questions and sending the answers back to Tokyo. For some time, his company refused to believe that U.S. tastes were different from their own. After many years of nagging, Mr. Katayama finally got a product that Americans liked, the 240Z. Eventually, the name *Datsun* was changed to *Nissan* in an attempt to remove the old quality image.

A second example is that of a U.S. appliance company whose ranges and refrigerators were admired by Japanese buyers. Unfortunately, the smaller living quarters of the typical Japanese home do not have enough space to accommodate the U.S. models. Some could not even pass through the narrow doors of Japanese kitchens. Although the products' performance characteristics were high, the products were simply not fit for use in Japan.

Value-Based Criteria

A fourth approach to defining quality is based on *value*; that is, the relationship of usefulness or satisfaction to price. From this perspective, a quality product is one that is as useful as competing products and is sold at a lower price or one that offers greater usefulness or satisfaction at a comparable price. Thus, one might purchase a generic product, rather than a brand-name one, if it performs as well as the brand-name product at a lower price.

Competing on the basis of value became a key business strategy in the early 1990s. Procter & Gamble, for example, instituted a concept it calls *value pricing*—offering products at "everyday" low prices in an attempt to counter the common consumer practice of buying whatever brand happens to be on special. In this way, P&G hoped to attain consumer brand loyalty and more consistent sales, which would provide significant advantages for its manufacturing system. Competition demands that businesses seek to satisfy consumers' needs at lower prices. The value approach to quality incorporates a firm's goal of balancing product characteristics (the customer side of quality) with internal efficiencies (the operations side).

■ Manufacturing-Based Criteria

A fifth definition of quality is a manufacturing-based definition. That is, quality is defined as the desirable outcome of engineering and manufacturing practice, or *conformance to specifications*. Specifications are targets and tolerances determined by designers of products and services. Targets are the ideal values for which production is to strive; tolerances are specified because designers recognize that it is impossible to meet targets all of the time in manufacturing. For example, a part dimension might be specified as "0.236 ± 0.003 cm." This would mean that the target, or ideal value, is 0.236 centimeters, and that the allowable variation is 0.003 centimeters. Thus, any dimension in the range 0.233 to 0.239 centimenters is deemed acceptable; is said to conform to specifications. Likewise, in services, "on-time arrival" for an airplane might be specified as within 15 minutes of the scheduled arrival time. The target is the scheduled time, and the tolerance is specified to be 15 minutes.

For the Coca-Cola Company (see Quality Profile), for example, quality is "about manufacturing a product that people can depend on every time they reach for it," according to Donald R. Keough, president and chief operations officer. The company ensures that its products will taste the same anywhere in the world a consumer might buy them through rigorous quality and packaging standards. Conformance to specifications is a key definition of quality, since it provides a means of measuring quality. Specifications are meaningless, however, if they do not reflect attributes that are deemed important to the consumer.

■ Integrating Perspectives on Quality

The diversity of definitions of quality can be explained by examining the eight principal quality dimensions defined by Garvin:[8]

1. *Performance:* a product's primary operating characteristics—Using an automobile as an example, these would include such things as acceleration, braking distance, steering, and handling.

2. *Features:* the "bells and whistles" of a product—A car may have power options, a tape or CD deck, antilock brakes, and reclining seats.

3. *Reliability:* the probability of a product's surviving over a specified period of time under stated conditions of use—A car's ability to start on cold days and the frequency of failures are reliability factors.

4. *Conformance:* the degree to which physical and performance characteristics of a product match preestablished standards—A car's fit and finish and freedom from noises and squeaks can reflect this.

5. *Durability:* the amount of use one gets from a product before it physically deteriorates or until replacement is preferable—For a car this might include corrosion resistance and the long wear of upholstery fabric.

6. *Serviceability:* the speed, courtesy, and competence of repair—An automobile owner might be concerned with access to spare parts, the number of miles between major maintenance service, and the expense of service.

7. *Aesthetics:* how a product looks, feels, sounds, tastes, or smells—A car's color, instrument panel design, control placement, and "feel of the road," for example, may make it aesthetically pleasing.

8. *Perceived quality:* subjective assessment of quality resulting from image, advertising, or brand names—For a car, this might be shaped by magazine reviews and manufacturers' brochures.

Each of the definitions of quality examined in this section focuses on different quality dimensions, and none fully captures all of them. Therefore, it is not surprising that conflicts exist among the definitions. (Note that the definitions and dimensions of quality discussed in this section appear to relate primarily to manufactured goods. The key dimensions of service quality are examined in the next chapter.)

Although product quality should be important to all individuals throughout a production–distribution system, how *quality* is defined may depend on one's position in the system; that is, whether one is the designer, manufacturer, distributor, or customer. To understand this more clearly, let us consider the production–distribution cycle that is illustrated in Figure 1.1. The customer is the driving force for the production of goods and services, and customers generally view quality from either the transcendent or the product-based perspective. The goods and services produced should meet customers' needs; indeed, business organizations' existences depend upon this. It is the role of the marketing function to determine these needs. A product that meets customer needs can rightly be described as "quality." Hence, the user-based definition of quality is meaningful to people who work in marketing.

The manufacturer must translate customer requirements into detailed product and process specifications. Making this "translation" is the role of research and development, product design, and engineering. Product specifications might address such attributes of the product as size, form, finish, taste, dimensions, tolerances, materials, operational characteristics, and safety features. Process specifications indicate the types of equipment, tools, and facilities to be used in production. Product designers must balance performance and cost to meet

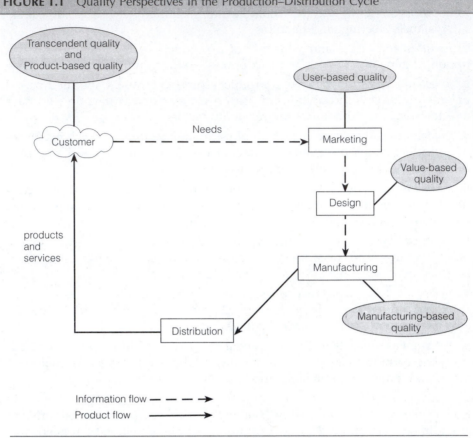

FIGURE 1.1   Quality Perspectives in the Production–Distribution Cycle

marketing objectives; thus, the value-based definition of quality is most useful at this stage.

A lot of variation can occur during manufacturing operations. Machine settings can fall out of adjustment; operators and assemblers can make mistakes; materials can be defective. Even in the most closely controlled process, specific variations in product output are inevitable and unpredictable. The manufacturing function is responsible for guaranteeing that design specifications are adhered to during production and that the final product performs as intended. Thus, for production personnel, quality is defined by the manufacturing-based definition. Conformance to product specifications is their goal.

The production–distribution cycle is completed when the product has been moved from the manufacturing plant, perhaps through wholesale and retail outlets, to the customer. Distribution does not end the customer's relationship with the manufacturer, however. The customer may need various services such as installation, user information, and special training. Such services are part of the product and cannot be ignored in quality management.

The quality of customer service is a key factor to the success of a business. This has been noted by Tom Peters and Robert Waterman in their best-selling book, *In Search of Excellence.* They observe that "excellent" companies "provide unparalleled quality, service, and reliability—things that work and last."[9] For such companies, service is the rule, not the exception. The growth of IBM (despite its recent financial setbacks) illustrates the value of good service. IBM's success in computers was a result of its strategy in the punched-card business. IBM knew the needs of data processing users. Focusing on software and service while other companies were focused on hardware, IBM built its good reputation.

The need for different views of what constitutes quality at different points inside and outside an organization is now clear. All of these perspectives are necessary—and must be embodied in an overall company philosophy—in order to result in a truly "quality" product that will satisfy customers' needs.

A good illustration of how the impact of the different views of quality can apply to a single product is hospital care. The transcendent definition of quality applies to the hospital's need to promote and maintain an image of excellence by ensuring the competency of its medical staff, the availability of treatments for rare or complicated disorders, or the availability of advanced medical technology. Subjective judgments of this kind of quality are made by patients and third-party organizations. Those who audit hospital efficiency and measure treatment consistency and resource consumption view quality according to product-based dimensions. This view of quality is predominant among government and health-care accrediting agencies.

Patients' perceptions of healthcare quality are focused on product-based and user-based criteria, and their expectations are high because of widely publicized improvements in medical care, advances in therapeutic drug treatments, and innovative surgery. This has increased the pressure on hospitals to provide the variety of services to meet these expectations. As demand for flawless service increases, the medical staff and ancillary services must turn their attention to a manufacturing-based definition of quality. This is the view of accrediting agencies and the medical profession, which mandate conformance to various practices and determine licensing requirements for practice.

■ Customer-Driven Quality

Official definitions of quality terminology were standardized in 1978 by the American National Standards Institute (ANSI) and the American Society for Quality Control (ASQC).[10] These groups defined quality as "the totality of features and characteristics of a product or service that bears on its ability to satisfy given needs." This definition draws heavily on the product- and user-based approaches and is driven by the need to contribute value to customers and thus to influence satisfaction and preference. By the end of the 1980s, many companies had begun using a simpler, yet powerful, customer-driven definition of quality:

> Quality is meeting or exceeding customer expectations.

To understand this definition, one must first understand the meanings of *customer*. Most people think of a "customer" as the ultimate purchaser of a product or service; for instance, the person who buys an automobile for personal use or the guest who registers at a hotel. These customers are more precisely referred to as **consumers.** Clearly, meeting the expectations of consumers is the ultimate goal of any business. Before a product reaches consumers, it may flow through a chain of many firms or departments, each of which add some value to the product. For example, an automobile engine plant may purchase steel from a steel company, produce engines, and then transport the engines to an assembly plant. The steel company is a supplier to the engine plant; the engine plant is a supplier to the assembly plant. The engine plant is thus a customer of the steel company, and the assembly plant is a customer of the engine plant. These customers are called **external customers.**

Every employee in a company also has **internal customers,** who receive goods or services from suppliers within the company. An assembly department, for example, is an internal customer of the machining department, and managers are internal customers of the secretarial pool. Most businesses consist of many such "chains of customers." Thus, the job of an employee is not simply to please his or her supervisor; it is to satisfy the needs of particular internal and external customers. Failure to meet the needs and expectations of internal customers can result in a poor-quality product. For example, a poor design for a computerized hotel reservation system makes it difficult for reservation clerks to do their job, and consequently affects consumers' satisfaction. Understanding who are one's customers and their expectations is fundamental to achieving customer satisfaction. This is a radical departure from traditional ways of thinking in a functionally oriented organization. It allows workers to understand their place in the larger system and their contribution to the final product. (Who are the customers of a university, its instructors, and its students?)

Quality as customer satisfaction has been fundamental to Japanese business approaches. The International Quality Study *Top Line Findings*[11] found that the percentage of businesses stating that they "always" or "almost always" develop new products and services based on customer expectations was 58 percent for Japanese firms, 40 percent for German firms, and only 22 percent for U.S. firms. The president and CEO of Fujitsu Network Transmission Systems, a U.S. subsidiary of Fujitsu, Ltd., stated, "Our customers are intelligent; they expect us to continuously evolve to meet their ever-changing needs. They can't afford to have a thousand mediocre suppliers in today's competitive environment. They want a few exceptional ones."

TOTAL QUALITY: A NEW APPROACH TO MANAGEMENT

In the 1970s a General Electric task force studied consumer perceptions of the quality of various GE product lines.[12] Lines with relatively poor reputations for quality were found to de-emphasize the customer's viewpoint, regard quality as synonymous with tight tolerance and conformance to specifications, tie quality objectives to manufacturing flow, express quality objectives as the number of defects per unit, and use formal quality control systems only in manufacturing. In contrast, product lines that received customer praise were found to emphasize satisfying customer expectations, determine customer needs through market research, use customer-based quality performance measures, and have formalized quality control systems in place for all business functions, not solely for manufacturing. The task force concluded that quality must not be viewed solely from a technical point of view; a significant emphasis must be placed on managerial activities.

As companies came to recognize the broad scope of quality, the concept of **total quality** emerged. A definition of total quality was endorsed in 1992 by the chairs and CEOs of nine major U.S. corporations in cooperation with deans of business and engineering departments of major universities, and recognized consultants:[13]

> Total Quality (TQ) is a people-focused management system that aims at continual increase in customer satisfaction at continually lower real cost. TQ is a total system approach (not a separate area or program) and an integral part of high-level strat-

egy; it works horizontally across functions and departments, involves all employees, top to bottom, and extends backward and forward to include the supply chain and the customer chain. TQ stresses learning and adaptation to continual change as keys to organizational success.

The foundation of total quality is philosophical: the scientific method. TQ includes systems, methods, and tools. The systems permit change; the philosophy stays the same. TQ is anchored in values that stress the dignity of the individual and the power of community action.

Procter & Gamble uses a concise definition: *Total quality is the unyielding and continually improving effort by everyone in an organization to understand, meet, and exceed the expectations of customers.*

The term *total quality management*, or *TQM*, is commonly used to denote the system of managing for total quality. The core principles of TQM are

- focusing on achieving customer satisfaction,
- striving for continuous improvement, and
- encouraging the full involvement of the entire work force.

These principles are quite different from traditional management practices. Historically, companies did little to understand external customer requirements, much less those of internal customers. A certain amount of waste and error was tolerable and was controlled by postproduction inspection. Improvements in quality resulted from technological breakthroughs. Managers and specialists solved problems in an ad hoc manner. With total quality, an organization actively seeks to identify customer needs and expectations, to build quality into work processes, and to improve every work function continuously through participative problem-solving efforts based on objective data. These issues are discussed in more depth in Chapter 4.

The total quality movement has fundamentally changed the practice of management in the 1990s. Tom Peters, author of several best-selling management books, captured the essence of the quality revolution in his *Thriving on Chaos*. In a related journal article,[14] Peters explained how business functions, processes, and concepts change, have been changing, and will be changing to meet the demands of the dynamic environment. Peters identified 10 specific areas of change: manufacturing, marketing, sales and service, international business, innovation, people, organization, management information systems (MIS), financial management and control, and leadership. Each of these areas is addressed at various points throughout this book. Here we provide a few examples of changes total quality thinking is bringing about in three of those areas—manufacturing, people, and leadership.

In manufacturing, Peters points out, the old mindset was focused on volume, cost, and efficiency to the detriment of quality, responsiveness, and people. Now, not only is there a shift to flexibility, but quality, responsiveness, and people have become much more important than capital. Manufacturing is being used as a primary marketing tool. Customers are invited into plants for inspection tours and team meetings. Exchange visits between plant personnel and customers are facilitated so that operating conditions in the customers' organizations may be better understood.

In the people area, Peters describes the old approach as focusing on capital rather than people and on tight control, close supervision, adversarial union relations, money as the only motivator, and minimal training (because turnover was a perennial problem). With the new focus on quality, service, and responsiveness, emphasis on the importance of people to organizational success is increasing. This has resulted in the development of individual and team participation programs; the elimination of one or more layers of supervision; and more employee involvement in budgeting, inventory management, day-to-day problem solving, and quality monitoring.

Finally, in the leadership area, the old approach was the detached, analytic "manager as leader." Strategic planning was centralized, with corporate decision making dominated by central corporate and group staffs. The new approach is decentralized, with values (such as quality) set at the top, but staff functions—planning, purchasing, personnel, MIS, and so on—decentralized. Top managers and a leaner staff are in touch with customers and operations, generally in the field, with the leader acting as dramatist, tone setter, and visionary.

TOTAL QUALITY AND COMPETITIVE ADVANTAGE

Competitive advantage denotes a firm's ability to achieve market superiority. In the long run, a sustainable competitive advantage provides above-average performance. S. C. Wheelwright identified six characteristics of a strong competitive advantage:[15]

1. It is driven by customer wants and needs. A company provides value to its customers that competitors do not.

2. It makes a significant contribution to the success of the business.

3. It matches the organization's unique resources with opportunities in the environment. No two companies have the same resources; a good strategy uses the firm's particular resources effectively.

4. It is durable and lasting, and difficult for competitors to copy. A superior research and development department, for example, can consistently develop new products or processes that enable the firm to remain ahead of competitors.

5. It provides a basis for further improvement.

6. It provides direction and motivation to the entire organization.

Each of these characteristics relates to quality, suggesting that quality is an important source of competitive advantage.

The importance of quality in achieving competitive advantage was demonstrated by several research studies during the 1980s. PIMS Associates, Inc., a subsidiary of the Strategic Planning Institute, maintains a database of 1200 companies and studies the impact of product quality on corporate performance.[16] PIMS researchers have found that:

■ Product quality is an important determinant of business profitability.

■ Businesses that offer premium-quality products and services usually have large market shares and were early entrants into their markets.

■ Quality is positively and significantly related to a higher return on investment for almost all kinds of products and market situations. (PIMS studies have shown that firms whose products are perceived as having superior quality have more than three times the return on sales of firms whose products are perceived as having inferior quality.)

■ Instituting a strategy of quality improvement usually leads to increased market share, but at the cost of reduced short-run profitability.

■ High-quality producers can usually charge premium prices.

General Systems Company, a prominent Pittsfield, Massachusetts quality-management consulting firm, has found that firms with TQM systems in place consistently exceed industry norms for return on investment. This is attributed to three factors. First, TQM reduces the direct costs associated with poor quality. Second, improvements in quality tend to lead to increases in productivity. Finally, the combination of improved quality and increased productivity leads to increases in market share.

These findings can be summarized as in Figure 1.2. A product's value in the marketplace is influenced by the quality of its design. Improvements in such aspects as performance, features, and reliability will differentiate the product from its competitors, improve a firm's quality reputation, and improve the perceived value of the product. This allows the company to command higher prices as well as to achieve a greater market share. This in turn leads to increased revenues, which offset the costs of improving the design.

Improved conformance in production leads to lower manufacturing and service costs through savings in rework, scrap, and warranty expenses. This viewpoint was popularized by Philip Crosby in his book *Quality is Free*.[17] Crosby states:

> Quality is not only free, it is an honest-to-everything profit maker. Every penny you don't spend on doing things wrong, over, or instead of, becomes half a penny right on the bottom line. In these days of "who knows what is going to happen to our business tomorrow," there aren't many ways left to make a profit improvement. If you concentrate on making quality certain, you can probably increase your profit by an amount equal to 5% to 10% of your sales. That is a lot of money for free.

The net effect of improved quality of design and conformance is increased profits.

As noted earlier, consumers make purchasing decisions on the basis of perceived value. When organizations provide less perceived value than their competitors, they lose market share. This is exactly what happened to U.S. automakers in the 1970s and 1980s. Thus, firms must focus their efforts on improving the quality of their design and service as well as reducing their costs.

FIGURE 1.2 Quality and Profitability

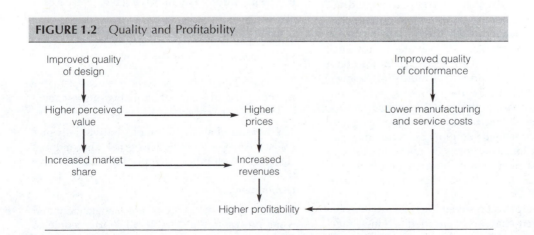

No longer can firms confine their quality efforts to defect elimination. In today's global marketplace, the absence of defects is a "given," rather than a source of competitive advantage. Quality is the result of a commitment to the never-ending cycle of improvements in market research, product development and design, production, and customer satisfaction.

QUALITY IN PRACTICE   **THE XEROX TRANSFORMATION**[18]

The Xerox 914, the first plain-paper copier, was introduced in 1959. Regarded by many people as the most successful business product ever introduced, it created a new industry. During the 1960s Xerox grew rapidly, selling all it could produce, and reached $1 billion in revenue in record-setting time. By the mid 1970s its return on assets was in the low twenty-percent range. Its competitive advantage was due to strong patents, a growing market, and little competition. In such an environment, there seemed to be little need to focus on customers.

During the 1970s, however, IBM and Kodak entered the high-volume copier business—Xerox's principal market. Several Japanese companies introduced high-quality low-volume copiers, a market that Xerox had virtually ignored, and established a foundation for moving into the high-volume market. In addition, the Federal Trade Commission accused Xerox of illegally monopolizing the copier business; after negotiations, Xerox agreed to open approximately 1700 patents to competitors. Xerox was soon losing market share to Japanese competitors, and by the early 1980s it faced a serious competitive threat from copy machine manufacturers in Japan; Xerox's market share had fallen to less than 50 percent. Some people even predicted that the company would not survive. Rework, scrap, excessive inspection, lost business, and other problems were estimated to be costing Xerox more than 20 percent of revenue, which in 1983 amounted to nearly $2 billion. Both the company and its primary union, the Amalgamated Clothing and Textile Workers, were concerned. In comparing itself with its competition, Xerox discovered that it had nine times as many suppliers, twice as many employees, cycle times that were twice as long, ten times as many rejects, and seven times as many manufacturing defects in finished products. It was clear that radical changes were required.

In 1983, company president David T. Kearns became convinced that Xerox needed a long-range, comprehensive quality strategy as well as a change in its traditional management culture. Kearns was aware of Japanese subsidiary Fuji Xerox's success in implementing quality-management practices and was approached by several Xerox employees about instituting total quality management. He commissioned a team to outline a TQM approach for Xerox. The team's report stated that instituting TQM would require changes in behaviors and attitudes throughout the company as well as operational changes in the company's business practices. Kearns determined that Xerox would initiate a total quality management approach, that they would take the time to "design it right the first time," and that the effort would involve all employees. Kearns and the company's top 25 managers wrote the Xerox Quality Policy which states:

■ Xerox is a quality company.

■ Quality is the basic business principle for Xerox.

■ Quality means providing our external and internal customers with innovative products and services that fully satisfy their requirements.

■ Quality improvement is the job of every Xerox employee.

This policy led to a process called *Leadership Through Quality*, which has three objectives:

1. To instill quality as the basic business principle in Xerox, and to ensure that quality improvement becomes the job of every Xerox person.

2. To ensure that Xerox people, individually and collectively, provide our external and internal customers with innovative products and services that fully satisfy their existing and latent requirements.

3. To establish as a way of life management and work processes that enable all Xerox people to continuously pursue quality improvement in meeting customer requirements.

In addition, Leadership Through Quality is directed at achieving four goals in all Xerox activities:

1. *Customer Goal:* To become an organization with whom customers are eager to do business.

2. *Employee Goal:* To create an environment where everyone can take pride in the organization and feel responsible for its success.

3. *Business Goal:* To increase profits and presence at a rate faster than the markets in which Xerox competes.

4. *Process Goal:* To use Leadership Through Quality principles in all Xerox does.

Leadership Through Quality radically changed the way Xerox did business. All activities, such as product planning, distribution, and establishing unit objectives, now begin with a focus on customer requirements. "Benchmarking"—identifying and studying the companies and organizations that best perform critical business functions and then incorporating those organizations' ideas into the firm's operations—became an important component of Xerox's quality efforts. Xerox benchmarked more than 200 processes with those of noncompetitive companies. For instance, ideas for improving production scheduling came from Cummins Engine Company, ideas for improving the distribution system came from L. L. Bean, and ideas for improving billing processes came from American Express.

Measuring customer satisfaction and training are important components of the program. Every month, 40,000 surveys are mailed to customers, seeking feedback on equipment performance, sales, service, and administrative support. Any reported dissatisfaction is dealt with immediately and is usually resolved in a matter of days. When the program was instituted every Xerox employee worldwide, and at all levels of the company, received the same training in quality principles. This began with top management and filtered down through each level of the firm. Five years, four million labor-hours, and more than $125 million later, all employees had received quality-related training. In 1988 about 79 percent of Xerox employees were involved in quality improvement teams.

Several other steps were taken. Xerox worked with suppliers to improve their processes, implement statistical methods and a total quality process, and to support a just-in-time inventory concept. Suppliers that joined in these efforts were involved in the earliest phases of new product designs and rewarded with long-term contracts.

Employee involvement and participation was also an important effort. Xerox had always had good relationships with its unions. In 1980 they signed a contract with their principal union, the Amalgamated Clothing and Textile Workers, encouraging union members' participation in quality improvement processes. This was the first program in the company that linked managers with employees in a mutual problem-solving approach and served as a model for other corporations. A subsequent contract included the provision that "every employee shall support the concept of continuous quality improvement while reducing quality costs through teamwork."

Most important, management became the role model for the new way of doing business. Managers are required to practice quality in their daily activities and to promote Leadership Through Quality among their peers and subordinates. Reward and recognition systems were modified to focus on teamwork and quality results. Managers became "coaches," involving their employees in the act of running the business on a routine basis.

From the initiation of Leadership Through Quality until Xerox's Business Products and Systems organization won the Malcolm Baldrige National Quality Award in 1989, some of the most obvious impacts of the Leadership Through Quality program included:

■ Reject rates on the assembly line fell from 10,000 parts per million to 300 parts per million.

■ Ninety-five percent of supplied parts no longer needed inspection; in 1989, 30 U.S. suppliers went the entire year defect-free.

■ The number of suppliers was cut from 5,000 to less than 500.

■ The cost of purchased parts was reduced by 45 percent.

■ Despite inflation, manufacturing costs dropped 20 percent.

■ Product development time decreased by 60 percent.

■ Overall product quality improved 93 percent.

Xerox has learned that customer satisfaction plus employee motivation and satisfaction results in increased market share and improved return on assets. In 1989, president David Kearns observed that quality is "a race without a finish line." The company continues to operate on the motto:

We are no longer the company we once were.
We are not yet the company we want to be.
We are a company dedicated to Continuous
   Quality Improvement.

Key Issues for Discussion

1. How are the core principles of total quality reflected in Xerox's management practices?

2. Discuss the meaning of *Quality is a race without a finish line.* What is its significance to Xerox, or to any organization?

QUALITY IN PRACTICE   THE CADILLAC QUALITY STORY[19]

Cadillac Motor Car Company is the flagship division of General Motors' North American Automotive Operations. Founded in 1902 by Henry Martin Leland, Cadillac was built on a legacy of superior craftsmanship and unsurpassed quality, which gave it recognition as "the standard of the world." Cadillac's first official quality recognition came in 1908, when it was awarded the Dewar Trophy, a prize sponsored annually by the Royal Automobile Club of England to encourage technical progress. Cadillac won the trophy for its demonstration of the complete interchangeability of parts. This was the first time a U.S. company had won this prestigious honor. Cadillac won the trophy again in 1915 for the first application of the electric self-starter.

Cadillac's quality leadership went unchallenged for decades. Then the early 1980s ushered in an era of progressively stringent emissions standards and fuel-economy requirements. Cadillac responded with new powertrain components and, ultimately, new exterior designs that did not completely meet customer expectations. By the mid 1980s, Cadillac's prestigious image was in jeopardy.

Since 1985, a turnaround has occurred. Cadillac has demonstrated continuous improvement in both quality and consumer satisfaction. The story of Cadillac's transformation—the people, systems, processes, and products responsible for the improvement—earned Cadillac the 1990 Malcolm Baldrige National Quality Award, the first U.S. automobile company so honored.

Three strategies are behind the transformation:

- A cultural change
- A constant focus on the customer
- A disciplined approach to planning

These three strategies support each other and are totally integrated. Together, they reflect Cadillac's total quality process.

Teamwork and employee involvement are at the heart of Cadillac's cultural change. Four initiatives that are primarily responsible for increasing teamwork and employee involvement are simultaneous

engineering, supplier partnerships, the UAW–GM Quality Network, and Cadillac's People Strategy.

Simultaneous engineering is a process in which appropriate disciplines are committed to work interactively to conceive, approve, develop, and implement product programs that meet predetermined objectives. Simultaneous engineering teams involving 700 employees, suppliers, and dealers are responsible for defining, engineering, marketing, and continuously improving all Cadillac vehicles.

In 1985, Cadillac began redefining its *supplier relationships* by asking suppliers to take on additional product-development responsibilities. This effort led to a reduction in the supply base and a closer, more focused relationship.

Since 1973, GM and the United Auto Workers (UAW) have worked together to improve product qualty and the quality of work life. In 1987 corporate management and the UAW recognized that a consistent, joint quality-improvement process was needed to improve competitiveness. The *UAW–GM Quality Network* comprises joint union and management quality councils at the corporate, group, division, and plant levels of the organization. These councils oversee all quality improvement efforts and assist in the implementation of the business plan.

The success of teamwork and employee involvement depends on people. At Cadillac, people are considered to be its greatest strength and the true differentiators of all successful organizations. *Cadillac's People Strategy* is designed to meet the needs of Cadillac employees while achieving business objectives. Selection processes are developed to place or reallocate people in concert with the needs of the business. Efforts are then made to develop employees, involve them in decision making, communicate to them in ways that ensure their understanding, and create an environment in which they can work effectively. These efforts are reinforced with recognition and reward systems that support the behaviors necessary to achieve the business plan.

At Cadillac, customer satisfaction is the master plan. Cadillac's cultural change broke down the walls between functions and allowed the company to focus on the customer—both internal and external. Each Cadillac employee is committed to providing the customer with products or services that exceed expectations. An example of the focus on internal customers is the Assembly Line Effectiveness Center, a simulated manufacturing environment used to evaluate the "buildability" of future models. In this environment, design teams hear and can understand the "voice of the assembler" much earlier than before.

The Cadillac Market Assurance Process integrates the needs of customers at every phase of product development. Cadillac uses extensive market research to collect information about its external customers. Much research is also conducted after the sale to collect data on Cadillac's target market, performance of the vehicles, and customer satisfaction. Customer service programs include Cadillac Roadside Service and Cadillac Consumer Relations Center, which are design to respond to emergencies, questions, and concerns of customers and potential customers. Cadillac was the first domestic manufacturer to offer a four-year 50,000-mile warranty without a deductible payment, reflecting Cadillac's confidence in the quality of its cars.

Cadillac's approach to business planning is focused on continuously improving the quality of Cadillac products, processes, and services. The business-planning process has four objectives.

1. To involve every employee in the running of the business.

2. To reinforce continually Cadillac's mission and long-term strategic objectives throughout the organization.

3. To align the short-term business objectives with the goals and action plans developed by every plant and functional staff.

4. To institutionalize continuous improvement of products and services.

Each staff and plant develops a quality plan that aligns with the overall Cadillac business plan. The business plan is distributed to all employees to make them aware of the organization's major objectives and as an attempt to ensure that all employees are moving in the same direction.

These strategies have resulted in continuous improvement in quality, productivity, and customer satisfaction measures. Between 1986 and 1990, warranty-related costs dropped nearly 30%. Productivity at the Detroit-Hamtramck Assembly Center increased by 58%. Lead time for a completely new model was cut by 40 weeks. Also, Cadillac was leading domestic makes on J. D. Power and Associates' Customer Satisfaction Index and Sales Satisfaction Index.

Key Issues for Discussion

1. Discuss the elements of the Cadillac quality story that relate to concepts presented in this chapter—for example, the definition of quality, the reasons for quality awareness, role of customers, and so on.

2. Explain why all three strategies behind the Cadillac quality transformation were necessary. What do you think might have happened if one of these had been assigned less importance?

SUMMARY OF KEY POINTS

■ *Quality assurance* refers to any action directed toward providing consumers with goods and services of appropriate quality. Although craftspersons were attentive to quality, the industrial revolution moved responsibility for quality away from the worker and into separate staff departments. This had the effect of making quality a technical, as opposed to managerial, function.

■ W. Edwards Deming and Joseph Juran taught techniques of quality control and management to the Japanese in the 1950s. Over the next 20 years, Japan made massive improvements in quality, while the quality of U.S. products increased at a much slower rate.

■ Four significant influences brought about the "quality revolution" in the United States in the 1980s: consumer pressure, changes in technology, outdated managerial thinking, and loss of national competitiveness. Quality assumed an unprecedented level of importance in the United States that continues today.

■ *Quality* is defined from many viewpoints. These include transcendent quality, product- and value-based quality, fitness for use, and conformance to specifications. The official definition of quality is "the totality of features and characteristics of a product or service that bears on its ability to satisfy given needs." Most businesses today define it as "meeting or exceeding customer expectations."

■ The key dimensions of quality are performance, features, reliability, conformance, durability, serviceability, and aesthetics. Each dimension influences customers' perceptions of quality.

■ Customers include consumers, who ultimately use a product; external customers, who may be intermediaries between the producer and the consumer; and internal customers, who are the recipients of goods and services from suppliers within the producing firm.

■ *Total quality* refers to the involvement of all employees in seeking to achieve customer satisfaction through continuous improvement activities. *Total Quality Management (TQM)* is commonly used to denote the system of managing for total quality.

■ *Competitive advantage* denotes a firm's ability to achieve market superiority over its competitors. Quality is a key source of competitive advantage, and studies have shown that quality is positively related to increased market share and profitability.

REVIEW QUESTIONS

1. Briefly summarize the history of quality before and since the industrial revolution.

2. What factors have contributed to the increased awareness of quality in modern business?

3. Discuss the importance of quality to the national interest.

4. Explain the various definitions of *quality*. Can a single definition suffice?

5. Distinguish among consumers, external customers, and internal customers. Illustrate how these concepts apply to a McDonald's restaurant, a Pizza Hut, or a similar franchise.

6. What is meant by *total quality*?

7. Explain the core principles of total quality management. How do these differ from traditional management principles?

8. Discuss the changes Tom Peters has recognized in the manufacturing, people, and leadership areas of organizations.

9. How does quality support the achievement of competitive advantage?

10. Explain the role of quality in improving a firm's profitability.

11. Contrast the experiences of Xerox and Cadillac in developing their quality focus. What similarities and differences do you see?

DISCUSSION QUESTIONS

1. What made the industrial revolution a key turning point in the history of quality? Do you believe the "Japanese revolution" will be viewed as a similar turning point?

2. Choose a product or service (such as the hospital example in this chapter) to illustrate how several definitions of quality can apply simultaneously within an organization.

3. Cite several examples from your own experience in which your expectations were met, exceeded, or not met when you purchased goods or services. Did your experience change your regard for the company and/or its product? How?

4. Select a product or a service. Develop a list of appropriate fitness-for-use criteria for it.

5. Select a service activity with which you are familiar. If you were the manager of this activity, what "conformance to specifications" criteria would you use to monitor it?

6. How might the definitions of quality apply to your college or university? Provide examples of its customers and ways their expectations can be met or exceeded.

7. Select three manufactured goods and three service organizations. Discuss how the key dimensions of quality (performance, features, etc.) apply to each.

8. How might you apply the concepts of total quality to your personal life? Consider your relations with others and your daily activities as a student, as a member of a social or professional organization, as a family member, and so on.

9. List ten businesses that you have read about or with which you have personal experience and describe their sources of competitive advantage. For each, state whether you believe that quality supports their strategy or does not support it.

10. Prepare a "Quality in Practice" case similar to the Xerox and Cadillac cases, using sources such as business periodicals, personal interviews, and so on. Focus your discussion on how their approach to total quality supports their competitive strategy.

CASES

I. Chrysler's Transmission Headache[20]

Chrysler pioneered its immensely popular minivan in 1984, which quickly became the best-selling product the company had ever built. Within five years, Chrysler held more than 50 percent of the market share for minivans. In 1989, Chrysler offered a new automatic transmission as an option in some of its top models of minivans and luxury automobiles. The transmission immediately became a headache for Chrysler when many customers reported serious problems.

Claiming that it had made improvements to reduce the initial problems, Chrysler continued to use the transmission. Meanwhile, the Center for Auto Safety, a consumer group that monitors the auto industry, charged that Chrysler had not tested the transmission before introducing it. Data on owner complaints and frequency of repairs supported the group's claim: about 20 percent of owners were reporting problems with the transmission during the first year of ownership.

For the 1991 model year, Chrysler extensively updated the design of the vehicle but continued to use the troublesome transmission as standard equipment with most of the larger engines in high demand. *Consumer Reports,* which had recommended the vehicle as its top choice for many years, placed it at the bottom of the list in 1991, citing the transmission in particular, as well as other signs of deteriorating quality. A new Toyota model captured the top spot that year.

Discussion Questions

1. To what factors might you attribute Chrysler's failure to maintain market leadership?

2. What might Chrysler have done differently?

3. How might a stronger focus on total quality principles have helped them?

II. Deere & Company

Deere & Company is a world-leading manufacturer of agricultural, industrial, and lawn and garden care equipment. Because of the company's close ties to the agricultural industry, corporate performance in both sales and profits suffered between 1984 and 1987. During that period, the company made adjustments in its product mix and manufacturing processes to enable it to better compete in the global environment. Deere's objective was to become the low-cost producer in the markets it serves. The paragraphs below are excerpts from Deere's annual reports.

1984

In spite of the industry environment of low demand, the challenge is to do what we do better. Provide more value per dollar of purchase price. To accomplish this will require cost-effectiveness in all facets of our business, which includes being more flexible and more aggressive in adopting the most modern design and manufacturing technologies.

Product design is being systematically reviewed to provide improved performance and quality at a lower cost.

New manufacturing technologies such as robot welding have enabled Deere employees to become more efficient while producing parts of higher and more consistent quality. Underlying most changes in the forestry equipment line was a special emphasis on increased reliability.

1986 (The Agricultural Economy Was Poor.)

Lower production volumes are forcing U.S. manufacturers to consider sourcing of parts and components. OEMs [original equipment manufacturers] are recognizing John Deere's technological advantage and are giving their accounts to John Deere, resulting in increased production volume.

As we improve our existing operations and expand into new but related businesses we are guided by the same principles we have followed throughout our history—those that express excellent value for our customers and fair dealing with all who come into contact with our company.

New products that offer features and quality of particular value to the customer, coupled with competitive pricing and excellent dealer service, have enhanced the company's position in the consumer products market.

The use of leveraged engineering has resulted in new products that meet the current needs of the market, do so promptly, and uphold the John Deere reputation for quality without compromise.

1987

John Deere is determined to be the lowest-cost producer in our industries and to sustain a competitive advantage on a global basis. However, we all must perpetuate the company's reputation for providing the best quality and value to our customers. While we're making structural changes in our operations we must continue to adhere to these business principles.

John Deere leadership in the agricultural equipment business is based on a line of products that has earned a reputation for excellent quality and reliability, on the skills and services we have to support the product line, and on our strong network of independent dealers.

In our continuing effort to improve the quality and performance of John Deere agricultural equipment, we have traditionally invested a higher percent of sales in product R&D than any of our major competitors.

The industrial equipment improvement reflects our strong product line and dedicated organization and our employees' determination to reduce costs, improve quality, and deliver the best value to the customer.

The total value of John Deere equipment is quality, reliability, dealer support, finance plans, resale value, and the company that stands behind it all.

1988

The company's productivity, whether measured in terms of production, sales, or net income per employee, has improved dramatically. Our products and manufacturing facilities are frequently cited as examples of industrial excellence.

This ongoing commitment to product excellence through large research and development expenditures has contributed to the recognition of John Deere products as the finest in the market.

These new products represent new standards of performance and quality consistent with the company's primary principle to give the customer greater value.

John Deere's advancements in engineering and manufacturing technology help hold the line against cost and allow the company to focus more primarily on what the customer wants.

1989

Many of the principles guiding this company are as old as the company itself—principles like integrity, the quality and value of our products and services, and the esteem in which the company holds its customers, dealers, and employees. Other principles that guide us have emerged more recently; we learned in the trials of the 1980s that cost reduction is not just a competitive necessity. It must become a way of life in all aspects of our business.

We must continue to ensure that John Deere products offer the customer the best value in all respects—in quality, reliability, features, resale price, and especially in the value added by an independent network of well-placed, full-servicing dealers people can rely on.

We must further improve manufacturing efficiencies, through both technology and the participation of wage and salaried employees.

Assignment

On the basis of this information, prepare a brief report discussing Deere & Company's view of quality and any changes you notice in its definition or approach during the 1980s. Relate your discussion to issues discussed in this chapter. You may also wish to study some more recent annual reports to see how the company is progressing through the 1990s.

III. Is Quality Good Marketing or Is Good Marketing Quality?[21]

Quality is important to the employees of a Fortune 500 leisure furniture manufacturer and retailer. Franchise owners are required to operate their stores with a focus on high quality, knowing that their license may be revoked if the corporation judges their quality to be adequate. Franchise owners recognize that commitment to quality begins with management and filters down to all areas of the business. Managers believe that if they cut corners, their employees are likely to do the same. They emphasize that things should be done correctly the first time and that there is always something that can be improved. They are never *totally* satisfied with the present level of quality. This commitment to the pursuit of excellence is passed down to every employee. The franchisor's quality motto is "Excellence and quality are not destinations; they are journeys."

Quality efforts are made in all areas of the business in an attempt to achieve "Zero Unsatisfied Customers." The first thing a customer notices at each franchise store is its "curb appeal." The parking lot is kept clean. An attractive sign displays the mission of the company, which explains the company's commitment to satisfying customers through service, selection, and value. When the customer enters the showroom, several displays of furniture are visible immediately. These displays, called *vignettes*, are small room settings including, for example, a sofa, one or two chairs, a coffee table, and an end table. Lamps and accessories are included in the vignettes, although the store carries very few such items and most are not available for purchase. Vignettes show the different styles (country, traditional, contempo-

rary, and transitional) that are available. The vignettes are intended to provide the customer with an "impression of quality" upon entering the store. Much care is taken in designing the vignettes, right down to the spacing between the pieces of furniture, and they are constantly monitored. The entire showroom is dusted and cleaned at least once a day; carpet and upholstered furniture are shampooed every month. The sales counter is kept neat and uncluttered. As one franchisee stated, "Never give a customer a reason not to buy."

Training and continuing education of a high-quality sales staff is a company priority. The salesperson must believe in the store's product and service quality and attempt to instill this in customers' minds. The salesperson must attempt to understand customers' needs and to satisfy them with the company's products. All salespersons seek five key pieces of information about the customer. The first concerns the customer's tastes, involving questions such as:

1. Have you been shopping for furniture recently?

2. How long have you been shopping?

3. Where have you been shopping?

4. What piece or pieces have you seen that you like?

5. What piece or pieces have you seen that you do not like?

The second is who the purchase-decision-maker is. (In many cases, this person is not present.) The third area is timing. Does the customer need the merchandise by a certain date or for a particular occasion? The fourth piece of information is how much the customer wants to *invest* (not *spend.*) Finally, the salesperson asks how the customer wishes to pay for the merchandise and offers several payment options. The salesperson sends each customer, whether a purchaser or not, a thank you note as a follow-up.

The franchisor also emphasizes quality in warehousing. This includes handling of the product from the point of receiving until its shipment from the warehouse. Furniture received at the warehouse is inspected for defects, such as rips and scratches. If a defect cannot be repaired, the unit is promptly shipped back to the manufacturer. The next step is to steam out any bumps or creases that occurred in shipping. When furniture is delivered to a franchisee's showroom, the vice president of merchandising is responsible for placing it in the showroom for proper price-tagging.

For customer delivery, the store rents professional-looking uniforms for its delivery personnel. The delivery equipment is well-maintained, clean, and reliable. Trucks are cleaned every day and repainted frequently. The trucks are on a tight maintenance schedule in order to maximize reliability. Customers can request a guaranteed two-hour delivery window. Delivery personnel call the day prior to the scheduled delivery to remind the customer of the time and to confirm that someone will be home. At the customer's residence, delivery personnel must complete tasks specified on a checklist, including placing the furniture exactly where the customer wants it, confirming that items such as recliners are in working order, demonstrating proper operation when appropriate, and other tasks. The delivery person is not permitted to leave until the customer is satisfied with the product and the service. If there are any problems or complaints that cannot be resolved by the delivery person, he or she must contact the manager and arrange a solution.

Customers receive numerous guarantees, including lifetime parts warranties, seven-day exchange privileges, and in-home consultations. Follow-up telephone calls ask customers about their feelings toward all aspects of their experience with the purchase. They are asked about store appearance, if the merchandise was in excellent condition when delivered, if it is sufficient to meet their needs, how the delivery personnel performed, and so on. As one franchise owner sums it up, "The best way to assure quality is through product inspection and market research."

Discussion Questions

1. Of what value in achieving quality are the actions this company takes in store appearance, warehousing, delivery, and customer relations? Can you think of other aspects of quality that have not been mentioned here?

2. Do you agree with the franchisee's statement at the end of the case? Why or why not?

3. How would you address the question posed by the case title?

■ NOTES

1. Early history is reported in Delmer C. Dague, "Quality—Historical Perspective," *Quality Control in Manufacturing* (Warrendale, PA: Society of Automotive Engineers, February 1981); and L. P. Provost and C. L. Norman, "Variation through the Ages," *Quality Progress* 23, no. 12 (December 1990), 39–44. Modern events are discussed in Nancy Karabatsos, "Quality in Transition, Part One: Account of the '80s," *Quality Progress* 22, no. 12 (December 1989), 22–26; and Joseph M. Juran, "The Upcoming Century of Quality," address to the ASQC Annual Quality Congress, Las Vegas, 24 May, 1994.

2. M. D. Fagan, ed., *A History of Engineering and Science in the Bell System: The Early Years, 1875–1925* (New York: Bell Telephone Laboratories, 1974).

3. "Manufacturing Tops List of Concerns among Executives," *Industrial Engineering* 22, no. 6 (June 1990), 8.

4. *International Quality Study: Top Line Findings* (Cleveland, OH: American Quality Foundation and Ernst & Young, 1991).

5. Three comprehensive reviews of the concept of quality are David A. Garvin, "What Does Product Quality Really Mean?" *Sloan Management Review* 26 (1984), no. 1, 25–43; Gerald F. Smith, "The Meaning of Quality," *Total Quality Management* 4 (1993), no. 3, 235–244; and Carol A. Reeves and David A. Bednar, "Defining Quality: Alternatives and Implications," *Academy of Management Review* 19 (1994), no. 3, 419–445.

6. Garvin, see note 5, 25.

7. Gregory M. Seal, "1990s—Years of Promise, Years of Peril for U.S. Manufacturers," *Industrial Engineering* 22, no. 1 (January 1990), 18–21.

8. Garvin, see note 5, 29–30.

9. Thomas J. Peters and Robert H. Waterman, Jr., *In Search of Excellence: Lessons from America's Best-Run Companies* (New York: Harper & Row, 1982), 14.

10. *ANSI/ASQC A3-1978, Quality Systems Terminology* (Milwaukee, WI: American Society for Quality Control, 1978).

11. *International Quality Study*, see note 4.

12. Lawrence Utzig, "Quality Reputation—A Precious Asset," *ASQC Technical Conference Transactions*, Atlanta, 1980, 145–154.

13. Procter & Gamble, *Report to the Total Quality Leadership Steering Committee and Working Councils* (Cincinnati, OH: Procter & Gamble, 1992).

14. Tom Peters, "A World Turned Upside Down," *The*

Academy of Management Executive 1 (1987), no. 3, 233–243.

15. S. C. Wheelwright, "Competing through Manufacturing," in Ray Wild, ed., *International Handbook of Production and Operations Management* (London: Cassell Educational, Ltd., 1989), 15–32.

16. *The PIMS Letter on Business Strategy*, no. 4, 1986 (Cambridge, MA): Strategic Planning Institute.

17. Philip Crosby, *Quality Is Free* (New York: McGraw-Hill, 1979).

18. Information for this case was obtained from "Xerox Quest for Quality and the Malcolm Baldrige National Quality Award" presentation script; Norman E. Rickard, Jr., "The Quest for Quality: A Race without a Finish Line," *Industrial Engineering*, January 1991, 25–27; Howard S. Gitlow and Elvira N. Loredo, "Total Quality

Management at Xerox: A Case Study," *Quality Engineering* 5 (1993), no. 3, 403–432; and Xerox Quality Solutions, *A World of Quality* (Milwaukee, WI: ASQC Quality Press, 1993). Reprinted with permission of the Xerox Corporation.

19. Adapted from "Cadillac, The Quality Story" (Detroit, MI: Cadillac Motor Car Division.)

20. Adapted from Sangit Chatterjee and Mustafa Yilmaz, "American Management Must Change Its View of Quality as a 'Necessary Evil,'" *Industrial Engineering*, October 1991, 44–48. Adapted from *IIE Solutions Magazine*, 25 Technology Park/Atlanta, Norcross, GA 30092 (404)449-0461. Copyright © 1991.

21. We thank students William Wenz and E. Allan Hilsinger for conducting the research from which this case is adapted.

■ BIBLIOGRAPHY

Freund, Richard A. "Definitions and Basic Quality Concepts." *Journal of Quality Technology*, January 1985, 50–56.

Garvin, David A. *Managing Quality*. New York: The Free Press, 1988.

Hayes, Glenn E. "Quality: Quandary and Quest." *Quality* 22, no. 7 (July 1983), 18.

Hiam, Alexander. *Closing the Quality Gap: Lessons from America's Leading Companies*. Englewood Cliffs, NJ: Prentice-Hall, 1992.

Hunt, V. Daniel. *Managing for Quality: Integrating Quality and Business Strategy*. Homewood, IL: Business One Irwin, 1993.

Page, Harold S. "A Quality Strategy for the '80s." *Quality Progress* 16, no. 11 (November 1983), 16–21.

Schmidt, Warren H., and Jerome P. Finnigan. *The Race without a Finish Line*. San Francisco: Jossey-Bass, 1992.

Van Gigch, John P. "Quality—Producer and Consumer Views." *Quality Progress* 10, no. 4 (April 1977), 30–33.

Wachniak, Ray. "World-Class Quality: An American Response to the Challenge." In *Quest for Quality: Managing the Total System*, ed. M. Sepehri. Norcross, GA: Institute of Industrial Engineers, 1987.

Quality in Manufacturing and Service Systems

As noted in Chapter 1, modern quality management in the United States began in the manufacturing sector. Global competition during the 1980s generated renewed interest in manufacturing quality, and many U.S. companies made tremendous strides in reducing the levels of defects in manufactured goods. Near the end of his tenure as CEO of Chrysler, Lee Iacocca exclaimed in television commercials, "Our cars are every bit as good as the Japanese." By the early 1990s, J. D. Power surveys found only one repair per unit difference between the highest-quality and the 75th-highest-quality automobile models. Although zero defects—or at most, a few defects per million—is now the goal of world-class manufacturers, Mazda chairman Kenichi Yamamoto was quoted in the October 1990 *Business Week* special issue on quality as saying, "*Any* manufacturer can produce according to statistics." Defect-free quality—conformance to specifications—is almost taken for granted today in many industries.

One of the outcomes of vastly improved manufacturing quality is continually rising consumer expectations. In particular, consumers have come to expect improvements in product designs and service. As companies have been achieving the quality that "meets and exceeds customers' expectations," they have realized that that level of quality is not sufficient; they have found that they must provide dimensions of quality that will *delight* the customer.

By the 1990s, businesses began to pay increased attention to service quality. Businesses discovered that customer retention is key to their survival, and that service quality is critical to retaining customers. Companies began to think in terms of "zero defections" and to explore new ways of developing customer loyalty. "Stand-alone" service organizations such as hospitals, banks, and educational institutions began to use total quality approaches in their operations. Manufacturing companies began to regard ancillary services such as order entry, delivery, and complaint response as new avenues for meeting and exceeding customer expectations. Managers now realize that the quality of *service* can be managed as a competitive weapon. A hospital in Detroit, for example, promises to attend to its emergency room patients in 20 minutes or less. If it is unable to do this, the care will be free.[1] Slogans such as "Whatever it takes" and service guarantees are becoming the norm in today's competitive service environment.

The concept of quality has moved far beyond a narrow manufacturing concept. It has broadened in scope to include nearly any organizational improvement, such as reducing the time needed to perform a task and improving employee skills and satisfaction. Anything that can help to satisfy or to delight customers is now regarded as an element of quality.

This chapter explores the role of quality in both manufacturing and service organizations, focusing on the importance of quality in every area of a business. The major categories of tasks that help companies to achieve quality are discussed, and then the relationship between quality and productivity is examined.

QUALITY IN PRODUCTION SYSTEMS

Production is the process of converting the resources available to an organization into products—goods and services. The collection of activities and operations involved in producing an organization's goods and services is referred to as a **production system.** Although production systems are often thought of in the context of manufacturing, service organizations also are production systems. In this section, the primary focus is on manufacturing; service organizations are the specific subject of a later section.

A production system consists of three major components:

1. *Inputs:* physical facilities, materials, capital, equipment, people, and energy

2. *Outputs:* the products and services produced by the system

3. *Processes:* machining, mixing, assembly, loan approval, and other activities that transform inputs into outputs

For many years, U.S. businesses viewed their production systems as essentially walled in; their views were focused internally on these three components and excluded consideration of customers (both internal and external) and suppliers. Japan built its production systems from a different viewpoint. In 1950, when W. Edwards Deming was helping Japan with its postwar rebuilding effort, he illustrated his vision of a production system to a group of Japanese industrialists (collectively representing about 80 percent of the nation's capital) with a sketch. His diagram, shown in Figure 2.1, depicts not only the relationships among inputs, processes, and outputs, but also the importance of customers and suppliers, the interdependency of organizational processes, the usefulness of consumer research, and mechanisms for continuous improvement.

Deming told the Japanese that understanding customers and suppliers was crucial to planning for quality. He advised them that continuous improvement of both products and processes through better understanding of customer requirements is the key to capturing world markets. Deming predicted that within five years, Japanese manufacturers would be producing products of the highest quality in the world and would have gained a large share of the world market. He was wrong. By applying these ideas, the Japanese penetrated several global markets in less than *four* years.

■ Three Levels of Quality[2]

Deming's view of a production system has changed business thinking forever. The traditional way of viewing an organization is by surveying the vertical dimension—by keeping an eye on an organization chart. This approach is an attempt to ensure that the organization is *effective*; that is, that it is "doing the right *things*." However, an organization is a *system* that employs various *processes* to convert inputs into outputs. Work gets done (or fails to get done) horizontally or cross-functionally, not hierarchically. Thus, the organization must focus on the horizontal dimension as well as the vertical to ensure that it is *efficient*; that is, that it is "doing things *right*." Every decision a manager makes, and every task a worker performs, can affect quality positively or adversely. To produce goods and services that meet or exceed customer expectations, a company must un-

FIGURE 2.1   Deming's View of a Production System

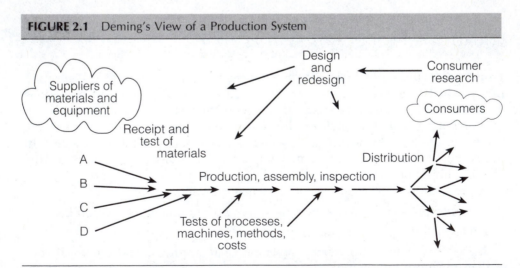

SOURCE: Reprinted from *Out of the Crisis*, p. 5, by W. Edwards Deming, by permission of M.I.T. and the W. Edwards Deming Institute. Publishing by MIT Center for Advanced Engineering Study, Cambridge, MA 02139. Copyright 1986 by W. Edwards Deming.

derstand the impacts of its entire system on quality. Many of the greatest opportunities for improving organizational performance lie in the organizational interfaces—those spaces between the boxes on an organization chart.

An organization that is committed to quality must examine quality at three levels: the organizational level, the process level, and the performer/job level. At the *organizational level*, quality concerns center on meeting external customer requirements. An organization must seek customer input on a regular basis. Questions such as the following help to define quality at the organizational level:

Which products and services meet your expectations?
Which do not?
What products or services do you need that you are not receiving?
Are you receiving products or services that you do not need?

Customer-driven performance standards should be used as bases for goal setting, problem solving, performance appraisal, incentive compensation, nonfinancial rewards, and resource allocation.

At the *process level*, organizational units are classified as functions or departments, such as marketing, design, product development, operations, finance, purchasing, billing, and so on. Since most processes are cross-functional, the danger exists that managers of particular organizational units will try to optimize the activities under their control, which can suboptimize activities for the organization as a whole. At this level, managers must ask questions such as:

What products or services are most important to the (external) customer?
What processes produce those products and services?
What are the key inputs to the process?
Which processes have the most significant effect on the organization's customer-driven performance standards?
Who are my internal customers and what are their needs?

At the *performer level* (sometimes called the job level or the task-design level), standards for output must be based on quality and customer-service requirements that originate at the organizational and process levels. These standards include requirements for such things as accuracy, completeness, innovation, timeliness, and cost. For each output of an individual's job, one must ask:

What is required by the customer, both internal and external?
How can the requirements be measured?
What is the specific standard for each measure?

These questions lead to the development of effective control systems.

Subsequent chapters expand on these ideas. To understand the interactions of functional organizational units on quality, let us examine their roles more closely. We first examine manufacturing systems.

QUALITY AND MANUFACTURING FUNCTIONS

■ Manufacturing Functions

Figure 2.2 illustrates the relationships among the key functions in a typical manufacturing system. The quality concerns of each component of the system are described in this section.

FIGURE 2.2   Functional Relationships in a Typical Manufacturing System

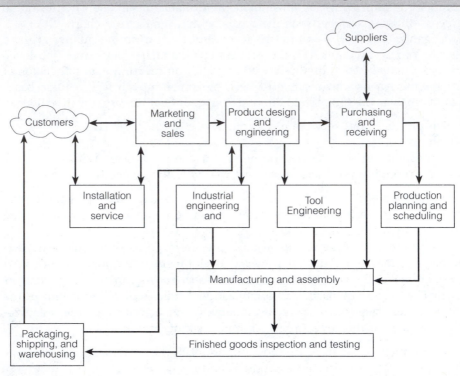

MARKETING AND SALES

Milton Hershey, the founder of Hershey Foods Corporation, understood the relationship between quality and sales. He used to say, "Give them quality. That's the best advertising in the world." For the first 68 years it was in business, Hershey Foods did not see a need to advertise its products in the mass media.[3] Marketing and sales is much more than advertising. Today, marketing and sales employees have important responsibilities for quality.

Marketing and sales personnel are responsible for determining the needs and expectations of consumers. This includes learning the products and product features consumers want and the price that consumers are willing to pay for them. This information enables a firm to define products that are fit for use and capable of being produced within the technological and budgetary constraints of the organization. Effective market research and active solicitation of customer feedback are necessary for developing quality products.

When a product goes into production, the sales and marketing staff can help a company achieve its quality goals. Salespeople seek feedback on product performance from customers. If a product is not performing up to customers' expectations, the salespeople make designers and engineers aware of the problems. When customers receive the products, sales personnel should help to ensure that customers receive adequate assistance. Marketing personnel can then actively participate in any needed corrective action programs to ensure customer satisfaction.

Sales representatives for Ames Rubber Corporation (see Quality Profile), a producer of rollers used in copiers, printers, and typewriters, take special note of such things as the volume of work a customer or prospective customer expects,

QUALITY PROFILE
Ames Rubber Corporation

Ames Rubber Corporation, based in Hamburg, New Jersey, produces rubber rollers used to feed paper, transfer toner, and fuse toner to paper in office machines such as copiers, printers, and typewriters. The company is the world's largest manufacturer of rollers for mid- to large-sized copiers. Ames also produces highly specialized parts for protecting the transaxles of front-wheel-drive vehicles. The company was founded in 1949 and by 1993 it employed 445 "Teammates" at four sites, and had won the Malcolm Baldrige National Quality Award.

The company's organization chart clearly states its approach to business. External customers are on top, above the firm's unit managers and other managers, which are above the president. The entire business strategy is designed to ensure that the customer drives Ames Rubber's operations and goals. All products are made to order to customer design and specification. Its

warranties are among the best in the industry and include a refund of the customer's portion of development costs for prototype parts if Ames fails to achieve the specifications.

Ames's total-quality initiative began in 1987 when it invited Xerox personnel to train the executive committee. The process came to involve all Teammates (employees) in pursuing a common goal: full satisfaction of internal and external customers' needs through total quality in every endeavor. Between 1989 and 1993, the defect rate for Ames's largest customer, Xerox was reduced from more than 30,000 parts per million to just 11. Over a five-year period, Teammate ideas saved the company more than $3 million. The company has demonstrated that total quality is not only good, it is profitable.

SOURCE: Malcolm Baldrige National Quality Award, *Profiles of Winners,* National Institute of Standards and Technology, Department of Commerce.

the product features the customer seeks, and the customers' cost, service, and delivery requirements. Ames's sales department also conducts quarterly customer satisfaction surveys and monthly customer contact surveys. Customer satisfaction surveys collect data in the areas of products, service, information, and relationships. Customer contact surveys, which take the form of informal conversations, explore quality, cost, delivery, and service. All this information is used by the company to improve customer satisfaction.

PRODUCT DESIGN AND ENGINEERING

The product design and engineering functions develop technical specifications for products and production processes to meet the requirements determined by the marketing function. Underengineered products will fail in the marketplace because they will not meet customer needs. Products that are overengineered, those that exceed the customer requirements, may not find a profitable market. Japanese automakers, for instance, discovered in the early 1990s that many consumers are unwilling to pay for some luxury features they had designed into their cars as standard features. Overengineering can also create a complacency that leads to poor quality. Poorly designed manufacturing processes result in poor quality or higher costs.

The landscape of business is littered with good and great design ideas that failed to arrive in the marketplace or failed to succeed because of design or quality problems. Some examples were pointed out in 1982 by Arnold Putnam:[4]

■ An electronics manufacturer assigned 600 engineers and two consulting companies to solve certain critical problems in order to meet a new product deadline. The deadline was met, but the product had heavy service and replacement demands during its first 12 months.

■ A textile machine manufacturer, playing catch-up with foreign competition, released a new product without model testing and had to withdraw it after shipping 50–100 units in the first two years.

■ The Air Force bought a jet engine based on the performance of a prototype (as most military products are), assuming that the prototype's design tolerances would be maintained. When produced with actual manufacturing tooling, many parts had to be rejected, which led to many delays and many changes. Little consideration was given to whether the production model could meet the output requirements as readily as the prototpye. Further examination revealed that the prototype did not satisfy the design tolerances.

Many similar examples could be cited to illustrate the importance of product and process design in achieving manufacturing quality. Such examples also demonstrate the difficulty of "getting it right the first time." Good design can help to prevent manufacturing defects and service errors and to reduce the need for the non-value-adding inspection practices that have dominated much of U.S. industry.

Motorola (see Quality Profile) has been a role model for improving manufacturing quality through its product and process design activities. Motorola set an ambitious goal of *six-sigma quality*—a level of quality representing no more than 3.4 defects per million opportunities—for every process in the company. To reach this goal, Motorola determined that before it manufactures a product it must first determine the product characteristics that will satisfy customers (marketing's role); determine if these characteristics can be controlled through the product's design, the manufacturing process, or the materials used; develop design tolerances that will assure successful product performance; conduct measurements to determine process variations from existing specifications; and then hone the product design, manufacturing process, or both in order to achieve the desired results. Quality in product and process design is considered further in Chapter 7.

Purchasing and Receiving

The quality of purchased parts and services and the timeliness of their delivery are critical. In many companies, however, purchasing managers are still evaluated only with regard to cost and delivery effectiveness. A purchasing agent should be responsible for all aspects of procurement, including quality. The purchasing department can help a firm achieve quality by:

■ selecting quality-conscious suppliers,

■ ensuring that purchase orders clearly define the quality requirements specified by product design and engineering,

■ bringing together technical staffs from both the buyer's and suppliers' companies to design products and solve technical problems,

■ establishing long-term supplier relationships based on trust,

■ providing quality-improvement training to suppliers,

■ informing suppliers of any problems encountered with their goods, and

■ maintaining good communication with suppliers as quality requirements and design changes occur.

QUALITY PROFILE

Motorola, Inc.

Motorola has the distinction of being a recipient of the Malcolm Baldrige National Quality Award in the Award's first year, 1988. Employing more than 130,000 workers at more than 50 facilities across the world, Motorola is among the 150 largest U.S. industrial corporations. Its principal product lines include communication systems and semiconductors, and it distributes its products through direct sales and service operations. An engineering-oriented company, it historically created new markets with innovative products—essentially telling customers what they wanted. As customers became more sophisticated and competition increased, Motorola shifted from a product focus to a customer focus, setting its fundamental objective as *total customer satisfaction.*

Two key beliefs guide the culture of the firm: respect for people and uncompromising integrity. Motorola's goals are to increase its global market share and to become the best in its class in all aspects—people, marketing, technology, product, manufacturing, and service. In terms of people, its objective is to be recognized worldwide as a company for which anyone would want to work.

Motorola was a pioneer in continual reduction of defects and cycle times in all processes of the company, such as design, order entry, manufacturing, marketing, and administrative functions. Employees in every function of the business record defects and use statistical techniques to analyze the results. Products that once took weeks to produce are now completed in less than an hour. Even the time needed for closing the financial books has been reduced. It used to take a month and had been reduced to four days at last count.

SOURCES: Ed Pena, "Motorola's Secret to Total Quality Control," *Quality Progress,* October 1990, pp. 43–45; A. William Wiggenhorn, "Stalking Quality at Motorola," presentation at the 1990 Council of Logistics Management Conference.

An example of the quality consciousness of Japanese customers was related to a college class by the manager of a U.S. plant that was supplying stock to a Japanese manufacturer of semiconductor devices for electronics applications. The U.S. manager was justifiably proud of having the best-quality material of this type available from any U.S. supplier, which was why his company had been chosen as a supplier. However, when the Japanese firm tested the first shipment of 9,000,000 parts, it was quite upset with the lack of quality and informed the U.S. firm that it would have to do better or face being replaced by a Japanese supplier. The incoming inspection had detected *five* bad parts in the total shipment!

One facet of Motorola's six-sigma quality program is the goal of reducing the number of suppliers and improving their capabilities and quality. Motorola provides extensive assistance and training to their suppliers and expects results in return. Motorola evaluates suppliers on the quality of delivered product and the timeliness of deliveries. Only those suppliers that meet the company's expectations for superior quality are retained.

The receiving department is the link between purchasing and production. It must ensure that the delivered items are of the quality specified by the purchase contract. It does this through various inspection and testing policies. If the incoming material is of high quality, extensive inspection and testing is not necessary. Many companies now require that their suppliers provide proof that their processes can consistently produce products of specified quality and give preferential treatment to those that can.

The quality of incoming materials and parts has become more critical as the use of flexible automation has increased. Many U.S. firms have implemented the

Japanese management concept of just-in-time (JIT) scheduling. JIT requires that inventories be reduced to the barest minimum. To maintain production, the quality of materials must be very high, since there are no buffer inventories to take up the slack.

PRODUCTION PLANNING AND SCHEDULING

A production plan specifies long-term and short-term production requirements for filling customer orders and meeting anticipated demand. The correct materials, tools, and equipment must be available at the proper time and in the proper places in order to maintain a smooth flow of production. Poor quality often results from time pressures due to insufficient planning and scheduling. Modern concepts of production planning and scheduling, such as JIT, have been shown to lead to quality improvements and cost savings.

MANUFACTURING AND ASSEMBLY

The role of manufacturing and assembly in producing quality is to ensure that the product is made correctly. The linkage to design and process engineering, as noted earlier, is obvious; manufacturing cannot do its job without a good product design and good process technology. Once in production, however, no defects should be acceptable. If and when they do occur, every effort must be made to identify their causes and eliminate them. Inspecting-out already defective items is costly and wasteful.

Both technology and people are essential to high-quality manufacturing. Ames Rubber Corporation, for example, produces more than 17,000 custom parts by means of a wide range of manufacturing operations such as casting, extrusion, spraying, and molding. Each operation requires appropriate measuring methods and devices that are capable of close scrutiny. Sophisticated measuring and testing equipment, such as laser-measuring devices, ensure in-line process control. All Ames manufacturing staff understand the importance and use of statistics in controlling processes. At each production step, operators, inspectors, and supervisors collect and evaluate performance data. This allows Ames to detect deviations from the processes immediately and to make the necessary adjustments.

TOOL ENGINEERING

The tool engineering function is responsible for designing and maintaining the tools used in manufacturing and inspection. Worn manufacturing tools result in defective parts, and improperly calibrated inspection gauges give misleading information. These and other tool problems result in poor quality and inefficiency. Engineers at Ames Rubber use statistical techniques to evaluate tooling and equipment and conduct periodic studies to ensure that Ames continues to meet or exceed product requirements.

INDUSTRIAL ENGINEERING AND PROCESS DESIGN

Manufacturing processes must be capable of producing items that meet specifications consistently. If they cannot, the result is excessive scrap, waste, and higher costs. The job of industrial engineers and process designers is to work with product design engineers to develop realistic specifications. In addition, they must select appropriate technologies, equipment, and work methods for producing quality products. Industrial engineers also work on designing facilities and arranging equipment to achieve smooth production flow and to reduce the opportunities for product damage. Recently, industrial engineering as a profession has been incorporating the types of activities more often taught in business schools.

FINISHED GOODS INSPECTION AND TEST

The purposes of final product inspection are to judge the quality of manufacturing, to discover and help to resolve production problems that may arise, and to ensure that no defective items reach the customer. If quality is built into the product properly, such inspection should be unnecessary except for auditing purposes and functional testing. Electronic components, for example, are subjected to extensive "burn-in" tests that assure proper operation and eliminate short-life items. In any case, inspection should be used as a means of gathering information that can be used to improve quality, not simply to remove defective items.

PACKAGING, SHIPPING, AND WAREHOUSING

Even good-quality items that leave the plant floor can be incorrectly labeled or damaged in transit. Packaging, shipping, and warehousing—often termed *logistics* activities—are the functions that protect quality after goods are produced.

INSTALLATION AND SERVICE

Products must be used correctly in order to benefit the customer. Users must understand a product and have adequate instructions for proper installation and operation. Should any problem occur, customer satisfaction depends on good after-the-sale service. In fact, service after the sale is one of the most important factors in establishing customer perception of quality and customer loyalty. At the Wallace Company (see Quality Profile), truck drivers saw the opportunity to do more than merely deliver materials to receiving docks. Where labor relations permit, they make deliveries to specific locations within plants and assist with unloading, stocking, and inventory counts. Many companies specify standards for customer service similar to the dimensions and tolerances prescribed for manufactured goods. At Wallace, for example, associates are expected to arrive for all appointments on time and to return customer phone calls within a prescribed time period. They are also responsible for knowing and observing their respective customers' rules and regulations, especially those regarding safety procedures.

■ Business Support Functions for Manufacturing

In addition to the functions directly related to manufacturing the product, certain business support activities are necessary for achieving quality. Some of them are discussed here.

GENERAL MANAGEMENT

General management has the overall responsibility for planning and executing the firm's quality assurance program. Top managers must provide leadership

QUALITY PROFILE

Wallace Company, Inc.

Wallace Company, Inc. was founded as a family-owned and -operated industrial distributor of pipe, valves, fittings, and specialty products to the refining, chemical, and petrochemical industries. Corporate offices are in Houston, Texas, and nine branch offices are located in Texas, Alabama, and Louisiana. In 1990, the year Wallace won the Malcolm Baldrige National Quality Award, the company employed 280 people and had sales of $90 million. Their achievement demonstrated that quality is as applicable to small, family-owned businesses as it is to large manufacturing and service organizations.

Wallace's "associates"—its employees—are responsible for devising and carrying out plans for accomplishing the company's quality objectives. Participation on quality improvement teams, whose membership is voluntary and cuts across departmental and district-office boundaries, increased dramatically after 1985. As involvement increased, absenteeism, turnover, and work-related injuries dropped sharply. Between 1985 and 1987, the firm's market share almost doubled, its on-time deliveries jumped from 75 to 92 percent, and its operating profits increased by 740 percent.

Unfortunately, not long after winning the Baldrige, Wallace was forced to file for bankruptcy under Chapter 11, primarily because of recalled bank loans as the Texas oil industry fell on hard economic times. Although quality may be necessary for competitiveness in today's business environment, it does not guarantee an organization's survival.

SOURCE: Malcolm Baldrige National Quality Award, *Profiles of Winners,* National Institute of Standards and Technology, Department of Commerce.

that motivates the entire organization, develop strategic quality plans, and ensure that quality initiatives permeate every process and involve every individual in the organization. These issues are discussed further in Chapter 6.

FINANCE AND ACCOUNTING

The finance function is responsible for obtaining funds, controlling their use, analyzing investment opportunities, and ensuring that the firm operates cost-effectively and—ideally—profitably. Financial decisions affect manufacturing equipment purchases, cost-control policies, price–volume decisions, and nearly all facets of the organization. In many organizations, however, financial managers do not understand how they can influence quality. Finance must authorize sufficient budgeting for equipment, training, and other means of assuring quality. Financial studies can help to expose the costs of poor quality and opportunities for reducing it. Accounting data are useful in identifying areas for quality improvement and tracking the progress of quality improvement programs. Furthermore, inappropriate accounting approaches can hide poor quality.

Financial and accounting personnel who have contacts with customers can directly influence the service their company provides. At many companies, employees chart invoice accuracy, the time needed to process invoices, and the time needed to pay bills, for example. In addition, they can apply quality improvement techniques to improve their own operations. Financial personnel at Motorola, for example, were able to reduce the time needed to close the books from one month to four days.

HUMAN RESOURCE MANAGEMENT

Human resource management is receiving increased attention because many U.S. firms have recognized that the high quality achieved by some foreign competitors is not due to special technology but, rather, to their human resource practices. Because people are the most important resource in any organization, the human resource function plays an essential role in quality management. Employees must have the proper skills (and hence training) and motivation in order to do quality work, and they should be recognized and rewarded for doing it. They must be given the authority and responsibility to make critical quality decisions when necessary. Teamwork has been shown to be highly effective in resolving complex quality issues. All managers play an important role in developing the people resource.

Solectron Corporation (see Quality Profile), a San Jose–based contract manufacturer of computer components, took major steps to improve its human resources capabilities. For example, to improve communications within the company, Solectron instituted a formal language and skills training program. Courses included Basic Electrical Assembly, American Culture, and English. The program fostered enthusiasm among the firm's employees as well as facilitated its quality efforts. The human resource department developed a customer satisfaction index and a mechanism for assessing the performance of department directors based on feedback from colleagues and subordinates. The approximately 75 department managers meet three times a week to monitor quality results, training procedures, and customer feedback. The role of human resource management and teamwork in the total quality effort is treated more extensively in Chapters 10 and 11.

QUALITY ASSURANCE

Every manager is responsible for studying and improving the quality of the process for which he or she is responsible. Because some managers lack the technical expertise required for performing needed statistical tests or data analyses, technical specialists—usually in the "quality assurance department"—assist the managers in these tasks. Quality assurance specialists perform special statistical studies and analyses and may be assigned to work with any of the manufacturing or business support functions. It must be remembered that a firm's quality assurance department cannot *assure quality* in the organization. Its proper role is to provide guidance and support for the firm's total effort toward this goal.

LEGAL SERVICES

A firm's legal department attempts to guarantee that the firm complies with laws and regulations regarding such things as product labeling, packaging, safety, and transportation; designs and words its warranties properly; satisfies its contractual requirements; and has proper procedures and documentation in place in the event of liability claims against it. The rapid increase in liability suits has made legal services an important aspect of quality assurance.

SUMMARY

It is clear that a manufacturing system is actually an integrated collection of *services*. When a manufacturing system is viewed as a "chain of customers," the concept of quality as meeting or exceeding customer expectations has wide-ranging implications. A "customer-driven" quality focus must involve *everyone* in the organization. Thus, not only must the firm pay attention to its manufacturing quality, it must scrutinize all activities that can help it to meet and exceed customer expectations. Quality is indeed everyone's responsibility.

QUALITY PROFILE
Solectron Corporation

Solectron Corporation of San Jose, California, a winner of the Malcolm Baldrige National Quality Award in 1991, was founded in 1977 as a small-assembly job shop. The firm specializes in assembling complex printed circuit boards and subsystems for computers and other electronic products. In addition, the company provides system-level assembly services. Most of its output is customer-designed products.

To ensure quality performance and on-time delivery, two teams work with each customer: a project planning team that plans, schedules, and defines material requirements and product lead times, and a total quality control team that monitors and evaluates production in order to anticipate potential problems and improve process yields. All customers are surveyed weekly, and the results are compiled in a customer satisfaction index, which senior executives review at one of their three weekly meetings on quality-related issues. Most of the 2100 employees, representing more than 20 different cultures, are trained in statistical tools and problem solving and are empowered to improve processes and take corrective action when necessary. By 1991 Solectron's total quality efforts had reduced its defect rates to 233 parts per million, and its on-time delivery rate was over 97 percent.

SOURCE: Karen Bemowski, "Three Electronics Firms Win 1991 Baldrige Award," *Quality Progress* 24, no. 11 (November 1991), 39–41. Copyright © 1990, American Society for Quality Control. Reprinted with permission.

Figure 2.3 summarizes some relationships between quality responsibility and organizational functions. Such a chart is useful for analyzing, identifying, and establishing an effective quality organization.

QUALITY IN SERVICES

Service has been defined as "a social act which takes place in direct contact between the customer and representatives of the service company."[5] A service might be as simple as handling a complaint or as complex as a home mortgage. Many organizations are pure service businesses; their products are intangible. Examples would include a law firm, whose product is legal advice, and a health care facility, whose product is comfort and better health. Service organizations include all nonmanufacturing organizations except such industries as agriculture, mining, and construction. The U.S. government's Standard Industrial Classification system describes service organizations as those

> primarily engaged in providing a wide variety of services for individuals, business and government establishments, and other organizations. Hotels and other lodging places, establishments providing personal, business, repair, and amusement services; health, legal, engineering, and other professional services; educational institutions, membership organizations, and other miscellaneous services are included.

Also usually included in this category are real estate, financial services, retailers, transportation, and public utilities.

The service sector has grown rapidly in recent years. In 1945, 22.9 million people were employed by service-producing industries, and 18.5 million people were employed by goods-producing industries. By 1985, the number of people employed in services had grown to 72.5 million, while the number employed in

FIGURE 2.3 Quality Function Relationship Chart

Code: (R) = Responsible
 C = Must contribute
 M = May contribute
 I = Is informed

Areas of Responsibility	General Manager	Finance	Marketing	Engineering	Manager Manufacturing	Manufacturing Engineering	Quality Control	Materials	Shop Operations
Determine needs of customer			(R)						
Establish quality level for business	(R)		C	C	C				
Establish product design specs				(R)					
Establish manufacturing process design				C	M	(R)	M	M	C
Produce products to design specs			M	C	C	C	C	C	(R)
Determine process capabilities					I	C	(R)	M	C
Qualify suppliers on quality							C	(R)	
Plan the quality system	(R)		C	C	C	C	(R)	C	C
Plan inspection and test procedures						C	(R)	C	C
Design test and inspection equipment						C	(R)		M
Feed back quality information			C	C	I	M	(R)	C	C
Gather complaint data			(R)						
Analyze complaint data			M	M.			(R)		
Obtain corrective action			M	C	C	C	(R)	C	C
Compile quality costs		(R)	C	C	C				
Analyze quality costs		M					(R)		
In-process quality measurements							(R)		C
In-process quality audit				C		C	(R)		
Final product inspection				C	C	M	C	(R)	

SOURCE: A. V. Feigenbaum, *Total Quality Control*, 3d ed. (New York: McGraw-Hill, 1983), 161.

goods-producing industries had grown to only 25.0 million. Much of the growth in the service sector occurred in the 1970s.

Service quality includes both the quality of *core services* and *facilitating services*. For example, all banks provide checking account services. A checking account is a core service product, and all banks can be expected to provide accurate account statements. In addition, many banks provide such services as automated teller service, rapid clearing of check deposits, and 24-hour telephone access to account information. These represent facilitating services. They enhance the value of the core service to the customer.

Facilitating services are also provided by businesses that produce tangible goods, and their value to customers may even exceed the value of the firm's core products. For instance, a fast-food restaurant may produce tangible goods in the form of burgers and fries. These are the restaurant's core products. However, the restaurant's distinguishing features may be the speed and friendliness of its service. (In fact, many now call these establishments *quick-service*, instead of *fast-*

food, restaurants.) We tend to classify such organizations as service (rather than manufacturing) organizations, since they compete primarily on the basis of service. Similarly, service is a key element for many traditional manufacturing companies. For instance, a computer equipment manufacturer such as IBM may provide extensive maintenance and consulting services, which may be more important to the customer than the core product.

The importance of quality in services cannot be underestimated. The American Management Association estimates that the average company loses as many as 35 percent of its customers each year, and that about two thirds of these are lost because of poor customer service. Studies have shown that companies can boost their profits by almost 100 percent by retaining just 5 percent more of their customers than their competitors retain.[6] This is because the cost of acquiring new customers is much higher than the costs associated with retaining customers. Companies with loyal, long-time customers can financially outperform competitors with higher customer turnover even when their unit costs are higher and their market share is smaller.

■ Comparison of Manufacturing and Service Systems

Deming's view of a production system (see Figure 2.1) can be applied to service organizations as well as to manufacturing organizations. Figure 2.4 extends Deming's model to the system of higher education. Suppliers include families, high schools, two-year colleges, and businesses. The inputs to the system are students, faculty, support staff, and so on. Outputs include people with new knowledge and abilities and research findings that are useful to organizations. The customers include the business community, graduate schools, society, students, and families. Processes include teaching, student counseling, and scientific research. Similar to manufacturing systems, educational systems can conduct customer research for evaluation and improvement. For example, by observing students, analyzing test results, and using other sources of student feedback, instructors assess their effectiveness and develop strategies for improving it. Some colleges and universities survey their graduates and their graduates' employers to assess consumer satisfaction with their product. Such feedback helps colleges, departments, and faculty members to redesign curriculum, improve course content, and improve facilitating services such as academic advising. A

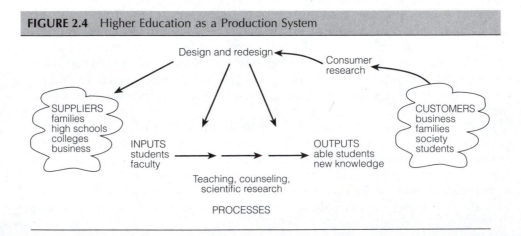

FIGURE 2.4   Higher Education as a Production System

similar model could be developed for an individual classroom. (Who are the customers and suppliers? What are the key processes? What types of "consumer research" might be appropriate?)

The definitions of quality that apply to manufactured products apply equally to service products. The very nature of service implies that it must respond to the needs of the customer; that is, the service must "meet or exceed customer expectations." These expectations must be translated into performance standards and specifications similar to standards of conformance that direct manufacturing activities. For example, a quick-service restaurant might be expected to serve a complete dinner within 5 minutes. In a fine restaurant, however, one might expect to have 10 to 15 minutes between courses, and might regard the service as poor if the time between courses is too short.

The production of services differs from manufacturing in many ways, however, and these differences have important implications for quality management. The most critical differences are described here.

■ Customer needs and performance standards are often difficult to identify and measure, primarily because customers define them, and each customer is different. Important dimensions of service quality include:

Time. How long must a customer wait for the service and for completion of the service?

Timeliness. Will the package be delivered by 10:30 the next morning?

Completeness. Are all ordered items delivered?

Courtesy. Do front-line employees greet each customer?

Consistency. Are services delivered in the same fashion each time for each customer?

Accessibility and convenience. Is the service easy to obtain?

Accuracy. Is the service performed correctly the first time?

Responsiveness. Can service personnel react quickly to unexpected problems?

In addition, the production of services typically requires a higher degree of customization than does manufacturing. Doctors, lawyers, insurance salespeople, and food-service employees must tailor their services to individual customers. In manufacturing, the goal is uniformity.

■ The output of many service systems is intangible, whereas manufacturing produces tangible, visible products. Manufacturing quality can be assessed against firm design specifications (for example, the depth of cut should be .125"), but service quality can only be assessed against customers' subjective, nebulous expectations and past experiences. (What is a "good" sales experience?) Also, the customer can "have and hold" a manufactured product, but can only remember a service. Manufactured goods can be recalled or replaced by the manufacturer, but poor service can only be followed up by apologies and reparations.

■ Services are produced and consumed simultaneously, whereas manufactured goods are produced prior to consumption. In addition, many services must be performed at the convenience of the customer. Therefore, services cannot be stored, inventoried, or inspected prior to delivery as manufactured goods are. Much more attention must be paid to training and building quality into the service as means of quality assurance.

■ Customers often are involved in the service process and present while it is being performed, whereas manufacturing is performed away from the customer. For example, customers of a quick-service restaurant place their own orders, carry their food to the table, and are expected to clear the table when they have finished eating.

■ Services are generally labor intensive, whereas manufacturing is more capital intensive. The quality of human interaction is a vital factor for services that involve human contact. For example, the quality of hospital care depends heavily on interactions among the patient, nurses, doctors, and other medical staff. Banks have found that tellers' friendliness is a key factor in retaining depositors. Hence, the behavior and morale of service employees is critical in delivering a quality service experience.

■ Many service organizations must handle very large numbers of customer transactions. For example, on a given business day, the Royal Bank of Canada handles more than 5.5 million transactions for 7.5 million customers through 1600 branches and more than 3500 banking machines, and Federal Express handles 1.5 million shipments at 1650 sites in 127 countries. Such large volumes increase the opportunity for error.

■ Components of Service System Quality

The differences between manufacturing and service organizations create distinct challenges for managing quality. Many service organizations such as airlines, banks, and hotels have well-developed quality assurance systems. Most are based on manufacturing analogies, however, and are thus more product-oriented than service-oriented. For instance, a hotel's quality assurance system may be limited to technical standards such as the components of a properly made up guest room. Standards for intangible quality characteristics are difficult to establish. Often they must be set judgmentally and then tested for satisfactory levels. Because employee performance and behavior and service transaction speed are the strongest determinants of perceived service quality, the two key components of service system quality are employees and information technology. This does not imply that these factors are not important in manufacturing, of course, but they have special significance in services—just as engineering technology might have in manufacturing.

EMPLOYEES

Customers evaluate a service primarily by the quality of the human contact. A *Wall Street Journal* survey found that Americans' biggest complaints about service employees are of delivery people or salespeople who fail to show up when you have stayed home at a scheduled time for them; salespeople who are poorly informed; and salesclerks who talk on the phone while waiting on you, say "It's not my department," talk down to you, or cannot describe how a product works.

Researchers have repeatedly demonstrated that when service employee job satisfaction is high, customer satisfaction is high, and that when job satisfaction is low, customer satisfaction is low.[7] Many service companies act on the motto "If we take care of our employees, they will take care of our customers." At Federal Express (see Quality Profile), for instance, the company credo is stated simply as "People, Service, Profits." All potential decisions in the company are evaluated on their effects on the employees (people), on their customers (service),

---

QUALITY PROFILE

Federal Express Corporation

Conceived by Chairman and Chief Executive Officer Frederick W. Smith, FedEx launched operations in 1973 with a fleet of eight small aircraft. Five years later, the company employed 10,000 people and handled a daily volume of 35,000 shipments. By 1990, when FedEx was the first service company to win the Malcolm Baldrige National Quality Award, 90,000 employees at more than 1650 sites were processing 1.5 million shipments daily, each one tracked by a central information system and delivered by a highly decentralized distribution network. By constantly adhering to a management philosophy that emphasizes people, service, and profit, in that order, FedEx has achieved high levels of customer satisfaction and rapid sales growth. Extensive customer and internal data are used by cross-functional teams involved in the company's new product introduction process. Employees are encouraged to be innovative and to make decisions that advance quality and customer satisfaction goals. FedEx management continually sets higher goals for quality performance and customer satisfaction, investing heavily in state-of-the-art technology, and building on its reputation as an excellent employer. Company leaders are committed to management by fact, analysis, and improvement.

SOURCES: Malcolm Baldrige National Quality Award, *Profiles of Winners,* National Institute of Standards and Technology, Department of Commerce; Federal Express Corporation Information Book.

---

and the company's financial performance (profits), *in that order.* Federal Express has a "no lay-off" philosophy, and its "guaranteed fair treatment procedure" (discussed in Chapter 10) for handling employee grievances is used by firms in many industries as a model. Front-line workers can qualify for promotion to management positions, and the company has a well-developed recognition program for team and individual contributions to company performance.

In many companies, unfortunately, the front-line employees—salesclerks, receptionists, delivery personnel, and so on, who have the most contact with customers—receive the lowest pay, minimal training, little decision making authority, and little responsibility (what is termed *empowerment*). High-quality service employees require reward systems that recognize customer satisfaction results and customer-focused behaviors, appropriate skills and abilities for performing the job, and supervisors who act more as coaches and mentors than as administrators. Training is particularly important, as service employees need to be skilled in handling every customer interaction, from greeting customers to asking the right questions. These issues are discussed further in Chapter 10.

Avis (see Quality Profile) is another service company that pays close attention to its human resources.[8] Called one of the "100 best companies to work for in America," Avis has ranked high in the Malcolm Baldrige National Quality Award competition but had not yet won the award as of early 1995. Baldrige Award examiners have noted that "Customer relationship management is a major strength of the company" and that "there is substantial evidence of a high level of customer satisfaction." Avis's commitment to maintaining a "propeople" corporate culture is backed up by policies of retaining its employees and promoting from within. Attempting to improve customer service and internal performance and efficiency by improving the workplace environment and employee–management communications is a key objective of Avis's Employee Participation Group (EPG) program. Employee empowerment is credited for improvements in employee productivity and job satisfaction. EPG representatives, along with senior and middle management, meet annually to plot customer service and quality improvement strategies for the fiscal year. Avis's Training

---

QUALITY PROFILE

Avis, Inc.

Avis, Inc., is a worldwide corporation that includes the U.S. Rent A Car Division, with more than 14,000 employees; the International Division, which has corporate and joint-venture holdings in 10 countries and licensee operations in 60 countries; WizCom, a subsidiary that provides advanced computer systems to the travel industry; and partial ownership of Avis Europe. The firm's "We try harder" slogan appeared in 1962 as part of an advertising campaign. It proved to be so effective that it quickly became a part of the company's culture. Today, Avis is on the cutting edge of quality management. Its strong team of empowered employees is eager to serve customers with the best product in the most comfortable, agreeable environment with the fastest speed at the right price.

In 1993, Avis received recognition from Robert Levering and Milton Moskowitz as one of the "100 Best Companies to Work for in America." Although the company had not yet won a Baldrige Award by 1995, it had scored high enough to receive a site visit in 1991. In 1992, Baldrige examiners noted that "Customer-relationship management is a major strength of the company" and that Avis's product and service quality results are due to "the company's intentional efforts to improve performance. . . . that the results are intended and not just a result of luck."

The Avis "Quest for Excellence" mission is to maximize customer satisfaction, quality of service, and return to equity-holders. The firm believes that quality service is linked to quality financial performance. The corporate strategic plan has four primary goals: to achieve financial targets, to maintain strong market position in the United States and around the world, to stand apart from the competition as a leader in quality of service and customer satisfaction, and to enhance its pro-people corporate culture. In short, Avis intends to be the best.

SOURCE: Avis Rent A Car System, Inc. *1993 Employee-Owners' Annual Report and Quality Review.* © 1993 Wizard Co., Inc.

Services Department continually creates new programs to keep pace with changes in customer needs and the workforce. Each year, the 1000-plus employees at the Worldwide Reservation Center take on a wide range of customer service, company performance, and quality of work projects aimed at "putting people first." Perhaps the major reason Avis's owners pay such close attention to the employees is that they are one and the same; Avis is an employee-owned company.

INFORMATION TECHNOLOGY

Information technology incorporates computing, communication, data processing, and various other means of converting data into useful information. Information technology is essential in modern service organizations because of the high volumes of information they must process and because customers demand service at ever-increasing speeds. Intelligent use of information technology not only leads to improved quality and productivity, but also to competitive advantage. This is particularly true when technology is used to better serve the customer and to make it easier for customers to do business with the company.

Every service industry is exploiting information technology to improve customer service. Restaurants, for example, use hand-held order-entry computer terminals to speed up the ordering process. An order is instantaneously transmitted to the kitchen or bar, where it is displayed and the guest check is printed. In addition to saving time, such systems improve accuracy by standardizing the order-taking, billing, and inventory procedures and reducing the need for handwriting. Credit authorizations, which once took several minutes by telephone, are now accomplished in seconds through computerized authorization systems. Customers can shop from electronic catalogues at retail stores and use videodisc systems at automobile showrooms to select options from thousands of possible combinations. Federal Express's hand-held "SuperTracker" scans packages' bar codes every time packages change hands between pickup and delivery.

Avis's Worldwide Reservation Center handled 23 million calls in 1994 and booked more than 6.5 million reservations.[9] Special computer terminals enhance convenience for the reservation agents and increase their productivity, because key rules, regulations, and other information are programmed into the system. "Scripts" have been developed for the usual customer situations, and the system provides prompts to guide the agent. Avis's "Wizard" system was the first fully integrated reservation, rental, and management information system in the car rental industry, and it has grown with the company. In 1981, the system could handle a million instructions per second and store 20 million characters per drive; its cost was $194,000 per billion characters. In 1993, the system's capabilities were 127 million instructions per second and 1.8 billion characters per drive, and its cost was down to $11,621 per billion characters. Wizard is connected to every major credit card company and processes more than 1.5 million credit card transactions per month. The system enables customer service agents to handle between 75 and 85 percent of queries on the first call with no delay or needed follow-up. In 1993, Avis made more than 100 upgrades to the system in order to keep it on the cutting edge of reservation-system technology. WizCom International, Ltd., a subsidiary of Avis, Inc., applies computer technologies to the hotel and travel industries in 33 countries.

Another example is provided by Fidelity Investments.[10] Fidelity receives about 200,000 telephone calls each day, more than two thirds of which are handled by a computer system without human intervention. A computer switching system monitors the call loads at Fidelity's four telephone centers and distributes calls among its more than 2000 representatives. Fidelity is developing a "workstation of the future" that will allow its representatives to call up any customer's account on their terminal screen. Using this, Fidelity will be able to offer its customers up-to-the-second, personalized information and service while improving internal productivity.

Information technology is reducing the labor intensity of many service operations. Automated teller machines, for instance, have eliminated some banking-industry jobs. While information technology reduces labor intensity and increases the speed of service, it can have adverse effects on other dimensions of quality. Some people, including some customers, will argue that customer satisfaction is decreased when there is less personal interaction. Thus, service providers must balance conflicting quality concerns.

QUALITY AND PRODUCTIVITY

The relationship between quality and productivity poses a dilemma for many managers. Traditionally, quality and productivity have been seen as conflicting, and production efficiency has been the primary consideration in manufacturing decisions. Many managers believe that quality cannot be improved without significant losses in production efficiency and profitability. The modern view is that quality improvements lead to improved productivity.

Productivity—a measure of how well the resources of a firm are being used—has been an important concern of U.S. manufacturers in recent years, particularly because the rate of U.S. productivity growth has fallen behind that of other countries, such as Japan and Germany, even though our overall level is still the highest. In its general form,

Productivity = output/input

Input usually includes labor, capital, material, and energy or some subset of these. As output increases for a constant level of input, or as input decreases for a constant level of output, productivity is increased. The U.S. Bureau of Labor Statistics uses the productivity measure "total economic output/total worker-hours expended" in computing national productivity. Other examples of productivity measures include labor productivity (units of output per labor hour), machine productivity (units of output per machine-hour), capital productivity (units of output per dollar input), and energy productivity (units of output per unit of energy consumed).

To illustrate a productivity measure, suppose that a company produces 400 printed circuit boards per eight-hour day using 50 employees. The labor productivity would be computed as

400 boards/(50 persons)(8 hours) = 1 board per labor-hour

If the company increased its production to 600 circuit boards per day by hiring 25 additional employees, the labor productivity would be

600 boards/(75 persons) (8 hours) = 1 board per labor-hour

Even though production would have increased, productivity would be the same, since the labor input was increased proportionately.

This example does not take quality into account. Making a bad product requires just as many resources, and perhaps more, as making a good one. Spending more labor on reworking poor quality increases the denominator of this measure; producing more scrap decreases the numerator. Thus, productivity can increase dramatically if a product is made right the first time. High productivity does not necessarily imply good quality, however. Some managers report good productivity measures by playing numbers games. Reporting total output rather than only good output, for example, can mask quality problems.

Productivity measures provide managers with an indication of how to improve productivity: increase the numerator, decrease the denominator, or do both. Many managers still associate productivity improvement with improvements in technology, such as automation and specialization, and certainly, technology is vitally important. Robots, for example, can perform repetitive tasks that would be boring or hazardous to humans. Other forms of automated manufacturing provide advances in speed and accuracy. Many times, however, quality improvement is overlooked as a potential means of increasing productivity. When productivity measurement is viewed from a narrow perspective, it may seem that quality improvements lead to lower levels of productivity. For example, consider a financial services employee who transcribes applications into a computer database. A typical productivity measure for such an operation might be "number of applications per hour." If quality is measured as the rate of errors in transcription, it is clear that an inverse relationship will exist between speed and error rate. Efforts to improve quality by reducing time pressures for output or adding some self-checking activities will clearly decrease productivity as it is measured. However, managers who focus solely on such an analysis are missing the big picture. Increased errors will cause decreased customer satisfaction, increased rework, increased inspection, and low employee morale. Eventually the costs associated with these activities will outweigh the benefits of higher output rates. Thus, managers must not view productivity measurement in isolation, but in the global context of quality, cost, and customer satisfaction.

The term **hidden factory** is often used to refer to the portion of plant capacity that exists to rework unsatisfactory parts, to replace products recalled from the field, or to retest and reinspect rejected units. The hidden factory can account for 15 to 40 percent of a plant's capacity. Clearly, eliminating such unnecessary operations will increase productivity significantly.

Many business decisions have a positive influence on both productivity and quality. For instance, a simple and easy-to-make product design should reduce defects and increase productivity at the same time. Streamlining production processes has a similar effect; productivity is improved, because chances for errors are eliminated and unnecessary operations are removed. Improved equipment, worker training, and preventive maintenance also contribute to improved productivity and quality. Leonard and Sasser provide some examples for which quality improvements have led to increased productivity:[11]

■ One company's installation of a new "clean room" reduced contaminants on printed circuit boards and boosted output by almost 35 percent.

■ Elimination of rework stations at one television factory forced assembly workers to find and solve their own quality mistakes. These adjustments resulted in an increased production rate per hour of direct labor and in the elimination of thousands of dollars of rework costs.

■ One company, using precision assembly equipment, designed components that would not fit together unless they were "right." This arrangement raised production rates as well as distribution efficiencies. It also improved the productivity of the sales force, who no longer had to spend time collecting, boxing, and replacing returned components.

Y. K. Shetty studied the productivity improvement programs of 171 of the 1300 largest U.S. companies in 1983 and 1984.[12] Shetty found that quality improvement ranked sixth in preference as a tool for improving productivity, behind cost reduction, employee participation, productivity incentives, goal setting, and increased automation. Just a few years later, the potential of quality as a productivity improvement tool was widely recognized by U.S. businesses.

QUALITY IN PRACTICE   THE SPARE PARTS QUALITY SYSTEM AT DEC[13]

Digital Equipment Corporation (DEC) is one of the world's largest computer manufacturers. The reputation of DEC's Field Service Organization depends mostly on the quality of the spare parts provided to customers. At DEC, spare parts are referred to as *field replaceable units* or *FRUs*. To prevent problems from occurring or to correct those that do occur, DEC created a field service logistics quality assurance group, which was responsible for providing the field with functional and reliable FRUs. The group consists of five functional units within the organization; these units and their responsibilities are listed in Table 2.1.

Maintaining a high level of service requires continual planning and revision through all the stages of a product's life. DEC can see how well it has performed each task by using measurements that include the mean time to repair, the mean time between failures, and defective FRU percentage. Predictive measurements are also available from internal sources. For example, manufacturing provides quality measures that indicate their contribution to any problem that may arise.

Because design problems are the most difficult and expensive to correct, DEC emphasizes FRU development early in a product's design. To provide high-quality FRUs, DEC uses several different tools and techniques, including quality contracts, FRU manufacturing certifications, and detailed information about activities to be completed before FRUs are shipped. The emphasis is on prevention, rather than detection and correction. The company also employs statistical tools to track FRU performance in the field—to spot trends, signify differences, forecast future activity, and show geographic differences in FRU usage.

An application of this spare-parts quality system is in DEC's family of personal computers. The maintenance strategy formulated during product design and development took into account that customers were expected to install and maintain the new products. Therefore, it was necessary to incorporate the needs and the level of computer sophistication of this new customer base into a maintenance strategy and into quality and reliability requirements for FRUs.

Design engineers were given certain constraints. The system had to be able to self-diagnose faults down to the FRU level and to communicate this information to the user. The user then had to be able to remove the defective part and install the replacement without worrying about compatibility or the need for adjustments.

Manufacturing had to be able to mass-produce this design at very high quality levels. DEC knows that it has more to lose when a customer finds a defective spare part than when a field service engineer encounters a problem with a FRU. The quality of spare parts can become a competitive edge, and the manufacturing process must reflect this fact in such areas as process control, test capability, and length of burn-in.

The packaging, storage, and distribution of replacement parts for personal computers become increasingly important as more and more customers perform their own maintenance. To ensure that spare parts are available to customers, the parts are stocked at many more locations. This procedure increases transportation and handling by individuals unfamiliar with electronics components and thus increases the potential for damage to the components.

The personal computer market makes spare-parts performance reporting more complex, but it also necessitates that reports be timely. Each location where parts are stocked has information about how customers currently perceive FRU performance. A summary of that information is available at DEC corporate headquarters, allowing the company to react rapidly to trends so that it can isolate problems, determine causes, and implement solutions.

TABLE 2.1	Management Responsibilities for Spare Parts Quality Assurance at DEC
Group	**Responsibility**
Marketing	Define end-user needs and abilities
Engineering	Understand end-user application
	Component selection
	Assembly layout
	Repairability
	Maintainability
Manufacturing	Process quality
	Process control
	Test coverage
	Infancy failures removal
Logistics	Packaging
	Handling
	Storage
	Revision control
Field service	Training
	Handling
	Storage
	Adjustments
	Diagnosing

Key Issues for Discussion

1. Discuss how the management responsibilities for the various functional groups at DEC support total quality management.

2. Describe how the DEC field service organization addresses the various issues of quality in service organizations identified in the chapter.

QUALITY IN PRACTICE   SERVICE QUALITY AT THE RITZ-CARLTON HOTEL COMPANY[14]

In 1992, the Ritz-Carlton Hotel Company became the first hospitality organization to receive the Malcolm Baldrige National Quality Award. The hotel industry is a very competitive business, one in which consumers place high emphases on reliability, timely delivery, and value. Ritz-Carlton focuses on the principal concerns of its main customers and strives to provide them with highly personalized, caring service. Attention to employee performance and information technology are two of the company's many strengths that helped it to achieve superior quality.

The Ritz-Carlton operates from an easy-to-understand definition of service quality that is aggressively communicated and internalized at all levels of the organization. Its "Three Steps of Service," motto, and credo, shown in Figure 2.5, are instilled in all employees. To provide the personalized service demanded by customers, the human-resource function works closely with the other operational functions. Each hotel has a director of human resources and a training manager, who are assisted by the hotel's quality leader. Each work area has a departmental trainer that is responsible for training and certifying new employees in his or her unit. Ritz-Carlton uses a highly predictive "character-trait recruiting" instrument for determining candidates' fitness for each of 120 job positions. New employees receive two days' orientation in which senior executives demonstrate Ritz-Carlton methods and instill Ritz-Carlton values. Three weeks later, managers monitor the effectiveness of the instruction and then conduct a follow-up training session. Later, new employees must pass written and skill-demonstration tests in order to become certified in their work areas.

Every day, in each work area, each shift supervisor conducts a quality line-up meeting and briefing session. Employees receive instruction for becoming certified as quality engineers capable of identifying waste in their work. Through these and other mechanisms, employees receive more than 100 hours of quality education aimed at fostering a commitment to premium service, solving problems, setting strategic quality plans, and generating new ideas.

Employees are empowered to "move heaven and earth to satisfy a customer," to enlist the aid of other employees to resolve a problem swiftly, to spend up to $2000 to satisfy a guest, to decide the business terms of a sale, to be involved in setting plans for their particular work area, and to speak with anyone in the company regarding any problem.

The Ritz-Carlton uses information technology on a daily basis to gather and use customer-satisfaction and quality-related data. Information systems involve every employee and provide critical, responsive data on guest-preferences, quantity of error-free products and services, and opportunities for quality improvement. The guest-profiling system records the individual preferences of the hundreds of thousands of guests who have stayed at least three times at any of the hotels. It gives front-desk employees immediate access to such information as

FIGURE 2.5   The Ritz-Carlton Three Steps of Service, Motto, and Credo

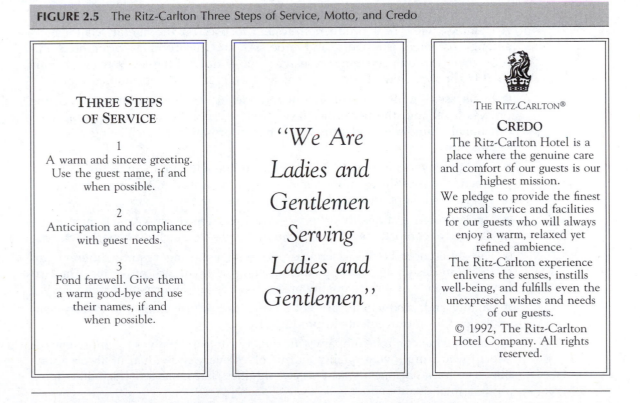

THREE STEPS OF SERVICE

1
A warm and sincere greeting. Use the guest name, if and when possible.

2
Anticipation and compliance with guest needs.

3
Fond farewell. Give them a warm good-bye and use their names, if and when possible.

"We Are Ladies and Gentlemen Serving Ladies and Gentlemen"

THE RITZ-CARLTON®

CREDO

The Ritz-Carlton Hotel is a place where the genuine care and comfort of our guests is our highest mission.

We pledge to provide the finest personal service and facilities for our guests who will always enjoy a warm, relaxed yet refined ambience.

The Ritz-Carlton experience enlivens the senses, instills well-being, and fulfills even the unexpressed wishes and needs of our guests.

© 1992, The Ritz-Carlton Hotel Company. All rights reserved.

whether the guest smokes, whether he or she prefers wine or a rose in the evening, and what kind of pillow he or she prefers.

These are only a few of Ritz-Carlton's quality practices and the results have been impressive. At the time of winning the Baldrige Award, customer satisfaction was upwards of 95 percent. Employee turnover was 48 percent, in an industry where the average is more than 100 percent. One hundred percent of key group accounts were retained in 1991. The number of employees needed per guest room during preopening activities of a new hotel was reduced 12 percent. Within a 3-year period, Ritz-Carlton reduced the number of labor-hours per guest room by 8 percent. Housekeeping costs per occupied room were reduced from $7.90 to $7.30 in less than one year. The average time required to clean a room was decreased from 30 to 28.5 minutes,

and elevator waiting time was reduced by 33 percent. Departmental profits per available guest room were nearly five times the industry average. One lesson the hotel has learned is not to underestimate the value of even one idea or quality improvement effort.

RITZ-CARLTON is a federally-registered trademark of the Ritz-Carlton Hotel Company.

Key Issues for Discussion

1. What are the benefits of the character-trait recruiting instrument to the company?

2. In what ways does information technology support the company's values?

3. What productivity improvements are cited? Have the company's quality efforts had a direct impact on productivity? An indirect impact? Explain.

SUMMARY OF KEY POINTS

■ Manufacturing quality improved dramatically during the 1980s; by the 1990s, service providers were paying more attention to quality issues.

■ A production system consists of all the activities and operations involved in producing an organization's goods or services. It has three major components: inputs, outputs, and processes.

■ Deming's view of a production system focuses on the lateral relationships among customers, suppliers, and processes and incorporates continuous improvement through consumer research. This is quite different from the hierarchial traditional view of organizations as portrayed by organizational charts.

■ Businesses should view quality at three levels: the organizational level, the process level, and the performer level. This perspective cuts across traditional functional boundaries and provides better information for achieving customer satisfaction.

■ Quality plays an important role in each component of a manufacturing firm's production and business-support systems. All are linked together as a collection of services that support the organization's objectives.

■ The importance of quality in services has grown in recent years. It may be the key source of competitive advantage for all businesses, including manufacturers.

■ The differences between services and manufacturing require different approaches in designing and implementing quality assurance programs. The two key components of service quality are employees and information technology.

■ Quality and productivity are not antithetical; improvements in quality generally lead to improvements in productivity.

■ Total quality control (companywide quality control) involves a comprehensive effort toward improving quality and involves every individual in an organization. The term *total quality management* signifies that managerial activities must guide a total quality effort.

REVIEW QUESTIONS

1. Explain the components of a production system. How does Deming's view of a production system differ from the traditional "input–process–output" model?

2. Explain the three levels of quality and the key issues that must be addressed at each level.

3. Explain the quality concerns of each major function of a manufacturing system.

4. How can business support systems help to sustain quality in an organization?

5. Distinguish between *facilitating* services and *core* services and give examples.

6. Why is service quality especially important in today's business environment?

7. Discuss the differences between manufacturing and service organizations. What are the implications of these differences for quality assurance?

8. Explain the roles of employees and information technology in providing quality service. How are they reflected in Avis's motto of "We try harder"?

9. What is productivity?

10. What is meant by the term *hidden factory?*

11. Discuss the ideal relationship between productivity and quality.

DISCUSSION QUESTIONS

1. Could it be argued that Deming's model of a production system is another way of representing an organization chart? Explain.

2. Explain how the "three levels of quality" might apply to a college or university.

3. Interview some key managers at a nearby manufacturing company and construct a diagram similar to Figure 2.2 showing the company's key functions and their relationships. Summarize the major quality converns of each function and develop a relationship chart similar to that of Figure 2.3.

4. Discuss some good and bad service experiences that you have had. How did they affect your loyalty as a customer?

5. This chapter listed several dimensions of service quality (time, timeliness, and so on). List ten service organizations and specify which dimension(s) each organization emphasizes. State whether you believe the emphasis gives the firm competitive advantage.

6. Cite some examples from your own experience in which you felt employees were truly empowered to serve you better.

7. How is information technology used to improve service in your college or university?

8. How might a company determine its hidden factory?

9. Consider these scenarios:[15]

   a. An organization inspects incoming resources on receipt, inspects at key partial product completion states, and final inspects. Unacceptable output at each stage is rejected and dealt with appropriately. Rework is possible, and defects identified as correctable are corrected.

   b. A group of five spray painters on an assembly line operates with basic job training but little feedback as to their job performance. Inspectors down the line, isolated from the direct-line personnel, evaluate the output from the painting department on the basis of specific quality attributes (runs, too wide or narrow shading, stripes, etc.). These quality attributes are clear to the inspectors but virtually unknown to the painters themselves. Painters never talk to the inspectors for a variety of reasons (job classifications, physical location, no time for it).

c. A firm is committed to achieving high quality in the goods and services it produces. The quality control department has convinced management that the best way to accomplish this is to have the department inspect all goods and services produced. A significant amount of effort and other resources has been devoted to building and developing a large, quality organization that emphasizes inspection, correction, and zero defects.

Briefly describe the productivity/quality interaction in each scenario, and suggest steps that management could take to improve it in each situation.

CASES

I. Shiny Hill Farms[16]

Shiny Hill Farms is a major pork processor, specializing in smoked meats, hams, sausages, and luncheon meats. The firm's largest facility slaughters more than 5000 hogs each day. Throughout the food industry, quality is a high priority, and Shiny Hill Farms is no exception.

The quality assurance department (QA) seeks to prevent *any* defective products from reaching the consumer. QA's primary concern is for controlling product weight, appearance, and shelf life throughout the manufacturing operations. Production operators are held accountable for their cuts on specific meat products. The cuts must be performed according to quality assurance specifications in order to obtain high yields. (*Yield* is the percentage of the live weight of the hog that can be sold.)

Quality Assurance monitors all operations, from the killing of hogs through packaging. QA personnel inspect incoming animals, work with USDA inspectors, and monitor cooking temperatures. They check scales daily to ensure they are providing correct weights. If products fall outside specifications, it is the responsibility of QA personnel to notify operators that changes need to be made to bring quality up to standard. Many QA personnel monitor weights of packaged boxes continuously to ensure that they conform to weight specifications. They open boxes and weigh the packages as well as check them for defects such as rips, leaks, and pin holes. Weights of packages near the bottom, middle, and top of each skid (pallet) are inspected. If these packages conform to weight specifications, then the entire skid is accepted and sent to the warehouse. If not, the skid is tagged for 100 percent inspection, and the process is studied to determine why the var-

iations occurred. QA personnel analyze graphs of yields and packaging waste weekly.

Other functions throughout the company focus on quality. The sanitation department, for example, sanitizes all manufacturing machines and work surfaces before initial production runs each day. The research and development department plays an important role in improving quality. For example, it is continually seeking out and testing new methods of curing meat and of killing bacteria more effectively and efficiently. R&D also helps to develop new packaging that may improve consumers' perception of quality. In addition, it develops new products, such as "lite" luncheon meats that contain less fat and cholesterol, enlisting the aid of focus groups and taste panels.

A food processing plant is an intense, high-speed manufacturing setting. Shiny Hill Farms operators may have to make as many as 10 cuts each minute on a conveyor line. Engineering personnel replaced all old manufacturing lines with ergonomically correct lines. The production line was redesigned to a standard height with adjustable-height work stations to better meet operators' needs. Turnover of meat cutters averages between 30 and 40 percent. New cutters are shown a video on how to use machines and knives correctly in order to make quality cuts. On the line, they are expected to learn from experience—watching others and learning from their mistakes.

Discussion Questions

1. Describe the scope of quality efforts in this organization.

2. What is the role of the quality assurance department at Shiny Hill Farms? Does it promote the concept of total quality?

3. What suggestions do you have for improving Shiny Hill Farms's quality effort?

II. Mercantile Stores[17]

Mercantile Stores are located throughout the Southeast, Midwest, and Gulf Coast and include seven divisions: Gayfers, Masion Blanche, Castner Knott, McAlpin's, Jones, Joslins, and J. B. White. Mercantile's mission statement states that "Mercantile Stores is dedicated to creating excitement in merchandising by providing the highest level of service to our customers and a broad assortment of fashionable products that offer superior quality and value." In 1983 Mercantile initiated a program for processing incoming merchandise at regional distribution centers. This was seen as more efficient than to receiving merchandise in the individual stores. In 1986, they remodeled and expanded existing stores to accommodate a greater selection of fashion merchandise. Designer apparel offerings were increased in 1987.

In 1989 a major technological initiative called *Quick Response* was instituted. It integrated all facets of operations, from inventory planning to purchasing and inventory control, to provide customers with better service. Some of the technologies introduced were price look-up and point-of-sale laser scanning systems, electronic purchase ordering and replenishment, and electronic invoicing and funds transfer. Stronger partnerships were developed with suppliers to help ensure that suppliers have sufficient merchandise for stocking the stores. The company is in constant contact with its suppliers for mutual benefit. For example, Hanes hosiery used selling information furnished electronically and shipped 97 percent of Quick Response orders. Sales increased 17 percent, and the inventory level decreased by 15 percent.

The Quick Response program eliminated bottlenecks within the merchandise processing functions. Previously, shipments had required a high amount of labor-intensive efforts: opening cartons, physical counts, sorting, and manual ticketing. Advance shipping notice capability now provides the means of knowing exactly what is coming and when. Shipments arrive preticketed by suppliers with external shipping container marking. Entire containers are scanned for contents and matched to purchase orders.

Mercantile Stores established a University Business School for training its management associates to implement quality practices within the company. The school's motto, "Investing in excellence through education," reflects the company's commitment to the development of its people. Sales associates, department managers, and store managers are empowered and challenged to embrace ownership and responsibility in their jobs. They plan and monitor their own forecasts from start to finish, for example. Complete customer satisfaction is seen as the responsibility of all associates. Decisions are made as close to the customer as possible, and promotions are made from within the company.

Discussion Questions

1. How does Mercantile view quality? Explain the roles of people and information technology in achieving quality in the Mercantile organization.

2. Compare the importance of "internal quality" (what the company sees) and "external quality" (what the customer sees). Do they conflict? What is needed to ensure that they are consistent?

■ NOTES

1. "Michigan Hospital Promises to Deliver," *The Cincinnati Enquirer,* 17 July, 1991, A2.

2. Adapted from Alan P. Brache and Geary A. Rummler, "The Three Levels of Quality," *Quality Progress* 21, no. 10 (October 1988), 46–51.

3. "A Profile of Hershey Foods Corporation" (Hershey Foods Corporation, Hershey, PA 17033), 7.

4. Arnold O. Putnam, "Three Quality Issues Management Still Avoids," *Quality Progress* 16, no. 12 (December 1982), 12.

5. Richard Norman, *Service Management Strategy and Leadership* (New York: John Wiley & Sons, 1984).

6. Frederick F. Reichheld and W. Earl Sasser, Jr., "Zero Defections: Quality Comes to Services," *Harvard Business Review* 68, no. 5 (September–October 1990), 105–112.

7. Ron Zemke, "Auditing Customer Service: Look Inside as Well as Out," *Employee Relations Today* 16 (1989), Autumn, 197–203.

8. Avis Rent A Car System, Inc., *1993 Employee–Owners' Annual Report and Quality Review.* © 1993 Wizard Co., Inc.

9. Avis, see note 8.
10. *Quality '93: Empowering People with Technology,* Advertisement in *Fortune* (September 20, 1993).
11. Frank S. Leonard and W. Earl Sasser, "The Incline of Quality," *Harvard Business Review* 60, no. 5 (September/October 1982), 163–171. Copyright © 1982 by the President and Fellows of Harvard College; all rights reserved.
12. Y. K. Shetty, "Corporate Response to Productivity Challenges," *National Productivity Review,* Winter 1984–85, 7–14.
13. Adapted from Robert Rosenthal, "Spare Part Quality Assurance," *Quality Progress* 16, no. 5 (May 1983) 24–27.
14. Adapted from Ritz-Carlton's Malcolm Baldrige National Quality Award application summary and Cheri Henderson, "Putting On the Ritz," *The TQM Magazine* 2, no. 5 (November–December 1992), 292–296.
15. Adapted from D. Scott Sink and J. Bert Keats, "Productivity and Quality: What Is the Connection?" *1982 Fall Industrial Engineering Conference Proceedings* (Norcross, GA: Institute of Industrial Engineers), 277–283.
16. Based on a student project prepared by Burton Phillips and Stefanie Steward. Their contribution is gratefully acknowledged.
17. Based on Mercantile annual reports from 1983 to 1992. The authors are grateful to Michelle Marsh for her research leading to this case.

■ BIBLIOGRAPHY

Berry, Leonard L.; Valarie A. Zeithaml; and A. Parasuraman. "Five Imperatives for Improving Service Quality." *Sloan Management Review,* Summer 1990, 29–38.

Chowdhury, A. R. "The Basics of Productivity Analysis." *Quality Progress* 19, no. 10 (October 1986), 68–70.

Freund, Richard A. "The Role of Quality Technology." In *Quality Assurance: Methods, Management, and Motivation,* ed. H. J. Bajaria, 10–13, Dearborn, MI: Society of Manufacturing Engineers, 1981.

Garvin, David A . *Managing Quality.* New York: The Free Press, 1988.

Harris, Adrienne. "The Customer's Always Right." *Black Enterprise* 21 (1991), June, 233–242.

Haywood-Farmer, John. "A Conceptual Model of Service Quality." *International Journal of Operations and Production Management* 8 (1988), no. 6, 19–29.

King, Carol A. "Service Quality Assurance Is Different." *Quality Progress* 18, no. 6 (June 1985), 14–18.

Lewis, Barbara R. "Quality in the Service Sector: A Review." *International Journal of Bank Marketing* 7 (1989), no. 5, 4–12.

Midas, Michael T., Jr. "The Quality/Productivity Connection." *Quality* 21, no. 2 (February 1982), 22–23.

Murray, David J. "Quality Assurance and Other Departments." In *Quality Assurance: Methods, Management, and Motivation,* ed. H. J. Bajaria, 41–46, Dearborn, MI: Society of Manufacturing Engineers, 1981.

Rosander, A. C. "Service Industry QC—Is the Challenge Being Met?" *Quality Progress* 13, no. 9 (September 1980), 33–34.

Scanlon, Frank, and John T. Hagan. "Quality Management for the Service Industries—Part 1." *Quality Progress* 16, no. 5 (May 1983), 18–23.

Shetty, Y. K., and Joel E. Ross. "Quality and Its Management in Service Businesses." *Industrial Management,* November/December 1985.

Sink, D. Scott, and J. Bert Keats. "Productivity and Quality: What Is the Connection?" *1982 Fall Industrial Engineering Conference Proceedings,* 277–283. Norcross, GA: Institute of Industrial Engineers.

Thompson, Phillip; Glenn DeSouza; and Bradley T. Gale. "The Strategic Management of Service Quality." *Quality Progress* 18, no. 6 (June 1985), 20–25.

Williams, Roy H., and Ronald M. Zigli. "Ambiguity Impedes Quality in the Service Industries." *Quality Progress* 20, no. 7 (July 1987), 14–17.

Zemke, Ron. "The Emerging Art of Service Management." *Training* 29 (1992), January, 36–42.

Quality Management Philosophies

Although scores of individuals have made substantial contributions to the theory and practice of quality management, three individuals—W. Edwards Deming, Joseph M. Juran, and Philip B. Crosby—are regarded as true "management gurus" in the quality revolution. Their insights on measuring, managing, and improving quality have had profound impacts on countless managers and entire corporations around the world. Because of their personalities, Deming, Juran, and Crosby have been likened, respectively, to a fire-and-brimstone preacher, a theologian, and an evangelist. Deming's gruff demeanor reportedly struck fear into many of the corporate executives who attended his seminars; Juran's *Quality Control Handbook* is often called the "bible" of quality; and Crosby is noted for his inspiring, motivational speaking. This chapter presents the philosophies of these three leaders and examines their individual contributions as well as their philosophical similarities and differences. In addition, it discusses the contributions of two other individuals who have helped to shape current thinking in quality management, Armand V. Feigenbaum and Kaoru Ishikawa.

THE DEMING PHILOSOPHY

No individual has had more influence on quality management than Dr. W. Edwards Deming. Deming received a Ph.D. in physics and was trained as a statistician, so much of his philosophy can be traced to these roots. He worked for Western Electric during its pioneering era of statistical quality control in the 1920s and 1930s. Deming recognized the importance of viewing management processes statistically. During World War II he taught quality control courses as part of the U.S. national defense effort, but he realized that teaching statistics only to engineers and factory workers would never solve the fundamental quality problems that manufacturing needed to address. Despite numerous efforts, his attempts to convey the message of quality to upper-level managers in the United States were ignored.

Shortly after World War II Deming was invited to Japan to help the country take a census. The Japanese had heard about his theories and their usefulness to U.S. companies during the war. Consequently, he soon began to teach them statistical quality control. His thinking went beyond mere statistics, however. Deming preached the importance of top-management leadership, customer/supplier partnerships, and continuous improvement in product development and manufacturing processes. Japanese managers embraced these ideas, and the rest, as they say, is history. Deming's influence on Japanese industry was so great that the Union of Japanese Scientists and Engineers established the Deming Application Prize in 1951 to recognize companies that show a high level of achievement in quality practices. Deming also received Japan's highest honor, the Royal Order of the Sacred Treasurer, from the Emperor. The former chairman of NEC Electronics once said, "There is not a day I don't think about what Dr. Deming meant to us."

Although Deming lived in Washington, D.C., he remained virtually unknown in the United States until 1980, when NBC telecast a program entitled "If Japan Can . . . Why Can't We?" The documentary highlighted Deming's contributions in Japan and his later work with Nashua Corporation. Shortly afterward, his name was frequently on the lips of U.S. corporate executives. Companies such as Ford, GM, and Procter & Gamble invited him to work with them to improve their quality. To their initial surprise, Deming did not lay out "a quality improvement program" for them. His goal was to change entire *perspectives* in management, and often radically. Deming worked with passion until his death in December 1993 at the age of 93, knowing he had little time left to make a difference in his home country. When asked how he would like to be remembered, Deming replied, "I probably won't even be remembered." Then after a long pause, he added, "Well, maybe . . . as someone who spent his life trying to keep America from committing suicide."[1]

■ Foundations of the Deming Philosophy

Unlike other management gurus and consultants, Deming never defined or described quality precisely. In his last book, he stated, "A product or a service possesses quality if it helps somebody and enjoys a good and sustainable market."[2] The Deming philosophy focuses on bringing about improvements in product and service quality by reducing uncertainty and variability in the design and manufacturing process. In Deming's view, variation is the chief culprit of poor quality. In mechanical assemblies, for example, variations from specifications for part dimensions lead to inconsistent performance and premature wear and failure. Likewise, inconsistencies in service frustrate customers and hurt companies' reputations. To accomplish reductions in variation, Deming advocated a never-ending cycle of product design, manufacture, test, and sales, followed by market surveys and then redesign and so forth. He claimed that higher quality leads to higher productivity, which in turn leads to long-term competitive strength. The Deming "chain reaction" theory (Figure 3.1) summarizes this view. The theory is that improvements in quality lead to lower costs because they result in less rework, fewer mistakes, fewer delays and snags, and better use of time and materials. Lower costs, in turn, lead to productivity improvements. With better quality and lower prices, a firm can achieve a higher market share and thus stay in business, providing more and more jobs. Deming stressed that top management has the overriding responsibility for quality improvement.

Deming's philosophy underwent many changes as he continued to learn. In his early work in the United States, he preached his "14 Points" (Table 3.1), which are discussed in detail later in the chapter. The 14 Points caused some confusion and misunderstanding among businesspeople, because Deming did not provide a clear rationale for them. Near the end of his life, however, he synthesized the underlying foundations of the 14 Points in what he called "A System of Profound Knowledge." Understanding the elements of this "system" provides critical insights needed for understanding and appreciating the 14 Points.

Deming's Profound Knowledge system consists of four interrelated parts:

FIGURE 3.1   The Deming Chain Reaction

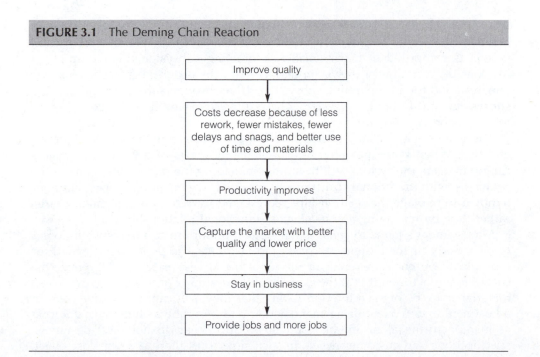

TABLE 3.1 Deming's 14 Points

1. Create and publish to all employees a statement of the aims and purposes of the company or other organization. The management must demonstrate constantly their commitment to this statement.
2. Learn the new philosophy, top management and everybody.
3. Understand the purpose of inspection, for improvement of processes and reduction of cost.
4. End the practice of awarding business on the basis of price tag alone.
5. Improve constantly and forever the system of production and service.
6. Institute training.
7. Teach and institute leadership.
8. Drive out fear. Create trust. Create a climate for innovation.
9. Optimize toward the aims and purposes of the company the efforts of teams, groups, staff areas.
10. Eliminate exhortations for the work force.
11. (a) Eliminate numerical quotas for production. Instead, learn and institute methods for improvement.
    (b) Eliminate M.B.O. [management by objective]. Instead, learn the capabilities of processes and how to improve them.
12. Remove barriers that rob people of pride of workmanship.
13. Encourage education and self-improvement for everyone.
14. Take action to accomplish the transformation.

SOURCE: Originally published in *Out of the Crisis* by W. Edwards Deming. Published by M.I.T. Center for Advanced Engineering Study, Cambridge, MA 02139. Copyright 1986 by W. Edwards Deming. Revised by W. Edwards Deming in January 1990. Reprinted by permission of M.I.T. and the W. Edwards Deming Institute.

1. appreciation for a system,

2. understanding of variation,

3. theory of knowledge, and

4. psychology.

Each of these parts is explained here.

SYSTEMS

A system is a set of functions or activities within an organization that work together for the aim of the organization. As explained in Chapter 2, a production system is composed of many smaller, interacting subsystems. For example, a McDonald's restaurant is a system that includes the order-taker/cashier subsystem, grill and food preparation subsystem, drive-through subsystem, purchasing subsystem, and training subsystem. These subsystems are linked together as internal customers and suppliers.

The components of any system must work together if the system is to be effective. When there are interactions among the parts of a system, managers cannot manage the system well by simply managing the parts. This is one of the problems with traditional, functionally oriented organizations. They have attempted to manage the relationships represented by *vertical* organization charts, rather than by managing *horizontal*, cross-functional relationships.

Management's job is to *optimize* the system. Suboptimization results in losses to everybody in the system. According to Deming, it is poor management, for example, to purchase materials or service at the lowest price or to minimize the cost of manufacture if it is at the expense of the system. For instance, inexpensive materials may be of such inferior quality that they will cause excessive costs in adjustment and repair during manufacture and assembly. Minimizing the cost of manufacturing alone might result in products that do not meet designers' specifications and customer needs. In such situations, there is a win–lose effect.

Purchasing wins, manufacturing loses; manufacturing wins, customers lose, and so on. Any system that results in a win–lose outcome is suboptimal. To manage any system, managers must understand the interrelationships among the systems's components and among the people that work in it.

Management must have an *aim*, a purpose toward which the system continually strives. Deming believes that the aim of any system should be for everybody—stockholders, employees, customers, community—and the environment to gain over the long term. Stockholders can realize financial benefits, employees can receive opportunities for training and education, customers can receive products and services that meet their needs and create satisfaction, the community can benefit from business leadership, and the environment can benefit from responsible management.

This theory applies to managing people also. All the people who work within a system can contribute to improvement, which will enhance their joy in work. Many factors within the system affect an individual employee's performance; for example:

- the training received,
- the information and resources provided,
- the leadership of supervisors and managers,
- disruptions on the job, and
- management policies and practices.

Few performance appraisals recognize such factors. Pitting individuals or departments against each other for resources is self-destructive to an organization. The individuals or departments will perform to maximize their own expected gain, not that of the entire firm. Therefore, optimizing the system requires internal cooperation. Similarly, using sales quotas or arbitrary cost-reduction goals will not motivate people to improve the system and customer satisfaction; the people will perform only to meet the quotas or goals.

VARIATION

The second part of Profound Knowledge is a basic understanding of statistical theory and variation. We see variation everywhere, from hitting golf balls to being served in a restaurant. A device called a *quincunx* illustrates a natural process of variation. A computer-simulated quincunx is shown in Figure 3.2.[3] In the simulation, small balls are dropped from a hole in the top and hit a series of pins as they fall toward collection boxes. The pins cause each ball to move randomly to the left or right as it strikes each pin on its way down. Note that most balls end up toward the middle of the box. Figure 3.3 shows the frequency distribution of where the balls landed in one simulation. Note the roughly symmetrical, bell shape of the distribution. A normal distribution is bell-shaped. Even though all balls are dropped from the same position, the end result shows variation.

The same kind of variation exists in production processes. Actually, a production process contains many sources of variation, as illustrated in Figure 3.4. Different lots of material vary in strength, thickness, or moisture content, for example. Cutting tools have inherent variation in their strength and composition. During manufacturing, tools experience wear, vibrations cause changes in machine settings, and electrical fluctuations cause variations in power. Operators do not position parts on fixtures consistently, and physical and emotional stress

FIGURE 3.2   A Quincunx in Action

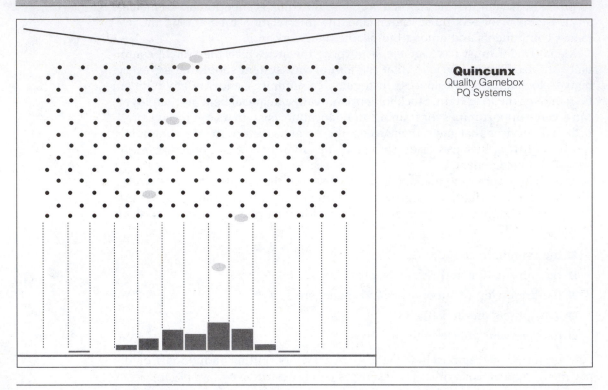

affect operators' consistency. In addition, measurement gauges and human inspection capabilities are not uniform. Even when measurements of several items by the same instrument are the same, it is due to a lack of precision in the measurement instrument; extremely precise instruments always reveal slight differences.

The complex interactions of these variations in materials, tools, machines, operators, and the environment are not easily understood. Variation due to any of these individual sources appears at random; however their combined effect is stable and can usually be predicted statistically. These factors that are present as a natural part of a process are referred to as *common causes of variation.*

Common causes of variation generally account for about 80 to 90 percent of the observed variation in a production process. The remaining 10 to 20 percent are the result of *special causes of variation,* often called *assignable causes.* Special causes arise from external sources that are not inherent in the process. Factors such as a bad batch of material from a supplier, a poorly trained operator, excessive tool wear, or miscalibration of measuring instruments are examples of special causes. Special causes result in unnatural variation that disrupts the random pattern of common causes. Hence, they tend to be easily detectable using statistical methods, and usually economical to correct.

Common causes are a result of the design of the system—as management has designed it. For instance, suppose that boards are to be cut to the precise length of 25.35 inches. If the worker is provided with only a hand saw, a table, and a yardstick, it will be virtually impossible for him or her to cut lengths of this precision consistently. Improvements in conformance can only be achieved if management provides more accurate equipment and training in the correct work

FIGURE 3.3 Results from a Quincunx Experiment

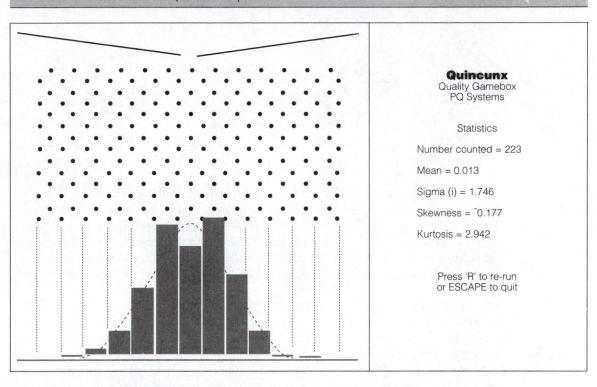

Quincunx
Quality Gamebox
PQ Systems

Statistics

Number counted = 223

Mean = 0.013

Sigma (i) = 1.746

Skewness = ‾0.177

Kurtosis = 2.942

Press 'R' to re-run
or ESCAPE to quit

methods. On the other hand, suppose that an accurate measurement instrument, a fixture for holding the boards, and an electric saw are available. Clearly, the output from this system will have less variability and more consistent quality. If the saw blade becomes worn or chipped, the quality will deteriorate. This would be a special cause of variation, which should be identified and corrected by the worker.

A system governed only by common causes is labeled a stable system. Understanding a stable system and the differences between special and common causes of variation is essential for managing any system. Management can make two fundamental mistakes in attempting to improve a process:

1. To treat as a special cause any fault, complaint, mistake, breakdown, accident, or shortage when it actually is due to common causes.

2. To attribute to common causes any fault, complaint, mistake, breakdown, accident, or shortage when it actually is due to a special cause.

In the first case, tampering with a stable system can increase the variation in the system. In the second case, the opportunity to reduce variation is missed because the amount of variation is mistakenly assumed to be uncontrollable.

Deming suggests that management always work to reduce variation. With less variation, both the producer and consumer benefit. The producer benefits by needing less inspection, experiencing less scrap and rework, and having higher productivity. The consumer has the advantage of knowing that all products have similar quality characteristics. This advantage can be especially critical when the consumer is another firm using large quantities of the product in its own manufacturing or service operations.

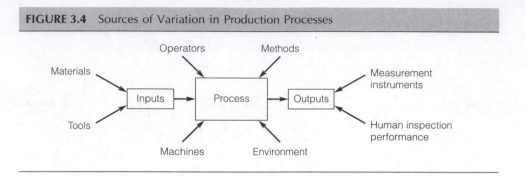

FIGURE 3.4   Sources of Variation in Production Processes

A Japanese engineer, Genichi Taguchi—whose philosophy was strongly advocated by Deming—explained the economic value of reducing variation. Taguchi measured quality as the variation from the target value of a design specification, and then translated that variation into an economic "loss function" that expresses the cost of variation in monetary terms. To understand Taguchi's philosophy better, let us reconsider the manufacturing-based definition of quality as "conformance to specifications."

Suppose that a specification for some quality characteristic is 0.500 ± 0.020. Using this definition, the actual value of the quality characteristic can fall anywhere in a range from 0.480 to 0.520. This approach assumes that the customer, either the consumer or the next department in the production process, would accept any value within the 0.480 to 0.520 range, but not be satisfied with a value outside this tolerance range. Also, this approach assumes that costs do not depend on the actual value of the quality characteristic as long as it falls within the tolerance specified (see Figure 3.5).

But what is the real difference between 0.479 and 0.481? The former would be considered as "out of specification" and either reworked or scrapped while the latter would be acceptable. Actually, the impact of either value on the performance characteristic of the product would be about the same. Neither value is close to the nominal specification 0.500. The nominal specification is the ideal target value for the critical quality characteristic. Taguchi's approach assumes that the smaller the variation about the nominal specification, the better is the quality. In turn, products are more consistent, and total costs are less. The following example illustrates this notion.

The Japanese newspaper *Ashai* published an example comparing the cost and quality of Sony televisions at two plants in Japan and San Diego.[4] The color density of all the units produced at the San Diego plant were within specifica-

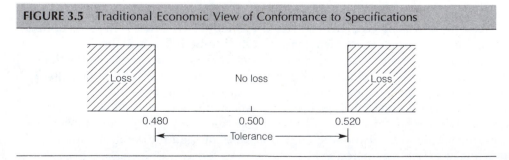

FIGURE 3.5   Traditional Economic View of Conformance to Specifications

tions, while some of those shipped from the Japanese plant were not (see Figure 3.6). However, the average loss per unit of the San Diego plant was $0.89 greater than that of the Japanese plant. This increased cost occurred because workers adjusted units that were out of specification at the San Diego plant, adding cost to the process. Furthermore, a unit adjusted to minimally meet specifications was more likely to generate customer complaints than a unit close to the original target value, therefore incurring higher field service costs. Figure 3.6 shows that fewer U.S.–produced sets met the target value for color density. The distribution of quality in the Japanese plant was more uniform around the target value, and though some units were out of specification, the total cost was less.

The only way to reduce common cause variation is to change the technology of the process. The process technology—machines, people, materials, methods, or measurement process—is under control of *management*, not the production operators. Putting pressure on operators to perform at higher quality levels may simply not be possible, and may even be counterproductive.

Statistical methods are the primary tool used to identify the occurrence of variation due to special causes. Once special cause variations are identified, they can be corrected. The responsibility for this identification and correction should lie with the production operators and their immediate supervisors, not quality assurance staff. Deming proposes that every employee in the firm be familiar with statistical techniques and other problem-solving tools. Statistics can then become the common language that every employee—from top executives to line workers—uses to communicate with one another. Its value lies in its objectivity; statistics leaves little room for ambiguity or misunderstanding.

THEORY OF KNOWLEDGE

The third part of Profound Knowledge is the theory of knowledge, the branch of philosophy concerned with the nature and scope of knowledge, its presuppositions and basis, and the general reliability of claims to knowledge. Deming's system was influenced greatly by Clarence Irving Lewis, author of *Mind and the World*, (Mineola, NY: Dover, 1929). Lewis stated "There is no knowledge without interpretation. If interpretation, which represents an activity of the mind, is always subject to the check of further experience, how is knowledge possible at all? . . . An argument from past to future at best is probable only, and even this probability must rest upon principles which are themselves more than probable."

Deming emphasized that knowledge is not possible without theory, and experience alone does not establish a theory. Any rational plan, however simple,

---

FIGURE 3.6   Variation in U.S.- versus Japanese-Made Television Components

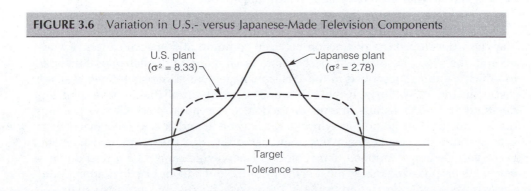

requires prediction concerning conditions, behavior, and comparison of performance. A statement devoid of prediction or explanation of past events conveys no knowledge. Experience only *describes*—it cannot be tested or validated—and alone is no help in management. Theory, on the other hand, shows a cause and effect relationship that can be used for prediction. Copying an example of success, without understanding it with theory, may lead to disaster. Many companies have jumped on the latest popular approach advocated by business consultants, only to see the approach fail. Methods that have sustained success are grounded in theory. This notion implies that management decisions must be based on facts, not instincts. Objective data and a systematic problem-solving process provide a rational basis for making decisions. Thus, the purpose of theory is to develop a science, and the purpose of science is to describe, predict, and control practice. (This discussion is continued in a later chapter, particularly in the context of "learning organizations.")

PSYCHOLOGY

Psychology helps us understand people, interactions between people and circumstances, interactions between leaders and employees, and any system of management. Much of Deming's philosophy is based on understanding human behavior and treating people fairly. People differ from one another. A leader must be aware of these differences and work toward optimizing everybody's abilities and preferences. Most managers operate under the assumption that all people are alike. However, a true leader understands that people learn in different ways and at different speeds, and manages the system accordingly.

People are motivated intrinsicly and extrinsicly. Fear does not motivate people; instead, it prevents the system from reaching its full potential. People are born with a need for love and esteem in their relationships with other people. Some circumstances provide people with dignity and self-esteem. Conversely, circumstances that deny people these advantages will smother intrinsic motivation. If people cannot enjoy their work, they will not be productive and focused on quality principles. Psychology helps us to nurture and preserve these positive innate attributes of people.

One of Deming's more controversial beliefs is that pay is not a motivator, although industrial psychologists have said this for decades. The chairman of General Motors once stated if GM doubled the salary of every employee, nothing would change. Monetary rewards are a way out for managers who do not understand how to manage intrinsic motivation. When joy in work becomes secondary to getting good ratings, employees are ruled by external forces and must act to protect what they have and avoid punishment.

Very little in Deming's system of Profound Knowledge is original. Walter Shewhart developed the distinction between common and special causes of variation in the 1920s; business schools began to teach many of the behavioral theories to which Deming subscribed in the 1960s; management scientists refined systems theory in the 1950s through the 1970s; and scientists in all fields have long understood the relationships among prediction, observation, and theory. Deming made a major contribution in tying these concepts together. He recognized their synergy and developed them into a unified universal theory of management. However, Deming cautioned that Profound Knowledge cannot be forced on anybody. He emphasized that it must come from the outside and by invitation. Managers must want to learn and apply it. Otherwise, it's just business as usual.

■ The Red Bead and Funnel Experiments[5]

In his four-day management seminars, Deming used two simple, yet powerful experiments to educate his audience. The first is the "Red Bead" experiment, which proceeds as follows. A Foreman (usually Deming) selects several volunteers from the audience: Six Willing Workers, a Recorder, two Inspectors, and a Chief Inspector. The materials for the experiment include 4000 wooden beads—800 red and 3200 white—and two Tupperware boxes, one slightly smaller than the other. Also, a paddle with 50 holes or depressions is used to scoop up 50 beads, which is the prescribed workload. In this experiment, the company is "producing" beads for a new customer who needs only white beads and will not take red beads. The Foreman explains that everyone will be an apprentice for three days to learn the job. During apprenticeship, the workers may ask questions. Once production starts, however, no questions are allowed. The procedures are rigid; no departures from procedures are permitted so that no variation in performance will occur. The Foreman explains to the Willing Workers that their jobs depend on their performance and if they are dismissed, many others are willing to replace them. Furthermore, no resignations are allowed.

The company's work standard, the Foreman explains, is 50 beads per day. The production process is simple: Mix the raw material and pour it into the smaller box. Repeat this procedure, returning the beads from the smaller box to the larger one. Grasp the paddle and insert it into the bead mixture. Raise the paddle at a 44-degree angle so that every depression will hold a bead. The two Inspectors count the beads independently and record the counts. The Chief Inspector checks the counts and announces the results, which are written down by the Recorder. The Chief Inspector then dismisses the worker. When all six Willing Workers have produced the day's quota, the Foreman evaluates the results.

Figure 3.7 shows the results of the first day's production generated with the *Quality Gamebox* computer simulation software. The Foreman is disappointed. He reminds the Willing Workers that their job is to make white beads, not red

---

FIGURE 3.7   First Day's Production (The paddle shows the result of the last Willing Worker, Ann.)

Bead Box
Quality Gamebox
PQ Systems

Percentage of red beads = 20

Player	Rounds	Reds	p
Jeff	1	10	0.200
Dave	1	11	0.220
Tom	1	11	0.220
Dennis	1	14	0.280
Marty	1	7	0.140
Ann	1	11	0.220

Statistics
pbar = 0.21
UCL = 0.39   LCL = 0.04
p - p-chart, <Enter> - continue

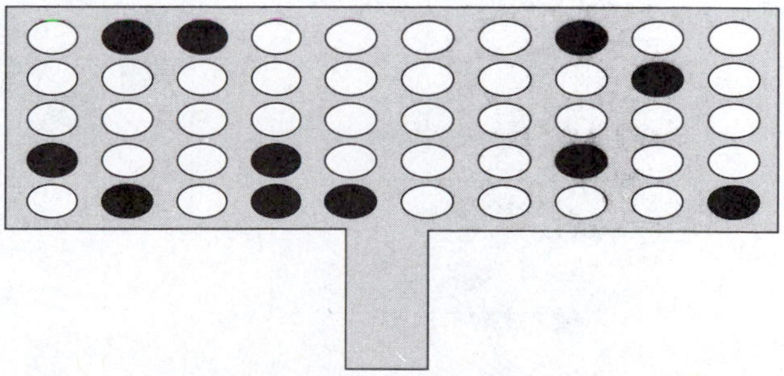

ones. The company is on a merit system, and it rewards only good performance. Marty only made 7 red beads and deserves a pay increase. The data do not lie; he is the best worker. Dennis made 14 red beads. Everyone likes him, but he must be placed on probation. The Foreman announces that management has set a goal of no more than 7 red beads per day per worker, and sees no reason why everyone cannot be as good as Marty.

Figure 3.8 shows the cumulative results for the second day. We see that after two days, Jeff had produced 23 red beads, Dave 23, Tom 20, Dennis 21, Marty 17, and Ann 23. (The second day's results can be found by subtraction: Jeff produces 13 beads, Dave 13, Tom 9, Dennis 7, Marty 10, and Ann 12.) The overall performance was not good. Management is watching carefully. The Foreman reminds them again that their jobs depend on performance. Marty is a big disappointment. The merit increase obviously went to his head. The Foreman chastises him in front of the other workers. Dennis, on the other hand, showed remarkable improvement; probation and the threat of losing his job made him a better worker—only 7 red beads—a 50 percent reduction in defects! He met the goal; if he can do it, anyone can. Dennis gets a special commendation from the plant manager.

At the beginning of the third day, management announces a Zero Defects Day. Everyone will do their best on this last day of the apprenticeship program. The Foreman is desperate and he tells the Willing Workers again that their jobs are their own responsibility. From Figure 3.9, production figures can be determined (by computing the difference between the cumulative output of day 3 and day 2), and shows that Jeff produces 12 red beads, Dave 18, Tom 17, Dennis 9, Marty 6, and Ann 11. Clearly, Marty learned a lesson the day before, but the group's overall performance is not good. Management is bitterly disappointed at the results. The Zero Defect Day program did not improve quality substantially; in fact, more red beads were produced today than ever before. Costs are getting out of control, and there is talk of shutting down the entire plant. Dave and Tom receive pink slips informing them that tomorrow will be their last day; their

FIGURE 3.8   Second Day's Cumulative Results

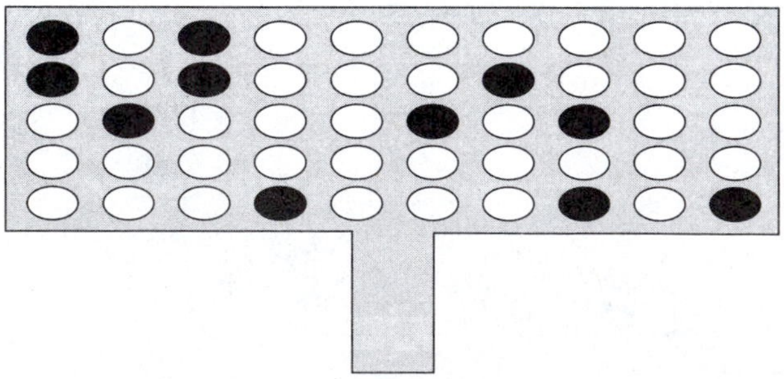

FIGURE 3.9 Third Day's Cumulative Results

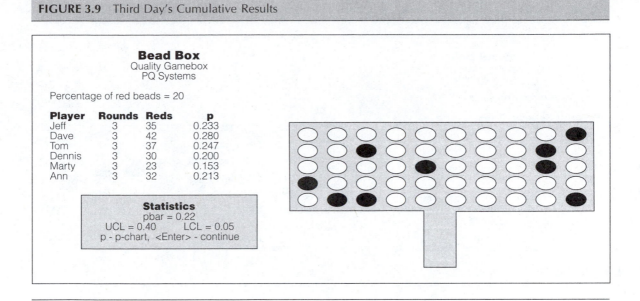

Bead Box
Quality Gamebox
PQ Systems

Percentage of red beads = 20

Player	Rounds	Reds	p
Jeff	3	35	0.233
Dave	3	42	0.280
Tom	3	37	0.247
Dennis	3	30	0.200
Marty	3	23	0.153
Ann	3	32	0.213

Statistics
pbar = 0.22
UCL = 0.40   LCL = 0.05
p - p-chart, <Enter> - continue

work is clearly much worse than the others. But the Foreman is optimistic. He puts up a poster saying ''Be a Quality Worker!'' to encourage the others to reach the goal.

On the fourth day (see Figure 3.10), we find that the number of red beads produced by the six Willing Workers is 8, 11, 8, 9, 8, and 9. The production is still not good enough. The Foreman announces that management has decided to close the plant after all.

The Red Bead experiment offers several important lessons for managers:

■ *Variation exists in systems and, if stable, can be predicted.* If we plot the fraction of red beads produced by each worker each day, we can observe this variation easily. Figure 3.11 is a *run chart* of these data, which simply shows a plot of the fraction of red beads produced over time. All points fluctuate about the overall average, which is 0.21, falling roughly between 0.10 and 0.40. In Chapter 15 we will learn to calculate statistical limits of variation (0.04 and 0.38) and show that all points come from a stable system; that is, the variation arises from common causes. Although the exact number of red beads in any particular paddle is not predictable, we can describe statistically what we expect from the system.

■ *All the variation in the production of red beads, and the variation from day to day of any Willing Worker, came entirely from the process itself.* In this experiment, Deming deliberately eliminated the source of variability that managers usually believe is the most significant: people. Each worker was basically identical, and no evidence showed that any one of them was better than another. They could not control the number of red beads produced, and could do no better than the system would allow. Neither motivation nor threats had any influence. Unfortunately, many managers believe that all variation is controllable and place blame on those who cannot do anything about it.

■ *Numerical goals are often meaningless.* A Foreman who gives out merit pay and puts people on probation, supposedly as rewards and punishment of performance, actually, rewards and punishes the performance of the *process,*

FIGURE 3.10   Fourth Day's Cumulative Results

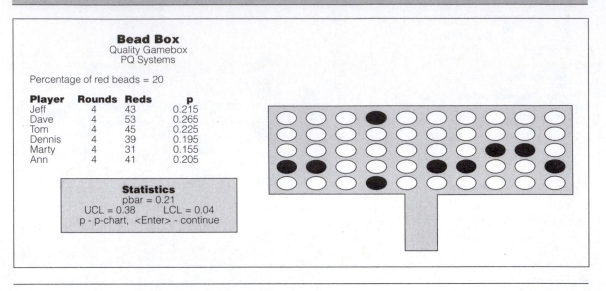

not the Willing Workers. To rank or appraise people arbitrarily is demoralizing, especially when workers cannot influence the outcomes. No matter what the goal is, it has no effect on the actual number of red beads produced. Exhorting workers to "Do their best" only leads to frustration. Management has no basis to assume that the best Willing Workers of the past will be the best in the future.

■ *Management is responsible for the system.* The experiment shows bad management. Procedures are rigid. The Willing Workers have no say in improving the process. Management is responsible for the incoming material, but does not work with the supplier to improve the inputs to the system. Management designed the production system and decided to rely on inspection to control the process. These decisions have far more influence on the outcomes than the efforts of the workers. Three inspectors are probably as costly as the six workers and add practically no value to the output.

Deming's second experiment is the Funnel Experiment. Its purpose is to show that people can and do affect the outcomes of many processes and create unwanted variation by "tampering" with the process, or indiscriminately trying to remove common causes of variation. In this experiment, a funnel is suspended above a table with a target drawn on a tablecloth. The goal is to hit the target. Participants drop a marble through the funnel and mark the place where the marble eventually lands. Rarely will the marble rest on the target. This variation is due to common causes in the process. One strategy is to simply leave the funnel alone, which creates some variation of points around the target. However, many people believe they can improve the results by adjusting the location of the funnel. Three possible rules for adjusting the funnel are:

Rule 2. Measure the deviation from the point at which the marble comes to rest and the target. Move the funnel an equal distance in the opposite direction *from its current position* [Figure 3.12(a)].

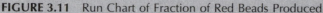

FIGURE 3.11   Run Chart of Fraction of Red Beads Produced

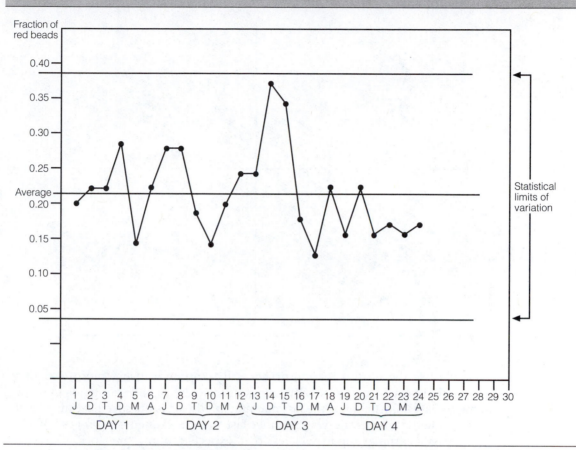

Rule 3. Measure the deviation from the point at which the marble comes to rest and the target. Set the funnel an equal distance in the opposite direction of the error *from the target* [Figure 3.12(b)].

Rule 4. Place the funnel over the spot where the marble last came to rest.

Figure 3.13 shows a computer simulation of these strategies using the *Quality Game-box*. Clearly the first rule—leave the funnel alone—results in the least variation.

FIGURE 3.12   Two Rules for Adjusting the Funnel

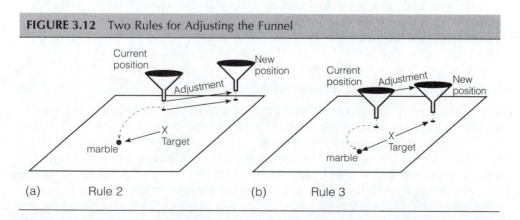

FIGURE 3.13   Results of the Funnel Experiment

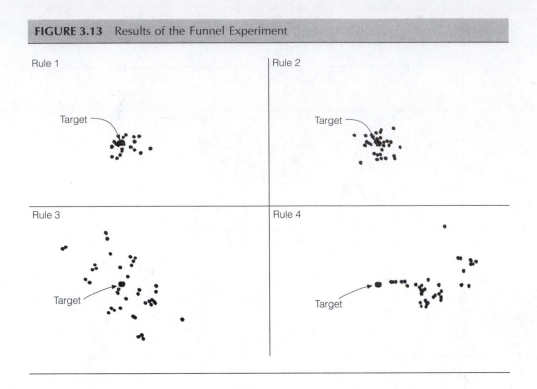

People use these rules inappropriately all the time, causing more variation that would normally occur. An amateur golfer who hits a bad shot tends to make an immediate adjustment. If the last manufactured part is off-specification, adjust the machine. If a schedule was not met last month, change the process. If the last quarter's earnings report was less than expected, dump the stock. If an employee's performance last week was subpar (or exceptional), punish (or reward) the employee. In all these cases, the error is usually compounded by an inappropriate reaction. All of these policies stem from a lack of understanding of variation, which originates from not understanding the process.

■ Deming's 14 Points

Deming was emphatic in his belief that managerial practices needed a radical overhaul. His 14 Points listed in Table 3.1 constitute the core of his program for achieving quality excellence. According to Deming, the 14 Points cannot be implemented selectively; they are an all-or-nothing commitment. We will consider each in turn.

POINT 1: CREATE A VISION AND DEMONSTRATE COMMITMENT

Deming believed that businesses should not exist simply for profit; they are social entities whose basic purpose is to serve their customers and employees. To do this, they must take a long-term view and invest in innovation, training, and research. In Japan, for instance, companies spend considerably more on research and development than in the United States. They willingly give up short-term profits knowing they will achieve a greater market share in the future.

The emphasis on short-term profits has eroded American industry. Short-term thinking is driven by quarterly dividends, annual performance appraisals, monthly sales quotas, and the fear of hostile takeovers. Job-hopping, where personal career advancement is placed ahead of the welfare of the firm, is one of Deming's "Deadly Diseases." The costs due to lost knowledge and experience, as well as the investments in hiring and training, are staggering. Take American sports, for example. How many teams can build a dynasty with free agency? Many players go to the highest bidder with little team loyalty. Consequently, employees work only for their boss or individual rewards, and not for the company's future.

Today's corporations frequently "downsize" in a desperate attempt to overcome the problems brought about by long-term ineffective management. Often, the problems result from a competitive crisis or financial losses. Wayne Cascio has defined downsizing as "the planned elimination of positions or jobs."[6] Cascio points out that "Downsizing may occur by reducing work (not just employees) . . . [or by] implementing cost-containment strategies that streamline activities such as transaction processing, information systems or sign-off policies." Too often, managers equate downsizing with massive layoffs.

Edmund Faltermayer points out a number of creative approaches that companies may take to reduce or eliminate layoffs.[7]

- Hiring freezes
- Restricting overtime
- Retraining/redeploying excess workers
- Switching positions to temporary/part-time
- Job sharing
- Employ consultants, instead of permanent staff
- Use voluntary leave/unpaid vacations
- Shorten the workweek
- Reduce pay
- Encourage early retirement
- Start lean and stay lean

Successful use of such strategies takes careful planning and disciplined management, but generally such alternatives are superior to wholesale layoffs.

Deming understood that business must adopt a long-term perspective and take responsibility for providing jobs and improving a firm's competitive position. This responsibility lies with top management, who must develop a vision and set the policies and mission of the organization. They must then act on the policies and show commitment.

POINT 2: LEARN THE NEW PHILOSOPHY

The world has changed in the last few decades. Old methods of management built on Frederick Taylor's principles, such as quota-driven production, work measurement, and adversarial work relationships will not work in today's global business environment. They create mistrust, fear, and anxiety and a focus on "satisficing," rather than "optimizing."

Production and service processes often contain considerable waste and inefficiencies. For example, several years ago one of the authors purchased a new dining room set, delivered directly from the factory. A brass knob was missing from one of the doors. The company was prompt in sending a replacement knob. In fact, a package containing six knobs arrived the following week. Later, another

package of six arrived. A few weeks later a third package came. Imagine the cost
to the company of administrative time as well as the items themselves! Eliminating defects is not enough. Companies must develop a quality consciousness
and a new attitude that "good enough" just *isn't*.

Companies cannot survive if products of poor quality of conformance or poor
fitness for use leave their customers dissatisfied. Instead, companies must take a
customer-driven approach based on mutual cooperation between labor and management and a never-ending cycle of improvement. Everyone, from the board-
room to the stockroom, must learn the new philosophy.

POINT 3: UNDERSTAND INSPECTION

Routine inspection acknowledges that defects are present, but does not add value
to the product. Rather, it is rarely accurate, and encourages the production of
defective products by letting someone else catch and fix the problem. The rework
and disposition of defective material decreases productivity and increases costs.
In service industries, rework cannot be performed; external failures are the most
damaging to business.

Workers must take responsibility for their work, rather than leave the problems for someone else down the production line. Managers need to understand
the concept of variation and how it affects their processes and seek to reduce the
common causes of variation. Simple statistical tools can be used to help control
processes and eliminate mass inspection as the principal activity in quality control. Inspection should be used as an information-gathering tool for improvement, not as a means of "assuring" quality or blaming workers.

POINT 4: STOP MAKING DECISIONS PURELY ON THE BASIS OF COST

Purchasing departments have long been driven by cost minimization without
regard for quality. In 1931 Walter Shewhart noted that price has no meaning
without quality.[8] Yet, by tradition, the purchasing manager's performance is
evaluated by cost. What is the true cost of purchasing substandard materials?
The direct costs of poor quality materials that arise during production or during
warranty periods, as well as the loss of customer goodwill, can far exceed the
cost "savings" perceived by purchasing. Purchasing must understand its role as
a supplier to production. This relationship causes individuals to rethink the
meaning of an "organizational boundary." It is not simply the four walls around
the production floor. The supplier and manufacturer must be considered as a
"macro organization."

Deming urged businesses to establish long-term relationships with a few suppliers, leading to loyalty and opportunities for mutual improvement. Management has long justified multiple suppliers for reasons such as providing
protection against strikes or natural disasters but has ignored "hidden" costs
such as increased travel to visit suppliers, loss of volume discounts, increased
setup charges resulting in higher unit costs, and increased inventory and administrative expense. Most importantly, constantly changing suppliers solely on the
basis of price increases the variation in the material supplied to production, since
each supplier's process is different.

In contrast, a reduced supply base decreases the variation coming into the
process, thus reducing scrap, rework, and the need for adjustment to accommodate this variation. A long-term relationship strengthens the supplier–customer bond, allows the supplier to produce in greater quantity, improves

communication with the customer, and therefore enhances opportunities for process improvement. Suppliers know only quality goods are acceptable if they want to maintain a long-term relationship. Statistical methods provide a common language for communication within that relationship.

POINT 5: IMPROVE CONSTANTLY AND FOREVER

Quality improvement will be discussed extensively in Chapter 9. Traditionally, Western management has viewed improvement in the context of large, expensive innovations such as robotics and computer-integrated manufacturing. Yet the success of Japanese manufacturers is due primarily to continuous incremental improvements. In Japan, improvement is a way of life.

Improvements are necessary in both design and production. Improved design comes from understanding customer needs and continual market surveys and other sources of feedback, and from understanding the manufacturing process and developing manufacturable designs. Improved production is achieved by reducing the causes of variation and establishing stable, predictable processes. Statistical methods provide a tool for improvement, which goes beyond production and includes transportation, engineering, maintenance, sales, service, and administration. When quality improves, productivity improves and costs decrease.

Improvement means reducing variation by eliminating special causes and reducing the effects of common causes. As the Red Bead and Funnel experiments demonstrate, confusion about special and common causes of variation leads to frustration for both managers and workers. Management blames workers for problems beyond worker control—the common causes. Workers who may be trying their best don't understand why they cannot do a better job. Eliminating special causes of variation permits a more stable and predictable process. Using statistical methods, workers can identify special causes when they occur and take corrective action, which is their responsibility; however, common causes of variation are due to the system that management designs. Deming estimated that 85–95 percent of variation results from the system. Statistical methods can be used by managers to understand common causes and lead to their reduction.

POINT 6: INSTITUTE TRAINING

For continuous improvement, employees—both management and workers—require the proper tools and knowledge. People are an organization's most valuable resource; they want to do a good job, but they often do not know how. Management must take responsibility for helping them. Deming noted that in Japan, entry-level managers spend 4 to 12 years on the factory floor and in other activities to learn the aspects of production. All employees should be trained in statistical tools for quality problem solving. Not only does training result in improvements in quality and productivity, but it adds to worker morale, and demonstrates to workers that the company is dedicated to helping them and investing in their future. In addition, training reduces barriers between workers and supervisors, giving both more incentive to improve further. For example, at Honda of America in Marysville, Ohio, all employees start out on the production floor, regardless of their job classification.

POINT 7: INSTITUTE LEADERSHIP

The job of management is leadership, not supervision. Supervision is simply overseeing and directing work; leadership means providing guidance to help employees do their jobs better with less effort. In many companies, supervisors know little about the job itself because the position is often used as an entry-level job for college graduates. The supervisors have never worked in the department and cannot train the workers, so their principal responsibility is to get the product out the door.

Supervision should provide the link between management and the workforce. Good supervisors are not police or paper-pushers, but rather coaches, helping workers to do a better job and develop their skills. Leadership can help to eliminate the element of fear from the job and encourage teamwork.

POINT 8: DRIVE OUT FEAR

Driving out fear underlies many of Deming's 14 Points. Fear is manifested in many ways: fear of reprisal, fear of failure, fear of the unknown, fear of relinquishing control, and fear of change. No system can work without the mutual respect of managers and workers. Workers are often afraid to report quality problems because they might not meet their quotas, their incentive pay might be reduced, or they might be blamed for problems in the system. One of Deming's classic stories involved a foreman who would not stop production to repair a worn out piece of machinery. Stopping production would mean missing his daily quota. He said nothing, and the machine failed, causing the line to shut down for four days. Managers are also afraid to cooperate with other departments, because the other managers might receive higher performance ratings and bonuses, or because they fear takeovers or reorganizations. Fear encourages short-term thinking.

Managers fear losing power. One example is presented by Bushe.[9] After a statistical quality control program was implemented in an automotive plant, worker groups were sometimes able to offer better advice about system improvements than the corporate engineering staff, which ran counter to the plant's well-established culture. Middle managers were no longer the "experts." Their fear diminished their support for the program, which was eventually eliminated.

POINT 9: OPTIMIZE THE EFFORTS OF TEAMS

Teamwork helps to break down barriers between departments and individuals. Barriers between functional areas occur when managers fear they might lose power. Internal competition for raises and performance ratings contributes to building barriers. The lack of cooperation leads to poor quality because other departments cannot understand what their "customers" want and do not get what they need from their "suppliers." In Japan, companies emphasize that the next department or individual in the production process is actually the customer, and train their workers to manage such customer relationships.

Perhaps the biggest barrier to team efforts in the United States results from issues between union and management. With some notable exceptions, the history of management-labor relations in U.S. firms has been largely adversarial. Lack of sensitivity to worker needs, exploitation of workers, and poor management practices and policies have frequently resulted in strained relations between managers and their subordinates. Labor leaders also must bear their share of the blame. They have resisted many management efforts to reduce rigid, rule-based tasks, preferring to adhere to the structured approaches rooted in Frederick W. Taylor's historical principles of scientific management.[10]

An example of how adversarial relations can affect labor and management in the workplace is presented in Table 3.2, which shows actual comments of hourly

TABLE 3.2 Perceived Labor versus Management Attitudes	
Hourly Employee Perceptions (related to company and management) ⟶ ⟵	**Management Perceptions** (related to hourly employees)
Unionization	Labor agreement
Grievance procedures	Excuse makers
Job duties and assignments	Untrustworthy
Poor basic skill development	Ignorant
Poor training	Lazy
Poor working conditions	Step-children
Low morale	No team players
Untrained leadership	No goals
Suspicious (of management)	"Bus driver" orientation
No information (from management)	No sound basis for improvement

maintenance employees of a transit company. Both columns of descriptive adjectives were provided by hourly employees to the director of maintenance education and development. The director, who later successfully developed an employee involvement program to reverse the attitudes, confirmed that the employees' perceptions of how hourly employees regarded management and how management regarded them were generally accurate. However, the contrast between the conditions viewed by the workers and the same conditions seen through the eyes of the managers is quite revealing. For example, managers frequently thought of the workers as ignorant (unable to learn) or lazy, while the workers merely viewed themselves as having poor basic skills (math, reading, etc.) and poor training. When management acknowledged the truth in the workers' perceptions and instituted courses in basic skill development, job-related skills, and participative problem solving, employee attitudes quickly became more positive.[11] This illustration shows that training and employee involvement are important means of removing such barriers. The subject of employee involvement is covered in greater detail in Chapter 11.

POINT 10: ELIMINATE EXHORTATIONS

Posters, slogans, and motivational programs calling for "Zero Defects," "Do It Right the First Time," "Improve Productivity and Quality," and so on, are directed at the wrong people. These motivational programs assume that all quality problems are due to human behavior and that workers can improve simply through motivational methods. Workers become frustrated when they cannot improve or are penalized for defects.

Motivational approaches overlook the source of many problems—the system. Common causes of variation stemming from the design of the system are management's problem, not the workers'. If anything, workers' attempts to fix problems only increase the variation. Improvement occurs by understanding the nature of special and common causes. Thus, statistical thinking and training, not slogans, are the best route to improving quality. Motivation can be better achieved from trust and leadership than from slogans and goals.

POINT 11: ELIMINATE NUMERICAL QUOTAS AND MANAGEMENT BY OBJECTIVE (M.B.O.)

Measurement has been, and often still is, used punitively. Standards and quotas are born of short-term perspectives and create fear. They do not encourage improvement, particularly if rewards or performance appraisals are tied to meeting quotas. Workers may short-cut quality to reach the goal. Once a standard is reached, little incentive remains for workers to continue production or to improve quality; they will do no more than they are asked to do.

Arbitrary management goals, such as increasing sales by 5 percent next year or decreasing costs next quarter by 10 percent, have no meaning without a method to achieve them. Deming acknowledged that goals are useful, but numerical goals set for others without incorporating a method to reach the goal generate frustration and resentment. Further, variation in the system year to year or quarter to quarter —5 percent increase or a 6 percent decrease, for example—makes comparisons meaningless. Management must understand the system and continually try to improve it, rather than focus on short-term goals.

POINT 12: REMOVE BARRIERS TO PRIDE IN WORKMANSHIP

People on the factory floor and even in management have become, in Deming's words, "a commodity." Factory workers are given monotonous tasks, provided with inferior machines, tools, or materials, told to run defective items to meet sales pressures, and report to supervisors who know nothing about the job. Salaried employees are expected to work evenings and weekends to make up for cost-cutting measures that resulted in layoffs of their colleagues. Many are given the title of "management" so that overtime need not be paid. Even employees in the quality profession are not immune.[12] An inspection technician stated, "This profession always seems to end up being called the troublemakers." A quality engineer stated, "The managers over me now give little direction, are very resistant to change, and do little to advance their people." A quality supervisor said, "Someone less qualified could perform my job . . . for less money." How can these individuals take pride in their work? Many cannot be certain they will have a job next year.

Deming believed that one of the biggest barriers to pride in workmanship is performance appraisal. Performance appraisal destroys teamwork by promoting competition for limited resources, fosters mediocrity because objectives typically are driven by numbers and what the boss wants rather than by quality, focuses on the short term and discourages risk-taking, and confounds the "people resources" with other resources. If all individuals are working within the system, then they should not be singled out of the system to be ranked. Some people have to be "below average," which can only result in frustration if those individuals are working within the confines of the system. Deming sorted performance into three categories: the majority of performances that are within the system, performances outside the system on the superior side, and performances outside the system on the inferior side. Statistical methods provide the basis for these classifications. Superior performers should be compensated specially; inferior performers need extra training or replacement.

Although many companies will not eliminate performance appraisals completely, some have made substantial changes. The Xerox "Green Book" developed in 1983, their documentation of Leadership Through Quality (see the Quality in Practice case in Chapter 1), cites one example:

Xerox will separate performance appraisal from annual salary reviews. The primary focus of appraisal will be recognition of both the accomplishment of results and the use of the Quality Improvement Process. The current Merit Increase Planning (MIP) system requires a prescribed distribution of appraisal results, which leads to stack ranking. This makes people feel like "numbers" and leads to competition within the group. Separating pay from appraisal allows managers to evaluate individual performance more constructively and eliminates competition. Performance appraisals will be separated from annual salary reviews by a minimum of three months. In conjunction with corporate personnel, existing appraisal systems will be examined for their suitability to achieve the objective appraisals described here. Where necessary, they will be modified.[13]

POINT 13: ENCOURAGE EDUCATION AND SELF-IMPROVEMENT

The difference between this point and Point 6 is subtle. Point 6 refers to training in specific job skills; Point 13 refers to continuing, broad education for self-development. Organizations must invest in their people at all levels to ensure success in the long term. A fundamental mission of business is to provide jobs as stated in Point 1, but business and society also have the responsibility to improve the value of the individual. Developing the worth of the individual is a powerful motivation method.

POINT 14: TAKE ACTION

The transformation begins with top management and includes everyone. Applying the Deming philosophy launches a major cultural change that many firms find difficult, particularly when many of the traditional management practices Deming felt must be eliminated are deeply ingrained in the organization's culture. Ford Motor Company, for example, has embraced the Deming philosophy totally. Their experience is discussed in the Quality in Practice section later in this chapter.

In addition to the 14 Points, Deming proposed "Seven Deadly Diseases" that obstruct the quest for quality:

1. *Lack of constancy of purpose:* This "disease" is the antithesis of the first of his 14 Points. Many companies have only short-term quality programs. They do not look toward the long term, nor do they ingrain the quality philosophy into the corporate culture. As soon as the quality champion leaves or retires, the quality focus begins to crumble.

2. *Emphasis on short-term profits:* Firms seeking only to increase the quarterly dividend undermine quality. Japanese firms invest heavily in research and development, forsaking short-term profits with the goal of capturing market share five to ten years later. Short-term thinking is fed by fear of unfriendly takeovers and leveraged buy-outs.

3. *Evaluation of performance, merit rating, or annual review of performance:* Deming clearly spelled out this negative practice in his 14 Points. Such activity destroys teamwork, builds fear, and encourages defection from management. Deming called this "management by fear."

4. *Mobility of management:* Managers who continually job-hop fail to understand the companies for which they work, focus on the short term, and are unable to implement the long-term changes necessary for lasting quality improvement.

5. *Running a company on visible figures alone:* The most important figures are unknown and often unknowable, such as the effect of a satisfied customer.

6. *Excessive medical costs for employee health care that increase the final costs of goods and services:* Health care costs and the rate of absenteeism due to illness have increased at a phenomenal rate over the years. The long-term effect has been a deterioration in competitiveness.

7. *Excessive costs of warranty, fueled by lawyers who work on the basis of contingency fees:* Consider the amount of malpractice insurance that medical professionals must now pay, due to a proliferation of lawsuits and multimillion dollar judgments. The fear built into the system is driving many doctors, such as obstetricians, to abandon their practices.

Many people have criticized Deming because his philosophy is just that: a philosophy. It lacks specific direction and prescriptive approaches and does not fit into the traditional American business culture. Many behavioral scientists contend that Deming's ideas are contrary to research findings. Fueling this attitude is the almost cult-like fervor and devotion of "Deming's disciples" who believe that his is the only way to approach quality.

Deming did not propose specific methods for implementation because he wanted people to study his ideas and derive their own approaches. As he often stated, "There is no instant pudding." Despite the controversy, many firms have organized their quality approaches around Deming's philosophy. Some companies, such as 1991 Baldrige Award winner Zytec Corporation (see Quality in Practice later in the chapter) have been very successful. Chapter 13 discusses further the importance of considering other approaches to quality and adapting those that best fit a firm's individual culture.

THE JURAN PHILOSOPHY

Joseph Juran joined Western Electric in the 1920s as it pioneered in the development of statistical methods for quality. He spent much of his time as a corporate industrial engineer and, in 1951, did most of the writing, editing, and publishing of the *Quality Control Handbook.* This book, one of the most comprehensive quality manuals ever written, has been revised several times and continues to be a popular reference.

Like Deming, Juran taught quality principles to the Japanese in the 1950s and was a principal force in their quality reorganization. Juran also echoed Deming's conclusion that U.S. businesses face a major crisis in quality due to the huge costs of poor quality and the loss of sales to foreign competition. Both men felt the solution to this crisis depends on new thinking about quality that includes all levels of the managerial hierarchy. Upper management in particular requires training and experience in managing for quality.

Unlike Deming, however, Juran did not propose a major cultural change in the organization, but rather sought to improve quality by working within the system familiar to U.S. managers. Thus, his programs were designed to fit into a company's current strategic business planning with minimal risk of rejection. He argued that employees at different levels of an organization speak in their own "languages." (Deming, on the other hand, believed statistics should be the common language.) Juran stated that top management speaks in the language of dollars; workers speak in the language of things; and middle management must be able to speak both languages and translate between dollars and things. Thus, to get top management's attention, quality issues must be cast in the language they understand—dollars. Hence, Juran advocated the use of quality cost accounting and analysis to focus attention on quality problems. At the operational level, Juran focused on increasing conformance to specifications through elimination of defects, supported extensively by statistical tools for analysis. Thus, his philosophy fit well into existing management systems.

Juran defined quality as "(1) product performance that results in customer satisfaction; (2) freedom from product deficiencies, which avoids customer dissatisfaction"—simply summarized as "fitness for use." This definition can be broken down into four categories: quality of design, quality of conformance, availability, and field service. Quality of design concentrates on market research, the product concept, and design specifications. Quality of conformance includes technology, manpower, and management. Availability focuses on reliability, maintainability, and logistical support. Field service quality comprises promptness, competence, and integrity.

The pursuit of quality is viewed on two levels: (1) The mission of the firm as a whole is to achieve high product quality; and (2) the mission of each department in the firm is to achieve high production quality. Like Deming, Juran advocated a never-ending spiral of activities that includes market research, product development, design, planning for manufacture, purchasing, production process control, inspection and testing, and sales, followed by customer feedback. The interdependency of these functions emphasizes the need for competent company-wide quality management. Senior management must play an active and enthusiastic leadership role in the quality management process.

Juran's prescriptions focus on three major quality processes, called the Quality Trilogy: (1) *quality planning*—the process of preparing to meet quality goals; (2) *quality control*—the process of meeting quality goals during operations; and (3) *quality improvement*—the process of breaking through to unprecedented levels of performance.

Quality planning begins with identifying customers, both external and internal, determining their needs, and developing product features that respond to those needs. Thus, like Deming, Juran wanted employees to know who uses their products, whether in the next department or in another organization. Quality goals based on meeting the needs of customers and suppliers alike at a minimum combined cost are then established. Next, the process that can produce the product to satisfy customers' needs and meet quality goals under operating conditions must be designed. Strategic planning for quality—similar to the firm's financial planning process—determines short-term and long-term goals, sets priorities, compares results with previous plans, and meshes the plans with other corporate strategic objectives.

As a parallel to Deming's emphasis on identifying and reducing sources of variation, Juran stated that quality control involves determining what to control, establishing units of measurement to evaluate data objectively, establishing standards of performance, measuring actual performance, interpreting the difference between actual performance and the standard, and taking action on the difference.

Unlike Deming, however, Juran specified a detailed program for quality improvement. Such a program involves proving the need for improvement, identifying specific projects for improvement, organizing support for the projects, diagnosing the causes, providing remedies for the causes, proving that the remedies are effective under operating conditions, and providing control to maintain improvements. At any given point in time, hundreds or even thousands of quality improvement projects should be under way in all areas of the firm. In Chapter 9, we discuss the specifics of Juran's quality improvement approach.

Juran's assessment of most companies revealed that quality control receives top priority among the trilogy; most companies feel strong in this category. Quality planning and quality improvement, however, do not receive priority attention and are significantly weaker in most organizations. Juran felt that more effort should go into quality planning and, especially, quality improvement.

Juran supported these conclusions with several case examples in which Japanese firms using technology, materials, and processes identical to those of U.S. firms had much higher levels of quality and productivity. Beginning around 1950, upper management in Japan took responsibility for managing quality, trained employees at every level of the firm, and added quality goals to their business plans. They implemented quality improvement projects at a far greater pace than their Western counterparts, and fully involved the entire work force. As a result, in the 1970s, Japanese product quality exceeded Western quality and continues to improve at a greater pace (see Figure 3.14).

Japanese efforts at quality improvement were supported by massive training programs and top management leadership. Training in managerial quality-oriented concepts as well as training in the tools used to achieve quality improvement, cost reduction, data collection, and analysis represents important components of Juran's philosophy. Juran maintained that the Japanese experience emphasizes the significance of quality training in competitive advantage, reduced failure costs, higher productivity, smaller inventories, and better delivery performance. The Juran Institute, founded by Dr. Juran, provides substantial training in the form of seminars, videotapes, and other materials.

Many aspects of the Juran and Deming philosophies are similar. The focus on top management commitment, the need for improvement, the use of quality control techniques, and the importance of training are fundamental to both philosophies. However, they did not agree on all points. For instance, Juran believed that Deming was wrong to tell management to drive out fear. According to Juran, "Fear can bring out the best in people."[14]

FIGURE 3.14   Quality Improvements in Japan and the West

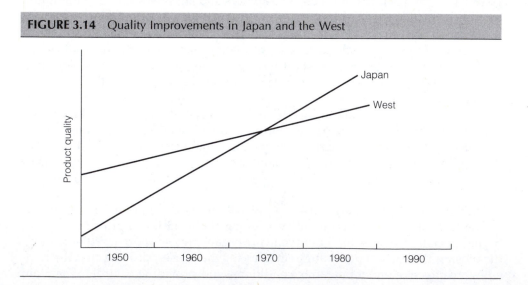

THE CROSBY PHILOSOPHY

Philip B. Crosby was corporate vice president for quality at International Telephone and Telegraph (ITT) for 14 years after working his way up from line inspector. After leaving ITT, he established Philip Crosby Associates in 1979 to develop and offer training programs. He also authored several popular books. His first book, *Quality is Free*, sold about one million copies.

The essence of Crosby's quality philosophy is embodied in what he calls the "Absolutes of Quality Management" and the "Basic Elements of Improvement." Crosby's Absolutes of Quality Management include the following points:

■ *Quality means conformance to requirements, not elegance.* Crosby quickly dispels the myth that quality follows the transcendent definition discussed in Chapter 1. Requirements must be clearly stated so that they cannot be misunderstood. Requirements act as communication devices and are ironclad. Once requirements are established, then one can take measurements to determine conformance to those requirements. The nonconformance detected is the absence of quality. Quality problems become nonconformance problems, that is, variation in output. Setting requirements is the responsibility of management.

■ *There is no such thing as a quality problem.* Problems must be identified by those individuals or departments that cause them. Thus, a firm may experience accounting problems, manufacturing problems, design problems, front-desk problems, and so on. In other words, quality originates in functional departments, not in the quality department, and therefore the burden of responsibility for such problems falls on these functional departments. The quality department should measure conformance, report results, and lead the drive to develop a positive attitude toward quality improvement. This Absolute is similar to Deming's third point.

■ *There is no such thing as the economics of quality; doing the job right the first time is always cheaper.* Crosby supports the premise that "economics of quality" has no meaning. Quality is free. What costs money are all actions that involve not doing jobs right the first time. The Deming chain reaction sends a similar message.

■ *The only performance measurement is the cost of quality, which is the expense of nonconformance.* Crosby notes that most companies spend 15 to 20 percent of their sales dollars on quality costs. A company with a well-run quality management program can achieve a cost of quality that is less than 2.5 percent of sales, primarily in the prevention and appraisal categories. Crosby's program calls for measuring and publicizing the cost of poor quality. Quality cost data are useful to call problems to management's attention, to select opportunities for corrective action, and to track quality improvement over time. Such data provide visible proof of improvement and recognition of achievement. Juran supported this approach.

■ *The only performance standard is "Zero Defects (ZD)."* Crosby feels that the Zero Defects concept is widely misunderstood and resisted. Zero Defects is not a motivational program. It is described as follows:

Zero Defects is a performance standard. It is the standard of the craftsperson regardless of his or her assignment. . . . The theme of ZD is do it right the first time. That means concentrating on preventing defects rather than just finding and fixing them.

People are conditioned to believe that error is inevitable; thus they not only accept error, they anticipate it. It does not bother us to make a few errors in our work . . . to err is human. We all have our own standards in business or academic life—our own points at which errors begin to bother us. It is good to get an A in school, but it may be OK to pass with a C.

We do not maintain these standards, however, when it comes to our personal life. If we did, we should expect to be shortchanged every now and then when we cash our paycheck; we should expect hospital nurses to drop a constant percentage of newborn babies. . . . We as individuals do not tolerate these things. We have a dual standard: one for ourselves and one for our work.

Most human error is caused by lack of attention rather than lack of knowledge. Lack of attention is created when we assume that error is inevitable. If we consider this condition carefully, and pledge ourselves to make a constant conscious effort to do our jobs right the first time, we will take a giant step toward eliminating the waste of rework, scrap, and repair that increases cost and reduces individual opportunity.[15]

Juran and Deming, on the other hand, would point out the uselessness, or even hypocrisy of exhorting a line worker to produce perfection since the overwhelming majority of imperfections stem from poorly designed manufacturing systems beyond the workers' control.

Crosby's Basic Elements of Improvement include determination, education, and implementation. Determination means that top management must take quality improvement seriously. Everyone should understand the Absolutes, which can be accomplished only through education. Finally, every member of the management team must understand the implementation process.

Unlike Juran and Deming, Crosby's program is primarily behavioral. He emphasizes using management and organizational processes rather than statistical techniques to change corporate culture and attitudes. Like Juran and unlike Deming, his approach fits well within existing organizational structures.

Crosby's approach, however, provides relatively few details about how firms should address the finer points of quality management. It focuses on managerial thinking rather than on organizational systems. By allowing managers to determine the best methods to apply in their own firm's situations, his approach tends to avoid some of the implementation problems experienced by firms that have adopted the Deming philosophy.

Crosby's philosophy has not earned the respect of his rivals.[16] Even though they agree that he is an entertaining speaker and a great motivator, they say his approach lacks substance in the methods of achieving quality improvement. Nevertheless, hundreds of thousands have taken his courses in-house or at his Quality College in Winter Park, Florida.

OTHER QUALITY PHILOSOPHERS

A. V. Feigenbaum and Kaoru Ishikawa were both awarded the title of Honorary Members of the American Society for Quality Control in 1986.[17] At that time the society had only four living honorary members, two of whom were W. Edwards Deming and Joseph M. Juran. Obviously, the title of "Honorary Member" is not given lightly by the ASQC, and therefore validates the premise that Feigenbaum and Ishikawa are among the world-class leaders of the quality movement. In this section we briefly review the accomplishments that have made them part of this elite group.

■ A. V. Feigenbaum

A. V. Feigenbaum's career in quality began more than 40 years ago. For 10 years, he was the manager of worldwide manufacturing and quality control at General Electric. In 1968 he founded General Systems Company of Pittsfield, Massachusetts, and serves as president. Feigenbaum has traveled and spoken to various audiences and groups around the world over the years. He was elected as the founding chairman of the board of the International Academy of Quality, which has attracted active participation from the European Organization for Quality Control, the Union of Japanese Scientists and Engineers (JUSE), as well as the American Society for Quality Control.

Feigenbaum is best known for coining the phrase *total quality control* in the United States. His book *Total Quality Control* was first published in 1951 under the title *Quality Control: Principles, Practice, and Administration.* He viewed quality as a strategic business tool that requires involvement from everyone in the organization, and promoted the use of quality costs as a measurement and evaluation tool. Feigenbaum's philosophy is summarized in his Three Steps to Quality:

1. *Quality Leadership:* A continuous management emphasis is grounded on sound planning rather than reaction to failures. Management must maintain a constant focus and lead the quality effort.
2. *Modern Quality Technology:* The traditional quality department cannot resolve 80 to 90 percent of quality problems. This task requires the integration of office staff as well as engineers and shopfloor workers in the process who continually evaluate and implement new techniques to satisfy customers in the future.
3. *Organizational Commitment:* Continuous training and motivation of the entire workforce as well as an integration of quality in business planning indicate the importance of quality and provide the means for including it in all aspects of the firm's activities.

The Japanese latched on to this concept of total quality control as the foundation for their practice called Company-Wide Quality Control (CWQC), which began in the 1960s. Feigenbaum's ideas also have become important elements of the Malcolm Baldrige National Quality Award Criteria.

■ Kaoru Ishikawa

An early pioneer in the quality revolution in Japan, Kaoru Ishikawa was the foremost figure in Japanese quality until his death in 1989. Without his leadership, the Japanese quality movement would not enjoy the worldwide acclaim and success that it has today. Dr. Ishikawa was a professor of engineering at Tokyo University for many years. Ishikawa was instrumental in the development of the broad outlines of Japanese quality strategy, the concept of CWQC, the audit process used for determining whether a company will be selected to receive the Deming Award, team-based problem solving, and a variety of problem-solving tools that he thought any worker could use.

As a member of the editorial review board for the Japanese journal *Quality Control for Foremen,* founded in 1962, and later as the chief executive director of the QC Circle Headquarters at the Union of Japanese Scientists and Engineers (JUSE), Dr. Ishikawa influenced the development of a participative, bottom-up view of quality, which became the trademark of the Japanese approach to quality management. However, Ishikawa was also able to get the attention of top management and persuade them that a companywide approach to quality control was necessary for total success.

Some key elements of his philosophy are summarized here.

1. Quality begins with education and ends with education.

2. The first step in quality is to know the requirements of customers.

3. The ideal state of quality control occurs when inspection is no longer necessary.

4. Remove the root cause, not the symptoms.

5. Quality control is the responsibility of all workers and all divisions.

6. Do not confuse the means with the objectives.

7. Put quality first and set your sights on long-term profits.

8. Marketing is the entrance and exit of quality.

9. Top management must not show anger when facts are presented by subordinates.

10. Ninety-five percent of problems in a company can be solved with simple tools for analysis and problem solving.

11. Data without dispersion information (i.e., variability) is false data.

COMPARISONS OF QUALITY PHILOSOPHIES

Even though Deming, Juran, and Crosby all view quality as imperative in the future competitiveness of Western industry, they have significantly different approaches to implementing organizational change. In each philosophy, quality clearly requires a total commitment from everyone in an organization. Any organizational activity can be viewed in one of three ways, depending on the intensity of commitment to the activity:

1. Function: a task or group of tasks to be performed that contribute to the mission or purpose of an organization.

2. Process: a set of steps, procedures, or policies that define how a function is to be performed and what results are expected.

3. Ideology: a set of values or beliefs that guide an organization in the establishment of its mission, processes, and functions.

Many managers view quality as a set of tasks to be performed by specialists in quality control. Other managers have a broader perspective and see quality as a process in which many people at the operating level from a number of functional areas of the organization are involved. Still other managers take the broadest viewpoint in which quality is an ideology or philosophy that pervades the entire organization: Everyone must believe in it and support it.

In spite of the differences in their perspectives, the philosophies of Deming, Juran, and Crosby are more alike than different. Each views top management commitment as an absolute necessity; demonstrates that quality management practices will save, not cost money; places responsibility for quality on management, not the workers; stresses the need for continuous, never-ending improvement; acknowledges the importance of the customer and strong management–worker partnerships; and recognizes the need for and difficulties associated with changing the organizational culture.

The individual nature of business firms complicates the strict application of one specific philosophy as advocated by Deming, Juran, or Crosby. Although each of these philosophies can be highly effective, a firm must first understand the nature and differences of the philosophies and then develop a quality management approach that is tailored to its individual organization. Any approach should include goals and objectives, allocation of responsibilities, a measurement system and description of tools to be employed, an outline of the management style that will be used, and a strategy for implementation. After taking these steps, the management team is responsible for leading the organization through successful execution.

QUALITY IN PRACTICE   FORD BECOMES A "DEMING COMPANY"

Ford Motor Company has been one of the leaders in adopting the Deming philosophy. Dr. Deming came to Ford in 1981 to meet with President Donald Petersen and other company officials, who were stimulated by NBC's program "If Japan Can, Why Can't We?" Actually, or so the story goes, Deming was first approached by one of Ford's vice presidents. Deming's response was that he would not come unless invited by the CEO as an indication of top management commitment.

Deming began by giving seminars for top executives and meeting with various employees, suggesting changes corresponding to his 14 Points. Ford managers visited Nashua Corporation to learn how statistical methods were used. Chief executives from many of Ford's major suppliers visited Japan. Petersen himself took a course on statistical methods. The 14 Points became the basis for a transformation of Ford's philosophy. Management commitment is evident in statements found in various annual reports:

Last year [1982] we pledged our efforts to continuous improvement. . . . We renew that pledge. In product, this means unqualified commitment to customer-response excellence worldwide . . . we made quality our No. 1 objective several years ago. We have achieved steady and substantial quality improvement in the United States, where Ford now leads its major domestic competition. . . . Ford's quality goals also include leadership in customer service. . . . Our key to continued success in the quest for product quality is establishing an effective long-term relationship with our suppliers. . . . Ford is involving suppliers far earlier in the design process. . . . This helps reduce engineering and production costs and ensures uninterrupted improvement in quality. Ford has instituted a system that makes quality considerations a critical factor in every supplier-selection decision and establishes formal quality ratings for every supplier. The Q1 Preferred Quality Award recognizes suppliers who achieve and maintain a consistently high level of quality and prove their commitment to continuing improvement. (Ford Motor Company 1983 Annual Report)

Company Mission, Values, and Guiding Principles

MISSION
Ford Motor Company is a worldwide leader in automotive and automotive-related products and services as well as in newer industries such as aerospace, communications, and financial services. Our mission is to improve continually our products and services to meet our customers' needs, allowing us to prosper as a business and to provide a reasonable return for our stockholders, the owners of our business.

VALUES
How we accomplish our mission is as important as the mission itself. Fundamental to success for the company are these basic values:
- *People.* Our people are the source of our strength. They provide our corporate intelligence and determine our reputation and vitality. Involvement and teamwork are our core human values.

■ *Products*. Our products are the end result of our efforts, and they should be the best in serving customers worldwide. As our products are viewed, so are we viewed.

■ *Profits*. Profits are the ultimate measure of how efficiently we provide customers with the best products for their needs. Profits are required to survive and grow.

GUIDING PRINCIPLES

■ *Quality comes first.* To achieve customer satisfaction, the quality of our products and services must be our number one priority.

■ *Customers are the focus of everything we do.* Our work must be done with customers in mind, providing better products and services than our competition.

■ *Continuous improvement is essential to our success.* We must strive for excellence in everything we do; in our products, in their safety and value—and in our services, our human relations, our competitiveness and our profitability.

■ *Employee involvement is our way of life.* We are a team. We must treat each other with trust and respect.

■ *Dealers and suppliers are our partners.* The Company must maintain mutually beneficial relationships with dealers, suppliers, and our other business associates.

■ *Integrity is never compromised.* The conduct of our Company worldwide must be pursued in a manner that is socially responsible and commands respect for its integrity and for its positive contributions to society. Our doors are open to men and women alike without discrimination and without regard to ethnic origin or personal beliefs. (Ford Motor Company 1984 Annual Report)

After the industry-wide crisis at the turn of the decade, Ford embarked on an intensive quality improvement process. Results have been dramatic. Customer research shows that the quality of our 1986 cars and trucks is more than 50 percent better than that of our 1980 models. . . . We have explored new approaches to accelerate the rate of improvement. This led us to focus on strategic issues related to our quality effort. The strategy that evolved was to concentrate on developing and implementing fundamental changes in the overall quality/customer satisfaction process. . . . Quality includes every aspect of the vehicle that determines customer satisfaction and provides fundamental value. This means how well the

vehicle is made, how well it performs, how well it lasts, and how well the customer is treated by both the Company and the dealer. There will be no compromise in our quest for quality. (Ford Motor Company 1985 Annual Report)

Ford's 1987 earnings were the highest for any company in automotive history, despite a seven percent drop in U.S. car and truck industry sales, higher capital spending, and increased marketing costs. (Ford Motor Company 1987 Annual Report)

Ford has developed a policy of Total Quality Excellence that emphasizes the importance of quality in every action, operation, and product associated with Ford Motor Company. The fundamental precepts of this policy are:

■ Quality is defined by the customer; the customer wants products and services that, throughout their life, meet his or her needs and expectations at a cost that represents value.

■ Quality excellence can best be achieved by preventing problems rather than by detecting and correcting them after they occur.

■ All work that is done by Company employees, suppliers, and dealers is part of a process that creates a product or service for a customer. Each person can influence some part of that process and, therefore, affects the quality of its output and the ultimate customer's satisfaction with our products and services.

■ Sustained quality excellence requires continuous process improvement. This means, regardless of how good present performance may be, it can become even better.

■ People provide the intelligence and generate the actions that are necessary to realize these improvements.

■ Each employee is a customer for work done by other employees or suppliers, with a right to expect good work from others and an obligation to contribute work of high caliber to those who, in turn, are his or her customers.

The goal of Ford Total Quality Excellence is to achieve superior external and internal customer satisfaction levels. Each employee's commitment to the precepts of Ford Total Quality Excellence and management's further commitment to implementation of supporting managerial and operating systems is essential to realizing that goal.

Donald Petersen has stated:

The work of Dr. Deming has definitely helped change Ford's corporate leadership. It is management's responsibility to create the environment in which everyone can contribute to continuous improvement in processes and systems. We're making good progress along these lines with employee involvement and participative management. Real gains of the new management system are shared with employees through job security, recognition of contribution, and compensation.

While employees have benefited, so has the company and our customers. For example, we are running well over 60 percent better levels of quality in our products today. I dare say we would not have predicted that much improvement in that short a time. Dr. Deming has influenced my thinking in a variety of ways. What stands out is that he helped me crystal-lize my ideas concerning the value of teamwork, process improvement and the pervasive power of the concept of continuous improvement.[18]

Key Issues for Discussion

1. Discuss specific themes in the Deming philosophy that are evident in statements made in Ford's annual reports.

2. Which definition of quality (see Chapter 1) is used in the 1985 Annual Report? Which of Garvin's eight dimensions of quality are stressed?

3. Review recent Ford annual reports and summarize their quality efforts. What changes, if any, are evident?

QUALITY IN PRACTICE   ZYTEC CORPORATION[19]

Zytec Corporation designs and manufactures electronic power supplies and repairs power supplies and CRT monitors. Most of its customers are large multinational companies, and Zytec competes for business with Far East and European companies as well as approximately 400 U.S. companies. Founded in 1984, Zytec is the fastest growing U.S. electronic power supply company, and the largest power supply repair company in North America. In 1991, Zytec won the Malcolm Baldrige National Quality Award.

Since its start, Zytec has used quality and reliability of its products and services as the key strategy to differentiate itself from its competition. The company's view of quality is simply stated in its mission statement:

Zytec is a company that competes on value, provides technical excellence in its products and services, and believes in the importance of execution. We believe in a simple form and lean staff, the importance of people as individuals, and the development of productive employees through training and capital investment. We focus on what we know best, thereby making a fair profit on current operations to meet our obligations and perpetuate our continued growth.

To carry out its mission, Zytec's senior executives embraced Dr. Deming's 14 Points as the cornerstone of the company's quality improvement culture. They established the Deming Steering Committee to guide the Deming process and champion individual Deming Points. To demonstrate their commitment, senior management acted as advisors to the three Deming Implementation Teams. All Zytec employees attended meetings to increase their knowledge of Deming's Points. Many employees also attended Deming seminars. From long-range strategic planning and employee empowerment to leadership, Deming's 14 Points guide Zytec's actions.

In the Deming approach, data supply the basis for setting goals and developing plans for quality leadership. Zytec collects data by soliciting customer feedback, conducting market research, and studying its customers, suppliers, competitors, and industry leaders. Cross-functional teams use the data to formulate long-range strategic planning goals. Departmental planning teams then develop detailed action plans to implement these goals.

The strategic plan, along with Deming's 14 Points, guides human resource planning. For example, Point 7 demands that companies institute leadership. Zytec's long-range strategic plan includes the implementation of "self-managed work groups in which employees make most day-to-day decisions while management focuses on coaching and process improvement." A long-range strategic objective that derives from this plan is "Managers will be trained to become better coaches/facilitators." A short-range human resources objective is "Managers will become facilitators of self-managed work groups."

Employees in these self-managed work groups, in cross-functional teams, and as individuals are granted broad authority to achieve their team and personal goals. For example, any employee can spend up to $1000 to resolve a customer complaint without prior authority; hourly workers can make process changes with the agreement of only one other person; and sales people are authorized to travel whenever necessary to improve customer service.

Zytec provides extensive quality-oriented training to employees as well as opportunities for them to grow and participate. In turn, employee participation contributes to continuous improvement. As of February 1991, the average employee had received 72 hours of internal quality-related training. New skills are reinforced by giving employees the opportunity and authority to use them. Ongoing assistance is available through in-line trainers in each production line, the training department, and managers at all levels and in all departments.

Zytec views all employees as customer-contact personnel. In 1990, more than half of its employees had direct customer contact. All employees, therefore,

receive customer relationship training. Sales representatives and account managers participate in specialized training. Zytec improves its role in customer relationships by listening to and surveying customers, and comparing its sales/service practices against eleven world-class organizations. Complaints are formally monitored, measured, and resolved through Zytec's Customer Action Request process, which then determines the root causes of complaints and improves the processes by eliminating the cause.

As Zytec's employees experience the results of training, involvement, and empowerment, Dr. Deming's 14 Points become more than vague guidelines. Each year—beginning in 1984—Zytec surveys its employees to gauge how effectively the company implements Deming's Points. Figure 3.15 shows how employee's perception scores improved through 1990.

Zytec sets three principal quality goals for its suppliers: (1) 3.4 defectives per million opportunities, (2) 96 percent on-time delivery to the day, and (3) a 25-day lead time. These requirements are underscored in all communications with suppliers and supported by technical assistance and training. Zytec commits itself to open communication and development of true partnerships with its suppliers

FIGURE 3.15 Results of Employee Deming 14 Points Implementation Surveys

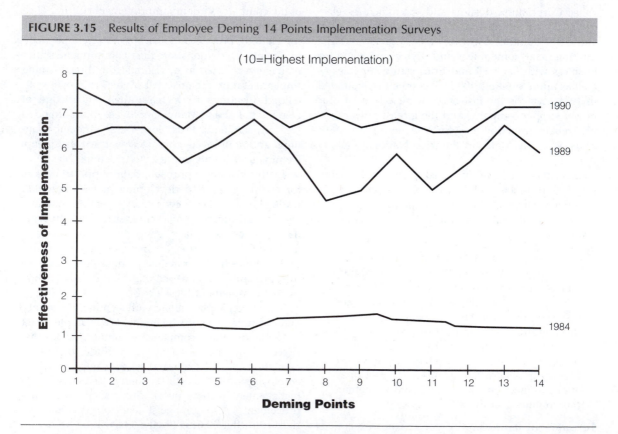

and often involves them in the early stages of a development program to benefit from their knowledge.

The results of Zytec's attention to Deming's philosophy are impressive. Product quality improved from 99 percent in 1988 to 99.7 percent in 1990. Product reliability—measured as mean time between failures in hours—improved by a magnitude of 10 in just five years and ranks among the world's leaders. In a two-year period, warranty costs fell 48 percent, repair cycle time was reduced 31 percent, product costs were cut 30 to 40 percent, internal yields improved 51 percent, manufacturing cycle time fell 26 percent, and scrap rate was cut in half. In an independent survey of power supply manufacturers, Zytec ranked number one against its competitors and exceeded the industry average in 21 of 22 attributes deemed important to its customers.

Key Issues for Discussion

1. Explain how Zytec has adopted Deming's view of a production system as introduced in Chapter 2.

2. From the limited information presented in this Quality in Practice case, describe which of Deming's 14 Points are addressed by Zytec, and how the company supports the underlying philosophy of that Point.

SUMMARY OF KEY POINTS

■ W. Edwards Deming, Joseph Juran, and Philip Crosby are recognized as the top three international leaders of modern quality thinking. A. V. Feigenbaum and Kaoru Ishikawa have also made significant contributions to quality leadership.

■ Deming's philosophy is based on improving products and services by reducing uncertainty and variation. Systems thinking, statistical understanding of variation, the theory of knowledge, and psychology are the foundation of his philosophy. He advocates a radical cultural change in organizations, which is embodied in his 14 Points.

■ The Deming chain reaction states that quality improvement reduces cost, increases productivity, increases market share, and allows firms to stay in business and provide jobs.

■ Two sources of variation occur in production processes: variation that is present as a natural part of the process (common causes), and variation that arises from external sources (special causes). Common causes are the responsibility of management and generally account for 85 to 95 percent of the total variation. Special causes can be identified and corrected by the workforce.

■ The Red Bead and Funnel Experiments illustrate the dangers of misunderstanding variation in a system and the poor decisions that may result.

■ Joseph Juran's philosophy seeks to provide change within the current American management system. Quality is defined as fitness for use. The Quality Trilogy—planning, control, and improvement—provides a direction for quality assurance in organizations.

■ Philip Crosby's approach to quality is summarized in his Absolutes of Quality Management. He places more emphasis on behavioral change rather than on the use of statistical techniques as advocated by Deming and Juran.

■ A. V. Feigenbaum views quality as a strategic business tool and coined the phrase "total quality control." He promoted the importance of shifting quality responsibility to everyone in an organization and developing cost of quality approaches.

■ Kaoru Ishikawa was instrumental in the Japanese quality movement, particularly in advocating a companywide quality control approach, the use of employee teams, and the use of problem-solving tools for quality improvement.

■ Managers need to understand the differences and similarities in the leading quality philosophies and develop a quality management approach tailored to their organizations.

REVIEW QUESTIONS

1. Explain the Deming Chain Reaction. Can you point to any examples of companies you have read about in business periodicals for which this theory appears to hold?

2. Summarize the four components of Profound Knowledge. How do they mutually support each other?

3. Explain the difference between common and special causes of variation.

4. Explain the two fundamental mistakes that managers make when attempting to improve a process. Can you cite any examples in your personal experience in which such mistakes were made?

5. How does Taguchi's approach to measuring variation support the Deming philosophy?

6. Explain the Theory of Knowledge. What implications might this have for Wall Street analysts who react to quarterly earnings reports?

7. Discuss the lessons of the Red Bead and Funnel Experiments. Can you cite any examples in your experience where someone acted counter to these lessons?

8. Explain the interrelationships among Deming's 14 Points. How do they support each other? Why must they be viewed as a whole rather than separately?

9. The following themes form the basis for Deming's philosophy. Classify the 14 Points into these categories and discuss the commonalties within each category.

    a. Organizational purpose and mission

    b. Quantitative goals

    c. Revolution of management philosophy

    d. Elimination of seat-of-the-pants decisions

    e. Cooperation building

    f. Improvement of manager-worker relations

10. What are Deming's Deadly Diseases? How do they relate to the 14 Points?

11. Explain Juran's Quality Trilogy.

12. How is Juran's philosophy similar or different from Deming's?

13. What are Crosby's Absolutes of Quality Management and Basic Elements of Improvement? How are they similar or different from Deming's 14 Points?

14. What were the contributions of A. V. Feigenbaum and Kaoru Ishikawa?

DISCUSSION QUESTIONS

1. How does Deming's definition of quality compare with the definitions discussed in Chapter 1?

2. Think of a system with which you are familiar, such as your college, fraternity, or a student organization. What is the purpose of that system? What would it mean to *optimize* that system?

3. List some examples of variation that you observe in your daily life. How might they be reduced?

4. How might the Red Bead Experiment be used to understand and improve education?

5. The following represent examples of tampering with a stable process as Deming illustrates with the Funnel Experiment. Which funnel adjustment rule (2, 3, or 4) does each example represent?

   a. Adjust the process when a piece goes out of specification

   b. Match the color to the last batch

   c. Trade barriers

   d. Musicians' instruments tune sequentially, not against the same source

   e. Adjustments by the Federal Reserve Board

   f. Gambler increases a bet to cover losses

   g. Reaction to stock market news

   h. Hanging wallpaper

6. Suggest ways that management can recognize the existence of fear in an organization. What strategies might managers use to deal with and eliminate fear?

7. Which of Deming's 14 Points do you think are most controversial to current managers in the United States? Why?

8. Discuss how Deming's 14 Points can apply to an academic environment. How can learning and classroom performance be improved by applying Deming's philosophy?

9. In a videotape made in 1993, Deming related a story of a woman executive who spent an entire day flying from city to city, changing planes several times, because her company's travel department received a cheaper fare than if she had taken a direct flight. How does this example violate the concepts of Profound Knowledge and the 14 Points, and what should the company do about it?

10. The original version of Deming's 14 Points (developed in the early 1980s) is given in Table 3.3. Contrast each of these with the revised version in Table 3.1 early in the chapter. Explain the implications of the changes. Why might Deming have made these changes?

11. Considering the international outlook and contributions of Feigenbaum and Ishikawa, would you say that any firm today could have an effective quality process if they ignored the international changes occurring in the quality arena? Why or why not?

12. Study the annual reports of some major companies issued over a period of several years. Using liberal quotations, discuss the role of quality in these companies. How have their perspectives on quality changed over the years? Do you see evidence of implementation of the quality philosophies discussed in this chapter?

13. Design a questionnaire or survey instrument to determine the degree to which an organization is ''Demingized''? Explain how you developed the questions.

TABLE 3.3   Original Version of Deming's 14 Points

1. Create constancy of purpose toward improvement of product and service, with the aim of becoming competitive and to stay in business and to provide jobs.
2. Adopt the new philosophy. We are in a new economic age. Western management must awaken to the challenge, must learn their responsibilities, and take on leadership for change.
3. Cease dependence on inspection to achieve quality. Eliminate the need for inspection on a mass basis by building quality into the product in the first place.
4. End the practice of awarding business on the basis of price tag alone. Instead, minimize total cost. Move toward a single supplier for any one item, on a long-term relationship of loyalty and trust.
5. Improve constantly and forever the system of production and service to improve quality and productivity, and thus constantly decrease costs.
6. Institute training on the job.
7. Institute leadership. The aim of supervision should be to help people and machines and gadgets do a better job. Supervision of management is in need of overhaul, as well as the supervision of production workers.
8. Drive out fear so everyone can work effectively for the company.
9. Break down barriers between departments. People in research, design, sales, and production must work as a team, to foresee problems of production and those that may be encountered with the product or service.
10. Eliminate slogans, exhortations, and targets for the work force that ask for zero defects or new levels of productivity. Such exhortations only create adversarial relationships, as the bulk of the causes of low quality and low productivity belong to the system and thus lie beyond the power of the work force.
11a. Eliminate work standards (quotas) on the factory floor. Substitute leadership.
11b. Eliminate management by objective. Eliminate management by numbers, numerical goals. Substitute leadership.
12a. Remove barriers that rob hourly workers of their right to pride of workmanship. The responsibility of supervisors must be changed from sheer numbers to quality.
12b. Remove barriers that rob people in management and engineering of their right to pride in workmanship. This means, *inter alia,* abolishment of the annual or merit rating and of management by objective.
13. Institute a vigorous program of education and self-improvement.
14. Put everybody in the company to work to accomplish the transformation. The transformation is everybody's job.

CASES

I. The Disciplinary Citation

A local delivery service has 40 drivers who deliver packages throughout the metropolitan area. Occasionally, drivers make mistakes, such as entering the wrong package number on a shipping document, failing to get a signature, and so on. A total of 240 mistakes were made in one year as shown in Table 3.4. The manager in charge of this operation has is-sued a disciplinary citation to drivers for each mistake.

Discussion Questions

1. What is your opinion of the manager's approach? How does it compare with the Deming philosophy?

TABLE 3.4

Driver No.	1	2	3	4	5	6	7	8	9	10	11	12	13	14
Mistakes	6	1	0	14	0	2	18	2	5	13	1	4	6	5
Driver No.	15	16	17	18	19	20	21	22	23	24	25	26	27	28
Mistakes	0	0	1	3	15	24	3	4	1	2	3	22	4	8
Driver No.	29	30	31	32	33	34	35	36	37	38	39	40		
Mistakes	2	6	8	0	9	20	9	0	3	14	1	1		

2. How might the analysis of these data help the manager to understand the variation in the system? Do you think that all variation stems from common causes? If not, why not? How can the data help the manager to improve the performance of this system or be used to reward good performance?

II. Value Pricing at Procter & Gamble[20]

"Consumers won't pay for a company's inefficiency." Thus, Edwin L. Artzt, chairman of Procter & Gamble, one of the world's leading consumer products companies, leads P&G's crusade to reduce product prices and give consumers better value. "Value pricing" is a controversial policy that, contrary to some reports, is not a short-term reaction to competitive pressures, but a fundamental change in long-term strategy. The concept of value pricing is to price products at a reasonable "everyday low price" rate, somewhere between the normal retail price and sale prices that are frequently offered. P&G learned through consumer research that up-and-down pricing policies were eroding the brands' perceived value. In other words, consumers began to think that P&G's brands were only worth their discount prices. When P&G discounted products, consumers stocked up and then substituted competitors' products when P&G's products were not on sale.

But the reasons for the switch to value pricing go deeper than consumer perceptions. Within the company, the frequent promotions sent costs spiraling. At one point, the company made 55 daily price changes on some 80 brands, which necessitated rework on every third order. Often, special packaging and handling were required. Ordering peaked during the promotions as distributors stockpiled huge quantities of goods (known as forward buying), which resulted in excessive overtime in the factories followed by periods of underutilization. Plants ran at 55 to 60 percent of rated efficiency with huge swings in output. These fluctuations strained the distribution system as well, loading up warehouses during slow periods and overworking the transportation systems during peak times.

With value pricing, demand rates are much smoother. Retailers automatically order products as they sell them. When 100 cases of Cheer detergent leave a retailer's warehouse, a computer orders 100 more. Both P&G and retailers save money. Plant efficiency rates have increased to over 80 percent across the company at the same time North American inventories dropped 10 percent, an improvement that the company expects to double in one year. One grocery store chain saved $500,000 by ordering toilet paper, tissues, and towels in this fashion; another experienced a 10 percent increase in sales of Pampers and Luvs diapers because the ordering system kept its shelves fully stocked.

Discussion Questions

1. Describe the chain of events in the logistics system (suppliers, manufacturing, warehousing, distribution, and retailing) under the old, highly variable pricing structure. Draw a diagram to show how inventory levels fluctuate when prices increase and decrease.

2. Explain Procter & Gamble's experience within the context of the Deming philosophy. Specifically, what aspects of Profound Knowledge seem to be evident in this case? Would you be surprised to learn that the company consulted with Dr. Deming extensively and sent their top managers to Deming seminars? Why or why not?

III. The Reservation Clerk[21]

Mary Matthews works for an airline as a reservation clerk. Her duties include answering the telephone, making reservations, and providing information to customers. Her supervisor told her to be courteous and not to rush callers. However, the supervisor also told her that she must answer 25 calls per hour so that the department's account manager can prepare an adequate budget. Mary comes home each day, frustrated because the computer is slow in delivering information that she needs, and sometimes reports no information. Without information from the computer, she is forced to use printed directories and guides.

Discussion Questions

1. What is Mary's job?

2. Drawing upon Deming's principles, outline a plan to improve this situation.

■ NOTES

1. John Hillkirk, "World-famous Quality Expert Dead at 93," *USA Today*, 21 December, 1993.
2. W. Edwards Deming, *The New Economics for Industry, Government, Education* (Cambridge, MA: MIT Center for Advanced Engineering Study, 1993).
3. The quincunx simulator is contained in the *Quality Gamebox*, a registered trademark of Productivity-Quality Systems, Inc., 10468 Miamisburg–Springboro Road, Miamisburg, Ohio 45342; (513) 885–2255; (800) 777–3020. The *Quality Gamebox* software is distributed with the Instructor's Manual for this book with permission of PQ Systems.
4. April 17, 1979; cited in L.P. Sullivan, "Reducing Variability: A New Approach to Quality," *Quality Progress* 17, no. 7 (July 1984), 15–21.
5. Based on the descriptions given in Deming, see note 2.
6. Wayne F. Cascio, "Downsizing: What Do We Know? What Have We Learned?" *Academy of Management Executive* 7, no. 1 (February 1993), 95–104.
7. Edmund Faltermayer "Is This Layoff Necessary?" *Fortune*, 1 June, 1992, 71–86.
8. Walter A. Shewhart, *Economic Control of Quality of a Manufactured Product* (New York: Van Nostrand, 1931).
9. Gervase R. Bushe, "Cultural Contradictions of Statistical Process Control in American Manufacturing Organizations," *Journal of Management* 14 (May 1988), 19–31.
10. "Detroit vs. the UAW: At Odds over Teamwork," *Business Week*, 24 August, 1987, 54–55.
11. William M. Lindsay, Kent Curtis, and Ralph C. Hennie, "Houston Metropolitan Transit Authority: Where Cooperative Team Efforts Produce Measurable Results," Presentation at the IAQC Fall Conference, Orlando, FL, 1986.
12. Brad Stratton, "The Price Is Right: ASQC Annual Salary Survey," *Quality Progress* 21, no. 9 (September 1988), 24–29.
13. Xerox Quality Solutions, *A World of Quality: The Timeless Passport* (Milwaukee, WI: ASQC Quality Press, 1993), 54.
14. Jeremy Main, "Under the Spell of the Quality Gurus," *Fortune*, 18 August, 1986, 30–34.
15. Philip B. Crosby, *Quality Is Free* (New York: McGraw-Hill, 1979), 200–201.
16. Main, see note 14.
17. Facts in this section were obtained from "Profile: the ASQC Honorary Members A. V. Feigenbaum and Kaoru Ishikawa," *Quality Progress* 19, no. 8 (August 1986), 43–45; and Bruce Brocka and M. Suzanne Brocka, *Quality Management: Implementing the Best Ideas of the Masters* (Homewood, IL: Business One Irwin, 1992).
18. Donald R. Katz, "Coming Home" *Business Month*, October 1988, 58.
19. Adapted from Zytec Malcolm Baldrige National Quality Award Application Summary.
20. Facts in this case were drawn from Patricia Gallagher, "Value Pricing for Profits," *The Cincinnati Enquirer*, 21 December, 1992, D-1, D-6; "Procter & Gamble Hits Back," *Business Week*, 19 July, 1993, 20–22; and Bill Saporito, "Behind the Tumult at P&G," *Fortune*, 7 March, 1994, 75–82.
21. Based on an anecdote in W. Edwards Deming, *Out of the Crisis* (Cambridge, MA: MIT Center for Advanced Engineering Study, 1986).

■ BIBLIOGRAPHY

Brocka, Bruce, and M. Suzanne Brocka. *Quality Management: Implementing the Best Ideas of the Masters.* Homewood, IL: Business One Irwin, 1992.

Deming, W. Edwards. *The New Economics for Industry, Government, Education.* Cambridge, MA: MIT Center for Advanced Engineering Study, 1993.

————. *Out of the Crisis.* Cambridge, MA: MIT Center for Advanced Engineering Study, 1986.

Duncan, W. Jack, and Joseph G. Van Matre. "The Gospel According to Deming: Is It Really New?" *Business Ho-*

rizons, July–August 1990, 3–9.

Hunt, V. Daniel. *Managing for Quality.* Homewood, IL: Business One Irwin, 1993.

Juran, J. M. *Juran on Quality by Design.* New York: The Free Press, 1992.

_____ . ''Product Quality—A Prescription for the West.'' *Management Review,* June–July 1981.

_____ . ''The Quality Trilogy.'' *Quality Progress* 19 (August 1986), 19–24.

Kivenko, Ken. ''Improve Performance by Driving Out Fear.'' *Quality Progress* 27, no. 10 (October 1994), 77–79.

Ohio Quality and Productivity Forum Roundtable. ''Deming's Point Four: A Study.'' *Quality Progress,* December 1988, 31–35.

Raturi, A., and D. McCutcheon. ''An Epistemological Framework for Quality Management,'' Working Paper. Cincinnati, OH: University of Cincinnati, Department of Quantitative Analysis and Information Systems, March 1990.

Scherkenbach, William W. *Deming's Road to Continual Improvement.* Knoxville, TN: SPC Press, 1991.

Management Issues in Quality

For quality to succeed in an organization, it must become a part of everyone's daily activities. All people are managers of their own work—production operators and front-line service workers as well as top and middle managers. A total quality system must be built on sound managerial practices that focus on customers; provide leadership and motivation to employees; integrate quality into business planning, products, and processes; provide useful information to maintain performance and continuously improve; involve everyone and foster teamwork; and permit effective evaluation of quality efforts. Accomplishing these tasks requires a well-structured organization and implementation approach.

Part 2 of this book addresses the management system for achieving total quality. Chapter 4 discusses the key elements of TQM, how it differs from traditional management, and its applications in manufacturing, service, and the public sector. Chapter 5 examines the role and importance of customer focus in achieving strategic business objectives. A customer focus provides the basis for a total quality organization's strategic planning and leadership activities—the subject of Chapter 6.

Chapter 7 examines the role of quality in product and process design. Chapters 8 and 9 deal with how information is used to support total quality. Specifically, Chapter 8 discusses the role of measurement and strategic information management, and Chapter 9 introduces approaches for managing and continuously improving processes.

Chapters 10 and 11 address human resource issues. Chapter 10 discusses the modern role of human resource management in a quality system. Chapter 11 examines issues of teamwork and employee participation for achieving high performance. Chapter 12 describes approaches for evaluating and assessing quality management systems, focusing particularly on ISO 9000 standards and the Malcolm Baldrige National Quality Award. Finally, Chapter 13 discusses how to build organizations that have a quality focus and how to implement quality efforts successfully.

CHAPTER 4

Total Quality Management

In the early 1980s, Polaroid conducted an internal survey of its operations and identified seven major areas of concern:[1]

1. Quality only became a consideration at final assembly, rather than early in the design and development stages of the production system.

2. Polaroid employees did not fully understand customer needs and satisfaction.

3. Quality issues failed to gain much attention until problems developed.

4. Management seemed willing to sacrifice quality when it conflicted with costs or scheduling.

5. Operators lacked sufficient training in their jobs and in quality issues.

6. Suppliers also contributed their own quality problems to the system.

7. High quality costs were common.

These issues are not *quality* problems. They are *design* problems, *marketing* problems, *manufacturing* problems, *human resource* problems, *supplier relations* problems, and *financial* problems. They involve people, technology, information, and management. In other words, businesses must integrate quality into all its operations. Polaroid responded to the identified areas of concern by formulating a comprehensive and integrated management strategy centered on quality.

Polaroid's experience was not unique. Many U.S. companies like Motorola, Xerox, and the Big Three automobile makers found themselves in similar circumstances about 1980. After serious soul searching, these companies realized that survival depended on quality, and not just as control of product defects. Quality had to permeate every facet of their businesses. With the help of Deming, Juran, and Crosby, top managers began to recognize that competitive success depends on improving quality. Quality became the central focus of management strategy and decision making.

Today, the term *total quality management (TQM)* conveys the total, company-wide effort—through full involvement of the entire workforce and a focus on continuous improvement—that companies use to achieve customer satisfaction. TQM is both a comprehensive managerial philosophy and a collection of tools and approaches for its implementation.

Unfortunately, a three-letter acronym cannot fully represent the philosophy embodied by TQM. Such acronyms tend to suggest the latest business fad that will eventually fade. For TQM, however, the name may change, but the principles will remain universal. The goals of TQM are to satisfy the needs of customers, prevent poor quality rather than correcting problems after the fact, develop an attitude of continuous improvement in operations, understand the value of measuring performance to identify opportunities and maintain improvements, and eliminate chronic sources of inefficiencies and costs. There are probably as many different approaches to TQM as there are business firms. Even though no one approach can be labelled ideal, successful approaches share many common attributes. This chapter discusses principles of TQM used by successful companies.

THE EVOLUTION OF TOTAL QUALITY MANAGEMENT

The notion that quality is a total organization-wide effort has been around for many years. A. V. Feigenbaum recognized the importance of a comprehensive approach to quality in the 1950s and coined the term *total quality control*. Feigenbaum defined four characteristics of the "engineered total quality system."[2]

1. It represents a point of view for thinking about the way quality really works in a modern business company or governmental agency and how quality decisions can best be made.

2. It represents the basis for the deeply thought-through documentation . . . of the key, enduring quality activities and the integrated people-machine-information relationships which make a particular activity viable and communicable throughout the firm.

3. It is the foundation for making the broader scope quality activities of the company manageable because it permits the management and employees of the plant and company to get their arms firmly around their customer-requirements-to-customer-satisfaction quality activities.

4. It is the basis for systematic engineering of order-of-magnitude improvements throughout the major quality activities of the company.

Feigenbaum observed that the quality of products and services is directly influenced by what he terms the *9 M's*: markets, money, management, men and women, motivation, materials, machines and mechanization, modern information methods, and mounting product requirements. Although he developed his ideas from an engineering perspective, his concepts apply more broadly to general management.

The Japanese adopted Feigenbaum's concept and renamed it **companywide quality control.** Reiker listed five aspects of total quality control practiced in Japan.[3]

1. Quality emphasis extends through market analysis, design, and customer service rather than only the production stages of making a product.

2. Quality emphasis is directed toward operations in every department from executives to clerical personnel.

3. Quality is the responsibility of the individual and the work group, not some other group, such as inspection.

4. There are two types of quality characteristics as viewed by customers: those that satisfy and those that motivate. Only the latter are strongly related to repeat sales and a "quality" image.

5. The first customer for a part or piece of information is usually the next department in the production process.

Reiker emphasized that with the use of total quality control, a company achieves objectives more efficiently at every level of the company from daily work to managing the entire enterprise. Total quality control was successful in Japan for three key reasons: (1) upper managers personally took charge of leading the quality revolution; (2) all levels of employees and functions underwent training in managing for quality; and (3) quality improvement was undertaken at a continuing, rapid pace.[4]

The strong influence of Deming's philosophy is evident in these characteristics. As noted in the last chapter, Deming's influence—as well as that of Juran and Crosby—moved quality from a purely technical issue to a management issue. From this viewpoint, the concept of total quality *management* was born. (The term *TQM* was actually developed within the Department of Defense. It has since been renamed *Total Quality Leadership,* since leadership outranks management in military thought.)

Japan promoted total quality since 1951, when the Union of Japanese Scientists and Engineers (JUSE) instituted the Deming Prize to award individuals and companies who meet stringent criteria for quality management practice. The United States developed its own award, the Malcolm Baldrige National Quality Award, but not until 1987. The Baldrige Award was instituted by an act of Congress. It recognizes U.S. companies with exemplary quality management practices and provides role models to the rest of the nation.

Perhaps more than any single activity, the Baldrige Award has drawn unprecedented attention to quality throughout U.S. business. The intent of the award is not to signify "winning." Rather, its purpose is to improve the competitiveness of industry in the United States by recognizing world-class quality management practices and sharing this knowledge. The Baldrige Award has stimulated study and education in world-class TQM practices, and has provided a common vocabulary that facilitates communication among firms in all sectors of the economy. The award criteria provide a comprehensive set of guidelines for companies to use in assessing their own quality management practices. Most importantly, the Baldrige Award creates a sense of excitement about quality among top executives throughout the nation. Both the Deming Prize and the Baldrige Award are discussed in greater detail in Chapter 12.

FOUNDATIONS OF TOTAL QUALITY MANAGEMENT

Total Quality Management is a philosophy or approach to management that is grounded on three core principles:

1. A focus on the customer
2. Participation and teamwork
3. Continuous improvement

These principles are supported and implemented by an integrated organizational infrastructure, a set of management practices, and a wide variety of tools and techniques, which all must work together and support each other as suggested in Figure 4.1.

■ Customer Focus

The modern definition of quality centers on meeting or exceeding customer expectations. Thus, the customer is the principal judge of quality. Both Deming

FIGURE 4.1 The Scope of Total Quality Management

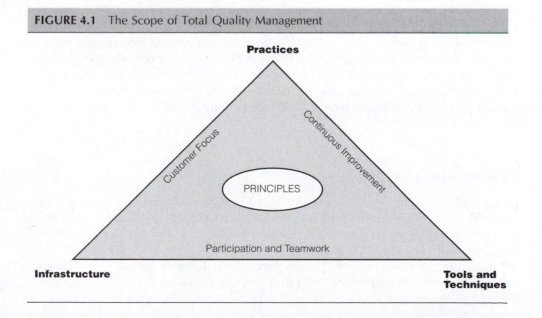

and Juran stress this point in their philosophies. The importance of customers is also stressed in the Malcolm Baldrige National Quality Award criteria—25 percent of the score is based on how well the company focuses on its customers and on achieving customer satisfaction.

Perceptions of value and satisfaction are influenced by many factors throughout the customer's overall purchase, ownership, and service experiences. Companies must focus on all product and service attributes that contribute to perceived value to the customer and lead to customer satisfaction. To accomplish this task, a company's efforts need to extend well beyond merely meeting specifications, defect and error reduction, or reducing complaints. They must include the design of new products that truly delight the customer and respond rapidly to changing consumer and market demands.

All strategic decisions a company concerned with quality makes are "customer-driven." In other words, the company shows constant sensitivity to emerging customer and market requirements; it also measures the factors that drive customer satisfaction. A company close to its customer knows what the customer wants, how the customer uses its products, and anticipates the needs that the customer may not even be able to express. To accomplish this task a company can and should use various means, such as customer opinion surveys and focus groups, to understand customer requirements and values. These companies continually develop new techniques to obtain customer feedback. Many companies have established toll-free telephone numbers, for example. In other companies, sales and marketing executives meet with random groups of key customers on a regular basis. Creative product design and development staffs and effective market research capabilities are also essential attributes of a customer-driven company.

A firm also must recognize that internal customers are as important in assuring quality as are external customers who purchase the product. Employees who view themselves as both customers of and suppliers to other employees understand how their work links to the final product. After all, the responsibility of any supplier is to understand and meet customer requirements in the most efficient *and* effective manner possible.

Customer focus extends beyond the consumer and internal relationships, however. Society represents an important customer of business. A world-class company, by definition, is an exemplary corporate citizen. Business ethics, public health and safety, environment, and sharing of quality-related information in the company's business and geographic communities are necessary activities. In addition, company support—within reasonable limits of its resources—of national, industry, trade, and community activities and the sharing of nonproprietary quality-related information demonstrate far-reaching benefits. Customer focus is the subject of Chapter 5.

■ Participation and Teamwork

Juran credited Japanese managers' full use of the knowledge and creativity of the entire workforce as one of the reasons for Japan's rapid quality achievements. When managers give employees the tools to make good decisions and the freedom and encouragement to make contributions, they virtually guarantee that better quality products and production processes will result. Employees allowed to participate—both individually and in teams—in decisions that affect their jobs and the customer can make substantial quality contributions. In any organization, the person who best understands his or her job and how to improve both the product and the process is the one performing it. By training employees to think creatively and rewarding good suggestions, managers can develop loyalty and trust. This attitude represents a profound shift in the typical philosophy of senior management; the traditional view was that the workforce should be "managed"—or to put it less formally, the workforce should leave their brains at the door. Good intentions alone are not enough to encourage employee involvement. Management's task includes formulating the systems and procedures and then putting them in place to ensure that participation becomes a part of the culture. Managers can encourage participation by implementing suggestion systems that act rapidly, provide feedback, and reward good ideas. These systems should also recognize team and individual accomplishments, share success stories throughout the organization, encourage risk taking by removing the fear of failure, promote the formation of employee involvement teams, and provide financial and technical support to employees to develop their ideas.

Empowering employees to make decisions that satisfy customers without constraining them with bureaucratic rules shows the highest level of trust. True empowerment can only occur in a customer-driven organization that embraces the ideals of total quality management. Marriott and American Express are examples of two companies that empower and reward their employees for service quality. Marriott calls its customer service representatives "associates." Associates are permitted wide discretion to call on any part of the company to help customers and can earn lush bonuses for extraordinary work. American Express gives cash awards—up to $1,000—to "Great Performers" such as Barbara Weber who, in 1986, cut through miles of State Department and Treasury Department red tape to refund $980 of stolen traveler's checks to a customer stranded in Cuba.

Another important element of total quality management is teamwork, which focuses attention on customer–supplier relationships and encourages the involvement of the total workforce in attacking systemic problems, particularly those that cross functional boundaries. Ironically, although problem-solving teams were introduced in the United States in the 1940s to help solve problems on the factory floor, they failed, primarily because of management resistance to workers' suggestions. The Japanese, however, began widespread implementation of similar teams, called *quality circles*, in 1962 with dramatic results. Eventually, the concept returned to the United States. Today, the use of *self-managed teams* is growing. These teams combine teamwork and empowerment into a powerful method of employee involvement.

An important type of team is the *cross-functional team*. Traditionally, organizations were integrated vertically by linking all the levels of management in a hierarchical fashion (consider the traditional organization chart). TQM requires horizontal coordination between organizational units (as in Deming's picture of a production system in Chapter 1). Poor quality often results from breakdowns in responsibility that occur when an organization focuses solely on vertical structures, and fails to recognize the horizontal interactions (such as those between design and engineering, engineering and manufacturing, manufacturing and shipping, shipping and sales). Vertical structures lead to internal competition rather than promoting the good of the whole organization. A process focus on the other hand, which concentrates on creating outputs from inputs, provides better insights into how the organization actually operates.

General Motors, for example, tries to eliminate the practice of competing internally and instead promotes teamwork. One manager characterized GM as one of the most fiercely internally competitive companies that ever existed. To counter internal competition, GM developed a system called the Quality Network, made up of joint union–management Quality Councils at the corporate, division, and plant levels. This system is common across all of General Motors. The heart of the Quality Network is a customer satisfaction model that encourages teamwork and cooperation (see Figure 4.2). For example, plants hold periodic corporate analysis meetings during which entire plants shut down operations briefly for thorough audits of the quality system. Hundreds of plant-level work teams with thousands of workers focus on ways to improve quality and productivity.

Partnerships are an additional way of promoting teamwork. Partnerships between a company and organized labor and between customers and suppliers are common among companies practicing TQM. Motorola, for instance, seeks suppliers that share its values. Then Motorola sharpens supplier skills by teaching them Motorola TQM techniques, even requiring suppliers to take courses in customer satisfaction and cycle time reduction at Motorola University. In this way, Motorola is teaching, coaching, and pushing its suppliers in a direction that has been successful for Motorola. If suppliers get better, then so will Motorola. On the other side of the coin, Motorola established a fifteen-member council of suppliers to rate Motorola's own practices and offer suggestions for improvement.[5]

Partnerships can also serve larger community interests by linking with educational organizations. Many Baldrige Award winners have adopted colleges and universities and trained faculty and administrators in total quality or are working with community school systems to improve primary and secondary education. Teamwork and participation involving everyone in the organization, as well as suppliers and customers, leads to creativity, innovation, and mutual benefits. Chapters 10 and 11 focus on participation and teamwork.

■ Continuous Improvement

Continuous improvement has its roots in the industrial revolution. In the early 1900s, Frederick Taylor, often called the Father of Scientific Management, believed that management had a responsibility to find the best way to do a job and train workers in the appropriate procedures. Time and motion study became the staple of the industrial engineer who sought to break down work into its

FIGURE 4.2 The General Motors Quality Network Process Model

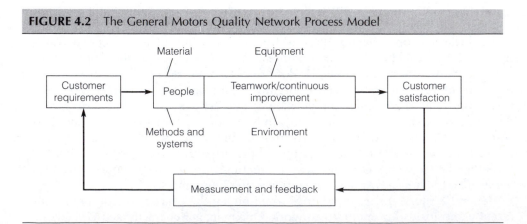

fundamental elements and eliminate wasted motion and operations. The industrial engineer acted as the expert who defined how jobs should be performed; supervision was the means of ensuring that workers did as they were told. In Taylor's philosophy, the focus was on efficiency and productivity. This approach helped revolutionized manufacturing and made the United States the world's leading industrial power.

Continuous improvement is an integral part of the management of all systems and processes. Deming introduced the notion of continuous improvement in his diagram of a production system and ingrained this thinking into Japanese management. Juran suggested that companies develop annual improvement targets and engage in hundreds of quality improvement projects continuously. Crosby's 14-point improvement plan ended with "Do it over again." Under a TQM framework, however, responsibility for quality lies with the individual worker and teams of workers and quality is the principal focus. Management plays a facilitating role in TQM. Achieving the highest levels of quality requires a well-defined and well-executed approach to continuous improvement. The process of continuous improvement requires systematic planning, execution, and evaluation.

Improvement is a critical aspect of all operations and of all work unit activities of a company. Improvements may take any one of several forms:

■ Enhancing value to the customer through new and improved products and services

■ Reducing errors, defects, and waste

■ Improving productivity and effectiveness in the use of all resources

■ Improving responsiveness and cycle time performance

The need to improve products and services to gain market advantage, reduce errors and defects, and improve productivity are basic business objectives. The importance of responsiveness and cycle time performance is rather new. As more businesses compete on service, success in competitive markets demands ever-shorter product and service introduction cycles and more rapid response to customers. These aspects result when work processes meet both quality and response goals. Accordingly, response time improvement should be a major focus within all quality improvement processes of work units. As part of this focus, all designs, objectives, and work unit activities need to include measurement of cycle time and responsiveness. Major improvements in response time may require significant simplification of work processes. Response time improvements often drive simultaneous improvements in quality and productivity. Because of their interrelatedness, response time, quality, and productivity objectives should be considered together. Chapter 9 discusses continuous improvement in greater detail.

■ Infrastructure, Practices, and Tools

Infrastructure refers to the basic management systems that enable a firm to realize the core principles of TQM. A TQM infrastructure includes the following elements:

■ leadership

■ strategic planning

■ data and information management

- process management
- supplier management
- human resources management

Practices are those activities that occur within a management system to achieve its objectives. For example, performance appraisal and training are human resources management practices. *Tools* include a wide variety of graphical and statistical methods employees use to plan strategies, collect data, solve problems, and analyze results. For instance, a chart showing trends in manufacturing defects as workers progress through a training program is a simple tool to monitor the effectiveness of the training. The relationships among infrastructure, practices, and tools are illustrated in Figure 4.3. This section gives a brief overview of the major elements of a TQM infrastructure. Specific practices, however, are described in subsequent chapters, in which various tools are introduced as appropriate. Total quality management practices and helpful tools continually evolve and improve. Therefore, discussion of each and every useful practice or tool is not possible within the scope of this book. The most important practices and tools, which have gained widespread acceptance in business, are described here.

LEADERSHIP

The success of any organization depends on the performance of the workers at the bottom of the pyramid. Ross Perot once said that inventories can be managed, but people must be led. All managers, ideally starting with the CEO, must act as the organization's leaders for quality. Their task is to create clear quality values and high expectations, and then build these into the company's operations. Through management initiation and support, strategies, systems, and methods for achieving excellence are created. Senior management's regular personal involvement in visible activities—planning, reviewing company quality performance, serving on quality improvement teams, interacting with customers, and recognizing employees for quality achievement—serves as a role model for reinforcing the values and encouraging leadership in all levels of management. As the focal point, senior management provides broad perspectives and vision, encouragement, and recognition. If commitment to quality is not a priority, any

FIGURE 4.3   Relationships Among Infrastructure, Practices, and Tools

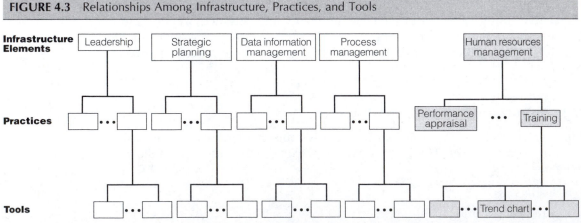

initiative can easily fail. When the Ritz-Carlton Hotel opens a new facility, the CEO works alongside the housekeeping and kitchen staffs making beds and washing dishes. Imagine the message these actions send to the workers! The CEO of Motorola, for instance, placed quality first on the agenda at every board meeting. He frequently left the meeting after discussing quality, sending the message that once the directors took care of quality, financial issues and other matters would take care of themselves. Most TQ-focused companies use quality councils to guide the deployment of quality initiatives. These councils set quality policy and review performance goals within the company.

STRATEGIC PLANNING

Achieving quality and market leadership requires a strategy that reflects long-term commitments to customers, employees, stockholders, and suppliers. The organization must first address some fundamental questions.

- Who are our customers?
- What is our mission?
- What principles do we value?
- What are our long-range and short-range goals?

A company cannot ignore quality in its strategic planning processes. In fact, if a company views quality from the customer satisfaction perspective, their strategic business planning *is* quality planning.

Quality improvements do not happen instantaneously. Unfortunately, most people in the United States hate to wait. They tend to seek immediate results and move on to other approaches when results are not imminent, which also explains the string of three-letter acronyms that pop up persistently in business circles. Thus, unless an organization takes steps to ensure that TQM remains a priority, the organization risks losing the commitment of its employees. TQM is not a short-term *program,* but rather it is a part of the corporate culture. The success of Japanese manufacturers evolved over several decades. They willingly sacrificed short-term profits in anticipation of long-term benefits. Clearly, their strategy paid off. On the other hand, the longer an organization takes to carry out TQM, the further behind its competitors it falls. Thus, a firm stands to benefit most by moving rapidly yet carefully when developing a TQM culture.

Effective quality systems place a strong emphasis on prevention. Prevention is best achieved by designing quality into products and services and into the processes that produce them. Superior design quality can significantly reduce production errors and waste, customer dissatisfaction, and associated costs. Often this type of improvement requires a sweeping overhaul of existing practices, as was the case with Scandinavian Airlines System.[6]

Improving the design of its service system transformed Scandinavian Airlines System (SAS) in Sweden. When president and CEO Jan Carlzon took over SAS in 1980, the company was suffering from the effects of an oil shock, two years of financial losses, and high labor costs. These factors prevented the company from competing on price alone with U.S. and Asian airlines. Carlzon set about creating a quality image by instituting low standby fares for passengers under age 27; reconfiguring airplanes to give more comfort and amenities to business-class passengers; training and empowering employees to handle problems swiftly, competently, and without excessive red tape; and improving ground service. Changes included better express check-in service, new business facilities such as computers and fax machines, and automatic delivery of luggage to hotels owned by or linked to SAS's full-service travel agency. To attain SAS's quality goals, Carlzon stresses the need to have behavioral change take place at the "moment of truth" when the employee comes into contact with the customer during the process of delivering the company's service.

DATA AND INFORMATION MANAGEMENT

To understand variation, identify causes of quality problems, and achieve lasting improvements in products and processes, managers start with reliable information, data, and analysis. To obtain reliable data, managers measure the quality of products, internal processes, and customer satisfaction. Many types of facts and data are needed for quality assessment and quality improvement:

- customer needs
- product and service performance
- operations performance
- market assessments
- competitive comparisons
- supplier performance
- employee performance
- cost and financial performance

The data and indicators used should represent the factors that determine customer satisfaction and operational performance—the *key business factors* of the company. A system of indicators tied to customer and company performance requirements represents a clear and objective basis for aligning all activities of the company toward common goals. Management uses facts, data, and analysis to support a variety of company purposes: planning, reviewing company performance, improving operations, and comparing company quality performance with competitors' performance. Statistical reasoning with factual data provides the basis for problem solving and continuous improvement.

Companies need accurate measures to assess quality improvement. The usefulness of accurate measures demands accurate and timely reporting of information and a systematic measurement and evaluation process. Traditional information systems focus on cost and financial accounting, sales, marketing, purchasing, and scheduling. To improve overall quality, quality measures must become part of the reports provided to middle and upper management. Line workers and supervisors also require quality reports to identify, analyze, and solve problems.

PROCESS MANAGEMENT

According to AT&T, a process is how work creates value for customers.[7] The focus on processes, rather than on the organizational hierarchy, was noted in Chapter 3 in the context of Deming's view of production systems, and is shown in Figure 4.4. Nearly every major activity within a business involves some form of cross-functional cooperation. A process perspective links all parts of an organization together and increases employee understanding of the entire system, rather than focusing on only a small part. In addition, it helps managers to recognize that problems arise from processes, not people.

FIGURE 4.4 Process versus Function

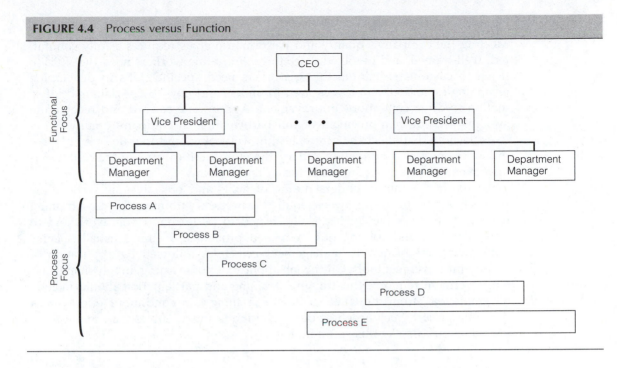

Within the context of TQM, businesses focus on the *design* of processes to develop and deliver products that meet the needs of customers, as well as the *improvement* of processes to improve continually efficiency and effectiveness. Process management requires that organizations anticipate and understand customer needs as well as control processes to eliminate unwanted variation. Practices such as failsafing and preventive maintenance reduce the opportunities for defects and errors. Improved processes lead to better quality products and services and less waste and rework. This improvement eventually translates into more satisfied customers and higher profits, and, following the Deming Chain Reaction, the ability to stay in business and provide jobs. By viewing the system as processes rather than functions, management finds that improvement ideas literally jump right out. Many of these ideas significantly reduce the time needed to perform the process, enabling companies to respond to customers much more quickly. As time and process complexity decreases, the opportunities for defects and errors also decrease, thus improving quality.

SUPPLIER MANAGEMENT

An important aspect of process management is working with suppliers—the external providers of goods and services. Only when organizations convey their principal requirements and expectations to suppliers can they determine whether their requirements are met and provide feedback on performance. For many companies, suppliers play an increasingly important role in achieving high performance and low costs, as well as in meeting strategic objectives. Key suppliers might provide unique design or marketing capabilities. By partnering with suppliers, an organization can improve its ability to satisfy customers and boost productivity and quality. One example of how supplier partnership can improve fundamental business processes is given in the AT&T Quality in Practice case at the end of this chapter.

HUMAN RESOURCES MANAGEMENT

Meeting the company's quality and performance goals requires a fully committed, well-trained, and involved work force. Front-line workers need the skills to listen to customers; manufacturing workers need specific skills in developing technologies; and all employees need to understand how to use data and information to drive continuous improvement. Appropriate reward and recognition systems provide reinforcement of full participation in company quality objectives. Factors that affect the safety, health, well-being, and morale of employees influence employee motivation and are therefore a critical part of the continuous improvement objectives and activities of the company.

To reach a common understanding of goals and objectives as well as the means to attain them, employees require the necessary training. Effective training teaches employees the quality skills related to performing their work and to understanding and solving quality-related problems. Training usually begins with awareness of quality management principles followed by application of quality improvement tools. On-the-job applications of learning, involvement, and empowerment reinforce this training. Training and participation should include all employees, from the CEO on down. Training is a continuous effort, not a one-time project. Such an effort demands significant resources, and many firms are reluctant to make this commitment.

■ Corporate Culture

Corporate culture can be simply described as "This is the way we do things at XYZ Company." Peters and Waterman, in their classic work *In Search of Excellence*, pointed out a number of companies such as Procter & Gamble, Digital Equipment, and Walt Disney Productions as examples of firms that have developed a unique corporate culture, which contributes to their overall excellence.[8] Peters and Waterman give eight prescriptions for excellence:

1. A bias for action
2. Staying close to the customer
3. Autonomy and entrepreneurship
4. Productivity through people
5. Hands-on, value-driven operations
6. Sticking to knitting (translation: focus on doing what you do best)
7. Simple form, lean staff
8. Simultaneous loose–tight controls.

All of these characteristics contribute to total quality in various ways. For example, a "bias for action" implies that a firm takes a proactive approach toward quality. Instead of talking about quality improvement, people *move* to make things happen. "Staying close to the customer" is a core principle of total quality management. Today's concepts of empowerment reflect "autonomy and entrepreneurship." The other points are similar to the core principles of teamwork and continuous improvement. Even "simultaneous loose–tight controls" can be applied to quality advantageously. For instance, inspections upon receipt of goods from suppliers who provide consistently high quality can often be eliminated, which saves the customer money and encourages the supplier to continue to maintain high quality levels. Suppliers who cannot provide high quality will be tightly controlled or even dropped if they cannot improve. In retrospect, Peters and Waterman can be considered "prophets" of the quality movement that began in the 1980s and is still going on today.

Philip Crosby pointed out the importance of a cultural revolution within a firm attempting to establish total quality. He stated, "One of the reasons I cheerfully share these [quality improvement] programs with other companies is that I know that many will probably not be able to use them. Not because they are not capable, but because they do not have a top management willing to be patient while the program is ground out four yards at a time. It took five to seven years of unrelenting effort to achieve the cultural revolution at ITT and I seriously doubt if it will ever be eliminated there."[9]

The principles of total quality must become a living, breathing part of the organization's culture. They are embodied in the strategies and leadership philosophies of nearly every major company. For example, the total quality philosophy at Procter & Gamble focuses on delivering superior consumer satisfaction and boils down to four principles:[10]

- *Really know our customers and consumers.* Know those who resell our products and those who finally use them—and then meet and exceed their expectations.

- *Do right things right.* This requires hard data and sound statistical analysis to select the "right things" and to direct continual improvement in how well we do those things.

- *Concentrate on improving systems.* In order to achieve superior customer and consumer satisfaction and leadership financial goals, we must continually analyze and improve the capability of our basic business systems and subsystems.

- *Empower people.* This means removing barriers and providing a climate in which everyone in the enterprise is encouraged and trained to make his or her maximum contribution to business objectives.

The *P&G Statement of Purpose* captures the "what," "how," and expected "results" of their quality efforts.

We will provide products of superior quality and value that best fill the needs of the world's consumers.

We will achieve that purpose through an organization and a working environment which attracts the finest people; fully develops and challenges our individual talents; encourages our free and spirited collaboration to drive the business ahead; and maintains the Company's historic principles of integrity, and doing the right thing.

Through the successful pursuit of our commitment, we expect our brands to achieve leadership share and profit positions so that, as a result, our business, our people, our shareholders, and the communities in which we live and work, will prosper.

A similar philosophy is described by the American Express Quality Leadership approach. The fundamental beliefs about quality that provide the philosophical underpinnings and guide decision making at American Express are

- Quality is the foundation of continued success.

- Quality is a journey of continuous improvement and innovation.

- Quality provides a high return, but requires the investment of time and resources.

■ Quality requires committed leadership.

■ Quality begins by meeting or exceeding the expectations of customers and employees.

■ Quality requires teamwork and learning at all levels.

■ Quality comes from the energy of a diverse community of motivated and skilled people who are given and take responsibility.

Moving from a traditional to a TQM culture requires significant changes in management attitudes and practices. The next section addresses the key differences between a traditional culture and a culture of TQM. Overcoming the deep resistance to change that often accompanies the establishment of total quality practices can only take place when management understands these differences.

BENEFITS OF TOTAL QUALITY MANAGEMENT

Companies that subscribe to total quality management principles experience outstanding returns on their investment. The General Accounting Office (GAO) of the U.S. government studied 20 companies that were among the highest scoring applicants in the 1988 and 1989 Baldrige Award competition. The study indicated that companies that adopted total quality management practices experienced an overall improvement in corporate performance.[11] In nearly all cases, companies that used TQM achieved better employee relations, higher productivity, greater customer satisfaction, increased market share, and improved profitability.

The GAO developed a general framework, shown in Figure 4.5, that describes total quality management and the benefits that accrue. The solid line shows the direction of the total quality processes to improve competitiveness. The process begins with a leadership dedicated to improving products and services as well as the quality systems. Improvements in these areas lead to customer satisfaction and benefits to the organization, both of which improve competitiveness. The dotted lines indicate the information feedback necessary for continuous improvement. The arrows in the boxes show the expected direction of the performance indicators.

The following list includes some of the specific results achieved by companies that won the Malcolm Baldrige National Quality Award.

■ Customer accounts at Granite Rock, a small California supplier to the construction industry (profiled in a Quality in Practice in Chapter 5), have increased 38 percent during the period from 1989 through mid-1993, while overall construction spending in its market area declined over 40 percent.

■ In 1992, Texas Instruments Defense Systems & Electronics Group (see Quality Profile) had a 21 percent reduction in production cycle time with a 56 percent reduction in stock-to-production time.

■ From 1988 to 1992, Zytec's internal manufacturing process yields improved five-fold. Its customer out-of-box quality rose from 99 percent to 99.8 percent, and on-time delivery improved from 75 percent to 98 percent.

■ Motorola's employee productivity improved 100 percent during the time period from 1988 to 1994—an annual compounded rate of 12.2 percent—through better design, continuous improvement in defect reduction, and employee education and empowerment.

FIGURE 4.5 The GAO Total Quality Management Model

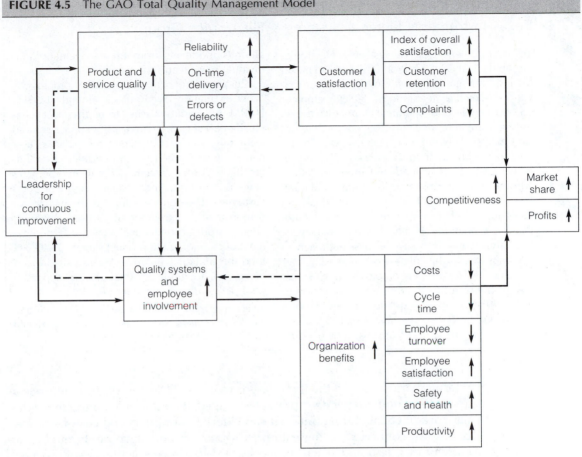

■ Solectron, by focusing on customer satisfaction, experienced average yearly revenue growth of 46.8 percent, and by focusing on process quality saw average yearly net income growth of 57.3 percent over five years.

■ At Globe Metallurgical (see Quality Profile), from 1988 to 1992, exports grew from 2 percent to 20 percent of sales, while overall sales grew by 24 percent.

■ According to a Commerce Department study, the five publicly traded, whole-company Baldrige Award winners outperformed the Standard & Poor's 500 from the time of their winning through October 3, 1994 by 6.5 to 1. Eight other companies that received site visits during 1990 through 1993 outperformed the S&P 500 by 4.5 to 1.

■ TQM and Traditional Management Practices

TQM is quite different from traditional management practices. Some of the key differences are described in the following list.[12]

■ *Organizational structures:* Traditional management views an enterprise as a collection of separate, highly specialized individual performers and units, linked within a functional hierarchy. Lateral connections are made by

QUALITY PROFILE
Texas Instruments Defense Systems & Electronics Group

Texas Instruments Defense Systems & Electronics Group (DSEG) is a $2 billion Dallas-based maker of precision-guided weapons and other advanced defense technology. DSEG employs 15,000 people and operates 11 manufacturing, testing, research, and distribution facilities at sites located in North and Central Texas. The individuals who founded TI created a culture in which people are valued and involved, ethics and integrity are more important than profit and loss, customer focus is stressed, individuals are recognized and rewarded, and technical innovators are prized as highly as skilled managers. Executives view TQM as the best approach to accomplish any objective—from increasing market share to controlling employee health care costs—and teams as the most effective means to execute the company's quality strategy. From a pilot group of four worker teams in 1983, a network of more than 1900 teams has grown to link all units and levels, from top management to individual work teams.

Customers recognize TI's quality progress. A Navy evaluation of 17 missiles found TI-DSEG HARM and Shrike missiles to be the most reliable. Since 1986, more than 100 TI processes and techniques were designated by the Navy as "best manufacturing practices," more than any other company. Formal customer complaints fell by 62 percent, and in an independent survey of 2000 customers, the company topped its main competitors in all 11 customer satisfaction categories, ranging from cost-effective pricing and deployment of technology to product support. TI-DSEG used the Malcolm Baldrige Award Criteria as a framework to guide its total quality approach since 1989; it won the award in 1992.

SOURCE: Malcolm Baldrige National Quality Award, *Profiles of Winners,* National Institute of Standards and Technology, Department of Commerce.

intermediaries close to the top of the provinces. TQM views the enterprise as a system of interdependent processes, linked laterally, over time, through a network of collaborating (internal and external) suppliers and customers. Processes are connected to the enterprise's mission and purpose, through a hierarchy of micro and macro processes. Every process contains subprocesses and is also contained within a higher order process. This structure of processes is repeated throughout the hierarchy.

■ *Role of people:* Traditional management views people as a commodity, interchangeable, and developed based on the perceived needs of the enterprise. People are passive contributors, with little autonomy, doing what they are told and nothing more. TQM views people as the enterprise's true competitive edge. Leadership provides people with opportunities for personal growth and development. People take joy and pride through learning and accomplishment, and enhance the capability of the enterprise to succeed. People are active contributors, valued for their creativity and intelligence. Every person is a process manager, presiding over the transformation of inputs to outputs of greater value to the enterprise and to the consumer.

■ *Definition of quality:* In traditional management, quality is the adherence to internal specifications and standards. The absence of defects, therefore, defines quality. Inspection of people's work by others is necessary to control defects. Innovation is not required. In TQM, quality is defined in a positive sense as products and services that go beyond present needs and expectations of customers. Innovation is required.

■ *Goals and objectives:* In traditional management, the functional provinces are in a zero-sum game in which there must be a loser for every winner. People do not cooperate unless it serves their own or their unit's best interests. Parochialism is a fact of business life. In TQM, self-interest and the greater good

QUALITY PROFILE

Globe Metallurgical, Inc.

Globe Metallurgical, Inc., a small-business winner of the Malcolm Baldrige National Quality Award in 1988, has plants in Beverly, Ohio, and Selma, Alabama. The plants produce about 100,000 tons of alloys for more than 300 customers. In the early 1980s, the company found itself faced with threats from foreign manufacturers. Globe's quality initiative was motivated by Ford Motor Company's Q-1 supplier program. To be considered as a long-term supplier for Ford, Globe launched a total quality approach. To begin, managers and supervisors viewed videotape lectures by W. Edwards Deming. The entire work force was trained in statistical methods. Globe also developed a quality manual and offered quality-related education and training to its suppliers. It instituted practices to improve employee morale, such as improved benefit and pension plans, elimination of time clocks, and

profit sharing plans. A Quality-Efficiency-Cost steering committee led the total quality approach effort, supported by a variety of teams in which workers generated ideas for improvements.

Teamwork and statistical methods helped Globe achieve significant improvements in product quality. Greater consistency in final products—achieving specifications that fall within ranges more demanding than those imposed by customers—significantly lowered the chance of an out-of-specification shipment. This improvement also resulted in increased production rates and lower energy consumption. From 1985 to 1987, customer complaints decreased by 91 percent, and the accident rate, near the industry average in 1985, fell while the industry average rose.

SOURCE: Malcolm Baldrige National Quality Award, *Profiles of Winners,* National Institute of Standards and Technology, Department of Commerce.

are served simultaneously by serving one's customers. Everyone wins or no one wins. Cooperation takes the place of competition.

■ *Knowledge:* In traditional management, quality embodies knowledge applicable only to manufacturing and engineering. In TQM, quality embodies knowledge applicable to all the disciplines of the enterprise. All levels of management and the workforce must, as Deming often said, "learn the new philosophy."

■ *Management systems:* In traditional management, managers oversee departments or functions or collections of individuals. The pieces do not know they are interdependent. They each act as if they are the whole. Quality problems occur when individual people or departments do not do their best. In TQM, managers oversee interdependent systems and processes and exercise managerial leadership through participative management. Their roles are to act as mentors, facilitators, and innovators. Quality results from the enterprises' systems and individuals working together. People working in the system cannot do better than the system allows (recall the Red Bead Experiment). The majority of problems are prevented and improvement promoted when people understand how they fit in, and have the knowledge to maximize their contribution to the whole system. Only management can create an environment that nurtures a team-oriented culture, which focuses on problem prevention and continuous improvement.

■ *Reward systems:* In traditional management, performance appraisal, recognition, and reward systems place people in an internally competitive environment. This environment reinforces individualism to the detriment of teamwork. In TQM, reward systems recognize individual as well as team contributions and reinforce cooperation.

■ *Management's role:* Once the organization has found a formula for success it is reluctant to change it. Management's job, therefore, is to maintain the status quo by preventing change. In TQM, the environment in which the enterprise interacts constantly changes. If the enterprise continues to do what it has done in the past, its future performance, relative to the competition, will deteriorate. Management's job, therefore, is to provide the leadership for continual improvement and innovation in processes and systems, products, and services. External change is inevitable, but a favorable future can be shaped.

■ *Union–management relations:* In traditional management, the adversarial relationship between union and management is inevitable. The only area for negotiation lies in traditional issues, such as wages, health, and safety. In TQM, the union becomes a partner and a stakeholder in the success of the enterprise. The potential for partnership and collaboration is unlimited, particularly in the areas of education, training, and meaningful involvement of employees in process improvement.

■ *Teamwork:* In traditional management, hierarchical "chimney" organization structures promote identification with functions and tend to create competition, conflict, and adversarial relations between functions. In TQM, formal and informal mechanisms encourage and facilitate teamwork and team development across the entire enterprise.

■ *Supplier relationships:* In traditional management, suppliers are pitted against each other to obtain the lowest price. The more suppliers competing against each other the better it is for the customer company. In TQM, suppliers are partners with their customers. Partnership aims to encourage innovation, reduce variation of critical characteristics, lower costs, and improve quality. Reducing the number of suppliers and establishing long-term relationships helps to achieve this aim.

■ *Control:* In traditional management, control is achieved by preestablished inflexible responsive patterns given in the book of rules and procedures. People are customers of the "book" which prescribes appropriate behaviors. In TQM, control results from shared values and beliefs, as well as knowledge of mission, purpose, and customer requirements.

■ *Customers:* In traditional management, customers are outside the enterprise and within the domain of marketing and sales. In TQM, everyone inside the enterprise is a customer of an internal or external supplier. Marketing concepts and tools can be used to assess internal customer needs and communicate internal supplier capabilities.

■ *Responsibility:* In traditional management, the manager's job is to do the subordinates' planning, and inspect the work to make sure the plans are followed. In TQM, the manager's job is to manage his or her own process and relationships with others and give subordinates the capability to do the same through empowerment. The manager must be a coach and facilitator rather than a director.

■ *Motivation:* In traditional management, motivation is achieved by aversive control. People are motivated to do what they do to avoid failure and punishment, rather than contribute something of value to the enterprise. People are afraid to do anything that would displease their supervisor or not be in compliance with company regulations. The system makes people feel like losers. In TQM, managers provide leadership rather than overt intervention in the processes of their subordinates, who are viewed as process managers rather than functional specialists. People are motivated to make meaningful contributions to what they believe is an important and noble cause and of value to the enterprise and society. The system enables people to feel like winners.

■ *Competition:* In traditional management, competition is inevitable and inherent in human nature. In TQM, competitive behavior—one person against another or one group against another—is not a natural state. Instead, competitive behavior seeks to improve the methods for pleasing the customer, eliminating waste of nonrenewable resources, or preventing passing on to future generations a damaged planet, incapable of sustaining human life.

■ The Impact of TQM on Management

TQM demands new styles of managing and an entirely new set of skills.[13] These new styles include the following characteristics:

- Thinking in terms of systems
- Defining customer requirements
- Planning for quality improvement with each customer
- Dealing with customer dissatisfaction
- Ensuring ongoing quality efforts
- Developing a life-long learning style
- Teambuilding
- Encouraging openness
- Creating climates of trust and eliminating fear
- Listening and providing feedback
- Leading and participating in group meetings
- Solving problems with data
- Clarifying goals and resolving conflicts
- Delegating and coaching
- Implementing change
- Making continuous improvement a way of life

TQM also requires that managers learn new "languages." William Wiggenhorn, corporate vice president for training and education at Motorola, discussed the new "language of quality."[14] He discussed the need to teach basic concepts of statistics, such as "bell curves, probabilities, and standard deviations expressed in multiples of the Greek letter sigma," to all 102,000 employees in his company. Deming, as noted in the last chapter, promoted similar education in statistical thinking. In addition to the language of statistics, "new dialects" have been developed by marketing and customer service experts, organizational behavior specialists, industrial and mechanical engineers, cost accountants, participative (employee involvement) team coordinators, and others. Meeting the needs of customers necessitates new tools and a vocabulary to gather, analyze, interpret, and act. This new dialect contains terms such as the "voice of the customer" and "quality function deployment."

Organization behavior specialists apply their theories to solve leadership and motivation problems in dynamic, fast-moving organizations. Their language and tools facilitate communication between managers and TQM workers. One specific concept stresses attention to the details of the task. Attention to detail helps managers design jobs and purposefully build in the motivation and interest that will enhance quality of worklife and develop team approaches to problem solving. Training and work-related projects challenge managers and first-line employees to be "self-managed." The characteristic of self-management demands creativity, problem-solving skills, and a constant effort and desire to increase personal knowledge, skills, and value to the organization.

Technical advances have required industrial and mechanical engineers to assume the role of "on-the-spot" troubleshooters rather than aloof "gurus" of technology. Even design engineers must now interact and coordinate more with process engineers, sales people, and customers to design better products that meet customer needs. In addition, tools developed by industrial engineers over the years are now being adapted for use as group problem-solving techniques.

Historically, cost accountants have been in charge of controlling costs. Within a TQM system, cost accountants are now being asked to provide explicit numbers, analysis, and guidance on reducing quality costs. Frequently, they find themselves being called on to provide figures to update line workers and managers on the competitive position of the company. They are also in a position to provide information and expertise to assist problem-solving teams with their projects.

Last, but not least, employee involvement team coordinators lead the task of developing, training, and evaluating the results of teams. These specialists may be drawn from any of the areas discussed in the preceding paragraphs; however, they need a thorough grounding in both technical and human resources areas. The teams that they coordinate or facilitate use structured problem-solving techniques to make significant improvements in quality improvement, cost reduction, and process simplification.

You may already have learned the basics of many of these dialects in your earlier studies. However, the importance of the universal language of quality lies in its ability to sharpen the focus on what may otherwise simply be interesting theories. By focusing on quality applications, the theories developed in marketing, accounting, operations management, information systems, and organizational behavior courses, seminars, and texts can take on new meaning. The person who learns to adapt his or her vocabulary and expertise to the requirements of TQM is bound to be valuable to its implementation.

THE GROWTH AND ADOPTION OF TQM

TQM originally matured in the manufacturing sector. During the 1980s, industry in the United States faced a serious competitive crisis. The percentage of nonagricultural workers employed in manufacturing dropped from 35.2 percent in 1947 to 18.7 percent in 1987. The balance of trade in manufacturing goods dropped from a surplus of $18.1 billion in 1981 to a deficit of $151 billion in 1987. Many manufacturers closed plants, which resulted in layoffs of millions of workers. The turnaround at Xerox, Motorola, Ford, and many other companies is directly attributable to an increased focus on quality, spurred on by the manufacturing crisis. As the success stories of manufacturing quality improvement spread, services, government agencies, and educational institutions began to look seriously at how to adapt the principles to their unique organizational cultures. Since then, TQM has permeated every aspect of our society. This section discusses some of the current initiatives in manufacturing, service, government, and education.

TQM in Manufacturing

Well-developed quality assurance systems have functioned in manufacturing for some time. However, these systems have focused on technical issues such as reliability, defect measurement, and process control. The transition to a customer-driven organization caused fundamental changes in manufacturing practices. These changes are particularly evident in product design, worker empowerment, and supplier relations. Product design, for example, integrates marketing, engineering, and manufacturing operations (see Chapter 7). Empowering workers to collect data, perform analyses, and take responsibility for continuous improvements moved the responsibility for quality from the quality control department onto the factory floor. Suppliers became partners in the product design and manufacturing efforts. Many of these efforts were stimulated by the automobile industry as Ford, GM, and Chrysler forced their network of suppliers to improve quality. In 1980, the average new U.S. car had more than seven defects. That statistic has fallen below two today.

Quality leaders in the manufacturing sector include Xerox, AT&T Transmission Systems, Cadillac Motor Car Company, Motorola Inc., Solectron Corporation, and many others. AT&T Transmission Systems (see Quality Profile) emphasizes automated data collection using bar codes and electronic links to provide real-time updates on process performance and ensure the accuracy of manufacturing data. Such information helps to reduce production time and speed development of new products. At Cadillac, more than 700 employees and supplier representatives participate on "simultaneous engineering" teams responsible for defining, engineering, marketing, and continuously improving all Cadillac products. Its product design and development begin with integrated knowledge of all essential elements, including performance targets, product features, systems and parts, processes, and maintenance requirements. This approach anticipates how changes in one functional area will affect the others, making it easier to prevent problems and bottlenecks.

Motorola's employees record defects found in every function of the business in an effort to reduce defects to a target of fewer than 3.4 defects per million opportunities. Motorola is a leader in efforts to reduce total cycle time—the time from when a customer places an order until it is delivered. Solectron specializes in the assembly of complex printed circuit boards and subsystems for makers of computers and other electronic products. As part of its quality efforts, it charts key performance and process control data in all departments. Workers, most of whom are trained in statistical process control methods, are empowered to make process improvements and take corrective actions.

One of the pressures facing many manufacturing industries is the pressure to meet strict quality standards that are required to do business with most European companies. The free trade agreement among the twelve countries of the European Economic Community that went into effect in 1992 had a major impact on standardization of quality systems. To standardize requirements for European countries within the common market and those wishing to do business with those countries, the International Organization for Standardization (ISO) adopted a series of written quality standards in 1987, called the ISO 9000 series of standards.[15] In some markets, companies will not buy from noncertified suppliers. Any telecommunications product that interfaces with the European telecommunications network, for instance, must be purchased from manufacturers that have been certified to be in compliance with ISO 9000. The standards have been adopted in the United States by the American National Standards Institute

(ANSI), with the endorsement and cooperation of the American Society for Quality Control (ASQC). The standards have rigorous documentation requirements for quality assurance systems, which help companies uncover problems and improve processes. The ISO 9000 standards are forcing many companies to reexamine their quality assurance systems. This topic is discussed in more depth in Chapter 12.

■ TQM in Services

The service sector joined the TQM movement several years after manufacturing. The lag in adopting TQM can be attributed to the fact that these industries had not confronted the same aggressive foreign competition that faced manufacturing. Another factor is the high turnover rate in the service industry jobs, which typically pay less than manufacturing jobs. Constantly changing personnel makes establishing a culture for continuous improvement more difficult. Also, the very nature of *quality* changed from a focus on product defects to customer satisfaction. Companies that have achieved national prominence in the service industry include AT&T Universal Card Services, Federal Express Corporation, and The Ritz-Carlton Hotel Company.

AT&T Universal Card Services (UCS) (see Quality Profile) won the Baldrige Award after being in existence for only two years, becoming the second largest credit card company in the industry. The company uses eight broad categories of "satisfiers" to define its quality focus. These satisfiers are linked to an exhaustive set of internal performance measures. UCS has determined what constitutes world-class performance and service, and sets its quality goals accordingly. UCS leads the industry in such areas as speed and accuracy of application processing and customer satisfaction. A list of the "10 most wanted" quality improvements is developed, and cross-functional teams create specific programs and performance measures that link progress to strategic goals.

QUALITY PROFILE
AT&T Universal Card Services

AT&T Universal Card Services (UCS) was launched on March 26, 1990. UCS markets and provides customer services for the AT&T Universal Card, a combined long-distance calling card and general purpose credit card. By September 1992, UCS had more than 10.2 million active accounts and nearly 16 million cardholders, making it the second largest bank card in the industry. The company, headquartered in Jacksonville, Florida, has 2500 associates in four cities across the United States. The values that guide UCS include customer delight, commitment, teamwork, continuous improvement, trust and integrity, mutual respect, and a sense of urgency. UCS continually evaluates and improves the tools and technologies they use to serve customers quickly and efficiently. The company is building a world-class integrated information analysis system to improve the quality of customer account inquiry, data access, and information analysis processes. These efforts translated into significant reductions in operating expenses, increases in productivity, and industry-leading customer satisfaction results.

Application processing cycle time improvements led UCS to an industry-leading consistent three-day processing cycle time, when the industry average is 24 days, and the best in-class competitor takes 10 days. In their first two years of business, UCS received numerous recognitions and awards—including Best Product of 1990 by *Business Week,* Top Banking Innovation by *American Banker,* and Compass Award from the American Marketing Association for outstanding performance—all culminating in a 1992 Baldrige Award.

SOURCE: Malcolm Baldrige National Quality Award, *Profiles of Winners,* National Institute of Standards and Technology, Department of Commerce.

FedEx (formerly Federal Express) measures quality in a similar fashion. FedEx uses a 10-component index that describes comprehensively how its performance is viewed by its customers. Performance data are gathered using advanced computer and tracking systems. Management meets daily to discuss the previous day's performance and tracks weekly, monthly, and annual trends. Training of front-line personnel is the responsibility of managers. Teams regularly assess training needs and devise programs to address those needs. In addition, FedEx uses a well-developed recognition program to acknowledge team and individual contributions.

The Ritz-Carlton Hotel Company operates 25 luxury hotels and pursues the distinction of being the best in its market. It relies on the strength of a comprehensive service quality program that is integrated into marketing and business objectives. This program includes participatory executive leadership, thorough information gathering, coordinated planning and execution, and a trained work force that is empowered to "move heaven and earth" to satisfy customers. Each employee is expected to understand the Ritz-Carlton credo, motto ("Ladies and Gentlemen Serving Ladies and Gentlemen"), three steps of service, and 20 "Ritz-Carlton Basics." Company studies prove the effectiveness of this emphasis, which pays dividends to customers, and ultimately to the company. Daily quality production reports—derived from data submitted from each of 720 work areas in the hotel system—serve as an early warning system that identifies problems and compares them with customer expectations in order to improve services.

These three companies are a minority in their industries. In general, financial services companies, transportation and shipping, and the hotel industry have a long way to go in adopting TQM. Each industry is rooted in traditional cultures that are difficult to change. One service industry that has garnered widespread support for TQM, however, is health care.

As more public and government attention focuses on the health care system, health care providers turn toward TQM as a means of achieving better performance and lower costs.[16] For example, Intermountain Health Care, a nonprofit system of 24 hospitals in Utah, has pursued total quality as a strategic objective since 1985. (In the health care industry, the term CQI—Continuous Quality Improvement—is preferred over TQM). One hospital lowered the rate of postsurgical infections to less than one-fifth of the acceptable national norms through its use of statistical tools for quality improvement. At Boston's New England Deaconess Hospital, teams identify problems that add unnecessary days to hospital stays. In two years, Deaconess achieved a 10 percent overall decrease in length of hospital stay. By reexamining fundamental health care processes, costs can be reduced and quality can be dramatically improved. In 1995, the Malcolm Baldrige National Quality Award initiated a pilot award program for the health care sector (as well as education), with the expectation that such a program will act as a catalyst for quality in healthcare, just as it has in business.

The International Quality Study, a research project conducted by the American Quality Foundation and Ernst & Young in 1991, found that the percentage of health care organizations using quality as a primary assessment criterion for senior management compensation will more than double from a 1991 level of 20 percent to 51 percent in the future, that the percentage of organizations using customer satisfaction as a primary criterion in strategic planning will increase from a 1991 level of 31 percent to 72 percent in the future, and that an increasing number of employees will be involved in quality-related teams. Additionally, the Joint Commission on Accreditation of Healthcare Organizations (JCAHO) issued new standards requiring all hospital CEOs to educate themselves on CQI methods.[17]Accreditation standards more fully incorporate quality improvement principles in areas such as surgical case review, blood usage evaluation, and drug usage evaluation.

■ TQM in the Public Sector

The federal government has a surprisingly long history of quality improvement activities. Quality circle programs—a form of team participation—were developed in the late 1970s at several Department of Defense installations, such as the Norfolk Naval Shipyard and the Cherry Point Naval Air Station. NASA began its quality improvement efforts in the early 1980s, both internally and with its suppliers.[18] However, only recently have senior elected officials and top civil servants begun to develop a total quality management focus. A General Accounting Office report on the "status, scope, and benefits of TQM efforts in the federal government (GGD-93-9BR; October 1, 1992) found that 68 percent of all federal organizations and installations surveyed had some type of TQM effort underway.

The TQM process caught the attention of a number of agencies and managers when Executive Order 12637, "Productivity Improvement for the Federal Government," was signed by President Ronald Reagan in 1988.[19] The order required senior managers to monitor and improve both quality and productivity. It also encouraged them to use employee involvement, training, and participation in decision making, along with the more traditional methods of incentives, recognition, and rewards, to enhance the process.

Fortunately, the changeover from a Republican to a Democratic administration with the inauguration of Bill Clinton as president in 1993 did not slow the advancement of TQM in the federal government. In fact, President Clinton had implemented a TQM process in the state government of Arkansas while he was the governor. Just before his election to the presidency, he wrote an article upholding the values of TQM as a way to enhance the operations of the federal government and to make it more customer-focussed.[20]

An initiative to streamline government was approved by President Clinton shortly after he assumed the presidency. Under the direction of Vice President Al Gore, a report entitled "Creating a Government That Works Better and Costs Less: Report of the National Performance Review" was written and published in the fall of 1993. In it, Vice President Gore made 384 recommendations and indicated 1214 specific actions that the federal government should take to improve government operations and reduce costs. This National Performance Review (NPR) report triggered 11 Executive Orders and Memoranda, signed by the President, to do such things as[21]

■ Eliminate one-half of Executive Branch internal regulations within three years.

■ Set customer service standards to ensure that service provided by agencies "equals the best in business."

■ Create a National Partnership Council to involve government employees and union representatives in championing changes called for by NPR.

■ Create the President's Community Advisory Board to help communities deliver integrated services instead of working out of fragmented federal grants.

■ Streamline bureaucracy by requiring federal agencies to reduce staff by 252,000 people within five years and cut the supervisory ratio from 1:7 to 1:15; also cut office staff in half.

■ Improve agency rulemaking procedures by streamlining the regulatory development process to save time and resources.

■ Implement management reform in the executive branch through newly designated Chief Operating Officers, who work through the President's Management Council to lead the reinvention efforts.

Whether the federal government will be able to "reinvent" itself, or whether this is just another of a long line of "rearrangements" of activities, remains to be seen. However, that TQM principles can have some positive impact on one of the most complex organizations in the world is indeed a refreshing notion.

One of the mechanisms set up to promote quality during the Reagan era was the Federal Quality Institute (FQI). The FQI was established within the U.S. Office of Personnel Management in Washington, D.C., as the "primary source of leadership, information, and consulting services on quality management in the federal government." The Institute provides such products and services as seminars, start-up assistance, national and regional conferences, support of quality awards, a listing of private sector consultants, an information network, and research and publications. The Institute's logo, reproduced in Figure 4.6, shows in graphic form that their concept is similar to that of private sector business.

FEDERAL QUALITY AWARDS

In 1990, the FQI was given responsibility for administering the Presidential Quality Award and the Quality Improvement Prototype Award, which are the federal government's equivalent of the Malcolm Baldrige National Quality Award given

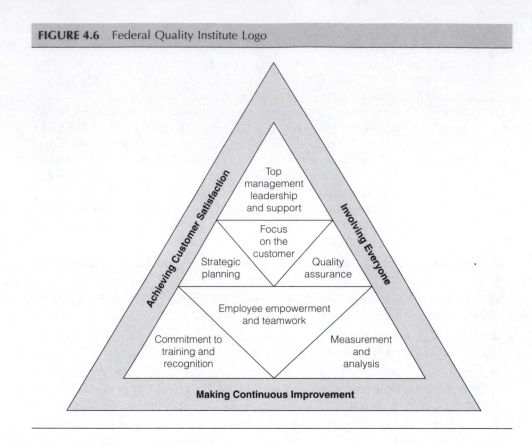

FIGURE 4.6   Federal Quality Institute Logo

to private sector businesses. The Baldrige Award will be discussed in greater detail in Chapter 12. In June 1993, Dick Obrien, administrator of the President's Federal Quality Awards Program, announced[22]

> We have changed the criteria for the Presidential Award for Quality so that they closely parallel the criteria for the Malcolm Baldrige National Quality Award. Our new scoring guidelines are in place for the 1994 award cycle. We made these changes to make the Government criteria more congruent with the criteria accepted in the private sector and to encourage private-public partnerships as we go about the business of reinventing government.

Table 4.1 lists the 1992–1994 Quality Improvement Prototype winners. These and earlier winners provide examples of what a concerted emphasis on TQM can accomplish within the federal government's vast agencies. For example, the Naval Aviation Depot at Cherry Point, North Carolina is the only two-time winner of the Quality Improvement Prototype award. This location is responsible for maintenance, engineering, and logistics support of military aircraft, engines and components and is operated by the U.S. Marine Corps. It employs approximately 3000 people in 144 skill trades represented by six unions. It must compete for work in the public and private sectors. Some of the Depot's accomplishments include:

- Increasing market share of the highly competitive aircraft maintenance work from $249 million in 1988 to $400 million in 1993.

- Realizing $185 million in savings and cost avoidance from 1988 to 1993.

- Providing almost $20 million in productivity gain-sharing awards to employees since 1988.

TABLE 4.1   The 1992–1994 Quality Improvement Prototype Award Winners

"A prototype organization demonstrates an extraordinary commitment to quality improvement, focuses attention on satisfying its customers and establishes high standards of quality, timeliness and efficiency. This kind of organization also serves as a model for the rest of government—showing how a commitment to quality leads to better and more efficient services and products for its customers."
    —James C. Miller, III, Director of the Office of Management and Budget, 1988.

1992

San Francisco Region Wage and Hour Division, Employment Standards Division, Department of Labor

Administration, Patent and Trademark Office, Department of Commerce, Arlington, VA

Regional Office and Insurance Center, Department of Veterans Affairs, Philadelphia, PA

Aeronautical Systems Division, Air Force Systems Command, Wright-Patterson Air Force Base, OH

Defense Contract Management District Northeast, Defense Logistics Agency, Boston, MA

1993

Arnold Engineering Development Center, Arnold Air Force Base, TN

Naval Air Warfare Center, Aircraft Division, Lakehurst, NJ

Naval Aviation Depot, Cherry Point, NC

1994

Army Tank/Automotive Research, Development and Engineering Center, MI

Air Force Electronics Systems Center, MA

Naval Undersea Warfare Center, WA

One of the 1991 winners, the Defense Industrial Supply Center (DISC) at Wright Patterson Air Force Base, undertook a quality turnaround after they experienced problems in supply availability and increased backorders. Although a quality circle program had been successfully established, managers realized that a TQM commitment was lacking. The turnaround results were evident in the improvements reported, including the reduction of backorders from 273,000 to 263,000, between fiscal year (FY) 1988 and FY 1989; an increase in supply availability (the percentage of time the customers' orders are filled the first time through the system) to 87.6 percent, the highest rate since 1984; and the development of an "introspection program" to identify, eliminate, and prevent problems. The story of the Cincinnati Service Center of the IRS, a 1990 award winner, will be presented as a Quality in Practice case in Chapter 11.

STATE AND CITY TQM EFFORTS

State governments have gained momentum in developing their own TQM programs and processes. A recent telephone survey by the National Governor's Association (NGA) showed that 36 of the 50 states have some type of quality management effort underway.[23] Massachusetts, for example, has formed a Quality Improvement Council to oversee and facilitate a broad TQM program. Governor Fife Symington of Arizona introduced TQM into state management processes as part of his Strategic Long-Term Improvement Management project. In North Carolina, pilot projects for improvement in the quality of services are underway in the Department of Administration and the Division of Motor Vehicles. New York announced a "Quality through Participation" program in August 1991, to improve service delivery in state operations. Firms such as Corning,

IBM, Kodak, and Xerox are cooperating in this effort. Many other states are investigating TQM and working with corporate partners in developing programs.

City governments have also recognized the potential of total quality management. One of the best documented examples of successful TQM development and use involved the city of Madison, Wisconsin. Joseph Sensenbrenner, mayor of Madison from 1983 to 1989, was one of the leaders in bringing TQM to city government.[24] After a 1983 audit disclosed problems at the city garage, such as long delays in repair and equipment unavailability, but offered no explanations as to the root causes of the problems, Sensenbrenner attended a seminar by W. Edwards Deming. Even though he agreed with the Deming philosophy, Sensenbrenner also recognized the ingrained bureaucratic culture of government.

He attempted to apply the Deming theory at the city garage, where the manager and mechanics were surprised to see "top management" personally visible and committed to their problems. Sensenbrenner obtained the cooperation of the union president and formed a team to gather data from individual mechanics and the repair process itself. The team found that many delays resulted from insufficient stocking of repair parts, which, in turn was caused by having more than 440 different types, makes, models, and years of equipment—all obtained by purchasing from the lowest bidder. When looking for the reason behind the problem, the team encountered a classic case of passing the buck: The parts purchaser said that central purchasing would not let him stock fewer parts from fewer reliable suppliers; central purchasing claimed the comptroller would not allow it; the comptroller was sure the city attorney would never approve it. The city attorney said, "Why, of course you can do that. All you need to do is write the specifications so they include the warranty, the ease of maintenance, the availability of parts, and the resale value over time. . . . I assumed you were doing it all along." As Deming stated, the problem was not caused by the workers; it was a result of the system.

Finding a solution meant introducing front-line employees to problem solving. Solving the problem required teamwork and breaking down barriers between departments. The concept of an internal customer was virtually unknown. When the 24-step purchasing policy was changed to 3 steps, employees were stunned and delighted that someone was listening to them. They studied the potential of a preventive maintenance program and discovered, for example, that city departments did not use truck-bed linings when hauling corrosive materials such as salt. Mechanics rode along on police patrols and learned that squad cars spent more time idling; this information was used to tune engines properly. Other departments helped gather data. As a result, the average vehicle turnaround time was reduced from nine days to three with a net annual savings of about $700,000.

The lessons learned in the city garage were expanded to other departments from painting to health. Although employee morale improved, middle management presented considerable resistance. At one point, all team members in one set of projects resigned, feeling that their managers—who should have been giving them guidance and support—were instead setting them up for failure and blame. Direct involvement by the mayor along with improved planning and communication solved the problem.

By the time Sensenbrenner left office in 1989, Madison's city departments each ran between 20 and 30 quality improvement projects at a time; five agencies focused on long-term commitment to new management practices, including continuous quality improvement skills and data-gathering techniques; the city provided training in quality to every employee; several state agencies eager to follow

Madison's approach initiated joint efforts; and city workers continued to invent service improvements for internal and external customers.

■ TQM in Education

Education represents one of the most interesting and challenging areas for TQM advocates. In many ways, education is the key to the future of TQM, just as it is to the future economic, social, political and societal well-being of any nation. Attacks on the quality of education in the United States, from kindergarten through the 12th grade (K–12) and at colleges and universities provided a rallying cry for education reform during the last decade.[25] Aside from a few notable exceptions and pockets of excellence, educators, educational institutions, political groups and leaders, and even the public generally have been slow to attack the problem of educational decline on a systematic basis. A comprehensive review of the subject is beyond the scope of this text; however, a few specific examples of how leadership of concerned educators and partnerships with business organizations that have a TQM focus have stimulated significant changes may be helpful here.

TQM in K–12: Mt. Edgecumbe High School

Perhaps the most widely publicized story of the successful use of TQM in a K–12 school is that of Mt. Edgecumbe High School in Sitka, Alaska.[26] Mt. Edgecumbe is a public boarding school with some 200 students, often from problem homes in rural Alaska. Many are Native Americans, who are struggling to keep their culture alive while learning to live and work in American society. David Langford, a teacher, brought the TQM concept to Mt. Edgecumbe after hearing about it at a meeting at McDonnell-Douglas Helicopter Co. After reading many books by quality gurus such as Deming, Juran, and Crosby, Langford took some students in a computer club on a trip to Gilbert (Arizona) High School. There, they observed how Delores Christiansen taught continuous improvement in her business classes. They also visited companies in the Phoenix area that were using TQM. The students, with the coaching of Langford, began to use TQM concepts to improve school processes. For example, the students tackled the problem of too many tardy classmates. By investigating the reasons for tardiness, the students persuaded the administration to drop the punishment for tardy students, and were able to reduce the average number of late occurrences per week from 35 to 5.

As an even more radical change, the school dropped the traditional grading system. Instead, students use statistical techniques to keep track of their own progress. No assignment is considered finished until it is perfect. Eliminating grades has had a positive effect. One student, James Penemarl reported, "I found myself learning a lot more. It's not the teacher having to check my progress, it's me having to check my progress. See, however much I learn is up to me, and if I want to learn, I'm going to go out and learn." Despite the obvious success of what they call CIP, the Continuous Improvement Process (approximately 50 percent of students now go on to college), the messages that David Langford gives in interviews about the school are (1) it takes time, effort, and persistence—it's not a "quick fix", and (2) there's always room for improvement.

TQM in Universities

The most publicized TQM success story at the university level is Oregon State University (OSU). The implementation process was documented in an article by

Dr. L. Edwin Coate, OSU's vice president of Finance and Administration, who took the leading role in bringing TQM to OSU.[27] With a commitment from the president, the university set a goal of implementing an institution-wide TQM process by 1994. After surveying 25 colleges and universities already involved in a TQM process, Coate and others at OSU decided that the basic tenets of TQM could be applied to universities. However, as Coate pointed out

> We must not, however, apply TQM principles without research, adaptation, training, and pilot testing in the actual university setting. Educators will need to be trained to collect and interpret data on program effectiveness and pupil achievement and to identify patterns that develop over a period of time.
>
> When a pattern is having a negative effect on the educational process, changes must be made. The quality improvement tools of TQM are available to do this.

After further study of TQM literature, a visit from Dr. W. Edwards Deming, company visits to Ford, Hewlett-Packard, and Dow, and attendance by the president and several top administrators at a seminar on problem-solving tools, administrators at OSU began the planning phase. They determined that the best approach to implementing TQM at OSU was to combine a strategic planning approach similar to the one used at Hewlett-Packard, along with the Baldrige Award criteria, in order to create a five-year plan.

The first pilot study at OSU was conducted in the physical plant area for a number of reasons: (1) TQM was considered a high-priority issue, (2) it had a high probability of success, (3) management agreed that it was important, (4) no one else was working on it, and (5) it was important to the customers of the organization. A multi-level team of twelve people chose to study the specific issue of ways to "decrease turnaround time in the remodeling process." Early on, they found that the complete process was too complex to be studied by a single team. They estimated that a chart covering the entire process would be 17 feet long. They also felt that more engineering representatives were required. Thus, two subteams—engineering, and design and construction—were formed. These teams made and implemented a number of recommendations, including the development of a project manager position, installation of a customer service center to enhance work scheduling, control and follow up, implementation of customer surveys to assess communications, more consultation at the beginning of the process with customers, identification of equipment and materials that can be purchased during the design phase, and shop participation to identify potential problems during the design phase. The first pilot project reduced the remodeling project time by 10 percent. These process changes improved employee attitudes and the work ethic in the physical plant area. In turn, customers were more satisfied and more understanding when delays were encountered. Using customer surveys, the team studied many other processes such as those in recruitment and admissions, which resulted in the formation of a cross-functional marketing committee. More detailed information about the work at OSU and the application of TQM principles can be found in Coate and Lewis and Smith.[28] However, note that most applications of TQM in higher education have focused on the administrative side, not in teaching or research.

BUSINESS–EDUCATION PARTNERSHIPS

Management and leaders in business have raised concerns about the quality of education in the United States. Many of their efforts have been focussed on the

K–12 problems, since they appear to be more widespread and have great impact. In 1992, *Fortune* magazine surveyed the amount of business contribution and support to all levels of education. Of the 342 *Fortune Industrial 500* and *Service 500* firms that responded, 84 percent indicated their top management was "very involved" or "fairly involved" in education. Sixty-five percent of respondents reported that their companies made donations to elementary school-related projects, 75 percent donated to high school related efforts, and 87 percent donated to colleges and universities.[29]

In May 1991, a consortium of professional associations, business associations, individual businesses, and universities incorporated as a nonprofit membership group called the National Education Quality Initiative (NEQI).[30] Its purpose is far-reaching, based on its mission statement:

> It is the purpose of the National Education Quality Initiative to foster three objectives by all practical means so that all residents of this nation will become wholly knowledgeable about quality:
>
> ■ To obtain the inclusion of appropriate portions of the quality sciences and associated arts into every course anyone takes from preschool through graduate school and in continuing education.
>
> ■ To obtain the incorporation of the quality sciences and associated arts into all aspects of the administration and operation of all schools in the country.
>
> ■ To improve the quality of the content and delivery of all material to students in the entire educational process.

Perhaps the largest single private grant of $500 million for school improvement was announced in December 1993, donated by media giant and philanthropist Walter Annenburg. With such efforts underway, substantial improvements can now be made in the K–12 educational system, although they will not be rapid or easy.

A consortium of businesses, including Procter & Gamble, American Express, General Motors, IBM, Milliken, Motorola, 3M, and Xerox, has explored ways in which universities can be persuaded to incorporate TQM into curricula in business and engineering.[31] The following list of businesses and educational institutions is only a small sampling of partnership arrangements for sharing experiences and TQM training that have developed over the past four years:

■ IBM, MIT, and Rochester Institute of Technology
■ Milliken, Georgia Tech, and N.C. State
■ Motorola and Purdue
■ P&G, University of Wisconsin–Madison, and Tuskegee Institute
■ Xerox and Carnegie Mellon

In addition, to encourage development of comprehensive approaches to TQM in colleges of business and engineering, IBM has given $1 million grants to each of eight universities. Part of IBM's motivation lies in their expectation of a return on their investment, that is, in the quality of graduates from these and other programs. These efforts demonstrate that businesses are serious about improving the quality of both content and delivery of instruction at colleges and universities through use of TQM methods.

CRITICISM AND DEBATE

Much criticism has arisen regarding TQM. In reference to Douglas Aircraft, a troubled subsidiary of McDonnell Douglas Corporation, *Newsweek* stated, "The aircraft maker three years ago embraced 'Total Quality Management,' a Japanese import that had become the American business cult of the 1980s. . . . At Douglas, TQM appeared to be just one more hothouse Japanese flower never meant to grow on rocky ground."[32] Other articles in *The Wall Street Journal* ("Quality Programs Show Shoddy Results," May 14, 1992) and the *New York Times* ("The Lemmings Who Love Total Quality," May 3, 1992) suggest that total quality approaches are passing fads and inherently flawed. The critics do support their opinions.[33] For example, a 1992 Rath & Strong survey found that only 20 percent of *Fortune 500* companies are satisfied with the results of their TQM initiatives. Applications for the Malcolm Baldrige National Quality Award have declined since peaking at 106 in 1991. A survey of 300 electronics companies by the American Electronics Association found that among the 73 percent of the companies that had quality programs in place, more than half noted that quality had not improved by even 10 percent.

Despite the critics, a recent study by the Conference Board indicates that TQM is alive and well.[34] Many companies have achieved astounding success through a total quality emphasis. The world has become more quality conscious, and companies that resist TQM may not be in business for long. In actuality, the quality management discipline is quite young. Companies that have invested millions of dollars in improving quality are not about to let their investment go to waste; however, they need to be both persistent and patient to achieve desired results. The Conference Board study, based on more than five years of research on hundreds of U.S. companies, found that companies need at least four years to persuade employees to buy into the TQM philosophy and eight to ten years to fully establish a TQM culture. When any company begins to think of how to improve quality, it will find itself looking at the various approaches united under the TQM concept. Today, total quality is a matter of survival.

Perhaps a three-letter acronym is inadequate to represent such a powerful management concept. Unfortunately, many people simply point to newspaper headlines and selected surveys as a generalizable condemnation of TQM. Reasons for failure of TQM usually are rooted in organizational approaches and management systems, many of which are addressed in Chapter 13 and throughout this book. As the editor of *Quality Digest* put it: "No, TQM isn't dead. TQM failures just prove that bad management is still alive and kicking."

The cases in the following section illustrate how entire organizations successfully apply the principles and practices of total quality management. Profiles of AT&T and the Saturn division of General Motors provide two excellent examples of incorporating the concepts of TQM within an organization's culture.

QUALITY IN PRACTICE   TOTAL QUALITY MANAGEMENT AT AT&T[35]

AT&T has been a pioneer in quality, revolutionizing industrial practices and helping to make AT&T products among the best in the world. In 1988, the company changed the direction of its management practices and concentrated on total quality. AT&T put customers at the top of the organization, began a process of structural and operational changes aimed at making it the best in the world at delivering the benefits of information technology. It reshaped the company into business units aligned directly with customers. In 1992, two divisions—the Network Transmission Systems and Universal Card Services—won the Malcolm Baldrige Award.

Certain fundamental principles guide AT&T:

- The customer comes first.
- Quality happens through people.
- All work is part of a process.
- Suppliers are an integral part of the business.
- Prevention is achieved through planning.
- Quality improvement never ends.

AT&T's Total Quality Approach, shown in Figure 4.7, is built on these principles, which determines company practices and guides the management of its business. It contains four elements: *Customer Focus, Management and Improvement, Supplier Partnership,* and the *Leadership and Involvement of Our People.* It has the power to direct change, align and focus their efforts, and ensure that they meet the needs of customers, employees, stockholders, suppliers, and communities. The Total Quality Approach has two dimensions. The horizontal dimension represents how the company manages work to add value for customers. The vertical dimension represents a new way for employees to work together, requiring full involvement of people and a new role for leadership.

AT&T defines quality as consistently meeting customer expectations. It challenges employees to identify customers, anticipate and understand what customers need and expect, and ensure that all they do contributes to their ability to deliver. One example of this customer focus occurred when a cardholder called AT&T Universal Card Services in hope that the office might have a record of a recent purchase by his wife, a victim of Alzheimer's disease who had disappeared on vacation. The AT&T associate who received the call verified the story and investigated. Each day he checked the account regularly. On the fifth day, he received a call from a merchant whose description fit the missing woman. He then notified the husband and police. A medical team was dispatched and the woman was returned safely to her family.

AT&T aligns its work processes to satisfy its customers, which include both large, cross-functional processes that deliver products and services to outside customers as well as the many internal processes whose suppliers and customers are inside the company. Throughout AT&T, cross-functional teams manage and improve processes, following the

---

FIGURE 4.7 AT&T Total Quality Approach

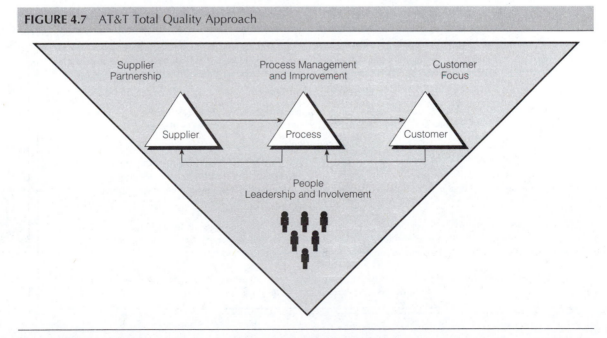

company's Process Quality Management and Improvement Methodology:

1. Establish process management responsibilities.

2. Baseline the current process and identify customer requirements.

3. Define and establish measures.

4. Assess conformance to customer requirements.

5. Investigate to find improvement opportunities.

6. Rank the opportunities and set objectives.

7. Continuously improve the process.

The AT&T Supplier Quality Policy states clearly the company's commitment to work in partnership with suppliers toward the common goal of customer satisfaction.

We view our suppliers as an integral part of our business. Relationships with our suppliers are driven by our customers and built on Total Quality Principles and Practices. We commit to a Supplier Management Process that continuously improves our ability to add value for AT&T customers.

One example of supplier partnerships involves local telephone companies who provide AT&T access to their customers. Following divestiture, AT&T established a Financial Assurance Organization to check the accuracy of access charges and to correct errors. By 1989, AT&T employed 1100 people working to duplicate the supplier's access-billing system, anticipate charges, and resolve problems. In 1990, AT&T began a joint effort with Pacific Bell to design a single access billing verification process—involving both supplier and customer—that shifted focus from correction to prevention, moved accountability for accuracy to the supplier, and replaced post-bill resolution with pre-bill certification. As a result, the

---

FIGURE 4.8 AT&T's Shared Values

OUR COMMON BOND

We commit to these values to guide our decisions and behavior:

Respect for Individuals

We treat each other with respect and dignity, valuing individual and cultural differences. We communicate frequently and with candor, listening to each other regardless of level or position. Recognizing that exceptional quality begins with people, we give individuals the authority to use their capabilities to the fullest to satisfy their customers. Our environment supports personal growth and continuous learning for all AT&T people.

Dedication to Helping Customers

We truly care for each customer. We build enduring relationships by understanding and anticipating our customers' needs and by serving them better each time than the time before. AT&T customers can count on us to consistently deliver superior products and services that help them achieve their personal and business goals.

Highest Standards of Integrity

We are honest and ethical in all our business dealings, starting with how we treat each other. We keep our promises and admit our mistakes. Our personal conduct ensures that AT&T's name is always worthy of trust.

Innovation

We believe innovation is the engine that will keep us vital and growing. Our culture embraces creativity, seeks different perspectives, and risks pursuing new opportunities. We create and rapidly convert technology into products and services, constantly searching for new ways to make technology more useful to customers.

Teamwork

We encourage and reward both individual and team achievements. We freely join with colleagues across organizational boundaries to advance the interests of customers and shareowners. Our team spirit extends to being responsible and caring partners in the communities where we live and work.

By living these values, AT&T aspires to set a standard of excellence world wide that will reward our shareowners, our customers, and all AT&T people.

time needed in the validation process declined from three months to 24 hours, accuracy went up, and costs came down.

The new role of leadership is represented by the inverted pyramid in Figure 4.7. Customers are at the top of the organization; leaders provide direction, empowerment, and support for the people who create value for those customers. AT&T's shared values—Respect for the Individual, Dedication to Helping Customers, Highest Standards of Integrity, Innovation, and Teamwork—influence decisions and define how employees work together (see Figure 4.8). A management executive committee, serving as the AT&T Quality Council, sets policy and strategy. The corporate quality office supports the council and helps develop and deploy methods, guidelines, and tools to advance efforts throughout the company. A quality steering committee, made up of quality managers from all units, fosters communication and guides companywide improvement efforts.

The Total Quality Approach calls for full involvement of all employees. Employees contribute beyond their natural work groups through quality councils, cross-functional process management teams, quality improvement teams in daily work, quality of work life teams, and through suggestion systems. Teamwork is the critical ingredient to achievement and improvement at AT&T. Throughout the company, teams apply the Total Quality Approach to improve their ability to serve customers. The results of these team efforts range from dramatic reductions in costs and time intervals, to small process changes that add up to increased customer satisfaction. For example, unreliable test and measurement equipment caused quality problems at the Reading Works. A team recommended a new calibration system built on a partnership between calibration engineers and the production line. The new system subsequently cut calibration costs in half and brought AT&T's test and measurement equipment to a level that exceeds industry standards. In addition, a Motorola Quality Assurance audit team recognized this new process as "best in industry worldwide."

Key Issues for Discussion

1. Explain how AT&T's Total Quality Approach supports the principles of TQM discussed in this chapter.

2. Discuss some of the key practices, techniques, and infrastructure that support AT&T's quality focus.

QUALITY IN PRACTICE   SATURN CORPORATION IS BUILT ON TOTAL QUALITY[36]

General Motors' Saturn project has become a test of whether U.S. industry can adapt and beat the Japanese automakers at what they do best. Saturn was born in June 1982, when GM began a top-secret project aimed at revolutionizing carmaking in the United States. They named it *Saturn* after the rocket that propelled the United States past the Soviets' lead in space exploration. About two-and-one-half years later, the Saturn Corporation was formed as a wholly owned subsidiary of General Motors in January 1985. GM's chairman Roger Smith called Saturn the "key to GM's long term competitiveness, survival, and success."

In the small car market in which Saturn vehicles compete, quality is a "must." Meeting and exceeding customers' requirements and expectations on a consistent basis is a key strategy in Saturn's success. To accomplish its objective, the Saturn project began with a clean slate. Nothing in GM's manufacturing past was required for building the Saturn; all design and engineering approaches were new. The Saturn manufacturing complex was built to be self-sufficient, with its own stamping plants, power train assembly, and foundries. Saturn was originally intended to be a high-tech factory full of automated equipment and robots. But GM's joint venture with Toyota proved that labor–management relations could do more for quality and productivity than automation. Workers are chosen more for their interpersonal skills than for technical skills.

Saturn machines and assembles both manual and automatic transmissions on the same line in any sequence, a first for a U.S. manufacturer. Cars move along the line on wooden pallets and workers travel with them, which is easier on workers' legs than standing on concrete floors and eliminates the need to walk down the line to install parts. GM even overhauled the administrative systems that operate within Saturn. As each finished car exits the plant, Saturn's computers automatically authorize payment to suppliers. Saturn uses only one data base for all its financial operations, including purchasing, payroll, and dealer billing.

Saturn does not have a formal quality department. There is no one director of quality. Saturn uses a series of quality councils to set quality goals and provide general direction. These councils are composed of both UAW union members and management team members who meet on a periodic basis. The highest quality council is chaired by the president of the local UAW union and the president of Saturn Corporation. In addition to quality councils, Saturn also has specific quality resource areas to aid and support the team members assembling the vehicles on the factory floor. These quality resource areas are also responsible for the development and audit of quality procedures, quality methods, and quality systems.

Saturn's corporate philosophy reads as follows:

We, the Saturn Team, in concert with the UAW and General Motors, believe that meeting the needs of customers, Saturn members, suppliers, dealers, and neighbors is fundamental to fulfilling our mission.

To meet our customers' needs:

■ Our products and services must be world leaders in value and satisfaction.

To meet our members' needs:

■ We will create a sense of belonging in an environment of mutual trust, respect and dignity.
■ We believe that all people want to be involved in decisions that affect them, care about their jobs, take pride in themselves and their contributions, and want to share in the success of their efforts.
■ We will develop the tools, training and education for each member, recognizing individual skills and knowledge.
■ We believe that creative, motivated and responsible team members who understand that change is critical to success are Saturn's most important asset.

To meet our suppliers' and dealers' needs:

■ We will create real partnerships with them.
■ We will be open and fair in our dealings, reflecting trust, respect and their importance to Saturn.

■ We want dealers and suppliers to feel ownership in Saturn's mission and philosophy as their own.

To meet the needs of our neighbors and the communities in which we live and operate:

■ We will be good citizens, protect the environment and conserve natural resources.
■ We will seek to cooperate with government at all levels and strive to be sensitive, open and candid in our public statements.

This statement represents a fundamental commitment not to be compromised or undermined by decisions that could be attractive in the short term but would lead the organization in an undesired direction in the long run. Every decision must fit Saturn's philosophy.

Starting from ground level, Saturn defined the values necessary to compete effectively and to attract the best GM managers and UAW workers willing to assume the challenges and risks associated with those values. Saturn's culture, created with these values, can be summed up in one word: *partnership*. A close partnership between GM and the UAW influences every strategic, tactical, and operational decision. Such sharing of decision making and building mutual trust is unique in the U.S. auto industry. Educational initiatives directed at improving union leaders' business knowledge and managers' people knowledge strengthen communication and contribute an important element to this partnership.

One of Saturn's major innovations is GM's agreement with the UAW. Teams of workers have broad decision-making powers and responsibilities. They undergo hundreds of hours of training and learn the economics behind each car. This UAW contract differs significantly from previous contracts. It includes the following features:

■ The contract has no specific expiration date. Exactly one year from the date that the first car comes off the line, management and labor may begin modifying the contract, if necessary, on a day-to-day basis.

■ Saturn workers have a hand in the design of the vehicle and the factory.

■ Job classifications, which number in the dozens in traditional automobile factories, have been cut to only a few. As a result, a production worker can do a simple repair without waiting for an electrician while production grinds to a halt.

■ Saturn employees work on salary and receive 80 percent of the wages other UAW members receive, but they are eligible for bonuses depending on the car's success.

Worker involvement is unprecedented. Intensive training and elimination of barriers between management and labor characterize Saturn. Teams of line workers do more than just assemble parts; they "hire" workers, approve parts from suppliers, choose their own equipment, and handle administrative matters such as their budgets. Workers and union representatives have a great deal of input on business issues. In 1991, when managers increased production that wound up raising the number of defects, line workers staged a slowdown during the visit of GM's chairman. The president of the UAW stated, "We are not going to sacrifice quality to get productivity." Managers eventually eased their production goals.

The heart of the organizational structure of Saturn is a *work unit,* a team of about 15 people who make decisions by consensus. Work units evolve, starting as conventional teams with an external union and management advisor. They then begin to assume the responsibilities traditionally assigned to a supervisor or foreman. As the team hires other members, it teaches them Saturn's mission, philosophy, and values, and ensures that they develop the necessary skills to perform the team's tasks. With increased group interaction, the team moves toward a completely self-directed team. Team members, most of whom have worked from five to twenty-five years in the auto industry, receive from 250 to 750 hours of intensive education and training just to prepare for their jobs. The education covers behavioral subjects, leadership, and team development, and even includes learning to read a balance sheet. Saturn opens its books internally and expects employees to know how much their operations add to the cost of the car.

Partnerships necessarily extend to suppliers and dealers. Saturn's goal is to establish a long-term partnership with only one supplier for each input based on mutual trust, high quality standards, just-in-time delivery, and continuous improvement. Saturn believes that each dealer must not be threatened by competition from other Saturn dealers, a practice that has proven to be counterproductive in the automobile industry. Instead, Saturn dealers have designated market areas and help other regions as needed. The no-dicker sticker price also reduces internal competition.

Day-to-day monitoring of product quality is accomplished through the use of statistical methods, adherence to Saturn quality systems and procedures, the appropriate use of various problem-solving tools, quality-related education in a team environment, and inherent team motivation and enthusiasm. Work unit members receive customer feedback from the field within 24 hours to facilitate rapid analysis and appropriate corrective action.

In 1993, Saturn captured 2.39 percent of the U.S. car market. Seventy-three percent of the buyers were classified as "plus business" to General Motors, meaning that had Saturn not been available, these buyers would not have purchased a GM product. Ongoing surveys show that 97 percent of Saturn owners say they would "enthusiastically recommend the purchase of a Saturn car" to a friend, relative, or neighbor.

Key Issues for Discussion

1. Explain how the infrastructure at Saturn was designed to support the principles of total quality management.

2. Discuss why a "clean sheet" approach to designing the Saturn organization can more successfully implement TQM than attempting to change a traditional organization.

SUMMARY OF KEY POINTS

■ Total quality management (TQM) is a total, companywide effort—through full involvement of the entire workforce and a focus on continuous improvement—that companies use to achieve customer satisfaction. TQM is both a comprehensive managerial philosophy and a collection of tools and approaches for its implementation.

■ TQM is an approach that is grounded on the three core principles of: a focus on customers; participation and teamwork; and continuous improvement.

■ Effective implementation of TQM is dependent on: infrastructure, practice and tools; leadership; strategic planning; data and information management;

process management; supplier management; human resource management; and development of a supportive corporate culture.

■ TQM represents a philosophy that is quite different from traditional management in many aspects, including organizational structures, role of people, management systems, rewards, teamwork, supplier relationships, control, customers, motivation, and competition.

■ TQM demands new styles of management, skills, and "languages" that must be spoken throughout the organization, with participation by all employees. Change and rising expectations cause setbacks and anxiety, which can be avoided through proper planning.

■ TQM has gone beyond the private sector and has become important in government operations. Many Federal quality awards have been established to recognize government agencies that have achieved high quality levels. The 1993 National Performance Review report set the stage for the Clinton administration's "reinventing government" initiative that uses many of the TQM concepts.

■ K–12 school systems, colleges and universities, supported and encouraged by business and industry groups, are beginning to adapt the TQM philosophy to their operations and administrative systems. Business-education partnerships have been formed to provide funding, research and a forum for discussion of the application of TQM to education.

■ TQM had been criticized in the media as a passing fad and a flawed philosophy. However, a number of objective studies have shown that TQM is alive and well and that its benefits far outweigh its weaknesses.

REVIEW QUESTIONS

1. Define total quality management.

2. What are the four characteristics of Feigenbaum's "engineered total quality system"? Do these same principles apply today as they did in the 1950s?

3. How does companywide quality control as practiced in Japan relate to our concept of total quality management?

4. Explain the core principles of TQM.

5. Define the elements of a TQM infrastructure.

6. Explain the difference between TQM principles, infrastructure, practices, and tools.

7. Describe the various types of facts and data needed for quality assessment and improvement.

8. Provide some examples of continuous improvement within a company.

9. What is corporate culture? How can TQM be integrated into a company's culture?

10. What aspects of the Procter & Gamble statement of quality principles and purpose capture the essence of total quality?

11. Explain the tangible benefits that can occur from a TQM focus.

12. Contrast the important differences between TQM and traditional management practices in the following areas:

a. Organizational structure

b. Role of people

c. Definition of quality

d. Goals and objectives

e. Knowledge

f. Management systems

g. Reward systems

h. Management's role

i. Union–management relations

j. Teamwork

k. Supplier relationships

l. Control

m. Customers

n. Responsibility

o. Motivation

p. Competition

13. What impacts has TQM had on modern management thinking and practices?

14. Explain the differences in the adoption and potential for success of TQM in manufacturing, service, the public sector, and education.

15. Why should TQM *not* be considered a short-term program?

DISCUSSION QUESTIONS

1. Think of some "quality" issues similar to the Polaroid case discussed in the introduction to this chapter that you have encountered in a job or within your school. How would you classify them as something other than "quality" issues?

2. Find or develop an organization chart for your college or university. List several key processes that contribute to the mission of the school and explain how they cut across functions in the organization chart.

3. Explain how the TQM philosophy might apply to the management of a fraternity or student organization.

4. How can you encourage and promote teamwork and participation within an organization?

5. How would you characterize the "corporate culture" of your college or university? How can it provide a foundation for total quality management, if it does not already do so?

6. Many companies are forging strategic alliances with international partners. Study this issue and discuss how it relates to TQM principles.[37]

7. Consider each of the management practices we discussed in this chapter in the context of TQM versus traditional management (see Review Question 12). Propose some approaches for how an organization might move from the traditional practice to a TQM focus. What changes would be necessary?

8. How can an instructor use TQM concepts in conducting a college class?

9. Has TQM been adopted by your local government? Interview some local politicians and managers to answer this question. Can you, as a customer, obtain easy access to these people?

10. What did the editor of *Quality Digest* mean when stating, "TQM failures just prove that bad management is still alive and kicking"?

C A S E S

I. Hillshire Farm/Kahn's[38]

In 1971, Consolidated Foods Incorporated (later renamed Sara Lee) acquired Quality Packing Company, the forerunner of Hillshire Farm, to complete the meat product lines for their Kahn's division and compete in the smoked sausage market. In 1988, Hillshire Farm merged with Kahn's to gain economies of scale and buying power.

Milton Schloss, president of Kahn's at the time of the acquisition, wanted to produce smoked sausage products that were equal to or superior to the market leader, Eckridge. Hillshire Farm surpassed Eckridge as the leader in the smoked sausage market. As president of Hillshire Farm and Kahn's, Schloss was a firm believer in "managing by walking around." He made a habit of taking a daily tour of the plant and asking employees "What's new?" One day an employee asked him if he really meant it. The question surprised Schloss, and he arranged to meet privately with the employee early the next morning. The employee arrived with a balsa wood model of a new plant layout he had been working on at home. Recognizing the superiority of his ideas, Schloss asked him why he never came forward before. The employee said that nobody had ever asked him. The design was implemented and portions are still in place at Hillshire Farm in Cincinnati. This event acted as a catalyst for further quality efforts.

Drawing from a similar program at Procter & Gamble, Hillshire Farm developed a system called Deliberate Methods Change (DMC) to seek ways for continually improving their processes. Using DMC, semi-voluntary groups of salaried employees met to improve current processes. By emphasizing the positive aspects of improvement and refusing to place blame on process design flaws, these groups built trust among the work force.

Schloss saw the importance of quality within the meat industry, and especially at Hillshire Farm. He used customer complaints as the basis for defining quality, or more accurately, what customers found unacceptable. Schloss personally answered all customer complaints promptly, a practice that was unheard of at the time. Frequently, customers were so surprised to hear from the company president that they apologized for their complaints. However, Schloss listened carefully to understand the nature of the complaint so that he could improve product quality. Also, he believed that a phone call from the company president would allow Hillshire Farm to keep the customer for life.

Schloss took a variety of steps to show his commitment and improve quality. He kept the plant grounds free of litter, all the walls freshly painted, and the grass and shrubbery neatly trimmed. With these extra touches, he communicated to employees the attitude they should adopt when they entered the building. Schloss also insisted that all telephone calls be answered after two rings, and that the caller not be kept on hold for long. The company defined four dimensions of quality—taste, particle definition, color, and packaging—and kept all employees continually informed of the standards required by the company along each dimension. The accounting and finance departments judged quality according to how promptly and accurately they could make invoices and payments. Marketing and sales identified the features of the product that the customer perceived as most valuable and differentiable, and then worked to convince the customer of Hillshire Farm's leadership in these features.

Schloss took personal responsibility for seeing that these activities were performed throughout the company. He believed that management must act immediately on new ideas and suggestions. Getting commitment from supervisors was the most difficult task. Management had to explain the "hows and whys" behind the changes, motivate the workers, and recognize the top performers.

When Bill Geoppinger became the CEO at Hillshire Farm and Kahn's, he realized that a great challenge lay ahead. He had inherited an organization that, while focused on quality, was essentially an autocracy. Employees were used to management making the decisions. Geoppinger realized that significant changes would be difficult to make because of the existing cultural tradition.

To implement a total quality effort successfully, Geoppinger knew that the corporate culture would have to change, to become more open, flexible, and responsive. He brought in a new management team that emphasized total quality and team approaches, and discontinued many of the personal initiatives devised by Milton Schloss. The 1988 merger of Hillshire Farm and Kahn's further served to alter the corporate culture. Empowerment of employees became a priority. Management held regular meetings with line employees to give them the opportunity to share their concerns. They encouraged line employees to participate as members of DMC teams. This open culture and emphasis on empowerment was adapted to all aspects of the business, including accounting, finance, and marketing. However, the most visible total quality effort occurred in production operations.

In 1991, the Deli Select Line implemented statistical process control (SPC). As market leader in this product category, the company wished to keep its competitive advantage in this low-margin business. The division was relatively new and had new employees who could be empowered with little resistance. Before implementing SPC, the only data they collected was yield, the "efficient use of inputs." The team decided that yield improvement would be a good objective for improving costs. However, quality could not be sacrificed for yield, so the team also monitored defect rates through adherence to product specifications of the output and tracking customer complaints.

Calculating product defects proved challenging. First, they quantified customers' perceptions of quality from complaint records. Through team efforts, they defined specifications for the product and its packaging. They inspected the product from the customer's point of view, as seen through the package window. Because they continually monitored incoming meat quality in identifying yields, they felt that this amount of inspection was sufficient.

To track defect rates, they pulled a box of finished products at random every hour and inspected it for product and packaging characteristics. Points for each characteristic were assigned based on severity, of the defect and graphed on a control chart. Using SPC, the company realized improvements in defects and yields. By statistically tracking customer complaints, the team determined which factors were the greatest cause of concern. For example, fat is a major concern because it is highly visible in darker meat products.

Assignment

Based on the facts presented in this case, perform an assessment of the company in the following areas:

> customer focus
>
> quality leadership
>
> continuous improvement
>
> fact-based management
>
> employee participation

List strengths and areas for improvement that you would suggest in each of these categories.

Would you state that Hillshire Farm/Kahn's has fully adopted TQM? Why or why not? What steps would you recommend that the company take next?

II. The Case of the Stalled Quality Program[39]

A manufacturer of electrical parts had installed a quality management program that never quite got off the ground. A conversation with two employees, a supervisor and an inspector who was not part of the management team is provided here:

Supervisor: "We have some problems in inspection. With a certain inspector, we have a large rejection rate. At first, we thought something was wrong with process variability. So we went in and did all kinds of trouble-shooting and found nothing. Having found no assignable cause, we were at a loss and we had to move the inspector to a different position."

Inspector: "Our inspection job is made up of two components: one part is visual and somewhat subjective; the other part uses measuring instruments and is usually objective provided the instruments are well calibrated. I have never had problems with anybody on the second part. Whenever a disagreement arises, we resolve our differences after recalibrating the measuring instrument. However, I have disagreed with the supervisor and other inspectors on the subjective part of the evaluation process. Their [other inspectors] overall rejection rate has been consistently lower than mine. Whenever I go on vacation or am absent, the overall defect rate in my shift goes down. I was constantly blamed for the high defect rates that were produced during my shifts.''

Consultant: "So how did you go about proving to your supervisor that you had a legitimate point?"

Inspector: "I did an informal study. I studied the final rejection rate downstream. I divided the data into two parts: the rejection rate for which I was the inspector, and the rejection rate for which other inspectors were responsible. I actually collected data, analyzed it, and prepared a report for my supervisor. What I found and reported tells the whole story. The nonconforming rates down-

stream were a good 10 percent higher for items passed in other shifts. I tried to stress the fact that the visual part of the inspection in the other shifts was not done properly, giving a false sense of productivity only to lead to a higher number of nonconforming items downstream. All my data and reasoning fell on deaf ears and I was shifted from my position to a lesser job with fewer responsibilities.''

Discussion Question

If you were the consultant to this company, what would you tell the senior management?

■ NOTES

1. Harold S. Page, "A Quality Strategy for the '80s," *Quality Progress,* 16, no. 11 (November 1983), 16–21.
2. A. V. Feigenbaum, *Total Quality Control,* 3rd ed. (New York: McGraw Hill, 1993), 85–86.
3. Wayne S. Reiker, "Integrating the Pieces for Total Quality Control," *The Quality Circles Journal* (now *The Journal for Quality and Participation*), 6, no. 4 (December 1983), 14–20.
4. J. M. Juran, "Managing for Quality," *The Journal for Quality and Participation,* 11, no. 1, (January/February 1988), 8–12.
5. Myron Magnet, "The New Golden Rule of Business," *Fortune,* 21 February, 1994, 60–64.
6. Kenneth Labich, "An Airline that Soars on Service," *Fortune,* 31 December, 1990, 94–96.
7. *AT&T's Total Quality Approach,* AT&T Corporate Quality Office (1992), 6.
8. Adapted from pp. 13–15 of *In Search of Excellence,* by Thomas J. Peters and Robert H. Waterman. Copyright © 1982 by Thomas J. Peters and Robert H. Waterman. Reprinted by permission of Harper & Row Publishers, Inc.
9. Philip Crosby, *Quality Is Free* (New York: McGraw-Hill, 1979), 17.
10. "Total Quality at Procter & Gamble," The Total Quality Forum, Cincinnati, OH, 6–8 August, 1991.
11. U.S. General Accounting Office, "Management Practices: U.S. Companies Improve Performance Through Quality Efforts," GA/NSIAD-91-190 (May 1991).
12. Ed Baker, "The Chief Executive Officer's Role in Total Quality: Preparing the Enterprise for Leadership in the New Economic Age," Proceedings of the William G. Hunter Conference on Quality, Madison, WI (1989).
13. Thomas H. Tappen, Jr., "Beyond Systems—The Politics of Managing in a TQM Environment," *National Productivity Review* (Winter 1991/92), 9–19.
14. William Wiggenhorn, "Motorola U: When Training Becomes Education," *Harvard Business Review* (July/August 1990), 74. Copyright © 1990 by the President and Fellows of Harvard College; all rights reserved.
15. "World Quality: Making Connections Through Standards," *Quality Progress,* 23, no. 6 (June 1990), 16–17.

16. "Reinventing Health Care," *Fortune,* 12 July, 1993, Advertisement section.
17. "New JCAHO Standards Emphasize Continuous Quality Improvement," *Hospitals,* 5 August, 1991, 41–44.
18. Ned Hamson. "The FQI Story: Today and Tomorrow," *The Journal for Quality and Participation* (July/August, 1990), 46–49.
19. Executive Order No. 12637, vol. 7 *United States Code Congressional and Administrative News,* 100th Congress—Second Session (St. Paul, MN: West Publishing Co.), B21–B23.
20. Bill Clinton, "Putting People First," *Journal of Quality and Participation* (October/November 1992), 10–12.
21. Adapted from "What's Happening With the National Performance Review Recommendations?" *Federal Quality News,* 2, no. 5 (December/January, 1994), 8–9.
22. "Presidential Award To Be . . ," *Federal Quality News,* 2, no. 2 (June 1993), 7.
23. Jennifer Jordan, "Everything You Wanted to Know About TQM," *The Public Manager* (Winter 1992–93), 45.
24. Joseph Sensenbrenner, "Quality Comes to City Hall," *Harvard Business Review* (March/April 1991), 64–75. Copyright © 1991 by the President and Fellows of Harvard College; all rights reserved.
25. See, for example, Christina Del Valle, "Readin', Writin', and Reform," *Business Week/Quality Special Issue,* 25 October, 1991, 140–142; Myron Tribus, "Quality Management in Education," *The Journal for Quality and Participation* (January/February 1993), 12–21. See also Christopher W.L. and Paula E. Morrison. "Students Aren't Learning Quality Principles in Business Schools," *Quality Progress,* 25, no. 1 (January 1992), 25–27; John A. Byrne. "Is Research in the Ivory Tower 'Fuzzy, Irrelevant, and Pretentious'?" *Business Week,* 29 October, 1990, 62–66.
26. This section is adapted from an extensive account in Lloyd Dobyns and Clare Crawford-Mason, *Quality or Else* (Boston: Houghton-Mifflin, 1991), 221–230.
27. L. Edwin Coate, "TQM at Oregon State University," Reprinted with permission from *The Journal for Quality and Participation* (December 1990), 56–65. Copyright ©

The Association for Quality and Participation, Cincinnati, Ohio.

28. L. Edward Coate, *Implementing Total Quality Management in a University Setting* (Corvallis, OR: Oregon State University, July 1990); Ralph G. Lewis and Douglas H. Smith, *Total Quality in Higher Education* (Delray Beach, FL: St. Lucie Press, 1994).

29. "How Businesses Can Help the Schools," *Fortune*, 16 November, 1992, 147–174.

30. Frank Caplan, "The National Education Quality Initiative," *Quality Progress* (October 1992), 63–65.

31. Robinson, James D., et al., "An Open Letter: TQM on the Campus," *Harvard Business Review* (November/December 1991), 94–95.

32. "The Cost of Quality," *Newsweek*, 7 September 1992, 48–49.

33. Scott Madison Paton, "Is TQM Dead?" *Quality Digest* (April 1994), 24–29.

34. Ronald E. Yates, "TQM is Alive and Well—and Not Just a Fad, Study Finds," *Chicago Tribune*, 9 February, 1994, 1, business section.

35. Adapted from *AT&T's Total Quality Approach*, Issue 1.1 (December 1992).

36. Based on a variety of materials provided by the Saturn Assistance Center, Saturn Corporation, Spring Hill, TN; Frederick Standish, "As Saturn's Debut Nears, Skepticism Still Abounds," *The Cincinnati Enquirer*, 7 July 1990, F-2; "Here Comes GM's Saturn," *Business Week*, 9 April, 1990, 56–62; "Saturn Workers Say 'No' to Speed Up," *APICS—The Performance Advantage* (February 1992), 11; "Saturn," *Business Week*, 17 August, 1992, 86–91. Richard G. LeFauve and Arnold C. Hax, "Managerial and Technological Innovations at Saturn Corporation," *MIT Management*, Spring 1992, 8–19.

37. Magazines such as *Fortune* and *Business Week* often are a good source for such research.

38. Appreciation is given to Dr. Reginald Bruce and his students at the University of Cincinnati for this case.

39. Adapted from Sangit Chatterjee and Mustafa Yilmaz, "American Management Must Change Its View of Quality as a 'Necessary Evil.'" *Industrial Engineering* (October 1991), 44–48.

■ BIBLIOGRAPHY

"The Cracks in Quality." *The Economist*, April 18, 1992, 67–68.

Rohan, Thomas M. "Why Quality Programs Drag." *Industry Week*, 241, no. 9, May 4, 1992, 47.

Fuchsberg, Gilbert. "Quality Programs Show Shoddy Results." *The Wall Street Journal*, May 14, 1992, B1.

Hunt, V. Daniel. *Managing for Quality: Integrating Quality and Business Strategy*. Homewood, IL: Business One Irwin, 1993.

"Profiles of Winners, 1988–1993," Malcolm Baldrige National Quality Award.

Schmidt, Warren H., and Jerome P. Finnigan. *The Race Without a Finish Line*. San Francisco: Jossey-Bass Publishers, 1992.

"Total Quality at Procter & Gamble." Cincinnati, OH: The Total Quality Forum, August 6–8, 1991.

United States General Accounting Office. *Management Practices: U.S. Companies Improve Performance Through Quality Efforts*, GAO/NSIAD-91-190, May 1991.

CHAPTER 5

Focusing on Customers

The rock-and-roll band, the Grateful Dead, may seem to be an unlikely example for the topic of focusing on customers, yet consider these facts.[1] The Grateful Dead has been going strong for over a quarter-century and commands one of the most loyal followings of any musical group. Instead of barring recording equipment from their concerts, a standard practice designed to protect record sales, the band sets aside a special area in concert halls to accommodate fans' equipment. The quality of lighting and sound exceeds that of most other bands. They keep the ticket prices at or below the average price of other rock concerts. Their concerts are often nearly twice as long as other performers—up to three-and-one-half hours—and no songs are repeated during a four-night stand in one city. Fans can obtain tickets by mail instead of waiting in long lines. With their tickets, fans also receive a list of inexpensive hotels, restaurants, and camping facilities in the area. The Dead have a loyal customer base, affectionately known as "Deadheads." And their customer focus has paid off handsomely: in recent years, estimates of annual ticket revenues have consistently exceeded $30 million.

In Japanese the same word—*okyakusama*—means both "customer" and "honorable guest." World-class organizations are obsessed with meeting and exceeding customer expectations. Many companies such as Disney and Nissan Motor Co.'s Infiniti division were built on the notion of satisfying the customer. Home Depot, cited by Wal-Mart's CEO as *the* best retail organization in the United States, ranked first in ten-year growth in earnings per share as of 1993.[2] Home Depot's service philosophy is "Every customer has to be treated like your mother, your father, your sister, or your brother."

Other firms have had to *learn* to be customer-focused, often in response to a competitive crisis. Motorola is one example. Like many innovative engineering firms, they created new markets by essentially telling customers what they wanted. But as customers became more sophisticated and competition increased, they told Motorola that the company needed to improve. As a consequence, Motorola changed its objectives from a product focus to a customer focus. In 1979, Motorola set *total customer satisfaction* as its fundamental goal. Less than 10 years later, they were among the first winners of the Malcolm Baldrige National Quality Award.

Within a quality-conscious company, both the planning of products and the planning of the system that makes or delivers those products focus on fulfilling the needs and expectations of customers. To achieve customer satisfaction, the organization identifies customers' needs, designs the production and service systems to meet those needs, and measures the results as the basis for improvement. The company also integrates customers into the strategic planning activities of all managers. This chapter focuses on this concept of customer-driven quality.

THE IMPORTANCE OF CUSTOMER FOCUS

Focusing on customers is not just a quality issue; it is sound business practice. The strategic management literature defines *competitive advantage* as a firm's ability to achieve market superiority over its competitors. A strong competitive advantage is characteristically driven by customer wants and needs.[3] A company's customer-driven focus actually addresses all stakeholders: customers, employees, suppliers, stockholders, the public, and the community.

Any business has four key goals:

1. To satisfy its customers
2. To achieve higher customer satisfaction than its competitors
3. To retain customers in the long run
4. To gain market share

To achieve these goals, a business must deliver ever-improving *value* to its customers. Value, as defined in Chapter 1, is quality related to price. Consumers no longer buy solely on the basis of price. They compare the total package of products and services that a business offers (sometimes called the *consumer benefit package*) with the price and with competitive offerings. The consumer benefit package influences the perception of quality and includes the physical product and its quality dimensions; pre-sale support, such as ease of ordering; rapid, on-time, and accurate delivery; and post-sale support, such as field service, warranties, and technical support. If competitors offer better choices for a similar price, consumers will naturally select the package with the highest perceived quality. Thus, understanding exactly what consumers want is absolutely crucial to competitive success. If a competitor offers the same package of goods and services at a lower price, customers make the choice. However, lower prices require lower costs if the firm is to continue to be profitable. Quality improvements in operations reduce costs. Therefore, businesses must focus on both continually improving product quality and reducing costs.

Customer satisfaction occurs when products and services respond to customers needs; that is, when products and services meet or exceed customer expectations—our principal definition of quality. Customer satisfaction translates directly into increased profits. Loyal customers spend more, refer new clients, and are less costly to do business with. Studies at IBM showed that each percentage point in improved customer satisfaction translates into $500 million more revenue over five years.[4] Although Home Depot customers spend only about $38 each visit, they shop 30 times annually and spend more than $25,000 throughout a lifetime.[5] Poor quality products and services, on the other hand, lead to customer dissatisfaction in the form of complaints, returns, and unfavorable word-of-mouth publicity. Dissatisfied customers purchase from competitors. One study found that customers are five times more likely to switch because of perceived service problems than for price concerns or product quality issues.[6] In addition, it costs about five times more to gain a new customer than to keep an existing one. Studies have also shown that dissatisfied customers tell at least twice as many friends about bad experiences than they tell about good ones.

In services, customer satisfaction or dissatisfaction takes place during *moments of truth*—every instance in which a customer comes in contact with an employee of the company. Moments of truth may be direct contacts with customer representatives or service personnel, or when customers read letters, invoices, or other company correspondence. Problems result from unkept promises, failure to provide full service, service not provided when needed, incorrectly or incompletely performed service, or failure to convey the correct information. At moments of truth, customers form perceptions about the quality of the service by comparing their expectations with the actual outcomes.

Consider an airline, for example. (The phrase "moment of truth" was actually popularized by the CEO of Scandinavian Airlines System, Jan Carlzon.) Moments of truth occur when a customer makes a reservation, buys tickets, checks baggage, boards a flight, orders a beverage, requests a magazine, deplanes, and picks up baggage. Multiply these instances by the number of passengers and the number of daily flights, and it is easy to see that hundreds of thousands of moments of truth occur each day. Each occurrence influences a positive or negative image about the company. Southwest Airlines recognizes the power of customer focus.[7] The company insists on capitalizing the word "Customer" in all its ads and brochures. Every one of the approximately 1000 customers who write to the airline get a personal response (not a form letter) within four weeks, and frequent fliers even get birthday cards. The airline even moved a flight up a quarter-hour when five medical students who commuted weekly to an out-of-state medical school complained that the flight got them to class 15 minutes late. To quote the CEO, "We dignify the customer." Southwest has been the only profitable major U.S. airline in recent years.

Customer retention is a key factor for competitive success and is closely tied to quality and customer satisfaction. Product features heavily influence the first sale to a customer. At this time, customers do not know what quality problems may result. However, product quality and the service rendered during the product's life determine the number of subsequent sales.[8] One study of a Tennessee commercial bank found that a one-tenth percentage point improvement in overall customer satisfaction translated into a six-tenth percentage point increase in customer retention. Another study found that companies with a 98 percent customer retention rate are twice as profitable as those at 94 percent.

Growth in market share is strongly correlated with customer satisfaction. Avis, for instance, recognizes that they have two ways to increase market share in the rental car business: (1) by buying large volumes of corporate business with extremely low rates, and (2) by improving customer satisfaction levels, thereby increasing repurchase intent and repeat business. Avis stated that they will not buy business at low rates for the sole purpose of increasing market share. Avis's marketing department uses a full range of research and analysis to keep pace with changing market trends and develop programs that respond to customers' needs. Through information technology, Avis queries all customers at car return to monitor trends and levels of customer satisfaction. It also calls 1500 customers each month to assess in detail satisfaction in each of nine service delivery areas.[9]

The importance of customer focus and satisfaction has grown in recent years. Ernst & Young and the American Quality Foundation reported in 1991 that the percentage of U.S. businesses that consider customer satisfaction to be a primary criterion in strategic planning was expected to leap from 37 to 69 percent within three years. In Japan, however, the comparable figures are 42 and 80 percent.[10]

CREATING SATISFIED CUSTOMERS

Customer satisfaction results from providing goods and services that meet or exceed customers' needs. Figure 5.1 provides a view of the process in which customer needs and expectations are translated into outputs during the design, production, and delivery processes. True customer needs and expectations are called *expected quality*. Expected quality is what the customer assumes will be received from the product. The producer identifies these needs and expectations and translates them into specifications for products and services. Actual quality is the outcome of the production process and what is delivered to the customer. Actual quality may differ considerably from expected quality. This difference happens when information gets lost or is misinterpreted from one step to the next. For instance, ineffective market research efforts may incorrectly assess the true customer needs and expectations. Designers of products and services may develop specifications that inadequately reflect these needs. Manufacturing operations or customer-contact personnel may not deliver according to the specifications. A further complication comes from the customer who sees and believes the quality of the product (perceived quality) as considerably different from what he or she actually receives (actual quality). Because perceived quality drives consumer behavior, this area is where producers should really center their concerns.

These different levels of quality can be summarized by a fundamental equation:

Perceived quality = Actual quality - Expected quality.

FIGURE 5.1   Customer-Driven Quality Cycle

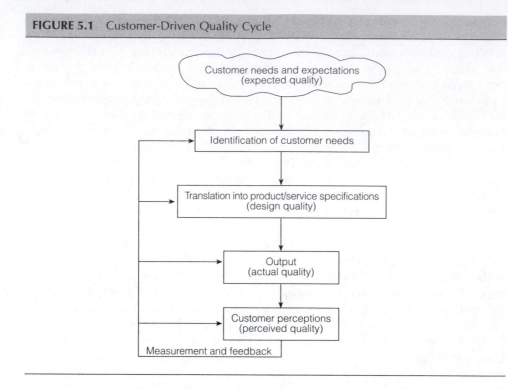

Any differences between the expected quality and actual quality can cause either unexpected satisfaction (actual quality is higher than expected quality) or dissatisfaction (actual quality is lower than expected quality). Understanding these relationships requires a system of customer satisfaction measurement and the ability to use customer feedback for improvement. This model suggests that producers must take great care to ensure that customer needs are met or exceeded both by the design and production process (discussed further in Chapter 7). However, the International Quality Study found that Japanese businesses were three times more likely than North American businesses to include customer expectations in the design of new products and services.[11]

■ Leading Practices

Successful companies in every industry engage in a variety of customer-oriented practices that lead to profitability and market share. These generic practices, and some specific examples from Malcolm Baldrige Award winners, are described in the following list.

1. *They understand both near-term and longer-term customer needs and expectations (the voice of the customer) and employ systematic processes for gathering customer needs and managing the information.* Cadillac, for example, has a network of more than 1600 dealers with primary responsibility for customer contact. The company collects customer information on new vehicle concepts in product and feature clinics. Customer councils bring current vehicle owners and vehicle team members together to talk about product satisfaction and areas for improvement. AT&T Universal Card Services has eight broad categories of 125 "satisfiers," each weighted to reflect its relative importance, that determine how customers perceive the value of credit card services. GTE Directories (see

---

QUALITY PROFILE

GTE Directories Corporation

GTE Directories Corporation, a 1994 winner of the Baldrige Award, publishes and sells advertising for telephone directories. It produces more than 1200 directory titles in 45 states and 17 countries. More than 5000 employees work at its Dallas/Ft. Worth headquarters and at dozens of other sites in North America and overseas.

In the 1980s, GTE Directories faced increased competition from other publishers and other media. The company responded by transforming itself from an organization that relied on experience, enthusiasm, and gut instincts to one focused on anticipating and satisfying customer needs based on concrete, systematic customer input. The company introduced formal quality improvement techniques in 1986, supported with strong leadership from the company's ex-

ecutive management. Their vision is "100 Percent Customer Satisfaction through Quality."

The results are impressive. In 1993, the published error ratio was just over 350 per million listings. In addition, it rates best-in-class in errors per thousand paid items. The number of advertisers handled by individual sales representatives has increased in each of the three years prior to 1994, and the number of sales hours spent with advertisers has jumped. Independent studies show that GTE directories are preferred in 271 of 274 primary markets, and the company has enjoyed sustained, increasing revenue growth.

SOURCE: Malcolm Baldrige National Quality Award, *Profiles of Winners,* National Institute of Standards and Technology, Department of Commerce.

Quality Profile) uses four basic approaches for identifying customer needs and monitoring satisfaction: (1) primary research, which includes focus groups, surveys, and interviews; (2) secondary research from monitoring competitors; (3) customer performance tracking that studies consumer behavior; and (4) customer feedback from sales representatives.

2. *They understand the linkages between the voice of the customer and design, production, and delivery processes.* This practice ensures that no critical requirements fall through the cracks, and minimizes the potential gaps between expected quality and actual quality. Ames Rubber Corporation uses a closed-loop communication system, called Continuous Supplier and Customer Involvement. New products begin with a series of customer meetings to create a product brief, which outlines technical, material, and operational requirements. The product brief is then forwarded to internal departments to select materials, processes, and procedures as approved by the customer. The customer evaluates prototypes until completely satisfied. Finally, a trial production run is made. Not until the customer approves the results does full-scale production commence.

3. *They make commitments to customers that promote trust and confidence in their products and services.* Eastman Chemical Company (see Quality Profile) has a no-fault return policy on its plastics products believed to be the only one of its kind in the chemical industry. A customer may return any plastics product for any reason for a full refund. This policy was a direct result of Eastman's customer surveys. AT&T Transmission Systems offers risk-free trials of new products and 24-hour technical support. Their new 2000 family of products is supported by a five-year warranty, the most extensive in the industry.

4. *They have effective customer relationship management processes by which customers can easily seek assistance, comment, complain, and receive prompt resolution of their concerns.* Eastman Chemical, for instance, provides a toll-free number through which customers can contact virtually anyone in the company—including the president—24 hours a day, seven days a week. Customer relationship management includes attention to training and developing customer-contact employees, and empowering them to do whatever necessary to satisfy the customer. All new Universal Card Services customer-contact associates attend an eight-week training program that emphasizes empowerment, technical training, and customer delight using an industry-leading instructional database that simulates the real customer-contact environment. Every customer relations representative at GTE Directories seeks to handle customer complaints on the first call. They are authorized to propose immediate solutions, including credit adjustments, free advertising, or even advertising in other media to offset omissions or misprints. If immediate resolution is not possible, they must resolve the complaint within 10 days.

5. *They measure customer satisfaction, compare the results relative to competitors, and use the information to evaluate and improve internal processes.* FedEx uses a 10-component Service Quality Indicator that comprehensively describes how its performance is viewed by customers. Management meets daily to discuss the previous day's performance and tracks weekly, monthly, and annual trends. A cross-functional team for each service component supports the evaluation and improvement initiatives. AT&T Universal Card Services maintains eight customer-related databases and eleven monthly surveys to track overall satisfaction and the quality of specific services.

The remainder of this chapter expands upon these important themes.

IDENTIFYING CUSTOMERS

To understand customer needs, a company must know *who* its customers are. Most employees think that "customers" are those people who ultimately purchase and use a company's products. These customers, or *consumers,* certainly are an important group. Identifying consumers is a top-management task related to the company's mission and vision. However, consumers are not the only customer group of concern to a business. The easiest way to identify customers is to think in terms of customer–supplier relationships.

AT&T uses a customer–supplier model as shown in Figure 5.2. Every process receives inputs from suppliers and creates outputs for customers. The feedback loops suggest that suppliers must also be considered as customers. They need appropriate information about the requirements they must meet. This model can be applied at the organization level, the process level, and the performer level (see the discussion of the "Three Levels of Quality" in Chapter 2.)

At the organization level, a business has various *external customers* (organizations not part of the company, but impacted by the company's activities) that may fall between the organization and the consumer. For example, manufacturers of consumer products distribute to retail stores such as Wal-Mart and grocery stores. The retail stores are external customers of the manufacturers. They have specific needs for timely delivery, appropriate product displays, accurate invoicing, and so forth. Since these stores allocate shelf space for the manufacturers' products, they represent important customers. The manufacturers are customers of the chemical companies, printing companies, and other suppliers of such things as materials and packaging materials.

At the process level, individual departments and key cross-functional processes within a company have *internal customers* who contribute to the company's mission and depend on the department's or function's products or services to ultimately serve consumers and external customers. For instance, manufacturing is a customer of purchasing, a nursing unit is a customer of the hospital laundry, and reservations is a customer of the information systems department for an airline or hotel. Figure 2.2 in Chapter 2 is a good example of the internal customer–supplier relationships within a typical manufacturing firm.

At the performer level, each employee receives inputs from others and produces some output to internal customers. A customer may be the assembly line worker at the next station, an executive's secretary, the order taker who passes along orders to the food preparer at McDonald's, or an x-ray technician who must meet a physician's request.

Identifying customers begins with asking some fundamental questions:

- What products or services are produced?
- Who uses these products and services?
- Who do employees call, write to, or answer questions for?
- Who supplies the inputs to the process?

FIGURE 5.2 AT&T's Customer–Supplier Model

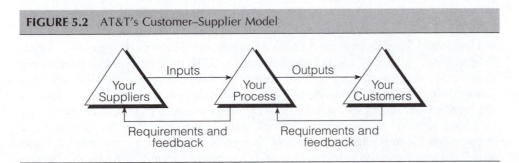

As individuals, departments, and functions develop their customer–supplier models, natural linkages become evident. These linkages build up the "chain of customers" throughout the company that connect every individual and function to the external customers and consumers. Eventually, everyone can better understand their role in satisfying not only their internal customers, but also the external customers.

If an organization remembers that its customers include its employees and the public, then it consciously maintains a work environment conducive to the well-being and growth of all employees. Efforts in this area should go beyond the expected training and job-related education. Health, safety, and ergonomics (the study of physical capabilities of people in the design of workplaces, tools, instruments, and so on) should be included in quality improvement activities. Many companies offer special services such as counseling, recreational and cultural activities, nonwork related education, day care, flexible work hours, and outplacement to their employees. Texas Instruments, for instance, provides preventive health screenings at little or no cost to encourage personal involvement in health management. The company-sponsored employee association, called "Texins," uses fitness activities, recreational clubs, and family events to promote employee well-being.

The public is also an important customer of business. A company must look ahead to anticipate public concerns and assess possible impacts on society of its products, services, and operations. Business ethics, environmental concerns, and safety are important societal issues. Companies can have a powerful influence on communities as corporate citizens through their contributions to charitable activities and the personal involvement of its employees. Based on a company's actions in promoting education, health care, and ethical conduct, the public judges a company's community behavior, which, in turn, can impact sales and profitability. For example, AT&T announced in August 1989 that they would eliminate emissions of chlorofluorocarbons from all manufacturing processes by 1994, and the Texas Instruments Defense Systems and Electronics Group's waste management program began with scrap metals recycling and has expanded to include white paper, plastic, corrugated paper, and wood. They also encourage their employees to participate in volunteer activities within local communities, particularly in helping schools prepare students to meet technical and quality challenges of business.

Finally, everyone is his or her own customer. Quality must be personalized, or it will have little meaning at any other level. This message has been promoted recently by Dr. Harry V. Roberts and Bernie Sergesketter.[12] They quoted Robert Galvin, former CEO of Motorola, who said in a speech to the Economic Club of Chicago "Quality is a very personal obligation. If you can't talk about quality in the first person . . . then you have not moved to the level of involvement of quality that is absolutely essential." Actually, similar ideas can be found in the writings of Benjamin Franklin, who used 13 standards to measure his character and behavior. Sergesketter, an AT&T vice president, developed a "personal quality checklist" to count his personal business "defects," such as not returning phone calls on time, being late for meetings, keeping a messy desk, and not clearing his voice mail the same day. He even included personal defects such as not exercising three times each week, being unpleasant to others, and not having his shoes shined. As he began to track these, he found the checklist to be a tremendous incentive to improve and change his behavior. Other employees at AT&T began doing the same, and found that paying attention to themselves as customers allowed them to become more organized and reduce stress, thereby improving their quality performance in business. Chapter 9 will address this issue further.

Customer Segmentation

Customers generally have different requirements and expectations. A company usually cannot satisfy all customers with the same products or services. This issue is particularly important for companies that do business globally (just think of the differences in regulations for automobiles in various countries or the differences in electrical power systems in the United States versus Europe). Therefore, companies that segment customers into natural groups and customize the products or services are better able to respond to customers' needs.

Juran suggests classifying customers into two main groups: the *vital few* and the *useful many*.[13] For example, organizers of conventions and meetings book large blocks of hotel rooms and have large catering needs. They represent the vital few and deserve special attention on an individual basis. Individual travelers and families are the useful many and typically need only standardized attention as a group.

Customer segmentation might be based on geography, demographic factors, ways in which products are used, volumes, or expected levels of service. For example, telecommunications services might be segmented by

- Residential customers, grouped according to dollar amount billed.
- Business customers, grouped according to size of business, number of different services used, and volume of usage.
- Third-party resellers, who purchase telecommunications capacity in bulk and manage their own customer groups.[14]

Such segmentation allows a company to prioritize customer groups. One way to prioritize segments is to consider, for each group, the benefits of satisfying their requirements and the consequences of failing to satisfy their requirements. This determination of benefits and consequences allows the company to align its internal processes according to the most important customer expectations.

UNDERSTANDING CUSTOMER NEEDS

As discussed in Chapter 1, quality has many dimensions, all of which are difficult for a producer to satisfy simultaneously. Table 5.1 gives some examples of the quality dimensions for both a manufactured product and a service product. The firm's concentration on the key drivers of customer satisfaction lead to business success. Considerable marketing efforts go into correctly identifying customer needs. Ford, for example, identified about 90 features that customers want in sales and service, including a ride to their next stop when they drop off a car for service and appointments within one day of a desired date. Ford then trimmed the list to seven service standards and six sales standards against which dealers have begun to measure themselves.[15]

In addition to technical quality characteristics of a product, customers have other needs and expectations throughout the life cycle of product purchase and use.[16] Before the sale, for instance, sales personnel need clear, unambiguous specifications that can be communicated to customers. The product characteristics relate to the product's intended application. The product functions correctly in

TABLE 5.1 Quality Dimensions of a Manufactured Product and Service

Quality Dimension	Manufactured Product (Stereo Amplifier)	Service Product (Checking Account)
Performance	Signal-to-noise ratio; power	Time to process customer requests
Features	Remote control	Automatic bill paying
Conformance	Workmanship	Accuracy
Reliability	Mean time to failure	Variability of time to process requests
Durability	Useful life	Keeping pace with industry trends
Serviceability	Ease of repair	Resolution of errors
Aesthetics	Oak cabinet	Appearance of bank lobby

SOURCE: Adapted from Paul E. Pisek, "Defining Quality at the Marketing/Development Interface," *Quality Progress* 20, no. 6 (June 1987), 28–36.

the environment in which the customer intends to use it. Delivery information proves reliable. After delivery, receipt of the product occurs when promised, and the shipment contains everything expected and needed to use the product. The product comes with clear and complete operating and setup instructions. The product functions as expected without defects. Consumers can easily learn to use the product. During use, the product continually meets specifications, a characteristic that is easy to verify. As the product ages, preventive maintenance is easy and economical. Factory and service centers handled repairs promptly. Finally, spare parts are available at reasonable cost over the life of the product.

For services, research has shown that five key dimensions of service quality contribute to customer perceptions:

1. *Reliability:* the ability to provide what was promised, dependably and accurately. Examples include customer service representatives responding in the promised time, following customer instructions, providing error-free invoices and statements, and making repairs correctly the first time.

2. *Assurance:* the knowledge and courtesy of employees, and their ability to convey trust and confidence. Examples include the ability to answer questions, having the capabilities to do the necessary work, monitoring credit card transactions to avoid possible fraud, and being polite and pleasant during customer transactions.

3. *Tangibles:* the physical facilities and equipment, and the appearance of personnel. Tangibles include attractive facilities, appropriately dressed employees, and well-designed forms that are easy to read and interpret.

4. *Empathy:* the degree of caring and individual attention provided to customers. Some examples might be the willingness to schedule deliveries at the customer's convenience, explaining technical jargon in layperson's language, and recognizing regular customers by name.

5. *Responsiveness:* the willingness to help customers and provide prompt service. Examples include acting quickly to resolve problems, promptly crediting returned merchandise, and rapidly replacing defective products.

A Japanese professor, Noriaki Kano, suggested three classes of customer requirements:

■ *Dissatisfiers:* requirements that are *expected* in a product or service. In an automobile, a radio, heater, and required safety features are examples, which are generally not stated by customers but assumed as given. If these features are not present, the customer is dissatisfied.

■ *Satisfiers:* requirements that customers say they want. Many car buyers want a sunroof or power windows. Although these requirements are generally not expected, fullfilling them creates satisfaction.

■ *Exciters/delighters:* new or innovative features that customers do not expect. One example, is Avis's Satellite Guidance[SM] System which began road-testing in California in 1994. The system has moving on-screen maps to help drivers pinpoint their location and follow the most direct route. The presence of un-expected features, such as the example shown in Figure 5.3, leads to high perceptions of quality.

In this particular classification system, satisfiers are relatively easy to deter-mine through routine marketing research; however, a company must make spe-cial effort to elicit customer perceptions about dissatisfiers and exciters/delighters. Sony and Seiko, for instance, go beyond traditional market research and produces dozens, even hundreds, of Walkman audio products and wrist watches with a variety of features to help them understand what excites and delights the customer. Those models that do not sell are simply dropped from the product lines. To practice this strategy effectively, marketing efforts must be supported by highly flexible manufacturing systems that permit rapid set up and quick response. As customers become familiar with them, exciters/delighters become satisfiers over time. Eventually, satisfiers become dissatisfiers. For in-stance, antilock brakes and air bags certainly were exciters/delighters when they were first introduced. Now, most car buyers expect them. Collision avoidance systems, however, may be an automotive exciter/delighter soon. Meeting cus-tomer expectations is often considered the minimum required to stay in business. To be truly competitive, companies must surprise and delight customers by go-ing beyond the expected. Thus, successful companies continually innovate and study customer perceptions to ensure that needs are being met.

Perhaps one of the best examples of understanding customer needs and using this information to improve competitiveness is Frank Perdue's chicken busi-ness.[17] Perdue learned what customers' key purchase criteria were; these in-cluded a yellow bird, high meat-to-bone ratio, no pinfeathers, freshness, availability, and brand image. He also determined the relative importance of each criterion, and how well the company and its competitors were meeting each of them. By systematically improving his ability to exceed customers' expectations relative to the competition, Perdue gained market share even though his chickens were premium-priced. Among Perdue's innovations was a used jet engine that dried the chickens, allowing the pinfeathers to be singed off.

GATHERING CUSTOMER INFORMATION

Companies use a variety of methods, or "listening posts," to collect information about customer needs and expectations, their importance, and customer satisfac-tion with the company's performance on these measures. Zytec (see the Quality in Practice case in Chapter 3) relies on 18 different processes to gather data and

FIGURE 5.3   An Example of an Exciter/Delighter in the Hotel Industry

> **MARRIOTT'S**
>
> **Orlando World Center**
> RESORT AND CONVENTION CENTER
>
> Room Number _____
>
> Welcome to Marriott's Orlando World Center!
>
> We hope your stay will be an enjoyable one. As an added convenience, we have provided this service card.
>
> Please check the appropriate box and we will gladly service your room daily at the time you have requested throughout your stay.
>
> ☐ 8 - 10 a.m.   ☐ 12 - 2 p.m.
>
> ☐ 10 - 12 a.m.   ☐ 2 - 4 p.m.
>
> ☐ For today only   ☐ After 4 p.m.
> _____
>
> ☐ For the remainder   ☐ Do Not Disturb
>   of my stay _____
>   _____
>   _____
>   _____
>
> Departure date _____
>
> Please hang outside your door before retiring.
>
>   Thank you very much,
>   Housekeeping Staff

SOURCE: Courtesy Marriott International, Inc.

information from and about customers, as shown in Figure 5.4. Notice how the number and sophistication of these processes increased over the years.

Some of the key approaches to gathering customer information include:

■ *Comment cards and formal surveys:* Comment cards and formal surveys are easy ways to solicit customer information. These approaches typically concentrate on measuring customer satisfaction, which is discussed later in this chapter. However, they often include questions pertaining to the customers' perception of the *importance* of particular quality dimensions as well as open-ended questions. Figure 5.5 shows one example; note that question 5 seeks ideas for improvements. Generally few customers will respond to comment

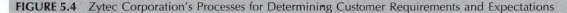

FIGURE 5.4 Zytec Corporation's Processes for Determining Customer Requirements and Expectations

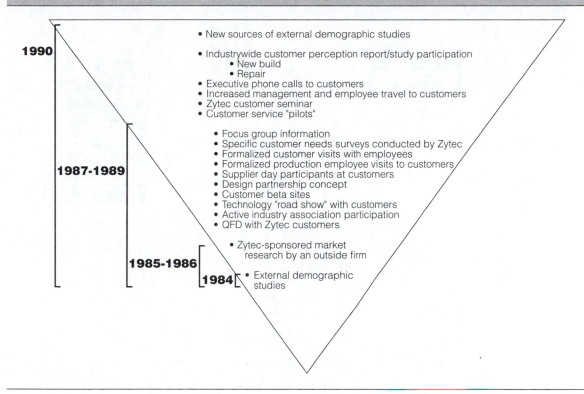

cards placed at restaurant tables or in hotel rooms, and those who do may not represent the typical customer.

Formal surveys can be designed to scientifically sample a customer base, but usually only a small proportion of customers respond. However, some companies find that they work well. USAA, a San Antonio financial services company mails 500,000 surveys to customers from a base of 2.5 million to inquire about satisfaction, future needs, and ideas for new products, and get a 60 percent return. BASF Corporation includes a self-addressed stamped card with each product shipment, asking customers if the shipment arrived on time, its condition and conformance to requirements, whether paperwork was included, if the correct fittings and equipment were on the truck, and if the truck driver was courteous and helpful.[18] Intel Corporation created the Vendor of Choice system to gather customer information. This survey asks customers what they want from a supplier and covers areas of service, price, delivery, quality, and technology.

■ *Focus groups:* A focus group is a panel of individuals (customers or noncustomers) who answer questions about a company's products and services as well as those of competitors. This interview approach allows a company to carefully select the composition of the panel and probe panel members about important issues, such as comparing experiences with expectations, in depth. Key questions that companies ask include: What do you like about the product or service? What pleases or delights you? What do you dislike? What problems have you encountered? If you had the ability, how would you change the product or service? Binney & Smith, maker of Crayolas®, conducts focus groups with the ultimate customer: young children.

FIGURE 5.5 Comment Card

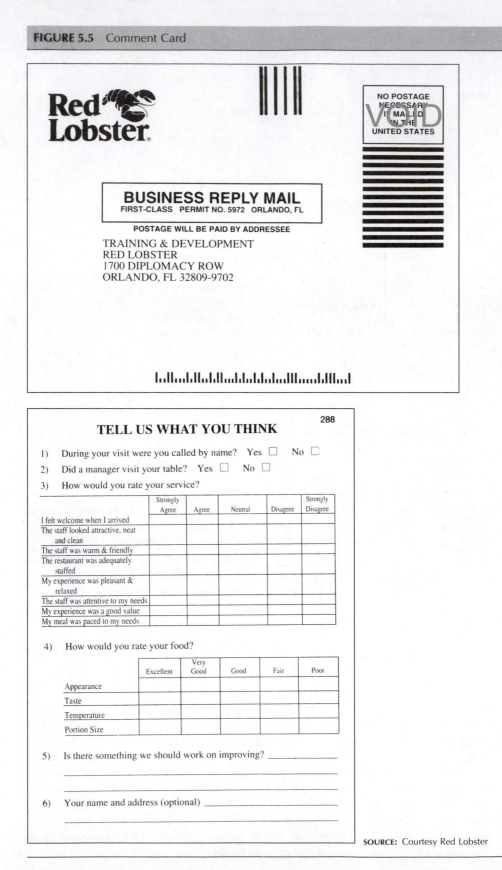

SOURCE: Courtesy Red Lobster

Although customers generally like to fill out surveys and comment cards, by doing so they are simply responding to the perspective of the people who designed the survey. Focus groups offer a substantial advantage by providing the direct voice of the customer to an organization. A disadvantage of focus groups is their higher cost of implementation compared to other approaches.

■ *Direct customer contact:* In customer-driven companies, top executives commonly visit with customers personally. Hearing issues and complaints first-hand is often an eye-opening experience. For example, top managers at Xerox spend one day each month answering customer service phones to interface with customers directly. Black and Decker executives go to homeowners' workshops to watch how customers use their tools, ask why they like or dislike certain ones, and even observe how they clean up their work space when they finish.[19] This approach also works well with rank-and-file employees. In 1992, Honda factory workers called more than 47,000 recent Accord buyers, about half of the owners who registered their cars with the company the previous spring, to find out whether customers were happy and to get ideas for improvements. Globe Metallurgical sends individual workers or teams to customers' facilities to find out which product characteristics are important to the customer and how customers use the products.

■ *Field intelligence:* Any employee who comes in direct contact with customers, such as salespeople, repair technicians, telephone operators, and receptionists, can obtain useful information simply by engaging in conversation and listening to customers. The effectiveness of this method depends upon a culture that encourages open communication with superiors. As another approach, employees simply observe customer behavior. One hotel noticed that customers did not use complementary bath crystals, so they eliminated the crystals (saving costs) and added other features that customers wanted. Honda frequently videotapes drivers as they test new cars.

■ *Study complaints:* Complaints, although undesirable from a service point of view, can be a key source of customer information. Complaints allow an organization to learn about product failures and service problems, particularly the gaps between expectations and performance. Hewlett-Packard, for example, assigns every piece of customer feedback to an "owner" in the company who must act on the information and report back to the person who called. If a customer complains about a printer, someone will check the company's database to see if the complaint is widespread and what the company is doing about it. AT&T Transmission Systems uses cross-functional teams to address customer complaints and collect data for further analysis.

Studies indicate that approximately one out of 25 customers complains. Thus, to take full advantage of complaints, companies must make it easy for customers to complain. The Coca-Cola Company, for instance, was among the first in the soft drink industry to set up a toll-free consumer hotline, which is printed on all product packages. Representatives log every contact into a computer system, which allows any quality problems to be tracked and resolved. Many companies use this practice today.

Customer requirements, as expressed in the customer's own terms, are called the *voice of the customer*. However, the customer's meaning is the crucial part of the message. As the vice president of marketing at Whirlpool stated, "The consumer speaks in code."[20] Whirlpool's research showed that customers wanted clean refrigerators, which could be interpreted to mean that they wanted easy-to-clean refrigerators. After analyzing the data and asking more questions, Whirlpool found out what most consumers actually wanted was refrigerators that *looked* clean with minimum fuss. As a result, Whirlpool's latest models have stucco-like fronts and sides that hide fingerprints.

■ Tools for Classifying Customer Requirements

Throughout this book various graphical tools to help manage information for quality are introduced. These tools are simple to use and understand, and being graphical in nature, provide a visual means of communication, particularly when used by teams. This section presents *affinity diagrams* and *tree diagrams*. Although they are used to classifying customer requirements, these tools can be applied in any setting that requires efficiently organized information. Other applications are described in later chapters.

The affinity diagram—a main ingredient of the *KJ method*, developed in the 1960s by Kawakita Jiro, a Japanese anthropologist—is a technique for gathering and organizing a large number of ideas or facts.[21] Its purpose is to allow teams to sift through large volumes of information efficiently and identify natural patterns or groupings in the information. With an affinity diagram, managers can more easily focus on the key issues and their elements rather than an unorganized collection of information. A tree diagram shows a hierarchical structure of facts and ideas. It is similar to an affinity diagram in that it categorizes concepts into natural groups. (Tree diagrams are also used in designing implementation plans for projects, which is shown in a later chapter.)

Affinity diagrams and tree diagrams are often used to organize customer requirements into logical categories, particularly after a variety of input is captured from interviews, field intelligence, and so on. For example, suppose that a banking team determined that the most important requirement for mortgage customers is timely closings.[22] Through focus groups and other customer interviews, customers listed the following as key elements of timely closings:

- Expeditious processes
- Reliability
- Consistent and accurate information
- Competitive rates
- Notification of industry changes
- Prior approvals
- Innovation
- Modem link between computers
- Buyer orientation
- Diversity of programs
- Mutual job understanding
- Flexibility
- Professionalism
- Timely and accurate status reports

The company's team would group these items into logical categories (Post-it® Notes are often used since they can be easily moved around on a wall) and provide a descriptive title for each category. The result is an affinity diagram, shown in Figure 5.6, which indicates that the key customer requirements for timely closings are communication, effective service, and loan products. Through organization of an affinity diagram, information can be used to better design a company's products and processes to meet customer requirements. A treediagram organizes the information in a slightly different fashion as shown in Figure 5.7.

CUSTOMER RELATIONSHIP MANAGEMENT

A company builds customer loyalty by developing trust and effectively managing the interactions and relationships with customers through customer-contact employees. Truly excellent companies foster close and total relationships with customers. To attain this kind of rapport, everyone in the company at all levels and functions is in contact with the customer. *Customer-contact employees* are particularly important. They are the people whose main responsibilities bring them into regular contact with customers—in person, by telephone, or through other means. Companies must carefully select these employees who are then extensively trained and empowered to meet and exceed customer expectations. These companies also provide easy access to their employees. AT&T Universal Card Services, for instance, has an 800 number, fax, and access for the hearing impaired 24 hours every day throughout the year, translation services for 140 languages, and bilingual Spanish/English operators. Customers are also informed if they will have to wait more than a minute. Globe Metallurgical and Westinghouse, for example, allow customers to conduct quality audits of the company facilities. Customers of Ames Rubber Corporation have immediate access to top division management, manufacturing personnel, quality engineers, sales and service representatives, and technical support staff.

FIGURE 5.6 Affinity Diagram

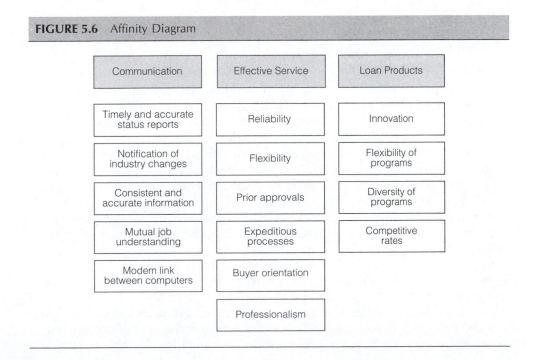

Communication	Effective Service	Loan Products
Timely and accurate status reports	Reliability	Innovation
Notification of industry changes	Flexibility	Flexibility of programs
Consistent and accurate information	Prior approvals	Diversity of programs
Mutual job understanding	Expeditious processes	Competitive rates
Modem link between computers	Buyer orientation	
	Professionalism	

FIGURE 5.7 Tree Diagram

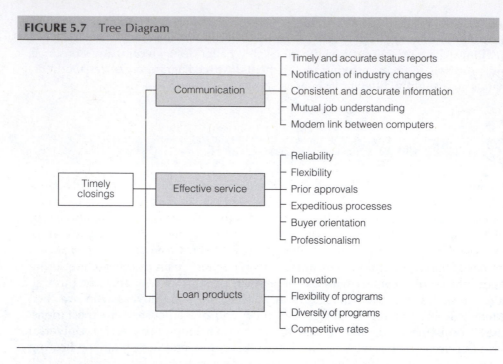

Excellent customer relationship management depends on four aspects:

1. Commitments to customers
2. Customer-focused service standards
3. Training and empowerment
4. Effective complaint management

Each aspect is addressed in the next sections.

■ Commitments to Customers

Companies that truly believe in the quality of their products make strong commitments to their customers. Commitments address the principal concerns of customers, are free from conditions that might weaken customers' trust and confidence, and are communicated clearly and simply to customers. Many commitments take the form of explicit guarantees and warranties. FedEx is highly recognized for its guarantee, which refunds full charges if a shipment is even a minute late. Xerox replaces any product that a customer does not find satisfactory, for any reason, within three years of purchase. Texas Instruments Defense Systems and Electronics Group pioneered the first product warranty for a missile product in its HARM warranty that allowed customers to return any system that failed within the first year after delivery. This practice was unheard of in the defense industry at that time. Similarly, Zaring Homes, a Cincinnati-based builder, promises that its homes will be built on time, on budget, and within specified quality standards, or the home is free—an extremely bold step for the housing industry.

AT&T Universal Card Services' most important commitment to all its customers is the linkage between the card's interest rate and the prime lending rate. The second commitment is the "free-for-life" commitment, by which charter members who applied during the first year and other potential customers the company solicits will never pay an annual fee, provided the card is used once per year. Their third commitment is an explicit service quality warranty, shown in Figure 5.8.

Extraordinary guarantees promising exceptional, uncompromising quality and customer satisfaction, and backing that promise with a payout intended to fully recapture the customer's good will with few if any strings attached—are one of the strongest actions a company can take to improve itself.[23] L.L. Bean's guarantee is a good example: "Everything we sell is backed by a 100 percent unconditional guarantee. We do not want you to have anything from L.L. Bean that is not completely satisfactory. Return anything you buy from us at any time for any reason it proves otherwise." By translating every element of customer dissatisfaction into financial costs, such guarantees quickly alert the company to problems and direct priorities. Workers gain better knowledge of the business and quality improves, which, in turn, results in increased sales and higher profits.

■ Customer-Focused Service Standards

Service standards are measurable performance levels or expectations that define the quality of customer contact. Service standards might include technical standards such as response time, (answering the telephone within two rings), or behavioral standards (using a customer's name whenever possible). Cadillac, for example, has well over 200 standards in its annual dealer service evaluation that measure dealer's customer satisfaction and service operation effectiveness. Customer needs and expectations form the basis of measurable service standards. For example, a customer needs and expects a rapid response to an inquiry. In this case, the service standard might be to return the customer's call within two hours with the information requested, even if the call is received near the end of the business day. The Quality in Practice case about Florida Power and Light at the end of the chapter provides a good example of how customer expectations determine service standards.

FIGURE 5.8   AT&T Universal Card Services Service Quality Warranty

---

Our customers can expect:

- *A Trusted Partner:* Each Universal cardmember customer will be treated as a trustworthy and respected individual whose problems are legitimate and whose point of view is valued.

- *Entitlement to Error-Free Service:* Our customers are entitled to 100% error-free service; no excuses.

- *Availability When You Need Us:* Our service staff is a phone call away, 24 hours a day, 365 days a year, and we will always tell the customers if they have to wait longer than a minute for service.

- *Quick Action to Protect Your Interests:* Any problem with a transaction made with the AT&T Universal Card can be solved with a call, and we will take immediate action to protect customer billing rights.

- *More Than Just Plastic:* If a Universal cardmember's card is lost or stolen, in most cases we will replace it in 24 hours anywhere in the U.S. and in most worldwide locations. In addition, we will provide emergency charge capability, access to cash and calling card capability until the new card is received.

Companies need to communicate service standards to all customer-contact employees. This communication often initially takes place during new employee orientations. However, to maintain the consistency and effectiveness of these standards, companies need to continually reinforce their service standards. Also, many customer-contact employees depend on internal customers for support, who also must understand the role they play in meeting service standards. The key to satisfying external customers is to satisfy internal customers first. At Southwest Airlines, for example, the philosophy is that if employees can provide the same service to one another as they do to passengers, the airline will benefit.[24] Each operating division identifies an internal customer. Mechanics who service planes target the pilots who fly them, and marketers treat reservation agents as customers. Departments even provide free ice cream or pizza as tokens of customer appreciation or for a job well done. Use of the customer–supplier model approach effectively communicates the importance of these relationships.

Finally, a company should implement a process for tracking adherence to the standards and providing feedback to the employees to improve their performance. Information technology supplies the data for effectively tracking conformance to customer service standards.

■ Training and Empowerment

Good customer relationship management depends on the quality of training of customer-contact personnel. Many companies begin with the recruiting process, selecting those employees who show the ability and desire to develop good customer relationships. Job applicants often go through rigorous screening processes. At Universal Card Services, for instance, every applicant completes a two-part general aptitude test. The company then invites successful candidates to participate in additional testing, which includes a customer-service role-playing exercise. Each applicant is asked to handle simulated incoming and outgoing calls. After completing the initial screening test, each candidate must pass a background check, credit check, and a medical evaluation, including drug testing, before being hired.

Companies committed to customer relationship management ensure that customer-contact employees understand the products and services well enough to answer any question, develop good listening and problem recovery skills, and feel able to handle problems. The Ritz-Carlton Hotel Company follows orientation training with on-the-job training and, subsequently, job certification. The company reinforces its values daily, recognizes extraordinary achievement, and appraises performance based on expectations explained during the orientation, training, and certification processes. For many companies, customer relationship training includes *every* person who comes in contact with customers, even receptionists.

Customer-contact employees also need access to a variety of company information to do their jobs, which requires support from the information technology component of the organization. FedEx, for example, furnishes employees with the information and technology they need to continually improve their performance. The Digitally Assisted Dispatch System (DADS) communicates to all couriers through screens in their vans, enabling quick response to pickup and delivery dispatches; it allows couriers to manage their time and routes with high efficiency.

Customers dislike being transferred to a seemingly endless number of employees to obtain information or resolve a problem. Empowered employees are able to make decisions on their own to satisfy the customer. TQM-focused companies empower their front-line people to do whatever is necessary to satisfy the customer. At the Ritz-Carlton, all employees are empowered to do whatever it takes to provide "instant pacification." No matter what their normal duties are, other employees must assist if aid is requested by a fellow worker who is responding to a guest's complaint or wish. Universal Card Services customer-contact associates may award a customer a $10 service guarantee certificate to apply to their bill if they perceive that the company inconvenienced the customer. However, the actions of empowered employees should be guided by a common vision. That is, employees require a consistent understanding of what actions they may or should take.

◾ Complaint Management

Despite all efforts to satisfy customers, every business experiences unhappy customers. Complaints can adversely affect business if not dealt with effectively. A company called Technical Assistance Research Programs, Inc., conducted studies that revealed the following information:

- The average company never hears from 96 percent of its unhappy customers. For every complaint received, the company has 26 customers with problems, six of which are serious.

- Of the customers who make a complaint, more than half will again do business with that organization if their complaint is resolved. If the customer feels that the complaint was resolved quickly, the figure jumps to 95 percent.

- The average customer who has had a problem will tell nine or ten others about it. Customers who have had complaints resolved satisfactorily will only tell about five others of the problem resolution.[25]

Effective resolution of complaints increases customer loyalty and retention. Many customers do not complain because they feel it wouldn't do any good or they are uncomfortable with the process. World-class organizations make it *easy* for customers to complain. Besides providing easy access to the company using toll-free telephone numbers (which should be adequately staffed and supported), many firms actively solicit complaints. Nissan, for instance, telephones each person who buys a new car or brings one in for significant warranty work. Its objective is to resolve all dissatisfaction within 24 hours.[26]

Companies involved in customer relationship management train customer-contact personnel to deal with angry customers. Customer service personnel need to listen carefully to determine the customer's feelings and then respond sympathetically, ensuring that the complaint is understood. They should make every effort to resolve the problem quickly. At the Ritz-Carlton Hotel Company, for example, employees can spend up to $2000 to resolve complaints with no questions asked.

Complaints provide a source of product and process improvement ideas. To improve products and processes effectively, companies must do more than simply fix the immediate problem. They need a systematic process for collecting and analyzing complaint data and then using that information for improvements. Typically, cross-functional teams study the information, determine the real source of the complaints, and make recommendations. In addition, the complaint process itself needs to be monitored, evaluated, and improved. Companies typically track the percent of customers who are satisfied with complaint resolution, the cost of resolving complaints, and the time required to resolve them.

■ Customer Partnerships

Today, suppliers are being asked to take on greater responsibilities to help their customers. As companies focus more on their core competencies—the things they do best—they are looking outside their organizations for assistance with non-critical support processes. Customer–supplier partnerships represent an important strategic alliance in achieving excellence and business success. Benefits of such partnerships include access to technology or distribution channels not available internally, shared risks in new investments and product development, improved products through early design recommendfations based on supplier capabilities, and reduced operations costs through better communications. For example, FedEx and Jostens formed a strategic partnership that enabled both to benefit from new sales of scholastic jewelry and yearbooks.[27] They took advantage of each others' strengths: Josten provided a high quality product with superior service, and FedEx provided reliable high-volume, short-interval delivery for these time-critical products.

Many companies work closely with suppliers that share common values. This close relationship improves supplier capabilities by teaching them quality-related tools and approaches. Although many companies have supplier certification programs (discussed in Chapter 12), some, such as Motorola, have suppliers rate them as customers. Motorola uses a 15-member council of suppliers that rates Motorola's practices and offer suggestions for improving, for example, the accuracy of production schedules or design layouts that Motorola provides.[28]

MEASURING CUSTOMER SATISFACTION

Customer feedback is vital to a business. Through feedback, a company learns how satisfied its customers are with its products and services and sometimes about competitors' products and services. Measurement of customer satisfaction completes the loop shown in Figure 5.1. Measures of customer satisfaction allow a business to

- ■ discover customer perceptions of how well the business is doing in meeting customer needs,
- ■ discover areas for improvement, both in the design and delivery of products and services, and
- ■ track trends to determine if changes actually result in improvements.

An effective customer satisfaction measurement system results in reliable information about customer ratings of specific product and service features and about the relationship between these ratings and the customer's likely future market behavior.

Customer service standards form the basis of customer satisfaction measures. Customer satisfaction measures may include product attributes such as product quality, product performance, usability, and maintainability; service attributes such as attitude, lead time, on-time delivery, exception handling, accountability, and technical support; image attributes such as reliability and price; and overall satisfaction measures. At FedEx, customers are asked to rate everything from billing to the performance of couriers, package condition, tracking and tracing capabilities, complaint handling, and helpfulness of employees. Measurements are based on a bona fide customer requirement or need.

The most helpful customer data include comparisons with key competitors. Companies often rely on third parties to conduct blind surveys to determine who key competitors are and how their products and services compare. Competitive comparisons often clarify how improvements in quality can translate into better customer satisfaction or whether key quality characteristics are being overlooked.

Data collection techniques should be easy to understand and use. Comment cards and formal surveys are the most common means of measuring customer satisfaction, although other techniques, such as face-to-face interviews and telephone interviews are used. Mail questionnaires have the advantage of low costs and self-administration, and can probe deeply into the issues. However they suffer from high nonresponse bias and are a slow means to obtain results because they measure predetermined perceptions of what is important to customers. Telephone interviews, while having a higher cost, have greater speed in execution and lower nonresponse bias.

Most customer satisfaction measures evaluate service characteristics. Developing measurable service quality characteristics can be difficult. A quality characteristic such as "availability" is ambiguous and not as easy to measure as the accuracy of order filling. Typically, such quality characteristics are translated into specific statements that clearly describe the concept. For example, any of the following statements could be used to describe "availability."

1. The doctor was available to schedule me at a good time.
2. I could get an appointment with the doctor at a time I desired.
3. My appointment was at a convenient time.

A "Likert" scale is used to measure the response (see Table 5.2). Responses in the "5" range tell a company what they are doing very well. Responses in the "4" range suggest that customer expectations are being met, but that the company may be vulnerable to competitors. Responses in the "3" range mean that the product or service barely meets customer expectations and that much room for improvement exists. Responses in the "1" or "2" range indicate serious problems.

TABLE 5.2 Examples of Likert Scales Used for Customer Satisfaction Measurement

Very Poor	Poor	Neither Poor nor Good	Good	Very Good
1	2	3	4	5
Strongly Disagree	Disagree	Neither Agree nor Disagree	Agree	Strongly Agree
1	2	3	4	5
Very Dissatisfied	Dissatisfied	Neither Satisfied nor Dissatisfied	Satisfied	Very Satisfied
1	2	3	4	5

The task of questionnaires is to detect differences in satisfaction levels and point out significant relationships between variables that are truly related to each other. To accomplish this task, scientifically designed questionnaires are required. A company uses these questionnaires to collect data on a frequent and systematic basis. Modern technology, such as computer databases in conjunction with a variety of statistical analysis tools, assists in tracking customer satisfaction and provides information for continuous improvement.

For example, the Marriott Corporation conducts extensive surveys of randomly selected hotel guests. The cover letter accompanying the survey, signed by J.W. Marriott, Jr., chairman of the board and president, includes the following:

> I want to assure you, as a valued patron of Marriott Hotels and Resorts, we are committed to providing you a consistently high level of quality guest service at all our lodging products. To help us achieve our commitment, we are asking you, and other randomly selected Marriott guests, to participate in the enclosed guest survey. By your evaluating our hospitality—telling us what we do right as well as what we must improve—you will help us meet your expectations. I personally will review some of the comments as well as the results compiled from all of the surveys. Your comments will be shared with each hotel's General Manager, to ensure follow-up is taken on any service or product shortcomings.

The survey consists of more than 30 multiple-section questions with additional space for comments. Figure 5.9 shows selected portions of the survey.

■ Analyzing and Using Customer Feedback

Deming stressed the importance of using customer feedback to improve a company's products and processes (refer to Figure 1.1 in Chapter 1). By examining trends in customer satisfaction measures and linking satisfaction data to its internal processes, a business can see its progress and areas for improvement. As the next step, the company assigns to an employee or group of employees the responsibility and accountability for developing improvement plans based on customer satisfaction results. Many companies, for example, tie managers' annual bonuses to customer satisfaction results. This practice acts as an incentive for managers and a direction for their efforts.

Appropriate customer satisfaction measurement distinguishes between processes that have high impact on satisfaction and low performance and those that are performing well. One way to assure measurement is appropriate is to collect information on both the *importance* and the *performance* of key quality characteristics. For example, in the Marriott survey, question 8 asks about the overall efficiency (performance) of the hotel staff; part of question 13 seeks the respondent's perception of the importance of overall staff efficiency. Evaluation of such data can be accomplished using a grid similar to the one shown in Figure 5.10. Results in the diagonal quadrants (the shaded areas) are good. A firm ideally wants high performance on important characteristics and not to waste resources on characteristics of low importance. Results off the diagonal indicate that the firm either is wasting resources to achieve high performance on unimportant customer attributes (overkill), or is not performing acceptably on important customer attributes, leaving the firm vulnerable to competition. The results of such an analysis can help target areas for improvement and cost savings.

Many companies have integrated customer feedback into their continuous improvement activities. For example, by listening to customers, Bank One opened nearly 60 percent of its 1377 branches in Ohio and Texas on Saturdays, and 20

FIGURE 5.9   Selected Portions of the Marriott Guest Survey

1. How would you rate our hotel on an overall basis?

EXCELLENT									POOR
10	9	8	7	6	5	4	3	2	1

7. How would you rate our hotel on:

	EXCELLENT									POOR
Check-in speed	10	9	8	7	6	5	4	3	2	1
Cleanliness and servicing of your room during stay	10	9	8	7	6	5	4	3	2	1
Check-out speed	10	9	8	7	6	5	4	3	2	1
Value of room for price paid	10	9	8	7	6	5	4	3	2	1
Service overall	10	9	8	7	6	5	4	3	2	1
Overall staff attitude	10	9	8	7	6	5	4	3	2	1

8. How would you rate the <u>efficiency</u> of our staff on an overall basis?

EXCELLENT									POOR
10	9	8	7	6	5	4	3	2	1

9. Please rate the following in terms of their friendly service.

	EXCELLENT									POOR
Reservation staff	10	9	8	7	6	5	4	3	2	1
Front desk clerk	10	9	8	7	6	5	4	3	2	1
Bellstaff	10	9	8	7	6	5	4	3	2	1
Housekeeping staff	10	9	8	7	6	5	4	3	2	1
Telephone operators	10	9	8	7	6	5	4	3	2	1
Gift shop staff	10	9	8	7	6	5	4	3	2	1
Engineering staff	10	9	8	7	6	5	4	3	2	1
Front desk cashier	10	9	8	7	6	5	4	3	2	1
Concierge staff:										
Concierge Level*	10	9	8	7	6	5	4	3	2	1
Hotel lobby*	10	9	8	7	6	5	4	3	2	1
Pool staff*	10	9	8	7	6	5	4	3	2	1
Golf staff*	10	9	8	7	6	5	4	3	2	1
Tennis staff*	10	9	8	7	6	5	4	3	2	1
Valet parking staff*	10	9	8	7	6	5	4	3	2	1

*(*Not available at all hotels)*

12. Was everything in your room in working order?

◯ Yes   ◯ No

If "NO", which of the following items were not it working order?

◯ Room air conditioning   ◯ Television reception
◯ Room heating   ◯ Heat lamp
◯ Bathtub drain   ◯ Door latch
◯ Sink drain   ◯ Drapes
◯ Water temperature   ◯ Telephone
◯ Water pressure   ◯ TV in-room movies
◯ Other bathroom plumbing ◯ Light bulbs
◯ Television   ◯ Clock/clock radio

◯ Other (please specify)_____

13. How <u>important</u> were each of the following items in determining your overall satisfaction with your hotel stay?

	EXTREMELY IMPORTANT									NOT AT ALL IMPORTANT
Having correct reservation information	10	9	8	7	6	5	4	3	2	1
Honoring your reservation	10	9	8	7	6	5	4	3	2	1
Fulfilling any special room-type or location requests	10	9	8	7	6	5	4	3	2	1
Check-in speed	10	9	8	7	6	5	4	3	2	1
Cleanliness and servicing of your room during your stay	10	9	8	7	6	5	4	3	2	1
Check-out speed	10	9	8	7	6	5	4	3	2	1
Value of room for price paid	10	9	8	7	6	5	4	3	2	1
Service overall	10	9	8	7	6	5	4	3	2	1
Overall staff efficiency	10	9	8	7	6	5	4	3	2	1
Overall staff attitude	10	9	8	7	6	5	4	3	2	1
Overall maintenance and upkeep of hotel	10	9	8	7	6	5	4	3	2	1
Having all items in your room in working order	10	9	8	7	6	5	4	3	2	1

SOURCE: Courtesy Marriott International, Inc.

---

percent on Sundays. A 24-hour customer hotline is also available. Since the early 1980s, Xerox has surveyed tens of thousands of customers annually and tracked the results through its Customer Satisfaction Measurement System (CSMS).[29] The data guide continuous improvements within the corporation. For instance, the CSMS uncovered the fact that customers wanted one-call, one-person problem resolution. As a result, Xerox created six Customer Care Centers, staffed by specially trained customer care representatives who handle some 1.2 million telephone calls and about one million written inquiries each year. Employees are cross-trained and empowered to adjust bills, correct forms, or take other steps to solve problems single-handedly. Any problems that cannot be resolved instantly are given a ten-day resolution deadline. The files remain open until customers confirm that they are totally satisfied with Xerox actions. CSMS data also showed that customer satisfaction is linked to cycle time—the elapsed time be-

---

FIGURE 5.10   Performance-Importance Comparison

	Performance	
Importance	Low	High
Low	Who cares?	Overkill
High	Vulnerable	Strengths

---

tween the reporting phone call and the solution of the problem. The data also showed that simply knowing when a technician will arrive has a positive effect on customer satisfaction. Xerox modified the system to call customers shortly after problems are reported and give them an estimated time of arrival.

A critical question to consider when developing customer satisfaction measurement programs is *Who is the customer?* Managers, purchasing agents, end users, and others all may be affected by a company's products and services. Xerox, for instance, sends specific surveys to buyers, managers, and users. Buyers provide feedback on their perceptions of the sales processes, managers provide input on billing and other administrative processes, and users provide feedback on product performance and technical support. Customer satisfaction measurement should not be confined to external customers. Information from internal customers contributes to the assessment of the organization's strengths and weaknesses. Often, the problems that cause employee dissatisfaction are the same issues that cause dissatisfaction in external customers. Many companies use employee opinion surveys or similar vehicles to seek employee feedback on the work environment, benefits, compensation, management, team activities, rewards and recognition, and company plans and values. However, other indicators of employee satisfaction include absenteeism, turnover, grievances, and strikes. These indicators can often supply better information than surveys that many employees may not take seriously.

■ The American Customer Satisfaction Index[30]

In 1994, the University of Michigan and the American Society for Quality Control released the first American Customer Satisfaction Index (ACSI), a new economic indicator that measures customer satisfaction at the national level. ACSI is based on customer evaluations of the quality of goods and services purchased in the United States and produced by both domestic firms and foreign firms with a substantial U.S. market share. The 1994 ACSI provides a baseline against which customer satisfaction levels can be tracked over time. It is designed to answer the questions: Are customer satisfaction and evaluations improving or declining for the nation's output of goods and services? Are they improving or declining for particular sectors of industry or specific industries? The index quantifies the value that customers place on products, and thus drives quality improvement. Companies can use the data to assess customer loyalty, identify potential barriers to entry within markets, predict return on investments, and pinpoint areas in which customer expectations are not being satisfied.

The index uses a tested, multi-equation, econometric model to produce four levels of indices: a national customer satisfaction index and indexes for seven

FIGURE 5.11 ACSI Model

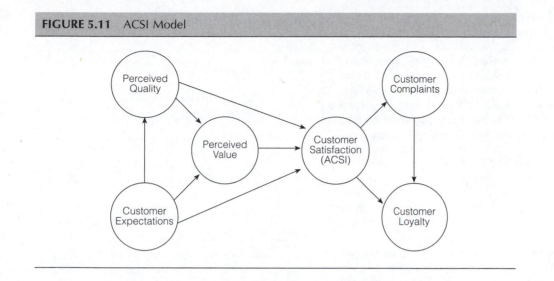

industrial sectors, 40 specific industries, and 203 companies and agencies within those industries. ACSI is based on results of telephone interviews conducted in a national sample of 46,000 consumers who have recently bought or used a company's product or service. The econometric model used to produce ACSI links customer satisfaction to its determinants: customer expectations, perceived quality, and perceived value. Customer satisfaction, in turn, is linked to customer loyalty, which has an impact on profitability. This process is summarized in Figure 5.11.

The initial index showed that nondurable manufacturing scored relatively high in customer satisfaction while public administration and government services scored relatively low. Over time, attention to the index could potentially raise the public's perception and understanding of quality, much like the consumer price index and other economic indicators. This increased awareness will help to interpret price and productivity measures and promote market-driven quality. More information on ACSI methodology and results can be obtained from ASQC at 1-800-248–1946.

QUALITY IN PRACTICE CUSTOMER FOCUS AT GRANITE ROCK[31]

Granite Rock Company is a California manufacturer of high-quality construction materials for road and highway construction and maintenance, and for residential and commercial building construction. Its major product lines include rock, sand and gravel aggregates, ready-mix concrete, blacktop, and other products. In an industry that typically buys from the lowest-bid supplier, Granite Rock is expanding the terms of competition to include high quality and speedy service. The strategy resulted in revenue

earned per employee that is about 30 percent above the industry average. Granite Rock won the Malcolm Baldrige National Quality Award in the Small Business category in 1992.

Granite Rock began its total quality program in 1985, stressing 100 percent satisfaction of customers' needs. Granite Rock's key customers are the contractor, who normally makes the purchasing decisions, and the end customer, who ultimately pays for the buildings or roads made with the company's materials. By emphasizing the hidden costs associated with slow service and substandard construction materials, such as rework and premature deterioration, Granite Rock has convinced a growing number of contractors of the value of using their high-quality materials and unmatched service. The company is so serious about satisfying customers that any customers need not pay their invoice unless completely satisfied. Granite Rock regularly surveys its customers, tracks and responds promptly to customer complaints, and ensures that its products arrive on time.

Surveying its principal customer groups is one of the key approaches Granite Rock uses to improve customer satisfaction. The surveys ask respondents to rate factors in buying concrete, not only from Granite Rock, but from competitors as well. (Figure 5.12 shows such a survey.) Through information obtained from the surveys, Granite Rock determined that the most important factors to customers in order of importance are on-time delivery, product quality, scheduling (ability to deliver products on short notice), problem resolution, price, credit terms, and salespeople's skills. Annually, the company surveys customers and noncustomers to obtain a "report card" on their service (Figure 5.13). Granite Rock repeats the survey every three or four years as priorities change, particularly if the economy changes. The results of the importance survey and competitive performance survey are summarized and plotted on an importance/performance graph to assess the strengths and vulnerabilities of the company and its competitors. Granite Rock looks at the distance between its ratings and the competitors. If the ratings are close, customers cannot differentiate Granite Rock from its competitors on that particular measure. By posting these graphs on bulletin boards at each plant, the company ensures that all employees, particularly salespeople, are fully informed of the survey results. However, salespeople do not use the results to downgrade the competition, but rather to understand the difference that Granite Rock can make to a contractor.

FIGURE 5.12 Granite Rock Customer Importance Survey

What is important to *YOU*?

Please rate each of the following on a scale from 1 to 5 with 5 being most important in your decision to purchase from a supplier.

Importance	Concrete Least . . . Most	Building Materials Least . . . Most
Responsive to special needs	1 2 3 4 5	1 2 3 4 5
Easy to place orders	1 2 3 4 5	1 2 3 4 5
Consistent product quality	1 2 3 4 5	1 2 3 4 5
On-time delivery	1 2 3 4 5	1 2 3 4 5
Accurate invoices	1 2 3 4 5	1 2 3 4 5
Lowest Prices	1 2 3 4 5	1 2 3 4 5
Attractive credit terms	1 2 3 4 5	1 2 3 4 5
Salespeople's skills	1 2 3 4 5	1 2 3 4 5
Helpful dispatchers	1 2 3 4 5	1 2 3 4 5
Courteous drivers	1 2 3 4 5	1 2 3 4 5
Supplier resolves problems fairly and quickly	1 2 3 4 5	1 2 3 4 5

Please write in any other items not listed above which are very important to you in making your purchase decision:

FIGURE 5.13 Granite Rock Customer Report Card

Please write in the names of the suppliers you use most often for concrete. Then grade each company using this scale:

A= The *Best*
B= Above Average
C= *Same* As Competition
D= Needs Improvement
F= *Terrible*

1 *Please write in the Concrete Supplier you use* MOST OFTEN
2 *Please write in your #2 Concrete Supplier*
3 *Please write in your #3 Concrete Supplier*

	1	2	3
1. Reliable Delivery			
A. Do your orders arrive on time?			
2. Consistent Quality			
A. How is their concrete's workability?			
B. How does it pump?			
C. Is the slump right?			
D. How about set time?			
E. How about psi strength?			
3. Dependable Service			
A. Are they responsive to special needs?			
B. Is it easy to place orders or requests with them?			
C. Are their invoices accurate?			
4. Competitive Pricing			
A. Are their prices competitive?			
B. Are their credit terms competitive?			
5. People Who Care			
A. Do their salespeople understand your needs?			
B. Are their dispatchers helpful?			
C. Are their drivers courteous?			
D. Do they address problems fairly and quickly?			
6. Overall Rating			

Surveys indicate a high correlation between quality service and employees' ability to understand the company's products and services. The results also help employees to align their priorities on improvements. Internal teams use the information to develop action plans to improve customer service. One of the customer-focused innovations that Granite Rock introduced is GraniteXpress, an automatic loading system—similar to an automated teller machine—at the A. R. Wilson Quarry. A customer inserts a credit card and requests the specific material. The truck is rapidly, accurately, and automatically loaded over a scale and automatically billed. The facility is open 24 hours a day, seven days a week. The subsequent reductions in trucking time can save customers thousands of dollars on a single project.

Key Issues for Discussion

1. How might Granite Rock's customers rank the importance of the following characteristics? Provide reasons for your opinions.

- **a.** problem resolution
- **b.** salespeople's skills
- **c.** on-time delivery
- **d.** scheduling
- **e.** price
- **f.** product quality
- **g.** credit terms

2. Explain the relationships between the customer importance survey and the customer report card. Do these surveys provide enough information to perform an importance–performance analysis?

QUALITY IN PRACTICE

WAITING TIME AND CUSTOMER SATISFACTION AT FLORIDA POWER AND LIGHT[32]

Florida Power and Light (FPL) is the third-largest investor-owned utility in the United States, with about 3.4 million customer accounts. Its customer service centers (call centers) are divided into four major business segments; each segment handles a logical bundle of call types. Depending on their experience, customer service representatives within each segment specialize in certain types of calls (see Figure 5.14). In the fall of 1991 the Service Assurance Systems group, which is responsible for improving the quality and customer satisfaction levels of FPL's phone operations, decided to find out what customers expect when they call to conduct business. Using focus groups and survey instruments, FPL discovered that its customers desired a pleasant experience while on hold, order taking conducted in a timely manner, and treatment typically accorded to valued customers. FPL wanted to keep costs down without increasing staff size. A cross-functional team suggested that providing customers with an estimate of the time they could expect to wait before being connected to a representative would help meet FPL's needs and increase customer satisfaction. To determine whether this idea had merit, FPL needed quantitative answers to the following questions:

■ How long do customers expect to wait?

■ What is the impact of a wait time announcement on customers' tolerance for waiting?

■ At what point does the wait time result in a significant decrease in customer satisfaction?

■ What is the relationship between wait time and the customer's satisfaction with the call itself?

■ Does wait time vary by type of call?

■ Are customers' stated wait time expectations congruent with the time they are actually willing to wait?

On a busy Monday, a random sample of 150 customers was taken. Wait time announcements were made manually from a control center and actual wait times were monitored. The customers were interviewed that evening to assess their reactions to the proposed service. The surveys showed that the average time customers expected to wait, without knowing the length of wait, was 94 seconds. But when the customers knew the length of wait, they were willing to wait an average of 105 seconds longer (a total of 199 seconds). Over 90 percent of customers in the sample indicated that the announcement was helpful. Customers were also asked to rate their level of satisfaction with their wait times (without advance knowledge). The

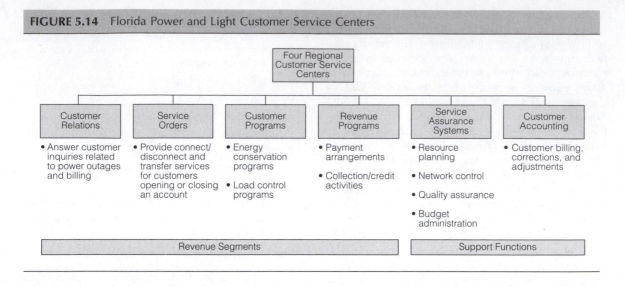

FIGURE 5.14 Florida Power and Light Customer Service Centers

results showed that a significant decrease in satisfaction occurred at two minutes. These results implied that FPL could buy more time without decreasing satisfaction by offering customers the choice of waiting for a predicted period or calling back later.

FPL knew that customer satisfaction relates directly to how callers perceive the quality of the phone representatives and wondered if this perception might be negatively biased due to a long wait. The survey revealed a 10 to 17 percent bias in customers' ratings of phone representatives due to excessive waiting time. If they could eliminate this bias, FPL could more accurately measure customers' satisfaction with the phone contact experience.

FPL segmented calls into three broad categories:

1. Routine calls for connecting or disconnecting service

2. Nonroutine and more complex calls regarding high bills and power outages

3. Calls regarding account-related financial arrangements, such as payment extension requests

After asking customers how long they would expect to wait for each type of call, FPL found that customers expected to wait significantly longer for the third category than for the others. FPL now had evidence that customers calling for different services had different wait time requirements. Finally, FPL discovered that customers thought they waited longer than they actually did.

From this research, FPL developed a system called "Smartqueue," which continuously updates the number of callers waiting and indicates the longest time a caller has been waiting for each department. The system then stores the information and compares it with earlier updates. This adjusted time is increased by a multiplier to account for customers' perceptions of the length of the wait. When a caller is transferred to the appropriate business segment, the unit tells the caller an approximate wait time and how many callers are waiting ahead of him or her. A pilot test of the system in Miami found that customers overwhelmingly perceived Smartqueue to be reasonably accurate in predicting waiting time; virtually all customers thought it was helpful and took the frustration out of waiting.

Key Issues for Discussion

1. Have one of your friends time you while you wait for varying amounts of time between 30 seconds and 3 minutes. Try not to count the seconds! Estimate the amount of time you waited. Did you find that your actual waiting times were longer or shorter than your estimates? Compare these results with your classmates. What does this experiment mean for organizations that are trying to set service standards?

2. What key lessons can be learned by other organizations from FPL's experience?

SUMMARY OF KEY POINTS

■ Satisfying customers is perhaps the most important competitive goal of any business. To achieve customer satisfaction, an organization identifies customers' needs, designs the production and service systems to meet those needs, and measure the results as a basis for improvement.

■ Customer satisfaction or dissatisfaction occurs during *moments of truth* when a customer comes in contact with an employee of the company. Customers form perceptions of the quality of service by comparing their expectations with actual outcomes.

■ The leading practices for achieving customer satisfaction include identifying customer needs and expectations, understanding the linkages between customer needs and design/production/delivery processes, making extraordinary commitments, managing the customer relationship process effectively, and measuring customer satisfaction and acting on the results.

■ The customer–supplier model advocated by AT&T facilitates the identification of customers. Customers include consumers, external customers, internal customers, the public, and oneself.

■ Customer needs differ. The Kano model segments customer requirements into dissatisfiers, satisfiers, and exciters/delighters. Most successful companies take special efforts to understand the last category and develop products and services that truly delight customers.

■ Gathering customer information is accomplished by various methods, including comment cards and formal surveys, focus groups, direct customer contact, field intelligence, and complaint analysis.

■ Affinity diagrams and tree diagrams are helpful tools for classifying customer requirements.

■ Customer relationship management includes establishing commitments, developing customer-focused service standards, training and empowering customer contact employees, and effectively dealing with complaints.

■ A good customer satisfaction measurement process is scientifically designed, includes performance and importance measures, and provides useful information to improve a company's operations and products to further satisfy its customers.

REVIEW QUESTIONS

1. What are the four key customer-related goals of any business?

2. How does customer satisfaction translate into profits?

3. Explain the concept of *moments of truth*.

4. Explain the customer-driven quality cycle. What are *expected quality, actual quality,* and *perceived quality?*

5. List and provide an example of the five leading practices of customer-focused quality.

6. Define the principal types of customers that an organization encounters.

7. Explain the AT&T customer–supplier model.

8. Why is it important to segment customers?

9. Explain the five key dimensions of service quality.

10. What is the Kano model, and what are its implications for quality management?

11. List the major approaches to gathering customer information. What are the advantages and disadvantages of each?

12. Describe how affinity diagrams and tree diagrams are used to organize and work with customer-related information.

13. What is an extraordinary commitment? Provide an example.

14. Define the term *service standards*. Why are service standards necessary?

15. Explain the role of training and empowerment of customer-contact employees in achieving customer satisfaction.

16. Why should a company make it easy for customers to complain?

17. Why does an organization measure customer satisfaction?

18. Explain the concept of importance–performance analysis and its benefit to an organization.

DISCUSSION QUESTIONS

1. Why do you think that many firms fail to recognize the importance of customers until they are faced with a crisis?

2. Prepare a list of moments of truth that you encounter during a typical quarter or semester at your college or university.

3. How might your school use the customer-driven quality cycle in Figure 5.1?

4. Determine whether your school implements any of the leading practices of a customer orientation in a systematic manner.

5. Consider a fraternity or other student organization and make a list of all of its customers.

6. Identify the "defects" in your personal life, and prepare a personal quality checklist of your own. Track your performance over several weeks. Do you observe any noticeable improvement?

7. How might a college or university segment its customers? What specific needs might each of these customer groups have?

8. Which of the five key dimensions of service quality—reliability, assurance, tangibles, empathy, or responsiveness—would the following survey items from a retail banking customer survey address?

   a. Following through on their promises

   b. Offering convenient banking hours

   c. Providing prompt customer service

   d. Properly handling any problems that arise

   e. Maintaining clean and pleasant branch office facilities

   f. Demonstrating knowledge of bank products and services

    g. Giving undivided attention to the customer

    h. Never being too busy to respond to customer requests

    i. Charging reasonable service fees

    j. Maintaining a professional appearance

    k. Providing error-free bank statements

    l. Keeping customer transactions confidential

  9. Provide several examples of dissatisfiers, satisfiers, and exciters/delighters in products or services that you have recently purchased. Why did you classify them into these categories?

10. Based on the information in this chapter, propose new approaches for measuring customer satisfaction for your faculty and instructors that go beyond the traditional course evaluation processes that your school may use.

11. You may have visited or purchased items from large computer and software retail stores. In a group brainstorming session, identify those characteristics of such a store that would be most important to you, and design a customer survey to evaluate customers' importance and the store's performance.

CASES

I. The Case of the Missing Reservation

Mark, Donna, and their children, along with another family, traditionally attended Easter brunch at a large downtown hotel. This year, as in the past, Donna called and made a reservation about three weeks prior to Easter. Because half the party consisted of small children, they arrived 20 minutes prior to the 11:30 reservation to assure being seated early. When they arrived, however, the hostess said that they did not have a reservation. The hostess explained that guests sometimes failed to show and that she would probably have a table available for them before long. Mark and Donna were quite upset and insisted that they had made a reservation and expected to be seated promptly. The hostess told them, "I believe that you made a reservation, but I can't seat you until all the people on the reservation list are seated. You are welcome to go to the lounge for complimentary coffee and punch while you wait." When Mark asked to see the manager, the hostess replied, "I am the manager," and turned to other duties. The party was eventually seated at 11:45, but was not at all happy with the experience.

    The next day, Mark wrote a letter to the hotel manager explaining the entire incident. Mark was in the MBA program at the local university and taking a course on total quality management. In the class, they had just studied issues of customer focus and some of the approaches used at the Ritz-Carlton Hotel, a 1992 Baldrige Award winner. Mark concluded his letter with the statement, "I doubt that we would have experienced this situation at a hotel that truly believes in quality." About a week later, he received the following letter:

    We enjoy hearing from our valued guests, but wish you had experienced the level of service and accommodations that we strive to achieve here at our hotel. Our restaurant manager received your letter and asked me to respond as Total Quality Lead.

    Looking back at our records we did not show a reservation on the books for your family. I have addressed your comments with the appropriate department head so that others will not have to experience the same inconveniences that you did.

    Thank you once again for sharing your thoughts with us. We believe in a philosophy of "continuous improvement," and it is through feedback such as yours that we can continue to improve the service to our guests.

Discussion Questions

1. Were the hostess's actions consistent with a customer-focused quality philosophy? What might she have done differently?

2. How would you have reacted to the letter that Mark received? Could the Total Quality Lead have responded differently? What does the fact that the hotel manager did not personally respond to the customer tell you?

II. Western America Airlines

Table 5.3 lists customer requirements as determined through a focus group conducted by Western America Airlines.

Assignment

1. Develop an affinity diagram and classify these requirements into appropriate categories.

2. Design a questionnaire to survey customers. Be sure to address any other pertinent issues/questions as well as customer information that would be appropriate to include in the questionnaire.

III. Valentine Laboratories[33]

Valentine Laboratories was founded in 1969 by B. Milo Valentino, a former aerospace engineer, who applied his talents to the needs of cardiothoracic medicine. Milo Valentino started with a single, patented idea in a garage in Hollywood, California. The first product was a simple, single-stage pump that could be used to support a patient undergoing open heart surgery. This first left-ventricular–assist device was continuously modified and improved, evolving into the world's first 100 percent portable, replacement for the human heart.

Valentine Labs manufactures and distributes a wide range of products and services for the treatment of heart patients worldwide. As a pioneer and

---

TABLE 5.3   Airline Customer Requirements

- Quality food
- Ability to solve problems and answer questions during flight
- Efficient boarding procedures
- Appealing interior appearance
- Well-maintained seats
- Reservation calls answered promptly
- Timely and accurate communication of information prior to boarding
- Good selection of magazines and newspapers
- Efficient and attentive flight attendants
- Good beverage selection
- Clean lavatories
- Efficient ticket line and waiting procedures
- Convenient ground transportation
- Courteous reservation personnel
- Good quality audio/visual system
- Sufficient quantity of food
- Interesting in-flight magazine
- Courteous and efficient gate personnel
- In-flight telephone access
- Good variety of audio/visual programming
- Flight attendants knowledgeable of airline programs and policies
- Correct explanation of fares and schedules
- Efficient seat selection process
- Courteous and efficient sky cap
- Timely and accurate communication of flight information (in-flight)
- Convenient baggage check-in
- Timely baggage claim upon arrival
- Comfortable seating and leg room
- Assistance for passengers with special needs
- Courteous ticket counter personnel
- Convenient parking close to terminal
- Ability to solve baggage claim problems
- Ability of reservation agents to answer questions

a leader in its field, Valentine Labs developed heart replacements that use innovative technologies, including its unique clot-free *Bloodline*™ Self-Cleaning Heart (SCH). Valentine's heart systems are devices consisting of synthetic materials in an electromechanical assembly, and are therefore able to avoid the common side effects (including rutting and climbing injuries) associated with its competitors' products, which are based on porcine- and primate-sourced materials. Only Valentine's heart replacement system functions without the need of strong anticlotting and antirejection drugs. For removing clots, the original technology required weekly blood letting and the use of suctioning-up-of-clots (SUC) machines at hospitals or local heart centers. These products and services were commercialized in the 1970s and are still the preferred treatment for older, more feeble patients or patients debilitated by heart disease and its associated complications. New technology developed in the mid '80s allowed the enhancement of the original *Bloodline* SCH with a replaceable filter and clot trap. Younger patients and patients without other primary or secondary incapacitating conditions are able to self-administer the 72-hour filter changes of these *Bloodline* products. State-of-the-art lithium/thyristor circuitry allow long battery life and enhanced portability. These products have provided a new freedom and an enhanced quality of life that permits a near-normal lifestyle for the majority of patients.

The company employs over 4800 employees in more than a dozen countries. Approximately 78 percent of its employees work in manufacturing plants located in Hollywood, California; Florence, Alabama; Tarpon Springs, Florida; Hit, Japan; Munich, Germany; and Vlad, Transylvania. Manufacturing of Solution and Disposable products takes place at plants in Alabama, Florida, and Transylvania. SUC machines are manufactured in California and Munich. SCH implantables are manufactured in plants in California and Japan.

Valentine Laboratories can trace its success to two key elements:

Emphasis on the customer

Strategy for managing the competition

Through its ability to leverage its global position in the marketplace and its global sourcing of critical raw materials, global manufacturing (in various tax havens), marketing, and strategic management of global competitors (e.g., Germany and Japan), the company has attained cardiac therapy leadership in its core business. It maintains a sensitivity to differing regional needs and employs the theme, "Think Global, Act Local, and Have a Heart," to gain strategic competitive advantage.

The company is managed as four global "regions," each with a president or general manager and functional organization. Revenues for 1993 were about $1.2 billion: 42 percent from North American sales, 28 percent from European sales, 16 percent from Japanese sales, and the remaining 14 percent from intercontinental sales.

Although the company divides its business into two market segments, its primary market consists of providing SCH products and support services for patients who care for themselves independently at home. Within its SCH business, Valentine has numerous competitors, but none with all the features of the *Bloodline* products. Valentine is the market leader with about 84 percent of the worldwide market share. The company's secondary market—SCH used with SUC (referred to simply as SUC hereafter in this report)—focuses on providing products used by professionals who care for patients in a hospital/ambulatory setting.

Self-Cleaning Heart system product requirements are tailored to meet the needs of patients and vary in terms of ease of use, labeling, packaging, and ease of disposal of the filters, tubing, solutions, and cleaning supplies necessary to maintain the system. Specialized ordering and distribution services are necessary in some regional markets. SCH is a highly sophisticated yet simple device whose major product features lend themselves to a high degree of standardization across geographical markets. Minor geographic differences in product requirements do exist, however, as do patient segment differences (e.g., geriatrics, diabetics, infection-prone patients). Service requirements are also tailored to this primarily homecare market. The company invests heavily in customer service, distribution, technical support, and education.

The company's business environment is characterized by the increasing intensity and complexity of international and domestic regulatory requirements and by the reimbursement policy of each country where the company markets its products. Reimbursement policy often determines the preferred treatment modality within a country, and therefore affects the company's ability to achieve market segment penetration.

The president of Valentine Laboratories and the company's global support groups are located in Hollywood, California. These global groups are composed of finance, human resources, quality and regulatory affairs, manufacturing, product development, research, and marketing.

For both the primary (SCH) and secondary (SUC) market segments, Valentine determines customer satisfaction based on the requirements model in Figure 5.15. Through statistical regression technique and analysis, Valentine found that quality and image determine value, which significantly influences buying behavior. Four major process areas (MPAs) drive overall satisfaction (''higher importance'' in Figure 5.15). In total, the eight MPAs of Figure 5.15 are further supported with 52 specific process attributes, or *moments of truth*, by which the customer determines satisfaction with overall quality. By way of example, process attributes supporting the four key MPAs and their underlying 25 MPAs are provided in Table 5.4.

The company employs a variety of methods to determine customer satisfaction, both through external processes (third-party customer satisfaction measurement (CSM) studies) and internal processes (daily reports from customer-contact employees and meetings/seminars). Methods, frequency, scales and objectivity/validity are noted in Table 5.5. Valentine places a high degree of confidence in third-party CSM studies, which are conducted ''blind'' to ensure objectivity and statistical validity at the 90 percent confidence level. Additionally, survey techniques employ a sample size of 200–300 customer accounts and up to fifty competitive accounts to assure validity and objectivity. Since all patients use a *Bloodline* Self-Cleaning Heart, some with replaceable filters and traps (SCH) and others requiring professional servicing at centers (SUC), all survey methods encompass both principal segment and the secondary segment, as well as regional segments of North America, Europe, and Japan.

As described in Table 5.3, Valentine uses third-party surveying techniques as the primary means of determining customer satisfaction relative to competitors. The company initiated customer retention studies to understand why specific customer ac-

counts chose competitive suppliers. Finally, product surveillance and technical services include competitive comparisons in independent surveys as well.

TABLE 5.4 Major Process Areas and Process Attributes
Products (SCH)
■ Solution consistency
■ Variety of formulations
■ Set reliability
■ Variety of ancillary products
Sales Representation
■ Knowledge of SCH therapy
■ Knowledge of products
■ Credible sales presentations
■ Accessibility/frequency
■ Professionalism
■ Problem resolution
■ Follow up on contract issues
■ Follow up on information
Education and Training
■ Product literature
■ Continuing education
■ Training materials—clinical
■ In-service/demonstrations
Order/Delivery
■ Call before delivery
■ On-time delivery
■ Inside delivery
■ Sufficient inventory
■ Order accuracy
■ Timeliness of returns
■ Emergency service
■ Travel service
■ Offering substitute/alternatives

FIGURE 5.15 Customer Requirements: Major Process Areas (MPAs)

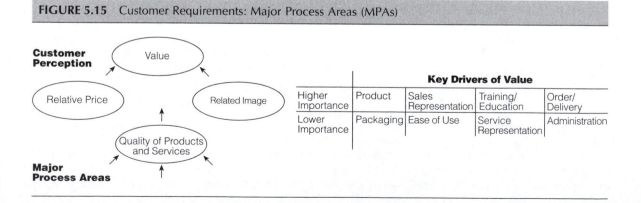

	Key Drivers of Value			
Higher Importance	Product	Sales Representation	Training/ Education	Order/ Delivery
Lower Importance	Packaging	Ease of Use	Service Representation	Administration

The company evaluates and improves its measurement processes for customer satisfaction through specific steps, as noted in Figure 5.16. In the case of external surveying techniques, not only major process areas, but process attributes are individually challenged, added or deleted by management, sales and customer focus groups. For instance, since 1985, Valentine expanded major process areas (from two to eight), developed a more critical rating scale, moved to a more critical respondent (patient to nurse), and changed its customer satisfaction goal from 95 percent to 100 percent.

Aggressive monitoring of customer dissatisfaction indicators also drives Valentine's process improvements. For example, low satisfaction ratings on "return goods, processing" led to further probing and clarification of gathered data (e.g., timeliness of pickup versus credit issuance). Furthermore, negative evaluation cards led to process improvements in the accuracy of data collection.

Discussion Questions

1. Summarize the key customers and customer requirements for Valentine Laboratories. What other factors are critical to this company's competitive success?

2. Summarize how the company determines customer satisfaction, what comparisons to competitors reveal to the company, and how processes for determining and measuring customer satisfaction are evaluated and improved.

3. How would you evaluate Valentine's approaches? Are they sound? Systematic? Are they based on factual data and information? Do they emphasize improvement over reaction to problems? Are they well-deployed throughout the company? Justify your answers.

TABLE 5.5 Customer Satisfaction Determination Methods

EXTERNAL

Method	Process	Scale	Frequency	Validity	Competitors
CSM (all)	Telephone survey of eight MPAs	1–5	Biannual	Third party (blind)	Includes competitors
Professional Services	Telephone survey	1–5	Quarterly	Third party (blind)	Includes competitors
Technical Services	Telephone survey	1–5	Biannual	Third party (blind)	Includes competitors
Customer Retention	Interview	1–5	Annual	Third party (blind)	Includes competitors

INTERNAL

Method	Process	Scale	Frequency	Validity	Competitors
General Reports	Sales generated	Issue/action	Ongoing (>100/month)	Direct from customer	Includes competitors
Call Sheets	Any customer-contact employee	Issue/action oriented	Ongoing (>100/month)	Direct from customer	Includes competitors
Evaluation Cards	Each patient delivery	Yes/No	Ongoing (>100/month)	Direct from customer	
Meetings/Field Visits	Reviews	Issue/action oriented	Ongoing	Direct from customer	

FIGURE 5.16 Process Evaluation Mode

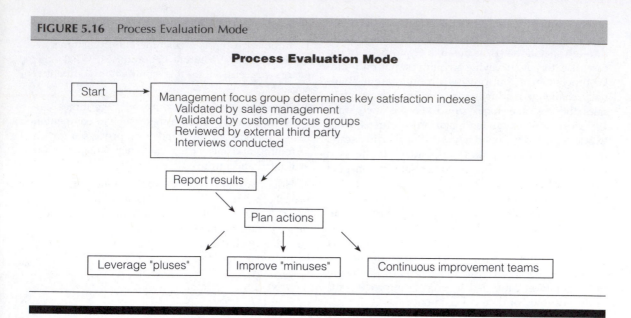

Process Evaluation Mode

Start → Management focus group determines key satisfaction indexes
 Validated by sales management
 Validated by customer focus groups
 Reviewed by external third party
 Interviews conducted

Report results

Plan actions

Leverage "pluses"   Improve "minuses"   Continuous improvement teams

■ NOTES

1. Brad Stratton, "Dead Quality," editorial comment, *Quality Progress* 24, no. 6 (June 1991), 5; Horne, Kim, "Quality and the Dead," letter to the editor, *Quality Progress* 24, no. 11 (November 1991), 6.
2. Patricia Sellers, "Companies That Serve You Best," *Fortune*, 31 May, 1993, 74–88.
3. S.C. Wheelwright, "Competing Through Manufacturing," in Ray Wild (ed.), *International Handbook of Production and Operations Management* (London: Cassell Educational, Ltd., 1989), 15–32.
4. David Kirkpatrick, "Breaking Up IBM," *Fortune,* 27 July, 1992, 44–58.
5. "Companies That Serve You Best," see note 2.
6. The Forum Corporation, *Customer Focus Research,* executive briefing, Boston, 1988.
7. Richard S. Teitelbaum, "Where Service Flies Right," *Fortune,* 24 August, 1992, 117–118.
8. J. M. Juran, *Juran on Quality by Design* (New York: The Free Press, 1992), 7.
9. *AVIS 1992 Annual Report and Quality Review.*
10. Ernst & Young and the American Quality Foundation, *International Quality Study*^{SM} Top Line Findings, 1991.
11. Ernst & Young, see note 10.
12. Harry V. Roberts and Bernie Sergesketter, *Quality Is Personal* (New York: The Free Press), 1993.
13. J. M. Juran, *Juran on Quality by Design* (New York: The Free Press, 1992), ch 3.
14. AT&T Quality Steering Committee, *Achieving Customer Satisfaction,* AT&T Bell Laboratories, 1990.
15. Rahul Jacob, "Why Some Customers Are More Equal Than Others," *Fortune,* 19 September, 1994, 215–224.
16. A. Richard Shores, *A TQM Approach to Achieving Manufacturing Excellence* (Milwaukee, WI: ASQC Quality Press, 1990), 99.

17. Robert D. Buzzell and Bradley T. Gale, *The PIMS Principles: Linking Strategy to Performance* (New York: The Free Press, 1987).
18. Manfred Buller, "Quality Improvement Process at BASF Polymers Group," in Jay Spechler (ed.), *When America Does it Right* (Norcross, GA: Industrial Engineering and Management Press, 1988), 55–63.
19. Susan Caminiti, "A Star Is Born," *Fortune* (Autumn/Winter 1993), 44–47.
20. "How to Listen to Consumers," *Fortune,* 11 January, 1993, 77.
21. "KJ" is a registered trademark of the Kawayoshida Research Center.
22. This example is adapted from Donald L. McLaurin and Shareen Bell, "Making Customer Service More Than Just a Slogan," *Quality Progress* 26, no. 11 (November 1993), 35–39.
23. Christopher Hart, "What Is an Extraordinary Guarantee?" *The Quality Observer* 3, no. 5 (March 1994), 15.
24. Teitelbaum, see note 7.
25. Karl Albrecht and Ronald E. Zemke, *Service America* (Homewood, IL: Dow Jones-Irwin, 1985).
26. "Focusing on the Customer," *Fortune,* 5 June, 1989, 226.
27. AT&T Corporate Quality Office, *Supplier Quality Management: Foundations* (1994), 52.
28. Myron Magnet, "The New Golden Rule of Business," *Fortune,* 21 February, 1994, 60–64.
29. "Quality '93: Empowering People With Technology," advertisement, *Fortune* (September, 1993).
30. Model developed by National Quality Research Center, University of Michigan Business School for the *American Customer Satisfaction Index, (ACSI).* Cosponsored with American Society for Quality Control, 1994.
31. Adapted from *Malcolm Baldrige National Quality Award*

Profiles of Winners, 1988–1993, and materials provided by Granite Rock, including the 1992 Malcolm Baldrige Application Summary; Edward O. Welles, "How're We Doing?" *Inc.* (May 1991); and Martha Heine, "Using Customer Report Cards Ups Service," undated reprint from *Concrete Trader.*

32. Adapted from Bob Graessel and Pete Zeidler, "Using Quality Function Deployment to Improve Customer Service," *Quality Progress* 26, no. 11 (November 1993), 59–63.

33. Adapted from "Valentine Laboratories," a case prepared for use in the 1994 Malcolm Baldrige National Quality Award Examiner Preparation Course. The case material is in the public domain.

■ BIBLIOGRAPHY

AT&T Quality Steering Committee. *Achieving Customer Satisfaction.* Quality Technology Center, AT&T Bell Laboratories, 1990.

Hayes, Bob E. *Measuring Customer Satisfaction.* Milwaukee, WI: ASQC Quality Press, 1990.

King, R. "Listening to the Voice of the Customer." *National Productivity Review* 6, no. 3 (1987), 277–281.

Malcolm Baldrige National Quality Award, 1994 Award Criteria.

Sanes, Christina. "Customer Complaints = Golden Opportunities." *1993 ASQC Quality Congress Transactions, Boston,* 45–51.

Toxell, Joseph R. "Service Time Quality Standards." *Quality Progress* 14, no. 9 (September 1981), 35–37.

Whitely, Richard C. *The Customer Driven Company.* Reading, MA: Addison-Wesley, 1991.

Zeithaml, A. Parasuraman, and Leonard L. Berry. *Delivering Quality Service.* New York: The Free Press, 1990.

Leadership and Strategic Planning

When Robert J. Eaton, the CEO of Chrysler, test-drove a prototype Cirrus sedan in March 1994, he observed poor fitting interior trim and engine noise on acceleration. He quickly launched a major campaign to boost the quality of Chrysler cars. As his first step he delayed production until corrections could be made.[1] Most quality experts agree that strong leadership, especially from the senior management of an organization, is absolutely necessary to develop and sustain a quality-based culture. *Leadership* is the right to exercise authority and the ability to achieve results from those people and systems under one's authority. Leaders may seek to motivate employees and develop enthusiasm for quality with rhetoric, but actions often speak louder than words. The former CEO of Motorola, Robert Galvin, made a habit of making quality the first item on the agenda of executive staff meetings—and then leaving the meeting before the discussion of financial issues. His leadership guided Motorola to become one of the first winners of the Malcolm Baldrige National Quality Award.

Leaders create clear and visible quality values, and integrate these values into the organization's strategy. *Strategy* is the pattern of decisions that determines and reveals a company's goals, policies, and plans to meet the needs of its stakeholders. Through an effective strategy, a business creates a sustainable competitive advantage. This process of envisioning the organization's future and developing the necessary procedures and operations to achieve that future is called *strategic planning.* In today's business environment, quality is a key element of strategic planning. This chapter describes the role of leadership and strategic planning for quality, with an emphasis on the application of leadership concepts in a TQM environment and the process of formulating and implementing TQM-based strategies.

LEADERSHIP FOR QUALITY

Despite its importance, leadership is one of the least-understood concepts in business. Even though many theories of leadership have been developed, no single approach adequately captures the essence of the concept. In practice, it can be as elusive as the notion of quality itself. This section briefly summarizes the principal concepts of leadership and the prominent leadership practices in quality management.

In order to achieve results, managers must persuade people to *act.* Many managers do this by wielding their power. *Power* can be defined as "the basic energy to initiate and sustain action, translating intention into reality; the quality without which leaders cannot lead."[2] A number of years ago, French and Raven developed a framework for understanding power.[3] Categories of power include:

■ *Legitimate power:* power based on formal position and authority in an organization.

■ *Reward power:* power to bestow recognition—tangible or psychological—upon followers.

■ *Expert power:* power obtained through the exercise of specialized skills and knowledge.

■ *Referent power:* power based on the follower's personal liking or admiration for the leader. Leaders frequently demonstrate charisma, personal characteristics, or reputation that the follower admires and wants to emulate.

■ *Coercive power:* power to obtain compliance through fear of punishment or sanctions.

This last type of power is much less likely to produce desired results than a combination of the others. Good leaders, through effective leadership skills, exert their power in appropriate, rather than inappropriate, ways.

In a recent article, Byrd described five core leadership skills exhibited by effective leaders: *vision, empowerment, intuition, self-understanding,* and *value congruence*.[4] Leaders are visionaries; they manage for the future, not the past (think back to the first of Deming's 14 Points). Vision is crucial during times of change. Leaders recognize radical organizational changes taking place today as opportunities to move closer to total quality. They create mental and verbal pictures of desirable future states and share these visions with the organizational partners, including customers, suppliers, and employees. For instance, the vision of individuals such as Bob Galvin and David Kearns led to the total quality transformations at Motorola and Xerox.

Leaders empower and encourage employees to participate in quality improvement efforts, and develop cross-functional teamwork and customer–supplier partnerships. At Motorola, for example, every department has Participative Management Process teams consisting of eight to twelve members who set objectives to support corporate goals. Individual employees develop goals and plans, track progress, and receive bonuses based on successful and timely achievement of goals. This type of empowerment may threaten many managers. True empowerment, however, means developing leadership at lower levels of the organization by spreading power downward and outward.

Leaders are not afraid to follow their intuition. Even in the face of uncertainty and change, leaders anticipate the future and willingly make difficult decisions that will help the organization to be successful. As newly appointed CEO of Xerox in 1982, David Kearns had already witnessed firsthand the implementation of TQM at Fuji Xerox. Once, when returning from Japan, he began listing the factors that made the Japanese better than their American counterparts. After eliminating those factors he felt were insignificant, three elements remained: cost, quality, and expectations.[5] His intuition in this case led him to develop the Leadership Through Quality initiative at Xerox.

Self-understanding requires the ability to look at one's self and then identify relationships with employees and within the organization. It requires an examination of one's weaknesses as well as strengths. One manager told Roger Milliken, chairman and CEO of Milliken & Co. (see Quality Profile), "There are only five managers [out of 400] in this room who know how to listen." Milliken recognized the need to do something. At the end of the meeting, Milliken stood up on a banquet chair, and raising his right arm, asked all of the assembled executives to repeat after him: "I will listen. I will not shoot the messenger. I recognize that management is the problem."[6] Many leaders have an insatiable appetite for knowledge and self-learning as well as a drive to develop their skills and use them effectively.

Finally, value congruence occurs when leaders integrate their values into the company's management system. Values are basic assumptions and beliefs about the nature of the business, mission, people, and relationships of an organization. Specifically, values include trust and respect for individuals, openness, teamwork, integrity, and commitment to quality. They become standards by which choices are made, and create an organizational structure in which quality is a routine part of activities and decisions throughout the organization. Employees quickly recognize leaders who do not apply the values they espouse or do so inconsistently. This incongruence causes employees to constantly doubt management's message.

These core skills—vision, empowerment, intuition, self-understanding, and value congruence—are reflected in the practices of quality leaders in organizations throughout the world.

QUALITY PROFILE
Milliken & Company

Milliken is a major textile manufacturer headquartered in Spartanburg, South Carolina. It is privately held and employs more than 14,000 associates at 47 facilities in the United States, with annual sales exceeding $1 billion. Its 28 businesses produce more than 48,000 different textile and chemical products, ranging from apparel fabrics to specialty chemicals and floor coverings. In the late 1970s, the company recognized that Japanese competitors were achieving higher quality, less waste, greater productivity, and fewer customer complaints with less advanced technology. This realization led to the conclusion that the company's management approaches and personnel practices were to blame. In 1981, senior management launched the Pursuit of Excellence process to focus on customer satisfaction throughout the company. This process led to a flatter management structure and a commitment to teamwork and human resources.

From 1984 to 1988, Milliken improved on-time delivery from 75 percent to an industry best of 99 percent. As a result, it received numerous customer awards, including a record number of General Motors' Mark of Excellence manufacturing awards. After winning the Malcolm Baldrige National Quality Award in 1989, Milliken set its sights on "Ten-Four" objectives—to achieve a tenfold improvement in key customer-focused quality measures over four years. Its long-range goal is to be fully responsive to customer needs, providing "products that customers want, in the quantity they want, when they want them."

SOURCE: Malcolm Baldrige National Quality Award, *Profiles of Winners,* National Institute of Standards and Technology, Department of Commerce, Courtesy Milliken & Co.

■ Leading Practices

In firms committed to total quality, various leadership practices share common elements. True leaders promote quality in several ways.

■ *They create a strategic vision and clear quality values that serve as a basis for business decisions at all levels of the organization.* An organization's vision and values revolve around customers—both external and internal. For example, FedEx's concise motto of People, Service, Profits conveys the commitment to the *people*—the employees of FedEx come first. If employees are happy, they will provide exceptional *service* to customers, and *profits* will follow. AT&T Universal Card Services' focus is engraved in the lobby of its headquarters—"Customers are the center of our universe." Rhetoric cannot stand alone; leaders must demonstrate commitment to the vision and values. At FedEx, every business decision is evaluated against the people-service-profits hierarchy—*in that order*. Successful leaders continually promote the vision throughout the organization using all forms of their communication: talks, newsletters, seminars, electronic mail, and video.

■ *They set high expectations.* A leader can inspire people to do things they do not believe they can do. Motorola set aggressive goals of reducing defects per unit of output in every operation by 100-fold in four years and reducing cycle time by 50 percent each year. One of Hewlett-Packard's goals is to reduce the interval between product concept and investment payback by one-half in five years. The 3M Company seeks to generate 25 percent of sales from products less than two years old. To promote such "stretch goals," leaders provide the resources and support necessary to meet them, especially training.

■ *They demonstrate substantial personal commitment and involvement in quality, often in a missionary-like fashion.* Leaders display a certain passion about quality and actively live the values. By "walking the talk," leaders serve as role models for the whole organization. Many CEOs lead quality training sessions, serve on quality improvement teams, work on projects that do not usually require top-level input, and personally visit customers. For example, senior managers at Texas Instruments Defense Systems and Electronics Group lead 150 of 1900 cross-functional teams. The president and CEO of AT&T Universal Card Services and his business team listen to customers' calls, review daily process measures, meet with suppliers, co-chair monthly Customer Listening Post meetings, host team sharing rallies, lead associate focus groups, and hold all-associate meetings quarterly. In small businesses, such as Marlow Industries (see Quality Profile), CEO and President Raymond Marlow chairs the TQM Council and has daily responsibility for quality-related matters.

■ *They integrate quality values into daily leadership and management.* At Zytec Corporation (see the Quality in Practice case in Chapter 3), senior executives formed a Deming Steering Committee to promote Deming's 14 Points. Members serve as advisors to Deming implementation teams. Leaders also evaluate and improve the effectiveness of their personal leadership processes. FedEx executives conduct surveys in which their leadership is evaluated by their employees. Managers then develop action plans to address weaknesses revealed by the survey and are held accountable for the leadership they provide. Leaders apply quality tools to improve their management processes. The chairman of Westinghouse (see Quality Profile) invited the Westinghouse Productivity and Quality Center to conduct a quality audit of the executive office, believing that if it was good enough for the rest of the company, it was good enough for him.

■ *They sustain an environment for quality excellence.* Leaders provide an environment with few bureaucratic rules and procedures. Such an environment encourages managers to experiment and take risks, permits employees to talk openly about problems, supports teamwork, and promotes employees' understanding of their responsibilities for quality. Solectron managers, for example, foster teamwork and give workers responsibility for meeting quality goals. They encourage a strong family atmosphere, promote clear and effective communications, and recognize and reward groups for exceptional performance. Besides monetary awards, Solectron often buys lunch for an entire division or brings in ice cream for the whole corporation.

Leaders ensure that middle managers and supervisors understand their principal roles and responsibilities for quality. Managers at all levels must communicate and reinforce the organization's quality values to the entire work force. Xerox, for example, redefined its promotion standards around quality. Managers will not be considered for promotions unless they visibly demonstrate support for the company's quality strategy; personally use quality processes and tools; consider customer satisfaction measures in business decisions; encourage feedback from peers, superiors, and customers; recognize and reward subordinates who practice quality improvement; and provide coaching and guidance to those requiring help.

From all these examples, we see that leadership is the "driver" of the entire quality system. Without leadership, TQM simply becomes the "flavor of the month," which is the major reason that total quality efforts fail in many organizations. Effective leadership practice, however, is built upon a sound foundation of theory.

QUALITY PROFILE
Marlow Industries

Marlow Industries received a Baldrige Award in 1991 in the small business category. Marlow Industries, based in Dallas, produces customized thermoelectric coolers—small, solid-state electronic devices that heat, cool, or stabilize the temperature of electronic equipment. In 1991, the company employed 160 people and had annual sales of $12 million. Their quality initiative dates back to 1987, when the company set out to improve a manufacturing and service operation that did not seem to need fixing, challenging itself to exceed its already demanding customer requirements. Since 1987, employee productivity increased at an average annual rate of 10 percent, the time between new product design and manufactured product trimmed, and the cost of scrap, rework, and other nonconformance errors cut nearly in half. Customers benefit with im-

proved on-time deliveries, extended warranties, and stable or decreasing prices.

Marlow describes its TQM system as a "top to bottom" approach to continuous improvement, led by the CEO and president, Raymond Marlow. All workers, from CEO to hourly employee, have taken Marlow's voluntary "Quality Pledge," committing to "Do it right today, better tomorrow." Extensive training, supplier partnerships, and information support contribute to meeting customer satisfaction objectives. Marlow has won numerous quality awards from customers, and in 1990, its top 10 customers rated the quality of Marlow products at 100 percent.

SOURCE: Malcolm Baldrige National Quality Award, *Profiles of Winners,* National Institute of Standards and Technology, Department of Commerce. Courtesy of Marlow Industries.

LEADERSHIP THEORIES

Dozens of leadership theories have been derived from literally thousands of leadership studies. A comprehensive review of these theories is well beyond the scope of this text. However, they are quite important within the context of TQM; therefore, this section provides a summary of the most popular leadership approaches and discusses their implications in a TQM environment.

Leadership theory can be studied from at least five perspectives: the trait approach, the behavioral view, situational (contingency) approaches, the role approach, and emerging theories.[7]

The **trait approach** involves discovering how to be a leader by examining the characteristics and methods of recognized leaders. Pioneering studies were performed several years ago.[8] Since then the trait approach has been discredited to some extent by academicians. Bennis and Nanus interviewed 90 successful manager/leaders and determined that the leaders do not necessarily share a common set of traits:

> They were right-brained and left-brained, tall and short, fat and thin, articulate and inarticulate, assertive and retiring, dressed for success and dressed for failure, participative and autocratic.[9]

Bennis and Nanus also discussed the need to lead others and manage oneself, thus separating the concept of leadership from management.

The **behavioral approach** attempts to determine the types of leadership behaviors that lead to successful task performance and employee satisfaction. Researchers at Ohio State University performed the most extensive series of leadership studies in developing this theory.[10] They showed that effective leadership depends on a proper blending of an employee relationship-centered approach to employees' needs with a production-centered approach to getting work done.

QUALITY PROFILE

Westinghouse Electric Commercial Nuclear Fuel Division

The Westinghouse Electric Corporation Commercial Nuclear Fuel Division (CNFD) is one of 26 such business units in the company and employs about 2000 people at three sites. The Specialty Metals Plant near Pittsburgh produces zircalloy tubes that encase pellets of uranium dioxide fuel processed at CNFD's plant in Columbia, South Carolina. CNFD uses state-of-the-art technology such as robots and other automated processing equipment, supercomputer simulations, and laser welding. Management, however, attributes substantial improvements in quality and efficiency not so much to advanced technology as to its work force and to CNFD's Total Quality approach to operations. A quality council of managers sets policies, plans, and strategies, and directs the quality improvement process. Quality is fully integrated into all design, production, and customer service activities. Progress is measured by a unique system called Pulse Points, which tracks improvements

in over 60 key performance areas and determines measurable goals within each unit of CNFD, down to the jobs of the hourly workers.

Although its eye is on the bottom line, CNFD management deliberately did not include cost concerns in its quality improvement program, believing that gains in quality would spawn cost reductions through increases in efficiency. Between 1984 and 1987, first-time-through yields in the manufacture of fuel rods increased from below 50 percent to 87 percent, substantially reducing scrap, rework, and manufacturing cycle time. This accomplishment helped them to achieve three consecutive years of 100 percent on-time delivery. CNFD was one of the first winners of the Malcolm Baldrige National Quality Award in 1988.

SOURCE: Malcolm Baldrige National Quality Award, *Profiles of Winners,* National Institute of Standards and Technology, Department of Commerce. Courtesy Westinghouse Productivity and Quality Center.

Other well-known behavioral leadership models included Douglas McGregor's *Theory X–Theory Y* model[11] and the Blake-Mouton *Managerial Grid* model.[12] McGregor explicitly defined contrasting assumptions that managers hold about workers and how those assumptions tend to influence the manager's behavior. Blake and Mouton defined five managerial styles that combined varying degrees of production-oriented and people-oriented concerns. Their contribution was to suggest that a high concern for both production and people was needed and that effective managers could be trained to develop a balanced concern for both.

The **contingency** or **situational approach** holds that there is no *universal* approach to leadership; rather, effective leadership behavior depends on situational factors that may change over time. Current leadership theory is based heavily on this approach, which states that effective leadership depends on three variables: the leader, the led, and the situation. One of the pioneering contingency theories of leadership was developed by Frederick E. Fiedler, a participant in the Ohio State research.[13] Fiedler's model, which is included in most principles of management texts, shows the effect of leadership styles on leader performance according to situational contingencies.

Vroom and Yetton developed a supervisory contingency model that was based in part on leadership propositions that follow from Vroom's VIE motivation theory[14] (see Chapter 10 for more discussion of motivation). The model, later updated and modified by Vroom and Jago,[15] prescribes an appropriate leadership style based on various contingencies in a decision-making situation. The model centers on the problem-solving function of leadership, and is based on the theory that the three major concerns of a leader in solving problems are (1) the quality of the decision, (2) the degree of acceptance of the decision by the subordinate(s), and (3) the time frame within which the decision must be made.

Two other contingency models of leadership—House's Path-Goal model and Hershey and Blanchard's Situational Leadership model—deserve special mention. Robert House developed his Path-Goal Leadership model based on expectancy theory.[16] Thus, the model bears some resemblance to the Vroom-Jago model. House's model states that the appropriate path to high performance and high job satisfaction is dependent on employee needs and abilities, the degree of structure of tasks to be performed, and the leadership style that is selected by the leader. Effective leaders choose one of four styles (achievement-oriented, directive, participative, or supportive) that matches the situational contingencies and helps team members along the path to their highest-value goals. The Hershey and Blanchard model relates the requirement for directive or supportive behavior of the leader to team members' readiness (relative maturity) to take responsibility and participate in decision making.[17]

The **role approach** suggests that leaders perform certain roles in order to be effective. The role approach is similar to the trait and behavioral approaches, but also takes into account situational factors. Thus, according to the theory, leaders at upper levels of the organization, or in large firms, may frequently be called upon to play the role of *figurehead* or *liaison* person between the firm and its outside environment. At a lower level, where spans of control are large, *motivational, coordinative,* or *disturbance handling* roles may be needed for effective leadership. Henry Mintzberg's various texts and articles provide the basis for this approach.[18]

Emerging theories enhance or extend current theory by attempting to answer questions raised, but not answered, by traditional contingency approaches. *Attributional theory* states that leaders' judgment on how to deal with subordinates in a specific situation is based on their attributions of the internal or external causes of the behaviors of followers. Readers who are interested in learning more about this approach are referred to Hellriegel et al.[19] *Transactional (charismatic) theory* assumes that certain leaders may develop the ability to inspire their subordinates to exert extraordinary efforts to achieve organizational goals, due to the leader's vision and understanding of how to tap into the developmental needs of the subordinates.

An emerging leadership theory that falls within the transactional category shows potential for dealing with the leadership needs of organizations that want to develop a total quality management process. This approach, called *Transformational Leadership Theory,* explains the impact of leadership in a TQM environment.[20] According to this model, leaders adopt many of the behaviors discussed earlier in this chapter. They take a long-term perspective, focus on customers, promote a shared vision and values, work to stimulate their organizations intellectually, invest in training, take some risks, and treat employees as individuals.

■ Quality Implications of Leadership Theories

Table 6.1 compares traditional *management* practice with true quality *leadership.* Traditional management too often relies on mechanistic planning and organizing, reacting to events, pushing products, and controlling people. This is exemplified in McGregor's Theory X-Y model, where the Theory X manager assumes that subordinates must be coerced and controlled in order to prevent quality problems and to obtain high productivity. Leadership, on the other hand, involves envisioning the future, coordinating the development of a coherent mission for the organization, overseeing the development and control of products and services that have exemplary quality and features, and providing a motivational

TABLE 6.1 TQM Leadership Contrasts

Managers	Leaders
Plan Projects	Practice
■ Make plans for the future (on paper) ■ Organize materials & methods ■ Preach management by objective	■ Envision the future ■ Optimize materials and methods ■ Use participative management
Push Products	Produce
■ Give "lip-service" to quality ■ Sell to customers ■ Cut costs ■ Perform R&D	■ Exemplary quality ■ Service to their customers ■ Less waste through better processes ■ Innovative products and services
Control People	Motivate People
■ Control people and things through systems ■ Reward conformance, punish deviation ■ Maintain status quo	■ Develop people's talents, control things with systems ■ Reward effort, skill development, and innovation; empower employees ■ Look to the future through continuous improvement

climate (corporate culture) for people. Thus, McGregor's Theory Y manager assumes that work is a natural activity, and people who are led well can be expected to be self-motivated to perform their best work if given the opportunity. Much of Deming's philosophy follows the principles in Theory Y.

According to the various contingency leadership theories, quality can be enhanced with the correct mix of the leader's style of management, characteristics of the led, and the situation. Emery Air Freight, for example, found that when the leader (supervisor) emphasized daily performance measures and used positive reinforcement, quality benefits resulted within that organization.[21] However, for a leader in an R&D laboratory—an entirely different situation—such an approach probably would not work. In fact, current leadership research suggests that the same outcome is unlikely. The R&D leader would probably be more effective by using a more participative approach, taking into consideration the *situation* of the higher technical skills and professional expertise of the employees. This approach is in agreement with the contingency model developed by Fiedler and others.

Mintzberg's role theory also suggests that appropriate roles for managers also depend on situational factors. For example, a line manager in an insurance firm who is moving away from a "command and control" management style in order to take a TQM approach to reorganizing would want to change some of the roles previously used in successful management. Some of the changes might involve a move away from the highly structuring roles of decision maker, disturbance handler, and entreprenuer, toward the more "facilitating" roles that assist subordinates, such as motivator, liason, and spokesperson. The subordinates, in turn would be expected to perform some of the former "managerial" type roles of making decisions, taking care of conflicts, and finding opportunities for improvement (an entrepreneurial activity) as part of self-managed teams.

As suggested earlier, senior managers must champion the *transformation* to a TQM culture. Thus, David Kearns, the CEO of Xerox, was the principal catalyst behind the transformation of the company (see Chapter 1). So was Bob Galvin at Motorola, Ray Marlow of Marlow Industries, and nearly every other Malcolm Baldrige Award recipient. Usually, the transformation depends on changing the view of the organization from a vertical perspective based on an organization chart, to a horizontal one based on a system and process perspective. Thus, transformational leadership may be the key ingredient in making the change to a TQM culture a lasting one.

Not all managers in TQM organizations should be transformational leaders, however. The charismatic transformational leader is rare, and most effective at the top. An organization pursuing TQM needs both those who establish visions and those who are effective at the day-to-day tasks needed to achieve them.[22] These transactional leaders play a critical role in promoting total quality. However, in the future, the characteristics of transformational leadership will have to be taught and practiced to a greater degree in order to deal with an increasingly dynamic business environment.

The purpose of leadership theories is to explain differences in leadership styles and contexts. The well-informed manager, engineer, or technician should be aware of such approaches and use them to broaden his or her understanding of how leadership can affect behavior in the workplace and lead to successful adoption of TQM. Although a succinct summary of the leadership dimensions and characteristics of all the theories is extremely difficult to develop, Table 6.2 categorizes the major theories of interest. Good leadership contributes substantially to high quality, while poor leadership often causes many quality problems in organizations.

One of the critical aspects of leadership is *strategic management*. Through strategic management, leaders mold an organization's future and manage change by focusing on an ideal vision of what the organization should and could be 5–10 years in the future. In the next section, some basic strategic management concepts are developed and then related to the total quality management process.

TABLE 6.2   Dimensions of Leadership Theories[23]

Leader

—Personal characteristics (abilities, skills, personalities)
—Roles (figurehead, liaison, decision maker, motivator)
—Behaviors (initiate structure, show consideration toward followers, adjust to situations)
—Sources and uses of power

Led

—Performance (outcomes in meeting goals)
—Behaviors (responses to leader and situation)
—Emotional state (excitement, arousal, efforts)

Situation (contingency factors)

—Correct diagnosis (group atmosphere, task structure, leader position power)
—Readiness (assessment of followers by leader)
—Subordinate/task characteristics
—Decisional and overall effectiveness (related to leadership style)
—Attribution (diagnosis of causes of behavior from/to leaders and followers)

STRATEGIC PLANNING

The concept of strategy has different meanings to different people. Quinn characterizes strategy this way:

> A strategy is a pattern or plan that integrates an organization's major goals, policies, and action sequences into a cohesive whole. A well-formulated strategy helps to marshal and allocate an organization's resources into a unique and viable posture based on its relative internal competencies and shortcomings, anticipated changes in the environment, and contingent moves by intelligent opponents.[24]

Formal strategies contain three elements:

1. Goals to be achieved
2. Policies that guide or limit action
3. Action sequences, or programs, that accomplish the goals

Effective strategies revolve around a few key concepts and thrusts—such as customer satisfaction—which provide focus. The objective of strategic planning is to build a posture that is so strong in selective ways that the organization can achieve its goals despite unforeseeable external forces.

Henry Mintzberg, an unconventional thinker when it comes to management, suggested that most corporate strategic planning is really *strategic programming*.[25] Such planning is numbers-driven and created by planners within the organization, instead of being led by top managers. Mintzberg argued that competitiveness requires more top-level strategic thinking and less mid-level strategic programming. Thus, the true (ideal) strategy-making process can be described as

> . . . capturing what the manager learns from all sources (both soft insights from his or her personal experiences and the experiences of others throughout the organization and the hard data from market research and the like) and then synthesizing that learning into a vision of the direction that the business should pursue.

Although Mintzberg did not specifically mention TQM, his description fits the conventional TQM wisdom that says vision and leadership are critical in the strategic planning and management process.

■ The Role of Quality in Strategic Planning

The literature on competitive strategy suggests that a firm can possess two basic types of competitive advantage: low cost and differentiation.[26] Thus, it is not surprising that strategic business planning typically revolved around financial and marketing goals. *Strategic quality planning*—a systematic approach to setting quality goals—has been viewed as separate and distinct from strategic business planning. Quality planning traditionally took place at low levels of the organization, and focused on manufacturing and technology.

The role of quality in business strategy has taken two significant steps since 1980. First, many firms recognized that a strategy driven by quality can lead to significant market advantages. Second, the line between a quality strategy and generic business strategies has become increasingly blurred. Customer-driven quality and operational performance excellence are key strategic business issues and an integral part of overall business planning. Quality improvement objectives like increasing customer satisfaction, reducing defects, and reducing process cycle times now generally receive as much attention as financial and marketing objectives. The current trend is to integrate quality planning within normal business planning, recognizing that quality drives financial and marketing success. Thus, *strategic quality planning* is synonymous with *strategic business planning*.

Through the use of strategic planning companies can accomplish several important tasks:

1. Understand key customer and operational requirements as input to setting strategic directions. This step aligns ongoing process improvements with the company's strategic directions.

2. Optimize the use of resources and ensure bridging between short-term and longer-term requirements, which may entail capital expenditures, training, etc.

3. Ensure that quality initiatives are understood at the three key levels of the organization: the company/organization level, the process level, and the individual level.

4. Ensure that work organizations and structures effectively facilitate the accomplishment of strategic plans and set the stage for integrating breakthrough and incremental improvement.

Complete integration of TQM into strategic business planning is most often the result of a natural evolution. For most new companies or those that have enjoyed a reasonable measure of success, quality takes a back seat to increasing sales, expanding capacity, or boosting production. In these companies, strategic planning usually centers on financial and marketing strategies.

However, as a company begins to face increasing competition and rising consumer expectations, cost-cutting objectives take precedence. Some departments or individuals may champion quality improvement efforts, but quality is not integrated in the company's strategic business plan. In the face of market crises experienced by many U.S. firms in the 1970s and 1980s, top management begins to realize the importance of quality as a strategic operating policy. In many cases, however, management still views quality as separate from financial and marketing plans. In companies that aspire to world-class status, quality becomes an integral part of the overall strategic plan as a central operating strategy. Consider the Xerox Corporation, which was profiled in a Quality in Practice case in Chapter 1. The Xerox Leadership Through Quality strategy is built on three elements:

1. Quality Principles
  - Quality as the basic business principle for Xerox in its leadership position
  - An understanding of customers' existing and latent requirements
  - Products and services that meet the requirements of all external and internal customers
  - Employee involvement, through participative problem solving, in improving quality
  - Error-free work as the most cost-effective way to improve quality

2. Management Actions and Behaviors
  - Assure strategic clarity and consistency
  - Provide visible supportive management practices, commitment, and leadership
  - Set quality objectives and measurement standards

- Establish and reinforce a management style of openness, trust, respect, patience, and discipline
- Develop an environment in which each person can be responsible for quality

3. Quality Tools
- The Xerox quality policy
- Competitive benchmarking and goal setting
- Systematic defect and error-prevention processes
- Training for leadership through quality
- Communication and recognition programs that reinforce leadership through quality
- A measure for the cost of quality (or its lack)

Following the formation of this strategy, senior executives at Xerox defined the goals they would strive to achieve and the activities necessary to implement these goals over the next five years.

■ Leading Practices

Effective organizations share several common approaches in their strategic planning efforts.

■ *Top management and employees all actively participate in the planning process.* Strong leadership is necessary to establish the credibility of a total quality focus and integrate quality into the business planning process. At the Ritz-Carlton Hotel Company, senior leadership also serves as the senior quality group. Similarly, senior executives at AT&T Transmission Systems compose the company's quality council. This council prioritizes quality objectives and reviews the progress of quality improvement efforts. Each member of the council chairs a separate steering committee responsible for the deployment of quality objectives.

Employees represent an important resource in strategic planning. Not only can the company capitalize on employee knowledge of customers and processes, but employee involvement greatly enhances the effectiveness of strategy implementation. Such "bottom-up" planning facilitates better understanding and assessment of customer needs. At Westinghouse Electric, employee teams study quality criteria for all processes and report findings to line and senior management. Customer teams study the needs of particular customers while other teams focus on production processes. The results of team studies are reviewed by the quality council, which then includes plans for improvement in the annual quality plan. At the Ritz-Carlton, teams at all levels—corporate, management, and employee—set objectives and devise action plans. Each hotel has a quality leader who serves as a resource and advisor to teams for developing and implementing plans.

■ *They use customer wants and needs to drive the strategy.* Strategic planning processes are aligned with the organizations' primary focus on customer satisfaction. The Ritz-Carlton, for instance, evaluates all action plans on how effectively they address customer requirements. A key goal is to become the first hospitality company with 100 percent customer retention; all plans must address this goal. The approaches for gathering customer information described in Chapter 5 are used in the annual planning processes. Similarly, AT&T Consumer Communication Services (see Quality Profile) identified five key determinants of customer satisfaction: call quality, customer service, billing, price, and company reputation. Company goals are directly aligned with these requirements and used to set targets for process improvements and new services.

■ *They involve suppliers in the strategic planning process.* Supplier partnerships are viewed as key long-term strategies. At AT&T Transmission Systems, managers negotiate five-year component quality goals with the company's suppliers. Suppliers, as well as customers, to the Wallace Company participate directly in the annual revision of the company's quality plan.

■ *They have well-established feedback systems for continuous measurement and re-evaluatation of the planning process.* Review and feedback ensure that planning remains effective despite changes in customer requirements and in the competitive environment. Granite Rock maintains a "Quality by Design Timeline" planning chart which tracks improvements in all of the company's objectives from 1985 to the present. It also lists company objectives into the future. Management reviews this chart regularly to identify areas needing additional effort or resources. AT&T Universal Card Services conducts a formal review annually of the key assumptions on which the current plans are based. Both internal and external industry experts assist in this effort. Motorola employs small teams from its corporate quality council to visit each of the company's divisions every year to audit its operations. The results are reviewed with division managers and reported to the corporate quality council to plan any necessary changes.

■ Strategy Formulation

Most companies follow some well-defined process for strategic planning. A generic strategic planning process is shown in Figure 6.1. The organization's leaders first explore and agree upon the *mission, vision,* and *guiding principles* of the organization, which form the foundation for the strategic plan.

The **mission** of a firm defines its reason for existence; it asks the question "Why are we in business?" It might include a definition of products and services the organization provides, technologies used to provide these products and services, types of markets, important customer needs, and distinctive competencies—the expertise that sets the firm apart from others. The mission of FedEx is to "produce outstanding financial returns by providing totally reliable, competitively superior global air-ground transportation of high priority goods and documents that require rapid, time-sensitive delivery." The mission of the Cadillac Motor Car Company is stated in a similar fashion: "to engineer, produce, and market the world's finest automobiles, known for uncompromised levels of distinctiveness, comfort, convenience, and refined performance."

A firm's mission guides the development of strategies by different groups within the firm. It establishes the context within which daily operating decisions are made and sets limits on available strategic options. In addition, it governs the tradeoffs among the various performance measures and between short- and long-term goals. Finally, it can inspire employees to focus their efforts towards the overall purpose of the organization.

The **vision** describes where the organization is headed and what it intends to be; it is a statement of the future that would not happen by itself. It articulates

QUALITY PROFILE
AT&T Consumer Communications Services

AT&T Consumer Communications Services (CCS), the largest of 22 AT&T units, provides long-distance communications services to more than 80 million residential customers. CCS operates in an intensely competitive, technology-driven industry that includes more than 500 long-distance companies today. CCS employs 44,000 associates at more than 900 sites throughout the United States.

With the aim of enhancing existing services, developing new ones, and distinguishing itself from competitors, CCS invests heavily in new technology, which has enabled it to expand the capabilities and increase the reliability of its Worldwide Intelligent Network. CCS has developed a highly automated system (FASTAR) that restores calling capacity within 10 minutes of a major facility outage. Real-time network monitoring and other technologies have strengthened CCS's ability to anticipate and prevent service disruptions.

In its 185 million daily interactions with customers, CCS measures its progress against the company's chief goal of achieving a perfect connection and contact for each customer, every time. Customer satisfaction levels have shown a steady upward trend, and more than 90 percent of customers rate the overall quality of the company's service as good or excellent. To deepen its understanding of customer needs, CCS revamped its customer-focused measurement system to provide greater detail and yield clearer targets for improvement. In 1994, CCS received the Malcolm Baldrige National Quality Award in the service category.

SOURCE: Malcolm Baldrige National Quality Award, *Profiles of Winners,* National Institute of Standards and Technology, Department of Commerce. Copyright 1995, AT&T. Reprinted with permission.

the basic characteristics that shape the organization's strategy. A vision should be clear and exciting to an organization's employees. It should be linked to customers' needs and convey a general strategy for achieving the mission. For example, PepsiCo states "We will be an outstanding company by exceeding customer expectations through empowered people, guided by shared values." Alcoa's vision is stated as: "Alcoa is a growing worldwide company dedicated to excellence through quality—creating value for customers, employees, and shareholders through innovation, technology, and operational expertise. Alcoa will be the best aluminum company in the world, and a leader in other businesses in which we choose to compete."

A vision must be consistent with the culture and values of the organization. **Values,** or **guiding principles** guide the journey to that vision by defining attitudes and policies for all employees, which are reinforced through conscious and subconscious behavior at all levels of the organization. PepsiCo's shared values are diversity (respecting for individual differences), integrity (doing what we say), honesty (speaking openly and working hard to understand and resolve issues), teamwork (working on real customer needs), accountability (committing fully to meeting expectations), and balance (respecting individual decisions to achieve professional and personal balance in life).

The mission, vision, and guiding principles serve as the foundation for strategic planning. They must be articulated by top management and others who lead, especially the CEO. They also have to be transmitted, practiced, and reinforced through symbolic and real action before they become "real" to the employees and the people, groups, and organizations in the external environment that do business with the firm.

FIGURE 6.1 Strategic Planning Process

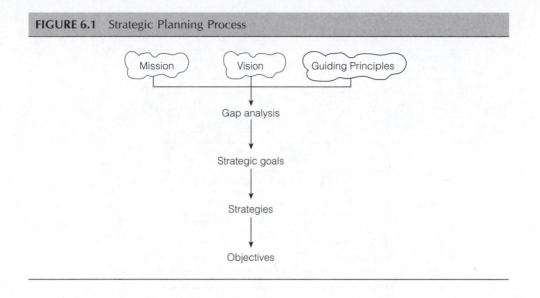

As the next step in the process, companies assess the gap between where it is now and where it wants to be as described in its vision. Using this assessment, an organization develops goals, strategies, and objectives that will enable it to bridge the gap. **Goals** are broad statements that set the direction for the organization to take in realizing its mission and closing the gap between where it is and where it wants to be. **Strategies** are key actions toward achieving the goals. **Objectives** are specific, measurable actions that support the strategies.

Goals need to be consistent with the key factors that drive the business. *Key business drivers* are those strategic elements of a business that drive the major elements of the quality system: strategic planning, design and management of process quality, human resources development and management, as well as information and analysis. Key business drivers set the direction for both the planning and deployment of a company's strategy. For example, suppose that one of a firm's product lines is in a declining market. A strategy of reducing the variation in the firm's manufacturing process would be inappropriate. On the other hand, a strategy of improving research and development efforts might be. Key business drivers should be consistent with important business factors such as

■ the nature of a company's products and services, its principal customers, major markets, and key customer quality requirements

■ position in market and competitive environment

■ facilities and technologies

■ suppliers

■ other factors, such as the regulatory environment, industry changes, etc.

The specific process by which strategic planning is performed varies among companies. For example, Figure 6.2 shows the strategic quality planning process for Eastman Chemical Company, a 1993 recipient of the Malcolm Baldrige National Quality Award.

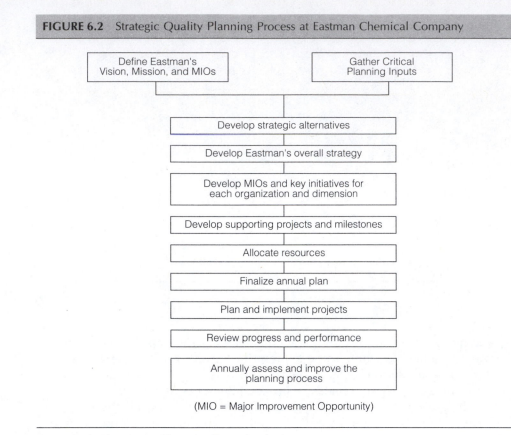

FIGURE 6.2   Strategic Quality Planning Process at Eastman Chemical Company

(MIO = Major Improvement Opportunity)

SOURCE: Used with permission of Eastman Chemical Company.

■ Strategy Deployment

Top management requires a method to ensure that their plans and strategies are executed successfully within the organization. This requirement is the equivalent of Mintzberg's concept of *strategic programming*. Managers determine specific responsibility for meeting objectives at lower levels of the organization and provide the resources necessary. The traditional approach to deploying strategy is top-down. From a TQM perspective, subordinates are both customers and suppliers, and therefore, their input is necessary. An iterative process in which senior management asks what lower levels of the organization can do, what they need, and what conflicts may arise can avoid many of the implementation problems that managers typically face.

The Japanese deploy strategy through a process known as *hoshin kanri*, or *hoshin planning*. In the United States, this process is often referred to as *policy deployment*, or *management by planning*. Many companies, most notably Florida Power and Light, Hewlett-Packard, and AT&T, have adopted this process. The literal Japanese translation of *hoshin kanri* is "pointing direction."[27] The idea is to point, or align, the entire organization in a common direction. Florida Power and Light defines policy deployment as "the executive deployment of selected policy-driven priorities and the necessary resources to achieve performance breakthroughs." Hewlett-Packard calls it "a process for annual planning and implementation which focuses on areas needing significant improvement." AT&T's definition is "an organization-wide and customer-focused management approach aimed at planning and executing breakthrough improvements in business performance." Regardless of the particular definition, policy deployment emphasizes organization-wide planning and setting of priorities, provides resources to meet objectives, and measures performance as a basis for improving performance. Policy deployment is essentially a TQ-based approach to executing a strategy.

Imai provides an example of policy deployment:

> To illustrate the need for policy deployment, let us consider the following case: The president of an airline company proclaims that he believes in safety and that his corporate goal is to make sure that safety is maintained throughout the company. This proclamation is prominently featured in the company's quarterly report and its advertising. Let us further suppose that the department managers also swear a firm belief in safety. The catering manager says he believes in safety. The pilots say they believe in safety. The flight crews say they believe in safety. Everyone in the company practices safety. True? Or might everyone simply be paying lip service to the idea of safety?
>
> On the other hand, if the president states that safety is company policy and works with his division managers to develop a plan for safety that defines their responsibilities, everyone will have a very specific subject to discuss. Safety will become a real concern. For the manager in charge of catering services, safety might mean maintaining the quality of food to avoid customer dissatisfaction or illness.
>
> In that case, how does he ensure that the food is of top quality? What sorts of control points and check points does he establish? How does he ensure that there is no deterioration of food quality in flight? Who checks the temperature of the refrigerators or the condition of the oven while the plane is in the air?
>
> Only when safety is translated into specific actions with specific control and check points established for each employee's job may safety be said to have been truly deployed as a policy. Policy deployment calls for everyone to interpret policy in light of his own responsibilities and for everyone to work out criteria to check his success in carrying out the policy.[28]

Figure 6.3 provides a simplified description of the policy deployment process.[29] With policy deployment, top management is responsible for developing and communicating a vision, then building organization-wide commitment to its achievement.[30] The long-term strategic plan forms the basis for shorter-term planning. This vision is deployed through the development and execution of annual objectives and plans. All levels of employees actively participate in generating strategy and action plans to attain the vision. At each level, progressively more detailed and concrete means to accomplish the objectives are determined. Objectives should be challenging, but people should feel that they are attainable. To this end, middle management negotiates with senior management regarding the objectives that will achieve the strategies, and what process changes and resources might be required to achieve those objectives. Middle management then negotiates with the implementation teams the final short-term objectives and the performance measures that are used to indicate progress toward accomplishing the objectives.

Management reviews at specific checkpoints ensure the effectiveness of individual elements of the strategy. The implementation teams are empowered to manage actions and schedule their activities. Periodic reviews (monthly or quarterly) track progress and diagnose problems. Management may modify objectives on the basis of these reviews, as evidenced by the feedback loop in the figure. Top management evaluates results as well as the deployment process itself through annual reviews, which serve as a basis for the next planning cycle.

Note, however, that top management does not develop action plans; they set overall guidelines and strategies. Departments and functional units develop specific implementation plans. Hence, the process in Figure 6.3 includes both

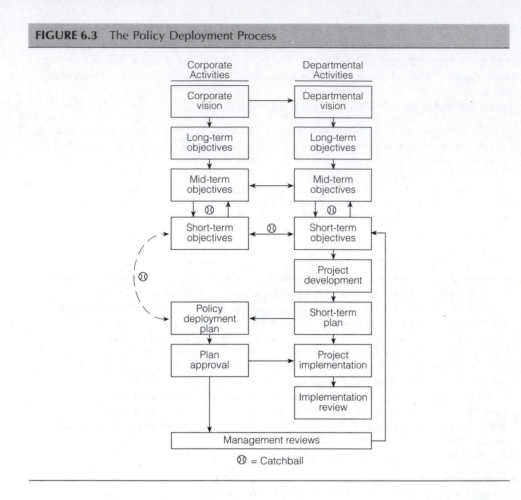

FIGURE 6.3   The Policy Deployment Process

corporate and departmental activities. In practice, policy deployment entails a high degree of detail, including the anticipation of possible problems during implementation. The emphasis is on the improvement of the process, as opposed to a results-only orientation.

The negotiation process is called *catchball* (represented by the baseball symbol in Figure 6.3). Leaders communicate mid-term objectives and measures to middle managers who develop short-term objectives and recommend necessary resources, targets, and roles/responsibilities. These issues are discussed and debated until agreement is reached. The objectives then cascade to lower levels of the organization where short-term plans are developed.

Catchball is an up, down, and sideways communication process as opposed to an autocratic, top-down management style. It marshalls the collective expertise of the whole organization and results in realistic and achievable objectives that do not conflict. In the spirit of Deming, the process focuses on optimizing the system rather than individual goals and objectives. Clearly, this process can only occur in a TQM culture that nourishes open communication.

■ MBO and Policy Deployment

Policy deployment bears some similarity to management by objective (MBO). MBO is ''a process by which the superior and subordinate managers of an organization jointly identify its common goals, define each individual's major areas of responsibility in terms of the results expected, and use these measures as guides for operating the unit and assessing the contribution of each of its members."[31] Both approaches are driven by objectives, involve employees, deploy the objectives, emphasize measurement and accountability, and rely on individual participation. However, they have some important differences. First, MBO objectives generally are not supportive of the company's vision but are set independently. MBO usually results in numerous objectives that focus on the management of individual employee performance rather than on improvement of the organization as a whole. Individual performance evaluation and rewards are closely tied to attainment of objectives. This practice tends to promote actions that optimize the individuals' gain, rather than organization improvement. (Think of Deming's philosophy. He was a strong opponent of MBO.) In contrast, policy deployment selects key objectives that represent the business capabilities critical for business competitiveness. These annual objectives are tied to the vision and strategic plan, and are defined with clear measures at every level of deployment. Each level of the management hierarchy is responsible for some project or program that contributes to one or more objectives. Objectives are broken down and deployed in such a way that all employees can see how their individual efforts are aligned with the organizational objectives.

Second, management uses MBO primarily as a means of tight control; in practice most subordinates succumb to their supervisor's wishes. In policy deployment, cross-functional teams are formed to ensure horizontal alignment. Bottom-up, top-down negotiations (catchball) are conducted throughout the planning process until all levels reach agreement.

Finally, MBO objectives are often not used in daily work; instead, they are only resurrected during performance reviews, which focus on results. In policy deployment, each team participates in regular reviews and diagnosis, using the same language and format. The periodic reviews also involve the process as well as results. This practice allows identification and correction of root causes of unsatisfactory results.

Beware, however, that various MBO approaches exist in the United States, and that it is practiced differently in Japan. Many smaller organizations with good internal communication have used MBO successfully. Thus, some approaches to MBO may not be as inconsistent with policy deployment as implied.

THE SEVEN MANAGEMENT AND PLANNING TOOLS

Managers may use a variety of tools and techniques, known as the *seven management and planning tools*, to implement policy deployment. These tools are particularly useful in structuring unstructured ideas, making strategic plans, and organizing and controlling large, complex projects. Thus, they can benefit all employees involved in quality planning and implementation.

These tools had their roots in post–World War II operations research developments in the United States, but were combined and refined by several Japanese companies over the past several decades as part of their planning processes. They were popularized in the United States by the consulting firm GOAL/QPC, and have been used by a number of firms since 1984 to improve their quality planning and improvement efforts. Many companies formally integrated these tools into policy deployment activities. Two of them—affinity diagrams and tree diagrams—were introduced in the previous chapter. The next section briefly describes the management and planning tools, and shows how they can be used in policy deployment. The text presents a hypothetical high-technology consumer electronics company, MicroTech, to illustrate the application of these tools. MicroTech's mission is

> To design and manufacture miniature electronics products utilizing radio frequency technologies, digital signal processing technologies, and state-of-the-art surface mount manufacturing techniques.

■ Affinity Diagrams

The affinity diagram was introduced in the last chapter as a tool for organizing a large number of ideas, opinions, and facts relating to a broad problem or subject area. In developing a vision statement, for example, senior management might conduct a brainstorming session to develop a list of ideas to incorporate into the vision. This list might include

low product maintenance	low production costs
satisfied employees	innovative product features
courteous order entry	high return on investment
low price	constant technology innovation
quick delivery	high quality
growth in shareholder value	motivated employees
teamwork	unique products
responsive technical support	small, lightweight designs
personal employee growth	

Once a large number of ideas have been generated, they can be grouped according to their "affinity" or relationship to each other. An affinity diagram for the preceding list is shown in Figure 6.4.

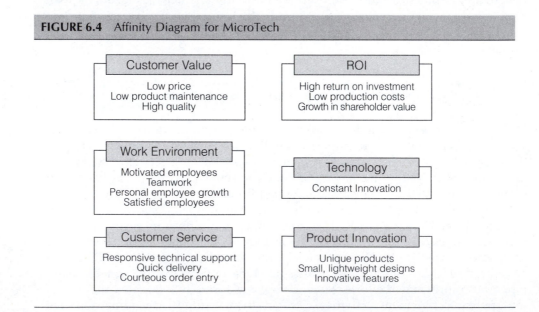

FIGURE 6.4   Affinity Diagram for MicroTech

■ Interrelationship Digraphs

An interrelationship digraph identifies and explores causal relationships among related concepts or ideas. It shows that every idea can be logically linked with more than one other idea at a time, and allows for "lateral thinking" rather than "linear thinking." This technique is often used after the affinity diagram has clarified issues and problems. Figure 6.5 shows an example of how the key strategic factors for MicroTech relate to one another. The elements having the most net outward-pointing arrows (number out minus number in) represent the primary drivers of the company's vision: in this case, work environment and customer service. As a result, MicroTech might develop the following vision statement:

> We will provide exceptional value to our customers in terms of cost-effective products and services of the highest quality, leading to superior value to our shareholders. We will provide a supportive work environment that promotes personal growth and the pursuit of excellence and allows each employee to achieve his or her full potential. We are committed to advancing the state-of-the-art in electronics miniaturization and related technologies and to developing market opportunities that are built upon our unique technical expertise.

■ Tree Diagrams

A tree diagram maps out the paths and tasks necessary to complete a specific project or reach a specified goal. Thus, the planner uses this technique to seek answers to such questions as "What sequence of tasks will address the issue?" or "What factors contribute to the existence of the key problem?"

A tree diagram brings the issues and problems revealed by the affinity diagram and the interrelationship digraph down to the operational planning stage. A clear statement specifies problem or process. From this general statement, a team can be established to recommend steps to solve the problem or implement the plan. The "product" produced by this group would be a tree diagram with activities and perhaps recommendations for timing the activities. Figure 6.6 shows an example of how a tree diagram can be used to map out key goals and strategies for MicroTech.

FIGURE 6.5   Interrelationship Digraph of MicroTech's Strategic Factors

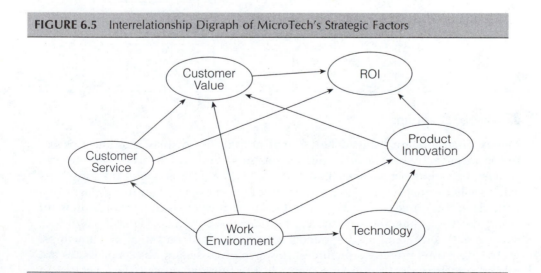

FIGURE 6.6 Tree Diagram of MicroTech Goals and Strategies

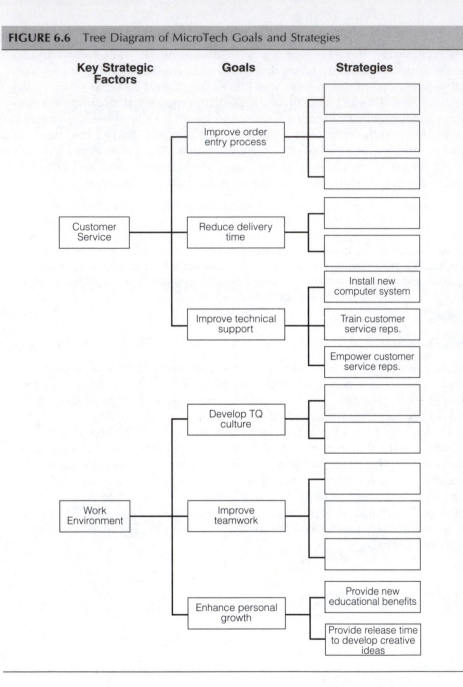

Matrix Diagrams

Matrix diagrams are "spreadsheets" that graphically display relationships between ideas, activities, or other dimensions in such a way as to provide logical connecting points between each item. A matrix diagram is one of the most versatile tools in quality planning. One example is shown in Figure 6.7. Here, we have listed the three principal goals articulated in MicroTech's vision statement along the rows, and the key strategies along the columns. Typically, symbols such as ●, ○, and △ are used to denote strong, medium, and weak relationships. Matrix diagrams provide a picture of how well two sets of objects or issues are related and can identify missing pieces in the thought process. For instance, a

FIGURE 6.7 Matrix Diagram for MicroTech's Goals and Strategies

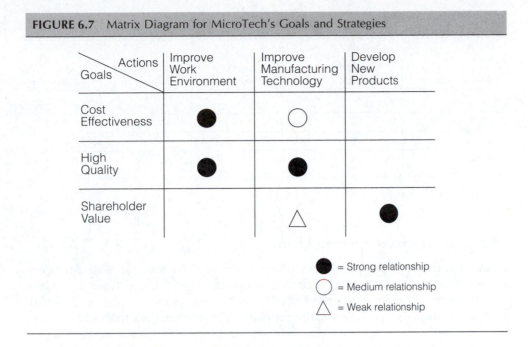

row without many relationships might indicate that the actions proposed will not meet the company's goals. In Figure 6.7, we see that focused attention to these three strategies should meet MicroTech's goals. Other matrices might relate short-term plans to medium-term objectives, or individual actions to short-term plans. These visual depictions can help managers set priorities on plans and actions.

■ Matrix Data Analysis

Matrix data analysis takes data and arranges it to display quantitative relationships among variables to make them more easily understood and analyzed. In its original form used in Japan, matrix data analysis is a rigorous, statistically based "factor analysis" technique. Many feel that this method, while worthwhile for many applications, is too quantitative to be used on a daily basis and have developed alternative tools that are easier to understand and implement. Some of these alternatives are similar to decision analysis matrixes that you may have studied in a quantitative methods course.

A small example of matrix data analysis is shown in Figure 6.8. In this example, MicroTech market research determined that the four most important consumer requirements are price, reliability, delivery, and technical support. Through market research, an importance weighting was developed for each. They also determined numerical ratings for the company and their best competitor. Such an analysis provides information as to which actions the company should deploy to better meet key customer requirements. For example, in Figure 6.8, reliability is the highest in importance, and MicroTech has a narrow lead over its best competitor; thus, they should continue to strive for improving product reliability. Also, technical support is of relatively high importance, but MicroTech is perceived to be inferior to its best competitor in this category. Thus, improving the quality of support services should be a major objective.

FIGURE 6.8   Matrix Data Analysis of Customer Requirements for MicroTech

Requirement	Importance Weight	Best Competitor Evaluation	MicroTech Evaluation	Difference*
Price	.2	6	8	+2
Reliability	.4	7	8	+1
Delivery	.1	8	5	−3
Technical Support	.3	7	5	−2

*MicroTech − Best Competitor

Process Decision Program Charts

A process decision program chart (PDPC) is a method for mapping out every conceivable event and contingency that can occur when moving from a problem statement to possible solutions. A PDPC takes each branch of a tree diagram, anticipates possible problems, and provides countermeasures that will (1) prevent the deviation from occurring, or (2) be in place if the deviation *does* occur. Figure 6.9 shows one example for implementing a strategy to educate and train all employees to use a new computer system.

Arrow Diagrams

For years, construction planners have used arrow diagrams in the form of CPM and PERT project planning techniques. Arrow diagramming has also been taught extensively in quantitative methods, operations management, and other business

FIGURE 6.9   A Process Decision Program Chart

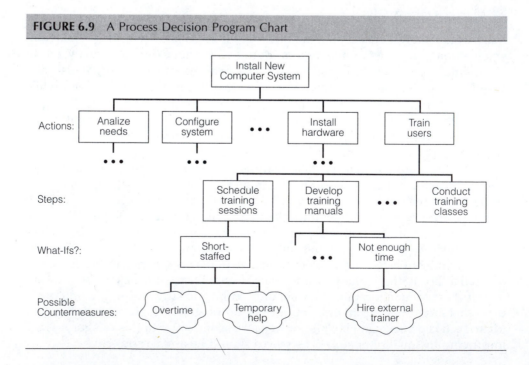

FIGURE 6.10   An Arrow Diagram for Project Planning

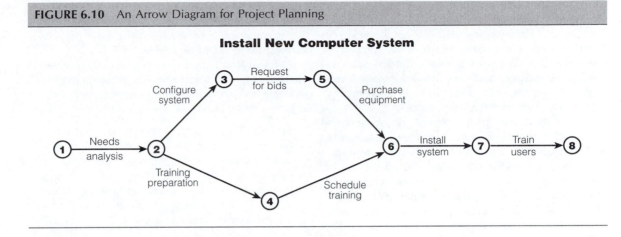

Install New Computer System

---

and engineering courses in the United States for a number of years. Unfortunately, their use has generally been confined to technical experts. By adding it to the "quality toolbox," it has become more widely available to general managers and other nontechnical personnel. Figure 6.10 shows an example. Time estimates can easily be added to each activity in order to schedule and control the project.

These seven tools provide managers with improved capability to make better decisions and facilitate the implementation process. With proper planning, managers can use their time more effectively to continuously improve and innovate.

QUALITY IN PRACTICE   **TEACHING THE BUFFALOS TO FLY: JOHNSONVILLE FOODS**[32]

Ralph C. Stayer, owner and CEO of Johnsonville Foods Co. in Sheboygan Falls, Wisconsin, has been profiled by Tom Peters in his book *Thriving on Chaos* and the PBS video program, *The Leadership Alliance*.[33] Stayer recently revealed his leadership secrets in the book that he co-authored with James A. Belasco under the intriguing title of *Flight of the Buffalo*.[34] Stayer was responsible for initiating the process that transformed a sleepy, family-owned sausage-making company into a nationally recognized firm that is using an innovative self-management process to remain healthy in an increasingly competitive industry. In the first chapter of his book, Stayer compares his company to a herd of buffalo that follows a single leader wherever the leader wants them to go. In the old West when buffalo hunters wanted to kill a lot of buffalo, they just killed the lead buffalo. The rest of the herd was easily cut down, since they would stop and mill around the fallen leader, waiting for him to lead them to safety.

Stayer wanted to change the leadership paradigm to encourage his employees to become responsible, interdependent workers, more like a flock of wild geese. Geese fly in their typical "V" formation, with different birds taking the lead at different points in time. Essentially, they share the leadership load. He stated that the leadership principles for the new paradigm include the following points:

■ Leaders transfer ownership of the work to those who execute the work.

■ Leaders create the environment for ownership where each person wants to be responsible.

■ Leaders coach the development of personal capabilities.

■ Leaders learn fast themselves and encourage others also to learn quickly.[35]

Ralph Stayer began to transform Johnsonville in the early 1980s before they reached a point of crisis.

They were a small regional meat packer that was strong in Wisconsin and beginning to make some inroads into surrounding states. Over the next ten years, through his and the efforts of the company's "associates," their return on assets doubled, sales increased nine times, and product and quality levels improved significantly, even though the company was in a mature and declining industry.

Stayer tried the "prescriptions" of job descriptions, MBO, communication improvement methods, and even an early version of quality circles to transform the company's culture. None stood the test of time nor his gut feel for what changes were needed in the company. He felt that his small entrepreneurial firm had the potential to be *great*, but was only performing up to the average measures in the industry.

The Palmer Sausage decision, detailed in a 1985 Harvard Business School case, was the turning point for employee learning and empowerment.[36] Palmer Sausage Co., a larger regional competitor, had a product that they wished to distribute, but they were consolidating plants and contacted Johnsonville about the possibility of providing some extra capacity. Although this "golden opportunity" would help the company grow, Johnsonville would have to build a new plant, hire additional workers, and make other improvements. Meanwhile, if Palmer didn't like Johnsonville's product they could cancel the contract with a 30-day notice, leaving Johnsonville in a vulnerable position with unused plant capacity and too many workers on the payroll. Instead of making an executive decision, Ralph Stayer empowered his workers and managers to study the problem and decide whether to accept Palmer's offer. Many small groups met and discussed the decision and decided to accept the offer.

The employees rose to the challenge. Initially, they worked six or seven days per week while the new plant was being built. The new employees were brought on board and trained, and the old employees rapidly learned new skills. The quality levels for both Johnsonville and Palmer products rose, despite the strain of high production. The new plant was successfully brought on line in 1987.

A result that is perhaps even more significant is the degree to which employees have taken over both strategic and operating management responsibilities at Johnsonville Foods. In Stayer's words:

> Profoundly, Johnsonville people learned what they needed to do. They learned to be responsible for more of the strategic decisions at Johnsonville. They changed the career tracking system and set new team performance standards. Then they went on transforming themselves from buffalo into geese.

Capital budgeting, new product development, scheduling, hiring and firing, quality and productivity measurement, and a number of other strategic and operating decisions are now made by teams of line employees at Johnsonville.

In summary, Stayer sees the key to leadership success as *doing* the job of changing the leadership paradigm, owning up to being part of the problem as a traditional manager, empowering employees to do the jobs that they are capable of doing and growing into, coaching and rewarding performance in multiple ways, and learning, learning, learning.

Key Issues for Discussion

1. From a strategic management standpoint, does Ralph Stayer provide sufficient planning and control to keep the company on track?

2. What type of management style does he seem to follow? Does it "fit" any of the leadership theories that were developed in the chapter?

3. How easy or difficult would it be for other companies to duplicate the leadership style of Stayer and the organizational systems practiced at Johnsonville Foods?

QUALITY IN PRACTICE   **LEADERSHIP AT RUBBERMAID, INC.**[37]

In 1994, *Fortune* magazine named Rubbermaid, Inc., America's most admired company by the 10,000 senior executives, outside directors, and financial analysts who participated in the publication's 12th annual "Corporate Reputations Survey." Rubbermaid's mission statement is

[To] be the leading world-class marketer of best value, brand-name, primarily plastic products for the consumer, institutional, office products, agricultural, and industrial markets. The Company is market-driven. We listen to customers and consumers and respond to the trends and changes in their needs and lifestyles. This strategy guides all of Rubbermaid's businesses in developing new products, leads us into new markets, allows us to apply relevant new technologies more effectively in creating value, and directs our efforts in developing working partnerships with all the Company's constituencies.

To accomplish this mission, Rubbermaid promotes a broad set of management principles:

We believe our primary responsibility is to the consumers and customers who buy our products and services. We will consistently delight them with our quality, innovation, and prompt and accurate service. We will utilize teamwork, new processes and technologies to compress time and improve our business processes. Every associate will contribute to reducing our costs and adding value to the business. We believe that by eliminating boundaries between business partners, we can best improve our value.

We believe that our partners are entitled to share in the economic benefit derived from our efforts to create, develop, produce, source, and market products worldwide. To this end,

For our consumers we will strive to
- understand and be creatively responsive to their needs
- always look to improve value for them
- stand behind our products and services
- help protect and improve the environment

For our [external] customers we will strive to
- work as partners with integrity and principled negotiation
- invest aggressively in research, new products, capacity and technology
- offer on-trend products of exceptional design, fashion, quality and utility
- work together to reduce or eliminate non-value activities
- provide mass customization and creative, aggressive marketing
- understand and respond innovatively to their changing requirements

For our suppliers we will strive to
- foster mutually beneficial long-term business partnerships
- utilize our mutual capabilities to create better value
- be objective and ethical in all transactions

For our associates we will strive to
- have management lead by example
- provide an environment which is positive and reinforces initiative
- reinforce experimentation, listening and risk taking
- nurture diversity and variety of thought
- develop with them a learning contract
- empower to the fullest extent with appropriate accountability
- offer equal opportunity for career growth and advancement
- create focused, decentralized operating units
- provide rewards and opportunity consistent with their contribution
- develop a global view of customers, consumers, vendors and opportunities

For our communities and governments we will strive to
- support the economy and general welfare
- conduct business in an ethical and responsible manner
- encourage our associates to participate actively with them
- communicate the many benefits of the free enterprise system
- be a good corporate citizen

For our shareholders we will strive to
- continually reinvent our people, products, processes, plans and plants
- optimize the full resources of the organization
- provide superior management with depth and continuity
- provide leadership which is proactive and demands excellence
- balance our incremental and leap growth strategies
- provide an attractive and consistent return on investment
- communicate effectively the Company's performance on a timely basis

For everyone we will strive to
- ensure that every Rubbermaid associate acts with high integrity and observes our shared ethical standards

Rubbermaid began as the Wooster Rubber Co., of Wooster, Ohio, a maker of toy balloons and dustpans. The founder's son, Stanley Gault, became CEO in 1980, and for 11 years led the company to achieve annual profit increases of 14 percent and share price increases of more than 25 percent. Gault retired in 1991 and became CEO of Goodyear, but still remains on the board. After a short period of transition, Wolfgang Schmitt became CEO in November 1992. Schmitt set goals that include entering a new product category every 12 to 18 months, getting 33 percent of sales from products introduced in the past five years, and increasing revenues from markets outside the United States from 18 to 25 percent by the year 2000.

Rubbermaid's success stems from exceptional leadership and the dedication of its workers and product teams. When Gault ran the company, a union trucker had heard about his open door policy and asked if it applied to him.[38] Gault told him that he would meet him at 6:00 A.M. and would make the coffee. The trucker discussed some issues that were bothering him including poor lighting at the docks and poor condition of older truck cabs. Gault told him that the Rubbermaid family comes first. The next morning, Gault made sure that the cabs were replaced and wanted the drivers involved in selecting the supplier. As he observed, it went through the system "like wildfire."

Twenty cross-functional teams, made up of people from marketing, manufacturing, research and development, finance, and other departments, focus on specific product lines and provide most of the ideas for products. When Schmitt and Richard Gates, head of business development, visited London, they came away with eleven product ideas from an exhibit of Egyptian antiquities. "They [the Egyptians] used a lot of kitchen utensils, some of which were very nice. Nice designs."

Although Rubbermaid introduces more than 365 new products each year, it does no formal market testing, except for small focus groups (twelve bass fishermen critiqued a new tacklebox). Schmitt does not believe in market testing. "We don't want to be copied. It's not that much riskier to just roll it out. Plus, it puts pressure on us to do it right the first time."

Key Issues for Discussion

1. How does Rubbermaid's mission and management principles provide a total quality focus for the company?

2. Could Rubbermaid accomplish its mission without strong executive leadership? What effect do you think that Gault's meeting with the trucker had on the rest of the company?

3. How does executive leadership contribute to the management principles stated for each category of the company's constituencies?

QUALITY IN PRACTICE | **STRATEGIC QUALITY PLANNING AT THE STROH BREWERY COMPANY[39]**

The Total Quality Management Program at The Stroh Brewery Company in Detroit is based in the fundamental belief that employees hold the key to achieving a comprehensive focus on Service-Quality—an organized concerted effort to add value to products, including those processes through which services are delivered—that will enable Stroh's to meet and exceed the expectations of its customers. Service-Quality means more than a quality product. It must be defined through customers' perception of value. The customer judges Stroh not just by the reliability of their basic product, but from the "total experience" of doing business with them. Every encounter with a company system or a company employee is a "moment of truth" when the customer will judge the Service-Quality efforts of Stroh. This philosophy is reflected in the company's strategic plan.

Vision
Our vision of The Stroh Brewery Company is one of a growing and prospering company with a dynamic and motivated organization providing our shareholders with reasonable return on their investment.

Mission
To achieve this vision, our mission is to produce, distribute and market a variety of high-quality beers in a manner that meets or exceeds the expectations of our customers.

Values
Our company values provide a constant point of reference for all of our efforts and confirm our commitment to Stroh employees and to all of our customers. The core values of *Quality*, *Integrity*, and *Teamwork* will serve as the foundation upon which we will build success.

■ *Quality*. We seek to continuously improve the level of quality in all that we do. We pursue having the finest products, efficient production and distribution facilities, innovative marketing and sales programs, and totally supportive administrative policies and procedures. These efforts are directed at meeting or exceeding our customers' expectations—both inside and outside the Company.

■ *Integrity*. We conduct all of our activities with integrity. We believe that the Stroh name stands for honesty and trust. We apply this belief to our relationship with all employees, our suppliers, wholesalers, and all others with whom we have business relationships. Our business activities will model our values, demonstrating that we are a responsible corporate citizen with a firm resolve to live up to our social and environmental responsibilities.

■ *Teamwork.* Teamwork is essential to our mutual success. Stroh employees are a valuable asset. Every employee is given respect and trust, regardless of position in the organization. All employees are encouraged to share their views and suggestions. It is through mutual respect, cooperation, and sharing of ideas with employees, suppliers, wholesalers, and retailers that the full potential of the company will be realized. We will fully support the submission and discussion of new ideas from all of our associates (employees, wholesalers, and suppliers). Commitment and innovation will be viewed as actions worthy of praise and recognition.

Strategy

In support of our vision and mission, the following strategies will be employed to achieve our Service-Quality goal. WE WILL:

■ Maintain a competitive brand portfolio that allows us to capture unique market opportunities and strive to realize the potential of our present brands, and new product introductions. Our goal is to increase unit volume. This does not mean, however, that every brand will experience unit growth every year. We will manage each brand based on its long-term growth potential, its strategic relevance, and its relationship to the company's overall business strategy.

■ Invest heavily in the development of our human resources through orientation and training, which will enable our employees to make better decisions and to improve processes. We will hire individuals who have the job-related skills and abilities that support Stroh's Service-Quality mode of operation.

■ Develop and introduce line extensions, new brands, and new packages, seeking to create innovative breakthroughs. New products are a critical element to Stroh's overall success. We will develop new products with a sense of urgency while maintaining a commitment to sound product concepts, excellent sales execution, and appropriate marketing support.

■ Maintain a flexible approach in the balance between national and regional marketing and sales efforts. Although there are aspects of marketing our products that have relevance to all markets (e.g. national advertising), we will always try to find ways to capitalize on regional strengths and opportunities.

■ Pursue opportunities to develop international markets. Our focus for the future extends to international markets where we believe there are significant opportunities to market our products both directly and in partnership with others.

■ Commit to maintaining the best distribution network in the industry along with our full support of the three-tier system. Our distribution system will function around the guiding principles of Service-Quality.

■ Strive to control production and administrative expenses which allow us to provide the maximum funds to market our products. We will do this by constantly seeking ways to improve our method of completing tasks necessary to our business.

■ Consider acquiring assets to build synergies and to reduce production costs. The acquisition of additional brands, manufacturing facilities, and other businesses that will improve the company's overall strategic position is viewed as highly desirable.

■ Invest in plant equipment and new technologies to produce new products and to maintain our production facilities to remain competitive.

■ Be comfortable with change. We will pursue change as a strategic weapon. There is no safety in standing still, nor is there any advantage in abiding by the rules set by our competitors. Change will not be pursued for its own sake, but neither will change be avoided because it is uncomfortable or because of the risks associated with change.

■ Be market and service driven. We will develop systems and processes to facilitate this strategy.

Key Issues for Discussion

1. Who are Stroh's customers? Would you say that The Stroh Brewery Company is a "customer-driven" company?

2. What aspects of Stroh's vision, mission, values, and strategy support the fundamental principles of TQM?

SUMMARY OF KEY POINTS

■ Leadership is the right to exercise authority and the ability to achieve results from the people and systems under one's authority. Leaders create clear and visible quality values and integrate these into the organization's strategy.

■ Five core leadership skills are vision, empowerment, intuition, self-understanding, and value congruence. These skills help true leaders to promote and practice total quality by creating a customer-driven vision, setting high expectations, demonstrating personal involvement, integrating quality into daily management, and sustaining an environment for quality excellence.

■ Leadership has been studied from at least five major perspectives: the trait approach, the behavioral view, the contingency approach, the role approach, and new perspectives such as transactional theory. Contemporary theories are based on contingency approaches, and include Fiedler's model, Vroom and Jago's model, and a variety of others.

■ A critical role of leadership is strategic management. Strategy is the pattern of decisions that determines and reveals a company's goals, policies, and plans, and is determined through strategic planning. Strategic quality planning includes understanding key customer requirements, optimizing the use of resources, ensuring that quality initiatives will be understood at all levels in the organization, and ensuring that the organization will plan for breakthrough and continuous improvements.

■ Key practices for effective strategic planning include active participation by both top management and lower-level employees, a strong customer focus, supplier involvement, and well-established measurement and feedback systems.

■ Strategy formulation begins with determining the organization's mission, vision, and guiding principles. These lead to goals and strategies that set the direction for achieving the mission. It is important that goals be consistent with the key business factors that lead to competitive success. Companies use various approaches to strategic planning.

■ Deploying strategy effectively is often done through a process called hoshin kanri, or policy deployment. Policy deployment emphasizes organization-wide planning and setting of priorities, providing resources to meet objectives, and measuring performance as a basis for improving it. It is essentially a total quality approach to executing a strategy.

■ The seven management and planning tools help managers to implement policy deployment and are useful in other areas of quality planning. These tools are the affinity diagram, interrelationship digraph, tree diagram, matrix diagram, matrix data analysis, process decision program chart, and arrow diagram.

REVIEW QUESTIONS

1. Define leadership. Why is it necessary for successful total quality management?

2. List the five core leadership skills. Of what value are these skills in TQM?

3. What are the leading practices of top managers in TQM-based organizations? Provide some examples of each.

4. What are the five common perspectives from which leadership theory is studied? Explain each.

5. Contrast Fiedler's contingency theory with the Vroom-Jago model. What are the similarities and differences?

6. What is transformational leadership theory? How does it explain leadership in a TQM environment?

7. What is a strategy? What elements do most strategies contain?

8. Explain the role of quality in strategic planning. Why should strategic quality planning be synonymous with strategic business planning?

9. What are the leading practices for effective strategic planning?

10. Define mission, vision, and guiding principles. What is the purpose of each?

11. Explain the basic strategic planning process.

12. What are the key business factors of most companies? How do these drive strategic planning?

13. What is hoshin kanri? Provide a simplified description of this process.

14. How does catchball play an important role in policy deployment?

15. Explain the differences between management by objective and policy deployment.

16. List and explain the major uses for the seven management and planning tools.

DISCUSSION QUESTIONS

1. We stated that leadership is the "driver" of a total quality system? What does this statement imply and what implications does this have for future CEOs? Middle managers? Supervisors?

2. Provide examples from your own experiences in which leaders (not necessarily company managers— consider academic unit heads, presidents of student organizations, and even family members) exhibited one or more of the five core leadership skills described in this chapter. What impacts did these have on the organization?

3. State some examples in which leaders you have worked for exhibited some of the leading practices described in this chapter. Can you provide examples for which they have not?

4. Discuss the implications of the various leadership theories described in this chapter for managers in TQM environments. What specific aspects of these theories affect the basic principles of TQM described in Chapter 4?

5. Review Deming's 14 Points. What aspects of leadership theories are evident in them, either individually or as a holistic philosophy?

6. Give examples of different "situational conditions" that would affect leadership styles according to Fiedler's model. As a company moves from a little to a high degree of TQM adoption, how do the situational conditions change? What does this mean for leadership?

7. In your role as a student, develop your own statements of mission, vision, and guiding principles. How would you create a strategy to achieve your mission and vision?

8. How does the Xerox Leadership Through Quality strategy support TQM?

9. Research the background of recent Baldrige Award winners. How do they integrate quality into their business strategies? Discuss different approaches that these firms use.

10. How can TQM improve the *process* of strategic planning?

11. Interview managers at some local companies to determine whether their businesses have well-defined mission, vision, and guiding principles. If they do, how are these translated into strategy? If not, what steps should they take?

12. Does your university or college have a mission and strategy? How might policy deployment be used in a university setting?

13. Contrast the following vision statements in terms of their usefulness to an organization.

a. To become the industry leader and achieve superior growth and market share.

b. To become the best-managed electric utility in the United States and an excellent company overall and be recognized as such.

c. Being the best at everything we do, exceeding customer expectations; growing our business to increase its value to customers, employees, shareowners, and communities in which we work.

14. Propose three applications for each of the seven management and planning tools discussed in the chapter. You might consider some applications around school, such as in the classroom, studying for exams, and so on.

CASES

I. Corryville Foundry Company[40]

Corryville Foundry Company (CFC) was founded in the mid 1940s in a 3000 square foot building with nine people as a small family business to produce castings. In the 1960s, as business grew, the company expanded its facilities and its capability to develop its own tooling patterns, eventually moving into a 40,000 square foot building. Over this time period, the foundry industry declined from more than 12,000 companies to about 4,000.

With such a shrinking market, CFC began to listen more to its customers. They discovered that customers were not happy with the quality of the products they had been receiving. In 1989, CFC made a commitment to quality by hiring a quality assurance manager, Ronald Chalmer. Mr. Chalmer felt that upper management was committed to quality and saw an opportunity to change the company's culture. He also firmly believed in Deming's philosophy. One of the first things he did was to work with upper management in developing a mission statement:

> Our mission at CFC is to improve the return on investment. We can accomplish this by changing attitudes and incorporating a quality/team environment. This will improve the quality of our products, enhance our productivity (which in turn will allow us to quote competitive prices) and elevate our service and response level to our customers. There are

several factors which make positive change imperative.

The standards for competitive levels of quality and service are becoming more demanding. The emergence of the "World Market" has brought on new challenges. We are in a low growth, mature market. In order for CFC to improve return on investment, we must develop a strategy to improve quality and responsiveness in all areas of the company. We need to have all employees recognize the importance of product quality and service and move toward more favorable pricing. We need to change thinking throughout the organization to get employees involved, to encourage teamwork, to develop a more flexible workforce and adaptable organization. We need to instill pride in the workplace and the product.

We believe that we can best achieve the desired future state by study of and adherence to the teachings of W. Edwards Deming.

Under Mr. Chalmer's direction, CFC made some substantial improvements in the quality of castings, particularly reducing scrap and reject rates. He worked closely with the factory workers directly responsible for the products, asking them what they needed to get the job done and ensuring management commitment to provide the necessary resources. For example, CFC invested in a new controller for the furnaces that provided a digital readout of temperature. With this technology, workers were able to categorize the metal temperatures needed for each casting type and were able to adjust the process as needed. The success of this project led the company to empower employees to control many other aspects of the system.

Three years later, the president and CEO retired. The new CEO, who had been a vice president of a major manufacturing company, did not feel that the mission statement provided a clear and vivid direction. Consequently, he set up a planning retreat for senior management (including Mr. Chalmer) to develop a new strategic vision.

Discussion Questions

1. Comment on the current mission statement. Does it provide the strategic direction necessary for success for this company?

2. How can the mission statement be improved? Suggest a better statement of mission, vision, and guiding principles.

II. Blue Genes Corporation[41]

Blue Genes Mission Statement

Blue Genes Corporation is a worldwide corporation applying a wide range of counseling and therapeutic services to addressing and eliminating clinical depression. The company is dedicated to improving the well-being of people around the world. The employees of Blue Genes have a shared commitment to:

- Provide customers with innovative and technologically advanced products and services.
- Deliver products and services of superior quality and value to our customers.
- Manage the company to achieve its profit objectives.
- Maintain the highest level of ethics, integrity, and excellence in all phases of our business.

Blue Genes recognizes the value of its employees to the success of the corporation. Blue Genes is dedicated to the fair and equitable treatment of its employees and to the promotion of a safe, stimulating, and challenging environment that supports teamwork and personal growth.

Blue Genes delivers the following products and services:

- Behavioral counseling (psychology)
- Behavioral medicine (psychiatric drugs)
- Genetic counseling (diagnostics)
- Genetic engineering (in-vitro fertilization)
- Genetic therapy (gene inhibiting drugs)

Blue Genes Corporation was formed to combat clinical depression in U.S. society. The company, recognizing that the causes of clinical depression are many and varied, delivers diversified products and services to the clinically depressed. Its structure is based upon the nature of the products and services it offers as reflected in the preceding list.

Most products and services offered in these areas are drawn from the existing technology base; Blue Genes acts as a distributor of appropriate technologies to customers. However, the company has developed specific technologies—specifically, the GenFo® product line—that allow early diagnosis of genetic faults linked to depression. Blue Genes has also developed specific drugs to treat depression through genetic suppression, sold under the Blue Bottle® label.

Blue Genes continues to build upon its core competencies in genetic research while keeping up with alternate offerings from the classical pharmaceutical companies. It strives to serve its customers as effectively as possible without regard to profit motives or proprietary positions. The company considers its true product to be a happy patient and does whatever is needed to deliver that product.

Blue Genes' 930 employees represent a broad spectrum of educational levels and cultures. They possess scientific expertise in the areas of genetics, behavioral science, psychiatry, immunology, molecular biology, molecular modeling, chemistry, physics, clinical medicine, mathematics, biostatistics, pharmacology, engineering, and business.

In 1989, Blue Genes initiated a formal total quality management process, Blue Skies. A major component of this quality process was a training and development program for all employees beginning with the senior executives, then extending to all employees. The program emphasizes customer focus and continuous improvement tools. As a result of the total quality management process, all employees have committed to making customers happy.

The key requirements for Blue Genes' offerings center on effectiveness and safety. Because the company, in many ways, experiences "soft results" of its services, it relies heavily on standard psychological testing instruments to determine whether services have been effective.

As a developer and distributor of drugs, Blue Genes is very sensitive to the dangers inherent with side effects and misuse or adulteration. Therefore, it complies with both mandatory and voluntary guidelines established by the governments of the countries in which it operates and the societies that represent the company's fields (such as the American Psychological Association).

Blue Genes' primary customers are health care professionals who use the products it manufactures and/or distributes and those patients it works with directly in counseling and clinical studies. The company also considers the patients of those using its products as customers and include them in its measurements of product effectiveness. Blue Genes extends its "customer-oriented" consideration to each component of the supply chain, considering the needs of all groups and individuals involved.

In keeping with the company's worldwide mission, Blue Genes established a global presence early in its history. Although it distributes to the worldwide market, Blue Genes currently provides direct counseling services at its Raleigh headquarters and research sites in New York and Richmond only. Approximately 20 percent of distribution revenues are derived from outside the United States.

Blue Genes is unique in its approach of offering diversified services and products to a single customer group. As such, it is difficult to compare overall operations to a specific industry. In general, Blue Genes rarely distributes more than five percent of any represented product's annual sales. Key competitors in the area of antidepressant drugs would include major drug companies, most notably Eli Lilly with their popular drug Prozac®.

However, for that portion of the market choosing to use the genetic approach to prevention and treatment of clinical depression, Blue Genes is considered the industry leader. Although other biotechnology companies, such as Gen-Chek and Startagene, are doing work in this area, Blue Genes' focused approach gives it a 75 percent share of this chosen market.

Blue Genes has three manufacturing and distribution buildings occupying over 180,000 square feet located in Raleigh, North Carolina. In addition, it maintains behavioral and clinical outreach centers in New York City and Richmond, Virginia.

Examples of specialized equipment used in its manufacturing operations include:

- Automated column chromatography system
- Stainless steel liquid fillers
- State-of-the-art freeze dryers
- Automated acid & base incubation systems
- Cleanrooms
- Fermenters

Key technologies include genetic engineering and expression; gene selection, development, generation, purification, and labeling; radioisotope technology; and robotics and automation.

Blue Genes does business with more than 1000 suppliers. Approximately 100 of these provide materials used in the manufacturing areas, 600 provide products that the company distributes, and the remainder provide indirect materials and services. Approximately 50 percent of Blue Genes' revenues are derived from the direct distribution of products that come from its suppliers.

Blue Genes management recognizes the critical nature of positive and long-term relations with suppliers. One example of its commitment to supplier quality is Blue Genes' supplier certification process. This process, created in 1989, is designed to maintain alignment with suppliers. Blue Genes' award program, *Supplier Celebration,* is another means by which it communicates to suppliers its commitment to total quality. These examples illustrate the desire to partner with suppliers in making customers happy.

The nature of its products demands that Blue Genes consistently meet all applicable health, safety, and environmental regulations (local, state, and federal). Specific examples of regulatory requirements include the Occupational Safety and Health Act (OSHA) and the Code of Federal Regulations.

All of Blue Genes' products are subject to approval and regulation by the Food and Drug Administration (FDA) and similar authorities in other countries. Medical products must perform according to customer-driven specifications. The FDA's charter is to ensure that a company's products are safe and effective and will not endanger public health. Therefore, Blue Genes complies with FDA regulations that include inspection; investigation and resolution of product failure, adverse event, or customer complaint; and auditing of the company's quality assurance program. In addition, new products must be submitted for review and clearance by the FDA prior to marketing; these submissions include establishment licenses and product licenses. Since the end customer, the patient, is the most important consideration in the entire system, clinical trials involving human subjects must meet established criteria to gain FDA approval. The need to meet the rigorous demands of the FDA for data forces an organization such as Blue Genes to base corporate decisions on facts and data.

The quality planning process at Blue Genes addresses a number of factors that are crucial to long-term success, such as rapid technological changes, breakthroughs in the understanding of clinical depression, economic demands, changes in clinical behavior, high cost of health care, or industry consolidation. By focusing on customer alignment—the honest and continual exchange, internally and externally, of information and ideas pertaining to process and product improvement—management can plan to master the future and to prosper. While the concepts of total involvement, measurement, systematic support, and continuous improvement are major forces in the TQM effort at Blue Genes, a customer focus and organizational alignment are what drive the company toward achieving its quality goal of making customers happy.

Blue Genes Definition of Quality
Making Customers Happy

Blue Genes' strategic intent is to eradicate clinical depression worldwide, to effectively bring joy to the world. Blue Skies, its TQM process, drives its efforts to meet that strategic intent.

Blue Genes Strategic Intent
Joy to the World

Strategic Quality and Company Performance Planning Process

Blue Genes develops plans and strategies for the short term and longer term through an annual quality planning process (QPP) shown in Figure 6.11. During this process, the company cycles through two phases: the long-term (five years) strategic quality plan (SQP) and the shorter-term (one year) tactical quality plan (TQP).

Company Challenges

1. Manage all aspects of the business using the principles of Blue Skies

2. Develop new products faster than any of our competitors

3. Be the earliest distributor of new technologies addressing clinical depression

4. Define and access core technologies necessary to meet the long-term needs of the organization

5. Be the best in the industry in developing and managing strategic alliances

6. Achieve defined financial goals

7. Provide a better quality of life to our customers, and improve our results in this arena significantly every year

First, Blue Genes actively reviews customer needs, key quality requirements, and available business opportunities against its guiding principles: its mission statement, strategic intent, definition of quality, and company challenges (which represent current long-term strategies, goals, and business plans). Our quality planning process facilitation team ensures that cross-functional strategy teams consider this information as well as company capabilities and the competitive environment.

These teams, with two types of focus, interact in the quality planning process, which has evolved into the matrix activity depicted in Figure 6.12. The columns of this grid represent market approaches and are addressed by customer-focused strategy teams. These teams consider many factors including those indicated by the rows of the grid. The rows represent capabilities and core competencies. Key functional areas must be managed to support the customer-focused strategy teams. These key areas are addressed through capability-focused strategy teams of their own. The participants in these two sets of teams meet regularly during the planning process to compare needs and capabilities, adjusting goals or expectations appropriately. The QPP facilitation team, which includes the CEO, his staff, and key individuals from strategic planning and human resources, provide direction, resources, and venues for this ongoing interaction.

The customer-focused strategy teams work with the QPP facilitation team and several capability-focused strategy teams to produce strategic goals, measures, and plans that match current and future customer needs to current and future company capabilities. Each strategy team is supported by subteams that address specific issues. Every Blue Genes employee is involved in at least one such subteam, and is kept informed of the status and activities of the parent strategy team. All strategy teams and subteams remain intact to retain the expertise of each group for the TQP and future QPP cycles.

The SQP forms the basis for the second phase of the quality planning process, the tactical quality plan. In the TQP, detailed resources are allocated, and goals, measures, and plans are established at all levels of the organization.

The QPP uses data and analysis results to develop business plans and priorities by considering the following areas:

1. *Customer requirements and the expected evolution of these requirements:* The evolving market and the company's commitment to innovation make customer awareness a major competitive advantage for Blue Genes. Several methods are used to maintain or improve customer satisfaction. Blue Genes is most influenced by its review of technological advances that provide more effective treatments for clinical depression. Development efforts include both improving current products and developing future products. Improvements to existing products play a large part in customer retention, the measure of which provides one of the corporate lead signs. The company stays in contact with its customers of the future through the new product committees and by research and development. Senior level scientists and consulting firms (both scientific and marketing) talk with

key experts and customers to project the future, to anticipate the capabilities that the industry may create, and to anticipate how these capabilities could benefit customers. These future projections of technologies and products result in product introduction schedules that are key goals for the organization.

2. *Projections of the competitive environment:* Blue Genes observes and responds to competitors, not

---

FIGURE 6.11 Blue Genes' Quality Planning Process

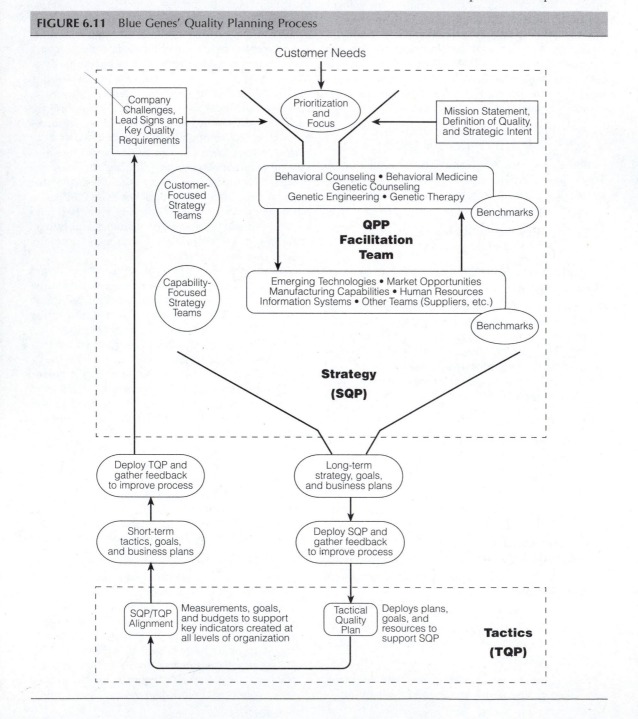

FIGURE 6.12   Quality Planning Process Strategy Team Grid

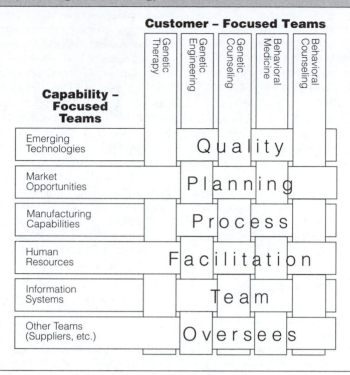

only because of the financial aspects of competition, but also because competitors' products may reflect the industry's evolving capabilities. Competitive product evaluations and participation in industry forums, such as the American Psychological Association's annual conference, provide opportunities to share nonproprietary information. Blue Genes' market research and competitive assessment groups communicate competitive information to appropriate strategy teams and management.

3. *Risks—financial, market, technological, and societal:* The future focus of Blue Genes requires a great deal of risk analysis. This analysis takes the form of contingency planning and multi-path development. Management also performs cost-versus-benefit and make-versus-buy analysis. Customer-focused teams regularly review existing products and processes to verify fit with the innovative, high-quality focus. Societal risk figures prominently in company plans. Management evaluates not only the societal risks of producing (environmental impact, etc.), but also the societal risks of failing to produce, and then focuses developmental resources on products with significant benefits.

4. *Company capabilities to address key new requirements or market leadership opportunities:* Capability-

focused teams ensure that all company resources are considered during the planning process. For example, the Human Resources team actively participates with each customer-focused strategy team in the SQP to ensure that needed competencies are matched with available skills. Human resources then coordinates plans to backfill personnel needs to ensure rapid resource deployment.

5. *Supplier capabilities:* Each strategy team prepares an analysis of needed supplier capabilities to support their activities. One capability-focused strategy team provides a holistic analysis matching these needed capabilities to the supplier base and develops plans to correct deficiencies and improve suppliers' capabilities. This team includes the representatives of critical suppliers, especially those companies that supply products for distribution. This interaction allows the formulation of mutually agreeable delivery and inventory policies.

Strategies to Improve Operational Performance During the Quality Planning Process

Maintaining the status quo is not enough in a rapidly changing industry. Thus, Blue Genes strongly encourages both continuous improvement and breakthrough thinking. Operational performance improvement opportunities are addressed in two ways:

1. *Realigning work processes ("reengineering") to improve customer focus and operational performance.* By including capability-focused teams in QPP, the company is able to address reallocation opportunities in processes, in proximity, and in organizational relationship.

2. *Productivity and cycle time improvement and reduction in waste.* During the quality planning process, Blue Genes holds brainstorming sessions to improve productivity and to reduce waste. Management then selects the best opportunities and adds them to the capability-focused teams' goals and plans. Over the past six years, Blue Genes achieved 45 percent cost reductions for manufactured products and more than doubled inventory turns for distributed products.

Implementing Overall Plans and Strategies

Management deploys plan requirements to all work units and to suppliers, and ensures alignment of work unit activities in several ways. Many company managers actively participate in the quality planning process, so a significant amount of deployment begins during the plan's creation. Once a plan (SQP or TQP) has been reviewed, all managers receive copies for reference. In addition, top managers hold small group meetings to present the contents of the plan and to field questions and receive feedback from individuals. These meetings are designed to include every Blue Genes employee.

Blue Genes communicates appropriate plan requirements to suppliers through its normal contact with them and through the supplier development survey and quarterly supplier information newsletter, *Blue News.*

Presentation of the SQP starts the TQP phase of the quality planning process. Measurements and goals at all levels of the organization are linked via the lead signs. The SQP defines long-term goals for the corporate lead signs, which in turn translate to goals for measures at all levels, down to individual goals and measurements. The strategic quality plan leads to functional plans which in turn become departmental plans and objectives. Individual employees then set their objectives to meet these departmental objectives. Thus, the quality planning process aligns day-to-day activities and measures in all areas of the company. By encouraging people to relate the SQP to actions under their direct control, via the TQP, Blue Genes achieves a strong connection from SQP to implementation. The measurement basis of this deployment also gives closed-loop feedback, allowing teams and management to identify

barriers and make decisions that may not have been specifically defined by the SQP, but that support the philosophies of the SQP. Thus, strategic quality planning is an evolving and continual process.

Management delegates resources to meet plan commitments at two levels. First, the SQP is a long-term plan, which commits resources for at least a five-year period. The shorter-term TQP allocates specific resources to support the SQP and to define measurable short-term goals to meet the longer-term goals of the SQP. Note that the TQP supports the directives agreed upon in the SQP. Basic long-term funding levels for both operating expenses and capital have already been committed in the strategic quality plan. The company commits personnel as well during the QPP; most teams involved in creating the SQP continue as guiding and implementing bodies. In addition, the quality council may charter new teams to address process improvements targeted by the plan.

Evaluating and Improving Blue Genes' Planning Processes

When management listens to feedback about the quality planning process, the result is a continuously evolving, continuously improving process. The QPP facilitation team evaluates feedback and actively encourages improvements to the planning process. Examples of improvements and the means by which they have been achieved include:

1. *The core planning process:* Each year, upon completion of a quality planning process cycle, Blue Genes' management conducts an appraisal to improve the process for the following year. All participants in the strategy teams are included in this analysis of what went well and what needed work. Individual satisfaction levels with the outcome are also considered. The feedback is then used extensively to improve the process. Some of the evolution involves the mechanics of the process itself. For example, top management now presents the plan to every employee and involves even more of the company and more suppliers and customers in the process. Other improvements resulting from the appraisal process include a stronger emphasis on measurements, keeping QPP strategy teams intact throughout the year, and creating the lead signs to improve both the quality of information and the ability to achieve a seamless roll-out of the QPP philosophies.

2. *Deploying plan requirements to work units:* The evaluation process resulted in adopting several improved deployment methods. Lead signs provide a strong way of relating overall requirements to individual and work unit activities. Blue Genes also instituted a personal communication method to deploy the content of both the SQP and the TQP. The QPP facilitation team meets with groups of about 60 employees, taking an hour to present the content of each of these plans and to answer general questions. These groups break into smaller groups who meet with a member of the QPP facilitation team to discuss questions about the process and the content of the plan. This practice clearly deploys the plan as it relates to the concerns of individuals. Additionally, Blue Genes improved its deployment process by creating the supplier development department and the supplier information newsletter, *Blue News*.

3. *Input from all levels of the company:* At the small group deployment sessions, the QPP facilitation team solicits input from each employee. They combine this input with the formal feedback from plan participants, the ongoing feedback from direct communication, and the suggestion system to ensure that they hear and consider each employee's voice.

Discussion Questions

1. Summarize how Blue Genes develops strategies and business plans to address quality and customer satisfaction for both the short and long term. How effectively do they address the following issues? State what you consider key strengths and deficiencies.

a. Customer requirements and the expected evolution of these requirements

b. Projections of the competitive environment

c. Financial, market, technological, and societal risks

d. Company capabilities, such as human resource and research and development, to address key new requirements or market leadership opportunities

e. Supplier capabilities

2. How well do their strategies and plans address operational performance improvement?

3. How well are the plans deployed? Comment specifically on how Blue Genes deploys its plans to work units and suppliers, how it ensures alignment of lower-level plans and activities with broader goals, and how resources are committed to meet plan requirements.

4. How effectively does the company *evaluate* and *improve* its planning process and its deployment process?

■ NOTES

1. David Woodruff, "Bug Control at Chrysler," *Business Week*, 22 August, 1994, 26.
2. Warren Bennis and Burt Nanus, *Leaders: the Strategies for Taking Charge* (New York: Harper and Row, 1985), 15.
3. J.R.P. French, Jr. and B.H. Raven. "The Bases of Social Power," in D. Cartwright and A. Zanders (eds.) *Group Dynamics: Research and Theory*, 2d ed. (New York: Harper & Row, 1960), 607–623.
4. R.E. Byrd, "Corporate Leadership Skills: A New Synthesis," *Organizational Dynamics* (Summer 1987), 34–43.
5. Xerox Quality Solutions, *A World of Quality: The Timeless Passport* (Milwaukee, WI: ASQC Quality Press, 1993), 5.
6. Robert Haavind and the editors of *Electronic Business, The Road to the Baldrige Award* (Boston: Butterworth-Heinemann, 1992), 50–51.
7. Judith R. Gordon, *A Diagnostic Approach to Organizational Behavior*, 3rd ed. (Boston: Allyn and Bacon, 1991), 341–370.
8. R.M. Stogdill, *Handbook of Leadership* (New York: Free Press, 1974).
9. Warren Bennis and Burt Nanus, *Leaders: The Strategies for Taking Charge* (New York: Harper & Row, 1985), 25–26.
10. R.M. Stogdill, see note 8; R. House and M. Baetz, "Leadership: Some Generalizations and New Research Directions," in B.M. Staw (ed.) *Research in Organizational Behavior* (Greenwich, CT: JAI Press, 1979), 359.
11. Douglas McGregor, *The Human Side of Enterprise* (New York: McGraw-Hill, 1960).
12. R.R. Blake and J.S. Mouton, *The Managerial Grid* (Houston: Gulf Publishing, 1965).
13. Frederick E. Fiedler, *A Theory of Leadership Effectiveness* (New York: McGraw-Hill, 1967).
14. Victor H. Vroom and Phillip W. Yetton, *Leadership and Decision Making* (Pittsburgh, PA: University of Pittsburgh Press, 1973).
15. V. H. Vroom and A.G. Jago, *The New Leadership*, (Englewood Cliffs, NJ: Prentice-Hall, 1988).
16. Robert J. House, "A Path-Goal Theory of Leadership Effectiveness," *Administrative Science Quarterly* 16 (1971), 321–328; R.J. House and T.R. Mitchell, "Path-Goal Theory of Leadership," *Journal of Contemporary Business* (Autumn 1974), 81–98.
17. P. Hershey and K.H. Blanchard, *Management of Organizational Behavior*, 5th ed. (Englewood Cliffs, NJ: Prentice-Hall, 1988).
18. Henry Mintzberg, *Mintzberg on Management: Inside Our Strange World of Organizations* (New York: Free Press, 1989). Also, *The Nature of Managerial Work* (New York: Harper and Row, 1973); "The Manager's Job: Folklore

and Fact," *Harvard Business Review* (July/August 1975).

19. Reprinted by permission from Don Hellriegel, John W. Slocum, Jr., and Richard W. Woodman, *Organizational Behavior*, 6th ed. (St. Paul, MN: West, 1992), 413–414. All rights reserved.

20. The term *transformational leadership* has been attributed to James M. Burns. See his book, *Leadership* (New York: Harper and Row, 1978). Other sources are: N.M. Tichy and D.O. Ulrich, "The Leadership Challenge: A Call For the Transformational Leader," *Sloan Management Review* 26 (1984), 59–68; N.M. Tichy and M.A. Devanna, *The Transformational Leader* (New York: John Wiley, 1986); B.M. Bass, *Leadership and Performance Beyond Expectations* (New York: Free Press, 1985).

21. Edward J. Feeney, "At Emery Air Freight: Positive Reinforcement Boosts Performance," *Organizational Dynamics* 1, no. 3 (1973), 41–50.

22. Philip Atkinson, "Leadership, Total Quality and Cultural Change," *Management Services* (June 1991), 16–19.

23. Adapted from Don Hellriegel et al., see note 19, 418–419.

24. James Brian Quinn, *Strategies for Change: Logical Incrementalism* (Homewood IL: Richard D. Irwin, 1980).

25. Henry Mintzberg. "The Fall and Rise of Strategic Planning," *Harvard Business Review* (January/February 1994), 107–114.

26. Michael E. Porter, *Competitive Advantage: Creating and Sustaining Superior Performance* (New York: The Free Press, 1985).

27. Bob King, *Hoshin Planning: The Developmental Approach* (Methuen, MA: GOAL/QPC, 1989).

28. M. Imai, *Kaizen: The Key to Japan's Competitive Success* (New York: McGraw-Hill, 1986), 144–145.

29. Adapted from Kersi F. Munshi, "Policy Deployment: A Key to Long-Term TQM Success," *ASQC Quality Congress Transactions* (Boston, 1993), 236–244.

30. The Ernst & Young Quality Improvement Consulting Group, *Total Quality: An Executive's Guide for the 1990s* (Homewood, IL: Dow Jones-Irwin, 1990).

31. G. Odiorne, *MBO: A System of Managerial Leadership for the '80s* (Belmont, CA: David S. Lake Publishers, 1979).

32. Information for this case study was adapted from several sources, including Ralph Stayer, "How I Learned to Let My Workers Lead," *Harvard Business Review* (November/December 1990), 66–83; James A. Belasco and Ralph C. Stayer, *Flight of the Buffalo* (New York: Warner Books, Inc., 1993); Tom Peters, *Thriving on Chaos: Handbook for a Management Revolution* (New York: Alfred A. Knopf, 1987). Additional information is also available in the Harvard cases by M.J. Roberts, *Johnsonville Sausage Co. (A)*, [#9-387-103]; *Johnsonville Sausage Co. (B)*, [#9-393-063]; HBR Videotape [9-888-517].

33. Tom Peters, *Thriving on Chaos: Handbook for a Management Revolution* (New York: Alfred A. Knopf, 1987); Tom Peters, "The Leadership Alliance," videotape, Video Publishing House, Inc., 1988.

34. James A. Belasco and Ralph C. Stayer, *Flight of the Buffalo: Soaring to Excellence, Learning To Let Employees Lead* (New York: Time-Warner, 1993).

35. James A. Belasco and Ralph C. Stayer, *Flight of the Buffalo: Soaring to Excellence, Learning To Let Employees Lead* (New York: Time-Warner, 1993), 19.

36. *Johnsonville Sausage,* Harvard Business School (1985), Cases #9-387-103 and #9-393-063.

37. Adapted from *Rubbermaid Philosophy, Management Principles, Mission, Objectives,* Rubbermaid 1993 Annual Report; Alan Farnham, "America's Most Admired Company," *Fortune,* 7 February, 1994, 50–54.

38. "Leaders of Corporate Change," *Fortune,* 14 December, 1992, 104–114.

39. Adapted with permission from "TQM," The Stroh Brewery Company.

40. This fictitious case stems from a real company. We thank our students John P. Rosiello and David Seilkop for contributing the research.

41. Adapted from a Case Item prepared for use in the 1994 Malcolm Baldrige National Quality Award Examiner Preparation Course. It describes a fictitious company with no connection to any existing company, either with the same name or otherwise.

■ BIBLIOGRAPHY

AT&T Quality Steering Committee. *Batting 1000: Using Baldrige Feedback to Improve Your Business.* AT&T Bell Laboratories, 1992.

AT&T Quality Steering Committee. *Policy Deployment.* AT&T Bell Laboratories, 1992.

Bass, B.M. *Leadership and Performance Beyond Expectations.* New York: Free Press, 1985.

Brager, Joan. "The Customer-Focused Quality Leader." *Quality Progress* 25, no. 5 (May 1992), 51–53.

Conger, J. and R. Kanugo. "Toward a Behavioral Theory of Charismatic Leadership in Organizational Settings." *Academy of Management Review* (October 1987), 637–647.

Dean, James W., Jr., and James R. Evans. *Total Quality: Management, Organization, and Strategy.* St. Paul, MN: West, 1994.

Hart, Christopher W.L., and Christopher E. Bogan. *The Baldrige.* New York: McGraw-Hill, 1992.

Juran, J.M. *Juran on Quality by Design.* New York: The Free Press, 1992.

Profiles of Malcolm Baldrige Award Winners. Boston: Allyn & Bacon, 1992.

St. Lawrence, Dennis, and Bob Stinnett. "Powerful Planning With Simple Techniques." *Quality Progress* 27, no. 7 (July 1994), 57–64.

Tedesco, Frank M. "Building Quality Goals into the Business Plan." *The Total Quality Review* 4, no. 1 (March/April 1994), 31–34.

U.S Department of Commerce and Booz-Allen & Hamilton, Inc. *Total Quality Management (TQM): Implementer's Workshop* (May 1990).

Waldman, David A. "A Theoretical Consideration of Leadership and Total Quality Management." *Leadership Quarterly* 4 (1993), 65–79.

Whiteley, Richard C. *The Customer Driven Company.* Reading, MA: Addison-Wesley, 1991.

7

Quality in Product and Process Design

In Deming's introductory lecture to Japanese managers, he contrasted the "old way" of product design—design it, make it, and try to sell it—with a "new way."

1. Design the product (with appropriate tests).
2. Make it and test it in the production line and in the laboratory.
3. Put it on the market.

4. Test it in service through market research; find out what the user thinks of it, and why the nonuser has not bought it.

5. Redesign the product, in light of consumer reactions to quality and price.[1]

 is a critical function of business. No matter how well a product is made, poor design will kill any market potential. Product design involves all activities performed to determine the functional specifications for a product and its fitness for use. Designers must translate the voice of the customer into a product that can be manufactured well or a service that can be delivered effectively. Quality of design, coupled with quality of conformance in production, determines the ultimate performance, reliability, and value of the product, and hence, the perceived quality. Design influences the efficiency of manufacture, speed of repair and service, and flexibility of sales strategies.

Process design is similar in nature to product design. Process design involves the planning of the physical facilities and the information and control systems required to manufacture a good or deliver a service. The goal of process design is to ensure that the product conforms to design specifications and is produced economically and productively. In this chapter the discussion centers on the important aspects of product and process design as they relate to quality.

AN OVERVIEW OF PRODUCT DEVELOPMENT

Most companies have some type of structured product development process. The typical product development process, shown in Figure 7.1, consists of idea generation, preliminary concept development, product/process development, full-scale production, and finally, market introduction. Clearly, the first step in product design is to come up with new ideas. As discussed in Chapter 5, new or redesigned product ideas should focus on customer needs and expectations. In the concept development phase, new ideas are studied for feasibility. Companies perform initial screenings and economic analyses to determine the market potential and financial impacts of new ideas and eliminate those without a high potential for success, thus avoiding expensive development costs. Design review

FIGURE 7.1   Structured Product Development Process

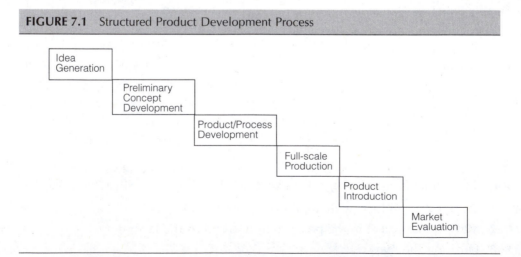

teams consider preliminary designs and ask such questions as: Will the product meet customers' requirements? Can it be manufactured economically with high quality?

If an idea survives the concept development stage—and many do not—detailed product and process development follows. For manufactured goods, the design process begins by determining engineering specifications for all materials, components, and parts. Engineering specifications consist of nominal or target values, as well as tolerances. The nominal specifications, sometimes called *product parameters*, determine the functional ability and performance characteristics of the product. Tolerances specify the precision required to achieve the desired performance. Product development includes prototype testing, in which a model (real or simulated) is constructed to test the product's physical properties or use under actual operating conditions. These tests might include performance tests, stress tests, environmental tests, wearout tests, and other reliability tests. Road testing an automobile or using a consumer panel to test a new food product are two examples. Such testing can uncover any problems and allow for correction prior to full-scale production. In addition to product development, companies develop and test the processes used in manufacturing, which includes selecting the appropriate technology, tooling, and suppliers, and performing pilot runs. If no serious problems are found, the company releases the product to full-scale production and introduces the product in the marketplace. Deming and Juran both advocated an ongoing product development process that relies on market evaluation and customer feedback to initiate continuous improvements.

One way to ensure success in product development is to involve customers in the process. Ames Rubber Company, for example, uses a four-step approach to product development that maintains close communication with the customer.[2] Typically, Ames Rubber initiates a new product through a series of meetings with the customer and sales/marketing or the technical services group. From these meetings, management prepares a product brief listing all technical, material, and operational requirements. The brief is forwarded to internal departments, such as engineering, quality, and manufacturing. The technical staff then selects materials, processes, and procedures, and submits their selections to the customer. Upon the customer's approval, a prototype is made. Ames delivers the prototype to the customer, who evaluates and tests it and reports results to the company. Ames makes the requested modifications and returns the prototype for further testing. This process continues until the customer is completely satisfied. Next, Ames makes a limited preproduction run. Data collected during the run are analyzed and shared with the customer. Upon approval, full-scale production commences.

Despite such structured attention to product development, companies invariably make numerous design changes after full-scale production begins. Design changes cost both time and money. Time rather than money has become perhaps the most important element of competitive strategy in the last decade. As companies continually develop new and improved products and competitors shorten product life cycles, the pressure to reduce the time to market increases each day. Any delay, such as design changes, that lengthen the time until the product can be released to the market can result in a significant competitive disadvantage. Furthermore, design changes grow more costly as the product moves through the product development cycle. Design changes often are the result of poor planning in the development process, which can be improved through various techniques, discussed in this chapter.

Thus, companies face two major issues related to quality in the product development phase: (1) designing products for quality and (2) shortening the cycle time from design to product introduction. Both are critical for competitive success.

◼ Leading Practices

World-class companies design new products and services—and the processes that produce them—to meet both quality requirements and company operational performance requirements. The key practices that organizations employ for efficient and effective product development include the following:

◼ *They address all product and service quality requirements early in the design process, taking into account cost and manufacturability, supplier requirements, and legal and environmental issues.* Good designs are easy and economical to manufacture, if properly coordinated with manufacturing and supplier capabilities. AT&T Transmission Systems, for example, has a new product introduction center that evaluates designs based on manufacturing capabilities. The Bell Laboratories engineering research center supports the introduction of new processes by simulating the manufacturing environment to evaluate new technologies. At Cadillac, product development and improvement teams include assembly operators and supplier representatives. In addition, companies need to address any legal or environmental issues associated with potential products. AT&T Universal Card Services evaluates possible new services against screening criteria before beginning its formal development process. This practice ensures that service designs meet consumer needs, strategic and financial objectives, risk parameters and legal requirements, and core competencies. The criteria are designed by the strategic planning group and coordinated with the company's strategic plan. Eastman Chemical reviews designs for safety, reliability, waste minimization, patent position, toxicity information, environmental risks, product disposal, and other customer needs. They also conduct a market analysis of key suppliers' abilities to manage costs, obtain materials, maintain production, and ship reliably.

◼ *They ensure that quality is built into products and services and use appropriate engineering and statistical tools and approaches during the development process.* Products must perform as they are intended. *Quality engineering* is concerned with the plans, procedures, and methods for designing and evaluating quality in goods and services. The goal of quality engineering approaches is to build quality into products during design. Eastman Chemical, for instance, uses laboratory modeling of processes, computer simulation, designed statistical experiments, and evaluation in customers' plants to assess the quality of its products prior to production. Texas Instruments locates its design centers strategically throughout its facilities. These centers offer expertise and systems with extensive capability for electrical and mechanical computer-aided design, system engineering, and manufacturing, and allow evaluation of parts with the best quality history, producibility, reliability, and other special engineering requirements. AT&T Universal Card Services uses qualitative and quantitative research and testing to verify how accurately they understand customer needs. Before introducing new products or services, they conduct market trials to determine whether they meet customer and business requirements. Their program management process has guidelines for deliverables, which addresses all quality requirements. Each phase of the process fulfills specific require-

QUALITY PROFILE
IBM Rochester, Minnesota

The Malcolm Baldrige National Quality Award can be awarded to entire corporations or to individual business units and divisions. Despite the ups and downs that IBM Corporation has experienced in recent history, a shining star is IBM Rochester, a 1990 Baldrige Award recipient. IBM Rochester manufactures and develops AS 400 intermediate computer systems and develops hard disk drives for PS/2, RISC/6000, and AS 400 computers in Rochester, Minnesota. In 1995, the facility employed 5100 people. Its strategic quality initiatives are based on six critical success factors: (1) improved product and service requirements definition, (2) an enhanced product strategy, (3) a defect elimination strategy, (4) cycle time reductions, (5) improved education, and (6) increased employee involvement and ownership. The Rochester quality process is a continuous loop that begins, ends, and begins again with the customer. Of approximately 40 data sources analyzed to guide improvement efforts, most either provide information on customers' product and service requirements or guide steps to refine these expectations into detailed specifications for new IBM offerings.

Between 1986 and 1989, IBM invested more than $300 million in improving its processes and information systems, and focused on improving problem-solving capabilities to prevent rather than detect defects. During that period, productivity improved 30 percent, product development time declined by more than half, manufacturing cycle time increased 60 percent, and product reliability rose threefold.

SOURCE: Malcolm Baldrige National Quality Award, *Profiles of Winners,* National Institute of Standards and Technology, Department of Commerce, and IBM Corporation.

ments, which must be completed, reviewed, and approved before the next phase of development begins. IBM Rochester (see Quality Profile) uses statistical techniques to study customers' priorities and tradeoffs; validates this information with customer councils, satisfaction surveys and other forms of feedback; and maintains a Software Partner Laboratory in which customers can certify that requirements are being met and that programs will operate correctly on their systems.

■ *They fully understand customer requirements and translate them into product and service design requirements.* Chapter 5 emphasized the need to understand customer requirements, particularly in terms of Figure 5.1. Product development must be driven by customer needs. At Ames Rubber Corporation, discussed earlier, and at many other companies, customers work directly with design engineers on new product development teams. At Whirlpool, when customers rate a competitor's product higher in satisfaction surveys, engineers take it apart to find out why. They also have hundreds of consumers fiddle with computer-simulated products while engineers record the users' reactions on videotape. When consumers said they wanted refrigerators to look clean with minimum fuss, Whirlpool designed models with stucco-like fronts and sides that hide fingerprints.[3] Texas Instruments Defense Systems and Electronics Group deliberately hires former military personnel to help the company relate to the ultimate customers' (soldier, sailor, or aircrew) needs and expectations.

However, even after collecting a lot of information, designers and engineers sometimes misunderstand customer requirements or overlook important ones. This widens, rather than reduces, the gap between expected quality and design quality in Figure 5.1. Leading companies establish procedures to effectively translate customer needs into the product specifications, particularly as needs change. A methodology called *quality function deployment* can help translate the "voice of the customer" into good designs.

■ *They develop linkages between product design requirements and process require-ments.* The job of designers and engineers is to develop standards and specifications that both meet consumer requirements and allow production with minimum incidence of any defects. This goal requires close attention to the production and delivery processes. Leading companies translate design requirements into production/delivery processes while increasing efficiency and effectiveness through waste reduction and cycle time improvement. For example, easily assembled designs reduce the risk of manufacturing defects and improve productivity. Processes must be capable of meeting design performance requirements. An operational policy developed at Eastman Chemical encourages employees to maximize product value by operating the process at target levels, not just within some specification limits.

■ *They manage the product development process to enhance cross-functional communication and reduce product development time.* Leading companies use cross-functional teams to coordinate all phases of product development and reduce development times. They establish standards, procedures, and training for cross-functional communication that prevents problems from occurring. At the Ritz-Carlton Hotel Company, for instance, the interface of all design, marketing, operations, and legal functions throughout each project allows the company to anticipate requirements and evaluate progress. Customized hotel products and services, such as meetings and banquet events, receive the full attention of local hotel cross-functional teams. These teams involve all internal and external suppliers, verify production and delivery capabilities before each event, critique samples, and assess results. At Globe Metallurgical, a team consisting of employees from customer service, engineering, and quality assurance work together before product development even begins. Afterwards, a team of customers and employees from purchasing, engineering, and quality assurance work with the first team to manage the development process. Cadillac's simultaneous engineering approach is a "process in which appropriate disciplines are committed to work interactively to conceive, approve, develop, and implement product programs that meet predetermined Cadillac objectives." Vehicle engineering teams, manufacturing teams, financial teams, materials management teams, sales teams, and system management teams are all responsible for quality, cost, timing, and technology. AT&T established nine expert breakthrough teams—called Achieving Process Excellence Teams—that identify process improvements for developing and deploying products faster in the market.

Throughout this chapter, various approaches that support these leading practices are introduced and discussed. The next section addresses some of the key issues of product design that relate to quality.

QUALITY ISSUES IN PRODUCT DESIGN

The complexity of today's products makes design a difficult activity. For example, a single state-of-the-art integrated circuit may contain millions of transistors and involve hundreds of manufacturing steps. High quality can be achieved in such complex products only by starting at the source of the production cycle: the design of the product and the production process. In addition to meeting customer requirements, design quality affects the operational performance of a company, that is, cost and manufacturing productivity. Finally, legal and environmental concerns now force companies to pay closer attention to design quality.

■ Cost and Manufacturability

Product design affects the costs of manufacturing (direct and indirect labor, materials, and overhead), the costs of warranty and field repair, and the amount of redesign activities. General Electric, for example, found that 75 percent of its manufacturing costs are determined by design. With products in which parts alone represent 65–80 percent of the manufacturing cost, design may account for 90 percent or more of the total manufacturing cost. Other companies exhibit similar figures. For Rolls Royce, design determines 80 percent of the final production costs; at General Motors, 70 percent of the cost of truck transmissions is related to design. These statistics imply that significant reductions in manufacturing cost are possible through careful attention to design.

Simplifying the design often can improve both cost and quality. Simplicity of design leads to simplicity in manufacturing and assembly. By cutting the number of parts, material costs generally go down, inventory levels fall, the number of suppliers shrinks, and production time can be shortened. In addition, quality and reliability improve because fewer parts lead to fewer failures. IBM, for example, realized many benefits by designing a new dot matrix printer, the Proprinter. IBM had been buying its dot matrix printers from Seiko Epson Corporation, then the world's low-cost producer. When IBM developed a printer with 65 percent fewer parts that was designed to snap together during final assembly without the use of fasteners, the result was a 90 percent reduction in assembly time and major cost reductions.

Product designers are chiefly concerned with performance and cost. Their responsibility is to create a design that meets performance criteria based on customers' needs at the lowest possible cost. Traditionally, only direct material and labor costs concerned product designers. Such costs were minimized, but higher costs due to scrap, rework, or returns after the product was released to production were incurred. Additionally, the pressure to meet deadlines often resulted in an inferior design that, while meeting functional requirements, caused quality problems during or after manufacture. Designers must be aware that *total cost* is the important issue, not simply the cost of direct labor and material. The quality engineer's task is to provide the link between design and manufacturing, which serves to minimize total costs.

Design must be coordinated with manufacturing to produce products of consistent quality with minimum waste. For example, a company typically replaces failing parts with more expensive counterparts during product testing. This action only increases manufacturing costs. As an alternative, a company can *redesign* the product around the less expensive parts. A Japanese watchmaker, for example, found that using expensive quartz crystals was not necessary to achieve high accuracy. Instead, an inexpensive capacitor compensated for variations in cheaper crystals and still achieved high accuracy.

Many aspects of product design can adversely affect manufacturability and, hence, quality.[4] Some parts may be designed with features difficult to fabricate repeatedly or with unnecessarily tight tolerances. Some parts may lack details for self-alignment or features for correct insertion. In other cases, parts so fragile or so susceptible to corrosion or contamination may be damaged in shipping or by internal handling. Sometimes a design simply has more parts than needed to perform the desired functions, which increases the chance of assembly error. Thus, problems of poor design may show up as errors, poor yield, damage, or functional failure in fabrication, assembly, test, transport, and end use.

A product's design affects quality at the supplier's plant and in the manufacturer's own plant. A frequent cause of supplier quality problems is incomplete or inaccurate specification of the item they are to supply. This problem often occurs with custom parts due to weakness in the design process, engineers who do not follow set procedures, or sloppiness in the procurement and purchasing process. The greater the number of different parts and the more suppliers involved, the more likely is a supplier to receive an inaccurate or incomplete parts specification. Such problems can be reduced by designing a product around preferred parts (those already approved based on their reliability and qualified source of supply), minimizing the number of parts in the design, and procuring parts from a minimum number of vendors.

In manufacturing and assembly, many of the same problems described in the preceding paragraph can occur. In addition, a manufacturer encounters problems in the area of assembly and test. For instance, designs with numerous parts increase the incidence of part mixups, missing parts, and test failures. Parts that are similar but not identical raise the possibility an assembler will use the wrong part. Parts without details to prevent insertion in the wrong orientation lead to more frequent improper assembly. Complicated assembly steps or tricky joining processes can cause incorrect, incomplete, unreliable, or otherwise faulty assemblies. Finally, the designer's failure to consider conditions to which parts will be exposed during assembly such as temperature, humidity, vibration, static electricity, and dust, may result in failures during testing or use.

Design for manufacturability (DFM) is the process of designing a product for efficient production at the highest level of quality. The main goals of DFM are to improve product quality, increase productivity, reduce time-to-market and manufacturing lead times, and maintain adaptability to future market conditions. DFM is intended to prevent product designs that simplify assembly operations but require more complex and expensive components, designs that simplify component manufacture while complicating the assembly process, and designs that are simple and inexpensive to produce but difficult or expensive to service or support.

Table 7.1 summarizes important design guidelines for improving manufacturability and thus improving quality and reducing costs. Many industries have developed more specific guidelines. For example, guidelines for designing printed circuit boards include:

- Placing all components on the top side of the board.
- Grouping similar components whenever possible.
- Maintaining a 0.60 inch clearance for insertable components.

Legal Issues

Safety in consumer products represents a major issue in design. Liability concerns cause many companies to forego certain product development activities. For example, Unison Industries, Inc., of Rockford, Illinois, developed a new solid-state electronic ignition system for piston-engine aircraft. The company dropped the product after prototype testing. Unison says it was sued over crashes involving aircraft on which its products were not even installed. Getting removed from the lawsuits proved costly in itself.[5] In a survey of more than 500 chief

TABLE 7.1 Design Guidelines for Quality Assurance	
Minimize Number of Parts	
■ Fewer part and assembly drawings	→ Lower volume of drawings and instructions to control
■ Less complicated assemblies	→ Lower assembly error rate
■ Fewer parts to hold to required quality characteristics	→ Higher consistency of part quality
■ Fewer parts to fail	→ Higher reliability
Minimize Number of Part Numbers	
■ Fewer variations of like parts	→ Lower assembly error rate
Design for Robustness (Taguchi method)	
■ Low sensitivity to component variability	→ Higher first-pass yield; less degradation of performance with time
Eliminate Adjustments	
■ No assembly adjustment errors	→ Higher first-pass yield
■ Eliminates adjustable components with high failure rates	→ Lower failure rate
Make Assembly Easy and Foolproof	
■ Parts cannot be assembled wrong	→ Lower assembly error rate
■ Obvious when parts are missing	→ Lower assembly error rate
■ Assembly tooling designed into part	→ Lower assembly error rate
■ Parts are self-securing	→ Lower assembly error rate
■ No "force fitting" of parts	→ Less damage to parts; better serviceability
Use Repeatable, Well-Understood Processes	
■ Part quality easy to control	→ Higher part yield
■ Assembly quality easy to control	→ Higher assembly yield
Choose Parts that Can Survive Process Operations	
■ Less damage to parts	→ Higher yield
■ Less degradation of parts	→ Higher reliability
Design for Efficient and Adequate Testing	
■ Less mistaking "good" for "bad" product and vice versa	→ Truer assessment of quality; less unnecessary rework
Lay Out Parts for Reliable Process Completion	
■ Less damage to parts during handling and assembly	→ Higher yield; higher reliability
Eliminate Engineering Changes on Released Products	
■ Fewer errors due to changeovers & multiple revisions/versions	→ Lower assembly error rate

SOURCE: D. Daetz, "The Effect of Product Design on Product Quality and Product Cost," *Quality Progress* 20, no. 6 (June 1987), 63–67.

executives, more than one-third worked for firms that have canceled introduction of products because of liability concerns. Many companies have closed plants and laid off workers, and more than 20 percent of the executives believe their companies have lost market share to foreign competitors because of product liability costs.

All parties responsible for design, manufacture, sales, and service of a defective product are now liable for damages. According to the theory of strict liability, anyone who sells a product that is defective or unreasonably dangerous is subject to liability for any physical harm caused to the user, the consumer, or the property of either.[6] This law applies when the seller is in the business of selling the product, and the product reaches the consumer without a substantial change in condition even if the seller has exercised all possible care in the preparation and sale of the product. The principal issue is whether a defect, direct or indirect, exists. If the existence of a defect can be established, the manufacturer usually will be held liable. A plaintiff need prove only that (1) the product was defective, (2) the defect was present when the product changed ownership, and (3) the defect resulted in injury.

Strict liability was used as a basis for the 1978 ruling against Ford in the Pinto automobile case. In the initial product liability case, the plaintiff was awarded $125 million in punitive damages. Based on Ford's own engineering documents, the plaintiff's lawyers established evidence that the company had determined changing the fuel tank design was more expensive than paying a few product liability claims.

With the doctrine of strict liability, the manufacturer is required to prove innocence. That is, the manufacturer must prove that it would be highly unlikely a product would be shipped in defective condition. *Defective condition* could mean a design defect, poor design implementation, inadequate warnings, improper instructions, failure to anticipate misuse, improper materials, assembly errors, inadequate testing, or failure to take corrective action. Thus, we see that liability extends throughout all production stages.

Quality assurance can greatly reduce the possibility of product liability claims as well as provide supporting evidence in defense arguments. Liability makes documentation of quality control procedures a necessity. A firm should record all evidence that shows the designer has established test and monitoring procedures of critical product characteristics. Feedback on test and inspection results along with corrective actions taken must also be documented. Even adequate packaging and handling procedures are not immune to examination in liability suits, since packaging is still within the manufacturer's span of control.

■ Environmental Issues

Today's environmental concerns have an unprecedented impact on product and process designs. An estimated 350 million home and office appliances were disposed of in 1993. Personal care appliances such as hair dryers are discarded at the rate of 50 million per year.[7] Pressures from environmental groups clamoring for "socially responsive" designs, states and municipalities that are running out of space for landfills, and consumers who want the most for their money have caused designers and managers to look carefully at the concept of "design for disassembly."[8] Design for disassembly consists of two components—recyclability and repairability.

Recyclable products are designed to be taken apart and their components repaired, refurbished, melted down, or otherwise salvaged for reuse. *Business Week* cites several U.S. firms already working on or marketing such products, including Whirlpool, Digital Equipment, 3M, and General Electric.[9] The latter's plastics division, which serves the durable goods market, uses only thermoplastics in its products. Unlike many other varieties of plastics, thermoplastics can be melted down and recast into other shapes and products, thus making them recyclable.

The recyclability feature appeals to environmentalists as well as city and state officials, both of whom are fighting the effects of waste disposal. At the same time, however, it creates new issues for designers and consumers. For example, designers strive to use fewer types of materials, such as plastics, with certain characteristics, such as thermal properties, that allow for reuse. Designers must also refrain from using certain methods of fastening, such as glues and screws, in favor of quick connect-disconnect bolts or other such fasteners. These changes in design will have an impact on tolerances, durability, and quality of products. Such design changes affect consumers who will be asked to recycle products (perhaps to recover a deposit), in spite of inconveniences such as transporting them to a recycling center.

Repairable products are not a new idea, but the concept lost favor when, in the 1960s and 1970s, the United States became known as the "throwaway society." Many products are discarded simply because the cost of maintenance or repair is too high when compared with the cost of a new item. Now design for disassembly promises to bring back easy, affordable product repair. For example, Whirlpool Corporation is developing a new appliance designed for repairability, with its parts sorted for easy coding. Thus, repairability has the potential of pleasing customers, who frequently find it easier and less costly to repair a product, rather than discard it. At the same time, companies are challenged to consider new approaches to design that build both cost effectiveness and quality into the product. For instance, even though assembling an item using rivets instead of screws is more efficient, this approach is contrary to a design for disassembly philosophy. An alternative might be an entirely new design that eliminates the need for fasteners in the first place.

These issues need not be viewed as hinderances to manufacturers. On the contrary, design for recyclability and repairability can improve manufacturability, resulting in a win-win situation for consumers and producers alike.

QUALITY ENGINEERING: DESIGNING FOR QUALITY

Quality engineering provides a set of approaches and tools that design quality into products. Quality engineering consists of two principal methods: **on-line quality methods,** which focus on control in the production process, and **off-line quality methods,** technical aids for improving quality in product and process design. On-line quality control methods are studied in Chapters 15 and 16. The objectives of off-line quality methods are to improve product manufacturability and reliability and to reduce product development and lifetime costs. Thus, quality engineering techniques should be integrated in the design process.

Many modern approaches to quality engineering stem from the work of Genichi Taguchi. Taguchi views quality engineering as composed of three elements: system design, parameter design, and tolerance design. The discussion in this section is limited to manufactured goods; later in this chapter special considerations of service system design are addressed.

■ System Design

System design is the process of applying scientific and engineering knowledge to produce a basic functional design that meets both customer needs and manufacturing requirements. The first question a designer must ask is: What is the product intended to do? A product's function must be driven by customer requirements. For example, consumers expect a camera to take good pictures. In developing a new camera, Japanese engineers studied pictures developed at photo labs and talked with customers to determine the major causes of poor pictures. The three biggest problems were underexposures, out-of-focus, and out-of-film (attempting to take pictures past the end of the roll). They developed the first camera that included a built-in flash to prevent underexposure, an autofocus lens, and an automatic rewind feature. Today, most popular models have these features to meet the customer requirements. Other design considerations include the product's weight, size, appearance, safety, life, serviceability, and maintainability. When decisions about these factors are dominated by engineering considerations rather than by customer requirements, poor designs that fail in the market are often the result.

Developing a basic functional design involves translating customer requirements into *measurable* technical requirements and, subsequently, into design specifications. Technical features, sometimes called design characteristics, translate the voice of the customer into technical language, specifically into engineering measures of product performance. For example, consumers might want portable stereos with "good sound quality." Technical aspects of a stereo system that affect sound quality include the frequency response, flutter (the wavering in pitch), and the speed accuracy (inconsistency affects the pitch and tempo of the sound). Technical requirements are *actionable*; they lead to design specifications such as the dimensions of all parts in a stereo system. Developing such specifications is the task of parameter and tolerance design.

■ Parameter Design

Parameter design establishes specifications, which represent the transition from a designer's concept to a producible design. Manufacturing specifications consist of *nominal dimensions* and *tolerances*. Nominal refers to the ideal dimension or the target value that manufacturing seeks to meet; tolerance, the permissible variation in a dimension or other quality characteristic, is based on the difficulty of meeting a target consistently. To illustrate these concepts, consider a microprocessor. The drawing in Figure 7.2 shows some of the critical dimensions and tolerances for the microprocessor. The "ratio" notation (0.514/0.588) denotes the permissible range of the dimension. Unless otherwise stated, the nominal dimension is the midpoint. Thus, the specification of 0.514/0.588 may be interpreted as a nominal dimension of 0.551 with a tolerance of plus or minus 0.037. Usually, this is written as 0.551 ± 0.037.

Detailed engineering drawings, such as the one illustrated in Figure 7.2, provide the necessary technical specifications for manufacturing personnel to produce a part or for purchasing agents to procure an item from suppliers. For purchased parts, engineering drawings provide a legal basis for the contract

FIGURE 7.2   Microprocessor

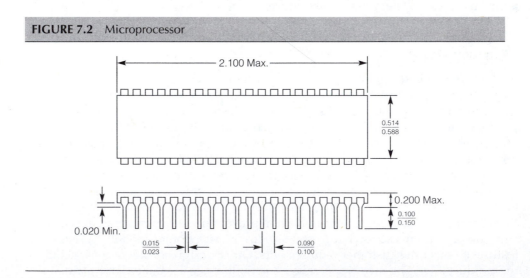

between the vendor and the company. Such drawings are also used to inspect finished parts and establish conformance to specifications. Assembly drawings and detailed drawings are important inputs to process design. They aid in determining what materials and machines are required, which in turn establishes the feasibility of production with existing equipment or the need for new equipment.

Both nominal specifications and tolerances relate design quality to quality of conformance. For managers and engineers they provide a focal point for discussing issues that relate design to manufacturing, manufacturing to plant engineering, plant operations to field service, and all of these back to redesign and product improvement. However, tolerances do not provide a license for simply meeting specifications. The goal is to meet nominal values as closely as possible.

While the specifications of mechanical products are determined by designers, government regulations often determine specifications for food and pharmaceutical products. For example, the U.S. Food and Drug Administration (FDA) sets quality standards regarding the number of unsavory items that find their way into food products.[10] Packaged mushrooms are allowed to contain up to 20 maggots of any size per 100 grams of drained mushrooms or 15 grams of dried mushrooms, while 100 grams of peanut butter may have an average of 30 insect fragments and one rodent hair. (Need we say more?)

ROBUST DESIGN

A product's performance is affected by manufacturing imperfections, environmental factors, and human variations in operating the product. Parameter design should take these issues into account. For example, military helicopters proved to be very sensitive to sand during the Iranian hostage rescue attempt because they simply were not designed for such an environment. A high-quality product performs near its performance target consistently throughout the product's life span and under all different operating conditions. Good parameter design identifies the settings of product or process parameters that minimize the sensitivity of designs to sources of variation in the factory and in use. Products that are insensitive to external sources of variation are called *robust*. For example, a television whose picture sharpness varies with environmental conditions such as room temperature and humidity would not be regarded as robust. An example of a robust design is the "gear effect" designed into modern golf clubs, which brings the ball back on line, even if it is hit off the "sweet spot" of the club. As another example, AT&T developed an integrated circuit that could be used in many products to amplify voice signals. As originally designed, the circuit had to be precisely manufactured to avoid variations in the strength of the signal. Such a circuit would have been costly to make because of stringent quality controls needed during the manufacturing process. But AT&T's engineers, after testing and analyzing the design, realized that if the resistance of the circuit were reduced—a minor change with no associated costs—the circuit would be far less sensitive to manufacturing variations. The result was a 40 percent improvement in quality.[11]

Taguchi proposes the use of statistically planned experiments for parameter design. A designed experiment is a test or series of tests that enables the experimenter to draw conclusions about the situation under study. For example, a paint company might be interested in determining whether different additives have an effect on the drying time of paint in order to select the additive that results in the shortest drying time. As another example, suppose that two machines produce the same part. The material used in processing can be loaded onto the machines either manually or with an automatic device. The experimenter might wish to determine whether the type of machine and the type of loading process affect the number of defectives and then to select the machine type and loading process combination that minimizes the number of defectives.

Experimental design techniques, developed by R. A. Fisher in England, date back to the 1920s. Historically, experimental design was not widely used in industrial quality improvement studies because engineers had trouble working with the large number of variables and their interactions on many different levels in industrial problems. In such situations, a large number of experiments had to be conducted. Taguchi, involved in improving the quality of the Japanese telephone system after World War II, recognized these limitations. He developed an approach to designing experiments that focused on the critical factors while deemphasizing their interactions, which greatly reduced the number of required experiments. In most applications of traditional methods of experimental design, the objective is to optimize the mean value of an important response variable, such as yield in a chemical process. Whereas using the Taguchi method, parameter design experiments aim to reduce the variability caused by manufacturing variations. In most industrial processes, controlling variability is much harder than controlling the average value.

Taguchi categorizes variables that affect the performance characteristics according to whether they are design parameters and sources of noise. Design parameters are those whose nominal settings can be chosen by the design engineer. The sources of noise are all those variables that cause performance characteristics to deviate from their target values. Noise factors can be systematically varied in a designed experiment. The key factors that affect the product's performance in the field as well as process performance in manufacturing should be identified and included in the experiment.

One objective of the experiment is to identify settings of design parameters at which the effect of noise factors on the performance characteristic is at a minimum. The minimum effect is determined by systematically varying the settings of the design parameters in the experiment and comparing the results. The experiments can be done either through physical experiments or by computer simulation using a program that relates performance characteristics to design parameters and noise factors.

In a celebrated case involving the Ina Tile Company, a Japanese ceramic tile manufacturer,[12] the company had purchased a $2 million kiln from West Germany in 1953. Tiles were stacked inside the kiln and baked. Tiles toward the outside of the stack tended to have a different average and more variation in dimensions than those inside the stack. The obvious cause was the uneven temperatures inside the kiln. Temperature was an uncontrollable factor, a noise factor. To try to eliminate the effects of temperature would require redesign of the kiln itself, a very costly alternative. A group of engineers, chemists, and others who were familiar with the manufacturing process brainstormed and identified seven major controllable variables that could affect the tile dimensions:

1. Limestone content
2. Fineness of additive
3. Content of agalmatolite
4. Type of agalmatolite
5. Raw material quantity

6. Content of waste return

7. Content of feldspar

The group designed and conducted an experiment using these factors. The experiment showed that the first factor, the limestone content, was the most significant factor; the other factors had smaller effects. By increasing the limestone content from one percent to five percent and choosing better levels for other factors, the percentage of size defects was reduced from 30 percent to less than 1 percent. Limestone was the cheapest material in the tile. In addition, the experiment revealed that a smaller amount of agalmatolite, the most expensive material in the tile, could be used without adversely affecting the tile dimension. Both the effect of the noise factor and the cost of the product were reduced at the same time! This discovery was a breakthrough in the ceramic tile industry.

Other objectives of Taguchi experiments include identifying the settings of design parameters that reduce cost without sacrificing quality, determining the design parameters that influence the mean value of the performance characteristic but have no effect on its variation, and identifying those design parameters that have no detectable influence on the performance characteristics. The tolerances on such parameters can be relaxed.

Another concept central to the Taguchi methods is the signal-to-noise (S/N) ratio, which measures the sensitivity of an effect (the signal) to the noise factors. The effect, or signal, is measured by its mean value, while the variability of the signal represents the noise factors, which are measured by the standard deviation. Thus the S/N ratio essentially is the ratio of the mean to the standard deviation. Such a measure incorporates both the controllable and uncontrollable factors. High signal-to-noise ratios mean that the sensitivity to noise factors is low.

The signal and noise terminology can be extended to any type of product or service. The signal is what the product or component is intended to deliver. Noise is interference created by outside environmental factors, or even internal components in the system, which affects the quality of the signal. For example, the signal for a package delivery service is on-time delivery of an undamaged package to its destination. Noise that might cause variations in the expected delivery time or conditions include internal factors such as misrouted, damaged, or incorrectly coded packages. External noise results from incorrect or incomplete addresses furnished by the sender or weather-related delays of aircraft or delivery vehicles. If the company takes steps to improve its systems and to guard against external noise-producing factors such as incorrect addresses, the signal will be stronger and clearer a higher percentage of the time, thus improving customer service and perceived quality.

As a practical tool for quality improvement the Taguchi methods have achieved considerable success in many industries. For example, ITT Avionics Division, a leading producer of electronic warfare systems, successfully used Taguchi methods.[13] ITT experienced a high defect rate when using a wave solder machine to solder assemblies on printed circuit boards. The wave solder machine, developed to eliminate hand soldering, transports printed circuit boards through a wave of solder under computer control. A brainstorming session identified fourteen process variables. From three sets of designed experiments the subsequent data resulted in decisions that lowered the defect rate from seven or eight to 1.5 per board. With 2500 solder connections per board, the defect rate now translates to 600 defects per million connections, a rate being constantly improved. ITT's Suprenant Company, an electrical wire and cable manufacturer and a supplier to Ford, saved an estimated $100,000 per year in scrap, reduced product variability by a factor of 10, and improved the run rate of an extruding operation by 30 percent using Taguchi methods. Many other companies such as Xerox and Ford have used Taguchi methods since the early 1980s.

However, Taguchi's approach to experimental design violates some traditional statistical principles and has been criticized by the statistical community.[14] To add to the shortcomings of his approach, Taguchi introduced some statistically invalid and misleading analyses, ignored modern graphical approaches to data analysis, and failed to advocate randomization in performing the experiments. Even though many of these issues are subject to debate, Taguchi's contributions include popularizing the concept of robust product design and attracting greater attention to education in quality engineering.

■ Tolerance Design

Tolerance design is the process of determining tolerances around the nominal settings identified by parameter design. Tolerances are necessary because it is a fact of life that not all parts can be produced exactly to nominal specifications, which results in natural variations (common causes) in production processes due to the "5 Ms": men and women, materials, machines, methods, and measurement. Common cause variation cannot be reduced unless the production technology (at least one of the 5 Ms) is changed. The natural variation resulting from a given combination of people, machinery, materials, methods, and measurements is known as *process capability*. If a process is incapable of producing within design specifications, management must weigh the cost of acquiring new technology against the consequences and related cost of allowing nonconformities in production. These costs may include, among others, 100 percent inspection, allowing nonconforming parts further in the production process, and possible loss of present and future customers. Process capability is explored in greater detail in Chapter 14.

To develop tolerance levels that specify how a part or product is produced, an engineer must understand the necessary tradeoffs. Narrow tolerances tend to raise manufacturing costs but they also increase the interchangeability of parts within the plant and in the field, product performance, durability, and appearance. Also, a tolerance reserve or factor of safety is needed to account for engineering uncertainty regarding the maximum variation allowable and compatibility with satisfactory product performance.

Wide tolerances, on the other hand, increase material utilization, machine throughput, and labor productivity, but have a negative impact on product characteristics as previously mentioned. Thus, factors operating to enlarge tolerances include production planning requirements; tool design, fabrication, and setup; tool adjustment and replacement, process yield; inspection and gauge control and maintenance; and labor and supervision requirements.

Setting inappropriate tolerances can also cause a high rate of defects. For instance, in one company, a bearing seat had to be machined on a large part costing more than $1000. Because of the precision tolerance specified by design engineers, one or two parts per month had to be scrapped when the tolerance was exceeded. The quality manager conducted a study which revealed that the bearings being used did not require such precise tolerances. When the tolerance was relaxed, the problem disappeared. This one design change resulted in approximately $20,000 in savings per year.

Traditionally, tolerances are set by convention rather than scientifically. A designer might use the tolerances specified on previous designs or base a design decision on judgment from past experience. All too often, tolerance settings fail to account for the impact of variation on product functionality, manufacturability, or economic consequences. A more scientific approach to tolerance design uses the Taguchi loss function.

The Taguchi Loss Function

Dr. Genichi Taguchi proposed a significantly different approach to viewing quality based on the economic implications of not meeting target specifications. Taguchi defined quality as the "[avoidance of] loss a product causes to society after being shipped, other than any losses caused by its intrinsic functions."[15] The loss to society includes costs incurred by the product's failure to meet customer expectations, the failure to meet performance characteristics, and harmful side effects caused by the product.

Failure to meet customer expectations precipitates numerous direct and indirect losses. For example, many years ago one of the authors purchased an automobile that was praised for its features, performance, and quality. (The car carried a two-year warranty when most other cars had only a one-year warranty, and it had even won a prestigious "car of the year" award.) Unfortunately, the automobile required frequent repair for numerous problems. Many of these occurred during the warranty period, which resulted in costs to the manufacturer and considerable inconvenience to the customer. Problems continued out of warranty, resulting in more cost and inconvenience. The dealer acknowledged that this particular model year had a poor quality record, but that quality had since improved considerably (and even suggested a trade-in for a new model!). The car was replaced (by a different make) much sooner than anticipated, with additional losses due to high depreciation. The manufacturer lost a repeat buyer, and the dealer eventually went out of business.

Failure to meet performance characteristics entails similar losses. If a product does not perform correctly when purchased, service costs must be borne by the dealer or manufacturer and the reputation of the manufacturer is damaged. Finally, poor quality may result in other societal losses, such as pollution or noise, which eventually lead to medical claims, worker compensation, and other costs affecting society in general.

Taguchi measures loss in monetary units and relates it to quantifiable product characteristics. In this way, he translates the language of the engineer into the language of the manager. To better understand Taguchi's philosophy as it influences tolerance design, reconsider the manufacturing-based definition of quality as "conformance to specifications." Suppose that a specification for some quality characteristic is 0.500 ± 0.020. Using this definition, it makes no difference whether the actual value of the quality characteristic is 0.480, 0.496, 0.500, or 0.520. This approach assumes that the customer, either the consumer or the next department in the production process, would be equally satisfied with any value between 0.480 and 0.520, but not satisfied outside of this tolerance range. Also, this approach assumes that costs do not depend on the actual value of the quality characteristic as long as it is within the tolerance specified, referred to as the "goalpost mentality" (see Figure 7.3).

But what is the real difference between 0.479 and 0.481? The former is considered "out of specification" and needs reworking or scrapping while the latter

FIGURE 7.3   Traditional Conformance to Specification Loss Function

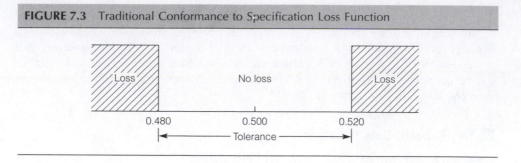

is acceptable. In reality, however, the impact of either on the performance characteristic of the product would be about the same. Neither is close to the nominal specification of 0.500. The designer sets the nominal specification, which is considered the ideal target value for the critical quality characteristic. Taguchi bases his approach on the assumption that the smaller the variation about the target value, the better the quality. In other words, the only meaningful specification is being on-target. The loss increases (as a quadratic function) as values move from the target, as illustrated in Figure 7.4. When nominal specifications are met, products are more consistent, which lowers total societal costs.

An example, published in the Japanese newspaper *Ashai,* compared the cost and quality of Sony televisions at two plants in Japan and San Diego.[16] The color density of all the units produced at the San Diego plant fell within specifications, while some of those shipped from the Japanese plant did not (see Figure 7.5). However, the average loss per unit of the San Diego plant was $0.89 greater than that of the Japanese plant. Units out of specification at the San Diego plant were adjusted within the plant, adding cost to the process. Furthermore, a unit adjusted to just within specifications was more likely to generate customer complaints than a unit that was closer to the original target value, therefore incurring higher field service costs. As demonstrated in Figure 7.5, fewer U.S.–produced sets met the target value for color density. The distribution of quality in the Japanese plant was more uniform around the target value; even though some units were out of specification, the total cost was less. Thus, any variation from the target value causes a loss to the customer. Generally, the larger the deviation,

FIGURE 7.4   Taguchi Loss Function

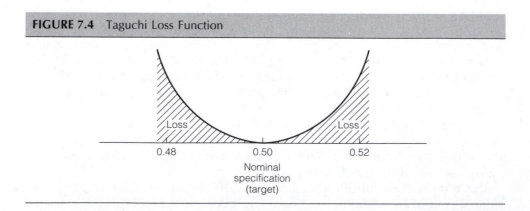

FIGURE 7.5   Color Density of TV Sets

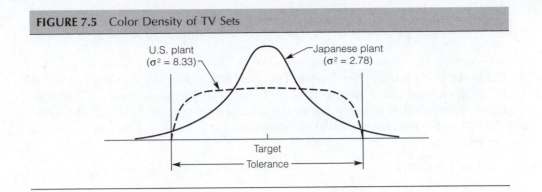

the larger the loss. Akio Morita, the chairman of Sony, explained the difference this way:

> When we tell one of our Japanese employees that the measurement of a certain part must be within a tolerance of plus or minus five, for example, he will automatically strive to get that part as close to zero tolerance as possible. When we started our plant in the United States, we found that the workers would follow instructions perfectly. But if we said make it between plus or minus five, they would get it somewhere near plus or minus five all right, but rarely as close to zero as the Japanese workers did.

COMPUTATIONS USING THE TAGUCHI LOSS FUNCTION[17]

The exact nature of the loss function for every quality characteristic is difficult to determine. Taguchi assumed that losses can be approximated by a quadratic function so that larger deviations from target cause increasingly larger losses. For the case in which a specific target value is best and quality deteriorates as the value moves away from the target on either side (called "nominal is best"), the loss function is represented by

$$L(x) = k(x - T)^2$$

where x is any value of the quality characteristic, T is the target value, and k is some constant. Figure 7.6 illustrates this equation.

FIGURE 7.6   Nominal-Is-Best Loss Function

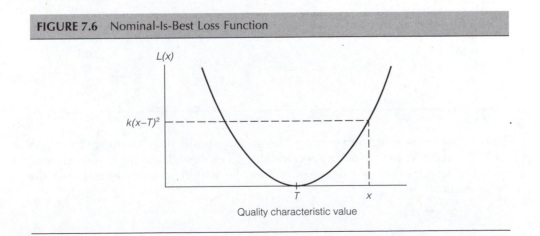

The constant k is estimated by determining the cost of repair or replacement if a certain deviation from the target occurs, as the following example illustrates.

EXAMPLE 1   Estimating the Taguchi Loss Function.   Assume that a certain quality characteristic has a specification of 0.500 ± 0.020. An analysis of company records reveals that if the value of the quality characteristic exceeds the target of 0.500 by the tolerance of 0.020 on either side, the product is likely to fail during the warranty period and costs $50 for repair. Then,

$$50 = k(0.020)^2$$

$$k = 50/0.0004 = 125,000$$

Therefore, the loss function is

$$L(x) = 125,000(x - T)^2$$

Thus, if the deviation is only 0.010, the estimated loss is

$$L(0.010) = 125,000(0.010)^2 = \$12.50$$

If the distribution of the variation about the target value is known, the average loss per unit can be computed by statistically averaging the loss associated with possible values of the quality characteristic. In statistical terminology, this average loss per unit is simply the expected value of the loss. To keep the mathematics simple, consider Example 2.

EXAMPLE 2   Computing Expected Loss with the Taguchi Loss Function.   Suppose that two processes, A and B, have the following distributions of a quality characteristic with specification 0.50 ± 0.02. In process A, the output of the process has values ranging from 0.48 to 0.52, all of which are equally likely. For process B, 60 percent of the output is expected to have a value of 0.50, 15 percent has a value of 0.49, and so on.

Value	Process A Probability	Process B Probability
0.47	0	0.02
0.48	0.20	0.03
0.49	0.20	0.15
0.50	0.20	0.60
0.51	0.20	0.15
0.52	0.20	0.03
0.53	0	0.02

Notice that the output from process A is spread equally over the range from 0.48 to 0.52 and lies entirely within specifications. In process B, output is concentrated near the target value, but does not entirely lie within specifications. Using the loss function

$$L(x) = 125,000(x - 0.50)^2$$

the expected loss for each process can be computed as follows:

Value, x	Loss	Process A Probability	Weighted Loss	Process B Probability	Weighted Loss
0.47	112.5	0.00	0	0.02	2.25
0.48	50.0	0.20	10	0.03	1.50
0.49	12.5	0.20	2.5	0.15	1.875
0.50	0.0	0.20	0	0.60	0
0.51	12.5	0.20	2.5	0.15	1.875
0.52	50.0	0.20	10	0.03	1.50
0.53	112.5	0.00	0	0.02	2.25
		Expected loss	25.0		11.25

Clearly process B incurs a smaller total expected loss even though some output falls outside specifications.

The expected loss is computed using a simple formula that involves the variance of the quality characteristic, σ^2, and the square of the deviation of the mean value from the target $D^2 = (\bar{x} - T)^2$. The expected loss is

$$EL(x) = k(\sigma^2 + D^2)$$

For instance, in process A, the variance of the quality characteristic is 0.0002 and $D^2 = 0$ since the mean value is equal to the target. Thus,

$$EL(x) = 125,000(0.0002 + 0) = 25$$

A similar computation can be used to determine the expected loss for process B.

In the Sony television example, k was determined to be 0.16. Since the mean of both distributions of color density fell on the target value, $D^2 = 0$ for both the U.S. and the Japanese plants. However, the variance of the distributions differed. For the San Diego plant, $\sigma^2 = 8.33$ and for the Japanese plant, $\sigma^2 = 2.78$. Thus the average loss per unit was computed to be

San Diego plant: $0.16(8.33) = \$1.33$

Japanese plant: $0.16(2.78) = \$0.44$

or a difference of $0.89 per unit.

The expected loss provides a measure of variation that is independent of specification limits. Such a measure stresses continuous improvement rather than acceptance of the status quo simply because a product "conforms to specifications."

Not all quality characteristics have nominal targets with tolerances on either side. In some cases, such as impurities in a chemical process or fuel consumption, "smaller is better." In other cases, "larger is better" as with breaking strength or product life. The loss function for the smaller-is-better case is

$$L(x) = kx^2$$

and for the larger-is-better case is

$$L(x) = k(1/x^2)$$

These formulas can be applied in a manner similar to the previous examples. The following example shows how the Taguchi loss function may be used to set tolerances.

EXAMPLE 3   Using the Taguchi Loss Function for Tolerance Design.   The desired speed of a cassette tape is 1.875 inches per second. Any deviation from this value causes a change in pitch and tempo and thus poor sound quality. Suppose that adjusting the tape speed under warranty when a customer complains and returns a cassette player costs a manufacturer $20. (This repair expense does not include other costs due to customer dissatisfaction and therefore is at best a lower bound on the actual loss.) Based on past information, the company knows the average customer will return a player if the tape speed is off the target by at least 0.15 inch per second. The loss function constant is computed as

$$20 = k(0.15)^2$$

$$k = 888.9$$

and thus the loss function is

$$L(x) = 888.9(x - 1.875)^2$$

At the factory, the adjustment can be made at a much lower cost of $3, which consists of the labor to make the adjustment and additional testing. What should the tolerance be before an adjustment is made at the factory?

To use the loss function, set $L(x) = \$3$ and solve for the tolerance:

$$3 = 888.9 \text{ (tolerance)}^2$$

$$\text{tolerance} = \sqrt{3/888.9} = 0.058$$

Therefore, if the tape speed is off by more than 0.058 inches per second, adjusting it at the factory is more economical. Thus, the specifications should be 1.875 ± 0.058 or 1.817 to 1.933.

QUALITY FUNCTION DEPLOYMENT

A major problem with the process illustrated in Figure 5.1 is that customers and engineers speak different languages. A customer might express a desire to own a car that is easy to start. The translation of this requirement into technical language might be "car will start within 10 seconds of continuous cranking." Or, a requirement that "soap leaves my skin feeling soft" demands translation into pH or hardness specifications for the bar of soap. The actual intended message can be lost in the translation and subsequent interpretation by design or production personnel.

The Japanese developed an approach called *quality function deployment (QFD)* to meet customers' requirements throughout the design process and also in the design of production systems. The term, a translation of the Kanji characters used to describe the process, can sound confusing. QFD is a customer-driven planning process to guide the design, manufacturing, and marketing of goods. Through QFD, every design, manufacturing, and control decision is made to meet the expressed needs of customers. It uses a type of matrix diagram (introduced in Chapter 5) to present data and information.

QFD originated in 1972 at Mitsubishi's Kobe shipyard site. Toyota began to develop the concept shortly thereafter, and has used it since 1977 with impressive results. Between January 1977 and October 1979, Toyota realized a 20 percent reduction in start-up costs on the launch of a new van. By 1982, start-up costs had fallen 38 percent from the 1977 baseline, and by 1984, were reduced by 61 percent. In addition, development time fell by one-third at the same time quality improved. Xerox and Ford initiated the use of QFD in the United States in 1986. Today, QFD is used successfully by manufacturers of electronics, appliances, clothing, and construction equipment, by firms such as General Motors, Ford, Mazda, Motorola, Xerox, Kodak, IBM, Procter & Gamble, Hewlett-Packard, and AT&T. The 1992 model Cadillac was planned and designed entirely with QFD. Two organizations, the American Supplier Institute, Inc., a nonprofit organization, and GOAL/QPC, a Massachusetts consulting firm, have publicized and developed the concept in the United States.

At the strategic level, QFD presents a challenge and the opportunity for top management to break out of its traditional narrow focus on "results," which can only be measured after the fact, and to view the broader process of how results are obtained. Under QFD, all operations of a company are driven by the voice of the customer, rather than by edicts of top management or the opinions or desires of design engineers. At the tactical and operational levels, QFD departs from the traditional product planning process in which product concepts are originated by design teams or research and development groups, tested and refined, produced, and marketed. A traditional approach gathers increasing amounts of information on customer perceptions, use, and problems, redesigns the product, modifies the production system, and then releases the improved product to the market. This approach has two problems. First, customers whose expectations and needs are not met by the original product are not likely to continue buying the product. Second, a considerable amount of wasted effort and time is spent redesigning products and production systems until customer needs are met. If customer needs can be identified properly in the first place, then such wasteful effort is eliminated, which is the principal focus of QFD.

QFD benefits companies through improved communication and teamwork between all constituencies in the production process, such as between marketing and design, between design and manufacturing, and between purchasing and suppliers. Product objectives are better understood and interpreted during the production process. Use of QFD determines the causes of customer dissatisfaction, making it a useful tool for competitive analysis of product quality by top management. Productivity as well as quality improvements generally follow QFD. Perhaps most significant, though, QFD reduces the time for new product development. QFD allows companies to simulate the effects of new design ideas and concepts. Through this benefit, companies can reduce product development time and bring new products into the market sooner, thus gaining competitive advantage. Details of the QFD process and its use are presented in the next section.

■ The Quality Function Deployment Process

A set of matrices is used to relate the voice of the customer to a product's technical requirements, component requirements, process control plans, and manufacturing operations. The first matrix, the *customer requirement planning matrix* shown in Figure 7.7, provides the basis for the QFD concept. The figure demonstrates why this matrix is often called the *House of Quality.*

FIGURE 7.7 The House of Quality

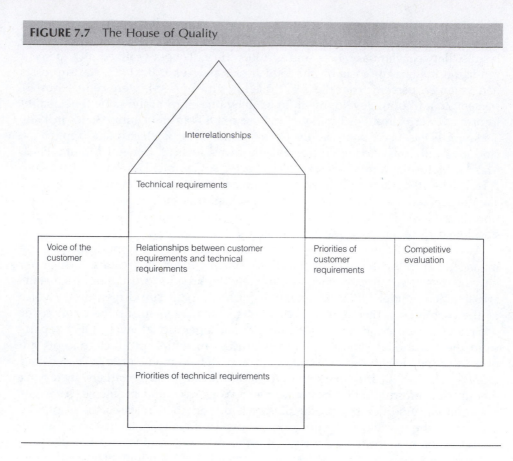

Building the House of Quality consists of six basic steps:

1. Identify customer requirements.

2. Identify technical requirements.

3. Relate the customer requirements to the technical requirements.

4. Conduct an evaluation of competing products.

5. Evaluate technical requirements and develop targets.

6. Determine which technical requirements to deploy in the remainder of the production process.

To illustrate the development of the House of Quality and the QFD process, the task of designing and developing a new textbook, such as an operations management or quality management text, is presented.

Step 1: Identify customer requirements. As discussed in Chapter 5, many methods can be used to gather valid customer information. In designing a textbook, for example, two primary customer requirements might be "meet instructional needs" and "enhance student ability to learn." Such descriptions are not technical specifications; they represent the voice of the customer, the professor who adopts the book and the student who uses it. Textbook publishers employ a number of techniques to gather information from customers. Since their primary customer is the professor teaching the course, they use manuscript reviews, discussions with sales representatives, discussions with convention representatives, and feedback cards in examination copies.

The voice of the customer is the primary input to the QFD process. The most critical and most difficult step of the process is to capture the essence of the customer's comments. The customer's own words are vitally important in preventing misinterpretation by designers and engineers. Listening to customers can open the door to creative opportunities.

Not all customers are end-users, however. For a manufacturer, customers might include government regulators, wholesalers, and retailers. In writing a textbook, authors must consider the needs of both instructors and students. While much is done to solicit input directly from professors, relatively little information is gathered from students, the end-users of texts. This situation is not unlike what happened in hospitals a few years ago when doctors, not patients, were considered the primary customers of hospitals.

Customer requirements normally expand into secondary and tertiary requirements. For a textbook, the primary attribute "meets instructional needs" might encompass secondary attributes of "good topical coverage," "appropriate level for the course," and "good exercises." "Good exercises" might be further subdivided into "sufficient quantity" and "range of difficulty." These desired product attributes are used as inputs to the QFD process. Figure 7.8 shows the voice of the customer in the House of Quality.

Step 2: List the product requirements necessary to meet the customer requirements. Product requirements are design characteristics that describe the customer requirements as expressed in the language of the designer and engineer. They must be measurable, since the output is controlled and compared to objective targets. Essentially, technical requirements are the "hows" by which the company will responds to the "whats"—customer requirements.

The author and publisher of a textbook have a variety of technical characteristics to consider, including the amount of research literature to cite, the amount of popular literature to reference, the number of numerical exercises, the number of open-ended exercises, the design and purpose of software ancillaries, the use of figures and tables, color, correctness of grammar, and size of the book.

The roof of the House of Quality shows the interrelationships between any pair of technical requirements. Various symbols denote these relationships. A typical scheme uses the symbol ◉ to denote a very strong relationship, ○ for a strong relationship, and Δ to denote a weak relationship. These relationships indicate answers to questions such as "How does one change of product characteristics affect others?" and assessment of tradeoffs between characteristics. For example, increasing one textbook characteristic such as the amount of popular literature coverage might expand the number of discussion questions that can be included in the book. However, it will probably increase the size of the book. Thus, strong relationships exist among these characteristics. This matrix process encourages one to view features collectively rather than individually. Figure 7.9 adds this information to the House of Quality.

Step 3: Develop a Relationship matrix between the customer requirements and the technical requirements. Customer requirements are listed down the left column; technical requirements are written across the top. In the matrix itself, symbols indicate the degree of relationship in a manner similar to that used in the roof of the House of Quality. The purpose of the relationship matrix is to show whether the final technical requirements adequately address customer requirements. This assessment is usually based on expert experience, customer responses, or controlled experiments.

The lack of a strong relationship between a customer requirement and any technical requirement shows that the customer needs either are not addressed or that the final product will have difficulty in meeting them. Similarly, if a technical requirement does not affect any customer requirement, it may be redundant or the designers may have missed some important customer need. For example, the amount of research literature referenced in a textbook bears a strong relationship (either positive or negative) to the customer requirements

FIGURE 7.8   Voice of the Customer

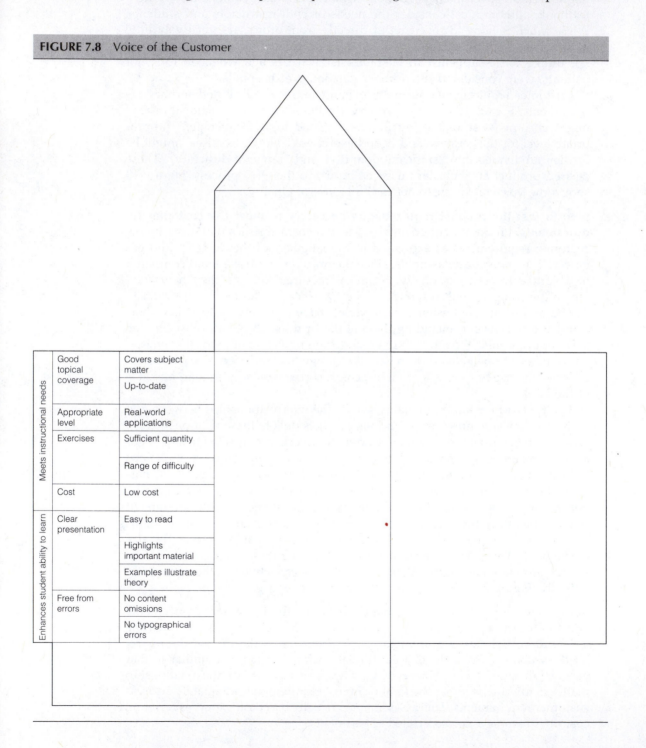

of "covers subject matter," "up-to-date," "no content omissions," "real-world applications," and "easy to read." Figure 7.10 shows an example of these relationships.

Step 4: Add market evaluation and key selling points. This step identifies importance ratings for each customer requirement and evaluates existing products for each of them. Customer importance ratings represent the areas of greatest interest and highest expectations as expressed by the customer.

FIGURE 7.9 Technical Requirements

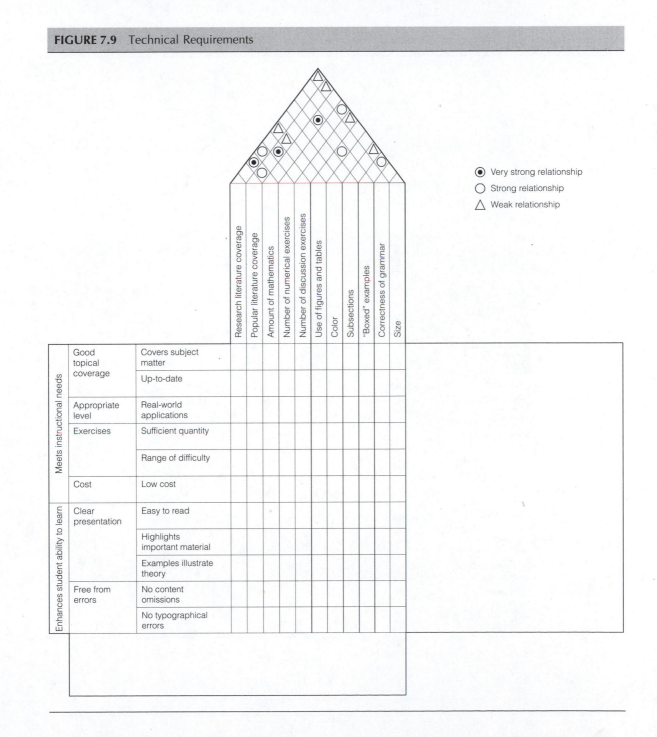

Competitive evaluation highlights the absolute strengths and weaknesses in competing products. By using this step, designers can discover opportunities for improvement. It also links QFD to a company's strategic vision and indicates priorities for the design process. For example, if a customer requirement receives a low evaluation on all competitors' products, then by focusing on this need a company can gain a competitive advantage. Such requirements become key selling points and the basis for formulating promotion strategies.

FIGURE 7.10 Relationship Matrix

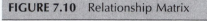

Legend:
- ◉ Very strong relationship
- ○ Strong relationship
- △ Weak relationship

			Research literature coverage	Popular literature coverage	Amount of mathematics	Number of numerical exercises	Number of discussion exercises	Use of figures and tables	Color	Subsections	"Boxed" examples	Correctness of grammar	Size
Meets instructional needs	Good topical coverage	Covers subject matter	◉	◉							△		○
		Up-to-date	◉	◉									○
	Appropriate level	Real-world applications		◉			○						
	Exercises	Sufficient quantity				◉	◉						△
		Range of difficulty				◉	○	○					
	Cost	Low cost	○	○	○			△	◉	○	○		◉
Enhances student ability to learn	Clear presentation	Easy to read	◉	△	◉			△	△	○	○	◉	
		Highlights important material						◉	○	△	◉		
		Examples illustrate theory	△	△							◉		
	Free from errors	No content omissions	◉	◉									
		No typographical errors			○			○					◉

In designing a textbook, the author and publisher might find that two major competing textbooks, A and B, are weak in applications, whereas customer surveys of instructors reveal applications to be a highly desirable attribute. By focusing on this attribute and using it as a key selling point, the author and publisher gain a competitive advantage, as demonstrated in Figure 7.11.

Step 5. Evaluate technical requirements of competitive products and develop targets. This step is usually accomplished through in-house testing and

FIGURE 7.11   Competitive Evaluation

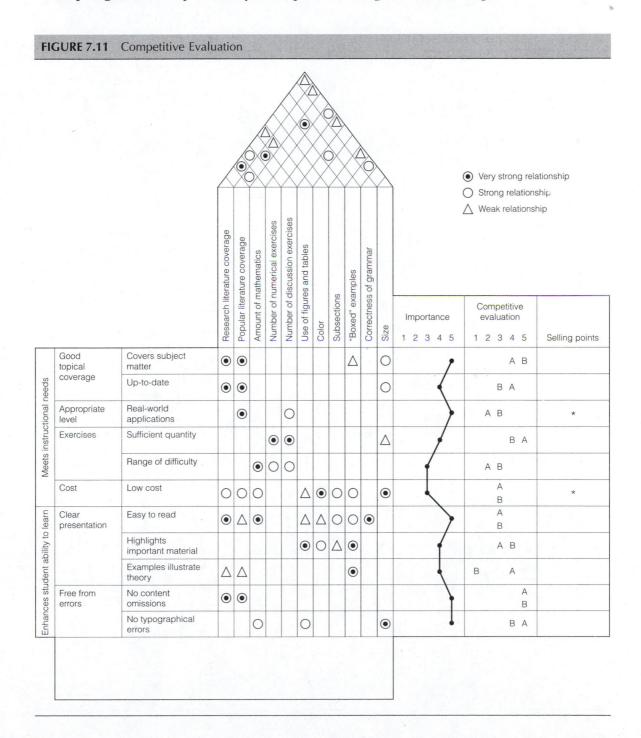

then translated into measurable terms. In-house evaluations are compared with the competitive evaluation of customer requirements to determine inconsistencies between customer requirements and technical requirements. If a competing product is found to best satisfy a customer requirement but the evaluation of the related technical requirements indicates otherwise, then either the measures used are faulty or else the product has an image difference (either positive toward the competitor or negative toward the company's

FIGURE 7.12 Completed House of Quality

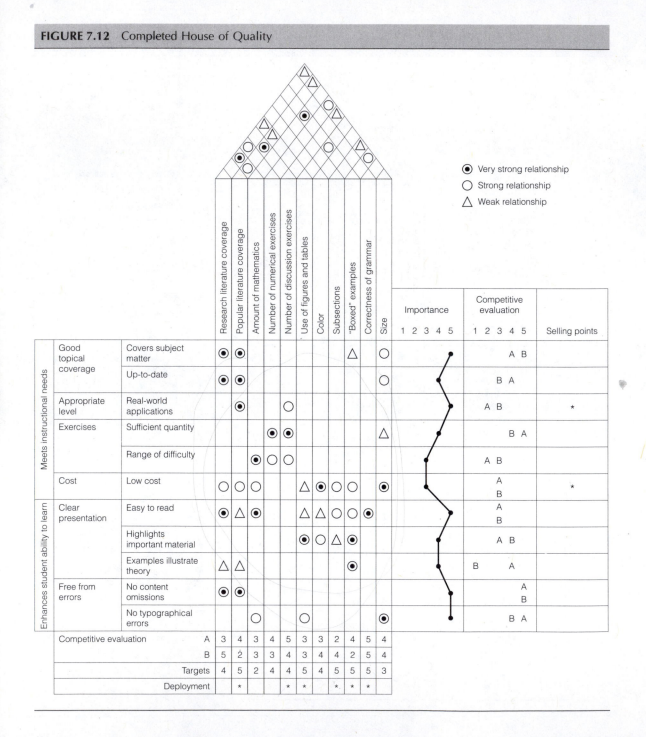

product), which affects customer perceptions. On the basis of customer importance ratings and existing product strengths and weaknesses, targets for each technical requirement are set, as shown in Figure 7.12.

For example, suppose that a number of instructors say that extensive research literature coverage is an important attribute. An evaluation of a competitor's text determines that it is extremely easy for undergraduates to read and comprehend. These two findings seem to be inconsistent with one another. Any one of several possible reasons might explain the discrepancy: (1) The text does not contain the level of research content that the adopting instructors think it does; or (2) the research literature is being presented in an extremely novel and readable way that could be adapted and/or improved on; or (3) the writer of the competing textbook is a known guru in the field and has an image as the expert whose text should be the primary one to be considered.

Step 6. Select technical requirements to be deployed in the remainder of the process. The technical requirements that have a strong relationship to customer needs, have poor competitive performance, or are strong selling points are identified during this step. These characteristics have the highest priority and need to be "deployed" throughout the remainder of the design and production process to maintain a responsiveness to the voice of the customer. Those characteristics not identified as critical do not need such rigorous attention.

For example, if "important material stands out" is an important customer attribute in a textbook, then an author and publisher must pay attention to the particular characteristics relating to chapter layout—the use of figures and tables, subsections, and color. In addition, if the attributes of "covers subject matter" and "up-to-date" are considered highly important, then the size of the book is of little concern. This step is also demonstrated in Figure 7.12.

■ Using the House of Quality

The House of Quality provides marketing with an important tool to understand customer needs and gives top management strategic direction. However, it is only the first step in the QFD process. The voice of the customer must be carried throughout the production process. Three other "houses of quality" are used to deploy the voice of the customer to component parts characteristics, process planning, and production planning. The following sections continue with the textbook development example to illustrate these concepts.

The textbook production process can be described in the following fashion:[18]

Stage	Functions
Acquisition	Proposal
	Review
	Contracting
Development	Writing
	Editing
Preproduction	Galleys
	Proofs
	Page makeup
	Cover design
Production	Printing

The textbook production process begins with a proposal, perhaps a draft chapter or two that the author sends to the publisher. After simultaneous reviews by professors who teach in that field, the idea is approved and the author proceeds with the writing stage. After further reviews and editing, the text goes into the preproduction stages of galleys, proofs, page makeup, and cover design. Galleys are used to check to ensure that wording, citations, and other details are correct. Proofs provide a check on the final typesetting process; page makeup involves adding pictures, figures, and complex tables; and cover design, of course, involves design of the cover. Then begins the relatively long and complex stage of production, which includes such processes as printing, cutting the pages, binding, and packaging the texts. The concept of QFD works in each of these stages to link the process back to the voice of the customer.

The second house is similar to the first house but applies to subsystems and components. The technical requirements from the first house are related to detailed requirements of subsystems and components (see Figure 7.13). At this stage, target values representing the best values for fit, function, and appearance are determined. For example, each chapter in a textbook could be considered as a component of the complete product with its own unique characteristics in terms of writing and style.

Most of the QFD activities represented by the first two houses of quality are performed by product development and engineering functions. At the next stage, the planning activities involve supervisors and production line operators. In the next house, the process plan relates the component characteristics to key process operations, the transition from planning to execution. If a product component parameter is critical and is created or affected during the process, it becomes a control point. A control point indicates what needs to be monitored and inspected. It forms the basis for a quality control plan delivering those critical characteristics that are crucial to achieving customer satisfaction.

In the textbook example, for instance, the characteristic "free from typographical errors" might relate to a component characteristic "correctness of numerical computations." A key process operation then would be an individual check of all numerical computations by a proofreader directly from the galley proofs, during the preproduction stage.

Finally, the last house relates the control points to specific requirements for quality control. At this point, a publisher would specify control methods, sample sizes, and so on to achieve the appropriate level of quality. These specifications

---

FIGURE 7.13   The Four Houses of Quality

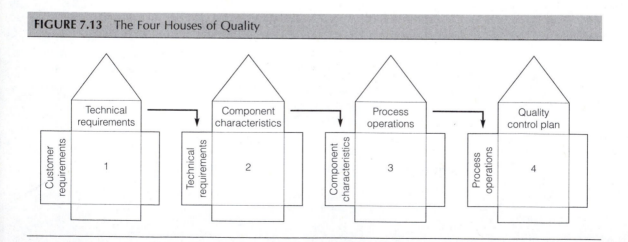

might include final page makeup checking in the preproduction stage and statistical process control steps taken by the printer and binder to ensure that a quality product is produced.

The vast majority of applications of QFD in the United States concentrate on the first and, to a lesser extent, the second houses of quality. Lawrence Sullivan, who brought QFD to the West, suggested that the third and fourth houses of quality offer far more significant benefits, especially in the United States.[19] In Japan, managers, engineers, and workers are more naturally cross-functional and tend to promote group effort and consensus thinking. In the United States, workers and managers are more vertically oriented and tend to suboptimize for individual and/or departmental achievements. Companies in the United States tend to promote breakthrough achievements, which often inhibits cross-functional interaction. If U.S. companies can maintain the breakthrough culture with emphasis on continuous improvement through more effective cross-functional interactions as supported by QFD, it can establish a competitive advantage over foreign competitors. The third and fourth houses of quality utilize the knowledge of about 80 percent of a company's employees—supervisors and operators. If their knowledge goes unused, this potential is wasted.

PROCESS DESIGN

As noted in Chapter 1, all work is performed by a process. Process design for manufacturing involves planning and designing the physical facilities, operations, work flows, and methods for producing goods to meet customer requirements. Many process decisions affect product quality and customer response time. For example, should operations be performed by human labor or by automated equipment? What is the capability of a piece of equipment or work method to produce defect-free output? Should the production facility use a process-based arrangement (in which all machines of a given type are in a common area), a product-based arrangement (in which entire production lines are dedicated to specific products), or a group-based arrangement (in which small "cells" of different machines produce a family of similar products)? By using quality function deployment, product and process designers can work together to develop products that not only meet customer needs, but can be produced efficiently and with high levels of quality.

A process design should also include information and control systems, which are important components of process planning but are sometimes viewed as secondary in importance to machines and hardware. This failure to give process design adequate attention is unfortunate, since like the design of physical facilities, the design of information and control systems revolves around productivity and quality issues. Routine documents such as operation sheets, route sheets, and flow process charts are used to communicate the details of a manufacturing process to shop floor personnel.[20] Methods and procedures for production scheduling are also required to control the flow of materials in production.

Efficient and effective reporting systems provide feedback on production activities. Written records—consisting of regular reports on critical variables relating to quality, scrap, and rework totals, process capability findings and recommendations, and employee involvement team presentations and reports—can all contribute to the internal intelligence system on how a process is running and where corrective actions need to take place.

An important part of process design is materials control. Inventory is any idle good that is held for future use. Inventory is a major contributor to poor quality because it hides quality problems; if a part is bad, a backup is always available. Large lot sizes that may have been produced hours, days, or even months ago do not provide proper feedback for identifying and correcting quality problems. With automation in particular, high-quality materials are essential. In addition, inventory causes excessive material handling, which contributes to cost and does not add value to the product. The Japanese consider inventory simply as waste.

George Stalk, Jr., vice president of the Boston Consulting Group, pointed out that many companies have discovered that traditional methods of forecasting, production scheduling, and control do not work in a dynamic, competitive environment.[21] He stated that excessive delays in receiving and acting on information from the marketplace distort the production system and create disruption, waste, and inefficiency. To alleviate these problems, he advocated correcting manufacturing techniques, sales and distribution, and innovation processes. The correction of manufacturing techniques involves the adoption of a variety of material management techniques that fall under the label of "time-based" innovations. Time-based techniques revolve around cutting delays in generating and processing paperwork, reducing costs, and improving customer service. It also involves decentralized design, cross-functional teams, simultaneous engineering where several groups work on various components of the product at the same time, and introducing small increments of improvement frequently, rather than large increments infrequently. All these activities become focused in the "just-in-time" philosophy at the operating level.

Just-in-time (JIT) is the Japanese approach to material management and control. JIT is more than a new method of material management; it represents a philosophy whose objective is to eliminate all sources of waste, including unnecessary inventory and scrap in production. Richard J. Schonberger describes JIT as a "quality and scrap control tool, as a streamlined plant configuration that raises process yield, as a production line balancing approach, and as an employee involvement and motivational mechanism."[22] The basic philosophy is to maintain inventories as close to zero as possible by producing only enough units to keep the next work station in a production process in operation. For example, grocery stores routinely receive only enough merchandise to keep their shelves stocked. They keep very little inventory in the stockroom. Because of product perishability, delivery trucks bring in milk and bread each day. Other trucks deliver canned goods every two or three days. In manufacturing operations, Japanese auto manufacturers in both Japan and the United States routinely encourage their suppliers to locate plants as near as possible to their factories so that frequent deliveries of small lots of parts can be made to the assembly lines.

JIT cannot function properly if production has a high rate of defective items. Implementation of JIT requires painstakingly careful attention to quality both in purchasing and in production. Since lot sizes are small, no safety stock is available to back up nonconforming items, and any quality problem disrupts the flow of materials through the plant. Conversely, a TQM philosophy can be strengthened by the immediate feedback on quality, which is a natural result of having a JIT system in place. A joint TQM/JIT philosophy focuses on continuous, intensive effort to coordinate closely all production activities into a single integrated system. Quality is the bonding force that holds the system together.

An excellent example of a world-class manufacturing process design is the Allen-Bradley advanced electronics manufacturing facility named EMS1 after the electronic manufacturing strategy that shaped its creation.[23] The $9.5 million facility produces solid-state products, including industrial terminals, machine vision systems, and radio frequency and bar code identification systems. The objectives in designing the facility included achieving unsurpassed product quality, reducing time to market, providing required manufacturing capacity, significantly improving internal and external customer satisfaction, and achieving the lowest possible total life cycle cost of a product. Any decision that did not meet these objectives was rejected. By benchmarking the best electronics manufacturers worldwide, Allen-Bradley identified the most advanced circuit board assembly machines. Some key elements of the process that now contribute to high productivity and rapid time to market are point-of-use storage of all components, smart scheduling, and a sequencing strategy in which insertion machines pull what they need on demand. Materials procurement systems are integrated with manufacturing systems under a just-in-time framework. Automatic identification tracks more than 1500 components. Bar code readers scan each panel and transmit the identification to a database which downloads instructions to the machine controls. To assure quality, the facility is static-free, and new lighting systems help employees perform and inspect operations.

■ Economic Models for Process Quality

One of the key issues that process designers face is how to incorporate quality considerations in process design. The old way of thinking is that higher quality costs more. Thus, for many years, books and articles about quality suggested that processes be designed to achieve an economic "optimum" level of conformance quality. Because this model has serious flaws and can be dangerously misleading, and is still used in some literature, a brief discussion of it follows here.

TRADITIONAL ECONOMIC MODEL

Quality costs are incurred by each activity devoted to conformance to specifications in a production system. For example, receiving inspects incoming materials; tool engineering maintains tools and gages in proper condition; inspectors evaluate and test work in process and finished goods. These costs are generally referred to as the **costs of quality assurance.** On the other hand, failure to conform to specifications will result in losses due to poor quality such as scrap, rework, and warranty adjustments. These costs are called **costs due to nonconformance.**

Figure 7.14 illustrates the classic relationship between the costs of quality assurance and the costs due to nonconformance. As the quality of conformance (measured by the percentage of defective products manufactured) increases as a result of improved quality assurance, the quality assurance costs increase and the costs due to nonconformance decrease. From a strict economic viewpoint, one seeks the optimal level of conformance that minimizes the total costs to the organization. This level shows the point that minimizes the total cost curve in Figure 7.14. The area to the left of the optimum point presents significant opportunity to improve quality through increased control. To the right, however, the cost of control outweighs the savings that are generated.

MODERN VIEWPOINTS

The model shown in Figure 7.14 has been used to justify operating at a level of quality conformance less than 100 percent. Many world-class firms, however,

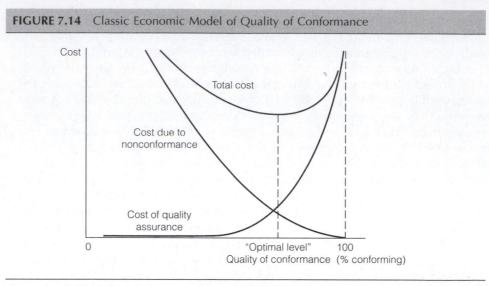

FIGURE 7.14   Classic Economic Model of Quality of Conformance

seemingly ignore the economic tradeoffs in an attempt to drive defects to zero. In reality, they are depending on increases in market share and consumer acceptance to offset the cost of "excess" quality control. This strategic decision tends to work best in expanding markets and less well in shrinking markets. To this end, Hsiang and Lee argued that the traditional quality cost model illustrated in Figure 7.14 ignores several important realities.[24] This model assumes that sales of the product are constant. Evidence shows, however, that quality improvement or degradation can significantly alter the demand for the product. Dissatisfied customers are less likely to be repeat purchasers than are satisfied customers. Word-of-mouth reputation can be significant in maintaining market share. Under the assumption that the firm seeks to maximize revenue, Hsiang and Lee show mathematically that the optimal level of conformance should be *higher* than that shown in Figure 7.14 when the revenue effect is considered (see Problem 4 at the end of the chapter).

As prevention of poor quality becomes a focus, the inherent failure rates of materials and products are reduced through new technologies, and improvements in automation reduce human error during production and appraisal. Thus, companies now have the ability to achieve perfection in quality at a finite cost; the cost of assuring quality does not extend to infinity as 100 percent conformance is reached. The total quality cost curve reaches its minimum at 100 percent conformance, justifying the philosophy of continuous improvement from an economic viewpoint. This new economic model is shown in Figure 7.15.

This model does not necessarily apply in every situation, such as when automation cannot be justified or used. It is, however, a long-term goal. The traditional model does help in assessing a firm's current position and in identifying quality improvement strategies. For example, if nonconformance costs greatly exceed quality assurance costs (to the left of the optimum), then the most sensible activity is to identify specific improvement projects that improve the quality of conformance and reduce the costs of poor quality. To the right of the optimum, the costs of quality assurance are high relative to the costs of nonconformance. In such situations, reducing the costs of quality assurance without sacrificing the level of conformance is possible. This reduction in costs might be achieved by improving technology, reducing inspection through more appropriate control

FIGURE 7.15   Modern Economic Model of Quality of Conformance

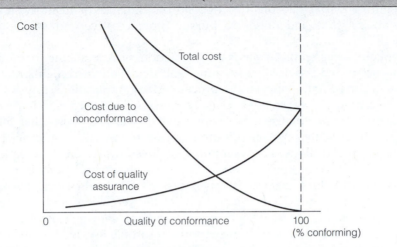

mechanisms, or relaxing unnecessarily tight quality standards relative to fitness-for-use criteria. The net effect of these activities is a continued shift of the "optimum" point to the right. Thus, the efforts toward zero defects make good economic sense. Strategies and methods for continuous improvement are found in Chapter 9.

Design for Defect Prevention

Typical sources of defects in production are omitted processing, processing errors, setup errors, missing parts, wrong parts, and adjustment errors. A good process design *prevents* defects from occurring at all.[25] The Japanese call this a **Zero (defect) Quality Control (ZQC)** system. ZQC consists of the following processes:

1. *Source inspection:* checking for factors that cause errors, not the resulting defect.

2. *100 percent inspection:* using 100 percent self-inspection, in which the operator inspects his or her own work, or in which inexpensive *poka-yoke* (mistake-proofing) devices inspect automatically for errors or defective operating conditions.

3. *Immediate action:* stopping operations instantly when a mistake is made and not resuming operations until the error is corrected. Feedback is provided through successive checks, in which the next person in the process immediately feeds back information to the supplying operator to stop production and fix the error.

ZQC is based on the fact that human beings tend to make mistakes inadvertently. Mistakes can result from forgetfulness, misunderstanding, errors in identification, lack of skill, absentmindedness, lack of standards, or equipment malfunctions. Blaming workers not only discourages them and lowers morale, but does not solve the problem. **Poka-yoke** is an approach for fail-safing processes using automatic devices or methods to avoid simple human error. The poka-yoke concept was developed and refined by the late Shigeo Shingo, a Japanese manufacturing engineer who developed the Toyota production system. The idea is to avoid repetitive tasks or actions that depend on vigilance or memory in order to free workers' time and minds to pursue more creative and value-adding activities.

Poka-yoke is focussed on two aspects: prediction, or recognizing that a defect is about to occur and providing a warning, and detection, or recognizing that a defect has occurred and stopping the process. Many applications of poka-yoke are deceptively simple, yet creative. Usually, they are inexpensive to implement. Many machines have limit switches connected to warning lights that tell the operator when parts are positioned improperly on the machine. Another example, a device on a drill counts the number of holes drilled in a workpiece; a buzzer sounds if the workpiece is removed before the correct number of holes has been drilled. A third example involves cassette covers that were frequently scratched when the screwdriver slipped out of the screw slot and slid against the plastic covers. The screw design was changed as shown in Figure 7.16 to prevent the screwdriver from slipping. Another example involved a metal roller used to laminate two surfaces bonded with hot melted glue. The glue tended to stick to the roller and cause defects in the laminate surface. An investigation showed that if the roller were dampened the glue would not stick. A secondary roller was added to dampen the steel roller during the process, preventing the glue from sticking. As a final example, one production step at Motorola involves putting alphabetic characters on a keyboard, then checking to make sure each key is placed correctly. A group of workers designed a clear template with the letters positioned slightly off center. By holding the template over the keyboard, assemblers can quickly spot mistakes.

QUALITY PLANNING AND DESIGN IN SERVICES

Service organizations do not have as well-defined products as do manufacturing firms. For example, even though all banks offer similar tangible goods such as checking, loans, automatic tellers, and so forth, the real differentiating factor among banks is the service provided. Thus, as in manufacturing, one must carefully define criteria that determine fitness for use and customer satisfaction. To do this, managers must talk with and listen to customers. Most service processes involve a greater interaction with the customer, often making it easier to identify needs and expectations. On the other hand, customers often cannot define their needs for service until after they have some point of reference or comparison.

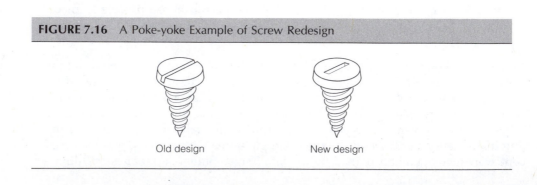

FIGURE 7.16 A Poke-yoke Example of Screw Redesign

Old design

New design

Also, needs are dynamic and frequently change. These factors can make identification of needs difficult.

One example of how customer needs lead to new service designs is the new check-in procedures introduced by Marriott.[26] Hotel guests do not like to wait to check in. Marriott established a new program called *1st 10* that virtually eliminates the front desk. Pertinent information such as time of arrival and credit card number is collected when the reservation is made, and materials are prepared prior to check in. The desk clerks need only pull the information and have guests sign the credit card slip, reducing the average check-in time from three minutes to a minute or less.

Researchers have suggested that services have three basic components: physical facilities, processes, and procedures; employees' behavior; and employees' professional judgment.[27] Designing a service essentially involves determining an effective balance of these components. The goal is to provide a service whose elements are internally consistent and directed at meeting the needs of a specific target market segment. Too much or too little emphasis on one component will lead to problems and poor customer perceptions. For example, too much emphasis on procedures might result in timely and efficient service, but might also suggest insensitivity and apathy toward the customer. Too much emphasis on behavior might provide a friendly and personable environment at the expense of slow, inconsistent, or chaotic service. Too much emphasis on professional judgment might lead to good solutions to customer problems but also to slow, inconsistent, or insensitive service.

A useful approach to designing effective services is first to recognize that services differ in the degree of customer contact and interaction, the degree of labor intensity, and the degree of customization. For example a railroad is low in all three dimensions. On the other hand, an interior design service would be high in all three dimensions. A fast-food restaurant would be high in customer contact and labor intensity, but low in customization.

Services low in all three dimensions of this classification are more similar to manufacturing organizations. The emphasis on quality should be focused on the physical facilities and procedures; behavior and professional judgment are relatively unimportant. As contact and interaction between the customer and the service system increases, two factors must be taken into account. In services low in labor intensity, the customer's impression of physical facilities, processes, and procedures is important. Service organizations must exercise special care in choosing and maintaining reliable and easy-to-use equipment. With higher levels of contact and interaction, appropriate staff behavior becomes increasingly important.

As labor intensity increases, variations between individuals become more important; however, the elements of personal behavior and professional judgment will remain relatively unimportant as long as the degrees of customization and contact and interaction remain low. As customization increases, professional judgment becomes a bigger factor in the customer's perception of service quality. In services high in all three dimensions, facilities, behavior, and professional judgment must be equally balanced.

In services, quality standards take the place of dimensions and tolerances applicable in manufacturing. Examples of standards by one of the airline industry leaders, Swissair, include:

- Ninety percent of calls are answered within 30 seconds.
- Ninety percent of passengers are checked in within three minutes of arrival.
- Baggage claim time is only ten minutes between the first and last customer.

However, service standards are inherently more difficult to define and measure than manufacturing specifications. They require extensive research into customer needs and attitudes regarding timeliness, consistency, accuracy, and other service requirements as discussed in previous chapters. While many product specifications developed for manufactured products are focused on meeting a target ("nominal is best" in the Taguchi philosophy), service targets typically are "smaller is better." Thus, the true service standard is zero defects, and any other standards (such as those of Swissair) should be construed as interim standards and targets only.

In planning for quality in services, Zimmerman and Enell suggest some questions for consideration:[28] What service standards are already in place? Which of these standards have been clearly communicated to all service personnel? Have these standards been communicated to the public? Which standards require refinement? What is the final result of the service provided? What should it ideally be?

With regard to time, some important questions include the following: What is the maximum access time that a patron will tolerate without feeling inconvenienced? How long should it take to perform the service itself? What is the maximum time for completion of service before the customer's view of the service is negatively affected? At what point does service begin, and what indicator signals the completion of the service? How many different people must the consumer deal with in completing the service?

Concerning completeness and consistency, a service organization should ask: What components of the service are essential? Desirable? Superfluous? What components or aspects of service must be controlled to deliver a service encounter of equal quality each time it occurs? Which components can differ from encounter to encounter while still leading to a total service encounter that meets standards? What products that affect its service performance does a service organization obtain from other sources?

Answers to such questions, while difficult to develop, provide information critical for quality planning. Techniques such as quality function deployment can be used effectively in service quality planning.

■ Service Process Design

When something goes wrong with a customer—if a meal is served late or a hotel guest finds billing errors—the server or front desk clerk usually gets the blame. The old phrase "Don't shoot the messenger," (in this case, of poor quality) often applies; the customer-contact person is usually only a small piece of a larger process. Deming and Juran noted many years ago that most quality problems are built into the system and are not the result of the workers.

A service product is a *process*; that is, a method of completing specific activities. Preparing an invoice, taking a telephone order, processing a credit card, preparing food, checking out of a hotel, and teaching a class are all examples of service processes. Service process designers must concentrate on doing things right the first time, minimizing process complexities, and making the process immune to inadvertent human errors, particularly during customer interactions. Service processes often involve both internal and external activities, a factor that complicates quality design. For example, in a bank, poor service can result from the way that tellers treat customers and also from poor quality of computers and communications equipment beyond the control of the tellers. Internal activities are primarily concerned with efficiency (quality of conformance), while external activities—with direct customer interaction—require attention to effectiveness (quality of design). All too often, workers involved in internal operations do not understand how their performance affects the customers they do not see. The success of the process depends on everyone—workers involved in internal as well as external activities—understanding they add value to the customer.

Dealing with symptoms of errors in internal operations by introducing extra inspection steps is usually less troublesome than seeking the root cause of errors and correcting them. However, this practice leads to inefficiencies and unnecessary costs. To prevent errors in external activities, work design should structure a task in such a way that it cannot be performed unless the person doing it devotes complete attention to the work. Effective design requires keen insight into the work process. The necessary insight can often be gained through suggestions from the people that do the work.

A service design is the specification of how the service should be delivered. The first phase in creating a service design is to list in detail the sequence of steps—value-adding activities and specific tasks—involved in delivering the service, usually depicted as a flowchart. Such a graphical representation provides an excellent communication device for visualizing and understanding the service operation. Flowcharts can become the basis for job descriptions, employee-training programs, and performance measurement. They help managers to estimate human resource, information systems, equipment, and facilities requirements. As design tools, they enable management to study and analyze services prior to implementation in order to improve quality and operational performance. Figure 7.17 shows the Ritz-Carlton's Three Steps of Service process. The process is highly structured and defines the procedures for anticipating and complying with customer needs. All employees who come in contact with customers are trained to follow this process.

FIGURE 7.17 The Ritz-Carlton Hotel Company: Three Steps of Service

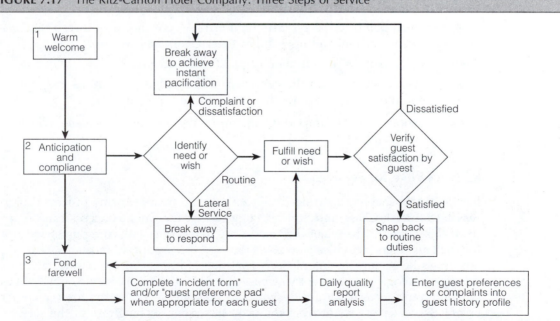

A good way to begin a service design is with the customer–supplier model we introduced in Chapter 5. Answers to questions such as "What is the purpose of the process?" "How does the process create customer satisfaction?" and "What are the essential inputs and outputs of the process?" provide useful starting information. Start with the outputs—customer requirements—and move backward through the process to identify the key steps needed to produce each output; stop when the process reaches the supplier input stage. AT&T calls this technique **backward chaining**.[29] AT&T suggests the following steps:

1. Begin with the process output and ask "What is the last essential subprocess that produces the output of the process?"

2. For that subprocess, ask, "What input does it need to produce the process output?" For each input, test its value to ensure that it is required.

3. For each input, identify its source. In many cases, the input will be the output of the previous subprocess. In some cases, the input may come from external suppliers.

4. Continue backward, one subprocess at a time, until each input comes from an external supplier.

This technique can be applied to each subprocess to create a more detailed process description.

Once a process is designed, several fundamental questions arise:

■ Are the steps in the process arranged in logical sequence?

■ Do all steps add value? Can some steps be eliminated and should others be added in order to improve quality or operational performance? Can some be combined? Should some be reordered?

■ Are capacities of each step in balance; that is, do bottlenecks exist for which customers will incur excessive waiting time?

■ What skills, equipment, and tools are required at each step of the process? Should some steps be automated?

■ At which points in the system might errors occur that would result in customer dissatisfaction, and how might these errors be corrected?

■ At which point or points should quality be measured?

■ Where interaction with the customer occurs, what procedures and guidelines should employees follow that will present a positive image?

These questions are also important in improving existing processes, which is discussed in Chapter 9.

■ Poka-Yoke for Services

Earlier in this chapter, the concept of *poka-yoke* for manufacturing process design was introduced. Chase and Stewart suggest that the same concepts can be applied to services.[30] The major differences are that service fail-safing must account for the customers' activities as well as those of the producer, and fail-safe methods must be set up for interactions conducted directly or by phone, mail, or other technologies, such as ATM. Chase and Stewart classify service poka-yokes by the type of error they are designed to prevent: server errors and customer errors. Server errors result from the task, treatment, or tangibles of the service. Customer errors occur during preparation, the service encounter, or during resolution.

Task errors include doing work incorrectly, work not requested, work in the wrong order, or too slowly. Some examples of poka-yoke devices for task errors are computer prompts, color-coded cash register keys, measuring tools such as McDonald's french-fry scoop, and signaling devices. Hospitals use trays for surgical instruments that have indentations for each instrument, preventing the surgeon from leaving one of them in the patient.

Treatment errors arise in the contact between the server and the customer, such as lack of courteous behavior, and failure to acknowledge, listen, or react appropriately to the customer. A bank encourages eye contact by requiring tellers to record the customer's eye color on a checklist as they start the transaction. To promote friendliness at a fast-food restaurant, trainers provide four specific cues for when to smile: when greeting the customer, when taking the order, when telling about the dessert special, and when giving the customer change. They encourage employees to observe whether the customer smiled back, a natural reinforcer for smiling.

Tangible errors are those in physical elements of the service, such as unclean facilities, dirty uniforms, inappropriate temperature, and document errors. Hotels wrap paper strips around towels to help the housekeeping staff identify clean linen and show which ones should be replaced. Spell-checkers in word processing software eliminate document misspellings (provided they are used!).

Customer errors in preparation include the failure to bring necessary materials to the encounter, to understand their role in the service transaction, and to engage the correct service. Digital Equipment provides a flowchart to specify how to place a service call. By guiding them through three yes-or-no questions, the flowchart prompts the customers to have the necessary information before calling.

Customer errors during an encounter can be due to inattention, misunderstanding, or simply a memory lapse, and include failure to remember steps in the process or to follow instructions. Poka-yoke examples include height bars at amusement rides that indicate rider size requirements, beepers that signal customers to remove cards from ATM machines, and locks on airplane lavatory doors that must be closed to turn on the lights. Some cashiers at restaurants fold back the top edge of credit card receipts holding together the restaurant's copies while revealing the customer's copy.

Customers may also make errors at the resolution stage of a service encounter. Errors include failure to signal service inadequacies, to learn from experience, to adjust expectations, and to execute appropriate post-encounter actions. Hotels might enclose a small gift certificate to encourage guests to provide feedback. Strategically placed tray-return stands and trash receptacles remind customers to return trays in fast-food facilities.

Fail-safing a service process requires identifying when and where failures generally occur. Once a failure is identified, the source must be found. The final step is to prevent the mistake from occurring through source inspection, self-inspection, or sequential checks.

MANAGING THE DESIGN PROCESS

Product development is a complex activity. It demands the involvement and cooperation of different functional groups within an organization to identify and solve design problems and seek to reduce product development and introduction times. Two techniques that assist in meeting these objectives are design reviews and concurrent engineering.

Design Reviews

To ensure that all important design objectives are taken into account during the design process, many companies use formal design reviews. The purpose of a **design review** is to stimulate discussion, raise questions, and generate new ideas and solutions to problems. The outcome of this process is a better product and lower costs. Design reviews facilitate standardization and reduce costs associated with frequent design changes by assisting designers to anticipate problems before they occur.

Design reviews, involving all aspects of the production system, should be planned, scheduled, and documented. Generally, a design review is conducted in three major stages: preliminary, intermediate, and final. The preliminary design review establishes early communication between marketing, engineering, manufacturing, and purchasing personnel and provides better coordination of their activities. It usually involves higher levels of management and concentrates on strategic issues in design that relate to customer requirements and thus the ultimate quality of the product. A preliminary design review evaluates such issues as the function of the product, conformance to customer's needs, completeness of specifications, manufacturing costs, and liability issues.

After the design is well established, an intermediate review takes place to study the design in greater detail to identify potential problems and suggest corrective action. Personnel at lower levels of the organization are more heavily involved at this stage. Finally, just before release to production, a final review is held. Materials lists, drawings, and other detailed design information are studied with the purpose of preventing costly changes after production setup.

Quality assurance professionals can play an important role in design reviews. Quality personnel have the expertise to classify quality characteristics and to determine quality levels and standards for verifying conformance to specifications. They can aid design engineers in the analysis of product function, life, interchangeability of components, and specifications; establish plans for inspection and testing and standardize criteria for product acceptance; assist engineering and production personnel in understanding customer requirements; help purchasing personnel select materials and parts; and analyze serviceability in the field.

An important component of design reviews is **value analysis/value engineering (VA/VE).** VA/VE involves assessing how the function of every component of a product, system, or service can be accomplished most economically without degrading the quality of the product or service. The term *value engineering* usually refers to cost avoidance or cost prevention before production; *value analysis* refers to cost reduction during production. Typical questions that are asked during VA/VE include: What are the functions of a particular component? Are they necessary? Can they be accomplished in a different way? What materials are used? Can a less costly material be substituted? For example, can off-the-shelf items be used in place of custom-specified components? How much material is wasted during manufacturing? Can waste be reduced by changing the design?

■ Concurrent Engineering

All departments play a crucial role in the design process. The designer's objective is to design a product that achieves the desired functional requirements. The manufacturing engineer's objective is to produce it efficiently. The salesperson's goal is to sell the product, and the finance person's goal is to make a profit. Purchasing seeks parts that meet quality requirements. Packaging and distribution deliver the product to the customer in good operating condition. Clearly all business functions have a stake in the product; therefore, all should work together.

Unfortunately, the product development process often is performed without such cooperation. In many large firms, product development is accomplished in a serial fashion as suggested in Figure 7.1. In the early stages of development, design engineers dominate the process. Later, the prototype is transferred to manufacturing for production. Finally, marketing and sales personnel are brought into the process. This approach has several disadvantages. First, product development time is long. Second, up to 90 percent of manufacturing costs may be committed before manufacturing engineers have any input to the design. Third, the final product may not be the best one for market conditions at the time of introduction.

An approach that alleviates these problems is called **concurrent engineering,** or **simultaneous engineering.** Concurrent engineering is a process in which all major functions involved with bringing a product to market are continuously involved with the product development from conception through sales. Such an approach achieves shorter product development cycles while simultaneously improving quality and lowering costs. Typical benefits include 30–70 percent less development time, 65–90 percent fewer engineering changes, 20–90 percent less time to market, 200–600 percent improvement in quality, 20–110 percent improvement in white collar productivity, and 20–120 percent higher return on assets.[31]

Concurrent engineering involves multifunctional teams, usually consisting of 4–20 members and including every specialty in the company. The functions of such teams are to determine the character of the product and decide what design methods and production methods are appropriate; analyze product functions so that all design decisions can be made with full knowledge of how the item is supposed to work; perform a design for manufacturability study to determine whether the design can be improved without affecting performance; formulate an assembly sequence; and design a factory system that fully involves workers.

Simultaneous engineering has been a major force behind the resurgence of U.S. automobile companies by enabling them to dramatically reduce product development time. In the past, automobile development followed a sequential process in which styling engineers dreamed up a concept and sent the concept to product engineers to design components. They in turn would send the designs to manufacturing and suppliers. This process was costly and inefficient; each handoff lost something in time and money. What appeared feasible for one group often proved impossible to accomplish by another. By the time the vehicle was finally produced, marketing was faced with selling a product for which they had no input. Often the vehicle was priced incorrectly for the target market.

In 1980, Ford launched Team Taurus, modeled after program management concepts in the aerospace industry. Program managers headed product teams that included representatives from design, engineering, purchasing, marketing, quality assurance, sales, and service. Cadillac adopted simultaneous engineering in 1985. Vehicle teams, composed of disciplines from every area of the organization, were responsible for managing all steps of product development. They defined the target market, and overall vehicle goals, and managed the timing, profitabilty, and continuous improvement of the vehicle's quality, reliability, durability, and performance. Chrysler's adaptation of simultaneous engineering enabled them to develop and introduce the celebrated Viper sports car in just two years.

Quality assurance personnel are in a uniquely qualified position to perform such design coordination. Quality engineers assist designers in developing products that can be consistently manufactured in conformance to specifications. They can better relate design standards to production, have access to supplier quality histories, and are aware of problem areas on the production floor. Quality personnel have knowledge of scrap, rework, and service records in the field. They also know the scope of various quality costs and assist the designer in determining specifications that balance such costs against design costs.

In summary, a total approach to product development and process design involves the following activities:

1. Constantly thinking in terms of how one can design or manufacture products better, not just solving or preventing problems.

2. Focusing on "things gone right" rather than "things gone wrong."

3. Defining customer expectations and going beyond them, not just barely meeting them or just matching competition.

4. Optimizing desirable features or results, not just incorporating them.

5. Minimizing the overall cost without compromising quality of function.

Quality engineering, QFD, and other techniques discussed in this chapter all contribute to achieving these objectives.[32]

QUALITY IN PRACTICE

QUALITY FUNCTION DEPLOYMENT AT DIGITAL EQUIPMENT CORPORATION[33]

Digital Equipment Corporation (DEC) was interested in developing direct access to an automated purchasing system for noncomputer-literate consumers. The system was to be made available in public places with accompanying telecommunications and terminal system development. DEC needed the right combination of features, pricing, distribution, and promotion for the system so that is could be used frequently and also be profitable. QFD was applied by taking the four houses of quality (see Figure 7.18), and changing their names so that software engineers would have a better understanding of the concepts.

They began the process by brainstorming ideas of what the service should achieve. (The individuals involved were typical consumers of the targeted service.) Examples included

■ I want to see a high-quality photo of every product.

■ I want my phone number, address, and other information kept secure.

■ I want to be able to access the system day or night.

■ I want a simple method of payment.

More than 100 requirements were created. Potential customers were then queried for their inputs and a few minor features were added.

The next step was to create functional specifications. For example, a security function was needed to meet the requirement that personal information be kept confidential. This specification was then broken down into more detailed functions. Another re-

FIGURE 7.18   Adaptation of the Houses of Quality to Software Development

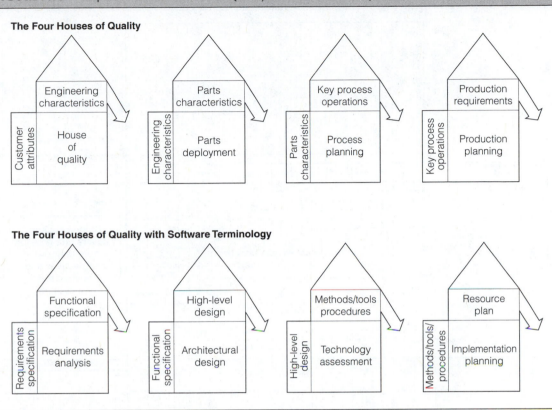

quirement concerned people who had never used a computer before: they must be able to use the service within 30 seconds without having to read any manuals or refer to on-line help.

At this point, they departed from the conventional QFD process and did not conduct any weighting exercise because observations have shown that weighting can delay the process, be difficult for customers to do if they cannot see a working prototype, and inhibit engineers' creativity. Figure 7.19 shows a high-level view of the matrix that the team developed.

The developers used the functional specifications as the basis for a test plan. Tests were written immediately from the first house of quality, independent of design implementation, which increased the amount of concurrency in the development process and led to a faster time to market.

The second house of quality consisted of determining high-level design elements for each functional specification. They would continually think that certain problems had not been considered, but discovered that they had already addressed the problem 99 percent of the time by looking at the matrix. The design was more than just a software design; it included distribution channels, pricing,

and selling the service as well as the required hardware terminals, telecommunications, and billing systems.

QFD enabled DEC to evaluate and make choices between critical design alternatives. For example, consider the following requirements:

■ It must be easy for the noncomputer customer to use.

■ It must perform well no matter how many people are using the system.

■ It must be inexpensive to order products through this service.

Some of the functional specifications might be:

■ Noncomputer-literate customers must be able to use the system within 30 seconds with no manuals or on-line help.

■ It must always respond to user input within one second.

■ The cost of use must be less than $15 per access.

Some of the design decisions to meet the ease-of-use requirement might be to:

FIGURE 7.19   QFD Requirements Analysis Matrix

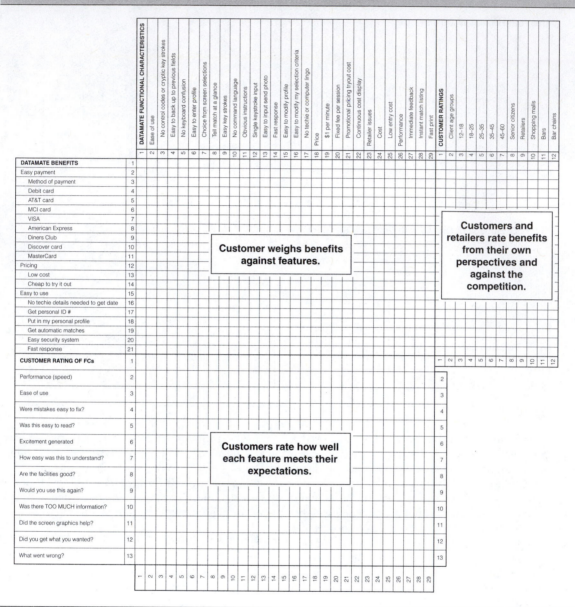

- Use a simple keyboard or no keyboard at all in order to eliminate confusion and computer phobia.
- Have the customer point at the desired option rather than use a keyboard or keyboard commands.
- Use a bit-mapped display with 3-D buttons on the screens for intuitive pressing to pick options, an approach with which most customers are already familiar.

However, bit-mapped displays cost more money, which affects the low cost of manufacture and capital equipment investment criteria. They also affect performance if each display is miles away from the central data base because it takes a long time to download bit maps through phone lines. In addition, bit-mapped graphics require a lot of computer resources, which increases the capital equipment investment. At this point, numbers can be put into the cells of the matrix to see the effect of one design feature on the other design features and requirements.

The third house of quality was used to resolve design alternative issues. Design features were mapped to the technology, procedures, and methods used to create the product. They looked at various pointing technologies to meet the ease-of-use criteria (cursor keys, mice, finger pads, touch screens). They also took into account such factors as an angry person yanking a mouse or smashing a fist on the keyboard, or someone spilling a drink on the keyboard. This analysis provided a clear record of the tradeoffs to be made.

The final house of quality matched the technology, methods, and procedures with people, time, equipment, building facilities, and money. If the requirements and the design are not complete and accurate, misjudgments of resources and time required can be quite costly. To reduce this risk, DEC created a prototype and test-marketed it, which allowed them to refine the first three houses before completing the fourth house. Building a prototype would require little rework if the initial requirements were mostly complete and accurate. With the prototype,

they could then ask customers to rate the service against the competition which would provide competitive weights in the first house of quality. At this point, the engineers could determine the importance of design features and make better tradeoffs.

DEC found that one of the benefits of QFD was that the first house of quality provided information to use in sales literature and advertisements, eliminating the need for this to be done by the marketing department. Engineers are now performing part of the marketing role, including surveys, prototype testing, and developing key items for advertising, and breaking down traditional barriers between marketing and engineers.

Key Issues for Discussion

1. Explain the relationships and analogies between the original four houses of quality and DEC's implementation. List similarities and differences.

2. DEC has suggested that marketing's role has been essentially eliminated. Can marketing's role be reduced in other industries? What limitations or implications does such an action present for business organizations?

SUMMARY OF KEY POINTS

■ Quality of design, coupled with quality of conformance in production, determines the ultimate performance, reliability, and value of a product. Product and process design must be coordinated to produce a quality product.

■ The product development process consists of idea generation, preliminary concept development, product/process development, full-scale production, product introduction, and market evaluation. Competitive pressures are forcing companies to reduce time to market, which can be accomplished by eliminating design changes and improving product manufacturability.

■ Leading practices in product design and development include addressing all product and service quality requirements early in the design process, building quality into products and services during the design stage, translating customer requirements into product and process designs effectively, linking product design and process design requirements, and managing the development process using cross-functional communication to reduce time to market.

■ Improvements in cost and quality often result from simplifying designs. Design for manufacturability is the process of designing a product so that it can be produced efficiently at the highest levels of quality.

■ Product liability has forced manufacturers to pay greater attention to quality in design. As one of Deming's Seven Deadly Diseases, liability is a serious threat to competitiveness.

■ Environmental concerns have made *design for disassembly* an important feature of products, which permits easy removal of components for recycling or repair.

■ Genichi Taguchi defined quality as the loss that a product causes to society after being shipped. The Taguchi loss function is a way of quantifying the costs due to variation from a target specification. This function has been used to demonstrate the economic value of meeting nominal specifications rather than simply staying within tolerances.

■ Taguchi's three principal tools for quality engineering are system design, parameter design, and tolerance design. System design focuses on producing a basic functional design. Parameter design identifies the nominal settings of product or process parameters that reduce variation. Tolerance design determines tolerances around the nominal settings. Tolerance design benefits by the application of statistical methods as well as the Taguchi loss function.

■ Customers and engineers/designers speak different languages. Quality function deployment (QFD) is a technique to used to carry the voice of the customer through the design and production process.

■ The major planning document in QFD is called the House of Quality and provides a planning structure for relating customers' needs to technical specifications and confirming that key specifications are identified and deployed throughout the subsequent production process.

■ Process design plans and configures physical facilities, operations, work flows, and methods for production. Just-in-time materials control brings process quality problems to the attention of management. Current thinking suggests that processes should be designed to achieve zero defects. Mistake-proofing, or *poka-yoke*, approaches reduce defects through simple inspection and prevention activities.

■ In designing services, one must consider physical facilities, processes, and procedures; behavior; and professional judgment. Classification of services along dimensions of customer contact and interaction, labor intensity, and degree of customization directs attention to the proper balance of these design elements. Backward chaining is a useful technique to design processes that add maximum product value and minimize waste. Poka-yoke concepts can also be applied to services to eliminate both server and customer errors.

■ Design reviews, value analysis/value engineering, and concurrent engineering are important approaches for managing the product development process. Multifunctional teams help to remove organizational barriers between departments and therefore reduce product development time.

REVIEW QUESTIONS

1. Describe the product design and development process.

2. What are nominal specifications and tolerances?

3. Discuss the importance of and impediments to reducing the time for product development.

4. Summarize the leading practices of world-class firms in the product development area.

5. Why are modern products more difficult to manufacture than traditional products like bicycles or hand tools?

6. What are some of the factors that must be considered in the design of a product, both technically and managerially?

7. Explain the concept and importance of design for manufacturability.

8. Summarize the key design practices for high quality in manufacturing and assembly.

9. Why should quality engineers at the design stage be concerned with product liability? What can be done to reduce the risk of product liability lawsuits?

10. Why is design for disassembly an important concept?

11. Explain the role of system, parameter, and tolerance design in quality engineering.

12. What are "Taguchi methods" and how are they used in product design?

13. Explain the concept of signal-to-noise ratio.

14. How does Taguchi define quality? How is quality measured according to his definition?

15. Explain how the Taguchi loss function differs from the traditional loss function assumed from specifications and tolerances?

16. Explain the basic principles of quality function deployment. How is it implemented in an organization?

17. What are the principal benefits of QFD?

18. Outline the process of building the House of Quality. What departments and functions within the company should be involved in each step of the process?

19. Explain the role of process design in producing a quality product. List and explain some of the key activities in process design.

20. Why is an economic optimum level of quality inappropriate? Describe the basis for the modern economic model of conformance quality.

21. Describe the Japanese concept of Zero (defect) Quality Control.

22. What is a poka-yoke? Provide some examples.

23. Explain the differences between designing manufactured products and services. How should the design of services be approached?

24. Explain the concept of backward chaining in designing service processes.

25. List some poka-yoke applications in services.

26. What is the purpose of a design review? What tools are used in design reviews?

27. What are value analysis and value engineering? How do they contribute to good design?

28. What is concurrent engineering? What functions do concurrent engineering teams perform?

DISCUSSION QUESTIONS

1. What is the "product development process" a school might use for designing and introducing a new course? How might it be improved to reduce "time to market"?

2. Examine some recently purchased product. Does it appear to be designed for disassembly or with concern for the environment?

3. Interview a plant manager at a local factory to determine his or her philosophy on meeting specifications. Is the manager familiar with the Taguchi loss function? Does he or she buy into the concept?

4. Using whatever "market research" techniques are appropriate, define a set of customer attributes for

  a. an "excellent cup of coffee"

  b. a picnic cooler

  c. a college registration process

For each case, determine a set of technical requirements and construct the relationship matrix for the House of Quality.

5. (This exercise would best be performed in a group.) Suppose that you were developing a small pizza restaurant with a dining area and local delivery. Develop a list of customer requirements and technical requirements and try to complete a House of Quality. What service standards might such an operation have?

6. Design a process using some of the approaches discussed in this chapter for

  a. preparing for an exam

  b. planning a vacation

  c. making breakfast for your family

Draw a flowchart for each process using the backward chaining approach and explain how to fail-safe these processes?

7. Provide some personal examples of poka-yoke in activities at school, home, or work.

8. Use the service quality planning questions suggested by Zimmerman and Enell to design a tutoring service for disadvantaged high school students in the community or for some other community service activity.

9. In a true story related by our colleague Professor James W. Dean, Jr., the general manager of an elevator company was frustrated with the lack of cooperation between the mechanical engineers who designed new elevators and the manufacturing engineers who determined how to produce them.[34] The mechanical engineers would often completely design a new elevator without any consulting with the manufacturing engineers, and then expect the factory to somehow figure out how to build it. Often the new products were difficult or nearly impossible to build, and their quality and cost suffered as a result. The designs were sent back to the mechanical engineers (often more than once) for engineering changes to improve their manufacturability, and customers sometimes waited for months for deliveries. The general manager believed that if the two groups of engineers would communicate early in the design process, many of the problems would be solved. At his wit's end, he found a large empty room in the plant and had both groups moved into it. The manager relaxed a bit, but a few weeks later, he returned to a surprise. The two groups of engineers had finally learned to cooperate—by building a wall of bookcases and file cabinets right down the middle of the room, separating them from each other! What would you do in this situation?

10. Legal Sea Foods operates several restaurants and fish markets in the Boston area. Their standards of excellence mandate that they serve only the freshest, highest-quality seafood. They guarantee the quality by buying only the "top of the catch" fish daily. Although Legal Sea Foods tries to make available the widest variety every day, certain species of fish are subject to migratory patterns and are not always present in New England waters. Weather conditions may also prevent local fishermen from fishing in certain areas.

Freshly caught fish are rushed to the company's quality control center where they are cut and filleted in an environmentally controlled state-of-the-art facility. All shellfish comes from government certified beds and are tested in an in-house microbiology laboratory for wholesomeness and purity. They even have special lobster storage tanks so that all lobsters are held under optimum conditions, in clean, pollution-free water. Every seafood item is inspected for quality eight separate times before it reaches the table.

At Legal Sea Foods' restaurants, every meal is cooked to order. While servers make every effort to deliver all meals within minutes of each other, they will not jeopardize the quality of an item by holding it beneath a heat lamp until the entire order is ready. The service staff is trained to work as a team for better service. More than one service person frequently delivers food to a table. When any item is ready, the closest available person serves it. Customer questions can be directed to any employee, not just the person who took the initial order.

a. What are the major processes performed by Legal Sea Foods? How does the process design support their goal of serving only the freshest, highest-quality seafood?

b. Where would Legal Sea Foods fall on the three-dimensional classification of service organizations? Is their process design consistent with this classification?

c. Based on the information provided, develop a list of customer requirements and a House of Quality.

PROBLEMS

1. A blueprint specification for the thickness of an automotive part is 0.120 ± 0.009 inch. It costs \$3 to scrap a part that is outside of the specifications. Determine the Taguchi loss function for this situation.

2. An electronic component has an output voltage specification of 75 ± 5 millivolts. Scrapping the component results in a \$300 loss.

a. What is the value of k in the Taguchi loss function?

b. If the process is centered on the target specification with a standard deviation of 2 millivolts, what is the expected loss per unit?

3. A computer chip is designed so that the distance between two adjacent pins has a specification of 2.000 ± 0.002 mm. The loss due to a defective chip is \$4. A sample of 25 chips was drawn from the production process and the results are shown below.

2.001	2.000	2.001	1.998	1.999
2.000	2.000	2.002	1.999	2.000
1.998	1.999	2.001	2.000	2.000
2.000	1.999	2.001	2.001	2.000
2.000	2.002	2.000	2.000	2.001

a. Compute the value of k in the Taguchi loss function.

b. What is the expected loss from this process based on the sample data?

4. Let $C(q)$ represent the total cost as a function of q, the quality of conformance, in Figure 7.14. Also, define p = unit price of the product, m = manufacturing cost (exclusive of quality-related costs) per unit of product (assumed constant with respect to volume), I = net income, and $D(q)$ = demand as a function of q. If $I = [p - C(q) - m]D(q)$, show that the value of q that maximizes I must be larger than the one that minimizes $C(q)$. (This rather difficult question requires calculus.)

5. In the production of transformers, any output voltage that exceeds ± 25 volts is unacceptable to the customer. Exceeding these limits results in an estimated loss of \$400. However, the manufacturer can adjust the voltage in the plant by changing a resistor that costs \$1.50.

a. Determine the Taguchi loss function.

b. Suppose the nominal specification is 120 volts. At what tolerance should the transformer be manufactured?

6. Fill in the partial House of Quality matrix below for a screwdriver. How would you prioritize the voice of the customer?

	Price	Interchangeable bits	Steel shaft	Rubber grip	Rachet capability	Plastic handle	Priority
Easy to use							
Does not rust							
Durable							
Comfortable							
Versatile							
Inexpensive							

7. Most children (and many adults) like to assemble and fly balsa wood gliders. From your own experiences (or from interviews with other students), define a set of customer requirements for a good glider. (Even better, buy one and test it to determine these requirements yourself.) If you were to design and manufacture such a product, how would you define a set of technical requirements for the design? Using your results, construct a relationship matrix for a House of Quality.

8. The *Hillsdale Observer*, a small-town newspaper in Hillsdale, Ohio, recently hired a quality consultant to conduct a study of the six mortgage lending institutions in town. The *Observer* then published it in the business section of the paper. Data from the study is listed in Table 7.2. A sample of customers who had obtained mortgages from each of the institutions was surveyed. The customer sample was asked to rate the importance of various quality factors that influenced their decision to get their mortgage loan from a particular institution. Weighting factors were calculated and appear in parentheses in the left column of the table. Another survey was then taken involving area realtors, who typically worked with all of the mortgage institutions. Realtors were asked to rate each

TABLE 7.2   Hillsdale Mortgage Institutions—Comparative Data

Customer Service Factors	LENDING INSTITUTIONS					
	National Mortgage	Sunset FSB	Local Bankcorp	Investor's Trust	Cities' Service FSB	Dewey, Cheatham Lenders
1. Competitive rates (1.10)	10	9	6	7	8	5
2. Accurate processing (1.05)	9	7	8	9	7	4
3. Timely completion (1.01)	8	6	7	7	8	7
4. Single point of contact* (0.95)	5	5	6	5	6	9
5. Courteous, knowledgeable personnel (0.89)	9	8	8	8	7	3
Total (weighted)	8.26	7.04	6.98	6.80	7.23	5.24

*Based on number of institutional representatives that customers had to deal with.

institution on each of the "customer" dimensions, using a scale of 0 to 10. The ratings (rounded) on each dimension are shown in the body of the table for the six institutions.

a. What information contained in the survey data applies to the quality function deployment process?

b. Develop a House of Quality matrix using this information. What further information is needed?

c. How could this information be used to develop a competing mortgage loan service?

CASES

I. A Case of Failure in Product Development[35]

In 1981, market share and profits in General Electric's appliance division were falling. The company's technology was antiquated compared to that of foreign competitors. For example, making a refrigerator compressor required 65 minutes of labor in comparison with just 25 minutes by competitors in Japan and Italy. Moreover, their labor costs were lower. The alternatives were obvious: Either purchase compressors from Japan or Italy or design and build a better model. By 1983, the decision to build a new rotary compressor in-house was made, along with a commitment for a new $120 million factory. GE was not a novice in rotary compressor technology; they had invented it and had been using it in air conditioners for many years. A rotary compressor weighed less, had one-third fewer parts, and was more energy-efficient than the current reciprocating compressors. Also, it took up less space, thus providing more room inside the refrigerators and therefore helped meet customer requirements better.

However, some engineers had argued against the change. Rotary compressors run hotter. In most air conditioners, this is not a problem since the coolant cools the compressor. In a refrigerator, the coolant flows only one-tenth as fast, and the unit runs about four times longer in one year than in an air conditioner. GE had problems with the early rotary compressors in air conditioners. Although the bugs had been eliminated in smaller units, GE quit using rotaries in larger units after frequent breakdowns in hot climates.

GE managers and design engineers were concerned about other issues. Rotary compressors make a high-pitched whine, and managers were afraid that this would adversely affect consumer acceptance. Many hours were spent by managers and consumer test panels on this issue. The new design also required key parts to work together with a tolerance of only 50 millionths of an inch. Nothing had been mass produced with such precision before, but manufacturing engineers felt sure they could do it.

The compressor they finally designed was nearly identical to that used in air conditioners, with one change. Two small parts inside the compressor were made out of powdered metal, rather than the hardened steel and cast iron used in air condnitioners. This was chosen because it could be machined to much closer tolerances and reduced machining costs. This was tried a decade earlier on air conditioners and did not work. This fact was told to the design engineers who were new to designing compressors, and they did not pay attention.

A consultant suggested that GE consider a joint venture with a Japanese company who had a rotary refrigerator compressor already on the market. This idea was rejected by management. The original designer of the air conditioning rotary compressor, who had left GE, had offered his services as a consultant. GE declined this offer, writing to him that they had sufficient technical expertise.

About 600 compressors were tested in 1983 without a single failure. They were run continuously for two months under elevated temperatures and pressures that were supposed to simulate five years of operation. GE normally conducts extensive field testing of new products; their original plan to test models in the field for two years was reduced to nine months to meet time pressures to complete the project.

After testing, the technician who disassembled and inspected the parts thought they did not look right. Parts of the motor were discolored, a sign of excessive heat. Bearings were worn, and it appeared that high heat was breaking down the lubricating oil. The technician's supervisors discounted these findings and did not relay them to upper levels of management. Another consultant who evaluated the test results believed that something was wrong because only one failure was found in two years, and he recommended that test conditions be intensified. This too was rejected by management.

By 1986, only 2.5 years after board approval, the new factory was producing compressors at a rate of 10 per minute. By the end of the year, over 1 million had been produced. Market share rose and the new refrigerator appeared to be a success. In July 1987 the first compressor failed. Soon after, reports of other failures in Puerto Rico arrived. By September, the appliance division knew it had a major problem. By December, the plant stopped making the compressor. It was not until 1988 that the problem was diagnosed as excessive wear in the two powdered-metal parts that burned up the oil. The cost in 1989 alone was $450 million. By mid-1990, GE had voluntarily replaced nearly 1.1 million compressors with new ones purchased from six suppliers, five of them foreign.

Discussion Questions

1. What factors in the product development process caused this disaster? What individuals were responsible?

2. Discuss how techniques of quality engineering might have improved the product development process for the compressor.

3. What lessons did GE probably learn for the future?

II. BurgerMate Corporation

A large national consumer products corporation recently acquired a regional chain of fast-food restaurants, BurgerMate, and plans to expand this chain nationally. As a result, they are seriously considering improved products and services development. Based on consumer surveys, the company determined that improving their basic burger is vital to capturing a significant share of market from competitors. They decided to approach this goal using quality function deployment.

Using focus groups and other market research methods, they found that consumers have four primary expectations for a hamburger. It should be tasty (moist and flavorful), healthy (nutritious), visually appealing (thick and "beefy"), and have good value for the money. Consumers placed the highest importance on nutrition, followed by value, followed by visual appeal and flavor. Moistness was only casually noted as an important attribute in the surveys.

BurgerMate faces three major competitors in this market: Grabby's, Queenburger, and Sandy's. Studies of their products have yielded the information shown in Table 7.3. Results of the consumer panel ratings for each of these competitors are shown in Table 7.4 (a 1-to-5 scale with 5 being the best).

Assignment

Using this information, construct a completed House of Quality and develop a deployment plan for a new burger. On what attributes should the company focus its marketing efforts?

TABLE 7.3 Competitors' Product Information

	Price	Size (oz.)	Calories	Sodium (mg)	Fat (%)
Grabby's	$1.45	5.5	492	576	15
Queenburger	$1.85	9.0	663	1081	16
Sandy's	$1.55	7.25	547	886	23

TABLE 7.4 Consumer Panel Ratings

Attribute	Grabby's	Queenburger	Sandy's
Moistness	4	4	5
Flavor	4	5	3
Nutrition	4	2	3
Visual appeal	3	5	4
Value	5	3	4

■ NOTES

1. Peter J. Kolesar, "What Deming Told the Japanese in 1950," *Quality Management Journal* 2, no. 1 (Fall 1994), 9–24.

2. Ames Rubber Corporation, *Application Summary for the 1993 Malcolm Baldrige National Quality Award.*

3. "How to Listen to Consumers," *Fortune,* 11 January, 1993, 77.

4. Adapted from Douglas Daetz, "The Effect of Product Design on Product Quality and Product Cost," *Quality Progress* (June 1987), 63–67. Copyright © 1987, Hewlett-Packard Co. All rights reserved. Reprinted with permission.

5. Carolyn Lochhead, "Liability's Creative Clamp Holds Firms to the Status Quo," *Insight,* 29 August, 1988, 38–40.

6. John H. Farrow, "Product Liability Requirements," *Quality Progress* (May 1980), 34–36; Mick Birmingham, "Product Liability: An Issue for Quality," *Quality* (February 1983), 41–42.

7. Peter Dewhurst, "Product Design for Manufacture: Design for Disassembly," *Industrial Engineering* (September 1993), 26–28.

8. Bruce Nussbaum and John Templeton, "Built to Last—Until It's Time to Take It Apart," *Business Week,* 17 September, 1990, 102–106.

9. Nussbaum and Templeton, see note 8.

10. Susan Dillingham, "A Little Gross Stuff in Food Is OK by FDA," *Insight,* 22 May, 1989, 25.

11. John Mayo, "Process Design as Important as Product Design," reprinted with permission from *The Wall Street Journal,* 29 October, 1984, 29, Dow Jones & Co., Inc. All rights reserved.

12. N. Raghu Kackar, "Off-Line Quality Control, Parameter Design, and the Taguchi Method," *Journal of Quality Technology* 17, no. 4 (October 1985), 176–188.

13. Bruce D. Nordwall, "ITT Uses Process Control Methods to Increase Plant Productivity," *Aviation Week & Space Technology,* 11 May, 1987, 69–74.

14. Joseph J. Pignatiello, Jr., and John S. Ramberg, "The Top 10 Triumphs and Tragedies of Genichi Taguchi," presented at the 35th ASQC/ASA Fall Technical Conference, Lexington, KY, 1991.

15. Genichi Taguchi, *Introduction to Quality Engineering* (Tokyo: Asian Productivity Organization, 1986), 1.

16. *Ashai,* 17 April, 1979; cited in L. P. Sullivan, "Reducing Variability: A New Approach to Quality," *Quality Progress* 17, no. 7 (July 1984), 15–21.

17. This section may be skipped without loss of continuity.

18. H. Richard Priesmeyer, "Integrating Educational Software and Textbook Development," *Academic Computing* (September 1988), 32–33, 50–51.

19. L. P. Sullivan, "Quality Function Deployment: The Latent Potential of Phases III and IV," in A. Richard Shores (ed.) *A TQM Approach to Achieving Manufacturing Excellence* (Milwaukee, WI: ASQC Quality Press, 1990), 265–279.

20. See James R. Evans, *Applied Production and Operations Management,* 5th ed. (St. Paul, MN: West Publishing Co., 1996), for a detailed description of these documents.

21. George Schalk Jr. "Time—The Next Source of Competitive Advantage," *Harvard Business Review* (July/August 1988). Copyright © 1988 by the President and Fellows of Harvard College; all rights reserved. Reprinted in *Quality Progress* (June 1989), 61–68.

22. Richard J. Schonberger, *Japanese Manufacturing Techniques* (New York: The Free Press, 1982), 17–18.

23. Adapted from Kim Blass, "World-Class Strategies Help Create a World-Class CIM Facility," *Industrial Engineering* 24, no. 11 (November 1992), 26–29.

24. C. Hsiang and L. Lee, "Zero Defects: A Quality Costs Approach," *Communications in Statistics—Theory and Methods* 14, no. 11 (1985), 2641–2655.

25. From *Poka-yoke: Improving Product Quality by Preventing Defects.* Edited by NKS/Factory Magazine, English translation copyright © 1988 by Productivity Press, Inc. P.O. Box 3007, Cambridge, MA 02140, (800) 394-6868. Reprinted by permission.

26. Faye Rice, "The New Rules of Superlative Service," *Fortune* (Autumn/Winter 1993), 50–53.

27. John Haywood-Farmer, "A Conceptual Model of Service Quality," *International Journal of Operations and Production Management* 8, no. 6 (1988), 19–29.

28. Charles D. Zimmerman, III, and John W. Enell, "Service Industries," Sec. 33 in J. M. Juran (ed.), *Juran's Quality Control Handbook,* 4th ed. (New York: McGraw-Hill, 1988).

29. AT&T Quality Steering Committee, *Reengineering Handbook,* AT&T Bell Laboratories (1991), 45.

30. Excerpts reprinted from Richard B. Chase and Douglas M. Stewart, "Make Your Service Fail-Safe," *Sloan Management Review* 35, no. 3 (Spring 1994), 35–44. Copyright 1994 by the Sloan Management Review Association. All rights reserved.

31. "A Smarter Way to Manufacture," *Business Week,* 30 April, 1990.

32. Don Clausing and Bruce H. Simpson, "Quality by Design," *Quality Progress* (January 1990), 41–44.

33. Adapted from George Van Treeck and Ray Thackeray, "Quality Function Deployment at Digital Equipment Corporation," *Concurrent Engineering* 1, no. 1 (January/February 1991), 14–20.

34. James W. Dean, Jr., and James R. Evans, *Total Quality: Management, Organization, and Strategy* (St. Paul, MN: West Publishing Co., 1994), 143.

35. Thomas F. O'Boyle, "GE Refrigerator Woes Illustrate the Hazards in Changing a Product." Reprinted by permission of *The Wall Street Journal,* © 7 May, 1990, A1, A6. Dow-Jones & Co., Inc. All rights reserved worldwide.

■ BIBLIOGRAPHY

Akao, Yoji (ed.) *Quality Function Deployment*. Cambridge, MA: Productivity Press, 1990.

Cohen, L. "QFD: An Application Perspective from DEC." *National Productivity Review* 7, no. 3 (1988), 197–208.

Conti, Tito. "Process Management and Quality Function Deployment." *Quality Progress* (December 1989), 45–48.

Davidow, William H., and Bro Uttal. *Total Customer Service*. New York: Harper & Row, 1989.

Day, Ronald G. *Quality Function Deployment*. Milwaukee, WI: ASQC Quality Press, 1993.

Eureka, William E., and Nancy E. Ryan. *The Customer-Driven Company*. Dearborn, MI: American Supplier Institute, 1988.

Fortuna, R. "Beyond Quality: Taking SPC Upstream." *Quality Progress*, 21, no. 6 (June 1988), 23–28.

Johnson, George. "Benchmarking to Success." *APICS—The Performance Advantage* (July 1991), 12–13.

Juran, J.M. *Juran on Quality by Design* New York: The Free Press, 1992.

King, R. "Listening to the Voice of the Customer." *National Productivity Review* 6, no. 3 (1987), 277–281.

Newcomb, John E. "Management by Policy Deployment." *Quality* (January 1989), 28–30.

Reid, R., and M. Hermann. "QFD . . . The Voice of the Customer." *The Journal for Quality and Participation* (December 1989), 44–46.

Sullivan, L. "Quality Function Deployment." *Quality Progress*, 19, no. 6 (June 1986), 39–50.

Walklet, R.H. "Cadillac Motor Car: Using Simultaneous Engineering to Ensure Quality and Continuous Improvement." In Jay W. Spechler (ed.), *Managing Quality in America's Most Admired Companies*. Norcross, GA: Industrial Engineering and Management Press, 1993.

CHAPTER

8

Measurement and Strategic Information Management

"In God we trust; all others use data" is a phrase one often hears in many companies. The principal goal of any employee is to make decisions that further the overall organizational goal of meeting or exceeding customer expectations as well as making productive use of the organization's resources. To make such decisions, employees need *information* about customers, products and services, processes, employees, suppliers, and competitors.

Information derives from analysis of data. Data, in turn, come from measurement. Thus, achieving quality excellence requires a framework of *measurement*, *data*, and *analysis*. *Measurement* is the act of determining whether an object possesses a certain quality characteristic (usually by visual inspection), or quantifying the amount of a quality characteristic using some type of measuring instrument. *Quality characteristics* are those properties of a product that are evaluated against specifications—whether an electronic item fails or passes a functional test, whether an employee followed an established procedure—or quantifiable characteristics such as the diameter, hardness, and weight of a ball bearing, or the time to fill a customer's order. Measurement allows assessment of the degree of conformance to a specification, which, in turn, enables managers and front-line workers to know how close they are to their targets and to set improvement priorities. Measurements provide a scorecard of business performance and make accomplishments visible to everyone. Knowing that one is doing a good job is a powerful motivator.

Measurements allow managers to make decisions on the basis of facts, not opinions. When Dr. Noriaki Kano consulted with Florida Power and Light (FP&L), the company told him that lightning was the principal cause of service interruptions. Kano asked why groundings or arresters had not prevented the interruptions; FP&L replied that these would not work with Florida's severe lightning. Kano asked for the data to back up this conclusion, but FP&L could not produce any. About eighteen months later when Kano next visited the company, they had collected data and found that interruptions occurred even when strong lightning was not present. In addition, they discovered that many utility poles did not have sufficient groundings, a situation they had not recognized until they collected the data.[1]

But measurement can also be dangerous. A phrase that one often hears is "How you are measured is how you perform." Analog Devices, a successful Massachusetts analog and digital equipment manufacturer, embraced TQM but found its stock price steadily declining. One of their key measures (on which managers were rewarded) was new product introduction time, with an objective of reducing it from 36 to six months. The product development team focused on this objective; as a result, engineers turned away from riskier new products and designed mundane derivatives of old products that no longer met customers' needs. The company subsequently scrapped that goal.[2] This example demonstrates the importance of selecting and using the *right* measures.

Inspection and measurement provide data, usually in the form of *quality and operational performance data*. Quality-related data such as defect rates and customer satisfaction results provide input needed for strategic planning, the design of products and services, human resource management, and process improvement. Operational performance data such as yields, cycle times, and productivity measures help managers determine if they are doing the right job, if they are using resources effectively, if they are improving, where problems are occurring, and where corrective action is needed.

Finally, data support analysis at all levels of an organization. Recall the discussion of the "three levels of quality" in Chapter 2. Data at the individual level provide workers with information to control machines and processes. *Control* is the continual process of evaluating performance, comparing that performance to a goal or standard, and taking corrective action when necessary. Control focuses on stability: the elimination of sporadic deviations from stable performance. Thus, control measures are are taken daily or more frequently and are nearly always expressed in nonmonetary terms.

At the process level, data collected through systematic measurement describe process performance and identify areas for improvement. Such data are expressed in both monetary and nonmonetary terms. Teams of workers, supervisors, and managers can use this data to determine causes of quality problems and recommend solutions. At the organization level, quality and operational performance data, along with relevant financial data, form the basis for strategic planning and decision making. They stress performance of the organization as a whole. In summary, data analysis is the foundation for control and improvement.

Although Deming believed in using data as a basis for problem solving, he was highly critical of overemphasizing measurement. He often stated that the most important figures, such as the value of a loyal customer, are unknown and unknowable. Although this is certainly true, considerable value lies in using objective data for planning and decision making. In their book, Osborne and Gaeble make three insightful observations:

1. If you don't measure results, you can't tell success from failure.

2. If you can't see success, you can't reward it—and if you can't reward success, you are probably rewarding failure.

3. If you can't recognize failure, you can't correct it.[3]

Good data and information management provide many benefits:

■ They help the company know that customers are receiving appropriate levels of service because indicators are used to measure it accurately.

■ They provide concrete feedback to workers to verify their progress.

■ They establish a basis for reward and recognition.

■ They provide a means of assessing progress and signaling the need for corrective action.

■ They reduce the costs of operations through better planning and improvement actions.

Despite the fact that more than half of the work force in the United States is engaged in the generation, processing, or dissemination of data and/or information, many companies do a poor job of systematically collecting appropriate data and analyzing it properly. Many managers experience more and more difficulty getting the information they really need, when they need it. Thus, not only are data and information essential to the development and operation of every facet of TQM, but TQM concepts also need to be applied to the generation of data and information. This chapter introduces basic concepts of quality measurement and strategic information management. Specific details of how information is used to control and improve quality by individual workers and teams at the operational level of an organization will be discussed in other chapters throughout the book.

THE STRATEGIC IMPORTANCE OF INFORMATION

Survival in today's competitive business world makes the sharing of information throughout an organization absolutely critical. A supply of consistent, accurate, and timely information across all functional areas facilitates a better organizational response to rapidly changing customer needs. With a comprehensive information strategy, organizations can work with customers and suppliers to reduce costs, improve products and processes, and shorten cycle times. As discussed in the last chapter, for example, new product development requires coordinated information from marketing, design and engineering, manufacturing, and sales. When information is available and accessible, tasks can be completed more quickly, and productivity increases.

Strong information systems tie people together as part of the organization structure. A good analogy for information systems within an organization might be the central nervous system in the body. The central nervous system sends messages to and from the brain to various points in the body where the work gets done, such as lifting, walking, thinking, or digesting food. Effective information systems provide information to the right people, when they need it. By having a central source of information accessible to everyone, individuals in manufacturing can have input to product design and sales; designers can obtain immediate feedback about manufacturing and financial implications of decisions; and everyone can share information for solving problems. Since knowledge translates into power, those who have the necessary information are *empowered* to make decisions and to take action to better serve customers.

One example of the impact of information sytems is the quasi-governmental financial corporation, the Federal National Mortgage Association (Fannie Mae).[4] Until the early 1990s their departmentalized organization and mainframe computer systems had been adequate to service their customers. However, Fannie Mae's management realized the organization was becoming bogged down in paperwork and decided to redesign the organization. They began by replacing rigid departmental structures with process teams that combined financial, marketing, and computer experts to work together on projects. They decentralized the necessary computing power by building a computer network, at a cost of some $10 million, tying together 2000 personal computers with software that made employee access to the information easier and more timely. The real test of the system and its superior productivity came with the falling interest rates in 1992. Fannie Mae managed to handle $257 billion in new loans—almost double their 1991 volume—while adding only 100 employees to their 3000-employee work force. In addition, their increased productivity allowed them to increase their profits by 13 percent to $1.6 billion. By concentrating on the strategic aspects of information, they more successfully met their customers' needs.

Daft discussed the importance of fitting the amount of information and its ''richness'' to organizational tasks and levels.[5] He defines **information richness** as the information-carrying capacity of data. Different media possess different amounts of information richness. For example:

1. Face-to-face is the richest medium. It provides many cues, such as body language and facial expression. Immediate feedback allows understanding to be checked and corrected. This channel is best for mitigating ambiguity, enabling managers to create a shared understanding.

2. Telephone and personal electronic media such as voice mail are next and represent a relatively rich channel because feedback is fast and messages are personally focused, although visual cues are missing.

3. Written, addressed documents—letters, memos, notes, and faxes—are lower in richness. Feedback is slow compared with richer media, and visual cues are minimal.

4. Written, impersonally addressed documents—bulletins, standard computer reports, computer databases, and printouts—are the leanest channels. These documents are not amenable to feedback and are often quantitative in nature. This channel is best for conveying a large amount of precise data to numerous people.

A variety of information richness needs at specific organizational levels can be matched with the type of technology used by those who are doing work at those levels. This matchup ensures that people receive the right kind of information to be effective in their jobs. For example, routine, repetitive jobs on factory production lines or in a bank check processing department might need lean communication channels consisting of bulletins, computerized quality reports, and digital readouts of part dimensions to provide immediate information on what is happening and how things are progressing. At middle levels of organizations, managers need aggregated information—daily or weekly scrap reports, customer complaint data from customer service representatives, or monthly sales and cost figures faxed in from field offices—provided by management information systems and decision support systems that have a moderate amount of information richness. Top management needs information from media with all levels of richness, including written executive information summaries showing performance against quality improvement goals; competitive information, obtained by managers or salespeople and transmitted verbally during a branch office visit; and requirements for work redesign and capital expenditures, transmitted verbally and with drawings during a project design meeting, all of which contribute to improving quality, productivity, and competitiveness.

At least three important trends are emerging in the development and use of information systems and performance management that will have a significant impact on the nature of total quality management. First, use of information technology will become even more pervasive throughout the organization, from the shop floor and the service representative's desk to the chief executive's suite. The second trend is changes in organization structures that empower people to take advantage of the strategic capabilities of information technologies and systems. The third trend is the use of information systems that move quality gains to the bottom line.

■ Leading Practices

Successful companies recognize the importance of reliable and appropriate data and information in strategic planning and daily customer-focused decision making. Data and information are the forces that drive quality excellence and improve operational and competitive performance. Some of the key practices are summarized below.

■ *They develop a comprehensive set of performance indicators that reflect internal and external customer requirements and the key factors that drive the business.* Performance indicators span the entire business operation, from suppliers to customers, and from front-line workers to top levels of management. AT&T Universal Card Services, for example, monitors key indicators for application processing, authorizations management, billing/statement processing, credit screening, credit card protection, payment processing, and relationship management. However, collecting data that no one uses or wants wastes valuable time and resources. Leading companies select appropriate measures and indicators using well-defined criteria. The Wallace Company, for example, has three standards for selecting the quality-related data maintained in its information base:

1. The data should meet internal customer needs, for example, sales reports, inventory records, and financial statements.

2. The data should meet external customer needs, for instance, on-time delivery to the right place.

3. The data should improve the company's quality leadership practices, such as human resource management.

■ *They push responsibility for inspection, measurement, and analysis down to the lowest levels of the organization using sound analytical methods to support analysis and decision making.* No longer do "quality control" departments perform inspection and measurement activities. Instead, organizations expect front-line workers to collect and analyze data from their individual processes as a basis for problem solving and improvement activities. Motorola, for instance, strives to measure every task performed by every one of its 120,000 employees. At GTE Directories, functional and cross-functional teams throughout the company work to maintain up-to-date scope, management, and quality of key operational measurement data. Strong analytical capability is the necessary precursor of good analysis. Leading companies employ a variety of statistical tools and structured approaches for analyzing data and turning it into useful information. They use structured problem-solving processes to study the information for improvement. For instance, FedEx developed a process called FADE: Focus, Analyze, Develop, and Execute, which is implemented through quality action teams.

■ *They ensure that data are reliable, accessible, and widely visible throughout the organization.* The instruments used to capture data must be reliable; that is, they must measure the true value consistently. Therefore, workers must give careful attention to instrument calibration and maintenance, as well as human factors associated with inspection and measurement activity. Most companies now rely on computer-based information systems for data processing and analysis. Texas Instruments, for instance, has a state-of-the art, on-line computer network that serves as the backbone of a comprehensive set of systems supplemented by local processing capabilities. The accuracy and reliability of support software is crucial in these systems. Texas Instruments uses standard formats and interfaces, a central group to conduct system performance review, and extensive training for developers and users.

Leading companies provide rapid access to data and information to all employees who need it. Xerox, for example, maintains one of the most extensive computer networks in the world, linking hundreds of sites on four continents to provide information 24 hours a day, seven days a week. At Milliken and other companies, databases are available to every associate throughout the computer network.

■ *They logically link key external indicators to internal indicators.* Wainwright Industries (see Quality Profile) aligns the company's business objectives with customers' critical success factors: price, line defects, delivery, and partnership. This alignment process prompted the development of five key strategic indicator categories: safety, internal customer satisfaction, external customer satisfaction, defect rate, and business performance. Within each category, Wainwright developed specific indicators and goals. For instance, for external

QUALITY PROFILE

Wainwright Industries, Inc.

Wainwright Industries, Inc., headquartered in St. Peters, Missouri, is a family-owned business that manufactures stamped and machined parts for U.S. and foreign customers in the automotive, aerospace, home security, and information processing industries. Annual sales total $30 million, and the company employs 275 associates. Craftsmanship, teamwork, and innovation have been commitments at Wainwright since its inception in 1947. Delivering products and services of unequaled quality that generate total customer satisfaction is Wainwright's principal objective. This commitment led the company to a Malcolm Baldrige National Quality Award in the small business category in 1994.

Wainwright constantly looks for ways to improve, searching inside and outside the organization for ideas and examples on how to streamline processes, cut delivery times, make training programs more effective, or enhance any other facet of its customer-focused operations. Its empowered work force provides a rich source of ideas; each associate averages more than one implemented improvement per week. From 1992 to 1994, overal customer satisfaction increased from 84 to 95 percent. Simultaneously, defect and scrap rates, manufacturing cycle time, and quality costs fell. Ninety-five percent of all purchase orders are processed within 24 hours. The lead time for making one of its principal products—drawn housings for electric motors—was reduced to 15 minutes from its former level of 8.75 days. Since initiating continuous improvement processes in 1991, the company reports steadily growing market share for its major products, productivity gains exceeding industry averages, and increasing profit margins.

SOURCE: Malcolm Baldrige National Quality Award, *Profiles of Winners,* National Institute of Standards and Technology, Department of Commerce.

customer satisfaction, they measure a satisfaction index and monthly complaints; for business performance, they track sales, capital expenditure, and market share for drawn housings. Data can also provide an indication of cause-and-effect relationships. Companies need to ask the key question: How do overall improvements in product and service quality and operational performance relate to changes in company financial performance and customer satisfaction? Understanding these linkages is vital to developing strategic goals and objectives. Fuji-Xerox, a Japanese subsidiary of Xerox, uses a variety of statistical techniques such as regression and analysis of variance to develop mathematical models relating such factors as copy quality, machine malfunctions, and maintenance time to customer satisfaction results.

■ *They continually refine information sources and their uses within the organization.* Poor data and analysis leads to poor decisions. Leading companies continually improve their analysis capabilities and training, staying abreast of new techniques. They conduct ongoing review and update their sources and uses of data, shorten the cycle time from data gathering to access, and broaden access to everyone who requires data for management and improvement. Xerox developed a Data Systems Quality Assurance approach for the design, development, and major upgrade of each data system. AT&T Universal Card Services uses cross-functional teams and computer technology to evaluate and improve continuously the cycle times from data acquisition through analysis, as well as improving the analysis processes themselves.

These practices encourage "management by fact," one of the key elements of total quality management.

THE SCOPE OF QUALITY AND OPERATIONAL PERFORMANCE DATA

Most businesses have traditionally relied on organizational performance data based on financial considerations, such as return on investment or earnings per share.[6] Unfortunately, many of the indicators are inaccurate and stress quantity over quality.[7] For example, traditional factory performance measurements such as direct labor efficiency and machine utilization promote building unnecessary inventory and overcontrol direct labor. This prevents workers from assuming responsibility for control and from focusing on process improvement. Focusing on machine utilization encourages having fewer, but larger, general purpose machines, resulting in more complex material flows and increasing inventory and throughput time. In traditional manufacturing and service operations, cost was the key measure of performance, particularly in highly competitive markets. Today, however, quality drives decisions. With the growing emphasis on customer satisfaction as a strategic dimension of performance, operational measures such as defect rates and response time take greater precedence.

The Deming flowchart of a production system (Figure 2.1) provides a convenient structure for managing quality-related data and information. The four key points in this system are supplier inputs, outputs, processes (both core and support), and customers, as well as the overall system itself. Thus, effective data and information management should address the following aspects:

1. Supplier performance: the inputs to the production system

2. Product and service quality: the outputs of the system and the core processes that create products and services

3. Business and support services: the functions and processes that support a company's core manufacturing or service capabilities

4. Company operational performance: customer-related and financial data for top-level planning

■ Supplier Performance

Suppliers are critical in achieving quality objectives. The term *supplier* refers to providers of goods and services. The use of these goods and services may occur at any stage during production, delivery, and consumption of the company's products and services. Thus, suppliers include businesses such as distributors, dealers, warranty repair services, contractors, and franchises as well as those providing materials and components.

Customers look for indicators of the quality of purchased goods and services. Clearly, if the quality of purchased materials and parts is poor, so will be the end product. Companies track various types of supplier product quality data: defect rates, functional performance, reliability, and maintainability. Also, service performance data such as timeliness, responsiveness, dependability, and technical support are necessary. Today, many companies go beyond simply evaluating suppliers' products and services to using auditing techniques to evaluate suppliers' systems.

■ Product and Service Quality

Customers demand defect-free products and responsive services. Product and service quality indicators focus on the outcomes of manufacturing and service processes that a company can assess without involving its customers. A common indicator of manufacturing quality is the *number of nonconformities per unit.* Historically, the term *defect* was used instead of *nonconformity.* Because of the negative connotation of *defect* and its potential implications in liability suits, *nonconformity* has become widely accepted. However, in this text, both terms are used interchangeably to be consistent with current literature and practice.

Many companies classify defects into three categories:

1. *Critical defect:* A critical defect is one that judgment and experience indicate will surely result in hazardous or unsafe conditions for individuals using, maintaining, or depending on the product and will prevent proper performance of the product.

2. *Major defect:* A major defect is one not critical but likely to result in failure or to materially reduce the usability of the unit for its intended purpose.

3. *Minor defect:* A minor defect is one not likely to materially reduce the usability of the item for its intended purpose, nor will it have any bearing on the effective use or operation of the unit.[8]

Inspection for critical defects should be conducted at all costs, particularly because critical defects may lead to serious consequences or product liability suits. Inspection of quality characteristics classified as major defects depends on the strategic quality goals of the firm. Any company wishing to remain in business and achieve a competitive advantage in the marketplace must avoid major defects as much as possible. Minor defects may escape inspection in many products, since they do not affect fitness for use. However, for many products, even minor defects can produce negative responses from customers. For example, a marred finish on a wrench would probably not cause much concern to a mechanic, while a similar defect on an automobile body would be unacceptable.

In services, a measure of quality analogous to defects is *errors per opportunity.* Each customer transaction provides an opportunity for many different types of errors. Service indicators linked closely to customer satisfaction provide a basis for improvement efforts. FedEx has an extensive quality measurement system that includes a composite measure, called the service quality indicator (SQI), which is a weighted sum of 10 factors that reflect customers' expectations of company performance. FedEx's SQI is shown in Table 8.1. Different weights reflect the importance of each failure; losing a package, for instance, is more serious that delivering it a few minutes late. The index is reported weekly and summarized on a monthly basis.

Nonconformities per unit and errors per opportunity are often reported as rates per thousand or million. A common measure is *dpmo*—defects per million opportunities. Thus, a defect rate of 2 per thousand is equivalent to 2000 dpmo. At some Motorola factories, quality is so good that they measure defects per *billion!*

In addition to product indicators, firms collect extensive data about the processes that create the products and services. Process data can reflect defect and error rates of intermediate operations, and also internal efficiency measures such as cost, time, and environmental impact. For example, Motorola measures nearly every process in the company, both in terms of defects and errors and time. One

TABLE 8.1   FedEx Service Quality Indicator Factors

Error Type	Description	Weight
1. *Complaints Reopened*—Customer complaints [on traces, invoices, missed pickups, etc.] reopened after an unsatisfactory resolution.		3
2. *Damaged packages*—packages with visible or concealed damage or spoilage due to weather or water damage, missed pickup, or late delivery.		10
3. *International*—a composite score of performance measures of international operations.		1
4. *Invoice adjustments*—customer requests for credit or refunds for real or perceived failures.		1
5. *Late pick-up stops*—packages that were picked up later than the stated pick-up time.		3
6. *Lost packages*—claims for missing packages or with contents missing.		10
7. *Missed proof of delivery*—invoices which lack written proof of delivery information		1
8. *Right Day Late*—delivery past promised time on the right day		1
9. *Traces*—Package status and proof of delivery requests not in the COSMOS IIB computer system (the FedEx "real time" tracking system).		3
10. *Wrong Day Late*—delivery on the wrong day.		5

SOURCE: Service Quality Indicators at Federal Express (internal company document)

of their key business objectives is to reduce total cycle time—the time from the point a customer expresses a need until the customer happily pays the company. All processes within the company, including design, order entry, manufacturing, and marketing, are measured for improvements in error rates and cycle times. Process data may also include operating performance, such as productivity, schedule performance, machine downtime, preventive maintenance activity, rates of problem resolution, energy efficiency, and raw material usage.

■ Business and Support Services

Business and support services are those that typically do not directly add value to a company's core products or services. They include units and operations involving finance and accounting, software services, sales, marketing, public relations, information services, purchasing, personnel, legal services, plant and facilities management, basic R&D, and secretarial and other administrative services. At AT&T Universal Card Services, key support services are collections, constituency management, customer acquisition, human resource management, information management, and financial management. These processes contribute to the quality of a company's core products and services, and are therefore subject to measurement of processing times, error rates, and other relevant performance indicators. A focus on *all* processes in an organization makes quality management "total," and everyone's responsibility.

■ Company Operational Results

Top management is typically most interested in the effectiveness of the overall system itself. Although they use the same types of information as people at lower organizational levels, they deal with data that is more aggregated and often expressed in dollars. Key measures of company operational performance include those that address productivity, efficiency, and effectiveness. Examples include generic indicators such as use of labor, materials, energy, capital, and assets.

Specific indicators might include productivity indexes, waste reduction, energy efficiency, and cycle time. Other important measures of company performance are the attitudes and opinions of employees (discussed further in Chapter 10), and measures of public responsibility, such as ethics, environmental protection, and corporate citizenship.

The two most important types of data in determining quality are customer-related data and financial data. **Customer-related data** can be external or internal. External customer satisfaction measures, discussed in Chapter 5, assess performance of the entire organization and define the internal measures that should be taken. Quality characteristics that are important to customers should drive internal measures. Internal measures might capture shipping effectiveness, response time, or returns. For example, American Express analysts monitor telephone conversations for politeness, tone of voice, accuracy of the transaction, and other customer service aspects. Comparisons between judgments of the analysts and judgments of customers in post-transaction interviews determine the relevance of specific internal measurements. When differences arise between customer satisfaction and internal measures of performance—for instance, when internal measures seem good yet customer satisfaction is low—the company takes it as an indication that it is measuring the wrong things. Thus, companies need to compare external data with internal data.

Top management makes most decisions with an eye toward the bottom line. Financial data relating to quality is necessary to making good decisions. A key financial performance indicator is the **cost of quality,** which managers use to prioritize improvement projects and gage the effectiveness of total quality efforts.

To illustrate the range of measurements that a company can take, Table 8.2 summarizes some of the key measurements taken by Texas Instruments.

TABLE 8.2 Key Quality Measurements at Texas Instruments

Customer-Related Measures
Percent shipping performance
Warehouse errors
Returned material cycle time

Product Quality Measures
Parts per million defective, electrical
Parts per million defective, visual/mechanical
Operating life test

Process Quality Measures
Cycle time
Rework at various stages
Final test yield

Supplier Performance Measures
Parts per million defective
Purity level
Functional test results

Company Operational Performance Measures
Cost of conformance
Cost of nonconformance
Total cost of quality

SOURCE: Cited in J.M. Juran, *Juran on Quality by Design* (New York: The Free Press, 1992), 143–144.

■ Attribute and Variable Measurements

Measurements can be classified in one of two categories. An **attribute** is a characteristic of quality either present or absent in the unit or product under consideration. Attributes assume the values of conformance or nonconformance, within tolerance or out of tolerance, complete or incomplete, or a similar dichotomy. An example would be the visual inspection of the color of an item from a printing process to determine whether it is acceptable. Another example is whether the correct ZIP code was used in shipping an order. A third example is whether the diameter of a shaft falls within specification limits of 1.60 ± 0.01". Attributes lead to discrete measurements such as counts of the fraction of nonconformances in a group, number of defects per unit, or rate of errors per opportunity.

The second type of quality characteristic is called a **variable.** Variables are appraised in terms of measurable values on a continuous scale, for instance, length or weight. Variables measurements are concerned with the *degree* of conformance to specifications. Thus, rather than determining whether the diameter of a shaft meets a specification of 1.60 ± 0.01", a measure of the actual value of the diameter is taken. Table 8.3 provides additional examples of both attribute and variables measurements.

Inspection by attributes is usually simpler than inspection by variables for several reasons. The inspection itself can be done more quickly and easily; less information needs to be recorded; and administration of the inspection is easier. In a statistical sense, however, attributes inspection is less efficient than variables inspection. Thus, attributes inspection requires a larger sample than variables inspection to obtain the same amount of statistical information about the quality of the product. (These issues are discussed further in Part III of this book.) This difference can become significant when inspection is time-consuming or expensive. Most quality characteristics in services are attributes, which is perhaps one reason why service organizations have been slow to adopt measurement-based quality management approaches.

DEVELOPING QUALITY PERFORMANCE INDICATORS

What quality performance indicators would the manager of a small pizza franchise that offers eat-in dining and local delivery use to monitor the business? Of the several dozen that come to mind, such a business would not have the time and resources to measure or observe all of them. In other words, any given business needs to select the most meaningful quality performance indicators.

Many companies collect the wrong data, if they collect data at all. Companies generally make two fundamental mistakes: (1) not measuring key characteristics critical to company performance or customer satisfaction, and (2) taking irrelevant or inappropriate measurements. In the first case, the company often fails to meet customer expectations to the fullest extent and possibly loses competitive advantage. In the second, the company directs attention to areas that are not important to customers, thus wasting time and resources. The number of performance indicators seems to grow with the size and complexity of the organization. Many performance indicators have been around for a long time, and few managers can probably say where, when, and why they developed. In most cases, somebody decided they were a good thing to have. For example, IDS

TABLE 8.3   Examples of Attributes and Variables Measurements

Attributes
  Percent accurate invoices
  Number of lost parcels
  Number of complaints
  Mistakes per week
  Percent shipments on time
  Errors per thousand lines of code
  Percent absenteeism

Variables
  Time waiting for service
  Hours per week correcting documents
  Time to process travel expense accounts
  Days from order receipt to shipment
  Cost of engineering changes per month
  Time between system crashes
  Cost of rush shipments

Financial Services, a subsidiary of American Express, used to measure more than 4000 individual tasks: functions like phone calls, mail coding, and application acceptance. Many of these tasks were subject to 100 percent inspection. Now, after redesigning their information management system, they measure 80 service processes and use statistical sampling.

Generally, product and service quality performance indicators should represent the most important factors that *predict* customer satisfaction and quality in customer use. This statement makes sense when referring back to Figure 5.1. The goal of production is to develop products and services that close the gap between customers' expected quality and actual quality. Customer needs lead to standards for product characteristics. Appropriate indicators then tell whether the standards are being met. The First National Bank of Chicago, for instance, asked its customers what they considered as good-quality features of a product and the delivery of those features.[9] Responses included timeliness, accuracy, operations efficiency, economics, and customer responsiveness. These responses initiated the development of 700 quality indicators such as lockbox processing time, bill keying accuracy, customer service inquiry resolution time, and money transfer timeliness. The right internal measurements provide timely information to take corrective action and anticipate problems before the customer encounters them.

In addition to a solid relationship to customer requirements, good indicators should be easy to understand and interpret, provide factual assistance for decision making, enable comparative analysis, and be economical to apply. Indicators for internal customers are just as important; a painting operation, for instance, depends on the results of a washing and cleaning operation.

Consider the pizza franchise. Suppose that market research determines that two of the key customer expectations are a tasty pizza and a pleasant eating environment. As discussed in the last chapter, customer expectations must be translated into product characteristics. Suppose that a product characteristic for a "tasty pizza" is fresh ingredients. One possible measure for "fresh ingredients" is time elapsed since purchase. Similarly, a product characteristic for "pleasant eating environment" might be a clean dining area, measured by the number of times that customers must wait for a table to be cleaned, number of clean tables available at 15-minute intervals, or frequency of washing the floor. An important question to ask is: Will an improvement in the performance of this quality indicator lead to more satisfied customers? If no apparent relationships can be distinguished, then perhaps new indicators should be used. Data that is preventive in nature enables the organization to pinpoint key problems and areas where something could go wrong or customers could become dissatisfied, or to identify opportunities to delight the customer.

Good indicators are also driven by other factors that determine what is important to the success of the business. **Key business factors** are those strategic elements of a business that drive all major elements of the quality system: strategic planning, design and management of process quality, human resources development and management, as well as information and analysis. Key business factors include

- the nature of a company's products and services
- principal customers
- major markets
- key customer quality requirements
- position in market and competitive environment
- facilities and technologies
- suppliers
- regulatory environment
- other factors, such as new company thrusts, industry changes, etc.

If managers can define the key factors that make the business run successfully, then they can more easily define the appropriate measurements and data requirements. For example, a computer software company does not need to collect extensive data on environmental quality issues whereas a chemical company certainly would. A pizza franchise that delivers bulk orders to fraternities and parties around a college campus would have a different set of key business factors than one in a quiet suburban residential neighborhood.

Most companies usually have a set of existing indicators. To assess their value, management must consider how these indicators relate to customer expectations and company operational performance. A convenient tool to help answer this question is a matrix diagram introduced in Chapter 5. Figure 8.1 shows an example. The rows correspond to customer requirements and key operational performance factors, and the columns correspond to existing indicators. A simple check mark can be used to designate that an indicator relates to a requirement. With such a matrix, managers can see whether all requirements are being measured, or if some indicators do not relate to key requirements and therefore can be eliminated. Quality function deployment, discussed in Chapter 7, is a more formal approach for accomplishing the task.

To generate useful performance measures a systematic process is required.[10]

1. *Identify all customers of the system and determine their requirements and expectations.* Organizations need answers to key questions: Who are my customers? and What do they expect? Many of the tools introduced in Chapter 5 can be used in this step, including customer surveys, focus groups, and user panels. Customer expectations change over time; thus, regular feedback must be obtained.

2. *Define the work process that provides the product or service.* Key questions include: What do I do that impacts customer needs? and What is my process?

FIGURE 8.1   Matrix Diagram for Evaluating Measurements and Customer Requirements

Requirements	Time Between Seating and Ordering	Time from Ordering to Delivery	Amount of toppings	. . .
Hot pizza		✓		
Tasty			✓	
Good service	✓			
Good value			✓	
Correct order				
. . .				
. . .				

The use of flowcharts described in Chapter 2 can stimulate the definition of work processes and internal customer–supplier relationships.

3. *Define the value-adding activities and outputs that compose the process.* This step—identifying each part in the system in which value is added and an intermediate output is produced—weeds out activities that do not add value to the process and contribute to waste and inefficiency. Analysis performed in this step identifies the internal customers within the process along with their needs and expectations.

4. *Develop performance measures or indicators.* Each key activity identified in step 3 represents a critical point where value is added to the output for the next (internal) customer until the final output is produced. At these checkpoints, performance can be measured. Key questions include: What factors determine how well the process is producing according to customer requirements? What deviations can occur? What sources of variability can occur?

5. *Evaluate the performance measures to ensure their usefulness.* Questions to consider include: Are measurements taken at critical points where value-adding activities occur? Are measurements controllable? Is it feasible to obtain the data needed for each measure? Have operational definitions for each measurement been established? *Operational definitions* are precise definitions of measurements that have no ambiguities. For example, when measuring "invoice errors," a precise definition of what is an error and what is not is needed. Does an error include an omission of information, wrong information, misspelling? Operational definitions provide a common understanding and enhance communication throughout the organization.

To illustrate this approach, consider the process of placing and filling a pizza order. Customer expectations include a quick response and a fair price. The process that provides this service is shown in Figure 8.2. To begin, the order taker is an (internal) customer of the caller (who provides the pizza order). Later, the caller is a customer of the deliverer (either at the pickup window or the caller's home). Also, the cook is a customer of the order taker (who prepares the documentation for the ordered pizza).

Some possible performance measures include:

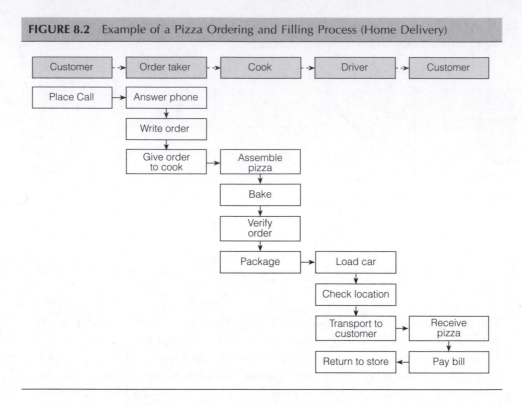

FIGURE 8.2 Example of a Pizza Ordering and Filling Process (Home Delivery)

■ Number of pizzas, by type per hour. If this number is high relative to the kitchen's capacity, then perhaps cooking time and/or preparation is being short-cut or delivery times are stretched out.

■ Order accuracy (as transmitted to the kitchen). This measure can indicate a lack of attention or knowledge on the part of the order taker.

■ Number of pizzas rejected per number prepared. A high number for this measure can indicate a lack of proper training of cooks, resulting in poor products and customer complaints.

■ Time to delivery. This measure might indicate a problem within the restaurant or inadequate training of the driver. (Of course, as happened with Domino's, measuring delivery time could encourage drivers to drive too fast and lead to safety problems.)

■ Number of errors in collections. Errors here can result in lost profits and higher prices.

■ Raw materials (dough, etc.) or finished pizzas inventory. A high number might result in spoilage and excess costs. Low inventory might result in lost orders or excessive customer waiting time.

Notice that these measures—only a few among many possible measures—are related to the customer expectations.

THE COST OF QUALITY

In most firms, cost accounting has been an important function. All organizations measure and report costs as a basis for control and improvement. The concept of the cost of quality emerged in the 1950s. Traditionally, the reporting of quality-related costs had been limited to inspection and testing; other costs were accumulated in overhead accounts. As managers began to define and isolate the full range of quality-related costs, a number of surprising facts emerged.[11] First, quality-related costs were much larger than previously reported, generally in the range of 20 to 40 percent of sales. Second, quality-related costs were not only related to manufacturing operations, but to ancillary services such as purchasing and customer service departments as well. Third, most of the costs resulted from poor quality and were avoidable. Finally, while the costs of poor quality were avoidable, no clear responsibility for action to reduce them was assigned, nor was any structured approach formulated to do so. As a result, many companies began to develop *cost of quality* programs. The "costs of quality"—or more specifically, the costs of *poor* quality—were associated with avoiding poor quality or incurred as a result of poor quality.

Quality cost programs have numerous objectives. Perhaps the most important objective is to translate quality problems into the "language" of upper management—the language of money. Juran noted that workers and supervisor speak in the "language of things"—units, defects, and so on. Unfortunately, quality problems expressed as the number of defects typically have little impact on top managers who are generally more concerned with financial performance. But if the magnitude of quality problems can be translated into monetary terms, such as "How much would it cost us to run this business if there were no quality problems?" the eyes of upper managers are opened. Dollar figures can be added meaningfully across departments or products and compared to other dollar measures. Middle managers who must deal with both workers and supervisors as well as top management must have the ability to speak in both languages.

Quality cost information serves a variety of other purposes. It helps management evaluate the relative importance of quality problems and thus identify major opportunities for cost reduction. It can aid in budgeting and cost control activities. Finally, it can serve as a scoreboard to evaluate the organization's success in achieving quality objectives.

To establish a cost of quality program, one must *identify* the activities that generate cost, *measure* them, *report* them in a way that is meaningful to managers, and *analyze* them to identify areas for improvement. The following sections discuss these activities in greater detail.

■ Quality Cost Classification

Quality costs can be organized into four major categories: prevention costs, appraisal costs, internal failure costs, and external failure costs. **Prevention costs** are expended in an effort to keep nonconforming products from occurring and reaching the customer, including the following specific costs:

■ *Quality planning costs*, such as salaries of individuals associated with quality planning and problem-solving teams, the development of new procedures, new equipment design, and reliability studies.

■ *Process control costs*, which include costs spent on analyzing production processes and implementing process control plans.

■ *Information systems costs* expended to develop data requirements and measurements.

■ *Training and general management costs*, including internal and external training programs, clerical staff expenses, and miscellaneous supplies.

Appraisal costs are expended on ascertaining quality levels through measurement and analysis of data in order to detect and correct problems. Categories of appraisal costs include

■ *Test and inspection costs* associated with incoming materials, work-in-process, and finished goods, including equipment costs and salaries.

■ *Instrument maintenance costs* due to calibration and repair of measuring instruments.

■ *Process measurement and control costs,* which involve the time spent by workers to gather and analyze quality measurements.

Internal failure costs are incurred as a result of unsatisfactory quality found before the delivery of a product to the customer; some examples include

■ *Scrap and rework costs,* including material, labor, and overhead.

■ *Costs of corrective action,* arising from time spent determining the causes of failure and correcting production problems.

■ *Downgrading costs,* such as revenue lost when selling a product at a lower price because it does not meet specifications.

■ *Process failures,* such as unplanned machine downtime or unplanned equipment repair.

External failure costs occur after poor quality products reach the customer, specifically

■ *Costs due to customer complaints and returns,* including rework on returned items, cancelled orders, and freight premiums.

■ *Product recall costs and warranty claims,* including the cost of repair or replacement as well as associated administrative costs.

■ *Product liability costs,* resulting from legal actions and settlements.

Experts estimate that 60 to 90 percent of total quality costs are the result of internal and external failure and are not easily controllable by management. In the past, managers reacted to high failure costs by increasing inspection. Such actions, however, only increase appraisal costs. The overall result is little, if any, improvement in quality or profitability. In practice, an increase in prevention usually generates larger savings in all other cost categories. In a typical scenario, the cost of replacing a poor-quality component in the field might be $500; the cost of replacement after assembly might be $50; the cost of testing and replacement during assembly might be $5; and the cost of changing the design to avoid the problem might be only 50 cents.

Better prevention of poor quality clearly reduces internal failure costs, since fewer defective items are made. External failure costs also decrease. In addition, less appraisal is required, since the products are made correctly the first time. However, since production is usually viewed in the short term, many managers fail to understand or implement these ideas.

A convenient way of reporting quality costs is through a breakdown by organizational function as shown in Figure 8.3. This matrix serves several purposes. First, it allows all departments to recognize their contributions to the cost of quality and participate in a cost of quality program. Second, it pinpoints areas of high quality cost and turns attention toward improvement efforts.

As with productivity measures, quality costs are often reported as an index; that is, the ratio of the current value to a base period. Index numbers increase

FIGURE 8.3 Cost of Quality Matrix

	Design Engineering	Purchasing	Production	...	Finance	...	Accounting	Totals
Prevention costs Quality planning Training ...								
Appraisal costs Test and inspection Instruments ...								
Internal failure costs Scrap Rework ...								
External failure costs Returns Recall costs ...								
Totals								

managers' understanding of the data, particularly how conditions in one period compare with those in other periods. A simple type of index is called a **relative index,** computed by dividing a current value by a base period value. Sometimes the result is multiplied by 100 to express it as a percentage. As an example, consider the following direct labor costs per quarter for a manufactured product:

Quarter	Cost
1	$1500
2	1800
3	1700
4	1750

If the first quarter is the base period, the cost relative indexes expressed as percentages are computed as

Quarter	Cost Relative Index
1	(1500/1500)(100) = 100
2	(1700/1500)(100) = 120
3	(1700/1500)(100) = 113.33
4	(1750/1500)(100) = 116.67

Costs and prices are often sensitive to changes in the firm. For example, if the number of units produced in each quarter differs, comparisons of direct labor costs are meaningless. However, a measure such as cost per unit would provide useful information for managers.

Quality costs themselves provide little information, since they may vary due to such factors as production volume or seasonality. Thus, index numbers can more effectively analyze quality cost data. Some common measurement bases are labor, manufacturing cost, sales, and units of product. Each is described here.

Labor Base Index *Quality cost per direct labor hour* represents a typical quality cost index that is easily understood by managers. Accounting departments can usually provide direct labor data—either total labor hours or standard labor hours. Standard hours often provide a better measure than total labor hours since they represent planned rather than actual production. Because labor-based indexes are drastically influenced by automation and other changes in technology, one must be careful in using them over long periods of time. Often quality cost per direct labor dollar is used to eliminate the effects of inflation.

Cost Base Index *Quality cost per manufacturing cost dollar* is a common index in this category. Manufacturing cost includes direct labor, material, and overhead costs that are usually available from accounting departments. Cost-based indexes are more stable than labor-based indexes, since they are not affected by price fluctuations or by changes in the level of automation.

Sales Base Index *Quality cost per sales dollar* is a popular index that appeals to top management. However, this measure is rather poor for short-term analysis, since sales usually lag behind production and are subject to seasonal variations. In addition, a sales base index is affected by changes in the selling price.

Unit Base Index A common measure in this category is *quality costs per unit of production.* This simple index is acceptable if the output of production lines is similar; however, it is a poor measure if many different products are made. In such a case, an alternative index of quality costs per equivalent unit of output is often used. To obtain this index, different product lines are weighted to approximate a standard or "average" product that is used as a common base.

All of these indexes, although used extensively in practice, have a fundamental problem. A change in the denominator can appear to be a change in the level of quality or productivity alone. For instance, if direct labor is decreased through managerial improvements, the direct labor-based index will increase even if quality does not change. Also, the common inclusion of overhead in manufacturing cost is certain to distort results. Nevertheless, use of such indexes is widespread and useful for comparing quality costs over time. Generally, sales bases are the most popular, followed by cost, labor, and unit bases.[12]

Quality cost data can be broken down by product line, process, department, work center, time, or cost category. This categorization makes data analysis more convenient and useful to management. For example, a company might collect quality costs by cost category and product for each time period, say one month. An example is given in the table below:

	JANUARY		FEBRUARY	
Cost category	Product A	Product B	Product A	Product B
Prevention	$ 2,000	$ 4,000	$ 2,000	$ 4,000
Appraisal	10,000	20,000	13,000	21,000
Internal failure	19,000	106,000	16,000	107,000
External failure	54,000	146,000	52,000	156,000
Total	85,000	276,000	83,000	288,000
Standard direct labor costs	35,000	90,000	28,000	86,000

A total quality cost index is

Quality cost index = total quality costs/direct labor costs

Alternatively, individual indexes can be computed by category, product, and time period, and are summarized in the following table.

	JANUARY		FEBRUARY	
Cost category	Product A	Product B	Product A	Product B
Prevention	.057	.044	.071	.047
Appraisal	.286	.222	.464	.244
Internal failure	.543	1.178	.571	1.244
External failure	1.543	1.622	1.857	1.814
Total	2.429	3.067	2.964	3.349

Such information can be used to identify trends or areas that require significant attention. Of course, such information can only signal areas for improvement; it cannot tell managers what the specific problems are. Teams of workers are responsible for uncovering the sources of problems and determining appropriate corrective action. For example, a steady rise in internal failure costs and decline in appraisal costs might indicate a problem in assembly, maintenance of testing equipment, or a lack of proper control of purchased parts.

A useful analysis tool is called **Pareto analysis.** This term was coined by Joseph Juran in the 1950s after observing that the majority of quality problems generally results from only a few causes. Juran named this technique after Vilfredo Pareto (1848–1923), an Italian economist who determined that 85 percent of the wealth in Milan was owned by only 15 percent of the people. In the context of quality costs, the sources of cost are rarely uniformly distributed. Pareto analysis consists of ordering cost categories from largest to smallest. For example, chances are that 70 or 80 percent of all internal failure costs are due to only one or two manufacturing problems. Identifying these "vital few" as they are called leads to corrective action that has a high return for a low dollar input. Pareto analysis, as discussed in the next chapter has many other applications in quality improvement.

For most companies embarking on a quality cost program, management typically finds that the highest costs occur in the external failure category, followed by internal failure, appraisal, and prevention, in that order. Clearly, the order should be reversed; that is, the bulk of quality costs should be found in prevention, some in appraisal, perhaps a little in internal failure, and virtually none in external failure. Thus, companies should first attempt to drive external failure costs to zero by investing in appraisal activities to discover the sources of failure and take corrective action. As quality improves, failure costs will decrease, and the amount of appraisal can be reduced with the shift of emphasis to prevention activities.

■ Establishing Cost of Quality Reporting Systems[13]

The Institute of Management Accountants recommends a 12-step process to establish a quality cost reporting system. The 12 steps are summarized here.

  1. *Obtain management commitment and support:* Establishing a quality cost system might be initiated by top management; in such cases, the commitment is clear. In other cases, the idea might arise from accounting or quality assurance personnel. Often, management must be convinced of its necessity. However, management can be easily persuaded through the development of an estimate of the cost of quality. Very often the magnitude of such costs will prompt immediate management support. Without management support, any initiatives are likely to fail and should not be pursued.

2. *Establish an installation team:* Individuals from throughout the organization should be selected for a quality cost team, including product managers, engineers, line workers, customer service representatives, and others who can identify specific quality cost elements. Users of the information also should participate actively.

3. *Select an organizational segment as a prototype:* As with any new program, start small and expand after gaining experience. The initial segment might be a specific product, department, or plant. It should be one believed to have high, measurable quality costs.

4. *Obtain cooperation and support of users and suppliers of information:* Both users and suppliers of information should be part of the installation team. Uncooperative suppliers can force delays in reporting information and render the system useless. Unused reports provide no benefit. Open communication is the key to obtaining cooperation. All parties must understand the nature and use of quality costs—a tool for improvement, not punishment.

5. *Define quality costs and quality cost categories:* The idea of quality costs is new to most individuals. The classifications of prevention, appraisal, internal failure, and external failure are most typical, but other suggestions should be considered. To avoid misunderstandings, operational definitions of each cost category should be written and distributed to all users and suppliers of quality cost information.

6. *Identify quality costs within each category:* As a starting point, ask users and suppliers of information to identify specific costs incurred because of poor quality. Considerable debate often surrounds the defining and classifying of specific quality costs. Sometimes several iterations are necessary before consensus is reached.

7. *Determine the sources of quality cost information:* Data may not be readily available in existing accounting systems. If the information is to be useful, quality costs must be visible and not buried within other accounts. Because some data may not be available, the team must determine if the extra effort necessary to collect such data is warranted or if estimates will suffice.

8. *Design quality cost reports and graphs:* Reports and visual aids must meet the needs of the users of the information. Lower organizational levels generally require more detailed information than upper levels. Appropriate stratification of the information by product line, department, or plant, for example, further aids analysis. Also, the form of quality cost indexes must be determined.

9. *Establish procedures to collect quality cost information:* Specific tasks are best assigned to individuals who understand what they are to do and how to do it. Forms can be designed to make the task as simple as possible, and computer system personnel should be consulted as necessary.

10. *Collect data, prepare and distribute reports:* If the preceding steps have been carefully performed, this step should become routine as users become familiar with the procedures.

11. *Eliminate bugs from the system:* In early trials, unreliable or unavailable data, employees who feel uncomfortable in collecting the data or interpreting the results, or computer system problems are all issues that may require attention and, eventually, resolution.

12. *Expand the system:* After the initial project has succeeded, plans should be developed to expand the system to other segments of the organization. Rotation of membership on the quality cost team broadens the base of persons who understand the system operation. Also, the system should be reviewed periodically and modified as necessary.

■ Quality Costs in Service Organizations

The nature of quality costs differs between service and manufacturing organizations. In manufacturing, quality costs are primarily product oriented; for services, however, they are generally labor dependent. Since quality in service organizations depends on employee–customer interaction, appraisal costs tend to account for a higher percentage of total quality costs than in manufacturing. In addition, internal failure costs tend to be much lower for service organizations with high customer contact, which have little opportunity to correct an error before it reaches the customer. By that time, the error becomes an external failure.

Since a far greater proportion of operating cost is attributed to people, a reduction in total quality costs often means a reduction in time worked and hence in personnel, particularly if a large proportion of time is built into the system for rework and other failure activities. Unless a positive strategy is developed to make alternative use of human talents, the threat of job losses will surely result in the lack of cooperation in developing and using a quality cost program.

External failure costs can become an extremely significant out-of-pocket expense to consumers of services. Consider the costs of interrupted service, such as telephone, electricity, or other utilities; delays in waiting to obtain service or excessive time in performing the service; errors made in billing, delivery, or installation; or unnecessary service. For example, a family moving from one city to another may have to pay additional costs for lodging and meals because the moving van does not arrive on the day promised; a doctor's prescription needs to be changed because of faulty diagnosis and the patient pays for unnecessary drugs; or a computer billing error requires several phone calls, letters, and copies of cancelled checks to correct.

Work measurement and sampling techniques are often used extensively to gather quality costs in service organizations. For example, work measurement can be used to determine how much time an employee spends on various quality-related activities. The proportion of time spent multiplied by the individual's salary represents an estimate of the quality cost for that activity. Consumer surveys and other means of customer feedback are also used to determine quality costs for services. In general, however, the intangible nature of the output makes quality cost accounting for services difficult.

■ Activity-Based Costing[14]

The importance of quality has had a major impact on the role of accounting systems in business. Standard accounting systems are generally able to provide quality cost data for direct labor, overhead, scrap, warranty expenses, product liability costs, and maintenance, repair, and calibration of test equipment. However, most accounting systems are not structured to capture important cost-of-quality information. Costs such as service effort, product design, remedial engineering effort, rework, in-process inspection, and engineering change losses must usually be estimated or collected through special efforts. Some costs due to external failure, such as customer dissatisfaction and future lost revenues are impossible to estimate accurately. Although prevention costs are the most important, appraisal costs, internal failure, external failure, and prevention costs (in that order) are usually easier to collect.

As Johnson and Kaplan noted, "Today's management information, driven by the procedures and cycle of the organization's financial reporting system is too late, too aggregated, and too distorted to be relevant for managers' planning and control decisions."[15] They summarize the consequences as follows:

■ Accounting information provides little help for reducing costs and improving productivity and quality. Indeed, the information might even be harmful.

■ The systems do not produce accurate product costs for pricing, sourcing, product mix, and responses to competition.

■ The system encourages managers to contract to the short-term cycle of the monthly profit-and-loss statement.

Traditional accounting systems focused on promoting the efficiency of mass production, particularly production with few standard products and high direct labor. Traditional systems accurately measure the resources that are consumed in proportion to the number of units produced of individual products. Today's products are characterized by much lower direct labor, and many activities that consume resources are unrelated to the volume of units produced. Due to automation, direct labor typically is only 15 percent of manufacturing cost and can be as low as five percent in high-tech industries. Meanwhile, overhead costs have grown to 55 percent or more, and are spread across all products using the same formula. Because of these changes, traditional accounting systems present an inadequate picture of manufacturing efficiency and effectiveness and do a poor job of allocating the expenses of these support resources to individual products. Moreover, they attach no value to such elements as rework or bottlenecks that impede processing. Since these costs are hidden, managers typically have little incentive to cut them.

A new approach to management accounting, called *activity-based costing*, organizes information about the work (or activity) that consumes resources and delivers value in a business. People consuming resources in work ultimately achieve the value that customers pay for. Examples of activities might be moving, inspecting, receiving, shipping, and order processing. To get a handle on these activities, cross-functional teams of workers, managers, and even secretaries map each step of every business process using flowcharts. These flowcharts pinpoint the operations that add value and reveal the ones that do not.

Activity-based costing allocates overhead costs to the products and services that use them. Knowing the costs of activities supports efforts to improve processes. Once activities can be traced to individual products or services, then additional strategic information is made available. The effects of delays and inefficiencies become readily apparent. The company can then focus on reducing these hidden costs.

The differences between traditional and activity-based cost accounting systems are reflected in Figures 8.4 and 8.5. In Figure 8.4, overhead costs are assigned to

FIGURE 8.4   Two-Stage Allocation Process: Traditional Cost System

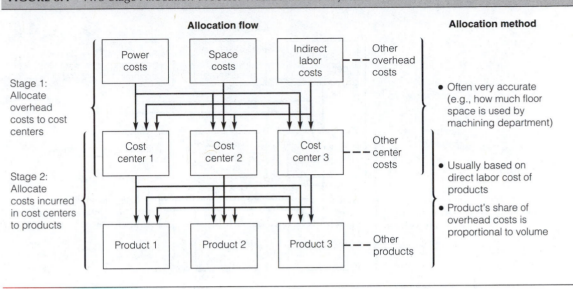

SOURCE: Robert S. Cooper and Robert S. Kaplan, *The Design of Cost Management Systems: Text and Readings* © 1991, p. 269. Reprinted by permission of Prentice-Hall, Englewood Cliffs, NJ.

cost centers, and then the accumulated costs are allocated to products proportional to elements such as direct labor or machine hours. In Figure 8.5, the expenses of support departments are assigned to the activities performed, such as machine setup, direct labor support, and parts administration. The expenses of each activity are then assigned to products based on the products' demand for the activities.

With the new information provided by activity-based costing, managers can make better decisions about product designs, process improvements, pricing, and product mix. Other benefits include the facilitation of continuous improvement activities to reduce overhead costs, and the ease with which relevant costs can be determined. For instance, Caterpillar Inc., used activity-based costing to determine the value of intangibles such as better quality and faster time-to-market to persuade the board to approve a $2 billion modernization effort in 1987. LTV has incorporated activity-based costing into its Integrated Process Management Methodology.[16] The accounting department supports the manufacturing and other departments by providing information on product costing and operating activities to evaluate performance, identify deficiencies, and quality costs arising from internal and external failure of products and customer product requirements. The system helps managers to integrate customer requirements with product improvement strategies.

An example of the power of activity-based costing involves Tektronix, Inc.[17] In late 1987, Gene Hendrickson, a plant manager of a printed circuit board plant in Forest Grove, Oregon, was concerned that unless profit-center performance improved, Tektronix would sell the operation. The plant had only recently adopted a just-in-time inventory system and rigorous quality controls that drastically improved reject rates. Using an activity-based cost management system, he found that high-volume, low-technology circuit boards produced mainly for internal consumption drew on so many resources that they generated negative profit margins of 46 percent and stole profits from other products. The system also uncovered other hidden costs stemming from delays in processing orders.

FIGURE 8.5 Two-Stage Assignment Process: Activity-Based Cost System

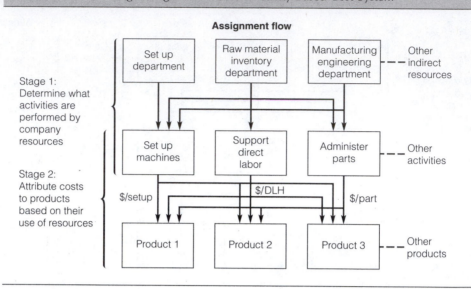

SOURCE: Robert S. Cooper and Robet S. Kaplan, *The Design of Cost Management Systems: Text and Readings* © 1991, p. 270. Reprinted by permission of Prentice-Hall, Englewood Cliffs, NJ.

With these findings, he persuaded the company to install new systems, such as an electronic link allowing customers to place orders directly with the plant's production scheduling computer. Factory operating margins improved to about four times the industry's average. Hendrickson observed that once activity-based costing revealed Tektronix's true costs, all their quality efforts came together.

This method can be easily adopted by service organizations in a straightforward manner. One of the major differences is that in manufacturing, demands for support resources arise from product volumes and mix. In services, many expenses stem from demands by individual customers. Large variations occur in the demands that different customers place on the organization even when they are using the same basic product. Thus, an organization must model customers' behavior when analyzing the source of demands for service functions.

The activity-based costing approach is gaining popularity as inexpensive computer software is developed to support it. Executives of the "Big Six" accounting firms believe that cost management is headed for sweeping reform based on this approach.

MANAGING DATA AND INFORMATION

Good information management is critical to business success. First, companies must ensure that data are reliable and accessible to all who need them. Second, they must use appropriate tools to analyze information.

■ Data Reliability

The familiar computer cliche, "Garbage in, garbage out," applies equally well to quality-related data. Any measurement is subject to error, and as a result, the credibility of the data can be suspect. For example, if two or more measurements are made of the same characteristic and the values are different, one might wonder what caused the variation, and more importantly, what is the correct value. A good measurement system must take into account the reliability of the data. **Reliability** of a measurement refers to how well the measuring instrument—manual instruments, automated equipment, or surveys and questionnaires—consistently measures the "true value" of the characteristic. Measurement reliability in manufacturing demands careful attention to metrology, the science of measurement. Metrology is discussed in Chapter 14.

In services, a useful approach to ensuring data reliability is periodic audits of the processes used to collect the data, conducted by internal cross-functional teams or external auditors, who assess the reliability of a company's data. Standardized forms, clear instructions, and adequate training lead to more consistent performance in data collection. At AT&T Universal Card Services, for example, standard data entry templates and procedures facilitate the consistency and uniform editing of manually input data. Data collected automatically from interfaces with other systems use standard record formats and edits, and are reconciled at each handoff. Also, a central data dictionary defines critical data elements according to source, meaning, format, and valid content of each. AT&T follows stringent guidelines and standards for developing, maintaining, documenting, and managing data systems.

Data Accessibility

A company's efforts are wasted if collected data are not available to the right employees when needed. In most companies, data are accessible to top managers and others on a need-to-know basis. In TQM-focused companies, quality-related data are accessible to everyone. A customer service representative who tells a customer that the rep needs to find some information and will call back the next day cannot satisfy that customer in a timely fashion. At Milliken, all databases, including product specifications, process data, supplier data, customer requirements, and environmental data are available to every associate throughout the computer network. Electronic charts displayed throughout the plant and in business support departments show key quality measures and trends. Salespeople at the Wallace Company can check inventory available at any district office. Data accessibility empowers employees and encourages their participation in quality improvement efforts.

Modern information technology plays a critical role in data accessibility. Many companies have state-of-the-art on-line computer networks supplemented by local processing capabilities. Prudential Insurance Company agents take portable computers to customer's homes or places of business.[18] This practice reduces the time needed to answer a client's questions and increases the accuracy and reliability of the answers. Sales and service offices are connected electronically. Each can obtain information about the current status of contracts being serviced by another office, and so, be of assistance to customers who contact them instead. They can also electronically forward requests for action to the appropriate office.

Analysis and Use of Quality-Related Data and Information

Data related to quality, customers, and operational performance support strategic planning and decision making. For such support to be effective, it must take the form of useful measures—an aggregation of a variety of data—that top management can understand and work with. Some companies develop an aggregate customer satisfaction index (CSI) by weighting satisfaction results, market share, and gains or losses of customers. Previous text discussed how FedEx aggregates different quality components into a single index. However, simply aggregating data is not enough. Managers must also understand the linkages between quality and key measures of business performance. For example, a company should understand how product and service quality improvement correlates with such business indicators as customer satisfaction, retention, market share, operating costs, revenues, and value-added per employee; how employee satisfaction relates to customer satisfaction; and how problem resolution affects costs and revenues. Establishing a clear cause and effect linkage between results and internal measures provides a visible and obvious direction for improvement. FedEx correlates the 10 quality components with customer satisfaction through extensive market research. Additionally, they conduct focus groups and other surveys to validate these relationships.

Interlinking is the term that describes the quantitative modeling of cause and effect relationships between external and internal performance criteria—such as the relationship of customer satisfaction measures to internal process measures.[19] A simple interlinking model was developed by Florida Power and Light.[20] In studying the telephone operation of their customer service centers, FP&L sampled customers to determine their level of satisfaction with waiting times on the telephone. Satisfaction began to fall significantly at about two minutes (see Figure 8.6). They also found that customer satisfaction is directly related to how callers perceive the competence of the phone representatives. Research showed that excessive waiting times caused a bias in the ratings. Eliminating this bias made a substantial contribution toward accurately measuring

FIGURE 8.6   Interlinking Model of Customer Satisfaction and Time on Hold

Customer Satisfaction Rating	Time on Hold
1.32	<30 sec.
1.57	30-60 sec.
1.67	1-2 min.
2.14	2-3 min.

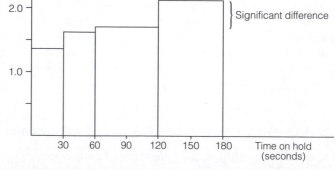

customer satisfaction with the phone contact experience. To improve customer satisfaction, FP&L developed a system to notify customers of the anticipated wait and give them a choice of holding or deferring the call to a later time. Customers were actually willing to wait longer if they knew the length of wait without being dissatisfied, thus improving customer satisfaction even when call traffic was heavy.

By using such interlinking models, managers can determine objectively the effects of additional resources or changes in the system to reduce waiting time. Improving the process is only appropriate once a linkage to customer satisfaction is established. This practice is "management by fact." The objectives and benefits of interlinking include:

- Screening out weak or misleading performance measures

- Focusing management attention on key performance measures that do make a difference

- Predicting performance such as customer satisfaction levels

- Setting target standards for performance

- Requiring areas such as marketing and operations to coordinate their data analysis efforts

- Making wise decisions faster than competitors do

- Seeing relationships among performance variables that competitors miss

- Enhancing communication within the organization based on good data analysis and management by fact.[21]

Even though interlinking can provide important benefits, the relationship between quality and financial performance is not always without controversy. A study of 19 recipients of the Malcolm Baldrige National Quality Award showed that even during poor economic conditions most firms performed financially as well or better than their competitors; many of these companies attribute a significant portion of financial improvements to their quality intitiatives.[22] However, a number of complicating factors make the link between quality indicators and financial performance somewhat tenuous. For example, short-term profits may be affected by factors such as accounting practices, business decisions, write-offs, dividends, and investments. Financial performance also depends on the performance of competitors and other external factors, such as local, national, and international economic conditions and business cycles. Thus, a TQM focus cannot guarantee financial success.

QUALITY IN PRACTICE

MEASUREMENT AND DATA MANAGEMENT AT XEROX[23]

In Chapter 1, the Quality in Practice feature described the quality transformation at Xerox. Measurement and data analysis is the cornerstone of their total quality effort. In 1989, Xerox had more than 375 major information systems supporting the business. Of these, 175 related specifically to the management, evaluation, and planning of quality,

and were used to support more than 300 specific applications of these tasks. Figure 8.7 illustrates the scope and depth of the data used to support a prevention-based approach to quality improvement.

The Xerox quality measurement system extends from suppliers to customers. Metrics are specified at key measurement points of the Xerox Delivery

FIGURE 8.7 Scope and Depth of Xerox Quality-Related Data

134 Data Uses to *EVALUATE* the Quality of All Xerox Work Processes

SCOPE ▶ / ▼ DEPTH	CUSTOMER 17	SUPPLIER 13	INTERNAL OPS 23	PRODUCT/ SERVICES 20	EMPLOYEES 17	COMPETI-TION 10	BENCH-MARK 15	SAFETY 18	ENVIRON-MENTAL 1
PLANNING 15	• Cust. sat. data	• Local cont validation	• L-T-Q assess • PDP phase	• Reliability data	• Employee attitude	• Prod assess • Dealer dist	• TQC benchmark-	• Occup illness data	
DESIGN 26									
MANUFAC-TURING 34									
SALES 12									
SERVICE 18									
ADMIN 14									
SUPPORT 15									

79 Data Uses to Enable *MANAGEMENT* Decisions for Continuous Improvement

SCOPE ▶ / ▼	CUSTOMER	SUPPLIER 9	INTERNAL OPS 28	PRODUCT/ SERVICES 17	EMPLOYEES 10	COMPETI-TION 3	BENCH-MARK	SAFETY
10	• Cust. sat. data	• Site and sourcing data	• L-T-Q assess • Team tracking	• Xerox Dev process	• Mgmt. styles scores	• Competitive news flash	• Org plng	• UL data
DESIGN 18								
MANUFAC- 16								
SALES 10								
SERVICE 9								
ADMIN 8								
SUPPORT 8								

92 Data Uses to *PLAN* for Continuous Quality Improvement

SCOPE ▶ / ▼ DEPTH	CUSTOMER 12	SUPPLIER 17	INTERNAL OPS 14	PRODUCT/ SERVICES 17	EMPLOYEES 14	COMPETI-TION 9	BENCH-MARK 9
PLANNING 27	• Customer requirements • Focus Group findings • Market research findings	• Supplier base • Technical plans • Product Array data • Quality history data	• Team excellence reports • Leadership through quality assessments	• Product - Quality - Reliability - Operability - Productivity - Planning • BRMS	• Training stats • Human resource data	• Trade assoc. reports • Trade show reports • Competitive scenarios	• Benc nws • Benc ref • Benc data
DESIGN 15	• Customer visits data • Problem ID data	• Commodity mix • Build site(s) • Technology data	• Cost of quality data • PDP test data	• Reliability • FMEA • Product life data • Config. data	• Mgmt. styles scores • Employee attitude survey	• Competitive support practices data	• Benc prac data
MANUFAC-TURING 12	• Customer visits data	• Commodity team surveys • Proc. capa-bility data • Source verif. data	• Suggestion system • Production line quality data	• Product quality data • In-line quality data	• Mgmt. styles scores • Employee attitude survey	• Competitive support practices data	• Benc prac data
SALES 10	• Customer sat. data • Problem ID data	N/A	• Establishment ping info sys • Int. mktg sys • Copy vol sys	• Demo skills profile	• Mgmt. styles scores • Employee attitude survey	• Competitive support practices data	• Benc prac data
SERVICE 11	• Customer sat. data	• Spares Demand Data	• Field service suggestions • Cancels data	• Serv call data • Field rel • Field perf data	• Mgmt. styles scores • Employee attitude survey	• Competitive support practices data	• Benc prac data
ADMIN 9	• Customer sat. data • Order-to-invoice data • Billing quality data	N/A	• Audit results	• Performance data	• Mgmt. styles scores • Employee attitude survey scores	• Competitive support practices data	• Benc prac data
SUPPORT 8	N/A	• Education - Total Quality Control - Stat Process Control	• Quality Team Results • Cost of Quality Data	• Grievance system reports	• Xerox employee assist prog. • Reward & recog. data	• Competitive support practices data	• Benc prac data

FIGURE 8.8 Data Systems Quality Assurance Steps

No.	Data Systems Quality Assurance Steps	VALIDITY	
		Data Accuracy	Data Timeliness
1	Is the specific data definition consistent with today's need?	Requirement check	
2	Is the process flow from data input to ultimate use defined and disciplined?	Process check	Timing check
3	Is the data integrity maintained under all possible test conditions?	Accuracy standard check	
4	Is there a mechanism for introducing change in the process flow without disrupting the system?		Improvement check
5	Is there a process for users to correct errors in the data?	Error correction check	
6	Is there a process for evaluating data errors for root cause and correction?	Root cause check	
7	Is a set of integrated performance standards and measurements in place for data input, processing and output?	Performance check	Performance check
8	Is there a system in place to improve the validity of, or eliminate the need for, this data?	Continuous improvement check	Continuous improvement check

Process. The answer to the question "What information can help us meet both internal and external customer requirements?" determines which information the company includes in their quality-related information systems. Each major operation such as the U.S. marketing group or development and manufacturing, has a system review board composed of senior managers with the responsibility of validating customer requirements and overseeing the process by which those requirements are transformed into detailed specifications. As requirements develop, line and MIS groups work closely together to meet any needs within the information/data system.

Xerox structures its data management system to enhance data accuracy, validity, timeliness, consistency, standardization, and easy access. It formulates procedures for the improved collection, retention, and security of data. Users—internal customers—work closely with the data management organizations to define requirements for the timely use, dissemination, and presentation of data and information. Validity, accuracy, and timeliness are emphasized by the data systems quality assurance steps, shown in Figure 8.8, during the design, construction, and major upgrade of each data system. The accessibility of one of the most extensive computer networks in the world provides an average end-to-end response time of 2.5 seconds (better than the industry average), linking hundreds of Xerox sites on four continents and supplying information 24 hours a day, seven days a week.

Xerox has several major systems for collecting, tracking, analyzing, and integrating data needed to make specific decisions. One, the Automated Installation Quality Report system, contains data on the installation and initial performance of every machine at a customer location anywhere in the United States. This database can be accessed from anywhere for quality analysis and action from the customer interface back to design. A second, called Technology Readiness, is a conceptual framework for bringing together all the technological information required for development of a new product. It prescribes data and data analysis requirements regarding failure modes, critical parameters, subsystem interactions, achievable manufacturing variances, and system performance against goals that reflect both internal and external customer satisfaction requirements.

The primary measure of product quality is defects per machine, defined as any variance from customer requirements. In the early 1980s, Xerox tracked only those defects attributable to internal operations. After the total quality effort, defects arising from all causes were given equal attention. Product teams use statistical tools and cost of quality analysis to track improvements. Beginning in 1985, Xerox manufacturing quality measurements became a mirror image of customer requirements. After a new machine is installed, quality results for product reliability are monitored via customer reports. To verify internal results, early unscheduled maintenance calls act as a key indicator. Other measures the company tracks include product development and delivery lead times, repair response time and efficiency, operability and productivity, total cost of ownership, billing accuracy, delivery of supplies, order entry, professionalism, sales representative attention, and administrative competence.

Key Issues for Discussion

1. Discuss how data captured by Xerox spans the entire scope of company performance.

2. This description of Xerox's data and information approaches was written before the concept of inter-

information might Xerox now employ based on the information presented here?

3. "Operability" means expanded features that are simple and easy to use, such as auto jam clearance, document handling, and easy-load paper and toner cartridges. Describe some methods to measure operability.

QUALITY IN PRACTICE   **QUALITY COST REPORTING AT NAP CONSUMER ELECTRONICS CORPORATION**[24]

North American Philips Consumer Electronics Corporation (NAPCEC) is a division of North American Philips Corporation, which ranks among the 100 largest industrial corporations in the United States. NAPCEC manufactures and sells a full line of consumer electronics products including televisions, tape players, VCRs, video cameras, and other types of audio systems. Because of the importance of quality in consumer electronics products, NAPCEC uses a wide variety of activities, including the measurement and reporting of quality costs, in its quality function. These activities are a part of North American Philips Corporation's quality improvement system, which represents an ongoing commitment to quality at every level of the organization.

NAPCEC began its quality cost system in 1976. The quality assurance group developed and implemented the system and today continues to be responsible for its operations. Quality cost data are collected by plant, product, and quality cost category. The financial accounting system then develops that data by determining which quality costs are recorded in the accounting system and identifying the specific accounts where they are recorded. Other quality costs that cannot be identified specifically in the accounts are developed through an estimation and allocation procedure in which department heads estimate the percentage of time spent on quality activities and then multiply the departmental costs by this percentage. An example of the quality cost accounts used by one of the plants is shown in Table 8.4. Each of these major accounts may be further divided into more detailed accounts as shown in Table 8.5.

The quality cost reports are usually in statement format. Graphs are used on occasion. In these reports, costs are broken down by quality cost cate-

gory and by product. Appraisal and internal failure costs are also reported as a percentage of direct labor and standard product cost. The format of the summary report, which is distributed to plant management and to higher levels of management, is shown in Table 8.6. Actual quality costs are compared to planned quality costs over each year, and a variance between planned and actual quality cost is computed. Quality costs as a percentage of standard manufacturing costs are shown for actual and planned costs for the current year and actual costs for the preceding year.

Table 8.7 shows the format of a direct labor quality cost report. Direct labor costs associated with appraisal and internal failure are reported by product. These reports are prepared for each operation, with the costs presented in dollar amounts and as a percentage of the total.

NAPCEC uses the data in the quality cost reports for budgeting activities, control activities, quality-related decisions, and trend analyses. A quality cost budget, which includes overhead costs, is developed from the manufacturing plan for the upcoming year. The budget for warranty and testing and repairs also makes extensive use of the data contained in the reports. Although the primary control feature limits service and warranty costs, appraisal and internal failure costs have been reduced significantly as a result of the quality cost program.

Key Issues for Discussion

1. Explain the various reports used by NAPCEC in their quality improvement system.

2. How are quality cost data used in preparing the budget for warranty, testing, and repairs?

TABLE 8.4 Quality Cost Accounts

Account Number	Account Title
100	**Prevention:**
110	Analysis and Planning for Quality and Reliability
120	Process Control
130	Specification Design and Development of Quality Information Equipment
140	Quality Training and Manpower Development
150	Product Design Verification
160	Systems Development and Management
170	Other Prevention Costs
180	Cost of Specific Plans and Actions Aimed at Preventing Administrative Errors and Management Systems Failures
200	**Appraisal:**
210	Test and Inspection of Purchased Direct Materials
220	Laboratory Testing of Purchased Materials
230	Laboratory or Other Measurement Services
240	Test and Inspection
250	Test and Inspection Equipment and Material
260	Quality and Quality System Audits
270	Outside Endorsements
280	Field Testing
290	Cost of Auditing and Inspection for Administrative Errors and Management System Failures Including Carrying out the Physical Inventories
300	**Internal Failure:**
310	Scrap
320	Repair
330	Rework
340	Scrap and Rework—Suppliers Fault
350	Salvage
360	Revisions and Corrective Actions
370	Down time Costs Due to Quality Reasons
380	Cost of Administrative Errors and Systems Failures
400	**External Failure:**
410	Complaints in Warranty
420	Complaints Out of Warranty
430	Product Liability Costs
440	Product Service
450	Traffic Damage
460	External Administrative Errors or Systems Failures Cost

TABLE 8.5 Internal Failure Costs of Administrative Errors and Systems Failures

Account Number	Account Title
381	Wasted Effort Due to Aborted Product Plans
382	Cancellation Due to Aborted Product Plans
383	Cost of Moving or Dumping Product that Did not Sell According to Plan
384	Cost of Missed Schedules
385	Cost of Redundant Staffing to "Catch" Administrative Errors and Systems Failures
386	Cost of Net Losses Found in Physical Inventories
387	Cost of Corrective Actions for Account 380

TABLE 8.6 Quality Cost Summary for the Month of September

| | | | | % OF MANUFACTURING STANDARD | | |
| | | | | Current Year | | Prior Year |
	Plan	Actual	Variance	Plan	Actual	Actual
Prevention						
Appraisal						
Internal failure						
External failure						

TABLE 8.7 Direct Labor Quality Cost Report

| | | APPRAISAL | | FAILURE | |
Category	Total Cost	Cost	%/Total	Cost	%/Total
Monochrome TV					
Color portable					
Color console					
Audio					
Odyssey					
VLP					
OEM					
Miscellaneous					
Plant total					

SUMMARY OF KEY POINTS

■ Achieving total quality depends on a framework of measurement and inspection, data, and analysis. Measurement quantifies the quality characteristic or determines whether the characteristic is present. With data, managers can make decisions based on facts and set improvement priorities.

■ Leading practices for information management include developing a set of performance indicators that reflect customer requirements and key business factors; pushing responsibility for data collection and analysis down to lower levels of the organization; ensuring reliable, accessible, and visible data; logically linking external indicators to internal indicators; and continually refining information sources and uses.

■ Quality and operational performance data include supplier performance, product and service quality, business and support services, and company operational performance. Data are either attribute (present or absent) or variable (measured on a continuous scale).

■ Performance indicators should represent the factors that predict customer satisfaction and are driven by key business factors. Close examination of the processes that create products and services is necessary in establishing good performance indicators.

■ Quality cost programs translate quality problems into the language of upper management—money. Through the use of quality cost information, management identifies opportunities for quality improvement. Quality cost information also aids in budgeting and cost control and serves as a scoreboard to evaluate an organization's success.

■ Quality costs generally are categorized into prevention, appraisal, internal failure, and external failure costs. These costs are often expressed as indexes using labor, manufacturing cost, sales, or unit measurement bases. Pareto analysis identifies quality problems that account for a large percentage of costs and that, if solved, result in high returns on investment.

■ Activity-based costing, a recent accounting approach, allocates overhead cost to the products and services that use them. This practice provides more useful information for quality improvement than traditional cost accounting systems.

■ Effective data management considers the reliability and accessibilty of data.

■ Interlinking is the quantitative modeling of cause and effect relationships between external and internal performance criteria. Interlinking allows managers to determine objectively the effects of internal variables under their control with external measures and hence make better managerial decisions.

REVIEW QUESTIONS

1. Explain the use of quality-related data at the "three levels of quality" in an organization.

2. What are the benefits and dangers of measurement and inspection?

3. Summarize the leading practices related to quality data and information management.

4. What are the four key areas on which data and information management should focus?

5. Why has the term *nonconformity* replaced *defect?*

6. Explain the difference between attribute and variable measurement and provide some examples.

7. What two basic mistakes do companies frequently make when collecting data?

8. What are key business factors? Summarize the major types.

9. Describe the process of defining quality performance indicators.

10. Why are quality cost programs valuable to managers?

11. List and explain the four major categories of quality costs. Give examples of each.

12. How are quality costs measured and collected in an organization?

13. Discuss how index numbers are often used to analyze quality cost data.

14. How do quality costs differ between service and manufacturing organizations? What collection techniques are more applicable to services?

15. Discuss the importance of each of the 12 steps suggested by the National Association of Accountants for implementing quality cost reporting systems.

16. What is Pareto analysis, and how is it used in analyzing quality cost data?

17. The percentage of total quality costs in a firm are distributed as follows:

Prevention 11%	Internal failure 38%
Appraisal 29%	External failure 22%

What conclusions are indicated by this data?

18. What conclusions can be drawn from the following data?

Cost Category	Amount
Equipment design	$ 20,000
Scrap	300,000
Reinspection and retest	360,000
Loss	90,000
Supplier quality surveys	8,000
Repair	80,000

19. Explain the concept of activity-based costing. How does it differ from traditional cost accounting? What role does it play in total quality?

20. Why is accessibility of data important? How does information technology improve accessibility?

21. What is interlinking? Provide an example.

22. Summarize the benefits and objectives of interlinking.

DISCUSSION QUESTIONS

1. Many restaurants and hotels use "table top" customer satisfaction surveys. Find several of these from local businesses and evaluate the types of questions and items included in the surveys. What internal performance indicators might be appropriate? How might this customer-related information be linked to internal performance indicators?

2. Many "course and instructor evaluation" systems consist of inappropriate or ineffective measurements. Discuss how the principles in this chapter can be used to develop an effective measurement system for instructor performance.

3. How can measurement be used to control and improve the daily operations of your college or university?

4. Discuss how quality measurements can be used in a fraternity or student organization.

5. What types of inspection are used in airline operations? Hospitals? Police departments? Universities? Talk with a manager or administrator to check your assumptions.

6. The use of universal product code (UPC) scanners in supermarkets has become common in recent years. The scanners read the UPC code, and the item description and price are read from a central computer. With a focus on quality, discuss the advantages and the disadvantages of these systems to both the stores and the customers.

7. Consider the following measurements for an airline. Would they be attributes or variables measurements? Explain your answers.

    a. passengers bumped per flight

    b. delay times of departures

    c. time spent at check-in counter

    d. customers with lost baggage

    e. delivery time for baggage

8. In a bank, the following measures are taken. Are these attributes or variables? Explain your answers.

   a. time spent waiting for a teller

   b. errors made in check handling

   c. customer inquiries

   d. turnaround time for mail transactions

   e. computer breakdowns

9. Interview managers at a local company to identify its key business factors. What quality indicators does the company measure? Are these indicators consistent with the key business factors?

10. In the making of cheese, companies test milk for somatic cell count to prevent diseases. They also test for bacteria to determine how clean the milk is, and perform a freezing-point test to see whether the milk was diluted with water (milk with water in it freezes at a lower temperature, increasing production costs since all excess water must be extracted). Final cheese products are subjected to weight, foreign elements, chemical, and taste and smell testing. What customer-related measures might interlink with these internal measures?

11. Ask some local business people if their companies conduct cost of quality evaluations. If they do, how do they use the information? If not, why?

12. What types of quality costs might be relevant to your college and university? Can they be measured?

13. Many quality experts like Joseph Juran and Philip Crosby advocate cost of quality evaluations. Deming, however, states that "the most important figures are unknown and unknowable." How can these conflicting opinions be resolved?

14. If you are familiar with spreadsheet software, discuss how such programs can be used by managers to analyze quality cost data. Design a spreadsheet that would be appropriate for this task.

15. Should a quality department have to cost-justify an expensive piece of measuring equipment based on estimated savings, or should the department manager simply point to "increased competition" as justification? To support your conclusion, try to find an actual situation in which each method was used.

PROBLEMS

1. Analyze the following cost data. What implications do these data suggest to management?

	PRODUCT		
	A	B	C
Total sales	$537,280	$233,600	$397,120
External failure	42%	20%	20%
Internal failure	45%	25%	45%
Appraisal	12%	52%	30%
Prevention	1%	3%	5%
(Figures represent percentages of quality costs by product.)			

2. Compute a sales dollar index base to analyze the following quality cost information and prepare a memo to management.

	QUARTER			
	1	2	3	4
Total sales	$4,120	$4,206	$4,454	$4,106
External failure	40.8	42.2	42.8	28.6
Internal failure	168.2	172.4	184.4	66.4
Appraisal	64.2	67.0	74.4	166.2
Prevention	28.4	29.2	30.2	40.2

3. Prepare a graph or chart showing the different quality cost categories and percentages for a printing company.

Cost Element	Amount
Proofreading	$710,000
Quality planning	10,000
Press downtime	405,000
Bindery waste	75,000
Checking and inspection	60,000
Customer complaint remakes	40,000
Printing plate revisions	40,000
Quality improvement projects	20,000
Other waste	55,000
Correction of typographical errors	300,000

4. Given the following cost elements, determine the total percentage in each of the four major quality cost categories.

Cost Element	Amount	Cost Element	Amount
Incoming test and inspection	$ 7,500	Material testing and inspection	$ 1,250
Scrap	35,000	Rework	70,000
Quality training	0	Quality problem solving by	
Inspection	25,000	product engineers	11,250
Test	5,000	Inspection equipment calibration	2,500
Adjustment cost of complaints	21,250	Writing procedures and	
Quality audits	2,500	instructions	2,500
Maintenance of tools and dies	9,200	Laboratory services	2,500
Quality control administration	5,000	Rework due to vendor faults	17,500
Laboratory testing	1,250	Correcting imperfections	6,250
Design of quality assurance		Setup for test and inspection	10,750
equipment	1,250	Formal complaints to vendors	10,000

5. Use Pareto analysis to investigate the following quality losses in a paper mill. What conclusions do you reach?

Category	Annual Loss
Downtime	$ 38,000
Testing costs	20,000
Rejected paper	560,000
Odd lot	79,000
Excess inspection	28,000
Customer complaints	125,000
High material costs	67,000

CASES

I. Ultra-Productivity Fasteners Company, Part I

The Ultra-Productivity Fasteners Company was founded in 1959 to supply a variety of fasteners—rivets, clips, and screws—to appliance manufacturers. These fasteners are used in the assembly of major appliances, including dishwashers, washing machines, clothes dryers, and ranges. In 1981, Ultra-Productivity successfully penetrated the automotive market. Currently the appliance market with three major OEM customers represents 60 percent of the annual sales. Two automotive customers account for approximately 30 percent of the sales; the remaining 10 percent of sales are made to a variety of smaller customers.

In the design phase, appliance manufacturers expect rapid response in the design and manufacture of special fasteners, and technical assistance in properly applying existing fastener designs. In the production and warranty phases, appliance manufacturers expect just-in-time delivery; fasteners that consistently meet specifications; fasteners that can be used on the production line without difficulty, and frequently with automated equipment; and fasteners that will not break during handling, shipping, or repair.

Requirements of the automotive customers are similar, but fasteners that will not break is more critical because of the additional vibration and safety considerations. Just-in-time delivery is a primary requirement for automotive customers since lack of a fastener may hold up assembly of an automobile.

Ultra-Productivity is one of three major manufacturers in the fastener market, in addition to a large number of small regional manufacturers. The market for fasteners is extremely competitive; price is a key consideration in the purchase decision.

Ultra-Productivity is headquartered in Louisville, Kentucky, with a major manufacturing plant at that location. Two other manufacturing plants are located at Lansing, Michigan and Atlanta, Georgia. The Louisville and Lansing plants are of comparable size, with approximately 300 production workers each. The Atlanta plant is only one-third the size of the other plants with approximately 100 production employees. Although quality has always been an important consideration, a formal, companywide quality improvement program was initiated in 1989 after a major automotive contract was lost.

Assignment

Summarize the key business factors for this company and define a set of quality performance indicators that would be consistent with these key business factors.

II. The Hamilton Bank Cost of Quality Report

The following cost of quality data was collected at an installment loan department at the Hamilton Bank. Classify these data into the appropriate cost of quality categories and analyze the results. What suggestions would you make to management?

Loan Processing

1. Run credit check: $26.13

2. Review documents: $3021.62

3. Make document corrections; gather additional information: $1013.65

4. Prepare tickler file; review and follow up on titles, insurance, second meetings: $156.75

5. Review all output: $2244.14

6. Correct rejects and incorrect output: $425.84

7. Reconcile incomplete collateral report: $78.34.

8. Respond to dealer calls; address associated problems; research and communicate information: $2418.88

9. Compensate for system downtime: $519.38

10. Conduct training: $1366.94

Loan Payment

1. Receive and process payments: $1045.00

2. Respond to inquiries when no coupon is presented with payments: $783.64

Loan Payoff

1. Receive and process payoff and release document: $13.92

2. Research payoff problems: $14.34

NOTES

1. Noriaki Kano, "A Perspective on Quality Activities in American Firms," *California Management Review* (Spring 1993), 12–31.
2. Jeremy Main, *Quality Wars* (New York: The Free Press, 1994), 130.
3. D. Osborne and T. Gaebler, *Reinventing Government: How the Entrepreneurial Spirit is Transforming the Public Sector* (Reading, MA: Addison-Wesley Publishing Co., 1992).
4. Howard Gleckman with John Carey, Russell Mitchell, Tim Smart, and Chris Roush. "The Technology Payoff," *Business Week*, 14 June, 1993, 57.
5. Reprinted by permission from Richard L. Daft, *Organization Theory and Design*, 4th ed. (St. Paul, MN: West Publishing Co., 1992), 286. All rights reserved.
6. Robert S. Kaplan and David P. Norton, "The Balanced Scorecard—Measures That Drive Performance," *Harvard Business Review* (January/February 1992), 71–79. Copyright 1992 by the President and Fellows of Harvard College; all rights reserved.
7. Ernest C. Huge, "Measuring and Rewarding Performance," in The Ernst & Young Quality Consulting Group, *Total Quality: An Executive's Guide for the 1990s* (Homewood IL: Irwin, 1990).
8. Glenn E. Hayes and Harry G. Romig, *Modern Quality Control* (Encino, CA: Benziger, Bruce & Glencoe, Inc., 1977).
9. "First National Bank of Chicago," *Profiles in Quality* (Boston, MA: Allyn and Bacon, 1991).
10. U.S. Office of Management and Budget, "How to Develop Quality Measures That Are Useful in Day-to-Day Measurement," U.S. Department of Commerce, National Technical Information Service (January 1989).
11. Frank M. Gryna, "Quality Costs," *Juran's Quality Control Handbook*, 4th ed. (New York: McGraw-Hill, 1988).
12. Edward Sullivan and Debra A. Owens, "Catching A Glimpse of Quality Costs Today," *Quality Progress* 16, no. 12 (December 1983), 21–24.
13. For further discussion, see Wayne J. Morse, Harold P. Roth, and Kay M. Poston, *Measuring, Planning, and Controlling Quality Costs* (Montvale, NJ: National Association of Accountants, 1987).
14. The reader is referred to the text by Cooper and Kaplan (1991) cited in the bibliography for a thorough treatment of this topic.
15. Thomas S. Johnson, and Robert S. Kaplan, *Relevance Lost* (Cambridge, MA: Harvard Business School Press, 1987), quoted in Joel E. Ross and David E. Wegman, "Quality Management and the Role of the Accountant," *Industrial Management* (July/August 1990), 21–23.
16. L. Reid, "Continuous Improvement Through Process Management," *Management Accounting* (September 1992), 37–44.
17. "A Bean-Counter's Best Friend," *Business Week/Quality 1991*, Special Issue, 25 October, 1991, 42.
18. Ethan I. Davis, "Quality Service at The Prudential," in Jay W. Spechler, *When America Does It Right* (Norcross, GA: Industrial Engineering and Management Press, 1988), 224–232.
19. David A. Collier, *The Service/Quality Solution* (Milwaukee, WI: ASQC Quality Press, and Burr Ridge, IL: Richard D. Irwin, 1994).
20. Bob Graessel and Pete Zeidler, "Using Quality Function Deployment to Improve Customer Service," *Quality Progress* 26, no. 11 (November 1993), 59–63.
21. Collier, 235–236, see note 19.
22. Joel D. Wisner, and Stan G. Eakins, "A Competitive Assessment of the Baldrige Winners," *The Total Quality Review* 4, no. 5 (November/December 1994), 15–24.
23. Adapted from *Xerox 1989 Malcolm Baldrige National Quality Award Application*, Xerox Corporation, 1993.
24. Morse et al., see note 13.

BIBLIOGRAPHY

American National Standard: Guide to Inspection Planning, ANSI/ASQC E-2-1984. Milwaukee, WI: American Society for Quality Control, 1984.

AT&T Quality Steering Committee. *Process Quality Management & Improvement Guidelines*. AT&T Bell Laboratories, 1987.

Case, Kenneth E., and Lynn L. Jones. *Profit Through Quality: Quality Assurance Programs for Manufacturers*. Norcross, GA: American Institute of Industrial Engineers, 1978.

Cooper, Robin, and Robert S. Kaplan. *The Design of Cost Management Systems: Text, Cases, and Readings*. New York: Prentice-Hall, 1991.

Cupello, James M. "A New Paradigm for Measuring TQM Progress," *Quality Progress* 27, no. 5 (May 1994), 79–82.

Davidow, William H., and Bro Uttal. *Total Customer Service*. New York: Harper & Row, 1989.

Donnell, Augustus, and Margaret Dellinger. *Analyzing Business Process Data: The Looking Glass*. AT&T Bell Laboratories, 1990.

Ferdeber, Charles J. "Measuring Quality and Productivity in a Service Environment," *Industrial Engineering* (July 1981), 193–201.

Haavind, Robert. *The Road to the Baldrige Award*. Boston: Butterworth-Heinemann, 1992.

Hart, Christopher W.L., and Christopher E. Bogan. *The Baldrige*. New York: McGraw-Hill, 1992.

Holm, Richard A. "Fulfilling the New Role of Inspection," *Manufacturing Engineering* (May 1988), 43–46.

Johnson, H. Thomas. "Activity-Based Information: A Blueprint for World-Class Management Accounting," *Management Accounting* (June 1988), 23–30.

Juran, Joseph M. *Juran on Quality By Design*. New York: The Free Press, 1992.

Kaplan, Robert S. "Yesterday's Accounting Undermines Production," *Harvard Business Review*, July-August, 1984.

Puma, Maurice. "Quality Technology in Manufacturing," *Quality Progress* 13, no. 8 (August, 1980), 16–19.

Rice, George O. "Metrology." In *Quality Management Handbook*, Loren Walsh, Ralph Wurster, and Raymond J. Kimber (eds.). New York: Marcel Dekker, 1986, 517–530.

Rosander, A.C. *The Quest for Quality in Services*. Milwaukee, WI: ASQC Quality Press, 1989.

Strong, Carol. "Measuring Performance Improves Service—If You Measure and Reward the Right Behaviors," *The Service Edge Newsletter* (October 1989).

Troxell, Joseph R. "Service Time Quality Standards," *Quality Progress* 14, no. 9 (September 1981), 35–37.

_____ . "Standards for Quality Control in Service Industries," *Quality Progess* 12, no. 1 (January 1979), 32–34.

Whitley, Richard C. *The Customer Driven Company*. Reading, MA: Addison-Wesley, 1991.

Wilkerson, David, and Clifton Cooksey. *Customer Service Measurement*. Arlington, VA: Coopers & Lybrand, 1994.

Yakhou, Mehenna, and Boubekeur Rahali. "Integration of Business Functions: Roles of Cross-Functional Information Systems," *APICS—The Performance Advantage* 2, no. 12 (December 1992), 35–37.

Process Management and Continuous Improvement

The president of Texas Instruments Defense Systems and Electronics Group has a sign in his office that reads: *"Unless you change the process, why would you expect the results to change?"* As a key principle of TQM, all work is performed by a process. Deming and Juran observed that the overwhelming majority of quality problems are associated with processes; few are due to the workers themselves. Thus, no purpose is served by blaming individuals for something over which they have no control. Rather, management is responsible—actually, they share responsibility with the work force—to continuously improve the processes with which individuals work.

Process management involves planning and administering the activities necessary to achieve a high level of performance in a process, and identifying opportunities for improving quality and operational performance, and ultimately, customer satisfaction. It involves collecting data; controlling the process by identifying, analyzing, and correcting abnormal conditions; identifying and implementing improvements; and maintaining these improvements. The distinction between control and improvement is illustrated in Figure 9.1. Any process performance measure naturally fluctuates around some average level. Abnormal conditions cause an unusual deviation from this pattern. Removing the causes of such abnormal conditions is the essence of control. Improvement, on the other hand, means changing the performance to a new level. Process management concentrates on preventing defects and errors, and eliminating such waste as nonvalue-added processing steps, waiting, and redundancy, which, in turn, result in better quality and improved company performance through shorter cycle times and faster customer responsiveness.

Nearly every leading company has a well-defined methodology for process management. AT&T, for example, bases its methodology on the following principles:

- Process quality improvement focuses on the end-to-end process.

- The mindset of quality is one of prevention and continuous improvement.

- Everyone manages a process at some level and is simultaneously a customer and a supplier.

- Customer needs drive process quality improvement.

- Corrective action focuses on removing the root cause of the problem rather than on treating its symptoms.

- Process simplification reduces opportunities for errors and rework.

- Process quality improvement results from a disciplined and structured application of the quality management principles.[1]

FIGURE 9.1   Control versus Improvement

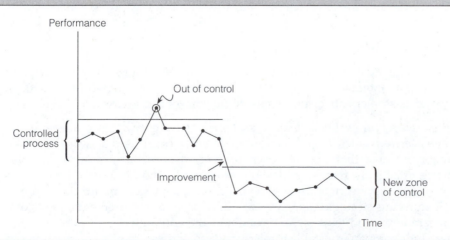

Because processes typically cut across traditional organizational boundaries, process management activities are best achieved through cross-functional teams, a topic discussed in Chapter 11.

This chapter discusses strategies for process *control* and *improvement* and introduces basic methodologies for quality improvement and problem solving. It also describes a variety of tools to support these methodologies.

THE SCOPE OF PROCESS MANAGEMENT

A **process** is sequence of activities that is intended to achieve some result, typically to create added value for a customer. Leading companies identify important business processes that affect customer satisfaction. They extend beyond core manufacturing or service processes to all business support processes such as marketing and technical support. Most companies define a set of **core processes** that drive the creation of its products and services, as well as a set of **support processes** critical to production and delivery. AT&T Consumer Communication Services, for example, defines its core processes as the network servicing process that addresses engineering, provisioning, and maintenance of the AT&T Worldwide Intelligent Network; the customer servicing process that guides customers to CCS employees for operator call completion, sales inquiries and assistance, billing inquiries, and account inquiries or billing adjustments; and the account management and billing process that manages the systems and interfaces for over 85 million customer accounts. Support processes include information and software services, human resources, public relations, law, regulatory, finance, marketing, and network security.

To apply techniques of process management, processes must be (1) repeatable, and (2) measurable. Repeatability means that the process must recur over time. The cycle may be long, as with product development processes or patent applications; or it may be short, as with a manufacturing operation or an order entry process. Repeatability ensures that enough data can be collected to reveal useful information. This information is obtained through measurement, as discussed in the last chapter. Information obtained through measurement reveals patterns about the process performance. The ability to predict performance facilitates the detection of out-of-control conditions and the search for improvements.

■ Leading Practices

Process management requires a disciplined effort involving all managers and workers in an organization. Companies that are recognized world leaders in quality and customer satisfaction share some common practices.

> ■ *They control the quality and operational performance of key processes used to produce and deliver products and services.* GTE Directories uses a series of cross-functional teams that manage each individual core business process. This practice effectively translates designs into goods and services. These teams also conduct appropriate process reviews, review process performance objectives, translate strategic quality plans into process requirements, and communicate new product designs throughout the company.

Leading companies establish measures and indicators to track quality and operational performance, and use them as a basis for controlling the processes and consistently meeting specifications and standards. At Eastman Chemical, manufacturing processes are monitored and controlled by collecting millions of pieces of process data each day. In the chemical business, equipment maintenance is crucial to safety, environmental protection, and quality. Eastman maintains a staff of highly qualified maintenance personnel who are trained to prevent and react to equipment breakdowns. Cadillac assesses in-process quality at every stage of the product development process. At the pre-production stage, prototype build checks are used to evaluate the assembly of the product; match checks verify the fit of sheet metal components and interior trim; engine tests ensure that the assembly plants are supplied with high-quality finished engines. Similar controls are used during and after assembly. Leading companies use statistical tools for understanding and controlling processes. Granite Rock, for instance, was the first in the construction materials industry to apply statistical process control in the management of production of aggregates, concrete, and asphalt products.

■ *They identify significant variations in processes and outputs, determine root causes, make corrections, and verify results.* Significant variations signal a lack of control. With a systematic method, leading companies identify, analyze, and solve quality problems. Xerox, for instance, uses a six-step problem-solving process:

1. Identify and select the problem
2. Analyze the problem
3. Generate potential solutions
4. Select and plan the solution
5. Implement the solution
6. Evaluate the solution

Procter & Gamble, on the other hand, follows an eight-step process that consists of issue selection, initial situation analysis, cause analysis, improvement planning, executing the plan, assessing results, standardizing improvements, and making future plans. Individual approaches might be slightly different, but all work toward identifying the root cause of problems. NCR Corporation defines **root cause** as "that condition (or interrelated set of conditions) having allowed or caused a defect to occur, which once corrected properly, permanently prevents recurrence of the defect in the same, or subsequent, product or service generated by the process."[2] Symptoms of problems can usually be reduced with temporary measures; eliminating the source of the problem, however, requires finding the root cause. Finding the root cause then permits a company to correct it for the long term, thereby eliminating defects and errors that result from the root cause. Various graphical tools are used extensively in these problem-solving processes.

An important aspect of control is empowering employees to stop production whenever significant variations are found. Not long ago, this type of employee control was unthinkable in many industries. Today, employees at the lowest level of the organization (who are most familiar with the process) have the responsibilities to identify and resolve process upsets. The Ritz-Carlton Hotel Company has a policy by which the first person who detects a problem is empowered to break away from routine duties, investigate and correct the problem immediately, document the incident, and then return to their routine.

AT&T Universal Card Services employs meetings, training, and a variety of media such as methods and procedures documents, newsletters, and elec-

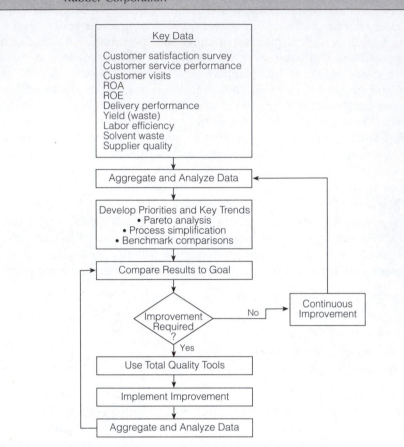

FIGURE 9.2 Data Analysis and Improvement Planning Process at Ames Rubber Corporation

tronic mail to prevent problems from occurring once root causes are identified. They verify corrective actions by reviewing measurement trends and increasing sampling efforts, by developing new measures targeting inconsistent processes, system changes, or enhancements, and by comparing internal results with customer-contact survey results.

■ *They continuously improve processes to achieve better quality, cycle time, and overall operational performance.* Leading companies employ systematic approaches for analyzing data and identifying improvements. Figure 9.2, for example, shows the process used at Ames Rubber Corporation. Note that this process relies heavily on the analysis of a variety of measurements and information. Leading companies use proven techniques such as process analysis and simplification and advanced technologies. Wainwright Industries, for example, evaluates each process after the first production run of a new product to identify and minimize all types of waste, such as unnecessary transportation, process steps, or waiting.

Leading companies include not only core production processes in improvement efforts, but also all business processes and support services such as finance and accounting, software services, sales, marketing, purchasing, facilities management, research and development, and secretarial and administrative services. At IBM Rochester, for instance, cross-functional teams examine all elements of production and support processes, from order entry to delivery and installation. The teams evaluate and remove, change, and improve steps in these processes. At AT&T Universal Card Services, management often raises internal standards when employees consistently meet a current standard and a margin for improvement remains. New technology is used creatively to improve customer service and reduce operating expenses through process and cycle time reductions, as well as fraud and credit-loss avoidance. Process owners visit world-class service providers and take advantage of the information to formulate action plans and set improvement goals and objectives.

The Ritz-Carlton has eight mechanisms devoted solely to the improvement of process, product, and service quality:

1. *New hotel start-up improvement process:* a cross-sectional team from the entire company that works together to identify and correct problem areas.

2. *Comprehensive performance evaluation process:* the work area team mechanism that empowers people who perform a job to develop the job procedures and performance standards.

3. *Quality network:* a mechanism of peer approval through which an individual employee can advance a good idea.

4. *Standing problem-solving team:* a standing work area team that addresses any problem it chooses.

5. *Quality improvement team:* special teams assembled to solve an assigned problem identified by an individual employee or leaders.

6. *Strategic quality planning:* annual work area teams that identify their missions, primary supplier objectives and action plans, internal objectives and action plans, and progress reviews.

7. *Streamlining process:* the annual hotel evaluation of processes, products, or services that are no longer valuable to the customer.

8. *Process improvement:* the team mechanism for corporate leaders, managers, and employees to improve the most critical processes.

■ *They set "stretch goals" and make extensive use of benchmarking and reengineering to achieve breakthrough performance. Stretch goals* push an organization to think differently. Such radical thinking results in dramatic innovation and quantum leaps in performance. Benchmarking and reengineering support innovation. *Benchmarking* is the search for best practices, in any company, in any industry, anywhere in the world. When Granite Rock could not find any company who was measuring on-time delivery of concrete, they talked with Domino's Pizza, a worldwide leader in on-time delivery of a rapidly perishable product (a characteristic similar to freshly mixed concrete) to acquire new ideas for measuring and improving their processes. AT&T has a corporate database to share benchmarking information among its business units. The database contains data from more than 100 companies and 250 benchmarking activities for key processes such as hardware and software development, manufacturing, financial planning and budgeting, international billing, and service delivery. AT&T obtains this information from customers, visits to other companies, trade shows and journals, professional societies, product brochures, and outside consultants. *Reengineering* is the radical redesign of business processes to achieve unprecedented improvements in performance. For example, Intel Corporation previously used a 91-step process costing thousands of dollars to purchase ballpoint pens—the same process that was used to purchase forklift trucks! The improved process was reduced to eight steps. In rethinking its purpose as a customer-driven, retail service company rather than a manufacturing company, Taco Bell eliminated the kitchen from its restaurants. Meat and beans are cooked outside the restaurant at central commissaries and reheated. Other food items such as diced tomatoes, onions, and olives are prepared off-site. This innovation saved about 11 million hours of work and $7 million per year over the entire chain.[3]

CONTROL SYSTEMS FOR QUALITY

Control is the continuing process of evaluating performance and taking corrective action when necessary. Any control system has three components: (1) a standard or goal, (2) a means of measuring accomplishment, and (3) comparison of actual results with the standard, along with feedback to form the basis for corrective action. Goals and standards are defined during planning and design processes. They establish what is supposed to be accomplished. These goals and standards are reflected by measurable quality characteristics, such as dimensions of machined parts, numbers of defectives, and waiting times. Methods for measuring these quality characteristics may be automated or performed manually by the work force. Measurements supply the information concerning what has actually been accomplished. Workers, supervisors, or managers then assess whether the actual results meet the goals and standards. If not, then remedial action must be taken. Remedial action is either short term, such as adjusting a machine setting, or long term, such as changing the technology of the process. Figure 9.3 illustrates a generic quality control system in production.

An example of a structured quality control process in the service industry is the "10-Step Monitoring and Evaluation Process" set forth by the Joint Commission on Accrediting Health Care Organizations. This process, shown in Table 9.1, provides a detailed sequence of activities for monitoring and evaluating the quality of health care in an effort to identify problems and improve care. Standards and goals are defined in steps 2 through 5; measurement is accomplished in step 6; and comparison and feedback is performed in the remaining steps.

Control is necessary for two reasons. First, companies need to maintain their high-quality processes. Control is a good check-and-balance system, which provides the discipline needed for continuous efficiency and effectiveness in processes that establish good quality. Second, a company must bring processes under control before any improvements can be made. The effect of potential improvements is impossible to measure if the process is affected by special causes of variation.

The need for control arises because of the inherent variation in any system or process. Sources of variation in production processes were discussed in Chapter 3 (specifically, Figure 3.4), which introduced the concepts of *common causes* and *special causes* of variation. Walter Shewhart is credited with recognizing the distinction between common and special causes of variation at Bell Laboratories in the 1920s. A process governed only by common causes is stable and remains essentially constant over time. The variation is predictable within established statistical limits. Prediction was the key idea in Shewhart's definition of control:

FIGURE 9.3   Generic Quality Control System

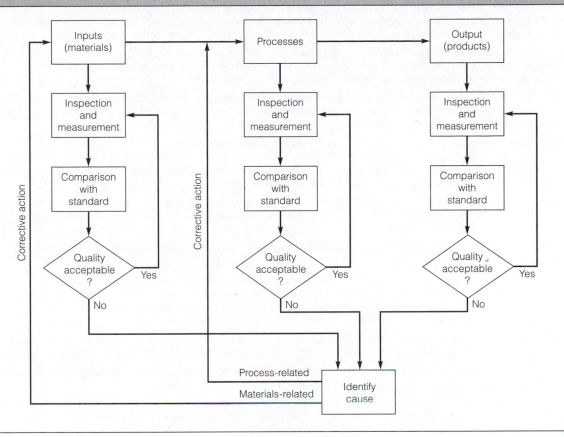

> A phenomenon will be said to be controlled when, through the use of past experience, we can predict, at least within limits, how the phenomenon may be expected to vary in the future.[4]

Controlling a process, therefore, is tantamount to identifying and removing special causes of variation.

Short-term remedial action often can be taken by workers on the shop floor. Long-term remedial action is the responsibility of management. The responsibility for control can be determined by checking three conditions. To be operator-controllable, (1) the operators must have the means of knowing what is expected of them through clear instructions and specifications; (2) they must have the means of determining their actual performance, typically through inspection and measurement, and (3) they must have a means of making corrections if they discover a variance between what is expected of them and their actual performance. If *any* of these criteria is not met, then the process is the responsibility of management, not the operators.

Both Juran and Deming made this important distinction. One of the major problems confronting American industry is the inability to distinguish between these two types of control. If operators are held accountable for or expected to act on problems beyond their control, they become frustrated and end up playing games with management. Juran and Deming stated that the majority of quality problems are management-controllable—the result of common cause variation. For the smaller proportion of operator-controllable problems resulting from

TABLE 9.1 10-Step Monitoring and Evaluation Process for Health Care Organizations

■ *Step 1: Assign Responsibility.* The emergency department director is responsible for, and actively participates in, monitoring and evaluation. The director assigns responsibility for the specific duties related to monitoring and evaluation.

■ *Step 2: Delineate Scope of Care.* The department considers the scope of care provided within emergency services to establish a basis for identifying important aspects of care to monitor and evaluate. The scope of care is a complete inventory of what the emergency department does.

■ *Step 3: Identify Important Aspects of Care.* Important aspects of care are those that are high-risk, high-volume, and/or problem-prone. Staff identify important aspects of care so that monitoring and evaluation focuses on emergency department activities with the greatest impact on patient care.

■ *Step 4: Identify Indicators.* Indicators of quality are identified for each important aspect of care. An indicator is a measurable variable related to a structure, process, or outcome of care. Examples of possible indicators (all of which would need to be further defined) include insufficient staffing for sudden surges in patient volume (structure), delays in physicians reporting to the emergency room (process), and transfusion errors (outcome).

■ *Step 5: Establish Thresholds for Evaluation.* A threshold for evaluation is the level or point at which intensive evaluation of care is triggered. A threshold may be 0% or 100% or any other appropriate level. Emergency department staff should establish a threshold for each indicator.

■ *Step 6: Collect and Organize Data.* Appropriate emergency department staff should collect data pertaining to the indicators. Data are organized to facilitate comparison with the thresholds for evaluation.

■ *Step 7: Evaluate Care.* When the cumulative data related to an indicator reach the threshold for evaluation, appropriate emergency department staff evaluate the care provided to determine whether a problem exists. This evaluation, which in many cases will take the form of peer review, should focus on possible trends and performance patterns. The evaluation is designed to identify causes of any problems or methods by which care or performance may be improved.

■ *Step 8: Take Actions to Solve Problems.* When problems are identified, action plans are developed, approved at appropriate levels, and enacted to solve the problem or take the opportunity to improve care.

■ *Step 9: Assess Actions and Document Improvement.* The effectiveness of any actions taken is assessed and documented. Further actions necessary to solve a problem are taken and their effectiveness is assessed.

■ *Step 10: Communicate Relevant Information to the Organization-wide Quality Assurance Program.* Findings from and conclusions of monitoring and evaluation, including actions taken to solve problems and improve care, are documented and reported monthly through the hospital's established channels of communication.

SOURCE: "Medical Staff Monitoring and Evaluation—Departmental Review," Chicago. Copyright by the Joint Commission on Accreditation of Health Care Organizations, Oakbrook Terrace, IL. Reprinted with permission (undated).

special causes, operators must be given the tools to identify them and the authority to take action. This philosophy has shifted the burden of assuring quality from inspection departments and quality control personnel to workers on the shop floor and in customer-contact positions.

■ Three Stages of Control

Terry and Franklin have provided a useful conceptualization of control by dividing it into three states: preliminary control, concurrent control, and feedback control.[5] This division is illustrated within the structure of the general control system model in Figure 9.4.

At the planning stage, **preliminary control** builds control into the process via systems for discovering potential quality problems prior to production. The second stage, called **concurrent control,** uses real-time feedback to recognize process variations quickly and to take corrective actions. Sometimes this process occurs automatically. For instance, in the production of plastic sheet stock, thickness depends on temperature. Sensors monitor the sheet thickness; if it begins to go out of tolerance, the system can adjust the temperature in order to change the thickness. In other cases, such feedback is accomplished by the production op-

FIGURE 9.4   Control System Structure

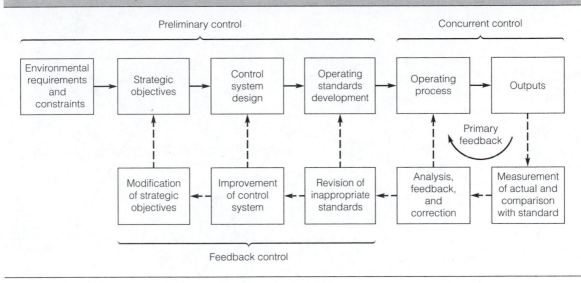

erators themselves. For example, workers might check the first few parts after a new production setup (called *setup verification*) to determine whether they conform to specifications. If not, the worker adjusts the setup. The third stage, **feedback control,** modifies the control system itself as strategies change, problems develop, or standards become obsolete.

Figure 9.5 relates the type of control to the level of management. Top managers are most concerned with preliminary control and the performance aspects of feedback control. Middle managers have more balanced interests in all areas of control but are charged with the responsibility of developing control systems and maintaining standards for concurrent control purposes. First-line managers have high concern for immediate feedback and correction through concurrent control. They are less concerned about establishing the overall mission in preliminary control or the analysis of results in feedback control except when day-to-day control factors are affected.

CONTINUOUS IMPROVEMENT

Prior to TQM, most U.S. managers simply *maintained* products and processes until they could be replaced by new technology. Japanese managers, on the other hand, focused on continually improving products and processes. The MIT Commission on Industrial Productivity observed this difference and stated:

> Another area in which U.S. firms have often lagged behind their overseas competitors is in exploiting the potential for continuous improvement in the quality and reliability of their products and processes. The cumulative effect of successive incremental improvements and modifications to established products and processes can be very large and may outpace efforts to achieve technological breakthroughs.[6]

Improvement should be a proactive task of management, not simply a reaction to problems and competitive threats. Many opportunities for improvement exist, including the obvious reduction in manufacturing defects and cycle times.

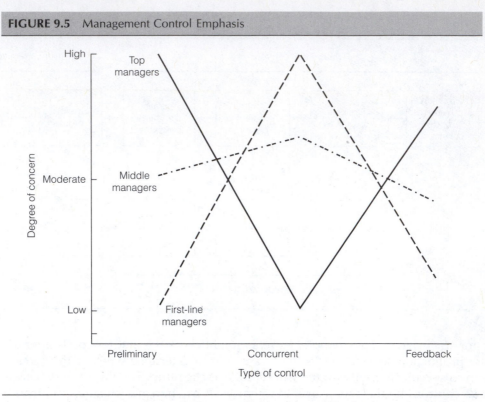

FIGURE 9.5 Management Control Emphasis

SOURCE: George R. Terry and Stephen G. Franklin, *Principles of Management,* 8th ed. (Homewood, IL: Irwin, 1982), 430.

Organizations should also consider improving employee morale, satisfaction, and cooperation; improving managerial practices; improving the design of products with features that better meet customers needs, and which achieve higher performance, higher reliability, and other market-driven dimensions of quality; and improving the efficiency of manufacturing systems by reducing worker idle time, and unnecessary motions, and by eliminating unnecessary inventory, unnecessary transportation and material handling, and scrap and rework.

The concept of continuous improvement was conceived and developed in the United States, yet it is often cited as the most important difference between Japanese and Western management.[7] One of the earliest examples in the United States was at National Cash Register Company (NCR). After a shipment of defective cash registers was returned in 1894, the company's founder discovered unpleasant and unsafe working conditions. He made many changes, including better lighting, new safety devices, ventilation, lounges, and lockers. The company offered extensive evening classes to improve employees' education and skills, and instituted a program for soliciting suggestions from factory workers. Workers received cash prizes and other recognitions for their best ideas; by the 1940s, the company was receiving an average of 3000 suggestions each year.

The Lincoln Electric Company, another early pioneer in continuous improvement, designed an "incentive management" system to promote continuous improvement. Workers were rewarded with compensation proportional to output and given increased status and publicity for their contributions. They were not penalized for finding more efficient ways to produce, but rather were rewarded for their ingenuity and increased productivity. The company profited because fixed overhead could be spread over the increased production. Workers had full responsibility for their work stations and were held accountable for quality. An employee advisory board elected by the work force met regularly with top management to discuss ideas and to identify problems.

While the experiences at NCR and Lincoln Electric were isolated, productivity improvement has always been the focal point of the profession of industrial engineering (IE). One productivity improvement program, called **work simplification,** was developed by Allan Mogensen. Mogensen believed that workers know their jobs better than anyone else. Therefore, if they are trained in the simple steps necessary to analyze and challenge the work they are doing, then they are more likely to be able to make improvements. In work simplification programs, workers receive training in the use of basic analytic techniques such as methods analysis, flowcharting, and diagramming to analyze work procedures for improvement. This concept helped the production effort during World War II greatly. Maytag and Texas Instruments were among the first companies to use work simplification.

Another approach, pioneered by Procter & Gamble, is called **planned methods change.** While work simplification emphasized continuous improvement, planned methods change went one step further, seeking not only to improve, but also to replace or eliminate unnecessary operations. This approach relied on forming teams of employees to study the operations, establishing specific dollar goals as to how much of their cost they would try to eliminate through planned change, and providing positive recognition for success.

Traditional improvement programs focused almost exclusively on productivity and cost. A focus on quality improvement, on the other hand, is relatively recent, stimulated by the success of the Japanese. During the rebuilding years after World War II in Japan, U.S. consultants taught the Japanese how to generate methods improvement ideas, and how to make sure they are implemented. At the same time, Japanese executives toured the United States and returned with numerous ideas. Many companies developed continuous improvement programs; some of the early ones included Toshiba in 1946, Matsushita Electric in 1950, and Toyota in 1951. Toyota, in particular, pioneered just-in-time (see Chapter 7). JIT showed that companies could make products with virtually zero defects, and reversed the thinking zero defects was a costly practice. In fact, JIT proved that producing extremely low defect levels typically saved money. Most importantly, JIT established a philosophy of improvement, which the Japanese call **kaizen** (pronounced kī - zen).

◼ Kaizen[8]

Kaizen is a philosophy, a way of life, that subsumes all business activities. Kaizen strategy has been called "the single most important concept in Japanese management—the key to Japanese competitive success." Often in the West, quality improvement is viewed simply as improvements in *product* quality. In the kaizen philosophy, improvement in all areas of business such as cost, meeting delivery schedules, employee safety and skill development, supplier relations, new product development, or productivity, all enhance the *quality of the firm*. Thus, any activity directed toward improvement falls under the kaizen umbrella. Activities to establish traditional quality control systems, install robotics and advanced technology, institute employee suggestion systems, maintain equipment, and implement just-in-time production systems all lead to improvement.

Kaizen is different from innovation. Innovation, which generally represents the focus of Western management, results in large, short-term, and radical changes in products or processes. Often innovation is the equivalent of substantial investment in equipment or technology with major rebuilding of entire plants. Innovation is dramatic and often championed by a few proponents. Formal economic analyses show large returns on investment. Major innovations such as material requirements planning (MRP) or flexible manufacturing systems (FMS) grab the attention of top managers. The American automotive industry, for example, believed that it could cure its quality and competitive problems in the 1970s by the introduction of robots and other types of automated equipment. They learned that innovative technologies are not the magic cure.

Kaizen, on the other hand, concentrates on small, gradual, though frequent, improvements over a long term. Financial investment is minimal. Everyone, not just top management, participates in the process; many improvements result from the know-how and experience of workers. People, not technology, are the principal asset. Kaizen is a process-oriented way of thinking rather than the results-oriented approach so characteristic of Western management thought. At Nissan Motor, for instance, any suggestion that saves at least 0.6 seconds in a production process is seriously considered by management. The concept of kaizen is so deeply ingrained in the minds of both managers and workers that they often do not even realize they are thinking in terms of improvement. Innovation is recognized as an important aspect of kaizen; however, it is emphasized far less in Japan than in the West.

In quality improvement, the first and foremost concern of the kaizen philosophy is the quality of people. If quality of people is improved, then the quality of products will follow. By instilling kaizen into people and training them in basic quality improvement tools, workers can build this philosophy into their work and continually seek improvement in their jobs. This process-oriented approach to improvement encourages constant communication among workers and managers.

Three things are required for a successful kaizen program: operating practices, total involvement, and training.[9] First, operating practices expose new improvement opportunities. Practices such as just-in-time reveal waste and inefficiency as well as poor quality. Second, in kaizen, every employee strives for improvement. Top management, for example, views improvement as an inherent component of corporate strategy and provides support to improvement activities by allocating resources effectively. They also build systems, procedures, and reward structures that are conducive to improvement. Middle management can implement top management's improvement goals by establishing, upgrading, and maintaining operating standards that reflect those goals; by improving cooperation between departments; and by making employees conscious of their responsibility for improvement and developing their problem solving skills through training. Supervisors can direct more of their attention to improvement rather than "supervision," which, in turn, facilitates communication and offers better guidance to workers. Finally, workers can engage in improvement through suggestion systems and small group activities, self-development programs that teach practical problem-solving techniques, and enhanced job performance skills. Motorola trains its employees to use a six-step approach for continuous improvement:

1. *Identify the product or service:* What work do I do?
2. *Identify the customer:* Who is the work for?

3. *Identify the supplier:* What do I need and from whom do I get it?

4. *Identify the process:* What steps or tasks are performed? What are the inputs and outputs for each step?

5. *Mistake-proof the process:* How can I eliminate or simplify tasks? What poka-yoke devices (see Chapter 7) can I use?

6. *Develop measurements and controls, and improvement goals:* How do I evaluate the process? How can I improve further?

This type of participative management approach and other employee involvement activities are fundamental to kaizen.

The essence of kaizen is simple and, upon reflection, just plain common sense. Much more can be said about kaizen; readers are encouraged to consult Imai's book. Kaizen is also present in the philosophies of other leaders in quality, such as Deming, Juran, and Crosby, as well as in other recent business trends, specifically benchmarking and reengineering, which are discussed in the next section.

STRETCH GOALS AND BREAKTHROUGH IMPROVEMENT

Motorola uses defects per unit as a quality measure throughout the company. A *unit* is any output of work, such as a line of computer code, a solder connection, or a page of a document. A defect is any failure to meet customer requirements. Motorola developed a concept called "six sigma" quality, which refers to allowing, at most, 3.4 defects per million units. (The statistical reasoning for six sigma is explained in Chapter 14.) In 1987, Motorola set the following goal:

> Improve product and services quality ten times by 1989, and at least one hundred fold by 1991. Achieve six sigma capability by 1992. With a deep sense of urgency, spread dedication to quality to every facet of the corporation, and achieve a culture of continuous improvement to assure total customer satisfaction. There is only one ultimate goal: zero defects—in everything we do.

These ambitious goals apply to all areas of the company, including order entry, sales, purchasing, manufacturing, and design. One of Motorola's current goals is a 10-fold improvement in cycle time every five years. The modern terminology for such goals is **stretch goals,** or **breakthrough objectives.** Stretch goals force an organization to think radically different, to encourage major improvements as well as incremental ones. When a goal of 10 percent improvement is set, managers or engineers can usually meet it with some minor improvements. However, when the goal is 1000 percent improvement, employees must be creative. The seemingly impossible is often achieved, yielding dramatic improvements and boosting morale. Two approaches that help companies accomplish such results are benchmarking and reengineering.

■ Benchmarking

The development and realization of improvement objectives, particularly stretch objectives, is often aided through a process known as **benchmarking.** Benchmarking is defined as "measuring your performance against that of best-in-class companies, determining how the best-in-class achieve those performance levels, and using the information as a basis for your own company's targets, strategies, and implementation."[10] Or more simply, "the search of industry best practices that lead to superior performance."[11] Through benchmarking, a company discovers its strengths and weaknesses and those of other industrial leaders and learns how to incorporate the best practices into its own operations.

The concept of benchmarking is not new.[12] In the early 1800s, Francis Lowell, a New England industrialist, traveled to England to study manufacturing techniques of the best British mill factories. Henry Ford created the assembly line after taking a tour of a Chicago slaughterhouse and watching carcasses, hung on hooks mounted on a monorail, move from one work station to another. Toyota's just-in-time production system was influenced by replenishment practices of U.S. supermarkets. Modern benchmarking was initiated by Xerox—an eventual winner of the Malcolm Baldrige National Quality Award (see the Quality in Practice in Chapter 1)—and has since become a common practice among leading firms.

Three major types of benchmarking have emerged in business. *Performance benchmarking* involves pricing, technical quality, features, and other quality or performance characteristics of products and services. Performance benchmarking is usually performed by direct comparisions or "reverse engineering," in which competitor's products are taken apart and analyzed. This practice is also called "competitive comparison," and involves studying products and processes of competitors in the same industry. *Process benchmarking* centers on work processes such as billing, order entry, or employee training. This type of benchmarking identifies the most effective practices in companies that perform similar functions, no matter what industry. For example, the warehousing and distribution practices of L. L. Bean were adapted by Xerox for its spare parts distribution system. Texas Instruments studied the kitting (order preparation) practices of six companies, including Mary Kay Cosmetics, and designed a process that captured the best practices of each of them, cutting kitting cycle time in half. Thus, companies should not aim benchmarking solely at direct competitors; in fact, they would be mistaken to do so. If a company simply benchmarks within its own industry, it may be competitive and have an edge in those areas in which it is the industry leader. However, if benchmarks are adopted from outside the industry, a company may learn ideas and processes as well as new applications that allow it to surpass the best within its own industry and to achieve distinctive superiority. Finally, *strategic benchmarking* examines how companies compete and seeks the winning strategies that have led to competitive advantage and market success.

The typical benchmarking process can be described by the process used at AT&T.

1. *Project conception:* identify the need and decide to benchmark.

2. *Planning:* determine the scope and objectives, and develop a benchmarking plan.

3. *Preliminary data collection:* Collect data on industry companies and similar processes as well as detailed data on your own processes.

4. *Best-in-class selection:* select companies with best-in-class processes.

5. *Best-in-class collection:* collect detailed data from companies with best-in-class processes.

6. *Assessment:* compare your own and best-in-class processes and develop recommendations.

7. *Implementation planning:* develop operational improvement plans to attain superior performance

8. *Implementation:* enact operational plans and monitor process improvements.

9. *Recalibration:* update benchmark findings and assess improvements in processes.[13]

Benchmarking has many benefits.[14] The best practices from any industry may be creatively incorporated into a company's operations. Benchmarking is motivating. It provides targets that have been achieved by others. Resistance to change may be lessened if ideas for improvement come from other industries. Technical breakthroughs from other industries that may be useful can be identified early. Benchmarking broadens peoples' experience base and increases knowledge. To be effective, it must be applied to all facets of a business. For example, Motorola encourages everyone in the organization to ask "Who is the best person in my own field and how might I use some of their techniques and characteristics to improve my own performance in order to be the best (executive, machine operator, chef, purchasing agent, etc.) in my 'class'?" Used in this fashion, benchmarking becomes a tool for continuous improvement.

◼ Reengineering

Reengineering has been defined as "the fundamental rethinking and radical redesign of business processes to achieve dramatic improvements in critical, contemporary measures of performance, such as cost, quality, service, and speed."[15] Reengineering involves asking basic questions about business processes: Why do we do it? and Why is it done this way? Such questioning often uncovers obsolete, erroneous, or inappropriate assumptions. Radical redesign involves tossing out existing procedures and reinventing the process, not just incrementally improving it. The goal is to achieve quantum leaps in performance. For example, IBM Credit Corporation cut the process of financing IBM computers, software, and services from seven days to four hours by rethinking the process. Originally, the process was designed to handle difficult applications and required four highly-trained specialists and a series of handoffs. The actual work took only about 1.5 hours; the rest of the time was spent in transit or delay. By questioning the assumption that every application was unique and difficult to process, IBM Credit Corporation was able to replace the specialists by a single individual supported by a user-friendly computer system that provided access to all the data and tools that the specialists would use.

Successful reengineering requires fundamental understanding of processes, creative thinking to break away from old traditions and assumptions, and effective use of information technology. Pepsi-Cola has embarked on a program to reengineer all of its key business processes, such as selling and delivery, equipment service and repair, procurement, and financial reporting. In the selling and delivery of its products, for example, customer reps typically experience stock outs of as much as 25 percent of product by the end of the day, resulting in late-day stops not getting full deliveries and the need to return to those accounts. Many other routes return with overstock of other products, increasing handling costs. By redesigning the system to include hand-held computers, customer reps can confirm and deliver that day's order and also take a future order for the next delivery to that customer.[16]

Benchmarking can greatly assist reengineering efforts. Reengineering without benchmarking probably will produce 5 to 10 percent improvements; benchmarking can increase this percentage to 50 or 75 percent. When GTE reengineered eight core processes of its telephone operations, it examined the best practices of some 84 companies from diverse industries. By studying outside best practices, a company can identify and import new technology, skills, structures, training, and capabilities.[17]

Contrary to the suggestions of many authors and consultants, reengineering is *not* completely different from TQM. The issue is not kaizen versus breakthrough improvement. In fact, Juran talked about breakthrough improvement long before Hammer and Champy popularized the term *reengineering*. Incremental and breakthrough improvement are complementary approaches that fall under the TQM umbrella; both are necessary to remain competitive. In fact, some suggest that reengineering requires TQM support to be successful.[18] Reengineering alone is often driven by upper management without the full support or understanding of the rest of the organization, and radical innovations may end up as failures. The TQM philosophy encourages participation and systematic study, measurement, and verification of results that support reengineering efforts.

QUALITY IMPROVEMENT AND PROBLEM SOLVING

Successful quality improvement depends on the ability to identify and solve problems. According to Kepner and Tregoe, a **problem** is a deviation between what should be happening and what actually is happening that is important enough to make someone think the deviation ought to be corrected.[19] Three conditions characterize a problem. First, several alternative courses of action from which to choose must be available. Second, the choice of a course of action can have a significant impact in the future. Third, some doubt exists as to which option to select. The selection of a course of action from several alternatives is called *decision making. Problem solving* is the activity associated with changing the state of what is actually happening to what should be happening.

Most problems can usually be categorized in one of three ways: structured, semistructured, or ill-structured. This classification is determined by the amount of information available about the problem. For structured problems, complete information about the problem—what is happening, what should be happening, and how to get there—is available. Ill-structured problems, on the other hand, are characterized by a high degree of fuzziness or vagueness. Semistructured problems fall somewhere in between. The usefulness of these classifications lies in their ability to prescribe a problem-solving aproach. Structured problems generally can be solved using routine, programmed decision-making techniques. Ill-structured and semistructured problems require more creative solutions and hence, a systematic process to find these solutions.

An example of a structured problem situation would be the case in which the diameter of a machined hole is smaller than the desired specification. The operator might be instructed to check the cutting tool for wear and replace it when necessary. Little problem-solving ability would be necessary to remedy this problem.

An example of a semistructured problem might be the case of determining what quality control actions to take when a new production setup on the shop floor has been initiated. This situation is certainly less routine and well-defined than the previous case. A solution to this problem might be to employ the following rules: Run the first five parts after the setup and compute the average dimension. If it is within one standard deviation of the target, continue production. If it is between one and two standard deviations of the target, take another sample. If it is beyond two standard deviations, stop and adjust the setup. Such problems can generally be solved using routine decision aids, although more creative effort may be needed to develop an acceptable solution.

Finally, an example of an ill-structured problem would be the situation in which 35 percent of final assemblies do not meet performance requirements. Here, considerably more ambiguity about the problem and how to go about solving it is involved than in either of the two previous cases. Simple, programmed decision rules cannot be developed. Such problems must be addressed individually using a systematic problem-solving methodology.

The following example shows how Hewlett-Packard dealt with a problem involving one of its suppliers.

EXAMPLE 1   Solving a Supplier Reject Problem.[20]   A supplier to Hewlett-Packard's Computer Division, in Cupertino, California, provided a unique assembly at a reasonable price but could not deliver the part without a high number of rejects. Management's first reaction was to consider a new supplier. However, since the supplier had been difficult to find, management made the decision to help the supplier do a better job.

A project team, headed by the procurement engineer and aided by the buyer and incoming inspection supervisor, was formed. Its goals were to eliminate incoming inspection and establish direct shipment of the supplier's assemblies into stock. The project team developed a three-stage plan to achieve these goals: investigation of why rejects occur, elimination of causes to gain quality confidence, and implementation of a plan to eliminate incoming inspection. Investigation was initiated by analyzing the vendor's production and quality assurance capabilities. HP had to make sure that the supplier had correct information on the product specifications required. It was found that the supplier's interpretation of the specification did not agree with HP's expectations for the part specified. The specification was therefore modified to better meet the objectives of both the supplier and HP.

Next, HP needed to ensure that the supplier's production process was capable of meeting HP's requirements. The supplier outlined the production process and noted several improvements it could make to improve quality. HP and its supplier established the same quality-measuring methods, materials, and equipment at the supplier's facility that were used at the HP plant. HP also videotaped the supplier's process for better communication and as a reference for future audits, and performed on-site inspections on production runs prior to shipment.

To gain confidence, HP closely monitored its own data and supplier data to confirm that the quality methods, materials, and equipment established earlier were being used. The supplier was encouraged to make corrections to its production processes. Communications improved and control charts verified that the processes were producing at an acceptable quality level.

Two of the major problems that were uncovered involved a disparity in specifications and measurement. The brightness specification for computer monitors was 47 foot lamberts (F.L.). For customers other than HP, the supplier's average brightness level was 38.25 F.L., with a minimum of 35 F.L. The supplier apparently misread or misunderstood HP's specification of 47. Also, a check revealed that measuring equipment and the adjustment instructions in the supplier's assembly stations were incompatible. The problems were corrected.

Eventually, HP stopped routine incoming inspection. HP monitored product quality by using control charts and by making yearly visits to the supplier's plant. When the charts indicated a quality problem, HP and the supplier made special inspections and took corrective measures. The benefits of this planning and action included a reduction in supplier appraisal costs and average lead times and the elimination of 100 percent inspection and rework returns.

The problem faced by Hewlett-Packard probably falls into the ill-structured category due to its complexity and lack of clear information, which is characteristic of many important problems in quality assurance. This case reveals some important aspects of problem solving. First, the number-of-rejects problem was not specific enough to be solved; it was a symptom of other problems, but not the problem in itself. This type of situation is often called a *mess*. HP and the supplier first had to identify specific problems, such as the misinterpretation of specifications, in order to correct the situation. Second, a project team was formed to address the problem. Third, the "gaining confidence" phase of the project relied on a significant amount of data collection and analysis, which enabled the problem-solving team to generate ideas for possible solutions. Fourth, both companies monitored and controlled the implementation of solutions.

Messy problems require a systematic process to develop and implement solutions. A structured process provides all employees with a common language and a set of tools to communicate with each other, particularly as members of cross-functional teams. "Speaking the same language" builds confidence and assures that solutions are developed objectively, rather than by intuition. Leaders in the quality revolution—Deming, Juran, and Crosby—have proposed specific methodologies for quality improvement. Each methodology is distinctive in its own right, yet they share many common themes. Most leading companies have adopted one of these or have developed their own unique version. This section reviews their approaches and then introduces a generic process for problem solving based on principles of creative thinking.

■ The Deming Cycle

Chapter 3 discussed W. Edwards Deming's 14 Points for management and his emphasis on the reduction of variation for quality improvement. The *Deming cycle* is a methodology for improvement. It was originally called the Shewhart cycle after its founder, Walter Shewhart, but was renamed the Deming cycle by the Japanese in 1950. The Deming cycle is composed of four stages: *plan, do, study,* and *act* (see Figure 9.6). (The third stage—study—was formerly called *check*, and the Deming cycle was known as the PDCA cycle. Deming made the change in 1990. Study is more appropriate; with only a "check," one might miss something. However, many people still use "check.") Much of the focus of the Deming cycle is on implementation. The plan stage consists of studying the current situation, gathering data, and planning for improvement. Its activities include defining the process, its inputs, outputs, customers, and suppliers; understanding customer expectations; identifying problems; testing theories of causes; and developing solutions. In the do stage, the plan is implemented on a trial basis, for example, in a laboratory, pilot production process, or with a small group of customers. This limited implementation is an experiment to evaluate a proposed solution and provide objective data. The study stage determines whether the trial plan is working correctly and if any further problems or op-

FIGURE 9.6   The Deming Cycle

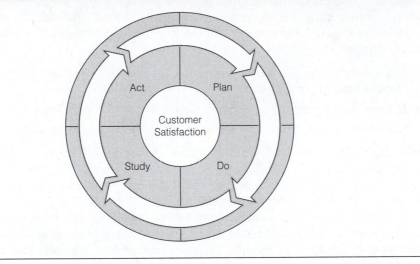

portunities are found. Often, a proposed solution must be modified or scrapped. New solutions are proposed and evaluated by returning to the do stage. In the last stage, act, the final plan is implemented and the improvements become standardized and practiced continuously. This process then leads back to the plan stage for further diagnosis and improvement. As Figure 9.6 illustrates, the cycle is never ending; that is, it is focused on continuous improvement. The improved process is only a springboard for further improvements. With its kaizen-like philosophy, one can easily see why the Deming cycle has been an essential element of Japanese quality improvement programs.

The Deming cycle is based on the premise that improvement comes from the application of knowledge.[21] This knowledge may be knowledge of engineering, management, or how a process operates that can make a job easier, more accurate, faster, less costly, safer, or better meet customer needs. Three fundamental questions to consider are

1. What are we trying to accomplish?
2. What changes can we make that will result in improvement?
3. How will we know that a change is an improvement?

Through a process of learning, knowledge is developed.

The following example demonstrates how the Deming cycle can be applied in practice.

EXAMPLE 2   Improving Service at a Restaurant.[22]   The co-owners of a luncheonette decided to do something about the long lines that occurred every day in their place of business. After discussions with their employees, several important facts came to light:

■ Customers waited in line for up to 15 minutes.

■ Usually, tables were available.

■ Many of their customers were regulars.

■ People taking orders and preparing food were getting in each other's way.

To measure the improvement that might result from any change they made, they decided to collect data on the number of customers in line, the number of empty tables, and the time until a customer received the food ordered.

In the plan stage, the owners wanted to test a few changes. They decided on three changes:

1. Provide a way for customers to fax their orders in ahead of time (rent a fax machine for one month).

2. Construct a preparation table in the kitchen with ample room for fax orders.

3. Devote one of their two cash registers to handling fax orders.

Both the length of the line and the number of empty tables was measured every 15 minutes during the lunch hour by one of the owners. In addition, when the 15 minute line check was done, she noted the last person in line and measured the time until that person got served.

In the do phase, the owners observed the results of the three measures for three weeks. In the study phase, they detected several improvements. Time in line went down from 15 minutes to an average of five minutes. The line length was cut to a peak average of 12 people, and the number of empty tables decreased slightly. In the act phase, the owners held a meeting with all employees to discuss the results. They decided to purchase the fax machine, prepare phone orders in the kitchen with the fax orders, and use both cash registers to handle walk-up and fax orders.

Juran's Improvement Program

Joseph Juran emphasized the importance of developing a habit of making annual improvements in quality and annual reductions in quality-related costs. Juran defined *breakthrough* as the accomplishment of any improvement that takes an organization to unprecedented levels of performance. Breakthrough attacks chronic losses or, in Deming's terminology, common causes of variation.

EXAMPLE 3   Breakthrough at INCO, Ltd.   An example of breakthrough was reported by the Manitoba Division of INCO Limited.[23] The data entry department employed a staff of six operators and a full-time working supervisor, yet still averaged 100 hours of overtime to handle the workload. After studying the processes and reviewing the needs with customers, the company simplified data entry procedures, employees cross-trained themselves in different skills, and work loads were smoothed. As a result, overtime was virtually eliminated (see Figure 9.7, p. 347) and the supervisor, who was an integral part of the improvement, was transferred to a more challenging and rewarding position in another department.

All breakthroughs follow a common sense sequence of discovery, organization, diagnosis, corrective action, and control. This "breakthrough sequence" is described and formalized in a 16-session videotape/workbook series entitled *Juran on Quality Improvement*, which is summarized below.

1. *Proof of the need:* Managers, especially top managers, need to be convinced that quality improvements are simply good economics. Through data collection efforts, information on poor quality, low productivity, or poor service can

FIGURE 9.7 Data Entry Overtime Hours

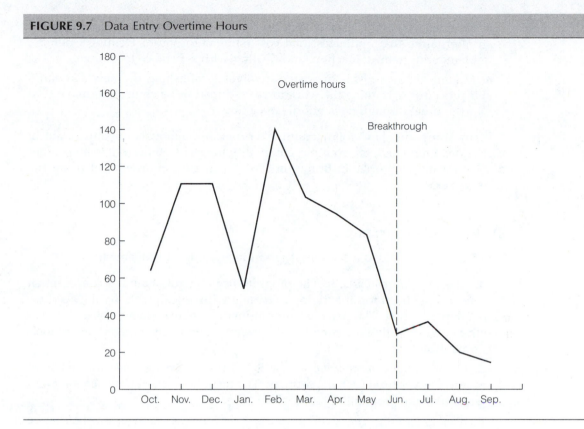

be translated into the language of money—the universal language of top management—to justify a request for resources to implement a quality improvement program.

2. *Project identification:* All breakthroughs are achieved project by project, and in no other way. By taking a project approach, management provides a forum for converting an atmosphere of defensiveness or blame into one of constructive action. Participation in a project increases the likelihood that the participant will act on the results.

3. *Organization for breakthrough:* Organization for improvement requires a clear responsibility for guiding the project. The responsibility for the project may be as broad as an entire division with formal committee structures or as narrow as a small group of workers at one production operation. These groups provide the definition and agreement as to the specific aims of the project, the authority to conduct experiments, and implementation strategies. The path from problem to solution consists of two journeys: one from symptom to cause (the diagnostic journey) and the other from cause to remedy (the remedial journey), which must be performed by different individuals with the appropriate skills.

4. *Diagnostic journey:* Diagnosticians skilled in data collection, statistics, and other problem-solving tools are needed at this stage. Some projects will require full-time, specialized experts while others can be performed by the work force. Management-controllable and operator-controllable problems require different methods of diagnosis and remedy.

5. *Remedial journey:* The remedial journey consists of several phases: choosing an alternative that optimizes total cost (similar to one of Deming's points), implementing remedial action, and dealing with resistance to change.

6. *Holding the gains:* This final step involves establishing the new standards and procedures, training the work force, and instituting controls to make sure that the breakthrough does not die over time.

Many companies have followed Juran's program religiously. A Xerox plant in Mitcheldean, England, for example, cut quality losses by 30 percent to 40 percent and won a national prize in Britain in 1984 for quality improvement using the Juran system.[24]

■ The Crosby Program

Philip Crosby proposed a 14-step program for quality improvement:

1. *Management commitment:* The program begins with obtaining commitment from management for quality improvement with an emphasis on the need for defect prevention. The personal commitment of management raises the visibility of a quality improvement program and encourages everyone's cooperation.

2. *Quality improvement team:* A quality improvement team is formed with representatives from each department. The team is oriented to the content and purpose of the program.

3. *Quality measurement:* Quality measurement for each activity must either be reviewed or established to show where improvement is possible, where corrective action is necessary, and to document actual improvement later.

4. *Cost of quality evaluation:* Accurate figures obtained on the cost of quality indicate where corrective action will be profitable. This step provides a companywide measurement of quality management performance.

5. *Quality awareness:* Share with employees the measurements of what a lack of quality is costing. This step gets supervisors and employees in the habit of talking positively about quality and changing existing attitudes.

6. *Corrective action:* As people are encouraged to talk about their problems, opportunities for correction come to light, particularly from the workers themselves. These problems must be brought to the attention of managers and resolved. As employees see that their problems are being corrected, they will get in the habit of identifying further problems.

7. *Establish an ad hoc committee for the zero defects program:* Three or four members of the team are selected to investigate the "zero defects" concept and ways to implement the program. It is not a motivation program, but a program to communicate the meaning of "zero defects" and the concept of doing it right the first time.

8. *Supervisor training:* All managers must understand each step well enough to explain it to their people. Training helps supervisors to understand the program and realize its value for themselves.

9. *Zero defects day:* The establishment of zero defects as the performance standard of the company should be done in one day so that everyone understands it the same way. It provides an emphasis and a long-lasting memory.

10. *Goal setting:* Each supervisor should establish goals to achieve that are specific and capable of being measured.

11. *Error cause removal:* Individuals are asked to describe any problem that keeps them from performing error-free work on a simple, one-page form. The appropriate functional group develops the answer. Problems should be acknowledged quickly. People need to know that problems will be heard and develop trust in management.

12. *Recognition:* Establish award programs to recognize those who meet their goals or perform outstanding acts. The prizes or awards should not be financial; recognition is what is important. People appreciate recognition of performance, which increases support of the program.

13. *Quality councils:* The quality professionals and team chairpersons meet regularly to discuss and determine actions necessary to upgrade and improve the quality program.

14. *Do it over again:* The typical program takes one year to 18 months. Changes in the organization require new organization efforts. Quality must be ingrained in the organization.

The quality improvement philosophies of Deming, Juran, and Crosby differ considerably. The Deming cycle is purposefully simple—to be understood and performed by individuals and groups at all levels of an organization. However, it concentrates more on verifying solutions rather than developing them. Juran's program is much more structured toward the project level and cast in traditional organizational language; it is replete with specific techniques and methods for implementing each step. Crosby's program is a formal, companywide program with a heavy emphasis on motivation.

Not every approach is appropriate for all organizations; one must be chosen or designed to fit the organization's culture and people. For example, at the Bethesda Hospitals of Cincinnati, Ohio, both the Juran and Deming approaches are integrated as shown in Figure 9.8. The left side of the figure incorporates the essential elements of Juran's diagnostic/remedial journeys. Once a solution is proposed, the Deming cycle is then used to evaluate the solution's effectiveness prior to implementation.

CREATIVE PROBLEM-SOLVING METHODOLOGY AND TOOLS FOR QUALITY IMPROVEMENT

Problem solving is a highly creative effort. Any problem-solving process has four major components:

1. Redefining and analyzing the problem
2. Generating ideas
3. Evaluating and selecting ideas
4. Implementing ideas[25]

In redefining and analyzing a problem, problem solvers collect and organize information, analyze the data and underlying assumptions, and reexamine the problem for new perspectives. At this stage, the goal of the problem solver is to

FIGURE 9.8 Bethesda Hospital Process Improvement Model

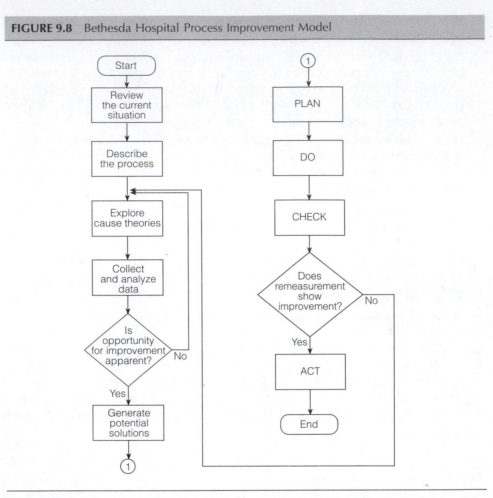

SOURCE: Reprinted with permission of Bethesda Hospital, Inc. 619 Oak Street, Cincinnati, Ohio 45241.

collect facts and achieve a workable problem definition. The purpose of generating ideas is to develop potential solutions. The two most important considerations in this step are to defer all judgment about the ideas and to use many different techniques to generate them. After ideas have been generated, the problem solvers evaluate them to identify and select the best ones. When problem solving is done in a group, as is most often the case with ill-structured problems, conflicts can easily develop. Thus, at this stage a good leader and facilitator is critical to reaching a consensus within the group. Finally, implementing ideas involves putting the solution to work, which requires a great deal of psychology in selling ideas and solutions and in gaining acceptance. All these components are evident in the Deming cycle and Juran's approach, although with different emphases.

An effective problem-solving process for quality improvement (and for any problem-solving activity, for that matter) is adapted from creative problem-solving concepts advocated by Osborn and by Parnes.[26] This strategy consists of the following steps:

1. Understanding the "mess"
2. Finding facts
3. Identifying specific problems
4. Generating ideas
5. Developing solutions
6. Implementation

The plan stage in the Deming cycle, for example, actually consists of the first five steps; the do, study, and act stages deal more with implementation. In Juran's program, the "diagnostic and remedial journeys" are essentially the same as this process. This process can easily be integrated into the Deming cycle, Juran's approach, and Crosby's program.

Seven simple tools—flowcharts, check sheets, histograms, Pareto diagrams, cause-and-effect diagrams, scatter diagrams, and control charts—termed the *Seven QC (quality control) Tools* by the Japanese, and the 7 Management and Planning Tools (discussed in Chapter 6) support this problem solving methodology. Table 9.2 shows the primary applications of each tool in the problem-solving process. They are designed simply so that workers at all levels can use them easily. The next sections examine how this methodology and tools can be applied to improve quality.

■ Mess Finding

Russell Ackoff, a noted authority on problem solving, defines a *mess* as a "system of external conditions that produces dissatisfaction."[27] Ackoff carefully distinguishes problems from messes. Managers in any organization generally deal with messes; problems must be identified and extracted from the "mess."

The mess in quality assurance is often a poor state of quality within an organization. High quality costs, high defect rates, and low customer satisfaction signify a mess. Messes arise from several sources:

■ A lack of knowledge about how a process works, which is particularly critical if the process is performed by different people. Such lack of knowledge results in inconsistency and increased variation in outputs.

■ A lack of knowledge about how a process *should* work, including understanding customer expectations and the goal of the process.

■ Errors in performing the steps involved in a process. In most cases, errors are inadvertent. The worker does not want to make errors and is unaware of having made them. Inadvertent errors occur randomly and because of lack of attention. In isolated cases, errors are willful, often the result of poor management practices.

■ Waste and complexity, which manifest themselves in many ways, such as unnecessary steps in a process and excess inventories.

■ Excess variation. Reducing variation is the foundation of the Deming and Juran philosophies.

TABLE 9.2   Creative Problem-Solving and Quality Improvement Tools

Problem-Solving Step	Principal Tools
Understanding the mess	Flowcharts, run charts, and control charts
Finding facts	Check sheets
Identifying problems	Pareto diagrams and histograms
Generating ideas	Cause-and-effect diagrams
Developing solutions	Scatter diagrams
Implementing the plan	The seven management and planning tools

Contributors to poor quality are often faults of the production system itself. They include hasty design and production of parts and assemblies; poor design specifications; inadequate testing of incoming materials and prototypes; failure to understand the capability of a process to meet specifications; failure to provide workers with statistical signals of control; inadequate training; lack of instrument calibration and false reporting of test results; and poor environmental characteristics such as light, temperature, and noise. Messes are a gold mine of opportunity for improvement. Work sampling can be used to help a manager understand the nature of activities being performed and opportunities for improvement.

EXAMPLE 4 Using Work Sampling to Identify Improvement Opportunities. One example involved about 30 clerical and professional people in a Hewlett-Packard office taking telephone orders.[28] Management felt that a large amount of the work being performed was related to resolving problems caused by mistakes in processing and shipping the orders. A work sampling study was performed to classify these activities and understand the nature of the problems better. The study, performed over three days, resulted in 130 observations of the activities of 10 people. The activities were grouped by major category and counted. The supervisor asked the following question about each activity: "If there were no errors in the process and everything were running perfectly, would you be working on this activity?" The results of the seven most frequently observed activities were:

Activity	Type	Frequency
Processing customer returns	Nonproductive	20
Entering orders into computer	Productive	14
Converting orders to fix a problem	Nonproductive	8
Making changes to orders	Productive	8
Expediting shipments	Nonproductive	7
Answering questions about order status	Nonproductive	6
Taking orders over the telephone	Productive	4

Sixty-one percent of these activities were classified as nonproductive work. The most frequent activity, processing customer returns, was a result of shipping the wrong product, duplicate shipment, or wrong quantity being delivered to customers. The amount of time spent on this activity was the equivalent of six people. The supervisor immediately made changes in the work procedures to improve the processing of returns. At the same time, a task force was formed to reduce the number of products returned.

In service organizations, customer complaints provide a starting point for identifying quality-related problems.[29] Focus groups can be used effectively to learn about customer's experiences with a particular service. Another technique often used is called the *critical incident technique,* which involves an in-depth interview to generate a complete story about a service interaction. This method often reveals numerous issues relating to quality.

To understand messes, one must first determine how a process works and what it is supposed to do. By clearly defining a process, all involved reach a common understanding and do not waste time collecting irrelevant data. Variation is reduced by eliminating inconsistencies in the process. Understanding how a process works also enables one to pinpoint obvious problems, error-proof the process and streamline it by eliminating nonvalue-added steps. Developing a flowchart of the process usually aids in understanding a mess.

Flowcharts are best developed by having the people involved in the process—employees, supervisors, managers, and customers—construct the flowchart. A facilitator provides objectivity in resolving conflicts. The facilitator can guide the discussion through questions such as "What happens next?", "Who makes the decision at this point?", and "What operation is performed at this point?" Quite often, the group does not universally agree on the answers to these questions due to misconceptions about the process itself or a lack of awareness of the "big picture."

Flowcharts help the people who are involved in the process understand it much better and more objectively. Employees realize how they fit into the process and who is their supplier and customers. This realization then leads to improved communication among all parties. By participating in the development of a flowchart, workers feel a sense of ownership in the process, and hence become more willing to work on improving it. If flowcharts are used in training employees, then more consistency will be achieved.

Once a flowchart is constructed, it can be used to identify quality problems as well as areas for productivity improvement. Questions such as "How does this operation affect the customer?", "Can we improve or even eliminate this operation?" or "Should we control a critical quality characteristic at this point?" trigger the identification of opportunities.

EXAMPLE 5 Parking Garage Operation Flowchart. Figure 9.9 (p. 354) shows a simple flowchart of a parking garage operation. For example, we see that customers can become dissatisfied if the ticket machine does not work properly, if they must wait a long time at the cashier, or if the cashier is not friendly or does not make the correct change. Once such aspects of the process become apparent, managers might make decisions regarding preventive maintenance for the ticket machine such as a daily check for an adequate supply of tickets, a full ink well, accuracy of the time clock, and proper functioning of all mechanical parts. New procedures for customer interaction can also be designed into the process. The cashier might be required to say hello, state the fee, and state the change returned.

RUN CHARTS AND CONTROL CHARTS

Control is a continuous activity, requiring that measurements be made periodically over time. Drawing a visual picture of the variation in a process enhances communications among operators and supervisors, production and design personnel, and suppliers and customers. By using a visual picture, participants can determine at what point a process goes out of control. Run charts and control charts, which provide this capability, were introduced briefly while discussing the Red Bead experiment in Chapter 3.

A **run chart** is a line graph in which data are plotted over time. The vertical axis represents the measurement; the horizontal axis is the time scale. The daily

FIGURE 9.9 Flowchart for Parking Garage Operation

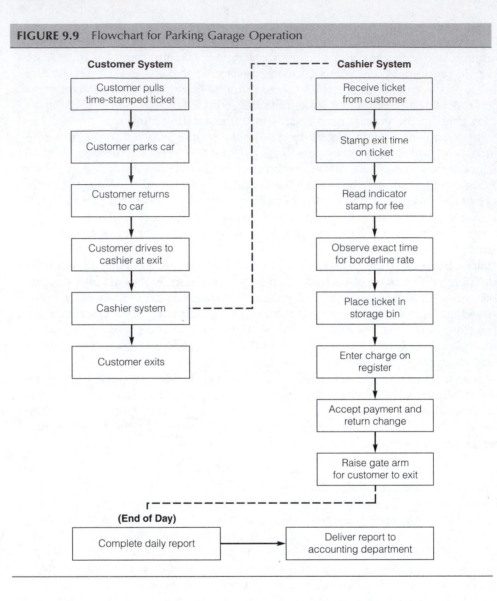

Customer System

Customer pulls time-stamped ticket

Customer parks car

Customer returns to car

Customer drives to cashier at exit

Cashier system

Customer exits

Cashier System

Receive ticket from customer

Stamp exit time on ticket

Read indicator stamp for fee

Observe exact time for borderline rate

Place ticket in storage bin

Enter charge on register

Accept payment and return change

Raise gate arm for customer to exit

(End of Day)

Complete daily report

Deliver report to accounting department

newspaper usually has several examples of run charts, such as the Dow Jones Industrial Average. Run charts show the performance and the variation of a process or some quality or productivity indicator over time. They can be used to track such things as production volume, costs, and customer satisfaction indexes. Run charts summarize data in a graphical fashion that is easy to understand and interpret, identify process changes and trends over time, and show the effects of corrective actions.

The first step in constructing a run chart is to identify the measurement or indicator to be monitored. Several options of how to take and report measurements are available. For variables data, one might measure the quality characteristics for each individual unit of process output. For low-volume processes, such as chemical production or surgeries, this particular type of measurement would be appropriate. However, for high-volume production processes or services with large numbers of customers or transactions, it would be impractical. Instead, samples taken on a periodic basis provide the data for computing basic statistical measures such as the mean and range or standard deviation. For attribute data, the number or proportion of items that do not conform to specifications can be counted. Another concern might be the number of nonconformances per unit.

Constructing the chart consists of the following steps:

Step 1. Collect the data. If samples are chosen, compute the relevant statistic for each sample, such as the average or proportion.

Step 2. Examine the range of the data. Scale the chart so that all data can be plotted on the vertical axis. Provide some additional room for new data as it is collected.

Step 3. Plot the points on the chart and connect them. Use graph paper if the chart is constructed by hand; a spreadsheet program is preferable.

Step 4. Compute the average of all plotted points and draw it as a horizontal line through the data. This line denoting the average is called the *center line (CL)* of the chart.

If the plotted points fluctuate in a stable pattern around the center line, with no large spikes, trends, or shifts, they indicate that the process is apparently under control. If unusual patterns exist, then the cause for lack of stability should be investigated and corrective action should be taken. Thus, run charts can identify messes caused by lack of control.

A **control chart** is simply a run chart to which two horizontal lines, called *control limits* are added: the *upper control limit (UCL)* and *lower control limit (LCL),* as illustrated in Figure 9.10 (p. 359). Control charts were first proposed by Walter Shewhart at Bell Laboratories in the 1920s and were strongly advocated by Deming. Control limits are chosen statistically so that there is a high probability (generally greater than 0.99) that points will fall between these limits if the process is in control. Control limits make it easier to interpret patterns in a run chart and draw conclusions about the state of control. Computing control limits is discussed in Chapters 15 and 16.

If sample values fall outside the control limits or if nonrandom patterns occur in the chart, then special causes may be affecting the process; the process is not stable. The process should be examined and corrective action taken as appro-

FIGURE 9.10 The Structure of a Control Chart

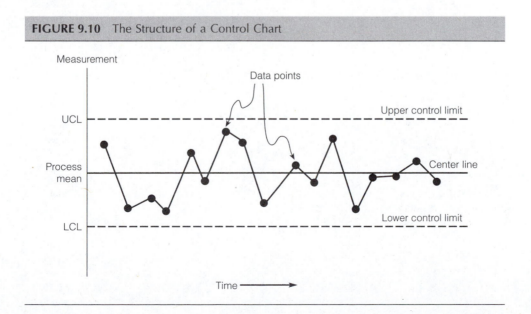

priate. If evaluation and correction are done in real time, then the chance of producing nonconforming product is minimized. Thus, as a problem-solving tool, control charts allow operators to identify quality problems as they occur. Of course, control charts alone cannot determine the source of the problem. Operators, supervisors, and engineers may have to resort to other problem-solving tools to seek the root cause.

EXAMPLE 6   Monitoring Surgery Infections.   The Joint Commission on Accreditation of Healthcare Organizations (JCAHO) monitors and evaluates health care providers according to strict standards and guidelines. Improvement in the quality of care is a principal concern. Hospitals are required to identify and monitor important quality indicators that affect patient care and establish "thresholds for evaluation" (TFE), which are levels at which special investigation of problems should occur. TFEs provide a means of focusing attention on nonrandom errors (that is, special causes of variation). A logical way to set TFEs is through control charts.

For instance, a hospital collects monthly data on the number of infections after surgeries. These data are shown in Table 9.3. Hospital administrators are concerned about whether the high percentages of infections (such as 1.76 percent in

TABLE 9.3   Monthly Data on Infections After Surgery

Month	Surgeries	Infections	Percent
1	208	1	0.48
2	225	3	1.33
3	201	3	1.49
4	236	1	0.42
5	220	3	1.36
6	244	1	0.41
7	247	1	0.40
8	245	1	0.41
9	250	1	0.40
10	227	0	0.00
11	234	2	0.85
12	227	4	1.76
13	213	2	0.94
14	212	1	0.47
15	193	2	1.04
16	182	0	0.00
17	140	1	0.71
18	230	1	0.43
19	187	1	0.53
20	252	2	0.79
21	201	1	0.50
22	226	0	0.00
23	222	2	0.90
24	212	2	0.94
25	219	1	0.46
26	223	2	0.90
27	191	1	0.52
28	222	0	0.00
29	231	3	1.30
30	239	1	0.42
31	217	2	0.92
32	241	1	0.41
33	220	3	1.36

Continued

Month	Surgeries	Infections	Percent
34	278	1	0.36
35	255	3	1.18
36	225	1	0.44
	7995	55	

month 12) are caused by factors other than randomness. A control chart constructed from these data is shown in Figure 9.11. (Note that if the control limits are removed, it becomes a simple run chart.) The average percent infections is 55/7995 = 0.688%. Using formulas described in Chapter 15, the upper control limit is computed to be 2.35 percent. None of the data points fall above the upper control limit, indicating that the variation each month is due purely to chance and that the process is stable. To reduce the infection rate, management would have to attack the common causes in the process. The upper control limit would be a logical TFE to use, since any value beyond this limit is unlikely to occur by chance. Management can continue to use this chart to monitor future data.

FIGURE 9.11   Control Chart for Surgery Infections

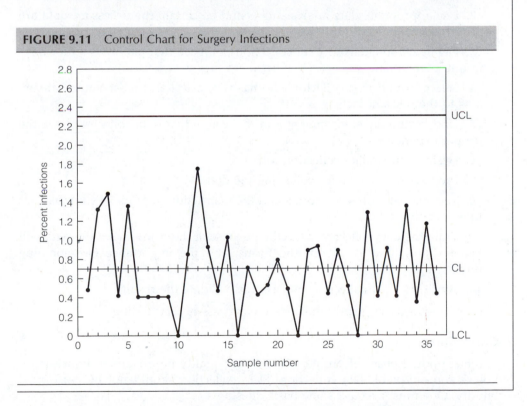

■ Fact Finding

Understanding the true state of quality—that is, fact finding—depends on data collection, observation, and careful listening. Past and current data is collected and analyzed to establish a base of information for problem identification and idea generation. As noted in Chapter 8, a good quality cost reporting system can provide important information for identifying quality problems. Many aspects of the quality information system—including control charts, process capability studies, analyses of customer complaints, and warranty claims—contribute to understanding the state of quality within an organization. As in the Hewlett-Packard example given earlier in this chapter, inspection of current production processes and practices often provides important information. The opinions of supervisors and workers are also a good source of information, as is feedback from customers and field service employees. Such opinions, however, must be based on fact and not on emotion. Proper design of the quality information system and the organizational structure is a prerequisite for effective problem solving for quality improvement.

The first step in data collection, which aids fact finding, is to develop operational definitions for all quality measures that will be collected. For example, what does it mean to have "on-time delivery"? Does it mean within one day of the promised time? One week? One hour? What is an error? Is it wrong information on an invoice, a typographical mistake, or either? Clearly, any data are meaningless unless they are well defined and understood without ambiguity.

The Juran Institute suggests 10 important considerations for data collection:

1. Formulate good questions that relate to the specific information needs of the project.

2. Use appropriate data analysis tools and be certain the necessary data are being collected.

3. Define comprehensive data collection points so that job flows suffer minimum interruption.

4. Select an unbiased collector who has the easiest and most immediate access to the relevant facts.

5. Understand the environment and make sure that data collectors have the proper experience.

6. Design simple data collection forms.

7. Prepare instructions for collecting the data.

8. Test the data collection forms and the instructions and make sure they are filled out properly.

9. Train the data collectors as to the purpose of the study, what the data will be used for, how to fill out the forms, and the importance of remaining unbiased.

10. Audit the data collection process and validate the results.[30]

These guidelines can greatly improve the process of fact finding.

CHECK SHEETS

The fact-finding phase of problem solving for quality improvement typically involves some type of data collection. Data collection should not be performed blindly. One must first ask some basic questions:

■ What questions are we trying to answer?

■ What type of data will we need to answer the question?

■ Where can we find the data?

■ Who can provide the data?

■ How can we collect the data with minimum effort and with minimum chance of error?

Nearly any kind of form may be used to collect data. **Data sheets** are simple columnar or tabular forms used to record data. To generate useful information from raw data, further processing generally is necessary. **Check sheets** are special types of data collection forms in which the results may be interpreted on the form directly without additional processing.

EXAMPLE 7   Parking Garage Data Collection Forms.   To collect data on parking garage rates, the cashier simply records the amount charged to each customer on a data sheet shown in Figure 9.12. If the rates are fixed at $0.50, $1.00, $1.30, $1.60, $1.90, to a maximum of $2.00, a more useful form for collecting this data is shown in Figure 9.13. If the data are tallied in this fashion, the rates occurring most often are readily apparent.

FIGURE 9.12   Data Collection Sheet for Parking Charges

Customer	Amount
1	1.00
2	0.50
3	1.30
4	1.30
5	2.00
6	1.60

FIGURE 9.13   Check Sheet for Garage Parking Rates

Amount	Tally
0.50	𝚰𝚮𝚮
1.00	𝚰𝚮𝚮 𝚰𝚮𝚮 ///
1.30	𝚰𝚮𝚮 𝚰𝚮𝚮 𝚰𝚮𝚮 𝚰𝚮𝚮 𝚰𝚮𝚮 //
1.60	𝚰𝚮𝚮 𝚰𝚮𝚮 𝚰𝚮𝚮 𝚰𝚮𝚮 //
2.00	𝚰𝚮𝚮 𝚰𝚮𝚮 ///

In manufacturing, check sheets similar to Figure 9.13 are simple to use and easily interpreted by shop personnel. Another example is given in Figure 9.14. Including information such as specification limits makes the number of nonconforming items easily observable and provides an immediate indication of the quality of the process. For example, in Figure 9.14 a significant proportion of dimensions is clearly out of specification, with a larger number on the high side than the low side.

A second type of check sheet for defective items is illustrated in Figure 9.15, which shows the type of defect and a tally in a resin production plant. Such a check sheet can be extended to include a time dimension so that data can be monitored and analyzed over time and trends and patterns, if any, can be detected.

Figure 9.16 shows an example of a defect location check sheet. Ishikawa relates how this check sheet was used to eliminate bubbles in laminated automobile windshield glass.[31] The location and form of bubbles were indicated on the check sheet; most of the bubbles occurred on the right side. Upon investigation, workers

FIGURE 9.14   Check Sheet for Data Collection

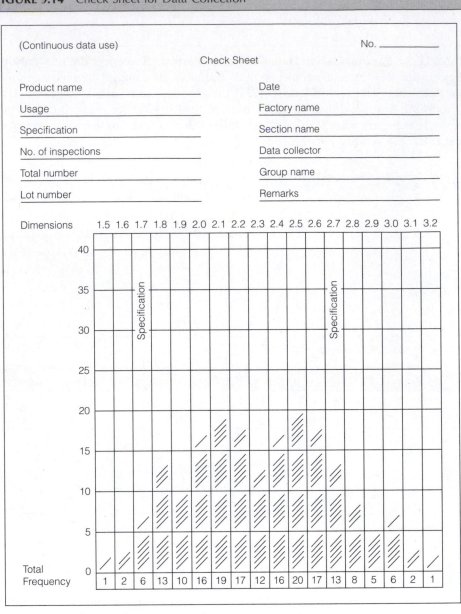

SOURCE: K. Ishikawa, *Guide to Quality Control* (Tokyo: Asian Productivity Organization, 1982), 31.

discovered that the pressure applied in laminating was off balance—the right side was receiving less pressure. The machine was adjusted, and the formation of bubbles was eliminated almost completely.

■ Problem Finding

An old proverb says that a problem clearly stated is half solved. The purpose of problem finding is to understand what the true problem is, that is, to identify the problem from the "mess." A major flaw in traditional problem-solving ap-

FIGURE 9.15   Defective Item Check Sheet

Check Sheet

Product: _____

Manufacturing stage: final insp. _____

Type of defect: scar, incomplete,
misshapen _____

Total no. inspected: 2530 _____

Remarks: all items inspected _____

Date: _____

Factory: _____

Section: _____

Inspector's
name: _____

Lot no. _____

Order no. _____

Type	Check	Subtotal
Surface scars	/// /// /// /// /// /// //	32
Cracks	/// /// /// /// ///	23
Incomplete	/// /// /// /// /// /// /// /// /// ///	48
Misshapen	////	4
Others	/// ///	8
	Grand total	115
Total rejects	/// /// /// /// /// /// /// /// /// /// /// /// /// /// /// /// /// /	86

SOURCE: K. Ishikawa, *Guide to Quality Control* (Tokyo: Asian Productivity Organization, 1982), 33.

proaches is a lack of emphasis on problem finding. Too often, action-oriented Americans want to jump to the solution phase of a problem without fully understanding the nature of the problem. Solving the wrong problem can happen if this step of the process is ignored.

The creative thinking literature emphasizes a redefinition of the problem, which is done by first asking "In what ways might I . . . ?" followed by "Why?" to redefine the problem. For example, consider the following simplified scenario for redefining "In what ways might I reduce the cost of final inspection?":

Ask why: Why do I want to reduce the cost of final inspection?

Answer: To reduce total quality costs.

Redefine: In what ways might I reduce total quality costs?

Ask why: Why do I want to reduce total quality costs?

Answer: To improve profitability.

Redefine: In what ways might I improve profitability?

As problems are restated in this fashion, new perspectives emerge. One must then converge to select the problem definition that best captures the real problem.

In services, a technique called *problem detection methodology* is often used to isolate critical problems.[32] Consumers assess each problem along several key dimensions such as frequency and bothersomeness. Consumers are asked to provide an estimate of how frequently they encounter a particular problem and also how bothersome the problem is to them. An example for food service problems

FIGURE 9.16 Defect Location Check Sheet

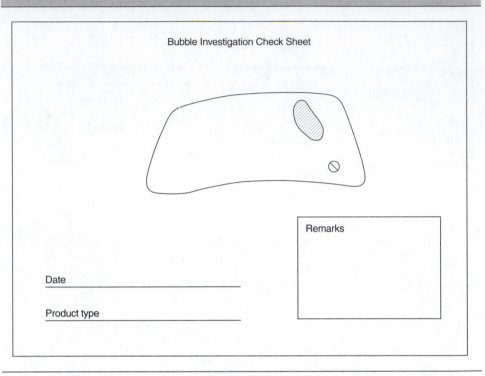

Bubble Investigation Check Sheet

Remarks

Date _____

Product type _____

SOURCE: K. Ishikawa, *Guide to Quality Control* (Tokyo: Asian Productivity Organization, 1982), 34.

is shown in Figure 9.17. In this example, poor food quality and discourteous employees are particularly bothersome, but occur only infrequently. Slow lines occur frequently, but are not perceived as highly bothersome. On the other hand, inflexible hours and empty vending machines were relatively frequent and bothersome. Management must direct attention to these problems.

FIGURE 9.17 Problem Detection Methodology in Food Service Assessment

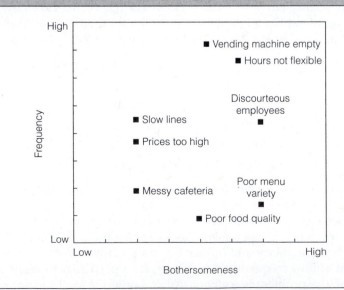

Although this methodology is useful, it has two significant limitations. First, the use of customer ratings to establish the relative impact on customer satisfaction and perceived quality yields ambiguous data. The problems customers find bothersome may not always be the ones that create the most dissatisfaction. Second, the ratings are subjective and not anchored to an absolute measurement system. More precise measures of customer satisfaction are needed.

HISTOGRAMS

Variation in a process always exists and generally displays some pattern. This pattern can be captured visually in a histogram. A **histogram** graphically represents the variation in a given set of data. It shows the frequency or number of observations of a particular value or within a specified group. Histograms provide clues about the characteristics of the parent population from which a sample is taken. Using a histogram, the shape of the distribution can be seen clearly and inferences can be made about the population. Patterns that would be difficult to see in an ordinary table of numbers become apparent.

EXAMPLE 8   Histogram of Parking Garage Charges.   A histogram of the parking garage charge data in Figure 9.13 (p. 359) is shown in Figure 9.18. The histogram shows that $1.30 is the most frequent parking charge, and that more than half the charges are either $1.30 or $1.60. How might this information lead to improvements in the process? The cashier probably spends a considerable amount of time making change for these amounts. If the rate structure were simplified, the waiting times of customers could be reduced and the accuracy of the change-making process improved. Since the rates are closely related to parking times, the histogram provides information that can be used to study the revenue implications of such changes.

FIGURE 9.18   Histogram of Parking Garage Charges

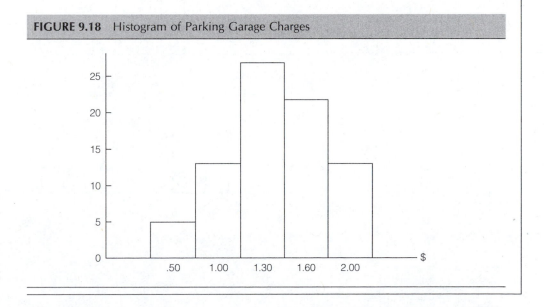

The check sheet in Figure 9.14 was designed to provide the visual appeal of a histogram as the data are tallied. For this data, one can easily determine the proportion of observations that fell outside of the specification limits. Histograms are extremely useful in process capability analysis, which is discussed in Chapter 14.

Figure 9.19 shows some typical patterns of histograms found in quality control applications. The bell-shaped pattern in Figure 9.19a is symmetrical in shape and is the most common form of variation in process output. The process is centered around some value and observations are less frequent the further away one moves from this central value. Any deviation from this pattern is usually the result of some external influence, which should be investigated. A bimodal pattern in Figure 9.19b suggests that two groups of bell-shaped measurements were combined. Isolation of the individual processes or conditions that cause this pattern is required. A uniform pattern in Figure 9.19c shows much wider variability with no central tendency. Often, this distribution is the result of combining the data of many different bell-shaped processes with different centers throughout the range of the data. A skewed pattern in Figure 9.19d is like the bell-shaped pattern, but not symmetrical; the distribution tails off in one direction. Skewed patterns arise when the data values are subject to a natural limit. For instance, time measurements of a manual task have a lower limit governed by the physical characteristics of the task and most will be close to this value. Infrequently, however, observations will be large due to disturbing influences on the process. If the task is related to customer service, then a long tail should be examined to

FIGURE 9.19   Typical Histogram Patterns in Quality Control

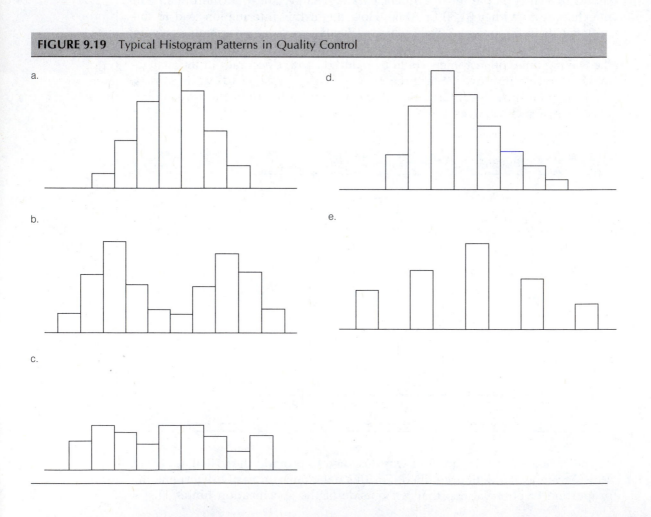

determine causes that result in long service times. Finally, a pattern such as that of Figure 9.19e with alternating high and low values often results from systematic measurement error, the way in which data are grouped, or bias due to rounding data values.

Some cautions should be heeded when interpreting histograms. First, the data should be representative of typical process conditions. If a new employee is now operating the equipment, or the equipment, material, method, etc., have changed, then new data should be collected. Second, the sample size should be large enough to provide good conclusions; the larger, the better. Various guidelines exist, but a suggested minimum of at least 50 observations should be drawn. Finally, any conclusions drawn should be confirmed through further study and analysis.

PARETO DIAGRAMS

Pareto analysis was introduced in Chapter 8 as a method for analyzing quality costs. The Pareto principle was observed by Joseph Juran in 1950. Juran found that most effects resulted from only a few causes. For instance, in analyzing costs in a paper mill, he found that 61 percent of total quality costs were attributable to one category—"broke," which is paper mill terminology for paper so defective that it is returned for reprocessing. In an analysis of 200 types of field failures of automotive engines, only five accounted for one-third of all failures; the top 25 accounted for two-thirds of the failures. In a textile mill, three of fifteen weavers were found to account for 74 percent of the defective cloth produced. Pareto analysis clearly separates the vital few from the trivial many and provides direction for selecting projects for improvement.

Pareto analysis is often used to analyze the data collected in check sheets. A Pareto distribution is one in which the characteristics observed are ordered from largest frequency to smallest.

EXAMPLE 9   Pareto Analysis of Defective Items.   In Figure 9.15 (p. 361), the types of defects are ordered by their relative percentage yield the following information:

	Number	Percent of Total
Incomplete	48	42%
Surface scars	32	28%
Cracks	23	20%
Others	8	7%
Misshapen	4	3%

The highest category of defects is "incomplete," accounting for 42 percent of the total. The top three categories account for 80 percent of defects.

A Pareto diagram is a histogram of the data from the largest frequency to the smallest. Often one also draws a cumulative frequency curve on the histogram as shown in Figure 9.20. Such a visual aid clearly shows the relative magnitude of defects and can be used to identify opportunities for improvement. The most costly or significant problems stand out. Pareto diagrams can also show the results of improvement programs over time. They are less intimidating to employees who are fearful of statistics.

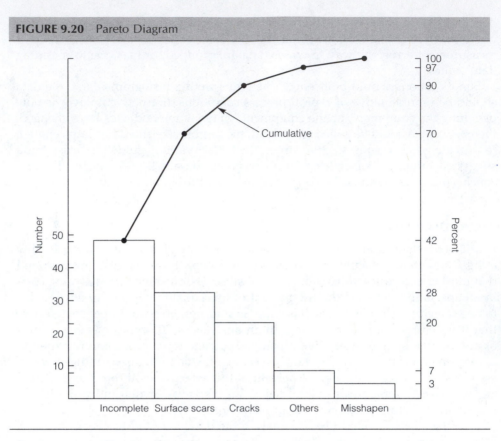

FIGURE 9.20 Pareto Diagram

■ Idea Finding

The purpose of the idea-finding step is to generate ideas for removing the problem. One of the difficulties in this task is the natural instinct to prejudge ideas before thoroughly evaluating them. Most people have a natural fear of proposing a "silly" idea or looking foolish. However, such ideas may actually form the basis for a creative and useful solution. Effective problem solvers must learn to *defer judgment* and *develop the ability to generate a large number of ideas* at this stage of the process. A number of processes and tools to facilitate idea generation can be used. One of the most popular is brainstorming.

Brainstorming, a useful group problem-solving procedure for generating ideas, was proposed by Alex Osborn[33] "for the sole purpose of producing checklists of ideas" that can be used in developing a solution to a problem. With brainstorming, no criticism is permitted, and people are encouraged to generate a large number of ideas through combination and enhancement of existing ideas. Wild ideas are encouraged and often trigger other good ideas from someone else.

The process often works in the following manner. Each individual in the group suggests an idea relating to the problem at hand, working in a round-robin fashion. If a person cannot think of anything, he or she passes. A facilitator writes down all ideas on a blackboard or easel so that everyone can see them. Only one idea is presented at a time by each individual. The process is repeated until no further ideas can be generated. By writing down the ideas in plain view of the group, new ideas are usually built from old ones by combining or extending previous suggestions.

For example, suppose that a group is examining the problem of the reasons for damage due to parts handling. The first individual might suggest "lack of storage"; the second, "poor placement of machines"; the third, "poor design of racks." The next individual might combine the previous two ideas and suggest "poor placement of parts on racks." In this fashion, one individual's idea might spawn a new idea from someone else.

Checklists are often used as a guide for generating ideas. Osborn proposed about 75 fundamental questions based on the following principles:

1. Put to other uses?
2. Adapt?
3. Modify?
4. Magnify?
5. Minify?
6. Substitute?
7. Rearrange?
8. Reverse?
9. Combine?

By consciously seeking ideas based on this list, one can generate many unusual, and often very useful, ideas.

Several other methods for generating ideas have been suggested. One is to change the wording of a problem statement. Simple modification of a single word can dramatically change the meaning. For example consider this statement: "In what ways might this company reduce quality costs by 30 percent?" Dropping the qualifier "by 30 percent" broadens the problem and potential solutions. Relaxing the "by 30 percent" to "by 5%" produces a similar effect. Changing the action verb or goal can also change the problem perspective. Turning a negative statement into a positive one leads to different ideas, such as "reducing quality costs" to "increasing quality value." Reversing the focus of the problem is another technique. For instance, "how to reduce costs due to excessive scrap" can be reversed to "how to use excessive scrap to reduce costs (by recycling, for example)."

CAUSE-AND-EFFECT DIAGRAMS

Variation in process output and other quality problems can occur for a variety of reasons, such as materials, machines, methods, people, and measurement. The goal of problem solving is to identify the *causes* of problems in order to correct them. The **cause-and-effect diagram** is an important tool in this task; it assists the generation of ideas for problem causes and, in turn, serves as a basis for solution finding.

The cause-and-effect diagram was introduced in Japan by Kaoru Ishikawa. It is a simple, graphical method for presenting a chain of causes and effects and for sorting out causes and organizing relationships between variables. Because of its structure, it is often called a *fishbone diagram.*

The general structure of a cause-and-effect diagram is shown in Figure 9.21. At the end of the horizontal line, a problem is listed. Each branch pointing into the main stem represents a possible cause. Branches pointing to the causes are contributors to these causes. The diagram identifies the most likely causes of a problem so that further data collection and analysis can be carried out.

FIGURE 9.21 General Structure of Cause-and-Effect Diagram

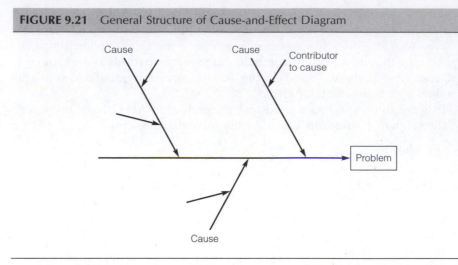

Two basic types of cause-and-effect diagrams are *dispersion analysis* and *process classification*. Dispersion analysis involves identifying and classifying possible causes for a specific quality problem. The fishbones in the diagram provide a chain of logical relationships among potential causes.

EXAMPLE 10 **Dispersion Analysis of Hospital Emergency Department Admissions.** A major hospital was concerned about the length of time required to get a patient from the emergency department to an in-patient bed. Significant delays appeared to be caused by beds not being available. A quality improvement team tackled this problem by developing a cause-and-effect diagram. They identified four major causes: environmental services, emergency department, medical/surgery unit, and admitting. Figure 9.22 (p. 369) shows a cause-and-effect diagram with several potential causes in each category. This diagram served as a basis for further investigations of contributing factors and data analysis to find the root cause of the problem.

A process classification cause-and-effect diagram is based on a flowchart of the process. The key factors that influence quality at each step are drawn on the flowchart.

EXAMPLE 11 **Process Classification Diagram for Parking Garage Operation.** Figure 9.23 (p. 370) shows the customer system portion of the flowchart for the parking garage operation discussed in Example 5. Potential contributors to poor quality are listed on the chart in a manner similar to the dispersion cause-and-effect diagram.

Cause-and-effect diagrams are constructed in a brainstorming type of atmosphere. Everyone can get involved and feel they are an important part of the problem-solving process. Usually small groups drawn from manufacturing or management work with a trained and experienced facilitator. The facilitator guides attention to discussion of the problem and its causes, not opinions. As a group technique, the cause-and-effect method requires significant interaction be-

FIGURE 9.22   Cause-and-Effect Diagram for Hospital Emergency Admission

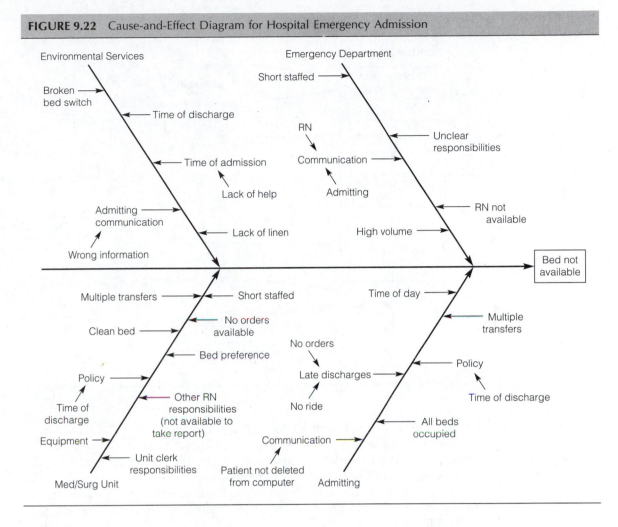

tween group members. The facilitator who listens carefully to the participants can capture the important ideas. A group can often be more effective by thinking of the problem broadly and considering environmental factors, political factors, employee issues, and even government policies if appropriate.

■ Solution Finding

The purpose of solution finding is to evaluate ideas that have been proposed and select a method to remove the problem. Questions that must be addressed include what facilities or equipment are needed, what are the costs, how much time is required for implementation, what is the effect on supervisors and workers, what results are expected, and what are the barriers to implementation.

SCATTER DIAGRAMS

Scatter diagrams are the graphical component of regression analysis. While they do not provide rigorous statistical analysis, they often point to important relationships between variables, such as the percent of an ingredient in an alloy and the hardness of the alloy. Typically, the variables in question represent possible

FIGURE 9.23 Process Classification Diagram

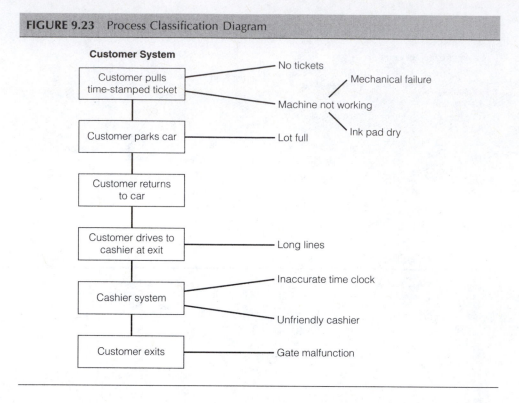

causes and effects obtained from Ishikawa diagrams. For example, if a manufacturer suspects that the percent of an ingredient in an alloy is causing quality problems in meeting hardness specifications, an employee group might collect data from samples on the amount of ingredient and hardness and plot the data on a scatter diagram as shown in Figure 9.24. The diagram shows the percentage has little effect on the hardness, and indicates that the group must investigate other possible causes.

Statistical correlation analysis is used to interpret scatter diagrams. Figure 9.25 shows three types of correlation. If the correlation is positive, an increase in variable x is related to an increase in variable y; if the correlation is negative, an increase in x is related to a decrease in y; and if the correlation is close to zero; the variables have no linear relationship.

■ Implementation

To implement a solution, responsibility must be assigned to a person or a group who will follow through on what must be done, where it will be done, when it will be done, and how it will be done. The potential consequences of each action should also be evaluated. The implementation phase of problem solving is often governed by consideration of personnel planning, budget issues, facilities, scheduling, and methods. Goals and milestones for evaluating improvement should be established. Plans for training personnel in new methods are often needed, along with a control mechanism for monitoring the process.

To implement a solution, changes are made in how things are done. A new procedure must be used, a new piece of equipment must be installed and debugged, or people must start paying attention to some aspect of quality that had

FIGURE 9.24 Scatter Diagram

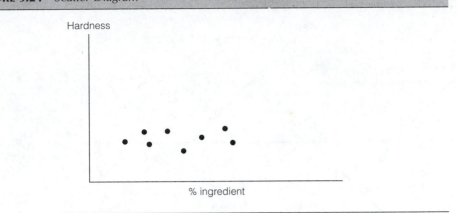

FIGURE 9.25 Three Types of Correlation

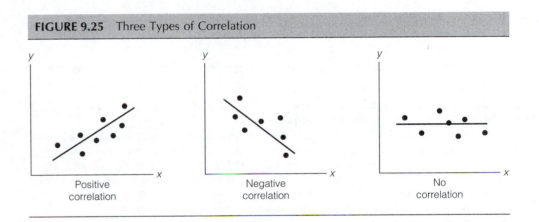

Positive correlation   Negative correlation   No correlation

been previously ignored. This step will be less painful if problem-solving teams have been properly organized.

The seven management and planning tools introduced in Chapter 6 are indispensable for implementation planning. Please refer back to that chapter for a discussion of these tools.

QUALITY IN PRACTICE

APPLICATIONS OF QUALITY IMPROVEMENT TOOLS AT ROTOR CLIP[34]

Rotor Clip Company, Inc., of Somerset, New Jersey, is a major manufacturer of retaining rings and self-tightening hose clamps and is a believer in the use of simple quality improvement tools. Several years ago, one of its clamps was failing stress testing during final inspections. No reason was evident, so managers and supervisors decided to develop a cause-and-effect diagram to search for a solution. Every employee involved with the part was called to a meeting to discuss the problem. The group was encouraged to brainstorm reasons for the problem, resulting in the fishbone diagram shown in Figure 9.26.

After reviewing all the probable causes, they concluded that the salt temperature of the quenching

FIGURE 9.26   The Fishbone Diagram for the Rotor Clip Clamp Problem

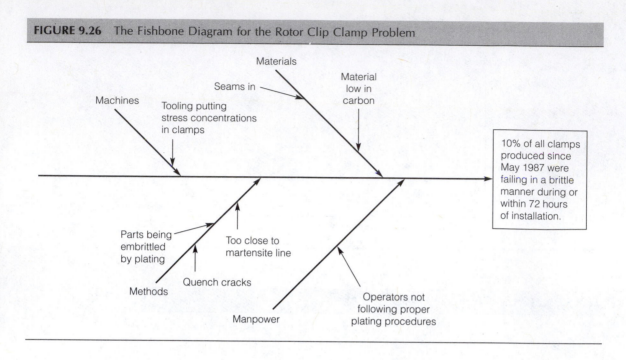

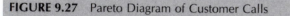

tank (a heat-treating step) was too close to the martensite line. This factor was selected for further study, but raising the salt temperature did not alleviate the problem. The group met again and agreed to pursue the second possibility, seams in one wire, as a possible cause. Wire samples that failed inspection were examined metallographically and seams were confirmed as the major cause of the defective parts. The material was returned to the supplier and new material yielded parts that passed the final inspection.

A second application involved the use of a Pareto diagram to study rising premium freight charges for shipping retaining rings. The study covered three months in order to collect enough data to draw conclusions. The Pareto diagram is shown in Figure 9.27. The results were startling. The most frequency cause of higher freight charges was customer requests. The

FIGURE 9.27   Pareto Diagram of Customer Calls

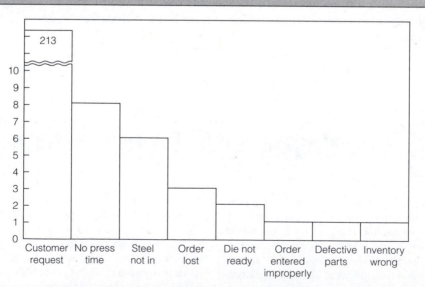

decision was made to continue the study to identify which customers consistently expedite their shipments and to work closely with them to find ways of reducing costs. The second largest contributor was the lack of available machine time. Once a die was installed in a stamping press, it ran until it produced the maximum number of parts (usually a million) before it was removed for routine maintenance. While this policy resulted in efficient utilization of tooling, it tied up the press and ultimately accounted for rush shipments. The policy was revised to limit die runs to fill orders more efficiently.

A third application was the use of a scatter diagram by the advertising department. Traditionally, the effect of advertising expenditures on the bottom line has been difficult to assess. Management wanted to learn if the number of advertising dollars spent correlated with the number of new customers gained in a given year. Advertising dollars spent by quarter were plotted against the number of new customers added for the same period for three consecutive years (see Figure 9.28). The positive correlation showed that heavy advertising was related to new customers. The results were fairly consistent from year to year except for the second quarter of 1988, in which an outlier clearly stood out from the rest. Advertising checked the media schedule and discovered that experimental image ads dominated that particular period. This discovery prompted the advertising department to eliminate image ads from its schedule.

Key Issues for Discussion

1. Once the seam problem in the clamps was understood, what controls could have been insti-

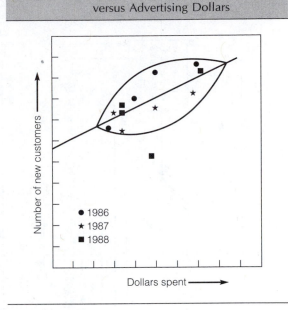

FIGURE 9.28 Scatter Diagram of New Customers versus Advertising Dollars

tuted to prevent the problem from occurring again?

2. In the freight charge example, what steps can the company take with customers who consistently expedite shipments?

3. How might the advertising department continue to use scatter diagrams in the future? How might the results be used to set budget priorities?

QUALITY IN PRACTICE   PROCESS IMPROVEMENT AT BOISE CASCADE[35]

The Timber and Wood Products Division of Boise Cascade formed a team of 11 people with diverse backgrounds from manufacturing, administration, and marketing to improve a customer claims processing and tracking system that affected all areas and customers in the six regions of the division. Although external customer surveys indicated that the company was not doing badly, internal opinions of the operation were far more critical.

The first eye-opener came when the process was flowcharted and the group discovered that more than 70 steps were performed for each claim. Figure 9.29 shows the original flowchart from the market-

ing and sales department. Combined division tasks numbered in the hundreds for a single claim; the marketing and sales portion of the flowchart alone consisted of up to 20 separate tasks and seven decisions, which sometimes took months to complete. Most of these steps added no value to the settlement outcome. The flowchart accomplished much more than just plotting Boise Cascade's time and efforts; it also helped build team members' confidence in each other and foster mutual respect. When they saw how each member was able to chart his or her part of the process and state individual concerns, everyone's reason for being on the team was validated.

FIGURE 9.29 Original Flowchart From the Marketing and Sales Department

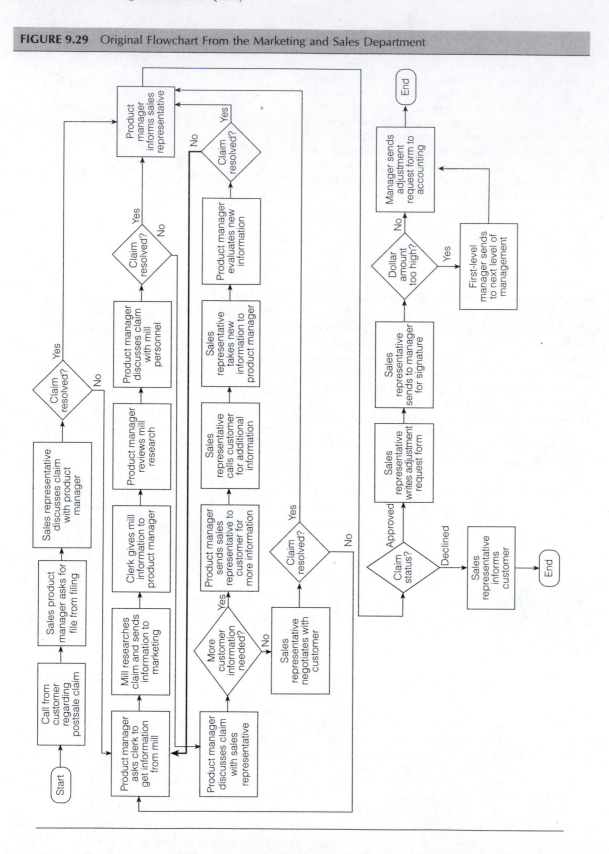

Although repetitious tasks and lack of uniform procedures were easy to identify, the group soon realized that data needed to be gathered. Their ultimate goal was to eliminate claims, but first the team needed specific information about the sources and causes of claims. Pareto charts identified the rate of incidence for 26 causes and linked them to a source either at the mill or in an administrative function (see Figure 9.30a). A histogram was used to sort claims by cost and frequency in different ranges of cost (Figure 9.30b). This visual depiction of the situation led the team to view it from an entirely

FIGURE 9.30   Pareto Charts Showing Mill and Administrative Causes of Claims

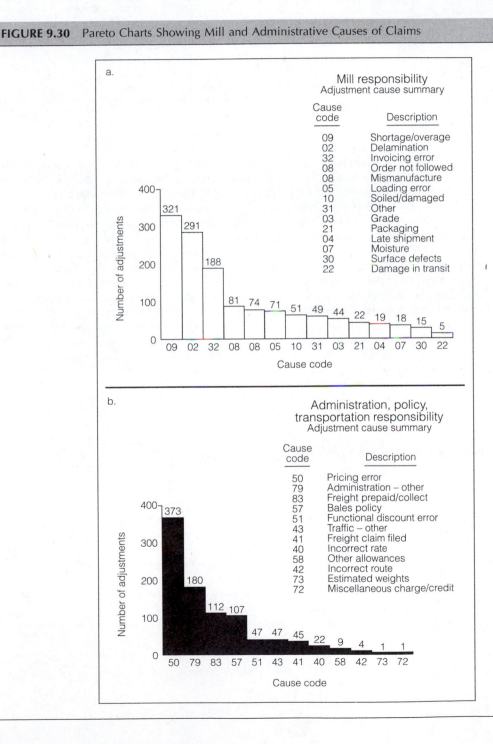

FIGURE 9.31 New Small Adjustment Request Form Process Flowchart for Marketing and Sales Department

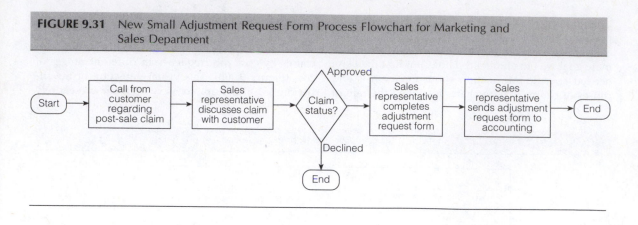

different point of view, contrary to the attitudes and practices they had embraced for many years. The data showed that 83 percent of claims accounted for only one-third of the total cost, and at least 95 percent of these claims were consistently settled in the customers' favor. Many claims cost the company as much or more to process than did the price of the settlement. The group then recommended that the sales representatives be given the authority to settle claims below a certain cost cutoff level, and be provided with additional training in claims settlement, documentation, and processing.

Surveys showed that external customers would be happy to receive a settlement within two weeks. The team members' ambition, however, was to exceed customers' expectations by as large a margin as possible, and recommended that the goal for processing claims under the cost cutoff be within 48 hours, with all others resolved within two weeks. The group eliminated seventy percent of the steps for small claims in the original flowchart as shown in Figure 9.31. Figure 9.32 shows a run chart that tracks the success rate of processing small claims within the targeted time period. Over 80 percent are now processed within 48 hours. Customers have complimented the company on the fairness and quickness of the settlement process and have actually decreased the number of claims. In addition, when customers receive a shipment not quite up to their expectations, they call the company—not to complain or file a claim—but to say, "I thought you'd like to know . . ."

FIGURE 9.32 Percentage of Small Claims Processed in 48 Hours

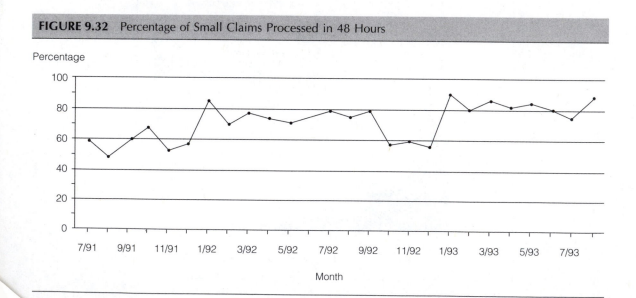

Key Issues for Discussion

1. What were the real benefits of flowcharting the claims process? Would other organizations experience similar results?

2. Contrast the two process flowcharts and discuss why the steps that were eliminated added no value to the outcome.

3. Estimate the average percentage of claims processed within 48 hours using the data points on the run chart during the first year and during the second year. Do the averages appear to be statistically different? How can this question be tested?

SUMMARY OF KEY POINTS

■ *Process management* involves planning and administration for controlling variation and continuously improving processes. To apply process management techniques, processes must be repeatable and measurable.

■ Leading process management practices include controlling quality and operational performance of all key business processes, seeking root causes of problems and correcting them, continuously improving processes using systematic problem-solving approaches, setting stretch goals, and employing benchmarking and reengineering to achieve breakthrough performance.

■ Control is the continuing process of evaluating performance, comparing outputs to goals or standards, and taking corrective action when necessary.

■ Any control system has three components: (1) a standard or goal, (2) a means of measuring accomplishment, and (3) comparison of actual results with the standard to provide feedback for corrective action.

■ A useful conceptualization of control divides it into three stages: preliminary control, concurrent control, and feedback control. Top managers are most involved in preliminary control; first-line managers and their subordinates in concurrent control; and middle managers coordinate all categories.

■ *Kaizen*, the Japanese term for improvement, is a philosophy of quality improvement in all areas of business using small, frequent, and gradual improvements over a long term.

■ Benchmarking is the search for best practices in any industry and using the information to set stretch goals and make improvements.

■ Reengineering is the fundamental rethinking and radical redesign of business processes to achieve dramatic improvements in performance. Reengineering complements continuous improvement efforts in a TQM culture.

■ A problem is a deviation between what is actually happening and what should be happening. Problem solving is a highly creative effort at the heart of quality improvement that encompasses problem redefinition and analysis, idea generation, evaluation and selection of ideas, and implementation.

■ The creative problem-solving process consists of mess finding, fact finding, problem finding, idea finding, solution finding, and implementation.

■ The Deming cycle is a problem-solving methodology that consists of four elements: plan, do, study, and act. It is based on continuous improvement and has been the foundation of most Japanese quality improvement efforts.

■ Juran's quality improvement approach is based on breakthrough—improvement that takes an organizaiton to unprecedented levels of performance. Breakthough attacks common causes of variation.

■ Crosby proposed a 14-step program for quality improvement based more on a managerial/behavioral approach than on the use of analytical tools.

■ The seven QC tools for quality improvement are flowcharts, run charts and control charts, check sheets, histograms, Pareto diagrams, cause-and-effect diagrams, and scatter diagrams. These tools support quality improvement processes and problem-solving efforts.

REVIEW QUESTIONS

1. What is *process management*? Why is it important to any business?

2. Explain the difference between innovation and continuous improvement. Why are both necessary to achieve competitive advantage?

3. Summarize the leading practices in process management.

4. Describe the three components of any control system.

5. Explain the concepts of preliminary control, concurrent control, and feedback control. How do they relate to one another and to the various levels of management?

6. What is meant by "operator-controllable"? What implications does it have for management?

7. What are work simplification and planned methods change? How do they differ from one another?

8. Explain the Japanese concept of *kaizen*. How does it differ from traditional Western approaches to improvement?

9. What is a *stretch goal*? How can stretch goals help an organization?

10. Define *benchmarking* and list its benefits. How does it differ from competitive comparison?

11. What is *reengineering*? How does it relate to TQM?

12. What is Kepner and Tregoe's definition of a problem? How does this definition apply to quality issues? Provide some examples.

13. Explain the difference between structured, semistructured, and ill-structured problems. What implications do these classifications have for solving problems?

14. What is the *Deming cycle*? How does it relate to the creative problem-solving process?

15. What is *breakthrough*? Describe Juran's breakthrough sequence for quality improvement.

16. Explain Crosby's program for quality improvement. How does it differ from the Deming cycle and Juran's breakthrough sequence?

17. Explain the four major components of problem solving. How can the seven QC tools support each step?

18. List and explain the six steps of the Osborn/Parnes problem-solving process.

19. Discuss some of the common sources of "messes."

20. Explain how work sampling can be used to identify quality improvement opportunities.

21. What techniques are useful to identify quality-related problems in service organizations?

22. Discuss the important considerations that must be taken into account when collecting data.

23. Describe a run chart and a control chart. What is the difference between them?

24. Describe different types of check sheets that are useful in quality improvement.

25. Explain the technique of problem detection methodology.

26. Describe various methods used for idea finding.

27. Explain the principles of brainstorming.

28. What is a cause-and-effect diagram? Describe the different types of cause-and-effect diagrams.

29. How do scatter diagrams assist in finding solutions to quality problems?

DISCUSSION QUESTIONS

1. Why is it necessary for a process to be repeatable and measurable? Provide some examples of processes that have these characteristics and some that do not.

2. List some of the common processes that a student performs. How can these processes be improved?

3. Are classroom examinations a means of control or improvement? What should they be?

4. Provide examples of common and special causes of variation in the following:

   a. taking a college examination

   b. grilling a hamburger

   c. meeting a scheduled appointment

5. Consider the following descriptions of two manufacturing facilities resulting from a quality audit.[36]
Company A: The PC board department uses no in-process inspection, no agitation in the plating tanks, uncalibrated timing devices, improper stacking, inadequate temperature control of drying oven, no solder analysis, no pin gauges for operators, and poor lighting for final 100 percent inspection; it experiences many rejects. Poor general housekeeping routines allow dust and corroded chemicals on shelves to contaminate the printed circuit boards placed on them.
Company B: Complete in-line QC program with quality data sheets stay with the lot from start to finish and records are neatly kept. Plating operations appear to be well instrumented. Safety regulations are enforced. All workers seem to be quality-minded. Every inspector is equipped with necessary gauges, and all gauges and instruments are calibrated. The entire plant is characterized by excellent housekeeping. Workers in critical areas wear white coats and gloves to reduce contamination.
   Discuss the differences in control strategies between these two firms. What recommendations would you make to the manager of company A?

6. How can kaizen be applied in a classroom?

7. Interview some faculty and determine whether they benchmark other educational programs. What types of information might they seek to improve curriculum and course content?

8. Identify some of the major processes a student encounters in a college or university. What types of noneducational institutions perform similar processes and might be candidates for benchmarking?

9. Write down the process for preparing for an exam. How could this process be reengineered to make it shorter or more effective?

10. State at least three applications of the Deming cycle in your personal life.

11. Identify two "messes" in your life and outline a plan for improving them.

12. State five different problems that you face as "In what ways might I . . .?" Use the why technique to redefine the problems. Have your initial problem definitions changed?

13. Provide two examples of each of the seven QC tools (different from those in the chapter) based on your own experience or research, such as in your personal life, school activities, or work.

14. A flowchart for a fast-food drive-through window is shown in Figure 9.33. Discuss the important quality characteristics inherent in this process and suggest possible improvements.

15. Develop a flowchart of your daily routine from getting up to going to school or work. How might you improve this routine?

16. Design a check sheet to help a high school student who is getting poor grades on a math quiz determine the source of his or her difficulty.

17. Develop an example of a process at your school—such as registering for classes—using problem detection methodology and interviewing other students. Based on the data collected, what are the critical problems? Can you suggest some solutions?

18. Develop cause-and-effect diagrams for the following problems:

   a. poor exam grade

   b. no job offers

FIGURE 9.33   Flowchart for Question 14

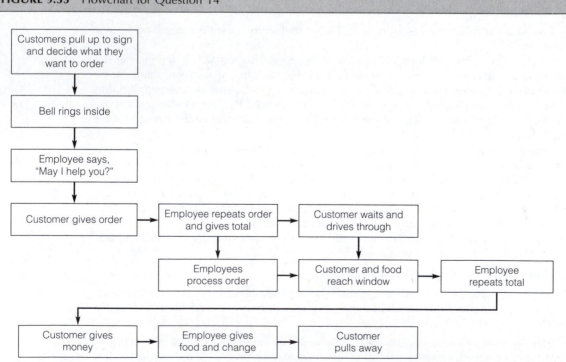

c. too many speeding tickets

d. late for work or school

19. Develop a list of improvement ideas to complete the following questions for any common business process:

a. What if operations are . . .?

b. What if employees are . . .?

c. What if information is . . .?

20. A pizza restaurant uses the following process:[37]

a. Customer telephones the restaurant to place an order.

b. Employee answers telephone, writes down order, and hands order to chef in the kitchen.

c. Chef assembles pizza by hand.

d. Chef bakes pizza in one of the four ovens.

e. Assistant verifies that the heated pizza matches the order and places it in a cardboard box and then in an insulated carrier.

f. Driver picks up pizza, gets small bills for change, checks map in store, gets in car, and drives to customer's location.

g. Driver gives pizza to customer, collects cash (no credit), and gives change to customer.

The president of the company wants to be able to deliver pizza to any customer in the city and keep investment in new technology to no more than 1.2 times current yearly profits. He has set some stretch goals:

■ Deliver pizza in half the time of competitors—customers want to have pizza delivered within approximately 10 minutes.

■ Deliver pizza that wins taste tests against both other delivered pizzas and restaurant pizzas.

■ Provide the extras typically found in restaurants, such as grated cheese, garlic, and hot peppers.

In a team of students, propose some reengineering solutions to this problem.

21. Figure 9.34 shows the Pepsi-Cola Company's three-step method for customer-valued process improvement. Discuss its differences and similarities to the Deming cycle or Juran's program.

22. A catalog order-filling process for personalized printed products can be described as follows:[38] Telephone orders are taken over a 12-hour period each day. Orders are collected from each person at the end of the day and checked for errors by the supervisor of the phone department, usually the following morning. The supervisor, who was busy on the phone, did not send this one-day batch of orders to the data processing department until after 1:00 p.m. In the next step—data processing—orders are invoiced in the one-day batches. Then they are printed and matched back to the original orders. At this point, if the order is a new customer order, it is sent to the person who did the customer verification and setup of new customer accounts. This process must to be completed before the order can be invoiced. The next step—order verification and proof-reading—occurs after invoicing is completed. The orders, with invoices attached, are given to a person who verifies that all required information is present and correct to permit typesetting. If the verifier has any questions, they are checked by computer or by calling the customer. Finally, the completed orders are sent to the typesetting department of the printshop.

a. Develop a flowchart for this process.

b. Discuss opportunities for improving the quality of service in this situation.

FIGURE 9.34 Pepsi-Cola Process Improvement Methodology

Steps	Actions
1. Start with the Customer	a. Understand and prioritize customer needs
	b. Establish customer measures and success criteria
	c. Select a process with most impact on customer needs
2. Understand Ourselves and Plan Improvements	a. Analyze the current process involving the performers in each step
	b. Design improved process
	c. Establish process measures
3. Do It	a. Pilot test improved process
	b. Implement improved process
	c. Stabilize process
	d. Go to Step 1 (continuously improve)

SOURCE: Courtesy of Pepsi-Cola Co. Reprinted with permission of The Forum Corporation.

23. An independent outplacement service helps unemployed executives find jobs. One of the major activities of the service is preparing resumes. Three word processors work at the service and type resumes and cover letters. They are assigned to individual clients, currently about 120. Turnaround time for typing is expected to be 24 hours. The word-processing operation begins with clients placing work in the assigned word processor's bin. When the word processor picks up the work (in batches), it is logged in using a timeclock stamp, and the work is typed and printed. After the batch is completed, the word processor returns the documents to the clients' bins, logs in the time delivered, and picks up new work. A supervisor tries to balance the workload for the three word processors. Lately, many of the clients have been complaining about errors in their documents—misspellings, missing lines, wrong formatting, and so on. The supervisor has told the word processors to be more careful, but the errors still persist.

    a. Develop a cause-and-effect diagram that might clarify the source of errors.

    b. What tools might the supervisor use to study ways to reduce the amount of errors?

24. Welz Business Machines sells and services a variety of copiers, computers, and other office equipment.[39] The company receives many calls each day for service, sales, accounting, and other departments. All calls are handled centrally through customer service representatives and routed to other individuals as appropriate. A number of customers complained about long waits when calling for service prompting a market research study, which found that customers became irritated if the call was not answered within five rings. Scott Welz, the company president, authorized the customer service department manager, Tim, to study this problem and find a method to shorten the call waiting time for its customers.

Tim met with the service representatives who answered the calls to attempt to determine the reasons for long waiting times. The following conversation ensued:

Tim: This is a serious problem; how a customer phone inquiry is answered is the first impression the customer receives from us. As you know, this company was founded on efficient and friendly service to all our customers. It's obvious why customers have to wait: you're on the phone with another customer. Can you think of any reasons that might keep you on the phone for an unnecessarily long time?

Survey of Customer Responses

We no longer buy Circle H products because:

The product is stale or soggy	0.9%
The flavor is poor	3.9%
The product is too expensive	16.0%
The packaging is inconvenient	24.5%
Delivery and restocking are too slow	21.3%
Preferred items aren't always available	20.0%
Incorrect quantities are often delivered	9.7%
Billing errors are often made	2.9%
Other reasons	0.8%

The president of Circle H has assigned you to perform a complete investigation to determine the causes of these quality problems and to recommend appropriate corrective action. You have authority to talk to any other person within the company.

The early stages of your investigation reveal that the three reasons most often cited by customers are symptomatic of some major quality problems in the company's operations. In proceeding with the audit, you decide to review all available data, which may yield indications of the root causes of these problems.

Further investigation reveals that, over a recent four-month period of time, a procedural change was made in the order approval process. You wish to find out whether this change caused a significant difference in the amount of time required to process an order from field sales through shipping. You therefore decide to investigate this particular situation.

On completion of your investigation into the problems with order processing, you determine that the change in procedures for order approval have led to an increase in the amount of time required to restock goods in the customers' stores. You want to recommend corrective action for this problem, but you first do additional investigation as to why the change was made. You learn that, because of large losses on delinquent accounts receivable, the change was made to require approval of restock orders by the credit manager. This change added an average of three hours to the amount of internal processing time needed for a restock order.

On review of your report, the president of Circle H takes note of administrative problems whose existence he had never suspected. To assure that corrective action will be effective and sustained, the president assigns you to take charge of the corrective action program.[40]

a. What types of data would be most useful to review for clues as to why the three major customer complaints occurred?

b. How would you investigate whether the change in the order approval process had a significant effect on order processing time?

c. Given your knowledge of problems in both order processing and accounts receivable, what should you do?

PROBLEMS

1. The number of seconds customers waited on the phone for a customer service representative are listed below. Construct a histogram. What do the data tell you?

5	7	7	15	21	15	22	10	10	6
8	18	14	5	7	8	3	8	4	10

Robin: I've noticed that quite often that the party to whom I need to route the call is not present. It takes time to transfer the call and wait to see if it is answered. If the party is not there, I end up apologizing and transferring the call to another extension.

Tim: You're right, Robin. Sales personnel often are out of the office for sales calls, absent on trips to preview new products, or not at their desks for a variety of reasons. What else might cause this problem?

Ravi: I get irritated at some customers who spend a great deal of time complaining about a problem that I cannot do anything about except to refer to someone else. Of course, I listen and sympathize with them, but this eats up a lot of time.

LaMarr: Some customers call so often that they think we're long lost friends and strike up a personal conversation.

Tim: That's not always a bad thing, you realize.

LaMarr: Sure, but it delays my answering other calls.

Nancy: It's not always the customer's fault. During lunch times, we're not all available to answer the phone.

Ravi: Right after we open at 9:00 a.m., we get a rush of calls. I think that many of the delays are caused by these peak periods.

Robin: I've noticed the same thing between 4 and 5 p.m.

Tim: I've had a few comments from department managers that they were routed calls that didn't fall in their areas of responsibility and had to be transferred again.

Mark: But that doesn't cause delays at our end.

Nancy: That's right, Mark, but I just realized that sometimes I simply don't understand what the customer's problem really is. I spend a lot of time trying to get him or her to explain it better. Often, I have to route it to *someone* because other calls are waiting.

Ravi: Perhaps we need to have more knowledge of our products.

Tim: Well, I think we've covered most of the major reasons as to why many customers have to wait. It seems to me that we have four major reasons: the phones are short-staffed, the receiving party is not present, the customer dominates the conversation, and you may not understand the customer's problem. Next, we need to collect some information next about these possible causes. I will set up a data collection sheet that you can use to track some of these things. Mark, would you help me on this?

Over the next two weeks, the staff collected data on the frequency of reasons why some callers had to wait. Their results are summarized as follows:

Reason	Total Number
Operators short-staffed	172
Receiving party not present	73
Customer dominates conversation	19
Lack of operator understanding	61
Other reasons	10

   a. From the conversation between Tim and his staff, draw a cause-and-effect diagram.

   b. Perform a Pareto analysis of the data collected.

   c. Discuss some actions the company might take to improve the situation.

25. You are an internal auditor at Circle H Company, a producer of snack foods. The company has lost three major customer accounts in the last six months, at a cost of $3.5 million in annual sales. A preliminary investigation in which customers were asked to list five main reasons why they no longer buy your product has revealed the following results:

2. The number of hours that a machine ran until failure is given below. Construct a histogram and discuss any conclusions that you might reach.

| 10.5 | 5.0 | 15.3 | 16.8 | 9.2 | 20.2 | 27.5 | 8.9 | 12.2 | 18.2 |
| 4.2 | 12.6 | 7.8 | 11.5 | 12.6 | 14.5 | 14.0 | 5.5 | 15.5 | 8.9 |

3. Analysis of customer complaints for a large mail-order house revealed the following:

billing errors: 867
shipping errors: 1960
unclear charges: 9650
long delay: 6672
delivery error: 452

Construct a Pareto diagram for these data. What conclusions would you reach?

4. In a manufacturing process, the production rate (parts/hour) was thought to affect the number of defectives found during a subsequent inspection. To test this theory, the production rate was varied and the number of defects were collected for the same batch sizes. The results were:

Production Rate	Number of Defectives
20	21
20	19
40	15
30	16
60	14
40	17

Construct a scatter diagram for these data. What conclusions can you reach?

5. The number of defects found in 30 samples of 100 electronic assemblies taken on a daily basis over one month is given below. Plot these data on a control chart, computing the average value (center line), but ignoring the control limits. Do you suspect that any special causes were present? Why?

| 1 | 6 | 5 | 5 | 4 | 3 | 2 | 2 | 4 | 6 | 2 | 1 | 3 | 1 | 4 |
| 5 | 4 | 1 | 6 | 15 | 12 | 6 | 3 | 4 | 3 | 3 | 2 | 5 | 7 | 4 |

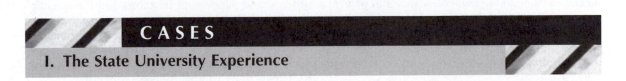

CASES

I. The State University Experience

Wow! That State University video was really cool. It has lots of majors; it's close to home so I can keep my job; and Mom and Dad loved it when they visited. I wish I could know what it's really like to be a student at State. Hmmm, I think I'll ask Mom and Dad to take a campus tour with me. . . .

I'm sure that we took our tour on the hottest day of the summer. The campus is huge—it took us about two hours to complete the tour and we didn't even see everything! I wasn't sure that the tour guide knew what he was doing. We went into a gigantic lecture hall and the lights weren't even on. Our tour guide couldn't find them so we had to hold the doors open so the sunlight could come in. About three-fourths of the way through the tour, our guide said, "State University isn't really a bad place to go to school; you just have to learn the system." I wonder what he meant by that?. . . .

This application is really confusing. How do I let the admissions office know that I am interested in physics, mechanical engineering, and industrial design? Even my parents can't figure it out. I guess I'll call the admissions office for some help. . . .

I'm so excited! Mom just handed me a letter from State! Maybe they've already accepted me. What? What's this? They say I need to send my transcript.

I did that when I mailed in my application two weeks ago. What's going on? I hope it won't affect my application. I better check with Admissions. . . .

You can't find my file? I thought you were only missing my transcript. I asked my counselor if she had sent it in yet. She told me that she sent it last week. Oh, you'll call me back when you locate my file? O.K. . . .

Finally, I've been accepted! Wait a minute. I didn't apply to University College; that's a two-year program. I wanted physics, M.E., or industrial design. Well, since my only choice is U. College and I really want to go to State, I guess I'll send in the confirmation form. It really looks a lot like the application. In fact, I know I gave them a lot of the same information. I wonder why they need it again? Seems like a waste of time. . . .

Orientation was a lot of fun. I'm glad they straightened out my acceptance at U. College. I think I will enjoy State after all. I met lots of other students. I saw my advisor and I signed up for classes. All I have left to do is pay my tuition bill. Whoops.

None of my financial aid is on this bill. I know I filled out all of the forms because I got an award letter from State. There is no way my parents and I can pay for this without financial aid. It says at the bottom, I'll lose all of my classes if I don't pay the bill on time. . . .

I'm not confirmed on the computer? I sent my form and the fee in a long time ago. What am I going to do? I don't want to lose all of my classes. I have to go to the admissions office or my college office and get a letter that says I am a confirmed student. O.K. If I do that tomorrow, will I still have all of my classes? . . .

I can't sleep; I'm so nervous about my first day. . . .

Discussion Questions

1. What breakdowns in service processes has this student experienced?

2. What types of process management activities should State University administrators undertake?

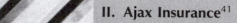

II. Ajax Insurance[41]

Ajax is a $4 billion life and health insurer operating in 30 states throughout the middle and southwestern United States. The company relies on the services of independent agents to sell its various coverages to the general public. The company has been particularly innovative in serving the needs of the small business market where service, value, and low-cost delivery confer a powerful competitive advantage. The key to maintaining low-cost status is to prevent excess losses through effective underwriting while minimizing expenses. Ajax has found that highly responsive service is the key to keeping customers, once it attracts them with highly competitive premiums.

Company leaders have utilized TQM approaches and training over the past five years to consolidate several smaller insurance companies Ajax acquired beginning in 1983. Originally the quality program was known as "Quality Altogether." The company has successfully developed a single culture with a shared vision and drive for excellence. The company's TQM system is moving to a higher level of effectiveness and integration. Quality Altogether has evolved from a job redesign effort into a broader, team-based, process-oriented TQM system.

Ajax top management believes strongly that automation is not the sole source of productivity and quality improvement. Management has embarked

on an aggressive companywide program of upgrading the training and effectiveness of Ajax's work force. Ajax's TQM program, renamed "The Quality Way," now serves as the overall system within which the company makes the best use of all its talent to obtain a lasting competitive advantage. Ajax now employs 600 people, of whom some 520 work in operations, policyholder servicing, information systems, and supporting functions. Most associates are white-collar workers with professional, administrative, and clerical functions. Through training and experience, these associates represent over 8000 years of insurance industry experience and nearly 3000 years of TQM application experience.

The company leases office space in two adjacent buildings of an office park in suburban Atlanta. The company is an equal opportunity employer and encourages work force diversity as reflected in the society at large.

Process Management: Product and Service Production and Delivery Processes

At Ajax Insurance, product and service delivery processes are carried out by highly trained and motivated operational and policyholder servicing teams. These teams own end-to-end responsibility for all aspects of the insurance product delivery and policyholder servicing from sales to claim payment.

Line management either owns, or has identified individual owners, for all product and service delivery processes. Key processes include:

- Processing applications for new coverage
- Entering new business into information processing systems
- Accounting
- Premium billing
- Servicing policyholder inquiries and requests.

Ajax manages quality and operational performance of its service processes at two levels. In the aggregate, each team requires the right number of people with the right work skills to meet customer demand within processing cycle time standards. Policies are monitored per full-time equivalent (FTE) to manage this aspect of process performance.

Ajax also controls daily quality from case to case by training and holding all associates accountable for quality and best processing procedures in their activities. Each work area is responsible for developing measures and standards that reflect customer-driven quality as well as company productivity targets. These standards and measurements of performance are posted in each work area for all associates and managers to see.

Processing applications for new coverage takes requests from sales agents or customers and decides eligibility, premium rates, and coverage. The key customer requirements are timeliness and accuracy. Information systems measure timeliness, and accuracy is determined through samples. Ajax's customer-driven timeliness standard varies by line of business but ranges from one day to five days, depending on complexity and customer expectations.

The process of entering new business into information processing systems focuses on installing new business into the company's service delivery processes. The key customer requirements of accuracy and timeliness are measured by work groups each day. Standards include on-line information input at the source and accuracy of data better than one defect per 10,000 opportunities.

Policy production manufactures and issues all of the policy and coverage documentation connected with the company's insurance product. Its principal requirements are aesthetic documents, produced accurately and on time.

Accounting processes supply sales information to the sales commission accounting team and control information to finance team. Its key requirements are timeliness and accuracy. Each work group team tracks these requirements either through processing systems or by means of sampling. Measurements are taken daily, weekly, and monthly. Ajax standards

call for reports within one day of the date of close and accuracy of less than three defects per million opportunities.

Premium billing processes operate largely automatically. However, many policyholder servicing tasks generate premium billing work that necessitates responsiveness to specific customer needs, as well as accuracy and timeliness. Ajax tracks billing adjustments, errors, and cycle time weekly and monthly. Customer-driven standards are for one defect per 100,000 opportunities and billing within 24 hours of implementing coverage.

Claim processing requires expertise in specific coverage offered, as well as accurate analysis of the eligibility of each claim under the coverage. Claim error rates are measured by weekly quality audit and cycle time is tracked daily and weekly. Customer-driven standards call for 90 percent claim completion within 10 days of first customer contact and require 95 percent claim accuracy on any amount paid as determined by an audit.

Servicing policyholder inquiries and requests requires prompt, courteous, responsive and satisfying personal treatment during each customer contact. Ajax tracks mail backlogs, phone waiting time, call abandonment rates, and other variables needed to exceed customer expectations. Most statistics are by-products of the automated telephone switching equipment. Calls are monitored and tracked per hour by associates. Standards have been set to equal or exceed customer expectations as determined by periodic surveys.

Ajax measures, aggregates and reports productivity, quality, timeliness, and accuracy of each service process in appropriate forms to all levels of management. Figure 9.35 summarizes the measurements which form a basis for managing major processes.

Because workloads vary and staff is relatively fixed, efficiency dictates that Ajax anticipates staffing needs before workloads arrive in order to totally satisfy customers by being right the first time and on time.

Production counts are maintained for most labor-intensive activities in order to identify bottlenecks. Productivity data also provides accurate trend information on policies processed per FTE (full-time equivalent) in each team and work group.

Ajax's goal is to constantly improve the accuracy of annual, monthly, and weekly workload forecasts by type of customer and service. Accurate forecasts are the key to minimum backlogs, no customer waiting, and avoiding excessive staffing due to unanticipated volume peaks.

Extensive pools of associates are trained in various skills. Personnel from these pools assist teams that become backlogged. In addition, teams lend and borrow members from each other, further improving

FIGURE 9.35   Key Processes and Customer Requirements

Key Process	Customer Requirements	Quality and Operational Performance	
		In Process D = Daily, W =	**End of Process** Weekly, M = Monthly
Process new applications	Timeliness, accuracy	D,W,M	W,M
Install new business	Accuracy, timeliness	D	D,W,M
Policy production	Aesthetics, timeliness, accuracy	D	W,M
Accounting	Accuracy, timeliness	D,W,M	D,W,M
Premium billing	Accuracy, timeliness	W,M	W,M
Claim processing	Accuracy, timeliness	D,W,M	M
Customer service	Responsiveness, timeliness, accuracy, courtesy	D	M

the ability to recover from workload forecast errors.

All processes are managed through daily and weekly measurement, comparisons to standard, and follow-up action. When measurements depart from the desired standards of performance, corrective action begins immediately.

Processes that go out of control may have quality problems driven by input from external agents or insureds. Other sources of upsets may be due to bottlenecks, systems upsets, unclear procedure, or employee turnover. Initially, teams closest to the process are empowered to act to restore a process to normal. If the team desires, or is unable to return service and productivity to normal, line management may become involved.

When a work team passes an out-of-control situation to a line manager, the manager typically joins the team and/or arranges for a quality assurance facilitator to join the team. In many cases managers find they must supplement the team with resources from information systems, finance, or the training department.

Once a team is capable of resolving the out-of-control situation, it follows a seven-step process to restore conditions to normal.

Step 1: Analyze what has gone wrong in the as-is process.

Step 2: Contain the problem to prevent customer upset.

Step 3: Drill into the process to find root causes.

Step 4: Brainstorm actions to reverse or prevent the problem at its cause.

Step 5: Plan actions to correct the process as it should be.

Step 6: Carry out the plan.

Step 7: Check with customers that service is back to normal, and document incident and action taken.

When the root cause of the out-of-control situation lies outside the processing operation, operations management invites sales force or agent participation in improvement teams—by conference call, if necessary—so sales can work with external customers to improve customer's quality of input to the work processes.

Quality assurance representatives facilitate process improvement teams to investigate strategically critical processes that remain out of control for more than three weeks. Improvement teams may recommend continuous improvement or process reengineering, or simply gather data on root causes of defects or interruptions and engage in continuous improvement.

QA facilitators receive formal training in team problem solving, team dynamics, cost/benefit analysis, and team leadership. They are qualified to give just-in-time training to work group teams that may encounter new problems.

Ajax integrates each corrective action into process management and control systems. Each improvement team files an improvement followup memo on each completed action. The memo outlines team participants and start and stop dates. The memo also identifies process, problems or opportunities, data gathered, root causes found, pilot tests run, and corrective action taken. Improvement memos also state performance metrics impacted and estimate the size and direction of impact on each measure. These memos are available on the same information network used for process documentation.

At Ajax, quality depends on all associates knowing the right way to do their work. The company coordinates its process flowcharts and task responsibilities to written procedures. Ajax procedures reside on over 200 online and up-to-date volumes of manuals accessible from any terminal. As part of the wrap-up on each corrective action project, the improvement team revises process documentation and alerts the training department to the potential need for retraining.

Process improvement teams and managers analyze customer satisfaction data and quality and productivity measures to drive the process improvement methodology. Improvement teams justify their existence by achieving better quality, performance, customer satisfaction, and cycle time. Middle management is responsible for coaching and supporting the teams in their improvement efforts.

Quality assurance keeps an on-line inventory of opportunities for improvement spotted by the improvement teams, assuring that teams always have plenty of work to do. Ajax classifies opportunities by process, type and scope of impact, suspected root cause, likely type of corrective action, recommended opportunity owner, and codes indicating size, difficulty, and riskiness of each opportunity.

Ajax inventory now identifies more than 1400 process improvement opportunities consisting of 15 percent process simplification; 20 percent rework and inspection reduction; 60 percent new systems functions or new technology, such as use of electronic imaging of documents; and 5 percent improvements generated through benchmarking efforts. Improvement teams refer to this inventory at the start of an improvement project to be sure they consider all aspects of their process quality or productivity opportunities.

Teams use process analysis (flowcharting) and simplification (combining or eliminating tasks) to reduce cycle time and increase productivity. One process improvement team redesigned jobs to reduce the number of steps to process new business from 55 to 23 while cutting the number of handoffs from 23 to 12.

Benchmarking information comes into play when teams learn how competitive firms perform similar functions. In such cases, the team reviews trade literature, conference speeches, and other sources of information to avoid repeating mistakes others have learned the hard way.

Process research and testing largely revolves around implementing new information systems applications. In such cases, the information systems department uses a structured approach to develop and test each new processing function. Operations and policyholder service personnel, who train associates in the new process, do the testing themselves.

Ajax participates in insurance industry operations groups to keep abreast of new developments in technology. The company monitors imaging systems and electronic data interchange for application in its processes. As a result of these efforts, employees now use E-mail extensively for communications with the field sales units.

Ajax gathers and uses voice of the customer and satisfaction information from both internal and external customers of its processes. The most critical use of customer information is in deciding on service standards. These standards then become the end-of-process metrics used to monitor process performance. Periodic data from customers influence whether standards are revised to exceed customer expectations or be competitive.

Stretch targets for all key productivity and quality metrics are based on the prior year's performance and on the amount of training or systems investment to be made in the coming year.

Discussion Questions

1. How well does Ajax maintain the quality and operational performance of its production and delivery processes? Evaluate the effectiveness of their control system, the process for identifying root causes of out-of-control variations, and the approaches to making, verifying, and integrating corrections into their processes. If you were an external consultant, what conclusions and recommendations would you make?

2. Evaluate Ajax's process improvement approach. How effectively do they use process analysis and simplification, benchmarking, process research and testing, alternative technologies, customer information, and stretch goals? Again, as an external consultant, what conclusions and recommendations would you make?

■ NOTES

1. AT&T Quality Steering Committee, *Process Quality Management & Improvement Guidelines*, AT&T Publication Center, AT&T Bell Laboratories (1987).

2. "NCR Corporation," in *Profiles in Quality* (Needham Heights, MA: Allyn and Bacon, 1991).

3. Michael Hammer and James Champy, *Reengineering the Corporation* (New York: HarperBusiness, 1993), 177–178.

4. Walter A. Shewhart, *Economic Control of Quality of Manufactured Product* (New York: Van Nostrand, 1931).

5. George R. Terry and Stephen G. Franklin, *Principles of Management*, 8th ed. (Homewood, IL: Richard D. Irwin, 1982), 426–428.

6. M.L. Dertouzos, R.K. Lester, R.M. Solow, and the MIT Commission on Industrial Productivity, *Made in America* (Cambridge, MA: MIT Press, 1989), 74.

7. Dean M. Schroeder and Alan G. Robinson, "America's Most Successful Export to Japan: Continuous Improvement Programs," *Sloan Management Review* 32, no. 2 (Spring 1991), 67–81.

8. Masaaki Imai, *KAIZEN—The Key to Japan's Competitive Success* (New York: McGraw-Hill, 1986).

9. Alan Robinson, ed., *Continuous Improvement in Operations* (Cambridge, MA: Productivity Press, 1991).

10. Lawrence S. Pryor, "Benchmarking: A Self-Improvement Strategy," *The Journal of Business Strategy* (November/December 1989), 28–32.

11. Robert C. Camp, *Benchmarking: The Search for Industry Best Practices That Lead to Superior Performance* (Milwaukee. WI: ASQC Quality Press and UNIPUB/Quality Resources, 1989).

12. Christopher E. Bogan and Michael J. English, "Benchmarking for Best Practices: Winning Through Innovative Adaptation," *Quality Digest* (August 1994), 52–62.

13. AT&T Consumer Communication Services *Summary of 1994 Application for the Malcolm Baldrige National Quality Award.*

14. Robert C. Camp, see note 11.

15. Hammer and Champy, see note 3, p. 32.

16. P. Kay Coleman, "Reengineering Pepsi's Road to the 'Right Side Up' Company," *Insights Quarterly* 5, no. 3 (Winter 1993), 18–35.

17. Bogan and English, see note 12.

18. Gerhard Plenert, "Process Re-Engineering: The Latest Fad Toward Failure," *APICS—The Performance Advantage* 4, no. 6 (June 1994), 22–24.

19. Charles H. Kepner and Benjamin B. Tregoe, *The Rational Manager* (New York: McGraw-Hill, 1965).

20. Adapted from John Flares and Constantine Pavsidis, "Help Your Supplier." Reprinted with permission from *Quality* 23 (September 1984), 42–43; a publication of Hitchcock Publishing, a Capital Cities/ABC, Inc., company.

21. Gerald Langley, Kevin Nolan, and Thomas Nolan, "The Foundation of Improvement," Sixth Annual International Deming User's Group Conference, Cincinnati, OH (August 1992).

22. Langley et al., see note 21.

23. L. M. Ames and W. D. Harwood, "People, Quality, and Process Improvement," Manitoba Division, INCO Limited (undated).

24. Jeremy Main, "Under the Spell of the Quality Gurus," *Fortune*, 18 August, 1986, 31.

25. A. VanGundy, "Comparing 'Little Known' Creative Problem-Solving Techniques," in *Creativity Week III, 1980 Proceedings* (Greensboro, NC: Center for Creative Leadership, 1981). The reader is also referred to James R. Evans, *Creative Thinking in the Decision and Management Sciences* (Cincinnati, OH: South-Western Publishing Co., 1991) for a thorough treatment of creative problem solving.

26. A. Osborn, *Applied Imagination*, 3rd ed. (New York: Scribner's, 1963); S. J. Parnes, R. B. Noller, and A M. Biondi (eds.), *Guide to Creative Action* (New York: Scribner's, 1977).

27. Russell Ackoff, "Beyond Problem Solving," presented at the Fifth Annual Meeting of the American Institute for Decision Sciences, Boston (16 November, 1973).

28. Adapted from F. Timothy Fuller, "Eliminating Complexity from Work: Improving Productivity by Enhancing Quality," *National Productivity Review* 4 (Autumn 1985), 327–344.

29. D. Randall Brandt and Kevin L. Reffett, "Focusing on Customer Problems to Improve Service Quality," *The Journal of Services Marketing* 3, no. 4 (Fall 1989), 5–14.

30. "The Tools of Quality Part V: Check Sheets," *Quality Progress* 23, no. 10 (October 1990), 53.

31. Ishikawa, Kaoru, *Guide to Quality Control*, 2nd revised ed., edited for clarity. (Tokyo: Asian Productivity Organization, 1986). Available from UNIPUB/Quality Resources, One Water Street, White Plains, NY 10601.

32. Brandt and Reffett, see note 29.

33. A. F. Osborn, *Applied Imagination* (New York: Scribner's, 1963).

34. Adapted from Bruce Rudin, "Simple Tools Solve Complex Problems." Reprinted with permission from *Quality* (April 1990), 50–51; a publication of Hitchcock Publishing, a Capital Cities/ABC, Inc., company.

35. Adapted from Dwight Kirscht and Jennifer M. Tunnell, "Boise Cascade Stakes a Claim on Quality," *Quality Progress* 26, no. 11 (November 1993), 91–96. With permission of Dwight M. Kirscht, Timber and Wood Products Division, Boise Cascade Corporation.

36. Edward A. Reynolds, "The Science (Art?) of Quality Audit and Evaluation," *Quality Progress* 23, no. 7 (July 1990), 55–56.

37. Adapted from AT&T Quality Steering Committee, *Reengineering Handbook*, AT&T Bell Laboratories (1991).

38. Adapted from Ronald G. Conant, "JIT in a Mail Order Operation Reduces Processing Time from Four Days to Four Hours," *Industrial Engineering* 20, no. 9 (September 1988), 34–37.

39. This problem was developed from a classic example published in "The Quest for Higher Quality: The Deming Prize and Quality Control," by RICOH of America, Inc.

40. Adapted from ASQC Quality Auditor Certification Brochure (July 1989).
41. Adapted from "Ajax Insurance," a case item prepared for the 1994 Malcolm Baldrige National Quality Award Preparation Course. This material is in the public domain.

■ BIBLIOGRAPHY

Ackoff, R.L., and Vergara, E. "Creativity in Problem Solving and Planning: A Review." *European Journal of Operations Research* 7 (1981), 1–13.

AT&T Quality Steering Committee. *Batting 1000.* AT&T Bell Laboratories, 1992.

_____. *Process Quality Management & Improvement Guidelines.* AT&T Bell Laboratories, 1987.

Box, G.E.P., and Bisgaard, S. "The Scientific Context of Quality Improvement." *Quality Progress* 20, no. 6 (June 1987), 54–61.

Brassard, Michael. *The Memory Jogger Plus+.* Methuen, MA: GOAL/QPC, 1989.

Burr, John T. "The Tools of Quality Part I: Going With the Flow(chart)." *Quality Progress* 23, no. 6 (June 1990), 64–67.

_____. "The Tools of Quality Part VI: Pareto Charts." *Quality Progress* 23, no. 11 (November 1990), 59–61.

_____. "The Tools of Quality Part VII: Scatter Diagrams." *Quality Progress* 23, no. 12 (December 1990), 87–89.

Cross, Kelvin, John Feather, and Richard Lynch. "TQM vs. Reengineering? There Should Be No Argument." *Quality Digest* (May 1994), 53–54.

Donnell, Augustus, and Margaret Dellinger. *Analyzing Business Process Data: The Looking Glass.* AT&T Bell Laboratories, 1990.

Freeman, N.B. "Quality on the Mend." *American Machinist and Automated Manufacturing* (April 1986), 102–112.

Gitlow, H., S. Gitlow, A. Oppenheim, and R. Oppenheim. *Tools and Methods for the Improvement of Quality.* Homewood, IL: Irwin, 1989.

Hradesky, John L. *Productivity and Quality Improvement.* New York: McGraw-Hill, 1988.

Juran Institute, Inc. "The Tools of Quality Part IV: Histograms." *Quality Progress* 23, no. 9 (September 1990), 75–78.

_____. "The Tools of Quality Part V: Check Sheets." *Quality Progress* 23, no. 10 (October 1990), 51–56.

Melan, E.H. "Process Management in Service and Administrative Operations." *Quality Progress* 18, no. 6 (June 1985), 52–59.

Mizuno, Shigeru. *Management for Quality Improvement: The 7 New QC Tools.* Cambridge MA: Productivity Press, 1988.

Sarazen, J. Stephen. "The Tools of Quality Part II: Cause-and-Effect Diagrams." *Quality Progress* 23, no. 7 (July 1990), 59–62.

Shainin, Peter D. "The Tools of Quality Part III: Control Charts." *Quality Progress* 23, no. 8 (August 1990), 79–82.

CHAPTER 10

Human Resource Management for Quality

All businesses have three principal resources: capital, physical, and human. Many global competitors, such as Japan, Taiwan, Singapore, and Switzerland, have few natural resources, but they use the same basic technologies as the United States. Companies in these countries have been forced to develop their competitive edge primarily through the human resource. The human resource is the only one that competitors cannot copy, the only one that can synergize, that is, produce output whose value is greater than the sum of its parts.

Deming emphasizes that no organization can survive without good people, people who are improving. The essence of Deming's Point 1 conveys his belief that profit should not be the ultimate objective of the firm. In Japan and in Europe, corporations are social entities, not simply money-making machines. The objective of these corporations is to serve customers and their own employees. Businesses in the United States are beginning to learn that to satisfy customers, they must first satisfy employees.

The role of human beings at work has changed as business and labor have changed over the years. Skilled craftspeople prior to the Industrial Revolution had a major stake in the quality of their products because their families' livelihoods depended on the sale of those products. They were motivated by pride in their work as well as the need for survival. The departure from the craftsmanship concept was promulgated by Frederick W. Taylor. Taylor concluded that a factory should be managed on a scientific basis. He focused on work methods design, the establishment of standards for daily work, selection and training of workers, and piecework incentives. Taylor separated planning from execution, concluding that foremen and workers of those days lacked the education necessary to plan their work. The foreman's role was to assure that the work force met productivity standards. Other pioneers of scientific management, such as Frank and Lilian Gilbreth and Henry Gantt, further refined the system through motion study, methods improvement, ergonomics, scheduling, and wage incentive systems.

The Taylor system dramatically improved productivity. However, as the pressures to achieve better productivity increased, quality eroded. The Taylor philosophy also contributed to the development of labor unions and established an adversarial relationship between labor and management that has yet to be completely overcome. Most significantly, the Taylor system failed to make use of an organization's most important asset—the knowledge and creativity of the work force. Japan, in particular, has marshaled this asset and clearly demonstrated that attention to the human resource can improve quality and productivity far more than robots and automation. Konosuke Matsushita told a group of U.S. executives in 1988:

> We will win, and you will lose. You cannot do anything about it because your failure is an internal disease. Your companies are based on Taylor's principles. Worse, your heads are Taylorized too. You firmly believe that good management means executives on one side, and workers on the other; on one side, men who think, and on the other side, men who can only work. For you, management is the art of smoothly transferring the executive's ideas to the workers' hands.
>
> We have passed the Taylor stage. . . . For us, management is the entire work force's intellectual commitment at the service of the company . . . without self-imposed functional or class barriers. . . . Only the intellects of all employees can permit a company to live with the ups and downs and requirements of its new environment. Yes, we will win and you will lose. For you are not able to rid your minds of the obsolete Taylorisms that we never had.[1]

The Taylor system philosophy assumes that (1) people are part of the process; (2) the process needs to be controlled externally to be productive; and (3) managers have to control carefully what people do. Recently, managers have begun to realize that these human resource practices no longer work very well. The new thinking is that (1) people design and improve the process; (2) workers who run the process must control it; and (3) managers must obtain the commitment of people to design, control, and improve processes so that they can remain productive. Thus, human resource management has shifted from a "control philosophy" to a "commitment philosophy." Studies have shown that such a shift results in higher quality, lower costs, less waste, better utilization, increased capacity, reduced turnover and absenteeism, faster implementation of change, greater human skill development, and better individual self-esteem.[2] However, managers are faced with such new responsibilities as investing extra effort, developing new skills and relationships, coping with higher levels of ambiguity and uncertainty as well as obsolete skills and careers that are casualties of change. Workers also face discomfort caused by changing attitudes and skill requirements and increased responsibility.

The revolution in industrial psychology and human relations began at the Hawthorne Works of Western Electric Company in the late 1920s by a Harvard team that included Elton Mayo, Fritz Roethlisberger, and William Dickson. Both Deming and Juran were working for Western Electric at the time, which may have influenced their views on quality and the work force. A few years later, the work of Abraham Maslow, Douglas McGregor, and Frederick Herzberg helped to develop the concepts of motivation, employee development, and individual and group approaches to job design with an emphasis on human relations. New theories are continually proposed. The challenge is how to use these theories properly for quality improvement.

In addition, information technology has dramatically changed the working environment. The flood of personal computers and computer networks requires highly trained and flexible employees. Because educational institutions are typically slow to respond to changes in the business environment, companies must train, retrain, and develop employees in rapidly developing technologies. Human resource practices must also encourage personal ownership of skill development and improvement. Clearly, businesses face a critical challenge in human resource management. In this chapter, the focus falls on human resource management within a total quality environment. The chapter also discusses quality-related issues in key personnel management practices, as well as the implications of motivation theories and models in a total quality environment.

THE SCOPE OF HUMAN RESOURCE MANAGEMENT

Human resource management (HRM) consists of those activities designed to provide for and coordinate the people of an organization.[3] HRM enables the work force to develop its full potential to pursue the company's quality and operational performance objectives. How the company builds and maintains an environment for quality excellence conducive to full participation and personal and organizational growth is the concern of HRM. Human resource functions include determining the organization's human resource needs; recruiting, selecting, developing, counseling, and rewarding employees; acting as a liaison with unions and government organizations; and handling other matters of employee well-being.

HRM is a modern term for what has been traditionally referred to as *personnel administration* or *personnel management.* In their traditional role, personnel managers in a business organization interviewed job applicants, negotiated contracts with the union, kept time cards on hourly workers, and occasionally taught a training course. Today, their role has changed dramatically. Human resource managers may still perform the traditional tasks of personnel managers, but the scope and importance of their area of responsibility have changed significantly. Human resource managers now take on a strategic role in their organizations.

They must consider and plan for the development of the organization's corporate culture at the same time they oversee day-to-day operations involved with maintenance of the HRM systems of their companies. If the organization commits itself to a total quality management philosophy, both the process and content of the human resource department—the way that it carries out its mission and responsibilities—will be drastically changed.

An example of the strategic use of HRM can be seen at the Prudential Insurance Company.[4] The Prudential identified five critical success factors that must be consistently implemented well in order to widen its lead over competitors. One of these factors is superior service to its customers and field force. The ability to deliver value-added service consistently requires superior performance in eight areas, which have been determined as key to becoming customer- and market-driven:

- People recruitment and retention
- Training
- Continuing education
- Creative use of information technologies
- Accessibility to customers
- Performance measuring and monitoring
- Recognition for superior performance
- Customer satisfaction monitoring

Five of these eight areas for superior performance involve HRM issues. All eight areas are related to quality issues of excellence in selection and retention, internal performance, customer service, and continuous improvement.

TQM and development of related skills has finally become an important priority in many companies. In a total quality environment employees need to understand the goal of customer satisfaction, be given the training and responsibilities to achieve this goal, and to feel that they indeed make a difference. For example, at the Coors Brewing Company in Golden, Colorado, the customer satisfaction improvement program is focused on giving employees the skills, and on creating the environment in which employees have one responsibility and one desired result: to satisfy and hopefully delight their customers, especially internal customers. Coors engaged in a massive training program to learn TQM principles, and then structured its organization systems (compensation, evaluation, and so on) to support the new effort. Coors successfully developed in its employees a passion for their jobs and pride in their work, which translate into measurable improvements in productivity, a remarkably low turnover rate, and the delivery of quality product and service throughout the system.[5]

A recent survey suggests that HRM managers recognize the development of employee involvement training, TQM skills, and related activities as necessary for corporate competitiveness. More than 1000 of *Human Resource Focus* readers from various industries and geographic regions were asked to rate key issues facing human resource (HR) professionals in 1993.[6] The top concerns were (1) employee involvement, with 46 percent of respondents rating it as one of their three top concerns; (2) customer service, with 39 percent of respondents ranking it among the top three items; and (3) total quality management (TQM), with 34 percent indicating it as an area critical to their job function. Respondents were also asked about the types of training offered by their companies. More than half said that their companies had increased training in customer service, teamwork, and TQM. Of the companies that offered such training, 67 percent increased training in customer service, 60 percent in teamwork, and 57 percent in TQM.

Just as all managers are responsible for quality even though their organizations may have quality professionals, all managers have a responsibility for human resources, even if the formal organizational structure has HRM professionals. Developing individual skills through on-the-job training, promoting teamwork and participation, motivating and recognizing employees, and providing meaningful communciation are important human resource skills that all managers must embrace for TQM to succeed. At Xerox, for instance, managers are directly accountable for the development and implementation of human resource plans that support quality goals of the company. Thus, understanding HRM practices is necessary for a total quality environment and a critical task of all managers.

■ Human Resource Management in a TQM Environment

The total quality management focus is changing the role of human resource management by changing the perspectives of employees, HRM professionals, and line-and-staff managers from an adversarial, control-oriented relationship to a cooperative position based on mutual organizational and individual goals, trust, and respect. Human resource managers tend to reflect the culture within which they are working, as well as influence it. Thus, values can and do play a key role in determining how the HRM function is carried out. Leading companies have revolutionized all (or nearly all) of their major human resource policies and procedures.[7] Table 10.1 contrasts traditional HRM policies with those policies found in companies recognized for successfully implementing total quality. In traditional organizations, HRM functions identify, prepare, direct, and reward employees for following rather narrow objectives. In TQM organizations, HRM units develop policies and procedures to ensure that employees can perform multiple roles, improvise when necessary, and direct themselves toward continuous improvement of both product quality and customer service. HRM has evolved from a support function to a leadership function in the organization.

The new HRM paradigm has been used successfully by many companies to develop a more cooperative, productive, flexible, and innovative work environment that recognizes the value of the human resource in meeting customer needs, with a focus on sharing information, responsibility, and rewards. It offers a way for everyone to search for a win-win solution, in contrast to the traditional win-lose mentality previously held by managers and workers.

■ Leading Practices

TQM-based HRM practices work to accomplish the following tasks:

1. Communicate the importance of each employee's contribution to total quality.

2. Stress quality-related synergies available through teamwork.

3. Empower employees to "make a difference."

4. Reinforce individual and team commitment to quality with a wide range of rewards and reinforcements.[8]

TABLE 10.1   Traditional Versus Total Quality Human Resource Paradigms

Corporate Context Dimension	Traditional Paradigm	Total Quality Paradigm
Corporate Culture	Individualism	Collective efforts
	Differentiation	Cross-functional work
	Autocratic leadership	Coaching/enabling
	Profits	Customer satisfaction
	Productivity	Quality

Human Resource Characteristics	Traditional Paradigm	Total Quality Paradigm
Communications	Top-down	Top-down
		Horizontal, lateral
		Multidirectional
Voice and involvement	Employment-at-will	Due process
	Suggestion systems	Quality circles
		Attitude surveys
Job design	Efficiency	Quality
	Productivity	Customization
	Standard procedures	Innovation
	Narrow span of control	Wide span of control
	Specific job descriptions	Autonomous work teams
		Empowerment
Training	Job related skills	Broad range of skills
	Functional, technical	Cross-functional
		Diagnostic, problem solving
	Productivity	Productive and quality
Performance measurement and evaluation	Individual goals	Team goals
	Supervisory review	Customer, peer, and supervisory review
	Emphasize financial performance	Emphasize quality and service
Rewards	Competition for individual merit increases and benefits	Team/group based rewards
		Financial rewards, financial and nonfinancial recognition
Health and safety	Treat problems	Prevent problems
		Safety programs
		Wellness programs
		Employee assistance
Selection/promotion career development	Selected by manager	Selected by peers
	Narrow job skills	Problem-solving skills
	Promotion based on individual accomplishment	Promotion based on group facilitation
	Linear career path	Horizontal career path

SOURCE: Blackburn and Rosen, "Total Quality and Human Resources Management: Lessons Learned from Baldrige Award-Winning Companies," *The Academy of Management Executive* 7, no. 3 (1993), 49–66.

These goals are realized by leading companies through the following practices:

■ *They integrate human resource plans with overall quality and operational perform-ance plans to fully address the needs and development of the entire work force.* Human resource plans should be driven by overall strategic plans. For example, a manufacturer of high-technology consumer electronics products, like the MicroTech example in Chapter 6, that has as key strategies product innovation and development of advanced technologies, might include in its human resource plans the goal of increasing the knowledge and skills of product design engineers and diagnostic technicians. AT&T, for instance, links its training and education to strategic plans to establish current and future competencies for both the organization and the individual. The Consumer Communications Services division develops long-term and short-term plans in four areas: competencies, organization effectiveness, performance, and people. Short-term plans in the first area include strengthening the linkage among competencies identification, assessment, employee development, and business needs; and refining roles and responsibilities to increase employee empowerment. Long-term plans center around the continuous learning environment and formulating new systems for empowering and developing employees.[9] Policy deployment, discussed in Chapter 6, provides a vehicle for ensuring that human resource plans are aligned with the overall strategic plans of the organization.

■ *They empower individuals and teams to make decisions that affect quality and customer satisfaction.* Many companies talk about empowerment, but few truly practice it. At AT&T, design engineers have the authority to stop a design, and line operators can stop the produciton line if they detect a quality problem. At the Ritz-Carlton Hotels, each employee can "move heaven and earth" and spend up to $2000 to satisfy a customer. In 1991, Texas Instruments began an organizational restructuring aimed at improving the environment for individual empowerment. By flattening the organization, that is, reducing management layers to five, TI reduced the ratio of supervisors to employees from 1:8 to 1:10. Empowerment is supported by increasing communication among employees, especially between different organizational levels and functions.

Empowerment requires substantial training. At Wainwright Industries associates are fully engaged in quality efforts beginning with their first day on the job. During new associate orientation, senior managers explain the importance of quality and customer satisfaction and outline the company's approaches to continuous improvement. Follow-up sessions are held 24 and 72 days after the start of employment. The company invests up to seven percent of its payroll in training and education. All associates take courses on quality values, communication techniques, problem solving, statistical process control, and synchronous manufacturing.

■ *They continually improve key personnel management processes such as recruitment, hiring, training, performance evaluation, and recognition.* A key approach to improving HRM practices is the use of employee surveys and measurement of key indicators. Surveys monitor employee satisfaction and identify problem areas. They might also ask employees to rate their supervisors on leadership, communication, and support. AT&T conducts an opinion survey every two years to measure employee attitudes and the effect of improvement efforts. Management compares the results within AT&T and with benchmarks of other high-performance companies. The Ritz-Carlton conducts an annual survey of all employees to determine their levels of satisfaction and also their understanding of basic quality standards. Texas Instruments targets for improvement all responses that are less than 65 percent favorable and any unfavorable year-to-year trends or themes. Employees then participate in focus groups to identify causes and work toward solutions. Surveys also evaluate performance and recognition systems. This information is used to tailor rewards to what is valued by employees. At Westinghouse Electric Corporation, each site within the division customizes its awards; some give mall gift certificates, while others give cash or other awards.

Many companies measure and track employee suggestion rates, time to respond to suggestions, cross-training, and team activities, as well as traditional measures such as absenteeism and turnover. Texas Instruments has a training council that uses a computerized system to monitor individualized training plans. Granite Rock has an employee evaluation system called an Individual Professional Development Plan for integrating the company's human resource needs and quality objectives with the individual's aspirations and abilities. This process, along with employee surveys, customer surveys, suggestions, and so on, helps to identify needs. AT&T uses a systematic methodology called the Instructional Technology Approach to assess, analyze, and develop curricula to identify and address skill and development gaps. Leading companies use benchmarking, discussed in Chapter 9, to assess human resource practices against best practices both inside and outside a given industry.

Motorola performs a week-long review of its quality system every two years, involving the entire organization. They evaluate the strengths and weaknesses, and provide recommendations for improvement. Part of this review looks at the human resource function to determine whether employees are capable and properly trained.

■ *They maintain a work environment conducive to the well-being and growth of all employees, and they measure employee satisfaction.* Satisfied employees are productive. As Hal Rosenbluth, president of Rosenbluth Travel puts it, "By maintaining an enjoyable, bureaucracy-free environment, one that encourages innovative thinking . . . and honest communication, people are free to concentrate solely on the needs of the clients."[10] Leading companies understand employee satisfaction, measure it, and use the results to improve the quality of worklife. Well-being factors such as health, safety, and ergonomics should be included in quality improvement activities. Ames Rubber Corporation, for example, has nine major long-range plans in effect, covering such areas as affirmative action, health benefits and safety, and accident reduction. FedEx teaches employees how to handle dangerous goods, lift heavy packages correctly, and drive safely. Leading companies also perform audits to identify risks and prevent accidents, focusing on root cause analysis. Texas Instruments, for example, uses safety, environmental, and ergonomic experts to institute preventive actions, investigate accidents, and provide training. At the Ritz-Carlton, project teams configure the best combination of technology and procedures to eliminate causes of safety and security problems.

Special services, such as counseling, recreational or cultural activities, non-work-related education, day care, flexible work hours, and outplacement activities contribute to employee satisfaction. Texas Instruments, for example, has a company-sponsored employee association called "Texins" that provides fitness activities, recreational clubs, and family events. Free counseling for personal and relationship problems is also provided. Granite Rock sponsors company picnics and parties. The effectiveness of such initiatives is measured using safety results, absenteeism, turnover rates, grievences, and attitude surveys.

■ *They promote ongoing employee contributions through individual and group participation.* The most common methods of employee involvement are suggestion systems and teams. AT&T Universal Card Services has a program called "Your Ideas . . . Your Universe," through which over 10,000 ideas were submitted in 1992 alone. Cadillac made a commitment to answer all suggestions within 24 hours; seventy percent of the suggestions they receive concern quality issues. Texas Instruments Defense Systems and Electronics Group employs a variety of teams such as corporate action teams to work on corporate-level goals, employee effectiveness teams to prevent potential problems in specific work areas, and department action teams to solve departmental problems. Texas Instruments set a stretch goal in 1992 to have every employee be a member of at least one team by the end of the year. Because employee involvement and teamwork are one of the fundamental principles of TQM, the next chapter is devoted entirely to this subject.

STRATEGIC PLANNING FOR HUMAN RESOURCE MANAGEMENT

Strategic planning for HRM focuses on employee development; work organization; reward, recognition, benefits, and compensation; and recruitment. Human resource plans typically include one or more of the following:

■ Mechanisms for promoting cooperation, such as internal customer/supplier relationships or other internal partnerships

■ Initiatives to promote labor–management cooperation, such as partnerships with unions

■ Creation and/or modification of recognition systems, compensation systems, or mechanisms for increasing or broadening employee responsibilities

■ Creating opportunities for employees to learn and use skills that go beyond current job assignments through redesigning processes

■ Education and training initiatives

■ Forming partnerships with educational institutions to develop employees or help ensure the future supply of well-prepared employees

Until recently, most organizations neglected the strategic aspects of human resource management, relegating HRM to a support function. Today, most progressive firms recognize that HRM plays the key role in developing a viable competitive strategy. Schuler and Jackson explored the linkage between strategy and HRM structure as shown in Table 10.2.[11] In general, managers must make choices in five areas that affect the design and operation of the HRM system: planning, staffing, appraising, compensating, and training and development. Each of these five areas has dimensions that can be viewed on a continuum from a structured environment with rigid practices to an unstructured environment with flexible practices.

Schuler and Jackson studied three typical competitive strategies: (1) cost reduction, (2) quality enhancement, and (3) innovation. Some companies, such as Honda of America, have pursued multiple strategies such as quality enhancement and innovation, although one of the three strategies tends to dominate in most organizations. They discussed specific employee role behaviors and human resource management practices needed to make each of the strategies fit within its competitive environment.

The cost reduction strategy fits a highly stable competitive environment, most often in a mature industry. The time frame, or strategic focus, is short term with routine, repetitive, predictable operations being the predominant work mode. Employees must "fit the mold," tolerate narrow skill use, be more concerned

TABLE 10.2	Human Resource Management Practice Continuae

Planning Choices

Informal	....	Formal
Short Term	....	Long Term
Explicit Job Analysis	....	Implicit Job Analysis
Job Simplification	....	Job Enrichment
Low Employee Involvement	....	High Employee Involvement

Staffing Choices

Internal Sources	....	External Sources
Narrow Paths	....	Broad Paths
Single Ladder	....	Multiple Ladders
Explicit Criteria	....	Implicit Criteria
Limited Socialization	....	Extensive Socialization
Closed Procedures	....	Open Procedures

Appraising Choices

Behavioral Criteria	....	Results Criteria

Purposes: Development, Remedial, Maintenance

Low Employee Participation	....	High Employee Participation
Short-Term Criteria	....	Long-Term Criteria
Individual Criteria	....	Group Criteria

Compensating Choices

Low Base Salaries	....	High Base Salaries
Internal Equity	....	External Equity
Few Perks	....	Many Perks
Standard, Fixed Package	....	Flexible Package
Low Participation	....	High Participation
No Incentives	....	Many Incentives
Short-Term Incentives	....	Long-Term Incentives
No Employment Security	....	High Employment Security
Hierarchical	....	High Participation

Training and Development Choices

Short Term	....	Long Term
Narrow Application	....	Broad Application
Productivity Emphasis	....	Quality of Work Life Emphasis
Spontaneous, Unplanned	....	Planned, Systematic
Individual Orientation	....	Group Orientation
Low Participation	....	High Participation

SOURCE: Adapted from R. S. Schuler, "Human Resource Management Practice Choices," in R. S. Schuler, S. A. Youngblood, and V. L. Huber (eds.), *Readings in Personnel and Human Resource Management,* 3rd ed. (St. Paul, MN: West Publishing Company, 1988).

about quantity than quality, be comfortable with stability, avoid risks, and have a tendency to resist change. They do, however, have to interact with other employees on the line in order to perform their jobs successfully, although this interaction is primarily reactive, rather than proactive. HRM practices generally fall on the left side of each continuum shown in Table 10.2. These more rigid choices correspond primarily to traditional HRM practices rather than TQM-based practices.

On the opposite side of the coin, an innovation strategy fits an unstable, unpredictable, turbulent environment and emphasizes creativity and flexibility. Employees must be comfortable with ambiguity and uncertainty, demonstrate a variety of skills, seek risks, and embrace change. Employees in a TQM environment tend to have a balanced concern for quality and quantity of output, high involvement with the job, and a very high concern for results. They also tend to be highly independent in their work, preferring the maximum possible level of autonomy. HRM choices that facilitate this strategy are on the right-hand side of each continuum in Table 10.2.

Most organizations do not find themselves in either a highly unstable or highly stable environment, but usually fall somewhere in between. Even the high-tech firms that typically experience unstable environments, such as Motorola, Apple Computer, and 3M, have many processes that benefit from an emphasis on systematic planning, control, and productivity enhancement rather than on continuous innovation. In this environment, a quality enhancement strategy is most appropriate.

To gain competitive advantage through a quality-enhancement strategy, a company can use key HRM practices such as (1) relatively fixed and explicit job descriptions, (2) high levels of employee participation in decisions relevant to immediate work conditions and the job itself, (3) a mix of individual and group criteria for performance appraisal that is mostly short-term and results-oriented, (4) egalitarian treatment of employees and some guarantees of employment security, and (5) extensive and continuous training and development of employees.

Although an emphasis on one or more of these factors may or may not be appropriate, as a whole they provide a generally accurate composite of individual and organizational requirements associated with an overall corporate strategy of quality enhancement. An organization wishing to implement this strategy would have to align its planning, staffing, appraising, compensating, and training and development systems and processes to support these HRM requirements.

Human resource plans should be aligned with overall company plans. Cadillac recognized the need to integrate human resource plans with its quality processes in 1987 when the executive staff charged the human resources staff with designing a people strategy to support the business/quality plan.[12] Figure 10.1 shows Cadillac's people strategy structure. At the top of the pyramid is the employee, the center of the process and reason for its existence. The employee is supported by seven People Strategy Teams with cross-functional, salaried, and hourly membership. These teams research, design, recommend, implement, and evaluate Cadillac's people processes. The People Strategy Teams receive policy

FIGURE 10.1   Cadillac's People Strategy Structure

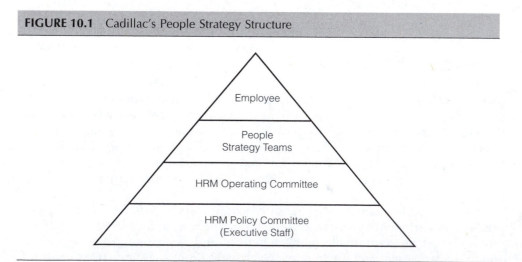

SOURCE: Courtesy Cadillac Motor Car Division

leadership and coaching from the human resource management operating committee. The executive staff acts as the human resource management policy committee, which provides direction and support.

EMPOWERMENT

The Malcolm Baldrige National Quality Award guidelines state, "Improving company performance requires improvements at all levels within a company. This, in turn, depends upon the skills and dedication of the entire workforce. Companies need to invest in the development of the workforce and to seek new avenues to involve employees in problem solving and decision making."[13] One of these avenues is empowerment. **Empowerment** simply means giving people authority and power to make decisions, gain greater control over their work, and thus more easily satisfy customers. Pete Coors, CEO of Coors Brewing, explained it simply: "We're moving from an environment where the supervisor says, 'This is the way it is going to be done and if you don't like it go someplace else,' to an environment where the supervisor can grow with the changes, get his troops together and say, 'Look, you guys are operating the equipment, what do *you* think we ought to do?'"[14]

Examples of empowerment abound. Workers in Coors' container operation give each other performance evaluations, and even screen, interview, and hire new people for the line. At Motorola, sales representatives have the authority to replace defective products up to six years after purchase, a decision that used to require top management approval. Hourly employees at GM's antilock brake system plant in Dayton, Ohio, can call in suppliers to help solve problems, and manage scrap, machine downtime, absences, and rework. At Globe Metallurgical, hourly group leaders take care of business on the weekends; no supervisors are needed. FedEx empowers employees to "do everything humanly possible to get the job done and to satisfy customers."

The need to empower the entire work force in order for quality to succeed has long been recognized, even if only recently put into practice. Juran wrote that "ideally, quality control should be delegated to the workforce to the maximum extent possible."[15] Empowerment resembles Juran's concept of "self-control," which was discussed in the last chapter. Five of Deming's 14 Points relate directly to the notion of empowerment.

Point 6: Institute training.

Point 7: Teach and institute leadership.

Point 8: Drive out fear. Create trust. Create a climate for innovation.

Point 10: Eliminate exhortations for the work force.

Point 13: Encourage education and self-improvement for everyone.[16]

These points suggest involving employees more directly in decision making processes, giving them the security and confidence to make decisions, and providing them with the necessary tools and training.

Successful empowerment of employees requires that

■ Employees be provided education, resources, and encouragement.

■ Policies and procedures be examined for needless restrictions on the ability of employees to serve customers.

■ An atmosphere of trust be fostered rather than resentment and punishment for failure.

■ Information be shared freely rather than closely guarded as a source of control and power.

■ Workers feel their efforts are desired and needed for the success of the organization.

■ Managers be given the required support and training to adopt a ''hands off'' leadership style.

■ Employees be trained in the amount of latitude they are allowed to take. Formulating decision rules and providing role playing scenarios are excellent ways of teaching employees.[17]

Empowerment means that leaders and managers must relinquish *some* of the power that they previously held. This power shift often creates management fears that workers will abuse this privilege. However, experience shows that front-line workers generally are more conservative than managers. For example, companies that have empowered employee groups to evaluate performance and grant pay raises to their peers have found that they are much tougher than managers were. Many companies require employees to report decisions they make or discuss them with their supervisors in a learning context. At McDonald's, employees have the freedom to make their own decisions, but only within certain parameters, allowing management to maintain a certain level of control. A regional vice president is quoted as saying, ''We've empowered [employees] to do whatever it takes—as long as it's based on fact-based customer research.''[18] New training methods emphasize customers first and the mechanics of doing the job second.

Empowerment gives managers new responsibilities. They must hire and develop people capable of handling empowerment, encourage risk-taking, and recognize achievements. Giving employees information of company finances and the financial implications of empowered decisions is also important. At DuPont's Delaware River plant, management shares cost figures with all workers. By sharing this information, management believes that workers will think more for themselves and identify with company goals.[19] Globe Metallurgical regularly conducts small group meetings with all employees to review financial performance. To help employees make decisions on issues affecting production, a department manager at Texas Eastman Chemicals Plant supplied operators with a daily financial report that showed how their decisions affected the bottom line. As a result, department profits doubled in four months and quality improved by 50 percent as employees began suggesting cost-saving improvements.[20]

Empowerment can be viewed as vertical teamwork between managerial and nonmanagerial personnel. It builds confidence in workers by showing them that the company has confidence in their ability to make decisions on their own. It generates commitment and pride. It also gives employees better experience and opportunity to advance their careers. It benefits customers who buy the products and services of organizations. For instance, empowered employees can often reduce bureaucratic red tape that customers encounter—such as seeking a supervisor's signature—which makes customer transactions speedier and more pleasant. John Akers, former chairman of IBM, said, ''Empowering our employees and inculcating a sense that everyone owns his or her piece of the business not only unleashes the talent and energy of our people, but also flattens the organization and reduces stifling bureaucracy."[21] Empowerment is an effective way of realizing one of Deming's 14 Points: Drive out fear.

PERSONNEL MANAGEMENT IN A TQM ENVIRONMENT[22]

The primary responsibilities of personnel management—recruitment and career development, performance appraisal, training and education, and recognition, reward, and compensation—can have a major impact on the success or failure of TQM efforts in an organization. All these issues are embedded in Deming's 14 Points, as well as in the writings of Juran and Crosby. In this section, the implications that total quality has for these human resource practices are discussed.

■ Recruitment and Career Development

Meeting and exceeding customer expectations begins with hiring the right people. Customer-contact employees make up one of the fastest-growing segments of the work force. Limited availability of people with the skills to perform complex, rapidly changing jobs is forcing HRM managers to rethink their selection strategies. Traditional hiring practices have been based on cognitive or technical rather than interpersonal skills. Today, the criterion is shifting to attributes such as enthusiasm, resourcefulness, creativity, and the flexibility to learn new skills rapidly. The concept of internal customers suggests that every employee needs good interpersonal skills. Even technical skill requirements are changing; to apply statistical process control principles on the job, all workers must have basic mathematics and logical-thinking abilities.

Customer-focused employees should exhibit certain characteristics.[23]

- The ability to remain calm under stressful situations
- Optimism, initiative, and a people-orientation
- The ability to listen well
- An orientation toward analysis and prevention
- The ability to solve problems

New approaches to evaluating candidates, such as psychological testing and situational role playing, are being used in the hiring process. Narrow job descriptions are being broadened. Many companies today seek the best available applicants and train them in TQM principles.

Motorola ties recruitment and selection activities to results in order to gauge the quality of their recruiting effort as they strive for TQM at every level.[24] Their recruiting department is measured by a new quality-oriented criterion: success of recruits on the job. Instead of using the old measure of how much it costs to hire each recruit, recruiters are now measured on whether new hires were well trained coming into the company, brought in at the right salary level, or left the company after the first six months for a better job. Based on these and other data, the department decided it had to increase, rather than decrease, the amount spent on each recruit. Thus, in recruiting activities, Motorola plans and sets objectives for recruiting, charts progress over time in order to reduce "defects" in the hiring process, and determines whether the "output" of the process (excellent employees) is under control, rather than just measuring inputs (dollar per recruit). Other major companies like Procter & Gamble seek entry level college graduates who understand total quality principles. They specifically want their new employees to think in terms of creating quality and value for consumers, to understand their customers and needs, and to work toward results despite obstacles.

Career development is also changing because of TQM. As managerial roles shift from directing and controlling to coaching and facilitating, managers, who must deal with cross-functional problems, benefit more from horizontal movement than from upward movement in narrow functional areas. Flatter organizations limit promotion opportunities. Thus, career development expands learning opportunities and creates more challenging assignments rather than increasing spans of managerial control.

■ Performance Appraisal

Considerable truth can be found in the statement, "How one is evaluated determines how one performs." Performance appraisal is an exceedingly difficult HRM activity. Organizations typically use performance appraisals for a number of reasons:

■ Appraisals provide feedback to employees who can then recognize and build on their strengths and work on their weaknesses.

■ Appraisals are used to determine salary increases.

■ Appraisals identify people for promotion.

■ Appraisals are used to deal with human resource legalities. As such, they can provide a paper trail to fight wrongful-discharge suits and act as a formal warning system to marginal employees.[25]

Conventional appraisal processes typically involve a manager or supervisor evaluating the work of a subordinate for a given time period. Steps and characteristics of these processes may include some or all of the following:

■ Objectives for a certain period of time (typically for the year ahead) are set unilaterally or jointly by the manager with his or her subordinate.

■ At the end of the review period, the manager sits down with the subordinate and reviews accomplishments, strengths and weaknesses, and/or personal characteristics of the subordinate related to the job.

■ Frequently, the form used for performance rating has 10 to 15 tangible and intangible categories, such as quantity of work, quality of work, works well with others, takes initiative, etc., to be rated on a five- or seven-point scale from "excellent" to "unsatisfactory" or "poor."

■ Usually, the manager appraises employees according to ratings distribution, based on company policies, such as "no more than 10 percent of any department's employees may be rated as excellent" or "merit raises or bonuses will only be paid to employees who are rated as excellent or very good."

■ The standard form generally asks the rater to evaluate the ratee's capacity to handle greater responsibility and/or readiness for promotion.

■ Often, the performance appraisal interview is accompanied by announcements of raises, bonuses, and/or promotions.

Dissatisfaction with conventional performance appraisal systems is common among both managers, who are the appraisers, and workers, who are the appraisees. General Motors, for example, discovered that 90 percent of its people believed they were in the top 10 percent. How discouraging is it to be rated lower? Many managers are inclined to give higher ratings because of potential negative impacts. Numerous research studies over the past several decades have pointed out the problems and pitfalls of performance appraisals.[26] Many legitimate objections can be made.[27] Appraisals nourish short-term performance and destroy long-term planning, discourage teamwork, foster mediocrity for those who meet or exceed performance expectations, assume that individuals are responsible for all results, are highly subjective and not measurable, and focus on detection rather than prevention. As such, they are contrary to fundamental TQM principles.

W. Edwards Deming strongly condemned the performance appraisal process because it is statistically unsound.[28] For example, many salespersons' compensation is based on a sales quota. However, sales depends on more than the individual's contribution. Factors such as the economy, competition, customer interaction with other aspects of the company, and prior relationships all affect sales. These system factors are outside the control of the individual salesperson. Thus, Deming would point out that sales (y) is a function of both system (S) and individual (I) performance factors.

$$y = f(S, I)$$

Solving an equation with two unknowns is impossible. Yet this impossible task is precisely what traditional performance appraisal systems attempt to do.

TQM assumes that people want to do better, and will if they are properly motivated and are given the opportunity to participate, along with adequate training and tools. From a shared vision of quality that goes beyond one's own workplace emerges a team concept in which trust, effective communication, and cooperation are necessary to achieve success. Performance appraisals are most effective when they are based on the objectives of the work teams that support the organization.[29] In this respect, they act as a diagnostic tool and review process for individual, team, and organizational development and achievement. The performance appraisal can also be a motivator when it is developed and used by the work team itself. Team efforts are harnessed when team members are empowered to monitor their own workplace activities.

In a TQM culture, quality improvement is one of the major dimensions on which employees are evaluated. Xerox, for instance, changed its performance review criteria by replacing traditional measures such as "follows procedures" and "meets standards" to evaluating employees on the basis of quality improvement, problem solving, and team contributions. Many companies use peer review, customer evaluations, and self-assessments as a part of the appraisal process.

In the spirit of Deming, many companies are replacing performance evaluation altogether with personal planning and development systems. Cadillac, for instance, replaced its traditional performance review with a personnel development planning process in which managers meet with employees to set future expectations, identify training needs, provide coaching, and reward continuous improvement. Eastman Chemical Company eliminated employee labeling, improved the focus on individual development planning, and encouraged employee involvement and ownership. Granite Rock does not emphasize past performance, but sets professional development goals in conjunction with the company's needs. No stigma is attached to failure; the thrust of the process is to develop each individual to the fullest. A TQM organization requires a closely monitored performance appraisal process that is oriented toward "best practices" and continuous improvement of quality.

■ Training and Education

Training is one of the largest initial costs in a total quality initiative, and not surprisingly, one in which many companies are reluctant to invest. Xerox Business Products and Systems invested more than $125 million in quality training. Even if companies make the investment, they often take great pains to measure the benefits against the costs. Motorola used to do this, but no longer. They *know* that the benefits of quality-based training outweigh the costs by at least 30 to 1. Training and education have become an essential responsibility of HRM departments in TQM organizations, particularly as empowered employees require new knowledge and skills.

Quality and related training and education provide and/or enhance the knowledge and skills employees need to do their jobs effectively and efficiently. Training includes quality awareness, leadership, project management, communications, teamwork, problem solving, interpreting and using data, meeting customer requirements, process analysis, process simplification, waste reduction, cycle time reduction, error-proofing, and other educational issues that affect employee effectiveness, efficiency, and safety. In many cases education also provides job enrichment skills and job rotation that enhance employees' career opportunities. Sometimes, training in basic skills such as reading, writing, language, and basic mathematics is needed for quality and operational performance improvement. Employees at Xerox learn a range of techniques, from the basic quality improvement tools introduced in Chapter 9 through benchmarking. Motorola employees learn statistical methods and defect reduction approaches. Other companies, such as FedEx and Wallace, train workers in team development and people issues.

Companies should assess the specific training needs of different employees. All employees need basic skills and quality orientation. However, advanced topics differ among employee categories and functions. For example, customer-contact personnel typically need a higher level of training in behavioral topics than manufacturing engineers, who need Taguchi methods. Customer needs should drive training strategies. At IBM Rochester, for example, managers tell the education department what they need, and programs are designed to meet those needs. By treating the training function as an internal supplier, the time to deliver training programs was reduced from five days to two.

The leaders in quality—Deming, Juran, and Crosby—actively promoted quality training and education. Two of Deming's 14 Points, for example, are devoted to these issues. The approaches of quality leaders are not based on sophisticated statistics or new technologies. Rather, they are focused on the philosophical importance of quality and simple tools and techniques that are easily applied and understood. Once the basics are in place, more advanced statistical methods can be taught and applied.

For example, the Juran Institute in Wilton, Connecticut, provides a variety of educational services and products devoted to quality improvement, including courses and seminars, public and on-site training, and consulting. The institute offers a video-based training program—called "Juran on Quality Improvement"—which is a structured, project-by-project process designed to produce annual improvement in quality and annual reduction in quality-related costs. The program features 16 video cassettes and supporting materials. More than 100,000 managers at 1000 locations have used the program; clients include General Motors, Eastman Kodak, and General Dynamics. Philip Crosby has engaged in similar ventures. Philip Crosby Associates (PCA) is widely regarded as the largest consulting and teaching firm in the quality area. Crosby opened Quality College in Winter Park, Florida, to teach his quality improvement philosophy to top management. During the last 15 years of his life, Deming conducted extensive programs for quality training, the most famous of which were his "Four-Day" seminars. These have been preserved on videotape and continue to be used for training in quality.

Companies committed to TQM invest heavily in training. Motorola and Texas Instruments, for example, provide at least 40 hours of training to every employee. The Cincinnati Service Center of the Internal Revenue Service devoted more than 420,000 hours (more than 70 hours and $500 per employee) in 1988 to classroom and on-the-job training as part of its quality improvement initiative. Cadillac sent more than 1400 employees to a four-day Deming seminar at a cost of nearly $1 million. Solectron increased its annual training hours from 85 to 150 between 1991 and 1995. Leading companies have formal training departments, whose systems and approaches evolved along with their overall quality systems. Training is usually based on the skills required to do a job, and needs are identified jointly by the employee and his or her supervisor. In many companies, managers train their workers directly in a top-down fashion; this approach was pioneered by Xerox, beginning with the CEO, David Kearns himself, during their transition to TQM.

Specific approaches vary by company. Most large companies have in-house training staffs with state-of-the-art facilities. The Federal Express Quality Academy, established in 1991, uses a television network that broadcasts courses in a "just-in-time" fashion at employees' work site. They also have a network of interactive video instruction, consisting of 1200 work stations at 700 locations. Over 2000 course titles are available for self-paced instruction. The Quality Academy tracks test scores, pass rates, and time on line.[30] Smaller companies often use outside consultants. The content should be customized to the company's needs; "packaged" seminars are often a waste of time. For example, AT&T developed a three-day training course for every manager.[31] The first day was aimed at creating an awareness of quality and productivity programs and progress throughout the world. Outside speakers reviewed the challenges to U.S. industry and the reasons for Japanese success. Company vice presidents discussed the challenges facing their lines of business. Other speakers talked about the methods used by other companies to manage quality and productivity. The second day focused on Juran's approach to quality and productivity improvement and how to organize and manage an annual improvement program. The final day dealt with tools, such as statistical methods, software, and project management. In addition, AT&T developed a number of courses specifically for product and process designers: a statistical reliability workshop, a reliability prediction workshop, an experimental design workshop, and a product and process design optimization workshop. Solectron Corporation, with a large multicultural work force, offers English as a second language, and training in communciations, interpersonal skills, and technical manufacturing skills, all with bilingual trainers.

Continual reinforcement of lessons learned in training programs is essential. Many companies send employees to courses, but then allow the knowledge to slip away. New knowledge can be reinforced in several ways. Motorola uses on-the-job coaching to reinforce training; the Ritz-Carlton has follow-up sessions to monitor instructional effectiveness. The Ritz-Carlton holds a "quality line-up" briefing session each day in every work area. During these sessions, employees receive instructions on achieving quality certification within the company. Work area teams set the quality certification performance standards of each position.

Finally, companies need an approach for evaluating training effectiveness. The Ritz-Carlton requires employees to pass written and skill demonstration tests. Other companies use on-the-job evaluation or tests in simulated work environments. Many measure behavior and attitude changes. However, the true test of training effectiveness is results. By establishing a linkage between training and results (see the discussion of interlinking in Chapter 8), companies can show the impact on customer satisfaction and also identify gaps in training.

■ Recognition and Reward

The topic of rewards has already been introduced in the context of performance appraisal. Motivation, leadership, performance review, training, and development all ultimately lead to the question of "What's in it for me?" for each individual in every organization. Without willing, sustained individual effort, coordinated team efforts, and the sum total of the individual efforts that meet organizational goals, TQM is an impossible dream. Recognition and rewards should reinforce quality relative to short-term financial considerations. They can be monetary or nonmonetary, formal or informal, individual or group. Employees should contribute to the company's performance and recognition approaches. Awards provide a visible means of promoting quality efforts and tell employees that the organization values their efforts, increasing their motivation to improve. Most importantly, rewards should lead to behaviors that increase customer satisfaction.

Extrinsic and intrinsic rewards are the key to sustained individual efforts. A well-designed pay and benefit system, which is discussed in the next section, can provide excellent extrinsic motivation. Other reward systems are nonmonetary. For instance, L.L. Bean gives dinners or certificates toward merchandise. "Bean's Best Awards" are selected by cross-functional teams based on innovative ideas, exceptional customer service, role modeling, expertise at their jobs, and exceptional management ability. The design of the job itself is vitally important to intrinsic rewards.[32] This aspect as part of motivation is addressed later in this chapter.

Certain key practices lead to effective employee recognition and rewards:

■ *Giving both individual and team awards.* At the Ritz-Carlton, individual awards include verbal and written praise and the most desirable job assignments. Team awards include bonus pools and sharing in the gratuity system. Many companies have formal corporate recognition programs, such as IBM's Market Driven Quality Award for outstanding individual and team achievements in quality improvement, or the Xerox President's Award and Team Excellence Award.

■ *Involving everyone.* Recognition programs involve both front-line employees and senior management. Westinghouse has a Wall of Fame to recognize quality achievers at each site. Solectron rewards groups by buying entire divisions lunch and bringing in ice cream for the entire plant.

■ *Tying rewards to quality based on measurable objectives.* Leading companies recognize and reward behavior, not just results. Zytec rewards employees for participating in the suggestion program by providing cash awards for each implemented suggestion. A group of peers selects the best improvement ideas each month, which are also rewarded with cash. Many rewards are linked to customer satisfaction measures. Awards that conflict with quality values are modified or eliminated. Continuous feedback reinforces good performance and identifies areas for improvement.

■ *Allowing peers and customers to nominate and recognize superior performance.* Texas Instruments, for example, has a Site Quality Award to recognize the top two percent on the basis of peer nomination. Employees at FedEx who receive favorable comments from a customer are automatically nominated for the Golden Falcon Award. Recipients chosen by a review committee receive a gold pin, a congratulatory call from the CEO, recognition in the company newsletter, and 10 shares of company stock.

■ *Publicizing extensively.* At the IRS, employee recognition takes place in a number of ways. Team and individual recognition is publicized in a newsletter; certificates and pins are awarded for cooperative effort; and the processing division conducts an awards breakfast and end-of-year picnic at which contributors and teams are recognized.

■ *Making recognition fun.* Domino's Pizza stages a national Olympics, in which teams from the company's three regions compete in 15 events based on 15 job categories, such as doughmaking, driving, answering the telephone, and delivery. Winners stand on platforms while the Olympic theme is played to receive medals, checks, and other forms of recognition. The finals are broadcast live to commissaries around the country. Domino's Olympics provides an excellent way to benchmark efforts throughout the corporation; winners attend three days of discussion with upper management to discuss what's good about the company, what needs improvement, and how those improvements can be made.[33]

Compensation

Compensation is always a sticky issue and ties closely to the subject of motivation. Money is a motivator when people are at the bottom of Maslow's hierarchy. Pay for performance can diminish intrinsic motivation. It causes most employees to believe they are being treated unfairly, and forces managers to deliver negative messages. Eventually, it creates win/lose situations. The objectives of a good compensation system should be to attract, retain, and not demotivate employees. Other objectives include reducing unexplainable variation in pay (think about Deming's principles) and encouraging internal cooperation rather than competition. New York-based Handy HRM Corporation conducted a study of 78 companies in 1992 and found that 71 percent used traditional financial measures, such as revenue growth, profitability, and cost management, as a basis for compensation. Only 54 percent used quality measures such as customer satisfaction, defect prevention, and cycle time reduction to make compensation decisions, although an additional 21 percent were considering doing so at the time of the study. The study also found that only one percent of respondents eliminated merit ratings from their salary programs as advocated by Deming.

Many TQM-focused companies now base compensation on the market rate for an individual with proven capabilities, and then make adjustments as capabilities are increased, along with enhanced responsibilities, seniority, and business results. For example, General Motors' Powertrain Division, influenced strongly by Deming, decoupled compensation from performance appraisals. Compensation is determined from a "maturity curve" that considers an individual's seniority, level of expertise, and market for his or her services. Peers and subordinates have input as to an individual's rating on this curve. Distinctions based on contributions are limited to truly exceptional individuals. Many companies link compensation to company track records, unit performance, team success, or individual achievement. A Monsanto Company chemical plant, for example, ties worker bonuses to results at individual units and rewards workers for helping to prevent accidents.[34] Interestingly, different programs exist in different Monsanto plants—all developed with the participation of workers. Plans that failed had been decreed by corporate headquarters, rather than formulated in cooperation with employees.

One method often used to separate individual compensation from performance appraisal is **gainsharing,** an approach in which all employees share savings equally. Xerox, for example, has both a gainsharing and profit-sharing plan. Another way to separate compensation and appraisal is to tie pay to the acquisition of new skills, often within the context of a continuous improvement program in which all employees are given opportunities to broaden their work-related competencies.

Walton described how an organization can move from a traditional control approach to a TQM-based approach.[35] Walton's model, summarized in Table 10.3, suggests that managers who are seriously concerned about moving from a traditional approach to a TQM approach modify the assumptions and structure of compensation systems. Pay policies must shift from an individual focus to a group focus using gainsharing and profit-sharing systems. Such programs reinforce the importance of group contributions instead of concentrating only on individual contributions. Since individual pay is not likely to be eliminated, it should be tied to development and mastery of skills, as opposed to traditional job evaluation. Finally in the new approach, when the economy turns down, the pain of layoffs and pay cuts is borne by managers and staff, not just by hourly employees.

The transition to a TQM approach to compensation is not an easy one, particularly in a hostile environment in which organizations may be trying to react

TABLE 10.3 Walton's Model: Characteristics of Compensation Management

	Traditional Control Approach	Transitional Approach	TQM/HRM Approach
1. Pay policies	Variable pay where possible to provide individual incentive	Typically no basic changes in compensation concepts	Variable rewards to create equity and to reinforce group achievements; gainsharing, profit sharing
2. Individual pay	Geared to job evaluation		Linked to skills, mastery
3. Effects of economic downturns	Cuts concentrated on hourly payroll, not staff	Equality of sacrifice among employee groups	Equality of sacrifice among employee groups

SOURCE: Adapted from Richard E. Walton, "Toward a Strategy," *HR Trends and Challenges,* Table 3–1, 38.

to competitors who already have demonstrated outstanding quality, high productivity, and lower wage rates. However, because of the aging work force, the need for general skills in broadly defined jobs, the trends toward group problem solving and team efforts, and continual economic pressures from foreign and domestic sources, managers may have no choice but to move to the TQM model.

Nucor Corporation has succeeded in attacking quality, productivity, participation, and compensation issues with only five levels of management: the president and COO, vice presidents and general manager, department managers, supervisors, and hourly workers.[36] Nucor has 6000 employees in 17 plants in the United States and had $2.3 billion in sales in 1993. Its corporate philosophy is reflected in a quote from Ken Iverson, chairman of the board:

> To keep a cooperative and productive work force you need, number one, to be completely honest about everything; number two, to allow each employee as much as possible to make decisions about that employee's work, to find easier and more productive ways to perform duties; and number three, to be as fair as possible to all employees.[37]

All employess, from the president on down, have the same benefits; the only differences in individual pay are related to responsibilities (suggested in Point 2 of Walton's model). Workers at Nucor's five nonunion steel mills earn base hourly rates that are less than half of the going rate for unionized steelworkers. Nucor uses pay incentives designed around groups of 40–50 workers, including secretaries and senior managers. Productivity and quality bonuses are based on the number of tons of steel of acceptable quality produced by a given production team, and typically range from 100 to 200 percent of base salary. The bonuses are paid every week to reinforce motivation. The average worker at Nucor earns several thousand dollars per year more than the average worker in the industry, while the company is able to sell its steel at competitive worldwide market prices. The company was producing a ton of steel for less than half the average costs of a U.S. steel company.[38] Nucor required fewer than four hours of labor per ton, Japanese companies required about five hours per ton, and other U.S. mills averaged more than six hours per ton. This comparison illustrates the use and benefits of team-based pay policies (Point 1 in Walton's model).

During downturns, managers at Nucor frequently find that their bonuses are cut, even while hourly workers continue to receive theirs, based on production rates (Point number 3 in Walton's model). In 1982, Nucor cut salaries for its 12 top executives by 5 percent and froze wages for its 3500 employees. However, despite the tough times, they maintained their policy of no layoffs as they had throughout the history of the current company. By March 1983, when the United Steelworkers Union signed a contract to reduce wages and benefits in order to improve the competitiveness of the basic steel industry, Iverson announced a 5 percent wage increase for Nucor's workers.

■ The Individual–System Interface

Bounds and Pace developed a model (see Figure 10.2) to show how individual activities of selection, performance, appraisal, development, and reward can be tied to the identical activities system within the overall company for a viable HRM process.[39] For example, a high-quality individual cannot be selected unless the HRM recruiter has determined what the relevant goals and objectives of the system or organization are, and how an individual's skills and characteristics will help to enhance the quality of that organization or department. As

FIGURE 10.2 Critical Individual-System Linkages: HRM Implications

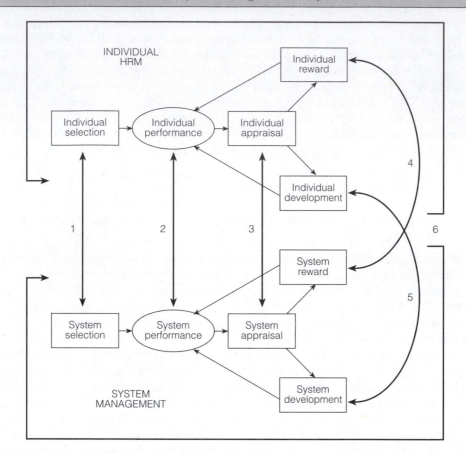

SOURCE: Bounds and Pace, "Human Resource Management." Copyright © 1990 by G. M. Bounds and L. A. Pace.

previously mentioned, Motorola defines the quality of their recruiting effort by how well selected individuals perform on the job in support of Motorola's system performance objectives.

As discussed earlier, individual performance appraisal has a number of pitfalls. To avoid these drawbacks, HRM systems that are geared primarily toward the individual in most organizations must be modified to encourage and reward individuals to support team initiatives.

Finally, in system development and organizational improvement, HRM managers must encourage individual development activities that support and enhance the systems. In one example, training in Japanese air conditioner manufacturing firms demonstrated the incredible commitment of those firms to the development of individuals to meet the corporate goal of quality improvement.

MOTIVATION

The issues discussed in the last section—career development, performance appraisal, training, rewards and recognition, and compensation—all contribute to individual motivation to achieve quality and operational performance objectives.

As managers in a TQM environment take on new roles as coaches and facilitators, their skills in motivating employees become even more crucial. Saul Gellerman, one of the pioneers in applying motivation theories to work, has written a practical and readable text on the subject.[40] Gellerman warns against four bogus concepts of motivation: (1) pumping up enthusiasm (recall Deming's warnings about slogans and exhortations); (2) making people happy (or at least less likely to complain); (3) a few easily memorized formulas that allegedly make people either more reasonable or less ornery; or (4) plain old bribery. Of course, one of the biggest motivators today is the need to stay in business. The intense competition from both domestic and foreign firms sends the simple message quoted from *Business Week* in the introduction to Part I: *Get better or get beat.*

Unfortunately, it's not that simple. If managers and workers are to be successful in organizational design, teamwork, and improvement activities, then simplistic knowledge and understanding of motivation is insufficient. To aid them in job design and organizational processes, managers and workers can apply appropriate motivational tools that are available.

Motivation and human behavior are major elements of Deming's Profound Knowledge discussed in Chapter 3. Quality depends on employee commitment at every level of the organization. If employees are not provided with the proper motivating climate to align their efforts to meet organizational goals, the result can be conflict, poor performance, and low quality levels. Managers must understand that there is no such thing as an unmotivated employee. The system within which employees work can seriously affect intrinsic motivation. Although thousands of studies have been performed over the years on human and animal subjects in attempts to define and refine the concept of motivation, it remains an extremely complex phenomenon that still is not fully understood. This section briefly reviews the major theories, models, and approaches, and their implications to TQM.

■ An Overview of Motivation Theories

Gellerman defined motivation as "the art of creating conditions that allow every one of us, warts and all, to get his work done at his own peak level of efficiency." A more formal definition of motivation is an individual's response to a felt need. Thus, some stimulus, or activating event, must spur the need to respond to that stimulus, generating the response itself. For example, an individual worker given the goal or quality task of achieving zero defects on the parts that he or she produces may feel a need to keep his or her job. Consequently, the worker is motivated by the stimulus of fear and responds by carefully producing parts to achieve the goal. Another less insecure worker may feel the need for approval of his or her work by peers or superiors and be motivated by the stimulus of pride. The worker then responds to that need and that stimulus by producing high-quality parts.

Researchers have proposed many theories and models as to how and why people are motivated. A theory is a way to describe, predict, and control what is observed in the world. Models graphically or symbolically show what a theory is saying in words. Often a model is so closely associated with a theory that the terms are used interchangeably. Theories and models are often classified according to common themes. Bowditch and Buono categorize motivation theories as content, process, and environmentally based theories.[41] These theories are often studied in traditional management courses and are summarized in Table 10.4.

TABLE 10.4 A Classification of Motivation Theories		
Motivation Theory	**Pioneer/Developer**	**Type of Theory**
Content Theories		
Hierarchy of Needs	Abraham Maslow	Need
Motivation and Maintenance	Frederick Herzberg	Need/satisfaction
Theory X-Y	Douglas MacGregor	Managerial expectations
n-Ach, n-Aff, n-Pow	David McClelland	Acquired need
Process Theories		
Preference–Expectancy	Victor Vroom	Expectancy
Contingency	Porter & Lawler	Expectancy/reward
Goal Setting	Edward Locke	Goal
Path–Goal Theory of Leadership	Robert J. House	Goal
Environmentally Based Theories		
Operant Conditioning	B.F. Skinner	Reinforcement
Equity	J. Stacy Adams	Equity
Social Learning/Self-Efficacy	A. Bandura	Social learning/self-efficacy
	Snyder & Williams	

In the behavioral sciences, as well as in the pure sciences, the originator of a theory is becoming more and more difficult to determine because many researchers' ideas often overlap. Thus, the information in Table 10.4 is merely suggestive of one or more names that have been associated with the development of the theory.

CONTENT THEORIES

Many of the theories of motivation developed by behavioral scientists over the past 75 years use simple *content* models that describe how and why people are motivated to work. Four of the best-known content models are those developed by Abraham Maslow, Douglas McGregor, Frederick Herzberg, and David McClelland.[42]

Maslow's *hierarchy of needs theory* and McGregor's *Theory X-Theory Y* model are well known. These theories greatly influenced Deming. Maslow's theory suggests that individual motivation is driven by unmet needs within the hierarchy of physiological, safety and security, social, esteem and status, and self-actualization needs. Under Theory X, workers dislike work and require close supervision and control. Under Theory Y, workers are self-motivated, seek responsibility, and exhibit a high degree of imagination and creativity at work. Deming consistently argued that incentive pay, compensation-based merit systems, and other forms of managerial control are destructive. Money is a motivator only when individuals are at the bottom of Maslow's hierarchy. In today's society, employees seek esteem and self-actualization and flourish in a Theory Y environment. This reasoning prompted the changes in General Motors' compensation system as discussed in the last section. Empowerment can succeed only if managers subscribe to Theory Y and emphasize the higher levels of Maslow's hierarchy.

Herzberg's *two-factor theory* suggests that two types of factors—maintenance factors and motivational factors—affect job performance. Maintenance factors are conditions that employees have come to expect, such as a safe working environment, job security, supervision, and pay. Workers in a situation with these conditions will not be dissatisfied, but maintenance factors generally do not provide any motivation to work harder. Motivational factors, such as recognition, advancement, achievement, and the nature of the work itself are less tangible, but do motivate people. From Herzberg's theory arose the concept of *job enrichment*, which is defined as increasing the areas of responsibility of workers so as to provide greater opportunities to use a range of skills and to see the "big picture"; employees gain a sense of fulfillment (satisfaction) from completion of every cycle of a task. Acquiring cross-functional skills, working in teams, and increased empowerment are forms of job enrichment.

Garvin presents an interesting example of how Japanese managers in the air conditioning industry view job enrichment as important to quality.[43] In Japan, newly hired workers are trained so that they can do every job on the line before eventually being assigned to only one job. Training frequently requires six to twelve months, in contrast to the standard training time of one to two days for newly hired production workers in U.S. air conditioning companies. The advantage to this "enriched" training is that workers are better able to track a defect to its source and can frequently suggest remedies to problems since they understand the entire process from start to finish.

Herzberg's theory has been criticized because it was developed solely from studies of accountants and engineers. Some later studies of lower-level workers cast doubt on the ability to generalize Herzberg's original findings.[44] However, the theory has been widely used and has stood the test of time.

David McClelland, a Harvard professor, has researched how the needs for achievement, power, and affiliation affect motivation to work. His *acquired needs theory*, sometimes called n-Ach, states that people with a high need for achievement are (1) satisfied when they attain their goals through good performance, (2) tend to set higher goals than those who do not have as high a need for achievement, and (3) generally will improve their performance when given feedback.[45]

Applying McClelland's theory to TQM practices has some advantages as well as drawbacks.[46] On the one hand, efforts to empower employees appeal to individuals who have a high need for power, since they are likely to feel that management is correcting a long-standing problem of not giving most employees sufficient power to influence conditions on the job. However, employees who have a high need for achievement may feel frustrated because they are being encouraged to work in groups, which makes their individual efforts less easily recognizable. In turn, unless new and more fulfilling roles are found for middle managers, they may feel that empowerment of their subordinates takes away their historical power and recognition for individual achievements, which helped to motivate them in traditional organizational settings.

PROCESS THEORIES

The second major thrust in motivation theories was the development of *process models*. Process theories and their models explain the dynamic process of how people make choices in an effort to obtain desired rewards. The most influential theories were developed by Victor Vroom, Lyman Porter and Edward Lawler, Edward Locke, and Robert House.

Victor H. Vroom proposed his *preference–expectancy theory* in 1964.[47] Vroom's work formed the basis for one of the better known process theories, the Porter and Lawler model, which is one of the most widely accepted process models of motivation available today. Porter and Lawler extended Vroom's work by examining more closely the traits and perceptions of the individual and the nature and impact of rewards on motivation. The Porter and Lawler model is a *contingency model* that explains the conditions and processes by which motivation to work takes place.[48] A contingency model defines the variables of a process, the interactions between those variables, and the dynamic conditions under which those variables work.

The Porter and Lawler model is shown in Figure 10.3. The flow of this model indicates that effort (Box 3) is dependent on value of reward (Box 1) and perceived effort-reward probability (Box 2). Effort leads to performance (Box 6), which is affected by the abilities and traits (Box 4) and the role perceptions (Box 5) of the individual. Performance (Box 6), in turn, influences actual rewards—intrinsic (Box 7A) or extrinsic (Box 7B)—perceived equitable rewards (Box 8), and a long-term influence (feedback) on perceived effort-reward probability. The rewards (Boxes 7A and 7B) and their perceived equity (Box 8) then influence satisfaction (Box 9), which has a long-term influence (feedback) on the value of reward (Box 1).

Components of the model are expectancy (which includes performance outcome expectancy and effort-performance expectancy), instrumentality (the combination of abilities, traits, and role perceptions), and valence (preference for anticipated outcomes). Valence is represented by the value of reward. Expectancy is included in the perceived effort-reward probability and is also related to perceived equitable rewards. Instrumentality is the linking of effort to performance (accomplishment), moderated by abilities and traits and role perceptions. Successful performance then results in intrinsic rewards (a feeling of accomplishment) and extrinsic rewards (raises or bonuses). Given that rewards are equitable, employees experience satisfaction, which in turn contributes to renewal of the motivation cycle. The model states that, depending on the actions of management, the expectations of employees, and the actual outcomes, a certain quantity and quality of employee motivation is present in an organization.

FIGURE 10.3 Porter and Lawler Expectancy Model

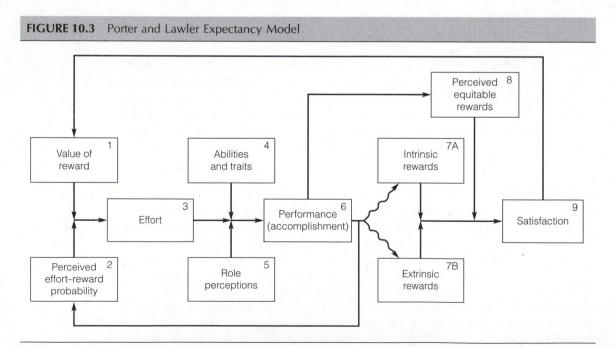

SOURCE: L. W. Porter and Edward E. Lawler, *Managerial Attidues and Performance,* (Burr Ridge, IL: Irwin, 1968); used with permission.

Porter and Lawler's model, while more complex than content models, accounts for the process dynamics that content models lack.

Two other closely related models are Locke's *goal-setting model* and House's *path-goal leadership model*.[49] Like the Porter and Lawler model, they are based on expectancy theory. Locke believed that individuals who have clear goals will work more quickly, perform better, and be more motivated that those who lack such goals. House built on this concept to show that employees who can see a clear path to reaching a goal, agree with the goal that is set, and are assisted by their leader's style in their effort to attain the goal, will be motivated to produce.

Both opportunities and questions surround the issue of how goal theories may be applied to TQM practices.[50] Obviously, continuous improvement activities suggest that managers and workers set challenging goals and try to reach them. At the same time, if quality is a "race without a finish line," then no clear path of goal attainment can be determined. Without that clear path, managers cannot assist their workers in setting and reaching ever higher goals toward improvement.

The debate between process and content theories of motivation centers on which theory is a more accurate representation of human motivation. Obviously, they represent two views of the same reality. The content approach provides a simple, static representation of components of motivation. The process approach focuses on the dynamic interaction between the components of effort, ability, rewards, and performance as perceived by individuals in the work environment. Understanding both content and process views can aid managers as they attempt to design work to enhance motivation for quality.

ENVIRONMENTALLY BASED THEORIES

Environmentally based theories are designed to alter the environment in which employees find themselves. The goal is to provide a more supportive climate within which individuals will be motivated to work. Pioneering work in this area was performed by B. F. Skinner, who developed his *theory of operant conditioning* (sometimes called *reinforcement theory*) in 1953.[51] Adams's *equity theory* and the theories of social learning and self-efficacy are also notable in this area.

Skinner's theory suggests that organisms (animals and humans) respond positively to positive stimuli presented in their environment and avoid negative stimuli. Thus, positive reinforcement of good work and concentrated effort leads to improved performance.

Skinner's work was put to practical use in the early 1970s.[52] One of the most far-reaching and dramatic examples of the use of positive reinforcement in a work environment took place at Emery Air Freight. Emery applied behavior modification techniques to areas with low performance levels, such as sales, customer service, and containerized shipping. The company used detailed measurement of performance factors coupled with daily feedback to their workers on their progress to increase performance and quality levels. Supervisors were taught to give positive reinforcement through praise and recognition of their employees' progress. They began applying this concept at least twice a week in the early stages of the program. Later, this reinforcement was put on a variable interval schedule as workers became more consistent in meeting high performance targets. Over a three-year period, Emery estimated savings of $3 million from a low-cost change.

Equity theory is concerned with individuals' beliefs about how fairly they are treated compared to their peers. Adams discovered that people tend to compare their own rewards or other outcomes to the efforts they have exerted.[53] They then compare their own reward to input ratio to others' ratios. This comparison allows individuals to determine if they have received more than, about the same, or less than others. To use a TQM analogy, this process may be considered a type of individual "benchmarking" of outcomes from work. If inequities exist people tend to take one of six actions:

1. Increase their inputs to justify higher rewards when they feel that they are overrewarded in comparison to others.

2. Decrease their inputs to compensate for lower rewards if they feel underrewarded.

3. Change the compensation that they receive through legal or other actions, such as leaving work early, stealing the company's supplies, and so on.

4. Modify their comparisons by choosing another person to compare themselves against.

5. Distort reality by rationalizing that the inequities are justified.

6. Leave the situation (quit the job) if the inequities cannot be resolved.[54]

The application of some motivation theories to quality necessitates caution. As Deming and Juran emphasized, workers are *intrinsically* motivated; management stands in the way. Management can motivate employees through good employee relations policies and practices, which include empowering employees to control their own work and make important decisions that affect quality, eliminating fear and blame for uncontrollable variation, recruiting employees who demonstrate the ability and willingness to meet quality standards, providing adequate training and education that explain the why as well as the how of doing quality work, changing the role of supervisors to coaches and teachers, and keeping workers informed of management decisions and actions that affect quality, as well as opportunities for participation in solving quality problems. Two trends that show promise for aligning numerous motivation theories with TQM practices are (1) the development of broad, integrative approaches to motivation and (2) an increasing emphasis on intrinsic (internal) motivation.

A relatively new set of promising approaches to motivation that brings both of these trends into focus is *social learning/self-efficacy theory*, developed by A. Bandura.[55] Similar concepts have been proposed by Snyder and Williams.[56] Bowditch and Buono suggest that these theories integrate operant conditioning theories based on assumptions that individuals are motivated primarily by *external* cues and consequences, with the individualistic theories of Maslow, McClelland, Vroom, and others who hold that motivation is determined by *internal* needs, satisfactions, and/or expectations.[57] It also considers processes of learning by observation and imitation (vicarious learning), anticipation of outcomes and consequences before they are experienced (mental symbolism), and controlling behavior and actions by managing the immediate environment, the individual's own cognitive processes (self-control), and the self-confidence (efficacy) that people have in their own abilities to perform well on the job.

■ Applying Motivation Theories to TQM

All the motivation theories reviewed here can be applied to support TQM in an organization. For example, Herzberg's simple theory suggests that ignoring maintenance factors such as supervison, working conditions, salary, peer relations, status, and security will produce dissatisfaction. Under such conditions, empowerment can be fruitless and even dangerous to the organization. Motivating factors such as achievement, recognition, and responsibility lead to personal satisfaction and sustained motivation for continuous improvement. Thus, to talk TQM without addressing these issues can easily result in failure. Understanding this point is certainly a prerequisite to implementation.

As an example of how the Porter and Lawler model might apply in TQM, suppose that a bank decides to install a statistical process control system in its check-clearing department. It performs the activities of planning the new system, organizing the work force, and training employees to use the new system. The bank even trains clerical workers in the details of recording information clearly and accurately. However, the bank emphasizes the detection of errors, the penalties for being caught making an error, and the advantages to the bank in reducing the costs brought on by the need to correct errors. No positive reinforcement is built into the system for making improvements in the process, reducing errors, or recording and using information. A few weeks after the system is installed, turnover and absentee rates have increased, new types of errors are being made, old error rates are increasing, and morale in the department is generally low.

For this situation, the Herzberg model would indicate that the motivating factors of status and the work (content) itself are missing. The Porter and Lawler model could be used to trace out the flaws in the motivating process. The model shows that the bank's system has a deficiency in perceived effort-reward probability and, perhaps, value of reward as well. Thus, if employees do not perceive a high effort-reward probability or do not see a high value in the rewards that are given, they will not apply their best efforts to the task. Their abilities and traits will not be exercised to the fullest, and their perceptions of their role in the firm will be either negative or confused. These factors combine to result in low performance which, in turn, will have a negative impact on extrinsic (tangible) rewards and intrinsic (intangible) rewards and on the perception of equitable (fair) rewards and overall satisfaction with accomplishment of the task. The negative cycle and consequences are renewed each time the task is performed. To turn the situation around, companies must introduce an upward rather than a downward spiral of motivation by providing a positive combination of expectancy, effort, and accomplishment.

In this example, the value of the reward ((Box 1) in the Porter and Lawler model in Figure 10.3), and the perceived effort-reward probability (Box 2) work in conjunction with intrinsic rewards, extrinsic rewards, and perceived equitable rewards (Boxes 7A, 7B, and 8) to produce motivated effort (Box 3), performance (Box 6), and satisfaction (Box 9). Thus, the attention to the details of job design can have a significant impact on the quality level in a work setting.

Bowditch and Buono suggested that an integrated theory of motivation could be developed by considering the types of behavior in a group of people that are of interest to management.[58] Since not all motivation theories are equally good in predicting a wide range of behavior, managers may need to consider situational factors and to apply the correct motivational tools to the specific situation in order to improve results. Table 10.5 shows a set of common management situations, with examples relating to TQM, and gives suggestions for the type of motivation theory that could be applied to understand individual motivation and to shape it to meet individual and organizational goals.

TABLE 10.5 Applying Motivation Theories to TQM

Situation	TQM Example	Applicable Motivation Theories
Choice of employees	Decisions to join employee involvement groups	Expectancy
Prediction of choices	Management desires employee "buy-in" for reengineering	Equity, goal-setting
Effort exerted on a task	Group members' responses in performing a process improvement project	Reinforcement, equity
Work satisfaction	Responses to a survey on how well employees are responding to empowerment initiatives encouraged by management	Need, equity
On-the-job performance	Reduction of customer complaints in a hospital billing department, due to reduction of errors	Reinforcement, equity, goal-setting
Withdrawal from the job	Absenteeism, turnover	Reinforcement, equity, or expencancy (often related to rewards/goals)

■ Work Design for Motivation[59]

The design of work is vital to job satisfaction, work effectivness, and personal motivation. Work must be designed to fit the technical needs of the organization and the human needs of the employees who must perform the task. When approached in a careful, systematic fashion, work design can improve quality and productivity as well as raise levels of employee motivation and morale.

An integrating theory that ties together many different perspectives was proposed by Hackman and Oldham. Their model, shown in Figure 10.4, explains the motivational properties of work design by combining technical and human components of a job. This model, an extremely effective operationalization of earlier motivation theories and research studies, draws heavily on the work of Herzberg and others and has been validated in numerous organizational settings.

The Hackman and Oldham model contains four major segments:

1. Critical psychological states
2. Core job characteristics
3. Moderating variables
4. Outcomes

Three critical psychological states drive the model. *Experienced meaningfulness* is the psychological need of workers to have the feeling that their work is a significant contribution to the organization and society. *Experienced responsibility* indicates the need of workers to be accountable for the quality and quantity of work produced. *Knowledge of results* implies that all workers feel the need to know how their work is evaluated and what the results of the evaluation are.

Five core job characteristics have been identified as having an impact on the critical psychological states:

1. *Task significance:* the degree to which the job gives the participant the feeling that it has a substantial impact on the organization or the world.

FIGURE 10.4   Hackman and Oldham Work Design Model

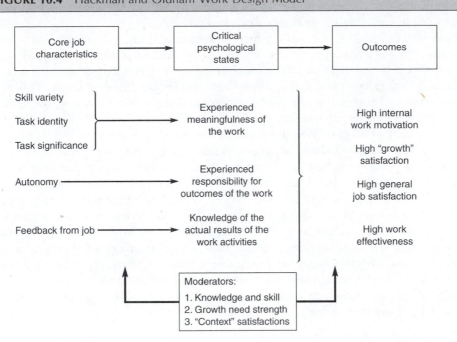

SOURCE: J. Richard Hackman and Greg R. Oldham, *Work Redesign,* p. 90. © 1980 by Addison-Wesley Publishing Co., Inc., Reading, MA. Reprinted by permission of the publisher.

2. *Task identity:* the degree to which the worker can perceive the task as a whole, identifiable piece of work from start to finish.

3. *Skill variety:* the degree to which the job requires the worker to use a variety of skills and talents.

4. *Autonomy:* the degree to which the task permits freedom, independence, and personal control to be exercised over the work.

5. *Feedback from the job:* the degree to which clear, timely information about the effectiveness of performance of the individual is available.

Quality is related in a primary or secondary sense to all five of the core job characteristics in the Hackman and Oldham model. Quality of a product or service is undoubtedly increased by a worker's dedicated application of skills, which is enhanced by task identity and a feeling of task significance. More directly, quality of work is enhanced by a job design that incorporates autonomy and feedback relating to quality characteristics. The key outcomes of high general job satisfaction and high work effectiveness can then be seen as results that define and reinforce excellent quality.

As an example illustrating characteristics of the Hackman and Oldham model, consider the case of workers in a small Delaware firm that produces space suits for astronauts. The work requires a great deal of handcrafting, using conventional sewing machinery as well as high technology in testing the suits for proper functioning. Task significance and task identity are evident in the workers' ability to see the job's extreme importance and its fit in the complete unit (a space suit for an individual astronaut). Skill variety and autonomy are somewhat limited since conventional sewing techniques must be used and rigid specifications must be precisely followed. However, other motivating aspects of the job may compensate for the lack of these characteristics. Feedback on results is timely and individualized. Comprehensive testing and inspection of the space suits is performed to assure that no defective units are produced.

Several approaches—job enlargement, job rotation, and job enrichment—can enhance the job characteristics in the Hackman and Oldham model. IBM was apparently the first user of **job enlargement,** in which workers' jobs were expanded to include several tasks rather than one single, low-level task. This approach reduced fragmentation of jobs and generally resulted in lower production costs, greater worker satisfaction, and higher quality, but it required higher wage rates and the purchase of more inspection equipment. **Job rotation** is a technique by which individual workers learn several tasks by rotating from one to another. The purpose of job rotation is to renew interest or motivation of the individual and to increase his or her complement of skills. However, several studies show that the main benefit was to increase workers' skills but that little, if any, motivational benefit could be expected.[60] Finally, **job enrichment** was developed by Frederick Herzberg as a strategy for implementing his two-factor theory of motivation. Job enrichment entails ''vertical job loading'' in which workers are given more authority, responsibility, and autonomy rather than simply more or different work to do. Job enrichment has been used successfully in a number of firms, notably AT&T—which experienced better employee attitudes and performance—as well as Texas Instruments, IBM, and General Foods.

LABOR RELATIONS IN A TQM ENVIRONMENT

In the rapidly changing environment of HRM, both managers and union leaders experience varying degrees of difficulty with sharing power with workers at every level. However, a TQM environment requires that unions and management cooperate in new and innovative ways if they are to survive.

Union leaders and their counterpart labor relations managers have their own culture. In the past, they have emphasized the following aspects of labor relations:

1. Collective bargaining
2. Work rules
3. Grievance procedures
4. Management and worker domains

Many of these procedures and work rules are legally binding on the company and have arisen through years of negotiation and policy-making. To simplify and/or eliminate them, labor and management must first agree that a new paradigm is desirable.

Leventhal suggested a joint problem-solving approach as a substitute for the traditional adversarial approach between labor and management in the new total quality-oriented work systems that are being put into place by many firms.[61] The following labor-management issues have become at least as important, if not more so, than the traditional issues:

- Work operations and design
- Pay systems (beyond rates and scales)
- Training
- System governance

Work operations and design affect the day-to-day tasks of union members. With a team approach to problem solving, many of the problems and frustrations of job design by third parties, such as industrial engineers with a limited understanding of the requirements of a specific job, can be reduced. Pay system design also requires input from the people who are affected by the system. This input can often prevent future headaches and grievances. Participation in training program development can help union members meet personal goals as well as corporate goals and objectives. For example, Lawrence Cable Company has a trainer as a member of every team in the company.[62] The company adopted a "pay for skills" approach, so the trainer is paid more after mastering certain training and analysis skills. Then the team trainer monitors the skills of the team members and helps design, refine, and deliver training courses in the needed skill areas. System governance works in many organizations after managers develop sufficient trust in their employees to turn over to them some of the traditional management functions. Nucor Corporation, the non-union steelmaker discussed earlier in this chapter, permits teams to select their own members and encourages workers to evaluate peers for bonuses and promotion opportunities. Other companies have peer review processes or committees that perform some of the disciplinary functions previously reserved for management.

To deal with these issues, both labor and management must become more flexible in their stance toward each other. This flexibility will require union members and leaders to (1) take new approaches toward dispute resolution, (2) develop flexible work rules and means for accommodation to such rules by union stewards, (3) initiate peer performance feedback methods designed to improve work operations, and (4) establish new contract language and ongoing labor-management negotiation. Management will also be required to adjust through the following actions:

■ Work with union representatives on how—or whether—new work systems will be adopted.

■ Examine values within a joint framework and adopt new ones to guide the transformed organization.

■ Include labor representation at every level at which process and job transformations are taking place.

■ Fill key training and employee involvement (EI) facilitator positions with both union and management representatives (Ford Motor Company has a parallel EI structure of union-management facilitators from the plant level up to corporate headquarters.)

■ Recognize union strengths, such as the ability to take the pulse of its membership on various issues.

An example of the new level of cooperation between unions and management is the historic agreement reached between LTV and the United Steelworkers (USW) union in 1985.[63] The terms of the contract at that time provided for

■ Workers paid on salaries, with built-in wage increases, but no provision for "cost of living allowance" (COLA) wage increases. Wage increases were based on learning new skills.

■ Twice-yearly performance bonuses of up to 25 percent of salary, starting in 1987.

■ Work divided into four skill levels, instead of rigid job classes; workers assigned to rotating teams of 10 to 12 workers on each shift.

■ Overtime paid after 40 hours per week, instead of after 8 hours per day, thus improving flexibility in scheduling.

■ Workers to have a voice in hiring, firing, grievance handling, work and vacation scheduling, and promotion.

■ Layoff pay plus unemployment compensation amounts to 100 percent of regular income. When unemployment compensation ceases, the company pays 60 percent of salary for a limited time.

■ Other benefits include nine holidays (versus ten previously), no vacations during first year of employment, pension program after two years, insurance "package" consisting of low-cost life insurance, medical and dental care.

This LTV–USW pact shows that change, when brought on by a competitive crisis, is possible, even in union-management systems once considered hopelessly adversarial.

Recent NLRB Rulings Affecting HRM Practices

The National Labor Relations Board (NLRB) ruled on two cases in 1993 and 1994 that complicate a company's determination of how far it can go legally to set up and use employee participation programs (EPPs) to make improvements in the workplace. These case decisions by a five-person board were based on interpretations of the 58-year-old National Labor Relations Act (NLRA, or Wagner Act) that prohibits unfair labor practices. The two cases involved a small, nonunion company, Electromation, and a large company, DuPont. The rulings are found in the NLRB proceedings as *Electromation vs. International Brotherhood of Teamsters* (309 N.L.R.B. - No. 163), and *E. I. duPont de Nemours and Company vs. Chemical Workers Association, Inc.* (311 N.L.R.B. - No. 88). In the Electromation case, the nonunion company's management set up five employee action committees to deal with policies concerning absenteeism, smoking, communications, pay for premium positions, and attendance bonuses. In duPont's case, management unilaterally (without bargaining with the union) changed the composition of safety and fitness committees to include nonmanagerial employees (where the committees had previously been composed only of management) at a unionized New Jersey plant. Without going into detail, the cases specified that "employer-dominated labor organizations" are prohibited. In both cases, the employee teams/committees were ruled to be "labor organizations" and to be "management dominated." Fink et al., in a recent series of articles, discussed the implications of the rulings for employee participation and labor-management cooperation.[64] They made four major points:

■ Most small to large U.S. companies fall under NLRB jurisdiction, and many employee participation programs would be declared labor organizations that were dominated by employers, if tested by the NLRB-established guidelines.

■ Companies with labor unions could probably establish "legal" EPPs by bargaining with the union and signing an agreement on how they would be structured and operated.

■ As long as unions see the EPP to be in accordance with their self-interest, management could likely get them to agree to the program.

■ Without the rulings of the NLRB being overturned in the courts, or legislation being passed to amend the NLRA, many nonunion companies could not withstand a challenge to their EPPs.

In summary, changes in union-management relations are critical where new work structures are considered vital to corporate survival or competitiveness. Good relations aid quality improvement and productivity at every level. On the other hand, poor relations produce changes that are cosmetic in nature, and guarantee that quality efforts will suffer.

QUALITY IN PRACTICE

HUMAN RESOURCE MANAGEMENT AT DISNEYLAND[65]

Walt Disney's original vision of Disneyland was "a place where adults and children can experience together some of the wonders of life, of adventure and feel better because of it." Achieving the vision required a constant effort and near-fanatical attention to detail. Every foreman or woman must present a maintenance report every afternoon. Every defect—from ride problems to pigeon droppings—gets coded to different craft areas. Then every night after the park closes, everything gets fixed. Every morning the painters scrape the lead off the back of the shooting gallery and repaint it. Every morning every window in the park is washed. Every morning three groups of two women each reapply makeup to every audio-animatronics figure in the park. The CEO observed:

> It is interesting to note that our guests' comments have been consistent. . . . First, they comment about the cleanliness of our operation; second, they comment about the friendliness and courtesy of our employees; and third, they remark that we offer a good show. Cleanliness and friendliness are qualities of operation which can only be achieved by people. A strong employee program cannot be built on lip service. It takes time and money and effort to develop and maintain an understanding of our "Disney Ways." And then we work hard to protect our investment in human resources. On our Disney team, we stress pride and dignity in their job, in their company and its traditions . . . and in themselves.
>
> Let me assure you that this is not just a responsibility to be handed off to personnel administrators and forgotten by presidents. It must start at the top. It must permeate everyone throughout the organization. It must be practiced by everyone. Motivation—pride—dedication—responsibility—reward, these are the cornerstones of the organization Walt Disney built.

Disney's Four Cs for success are curiosity, confidence, courage, and constancy. Disneyland interviews most prospective "cast members" (rather than "employees") in groups of three, a technique it adapted from the airline industry. For 45 to 60 minutes, the Disney interviewers ask the three a variety of questions. Although their answers are important, so are their attitudes. The interviewer watches how the interviewees interact. Those who pay attention to what the others say, respect others' responses, engage in thoughtful conversation, and smile are the kind of people that Disneyland seeks.

All new hires are given an eight-hour orientation describing the Disney experience, which includes a combination of presentations by highly trained in-costume cast members, slides and video presentations, and a tour of the park, both on stage and backstage. Disneyland wants cast members to know that they are a business, what the product is, and how their role contributes to the product. Also included is training in safety, courtesy, show, and standards of what they are expected to exemplify as Disney employees. New onstage cast members receive as many as 16 hours of classroom instruction, some of it after hours when the park is closed. Following this comes paired training, where experienced cast members work side by side with new ones for 16 to 48 hours.

At Disney, 85 percent of managers have been promoted from within. A management training program combines on-the-job with classroom training in areas such as Disney management perspective, labor laws, and management skills. As part of the program, the class is divided into smaller groups to develop a Disneyland improvement proposal that must be presented in both verbal and written form to Disneyland executives.

To audit the effectiveness of training programs, focus groups meet regularly. Groups might be made up of cast members leaving Disney to work for different companies or those with 30 days of on-the-job experience. They are surveyed on issues such as training, wages, and their relationship with management. Action plans are developed from survey results.

Current cast members are continually treated as special people. When a new orientation film was developed, it was shown to the cast first. When the introductory handbook was updated, it was mailed along with a personalized letter to their homes. When the Main Street electrical parade was refurbished, management felt it was important to preview the event before guests could see it, but there was no money budgeted for the preview. Instead, management decided to put on costumes and work the parade previews to avoid the cost.

The park sponsors the participation of hundreds of cast members in Disney-only sports leagues. Social events and after-hours treasure hunts based on Disney trivia build camaraderie and also raise money for charity.

Although the employees at the various Disney parks belong to nearly 30 unions, only one major strike has occurred in its 30+ year history. Many of the temporary Disney employees have worked regularly at the park during weekends, vacations, and holidays for periods of 20 years or longer.

Key Issues for Discussion

1. Discuss Disney's approach to building quality into their organization through human resource management. What lessons can be applied to other organizations?

2. Since Disney is a service firm, what special challenges does it face as it attempts to emphasize quality to its employees?

QUALITY IN PRACTICE   **TAKING CARE OF PEOPLE AT FEDEX[66]**

Take care of our people; they, in turn will deliver the impeccable service demanded by our customers who will reward us with the profitability necessary to secure our future
—*Federal Express Manager's Guide*

People are the first component of the FedEx corporate philosophy: People–Service–Profit. FedEx is dedicated to the principle that its employees are its "most important resource." Because the company believes in team effort and insists on an open atmosphere, it developed and refined a fair and equitable process for handling grievances, the Guaranteed Fair Treatment Procedure (GFTP). This process affirms an employee's right to appeal any eligible issue through a systematic review of progressively higher levels of management (see Figure 10.5), and provides an atmosphere for employees to discuss their complaints with management without fear of retaliation. Employees can have their concerns addressed through the management chain, all the way to the CEO, Frederick W. Smith, if necessary. In fact, Mr. Smith sits down every week with the executive vice president, chief personnel officer, and two other senior VPs to review GFTP cases that have progressed to the final stage. Employees are not assured of a judgment in their favor; however, the right to participate within the guidelines of the process is guaranteed.

One of the company's most effective quality tools is the SFA or Survey/Feedback/Action program which measures continuous leadership improvement. The SFA has been a part of the company's human resources commitment since 1980 and collects employee feedback about management's effectiveness and overall satisfaction about the company. Once a year, every member within every work group anonymously participates in the survey. The first 10 questions assess the immediate manager's leadership abilities as perceived by their customers—the people in their work group. Some examples include:

- My manager asks for my ideas about work.
- I can tell my manager what I think.
- My manager tells me when I do a good job.

While individual responses are kept confidential, overall survey results are passed on to the managers, who must then schedule a feedback session with their employees. Managers are encouraged to use quality improvement techniques to develop solutions to the problems identified in the survey. An action plan is developed and serves as an ongoing quality improvement plan for the issues identified during the feedback session. The results of the survey are then tallied as an overall corporate leadership score. The scores are subsequently used to

---

FIGURE 10.5   Federal Express Guaranteed Fair Treatment Procedure

---

Step 1: Management Review

- Employee has seven days in which to submit a GFT complaint. Management has 10 days to respond. An employee who doesn't agree with the decision has seven days to appeal.

  Over half of the GFTs filed are resolved in this first step.

Step 2: Officer Review

- May uphold the decision, overturn it, modify management's decision or initiate a Board of Review. Management has 10 days to render a decision. An employee who doesn't agree with the decision has seven days to appeal.

Step 3: Executive Review

- Five-member Appeals Board
  Frederick W. Smith, CEO;
  Thomas R. Oliver, Executive Vice President;
  James A. Perkins, CPO; and
  Two officers assigned on a rotating basis.

- May uphold, overturn, or initiate a Board of Review. Decision must be rendered within 14 days. Employee receives written response within three calendar days of the decision.

---

diagnose corporatewide leadership problems and, in addition, serve as a benchmark for setting the following year's corporate People goal.

The Open Door Policy at FedEx encourages employees to communicate their ideas and concerns directly to management, even when the subject is controversial. However, unlike with the GFTP, employees are not limited by time restrictions on filing or the number of Open Door issues that may be filed. If a manager receives an Open Door question, a response to the employee's inquiry must be handled as a top priority in accordance with the company's "People First" philosophy. The manager responding must also explain the reasoning behind the response.

FedEx's widely dispersed work force requires timely information. One of the most effective methods is the company's satellite-linked television network called FXTV. The special broadcasts, initiated to improve communication between senior management and the employee population, provide front-line feedback vital to the quality process. Employees are encouraged to call in during question-and-answer periods, which usually accompany all programs.

FedEx uses a variety of formal reward and recognition programs to encourage excellence in both individual and team performance.

■ *Bravo Zulu Award:* The name is U.S. Navy jargon for "well done." Any manager can bestow this award on any one for clearly going above and beyond specific job responsibilities.

■ *Golden Falcon Award:* With the highest honor given to nonmanagement employees, employees are recognized for demonstrating "exceptional performance achievements or unselfish acts that enhance customer service."

■ *Service Circle of Excellence Award:* On a monthly basis, the highest performing stations at FedEx are reviewed for selection as winners of this award.

■ *Star/Superstar:* Individual employees with consistently high job performance can be recognized through the Star/Superstar Program, which provides a percentage of salary as a lump sum cash award.

Training is a fundamental element of FedEx's quality process. More than $225 million is spent annually on skills and recurrent training. All customer-contact people receive extensive training before they assume their jobs. For example, call center agents participate in six weeks of training that include interactive videos, role-playing sessions, and lectures regarding features of service. Sales professionals receive extensive training emphasizing customer satisfaction.

The Leadership Institute provides leadership training and development for managers. The three basic curricular areas are core management principles, outdoor-based learning, and a leadership series. Participants study policies and procedures, leadership qualities, and management principles using experiential activities and group discussion. Participants share knowledge and gain insight into such topics as teamwork, risk-taking, diversity in the workplace, and situational leadership. After completing the courses, managers are encouraged to develop and communicate a departmental vision statement that empowers employees to achieve organizational goals and objectives.

The Quality Academy, established under the auspices of human resource development, assists in the continuing use of quality principles by educating participants about the processes and practical tools available to management and quality professionals. Courses are offered in the areas of quality action teams, benchmarking, cycle time reduction, facilitation skills, and statistical process control, as well as interactive video study. Generally, all employees can participate in these courses.

Key Issues for Discussion

1. Explain how human resource activities at FedEx work toward achieving the service and profit components of the company's philosophy.

2. How do HRM processes at FedEx support the fundamental principles of TQM: customer focus, participation and teamwork, and continuous improvement?

SUMMARY OF KEY POINTS

■ Human resource management (HRM) encompasses activities designed to provide for and coordinate the people of an organization. HRM is a modern term for what has been traditionally referred to as personnel administration or personnel management.

■ Human resource functions include determining the organization's human resource needs; recruiting, selecting, developing, counseling, and rewarding employees; acting as a liaison between unions and government organizations; and handling other matters of employee well-being. In a TQM environment, HR managers strategically support the organization's TQM approaches and deployment. This new paradigm requires a new emphasis and broader knowledge than before.

■ Goals of TQM-based HRM practices are to communicate the importance of each employee's contribution to total quality, to stress quality-related synergies available through teamwork, to empower employees to "make a difference," and to reinforce commitment through rewards and recognition.

■ Leading practices include integrating HR plans with overall business plans, empowering individuals and teams, continually improving key personnel management processes, maintaining the well-being and growth of all employees, measuring customer satisfaction, and promoting individual and group participation.

■ The TQM/HRM approach is a progressive approach designed to coordinate the human resources of an organization with the philosophy, values, and techniques of total quality management. This goal can be accomplished by adopting a strategic approach to HRM.

■ Empowerment—giving employees authority and autonomy to make decisions—can work to improve customer satisfaction. However, it requires new thinking to revise antiquated policies, as well as training and new management responsibilities.

■ HRM practices that support total quality concepts include employee selection and retention, performance appraisal, training and education, recognition and reward, and compensation.

■ Traditional performance appraisal processes often are at odds with a TQM philosophy. Performance appraisal should be based on quality-related issues, problem identification, coaching, and continuous improvement rather than tied to compensation and merit rating systems.

■ Training should meet the needs of different groups of employees, be reinforced on the job, and be evaluated for effectiveness.

■ Effective recognition and reward systems motivate employees and actively promote quality improvement efforts.

■ An effective and progressive compensation system depends on a policy of rewards that create equity and reinforce group achievements, and a system of individual pay linked to skills and mastery.

■ Understanding motivation and human behavior is a critical management skill in a TQM environment. Content, process, and environmentally based theories and models provide a theoretical basis for managerial leadership in a TQM environment.

■ Union and management must cooperate to make TQM effective. Recent rulings by the NLRB will likely force union and nonunion firms to examine their employee participation programs to determine whether they currently conform, or can be made to conform, to regulatory requirements.

REVIEW QUESTIONS

1. Discuss the impact of the Taylor system on quality, productivity, and human resource management.

2. Define *human resource management.* Contrast it with the traditional role of personnel management.

3. Contrast traditional HRM approaches with those required in a TQM environment.

4. Summarize the leading practices of TQM-based HRM practices.

5. What role does HRM play in supporting strategic business plans? Discuss the strategic choices that HR managers must consider.

6. What is empowerment? Discuss the changes that empowerment brings to organizations.

7. In a TQM-based organization, what is the role of recruitment and career development? What challenges does TQM pose in these areas?

8. Briefly summarize traditional performance appraisal processes. Within a TQM perspective, what objections have been raised concerning these processes? What steps can be taken to make performance appraisal more consistent with TQM principles?

9. Discuss the role of training and education in supporting total quality.

10. Summarize the key practices for good recognition and reward systems, and explain how they promote continuous improvement.

11. How have approaches to compensation changed as a result of a total quality focus?

12. Explain the linkages between individual human resource issues and system management.

13. Define the term *motivation* by listing its important components.

14. Outline the differences between process, content, and environmentally based theories of motivation. Which type is essential to quality managers?

15. What insights are provided by the Porter and Lawler model of motivation?

16. What are the major components of Hackman and Oldham's job characteristics model and how do they apply to quality?

17. How has TQM changed labor-management relations? What impacts have recent NLRB rulings had on HRM practices in a TQM environment?

DISCUSSION QUESTIONS

1. What is your reaction to Matsushita's statement "We will win, and you will lose."? Do you believe it is still true today (if it was accurate in 1988)?

2. Briefly review the history of HRM. Conduct a thorough literature search of one of the "branches" of HRM and relate it to current quality management issues.

3. How easily can a company shift from the traditional HRM approach to the TQM-based approach? Which of the areas—philosophy, business objectives, quality objectives, business information sharing, inclusion of constituencies, or employee involvement—might be the most difficult for companies to change? Why?

4. How can a fraternity or student organization use leading HRM practices of companies to develop its own strategic HRM plans? If you are involved in such an organization, develop a strategic HRM plan that supports total quality.

5. Cite some examples of empowerment or lack of empowerment from your own experiences.

6. How might the concept of empowerment be employed in a classroom?

7. Many companies today seek the best available applicants and train them in TQM principles. What implications does this have for designing college curricula and choosing elective courses in a given program?

8. Consider the statement "How one is evaluated determines how one performs." What does this mean for your classes? Would your performance change if grades were abolished (as Deming strongly advocated)?

9. Discuss the controversy over performance appraisal. Do you agree with Deming's approach, or do you take the more traditional viewpoint toward performance review? Why?

10. Most colleges and universities use a course/instructor evaluation system. If your school has one, how is it used? Does it support continuous improvement? How might the evaluation instrument or process be modified to better reflect TQM principles?

11. The Xerox training strategy is summarized as follows:

    a. The training is unform—common tools and processes are taught across all of Xerox, to all employees, creating a "common language within Xerox" that fosters cohesive team functioning.

    b. Training is conducted in family groups, with all members starting and finishing training at the same time to facilitate the change process.

    c. Training starts at the top of the organization with the CEO and cascades downward to all employees.[67]

What advantages does such strategy have? Do you see any possible disadvantages? Would this approach work in any business?

12. Design a (nonfinancial) recognition and reward system for your class. Would such a system improve instructor and student performance? Would you and your instructor support it, or would it simply be viewed as silly?

13. Discuss the conditions under which team incentives, gainsharing, and "pay for increased skills" reward systems may work. When is it a poor idea to install such systems?

14. What motivates you to study and perform in the classroom? Discuss how various motivation theories might lead to new ways of teaching and learning.

15. Survey several managers in one or two companies on the topic of motivation for quality. Try to find managers at each of the following levels to interview:

    a. quality control

    b. manufacturing or industrial engineering

    c. upper-level management

    d. first-line supervision

    e. line employees (perhaps a union steward or officer)

16. When simple theories such as Maslow's, Herzberg's, and McGregor's explain motivation, why does the search continue for more complex ones or for ones that integrate several different theories, such as Bandura's social learning/self-efficacy theory? What implications do they have for quality?

17. If you were a HRM manager at a *nonunion* TQM-oriented firm that had employee participation teams, what would you recommend to top management in light of the recent NLRB rulings? Read the sources listed in the text, and any others you may find and write a brief position paper justifying your answer.

CASES

I. HD Corporation[68]

HD Corporation, a manufacturer of heavy trucks, had a long, sad, and bitter history of employee relations. The company openly practiced management through terrorism. Engineers and technical people dominated the culture. One of the company's assembly plants devoted major resources to statistical process control. An entire department staffed with engineers justified its existence by keeping charts. The engineers collected and stored data on a computer and posted the charts in every production department once each week. They also posted lists of problems and defects attributable to each department. Another department busied itself with work redesign and assembly line balancing. The plant was highly product-focused. Material moved smoothly from one operation to the next. Subassemblies

flowed into assemblies like the tributaries of a river, all moving toward the final assembly line.

For all this effort, quality was mediocre at best. HD Corporation devoted more factory space to repair operations than they devoted to the original assembly. The individual and social side of the system was largely ignored. People lacked interpersonal skills, common goals, and trust, and they could not hope to attain these qualities under the existing power structure and reward system.

Assignment

If you were to take over as plant manager, what changes would you make? How would you begin?

II. Joy Industries[69]

Joy Industries' plastics products division (PPD) primarily manufactures and markets commercial and residential plastic components for a variety of end-use applications including toys, kitchen and home storage containers, and casings for control equipment. Its U.S. distribution system includes service to large national retailers such as Home Depot and

Wal-Mart for the home products and a network of 73 independent distributors for commercial products. Seven manufacturing plants are dispersed throughout the U.S. with a network of eight regional sales offices in major metropolitan areas.

Of the 5120 employees, 88 percent are in manufacturing. A corporate staff located in Landisville,

Pennsylvania, supports PPD in the legal, research, quality management, and engineering areas. Three of the seven plants are unionized. Relationships with these unions are excellent with a relatively low number of grievances and a high degree of cooperation in improving the business through employee involvement.

PPD is a market leader and has used its 10-year-old quality management process to continually improve its market position, quality, service, and costs. It has followed the Malcolm Baldrige National Quality Award Criteria for three years to further refine its approaches and achieve improved company performance.

The quality improvement process (QIP) is based as much on culture, behavior and values as on quality of product and service. Extensive changes have been implemented, redefining the internal customer/supplier relationships among all employees and their relationships to markets and customers. Nine of 14 quality improvement process actions are focused on human resource issues.

The 23 quality improvement teams use the 14 QIP actions to localize divisional strategies, which makes employees themselves—in all locations—the owners of change. Through the success of the quality improvement process and human resource strategies, the Plastics Products Division has significantly redefined an industry once steeped in tradition.

PPD's human resource strategy (Table 10.6) is based on the corporate quality goal:

To achieve total customer satisfaction by involving our employees in the improvement of

our business processes at a rate that sustains global leadership.

The leadership in this culture change has given the company a significant competitive advantage. In large part, leadership is the reason Joy Industries has been recognized for the second time by Robert Levering and Milton Moskowitz in *The 100 Best Companies to Work for in America.* (Only 55 companies were chosen for both the 1984 and 1993 editions.) Levering and Moskowitz cited several human resource issues: pay and benefits, career concept, security, fairness, camaraderie, pride in work and company openness.

Because of the maturity of our Quality Improvement Process, our approaches are fundamentally integrated into every aspect of our business. Pursuit of the ideals behind the concept of a high-performance organization are never-ending. Therefore, these approaches exist at various stages, are constantly refined and advanced, and have their own subset of tactics.

Specific short-term tactics are planned and implemented by each QIT to create a monolithic approach, but each QIT is empowered to interpret and manage what is best for their organization. This authority is especially important because of the different types of products made at each plant. (Eighty-eight percent of PPD employees work in manufacturing.)

For instance, at some plants (Seattle, Tulsa, and Akron), the manufacturing strategy creates a continuous-flow, integrated line for commodity products. Such lines require fewer people with higher process and team skills. The QIT takes the elements of the human resource strategy and 14 QIP

TABLE 10.6 Plastic Products Division Human Resource Strategy

Strategic Components	Plans and Approaches
Employee Involvement/Empowerment ■ Team-Based ■ Individual	■ Ongoing multifunctional teams ■ Ad hoc improvement teams ■ High performance organization ■ Process/function sharing ■ Opportunities for improvement
People Development	■ Performance reviews ■ Learning ■ Career concept
Recognition/Reward	■ Corporate awards ■ QIT recognition programs ■ Incentive rewards
Well-Being and Satisfaction	■ Communications ■ Employee feedback ■ Benefits ■ Compensation ■ Community interaction ■ Quality of life

actions that best enable them to achieve their goals. In plants that make higher-end speciality products (Tampa and Pittsburgh), the manufacturing strategy requires flexible manufacturing lines. At those plants, the QITs and human resource strategies focus on employees' capabilities in quick changeovers and a high degree of teamwork.

Longer-term plans involving all plants include flatter organizations, pay-for-knowledge systems, gainsharing, employee involvement, safety, and a size limit of 500 employees per plant for optimum flexibility.

Human Resource Improvement

Human resource plans and practices are improved through external and internal benchmarking, studying Baldrige winners, use of employee and QIT feedback, and corporate human resource experts in industrial relations and employment practices and services. The division's general management team (GMT) reviews all human resource goals to assure alignment with PPD's stretch goals and business plans. The plant managers, regional sales managers and their QITs implement activities toward the goals locally. A variety of performance indicators are used to measure improvement as outlined in Table 10.7.

Information about employees is collected on three levels.

1. *QIT Locations (plants, regional sales offices):* QITs collect data on a variety of approaches including employee interviews, team participation and results, gainsharing, safety, recognition, training and education, absenteeism, and grievances. These data are routinely shared with crews, QITs, and departments.

2. *Divisional (Plastic Products Division):* The division's general management team (GMT) routinely reviews results in person and by conference calls with plant managers. The general managers of manufacturing and sales and marketing each cross-reference their human resource data with goal achievements. Gainsharing and employee interviews accurately measure the effectiveness of employee involvement in improvement activities and serve as a basis for evaluation and refinement.

Global plant managers' meetings always include reports on key human resource initiatives. Once a year, QIT chairpersons attend the PPD Quality Council meeting to evaluate performance and plan the future initiatives. These are held at rotating sites so facility tours can be conducted. The group vice president visits every QIT yearly to review progress and future plans.

3. *Corporate (Joy Industries):* Using its corporate human resource information systems (CHRIS),

the company collects and maintains information about all employees in a permanent database. The data are used for numerous evaluations, including education and training, awards for excellence and other recognition, benefits preferences, performance reviews, and job histories. The CHRIS information is used by the GMT and corporate support departments.

At all levels, managers use the employee interview process established in 1960. Employee interviews are confidential, one-on-one efforts to determine satisfaction for all categories of employees. Nearly 9000 comments were made in 1992 interviews. Only one other company in the United States is known to use employee interviews the way Joy Industries does: not to "put out fires," but on a regular basis to prevent them.

Each location QIT analyzes the data and identifies not only overall employee satisfaction factors, but specific issues that directly impact absenteeism, turnover, grievances, and safety issues, as well as site-related concerns, and then develops plans for improvement.

In addition to employee interviews, Joy Industries uses employee satisfaction surveys. In May 1992, the company research and development center conducted a written employee satisfaction survey; employees inducated an exceptionally high 82 percent satisfaction level. Sales organizations conducted surveys, and employees had a satisfaction rating of 71.4 percent. QITs work closely to follow up this information. The appropriate general managers review the aggregated data and addresses division issues not handled locally.

Employee exit interviews are conducted in all cases, at the site involved. Issues not within the scope of a QIT are passed on to the general managers of manufacturing or sales and marketing for action, and to corporate recruiting for analysis and preventive action.

Assignment

Evaluate how the company's overall human resource management, plans, and processes are integrated with its overall quality operational performance plans, and how HR planning and management address the needs and development of the entire work force. Specifically,

- How do plans include (a) development, education, training, and empowerment, (b) mobility, flexibility, and changes in work organization, work proceses, or work schedules, (c) reward, recognition, benefits, and compensation, and (d) recruitment?
- How effectively does the company improve its key personnel processes?

TABLE 10.7   Plastic Products Division Performance Measurement

Strategies/Goals	Key Performance Indicators	QIT Initiatives (Sample)
Increase involvement of employees in improvement efforts	▪ # of corrective action teams ▪ # of process improvement teams ▪ # of opportunities for improvement ▪ # of gainsharing plants ▪ # of natural work teams	▪ Measure current level of involvement; develop plan for continued improvement ▪ Improve education/training for improvement teams ▪ Provide on-site facilitators to support teams ▪ Improve recognition effectiveness ▪ Improve communication of team activities
Improve safety	▪ Zero lost-time accidents ▪ Reduce OSHA recordables by 60% by 1996	▪ Provide S.T.O.P. safety training ▪ Benchmark—National Safety Council industries ▪ Increase effectiveness of safety autits
Flatter organizations	▪ # of layers reduced to four ▪ # of natural work teams	▪ Benchmark—Akron, Ohio, plant
Improve recruitment	▪ # of job offers ▪ Acceptance rate ▪ Rejection rate	▪ Improve process of selecting candidates ▪ Assess division's requirements ▪ Provide more accurate data to potential candidate about job
Improve recognition and reward systems to drive process improvement	▪ # of recognition systems ▪ % of employees recognized ▪ # of gainsharing plants ▪ # of pay-for-knowledge systems	▪ Encourage participation in improvement activities ▪ Provide timely recognition ▪ Develop use of day-to-day, informal and formal approaches ▪ Measure, assess and improve based on employee feedback ▪ Implement and monitor gainsharing
Improve employee satisfaction and feedback	▪ # of employee interviews ▪ # of comments favorable, unfavorable	▪ Develop follow-up plans ▪ Provide timely communication
Focus learning	▪ Extent of education/ training · ▪ Stretch goal and gainsharing achievement	▪ JIT training ▪ Improve needs assessment

▪ How effectively does the company evaluate and improve its human resource planning and management processes? Are selection, performance, recognition, job analysis, and training integrated to support improved performance and development of all categories and types of employees?

Are HR planning and management aligned with company strategies and plans?

Overall, are any significant gaps noticeable in their approaches or deployment throughout the organization? In what areas are they strongest? Weakest?

▪ NOTES

1. Cited in A. Richard Shores, *A TQM Approach to Achieving Manufacturing Excellence* (Milwaukee, WI: ASQC Quality Press, 1990), 270.

2. Richard E. Walton, "From Control to Commitment in the Workplace," *Harvard Business Review* 63, no. 2 (March/April 1985), 77–84. Copyright © by the President and Fellows of Harvard College; all rights reserved.

3. Lloyd L. Byars and Leslie W. Rue, *Human Resource Management,* 3rd ed. (Homewood, IL: Richard D. Irwin, 1991), 6.

4. Ethan Davis, "Quality Service at the Prudential," in

Spechler, Jay W. (ed.), *When America Does It Right* (Norcross, GA: Industrial Engineering and Management Press, 1988), 225–226.

5. Alan Wolf, "Coors' Customer Focus," *Beverage World* (March 1991).

6. Matthes, Karen, "A Look Ahead for '93," *Human Resource Focus* 70, no. 1 (January, 1993), 1, 4.

7. Richard Blackburn and Benson Rosen, "Total Quality and Human Resources Management: Lessons Learned from Baldrige Award-Winning Companies," *Academy of Management Executive* 7, no. 3 (1993), 49–66.

8. Blackburn and Rosen, see note 7.

9. AT&T Consumer Communication Services, *Summary of 1994 Application for the Malcolm Baldrige National Quality Award*.

10. Hal F. Rosenbluth, "Have Quality, Will Travel," *The TQM Magazine* (November/December 1992), 267–270.

11. Randall S. Schuler and Susan E. Jackson, "Linking Competitive Strategies With Human Resource Management Practice," *Academy of Management Executive* 1, no. 3 (1987), 207–219.

12. Cadillac Malcolm Baldrige Application Summary, 1990. Cadillac Motor Car Division, 2860 Clark Ave., Detroit, MI 48232.

13. Malcolm Baldrige National Quality Award Criteria (1993), 3.

14. Alan Wolf, "Golden Opportunities," *Beverage World*, (February 1991).

15. J.M. Juran, *Juran on Leadership for Quality: An Executive Handbook* (New York: The Free Press, 1989), 264.

16. Phillip A. Smith, William D. Anderson, and Stanley A. Brooking, "Employee Empowerment: A Case Study," *Production and Inventory Management* 34, no. 3 (1993), 45–50.

17. AT&T Quality Steering Committee, *Great Performances* (AT&T Bell Laboratories 1991), 39; and William Smitley and David Scott, "Empowerment: Unlocking the Potential of Your Work Force," *Quality Digest* 14, no. 8 (August 1994), 40–46.

18. Karen Jamrog Martel, "Best in Class: Fast Food," *The Quality Observer* 3, no. 6 (April 1994), 21.

19. "Changing a Culture: DuPont Tries to Make Sure That Its Research Wizardry Serves the Bottom Line," *The Wall Street Journal*, 27 March, 1992, A5.

20. Robert S. Kaplan, "Texas Eastman Company," Harvard Business School Case, No. 9-190-039.

21. John F. Akers, "World-Class Quality: Nothing Else Will Do," *Quality Progress* 24, no. 10 (October 1991), 26–27.

22. Many facts and examples in this section are reported in Blackburn and Rosen, see note 7.

23. *Great Performances*, see note 17.

24. Ronald Henkoff, "Make Your Office More Productive," *Fortune* 25 February, 1991, 76.

25. George Eckes, "Practical Alternatives to Performance Appraisals," *Quality Progress* 27, no. 11 (November 1994), 57–60.

26. Douglas McGregor, "An Uneasy Look at Performance Appraisal," *Harvard Business Review* (September/October 1972); Herbert H. Meyer, Emanuel Kay, and John R. P. French, Jr., "Split Roles in Performance Appraisal," *Harvard Business Review* (January/February 1965); Harry Levinson, "Appraisal of What Perfor-

mance?" *Harvard Business Review* (January/February 1965); A. M. Mohrman, *Deming Versus Performance Appraisal: Is There a Resolution?* (Los Angeles: Center for Effective Organizations, University of Southern California, 1989).

27. Eckes, see note 25.

28. W. Edwards Deming, *Out of the Crisis* (Cambridge, MA: MIT Center for Advanced Engineering Study, 1986).

29. Stanley M. Moss, "Appraise Your Performance Appraisal Process," *Quality Progress* (November 1989), 60.

30. Bill Wilson, "Quality Training At FedEx," *Quality Digest* 15, no. 1 (January 1995), 40–43.

31. A. Blanton Godfrey, "Training and Education in Quality and Reliability—A Modern Approach," *Communications in Statistics—Theory and Methods* 14 (1985), 2621–2638.

32. Dawn Anfuso, "L.L. Bean's TQM Efforts Put People Before Processes," *Personnel Journal* (July 1994), 73–83.

33. "Domino's Pizza, Inc." *Profiles in Quality* (Boston: Allyn and Bacon, 1991), 90–93.

34. "Bonus Pay: Buzzword or Bonanza?" *Business Week*, 14 November, 1994, 62–64.

35. Richard E. Walton, "Toward a Strategy of Eliciting Employee Commitment Based on Policies of Mutuality," in Richard E. Walton and Paul R Lawrence (eds.), *HR Trends and Challenges* (Boston, MA: Harvard Business School Press, 1985), 35–65.

36. Nancy J. Perry, "Here Come Richer, Riskier Pay Plans," *Fortune*, 19 December, 1988, 50–58.

37. Perry, 507, see note 36.

38. Frank C. Barnes, "Nucor (A)," in Robert R. Bell and John M. Burnham, *Managing Productivity and Change* (Cincinnati, OH: South-Western Publishing Company, 1991), 507.

39. Gregory M. Bounds and Larry A. Pace, "Human Resource Management for Competitive Capability," Chap. 26 in Michael J. Stahl and Gregory M. Bounds (eds.), *Competing Globally Through Customer Value* (New York: Quorum Books, 1991), 648–684.

40. Saul W. Gellerman, *Motivation in the Real World* (New York: Dutton, 1992), 4.

41. James L. Bowditch and Anthony F. Buono, *A Primer on Organizational Behavior*, 2d ed. (New York: John Wiley and Sons, 1990), 52.

42. See, for example, Abraham Maslow, "A Theory of Human Motivation," *Psychological Review* 50, no. 4 (July 1943), 370–396; Abraham Maslow, *Motivation and Personality* (New York: Harper and Row, 1954); F. Herzberg, B. Mausner, and B. Snyderman, *The Motivation to Work*, 2d. ed. (New York: John Wiley and Sons. 1959); Douglas McGregor, *The Human Side of Enterprise* (New York: McGraw-Hill, 1960); and D.C. McClelland, *Assessing Human Motivation* (Morristown, NJ: General Learning Press, 1971).

43. David A Garvin, *Managing Quality* (New York: The Free Press, 1988), 202–203.

44. J. Schneider and E. A Locke, "A Critique of Herzberg's Incident Classification System and a Suggested Revision," *Organizational Behavior and Human Performance* (1971), 441–457.

45. R.M. Steers and D.G. Spencer. "The Role of Achievement Motivation in Job Design," *Journal of Applied*

Psychology, 62, (1977), 472–479; G.A. Yukl and G.P. Latham, "Interrelationships Among Employee Participation, Individual Differences, Goal Difficulty, Instrumentality and Performance," *Personnel Psychology* 31 (1978), 305–324; and T. Matsui, A. Okada, and T. Kakuyama, "Influence of Achievement Need on Goal Setting, Performance and Feedback Effectiveness," *Journal of Applied Psychology* 67 (1982), 645–648, as cited in James L. Bowditch and Anthony F. Buono, 57, see note 41.

46. James W. Dean, Jr. and James R. Evans, *Total Quality: Management Organization and Strategy* (St. Paul, MN: West Publishing Co., 1994), 210.

47. Victor H. Vroom, *Work and Motivation* (New York: John Wiley and Sons, 1964).

48. L.W. Porter and Edward E. Lawler, *Managerial Attitudes and Performance* (Homewood, IL: Richard D. Irwin, 1968).

49. Edwin Locke, "Toward a Theory of Task Performance and Incentives," *Organizational Behavior and Human Performance* (Fall 1968), 157–189; R.J. House, "A Path-Goal Theory of Leadership Effectiveness," *Administrative Science Quarterly* 16, no. 3 (1971), 321–338.

50. James W. Dean, Jr. and James R. Evans, 211, see note 46.

51. B. F. Skinner, *Science and Human Behavior* (New York: Free Press, 1953). See also, *Beyond Freedom and Dignity* (New York: Bantam Books, 1971).

52. Edward J. Feeney, "At Emery Air Freight: Positive Reinforcement Boosts Performance," *Organizational Dynamics* (Winter 1973), 41–50.

53. J.S. Adams, "Toward an Understanding of Equity," *Journal of Abnormal and Social Psychology* 67 (1963), 422–436. Also see J. S. Adams and W.E. Rosenbaum, "The Relationship of Worker Productivity and Cognitive Dissonance About Wage Inequities," *Journal of Applied Psychology* 55, no. 1 (1971), 161–164.

54. Don Hellriegel and John W. Slocum, Jr., *Management,* 6th ed. (Reading, MA: Addison Wesley, 1992), 450.

55. A. Bandura, *Social Learning Theory* (Englewood Cliffs, NJ: Prentice-Hall, 1977). See also Marilyn Gist and Terence R. Mitchell, "Self-Efficacy: A Theoretical Analysis of Its Determinants and Malleability," *Academy of Management Review* 17, no. 2, (1992), 183–211; and R. Kreitner and F. Luthans, "A Social Learning Approach to Behavioral Management: Radical Behaviorists 'Mellowing Out'," *Organizational Dynamics* 13, no. 2 (1984), 47–65.

56. R.A. Snyder and Ronald R. Williams, "Self Theory: An Integrative Theory of Work Motivation," *Journal of Occupational Psychology* 55 (1982), 257–267.

57. Bowditch and Buono, 68–69, see note 41.

58. Bowditch and Buono, 73–74, see note 41.

59. Portions adapted from Chapter 4, "Motivation Through the Design of Work," in J. R. Hackman and G. R. Oldham, *Work Redesign* (Reading, MA: Addison-Wesley, 1980).

60. Hackman and Oldham, 25, see note 59.

61. Robert B. Leventhal, "Union Involvement in New Work Systems," *The Journal for Quality and Participation* (June 1991), 36–39.

62. Jack D. Orsburn, Linda Moran, Ed Musselwhite, and John H. Zenger, *Self-Directed Work Teams* (Homewood, IL: Business One-lrwin, 1990), 145–146.

63. John Hoerr, "LTV Steel Knocks the Rust Off Its Labor Relations," *Business Week*, 23 December, 1985, 57–58.

64. Ross L. Fink, Robert K. Robinson, and Ann Canty, "DuPont v. Chemical Workers Association: Further Limits on Employee Participation Programs," *Industrial Management* (March/April 1994), 3–5; Robert K. Robinson, Ross L. Fink, and Edward L. Gillenwater, "Do Employee Participation Programs Violate U.S. Labor Laws?" *Industrial Management* (May/June 1993), 3–5.

65. Adapted from Lee Branst, "Disneyland—A Kingdom of Service Quality," reprinted with permission from *Quality* 23 (February 1984), 16–18; a publication of Hitchcock Publishing, a Capital Cities/ABC Inc., company; and Brad Stratton, "How Disneyland Works," *Quality Progress* (July 1991), 17–30.

66. Adapted from *Federal Express Corporation Quality Profile*, Federal Express Corporation, 2005 Corporate Avenue, Memphis, TN 38132.

67. Xerox Business Products and Systems, *Malcolm Baldrige National Quality Award Submission Document* (1989).

68. Adapted from Quaterman Lee, "Quality in the Balance," *The Quality Observer* 3, no. 6 (April 1994). Reprinted with permission from The Quality Observer Corporation, P.O. Box 1111, Fairfax, VA 22030.

69. Adapted from "Joy Industries," a Case Item prepared for use in the 1994 Malcolm Baldrige National Quality Award Examiner Preparation Course. This material is in the public domain.

■ BIBLIOGRAPHY

AT&T Quality Steering Committee. *Batting 1000: Using Baldrige Feedback to Improve Your Business.* AT&T Bell Laboratories (1992).

—————. *Great Performances!* AT&T Bell Laboratories (1991).

Blackburn, Richard and Benjamin Rosen. "Total Quality and Human Resources Management: Lessons Learned from Baldrige Award-Winning Companies." *Academy of Management Executive* 7, no. 3 (1993), 49–66.

Christison, William L. "Financial Information is Key to Empowerment." *Quality Progress* 27, no. 7 (July 1994), 47–48.

Chung, Kae H., and Margaret Ann Gray. "Can We Adopt Japanese Methods of Human Resources Management?" *Personnel Administrator* 27 (May 1982), 43.

Dowling, William F. "Job Redesign on the Assembly Line: Farewell to the Blue-Collar Blues?" *Organizational Dynamics* 2, no. 2 (1973), 61.

General Motors Powertrain. "Application of Dr. Deming's Teachings to People Systems." Presentation slides (undated).

Griffin, R. W. "Toward an Integrated Theory of Task Design." In L.L. Cummings, and B.W. Staw, (eds.), *Research in Organizational Behavior* 9. Greenwich, CT: JAI Press, 1987, 79–120.

Hart, Christopher W.L., and Christopher E. Bogan. *The Baldrige.* New York: McGraw-Hill, 1992.

Herzberg, Frederick. *Work and the Nature of Man.* Cleveland, OH: World, 1966.

_____ . "One More Time: How Do You Motivate Employees?" *Harvard Business Review* 46, January/February 1968), 53–62.

Kanfer, Ruth. "Motivation Theory in Industrial and Organizational Psychology." In Marvin D. Dunnette and Leaeta M. Hough. *Handbook of Industrial and Organizational Psychology,* 2d. ed., vol. 1. Palo Alto, CA: Consulting Psychologists Press, Inc., 1990, 75–170.

Kern, Jill P., John J. Riley, and Louis N. Jones (eds.). *Human Resources Management.* Quality and Reliability Series, sponsored by the ASQC Human Resources Division. New York: Marcel Dekker, Inc., and Milwaukee: ASQC Quality Press, 1987.

Kilman, R.H., and T.J. Covin and Associates. *Corporate Transformation: Revitalizing Organizations for a Competitive World,* San Francisco: Jossey-Bass, 1988.

Lewin, Kurt. *A Dynamic Theory of Personality.* New York: McGraw-Hill, 1935.

Locke, E.A., and G.P. Latham. *Goal Setting: A Motivational Technique that Works!* Englewood Cliffs, NJ: Prentice-Hall, 1984.

Mayo, Elton. *The Human Problems of Industrial Civilization.* Cambridge, MA: Harvard Graduate School of Business, 1946.

Messmer, Max. "Rightsizing, Not Downsizing: How to Maintain Quality Through Strategic Staffing." *Industry Week,* 3 August, 1993, 23–26.

Miner, John B. *Theories of Organizational Behavior.* Hinsdale, IL: Dryden Press, 1980.

Olian, Judy D., and Sara L. Rynes. "Making Total Quality Work: Aligning Organizational Processes, Performance Measures, and Stakeholders." *Human Resource Management* (Fall 1991), 303–333.

Pierce, J. L., and R. B. Dunham. "The Measurement of Perceived Job Characteristics: The Job Diagnostic Survey Versus the Job Characteristics Inventory." *Academy of Management Journal* 21 (1978), 123–128.

Pierce, Jon L. "Job Design in Perspective." *Personnel Administrator* 25, no. 12 (1980), 67.

Powell, Cash, Jr. "Empowerment, the Stake in the Ground for ABS." *Target* (January/February 1992).

Rubinstein, Sidney P. "Quality and Democracy in the Workplace." *Quality Progress,* 21, no. 4 (April 1988), 25–28.

Ryan, John. "Labor/Management Participation: The A. O. Smith Experience." *Quality Progress,* 21, no. 4 (April 1988), 36–40.

Semerad, James M. "Create a New Learning Environment." *APICS—The Performance Advantage* (April 1993), 34–37.

Snell, Scott A., and James W. Dean. "Integrated Manufacturing and Human Resource Management: A Human Capital Perspective." *Academy of Management Journal* 35, no. 3 (1992), 467–504.

Taylor, Frederick W. *The Principles of Scientific Management.* New York: Harper & Row, 1911.

Teel, Kenneth S. "Performance Appraisal: Current Trends, Persistent Progress." *Personnel Journal* 59, no. 4 (April 1980), 296–301.

Wagel, William H. "Corning Zeros in on Total Quality." *Personnel* (July 1987).

Walton, Richard E. "From Control to Commitment in the Workplace." *Harvard Business Review* 63, no. 2 (March/April 1985), 77–85.

Yee, William, and Ed Musselwhite. "Living TQM With Workforce 2000." *1993 ASQC Quality Congress Transactions.* Boston, 141–146.

Yukl, Gary A. *Leadership in Organizations,* 2d ed. Englewood Cliffs, NJ: Prentice-Hall, 1989.

Participation and Teamwork

Rath & Strong, a Lexington, Massachusetts-based management consulting firm, polled almost 200 executives from *Fortune 500* companies about activities that foster superior performance results for an organization.[1] The survey revealed that personal initiative, when combined with a customer orientation and employee involvement, has a positive impact on business success and sales growth rate. However, although 79 percent of all respondents indicated that employees are increasingly expected to take initiative to bring about change in the company, 40 percent of the respondents replied that most people in their company *do not believe* that they can make a personal contribution to the company's success. Alan Frohman, a senior associate with Rath & Strong, stated, "These results are significant because they suggest that although people are being expected to take personal initiative, most organizations have not figured out how to translate those expectations into positive behaviors."

Participation and teamwork—the foundations of **employee involvement (EI)**—represent core principles of total quality management and are a natural extension of effective human resource management practices. Informal communication, open-door policies, suggestion systems, and teams encourage employees to share their knowledge and use their abilities to improve the processes that lead to customer satisfaction. In a TQM culture, employees are encouraged to challenge ineffective company policies and bring quality concerns directly to top management. Individual participation and team approaches involve transforming the culture of the entire organization to tap the creative energies of all employees and improve their motivation. Frohman emphasized that "the right corporate climate can have a tremendous impact on how comfortable people feel about taking action."

EI offers many advantages over traditional management practices:

- Replacing the adversarial mentality with trust and cooperation
- Developing the skills and leadership capability of individuals, creating a sense of mission and fostering trust
- Increasing employee morale and commitment to the organization
- Fostering creativity and innovation, the source of competitive advantage
- Helping people understand quality principles and instilling these principles into the corporate culture
- Allowing employees to solve problems at the source immediately
- Improving quality and productivity.[2]

Employee involvement should begin with a personal commitment to quality. If employees accept and commit to a quality philosophy, they are more apt to learn quality tools and techniques and use them in their daily work. As they begin to see the benefits of a commitment to quality, they will then be more receptive to working in teams. This team interaction, in turn, reinforces personal commitment, driving a never-ending cycle of improvement. Employee involvement also depends on the amount and type of information shared with employees, training, compensation and rewards, and the empowerment practices of the firms.[3] Thus, human resource management practices discussed in the last chapter must be designed to support and facilitate EI.

EI is exciting because it offers unprecedented possibilities for tapping the knowledge, enthusiasm, and expertise of the entire work force. Empowered employees take ownership of their jobs, improve processes they control, and make individual and team decisions. EI promises workers autonomy over their jobs and gives managers a powerful approach to improve quality and productivity. A study of *Fortune 1000* companies suggested that the vast majority of firms that use EI do so to improve the bottom line.[4] Productivity, quality, and employee motivation are the principal drivers behind EI efforts. Phillip Caldwell, former chief executive of Ford Motor Company stated:

> The magic of employee involvement [EI] is that it allows individuals to discover their own potential—and to put that potential to work in more creative ways. A survey last year of more than 750 EI participants at seven facilities found that a full 82 percent felt they had a chance to accomplish something worthwhile, compared with only 27 percent before EI was initiated. . . . People develop in themselves pride in workmanship, self-respect, self-reliance, and a heightened sense of responsibility.[5]

In many situations, especially when organized labor is involved, the work force tends to resist any effort to reduce rigid, rule-based tasks. Traditional labor managers, like their corporate management counterparts, prefer to adhere to the structured approaches that have their roots in Frederick W. Taylor's historical principles of scientific management.[6] A president of a United Paperworkers Local said:

> What the company wants is for us to work like the Japanese. Everybody go out and do jumping jacks in the morning and kiss each other when they go home at night. You work as a team, rat on each other, and lose control of your destiny. That's not going to work in this country.[7]

Thus, EI is also controversial because it threatens old ways of working and could undermine managerial and union control. If approached incorrectly by management, it could fail miserably.

Fortunately, such attitudes are changing. Employee involvement is gaining increased acceptance as an important component of modern quality management. Many experts, however, believe that the movement is not spreading fast enough, especially considering the potential benefits. Some suggest that the federal government should reinforce employee involvement in public policy. As pointed out in the last chapter, the government, when it is represented by the National Labor Relations Board, appears to be "muddying the water" rather than clearly reinforcing the use of employee involvement in corporations. At the same time, the Clinton administration's Secretary of Labor, Robert Reich, has promoted workplace cooperation.[8]

This chapter examines the history and development of employee involvement and discusses approaches for individual participation and teamwork and ways of measuring and evaluating these approaches.

THE IMPORTANCE AND SCOPE OF EMPLOYEE INVOLVEMENT

EI is rooted in the psychology of human needs. The motivation models of Maslow, Herzberg, and McGregor discussed in the last chapter form a rational basis for EI approaches. Employee involvement provides a powerful means of achieving the highest order needs of self-realization and fulfillment. Employees are motivated through exciting work, responsibility, and recognition. Companies gain many benefits by placing trust in people through the delegation of responsibility and self-control (Theory Y) aspects of employee involvement. Employee participation relies on empowerment and managers' sharing the tasks of setting goals, making decisions, and solving problems with subordinates. Sayles made an interesting observation:

> "Answers" [to business-related questions or problems] involve a mixture of manager and subordinate ideas and knowledge, formed in an interactive process. The synthesis is superior to what either could accomplish alone. Participation is not viewed primarily as a motivation technique but rather as an essential channel by which more senior managers learn about the realities and the operating details of the work situation.[9]

Human resource management has traditionally focused on individuals, as suggested in the previous chapter. This orientation makes sense since much of the work that gets done in organizations—assembly, order-filling, invoicing—is performed by individuals, who know their customers better than anyone else. However, a single person rarely has enough knowledge or experience to understand all aspects of the most important work processes (look back at Figure 4.4); thus team approaches are essential for process improvement.

Traditional HRM practices also encourage individual advancement. This mindset is built into the management system by such practices as management by objectives, individual performance evaluation, professional status and privileges, and individual promotion. Focusing on individuals contributes to rivalries, competition, favoritism, and self-centeredness, which collectively work against accomplishing the true mission of an organization: serving customers. Alfie Kohn, who studied issues of cooperation and competition among employees over five years, concluded that the ideal amount of competition in any company is none at all. Any informal competition that may develop is best discouraged; management should go out of the way to design cooperative work groups and incentive systems.[10] Research has shown that the effectiveness of supervisors and subordinates alike is positively related to cooperation and negatively related to competitiveness.

Employee involvement breaks down barriers between individuals, departments, and line and staff functions, an action prescribed by one of Deming's 14 Points. Typically, cooperation between such departments as design and manufacturing, doctors and hospital administrators, and business managers and orchestra conductors is not the norm. For example, when a problem between departments at IBM arose, employees investigated and documented the problem and then presented the information to their manager.[11] In typical bureaucratic fashion, the manager escalated the issue to the appropriate manager elsewhere in the company who then contacted the appropriate person in the "problem" department. The issue eventually found its way back to the owning department with a general request to resolve it and report back. The two departments finally met to discuss the problem. This process normally took weeks or months. In the interim, the problem may have resolved itself or changed. By fostering employee involvement and increasing empowerment, problem resolution times are slashed and better solutions result.

■ Historical Influences

EI programs are by no means new.[12] Many programs and experiments were initiated on a sporadic basis by industrial engineers, statisticians, and behavioral scientists. These early attempts influenced modern practices considerably. Unfortunately, these approaches lacked the complementary elements of TQM, such as a customer orientation, top management leadership and support, and a common set of tools for problem solving and continuous improvement.

Early work improvement activities at the Zeiss Company in Germany in the 1890s involved workers in work planning, design of precision machinery, and group problem solving.[13] In 1913, the Lincoln Electric Company began to develop its unique mix of work improvement and employee incentive plans, including an employee advisory board, employee stock ownership, year-end bonuses, and a benefit package[14] Lincoln Electric still boasts outstanding productivity, quality, and employee loyalty, some 85 years after beginning its experiment. Other productivity improvement initiatives discussed in Chapter 9, such as work simplification and planned methods change, relied on some form of employee involvement. All these approaches were based on a multifunctional process that cut across boundaries of disciplines and organizational levels.

Statistical quality control (SQC), described more fully in Chapters 14 through 16, involves employees in quality measurement and improvement activities.

Many of the statistical quality control techniques developed at AT&T's Bell Labs in the 1930s by Drs. Shewhart, Dodge, and Romig, as well as others, were the result of group participation. The company's *Statistical Quality Control Handbook*—designed for operations-level people—was written in 1956 by a manufacturing engineering team. The book, which is still in print, has been and continues to be used in numerous companies for training in SQC basics.[15] The authors recommended continued use of a quality team that consisted of a manufacturing supervisor, a quality control manager, a manufacturing engineer, and a statistical clerk for coordination of quality improvement and control projects.

W. Edwards Deming's approach to quality was always grounded in statistical quality control concepts but with a visionary recognition that, to make quality happen, individuals and groups of managers and operating level employees had to be involved. During the 1940s, Deming gave the same series of courses on statistical quality control in the United States that he gave in Japan during the 1950s. The only difference was that top management and technicians attended the courses in Japan, while only quality control staff, engineers, and technicians attended the U.S. sessions.[16] The results of this difference in commitment are strikingly clear.

During the 1940s and through the 1960s, a number of work innovation experiments that focused on worker motivation and productivity took place. These behavioral experiments frequently, though not exclusively, relied on the use of group participation at the operating level to achieve organizational change. One of the most publicized cases of work innovation was the Weldon Company, a division of Harwood Manufacturing, a garment manufacturing firm. Weldon engaged in a multifaceted program to improve productivity and effectiveness by a combination of (1) improving personnel practices for hiring, training, and termination, (2) instituting group problem-solving sessions with first-line supervisors and employees, and (3) conducting attitude surveys and acting on results to make beneficial improvements.[17]

Texas Instruments (TI) instituted several work innovations in the 1960s. Most production employees in the firm participated in a work simplification training program. All the people from a given line were trained at the same time to encourage group interaction and problem solving. A performance review system that emphasized individual goal setting was established. An annual opinion survey was also implemented with samples of 10–25 percent of TI employees. This survey measured employee attitudes for each of the factors identified in the Herzberg motivation maintenance theory.

Walton listed large and small firms that were leaders in work innovation experiments in the 1960s and 1970s.[18] He named General Motors, Procter & Gamble, Exxon, General Foods, TRW, Cummins Engine, Butler Manufacturing, Mars, Inc., Citibank, Prudential Insurance, Donnelly Mirrors, and Eaton Corporation. From a review of work improvement experiments conducted over a 10-year period, he concluded that (1) most such experiments were neither extreme successes nor extreme failures, (2) such innovations must take into account the interrelation of techniques, outcomes, and corporate culture, and (3) work improvement efforts that have balanced goals of both productivity and quality of worklife improvement are the most likely to succeed. Along the same lines, Werther, Ruch, and McClure provided an excellent set of readings and interpretation of productivity issues, organizational improvements, and recent innovations.[19]

■ Modern Employee Involvement Approaches

Employee involvement typically falls along a continuum as shown in Table 11.1, which ranges from simple information sharing to total self-direction. As total quality matures in an organization, higher levels of employee involvement are evident. In today's complex organizations, individuals are often called on to shift roles from individual "followers," to leaders, to system architects and back to followers again in a relatively short time. Thus, individuals must develop the flexibility to engage in team-based projects at all these levels.

A number of different labels have been applied to various EI approaches used in organizations. Some of the broad behavioral management approaches for individual participation include "quality of worklife (QWL)," "humanization of work," "work reform," "work restructuring," "work design," and "sociotechnical systems." Terms used to designate team approaches include *QWL teams, productivity action teams (PATs), quality circles,* and *self-managed teams.*

■ Leading Practices

Total quality leaders employ several key practices to foster employee involvement in their organizations:

■ *They involve all employees at all levels and in all functions.* Tom Peters suggested involving everyone in everything, in such activities as quality and productivity improvement, measuring and monitoring results, budget development, new technology assessment, recruiting and hiring, making customer calls, and participating in customer visits.[20] Many companies found that having production workers visit customers is a great way to help employees understand their role in customer satisfaction. Companies such as Saturn have

TABLE 11.1 Levels of Employee Involvement

Level	Action	Primary Outcome
1. Information sharing	Managers decide, then inform employees	Conformance
2. Dialogue	Managers get employee input, then decide	Acceptance
3. Special problem solving	Managers assign a one-time problem to selected employees	Contribution
4. Intragroup problem solving	Intact groups meet weekly to solve local problems	Commitment
5. Intergroup problem solving	Cross-functional groups meet to solve mutual problems	Cooperation
6. Focused problem solving	Intact groups deepen daily involvement in a specific issue	Concentration
7. Limited self-direction	Teams at selected sites function full time with minimum supervision	Accountability
8. Total self-direction	Executives facilitate self-management in an all-team company	Ownership

SOURCE: Copyright © Jack D. Orsburn, Linda Moran, Ed Musselwhite, and John H. Zenger, *Self-Directed Work Teams* (Burr Ridge, IL: Business One Irwin, 1990), 34. All rights reserved.

work teams that perform many basic HRM functions, including hiring and performance review. FedEx has call-in opportunities on the corporate television network for employees to interact with management. GTE Directories chartered a team to determine how the company should measure quality improvement team effectiveness. The team discovered that inconsistent evaluation guidelines made it difficult to manage the process, so they developed specific and measurable guidelines emphasizing customer satisfaction, measurable results, cross-functional involvement, and initiative. Having employees rate the quality of suppliers' items is another way of participating and improving quality. Leading companies do whatever they can to encourage upward communication throughout the company, such as having roundtable meetings with managers and open-door policies.

■ *They use suggestion systems effectively to promote involvement and motivate employees.* General Motors established a suggestion system more than 50 years ago, and Cadillac believes that it is one of the secrets to their quality success. Cadillac commits to answering all suggestions within 24 hours; 70 percent of the suggestions they receive involve quality issues. Milliken either implements or rejects every suggestion within three days. Although they give no rewards, employees still submit suggestions. In 1989, Milliken implemented 87 percent of the over 262,000 suggestions that were submitted. Nearly every other recipient of the Malcolm Baldrige National Quality Award has well-established suggestion systems.

■ *They emphasize and support teamwork throughout the organization.* Teams encourage free-flowing participation and interaction among its members. FedEx has more than 4000 Quality Action teams; at least 60 percent of Cadillac employees are members of some team. Texas Instruments set a stretch goal in 1992 to have every employee be a member of at least one team by the year's end. Granite Rock, with fewer than 400 employees, has about 100 functioning teams, ranging from ten corporate quality teams to project teams, purchasing teams, task forces, and function teams composed of people who do the same job at different locations. Special efforts keep the teams relevant and make sure that no teams exist for the sake of having them. Eastman Chemical Company encourages its teams to develop objectives and measures that are integrated with company and organizational goals defined by the company's strategic planning process. Each supervisor belongs to at least two teams: the one made up of his or her direct reports, and the team led by his or her immediate supervisor. Besides these "interlocking" teams, Eastman uses cross-functional process improvement teams, process management teams, internal customer–supplier partnership teams, focus groups, safety meetings, and employee surveys to promote involvement.

■ *They monitor the extent and effectiveness of employee involvement.* Indicators such as the number of teams, rate of growth, percentage of employees involved, number of suggestions implemented, time to respond to suggestions, and team activities provide a basis for evaluation and improvement. Leading companies also conduct extensive employee opinion and effectiveness assessments to improve employee involvement processes.

INDIVIDUAL COMMITMENT AND PERSONAL QUALITY

Individual commitment is vital to employee involvement efforts. Commitment leads to employee actions and goals that support those of the organization. Committed employees often go beyond what they're asked or normally expected to do in order to uphold a corporate goal or improve the value of a product or service for a customer.

A good example of commitment involved a young girl who laid her dental retainer on a picnic table at Disney World while eating lunch.[21] She forgot about it until later in the day. The family returned to the spot, found the table cleaned up, and were at a loss as to what to do. They spotted a custodian, told him the problem, and the custodian sought permission from his supervisor to have the garbage bags searched by the night crew that evening! Two weeks later, the family received a letter from the supervisor explaining that they had been unable to locate the retainer, despite their best efforts.

Peters and Waterman pointed to psychological studies that say "we simultaneously seek self-determination and security."[22] Many TQM practices provide employees with the first half of this goal. Companies are asking employees to take more responsibility for acting as the point of contact between the organization and the customer, to be team players as part of EI teams that seek ways to improve systems for better production and more effective and efficient customer service. Yet, the trend toward corporate downsizing, reengineering, and other changes in the workplace, many of which are driven by financial results alone, make security increasingly uncertain. The "exchange rate" (see discussion on the equity theory of motivation in the previous chapter), by which employees are rewarded with either tangible rewards (such as pay or bonuses) or intangible rewards (such as promotions or job security), is increasingly being called into question.

These trends make the type of commitment shown by the Disney employees more difficult to attain. As Wyatt pointed out in *Fortune*, the contract between individuals and companies has shifted dramatically in the last five years.[23] Previously, employees in large, prosperous companies could expect the company to provide a more or less paternalistic culture with job security or even lifetime employment, career paths with steady advancement, defined benefit pension plans, offices with various amenities for each level of the hierarchy, a 9-to-5 workday, and annual performances reviews with standard pay raises. Now, the best companies can only provide opportunities for their employees in the form of candor and communication about the direction the business is going and how that may affect job security and careers. Career paths are being replaced by project experiences and lateral moves, and defined benefit pension plans are giving way to defined contribution plans. Telecommuting is fast replacing offices, and the 9-to-5 workday is insufficient for even those who want to keep up, let alone get ahead. Annual performance reviews are supplemented or replaced by peer reviews and a variety of frequent evaluations, and standard pay raises are giving way to various types of incentive plans, pay for performance, or pay for skill plans.

So how does a company gain commitment in these situations? Gary Dessler examined 10 companies that show extraordinary concern for their employees, such as Saturn Corporation, Delta Airlines, Ben and Jerry's Homemade, Inc., FedEx, and IBM, to determine how they deal with the commitment problem.[24] During the turbulent business environment of the 1990s, several of these firms have had to scrap long-standing policies such as "lifetime employment" due to serious financial setbacks. Nevertheless, Dessler suggested that they still have the capability to inspire commitment in their employees by following many of his eight "Keys to Commitment":

■ *People-first values:* a total management commitment to employees that includes such things as fair treatment, written policies, hiring and indoctrination processes, managers who "walk the talk" in everyday actions, and elimination of trust barriers such as timeclocks.

■ *Double-talk:* a catchy way of saying that communication must flow up the organization as well as down. One example is the "Speak-up" programs used by companies such as Toyota, FedEx, IBM, and others to give employees a chance to air complaints and clarify misunderstandings about vital organization changes that affect them.

■ *Communion:* efforts to encourage people to take pride and develop a sense of ownership and belonging in their organization. It includes such practices as value-based hiring (hiring people who have team values, for example), eliminating status differences between managers and line employees (such as executive dining rooms), employee recognition rituals, regular group contact meetings, and having profit-sharing and risk-sharing plans that apply to both executives and employees.

■ *Transcendental meditation:* articulation and development of the ideologies, missions, and values, and communication mechanisms they require. For example, Mary Kay cosmetics emphasizes the Golden Rule, family values, and truth, sincerity, and honesty in customer dealings. Ben & Jerry's openly supports various political and social causes. The Saturn Corporation has tried to show that a U.S. approach to teamwork can support the development and manufacture of world-class cars.

■ *Value-based hiring:* careful attention to the hiring process by articulating the corporate values carefully, advertising widely, thorough (often multilevel, multiphase) interviewing, realistic job previews, and rigorous training and early job assignments under sometimes adverse conditions.

■ *Securitizing:* lifetime employment without guarantees, which seems to be a contradiction in terms but indicates that the company will do whatever it can to maintain permanent employment security through such practices as cross-training, use of part-time and temporary workers, bonuses given only if the company is profitable, and "sharing the pain" by salary and work week reductions during economic downturns.

■ *Hard-side rewards:* pay plans that support employees and provide incentives for them to help themselves while they help the organization. Such practices include bonus systems, "at risk" portions of pay packages, benefit and pension plans that give employees the idea that they are valued for the long term, and self-reporting of time worked.

■ *Actualizing:* giving employees the opportunity and incentives to use a wide variety of skills and knowledge to accomplish their jobs. This "key" is derived from the top of Maslow's Hierarchy of Needs—self-actualization.

■ Making Quality Personal

The Rath & Strong survey, cited in the opening section of this chapter, focused on personal initiative. Personal initiative means taking action to spot and fix problems, contribute to a company's goals, and bring about change. The responsibility for action lies with the individual and refers to how one manages oneself. Personal initiative is different from empowerment, which places responsibility on the organization or leaders to get people to act. It is also different from leadership, which refers to how one manages others. Rath & Strong suggest that "focusing too heavily on leadership or empowerment can actually undermine an organization's ability to affect change. . . . Ultimately, it is the personal initiative of an organization's employees that is responsible for enabling the company to create and sustain true change." If employees can develop a personal commitment to quality, they will persist in tasks, do them better, and commit to the goals and objectives of the organization.

The concept of "personal quality" has been promoted by Harry V. Roberts, Professor Emeritus at the University of Chicago's Graduate School of Business, and Bernard F. Sergesketter, Vice President of the Central Region of AT&T.[25] Personal quality may be thought of as personal empowerment, and is implemented by systematically keeping personal checklists for quality improvement. It can also be implemented through using Pareto analysis to evaluate the results and focus on improvements in much the same way as continuous improvement discussed in Chapter 9.

Roberts and Sergesketter developed the idea of a *personal quality checklist* to keep track of personal shortcomings, or defects, in personal work processes. The authors defended the use of a checklist to keep track of defects:

> The word "defect" has a negative connotation for some people who would like to keep track of the times we do things right rather than times we do things wrong. Fortunately, most of us do things right much more than we do things wrong, so it is easier in practice to count the defects. Moreover, we can get positive satisfaction from avoiding defects—witness accident prevention programs that count days without accidents.

An example of a personal quality checklist developed to improve professorial activities is provided in Figure 11.1. It can be used as a starting point for developing a personal quality checklist (see Case II at the end of the chapter). Note that each item on the checklist has a desired result, a way to measure each type of defect, and a time frame. Both work and personal defect categories are listed on the sheet.

Sergesketter plotted defects that he observed during the first 18 months of his use of his own personal quality checklist on a run chart as shown in Figure 11.2. Many of the results were surprising.[26] For instance, he was surprised at the extent to which he was not returning phone calls the same day. He discovered that he had no way to count defects related to correspondence. As a result, he started to date stamp correspondence when it arrived and date stamp the file copy of the response. None of the items he measured was in the "four-minute mile" category, and yet he started out at a rate of 100 defects per month, but dropped drastically simply because he was aware of them. He also observed that when a person shares a defect list with others, they can help in reducing defects.

Showing such personal commitment to quality improvement is one of the key signs of leadership discussed in Chapter 6. As Sergesketter noted, "I encourage and challenge you to start counting defects. It is impossible to reduce defects if we don't count them, and we can't reasonably ask our associates to count defects if we don't! I really believe that if several thousand of us here in the Central Region start counting defects, we will reduce them and differentiate ourselves from our competitors in a significant way."

Personal quality is an essential ingredient to make quality happen in the workplace, yet it has been neglected for a long time in the development of the quality movement. Perhaps management, in particular, has operated under the idea that promoting quality is something that companies *do to* employees, rather than something they *do with* employees. Until we come to grips with the personal aspects of quality and make it something that is an everyday consideration and

FIGURE 11.1 An Example of a Personal TQM Checklist

Week of: _____

Defect Category	M	T	W	TH	F	S	SU	Total
Search for something misplaced or lost, over 20 min.								
Failure to discard incoming junk by end of day								
Putting a small task on the "hold" pile, over 2 hours								
Failure to respond to letter or phone call in 24 hours								
Lack of clarity in setting requirements/deadlines								
Excessive "general interest" reading; over 30 min./weekday								
Failure to provide weekly opportunity for feedback from a class								
Less than two hours of writing per day, 4 days/week								
Less than 8 hrs of sleep on a weeknight								
Less than 3 exercise periods/week								
Take wife out for 1 meal/week								
Less than 0.5 hr. meditation per weekday								

FIGURE 11.2 Chart of Number of Defects/Month

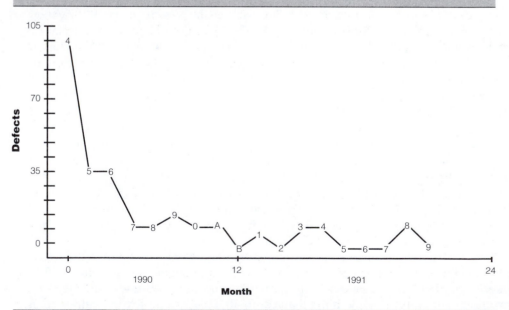

SOURCE: Harry V. Roberts and Bernard F. Sergesketter, *Quality Is Personal: A Foundation for Total Quality Management* (New York: The Free Press, 1993), 13.

a part of the way we do business, it is in constant danger of becoming a fad in every organization where it is tried. The good news is that, as Roberts and Sergesketter observed,

> Much of Deming's management philosophy is bound up in his famous 14 Points, which he advocates as a route for transformation of management. We found it interesting to see how a Personal Quality Checklist can aid one to understand what Deming is driving at in these points. To our surprise, we were able to trace valuable connections with all of them.

Perhaps in the daily attempt to bring about change in the individual parts of the organizational universe, managers, employees, professors, and students will find that personal quality is the key to unlock the door to a wider understanding of what TQM really is all about.

SUGGESTION SYSTEMS

Involving employees on a individual basis and increasing employee participation in quality improvement can be accomplished by many methods, including mentoring systems in which senior managers or employees counsel others at lower levels of the company, company newsletters, open-door policies of senior executives, employee surveys, and even video-based "town meetings" as done by FedEx. Perhaps the most refined form of individual participation for quality improvement is the suggestion system.

An employee suggestion system is a management tool for the submission, evaluation, and implementation of an employee's idea to save cost, increase quality, or improve other elements of work such as safety. Companies typically reward employees for implemented suggestions. At Toyota, for instance, employees generate nearly three million ideas each year—an average of 60 per employee—of which 85 percent are implemented by management. Cadillac asked teams of employees to tear apart the Seville and put it back together; they returned with 330 suggestions on how to improve it.

Fostering employee creativity has many benefits. Thinking makes even routine work enjoyable; writing down the suggestions improves workers' reasoning ability and writing skills. Satisfaction is the by-product of an implemented idea and a job made easier, safer, or better. Recognition for suggestions leads to higher levels of motivation, peer recognition, and possible monetary rewards. Workers gain an increased understanding of their work, which may lead to promotions and better interpersonal relationships in the workplace.

Suggestion systems, like most successful quality improvement methods, originated in the West but were refined in Japan. Most large Japanese firms and about half of the small and medium-sized firms have employee suggestion systems, which appear to be more extensive than those in the United States.[27] In fact, many U.S. plans have met with failure. One study found that about 90 percent of the suggestion plans begun in U.S. firms before 1977 have been abandoned.[28]

The relatively poor rates of participation in suggestion systems in the United States are due to a variety of reasons. (Experts estimate that the average number of suggestions per year made by U.S. employees in the automobile industry is about 0.1.) Most U.S. suggestion systems emphasize cost savings; it is the primary criterion for evaluation. U.S. systems favor significant, innovative ideas. Muse and Finster suggest that this focus effectively excludes fair consideration of suggestions that promise quality or productivity improvements over a longer period. Many employees perhaps feel they are unable to generate ideas that will save significant sums of money. Also, many managers typically take a passive approach, waiting for suggestions to be submitted. Additionally, many companies do not provide time for employees to develop suggestions during the regular work day, and employees are often unable to find time outside of their regular work schedules to develop ideas. A Swedish study found that the most common cause for withholding ideas is fear of a new time study and consequent loss of earnings or job security[29]

In addition to these reasons, the failure of many programs has also been attributed to

- unclear policies
- lack of continuous and enthusiastic promotion
- poor administration
- lack of management support

Suggestion systems in Japan are quite different. The Japanese modified U.S. suggestion systems to fit in their own culture, stressing participation and employee motivation over economic benefits. Japanese suggestion systems are similar to the kaizen concept: small, gradual, but continuous improvements. The number of suggestions per employee per year rose from about five to over 24 by 1987. In contrast, the average number of suggestions per employee in the United States was slightly more than one. The overall participation rate in Japan exceeds 65 percent, and many companies, such as Toyota, have participation rates above 90 percent, while that of typical U.S. firms is only about eight percent.[30]

Differences in suggestion systems between the United States and Japan have been attributed to several reasons. First, the suggestion process in Japan is included in formal training sessions and involves continual guidance from supervisors. Most U.S. systems revolve around a few posters or suggestion boxes. Second, management support in the United States is generally less than enthusiastic, in direct contrast to that in Japan. Third, American unions have not supported programs, especially if some jobs are at risk. In Japan, however, unions are company-based; thus any activity that is good for the company is good for the union and its employees. Finally, the group-centered culture in Japan facilitates cooperation rather than individual competition.

Suggestion systems should not simply be empty boxes for ideas; they must be carefully planned and executed. Management should encourage submissions with no restrictions, acknowledge all of them and respond promptly, evaluate the suggestions carefully, reward employees, and monitor suggestions that are implemented. Employees also need training in how to identify problems and develop solutions (see Chapter 9). Table 11.2 summarizes strategies that can foster the success of suggestion systems.

TEAMWORK

A **team** is a small number of people with complementary skills who are committed to a common purpose, set of performance goals, and approach for which

TABLE 11.2 Success Factors for Suggestion Systems

1. Ensure that management, first and foremost, is involved in the program. Involvement should begin at the top and filter down through all levels until all employees participate.

2. Push decision making regarding suggestion evaluation to lower levels.

3. Gain union support by pledging no layoffs due to productivity gains from adopted suggestions.

4. Train everyone in all facets of the suggestion system. Improve problem-solving capability by promoting creative problem solving through the use of the seven basic statistical tools.

5. Resolve all suggestions within one month.

6. Encourage all suggestors to personally describe their idea to a supervisor, engineer, or manager.

7. Promote pride in work, and quality and productivity gains from suggestions, rather than the big cash awards possible.

8. Remove ceilings on intangible suggestion awards. Revise evaluations of intangible suggestions to value them more on par with tangible suggestions.

9. Eliminate restrictions prohibiting suggestions regarding a worker's immediate work area.

10. Continuously promote the suggestion program, especially through supervisor support.

11. Trust employees enough to make allowances for generation, discussion, and submittal of suggestions during work hours.

12. Keep the program simple.

SOURCE: Muse and Finster, "A Comparison of Employee Suggestion Systems in Japan and the USA," University of Wisconsin Working Paper (1989).

they hold themselves mutually accountable.[31] Although organizations have traditionally been formed around task or work groups, the concept of teams and teamwork has taken on a new meaning in a TQM environment. Teams provide opportunities to individuals to solve problems that they may not be able to solve on their own. Teams may perform a variety of problem-solving activities, such as determining customer needs, developing a flowchart to study a process, brainstorming to discover improvement opportunities, selecting projects, recommending corrective actions, and tracking the effectiveness of solutions. Teams may also assume many traditional managerial functions. For example, an assembly team at GM's Saturn plant interviews and hires its own workers, approves parts from suppliers, chooses its equipment, and handles its own budget. Effective teams are goal-centered, independent, open, supportive, and empowered.

The central role of teams, and the need for such team skills as cooperation, interpersonal communications, cross-training, and group decision making, represents a fundamental shift in how the work of public and private organizations is performed in the United States and most countries in the Western world. Results from an ASQC/Gallup telephone survey in 1993 of 1293 randomly selected full-time employed adults showed the prevalence and impact of teamwork.[32] Eight out of ten employees reported that some type of team activities are taking place at work, and two out of three employees participated in team activities. Forty percent of those surveyed said that quality was the major goal of the teamwork; 22 percent said that efficiency and productivity was the major goal; 18 percent indicated that profitability or cost reduction was the goal; and 25 percent reported other or "don't know" goals. Employees who participate in team activities or who work in organizations that have formal quality improvement initiatives were found to feel more empowered, were more satisfied with the rate of improvement in quality in their companies, and were far more likely to have received training on both job-related and problem-solving/team-building skills. In fact, Dimock observes that a team "is a social system with its own structure and culture. Once a structure and culture are established, they may be fairly difficult to change and studies have shown it is often easier to start up a new group than to get an existing group to change."[33]

Many types of teams exist in different companies and industries. Among the most common are:

- *Quality Circles:* teams of workers and supervisors that meet regularly to address workplace problems involving quality and productivity.

- *Problem-Solving Teams:* teams whose members gather to solve a specific problem and then disband.

- *Management Teams:* teams consisting mainly of managers from various functions like sales and production that coordinate work among teams.

- *Work Teams:* teams organized to perform entire jobs, rather than specialized, assembly line-type work. When work teams are empowered, they are called *self-managed teams.*

- *Virtual Teams:* relatively new, these team members communicate by computer, take turns as leaders, and jump in and out as necessary.[34]

Work teams and quality circles typically are intraorganizational; that is, members usually come from the same department or function. Management teams, problem-solving teams, and virtual teams are cross-functional; they work on specific tasks or processes that cut across boundaries of several different departments regardless of their organizational home. Self-managed teams are the most advanced concept in teamwork. They are complex and vary a great deal in how they are structured and how they function. Self-managed teams are discussed further later in this section.

Problem solving drives the team concept. Figure 11.3 illustrates the process by which teams commonly operate. The three basic functions are to identify, analyze, and solve quality and productivity problems. The methodology is a process of creative problem solving as discussed in Chapter 9. Problem-solving techniques are taught to members by team leaders with the assistance of a facilitator, who is a full-time or part-time resource person.

One example of the power of teamwork is New York Life.[35] Throughout the New York Life organization, teams with such innovative names as Hot Pursuit, Watch Dogs, Just the Fax, French Connection, and Raiders of the Lost Transactions are streamlining operations. One of the most successful efforts was the work of an 18-person team formed to determine why 7000 letters a week—primarily premium notices—were being returned by the Post Office as "undeliverable." Called the Gravediggers because of their purpose of digging up addresses, the team, composed of employees from around the country, met weekly via teleconferences. Using problem-solving approaches, they discovered root causes such as policyholders moving and forgetting to notify the company; addresses that did not fit into the mailing envelope windows; addresses on applications that were difficult to read; and inadequate procedures for locating more accurate addresses. After implementing a variety of corrective measures, the volume of returned mail was reduced by more than 20 percent and saved over $600,000 through bar coding and sorting.

Another example is the platform team approach to automotive vehicle development introduced by Chrysler.[36] This cross-functional team approach brings together professionals from engineering, design, quality, manufacturing, business planning, program management, purchasing, sales, marketing, and finance

FIGURE 11.3   Functions of Employee Involvement Teams

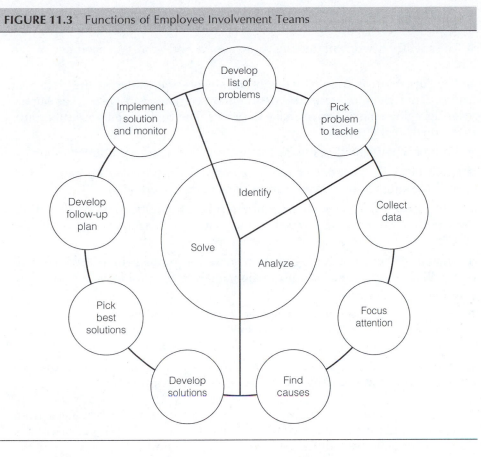

to work together to bring a new vehicle to market. The Dodge Viper, introduced in 1992, and the 1993 Jeep Grand Cherokee tested this approach and led to the development of the Chrysler Concorde, Dodge Intrepid, and Eagle Vision in just 39 months, not only on time and under budget, but exceeding 230 product excellence targets.

The team concept in quality was developed and refined through quality circles in Japan and evolved to powerful self-managed teams today. The next two sections present these two types of team approaches.

■ Quality (Control) Circles

The term **quality control circles (QCCs)** was coined in Japan in the early 1960s and brought to the United States in the early 1970s. After five years, the concept finally began to blossom in the United States. QCCs blend participative management approaches with classical problem solving, work simplification, and statistical quality control techniques to improve productivity as well as quality. The term *quality control circles* was shortened to *quality circles (QCs)*, which is in common use in the United States.

A **quality circle** is a small group of employees from the same work area who meet regularly and voluntarily to identify, solve, and implement solutions to work-related problems. Quality circles have some unique characteristics:

■ Quality circles are small groups, ranging from four to 15 members. Eight members is considered the norm.

■ All members come from the same shop or work area, which gives the circle its identity.

■ The members work under the same supervisor, who is a member of the circle.

■ The supervisor is usually, though not always, the leader of the circle. As leader, he or she moderates discussion and promotes consensus. The supervisor does not issue orders or make decisions. The circle members, as a group, make their own decisions.

■ Voluntary participation means that everyone has an opportunity to join.

■ Circles usually meet once every week on company time, with pay, and in special meeting rooms removed from their normal work area.

■ Circle members receive training in the rules of quality circle participation, the mechanics of running a meeting and making management presentations, and techniques of group problem solving.

■ Circle members, not management, choose the problems and projects that they will address, collect all information, analyze the problems, and develop solutions.

■ Technical specialists and management assist circles with information and expertise whenever asked to do so. Circles receive advice and guidance from an adviser who attends all meetings but is not a circle member.

■ Management presentations are given to those managers and technical specialists who would normally make the decision on a proposal.[37]

As mentioned earlier, the quality circle concept as defined here evolved from the quality control circles developed in Japan in the 1960s.[38] Quality control circles were an outgrowth of the postwar education effort in Japan. Prior to the visits of Deming and Juran, U.S. engineers worked with the Japanese to improve production methods, particularly in the development of high-quality communications equipment. Initially, quality training was limited to engineers and middle-level supervisors. This selectivity resulted from the traditional American way of thinking regarding division of labor but was in direct contrast to the Japanese philosophy of relying on production workers for creative ideas. Japanese manufacturers considered quality control to be the responsibility of all employees, including management and line workers. In Japan, foremen are considered to be "working supervisors," who are much closer to the workers than in the United States. Not only were top and middle managers attending seminars, but supervisors were being trained in basic quality concepts using nationwide radio broadcasts. Copies of the texts for quality control courses were sold on newsstands across the country. The push for quality was truly a national priority, and the results were dramatic.

This quality improvement effort and the cultural bias toward group activity resulted in the formation of the quality control circle concept, attributed to Dr. Kaoru Ishikawa, of the University of Tokyo. The initial growth of quality circles in Japan was phenomenal. The Union of Japanese Scientists and Engineers (JUSE) estimated that registration in quality circles grew from 400 members in 1962 to 200,000 members in 1968 to more than 700,000 members in 1978. Today, millions of workers are involved. Main cited results of recent surveys that estimated there were 743,000 circles in Japan in 1988, and that JUSE alone had 350,000 circles registered in 1992.[39]

Quality circle concepts were not only known but also used by some U.S. firms in the late 1960s according to existing evidence.[40] The quality of worklife programs developed in the early 1960s were related to circle concepts but tended to emphasize behavioral interventions, reorganization of groups or tasks, or efforts to build or enhance morale. The quality circle movement became established and began to grow when a team of managers for Lockheed Missiles and Space Division in California made a trip to Japan in 1973 to view quality control circles in action. A manufacturing manager for Lockheed, Wayne S. Rieker, headed this team of six managers who visited eight Japanese firms and returned with an enthusiastic report about the use of quality circle programs there.

After the success of the Lockheed program became known, many other manufacturing firms—including Westinghouse, General Electric, Cincinnati Milacron, Ford Motor Company, Dover Corporation, and Coors Beer Company—established quality circle programs or began using similar team problem-solving approaches. Later, service organizations such as hospitals, school systems, and state and federal governmental units started their quality circle programs.

In 1977, the International Association of Quality Circles (IAQC), now the Association for Quality and Participation (AQP), was formed. Evidence of the increasing importance of QC teams in the United States can be measured partly by attendance at the annual IAQC conference and in membership growth. According to a brochure produced by the association, conference attendance grew from 150 to 2700 registrants in the six years from 1978 through 1983.[41] During this same period, membership grew from 200 to 6000. During this time the word *control* was dropped from "quality control circles" and the standard designation of "quality circles" was established in the United States.

An extensive survey of 532 members of the IAQC (now AQP) provides insights into the nature of quality circle programs in the United States in the mid-1980s.[42] The survey responses covered a wide variety of manufacturing, service, government, and other organizations that had, or were planning to start, quality circle programs. The major purpose of the study was to analyze factors that contributed to effective versus less effective quality circle programs. Effectiveness factors were narrowed to three, including (1) size relationships, (2) savings-to-cost ratios, and (3) program factors. Effectiveness was defined primarily in terms of benefit-to-cost ratios. Large organizations with the most effective programs were in nonmanufacturing environments. Large organizations had a higher proportion of staff specialists who worked with quality circles and tended to have the longest-running quality circle programs.

Concerning savings/cost ratios, average annual savings per program was estimated to be $438,730, while average annual costs per program were estimated to be $132,300. This gives a benefit/cost ratio of about 3.3 to 1. Average savings per circle member were estimated at $1788, and average costs were $614. The benefit/cost ratio is estimated here at about 2.9 to 1. The two sets of figures do not yield the same ratio, because not all survey respondents responded to all questions on costs and savings.

The maturity of the program was directly related to the program's financial success—the older the program, the higher the per-member savings. Interestingly, 75 percent of the programs in the highest success category had per-circle-member costs of less than $400 and a 6:1 or higher benefit cost ratio.

Today, the term *quality circles* has become less popular as the notion of employee involvement has broadened in scope. However, the importance of QC-type teams should not be downplayed. One Cincinnati-area company with about

500 workers that still uses QC-type teams reported that they had received more than 10,000 suggestions from individuals and teams over an eight-year time span—an average of 2.5 suggestions per worker per year, with more than 70 percent of the suggestions having been implemented.

Quality circles are still strong in Japan as indicated by Main's 1988 survey, cited earlier.[43] Toyota, for example, uses the problem-solving skills of circles and engineers to their advantage. When Toyota found that 50 percent of its warranty losses were caused by 120 large problems and 4000 small problems, the set of large problems were assigned to their engineers. The set of small problems were given to their quality circles.[44]

■ Self-Managed Teams

Today, many companies are moving beyond the traditional team approaches to problem solving and decision making by adopting the self-managed team (SMT), or self-directed work team concept. In this participative management approach, employees are encouraged to take on many of the roles formerly held only by management. The emphasis on quality and improvement shifts from a passive, management-initiated process to a highly active, independent one.

A **self-managed team (SMT)** is defined as "a highly trained group of employees, from 6 to 18, on average, fully responsible for turning out a well-defined segment of finished work. The segment could be a final product, like a refrigerator or ball bearing; or a service, like a fully processed insurance claim. It could also be a complete but intermediate product or service, like a finished refrigerator motor, an aircraft fuselage, or the circuit plans for a television set."[45]

The SMT concept was developed in Britain and Sweden in the 1950s. One of the early companies to adopt SMTs was Volvo, the Swedish auto manufacturer. Pioneering efforts in SMT development were made by Procter & Gamble in 1962 and by General Motors in 1975. These U.S. developments were concurrent with the Japanese quality team developments that, in many cases, cannot be classified as true SMTs because of their limited autonomy. SMTs began to gain popularity in the United States in the late 1980s.

A 1991 study of workgroups in 22 manufacturing facilities in the United States and Canada showed a widespread use of SMTs.[46] SMTs were used in many industries, including food processing, auto-related businesses, petrochemicals, the glass industry, and other miscellaneous industries. The age of the teams ranged from one to 17 years. The average age was six years, and over half of the companies studied had established SMTs only within the past five years. Of the 22 cases studied, 15 (68 percent) established SMTs primarily for economic reasons (that is, to increase productivity, reduce costs, or improve product quality). Of these 15, four (all unionized) were established in response to threatened plant closures. Six of the cases (27 percent) established them primarily to improve the work environment or to increase employee satisfaction. One company adopted a team system specifically to avoid a union (ironically, that plant was organized a year after it opened and has remained union since).

SMTs exhibited the following characteristics:

■ They are empowered to share various management and leadership functions.

■ They plan, control, and improve their own work processes.

■ They set their own goals and inspect their own work.

- They often create their own schedules and review their performance as a group.
- They may prepare their own budgets and coordinate their work with other departments.
- They usually order materials, keep inventories, and deal with suppliers.
- They frequently are responsible for acquiring any new training they might need.
- They may hire their own replacements or assume responsibility for disciplining their own members.
- They take responsibility for the quality of their products and services.[47]

A good example of an SMT in action is found at AT&T Credit Corp.[48] In most financial companies, the jobs in the back offices consist of processing applications, claims, and customer accounts. These jobs are similar to manufacturing assembly lines: dull and repetitive. The division of labor into small tasks and the organization of work by function are characteristic of many service organizations. At AT&T Credit Corp., which was established in 1985 to provide financing for customers who lease equipment, for example, one department handled applications and checked the customer's credit standing, a second drew up contracts, and a third collected payments. No one person had responsibility for providing full service to a customer.

The company president recognized these drawbacks and decided to hire his own employees and give them ownership and accountability of the process. Although his first concern was to increase efficiency, his approach also provided more rewarding jobs as an additional benefit. In 1986, the company set up 11 teams of 10 to 15 newly hired workers in a high-volume division serving small business. The three major lease processing functions were combined in each team. The company also divided its national staff of field agents into seven regions and assigned two or three teams to handle business from each region. In this way, the same teams always worked with the same sales staff, establishing a personal relationship with them and their customers. Above all, team members took responsibility for solving customers' problems. Their slogan became, "Whoever gets the call owns the problem."

Members make most decisions on how to deal with customers, schedule their own time off, reassign work when people are absent, and interview prospective new employees. The teams process up to 800 lease applications daily versus half that amount under the old system, and have reduced the time for final credit approvals from several days to 24–48 hours.

Organizations consider self-directed teams for several reasons. First, such teams facilitate continuous improvement. Second, teams provide greater flexibility. They communicate more effectively, find better solutions, and implement recommendations more quickly than conventional approaches. Third, as organizations become flatter, self-directed teams can assume the decision-making powers relinquished by managers who have been eliminated. Finally, as the U.S. work force becomes more educated, self-directed teams offer employees a higher level of involvement and job satisfaction.

SMTs have achieved many positive results. In a Mercedes-Benz plant, defects were reduced by 50 percent. A study of 22 manufacturing plants using SMTs found that more than half of them made improvements in quality and productivity, removed at least one layer of management or supervision, and decreased their levels of grievances, absenteeism, and turnover.[49]

Too few objective studies of SMTs and other EI programs have been performed, which sounds a universal warning concerning their results. Also, those results that have been reported are frequently biased because of contamination with other improvement processes taking place in the same facility and/or the desire of those reporting the results to cast a favorable light on their efforts.

IMPLEMENTING EMPLOYEE INVOLVEMENT PROGRAMS

Quality circles as a formal concept can rightfully be labeled a fad of the 1980s. A number of articles written in the 1990s criticized the quality circle movement, branding it as a limited success or an outright failure.[50] However, many failures of quality circle programs have been based on management's false hopes of finding a panacea for all of the ills that plagued U.S. businesses in the 1970s. In essence, management believed that quality circles represented a quick fix without providing their full support and commitment. As expounded in the Deming philosophy, inadequate funding of the program, lack of proper training, resistance of staff or middle managers, and lack of proposal implementation by management are all elements of the system of management beyond the control of the workers. Under such circumstances, workers quickly lose interest and initiative.

In a study of quality and productivity improvement in two plants of a U.S. manufacturer of sausage casings, researchers discovered that the use of quality circles to deal with a problem of wire clips lost in the production process in one plant was superior to a "self-monitoring" approach applied to the same problem by workers in another plant.[51] Not only did the plant using quality circles show significant improvement in performance, but it experienced accompanying improvements in absenteeism and lost work time measures. The authors felt the need to defend the positive results found in their study in the face of much criticism of QC programs. They pointed out several factors that they believed led to poorly designed QC programs in the United States including:

■ Quality circles started out as a program designed to aid in improving quality and productivity in Japan and ended up being billed as a QWL program in the United States.

■ The idea of Deming's approach was to make powerful statistical quality control techniques and ideas available to every employee at every level and to make quality part of everyone's job. The American approach has been to set up a separate program under the control of nonline personnel, such as staff people from the human resources department.

■ Under the direction of HRM-oriented staff, the dominant theoretical orientation is not Deming's, but a blend of Maslow, Herzberg, and McGregor, thus stressing self-actualization, communication, and employee development, rather than measurable improvements in quality and productivity.

■ Sufficient reinforcement has not been built into the typical QC program for line management, middle management, facilitators, or participants to become strong supporters and believers in the process. Specifically, line management has frequently been asked to become involved without having adequate training as to how to shift responsibilities and redesign their own jobs. Middle managers have been asked for support, but have not been rewarded for or kept informed about the results of their efforts. Quality circle facilitators have frequently found that they are in a dead-end job, with no path to move up in the organization. Participants have found that their ideas were listened to, but only implemented after a long delay, if at all.[52]

The conclusion, then, is that the success of quality circles and similar employee involvement programs is situational and highly sensitive to management commitment and implementation strategies. If the organization is not ready to make changes and to struggle with the problems and opportunities of the philosophy, they will probably be dissatisfied with the results. If such an organization can develop patience, learn from its mistakes, and make evolutionary improvements, an EI approach will probably pay dividends in the long run.

In all fairness to management, failures can also be attributed to the teams themselves. For example, members may not be able to learn adequately the necessary problem-solving or group process skills. They may fail to reach agreement on problems to address or may propose inadequate solutions. Ideas may be poorly presented. Group versus nongroup friction, running out of ideas, and pressure for financial rewards for improvements suggested by groups may arise. If the EI program begins to decline, it can be killed by cynicism about the program and a terminal case of burnout.[53] Thus, EI programs should be monitored and controlled to determine the benefits that are derived and to decide whether to modify them.

◼ Planning for Employee Involvement

Fairly standard procedures exist for establishing EI team programs and training participants. Because any employee involvement program requires a major commitment to organizational change by management and workers, it is likely to fail unless a systems viewpoint is taken. Figure 11.4 illustrates the process of planning and implementing EI programs.

Jumping into EI approaches without adequate planning is an invitation to disaster. Initially, a company should engage in a period of investigation, reflection, and soul searching before buying into the concept of EI. Organizations begin by understanding the history and philosophy of EI. By learning how Japanese and American firms performed and the different types of teams that can be formed, an organization is in a better position to be its own expert rather than having to rely on the confusing, and sometimes contradictory, insights found in any single source written about the topic. Many companies rush out and form the wrong kind of teams for a specific job. For example, quality circle-type teams cannot achieve the same type of results as a cross-functional problem-solving team or a self-managed team.

After gathering background information, managers should examine their organization's goals, objectives, and culture to evaluate readiness to install EI programs. This step may be the most difficult portion of the process, because it requires a hard self-appraisal of the organization as a whole. One enthusiastic manager can often get teams going, but solid support of a number of managerial levels is necessary to keep them going. Managers should then analyze the work required. Teams take a lot of maintenance, and if the work can be done faster and better by a single person, then they should not be used.

Establishing a supportive culture for EI is crucial. A good example of laying the proper groundwork is Mack Trucks, Inc., as present in an editorial by Elios Pascual in the *Wall Street Journal*, which follows.

FIGURE 11.4 A Process Model for Establishing EI Programs

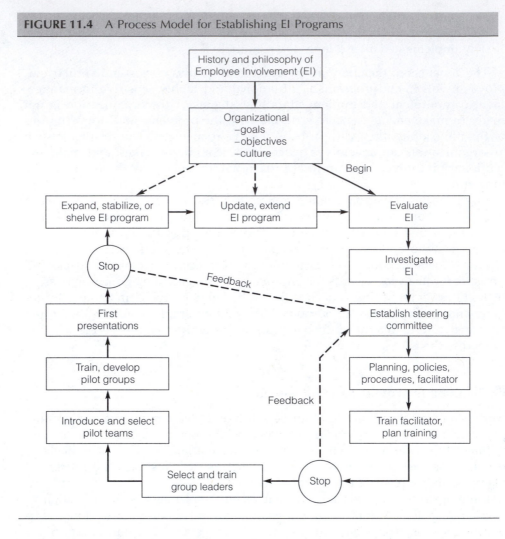

Mack Learns the Error of False Pride

Few traits can be as important to a company—or under the wrong conditions, as dangerous—as pride. When built on a foundation of excellent quality and service, pride can be the best of motivators. But if the foundation starts to deteriorate, the same pride can blind people to the need for radical change.

Perhaps no company better illustrates this truism than the company at which I work, Mack Trucks, Inc. The Mack name and the bulldog mascot are among the best recognized trademarks in the world. We say something's "Built like a Mack truck" when it's built to last.

A key to our reputation had always been the intense pride that Mack employees took in being part of the team that produced these quality vehicles, and their hard work paid off in a company that as recently as 1980 held more than 20 percent of the North American heavy-duty truck market and employed some 17,000 people.

But in the late 1980s, Mack's well-known slogans were beginning to ring hollow. Our quality was suffering, but we didn't know how badly because we weren't really measuring it. Our pride had deteriorated into arrogance that blinded us to the severity of our situation. By 1989, North American market penetration had dipped to 13 percent and employment had plummeted to 6500. That same year, the company lost $185 million—the first in a string of nearly five years in the red.

Perhaps the most important reason for this drop was the disappearance of the kind of teamwork that had built the company. Mack had become tied into the segregated, departmental organization that had discouraged people from talking to one another. The disconnection and frustration were apparent everywhere—from suppliers to employees. At one point, some 1200 partially assembled trucks at the company's Winnsboro, South Carolina plant had to be parked in nearby fields awaiting parts. Labor relations were so bad that when the new general manager of Mack's Macungie, Pennsylvania, assembly facility toured the plant on his first day on the job in 1990, an angry employee threw a bolt at him.

By 1991, the company was hovering near bankruptcy and we needed teamwork more than ever. It was at that point that we decided that unless we got everyone involved in the game, the game would soon be over.

Our first steps were somewhat symbolic. Sacred cows like the executive dining room were closed. Also gone was the restricted access to the executive floor and the private aircraft that shuttled Mack executives across the country.

But more substantive changes followed. Chief among them was an entirely new management team, unified by an effort to turn our employees from spectators into players. The first stsep was to convince them of the urgency of our situation. We began with the leadership of the United Auto Workers, our employees' largest union. We gave them a detailed honest assessment of our quality problems and perilous financial situation, and told them we needed their help.

Next, we took our message to the employee population as a whole. We sent out bulletins on personnel changes, our market position, our financial situation, and our priorities for internal improvements. Company managers attended open meetings in which we were given performance indicators and strategy guidelines to take back to their staffs. These meetings were supplemented with detailed monthly performance fact sheets posted at all the facilities.

But we still needed to get our players on the field—to make sure that the work process engendered genuine pride. To put this strategy into action, we focused on the development of dedicated teams. Since 1991, nearly 400 employee teams have been formed to study and improve everything from workstation design to order-cycle times; from clutch assembly to corporate culture.

Some of our most important initial work was done by Demerit Action Groups—employee teams charged with systematically auditing a vehicle's quality as it comes off the line, tracking down the cause of any "demerit," and implementing solutions. Since these audits began in 1990, we have reduced the average number of demerits by nearly 80 percent. And as the market once confirmed our quality problems, it is now confirming our quality improvements—warranty claims are down 53 percent from only three years ago.

As we've managed this change, we've learned that some of the easiest things to do are the most effective. For instance, when we began to evaluate our productivity, we included the UAW leadership in the same training sessions that our manufacturing engineers attended, so everyone had the same playbook and was dealing with the same knowledge base.

In our Macungie plant the line is stopped every day at 10:30 a.m. for a five minute staff meeting in which employees can ask about anything that is on their minds. If their immediate supervisor can't answer the question on the spot, he makes sure the question is answered within 24 hours.

There's more to this emphasis on teamwork and employee involvement than just good feelings. Since 1990, we've reduced the number of hours required to build a truck by 41 percent, and slashed in half both our inventories as a percentage of net sales and our break-even sales point. In 1993, we increased our U.S. market share and posted a sales increase of 38.5 percent, outpacing a market that increased 32.7 percent. And in April, we held celebrations in all our locations and took out a full-page ad in local papers to thank employees for boosting Mack into the black for the first time in nearly five years.

Employee teams have restored the right kind of pride to the Mack organization—pride built on a foundation of measurable achievements, absent any arrogance. That pride helped us to accelerate the steady improvement in our global performance, prepare for the next market downturn, and take full advantage of the opportunities the future is sure to bring.

(Mr. Pascual is chairman, president, and chief executive officer of Mack Trucks Inc., based in Allentown, Pennsylvania.)[54]

Most organizations benefit by establishing a steering committee made up of a group of interested, committed line and staff managers and, if a union exists, a union representative. The steering committee establishes initial policies and procedures for the EI program and chooses a person or persons to be the facilitator(s). Once first-line operative, clerical, or other candidate team members are given an introduction to team concepts, they are offered an opportunity to join a team.

If employees choose to join the team, they are given eight to 16 hours of initial or concurrent training before or during the first few group meetings. Usually, the facilitator or group leader will conduct the training. EI teams are taught to use brainstorming and the "Seven QC Tools" for problem solving, which were discussed at length in Chapter 9, as well as skills in presentation techniques and group leadership and motivation. Presentation skills are useful in presenting reports of solved problems to management; presentations are usually informal and serve to increase members' self-esteem. Leadership skills such as discussion leading, active listening, and role playing are taught as aids to enhance the effectiveness of team meetings. Failure to provide adequate training and other support, such as work design changes, electronic mail, and so on, leads to frustration in individuals who wonder why they are even on a team.

Peter Scholtes, a leading authority on teams for quality improvement, suggested 10 ingredients for a successful team:

1. *Clarity in team goals.* As a sound basis, a team agrees on a mission, purpose, and goals.

2. *An improvement plan.* A plan guides the team in determining schedules and mileposts by helping the team decide what advice, assistance, training, materials, and other resources it may need.

3. *Clearly defined roles.* All members must understand their duties and know who is responsible for what issues and tasks.

4. *Clear communication.* Team members should speak with clarity, listen actively, and share information.

5. *Beneficial team behaviors.* Teams should encourage members to use effective skills and practices to facilitate discussions and meetings.

6. *Well-defined decision procedures.* Teams should use data as the basis for decisions and learn to reach consensus on important issues.

7. *Balanced participation.* Everyone should participate, contribute their talents and share commitment to the team's success.

8. *Established ground rules.* The group outlines acceptable and unacceptable behaviors.

9. *Awareness of group process.* Team members exhibit sensitivity to nonverbal communication, understand group dynamics, and work on group process issues.

10. *Use of the scientific approach.* With structured problem-solving processes, teams can more easily find root causes of problems.[55]

Overcoming Resistance to Change

Even though the advantages of employee involvement are clear to the enlightened, many individuals resist change. Managers will not allow participation because it entails sharing power with employees. Low-level supervisors, whose interests tend to be ignored in EI, often fight it. Worker resistance is fostered by past management credibility problems and the "fad of the month" syndrome. Unions naturally resist such efforts, reading in ulterior motives of making employees work harder and trying to break up the union. Resistance to EI is driven by fear—fear of reprisal by management, fear of providing information, fear of change, fear of failure, fear of giving up control—as reflected in one of Deming's 14 Points. Fear limits the potential of people, and hence restricts the products and productivity of an organization.

Keys to overcoming resistance are early involvement by all parties, open and honest dialogue, and good planning. Management holds the key, however, as the organizational leaders. They must believe in workers and their ability to contribute. Managers, as leaders, must also show commitment to the practices of EI, such as training, rewards, and recognitions. Some specific suggestions include:

■ Design the change process to include significant management involvement in its implementation.

■ Create significant dissatisfaction with the status quo, stimulating a need for change. (For many companies, the crisis is usually there.)

■ Provide support to raise comfort levels with the new concepts.

■ Be consistent in the pursuit of participative management, continuously modeling the desired behavior.

■ Be intolerant of insubordination, and deal immediately and decisively with flagrant resisters.[56]

Transition to Self-Managed Teams

Self-managed teams represent the greatest challenge because they incorporate empowerment. Organizations that have SMTs have typically arrived at them through one of two routes—organizational start-up with SMTs in place, or transformations from more limited team structures. The latter is often a next logical step after other types of employee involvement programs have reached maturity.

Donovan outlined seven steps for the design of SMTs during a transition from a quality circle-type of program.[57] He recommended the establishment of a design team to analyze and change the work system of individual tasks, team tasks, and support functions. The steps involved include:

1. *Create a work unit responsible for an entire task.* This step requires defining a whole work unit based on identifying a customer, establishing a means of contact between the team and customer, and establishing the standard for the product or service.

2. *Establish specific measures of the work unit's output.* Establishing meaningful measures includes defining standards for outputs in terms of quality, quantity, cost, and timeliness, together with accountability and a feedback system.

3. *Design multiskilled jobs.* A systematic study of workflow functions and variances is followed by redesign of the jobs to enhance the development of multiple skills.

4. *Create internal management and coordination tasks.* The coordination of tasks of the work team, typically handled by managers in a conventional organization, is handled by the team and covers items such as scheduling, task assignments, hiring of new members, and cross-functional training, which must be addressed by designers and by the team itself.

5. *Create boundary management tasks.* Processes and procedures must be established to coordinate with managers, other departments, suppliers, and customers outside of the group.

6. *Establish access to information.* The group defines the information needed and the design of the processes, hardware, and software necessary to obtain direct, accurate, and timely performance-related feedback and information.

7. *Establish support systems.* The work team addresses consideration of how the teams are to be supported and involves the "hows" of training, career progression (based on skills developed and used), team interfacing with management, and payments and rewards.

The design process used in transforming an existing organization to a self-managed team approach does not appear to be considerably different from that used for development of a start-up work team organizational structure with one exception. Lazes and Falkenberg found that eight of eleven transformed plants had used shop floor-level workers on their design teams, while shop floor representatives were not generally included on the design team for start-up plants.[58] In summary, careful, systematic planning for both work design and coordination issues is apparently crucial to successful introduction of self-managed teams.

A study conducted by Development Dimensions International, the Association for Quality and Participation, and *Industry Week*, identified four key factors associated with successful SMTs.[59] First, the longer teams have been in place, the more positive are the reported results. This observation suggests that higher benefits occur with time, and that companies need to be patient. Second, a direct positive correlation could be made between the extent of job rotation and the reported results, which suggests that teams with a more complete understanding of their processes and business have a greater impact on quality and productivity. Third, effective leadership of supervisors and group leaders in providing direction, resources, and business information; coaching teams; and recognizing contributions led to increased member satisfaction, quality, and productivity. Finally, teams with responsibility for both production and personnel tasks reported the most positive results. These factors provide important guidelines for organizations that plan on using SMTs.

EVALUATING EMPLOYEE INVOLVEMENT AND HUMAN RESOURCE PRACTICES

Because many activities of EI programs are intangible and difficult to measure, EI program coordinators and facilitators have generally avoided setting up an explicit assessment and measurement systems. Despite the difficulties of measurement, the reasons why it should be performed are many, including the need to convince management to institute EI activities, to convince management and workers to continue to support EI efforts, to justify the allocation of resources to support efforts, and to determine ways to improve team effectiveness and efficiency.

Assessing the impact of EI and team activities can be accomplished in many ways. Both outcome and process measures provide data by which to assess EI effectiveness. Outcome measures might include cost savings, productivity improvements, defect rate reduction, customer satisfaction improvements, cycle time reductions, and employee turnover. One organization tracks team progress and effectiveness by periodically summarizing, for each team project, the number of suggested improvements, number of improvements implemented, percent implemented, baseline quality measure, percent change in quality measure, dollar savings, and current status.

Typical process measures of success are the number of suggestions that employees make for productivity and quality improvements and the numbers of participants in project teams and educational programs. Team process effectiveness can be assessed by tracking the average time it takes to complete a process improvement project, and determining if teams are getting better, smarter, and faster at performing improvements. Facilitators and program coordinators should also look for other indicators of success, such as improvements in team selection and planning processes, frequency of use of quality improvement tools by employees, employee understanding of problem-solving approaches, and senior management involvement. Employee surveys can also help in providing this information.

Team effectiveness surveys typically address important team and individual behaviors, such as unity for a common purpose, listening effectively and acknowledging others' contributions, obtaining participation of all members of the team, gathering and analyzing relevant data and information, sharing responsibility, using problem-solving processes and tools as described in Chapter 9, and meeting company objectives for quality improvement.

Employee surveys also help organizations better understand the "voice of the employee," particularly with regard to employee satisfaction, management policies, and their internal customers and suppliers. Such feedback helps organizations improve their human resource management practices. For example, Marlow Industries uses a survey that addresses a broad variety of issues, including management support, the company's total quality system, organizational effectiveness, training, and continuous improvement. Table 11.3 shows most of the questions included in their survey. All responses are made on a five-item scale ranging from TOTALLY DISAGREE to VERY MUCH AGREE.

Any measurement system should measure consistently, but be lenient, not rigid. Measurement should be tied to company objectives. Finally, trends and long-term results should be emphasized, and key results should be communicated to employees. Reporting of EI and HR program results must be tied in to the needs of management for information. A good system should report results on a regular basis, perhaps monthly or quarterly, with a summary year-end report, using graphical aids wherever possible. Detailed reports should go to lower-level managers, showing results at their level. Summary reports should go to higher management levels. Specific action, such as retraining in basic techniques, training in advanced techniques, contests, consideration of different types of rewards, or financial recognition, should be taken based on results.

TABLE 11.3 Employee Quality Survey—Marlow Industries

Management Support

1. The president is an active supporter of quality at Marlow Industries.
2. Senior management (VPs) are active supporters of quality at Marlow Industries.
3. My supervisor is an active supporter of quality at Marlow Industries.
4. My supervisor is concerned more about the quality of my work than the quantity of my work.
5. My supervisor can help me to do my job better.
6. My supervisor encourages good housekeeping efforts.
7. I receive recognition for a top quality job done.

Total Quality System

1. Marlow Industries' Total Quality System is not a fad. It will be active long into the future.
2. The Total Quality system had made an improvement in the performance of my work.
3. The Total Quality system has made an improvement in my ability to do my job right the first time.
4. I understand the meaning of the Quality Policy.
5. I believe in the meaning of the Quality Policy.
6. I understand the meaning of the Quality Pledge.
7. I believe in the meaning of the Quality Pledge.
8. All departments within Marlow Industries support the Total Quality system.
9. My co-workers support quality first.
10. My co-workers believe in the Quality Pledge.
11. My "supplier" co-worker treats me as his/her "customer" and meets my needs.
12. I know who my internal "customer" is.
13. I am able to meet the requirements of my internal customer.
14. I believe that improving quality is the key to maintaining Marlow Industries' success.

Organizational Effectiveness

1. I receive feedback that helps me perform my job better.
2. I am encouraged to stop and ask questions if something does not seem right.
3. There is a high level of quality in the products we ship to our external customers.
4. Marlow Industries provides reliable processes and equipment so that I can do my job right the first time.
5. I do not use defective materials.
6. I am provided proper procedures to do my job right.
7. My fellow workers have a high level of enthusiasm about Marlow Industries' quality.
8. I believe control charts will help us improve quality.
9. I believe Marlow Industries offers a high quality working environment.
10. I enjoy my job.

Training

1. I have received training to be able to do my job right the first time.
2. I have received training on how to determine if the work I do conforms to Marlow Industries' workmanship standards, and other requirements of the customer.
3. I receive adequate safety training so that I am aware of the safety and health requirements of my job.
4. My supervisor has received adequate training to be able to do his/her job right the first time.
5. My co-worker has received adequate training to be able to do his/her job right the first time.
6. I have received on-going training.
7. The training I have received has been very helpful to me in my job.

Job Satisfaction and Morale

1. I have a high level of personal job satisfaction.
2. My morale is high.
3. The morale of my work group is high.

Involvement

1. I feel involved at Marlow Industries.
2. I would like to be more involved at Marlow Industries.

SOURCE: Courtesy Marlow Industries.

CONCLUDING REMARKS ON EMPLOYEE INVOLVEMENT

Employee involvement appears to be closely related to overall TQM practices. That is, firms are more likely to adopt EI practices when they subscribe to other total quality practices. A 1992 study of 222 American and Japanese manufacturing firms operating in the United States supports this notion.[60] The survey respondents were asked if their employees had authority to stop the line to correct quality problems, whether machine operators were required to perform daily maintenance, and whether line workers carried the primary responsibility for quality (versus quality control inspectors). Traditional U.S firms—those that did not practice either JIT inventory control, TQM, TQC, or Deming management methods—were found to give their workers significantly less authority and responsibility for quality-related factors in manufacturing than the other two types of firms. Firms that used one or more Japanese-style management techniques were significantly different in their employee involvement practices.

A 1990 survey of *Fortune 1000* firms found that firm size was significantly related to greater use of various types of information sharing, knowledge development (through training in general and job-related skills), rewards, and power-sharing practices (using participation levels from surveys all the way to self-managed teams).[61] In other words, the larger the company, the more likely it is to use EI practices. Although the study did not seek information on financial payoffs, EI was seen as having a significant impact on performance indicators such as productivity, quality, worker satisfaction, turnover, absenteeism, competitiveness, and profitability, particularly in manufacturing firms. The authors pointed out some major differences between manufacturing and service firms' adoption of EI practices. They stated, "Employee involvement approaches are becoming increasingly common in some segments of the service sector, notably telecommunications and insurance. In general, however, it is difficult to find many prominent examples of firms that have made heavy use of employee involvement practices in banking, hotels, restaurants, transportation, utilities, and other service businesses."

An analysis of the findings of a large number of research studies on participation, job performance, and satisfaction showed that EI has many positive aspects, but that it is by no means a panacea for all of the problems of management.[62] Key studies of participation have concluded the following:

■ Participation is consistently and significantly related to job satisfaction.

■ People who have a high need for independence and low need for authoritarian control more strongly support and obtain satisfaction from the use of participative decision-making approaches.

■ Participation is generally associated with group or unit effectiveness. Effectiveness criteria may include decision quality, likelihood of implementation, and decision time.

■ Laboratory research on the quality of group versus individual decisions does not definitively answer the question of whether findings apply in the same manner within organizations.

■ Participation is consistently and positively related to how well decisions are implemented.

■ Participation takes time and money.

These findings generally support the advantages of EI listed earlier in this chapter. They suggest that the satisfaction of subordinates with their jobs depends significantly on the extent to which they participate in and exert influence on decisions affecting them in their work situation. People who have different personality characteristics will respond differently to involvement opportunities. Those who want to be told what to do may be initially uncomfortable in group problem-solving situations. However, the benefits of participation tend to enhance group or unit effectiveness.

Laboratory findings show persistent differences in content between group and individual decisions, and the group decisions tend to be superior. Numerous studies also show that participative decisions tend to be more readily accepted and efficiently carried out than those that are imposed. Finally, participation requires time and effort. Only those directly associated with the problems at hand can decide whether these costs are outweighed by the improvement in quality, the additional commitment to implementation, the presumed reduction in needed surveillance, and (if satisfaction is allowed some weight in the equation) the increase in satisfaction of human needs.

Organizational theorists such as Edward E. Lawler, co-developer of the Porter and Lawler motivation model presented in the previous chapter, have suggested that modern employee involvement practices have significantly enriched the concept of TQM.[63] Lawler differentiated between the traditional, Japanese-style TQM philosophy and the sociotechnical employee involvement philosophy (Table 11.4). Lawler argued that the TQM approach, as he defined it, is more structured and driven by a philosophy that assumes management direction and involvement, structured planning processes, and continuous improvement of processes through problem solving and incremental change. In contrast, the employee involvement approach is focused on various aspects of job design, organization design, pay systems, and organization change. It is more effectiveness-oriented and less efficiency-oriented than the structured TQM approach. He suggested that certain organizations may require a more quantified, measurement-oriented TQM approach, while others may require a less quantified employee involvement orientation.

For example, the traditional TQM approach may be best suited for high-volume production situations, such as automotive firms in the United States or for service companies such as FedEx. In environments where quick responsiveness to customer needs must be combined with cost-effective performance and quality, the EI approach, with its emphasis on empowerment and self-

TABLE 11.4   Traditional TQM and Employee Involvement Contrasts

Traditional TQM Philosophy	Employee Involvement Philosophy
Quality improvement	Organizational effectiveness
Management control	Self-management
Process improvement	Organization design
Work simplification	Enrichment/work teams
Work process codification	Employee discretion
Quality circles	Work teams
Internal customers	Feedback
Recognition rewards	Financial rewards

SOURCE: Lawler, ''Total Quality Management and Employee Involvement,'' *The Academy of Management Executive* 8, no.1 (February 1994), 71.

management may work best. Tom Peters, in his recent book, provided an example that seems to represent the EI approach. The Titeflex Hose plant in Springfield, Massachusetts, designs and fabricates specialty hoses for automotive and aircraft engines.[64] Before streamlining their operations, it took nine to eleven weeks to complete an average order and ship it to a customer. By empowering employees, developing autonomous teams that are designed to respond quickly to customer needs, and supporting them with information and expertise whenever the teams call for it, the time for standard orders to be completed now takes from two days to one week. Development time for new products has been cut by more than 50 percent. A rapid deployment team can now complete rush orders in three to four hours. In August 1988, 23 percent of the products were being shipped on time. By March 1989, 90 percent were shipped on time with fewer people and no new capital equipment being purchased to achieve the goal.

Lawler may have drawn too fine a line between TQM and EI approaches. Many people view the components of the Employee Involvement Philosophy in Table 11.4 as important elements of modern TQM practices and not distinct from TQM. In one sense, this opinion indicates that TQM is diffusing beyond its operations management roots to all disciplines of business. Lawler does not suggest that either approach is universally superior to the other, but that one or the other, or a blend of the two, may be best for various organizations, depending on environmental and other factors. This so-called "contingency approach" has long been at the core of management theory. In other words, no "one best way" exists to develop TQM in every organization.

QUALITY IN PRACTICE TOTAL EMPLOYEE INVOLVEMENT AT BURROUGHS WELLCOME CO.[65]

One of the keystones of success in TQM is ongoing employee involvement and genuine commitment to participative problem solving and decision making at every level. Burroughs Wellcome Co., a pharmaceutical firm, has achieved a high level of employee involvement over an extended period of time.

Burroughs Wellcome Co. (B. W. Co.) is a research-oriented U.S. pharmaceutical firm owned by the British firm, Wellcome, plc, whose stock, in turn, is 75 percent owned by The Wellcome Trust, a charitable organization in Britain that funds medical libraries and research. The company's administrative and research headquarters are in Research Triangle Park, North Carolina (abbreviated as RTP). Their major manufacturing facility is at Greenville, North Carolina.

Among hundreds of prescription and over-the-counter products that it produces, two of its best-known products are the over-the-counter antihistamine/decongestants, Actifed and Sudafed. A well-known, but highly controversial product, for which the company obtained generally positive reviews in a *Fortune* magazine article is AZT, the first drug approved for use on AIDS victims.[66]

B. W. Co. began their development of quality circles as an initial step in involving their employees in problem solving by starting six pilot circles at their manufacturing site in Greenville in 1981.

After going through the typical start-up process similar to that shown in Figure 11.3, the six pilot teams were put to work identifying, analyzing, and solving problems in their own work areas. Initial projects were slow in completion; the first team presentation was made to management approximately seven months after volunteers were recruited. However, management persevered in their efforts to establish the program. Within a year or so, the program was showing projected savings-to-expenditure ratios of between 1.28 and 2.27 to 1. By the end of the fifth year of the program, projected project savings were exceeding $1 million annually.

By late 1986, the program had grown to 63 circles, with 17 of those at the headquarters in RTP. In recent years, the process has evolved and fully matured to the point where most of the teams are self-managed and many are cross-functional (working across organizational boundaries with team membership including people from several departments, such as accounting, purchasing, and production). Most projects focus on "strategic areas of interest" to the firm.

The evolution of the process did not take place easily. Manning and Johnson identified four stages that characterized the development of EI at B. W. Co.[67]

- Resolving critical issues
- Employee buy-in
- Employee ownership
- Employee self-direction

Critical issues began to develop by the end of the first year of quality circle existence, including leader and facilitator appointments and length of service, the question of management support, and documentation of circle activities.

Leader and facilitator length of service became an issue when circle leaders who were first-line supervisors nominated by their supervisors for the pilot circles, began to joke and later complain about being "volunteered for life" for their EI jobs. This issue was overcome by providing for an assistant leader who was a line employee. After the group had made three project presentations to management, the assistant leader was eligible to be nominated as a group leader, if confirmed by the steering committee that oversees all aspects of the EI program. Facilitators were nominated by the EI coordinator or area managers, usually from the ranks of successful group leaders.

Management support became an issue during the second year. Managers in various areas of the plant reportedly were not supporting the groups in their areas. An investigation revealed that the reason for nonsupport was a lack of training, since managers had been appointed or transferred to their jobs after the EI process was under way. The solution to the problem involved regular training of new managers and a procedures manual to explain how the process worked and what their responsibilities were during various stages of group progress.

The third issue was documentation and administration of the progress of EI as more groups were added and projects mushroomed. Although many report forms were tried during the first couple of years, five reports are still consistently being used: (1) activity reports (meeting minutes), (2) attendance reports, (3) monthly reports, (4) annual reports, and (5) project summary reports (completed projects). Amazingly detailed, accurate records of every project under way and aggregate reports of all corporate EI activity are compiled on personal computers and stored within the coordinator's office by the coordinator and an assistant, with some clerical assistance.

After the pilot groups had completed their initial projects, they were surveyed and asked about their feelings toward circles. They said they had enjoyed the projects, felt good about their results and the opportunities for growth and development, and that they wanted to disband! However, by this time, many critical issues had been worked through, more circles were being formed, and management kept searching for solutions to make participation a permanent part of the way that the company does business. Soon, because of continued success, first-line supervisors began to ask to have awareness sessions presented in their areas, key staff people asked to become facilitators, and employees requested permission to develop the agenda for the annual Quality Circles Conference, a one-day companywide meeting. The "buy-in" stage was under way.

From there, a short step took the EI groups to the employee ownership stage. Three employee advisory committees that reported to the steering committee were formed: publicity, training, and policies and procedures. The committees took over EI publicity inside and outside the company, development and implementation of training on a wide variety of topics, and keeping handbooks and procedures up to date.

The EI process continues to evolve as employees come up with ways to improve the work environment, quality, productivity, and the EI process itself. They are essentially in control of the process, with management providing resources, guidance, and rewards for accomplishments.

The process of continuous improvement of employee involvement requires that the coordinator and responsible managers address the need to *communicate, motivate, educate,* and *administrate.* At B. W. Co., this task is accomplished by

- administrative efficiency
- extensive, effective communications
- support of managers/employees
- integration with corporate values, goals, and objectives
- establishing involvement as the highest priority management function.

The directive from top management, comes with support at every level:

Involvement will be made a part of the way that [this] company does business. Involvement must be approached the same way as any other business plan. It requires vision, a mission, goals and objectives, and strategies.[68]

EI caused a major change in the corporate culture at B. W. Co. Thus, it is not a process that is likely to be reversed in the future.

Key Issues for Discussion

1. Trace the development of EI at B. W. Co. from the program establishment to the current cross-functional EI teams working on "strategic areas of interest." Comment on how those steps conform to the "process model" for establishing EI programs that is shown in Figure 11.3.

2. What can you surmise about why the program at B. W. Co. has managed to stay in existence over a 10-year time frame when many other "quality circle" programs were abandoned after a year or two of operation? Do these results seem to be consistent with the findings on participation at the beginning of the chapter? Why or why not?

QUALITY IN PRACTICE   THE RIT/*USA TODAY* QUALITY CUP AWARDS[69]

The Rochester Institute of Technology and *USA Today* newspaper, together instituted the Quality Cup Award in 1991. This award honors individuals and teams in manufacturing, service, government, non-profit institutions, and small organizations who make significant improvements in their organizations. The Quality Cup is a national award and is different from other quality awards such as the Baldrige or state awards that recognize entire companies or divisions. The Quality Cup stresses that quality begins with the individual. Some of the recipients include the following:

■ *A team of hourly workers from U.S. Steel's Gary Works who visited automotive customers' plants to see firsthand the problems that bad steel was causing.* Both GM and Ford were threatening to cut U.S. Steel as a supplier in the late 1980s. Steel was bad, and it arrived late. A team of union workers, without management interference, were sent out to visit customers' plants. The team was given the freedom by management to change the system. They suggested rubber pads on flatbed trucks to cushion the steel; they created plastic rings to protect the rolls from crane damage; they persuaded other workers to take responsibility for the condition of the product by signing a tag attached to the shipment. Rejects went from 2.6 percent to 0.6 percent in only a few years.

■ *A team of nine employees and managers at Norfolk General Hospital who studied the process of ordering an X-ray, CAT scan, and other tests.* The average time between the ordering of an X-ray, CAT scan, or other radiological test and delivery of a written report to the doctor who ordered it was 72.5 hours. Three to five hundred tests were ordered each day. The chief radiologist was embarrassed at the turnaround. The team studied the process, identified 50 possible causes of delay, and reduced those to a few causing 80 percent of the problems. They uncovered hidden bottlenecks, eliminating 14 wasted steps from 40 steps in the process, and upgraded the technology. As a result, the average time was reduced to 13.8 hours. Their success depended on breaking turf barriers and having a diversity of representation, including managers, who could effect change. Even doctors report that faster information is allowing them to improve their own ways of practicing medicine.

■ *A team of administrators at Birmingham, Alabama's Wilkerson Middle School who attacked a key root cause of a multitude of problems in the school: poor reading skills.* They formed a small team of teachers and students that developed a radical solution— letting the kids teach. It created Readers Anonymous, a program that matches struggling sixth-graders with seventh- and eighth-graders who read well. Reading scores jumped 21, 31, and 26 percent for the sixth through eighth grades, respectively, from the previous year. Teachers working in teams identify "at-risk" students before they become academic problems. Teacher work teams meet each morning before school to discuss students. The new culture created a climate where kids and teachers want to come to school and learn more.

■ *A team at Pacific Bell Telephone who responded to a stretch goal challenge to reduce cable-related outages 25 percent in one year.* The team of 15 members included a lawyer, department managers, and three cable technicians. All volunteered, but some were skeptical. The lawyer viewed TQM as just "another fad." The team collected statistics on cable damage, which no one had done before. It learned that 41 percent of cable damage was caused by construction work, usually by a contractor cutting buried cable with a backhoe. In more than half the incidents, they had not contacted the Underground Service Alert 800-number to ask utilities to mark underground cables and pipes. New approaches developed included holding Contractor Awareness Nights, which included dinner and a raffle, publicizing in contractor journals and newspapers, direct contacts with the largest offenders, urging district attorneys to enforce a law penalizing contractors who do not contact the Underground Service Alert, and changing ways of marking the location of cables. The team also found that Pacific Bell's costs were not being reported accurately in the claims process, costing $3 million per year. As a result of these efforts, cable damage fell 24 percent in 1993, saving the company $6 million.

Key Issues for Discussion

1. Discuss the role of process management activities (discussed in Chapter 9) in these efforts.

2. Propose some criteria for evaluating Quality Cup applications and selecting the winners. What information should be included in the application?

SUMMARY OF KEY POINTS

■ Participation and teamwork are the foundations of employee involvement and encourage employees to challenge ineffective policies and use their creative energies to improve quality and productivity.

■ Employee involvement is a natural outgrowth of many motivation theories, and helps to break down barriers between individuals, departments, and line and staff functions. Many EI approaches have been proposed over the years and are still in use today. These approaches grew out of classical management and industrial engineering, statistical quality control, and behavioral management concepts, all developed in the United States. Modern approaches range from simple information sharing to total self-direction.

■ Leading practices that foster employee involvement include total involvement both vertically and horizontally in the organization, use of suggestion systems, teamwork, and measurement of involvement and success.

■ Employee involvement can lead to commitment. Commitment is fostered through a culture that puts people first and encourages open communication, a sense of ownership, a focus on values, "securitizing," rewards and incentives, and development of self actualization.

■ Quality begins at a personal level. The use of personal checklists is one way of reinforcing this idea and establishing commitment and ownership that paves the way to other forms of employee involvement.

■ Suggestion systems are popular forms of individual participation. Japan seems to have a much higher participation rate in formal suggestion systems, primarily due to management support and commitment and organizational culture.

■ A team is a small number of people with complimentary skills who are committed to a common purpose, set of performance goals, and approach for which they hold themselves mutually accountable. Teams exist in various forms, the most common being quality circles, problem-solving teams, management teams, work teams, and virtual teams.

■ The quality (control) circle concept evolved in Japan to allow employees to participate in the process of systematically analyzing and solving problems in their own workplaces. In the early 1980s many companies tried to import quality circles to the United States in the hope of getting the same positive benefits that the Japanese had obtained, but ineffective management limited the effectiveness of the movement until better understanding of TQM was developed.

■ Self-managed teams that take on many of the roles formerly reserved for management are having a positive impact on quality, continuous improvement, and effectiveness in more advanced organizations.

■ Implementing employee involvement initiatives requires the establishment of a supportive culture, effective planning and education, and overcoming resistance to change.

■ Evaluating EI practices is important to convince management and workers of their need and to monitor continued effectiveness. Both outcome and process measures provide useful data.

■ EI implementation appears to be closely related to overall TQM practices. Firms that subscribe to TQM principles are more likely to use EI approaches. Research shows that EI has many positive benefits and enhances the traditional practice of TQM.

REVIEW QUESTIONS

1. Discuss the advantages that EI offers over traditional management practices. Why is it so controversial?

2. Briefly summarize the roots of EI from its U.S. and Japanese origins.

3. Describe the various levels of employee involvement and their primary outcomes.

4. What are some of the leading practices that organizations use to foster employee involvement?

5. What benefits occur when quality is made personal?

6. Describe Dessler's eight Keys to Commitment. How do they support a TQM philosophy?

7. Explain how suggestion systems are typically implemented. Why have they been more successful in Japan than in the United States?

8. Summarize the key success factors for suggestion systems.

9. State the formal definition of a team. What advantages do teams provide to organizations?

10. Define the different types of teams that operate in modern organizations.

11. Describe the functions of EI teams. Explain how teams, often made up of people with limited technical expertise, can have any noticeable impact on product quality.

12. Define a quality circle. List the principal characteristics that differentiate quality circles from other group processes.

13. Summarize the history of quality control circles in Japan and quality circles in the United States.

14. What is a self-managed team? How does it differ from a quality circle? From a cross-functional team?

15. Summarize the unique features of self-managed teams.

16. Why did quality circles "die" in the United States during the 1980s?

17. Discuss how organizations go about instituting EI programs.

18. What are some of the key ingredients for successful teams?

19. What approaches can organizations use to overcome resistance to EI efforts?

20. Explain how self-managed teams can be developed using the EI model in the chapter. Does it matter whether an organization has had previous EI programs such as quality circles?

21. Describe some approaches to evaluating EI activities. List some of specific measures of effectiveness and tell why they are important to monitor.

22. Explain Lawler's distinction between traditional TQM and Employee Involvement philosophies?

DISCUSSION QUESTIONS

1. Could many failures of quality circles have been prevented had organizations fully adopted the Deming philosophy? Why or why not?

2. How might an organization make the transition from level 1 to level 8 in Table 11.1? What problems are they likely to encounter along the way?

3. How might EI approaches be applied in your college or university? To what functions? Who would be involved?

4. Describe how a teacher and students might work together as a team to improve classroom performance?

5. Find a company or plant in which quality circles, self-managed teams, or other forms of teamwork are used. Interview a manager or worker to determine how the team's program began and grew.

6. When Donald Peterson was CEO of Ford, he stated, "No matter what you are trying to do, teams are the most effective way to get the job done." Do you agree with this statement? Why or why not?

7. Discuss some of your experiences in working with teams. What problems did you encounter? What impacts do you think the team effort had that might not have otherwise resulted?

8. Do you think an organization can function entirely with self-managed teams; that is, with no additional layers of management?

9. Manufacturing and service firms measure work content and labor effectiveness using work standards derived from time and motion studies. Why can't similar concepts be used in the measurement of outputs of EI teams?

10. Japanese managers are reputed to be more people-oriented toward their workers than are American managers, yet they often set suggestion quotas for quality control circles in Japan. Speculate on why such measurement approaches are successfully used in Japan but are frequently avoided as demotivating in EI programs in the United States.

11. Are intrinsic rewards (satisfaction with a job well done) likely to be sufficient to keep employees interested in EI teamwork, or are more extrinsic rewards (cash or other tangible rewards) needed as the EI team movement matures? Why or why not?

12. Provide some additional examples in which the traditional TQM philosophy and EI philosophy defined by Lawler apply.

13. Conduct a telephone or personal interview of an EI coordinator at an organization that has had teams successfully in operation for three or more years. Compare their experiences to those at Burroughs Wellcome Co. in the Quality in Practice case to determine how they are similar or different. To what do they attribute their success?

14. How did Mack lose their quality focus? Was it due to the business environment, or due to management?

15. How did the formation of teams contribute to Mack's recovery? What was done after the crisis that was different from the earlier period?

CASES

I. The Frustrated Team Builder

Trent Humble, the director for quality training at the Oakton Plant of the Pineville Corporation, was trying to promote a TQM emphasis among staff personnel. The company had been successful in establishing employee involvement teams in the manufacturing areas, but the staff areas, such as accounting, engineering, purchasing, and production planning, were resistant to the ideas of applying TQM philosophies, principles, and techniques to their work. They claimed that they already worked closely together as a "team" and didn't need to learn about teamwork. Trent finally convinced the accounting superintendent, George Key, that some basic TQM training around the concept of using teamwork to do continuous process improvement (CPI) would be beneficial.

Trent decided to use a three-phase approach to the training, which was projected to include about 24 hours of classroom work, plus work on real projects in each of the accounting groups. The three phases would include: Phase I: introduction, team-building exercises, and an overview of process design concepts and techniques; Phase II: simulation of a process improvement project and choice of in-house projects within the accounting groups; Phase III: brief progress report meetings to report progress and plan for management presentations. After projects were completed and solutions were arrived at, formal presentations were to be made to the plant quality steering committee, who could approve the changes recommended by the project teams. The three project teams included one from accounts receivable (AR) and two from accounts payable (AP1 and AP2).

Things went along pretty well during Phase I. George Key, the accounting superintendent, was there to show support for the entire session. The AR supervisor, Helen Jackson, was there, as was the AP1 supervisor, James Jones, but the AP2 supervisor, Bob Greenshades, was dealing with a difficult supplier and never showed up for the training. Someone mentioned that people from purchasing had also been involved in the problem. The accountants and clerical support people seemed to easily understand the concepts of process design and improvement and were eager to start on their projects. Trent urged them to think about possible projects before their Phase II meeting.

Phase II was not as successful as Trent had hoped. George Key had to go out of town on a business trip. Jones, the AP1 supervisor was also out, but Greenshades, the AP2 supervisor was in attendance. George had tried to fill him in after the Phase I training, but it was obvious that the AP2 supervisor was absorbed with the supplier problem.

During the Phase II training, Trent emphasized the need to seek consensus on the project to be chosen. He also pointed out that the talents of everyone on the team needed to be tapped. To make starting easier and to ensure a successful project, Trent believed the group needed to choose an initial project that was directly within the teams' work sections and to avoid cross-functional projects that required coordination with other departments, at first. During the second half of the session, Trent guided the groups through the simulated projects so that they could obtain hands-on experience in using the process improvement methods and techniques. Greenshades went through the motions, but didn't seem to get into the exercise. At the end of the session, Trent had each team brainstorm ideas and narrow their lists to the top three. Since they were out of time, Trent suggested that each group meet and try to reach consensus on which project to adopt as a team project. He set a time when he would meet with each team to discuss progress.

At the meeting with the AP2 Team, he was surprised to learn that they had chosen to work on the supplier/purchasing problem that had been absorbing the energy of the AP2 supervisor. Trent tried to point out the difficulties of the project, but about half the team, plus the supervisor argued strongly to go ahead with it. The other half of the team was silent.

Six months later, the AR team and the AP1 team made management presentations on their completed projects. The first was extremely successful, having an estimated savings of $100,000 per year and cutting the time required to do an AR report in half. The AP1 team reported an estimated savings from their project of $25,000 per year, with other intangible benefits from an improved internal process. The AP2 team was still working on their project, but was having a hard time working with purchasing and the vendor on identifying and separating out the overlapping process problems that were at issue.

Assignment

Meet together in teams to discuss this case. Apply quality tools discussed in Chapter 9 to compress and expand the issues in this case, that is, to get down to root causes, key problems that need to be addressed, and the major environmental influences on the situation. For example, consider using the problem redefinition technique of repeatedly asking Why?: WHY did the AP2 group choose this problem? WHY was the training successful with two groups and not with the third group? and so on. Several people in the team should take a turn at being facilitator. Develop clear, specific recommendations for Trent on what he must do to "salvage" the EI process at Oakton.

II. A Personal TQM Project

Develop your own personal TQM checklist and analyze the results over an extended period of time. Users of this text come from a wide variety of backgrounds. They may be undergraduate students, graduate students in a regular or an executive MBA program, or employees in a company training and development program. In all cases, you are students. In many cases, you have work and family responsibilities. Use the guidelines listed below. After you have gathered data for a week or two, review the data for the purpose of analysis and improvement. Use run charts to plot weekly results. Later, you may wish to use Pareto analysis, cause and effect diagrams, or other tools to improve your personal analysis or work processes.

Personal TQM Project Guidelines[70]

1. Each participant should initiate a personal quality improvement project and maintain and improve it during the rest of the term.

2. Consistent effort, rather than elegant precision in pursing the project will be rewarded. That is, individual benefit, rather than "a grade," or perfection, is to be the major objective.

3. The personal quality checklist in Figure 11.5 provides a starting point for the project. Other tools and techniques (such as those listed in Chapter 9) may be incorporated at a later time.

4. Eight to ten items for personal tracking and improvement (see Table 11.5) should be chosen. The attached listing of possible checklist standards may be useful. However, participants are

TABLE 11.5   Suggested Standards for a Personal TQM Checklist

- Review class notes after each class
- Limit phone calls to ten minutes, where possible
- No more than 10 hours of TV per week
- Get up promptly—no snooze alarm
- Complete all reading assignments as due
- Plan by using a brief outline of what is to be accomplished daily
- Refer to daily plan, each day
- Use stairs instead of elevator
- Follow up on job contacts within 24 hours
- Work in library (or other quiet place) to avoid interruptions
- Stick to one subject at a time while studying
- Don't doggedly persist in trying to clear up a confusing point (or "bug" in a computer program) when stuck; set it aside and return later; for example, no more than 10 minutes searching for a problem
- Don't spend too much time on routine activities; for example, no more than 15 minutes for breakfast, decrease grooming time to no more than 20 minutes
- Remember names of people to whom you have been introduced
- In bed every night before midnight
- Good housekeeping standards around house, apartment, dorm room, by the end of the day
- Prompt payment of bills, before their due date
- Various dietary standards—eat vegetables, avoid fats (be specific!)
- Limit beer and/or cigarette consumption (be specific!)

SOURCE: Adapted from Harry V. Roberts and Bernard F. Sergesketter. *Quality is Personal: A Foundation for Total Quality Management.* New York: Free Press, 1993, p.35.

FIGURE 11.5 Personal Total Quality Management Checklist

Week of: _____

Defect Category	M	T	W	TH	F	S	SU	Total

not required to use only items from this list. Whatever is meaningful to you may be tracked.

5. After a week's data is gathered, a simple graph can be plotted to determine the level of "defects" encountered.

6. A suggested practice is that you share your personal checklist items and goals with your instructor, a colleague, spouse, or friend. Have that person ask you about your progress every week or so. If you are making regular progress, you should be happy to discuss it, and to show your charts and graphs. Even if your progress is uneven, you should be able to show that you've improved on one or two items, which is progress. Don't be too self-critical!

7. An intermediate progress report should be built into the process around the middle of the pilot study period. The final report on the pilot

project should be made at the end of the term. Consideration should be given to making personal TQM a permanent part of your personal planning and improvement process.

Discussion Questions

1. What did your graphical analysis reveal?

2. Did you experience the same thing that Sergesketter did when he found that certain items disappeared as problems in a short period of time, simply because he began to measure them?

3. How did you feel about discussing your "defects" with others?

4. How does the personal TQM process tie into TQM processes in a work environment? How does it fit with the concepts of "Quality in Daily Work," "Zero Defects," control of quality, and "Casting Out Fear," for example?

■ NOTES

1. Rath & Strong Executive Panel, Winter 1994 Survey on Personal Initiative, Summary of Findings.

2. Joseph J. Gufreda, Larry A. Maynard, and Lucy N. Lytle, "Employee Involvement in the Quality Process," in *The Ernst & Young Quality Improvement Consulting Group, Total Quality!: An Executive's Guide for the 1990s* (Homewood, IL: Richard D. Irwin, 1990).

3. Edward E. Lawler, III, Susan Albers Mohrman, and Gerald E. Ledford, Jr., *Employee Involvement and Total Quality Management: Practices and Results in* Fortune 1000 *Corporations* (San Francisco: Jossey-Bass, 1992), 33–36.

4. Lawler, Mohrman, and Ledford, see note 3.

5. Phillip Caldwell, "Cultivating Human Potential at Ford," *The Journal of Business Strategy* (Spring 1984), 75.

6. "Detroit vs. the UAW: At Odds Over Teamwork," *Business Week* 24 August, 1987, 54–55.

7. "The Payoff from Teamwork," *Business Week*, 10 July, 1989, 56.

8. "Quality Circle Busters," *The Wall Street Journal*, 9 June, 1993, A14.

9. Leonard R. Sayles, *The Working Leader* (New York: The Free Press, 1993), 98.

10. Alfie Kohn, *No Contest: The Case Against Competition* (Boston: Houghton Mifflin, 1986).

11. IBM Corporation, *The Transformation of IBM: A Market-Driven Quality Reference Guide*, Document Number G325–0670–00 (June 1992).

12. A more comprehensive review of history and the forerunners of quality circles from the early 1900s can be found in William M. Lindsay, "Quality Circles and Participative Work Improvement: A Cross-Disciplinary History," in Dennis F. Ray (ed.), *Southern Management Association Proceedings* (Mississippi State, MS: Mississippi State University, 1987), 220–222.

13. Sud Ingle, *Quality Circles Master Guide: Increasing Productivity with People Power* (Englewood Cliffs, NJ: Prentice-Hall, 1982), 7.

14. Leslie W. Rue and Lloyd L. Byars, *Management Theory and Application*, 3rd ed. (Homewood, IL: Irwin, 1983), 45.

15. *Statistical Quality Control Handbook*, AT&T (1956). Available from AT&T Technologies, Commercial Sales Clerk, Select Code 700–444, P.O. Box 19901, Indianapolis, IN 46219 or AT&T Customer Information Center, 1–800–432–6600.

16. W. Edwards Deming, "The Statistical Control of Quality," *Quality* (February 1980), 13–15.

17. Raymond A. Katzell and Daniel Yankelovich, *Work, Productivity, and Job Satisfaction* (New York: New York University, 1975), 336–339.

18. Richard E. Walton, "Work Innovations in the U.S.," *Harvard Business Review* (July/August 1979), 88, 91. Copyright © 1979 by the President and Fellows of Harvard College; all rights reserved.

19. William B. Werther, William A Ruch, and Lynne McClure, *Productivity Through People* (St. Paul, MN: West Publishing Company, 1986).

20. Peters, Tom J., *Thriving on Chaos: Handbook for a Management Revolution* (New York: Alfred A. Knopf, 1988).

21. David Armstrong, *Management by Storying Around* (New York: Doubleday Currency, 1992), 117–119.

22. Tom Peters and Robert H. Waterman, Jr., *In Search of Excellence: Lessons from America's Best-Run Companies* (New York: Harper and Row, 1982), 80–81.

23. John Wyatt, "The New Deal: What Companies and Employees Owe Each Other," *Fortune*, 13 June, 1994, 44–52.

24. This section is adapted from Gary Dessler, *Winning Commitment* (New York: McGraw-Hill, 1993), 153–163. Reproduced with permission of McGraw-Hill, Inc.

25. Harry V. Roberts and Bernard F. Sergesketter, *Quality Is Personal: A Foundation for Total Quality Management* (New York: The Free Press, 1993).

26. Roberts and Sergesketter, 13–14, see note 25.

27. Karen L. Muse and Mark P. Finster, "A Comparison of Employee Suggestion Systems in Japan and the USA," University of Wisconsin Working Paper (1989).

28. Jitenda Sharma, "Why Suggestion Systems Often Fail," *International Management* (1977).

29. Goran Ekvall, "Creativity at the Place of Work: Studies of Suggestors and Suggestion Systems in Industry," *Journal of Creative Behavior* vol. 10, no. 1 (1976), 52–54, 70.

30. Muse and Finster, see note 27.

31. Jon R. Katzenback and Douglas K. Smith, "The Discipline of Teams," *Harvard Business Review* (March/April 1993), 111–120.

32. John Ryan, "Employees Speak on Quality in ASQC/Gallup Survey," *Quality Progress* 26, no. 12 (December 1993), 51–53.

33. Hedley G. Dimock, *Groups: Leadership and Group Development* (San Diego: University Associates, 1987).

34. Brian Dumaine, "The Trouble With Teams," *Fortune* 5 September, 1994, 86–92.

35. "Gravedigging at New York Life," *Quality '92: Leading the World-Class Company*, Fortune Advertisement (21 September, 1992).

36. "Platform Approach at Chrysler," *Quality '93: Empowering People With Technology*, Fortune Advertisement, (20 September, 1993).

37. Philip C. Thompson, *Quality Circles: How To Make Them Work in America* (New York: AMACOM, 1982).

38. Much of the history in this section has been adapted from J. M. Juran, "The QC Circle Phenomenon," *Industrial Quality Control* (January 1967), 329–336.

39. Jeremy Main, *Quality Wars: The Triumphs and Defeats of American Business* (New York, The Free Press, 1994), 62.

40. Sidney P. Rubinstein, "QC Circles and U.S. Participative Movements," *1972 ASQC Technical Conference Transactions*, Washington, D.C., 391–396.

41. IAQC Exhibitor Brochure for the 6th Annual IAQC Conference and Exhibition, Cincinnati, Ohio (1984).

42. William M. Lindsay, *Measurement of Quality Circle Effectiveness: A Survey and Critique*, unpublished M.S. thesis, University of Cincinnati, College of Engineering (May 1986), 72, 117–120.

43. Jeremy Main. *Quality Wars* (New York: The Free Press, 1994), 62.

44. Main, see note 43.

45. Jack D. Orsburn, Linda Moran, Ed Musselwhite, and John H. Zenger, *Self-Directed Work Teams* (Homewood, IL: Business One-lrwin, 1990), 8.

46. Reprinted with permission from Peter Lazes and Marty Falkenberg, "Workgroups in America Today," *The Journal for Quality and Participation* 14, no. 3 (June 1991), 58–69. Copyright the Association for Quality and Participation, Cincinnati, Ohio.

47. Richard S. Wellins, William C. Byham, and Jeanne M. Wilson, *Empowered Teams* (San Francisco: Jossey-Bass, 1991).

48. Adapted from "Benefits for the Back Office, Too," *Business Week*, 10 July, 1989, 59.

49. Lazes and Falkenberg, see note 46.

50. For a thorough discussion and additional sources, see Richard E. Kopelman, *Managing Productivity in Organizations* (New York: McGraw-Hill, 1986), 133–135.

51. Paraphrased from: Naomi Krigsman and Richard M. Obrien, "Quality Circles, Feedback and Reinforcement: An Experimental Comparison and Behavioral Analysis," *Journal of Organizational/ Behavior Management* 9, no. 1 (1987), 77–78.

52. Krigsman and Obrien, see note 51.

53. Edward E. Lawler, and Susan A. Mohrman, "Quality Circles After the Fad," *Harvard Business Review* (January/February 1985), 65–71. Copyright © 1985 by the President and Fellows of Harvard College; all rights reserved.

54. Elios Pascual, "Mack Learns the Error of False Pride," Reprinted with permission from *The Wall Street Journal*, 11 July, 1994, A10. © 1994, Dow Jones & Co., Inc. All rights reserved.

55. Peter R. Scholtes, et al., *The Team Handbook: How to Use Teams to Improve Quality* (Madison, WI: Joiner Associates Inc., 1988), 6–10 to 6–22.

56. Peter B. Grazier, *Before It's Too Late* (Chadds Ford, PA: Teambuilding, Inc. 1989).

57. J. Michael Donovan, "Self-Managing Work Teams: Extending the Quality Circle Concept," *The Quality Circles Journal* (now *The Journal for Quality and Participation*) 9, no. 3 (March 1986), 15–20.

58. Lazes and Falkenberg, 59, see note 46.

59. Richard S. Wellins, Jeanne Wilson, Amy J. Katz, Patricia Laughlin, Charles R. Day, Jr., and Doreen Price, *Self-Directed Teams: A Study of Current Practice* (Cincinnati: AQP, 1990).

60. Maling Ebrahimpour and Barbara E. Withers. "Employee Involvement in Quality Improvement: A Comparison of American and Japanese Manufacturing Firms Operating in the U.S.," *IEEE Transactions in Engineering Management* 39, no. 2 (May, 1992), 142–148.

61. Lawler, Mohrman, and Ledford, 69–72, see note 3.

62. Robert L. Kahn, "In Search of the Hawthorne Effect," in Eugene Louis Cass and Frederick G. Zimmer (eds.), *Man and Work in Society* (New York: Van Nostrand Reinhold, 1975), 56–58.

63. Edward E. Lawler, III, "Total Quality Management and Employee Involvement: Are They Compatible?" *The Academy of Management Executive* 8, no. 1 (February, 1994), 68–76.

64. Tom Peters, *Liberation Management* (New York: Fawcett Columbine, 1994), 62–71.

65. Appreciation is expressed to Mitch Manning, Section Head of EI Administration at Burroughs Wellcome Co. for providing numerous papers, materials, and editorial suggestions on the EI program at B. W. Co.

66. Brian O'Reilly, "The Inside Story of the AIDS Drug," *Fortune*, 5 November, 1990, G112–129.

67. Mitchell W. Manning and G. Wesley Johnson, Jr., "Evolution in Involvement," undated working paper.

68. Mitch Manning, "Map Your Process," *Journal for Quality and Participation* (June 1989), 46–53.

69. Information about the Quality Cup can be obtained by writing to Quality Cup, *USA TODAY*, 1000 Wilson Blvd., 22nd Floor, Arlington, VA 22229. Adapted from "Description of Quality Cup Awards and Winners," *USA Today*, 8 April, 1994. Copyright 1994, *USA Today*. Reprinted with permission.

70. Adapted from Roberts and Sergesketter, see note 25.

■ BIBLIOGRAPHY

Bean, E., C. Ordowich, and A. Wesley. "Including the Supervisor in the Employee Involvement Effort." *National Productivity Review* (Winter 1985–1986), 64–77.

Belasco, James A., and Ralph C. Stayer. *Flight of the Buffalo: Soaring to Excellence, Learning To Let Employees Lead.* New York: Warner Books, 1993.

Benson, Tracy E. "Quality and Teamwork Get a Leg Up." *Industry Week*, 6 April, 1992, 66–68.

Bowen, D. E., and E. E. Lawler, III. "The Empowerment of Service Workers: What, How, Why and When" *Sloan Management Review* Vol. 33, no. 3 (1992), 31–39.

Bushe, G. R. "Cultural Contradictions of Statistical Process Control in American Manufacturing Organizations." *Journal of Management* 14 (1988), 19–31.

Dean, James W., and S. A. Snell. "Integrated Manufacturing and Job Design." *Academy of Management Journal* 34 (1991), 776–804.

Frangos, Stephen J., with Steven J. Bennett. *Team Zebra:*

How 1500 Partners Revitalized Eastman Kodak's Black & White Film-Making Flow. Essex Junction, VT: Omneo/ Oliver Wight, 1993.

Garvin, David A. "Quality Problems, Policies, and Attitudes in the United States and Japan: An Exploratory Study." *Academy of Management Journal* 29 (1986), 653–673.

Griffin, Ricky W. "Consequences of Quality Circles in an Industrial Setting: A Longitudinal Assessment." *Academy of Management Journal* (1988), 338–358.

Gryna, Frank M., Jr. *Quality Circles: A Team Approach to Problem Solving.* New York: AMACOM, 1981.

Johnson, Jack, and Jack T. Mollen. "Ten Tasks for Managers in the Empowered Workplace." *Journal for Quality and Participation* (December 1992), 18–20.

Lawler, E. E., and S. A. Mohrman. "Quality Circles: After the Honeymoon." *Organizational Dynamics* 15 (1987), 42–54.

Ledford, G. E., Jr. "Three Case Studies on Skill-Based Pay: An Overview." *Compensation and Benefits Review* 23 (1991), 11–23.

Mohr, William L., and Harriet Mohr. *Quality Circles: Changing Images of People at Work*. Reading, MA: Addison-Wesley, 1983.

Munchus, G. III. "Employer-Employee Based Quality Circles in Japan: Human Resources Policy Implications for American Firms." *Academy of Management Review* 8 (1983), 255–261.

Ouchi, William G. *Theory Z*. New York: Avon Books, 1981.

Pascale, Richard Tanney, and Anthony G. Athos. *The Art of Japanese Management*. New York: Warner Books Inc., 1981.

QC Sources: Selected Writings on Quality Circles. Cincinnati, OH: Association for Quality and Participation (formerly IAQC), 1983.

Schlesinger, L. A., and J. L. Heskett. "The Service-Driven Company." *Harvard Business Review* 69 (1991), 71–81.

Semler, Ricardo. "Managing Without Managers. *Harvard Business Review* 67 (September/October 1989), 76–84.

Waldman, David A. "The Contributions of Total Quality Management to a Theory of Work Performance." *Academy of Management Review* (1994), 510–532.

CHAPTER

12

Quality Management Evaluation and Assessment

OUTLINE

Quality Auditing
  Supplier Certification Audits
  Quality System Auditing
ISO 9000
  Structure of the ISO 9000 Standards
  Registration Process
  Perspectives on ISO 9000
The Malcolm Baldrige National Quality Award
  Baldrige Award Criteria
  The Baldrige Award Scoring System
  The Baldrige Award Evaluation Process
  Impacts of the Baldrige Award
  Using the Baldrige Award Criteria
  ISO 9000 and the Baldrige Award

  QS 9000
State Quality Awards
The Deming Prize
The European and Canadian Quality Awards
QUALITY IN PRACTICE: The Payoff from Baldrige at
  Texas Instruments
QUALITY IN PRACTICE: The Ford Q1 Award
QUALITY IN PRACTICE: Florida Power and Light
Summary of Key Points
Review Questions
Discussion Questions
CASES *World-Wide Appliances*
         Ultra-Productivity Fasteners, Part II

The past several chapters have described and illustrated the most important principles of total quality that provide the foundation for achieving customer satisfaction. Armand Feigenbaum, who pioneered the concept of total quality, recognized that any organization needs a clear and well-structured system that identifies, documents, coordinates, and maintains all the key quality-related activities throughout all relevant company and plant operations. Feigenbaum defined a **total quality system** as "the agreed companywide and plantwide operating work structure, documented in effective, integrated technical and managerial procedures, for guiding the coordinated actions of the work force, the

483

machines, and the information of the company and plant in the best and most practical ways to assure customer quality satisfaction and economical costs of quality."[1] Thus, a company needs both a framework for guiding quality-related actions by all employees as well as means of assessing how well these actions are carried out, particularly relative to the firm's competitors or world-class standards. Awards and certification procedures provide frameworks, and quality auditing and assessment procedures provide control processes. The most prominent frameworks for quality management are the United States' Malcolm Baldrige National Quality Award, Japan's Deming Prize, and the worldwide ISO 9000 standards. The Baldrige Award has been mentioned many times thus far; this chapter presents details about the award and its impact on U.S. business. In addition, information is given about ISO 9000, the Deming Prize, and the European and Canadian Quality Awards. To begin, this chapter discusses quality audits as a basis for understanding quality systems effectiveness.

QUALITY AUDITING

In any business, deviations from established procedures may occur. To reduce this type of variation and find opportunities for improvement, organizations conduct **audits**—independent, unbiased assessments of work activities. The most common type of assessment is the financial audit, with which most managers are familiar. A **quality audit** is a systematic and independent examination and evaluation to determine whether quality activities and results comply with planned arrangements and whether these arrangements are implemented effectively and are suitable to achieve objectives.[2] Quality audits provide several benefits:

1. Audits furnish benchmarks for determining whether a quality system is complete.

2. Periodic audits make everyone aware that the organization is serious about continually improving quality.

3. Audits often reveal activities that are innovative or performed in an exceptional fashion and can be highlighted and shared throughout the organization.

4. Audits point out areas that are inadequate or need improvement.

5. Audits become a permanent record of the progress in achieving the goals of the quality system.

6. Audits have become an important part of supplier quality certification systems.[3]

The three generic types of quality audits are policy, practice, and product.[4] *Policy audits* check written procedures and policies against standards and specifications. This audit usually involves reading manuals, records, and similar documents, and tells whether people in the organization know what they are supposed to be doing. *Practice audits* check actual practices against procedures or accepted good practices. For example, such an audit might assess whether gauges really are calibrated every month as required, or whether all welding is being done by certified welders. *Product audits* involve evaluation of the product: does it conform to specifications? This type of audit is used by many companies to evaluate a new supplier. Even though each of these audits is useful, quality auditing requires a broad view in which the organization focuses on the entire quality system.

The real benefit of quality auditing is in uncovering information to make improvements. Managers should not use audits as a means of punishment. The most effective use of audit findings is when employees participate in the process and are empowered to assume ownership of the problems and the solutions. Cross-functional teams are an excellent means of accomplishing this task.

Many companies perform internal quality assessments as a basis for improving quality management systems and practices. AT&T, for example, documents its quality system and business plans, surveys and interviews senior managers, employees, and customers; and gathers customer satisfaction, process performance, and financial data as a basis for evaluating its quality systems. This information, summarized in the form of a Baldrige Award application (to be discussed later in this chapter) forms the foundation for a quantitative measurement of the quality system and recommendations for improvement.[5]

Quality auditing is one of the most rapidly growing areas within the quality profession. The American Society for Quality Control certifies individuals as quality auditors. Certification consists of proof of practical experience and passing a comprehensive examination that covers five basic areas: (1) general knowledge, conduct, ethics, audit administration, (2) audit preparation, (3) audit performance, (4) audit reporting, corrective action, follow-up, and closure, and (5) auditing tools and techniques.[6] Many companies also perform external quality audits on suppliers, called supplier certification audits.

■ Supplier Certification Audits

The control of the quality of purchased materials is one of the principal responsibilities of quality assurance. The role of the purchasing department involves articulating clear and precise specifications that the supplier can and does understand. Also, purchasing requires good information on supplier performance, so it can select suppliers based on quality considerations, not solely on price.

Many different approaches are used to establish supplier quality. A drill bit manufacturer in Texas conducts quality evaluations at suppliers' plants. The inspections are always on short notice and are designed to see if the supplier is following appropriate quality control procedures. The Delco Moraine Division, a manufacturer of automotive brake controls, uses an awareness program that includes a videotape presentation shown at supplier plants. The tape emphasizes quality. After viewing the tape, supplier employees were better able to relate their work to Delco. At Bell Helicopter Textron, "quality alerts" are sent to subcontractors telling them of quality problems that have surfaced. They state the problem, outline corrective action, and require receipt to be acknowledged.

Formal programs typically are established to rate and certify suppliers who provide quality materials in a cost-effective and timely manner. A survey by *Purchasing* magazine reported that almost two-thirds of major manufacturing firms in the United States have supplier rating programs.[7] The reasons reported for rating suppliers were

- to improve quality: 91%
- to reduce costs: 56%
- to end inspections: 56%
- to reduce suppliers: 45%

■ to award/reward suppliers: 39%

■ to improve delivery: 15%

The Pharmaceutical Manufacturers Association defines a certified supplier to be one that, after extensive investigation, is found to supply material of such quality that routine testing on each lot received is unnecessary. Customers rely on sound in-process inspection, effective process controls, and inspection data generated by the supplier. Certification provides recognition for high-quality suppliers, which motivates them to improve continuously and attract more business.

Florida Power and Light has a three-tier vendor certification program.[8] Suppliers can be certified as a "Quality Vendor," "Certified Vendor," and "Excellent Vendor." To become a Quality Vendor, a supplier's products or services must meet basic requirements of quality, cost, delivery, and safety. In addition, the supplier must have a quality improvement process in place and must demonstrate that they have achieved significant improvements. They must also have an audit system to certify the process and the results. To become a Certified Vendor, the supplier must also have demonstrated the use of statistical process control and prove that their processes can meet FPL's specification requirements. They must also be able to document their capability and have a plan for continuous quality improvement. To achieve Excellent Vendor status, suppliers must demonstrate the ability to exceed FPL's specification requirements, employ reliability assurance techniques, and show that quality improvement is a central part of their management system.

Successful suppliers have a culture where employees and managers share in customers' goals, commitments, and risks to promote a long-term relationship (recall one of Deming's 14 Points about supplier relationships—not purchasing solely on the basis of price). At the Gillette Company, for example, the supplier certification program begins with Gillette identifying those suppliers with a proven ability to meet its specifications.[9] Once a supplier is selected to participate, Gillette expects them to establish a preproduction planning system to assess the capability of their process to meet Gillette's specifications. Feedback is offered in the form of recommended changes that will improve quality, reduce cost, or facilitate ease of manufacture. The responsibilities of Gillette's certified suppliers include the following:

1. To control production processes during manufacture to prevent nonconformities.

2. To control product and measure conformance against acceptance criteria to ensure that the product shipped will meet Gillette's requirements.

3. To provide suitable quantitative and/or qualitative inspection data with each lot.

4. To maintain the integrity of the production lot as well as traceability of inspection data to a specific lot.

5. To develop internal and external feedback systems to provide prompt and effective corrective actions when required.

The American Society for Quality Control's customer–supplier technical committee developed specific criteria for supplier certification.[10]

■ Certified suppliers experience virtually no product-related lot rejections for a significant time period, usually for 12 months, or in some cases two years.

■ Certified suppliers have no nonproduct-related rejections for a stated period of time. "Nonproduct-related" means mismarkings on a container, for example. Nonproduct-related problems require different types of corrective action than product-related problems. Typically, nonproduct-related problems can be corrected faster and easier.

■ Certified suppliers precipitate no production-related negative incidents for a stated period of time, usually six months. While incoming inspections determine conformance to specifications, specifications cannot possibly define every aspect of a product. Production-related problems are not always detectable by inspection and can result in latent defects that only become apparent later in the product's life.

■ Certified suppliers successfully pass on-site quality system evaluation (audit), conducted within the past year.

■ Certified suppliers operate according to an agreed-on specification. Documentation should not contain ambiguous phrases such as "free of flash" or "no characteristic odor."

■ Certified suppliers have a fully documented process and quality system, which should include the use of statistical process control and a program for continuous improvement.

■ Certified suppliers furnish timely copies of certificates of analysis, inspection data, and test results.

The details of supplier certification processes vary by company, and such programs are time-consuming and expensive to administer. Nevertheless, they are an important means of controlling incoming materials, particularly in a "just-in-time" environment.

Companies that have many suppliers spend large amounts of resources to certify every one of them. One approach to avoiding unnecessary audit costs and helping to assure buyers that specified practices are being followed is to create a uniform set of standards—an independent and transportable supplier qualification system. This system is the major focus of ISO 9000, which is discussed in an upcoming section.

■ Quality System Auditing

Product quality depends on many variables, such as the caliber of the components or materials used; the type of equipment used in design, production, handling, installation, testing, and shipping; the equipment calibration and maintenance procedures employed; the training and experience of production and supervisory personnel; the level of "workmanship"; and sometimes the environmental conditions in the work area. The process, organizational structure, procedures, and resources that manufacturers and suppliers use to control these variables to produce a product of consistent quality, which meets specifications and requirements, is called a *quality system*.[11] Quality system audits provide a comprehensive review in an effort to uncover problems and opportunities for improvement.

Typical issues covered in quality system audits include:

■ *Management involvement and leadership.* To what extent are all levels of management involved?

■ *Product and process design.* Do products meet customer needs? Are products designed for easy manufacturability?

■ *Product control.* Is a strong product control system in place that concentrates on defect *prevention*, before the fact, rather than defect removal after the product is made?

■ *Customer and supplier communications.* Does everyone understand who the customer is? To what extent do customers and suppliers communicate with each other?

■ *Quality improvement programs.* Is a quality improvement plan in place? What results have been achieved?

■ *Employee participation.* Are all employees actively involved in quality improvement?

■ *Education and training.* What is done to ensure that everyone understands his or her job and has the necessary skills? Are employees trained in quality improvement techniques?

■ *Quality information.* How is feedback on quality results collected and used?

Quality audits, performed in a timely fashion and in a positive spirit, can be invaluable in achieving quality excellence. Care must be taken not to allow audits to become a trivial exercise, but to provide valuable information to managers.

Two principal approaches have emerged as a basis for auditing quality systems and are based on the ISO 9000 international standards and the Malcolm Baldrige National Quality Award criteria.

ISO 9000

As quality became a major focus of businesses throughout the world, various organizations developed standards and guidelines. Terms such as *quality management, quality control, quality system,* and *quality assurance* acquired different, and sometimes conflicting meanings from country to country, within a country, and even within an industry.[12] As the European Community moved toward the European free trade agreement, which went into effect at the end of 1992, quality management became a key strategic objective. To standardize quality requirements for European countries within the common market and those wishing to do business with those countries, a specialized agency for standardization, the International Organization for Standardization, founded in 1946 and composed of representatives from the national standards bodies of 91 nations, adopted a series of written quality standards in 1987. The standards have been adopted in the United States by the American National Standards Institute (ANSI) with the endorsement and cooperation of the American Society for Quality Control (ASQC). The U.S. standards are called the ANSI/ASQC Q90-1987 series. The standards are recognized by about 100 countries, including Japan. In some foreign markets, companies will not buy from noncertified suppliers. Thus, meeting these standards is becoming a requirement for international competitiveness.

The ISO 9000 series of standards are different from the traditional notion of a standard. They are not engineering standards for measurement, terminology, test methods, or product specifications. They are *quality system standards* that guide a company's performance of specified requirements in the areas of design/development, production, installation, and service. They are based on the premise that certain generic characteristics of management practices can be standardized, and that a well-designed, well-implemented, and carefully managed quality system provides confidence that the outputs will meet customer expectations and requirements. The standards prescribe documentation for all processes affecting quality and suggest that compliance through auditing leads to continuous improvement.

Structure of the ISO 9000 Standards

The standards define three levels of quality assurance:

- Level 1 (ISO 9001) provides a model for quality assurance in firms that design, develop, produce, install, and service products.
- Level 2 (ISO 9002) provides a quality assurance model for firms engaged only in production and installation.
- Level 3 (ISO 9003) applies to firms engaged only in final inspection and test.

Two other standards, ISO 9000 and ISO 9004, define the basic elements of a comprehensive quality assurance system and provide guidance in applying the appropriate level. ISO 9004, specifically, guides the development and implementation of a quality system. It examines each of the elements of the quality system in detail and can be used for internal auditing purposes. Together, these standards are referred to as the ISO 9000 series.

The standards focus on 20 key requirements; those applicable to each level are shown in Table 12.1. To illustrate the scope of the requirements, consider the first one, *management responsibility*. The standards require that

- Management establishes, documents, and publicizes its policy, objectives, and commitment to quality and customer satisfaction.
- Management designates a representative with authority and responsibility for implementing and maintaining the requirements of the standard.
- Management defines the responsibility, authority, and relationships for all employees whose work affects quality.
- Management conducts in-house verification and review of the quality system. Management reviews should consider
  - the results of internal quality audits
  - management effectiveness
  - defects and irregularities
  - solutions to quality problems
  - implementation of past solutions
  - handling of nonconforming product
  - results of statistical scorekeeping tools
  - impact of quality methods on actual results

Auditors typically ask such questions as: Does a documented policy on quality exist? Have management objectives for quality been defined? Have the policy and objectives been transmitted and explained to all levels of the organization? Have job descriptions for people who manage or perform work affecting quality been documented? Are descriptions of functions that affect quality available? Has management designated a person or group with the authority to prevent

TABLE 12.1 ISO 9000 Series Requirements

Requirement	ISO 9001	ISO 9002	ISO 9003
Management responsibility	X	X	X
Quality system	X	X	X
Contract review	X	X	—
Design control	X	—	—
Document control	X	X	X
Purchasing	X	X	—
Purchaser supplied product	X	X	—
Product identification and traceability	X	X	X
Process control	X	X	—
Inspection and testing	X	X	X
Inspection, measurement, and test equipment	X	X	X
Inspection and test status	X	X	X
Control of nonconforming product	X	X	X
Corrective action	X	X	—
Handling, storage, packaging, and delivery	X	X	X
Quality records	X	X	X
Internal quality audits	X	X	X
Training	X	X	X
Servicing	X	—	—
Statistical control	X	X	X

nonconformities in products, identify and record quality problems, and recommend solutions? What means are used to verify the solutions?[13]

The basic requirements for the remaining elements of ISO 9001 are summarized below.

■ *Quality system.* The company must write and maintain a quality manual that meets the criteria of the applicable standard (9001, 9002, or 9003), which defines conformance to requirements.

■ *Contract review.* The company must review contracts to assess whether requirements are adequately defined and whether the capability exists to meet requirements.

■ *Design control.* The company must verify product design to ensure that requirements are being met and that procedures are in place for design planning and design changes.

■ *Document control.* The company must establish and maintain procedures for controlling documentation through approval, distribution, change, and modification.

■ *Purchasing.* The company must have procedures to ensure that purchased products conform to requirements.

■ *Purchaser supplied products.* Procedures to verify, store, and maintain items supplied by customers must be established.

■ *Product identification and traceability.* The company must identify and trace products during all stages of production, delivery, and installation.

■ *Process control.* The company must carry out production processes under controlled conditions. The processes must be documented and monitored, and workers must use approved equipment and have specified criteria for workmanship.

■ *Inspection, measurement, and test equipment.* The company must maintain records at all stages of inspection and testing.

■ *Inspection and test status.* The company must label products throughout all stages of production.

■ *Control of nonconforming product.* Procedures should ensure that the company avoids inadvertent use of nonconforming product.

■ *Corrective action.* The company should investigate causes of nonconformance and take action both to correct the problems and to prevent them in the future.

■ *Handling, storage, packaging, and delivery.* The company should properly handle, store, and deliver products.

■ *Quality records.* The company should identify, collect, index, file, and store all records relating to the quality system.

■ *Internal quality audits.* The company's system of internal audits determines whether its activities comply with requirements.

■ *Training.* Procedures are needed to identify needs and provide training of employees.

■ *Servicing.* The company must perform service as required by its contracts with customers.

■ *Statistical control.* Procedures should identify statistical techniques used to control processes, products, and services.

ISO requires that all published standards be reviewed on a periodic basis. Revised quality standards were published in 1994. The 1994 changes do not alter the basic approach but are designed to improve their usability. Many of the changes are improvements in language, such as clarifying a "product" to be "hardware, software, processed materials, or services," reducing the manufacturing focus of the standards (a college in England achieved ISO registration in 1994). The current set of complete standards can be purchased through the American Society for Quality Control in Milwaukee, Wisconsin.

■ Registration Process

The ISO 9000 standards originally were intended to be advisory in nature and to be used for two-party contractual situations (between a customer and supplier) and for internal auditing. However, they quickly evolved into a criteria for companies who wished to "certify" their quality management or achieve "registration" through a third-party auditor, usually a laboratory or some other accreditation agency (called a registrar). This process began in the United Kingdom. Rather than a supplier being audited for compliance to the standards by each customer, the registrar certifies the company, and this certification is accepted by all of the supplier's customers.

The registration process includes *document review* by the registrar of the quality system documents or quality manual; *preassessment*, which identifies potential noncompliance in the quality system or in the documentation, *assessment* by a team of two or three auditors of the quality system and its documentation; and *surveillance*, or periodic re-audits to verify conformity with the practices and systems registered. Recertification is required every three years. Individual sites—not entire companies—must achieve registration individually. All costs are borne by the applicant, so the process can be quite expensive.

◼ Perspectives on ISO 9000

Many misconceptions exist about what ISO 9000 actually is. The standards do not specify any measure of quality performance; specific product quality levels are set by the company. The standards are based on the principle that quality should be defined by the product or service's fitness for use, and that the customer has the right to receive appropriate quality. The standards only require that the supplier have a verifiable process in place to ensure that it consistently produces what it says it will produce, thus providing confidence to customers and company management that certain principles of good management are followed. The standards emphasize documenting conformance of quality systems to the company's quality manual and established quality system requirements. As one consultant explained it, "Document it, and do it like you document it. If it moves, train it. If not, calibrate it." Having an ISO 9000 certified supplier assures the customer that a consistent level of quality will be delivered. A supplier can comply with the standards and still produce a poor quality product—as long as it does so consistently! In addition, ISO 9000 does not consider activities such as leadership, strategic planning, or customer relationship management.

Having just read the preceding sentences, do not think that the standards are not useful. They provide a set of good common practices for quality assurance systems and are an excellent starting point for companies with no formal quality assurance program. Many companies find that their current quality systems already comply with most of the standards. For companies in the early stages of formal quality programs, the standards enforce the discipline of control that is necessary before they can seriously pursue continuous improvement. The requirements of periodic audits reinforce the stated quality system until it becomes ingrained in the company.

The rigorous documentation standards help companies uncover problems and improve their processes. At DuPont, for example, ISO 9000 has been credited with increasing on-time delivery from 70 to 90 percent, decreasing cycle time from 15 days to 1.5 days, increasing first-pass yields from 72 to 92 percent, and reducing the number of test procedures by one-third. In Canada, Toronto Plastics, Ltd. reduced defects from 150,000 per million to 15,000 after one year of ISO implementation.[14] Thus, using ISO 9000 as a basis for a quality system can improve productivity, decrease costs, and increase customer satisfaction.

In addition to improving internal operations, the most important reasons why companies seek ISO 9000 certification include:

◼ *Meeting contractual obligations.* Some customers now require certification of all their suppliers. Suppliers that do not pursue registration will eventually lose customers.

■ *Meeting trade regulations.* Many products sold in Europe, such as telecommunication terminal equipment, medical devices, gas appliances, toys, and construction products require product certifications to assure safety. Often, ISO certification is necessary to obtain product certification.

■ *Marketing goods in Europe.* ISO 9000 is widely accepted within the European Community. It is fast becoming a *de facto* requirement for doing business within the trading region.

■ *Gaining a competitive advantage.* Many customers use ISO registration as a basis for supplier selection. Companies without it may be at a market disadvantage.

The standards are intended to apply to all types of businesses, including electronics and chemicals, and to services such as health care, banking, and transportation. As of early 1993, only about 550 company sites in the United States were certified. In contrast, some 20,000 companies were certified in the United Kingdom. During the first nine months of 1993, registrations grew by 70 percent to about 45,000 worldwide, evidence of the growing global interest in the standards, driven primarily by marketplace demands. By June of 1994, the United States had almost 4000 registrations, and the United Kingdom had more than 36,000.

THE MALCOLM BALDRIGE NATIONAL QUALITY AWARD

Recognizing that U.S. productivity was declining, President Reagan signed legislation mandating a national study/conference on productivity in October 1982. The American Productivity and Quality Center (formerly the American Productivity Center) sponsored seven computer networking conferences in 1983 to prepare for an upcoming White House Conference on Productivity. The final report on these conferences recommended that "a National Quality Award, similar to the Deming Prize in Japan, be awarded annually to those firms that successfully challenge and meet the award requirements. These requirements and the accompanying examination process should be very similar to the Deming Prize system to be effective." The Baldrige Award was signed into law on August 20, 1987. The award is named after President Reagan's Secretary of Commerce who was killed in an accident shortly before the Senate acted on the legislation. Malcolm Baldrige was highly regarded by world leaders, having played a major role in carrying out the administration's trade policy, resolving technology transfer differences with China and India, and holding the first Cabinet-level talks with the Soviet Union in seven years that paved the way for increased access for U.S. firms in the Soviet market. Within the Commerce Department, he reduced the budget by more than 30 percent and administrative personnel by 25 percent.

The purposes of the Award are to

■ Help stimulate American companies to improve quality and productivity for the pride of recognition while obtaining a competitive edge through increased profits

■ Recognize the achievements of those companies that improve the quality of their goods and services and provide an example to others

■ Establish guidelines and criteria that can be used by business, industrial, governmental, and other enterprises in evaluating their own quality improvement efforts

■ Provide specific guidance for other American enterprises that wish to learn how to manage for high quality by making available detailed information on how winning enterprises were able to change their cultures and achieve eminence

The Baldrige Award recognizes U.S. companies that excel in quality management and quality achievement. The Baldrige Award does not exist simply to recognize product excellence, nor does it exist for the purpose of "winning." Its principal focus is on the management practices that lead to customer satisfaction and business results. The award promotes the awareness of quality as an increasingly important element in competitiveness, an understanding of the requirements for quality excellence, and sharing of information on successful quality strategies and the benefits derived from implementation of these strategies. Up to two companies can receive a Baldrige Award in each of the categories of manufacturing, small business, and service. Table 12.2 shows the recipients through 1994. In 1995, pilot programs in education and health care were instituted. As of this writing, it appears likely that Congress will approve awards in these sectors.

■ Baldrige Award Criteria

The award examination is based upon a rigorous set of criteria designed to encourage companies to enhance their competitiveness through efforts toward dual, results-oriented goals:

TABLE 12.2 Malcolm Baldrige Award Recipients

Year	Manufacturing	Small Business	Service
1988	Motorola, Inc. Westinghouse Commercial Nuclear Fuel Division	Globe Metallurgical, Inc.	
1989	Xerox Corp. Business Products and Systems Milliken & Co.		
1990	Cadillac Motor Car Division IBM Rochester	Wallace Co., Inc.	Federal Express
1991	Solectron Corp. Zytec Corp.	Marlow Industries	
1992	AT&T Network Systems Texas Instruments Defense Systems & Electronics Group	Granite Rock Co.	AT&T Universal Card Services The Ritz-Carlton Hotel Co.
1993	Eastman Chemical Co.	Ames Rubber Corp.	
1994		Wainwright Industries, Inc.	AT&T Consumer Communication Services GTE Directories Corp.

1. Delivery of ever-improving value to customers, resulting in improved marketplace success

2. Improvement of overall company performance and capabilities

The award criteria are built upon a set of core values and concepts that have been addressed in previous chapters:

- Customer-driven quality
- Leadership
- Continuous improvement and learning
- Employee participation and development
- Fast response
- Design quality and prevention
- Long-range view of the future
- Management by fact
- Partnership development
- Corporate responsibility and citizenship
- Results orientation

These core values are embodied in seven categories which form the basis for the assessment:

1.0 Leadership

2.0 Information and Analysis

3.0 Strategic Planning

4.0 Human Resource Development and Management

5.0 Process Management

6.0 Business Results

7.0 Customer Focus and Satisfaction

Figure 12.1 illustrates the dynamic relationships among the seven categories of criteria. This framework has four basic elements:

1. Senior executive leadership sets directions, creates values, goals, and systems, and guides the pursuit of customer value and company performance improvement.

2. The system comprises a set of well-defined and well-designed processes for meeting the company's customer and performance requirements.

3. Measures of progress establish a results-oriented basis for channeling actions to delivering ever-improving customer value and company performance.

4. The basic aims of the system are the delivery of ever-improving value to customers and success in the marketplace.

The seven categories in the Baldrige Award criteria and the elements on which examiners assess a company include:

1. *Leadership:* This category examines senior executives' leadership and personal involvement in setting strategic directions and building and maintaining a leadership system conducive to high performance, individual development, and organizational learning. The leadership category seeks evidence of how senior executives create values and expectations, set directions, develop and

FIGURE 12.1 Baldrige Award Criteria Framework

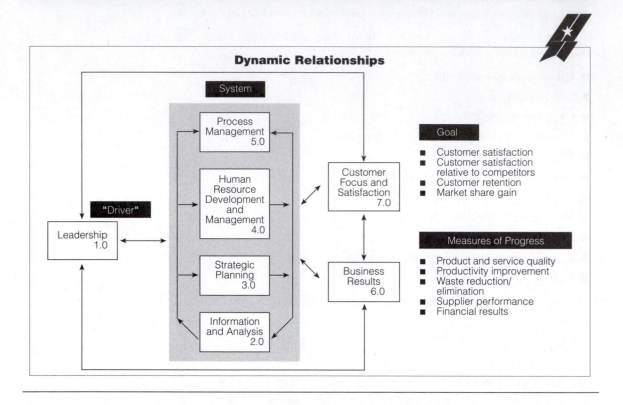

maintain an effective leadership system, build company capabilities, and evaluate and improve the effectiveness of the company's organization and leadership systems. It also seeks information on how the company's leadership system is translated into an effective overall organization and management system that is geared toward performance. Finally, the leadership category looks at how the company integrates its public responsibilities and corporate citizenship into its business planning and performance improvement practices.

2. *Information and Analysis:* This category addresses the information and analysis requirements for performance improvement based upon the improvement of key processes. It addresses the company's selection and management of data and information to support its overall business goals with primary emphasis on supporting process management and performance improvement. The selection and use of data and information related to competitive position—and to best practices—in driving improvement is a critical aspect of this category, as is the manner in which data and information from all parts of the company are aggregated and analyzed to support reviews, business decisions, and planning. Finally, this category addresses interlinking—how customer and market data, improvements in product and service quality, and improvements in operational performance relate to financial and/or market indicators.

3. *Strategic Planning:* This category focuses on the company's strategic and business planning and deployment of plans, along with the company's attention to customer and operational performance requirements. How the company develops its view of the future, sets strategic directions, and translates these into actionable key business drivers, including customer satisfaction and market leadership requirements, is the emphasis in this category. It is also concerned with how the company turns its key business drivers into action plans and measurements that permit tracking of performance.

4. *Human Resource Development and Management:* The areas addressed in this category are concerned with how well human resource practices tie into and are aligned with the company's strategic directions. Key issues are how human resource plans are derived from strategic plans and how the company evaluates and improves its HR planning and management; how the company's job design, compensation, and recognition approaches enable and encourage all employees to contribute effectively; how the company develops the work force via education and training; and how the work environment fosters well-being, satisfaction, and employee development.

5. *Process Management:* In this category the key issues of process management—effective design, a prevention orientation, evaluation and continuous improvement, linkage to suppliers, and overall high performance—are assessed. How the company designs and introduces products and services and integrates production and delivery requirements early in the design process, how it maintains and improves key production and delivery processes as well as support service processes, and how it manages the performance of suppliers are the primary aspects of this category.

6. *Business Results:* Business results provide an appropriate orientation for all processes and process improvement activities. This category addresses current levels and trends in product and service quality using key measures and indicators that relate to important customer and marketplace requirements. It also addresses the operational and financial performance of the company as well as comparative information so that results can be evaluated against competitors or other relevant markers of performance. Finally, it looks at current levels and trends in key measures of supplier performance.

7. *Customer Focus and Satisfaction:* The final category addresses how the company determines current and emerging customer requirements and expectations, provides effective customer relationship management, and determines customer satisfaction. This category also seeks results on customer satisfaction and dissatisfaction, and trends and current levels in key measures, relative to competitors.

In 1995, the seven categories consist of 24 examination items based on major quality system requirements. Each examination item includes a set of "areas to address" that illustrates and clarifies the intent of the items and describes the information that applicants provide. An application guidelines booklet is published each year and describes in detail the information that must be documented. (The *Instructor's Manual* that accompanies this text includes the 1995 criteria.) For example, the Leadership category consists of three examination items:

1. Senior Executive Leadership
2. Leadership System and Organization
3. Public Responsibility and Corporate Citizenship

The Senior Executive Leadership item has two areas that applicants must address:

a. How senior executives provide effective leadership and direction in building and improving company competitiveness, performance, and capabilities. Describe executives' roles in (1) creating and reinforcing values and expectations throughout the company's leadership system; (2) setting directions and performance excellence goals through strategic and business planning; and (3) reviewing overall company performance, including customer-related and operational performance.

b. How senior executives evaluate and improve the effectiveness of the company's leadership system and organization to pursue performance excellence goals.

For example, in the Senior Executive Leadership category, activities of senior executives appropriate for inclusion in part (a) are involvement with customers, employees, and suppliers, mentoring other executives, benchmarking, and employee recognition; and their personal leadership in their use of reviews to focus on key business objectives. Responses to part (b) might include assessment of executives by peers, direct reports, or a board of directors. It might also include results of surveys of company employees.

To illustrate the documentation process, consider some of the information provided by the Ritz-Carlton Hotel Company in their 1992 application (with a caveat that the scope of the criteria have been modified over the years) for the Leadership category. At the Ritz-Carlton, the senior leadership group doubles as the senior quality committee. The senior leaders personally devised the two original quality strategies to broaden the quality leadership of the Ritz-Carlton. The first course of action was new hotel start-up quality assurance. Since 1984, the senior leadership has personally assured that each new hotel product and service provides the characteristics expected by its main customers. An important aspect of this quality practice takes place during the concentrated and intense "seven-day countdown" when senior leaders work side by side with new employees. During these formative sessions, which all new employees must attend, the president and COO communicates company's principles. He personally creates the employee-guest interface image and facilitates each work area's first vision statement. Throughout the entire process, the senior leaders monitor work areas for "start-up," instill Gold Standards, model the company's relationship management, insist upon 100 percent compliance to customer's requirements, and recognize outstanding achievement.

The other initial course of action was the establishment of the Gold Standards. The Gold Standards, in their simplicity, represent an easy-to-understand definition of service quality, which is aggressively communicated and internalized at all levels of the organization. The constant and continuous reinforcement techniques of the Gold Standards, led by senior leaders, include training, daily line-up meetings, pocket cards outlining Ritz-Carlton principles, bulletin board postings, and other methods unique to each hotel. As a result, employees have an exceptional understanding and devotion to the company's vision, values, quality goals, and methods.

The Baldrige Award criteria have several key characteristics.

1. *The criteria are directed toward business results.* The criteria focus principally on seven key areas of business performance: customer satisfaction and retention; market share and new market development; product and service quality; financial indicators, productivity, operational effectiveness, and responsiveness; human resource performance and development; supplier performance and development; and public responsibility and corporate citizenship. Improvements in these seven areas contribute significantly to overall company performance—including financial performance. Emphasis on results balances strategies in such a way that they avoid inappropriate tradeoffs among important stakeholders or objectives.

2. *The criteria are nonprescriptive.* The criteria are a set of 24 basic interrelated, results-oriented requirements, but they do not prescribe specific quality tools, techniques, technologies, systems, or starting points. Companies are encouraged to develop and demonstrate creative, adaptive, and flexible approaches to meeting basic requirements.

3. *The criteria are comprehensive.* The criteria address all internal and external requirements of the company, including those related to fulfilling public responsibilities. Accordingly, all processes of all company work units are tied to these requirements.

4. *The criteria include interrelated learning cycles.* Learning takes place via feedback among the process and results elements. A learning cycle has four stages:

- planning, selection of indicators, and deployment of requirements

- execution of plans

- assessment of progress

- revision of plans based upon assessment findings

Note the similarity to the Deming Cycle (plan, do, study, act).

5. *The criteria emphasize alignment.* The criteria call for improvement at all levels and in all parts of the company. Such improvement is achieved via interconnecting and mutually reinforcing measures and indicators, derived from overall company requirements. These measures and indicators tie directly to customer value and operational performance and provide a communications tool and a basis for deploying consistent customer and operational performance requirements to all work units.

6. *The criteria are part of a diagnostic system.* Using the criteria provides a profile of strengths and areas for improvement that directs attention to processes and actions that contribute to business success.

■ The Baldrige Award Scoring System

Each examination item is assigned a point value that can be earned during the evaluation process. This scoring system is shown in Table 12.3. It is based upon three evaluation dimensions: approach, deployment, and results. *Approach* refers to the methods the company uses to achieve the requirements addressed in each category. The factors used to evaluate approaches include:

- The appropriateness of the methods, tools, and techniques to the requirements

- The effectiveness of methods, tools, and techniques

- The degree to which the approach is systematic, integrated, and consistently applied

- The degree to which the approach embodies effective evaluation/improvement cycles

- The degree to which the approach is based upon quantitative information that is objective and reliable

TABLE 12.3 Baldrige Award Scoring System

1995 Examination Categories/Items	Point Values
1.0 Leadership	**90**
1.1 Senior Executive Leadership	45
1.2 Leadership System and Organization	25
1.3 Public Responsibility and Corporate Citizenship	20
2.0 Information and Analysis	**75**
2.1 Management of Information and Data	20
2.2 Competitive Comparisons and Benchmarking	15
2.3 Analysis and Use of Company-Level Data	40
3.0 Strategic Planning	**55**
3.1 Strategy Development	35
3.2 Strategy Deployment	20
4.0 Human Resource Development and Management	**140**
4.1 Human Resource Planning and Evaluation	20
4.2 High Performance Work Systems	45
4.3 Employee Education, Training, and Development	50
4.4 Employee Well-Being and Satisfaction	25
5.0 Process Management	**140**
5.1 Design and Introduction of Products and Services	40
5.2 Process Management: Product and Service Production and Delivery	40
5.3 Process Management: Support Services	30
5.4 Management of Supplier Performance	30
6.0 Business Results	**250**
6.1 Product and Service Quality Results	75
6.2 Company Operational and Financial Results	130
6.3 Supplier Performance Results	45
7.0 Customer Focus and Satisfaction	**250**
7.1 Customer and Market Knowledge	30
7.2 Customer Relationship Management	30
7.3 Customer Satisfaction Determination	30
7.4 Customer Satisfaction Results	100
7.5 Customer Satisfaction Comparison	60
TOTAL POINTS	**1000**

SOURCE: 1995 Malcolm Baldrige National Quality Award Criteria, Department of Commerce.

■ Evidence of unique and innovative approaches, including the significant and effective new adaptations of tools and techniques used in other applications or types of businesses

Deployment refers to the extent to which the approaches are applied to all relevant areas and activities addressed and implied in each category. The factors used to evaluate deployment include:

■ Appropriate and effective use of the approach in key processes

■ Appropriate and effective application of the approach in the development and delivery of products and services

■ Appropriate and effective use of the approach in all interactions with customers, suppliers of goods and services, and the public

Results refers to the outcomes and effects in achieving the purposes addressed and implied in the criteria. The factors used to evaluate results include:

■ Current performance levels

■ Performance levels relative to appropriate comparisons and benchmarks

■ Rate of performance improvement

■ Breadth and importance of performance improvements

■ Demonstration of sustained improvement or sustained high-level performance

Examiners evaluate the applicant's response to each examination item, listing major strengths and areas for improvement relative to the criteria. Strengths demonstrate an effective and positive response to the criteria. Areas for improvement do not prescribe specific practices or examiners' opinions on what the company should be doing, but rather how management can better address the criteria. Based on these comments, a percentage score is given to each item. Each examination item is evaluated on approach/deployment or results. Table 12.4 summarizes the scoring guidelines.

Like quality itself, the specific award criteria are continually improved each year to better reflect the changing process of TQM. The initial set of criteria in 1988 had 62 items with 278 areas to address. By 1991, the criteria had only 32 items and 99 areas to address. The 1995 criteria were streamlined significantly to 24 items and 54 areas to address. More significantly, the word *quality* has been judiciously dropped throughout the document. For example, until 1994, Category 3 had been titled "Strategic Quality Planning." The change to "Strategic Planning" signifies that quality should be a part of business planning, not a separate issue. Throughout the document, the term *performance* has been substituted for quality as a deliberate attempt to recognize that the principles of TQM are the foundation for a company's management system, not just the quality system. As Curt Reimann, director of the Baldrige Award Program noted, "The things you do to win a Baldrige Award are exactly the things you'd do to win in the marketplace. Our strategy is to have the Baldrige Award criteria be a useful daily tool that simulates real competition."

The 1995 Criteria strengthened several themes: key business drivers of business development and cost reductions, financial data for priority setting, high performance work organizations, investment in work force development, continuous learning and improvement, and business results (including financial results). Results, which accounted for only 10 percent of the score in 1988 and 18 percent in 1994, now comprise 25 percent of the total score. The current year's criteria have undoubtedly been improved since this book was written; a free copy of the criteria can be obtained from the National Institute of Standards and Technology. (To obtain a free single copy, contact the Malcolm Baldrige National Quality Award, National Institute of Standards and Technology, Route 270 & Quince Orchard Road, Administration Building, Room A537, Gaithersburg, MD 20899 (301) 975-2036, FAX (301) 948-3716.)

■ The Baldrige Award Evaluation Process

The Baldrige evaluation process is rigorous. In the first stage, each application is thoroughly reviewed by five to eight examiners chosen from among leading quality professionals in business, academia, health care, and government (all of whom are volunteers). The scores are reviewed by a panel of nine judges without knowledge of the specific companies. The higher scoring applications enter a consensus stage in which the examiners discuss variations in individual scores and arrive at consensus scores for each item. The panel of judges then reviews the scores and selects the highest scoring applicants for site visits. At this point, five to eight examiners visit the company for up to a week to verify information contained in the written application and resolve issues that are unclear. The judges use the site visit reports to recommend award recipients. Final contenders each receive more than 400 hours of evaluation.

All applicants receive a feedback report that critically evaluates the company's strengths and areas for improvement relative to the award criteria. The feedback report, frequently 30 or more pages in length, contains the evaluation team's

TABLE 12.4   Baldrige Award Scoring Guidelines

Score	Approach/Deployment	Score	Results
0%	▪ no systematic approach evident, anecdotal information	0%	▪ no results or poor results in areas reported
10% to 30%	▪ beginning of a systematic approach to the primary purposes of the item ▪ early stages of a transition from reacting to problems to a general improvement orientation ▪ major gaps exist in deployment that would inhibit progress in achieving the primary purposes of the item	10% to 30%	▪ early stages of developing trends; some improvements and/or early good performance levels in a few areas ▪ results not reported for many to most areas of importance to the applicant's key business requirements
40% to 60%	▪ a sound, systematic approach, responsive to the primary purposes of the item ▪ a fact-based improvement process in place in key areas; more emphasis is placed on improvement than on reaction to problems ▪ no major gaps in deployment, though some areas or work units may be in very early stages of deployment	40% to 60%	▪ improvement trends and/or good performance levels reported for many to most areas of importance to the applicant's key business requirements ▪ no pattern of adverse trends and/or poor performance levels in areas of importance to the applicant's key business requirements ▪ some trends and/or current performance levels—evaluated against relevant comparisons and/or benchmarks—show areas of strength and/or good to very good relative performance levels
70% to 90%	▪ a sound, systematic approach, responsive to the overall purposes of the item ▪ a fact-based improvement process is a key management tool; clear evidence of refinement and improved integration as a result of improvement cycles and analysis ▪ approach is well-deployed, with no major gaps; deployment may vary in some areas or work units	70% to 90%	▪ current performance is good to excellent in most areas of importance to the applicant's key business requirements ▪ most improvement trends and/or performance levels are sustained ▪ many to most trends and/or current performance levels—evaluated against relevant comparisons and/or benchmarks—show areas of leadership and very good relative performance levels
100%	▪ a sound, systematic approach, fully responsive to all the requirements of the item ▪ a very strong, fact-based improvement process is a key management tool; strong refinement and integration—backed by excellent analysis ▪ approach is fully deployed without any significant weaknesses or gaps in any areas or work units	100%	▪ current performance is excellent in most areas of importance to the applicant's key business requirements ▪ excellent improvement trends and/or sustained excellent performance levels in most areas ▪ strong evidence of industry and benchmark leadership demonstrated in many areas

SOURCE: 1995 Malcolm Baldrige National Quality Award Criteria, Department of Commerce.

response to the written application. It includes a distribution of numerical scores of all applicants and a scoring summary of the individual applicant. This feedback is one of the most valuable aspects of the Baldrige Award program.

■ Impacts of the Baldrige Award

The Baldrige Award has generated an incredible amount of interest in quality, both within the United States and internationally. Winning companies have made thousands of presentations describing their quality management approaches and practices. Many states have instituted awards similar to the Baldrige and based on the Baldrige Criteria. The award criteria have been used to train hundreds of thousands of people and as a self-assessment tool within organizations.

In assessing the applications submitted for the Baldrige Award, several key strengths and common weaknesses are evident. Most companies that apply have strong senior management leadership and are driven by the needs of customers and the marketplace. These firms have aggressive goals and high expectations. Companies have strong information systems that provide an excellent basis for assessing the state of quality and that link external customer satisfaction measurements with internal measurements such as process quality and employee satisfaction. Most companies have invested heavily in human resource development, and employee involvement is continuing and expanding.

Common weaknesses among firms that do not score well include

- Weak information systems
- Delegation of quality responsibility to lower levels of the company
- A partial quality system, for example, strong in manufacturing but weak in support services
- An unclear definition of what quality means in the organization
- A lack of alignment among diverse functions within the firm; that is, not all processes are driven by common goals or use the same approaches
- Failure to use all listening posts to gather information critical to decision making

Among the more disappointing results found by Baldrige Award administrators is that relatively few organizations actually practice *total quality*. Many lack a quality vision or do not effectively translate this vision into a business strategy. Many companies still emphasize the negative side of quality—defect reduction, rather than customer focus. Finally, the gaps between the best and the average companies is quite large, indicating that much opportunity and hard work remains.

Baldrige Award–winning companies have shown excellent financial results. The Commerce Department reported that a person who had invested $1000 in each publicly traded winning company from the time the award was announced through October 3, 1994, would have gained a cumulative return of 188 percent, compared to a 28 percent return in the Standard & Poor's 500.[15]

■ Using the Baldrige Award Criteria

The Baldrige Award criteria form a blueprint for quality improvement in any organization. Hundreds of thousands of applications are distributed each year, yet only a handful of completed applications are received. Many companies are using the award criteria to evaluate their own quality programs, set up and implement TQM programs, communicate better with suppliers and partners, and for education and training. Even the U.S. Postal Service has decided to use the Baldrige Criteria as a basis to reestablish a quality system by identifying the areas that need the most improvement and providing a baseline to track progress. Using the award criteria as a self-assessment tool provides an objective framework, sets a high standard, and compares units that have different systems or organizations. It is also being used as a basis for giving awards within companies and at the local, state, and federal levels.

Many different philosophies and quality improvement programs exist. Organizations just getting started in quality improvement often have problems defining the quality system and setting objectives. The Baldrige Award addresses the full range of quality issues and can help those setting up new systems to get a complete picture of TQM.

The Baldrige Award criteria assist companies with internal communications, communications with suppliers, and communications with other companies seeking to share information. The criteria provide a focus on what to communicate and a framework for comparing strategies, methods, progress, and benchmarks. Finally, the Baldrige Award examination is being used for training and education, particularly for management, because it summarizes major issues that managers must understand. It draws the distinction between excellence and mediocrity.

ISO 9000 and the Baldrige Award[16]

With all the publicity surrounding the Baldrige Award and ISO 9000, many misconceptions about them have arisen. Two common misconceptions are that the Baldrige Award and ISO 9000 registration cover similar requirements, and that both address improvement and results. In reality, the Baldrige Award and ISO 9000 are distinctly different instruments that can reinforce one another when properly used. Table 12.5 contrasts the key differences between them. ISO 9000 is a minor subset of Baldrige. The Baldrige Criteria go far beyond ISO 9000, which does not deal directly with continuous improvement and customer satisfaction. Many companies are using the Baldrige Award criteria and ISO 9000 compatibly, sometimes sequentially and sometimes simultaneously.

Because of the growing focus on ISO 9000 as well as state quality awards (see the next major section), many companies who might have applied for the Baldrige Award have decided not to. Applications have fallen somewhat from the peak 106 in 1991 (although total applications to state and national award programs continue to increase). However, this decline in applications certainly does not mean that the Baldrige Award criteria or the award itself are less important, as demonstrated by the many state award programs and internal company assessments that are patterned after the Baldrige Award.

QS 9000

Late in 1994, the big three automobile manufacturers—Ford, Chrylser, and General Motors—released *QS 9000,* an interpretation and extension of ISO 9000 for automotive suppliers. QS 9000 is a collaborative effort of these firms to standardize their individual quality requirements while drawing upon the global ISO

TABLE 12.5 Contrasts Between the Baldrige Award and ISO 9000 Registration

	Baldrige Award Program	ISO 9000 Registration
Focus	Competitiveness; customer value and operational performance	Conformity to practices specified in the registrant's own quality system
Purpose	Educational; shares competitiveness learning	To provide a common basis for assuring buyers that specific practices conform with the providers' stated quality systems
Quality definition	Customer-driven	Conformity of specified operations to documented requirements
Improvement/results	Heavy dependence on results and improvement	Does not assess outcome-oriented results or improvement trends
Role in the marketplace	A form of recognition, but not intended to be a product endorsement or certification	Provides customers with assurances that a registered supplier has a documented quality system and follows it
Nature of assessment	Four-stage review process	Evaluation of quality manual and working documents and site audits to ensure conformance to stated practices
Feedback	Diagnostic feedback on approach, deployment, and results	Audit feedback on discrepancies and findings related to practices and documentation
Criteria improvement	Annual revision of criteria	Revisions of 1987 document issued in 1994, focusing on clarification
Responsibility for information sharing	Winners required to share quality strategies	No obligation to share information
Service quality	Service excellence a principal concern	Standards focused on repetitive processes, without a focus on critical service quality issues such as customer relationship management and human resource development
Scope of coverage	All operations and processes of all work units; includes all ISO 9001 requirements	Covers only design/development, production, installation, and servicing; address less than 10 percent of the Baldrige criteria
Documentation requirement	Not spelled out in criteria	A central audit requirement
Self-assessment	Principal use of criteria in the area of improvement practices	Standards primarily for "contractual situations" or other external audits

standards. Truck manufacturers—Mack Trucks, Freightliner, Navistar International, PACCAR Inc, and Volvo GM—also participated in the process. Their goal was to develop fundamental quality systems that provide for continuous improvement, emphasizing defect prevention and the reduction of variation and waste in the supply chain. This standardized quality will reduce the cost of doing business with suppliers and enhance the competitive position of the automakers and suppliers alike. QS 9000 applies to all internal and external suppliers of production and service parts and materials. Chrysler, Ford, GM, and truck manufacturers will require all suppliers to establish, document, and implement quality systems based on these standards according to individual customers' timing.

QS 9000 is based on ISO 9000 and includes all ISO requirements. However, QS 9000 goes well beyond ISO 9000 standards by including additional requirements such as continuous improvement, manufacturing capability, and production part approval processes. Many of the concepts in the Malcolm Baldrige

National Quality Award criteria are reflected in QS 9000. For example, under management responsibility (the first element in the ISO standards), suppliers are required to document trends in quality, operational performance (productivity, efficiency, and effectiveness), and current quality levels for key product and service features, and compare them with those of competitors and/or appropriate benchmarks. Suppliers are also required to have a documented process for determining customer satisfaction, including the frequency of determination and how objectivity and validity are assured. Trends in customer satisfaction and key indicators of customer dissatisfaction must be documented and supported by objective information, compared to competitors or benchmarks, and reviewed by senior management. The wording is almost identical to that found in the Baldrige Award criteria.

In addition, registration to QS 9000 requires demonstration of effectiveness in meeting the *intent* of the standards, rather than simply the "do it as you document it" philosophy. For instance, while ISO 9000 requires "suitable maintenance of equipment to ensure continuing process capability" under process control, QS 9000 requires suppliers to identify key process equipment and provide appropriate resources for maintenance, and develop an effective, planned total preventive maintenance system. The system should include a procedure that describes the planned maintenance activities, scheduled maintenance, and predictive maintenance methods. Also, extensive requirements for documenting process monitoring and operator instructions and process capability and performance requirements are built into the standards. Finally, additional requirements pertain specifically to Ford, Chrysler, and GM suppliers. Thus, registration under QS 9000 standards will also achieve ISO 9000 registration, but ISO-certified companies must meet the additional QS 9000 requirements to achieve QS certification.

STATE QUALITY AWARDS

Many states have developed award programs similar to the Baldrige Award. State award programs generally are designed to promote an awareness of productivity and quality, foster an information exchange, encourage firms to adopt quality and productivity improvement strategies, recognize firms that have instituted successful strategies, provide role models for other businesses in the state, encourage new industry to locate in the state, and establish a quality-of-life culture that will benefit all residents of the state.[17] Each state is unique, however, and thus the specific objectives will vary. For instance, the primary objectives of Minnesota's quality award are to encourage all Minnesota organizations to examine their current state of quality and to become more involved in the movement toward continuous quality improvement, as well as to recognize outstanding quality achievements in the state. Missouri, on the other hand, has as its objectives to educate all Missourians in quality improvement, to foster the pursuit of quality in all aspects of Missouri life, and to recognize quality leadership.

Award categories often extend beyond the Baldrige Award criteria. California, for example, is developing the Governor's Golden State Quality Awards, a joint project of the Trade and Commerce Agency and the Department of Consumer Affairs. The award is administered by the California Center for Quality, Education and Development, a private nonprofit corporation. It has five award categories:

1. *Quality in Management:* to recognize companies that excel in managing their core activity, be it manufacturing, services, or some combination

2. *Quality in the Marketplace:* to recognize companies that have translated an approach to quality into improved customer satisfaction and business results

3. *Quality in the Workplace:* to recognize companies that realize the full potential of the work force to achieve the company's performance objectives

4. *Quality in the Community:* to recognize companies that excel in their interaction with their communities

5. *The Governor's Golden State Quality Award:* to recognize companies that best exemplify the qualities described in the award application criteria for all of the individual awards. California's program embraces the Baldrige Award's concepts, but it presents and expresses them so as to appeal to the broadest possible spectrum of business enterprises.

The Massachusetts Quality Award is modeled after the Malcolm Baldrige National Quality Award, but generally requires less detailed responses to questions. The award is administered by the Massachusetts Council for Quality, Inc., a nonprofit organization affiliated with the University of Massachusetts at Lowell. The categories include service, manufacturing, small business, and nonprofit. The first award was presented in October 1992, and is named in honor of Armand V. Feigenbaum (see Chapter 3).

New York's Excelsior Award program departs the most from the Baldrige model.[18] It includes public sector agencies and educational institutions in addition to private companies. It goes further by stressing the importance of labor–management cooperation and human resource development in its criteria weighting scheme.

Many other states, including Connecticut, Delaware, Florida, Maine, North Carolina, New Jersey, New Mexico, Pennsylvania, Tennessee, and Texas, have similar awards, most of which are patterned after the Baldrige Award. In addition, Alabama, Louisiana, Maryland, Nevada, and Virginia have State Senate Productivity Awards that address quality issues. Other states are in the process of developing similar award programs.

THE DEMING PRIZE

The Deming Application Prize was instituted in 1951 by the Union of Japanese Scientists and Engineers (JUSE) in recognition and appreciation of W. Edwards Deming's achievements in statistical quality control and his friendship with the Japanese people. The Deming Prize has several categories, including prizes for individuals, factories, and small companies, and the Deming application prize, which is an annual award presented to a company or a division of a company that has achieved distinctive performance improvements through the application of companywide quality control (CWQC). As defined by JUSE, CWQC is

a system of activities to assure that quality products and services required by customers are economically designed, produced and supplied while respecting the principle of customer-orientation and the overall public well-being. These quality assurance activities involve market research, research and development, design, purchasing, production, inspection and sales, as well as all other related activities inside and outside the company. Through everyone in the company understanding both statistical concepts and methods, through their application to all the aspects of quality assurance and through repeating the cycle of rational planning, implementation, evaluation and action, CWQC aims to accomplish business objectives.[19]

The judging criteria consists of a checklist of 10 major categories as shown in Table 12.6. Each major category is divided into subcategories, or "checking points." For example, the policy category includes policies pursued for management, quality, and quality control; methods for establishing policies; appropriateness and consistency of policies; utilization of statistical methods; communication and dissemination of policies; checks of policies and the status of their achievement; and the relationship between policies and long- and short-term plans. Unlike the Baldrige Award, each category is weighted equally.

Hundreds of companies apply for the award each year. After an initial application is accepted as eligible for the process, the company must submit a detailed description of its quality practices. Sorting through and evaluating a large number of applications is an extraordinary effort in itself. Based on review of the written descriptions, only a few companies believed to be successful in CWQC are selected for a site visit. The site visit consists of a company presentation, in-depth questioning by the examiners, and an executive session with top managers. Examiners visit plants and are free to ask any worker any question. For example, at Florida Power and Light, the first non-Japanese company to win the Deming Prize, examiners asked questions of specific individuals such as "What are your main accountabilities?" "What are the important priority issues for the corporation?" "What indicators do you have for your performance? For your target?" "How are you doing today compared to your target?" They request examples of inadequate performance. Documentation must be made available immediately. The preparation is extensive and sometimes frustrating.

The Deming Prize is awarded to all companies that meet the prescribed standard, however, the small number of awards given each year is an indication of the difficulty of achieving the standard. The objectives are to ensure that a company has so thoroughly deployed a quality process that it will continue to improve long after a prize is awarded. The application process has no "losers." For companies that do not qualify, the examination process is automatically extended up to two times over three years.

As of 1992, 143 companies had won a Deming Prize, including the seven largest Japanese industrial corporations. Some winners of the Deming Prize include Toyota Motor Company, Ltd., NEC IC/Microcomputer Systems, Shimizu Construction Company, Ltd., and the Kansai Electric Power Company. Toyota has captured nearly 10 percent of the world's automotive market. NEC has earned a reputation for exceptional quality in a diverse set of electronics areas. Shimizu Construction is one of the top five construction firms in Japan and has entered the U.S. market by developing golf courses and condominium communities. Kansai Electric helped to bring recognition of total quality management into the service sector. Kansai offers electrical service at consistently low rates and has managed to shorten service interruptions significantly in comparison with other Japanese electric utilities. Kansai was the major benchmark firm for Florida Power and Light when it began to consider seriously making a bid for the prize.

TABLE 12.6   The Deming Application Prize Checklist

Items	Checking Points
1. Policies	(1) Management, quality and quality control/management policies (2) Methods for establishing policies (3) Appropriateness and consistency of policies (4) Utilization of statistical methods (5) Communication and dissemination of policies (6) Checks on policies and status of their achievement (7) Their relationship to long- and short-term plans
2. The Organization and its operations	(1) Clarity of authority and responsibility (2) Appropriateness of the delegation of authority (3) Inter-departmental coordination (4) Committee activities (5) Utilization of staff (6) Utilization of QC Circle activities (7) Quality control/management diagnosis
3. Education and dissemination	(1) Educational plan and results (2) Consciousness of quality and how it is managed, and understanding of quality control/management (3) Education on statistical concepts and methods and the degree to which they are disseminated (4) Grasp of effects (5) Education of associated companies (especially, group companies, vendors, contractors and distributors) (6) QC Circle activities (7) The system of improvement suggestions and its status
4. Information gathering, communication and its utilization	(1) Collection of external information (2) Inter-departmental communication (3) Speed of communication (utilization of computers) (4) Information processing, (statistical) analysis and utilization of information
5. Analysis	(1) Selection of important issues and improvement themes (2) Appropriateness of analytical methods (3) Utilization of statistical methods (4) Linkage with industry intrinsic technology (5) Quality analysis and process analysis (6) Utilization of analysis results (7) Action taken on improvement suggestions
6. Standardization	(1) System of standards (2) Methods of establishing, revising and abolishing standards (3) Actual performance in establishing, revising and abolishing standards (4) Contents of the standards (5) Utilization of statistical methods (6) Accumulation of technology (7) Utilization of standards
7. Control/management	(1) Management systems for quality and other-related elements, such as cost and delivery (quantity) (2) Control points and control items (3) Utilization of statistical methods and concepts, such as control charts (4) Contributions of QC Circle activities (5) Status of control/management activities (6) In-control situations
8. Quality assurance	(1) New product and service development methods (quality deployment and analysis, reliability testing and design review) (2) Preventive activities for safety and product liability (3) Degree of customer satisfaction (4) Process design, process analysis and process control and improvement

Continued

TABLE 12.6 The Deming Application Prize Checklist—*Continued*

Items	Checking Points
8. Quality assurance—*Cont.*	(5) Process capabilities (6) Instrumentation and inspection (7) Management of facilities, vendors, procurement and services (8) Quality assurance system and its diagnosis (9) Utilization of statistical methods (10) Quality evaluation and audit (11) Status of quality assurance
9. Effects	(1) Measurements of effects (2) Tangible effects such as quality, service, delivery, cost, profit, safety and environment (3) Intangible effects (4) Conformity of actual performance to planned effects
10. Future plans	(1) Concrete understanding of current situation (2) Measures for solving defect problems (3) Future promotion plans (4) Relationship between future plans and long-term plans

SOURCE: Compiled by the Deming Application Prize Subcommittee, revised 1984. The Deming Prize Guide for Oversea Companies, Union of Japanese Scientists and Engineers, 1992.

THE EUROPEAN AND CANADIAN QUALITY AWARDS

In October 1991, the European Foundation for Quality Management (EFQM) in partnership with the European Commission and the European Organization for Quality announced the creation of the European Quality Award. The award was designed to increase awareness throughout the European Community, and businesses in particular, of the growing importance of quality to their competitiveness in the increasingly global market and to their standards of life. The European Quality Award consists of two parts: the European Quality Prize, given to companies that demonstrate excellence in quality management practice by meeting the award criteria, and the European Quality Award, awarded to the most successful applicant. In 1992, four prizes and one award were granted for the first time.

Applicants must demonstrate that their TQM approach has contributed significantly to satisfying the expectations of customers, employees, and other constituencies. The award process is similar to the Deming Prize and Baldrige Award. The assessment is based on customer satisfaction, business results, processes, leadership, people satisfaction, resources, people management, policy and strategy, and impact on society. Figure 12.2 shows the framework for the European Quality Award. In comparing these elements with the Baldrige framework in Figure 12.1, many similarities and several differences are apparent. Results—including customer satisfaction, people (employee) satisfaction, and impact on society—constitute a higher percentage of the total score. These results, like the Baldrige Award, are driven by leadership and the quality system. The three criteria of people satisfaction, impact on society, and business results are somewhat different.[20]

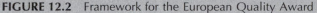

FIGURE 12.2 Framework for the European Quality Award

People satisfaction refers to how employees feel about the organization, including the working environment, perception of management style, career planning and development, and job security. Unlike Baldrige Award category 4.0, it is an independent results category. The impact on society category focuses on the perceptions of the company by the community at large and the company's approach to the quality of life, the environment, and the preservation of global resources. The European Quality Award criteria places greater emphasis on this category than is placed on the public responsibility item in the Baldrige Award criteria. The business results criterion explicitly addresses the financial performance of the firm, its market competitiveness, and its ability to satisfy shareholders' expectations. Other nonfinancial areas of performance, such as order processing time, new product design lead time, and time to break even are also considered.

Canada's National Quality Institute (NQI) recognizes Canada's foremost achievers of excellence through the prestigious Canada Awards for Excellence. NQI is a nonprofit organization designed to stimulate and support quality-driven innovation within all Canadian enterprises and institutions, including business, government, education, and health care. The Canadian Awards for Excellence quality criteria are similar in structure to the Baldrige Award criteria, with some key differences. The major categories and items within each category for 1995 are:

1. *Leadership (170 points):* strategic direction, leadership involvement, and outcomes.

2. *Customer focus (200 points):* voice of the customer, management of customer relationships, measurement, and outcomes.

3. *Planning for improvement (130 points):* development and content of improvement plan, assessment, and outcomes.

4. *People focus (200 points):* human resource planning, participatory environment, continuous learning environment, employee satisfaction, and outcomes.

5. *Process optimization (200 points):* process definition, process control, process improvement, and outcomes.

6. *Supplier focus (100 points):* partnering and outcomes.

These categories seek similar information as the Baldrige Award criteria. For example, the people focus category examines the development of human resource planning and implementation and operation of a strategy for achieving excellence through people. It also examines the organization's efforts to foster and support an environment that encourages and enables people to reach their full potential. A major difference is that measures and results are integrated into each category, whereas they appear separately in the Baldrige criteria. Outcomes (results) comprise 380 of the 1000 point total; less than Baldrige and the European criteria. Recipients of Canada's top quality award include Ford Electronics Manufacturing Corporation and the Toronto Manufacturing Plant of IBM Canada.

QUALITY IN PRACTICE   THE PAYOFF FROM BALDRIGE AT TEXAS INSTRUMENTS[21]

Texas Instruments (TI) Defense Systems & Electronics Group faced a critical issue that many businesses struggle with: Is the payoff of greater competitive advantage worth the effort of achieving total quality, specifically competing for the Baldrige Award? Their answer is a definite *yes*. TI understands firsthand that the real benefit of applying for the Baldrige Award lies in adopting its quality criteria. The application itself is the single-most powerful catalyst for the kinds of organizational and cultural changes that companies must make to compete.

TI's commitment to quality and productivity improvement dates back to the 1950s. But, like most corporations, most of its efforts were aimed at improving manufacturing and product quality. In the early 1980s, a total quality initiative was formalized across the entire corporation. Some business units made tremendous progress; the semiconductor operation in Japan won the Deming Prize in 1985.

When the Baldrige Award criteria appeared, TI used them to provide focus and coherence to the activities across the corporation. Using the criteria, they were able to tackle a part of total quality that previously had been unreachable: implementing quality efforts in staff, support, and nonmanufacturing areas. In 1989, TI asked every business unit to prepare a mock award application as a way of measuring its progress. This task represented a radical change for some operations because, until that time, most staff functions were not required to measure their processes or their results.

The Defense Systems & Electronics Group's self-assessment revealed that they were a long way from applying for and winning the Baldrige Award. But the group aggressively adopted the criteria as a blueprint for improving its business. Many executives did not believe that the criteria could be applied to defense contractors. Similarly, many executives today question whether small businesses can realistically meet the Baldrige Award criteria. TI discovered that all companies have one thing in common: customers. Focusing on customers to make the company more competitive provides meaning to the award.

The Baldrige Award application process changed almost everything within the Defense Systems & Electronics Group. Before applying, the group had no way of systematically measuring how well it understood its customers' concerns, captured customers' feedback, or made improvements in interacting with customers. Mountains of data were being collected, but most of the data measured internal criteria, not customer satisfaction. The structured, hierarchical management environment made it difficult to adopt ideas from outside sources.

The Baldrige Award process provided a way to make the customer the centerpiece of daily activities. It led to much better communication with customers and employees and accelerated progress toward less hierarchical, more functional work teams. It changed the management process from an individual activity to a team effort, leading to better decisions. Finally, it introduced two radical new ideas: benchmarking and stretch goals. Changing the culture was not easy and did not happen quickly. It took teamwork, consensus building, and buy in. At TI, it took about five years of dedicated pulling in the same direction to begin seeing measurable results.

Key Issues for Discussion

1. Explain the value of preparing a mock Baldrige Award application at Texas Instruments. Would other companies experience similar results?

2. As noted, some people question whether small businesses can realistically meet the Baldrige Award criteria. What aspects of the criteria would be more difficult for small businesses than large companies to address? How might a small business overcome these challenges?

QUALITY IN PRACTICE   THE FORD Q1 AWARD[22]

"A plant designated as Q1 is recognized as having achieved a level of excellence, and as having in place processes/systems for continuous improvement in meeting the customers' needs and expectations." This is Ford Motor Company's description of its Q1 Award for suppliers, the basis for their supplier certification program. The Q1 program was initiated in 1981 and expanded in 1984 to include Ford manufacturing plants worldwide.

Figure 12.3 illustrates the qualification process. It begins with a plant conducting a complete self-evaluation, using a set of criteria, assessment factors, and scoring guidelines. The purpose of the self-evaluation is to identify the areas in which a plant's quality system may be deficient so that corrections and improvement may be made and evaluated prior to petitioning for Q1 consideration. Ford's Safety Office and Corporate Quality Office then conduct in-plant reviews of safety compliance and process capability. Once the plant has completed its self-evaluation, made improvements, and had the in-plant reviews conducted, the plant can initiate a formal petition.

The criteria used to determine if a plant is qualified for the Q1 Award is based on five categories:

1. *Adequacy of the quality system:* includes indicators on how the plant manages change, employs teamwork and statistical methods, reviews incoming material, and rewards employees

2. *Process capability review:* a check of selected process parameters and product characteristics to determine stability and capability

3. *Internal quality indicators:* as measured by quality audits

4. *Customer satisfaction*

5. *Management commitment:* includes an evaluation of support and training

Specific items that are evaluated for the adequacy of the quality system include:

- advanced quality planning
- training for change
- organizational preparedness
- quality objectives during change periods
- change control procedures
- production responsibility for quality
- implementation of the team approach
- implementation support
- preliminary statistical studies
- measurement system variation studies
- statistical process control planning
- statistical control and capability implementation
- continuous improvement
- problem solving
- incoming material quality
- written procedures
- quality instructions
- gauges and test equipment
- repair procedures
- reward system

A scoring system is used to assess each of these criteria. For example, one of the items evaluated is "change control procedures." This item is concerned with written procedures developed by the plant to maintain and improve quality during change. Questions considered are as follows: Are there written procedures describing responsibilities and actions during change? Are they current? Are they readily accessible to all affected personnel? The plant must show how this procedure was implemented during recent changes. Examples of how points are awarded are described in the following list. Each plant may use varying approaches based on the nature of their processes, products, and work force. Any documented evidence that speaks to the intent of the questions will be considered.

- The plant has no procedure of any sort for managing change (0 points).

- The plant uses verbal procedures only for managing change (1 point).

- The plant has a written procedure on managing change, but there are major (2–4 points) or minor (5–6 points) shortcomings of a specific nature that should be resolved.

- The plant has an adequate written procedure on managing change, with some evidence (7 points) or comprehensive evidence (8 points) that the procedure is implemented as written.

- The plant's change management procedure is innovative and disseminated throughout the plant's organization (9–10 points).

FIGURE 12.3 Ford's Q1 Qualification Process

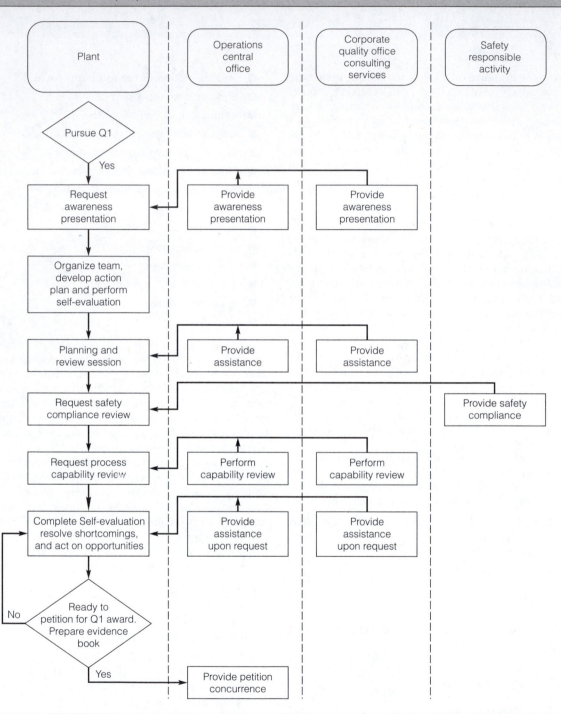

A second example is "measurement system variation studies." This question deals with the evaluation of and reaction to variation in the plant's measurement process. A Q1 plant will have statistical information on all of its major measurement systems and will have implemented improvement actions as appropriate. Questions that are considered include: Are measurement systems variation studies conducted on new and carryover devices, instruments, and systems for which the variation is not known? The scoring in this category is summarized as follows:

■ No studies have been conducted to assess variation on some of the plant's key measurement systems (0 points).

■ Variation studies have been run on several (1 point) or most (4 points) of the plant's measurement systems, but no verification of process stability has taken place.

■ Variation studies incorporating assessments or stability have been conducted on some (up to 30 percent—5 points) or most (31 percent to 90 percent—6 points) of the plant's measurement processes. Some of these studies have shown instability. Corrective actions have either not been incorporated or have not been in effect long enough to provide verification of effectiveness.

■ The plant has effectively implemented measurement systems variation studies of all major measurement processes and will have implemented improvement actions on several (1 to 4 processes—7 points) or many (5 or more processes—8 points) of its measurement processes.

■ The plant has been innovative in the understanding of measurement system variation and has advanced the state of the art of measurement of its processes (9–10 points).

A minimum weighted score is required for Q1 status. The focus of the overall qualification process is the *self-evaluation* by the plant. Ford provides consulting service to clarify, interpret, or provide additional information and assistance in the process.

Key Issues for Discussion

1. Describe the overall thrust of the Q1 criteria. How does it compare to the categories of the Baldrige Award?

2. How can the Q1 program help a plant develop and improve its quality system, even if it fails to qualify for the award?

QUALITY IN PRACTICE FLORIDA POWER AND LIGHT[23]

Florida Power and Light (FPL) is one of the largest electric utilities in the United States. Its territory covers 27,650 square miles, about half of Florida, and services a population of 5.7 million people. FPL has about 15,000 employees, operates 13 plants, 397 substations, and more than 53,000 miles of transmission and distribution lines.

During the 1970s, the company was forced to increase utility rates repeatedly because of increasing costs, slower sales growth, and stricter federal and state regulations. The company had become bureaucratic and inflexible. In 1981, Marshall McDonald, then chairman of the board, realized that the company had been concerned with keeping defects under control rather than improving quality. Due to his concern for quality, McDonald introduced quality improvement teams at FPL. Management knew this was a step in the right direction, but such teams alone would not bring about the change needed for the company to survive. McDonald tried to convince other executives that a total quality improvement process was needed, but all the experts that FPL talked to were in manufacturing, while FPL was primarily a service company. In 1983, while in Japan, McDonald met the president of Kansai Electric Power Company, a Deming Prize winner, who told

him about their total quality efforts. Company officials began to visit Kansai regularly, and with their help, FPL began its quality improvement program (QIP) in 1983.

"Policy deployment" was the driving force behind the QIP program. Policy deployment (see Chapter 6) is a method that takes corporate vision and determines priority issues that will make the vision a reality. For FPL, the issues involved improving reliability, customer satisfaction, and employee safety while keeping costs in control. Each department was then responsible for developing plans to improve in these areas. Once plans were determined, their status was checked regularly to make sure they were on schedule. Each department was limited to working on no more than three items that had the most influence on their department's performance, but the work on these was expected to be done in great detail.

"Quality in daily work" (QIDW) is the expression that FPL used for another concept for improving business systems quality. It involves standardizing work routines, removing waste from them, promoting the concept of internal customers, and enabling better practice to be replicated from one location to another. QIDW control systems consist of flowcharts, process and quality indicators, procedure standards, and computer systems. By examining and analyzing work over and over again, employees in every area contribute to simplifying their work and improving processes. They discover opportunities for computer systems to free line employees from repetitive tasks.

One illustration of how QIDW was used was the development of a computer system for processing customer trouble calls. In the system, the computer first checks to find out if the customer has been disconnected for nonpayment, then begins to locate places and devices that may be malfunctioning, and routes the call through a dispatcher to a troubleshooter. A repairperson heading to the scene may have a diagnosis before arrival. The information is stored in a database to be used for future improvement planning.

FPL revamped a centralized suggestion system it had been using for many years. Only about 600 suggestions had been submitted annually and it usually took six months for evaluation. A new decentralized system was proposed with simplified procedures to improve the response time. Employees participated in the implementation of their own suggestions. In 1988, 9000 suggestions were submitted; in 1989 this number increased to 25,000.

Training has played an important role in FPL's quality transformation. They found that training enhanced enthusiasm and participation. Supervisors are expected to train their employees and play a more active role as coaches and cheerleaders. As line employees have become more skilled in diagnosing and solving problems, issues that once required management attention are now handled by line employees. Problems are dealt with on a factual basis, not with intuition. All employees have developed a much broader view of the company and more flexibility in dealing with customers.

The management system has also changed. Customer satisfaction has become the focus of attention rather than cost control. Management reviews check on improvement progress monthly. Goals are now long term, but progress checks are frequent. Managers review progress with better statistical insight, recognizing that variation will exist, but seek to rid the system of common causes. Cross-functional teams are used to carry out large-scale improvement projects. Finally, the budget is integrated with quality improvement.

The influence of total quality control at FPL can be seen in Figure 12.4. The average length of service interruptions dropped from about 75 minutes in 1983 to about 47 minutes in 1989; the number of complaints per 1000 customers fell to one-third of

the 1983 level; safety has improved; and the price of electricity has stabilized.

After the Deming Prize[24]

Although winning the Deming Prize in 1989 was an honor of which the company and its employees were very proud, a number of employees were feeling that the quality improvement program, intensified by the Deming challenge, had become mechanical and inflexible. In fact, the bureaucratic features that had developed in the process were becoming barriers to continuous improvement in many instances.

At the same time, management had underestimated the speed and impact of the growing threat of deregulation and new competition in the electric utility industry. It was not preparing quickly enough to shift its structure and strategy to compete in this new environment, and needed to re-examine its vision and approach to the quality process. In 1990, the new chairman and CEO, James L. Broadhead, began to investigate both issues. He spoke personally to more than 500 employees in small groups and selected a team to make recommendations to address employees' concerns about the quality processes. The team suggested several changes, including retaining only those indicators, teams, and reports that contributed in a substantial way to achieving the objectives of the department and the company; eliminating many of the formal management reviews; no longer requiring a structured problem-solving process, but emphasizing continuous improvement and solutions that benefited the company and its customers; continuing to train all employees in the problem-solving process so they would have the appropriate tools and speak a common language; and dispersing the quality organizations within the company, making quality the responsibility of each business unit. In a letter to all employees, Mr. Broadhead reiterated management's commitment to continuous improvement in all aspects of FPL's business; nevertheless, some news media suggested that FPL was dismantling its quality efforts while attacking the TQM movement. Although the current and future focus is on cost reduction in an increasingly competitive environment, Mr. Broadhead has stated emphatically that "it is unacceptable to reduce costs at the expense of quality."

Five years after winning the Deming Prize, FPL still has an unwavering commitment to quality initiatives, which was noted by Dr. Noriaki Kano of the Union of Japanese Scientists and Engineers, after observing presentations from 11 FPL business units. Dr. Kano, who had served as a counselor to FPL

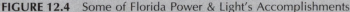

FIGURE 12.4 Some of Florida Power & Light's Accomplishments

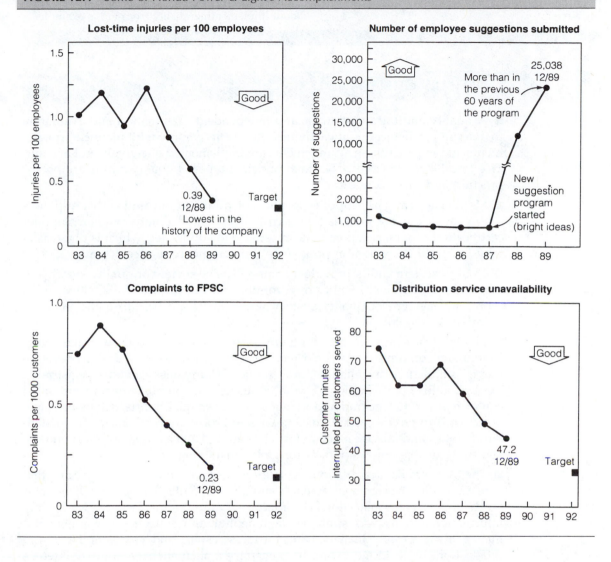

since 1986, was "pleasantly surprised" that FPL has simultaneously reduced costs and improved quality. Kano noted that recent improvements were based on skills developed through QIP practices. For example, one team improved service reliability by reducing transformer failures due to lightning. Before, an average of 23 transformers out of 761 on their worst-performing feeder failed each year. This number was reduced to zero failures, even though lightning strikes had increased 250 percent. Newly installed transformers incorporate the team's recommended changes, and existing transformers are modified as needed. The team leader stated that they found creative ways to use quality improvement tools and techniques to their best advantage without getting

caught up in excessive paperwork or attending compulsory meetings. "Like most employees, we're so familiar with the quality processes that it's almost second nature."

Key Issues for Discussion

1. What makes FPL unique in the types of quality problems its encounters? How is its product similar to and different from oil being processed in a refinery? From water being delivered by a city water department?

2. How did FPL use policy deployment to improve quality?

3. What was the role of QIP teams at FPL in developing quality, which enabled them to win the Deming Prize?

4. What lessons did FPL learn after winning the Deming Prize? What can other companies learn about implementing quality from FPL's example?

SUMMARY OF KEY POINTS

■ A quality audit is a systematic and independent examination and evaluation to determine whether quality activities and results comply with planned arrangements and whether these arrangements are implemented effectively and are suitable to achieve objectives. The three principal types of quality audits are policy, practice, and product audits.

■ Many companies use supplier certification audits to rate and certify suppliers who provide quality materials in a cost-effective and timely manner. Supplier certification programs can be quite expensive to administer, which is one reason why ISO 9000 has grown in popularity and acceptance in recent years.

■ Quality system audits provide a comprehensive review of quality systems to uncover problems and identify opportunities for improvement. ISO 9000 audits represent one type of quality system audit; others are based on the Malcolm Baldrige Award criteria.

■ ISO 9000 is a series of global quality system standards to ensure that a registered site conforms to specified requirements in the areas of design/development, production, installation, and service. Companies achieve registration through a third-party audit and periodic surveillance audits to ensure continued conformance. ISO registration does not guarantee a quality product; its principal objective is to ensure conformance to written procedures and documented standards. ISO standards are a good starting point to launch a quality effort and are becoming increasingly important for global marketing.

■ The Malcolm Baldrige National Quality Award recognizes U.S. companies that excel in quality management practices and quality results that achieve the highest levels of customer satisfaction. The Baldrige Award criteria focus on leadership, information and analysis, strategic planning, human resources development and management, process management, business results, and customer focus and satisfaction. The Baldrige Award has generated a phenomenal amount of interest, and many companies use its criteria as a basis for internal assessment of their quality systems. Many state award programs are patterned after the Baldrige Award. The Baldrige Award criteria differs considerably from ISO 9000, although they can be mutually reinforcing.

■ The Deming Prize was established in Japan in 1951 to recognize individuals, factories, and companies that distinctively apply companywide quality control and statistical principles advocated by W. Edwards Deming. Both Europe and Canada have established their own quality awards that are similar to the Baldrige in many respects.

REVIEW QUESTIONS

1. What is a quality audit? What benefits do quality audits provide?
2. Explain the differences among policy, practice, and product quality audits.

3. What issues are typically examined in a quality system audit?

4. What is the purpose of a supplier certification audit? Explain some of the common practices for supplier certification.

5. Summarize the history of the development of the ISO 9000 series of standards.

6. Explain the differences among ISO 9001, 9002, and 9003 standards. What is the purpose of ISO 9000 and 9004?

7. Briefly summarize the key elements of ISO 9000. Are these something that every company should be doing?

8. Explain the process of obtaining ISO 9000 registration. What is a registrar?

9. List the reasons companies pursue ISO 9000 registration. What benefits can registration provide?

10. Summarize the purposes of the Malcolm Baldrige National Quality Award.

11. Explain the Baldrige Award framework and why each element is important in any quality system.

12. Explain the significance of each of the key characteristics of the Baldrige Award.

13. Describe the Baldrige Award scoring system. What do we mean by "approach" and "deployment"?

14. Discuss some of the strengths and weaknesses that Baldrige Award administrators have observed among the applicants for the award.

15. How are the Baldrige Award criteria commonly used by companies that do not apply for the award?

16. Contrast the similarities and differences between ISO 9000 and the Baldrige Award.

17. What does JUSE mean by "company-wide quality control"? How does the Deming Prize criteria relate to the definition of CWQC?

18. Explain the differences between the Baldrige Award and the European and Canadian Quality Awards.

DISCUSSION QUESTIONS

1. How might you design a "quality audit" for your class? What information would you include in the audit? How would you perform it?

2. High schools might be considered as suppliers to colleges and universities. How might a college or university develop a "supplier certification program" for high schools?

3. Develop an affinity diagram that groups each of the 20 elements of ISO 9001 into one of the following categories:

   a. Administration

   b. Defining the quality system

   c. Controlling the quality system

   d. Measuring the quality system

   e. Quality system improvement

4. Contrast the ISO 9000 standards with the Baldrige Award criteria along each of the following dimensions:

   a. implementation time

   b. initial investment

   c. return on investment

    d. people building

    e. definition of quality

    f. customer relationships

    g. documentation

    h. use of quantitative techniques

    i. use of inspectors

    j. corrective action focus

5. Create a matrix diagram in which each row is a category of the Baldrige Award criteria and four columns correspond to

- Traditional management practices
- Growing awareness of the importance of quality
- Development of a solid quality management system
- Outstanding, world-class management practice

In each cell of the matrix, list two–five characteristics that you would expect to see for a company in each of the four situations above for that Baldrige Award category. How might this matrix be used as a self-assessment tool to provide directions for improvement?

6. Create a matrix diagram in which the rows correspond to each of Deming's 14 Points and the columns to each category of the Baldrige Award criteria. Use the symbols ●, ○, and △ to designate a strong, medium, or weak relationship (or none at all) between each of the 14 Points and each Baldrige Award category. How well do the Baldrige Award criteria support Deming's 14 Points?

7. Interview some managers at a local company that is pursuing or has pursued ISO 9000 registration. Report on the reasons for achieving registration, the perceived benefits, and the problems the company encountered during the process. How might various quality tools introduced in previous chapters be used to facilitate the process?

8. Discuss how the Baldrige Award criteria might be used as an internal assessment of the operation of a business school. Obtain a copy of the current year's criteria, select a category, and describe how it relates to the school's operation.

9. Contrast the categories of the Baldrige Award with the Deming Prize. How are they similar? Different?

10. Does your state have a quality award program? If so, obtain some current information about the program and report on it. If not, contact your state representative to see why not.

CASES

I. World-Wide Appliances

World-Wide Appliances (WWA) designs, manufactures, and markets large kitchen appliances—refrigerators, washers, dryers, and dishwashers—for the U.S. and international markets. WWA has plants in Durham, North Carolina; Birmingham, Alabama, and St. Louis, Missouri. All design activities are centralized in Durham. The Birmingham plant has approximately 2500 employees and operates two complete shifts, producing about 750,000 refrigerators each year under several brand names. The in-

ternational market is growing rapidly and is an important part of WWA strategy. However, domestic sales still account for the majority of revenue.

The Birmingham plant is currently working to obtain ISO 9002 registration. One of the motivations in becoming ISO 9002 certified is to streamline its European operations. In the past, refrigerators were shipped to retrofit companies in Europe that would modify them to meet local electrical requirements. Any certification that was necessary to sell the products in Europe was obtained by the retrofit company. WWA wanted to ship properly configured units directly to distributors in Europe. ISO registration could be a means of gaining this marketing advantage.

The registration effort is not directly opposed by any employees in the Birmingham plant. However, many people do not understand why they need to do certain things required by the standards. The quality manager assigned responsibility for the registration effort, Harold Glenn, does not feel that he has enough higher level support. The group-level managers who made the decision to seek registration have backed off and left it up to each individual location. Because of their lack of involvement, the upper-level plant management does not perceive it to be high priority. A lack of management support led to a general lack of support for the internal auditing team.

Although the work performed in the plant is highly labor intensive, few procedures in manufacturing are actually formally written. Harold feels that the most work will be needed in the areas of gauge calibration, record retention, and corrective action systems. Harold is not sure whether to use outside consultants to help the plant prepare for reg-

istration. If he does not, he feels that he will have to start a major training effort for internal employees.

An internal auditing structure is currently being formed. The plan calls for an internal audit in all areas twice a year. The plant plans to use a "bundling" technique to audit each area of the plant. Rather than audit the entire organization at one time, the plant will be divided into small areas, such as the foam injection operation. All requirements will be audited in each area by a small group of auditors. The results will be bundled together to get an overall assessment of the plant. The smaller audits will take place continuously according to an audit schedule. Harold hopes to have at least 50 employees trained to be internal auditors so that he can rotate the responsibilities among many people.

Discussion Questions

1. What criteria should Harold use to decide whether to use outside consultants? If he does not use outside consultants, what types of training should he consider for the plant employees?

2. Evaluate the proposed "bundling" auditing technique. What advantages or disadvantages might it have?

II. Ultra-Productivity Fasteners, Part II

Part I of the Ultra-Productivity Fasteners case was presented in Chapter 8. You should read the overview of the key business factors before proceeding. In this part, you are to play the role of a Malcolm Baldrige National Quality Award examiner and evaluate the company's response to item 6.1—Product and Service Quality Results. The Baldrige Award criteria for this item is shown in Figure 12.5. Note that this item asks for results, not approach and deployment. Some additional information from the 1994 Baldrige Award criteria about reporting and interpreting results is provided in Figure 12.6.

Assignment

Two versions of the company's response are provided. Read Version A first and identify the *strengths* and *areas for improvement* relative to the criteria. Strengths should reflect positive responses to the Areas to Address in the criteria. Areas for improvement should highlight issues that do not respond adequately to the Areas to Address. Then, using the scoring guidelines in Table 12.4 (results section), assign a score to this item. Repeat this process for Version B. What differences do you find? Why did your scores differ between versions?

Version A

Category 6.0: Quality and Operational Results

6.1: Product and Service Quality Results

Based on extensive regression analysis, our key internal measure of product quality which predicts customer satisfaction is "Lots Accepted at Test" the first time submitted. This measure has shown a steady, favorable trend (see Figure 12.7) and has exceeded the target set by the production VP, who has over 40 years of experience in this type of manufacturing.

Two key service quality measures for our just-in-time customers are "Shipments Reliability Index" and "Delivery Satisfaction Index." The Shipment Reliability Index (Figure 12.8) tracks delivery against the original, promised date established at the monthly "three-month schedule projection" meeting with the customer. Trends have been favorable and show us to be highly competitive with the two competitors tracked through feedback from automotive customers.

With the high-volume customers served, frequent last-minute changes occur in production model

FIGURE 12.5   Baldrige Award Product and Service Quality Results Criteria (for 1994)

6.1 Product and Service Quality Results *(70 pts.)*
Summarize trends and current quality levels for key product and service features; compare current levels with those of competitors and/or appropriate benchmarks.

Areas to Address

a. trends and current levels for the key measures and/or indicators of product and service quality
b. comparisons of current quality levels with that of principal competitors in the company's key markets, industry averages, industry leaders, and appropriate benchmarks

A   D   R

□—□   ☑

Notes:
1. Key product and service measures are measures relative to the set of all important features of the company's products and services. These measures, taken together, best represent the *most important factors that predict customer satisfaction and quality in customer use.* Examples include measures of accuracy, reliability, timeliness, performance, behavior, delivery, after-sales services, documentation, appearance, and effective complaint management.
2. Results reported in Item 6.1 should reflect all key product and service features described in the Business Overview and addressed in Items 7.1 and 5.1.
3. Data reported in Item 6.1 are intended to be objective measures of product and service quality, not the customers' satisfaction or reaction to the products and/or services.

Such data might be of several types, including: (a) internal (company) measurements; (b) field performance (when applicable); (c) proactive checks by the company of specific product and service features; and (d) data routinely collected by other organizations or on behalf of the company. Data reported in Item 6.1 should provide information on the company's performance relative to the specific product and service features that best *predict* customer satisfaction. These data, collected regularly, are then part of a process for monitoring and improving quality.
4. Bases for comparison might include independent surveys, studies, or laboratory testing; benchmarks; and company evaluations and testing.

schedules, which generate last-minute changes in delivery schedules. The "Delivery Satisfaction Index" (Figure 12.9) tracks shipments against original promised dates or changes made by customer request. This index reflects our ability to respond to customers' last-minute changes. It is much more rigorous than the "Shipment Reliability Index" and has shown a positive trend that reflects our "customer first" quality value.

The improvements in both "Shipments Reliability Index" and "Delivery Satisfaction Index" are directly related to our ability to measure and improve the performance of the process contributing to order fulfillment. The quality improvement team responsible for improvement of these two indices found that the major contributor to orders not shipped on time was order entry errors. A tracking system for "Order Entry Error Rate" was put in place in 1990 and has provided dramatic improvement (see Figure 12.10).

The measure of "Complaints Resolved on First Contact" (Figure 12.11) has shown a dramatic improvement since the Customer Service Associate training program was introduced in 1991. This improvement, coupled with a reduction in overall com-

plaints, has been a major contributor to improved customer satisfaction.

The percentage of invoice errors is another internal measure of our ability to deliver outstanding products and services that meet our customer's requirements and expectations. Figure 12.12 shows improvement in this area since 1991. A longer-range objective is to be equal to "World-class" companies that are down to 0.2 percent invoice errors.

Version B

Category 6.0: Quality and Operational Results

6.1: Product and Service Quality Results

Extensive regression analysis has shown that the level of product quality as perceived by the customer is actually a function of meeting both dimensional characteristics and meeting hardness specifications. Therefore, levels of compliance are tracked separately for these two important characteristics. "Lots Accepted at Test—Dimensional" first time submitted, trends are shown in Figure 12.13. A positive trend is shown and compares well with the best-manufacturer-benchmark level established by

---

FIGURE 12.6   Reporting Results and Trend Data in the Baldrige Award

1. Results Items require data to demonstrate progress (trend data), achievement (performance levels), and breadth of deployment. Evaluation of achievement is usually based upon two factors: (1) that the performance level has been sustained or is the current result of a favorable trend; and (2) that the performance level can be compared with that of other appropriate organizations.

2. Applicants are required to report trend data to show progress and to show that improvements or outstanding performance levels are sustained. No minimum period of time is specified for trend data. Time periods may span five years or more for some results. Trends may be much shorter in areas where improvement efforts are new. In cases where the trend line is short, the examiners' evaluation will take into account the demonstrated levels of performance.

3. The spacing between data points on a trend line (annual, monthly, etc.) should reflect a natural measurement/use scheme for such results. That is, how the data are used in process management should determine the spacing between data points. For example, measurement frequency should support timely improvement.

4. In reporting trend data, applicants should be aware that breadth of results is a major factor in the examiners' evaluation. For this reason, it is important to report data reflecting wide deployment of improvement activities. Use of graphs and tables offers a good means to present many results compactly.

5. Graphs and tables should be integrated into the body of the text, wherever possible.

The following graph illustrates data an applicant might present as part of a response to Item 6.1, Product and Service Quality Results. (The applicant has indicated, in the Business Overview and in Item 7.1, on-time delivery as a key customer requirement.)

Using the graph, the following characteristics of clear and effective data presentation are illustrated:

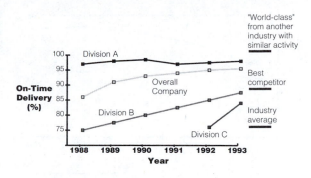

- the trend lines report data for a key business requirement
- both axes and units of measure are clearly labeled
- results are presented for several years
- meaningful comparisons are clearly shown
- the company shows, using a single graph, that its three divisions separately track on-time delivery

To help interpret the scoring guidelines, the following comments on the graphed results would be appropriate:

- The current overall company performance level is excellent. This conclusion is supported by the comparison with competitors and with a "world-class" level.

- The company exhibits an overall excellent improvement record.

- Division A is the current performance leader, showing sustained high performance and a slightly positive trend. Division B shows rapid improvement. Its current performance is near that of the best industry competitor, but trails the "world-class" level.

- Division C—a new division—shows rapid progress. Its current performance is not yet at the level of the best industry competitor.

---

the Automated Machines Council, which represents manufacturers using equipment similar to that installed in Ultra-Productivity shops.

"Lots Accepted at Test—Hardness" data is shown in Figure 12.14. Data plotted by plant, for each of our plants, proved to be a real revelation since the Louisville plant was obviously poorer in performance. Investigation showed that the hardening furnaces installed when the Louisville plant opened required excessive maintenance and lacked the sophisticated temperature control systems used in the other plants. In 1991, a major capital investment was made to replace the Lousiville hardening furnaces with state-of-the-art equipment. Data in

FIGURE 12.7   Lots Accepted at Test

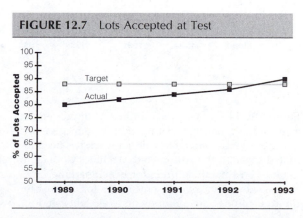

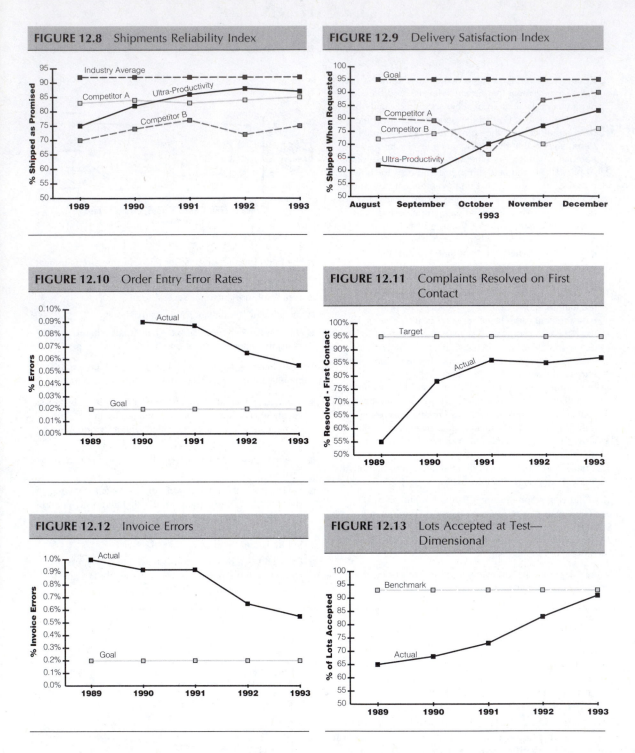

FIGURE 12.8   Shipments Reliability Index

FIGURE 12.9   Delivery Satisfaction Index

FIGURE 12.10   Order Entry Error Rates

FIGURE 12.11   Complaints Resolved on First Contact

FIGURE 12.12   Invoice Errors

FIGURE 12.13   Lots Accepted at Test— Dimensional

Figure 12.14 shows the dramatic improvement achieved. No benchmarks have been found for this hardness control characteristic, so work has been initiated through the Automated Machines Council to identify best manufacturers for benchmarking.

Two key service quality measures for our just-in-time customers are "Shipments Reliability Index" and "Delivery Satisfaction Index." The "Shipments Reliability Index" (Figure 12.15) tracks delivery against the original, promised date established at the monthly "three-month schedule projection" meeting with the customer. Trends have been favorable and show us to be highly competitive with the two best

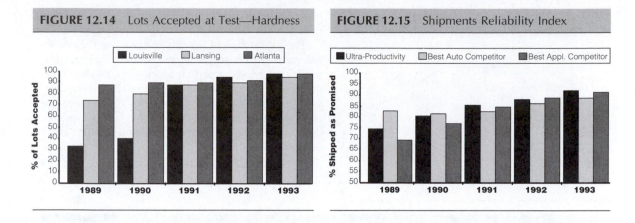

FIGURE 12.14 Lots Accepted at Test—Hardness

FIGURE 12.15 Shipments Reliability Index

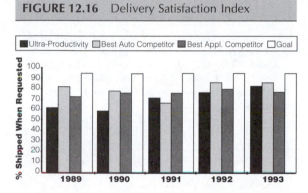

FIGURE 12.16 Delivery Satisfaction Index

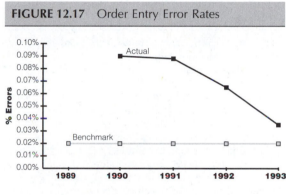

FIGURE 12.17 Order Entry Error Rates

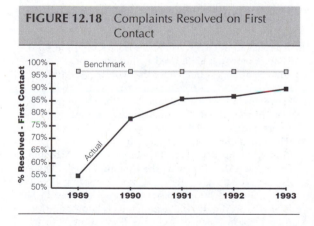

FIGURE 12.18 Complaints Resolved on First Contact

competitors tracked through feedback from one automotive and one major appliance customer.

With the high-volume customers served, frequent last-minute changes occur in production model schedules, which generate last-minute changes in delivery schedules. The "Delivery Satisfaction Index" (Figure 12.16) tracks shipments against original promised dates or changes made by customer request. This index reflects our ability to respond to customers' last-minute changes. It is much more rigorous than the "Shipment Reliability Index" and has shown a positive trend, which reflects our "customer first" quality value.

The improvements in both "Shipments Reliability Index" and "Delivery Satisfaction Index" are directly related to our ability to measure and improve the performance of the process contributing to order fulfillment. The quality improvement team responsible for improvement of these two indices found that the major contributor to orders not shipped on time was order entry errors. A tracking system for "Order Entry Error Rate" was put in place in 1990 and has provided dramatic improvement (see Figure 12.17).

The measure of "Complaints Resolved on First Contact" (Figure 12.18) has shown a dramatic improvement since the Customer Service Associate training program was introduced in 1991. This improvement, coupled with a reduction in overall complaints, has been a major contributor to improved customer satisfaction. A benchmark of 96 percent for

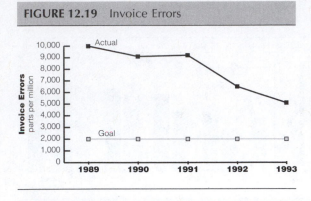

FIGURE 12.19 Invoice Errors

best performance in similar customer–supplied companies was established.

The percentage of invoice errors is another internal measure of our ability to deliver outstanding products and services that meet our customer's requirements and expectations. Figure 12.19 shows improvement in this area since 1990. A longer-range objective is to be equal to "World-class" companies that have 2000 ppm (parts per million) invoice error rates.

■ NOTES

1. A.V. Feigenbaum, *Total Quality Control,* 3rd ed., rev. (New York: McGraw-Hill, 1991), 77, 78.
2. ANSI/ASQC A3-1987, "Quality Systems Terminology" (Milwaukee, WI: ASQC, 1987).
3. Joseph R. Tunner, *A Quality Technology Primer for Managers* (Milwaukee, WI: ASQC Quality Press, 1990).
4. Edward A. Reynolds, "The Science (Art?) of Quality Audit and Evaluation," *Quality Progress* (July 1990), 55–56.
5. AT&T Quality Steering Committee, *AT&T Quality Manager's Handbook,* AT&T Bell Laboratories (1990).
6. American Society for Quality Control, *Certified Quality Auditor* (Milwaukee, WI: ASQC, 1993).
7. Tom Stundza, "Suppliers on the Hot Seat," *Purchasing* (17 January 1991), 92–98.
8. John J. Hudiburg, *Winning With Quality: The FPL Story* (White Plains, NY: Quality Resources, 1991).
9. Mike Lovitt, "Responsive Suppliers Are Smart Suppliers," *Quality Progress* (June 1989), 50–53.
10. Richard A. Maass, "Supplier Certification—A Positive Response to Just-in-Time," *Quality Progress* 21, no. 9 (September 1988), 75–80.
11. U.S. Department of Commerce, National Institute of Standards and Technology, *Questions and Answers on Quality, the ISO 9000 Standard Series, Quality System Registration, and Related Issues* (NISTIR 4721, April 1993).
12. Michael J. Timbers, "ISO 9000 and Europe's Attempts to Mandate Quality," *The Journal of European Business* (March/April 1992), 14–25.
13. AT&T Corporate Quality Office, *Using ISO 9000 to Improve Business Processes* (July 1994).
14. Astrid L.H. Eckstein, and Jaydeep Balakrishnan, "The ISO 9000 Series: Quality Management Systems for the Global Economy," *Production and Inventory Management Journal* 34, no. 4 (Fourth Quarter 1993), 66–71.
15. U.S. Department of Commerce News, February 3, 1995.
16. Curt W. Reimann, and Harry S. Hertz, "The Malcolm Baldrige National Quality Award and ISO 9000 Registration," *ASTM Standardization News* (November 1993), 42–53. This paper is a contribution of the U.S. Government not subject to copyright.
17. Paul M. Bobrowski, and John H. Bantham, "State Quality Initiatives: Mini-Baldrige to Baldrige Plus," *National Productivity Review* 13, no. 3 (Summer 1994), 423–438.
18. Bobrowski and Bantham, see note 17.
19. JUSE, *The Deming Prize Guide for Oversea Companies* (Tokyo, 1992), 5.
20. B. Nakkai, and J. Neves, "The Deming, Baldrige, and European Quality Awards," *Quality Progress* (April 1994), 33–37.
21. Adapted from Jerry R. Junkins, "Insights of a Baldrige Award Winner," *Quality Progress* (March 1994), 57–58. Used with permission of Texas Instruments.
22. Adapted from *Q1 for Assembly Plants.* Copyright Ford Motor Company, 1989. Used with permission.
23. Brad Stratton, "A Beacon for the World," *Quality Progress* (May 1990), 60–65; Al Henderson and *Target* Staff, "For Florida Power and Light After the Deming Prize: The "Music" Builds . . . And Builds . . . And Builds," *Target* (Summer 1990), 10–21.
24. The remainder of this Quality in Practice is adapted from "A Status Report on FPL's Improvement Activities Four Years After Receiving the Deming Prize," "Quality at Work," *FPL Today* 2, no. 1 (Spring 1993), and "Quality Effort Yields 'Impressive Results'," *INSIDEFPL* (May 1994). We gratefully acknowledge Mr. Alan E. Siebe, Manager, Quality Services at FPL, for providing these materials.

■ BIBLIOGRAPHY

Application Guidelines. Malcolm Baldrige National Quality Award. U.S. Department of Commerce, National Institute of Standards and Technology, 1995.

Boznak, Rudolph. "Manufacturers Must Prepare for International Quality Initiative." *Industrial Engineering* 23, no. 10 (October 1991), 13–14.

Bureau of Business Practice. *ISO 9000: Handbook of Quality Standards and Compliance*. New York: Simon & Schuster, 1992.

Bush, David, and Kevin Dooley. "The Deming Prize and Baldrige Award: How They Compare," *Quality Progress* 22, no. 1 (January 1989), 28–30.

Clements, Richard Barrett. *Quality Manager's Complete Guide to ISO 9000*. Englewood Cliffs, NJ: Prentice-Hall, 1993.

DeCarly, Neil J., and W. Kent Sterett. "History of the Malcolm Baldrige Award." *Quality Progress* 23, no. 3 (March 1990), 21–27.

Johnson, Perry L. *ISO 9000: Meeting the New International Standards*. New York: McGraw-Hill, 1993.

Main, Jeremy. "How To Win the Baldrige Award." *Fortune* (23 April, 1990), 101–116.

Ramsay, Martin. "ISO 9000: The Myths and Misconception." *APICS—The Performance Advantage* (June 1992), 55–57.

Reimann, Curt W. "The Baldrige Award: Leading the Way in Quality Initiatives." *Quality Progress* 22, no. 7 (July 1989), 35–39.

CHAPTER

13

Organizing and Implementing TQM

OUTLINE

At the Seventh Annual National Conference on Federal Quality in July 1994, 12-year-old Kelly Potter addressed the luncheon crowd of 2000 participants.[1] Kelly's elementary school in Nazareth, Pennsylvania, participates in Koality Kid, a program sponsored by the American Society for Quality Control, which promotes teaching of quality principles in elementary schools. Her message was not earthshaking. She thanked her family and school system members for their support and discussed how quality improvement techniques were used in her school for such things as cafeteria operations and homework assignments. She even applied these techniques to prepare her speech. The audience exploded with a standing ovation. Brad Stratton, editor of *Quality Progress*, observed, "I don't think they were applauding her verbal message, as much as her nonverbal message which was this: *Hey people! This stuff is so simple that kids can do it! Kids!"*

The principles of total quality—focus on the customer, involve everyone, and strive for continuous improvement—are simple to understand and represent common sense. Yet, many companies have experienced great difficulty in implementing total quality and even deciding whether to do it. This difficulty often results from some common misconceptions, such as TQM means doing lots of "things" like collecting data and organizing teams, or picking and choosing only those elements of TQM with which companies feel comfortable. Implementing total quality requires significant changes in organization design, processes, and culture. Such broad change has been a stumbling block for many companies.

The first question that every organization inevitably wrestles with is whether to even adopt TQM. Companies make the decision to use TQM for two basic reasons:

1. A firm reacts to competition that poses a threat to its profitable survival by turning to TQM.

2. TQM represents an opportunity to improve.

Most firms—even Baldrige Award winners—have moved toward TQM because of the first reason. Xerox, for example, watched its market share fall from 90 percent to less than 15 percent in a decade (see the Quality in Practice case in Chapter 1); Milliken faced increased competition from Asian textile manufacturers; Zytec Corporation found itself in financial difficulties because of reliance on a single customer. While not facing dire crises, perceived future threats were the impetus for FedEx and Solectron.

When faced with a threat to survival, a company effects cultural change more easily; under these circumstances, organizations generally implement TQM effectively. A company will generally have more difficulty gaining support for change when not facing a crisis. This reluctance is a reflection of the attitude "If it ain't broke, don't fix it." In such cases, a company might attempt to manufacture a crisis mentality to effect change.[2] This TQM task requires conviction (that is, *guts*) and leadership of top managers.

Firms have used a variety of approaches to implement quality within their organizations. Many of these approaches are one-dimensional and consequently, prone to failure. For example, some firms emphasize the use of quality tools such as statistical process control, but may only deploy them in a narrow part of the organization such as manufacturing. These firms will see some improvement, but because the entire organization is not involved, success will be limited. Others take a problem-solving approach in which defects in both production and customer service are identified and corrected through quality circles or other team approaches. However, they may ignore customer relationship management processes or strategic planning issues. Again, improvements will be achieved, but they will be sporadic and limited. By essentially delegating quality to front-line employees, management demonstrates a lack of leadership, which will not create the sustained culture required for longevity. A third approach might emphasize design, but ignore many potential means for continuous process improvement. Total quality requires a comprehensive effort that encompasses all of the elements discussed in this book thus far. What is really required is a total change in thinking, not a new collection of tools. A focus on tools and techniques is easy, what is hard is understanding and achieving the changes in human attitudes and behavior that are necessary.

The biggest dangers lie in the lack of complete understanding and the tendency to imitate—the easy way out. Many of the experts and consultants have rewritten total quality management around their own discipline, such as accounting, engineering, human resources, or statistics. The "one best model" of TQM may not mesh with an organization's culture; most successful companies have developed their own unique approaches to fit their own requirements. Research has shown that imitation of TQM efforts made by one successful organization may not lead to good results in another. To go back to Deming, no knowledge is possible without theory, or to use one of his more descriptive phrases, "There is no instant pudding." Successful TQM implementation requires a readiness for change, the adoption of sound practices and implementation strategies, and an effective organization. These issues are the topics of this chapter.

CORPORATE CULTURE AND ORGANIZATIONAL CHANGE

Why can some companies like Motorola and Xerox make radical changes while others fail miserably? Many TQM efforts fail simply because organizations are unable to adapt to change. A prerequisite to implementing TQM is a corporate culture that will allow change. A corporate culture is a company's value system and its collection of guiding principles backed by management policies and actions. A survey conducted by the Wyatt Co., a Washington, D.C., consulting firm, found that the barriers to change cited most often were employee resistance and "dysfunctional corporate culture"—one whose shared values and behavior are at odds with its long-term health.[3] An example of a dysfunctional culture is a high-tech company that stresses individual rewards while innovation depends on teamwork. Readiness for change is influenced by senior management leadership with a clear vision and strategic goals, a culture emphasizing customer satisfaction and continuous improvement, strong quality and operational performance measurements and benchmarking, a cross-functional orientation with good two-way communication among all levels, rewards for taking risks and innovating, a flexible but stable organization with relatively few layers of management, high employee morale, and the atmosphere to consider a wide variety of suggestions while making decisions quickly. The study suggests the obvious: change is easier in organizations that embrace TQM principles! Traditional organizations, as discussed in Chapter 4, are generally ill-prepared to accept change, not only with respect to TQM.

The importance of corporate culture and organizational change to quality can be illustrated by an example involving the First National Bank of Chicago.[4] Since 1971 the required return on equity of the banking industry has declined. Research showed that quality is the key buying determinant in noncredit services. First Chicago was determined to become the best in the noncredit services business. The bank began its quality transformation by altering its organizational framework. Separate strategic business units were created, each based on an individual product family. The strategic business unit manager suddenly became an entrepreneur. The manager was vested with the power to control not only expenses, but also product features, pricing, promotion, and quality. This framework brought the managers closer to the customer and made them more accountable for the quality of the products. Each business unit had its own customer service representatives to handle inquiries and problems. Because the customer service function and the production area were in the same location, the representatives could respond more efficiently to problems.

Pieters has suggested several ways in which a corporate culture change to a TQM environment can be made permanent.[5] They include:

1. Making involvement in TQ a required part of people's responsibility. Making it voluntary implies that it is less important than things that are required.

2. Using the existing organization to implement TQ. Special task forces and committees can disband; TQ should be part of the permanent organization.

3. Ensuring everyone spends at least one hour per week working on quality issues. Enforcing this rule gets people accustomed to the idea of devoting time to quality and keeps other priorities from crowding out TQ.

4. Changing the measurement and information systems. Without appropriate measurements and information systems, quality cannot become a part of the fabric of the organization. For example, AT&T Universal Card Services spent $20 million on computer workstations for associates to provide customer support with easy access to detailed card member information.

■ Leading Practices

Studies of highly successful companies suggest that certain key practices in their organizational culture have contributed to their success.[6] Although these issues have been discussed at length in previous chapters, bringing them together emphasizes the need for a *total* quality effort. These leading practices are described here.

■ *They focus on quality through strategic planning, which is deployed throughout the organization.* Successful companies develop detailed, well-communicated plans and reinforce them by visual aids posted throughout the company. These firms have a guiding vision, identify a few critical annual objectives, and frequently review progress. Goals might include both defensive goals (such as cost reduction) and offensive goals (such as building market share). These goals are long-term in nature and focus on investment in R&D, training, process design, and continuous improvement, which contribute to long-run effectiveness instead of just short-term efficiency. For example, Motorola has two major goals: defect prevention (their goal is two defects per billion by the year 2000), and cycle time reduction in all processes. Wainwright Industries identified four critical customer requirements: price, line defects, delivery, and partnership. These requirements are aligned with Wainwright objectives: ensuring consistent profitability, six sigma quality, best in class delivery, and associate job security. These objectives, in turn, lead to specific measurable indicators and stretch goals. Their "mission control" room, open to everyone, provides a daily update on customer satisfaction using red and green flags that indicate whether problems exist with individual customers.

■ *They have the commitment and involvement of top management.* Without exception, committed top management leadership is the key "driver" in the successful implementation of TQM. Many of the management principles and practices required in a TQM environment may be contrary to a company's long-standing practices. Top managers, ideally starting with the CEO, must become the organization's TQM leaders and provide the vision, encouragement, and recognition. Speeches and rhetoric are not enough; senior managers must be actively involved in setting the organization's mission and vision, and then "walk the talk."

■ *They integrate customer satisfaction across functions.* Customer satisfaction drives the quality effort. TQM implementation requires that everyone inside an organization be viewed as a customer of an internal or external supplier, and that the final customer be seen as the final arbiter of quality. Successful firms assign specific tasks and responsibilities for achieving customer satisfaction to all departments. Many companies use techniques such as quality function deployment to develop a cross-functional emphasis. Such integration necessitates a systems view, rather than the traditional functional focus, supported by sound measurement and reporting processes. It also requires improved communications. People need to communicate across organizational levels, functions, product lines, and locations to solve problems and implement change.

■ *They emphasize employee participation and training.* Everyone must participate in the improvement efforts. Employees must be empowered to make decisions that affect quality and develop and implement new and better systems. Participation can be encouraged by recognizing team and individual accomplishments, sharing success stories throughout the organization, encouraging risk-taking by removing the fear of failure; encouraging the formation of employee involvement teams; implementing suggestion systems that act rapidly, provide feedback, and reward implemented suggestions; and providing financial and technical support to employees to develop their ideas. Training involves everyone in the company; every employee, from entry-level workers to the CEO, receives training in TQM philosophies and techniques. Training is viewed as a steady and continuous effort, not a one-time project, which requires the commitment of significant resources—a move many firms are reluctant to make.

■ *They customize their quality efforts.* Managers usually are impatient and seek immediate successes, often by adopting off-the-shelf quality programs and practices, or imitating Japanese approaches. Joshua Hammond of the American Quality Foundation urges business leaders in the United States to develop approaches that maximize their own cultural strengths. How we implement quality efforts should be built on American strengths, and not simply be imitations of Japanese approaches. A successful quality strategy needs to fit within the existing organization culture, which is the reason the Baldrige Award guidelines are nonprescriptive. No magic formula works for everyone. At Zytec, for instance, Deming's 14 Points was chosen as the cornerstone of the company's quality improvement culture. They established a Deming Steering Committee to guide the Deming process, championed individual Deming Points, and acted as advisors to three Deming Implementation Teams. Motorola, on the other hand, invited numerous consultants. In the end, they decided to develop their own quality approach that fit their needs.

One study of Baldrige Award winners concluded that each has a unique "quality engine" that drives the quality activities of the organization.[7] These individual strengths are summarized in Table 13.1. This table does not suggest that all other aspects of TQM are ignored; they are not. The quality engine customizes the quality effort to the organizational culture and provides focus.

■ *They link quality to financial returns.* A successful quality initiative does not guarantee financial success. (However, many argue that without it, a company will eventually be doomed to failure.) Because quality often requires a substantial investment, companies should pay closer attention to the financial returns on quality investments. AT&T's chairman receives a quarterly report

TABLE 13.1 Quality Engines of Baldrige Award Recipients		
Company	**Quality Engine**	**Focus**
IBM Rochester	Market-driven quality	Customer needs early in the planning and design process
Motorola	Process control	Defect prevention; six-sigma quality
Cadillac	Product development	Integrating manufacturing and design, and partnering with customers and suppliers
Xerox	Benchmarking	Competitive and best-in class benchmarks (Xerox)
FedEx	Technology	Using technology to speed processes and improve customer service
Milliken	Employee empowerment and involvement	Self-managed teams and active participation of employees in all aspects of the business
Zytec	Strategic planning	Involvement of cross-functional teams, customers, and suppliers in the planning process
Westinghouse	Management by data and facts	Use of measurements to track and improve quality

from each business unit that describes quality improvements and their financial impacts. Quality, like any business decision, should add value to the organization. A prescription for implementing quality within an organization with a focus on ROQ—return on quality—was described in *Business Week*:

1. Start with an effective quality approach. Companies that don't have the basics, such as process and inventory controls and other building blocks, will find a healthy return on quality elusive.

2. Calculate the cost of current quality initiatives. Cost of warranties, problem prevention, and monitoring activities all count. Measure these against the returns for delivering a product or service to the customer.

3. Determine what key factors retain customers and what drives them away. Conduct detailed surveys. Forecast market changes, especially quality and new-product initiatives of competitors.

4. Focus on quality efforts most likely to improve customer satisfaction at a reasonable cost. Figure the link between each dollar spent on quality and its effect on customer retention and market share.

5. Roll out successful approaches after pilot-testing the most promising efforts and cutting the ones that don't have a big impact. Closely monitor results. Build word of mouth by publicizing success stories.

6. Improve quality efforts continually. Measure results against anticipated gains. Beware of the competition's initiative and don't hesitate to revamp approaches accordingly. Quality never rests.[8]

PLANNING FOR TQM IMPLEMENTATION

Implementing TQM successfully requires effective planning and organization. A good plan should begin with an assessment of where the organization is with respect to quality. This assessment identifies strengths and areas for improvement and determines what practices will yield the most benefit.

■ Self-Assessment

Many self-assessment instruments that provide a picture of the state of quality in the organization are available. The most complete instrument is the Malcolm Baldrige National Quality Award criteria, discussed in the previous chapter. Other, simpler instruments provide a quick picture of an organization's quality health. For example, Coopers & Lybrand developed a simple Quality Maturity Profile to assess a company's quality efforts.[9] (A similar matrix was proposed by Philip Crosby.) They have learned that a company typically moves through increasing levels of maturity:

■ *Innocence*, in which the organization does not recognize the need for improved product and service quality. Quality is considered a tradeoff for increased costs.

■ *Awareness*, which is typically achieved after the organization has lost sales due to quality problems. The company recognizes the need to act.

■ *Understanding*, in which the company receives quality training and implemented basic quality improvement systems. Management is an active supporter of the movement.

■ *Competence*, in which the organization operates with an integrated quality system providing regular and timely feedback. Advanced quality techniques are used.

■ *Excellence*, in which the company provides customer-oriented products and services in a world-class effort. The organization is totally responsive to market demands and delivers products on time at the lowest cost.

The matrix, shown in Table 13.2, can be used to assess the level of a firm's maturity in relation to typical measures of the firm's quality effort: approach, role of top management, quality responsibility, process, customer relations, supplier relations, quality cost, training, and transition strategy.

■ Best Practices

From a self-assessment, companies can develop effective implementation strategies. Research performed in 1992 by Ernst & Young and the American Quality Foundation, called the International Quality Study, suggested that trying to implement all the practices of world- class organizations may not always be the best strategy for TQM.[10] In fact, it can actually hurt, wasting time and money on the wrong things. The study indicated that best practices depend on the current level of performance of a company. Two measures of performance are the ROA (return on assets: aftertax income divided by total assets) and VAE (value added per employee: sales less the costs of materials, supplies, and work done by outside contractors). Low performers—those with less than two percent ROA and $47,000 VAE—can reap the highest benefits by concentrating on fundamentals. Such an effort includes identifying processes that add value and then simplifying them to improve response to customer and market demands. In addition, training and teamwork—particularly in resolving customer complaints—can lead to significant improvements. More advanced concepts like self-managed teams take too much preparation and time to be worthwhile for these companies. Other suggestions include benchmarking competitors rather than world-class companies, listening to the customer for ideas, selecting suppliers on the basis of price and reliability, buying turnkey technology that reduces costs, and rewarding front-line workers for teamwork and quality.

Medium performers—those with ROA from two percent to 6.9 percent and VAE between $47,000 and $73,999—achieve the most benefits from meticulously documenting gains and further refining practices to improve value added per employee, time to market, and customer satisfaction. Another fundamental action is to encourage employees at every level to find ways to improve their jobs. A separate quality assurance staff is recommended. These companies should also emulate market leaders and selected world-class companies; use customer input, formal market research, and internal ideas for new products; select suppliers first by quality certification, then price; find ways to use facilities more flexibly to produce a wider variety of products and services; and base compensation for workers and middle managers on contributions to teamwork and quality.

High performers—with ROA and VAE exceeding seven percent and $74,000 respectively—gain the most from using self-managed teams and cross-functional teams that concentrate on horizontal processes such as logistics and product development. Benchmarking product development, distribution, and customer service against world-class firms can be highly beneficial. Additional training,

TABLE 13.2   Coopers & Lybrand Quality Maturity Matrix

Characteristic	Innocence	Awareness	Understanding	Competence	Excellence
Approach	Reactive; fire fighting	Quality improvement	Prevention	Designed in	Innovation
Role of top management	Not involved	Assumes responsibility	Supports process focus	Measures total performance	Stimulates creative response to market evolution
Quality responsibility	Quality department	Management	Knolwedge transfer to operators	Quality at the source	Shared companywide
Process	Inspect and correct	Try new procedures	Process control	Real-time market feedback	Innovative improvement
Customer relations	React to worst complaints	Internal customer recognized	Plan to requirements of main customers	Improvement plans linked to customer	Customers aid innovation for future benefit
Supplier relations	React to worst defects	Education; reduce receiving inspection	Joint quality activities	Long-term strategic partnerships	Mutual work to prepare for market evolution
Quality cost (% of sales)	Over 20%	15–20%	8–15%	3–8%	Under 3%
Training	Little	Techniques	Planned	Continuous; companywide	Research
Transition strategy	Stabilization	Development	Technology transfer	Technology transfer	Organization

SOURCE: Coopers & Lybrand, *Integrated Quality* (New York: 1988).

except for new hires, is of limited value. In addition, new products should be based on customer input, benchmarking, and internal research and development. Suppliers should be chosen primarily for their technology and quality. Strategic partnerships should be considered to diversify manufacturing. Senior managers should be included in compensation schemes pegged to teamwork and quality. Finally, these firms should further refine practices to improve VAE, market response, and customer satisfaction.

Strangely, the IQS Best Practices Report has been interpreted by some news media as a criticism of TQM.[11] They translate the report as simply saying that many quality practices are a waste of time and ineffective. On the contrary, the results are the first significant effort to develop a prescriptive theory (back to Deming again) of TQM implementation, rather than relying on intuition and anecdotal evidence. This viewpoint is similar to the contingency approaches in motivation and leadership theory and contradicts the notion of one magic quick fix for quality. Rather, companies advance in stages along a learning curve in their application of TQM and must carefully design their programs to optimize its effect.

THE ROLE OF EMPLOYEES IN TQM IMPLEMENTATION

Three key players for successful TQM implementation are *senior management*, *middle management*, and *the work force*. Each plays a critical role in the implementation process. Senior managers must ensure that their plans and strategies are successfully executed within the organization. Middle managers provide the leadership by which the vision of senior management is translated into the operations of the organization. In the end, the work force delivers quality and, for TQM to succeed, must feel not only empowerment, but ownership.

■ Senior Management

Many organizations today find themselves in a leadership vacuum because the environment has changed more rapidly than they ever imagined. Their leadership styles have not kept pace, and they find themselves falling back on approaches that were "good enough" for their predecessors, but frequently inadequate today.

In an extensive research project, Henry Mintzberg studied managers who had formal authority and defined ten managerial roles that leaders must play.[12] These roles included (1) figurehead, (2) leader, (3) liaison, (4) monitor, (5) disseminator, (6) spokesperson, (7) entrepreneur, (8) disturbance handler, (9) resource allocator, and (10) negotiator. Mintzberg pointed out that the importance of each role is contingent on the environmental and organizational factors that face managers who must lead. These contingencies include the industry or environmental surroundings of the organization, its age and size, the organizational level at which the leader operates, and the part of the organization (e.g., operating core, technostructure, or support structure) in which the leader resides. For example, in a pharmaceutical firm, where government regulation and the need for constant protection of the "ethical" quality image abounds, the top management leader must spend a tremendous amount of time as figurehead, liaison, and spokesperson. In a small, family-owned foundry with a history of labor unrest, the CEO would tend to spend much more time as entrepreneur, disturbance handler, and negotiator in order to develop a quality product and image.

Senior managers' responsibilities include the following tasks:

1. Ensure that the organization focuses on the needs of the customer.

2. Cascade the mission, vision, and values of the organization throughout the organization.

3. Identify the critical processes that need attention and improvement.

4. Identify the resources and tradeoffs that must be made to fund the TQM activity.

5. Review progress and remove any identified barriers.

6. Improve the macroprocesses in which they are involved, both to improve the performance of the process and to demonstrate their ability to use quality tools for problem solving.[13]

These responsibilities require a commitment of time that is often perceived to take away from other duties. However, if senior managers recognize that quality management is simply good business management, then they are less likely to encounter conflict.

■ Middle Management

Leonard Sayles, a veteran leadership consultant and researcher, observed that middle managers are not expected to be leaders, but to be guardians of generally approved management principles (GAMP).[14] GAMP rests on time-honored assumptions and practices:

- Clear and fixed work goals and technology
- Relying on centralized specialist groups
- Focusing on numbers, such as meeting budgeted targets
- Being as autonomous as possible and ignoring the work system
- Delegating as much as possible and managing solely by results
- Compartmentalizing people issues and technology issues

Sayles notes that GAMP no longer works. They were probably effective in simple, stable organizations and the business environment of 30 or 40 years ago. Critical leadership roles in today's rapidly changing business environment involve coordination, technology development, system and process integration, and continuous improvement. Coordination involves ensuring that strategies and plans are actually carried out at the operating levels of the firm. In the past, employees required direction in the form of precise instructions on what to do and how to do it. Today, managers find themselves monitoring progress, disseminating information and suggestions between local and distant line, staff, and outside experts, and acting as a spokesperson inside and outside the firm. Technology development requires that managers constantly scan the environment to be aware of technological developments that may threaten or enhance the operations of the company. System and process integration means optimizing the system to meet strategic goals such as customer service, and using tools of quality measurement and continuous improvement.

Middle management has been tagged by many as a direct obstacle to creating a supportive environment for TQM.[15] Because of their position in the company, middle managers have been accused of feeding territorial competition and stifling information flow. They have also been blamed for not developing and/or preparing employees for change. Unwilling to take initiatives that contribute to continuous improvement, middle managers appear to be threatened by continuous improvement efforts. However, middle management's role in creating and sustaining a TQM culture is critical. Middle managers improve the operational processes that are the foundation of customer satisfaction. They can make or break cooperation and teamwork; and they are the principal means by which the remaining work force prepares for change.

Samuel suggests that transforming middle managers into change agents requires a systematic process which dissolves traditional management boundaries and replaces them with an empowered and team-oriented state of accountability for organizational performance. This process involves:

1. *Empowerment:* Middle managers must be accountable for the performance of the organization in meeting objectives.

2. *Creating a common vision of excellence:* This vision is then transformed into critical success factors which describe key areas of performance that relate to internal and external customer satisfaction.

3. *New rules for playing the organizational game:* Territorial walls must be broken, yielding a spirit of teamwork. Today's managers must assume the role of coach. One new approach is "interlocking accountability," in which managers are accountable to one another for their performance. The second is "team representation," in which each manager is responsible for accurately representing the ideas and decisions of the team to others outside the team.

4. *Implementing a continuous improvement process:* These projects should improve their operational systems and processes.

5. *Developing and retaining peak performers:* Middle managers must identify and develop future leaders of the organization.

Middle managers must also exhibit behaviors that are supportive of total quality, such as listening to employees as customers, creating a positive work environment, implementing quality improvements enthusiastically, challenging people to develop new ideas and reach their potential, setting challenging goals and providing positive feedback, and following through on promises. These changes are often difficult for middle managers to accept. The perceived threats from an empowered work force, which often leads to flatter organizations are indeed serious issues that organizations must tackle.

■ The Work Force

If total quality does not occur at the work-force level, it will not occur at all. The work force implements quality policies. This task requires **ownership.** Ownership goes beyond empowerment; it gives the employee the right to have a voice in deciding what needs to be done and how to do it.[16] It is based on a belief that what is good for the organization is also good for the individual and vice-versa. At Westinghouse, they define ownership as "taking personal responsibility for our jobs. . . for assuring that we meet or exceed our customers' standards and our own. We believe that ownership is a state of mind and heart that is characterized by a personal and emotional commitment to approach every decision and task with the confidence and leadership of an owner." Self-managed teams, discussed in Chapter 11, represent one form of ownership.

Increased ownership requires increased sharing of information with the work force and a commitment to the work force in good times and in bad. Wainwright Industries develops trust and belief in each associate. Although family-owned, its financial books were opened to everyone. After hourly wages and time clocks were eliminated; all associates became salaried. The company has maintained over 99 percent attendance since this change. Their continuous improvement process involves everyone and is associate-driven. Although Wainwright cannot guarantee a job for life, their commitment to job security is based on the philosophy that the training and development that Wainwright gives to its employees makes them highly employable and marketable, even if the company should suffer financial hardship. With such commitments, the company can more easily develop the loyalty and commitment needed within the work force as they strive to apply the principles of total quality. One measure of Wainwright's success is that the number of implemented suggestions per person per year exceeds 50, while the previous benchmark that Wainwright identified (Milliken) was 15!

■ Union–Management Relations

A major stumbling block in the United States in implementing TQM has been the traditional adversarial relationship between unions and management.[17] For example, in 1986 General Motors introduced a team concept for quality improvement in Van Nuys, California, which just barely passed a union membership vote with only 53 percent in support. Since then, the opposition has worked to oppose the concept. In many cases, management must share the responsibility in working with unions as equal partners. Both union and management have important roles in TQM.

Labor's role is first to recognize the need for changing its relationship with management and then to educate its members as to how cooperation will affect the organization. This information includes what its members can expect, and how working conditions and job security might change. Labor must carefully select members for such a program and maintain a positive attitude. TQM initiatives must be separated from collective bargaining.

Management must realize that the skills and knowledge of all employees are needed to improve quality and meet competitive challenges. Management must be willing to develop a closer working relationship with labor and be ready to address union concerns and cultivate trust. Both sides should receive training in communication and problem-solving skills. Union and management should have equal representation in committees. External consultants can provide an important role as facilitators and mediators in such efforts.

CREATING THE QUALITY ORGANIZATION

Organization links planning with doing. **Organizing** is the process of assigning work and responsibility to functions, teams, and individuals, along with the appropriate delegation of authority. Organizing establishes lines of authority and responsibility, improves efficiency and quality of work through synergism, and improves communication.

Organization to achieve quality has been important throughout history. The basic organizational unit in all societies is the family. People in families learned to cooperate in various tasks and activities at a very early time to survive and prosper. Typical tasks of these early "organizations" included the following:

- Obtaining basic resources such as food and materials for clothing
- Processing materials; for example, cooking, making clothes, creating weapons
- Developing human resources; for example, teaching children to do the two preceding tasks
- Trading processed products for basic resources
- Defending against attacks by animals or hostile humans
- Passing on the "culture" of the organization: language, history, religion, ethics, etc.

Generally, each individual performed all of these tasks at one time or another. Quality control was automatic, and lack of quality was potentially deadly; anyone who did not do the task properly was subject to starvation, injury, or calamity.

In the early days of manufacturing, work was performed by skilled craftspeople (men and women) who were responsible for most manufacturing tasks such as procurement, production, inspection, and sales. With the industrial revolution, organizations grew and became more complex. Different individuals assumed responsibility for different tasks; and they organized themselves into work groups, departments, and different functional units. Today, creating an effective organization for quality is essential.

Several factors having to do with *context* of the organization (and consequently, the quality organization) must be addressed in any organizing effort.[18] These issues impact how work is organized and include:

- *Company operational and organizational guidelines.* Standard practices that have developed over the firm's history often dictate how a company organizes and operates.

- *Management style.* The management team operates in a manner unique to a given company. For example, management style might be formal or informal, or democratic or autocratic. If the organization operates in a highly structured, formal atmosphere, organizing a quality effort around informal meetings would probably meet with little success.

- *Customer influences.* Formal specifications or administrative controls may be required by customers, particularly governmental agencies. Thus, the quality organization needs to understand and respond to these requirements.

- *Company size.* Large companies have the ability to maintain formal systems and records, whereas smaller companies may not.

- *Diversity and complexity of product line.* An organization suitable for the manufacture of a small number of highly sophisticated products may differ dramatically from an organization that produces a high volume of standard products.

- *Stability of the product line.* Stable product lines generate economies of scale that influence supervision, corrective action, and other quality-related issues. Frequent changes in products necessitate more control and changes to the quality system.

- *Financial stability.* Quality managers need to recognize that their efforts must fit within the overall budget of the firm.

■ *Availability of personnel.* The lack of certain skills may require other personnel, such as supervisors, to assume duties they ordinarily would not be assigned.

These issues suggest that a "one-size fits all" quality organization is inappropriate. The organization must be tailored to reflect individual company differences and provide the flexibility and the ability to change.

The primary elements of organizing are to decide *what* processes and tasks must be performed, and *who* will carry them out. The formal link between the what and the who of organizing is called the **organizational structure.** It consists of clarifying authority, responsibility, reporting lines, and performance standards between individuals at each level of the organization. An effective organization also depends on selecting the right projects and providing support to get the tasks done, along with adequate communication and cooperation between workers and managers, which is accomplished through quality councils and steering committees. Finally, the processes, policies, procedures, tools must be formalized, documented, and communicated. Proper organization can create the type of corporate culture that will enable total quality to be successful. These issues are addressed in the remainder of this section.

■ Quality and Organizational Structure

Traditional organizations tend to develop structures that help them to maintain stability. They tend to be rather highly structured, both in terms of rules and regulations, as well as the height of the "corporate ladder," with seven or more layers of managers between the CEO and the first-line worker. In contrast, organizations in rapidly changing environments, which characterizes modern organizations, have to build flexibility into their organization structures. Hence, they tend to have fewer written rules and regulations and flatter organizational structures.

An organization chart shows the *apparent structure* of the formal organization. However, some organizations refuse to be tied down by a conventional organization chart, even to the extent that employees make a running joke of titles. For example, Semco, Inc., a radically unconventional manufacturer of industrial equipment (mixers, washers, air conditioners, bakery plant units) located in Sao Paulo, Brazil, has what is called a "circular" organization chart with four concentric circles (they avoid the use of the term "levels"). The titles that go with these are Counselors (CEO and the equivalent of vice presidents), Partners (business unit heads), Coordinators (supervisory specialists and functional leaders), and Associates (everyone else). If anyone desires, he or she can think up a title for external use that describes their area or job responsibility. As the owner and CEO, Ricardo Simler, explains:

> Consistent with this philosophy, when a promotion takes place now at Semco we simply supply blank business cards and tell the newly elevated individual: "Think of a title that signals externally your area of operation and responsibility and have it printed." If the person likes "Procurement Manager," fine. If he wants something more elegant, he can print up cards saying, "First Pharaoh in Charge of Royal Supplies." Whatever he wants. But inside the company, there are only four options. (Anyway, almost all choose to print only their name.)[19]

Although thousands of different organization structures exist, the most conventional ones are variations or combinations of three basic types: (1) the line organization, (2) the line and staff organization, and (3) the matrix organization.

The line organization is a functional form, with departments that are responsible for marketing, finance, and operations. In the traditional organization, the quality department is generally distinct from other departments. In a TQ organization, the role of quality should be invisible in the organization chart, since quality planning and assurance are part of the responsibility of each operating manager and employee at every level. In theory, this organizational form could exist in a fairly large organization if all employees were thoroughly indoctrinated in the philosophy of quality and could be counted on to place quality as the top priority in all aspects of their daily work. In practice, this organization structure is not generally successful except when used in small firms.

The line and staff organization is the most prevalent type of organization structure for medium-sized to large firms. In such organizations, line departments carry out the functions of marketing, finance, and production for the organization. Staff personnel, including quality managers and technical specialists, assist the line managers in carrying out their jobs by providing technical assistance and advice. Variations on the basic line and staff organization can include geographic or customer organizations. In this traditional form of organization structure, quality managers and inspectors may take on the role of guardians of quality instead of technical experts who assist line managers and workers in attaining quality. This guardian-type role also happens when the quality assurance function is placed too low in the organization or when pressure from higher levels of the organization forces quality inspectors to ease up on quality so that more products can be shipped. The major cause of this problem is too much responsibility with insufficient authority.

The matrix type of organization is a relatively new form developed for use in situations where large, complex projects are designed and carried out, such as defense weapons systems or large construction projects. Firms that do such work have a basic need to develop an organization structure that will permit the efficient use of human resources while maintaining control over the many facets of the project being developed. In a matrix-type organization, each project has a project manager and each department that is providing personnel to work on various projects has a technical or administrative manager. Thus, a quality assurance technician might be assigned to the quality assurance department for technical and administrative activities but would be attached to Project A for day-to-day job assignments. The technician would report to the project manager of Project A and to his or her "technical boss" in the quality assurance department. When Project A is completed, the technician might be reassigned to Project B under a new project manager. He or she would still be reporting to the "technical boss" in quality assurance, however.

The matrix type of organization for project work has a number of advantages. It generally improves coordination in complex project work as well as improves the efficiency of personnel use. It has a major drawback in requiring split loyalty for people who report to two supervisors. This division of loyalty can be especially troublesome or even dangerous in a quality assurance area. For example, in a nuclear power plant project, a project manager who is under pressure to complete a project by a certain deadline might try to influence QA inspectors to take shortcuts in completing the inspection phase of the project. The QA manager, who might be hundreds of miles away from the site, would often not have the influence over the inspectors that the project manager would have.

Feigenbaum suggests three important considerations in structuring the quality control component of an organization, along with an added fourth criterion (illustrated in the organization chart in Figure 13.1):

1. Keep "layers" of supervision to a minimum so that lines of communication can be kept as short as possible.

2. Keep "spans" of supervision as broad as possible, which naturally follows if "layers" are to be kept at a minimum. The "span" is the number of persons reporting directly to a supervisor or manager. The lower in the organization one goes, the greater the spans should become, because the work of the reporting positions usually becomes more uniform in nature.

3. Place similar portions of work into a similar work package that can be handled by a person in the position considered.

4. Ensure that the top reporting level of the quality organization is sufficiently high to indicate the importance of the quality function and to ensure ready access to the key decision makers in the organization.[20]

The chart in Figure 13.1 shows a typical quality control organization based on a line and staff organizational form within a manufacturing organization. It shows how personnel in the staff function of quality assurance report to a manager for control of day-to-day projects, assignments, and work activities, and

FIGURE 13.1 A Typical Line-Staff Quality Organization Chart

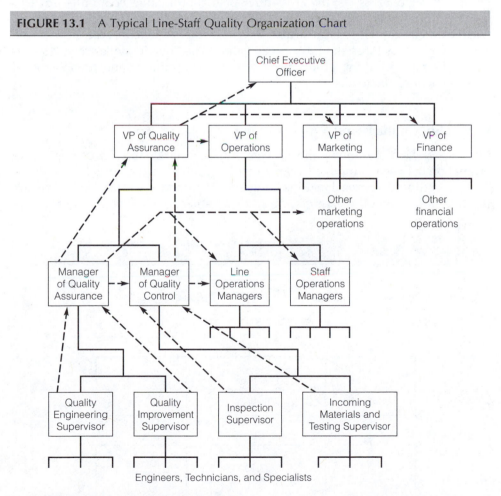

Solid lines show formal authority relationships.
Dotted lines show semiformal advisory relationships.

represents the *formal* organizational relationship. However, the semiformal advisory relationship can often be crucial to a successful quality program. In a way, the subordinate may be the superior (in a technical sense) of a manager in operations, marketing, or even his or her own department. Because of superior technical expertise about how to run a certain quality test or develop an employee involvement group solution, the subordinate gains the *expert* label, which increases the power of the subordinate's suggestions.

As more and more companies accept the process view of organizations, they are structuring the quality organization around functional or cross-functional teams. Thus, rather than view the organization in the formal hierarchy as suggested in Figure 13.1, the organizational chart looks more like the one of GTE Directories—shown in Figure 13.2. In this organizational structure, the management board leads the quality effort, meeting twice each month to discuss and review management and quality issues. Quality is implemented through various teams: core process business team, cross-functional coordinating committee, regional management councils, major business process management teams (PMTs), Malcolm Baldrige National Quality Award (MBNQA) teams, and quality improvement teams. The regional management councils identify and address key regional issues; the cross-functional coordinating committee reviews major proposals for consistency with the strategic plan and business priorities. Such team-based organization structures spread the ownership, and the accountability, for quality throughout the organization. The "quality department" serves as an internal consulting group, providing advice, training, and organizational development to the teams.

Quality Councils and Support Teams

Complex tasks of designing and implementing a total quality effort require coordination between individuals with a variety of interests and specialized talents. Multidisciplinary approaches to solving problems and coordinating efforts are the rule rather than the exception in most organizations today. A common ap-

FIGURE 13.2 GTE Directories Management Structure

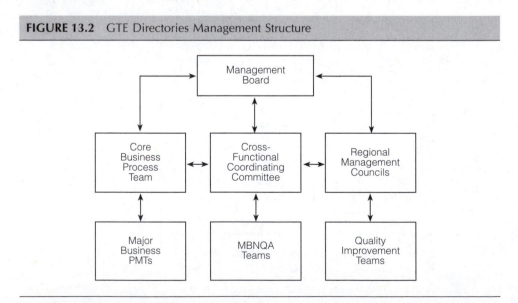

SOURCE: Courtesy of GTE Directories Corporation.

proach that has been used successfully to implement TQM is the formation of one or more steering teams of senior managers, which Juran terms *quality councils*. The AT&T Network Operations Group, for example, has an executive quality council, vice president quality councils, director quality councils, and division/district manager quality councils, all of which are networked together. Quality councils assume many responsibilities such as incorporating TQM into the company's strategic planning process and coordinating the overall effort. At AT&T, the quality council is characterized by several essential elements.[21]

■ *Leadership:* promoting and articulating the quality vision, communicating responsibilities and expectations for management action, aligning the business management process with the quality approach, maintaining high visibility for commitment and involvement, and ensuring that businesswide support is available in the form of education, consulting, methods, and tools.

■ *Planning:* planning strategic quality goals, understanding basic customer needs and business capabilities, developing long-term goals and near-term priorities, formulating human resource goals and policies, understanding employees' perceptions about quality and work, ensuring that all employees have the opportunity and skills to participate, and aligning reward and recognition systems to support the quality approach.

■ *Implementation:* forming key business process teams, chartering teams to manage and improve these processes, reviewing improvement plans, providing resources for improvement, enlisting all managers in the process, reviewing quality plans of major organizational units, and working with suppliers and business partners in joint quality planning.

■ *Review:* tracking progress through customer satisfaction and internal measures of quality, monitoring progress in attaining improvement objectives, celebrating successes, improving the quality system through auditing and identifying improvement opportunities, planning improvements, and validating the impact of improvements.

Other types of administrative teams support the quality organization. Two of the many examples include material review boards and employee involvement program steering teams. Material review boards were originally conceived for the specific purpose of expediting decisions on nonconforming lots of material for defense contracts.[22] There, board membership consisted of a military representative, a quality control specialist, and the component's designer. If the product was to be shipped, the board was required to examine the nonconformity to product specifications and to make a unanimous decision that the product's defect would not materially affect the product's proper functioning or fitness for use.

The scope of the material review board has been broadened to include recommending the disposition of raw materials or semifinished or finished products that are nonconforming to standards. Today's boards might consist of process engineers, QA personnel, and line supervisors. They may recommend that the products in question be returned to the supplier, reworked, scrapped, or sold as seconds. Once it has made its recommendation on a particular problem, the material review board turns the issue over to a high-level line manager to make the final decision concerning disposition of the material.

EI program steering teams have the responsibility of ensuring that the processes, approaches, and progress of an EI program are on track. Such a team might be composed of a quality manager, human resources manager, union representatives, and other representatives from management and the work force.

When well managed, administrative teams can be used to transmit information, gather opinions, and gain support for decisions. If misused, they can block progress, foster dissension, and diffuse responsibility to the point of meaninglessness.

■ Documentation and Procedures

The documents related to quality in organizations are many and varied. They are used to show standard practices and relationships between various departments and functions. The ideal situation would be organizations that started out with a systematic plan and process for documentation of quality plans, policies, and procedures. However, this situation generally does not happen in reality. Deployment of quality plans often takes place over a considerable period of time in an evolutionary fashion and requires skill, effort, and constant work to achieve desirable results.

The basic form of documenting quality-related policies and procedures is the **quality manual.** The purpose of a quality manual is to provide the organization with a central reference source of quality plans and procedures that result from mutual agreement. Thus, a quality manual serves as the official corporate memory, after careful preparation by members of the organization who agree it represents the best procedures or practices to follow. Such documents are only beneficial when kept up to date and used for their intended purpose.

A quality manual is generally organized into modular sections.[23] A general section deals with broad administration of the manual along with aids to its use. Managerial sections, or subsystems, deal with specific aspects of the quality system, such as customer relations, manufacturing, supplier relations, inspection and test, field service, statistical methodology, quality improvement, and human relations. Technological sections deal with materials, processes, products, and other elements that are special to the company.

A quality manual is often necessary to do business with federal, state, and/or local governments, or be a supplier to a major automotive or other industrial customer who demands to see a quality plan. It also is a first step in preparing an assessment of quality processes and procedures required for ISO 9000 certification.

ISO 9000 has put more stringent requirements on documentation for quality. *Documentation* that is prepared to support ISO 9000 registration generally consists of a high level quality manual that provides an overview of the quality system and how the various elements fit together. At the next level, a *procedures* section provides details of how each activity in different functional areas is performed. For example, a purchasing procedure would define how suppliers are selected and how a purchase order is written and approved. The third level is *work instructions,* often known as "standard operating procedures." These are step-by-step instructions of how particular jobs get done. Finally, a *forms and records* level compiles proof of what is actually done to ensure compliance with the stated procedures and work instructions.

As discussed in Chapter 12, the Baldrige Award criteria provides a more comprehensive framework for total quality than the ISO 9000 series of standards. As a result, many companies define their quality procedures relative to the Baldrige Award criteria.

SUSTAINING THE QUALITY ORGANIZATION

Getting started is often easy when compared to sustaining a quality focus. Numerous organizational barriers and challenges get in the way. New efforts usually begin with much enthusiasm, in part because of the sheer novelty of the effort. After a while, reality sets in and doubts surface. Real problems develop as early supporters begin to question the process. At this point, the organization can resign itself to inevitable failure or persist and seek to overcome the obstacles. Sustaining total quality requires an understanding of implementation barriers, the ability to deal with crises, and the ability to develop into a "learning organization."

■ Implementation Barriers

Numerous barriers to successfully implementing total quality exist in organizations:

- Lack of consistent top management support
- Inadequate knowledge and understanding about TQM
- Fear and resistance to change
- Lack of a long-term focus
- Politics and turf battles
- Employee apathy
- Inadequate planning

The people who implement quality initiatives often have conflicting goals and priorities. For example, the general manager of a large defense electronics contractor unveiled a big quality program, then plunged into dealing with the unit's plummeting revenues and layoffs. Quality went nowhere. At Florida Power and Light (see the Quality in Practice in Chapter 12), John J. Hudiburg drove hard to win the Deming Prize, but created a large bureaucracy in which morale fell as workers and managers had to compile hundreds of pages of analysis. The new CEO reduced the scope of the quality effort.[24]

Implementation of TQM is often attempted without a full grasp of its nature. Certain mistakes are made repeatedly.[25] Some of the more common mistakes include the following:

1. TQM is regarded as a "program," despite the rhetoric that may be made to the contrary.

2. Short-term results are not obtained, causing management to lose interest—often either no attempt is made to get short-term results, or management believes that measurable benefits lie *only* in the distant future.

3. The process is not driven by a focus on the customer, a connection to strategic business issues, and support from senior management.

4. Structural elements in the organization block change—such as compensation systems, promotion systems, accounting systems, rigid policies and procedures, specialization and functionalization, and status symbols such as offices and perks.

5. Goals are set too low. Management does not shoot for stretch goals or use outside benchmarks as targets.

6. The organizational culture remains one of "command and control" and is driven by fear or game-playing, budgets, schedules, or bureaucracy.

7. Training is not properly addressed. Too little training is offered to the work force. Training may be of the wrong kind, such as only classroom training or a focus on tools and not problems.

8. The focus is mainly on products, not processes.

9. Little real empowerment is given and is not supported in actions.

10. The organization is too successful and complacent. It is not receptive to change and learning, and clings to the "not invented here" syndrome.

11. The organization fails to address three fundamental questions: Is this another program? What's in it for me? How can I do this on top of everything else?

12. Senior management is not personally and visibly committed and actively participating.

13. An overemphasis on teams for cross-functional problems, which leads to the neglect of individual efforts for local improvements.

14. Employees operate under the belief that more data are always desirable, regardless of relevance—"paralysis by analysis."

15. Management fails to recognize that quality improvement is a personal responsibility at all levels of the organization.

16. The organization does not see itself as a collection of interrelated processes making up an overall system. Both the individual processes and the overall system need to be identified and understood.

While this list is extensive, it is by no means exhaustive. It reflects the still immature development of TQM. TQM requires a new set of skills and learning, including interpersonal awareness and competence, teambuilding, encouraging openness and trust, listening, giving and getting feedback, group participation, problem solving, clarifying goals, resolving conflicts, delegating and coaching, empowerment, and continuous improvement as a way of life.[26] The process must begin by creating a set of feelings and attitudes that lead to lasting values and organizational commitment. It must develop by planning a TQM strategy for the long term. Finally, it must be realized through training, continuous feedback and open communications, and empowerment.

■ Managing Crises

Implementing TQM has been likened to a marriage; the first year can be trying and crises inevitably arise.[27] Xerox described its pursuit of quality as three steps forward and one step back. The initial period centers on quality awareness, infrastructure, measurement systems, and new skills. After about a year, the quality message is no longer new and has lost some of its excitement. As measurement improves, companies begin to see problems more clearly. The realization that things are not going as well as expected causes disappointment, anxiety, and sometimes, panic. Companies tend to look for quick results, rather than at long-term improvement. First-year objectives typically are not achieved until the third or fourth year.

Perceived crises in implementing TQM programs arise from two sources. The first is change. TQM requires significant changes to an organization, in methods, processes, attitudes, and behavior. Organizations need time for this realization to set in, and sometimes change is painful. Line workers receive more responsibility and authority and become more accountable for their own work. Supervisors who were experts and order-givers are now forced to become facilitators and coaches. Middle managers who maintained processes are now problem solvers. Top managers must think differently, to become more aware of and interact with customers.

The second cause of a quality crisis is rising expectations. As people become more knowledgeable about what a quality organization should look like, they become more sensitive to problems within the organization and in their own behavior. This sensitivity can create anxiety. Such situations can be avoided through proper planning. At the beginning of the process, expectations should be kept simple. Everyone needs to recognize that setbacks will occur as a normal evolution. Managers should be trained to use interpersonal skills so that they can manage the human issues associated with change. First-year projects should be simple and have a high probability of success. All improvements, no matter how small, should be documented and publicized. Progress should be reviewed periodically, and goals revised accordingly.

◼ The Learning Organization

Psychologists suggest that individuals go through four stages of learning:

1. *Unconscious incompetence:* You don't know that you don't know.
2. *Conscious incompetence:* You realize that you don't know.
3. *Conscious competence:* You learn to do, but with conscious effort.
4. *Unconscious competence:* Performance comes effortlessly.

As discussed in Chapter 1, many companies in the United States languished in stage 1 until receiving a wake-up call in the 1980s with regard to quality. Unfortunately, as many organizations move into stage 2, they tend to shoot the messenger and refuse to accept the state of incompetence. This attitude can be explained by recognizing that organizations have both static and dynamic components. If organizations exist to structure the work of groups of people, then they must be expected to produce some tangible product or provide some service. The static part of the organization is intended to document, regularize, and maintain the rational requirements for work through relatively stable processes, policies, procedures, rules, and communications on which everyone, at least tacitly, agrees and depends. The static part of an organization thus inherently resists change.

However, organizations are also dynamic entities. Managers must consider the dynamic component in order to deal with instability in the environment, imperfect plans, the need for innovation, and the common human desire for variety and change. The degree of dynamism in organizations is moderated by factors such as culture, leadership, learning, and linkages between people and structures.

Therefore, both the culture and organizational structure should be designed to support the established direction in which the organization is moving, and modified whenever that direction changes significantly. Managers, especially those who do not understand the nature of leadership, are often hesitant to make needed organizational changes as the organization grows, even when the need for change becomes obvious. This need to change, to move through the four stages of learning *repeatedly*, is embodied in a concept called *the learning organization*.

The concept of organizational learning is not new. It has its roots in general systems theory[28] and systems dynamics[29] developed in the 1950s and 1960s, as well as theories of learning from organizational psychology. Peter Senge, a professor at the Massachusetts Institute of Technology (MIT), has become the major advocate of the learning organization movement. He defines the learning organization as:

> . . . an organization that is continually expanding its capacity to create its future. For such an organization, it is not enough merely to survive. "Survival learning" or what is more often termed "adaptive learning" is important—indeed it is necessary. But for a learning organization, "adaptive learning" must be joined by "generative learning," learning that enhances our capacity to create.[30]

The conceptual framework behind this definition requires an understanding and integration of many of the concepts and principles that are part of the TQM philosophy. Senge repeatedly points out, "Over the long run, superior performance depends on superior learning." What he means is that organizations cannot count on being successful in the long run if they merely have committed leaders who use TQM principles for strategic planning and policy deployment, practice TQM in daily operations, and use it for continuous improvement of the current process. These activities might be called "first generation" TQM. The key to developing learning organizations, according to Senge, is a new approach to leadership.

Instead of the *adaptive* approach to learning (first generation TQM), leaders must use a *generative* approach—constantly anticipating the needs of customers to the point of determining what products or services they would truly value but have never experienced and would never think of asking for them. Leaders must develop the capability to integrate creative thinking and problem solving throughout the organization. In the words of Walter Wriston, former CEO of Citibank, "The person who figures out how to harness the collective genius of the people in his or her organization is going to blow the competition away." Finally, leaders in learning organizations must help people to restructure their views of reality. Instead of the traditional focus on reacting to events and responding to historical trends, leaders must encourage and model decision making based on understanding the causes of events and behavior behind the trends in order to make positive changes to the system. Thus, real improvements (second generation TQM) can only be made by understanding the root causes, instead of treating the symptoms.

Garvin criticizes Senge and others for not providing an operational framework for implementing a learning organization (something that Senge attempts to correct in a recent book[31]). Garvin defines the learning organization as:

> . . . an organization that is skilled at creating, acquiring, and transferring knowledge, and at modifying its behavior to reflect new knowledge and insights.[32]

Interestingly, Garvin observes that simply trying to change and make improvements is not enough. Thus, companies, such as GM, that are trying but failing to make significant changes, have not yet become skilled learning organizations. Also, colleges and universities who know and teach about TQM but don't put the concepts into practice to improve their teaching, research, and administrative processes, are not exhibiting the characteristics of learning organizations. Companies that are successfully exhibiting the characteristics of learning organizations include Honda, Corning, and General Electric. Through active management of the learning process, they have become skilled in creating, acquiring, and transferring knowledge and in modifying behavior of their employees and other contributors to their enterprises.

Garvin points out that learning organizations have to become good at performing five main activities, including: "systematic problem solving, experimentation with new approaches, learning from their own experiences and history, learning from the experiences and best practices of others, and transferring knowledge quickly and efficiently throughout the organization."[33] Virtually all of these skills have been defined as TQM terms with the same basic meanings as Garvin suggests:

- Kaizen—continuous quality improvement
- Experimental design
- Santayana review[34]
- Benchmarking
- Dissemination and "holding the gains"

No single aspect works well for everyone. Although enthusiastic advocates of TQM would like to claim that all aspects of TQM are universal and can be applied to all organizations, all organizations will experience their own specific limitations in what can be achieved via the implementation of TQM practices. Sitkin and others proposed that a sharp distinction lies between the concepts of what they called "Total Quality Control" (TQC) and "Total Quality Learning" (TQL) approaches (see Table 13.3).[35] They argued that TQC practices applied to the quality precepts of customer satisfaction, continuous improvement, and treating the organization as a system result in a traditional closed cybernetic control system. A closed-loop control system has a standard, a way of measuring actual performance versus the standard, feedback on variances between actual versus standard, and a way to modify the system. The TQL approach, in contrast, applies practices to the precepts in an open-system way

TABLE 13.3   Linking the Distinctive Principles Associated With TQC and TQL to Common Underlying TQM Precepts

Shared TQM Precepts	PRINCIPLES DERIVED FROM COMMON PRECEPTS	
	Control-Oriented Principles (TQC)	Learning-Oriented Principles (TQL)
Customer Satisfaction	Monitor and assess known customer needs	Scan for new customers, needs, or issues
	Benchmark to better understand existing customer needs	Test customer need definitions
	Respond to customer needs	Stimulate new customer need definitions and levels
Continuous Improvement	Exploit existing skills and resources	Explore new skills and resources
	Increase control and reliability	Increase learning and resilience
Treating the Organization as a Total System	First-order learning (cybernetic feedback)	Second-order learning
	Participation enhancement focus	Diversity enhancement focus

that is experimentally oriented, rather than control oriented. The authors argued that the control aspects of TQC are appropriate to stable, routine environments where repetitive operations (such as high-volume manufacturing or service delivery) take place. The environment that contains innovative, highly uncertain operations (such as production of newly designed semiconductors or research and engineering departments) would require a TQL focus that was experimentally oriented and tolerant of mistakes in order to successfully invent new products and approaches. Their theory suggests that TQM implementation practices need to be modified in order to fit various environmental and contextual factors such as stage of the life-cycle of the product, industry in which the company operates, and level of education and training of the work force. Indeed, the Ernst & Young *Best Practices* report discussed earlier in this chapter confirmed the importance of exploring contingent factors in the implementation of TQM practices.

■ The Effects of Downsizing

Faced with severe financial pressures, many organizations have recently "downsized." Stowell pointed out that downsizing contains numerous pitfalls that managers frequently do not prepare for, or recognize as significant hazards.[36] He summarized a number of studies that showed that downsizing rarely accomplishes the goals managers have set for the effort. For example, a 1993 American Management Association study reported that only half the companies surveyed had increased profits and only one-third of the companies had improved their productivity by downsizing. Employee morale was reported to be lower in 80 percent of the firms. However, in spite of the poor results, two-thirds of the companies were planning on further cuts. Basically, he argued, most managers don't understand the long-term system effects of downsizing. Consequently, they take the "slash and burn" approach, which frequently ends up making things worse rather than better in the organization. When the system is not considered, job cuts result in temporarily positive changes, such as lower costs and higher stock prices. However, because such programs tend to overshoot their targets for personnel reduction, companies end up with higher costs for rehiring and training people for essential positions. In turn, headcounts creep, and, within a short period of time, more people than before the downsizing are on board; but now lower morale, lower productivity, lower quality, and lower stock price are also a part of the equation.

A serious problem is that downsizing is often mistakenly viewed as an result of TQM. One of the worst things an organization can do is to downsize shortly after implementing TQM. A much better approach is to downsize first, then use TQM as an opportunity to re-energize the company and make it more efficient. TQM tools can be used to build a new strategy for the company. Employees must recognize that TQM is not a separate effort, but the core approach for managing the business. Involved employees are more easily able to overcome the anxiety that accompanies downsizing. If it is inevitable, management must do everything possible to separate downsizing from TQM efforts. The keys to dealing with the dynamics of organizational change and quality implementation are understanding and shaping the corporate culture. This evolution of the corporate culture is embodied in the concept of the learning organization.

QUALITY IN PRACTICE

CHANGING THE ORGANIZATIONAL ARCHITECTURE AT XEROX[37]

Xerox Corporation's remarkable recovery of global competitiveness was profiled in a Quality in Practice in Chapter 1. However, both David Kearns, the CEO who helped to engineer Xerox's successful turnaround, and his successor Paul Allaire, realized that simply establishing TQM as part of the corporate culture was only the first critical step in the total quality "race without a finish line."

Part of Xerox's problem in the early 1980s was a too narrow view of their business strategy. Instead of creating a vision that focused on their core competency in image processing, Kearns' predecessor, Peter McColough, and Kearns himself, chose to diversify into other businesses. The largest of these was the insurance business. Xerox bought Crum and Forster in 1982 for $1.6 billion in cash and stock, which was then one of the largest corporate acquisitions in history. Because the Crum and Forster purchase occurred right after a massive layoff due to the declining copier business, Xerox employees and the financial community were less than enthusiastic about the deal. In hindsight, the decision was not a very good one. Even though financial services generated 40 percent of the company's profits in 1987, Crum and Forster and other financial ventures were not very profitable or a good fit with Xerox's core business.[38] However, Kearns insisted in his 1992 book that Xerox would have been considerably worse off in the mid-1980s had they not had the financial services business.[39] The financial service divisions have since been sold off.

The emerging vision of Xerox as "The Document Company" began to take place in the early 1990s. Kearns and Paul Allaire agreed that the corporate structure (the "organizational architecture" as it is now called by Xerox managers) needed radical change. Allaire believes the company must become even more customer focused, that employees must be given even more power and work on processes using teams, and that the company must change more in the next five years than it did in the previous ten (a concept that he calls 2X).[40]

How can a massive restructuring of a company as big and complex as Xerox take place? The blueprint for the change was described by the chief architect, Paul Allaire.[41] In 1990, he asked a group of six young managers to examine the kind of structure and practices that the company would need to be successful. The team, which became know as the "Futuretecture" team reported back three months

later to senior management of the company. They presented three scenarios—all variations of the existing Xerox structure—and a fourth radically different scenario. The fourth scenario was their preferred one and involved establishing independent global business divisions. They also transmitted a warning that the structure was less important than the informal behaviors, values, and attitudes that guided people within it.

To flesh out the changes and principles that were required, Allaire chartered another team, the Organizational Transformation Board (OTB), consisting of 15 managers and five support staff. Their task entailed establishing principles for redesigning the company and creating an understanding among key managers as to the direction Xerox was heading. The challenge was not so much in defining the structure, but in dealing with the "people issues" of coordination and support between units, which were vital to the new architecture. Within five months, the OTB had established the outlines of the structure toward which Xerox is now working.

Kearns and Nadler suggested some of the ways in which the new organizational design might differ from the old.[42] The new design would probably include the following aspects:

■ *Autonomous work teams:* self-managing groups, given real power, that undertake whole pieces of work.

■ *High-performance work systems:* sets of autonomous teams linked by technology into total work systems designed to support autonomy. In other words, whole factories can be created around these teams.

■ *Alliances and joint ventures:* cooperative efforts conducted at the tops of organizations that allow an organization to leverage its true competitive advantage and combine with others who have complementary advantages.

■ *Spin-outs:* creating new entities outside of the parent company—in essence, staking entrepreneurs.

■ *Networks:* combinations of different organizational forms—joint ventures, subsidiaries, spin-outs—with various tight and loose linkages. Scale without mass is achieved.

■ *Self-defining organizations:* organizations capable of rapid change that can reconfigure in response to or in anticipation of change.

■ *Fuzzy boundaries:* reducing the boundaries between the inside and outside of the organization. It means including customers and suppliers as part of the organization. Customers actually become codesigners of the product.

■ *Teamwork at the top:* creating teams to actually run the business. Sets of people thus play the traditional chief operating officer role, which allows management of diversity with different skills.

Based on information provided by Allaire in the *Harvard Business Review* article, the new Xerox architecture looks somewhat like the model provided in Figure 13.3. When asked what the "new model" was intended to accomplish, Allaire stated:

We are trying to break the bonds that tie up energy and commitment in a big company. Our goal is to make this $17 billion company more entrepreneurial, more innovative, and more responsive to the marketplace. In fact, we intend to create a company that combines the best of both worlds—the speed, flexibility, accountability, and creativity that come from being part of a small, highly focused organi-

zation, and the economies of scale, the access to resources, and the strategic vision that a large corporation can provide.

Whether this new organizational architecture can hold up the weight of a massive, worldwide, technologically driven organization over time remains to be seen.

Key Issues for Discussion

1. How did the *context* factors listed in the chapter affect Xerox's decision to go into the insurance business in the early 1980s when it was under attack by the Japanese copier companies in worldwide markets?

2. Explain how the new organizational structure as shown in Figure 13.3 resembles, or contrasts with the (1) line, (2) line and staff, (3) matrix, or (4) radical organization of Semco, as discussed in the chapter.

3. Discuss how successful this new structure is likely to be.

4. What TQM concepts play a part in the redesign of the organization and its effects on employees?

FIGURE 13.3   New Corporate Structure at Xerox

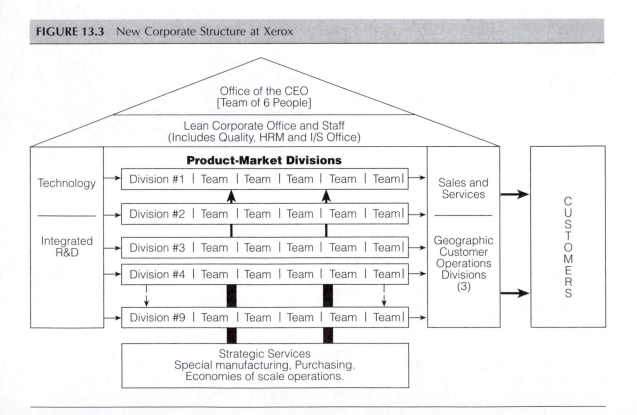

QUALITY IN PRACTICE

QUALITY ORGANIZATION AT THE IRS[43]

Like Rodney Dangerfield, the Internal Revenue Service (IRS) frequently "gets no respect." Very few people *enjoy* paying their taxes! Yet, from the viewpoint of a production system, one finds that conformance to specifications is high within the IRS. Also, from the standpoint of at least *one* of its customers, the U.S. Congress, it is achieving fitness for use. The IRS estimates a "compliance rate" of more than 90 percent; that is, more than 90 percent of all the taxes owed are paid.

The importance of quality at the IRS is revealed in an examination of the Quality Improvement Prototype initiative undertaken at the Cincinnati Service Center (CSC) in Covington, Kentucky. Because of this initiative, the center was designated as a "Quality Prototype" facility in 1990 by the Office of Management and Budget (OMB), which oversees the operations of all federal agencies.

The Cincinnati Service Center is one of 10 tax return processing centers within the United States. It conducts operations at seven sites in the immediate area using almost 600,000 square feet of office space and employing up to 6000 people at peak periods. It processes approximately 22 million returns per year from the states of Indiana, Kentucky, Michigan, Ohio, and West Virginia, and also handles taxpayer correspondence, correction, updating, compliance, storage, warehousing, and forms distribution responsibilities for the region. The CSC considers its external and internal customers to be taxpayers and tax practitioners in five states, six IRS district offices, and employees located in seven separate buildings.

CSC center managers clearly articulate its mission which is derived from the overall mission statement of the IRS:

The goal of the Cincinnati Service Center is to do a superior job of meeting customers' needs and expectations with products and services of the highest quality and value.

The CSC formally began its quest for quality in 1981 when quality circles, an early type of EI program discussed in Chapter 11, were initiated at the center. Even though as many as 15 such groups were created, this program did not represent a comprehensive approach to quality. In 1987, the active quality circle teams were integrated into a broader framework called the Quality Improvement Program (QIP). This new program was initiated in the top echelons of the IRS as a comprehensive, customer-driven adaptation of the Juran approach to quality. One particularly successful employee involvement team of clerical employees redesigned a tax forms cart to assist them in carrying and filing tax forms on shelves in a large storage facility.[44]

An extensive effort to publicize the program throughout the seven off-site CSC facilities began in 1988. Some of the types of publicity included a special QIP edition of the center's newsletter, and development of problem identification forms and volunteer signup sheets that were made available in all parts of the organization. To heighten interest and add a little humor, a mascot, "Captain Q," was designed and cloned. Fashioned of plywood, painted in bright colors, and clothed in jeans and a captain's hat, Captain Q called attention to the QIP boxes placed around the center's main and off-site buildings.

The center develops an annual business plan that includes quality targets and projects personnel and training requirements for the fiscal year, based on quality and productivity estimates. Some quality goals for the 1990 fiscal year included:

■ Improving the timeliness and quality of correspondence to taxpayers.

■ Improving the quality of the Underreporter Program, which involves center correspondence with taxpayers.

■ Continuing innovations in the Electronic Filing Program (ELF).

■ Emphasizing product quality throughout pipeline processing.

■ Continuing the Performance Indicator Program as a weekly monitoring tool.

Internal goals included:

■ Expanding the child-care center to include kindergarten and, if demand justifies, expanding care to nonprime shifts.

■ Expanding an existing Employee Assistance Program to address the needs of employees faced with the care of elderly family members.

■ Providing additional health-related programs and referrals to professional programs, such as health and exercise programs; referrals to substance abuse, drug abuse, and smoking cessation programs; stress reduction; and financial assistance programs.

■ Adding at least 12 QIP teams during the year.

The CSC is organized in a typical line and staff form. The center is headed by a director, who is responsible for accomplishing the mission and carrying out the programs related to tax collection. In his office is the assistant director, who acts as the center's chief operating officer, overseeing the day-to-day operations of the CSC. Six major program areas are managed by division chiefs, with responsibilities subdivided into branches, sections, and units within each of the program areas. On a separate reporting path to the director is a Problem Resolution Unit whose staff serves as an ombudsman for the center's external taxpayer customers. The QIP coordinator is responsible for purchasing training materials, promotional items and team awards, professional association memberships for coordinators, and planning of the annual QIP Recognition day.

An innovative structure, having mixed IRS/National Treasury Employee's Union (NTEU) representation, was developed to guide the QIP at each level in CSC. At the top management level, a Quality Council was established, consisting of the director, assistant director, NTEU president and vice president, members of the director's staff of division chiefs, and the QIP coordinator. Quality subcouncils, consisting of a mix of managers and bargaining unit employees, were selected from a list of volunteers. They are responsible for creating and appointing QIP teams and monitoring their progress. As of the end of 1990, there were 45 trained QIP teams.

CSC makes extensive efforts to communicate with employees on various levels. Reports on progress, problems, and results of the QIP originate at the top of the local IRS organization. Center managers meet regularly for an update on CSC activities. The vision is constantly communicated and reinforced by the center's director and management team. A cascade system is used to transmit information downward to division, branch, section, and unit levels. In addition to the director's and managers' attendance at project presentation and award ceremonies, articles on quality and participation are written for the employee publication, and such symbols as QIP-imprinted pens, notepads, quality logos, and the director's announcements over the public address system are constant reminders of the stress on quality.

The center now has a different focus on quality as contrasted with pre-QIP years, with an emphasis on "productivity, not *production*." Consequently, the Quality Assurance Branch has been charged with the responsibility of devising a system that will generate data to measure quality and assist in identifying root causes of problems in each operation. This task is accomplished through a variety of systems, reports, process reviews, and demonstration projects. Communications via such information sheets as "Quality Alerts" and "The Daily Wire" as well as individual and group reports keep employees and managers informed of where "hot spots" in a process or program are trending incorrectly.

Most of the quality objectives that were set in FY 1990 have been achieved at the CSC. With the advent of Vice President Al Gore's "Re-inventing Government" initiative in 1993, many changes have taken place at the CSC. The latest approach in their TQM journey encompasses efforts to develop a total quality organization (TQO), defined as:

■ Everyone working together for continuous improvement to product quality, productivity, and customer satisfaction.

■ NTEU and CSC are choosing to become a TQO in the mutual interest of both parties. While the IRS and NTEU will continue to perform their traditional responsibilities, both are committed to up-front resolution of differences.

Many of the organizational changes are technology driven; CSC is heavily involved in electronic filing, Tele-Tax filing (filing of simple returns by telephone entry), and a new pilot-stage system for electronic scanning of tax return information. Thus, the TQO approach is designed to increase empowerment of employees, improve QWL and labor-management relationships, and involve employees at early stages of work redesign and system changes to meet organization goals. The CSC and other centers around the United States will concentrate on four critical elements to certify whether they have become a TQO, including systems management, empowerment, labor-management relations, and quality of work life.

The obvious difficulty in the IRS's efforts to enhance customer satisfaction is that it has no natural demand for its product. However, given that everyone pays taxes, like it or not, the IRS goals of (1) increasing voluntary compliance, (2) reducing the burden on the taxpayer (now called "the customer" at the IRS), and (3) improving customer satisfaction, should make the taxpaying process a little less painful and build higher quality into IRS internal processes.

Key Issues for Discussion

1. How is the total quality management concept integrated throughout the CSC?

2. What inferences can you make about the effects of the organization structure on the QIP process? How could a structure such as is found in the IRS help or hinder a total quality management philosophy?

SUMMARY OF KEY POINTS

■ Companies adopt TQM to react to competitive threats or take advantage of perceived opportunities. In most cases, threats have provided the incentive to act and change the company's culture.

■ Successful adoption of TQM requires a readiness for change, sound practices and implementation strategies, and an effective organization.

■ Changing the corporate culture is necessary if TQM is to take root in an organization. Change is easier when management has a clear vision, a focus on customers and continuous improvement, strong measurement, cross-functional orientation, and high employee morale.

■ Key strategies for successfully implementing TQM include a focus on quality through planning, commitment and involvement of top management, integration of customer satisfaction across functions, and employee participation and training. However, no one model works for every organization. The "engines" that drive quality are unique and must fit into the organization's culture.

■ Self-assessment provides a starting point to initiate a quality effort. Best practices depend on the level of performance. Low performers must stick to basics such as process simplification, training, and teamwork, while high performers can benefit from benchmarking world-class organizations and using more advanced approaches. Many companies have wasted millions of dollars on quality programs; companies should consider the return on investment carefully when phasing in new approaches.

■ All employees play a role in TQM implementation. Senior managers must lead the effort and provide resources; middle managers must act as change agents to ensure that strategic goals are met; and the work force must take personal responsibility for making it happen. Unions must play a part in ensuring the welfare of the organization and work cooperatively with management.

■ Organizing is the process of assigning work and responsibility to functions, teams, and individuals, along with the appropriate delegation of authority. The quality organization must reflect individual company differences and provide the flexibility and ability to change.

■ The formal organizational structure should be as flat as possible with broad spans of supervision with the top reporting level of quality being high in the organization. Companies must understand that processes, rather than hierarchical reporting relationships, drive quality within the organization.

■ Quality councils, committees, and documented procedures are important parts of a modern quality organization, particularly as companies strive for ISO 9000 certification.

■ Organizations encounter numerous barriers to successful implementation. Companies need to recognize these barriers and avoid the common mistakes that stifle quality efforts.

■ Organizations must continue to learn and adapt to changing environments. The trend toward downsizing poses many problems in implementing TQM. Organizations should not underestimate the importance of making sure that TQM is not associated with downsizing.

REVIEW QUESTIONS

1. Why do companies decide to adopt TQM? What approach to TQM is more prevalent? Why?

2. Explain the problems associated with "one-dimensional" approaches to implementing quality.

3. Explain the term *dysfunctional corporate culture.* What implications does it have regarding quality?

4. How can an organization make permanent a corporate culture change to TQM?

5. Summarize the practices that researchers have observed as key to successful TQM implementation.

6. Discuss the "quality engines" of Baldrige Award winners. Why do they differ?

7. How can the "Quality Maturity Profile" be used to design an implementation plan?

8. What are the major conclusions and implications of the *Best Practices* report of Ernst & Young and the American Quality Foundation? How do they relate to Deming's philosophy?

9. Explain the importance of "return on quality" and the implications of ignoring it.

10. Describe the role of senior management, middle management, the work force, and unions in TQM implementation. Describe the responsibilities of each group and how they can support one another.

11. Define the term *organizing.* What is the purpose of organizing for quality?

12. Describe key contextual factors that affect organization. What implications do they have?

13. Describe the types of organization structure commonly used. What are the advantages or disadvantages of each?

14. Discuss important guidelines for structuring organizations to support total quality.

15. Explain the role of quality councils, steering committees, and documentation.

16. Discuss the barriers to successful TQM implementation.

17. What are some of the common mistakes that organizations make when attempting to implement TQM?

18. What common crises do organizations typically face early in the implementation process? How can they be avoided?

19. What is a *learning organization?* Why is this concept important to total quality?

20. Explain the impact of downsizing on TQM and the role that TQM can play when downsizing is necessary.

DISCUSSION QUESTIONS

1. How might total quality be implemented in an elementary school? Locate a school or district in your area that has or is implementing total quality principles as an example.

2. Study one or two companies in your area that have implemented TQM. What approaches have they used? Are they one-dimensional or multidimensional? What are their "quality engines"?

3. Interview some managers at a local company and use the Quality Maturity Matrix to assess their state of quality.

4. Develop a hierarchy of the Baldrige Award criteria's Areas to Address that would guide an organization from the "innocence" stage to quality excellence. In other words, what Areas to Address would be more appropriate for new organizations to concentrate on, and in what sequence should they progress toward fully meeting the Baldrige Award criteria?

5. List some key factors that differentiate quality implementation among small and large companies. If possible, study some companies to verify your hypotheses.

6. Compare the organizational structures of several companies. What differences are reflected in their quality approaches and results?

7. What steps might an organization take to overcome the implementation barriers and common mistakes cited in this chapter?

8. Discuss typical reasons for each of the following barriers to TQM implementation:

  a. poor planning

  b. lack of top management commitment

  c. work force resistance

  d. lack of proper training

  e. teamwork complacency

  f. failure to change the organization properly

  g. ineffective measurement of quality improvement

9. What might the "learning organization" concept mean to a college or university?

10. In one company, the overriding focus of implementing TQM was ability to reduce costs. How does this narrow view of TQM inhibit the effectiveness of the organization?

CASES

I. The Parable of the Green Lawn[45]

A new housing development has lots of packed earth and weeds, but no grass. Two neighbors make a wager on who will be the first to have a lush lawn.

Mr. Fast N. Furious knows that a lawn will not grow without grass seed, so he immediately buys the most expensive seed he can find because everyone knows that quality improves with price. Besides, he'll recover the cost of the seed through his wager. Next, he stands knee deep in his weeds and tosses the seed around his yard. Confident that he has a head start on his neighbor, who is not making much visible progress, he begins his next project.

Ms. Slo N. Steady, having grown up in the country, proceeds to clear the lot, till the soil, and even alter the slope of the terrain to provide better drainage. She checks the soil's pH, applied weed killer and fertilizer, and then distributes the grass seed evenly with a spreader. She applies a mulch cover and waters the lawn appropriately. She finishes several days after her neighbor, who asks if she would

like to concede defeat. After all, he does have some blades of grass poking up already.

Mr. Furious is encouraged by the few clumps of grass that sprout. While these small, green islands are better developed than Ms. Steady's fledgling lawn, they are surrounded by bare spots and weeds. If he maintains these footholds, he reasons, they should spread to the rest of the yard.

He notices that his neighbor's lawn is more uniform and is really starting to grow. He attributes this to the Steady children, who water the lawn each evening. Not wanting to appear to be imitating his neighbor, Mr. Furious instructs his children to water his lawn at noon.

The noon watering proves to be detrimental, so he decides to fertilize the remaining patches of grass. Since he wants to make up for the losses the noon watering caused, he applies the fertilizer at twice the recommended application rate. Most of the patches of grass that escape being burned by the fertilizer, however, are eventually choked out by the weeds.

After winning the wager with Mr. Furious, Ms. Steady lounges on the deck enjoying her new grill, which she paid for with the money from the wager. Her lawn requires minimal maintenance, so she is free to attend to the landscaping. The combination of the lawn and landscaping also results in an award from a neighborhood committee that determines that her lawn is a true showplace.

Mr. Furious still labors on his lawn. He blames the poor performance on his children's inability to properly water the lawn, nonconforming grass seed, insufficient sunlight, and poor soil. He claims that his neighbor has an unfair advantage and her success is based on conditions unique to her plot of land. He views the loss as grossly unfair; after all, he spends more time and money on his lawn than Ms. Steady does.

He continues to complain about how expensive the seed is and how much time he spends moving the sprinkler around to the few remaining clumps of grass that continue to grow. But Mr. Furious thinks that things will be better for him next year, because he plans to install an automatic sprinkler system and make a double-or-nothing wager with Ms. Steady.

© 1994 American Society for Quality Control. Reprinted with permission.

Discussion Questions

1. Within the context of the continual struggles to create a "world-class" lawn and "world-class" business, draw analogies between the events when total quality is implemented.

2. Specifically, translate the problems described here in business language. What are the implementation barriers to achieving total quality?

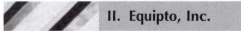

II. Equipto, Inc.

Equipto, Inc., a division of a *Fortune 500* corporation, is located in the Midwest. The Industrial Motor Division (IMD) makes motor units that are part of the installation package for large-scale industrial systems. The company has two major competitors in the United States and several smaller competitors abroad. Although their market share has shown a slight decrease, they remain second in U.S. market share and first worldwide.

Three years earlier, management had foreseen the need for adoption of a TQM philosophy. With much fanfare at the corporate level, the new TQM program, called "Quality or Else," had been rolled out. It soon became known by its initials QOE. Initial skepticism surfaced within various divisions about whether such a program would help to arrest the progress of Equipto's competitors, especially a rapidly growing Japanese firm that had recently announced plans to build a plant in the United States. However, an enthusiastic middle level production manager, Bob Green, who had a great deal of creativity as well as credibility, was shortly appointed as division director of TQM. He had a vision of TQM that was people-driven, but he had little knowledge of the details of statistical process control (SPC), since his degree was in liberal arts. Also at his level was a division director of quality assurance, Harry Rule, who was steeped in traditional SPC techniques and had many years of quality control experience in the company. Managers and staff alike viewed him as a statistical genius. Although he talked a good game about embracing TQM, empowerment, teamwork, listening to the voice of the customer, and other such rhetoric, he acted somewhat condescendingly toward anyone who wasn't his equal in SPC.

The EI program began with three days of top management training—led by an outside consulting firm—in TQM philosophy and techniques at the corporate level. All corporate and divisional top managers (the CEO, corporate VPs, divisional presidents and VPs, and a few selected staff people) were included in the executive training session. This TQM training was cascaded down through the divisions, such that every employee received two to five days of training. Much of the training was conducted in-house by facilitators at each plant in every division. Divisions could choose the depth of training in SPC techniques and were encouraged to hire local consultants to help them in this phase of the development. After the "up-front" training, EI groups were started so that employees could begin to practice their newly learned skills. These activities pretty much consumed the first year of the process.

During the second year, the company began to see some results. Employee skepticism, which had been a major problem in the rank-and-file unionized work force, began to subside due to three factors:

1. Recognition of teams and team members who had accomplished some significant results. One project that was completed after a nine month study showed paper savings of $100,000.

2. The enthusiasm of Bob Green, Corporate Director of TQM. He went around to all the plants in the division to beat the drum for quality about every three or four months.

3. Emphasis on the human relations aspects of quality, with little being said about SPC, standards, or quantitative analysis of the production processes. However, middle managers in the divisions had been given little training in how to handle an "empowered" work force, so they felt somewhat resentful of the process and were left out of team activities.

Equipto and its IMD were in trouble at the beginning of the new fiscal year. Although the EI teams had been going strong for over a year, and they had about 20 percent of the hourly work force involved, nothing tangible seemed to be happening. A cyclical downturn was apparently under way, and the company was scrambling for any business that it could get. Middle managers and line supervisors felt pressure to deliver *immediate* results. The pressure extended up and down the line. Green and Rule at corporate headquarters began to question each other's commitment to TQM, which led to speculation about the outbreak of a major turf war. Green was certain that more training of middle managers could help to turn the corner on quality. Rule was equally certain that more emphasis on SPC was needed at every level in the division.

The IMD had been the most successful division in implementing TQM of any in Equipto. Half the IMD's people in the plants were on a team, and a white-collar accounting department team was just being formed. Estimated savings during the first full year of team operation was $200,000 (including the one project that had saved $100,000). Since only about $40,000 in direct out-of-pocket expenses had been made for TQM program development, everyone felt that TQM gave a pretty good return.

At the middle of the year, top management announced that the company had sustained its largest quarterly loss in history. Division managers were told to pare expenses by 15 percent. Bob Green resigned to accept a job with another firm, and Harry Rule was named Corporate VP for quality with all phases of TQM and quality assurance under his direction. The divisions were given no specific directives on TQM programs or projects, but many thought that the changes might spell the death of the employee-focused quality program. Others decided to just wait and see. Still others began polishing up their resumes.

Discussion Questions

1. Discuss the way in which the TQM program was launched. Could it have been done differently, and perhaps better?

2. What are the pros and cons of up-front training (training before any projects are begun) versus just-in-time training (training which is done concurrently with development of projects). Do you think that some momentum might have been lost because employees were trained before they were sent out to work on projects?

3. When and in what form should SPC be introduced to employees at the operating levels in the firm? Was it time for Equipto to do so, or past time?

4. Is it possible for TQM to be a success, and the company to be unprofitable, or worse? What has happened in the recent history of Baldrige Award winners along that line?

5. What should the company do about its TQM process now? Scrap the program, keep the same emphasis, or change to a SPC focus? Why?

III. The Downsizing Dilemma[46]

A large international corporation implemented TQM about five years ago, quite successfully. They reduced the time to market substantially and drove down the cost of poor quality. The TQM efforts were supported by managers, supervisors, and hourly workers. The head of total quality had recently assumed responsibility for organizational development and training and saw further opportunities to increase the impact of TQM in the company.

A few months earlier, however, the corporate office decided that a downsizing effort would be necessary. Profits and market shares had declined in several divisions. Recently, the CEO sent out a year-

end letter to all employees where he touted the success of the TQM efforts and then wrote that because of its success, the downsizing effort could proceed even faster and more employees would leave the company than had been previously planned. The credibility of TQM was destroyed, perhaps irreversibly so.

Discussion Questions

1. What factors might have contributed to the manner in which downsizing occurred?

2. How might a company go about a necessary downsizing in a total quality manner?

■ NOTES

1. Brad Stratton, "Cynicism vs. Kelly Potter," Editorial Comment, *Quality Progress* 27, no. 9 (September 1994), 5.
2. Brian Dumaine, "Times Are Good? Create a Crisis," *Fortune* 28 June, 1993, 123–130.
3. Thomas A. Stewart, "Rate Your Readiness to Change," *Fortune* 7 February, 1994, 106–110.
4. "Banking on Quality," *Incentive* (September 1988), 62–75.
5. G.R. Pieters, "Behaving Responsibly," *TQM Magazine* 2, no. 2 (March/April, 1992), 25–29.
6. George H. Labovitz, and Yu Sang Chang, "Learn from the Best," *Quality Progress* (May 1990), 81–85; J.M. Juran, "Strategies for World-Class Quality," *Quality Progress* (March 1991), 81–85; Thomas H. Berry, *Managing the Total Quality Transformation* (New York: McGraw-Hill, 1991), ch. 9; Rahul Jacob, "TQM—More than a Dying Fad?" *Fortune* 18 October, 1993, 66–72.
7. James H. Davis, "Who Owns Your Quality Program? Lessons from Baldrige Award Winners," (New York: Coopers & Lybrand, undated).
8. "Quality: How to Make it Pay," *Business Week*, 8 August, 1994, 54–59.
9. Coopers & Lybrand, *Integrated Quality* (New York, 1988).
10. "Special Report: Quality," *Business Week*, 30 November, 1992, 66–75.
11. Cyndee Miller, "TQM's Value Criticized in New Report," *Marketing News* (1992); Gilbert Fuchsberg, "'Total Quality' Is Termed Only Partial Success," *The Wall Street Journal*, 1 October, 1992, B1, B7.
12. Henry Mintzberg, *Mintzberg on Management* (New York: The Free Press, 1989), 15–21.
13. Arthur R. Tenner, and Irving J. DeToro, *Total Quality Management: Three Steps to Continuous Improvement*, (Reading, MA: Addison-Wesley, 1992).
14. Leonard Sayles, *The Working Manager* (New York: The Free Press, 1993), 25–32.
15. Mark Samuel, "Catalysts for Change," *The TQM Magazine* (1992).
16. Davis, see note 7.
17. John Persico, Jr., Betty L. Bednarczyk, and David P. Negus, "Three Routes to the Same Destination: TQM, Part 1," *Quality Progress* 23, no. 1 (January 1990), 29–33.
18. Kermit F. Wasmuth, "Organization and Planning," in Loren Walsh, Ralph Wurster, and Raymond J. Kimber (eds.), *Quality Management Handbook* (Wheaton, IL: Hitchcock Publishing Company, 1986), 9–34.
19. Ricardo Simler, *Maverick* (New York: Warner Books, 1993), 196.
20. A V. Feigenbaum, *Total Quality Control*, 3rd ed. (New York: McGraw-Hill, 1983), 182.
21. Leading the Quality Initiative, op. cit., 13–14.
22. J.M. Juran and Frank M. Gryna, Jr., *Quality Planning and Analysis*, 2nd ed. (New York: McGraw-Hill, 1980), 371.
23. J.M. Juran and Frank M. Gryna, *Juran's Quality Control Handbook* (New York: McGraw-Hill, 1988), ch. 6.
24. *Business Week*, 25 October, 1991.
25. Core body of knowledge working council findings, "Issues in Implementation of TQ," *A Report of the Total Quality Leadership Steering Committee and Working Council*, Total Quality Forum, Cincinnati, Ohio (November 1992), 2–55 to 2–57.
26. Thomas H. Patten, Jr., "Beyond Systems—The Politics of Managing in a TQM Environment," *National Productivity Review* (1991/1992).
27. Barry Sheehy, "Hitting the Wall: How to Survive Your Quality Program's First Crisis," *National Productivity Review* 9, no. 3 (Summer 1990), 329–335.
28. L. von Bertalanffy, "The Theory of Open Systems in Physics and Biology," *Science* 111 (1950), 23–29.
29. J.W. Forrester, *Industrial Dynamics* (New York: John Wiley & Sons, 1961).
30. Peter M. Senge, *The Fifth Discipline: The Art and Practice of the Learning Organization* (New York: Doubleday Currency, 1990), 14.
31. Peter M. Senge, Charlotte Roberts, Richard B. Ross, Brian J. Smith, and Art Kleiner, *The Fifth Discipline Field Book: Strategies and Tools for Building a Learning Organization* (New York: Currency-Doubleday, 1994).
32. David A. Garvin. "Building a Learning Organization," *Harvard Business Review* (July/August, 1993), 80.
33. Garvin, see note 32.
34. This intriguing label deserves a special explanation. It was coined by Joseph Juran in *Juran on Quality by Design* (New York: Free Press, 1992), 409–413. It refers to the remark once made by philosopher George Santayana, who said, "Those who cannot remember the past are condemned to repeat it."
35. Sim B. Sitkin, Kathleen M. Sutcliffe, and Roger G. Schroeder. "Distinguishing Control from Learning in Total Quality Management: A Contingency Perspective," *Academy of Management Review* 19, no. 3 (1994), 537–564.
36. Daniel M. Stowell. "Innovative Approaches to Quality and Downsizing," *Quality Digest* (April, 1994), 46–52.
37. Primary sources for the information in this section include: Robert Howard, "The CEO as Organizational Architect: An Interview with Paul Allaire," *Harvard Business Review* (September/October, 1992), 107–119 and excerpts from pages 297–298 from *Prophets in the Dark* by David T. Kearns and David A. Nadler. Copyright © 1992 David T. Kearns and David A. Nadler. Reprinted by permission of HarperCollins Publishers, Inc.
38. James R. Norman, "Xerox on the Move," *Forbes* 10 June, 1991, 70.
39. Kearns and Nadler, 260, see note 37.
40. Karns and Nadler, 262–264, see note 37.
41. Robert Howard, see note 37.
42. Kearns and Nadler, 297–298, see note 37.
43. Adapted from Martha Curry, "Application Package Quality Improvement Prototype," Cincinnati Service Center (September 1989). The CSC won the Federal OMB Award in 1990. Appreciation is expressed to Martha Curry, QIP Coordinator, who assisted in editing this case.
44. "IRS Team Designs New Tax Form Cart," *IAQC Circle Reporter* (May/June 1987).
45. Adapted from James A. Alloway, Jr., "Laying Groundwork for Total Quality," *Quality Progress* 27, no. 1 (Jan-

uary 1994), 65–67. © 1994 American Society for Quality Control. Reprinted with permission.

46. Inspired by Dan Ciampa, "It's All Down to TQ," *The TQM Magazine* 3, no. 1 (March/April 1993), 17–21.

■ BIBLIOGRAPHY

AT&T Quality Steering Committee. *Batting 1000: Using Baldrige Feedback to Improve Your Business* AT&T Bell Laboratories (1992).

AT&T Quality Steering Committee. *Quality Manager's Handbook.* AT&T Bell Laboratories (1990).

Burns, T., and Stalker, G. M. *The Management of Innovation.* London: Tavistock, 1961.

Coud, Dana M. "The Function of Organizational Principles and Process," in *Quality Control and Reliability Management,* ASQC Education and Training Institute. Milwaukee: ASQC, 1969, 6–1 to 6–3.

Emery, F. E., Trist, E. L., and Woodward, J. *Management and Technology.* London: Her Majesty's Stationery Office, 1958.

Kukla, R. E. "Organizing a Manufacturing Improvement Program." *Quality Progress* (November 1983), 28.

Lawrence, P. R., and Lorsch, J. W. *Organization and Environment.* Boston: Harvard University, Division of Research, Graduate School of Business Administration, 1967.

Niven, Daniel. "When Times Get Tough, What Happens to TQM?" *Harvard Business Review* (May/June 1993), 20–33.

Profile of ISO 9000. Needham Heights, MA: Allyn and Bacon, 1992.

Rue, L. W., and Byars, L. *Management Theory and Application,* 4th ed. Homewood, IL: Richard D. Irwin, 1986.

Schmidt, Warren H., and Jerome P. Finnigan. *A Race Without a Finish Line.* San Francisco: Jossey-Bass Publishers, 1992.

Sinha, Madhav N., and Willborn, Walter W. O. *The Management of Quality Assurance.* New York: John Wiley & Sons, 1985.

Whalen M.J., and M.A. Rahim. "Common Barriers to Implementation and Development of a TQM Program." *Industrial Management* 36, no. 2 (March/April 1994), 19–22.

Technical Issues in Quality

PART

3

Although TQM represents a revolution in management thought, the assurance of quality on the factory floor and in the front lines of service depends on sound analytical techniques. These techniques have played an important role in quality assurance for nearly 70 years, and continue to figure prominently in the methods organizations use to reduce defects and better satisfy customers.

Part 3 of this book addresses some fundamental technical issues for assuring quality in manufactured goods and services. Chapter 14 describes foundations of quality control and the application of statistics to quality assurance. Chapters 15 and 16 present a comprehensive overview of statistical process control, with details of constructing and using control charts. Finally, Chapter 17 addresses reliability, particularly as it applies to the design of products and production processes.

CHAPTER 14

Quality Assurance and Control

Manufacturers can, and should, place a priority on their efforts to design quality into products and develop total quality management systems. But in the end, the actual quality of the final product is determined on the shop floor. The goal of manufacturing is to produce a defect-free finished product that consistently meets specifications. **Quality assurance and control** provide the basis for this task. Quality assurance identifies appropriate quality characteristics of final products, the factors that contribute to these characteristics, and procedures for quantitatively evaluating and controlling these factors. Control, as defined in

Chapter 9, consists of inspecting and/or measuring quality characteristics, comparing them to a standard, and providing feedback for corrective action.

Much controversy has surrounded the role of inspection in quality assurance. An early version of one of Deming's 14 Points was "eliminate mass inspection." When Deming revised the 14 Points in 1990 (Deming himself might be considered a model of the "learning organization"), he changed this point to "understand the purpose of inspection." What Deming was trying to convey in the early version was the need to eliminate quality assurance *solely* through final inspection, as was common industrial practice.

Heavy reliance on inspection proliferated because of the industrial revolution. The task of the inspection department was to seek out defective items in production and remove them prior to shipment. The bad product was either reworked or scrapped. During the manufacturing process, inspectors typically make the rounds periodically, pick up some parts, take them back to an inspection area, and check them. By the time the inspector determines that a problem exists, similar parts have probably already made their way downstream in the production process or have been mixed with good parts waiting for transfer to the next operation. In the second case, a "hold for inspection" tag is placed on the parts, which are then moved to an inspection area for 100 percent inspection to separate the good parts from the bad. In both cases, no information is fed back to the production workers to improve the process.

In either case, the firm incurs unnecessary expenses. In the case of rework, production flow must be disrupted, which adds unnecessary complexity to production control activities. Everyone knows that inspection is the mechanism to ensure that only good products are shipped; the pressure from management is for output, not quality. Inspectors become equivalent to "police" who are to catch "lawbreakers"—the operators and others who contributed to poor quality products.

Unfortunately, this scenario is still all too common in many companies. Not only does it often result in poor quality, but it can also affect interpersonal relations. Inspectors are often promoted from the ranks of production workers and have close associations with shop personnel. If a part borders on being defective, an inspector may tend to err in favor of the operators to preserve their friendship and protect them from criticism or even loss of jobs because of consistently poor quality production. Conversely, the operators, believing that the inspection department will catch any nonconforming parts, may not take their own roles in producing quality products seriously.

Just as there are never enough officers to patrol every highway, there are never enough inspectors to inspect every part and catch every defect. Thus, the practice of inspection to separate good from bad is inefficient and ineffective. The true purpose of inspection is to provide information for process management—to control and improve the process effectively. However, even if the results of final inspection are used to identify causes of poor quality, the problems have already occurred upstream in the production process. Any corrective action would occur far beyond the source of the problem. In addition, quality problems generally become more expensive as they move downstream in the production process. The cost of corrective action is directly related to the proximity to a problem. This relationship suggests that inspection activities be integrated throughout the production process as elements of effective process management systems. The essence of quality control is to choose the inspection points that provide the best information and improvement opportunities. Statistical analysis plays an important role in the analysis of inspection data. The strategic issues of data management and control were the topics in Chapters 8 and 9. In this and the following chapters, the focus falls on operational issues.

GAUGES AND MEASURING INSTRUMENTS

Measuring quality characteristics for manufactured items generally requires the use of the human senses—seeing, hearing, feeling, tasting, and smelling—and the use of some type of instrument or gauge to measure the magnitude of the characteristic. Manufacturing today uses a number of "low-technology" and "high-technology" gauges and measuring instruments. The term *low-technology instruments* generally describes primarily manual devices that have been available for a number of years and that do not include recent advances such as microprocessors, lasers, or advanced optical devices.

Gauges can generally be divided into two basic categories: **variable gauges** and **fixed gauges.** Variable gauges, used for variables inspection, are adjusted to measure each individual part or dimension being inspected. Fixed gauges, used for attribute inspection, are preset to a certain dimension; parts being measured are classified according to whether they meet this dimension. The terms *go* and *no-go* are often used to signify this classification. The photographs in Figure 14.1 illustrate many of the types of gauges discussed in this section.

Several types of gauges are used in variables inspection. **Line-graduated gauges** have graduated spacings representing known distances. They include rulers and tapes, various types of inside and outside calipers, and micrometers. Each instrument varies by function and precision of measurement. Rulers and tapes are used to measure length. They are generally accurate to within 1/64 inch. Vernier calipers are used to measure inside and outside diameters and are accurate to within 0.001 inch. Because of their construction, they require a considerable amount of skill to obtain accurate readings. Micrometers are also used to measure outside and inside diameters. Their usual accuracy is 0.001 inch, although some are made to measure in 0.0001-inch graduations. Micrometers have higher reliability in measuring than do vernier calipers.

Dial, digital, and **optical gauges** show variations using a mechanical, electronic, or optical system to obtain dimensional readings. Dial gauges use a mechanical system in which a movable contact touches the part to be measured and translates the dimensional characteristic through a gear train to the dial. The dimension is read from the face of the dial. Digital gauges use electronic systems to translate the movement of the contact touching the part to be measured directly into a number or reading on a dial. This level of sensitivity generally results in greater accuracy than a mechanical dial gauge can provide. Optical gauges use a lens system to magnify the profile of an object and project it onto a screen so that it can be viewed and measured.

Fixed gauges are much simpler than variable gauges. Once they are set for a particular dimension, no adjustment is required as long as wear or deposits on the measuring surfaces are negligible. Types of fixed gauges include plug gauges, ring gauges, snap gauges, and gauge blocks.

Plug gauges measure the inside diameters of bores. They have a machined diameter on one or both ends corresponding to go/no-go dimensions that have been specified for the bore being inspected. If the bore is larger than the no-go dimension of the plug gauge, the part is rejected. If the bore is smaller than the go dimension, it must be rebored to meet the minimum size specification. **Ring**

FIGURE 14.1   Various Types of Gauges

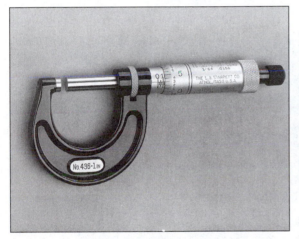

Line-graduated gauge

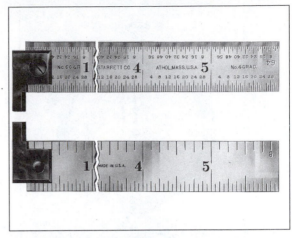

Steel hook rules

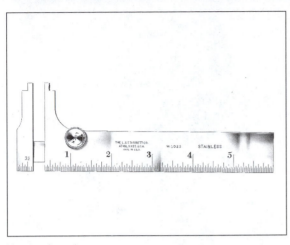

Micrometer

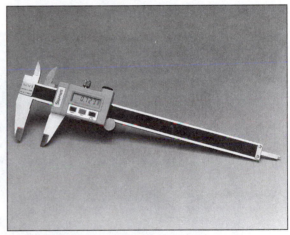

Digital caliper

One-inch digital electronic micrometer

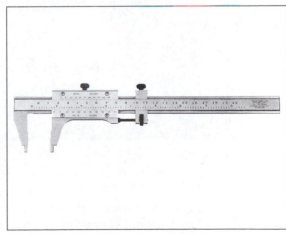

Vernier caliper

Continued

FIGURE 14.1   Various Types of Gauges—*Continued*

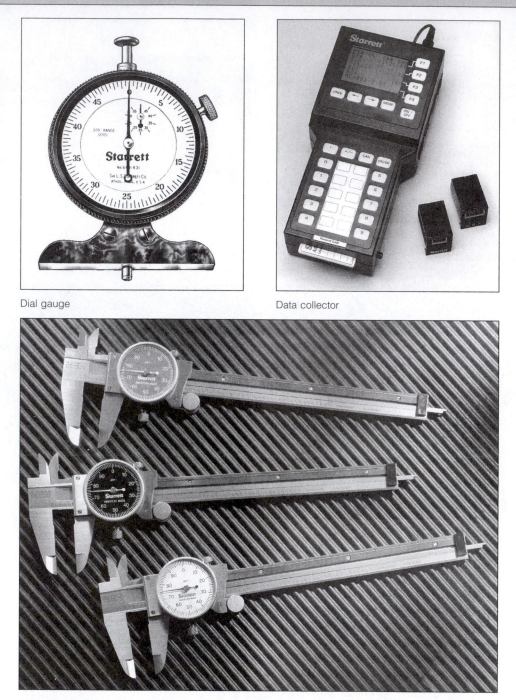

Dial gauge

Data collector

Dial calipers

SOURCE: Courtesy of the L. S. Starrett Company.

gauges measure outside diameters of parts using a go/no-go principle. Typically, they are made in pairs, with a no-go ring being used for the minimum dimension and a go ring being used for the maximum size limit. **Snap gauges** are similar to ring gauges in purpose but operate in a different fashion. They measure outside diameters of parts but have an open-ended construction allowing them to snap onto the diameter of the part.

Gauge blocks are special types of fixed gauges designed as a precision measurement standard for calibration of other measuring and inspection instruments. Gauge blocks are constructed of special steel in various lengths and have carefully machined, perfectly parallel, and highly polished measuring end surfaces. When stacked together, various combinations of lengths can be used to produce accurately any desired dimension to the nearest 0.0001 inch.

■ Automated Inspection Technology

Microprocessor technology has revolutionized the tasks of inspection and measurement. The potential uses of microprocessors in quality management and control are being developed at an astonishing rate today. Processes as diverse as manufacturing and microwave cooking can be monitored for correct temperature and timing. Heart monitors and grocery checkout scanners automatically store data for later analysis. Handheld micrometers can run "instant" statistical studies from readings taken on the shop floor. If desired, the readings can be loaded into a desktop personal computer for more thorough analysis.

A variety of automated testing and measuring equipment has been introduced in recent years. One of the most highly accurate and sophisticated instruments with digital readouts is the **coordinate measuring machine.** This versatile machine, often costing $50,000 to $100,000 or more, combines optics and computer technology in measuring dimensional characteristics that would be impossible to measure using conventional measuring instruments. *Photogrammetry* is an indirect, noncontact measurement process by which three-dimensional relationships in real space are determined through mathematical analysis of data extracted from photographic images. This process has applications in periodic inspection and real-time realignment of assembly tools.

Electro-optical measurements are based on *optical digitizing.* This technique transforms the optical field of view into an n-dimensional matrix. The system requires an average of one second per measurement with an accuracy of $+0.001$ inch or less over a 24×24-inch measuring range. *Fluorescent penetrant inspection* consists of treating parts with an electrostatic penetrant spray and then inspecting them by blacklight.

Vision systems consist of a camera and video analyzer, a microcomputer, and a display screen. Computer vision systems can read symbols, identify objects, measure dimensions, and inspect parts for flaws. In quality control applications, vision systems measure, verify, or inspect parts for dimensional tolerances, completeness of assembly, or mechanical defects.

In the automotive industry, vision systems are used in conjunction with robots to weld body seams of varying widths, tighten imprecisely located bolts, and mark identification numbers on engines and transmissions using lasers. At a General Motors plant in Lansing, Michigan, a vision-equipped robot system finds the exact location of a dozen lower suspension-rail bolts, then uses a pneumatic nut-runner attachment to tighten the bolts to precise torque specifications. The system works by visually locating two gauge holes on the underbody of the car. From these two points, the robot's control computer can calculate the exact locations of the 12 bolts and guide wrench sockets to the bolt heads. The system has resulted in more accurate bolt torquing and less manual rework downstream on the assembly line.[1]

A Massachusetts company, Cognex, developed a Windows-based image analysis and processing system called Checkpoint that uses point-and-click menus to facilitate its use.[2] A computer can inspect parts on an assembly line in as little as ten milliseconds and measure each one precisely. The system can be used anywhere along the line to spot missing parts, such as keys from a keyboard, and can also read numbers and characters and store information, allowing it to remember an individual part's movement through the assembly process. This precise information allows the company to track the serial number and manufacturing history in case a critical part fails in use.

STATISTICAL METHODS IN QUALITY CONTROL

Statistics is a science concerned with "the collection, organization, analysis, interpretation, and presentation of data."[3] Measurement processes provide data. The data may be dimensions of bolts being produced on a production line, order entry errors per day in an order entry department, or numbers of flight delays per week at an airport. Raw data such as the individual lengths of bolts does not provide information necessary for quality control or problem solving. Data must be organized, analyzed, and interpreted for quality control or problem solving. Statistics provides an efficient and effective way of obtaining meaningful information from data, allowing managers and workers to control and improve processes.

The importance of statistical concepts in quality assurance cannot be overemphasized. Indeed, statistics is basic to the understanding and implementation of quality assurance. Frank H. Squires, a well-known expert in quality, has credited W. Edwards Deming with keeping statistics in the forefront on the worldwide quality improvement movement. Squires states:

> The triumph of statistics is the triumph of Dr. Deming. When others have wavered or been lukewarm in their support for statistics, Dr. Deming has stood firm in his conviction that statistics is the heart of quality control. Indeed, he goes further and makes statistical principles central to the whole production process.[4]

All managers, supervisors, and production and clerical workers must have some knowledge of the technical aspects of statistical quality control. Successful companies around the world have shown that if a total quality control philosophy is to be implemented, employees at every level need to be trained in basic statistical problem-solving techniques.

The purpose of statistics in quality assurance is to assist managers, supervisors, and operators in controlling and improving the quality of manufacturing or service products. Readers of this text are assumed to have prior knowledge of elementary statistics. This section provides a brief review of some important statistical concepts used in quality control.

■ Statistical Methodology

The first major component of statistical methodology is the efficient collection, organization, and description of data, commonly referred to as **descriptive statistics.** Frequency distributions and histograms are used to organize and present data. Measures of central tendency (means, medians, proportions) and measures of dispersion (range, standard deviation, variance) provide important quantitative information about the nature of the data. For example, an airline might investigate the problem of lost baggage and determine that the major causes of the problem are lost or damaged identification tags, incorrect tags on the bags, and misrouting to baggage claim areas. An examination of frequencies for each of these categories might show that lost or damaged tags accounted for 50 percent of the problems, incorrect tags for 30 percent, and misrouting for only 20 percent. The airline might also compute the average number of baggage errors per 1000 passengers each month. Such information is useful in identifying quality problems and as a means of measuring improvement.

The second component of statistical problem solving is **statistical inference.** Statistical inference is the process of drawing conclusions about unknown characteristics of a population from which data were taken. Techniques used in this phase include hypothesis testing and experimental design. For example, a chemical manufacturer might be interested in determining the effect of temperature on the yield of a new manufacturing process. In a controlled experiment, the manufacturer might test the hypothesis that the temperature has an effect on the yield against the alternative hypothesis that temperature has no effect. If the temperature is, in fact, a critical variable, steps will be required to maintain the temperature at the proper level and to draw inferences as to whether the process remains under control, based on samples taken from it.

The third component in statistical methodology is **predictive statistics,** the purpose of which is to develop predictions of future values based on historical data. Correlation and regression analysis are two useful techniques. Frequently, these techniques can clarify the characteristics of a process as well as predict future results. For example, in quality assurance, correlation is frequently used in test instrument calibration studies. In such studies, an instrument is used to measure a standard test sample that has known characteristics. The actual results are compared to standard results, and adjustments are made to compensate for errors. Figure 14.2 summarizes statistical processes and methods commonly used in quality assurance.

■ Random Variables and Probability Distributions

The collectively exhaustive set of outcomes from an experiment makes up a **sample space.** A mathematical function that assigns numerical values to every possible outcome in a sample space is called a **random variable.** A random variable can be either **discrete** or **continuous,** depending on the specific numerical values it may assume. A discrete random variable can take on only finite values. An example would be the number of defects observed in a sample. A continuous random variable can take on any real value over a specified interval of real numbers. An example would be the diameters of bearings being manufactured in a factory. Of course, the actual observed values for the variable are limited by the precision of the measuring device. Hence, only a finite number of actual observations would occur. In theory, this result would still be a continuous random variable. Random variables are the key component used in the development of probability distributions.

A **probability distribution** represents a theoretical model of the relative frequency of a random variable. Relating probability distributions to the random variables that they represent allows a classification of the distributions as either discrete or continuous. The appendix to this chapter provides a review of the more useful probability distributions in quality assurance and control.

FIGURE 14.2   Statistical Methodology in Quality Assurance

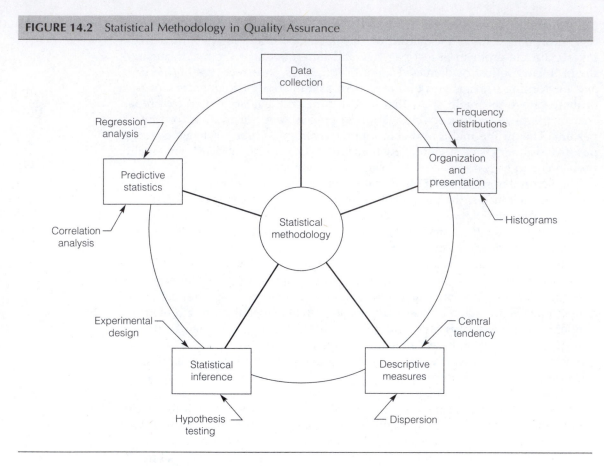

Sampling Theory and Distributions

Sampling techniques are essential in quality control. A **population** is a complete set or collection of objects of interest; a **sample** is a subset of objects taken from the population. The purpose of sampling is to gain knowledge about the characteristics of the population from the information that is contained in a sample. Characteristics of a population, such as the mean μ, standard deviation σ, or proportion π, are generally known as **parameters** of the population. In statistical notation, they are written as follows:

$$\text{population mean: } \mu = \frac{1}{N} \sum_{i=1}^{N} x_i$$

$$\text{population standard deviation: } \sigma = \sqrt{\frac{\sum_{i=1}^{N} (x_i - \mu)^2}{N}}$$

$$\text{population proportion: } \pi = \frac{Q}{N}$$

where x_i is the value of the ith observation, N is the number of items in a population, and Q is the number of items exhibiting a criterion of interest, such as manufacturing defects or on-time departures of aircraft.

The *sample mean, sample standard deviation* and *sample proportion* are computed as follows:

sample mean:
$$\bar{x} = \frac{1}{n} \sum_{i=1}^{n} x_i$$

sample standard deviation:
$$s = \sqrt{\frac{\sum_{i=1}^{n} (x_i - \bar{x})^2}{n - 1}}$$

sample proportion:
$$p = \frac{q}{n}$$

where n is the number of items in a sample, and q is the number of items in a sample exhibiting a criterion of interest.

Statistical theory is devoted to exploring the relationship between such *sample statistics* ($\bar{x}$, s, and p) and their corresponding *population parameters* (μ, σ, and π). For instance, the sample statistic $\bar{x}$ is generally used as a point estimator for the population parameter μ, and s as a point estimator for σ. The actual numerical values of $\bar{x}$ and s, which represent the single "best guess" for each unknown population parameter, are called **point estimates.**

SAMPLING DISTRIBUTIONS

Different samples will produce different estimates of the population parameters. Therefore, sample statistics such as $\bar{x}$, s, and p are random variables that have their own probability distribution, mean, and variance. These probability distributions are called **sampling distributions.** Knowledge of these sampling distributions will help in making probability statements about the relationship between sample statistics and population parameters. In quality control, the sampling distributions of $\bar{x}$ and p are of the most interest.

When using simple random sampling, the expected value of $\bar{x}$ is the population mean μ, or

$$E(\bar{x}) = \mu$$

The standard deviation of $\bar{x}$ (often called the **standard error of the mean**) is given by the formula

$$\sigma_{\bar{x}} = \frac{\sigma}{\sqrt{n}} \qquad \text{(for infinite populations or sampling with replacement from an infinite population)}$$

$$\sigma_{\bar{x}} = \sqrt{\frac{N - n}{N - 1}} \frac{\sigma}{\sqrt{n}} \qquad \text{(for finite populations)}$$

When $n/N \leq 0.05$, $\sigma_{\bar{x}} = \sigma/\sqrt{n}$ provides a good approximation for finite populations.

The last step is to develop the form of the probability distribution of $\bar{x}$. If the true population distribution is unknown, the **central limit theorem** can provide some useful insights. The central limit theorem (CLT) is stated as follows:

> If simple random samples of size n are taken from any population having a mean μ and a standard deviation σ, the probability distribution of the sample means approaches a normal distribution with mean μ and standard deviation (standard error) $\sigma_{\bar{x}} = \sigma/\sqrt{n}$ as n becomes very large. In more precise mathematical terms:

As $n \to \infty$ the distribution of the random variable $z = (\bar{x} - \mu)/(\sigma/\sqrt{n})$ approaches that of a standard normal distribution.

The power of the central limit theorem can be seen through computer simulation using the *Quality Gamebox* (see Chapter 3). Figure 14.3 shows the results of sampling from a triangular distribution for sample sizes of 1, 2, 5, and 10. For samples as small as five, the sampling distribution begins to develop into the symmetric bell-shaped form of a normal distribution.

The approximation to a normal distribution can be assumed for sample sizes of 30 or more. If the population is *known* to be normal, the sampling distribution of $\bar{x}$ is normal for any sample size.

Next, consider the sampling distribution of p, in which the expected value of p, $E(p) = \pi$. Here π is used as the population parameter and is not related to the *number* $\pi = 3.14159 \ldots$.

The standard deviation of p is

$$s_p = \sqrt{\frac{\pi(1 - \pi)}{n}}$$

for infinite populations.

For finite populations or when $n/N > 0.05$, modify s_p by

$$s_p = \sqrt{\frac{N - n}{N - 1}} \sqrt{\frac{\pi(1 - \pi)}{n}}$$

In applying the central limit theorem (CLT) to p, the sampling distribution of p can be approximated by a normal distribution for large sample sizes (see the chapter appendix).

This and subsequent chapters explore various applications of the CLT to statistical quality control in the areas of process capability determination and control

FIGURE 14.3 Illustration of Central Limit Theorem

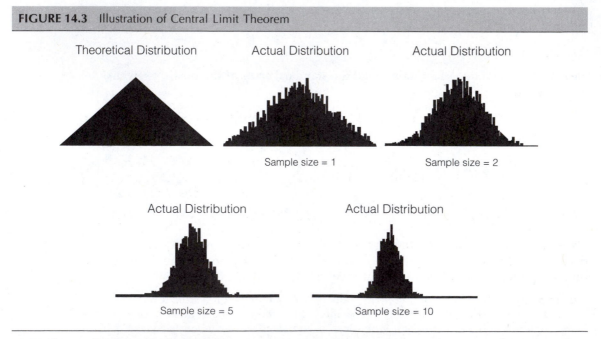

SOURCE: Courtesy of Productivity-Quality Systems, Inc.

charting. The following example illustrates an application of sampling distributions.

EXAMPLE 1   Sampling Distribution of Shaft Lengths.   The mean length of shafts produced on a lathe has historically been 50 inches, with a standard deviation of 0.12 inch. If a sample of 36 shafts is taken, what is the probability that the sample mean would be greater than 50.04 inches?

The sampling distribution of the mean is approximately normal with mean 50 and standard deviation $0.12/\sqrt{36}$. Thus,

$$z = \frac{\bar{x} - \mu}{\sigma/\sqrt{n}} = \frac{50.04 - 50}{0.12/\sqrt{36}} = 2.0$$

In the standard normal table, the value of 2.0 yields the probability of 0.4772 between the mean and this value. The area for $z \geqslant 2.0$ then is found by

$$P(z \geqslant 2.0) = 0.5000 - 0.4772 = 0.0228$$

Thus, the probability of a value equal to or greater than 50.04 inches as the mean of a sample of 36 items is only 0.0228 if the population mean is 50 inches. The applicability of sampling distributions to statistical quality control is that "shifts" in the population mean can quickly be detected using small representative samples to monitor the process. The procedure for finding the area under the curve is exactly the same as previously covered. However, the procedure for finding the z value differs in that the standard error term ($\sigma/\sqrt{n} = 0.12/\sqrt{36} = 0.02$) is substituted in the denominator of the equation for z.

Similarly, if a sample size of 64 is used, $\sigma/\sqrt{n} = 0.12/8 = 0.015$ and

$$z = \frac{\bar{x} - \mu}{\sigma/\sqrt{n}} = \frac{50.04 - 50}{0.015} = 2.67$$

and $P(z \geqslant 2.67) = 0.5000 - 0.4962 = 0.0038$. As the sample size increases, it is less likely that a mean value of at least 50.04 will be observed purely by chance. If it did, some special cause would likely be present.

■ Enumerative and Analytic Studies[5]

Deming emphasized the difference between *enumerative* and *analytic* studies. An enumerative study deals with a finite, identifiable, unchanging collection of units (a population) from which a sample is drawn for the purpose of making inferences or predictions. Examples of enumerative studies include:

■ Sample audits to assess the correctness of last month's bills and to estimate the total error in such bills. In this case, the population of interest consists of all of last month's bills.

■ Product acceptance sampling to decide on the disposition of a particular production lot. Here, the population consists of all units in the production lot.

In both these cases, the population is finite, identifiable, and unchanging. In an enumerative study, the correctness of statistical inferences requires a random sample from the population.

In contrast, analytic studies refer to situations that do *not* contain an existing, finite, well-defined, and unchanging population. Examples include:

■ A comparison of the average tensile strengths of the production units *that would be built* in a factory *some time in the future* using two different materials.

■ The efficiency of turbine engines *as yet not manufactured*.

In these cases, actions to improve or make predictions about the output of a (sometimes) hypothetical future are desired. However, data can be obtained only from the existing process, which is likely to be different. The interest centers on a process, rather than a population.

The distinction is important since the majority of industrial applications involve analytic, rather than enumerative, studies. Unfortunately, drawing conclusions from analytic studies is inherently more complex than assessing enumerative studies. Analytic studies require the critical and often unverifiable assumption that the process is statistically identical to that from which a sample is selected. This distinction brings about many other statistical ramifications. In other words, any time you are unsure of the proper procedures for analysis for a particular application, consult a qualified statistician!

QUALITY CONTROL PRACTICES IN MANUFACTURING

Quality control generally is performed at three major points in the production process: at the receipt of incoming materials, during the manufacturing process, and upon completion of production.

■ Receiving Inspection

Clearly, the receipt of incoming materials is the first point in the production process. If materials are of poor quality, then the final product will certainly be no better. Quality control in receiving allows a company to identify poor quality materials before value-adding operations begin.

Historically, the quality of incoming materials has been evaluated by the receiving function through reliance on **acceptance inspection.** The purpose of acceptance inspection is to make decisions on whether to *accept* or *reject* a group of items (formally called a *lot*) based on specified quality characteristics. Several different types of acceptance inspection methods are used in industry. The most common are spot checks, 100 percent inspection, and acceptance sampling.

Spot-check procedures select a fixed percentage of a lot for inspection. This amount might typically be 10 percent of the lot, or periodic removal of every tenth (or other specified interval) box of items that is delivered. The problem with spot checking is its lack of scientific basis. Because spot checking is not based on statistical principles, it does not give an assessment of the risks of making an incorrect decision. In fact, a fixed percentage method gives different levels of risk for different lot sizes. Spot checking is more useful as a quantity-verification tool to reconcile billing invoices than as a decision tool for quality verification.

One hundred percent inspection is essentially a sorting method and theoretically will eliminate all nonconforming items from a lot. However, it is usually costly and impractical for large lot sizes or when destructive tests are used. One hundred percent inspection may even give false results, because the monotony and repetition associated with the task can create boredom and fatigue in inspectors.

Situations exist where 100 percent inspection is necessary, however. They include inspection of products with critical safety requirements or those with high costs associated with failure.

The third method, which has been used quite extensively since the 1940s, is *acceptance sampling*. With this method, inspectors take a statistically determined random sample and use a decision rule to determine acceptance or rejection of the lot based on the observed number of nonconforming items. The general acceptance sampling procedure is shown in Figure 14.4. A lot is received from a supplier, items from the lot are inspected, and the results are compared with acceptance criteria. If these criteria are satisfied, the lot is accepted and sent to production or shipped to the customers; otherwise, the lot is rejected. Determination of whether to accept or reject a lot is often called **lot sentencing,** which is the true purpose of acceptance sampling. Acceptance sampling is not appropriate for estimating the quality of lots. That is, acceptance sampling techniques should not be used to attempt to determine the percentage of good items or the average value of a quality characteristic. Other statistical sampling schemes are appropriate for those tasks.

Acceptance sampling is based on statistical principles and, therefore, provides an assessment of risk in the decision. In addition, advocates cite other advantages. Acceptance sampling is relatively inexpensive and particularly well suited to destructive testing situations. It takes less time than 100 percent inspection, thus reducing the workload of inspectors. It also requires less handling, decreasing the chance of damage. Finally, acceptance sampling generally does not lead to inspector fatigue as does 100 percent inspection. Acceptance sampling also affords flexibility; the amount of inspection can be varied depending on the quality history. Since entire lots are rejected, suppliers feel economic and psychological

FIGURE 14.4   Acceptance Sampling Procedure

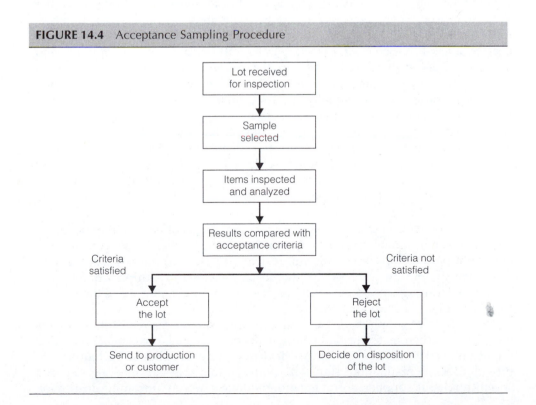

pressure to improve quality rather than simply to replace the nonconforming items.

Acceptance sampling, which was used extensively during World War II and contributed immensely to improving the quality of manufactured goods to support the war effort, became the foundation of quality control in the decades following the war. Then along came Deming, who condemned acceptance sampling as guaranteeing that "some customers will get defective product." Deming's argument depends on whether the supplier's process is a stable system (discussion of this concept can be found in Chapter 3). In a process that is stable, the only changes in the process are caused by random variation—common causes. Since the only difference between "good" lots and "bad" lots is random variation, the likelihood of another bad lot occurring after one bad lot is no greater than a bad lot occurring after a good one. Thus, nothing can be gained by accepting or rejecting lots that are, in reality, statistically indistinguishable.

If a supplier's process is not stable, variation in lots is due to a special cause outside of the system of common causes. In this case, the likelihood that a bad lot will occur after one bad lot is much greater than after a good one. Thus, a customer is reasonably motivated to inspect the lot, as well as subsequent lots, more carefully. Sampling inspection only makes sense when something can be learned from it.

Another argument against acceptance sampling is that it can only detect poor quality, not prevent it. The labor cost and tied-up inventory add no value to the product. There is no implicit trust in the supplier's ability to do what they are paid to do—supply conforming items. If a purchased lot is unacceptable, the customer must either (1) keep the lot (often at a reduced price to compensate for lower quality) and remove nonconforming items during production, or (2) return the rejected lot to the supplier. The first alternative is not a good one, since it will inevitably result in higher production costs and delays. However, if no other sources of product are available, it may be preferable to a production stoppage. With the second alternative, the supplier must pay the shipping cost, and the rejected lot will be screened, defective units will be reworked or replaced, and the lot will be resubmitted by the supplier. Some argue that the extra burden placed on the supplier often provides good motivation to improve quality. However, the extra costs will eventually be passed on to the customers and ultimately, to the consumer—a classic lose-lose situation.

As a temporary measure for quality control, however, acceptance sampling can serve a critical role.[6] In addition, it is useful when testing is destructive, when 100 percent inspection is not feasible, when a supplier has an excellent quality history but its process capability ratio is sufficiently low to make no inspection risky, and when potentially serious product liability risks are involved.[7]

In a TQM environment, however, customers should not have to rely on heavy inspection of incoming materials. Customers and suppliers both benefit from long-term partnerships built with mutual trust. Thus, if suppliers are doing their jobs correctly, incoming inspection should be unnecessary. Supplier quality can be assured through periodic audits as discussed in Chapter 12, either at the supplier's plant or with spot checks.

The burden of supplying high quality product should rest with the suppliers themselves. When materials and components are received, occasional inspection might be used to audit compliance. However, suppliers should be required to provide documentation and statistical evidence that they are meeting required specifications. If supplier documentation is done properly, incoming inspection can be completely eliminated. Japan has been doing this for years, and many companies in the West now follow this practice. To ensure that suppliers can provide high quality and reduce incoming inspection or testing, many companies provide free assistance to their suppliers in developing quality assurance programs or solving quality problems. Joint partnerships, training, incentives, recognition, and long-term agreement help to improve suppliers' abilities to meet key quality requirements.

The Texas Instruments Defense Systems and Electronics Group, for example, ensures that suppliers meet requirements and continuously improve through an extensive, prevention-based procurement system.[8] Their strategy is "to obtain defect-free materials, components, and services for the lowest total cost of ownership." The procurement process centers around multifunctional material management teams. Key supplier quality requirements include total cost conformance to company requirements, 100 percent on-time delivery, and lowest total cost of ownership. Texas Instruments measures suppliers' quality performance by parts per million defective, percentage of on-time deliveries, and cost of ownership. An electronic requisitioning system allows a paperless procurement process. More than 800 suppliers are linked to Texas Instruments through an information exchange system. Integrated data systems track the incoming quality and timeliness of deliveries as materials are received. Analytical reports and on-line data are used to identify material defect trends. Performance reports are sent each month to key suppliers. Joint customer–supplier teams are formed to communicate and improve performance. TI uses teaming relationships, certification programs, training workshops, supplier conferences, technical assistance, contract incentives, and special recognition programs to motivate suppliers to improve continuously. A supplier management task force of top managers directs current and strategic approaches to improving supplier management practices.

■ In-Process Inspection

Because unwanted variation can arise during production, for example, from machines going out of adjustment, worker inattention, or environmental conditions, quality control procedures are needed throughout the production process. Controlling quality while a process is operating is called **process control.** Process control helps operators to quickly recognize the occurrence of special causes of variation and make immediate adjustments to stabilize the process. Done properly, process control can eliminate the need for independent inspection activity. With process control, the production operator and inspector become one again, as was the case before the industrial revolution. Chapters 15 and 16 introduce statistical methods for process control.

In designing a process control system, consideration of three key questions is necessary: what to inspect, where to inspect, and how much to inspect. Thomas Pyzdek, an experienced consultant in quality, summed up the importance of control: "The objective of SPC [statistical process control] is to control all *process factors* which cause variation in *product features*."[9] The critical task is to control the processes that create the products, not the products that result from the processes. Production is costly and will not improve quality. The primary focus is *understanding* the processes. The use of flowcharts, cause-and-effect diagrams, and other tools as described in Chapter 9 is the best way to improve understanding of a process and the factors that may cause variation in the output.

Many organizations fall into the trap of trying to control every possible quality characteristic. Time and resources preclude this goal. Pyzdek suggests some guidelines for selection:

■ The indicator should be closely related to cost or quality.

■ The indicator should be easy to measure economically.

■ The indicator should show measurable variation.

■ The indicator should provide information to help the organization improve quality.

These guidelines and good engineering and managerial judgment will help to define a small, but critical, set of control indicators.

The decision of where to inspect in-process production is fundamentally an economic one. An organization must consider tradeoffs between the explicit costs of detection, repair, or replacement and the implicit costs of allowing a nonconformity to continue through the production process. These costs are sometimes difficult or even impossible to quantify. As a result, several rules of thumb influence the location decision. The more popular rules include the following:

■ Locate inspection before all processing operations, such as before every machine or assembly operation.

■ Locate inspection before relatively high-cost operations or where significant value is added to the product.

■ Locate inspection before processing operations that may make detection of defectives difficult or costly, such as operations that may mask or obscure faulty attributes, for example, painting.

■ Locate inspection after operations likely to generate a high proportion of defectives.

■ Locate inspection after the finished product is completed.

No one rule is best in all situations. Experience and common sense usually lead to good decisions; however, simulation, economic analysis, and other quantitative tools often are used to evaluate a particular design for inspection activities.

The final question is how much to inspect; that is, whether to inspect all outputs or just a sample. One must first ask: What would be the result of allowing a nonconforming item to continue through production or on to the consumer? If the result might be a safety hazard, costly repairs or correction, or some other intolerable condition, the conclusion would probably be to use 100 percent inspection. If the sampling plan is properly chosen and implemented, lots of good quality will be accepted more often than rejected, and lots of poor quality will be rejected more often than accepted. Remember, however, that inherent in sampling is a risk that a small percentage of nonconforming items will be passed.

Unless a product requires destructive testing (in which case, sampling is necessary) or faces critical safety concerns (in which case, 100 percent inspection is warranted), the choice among the three options (no inspection, 100 percent inspection, and sampling) can be addressed economically. In fact, on a strict economic basis, the choice is to have either no inspection or 100 percent inspection. Deming strongly advocated this viewpoint.

Let C_1 = cost of inspection and removal of a nonconforming item, C_2 = cost of repair if a nonconforming item is allowed to continue to the next point in the production process, and p = the true fraction of nonconforming items in the lot. The expected cost per item for 100 percent inspection is clearly C_1; the expected cost per item for no inspection is pC_2. Setting these equal to each other yields the breakeven value for p.

$$pC_2 = C_1$$

$$p = C_1/C_2$$

Thus, if $p > C_1/C_2$, the best decision is to use 100 percent inspection; if $p < C_1/C_2$, doing nothing at all is more economical.

In practice, however, both the costs C_1 and C_2 and the true fraction nonconforming, p, are difficult to determine accurately. The value of C_1 includes the capital cost of equipment used in the inspection process, depreciation, and residual value, and operating costs including labor, rent, utilities, maintenance, and replacement parts. Included in C_2 are the costs of disassembly and repair, sorting products to find the nonconformances, warranty repair costs if the products are shipped, and cost of lost sales. Many of these costs change over time. In addition, finding p requires sampling inspection in the first place. A useful rule of thumb is that if p is known to be much greater than C_1/C_2, use 100 percent inspection; if p is much less than this ratio, do not inspect. If p is close to C_1/C_2 or is highly variable, use sampling for protection and auditing purposes. In any case, sampling can actually increase costs if performed indiscriminately.

The choice of an acceptance inspection method should be based on the quality history of the supplier. If the quality history is excellent—as evidenced by good statistical control of the supplier's processes and a low process average—no inspection is needed. If, on the other hand, quality history is poor or the supplier shows evidence of lack of statistical control, some form of acceptance sampling should be used.

Motorola, one of the first recipients of the Malcolm Baldrige National Quality Award, uses sampling inspection as a temporary means of quality control until permanent corrective actions can be implemented.[10] Statistical sampling plans are used to inspect each lot as each operation is finished. Historical data on defects per million are used to select a sampling plan that has a high confidence level of rejecting lots that do not meet requirements. Each operator can decide to either scrap or to 100 percent inspect the product in question before sending it to the next operation. The result is that each operation receives only product known to be good and can therefore concentrate on process control and avoiding defects. While no sampling plan or 100 percent inspection can guarantee that all defects are eliminated, the combination of these techniques makes near-perfection possible.

Final Inspection

Although final inspection should not be the primary means of quality control, it is still an important part of the overall quality control system. Final inspection represents the last point in the manufacturing process at which the producer can verify that the product meets customer requirements and avoid external failure costs. For many consumer products, final inspection consists of functional testing. For instance, a manufacturer of televisions might do a simple test on every unit to make sure it operates properly. However, the company might not test every aspect of the television, such as picture sharpness or other characteristics. These aspects might have been evaluated through in-process controls. Computerized test equipment is quite widespread, allowing for 100 percent inspection to be conducted rapidly and cost-effectively.

Visual inspections for asthetic characteristics such as cosmetic defects often accompany final inspection. Visual inspection is challenging because specifications are subject to interpretation by individual inspectors who may view them in different ways. Considerable training is often required. Inspection error rates of 10–50 percent are not uncommon. Ask three people to proofread a lengthy manuscript for typographical errors as an experiment. Rarely will everyone discover all errors, much less the same ones. The same is true of complicated industrial inspection tasks, especially those involving detailed microelectronics.

Visual inspection tasks are affected by several factors:

■ *Complexity:* The number of defects caught by an inspector decreases with more parts and less orderly arrangement.

■ *Defect rate:* When the product defect rate is low, inspectors tend to miss more defects than when the defect rate is higher. (This factor applies to the proofreading task.)

■ *Repeated inspections:* Different inspectors will not miss the same defects. Therefore, if the same item is inspected by a number of different inspectors, a higher percentage of total defects will be caught.

■ *Inspection rate:* The inspector's performance degrades rapidly as the inspection rate increases.[11]

Understanding these factors leads to several ways to improve inspection:

■ Minimize the number of quality characteristics considered in an inspection task. Five to six different types are approximately the maximum amount that the human mind can handle well at one time.

■ Minimize disturbing influences and time pressures.

■ Provide clear, detailed instructions for the inspection task.

■ Design the workspace to facilitate the inspection task, and provide good lighting.

Automated technology such as vision systems have eliminated many manual inspection tasks and improved the quality of the inspection process.

METROLOGY

Chapter 8 discussed the importance of data reliability. Gauges and instruments used to measure quality characteristics must provide correct information, which is assured through **metrology**—the science of measurement. Originally, metrology only measured the physical attributes of an object. Today, metrology is defined broadly and is the collection of people, equipment, facilities, methods, and procedures used to assure correctness or adequacy of measurements. Metrology is vital to quality assurance because of the increasing emphasis on quality by government agencies, the implications of measurement error on safety and product liability, and the reliance on improved quality control methods such as statistical process control.

Every measurement is subject to error. Whenever variation is observed in measurements, some portion is due to measurement system error. Some errors are systematic (called *bias*); others are random. The size of the errors relative to the measurement value can significantly affect the quality of the data and resulting decisions. The evaluation of data obtained from inspection and measurement is not meaningful unless the measurement instruments are accurate, precise, and reproducible.

Accuracy is defined as the closeness of agreement between an observed value and an accepted reference value or standard. The lack of accuracy reflects a systematic bias in the measurement such as a gauge out of calibration, worn, or used improperly by the operator. Accuracy is measured as the amount of error in a measurement in proportion to the total size of the measurement. One measurement is more accurate than another if it has a smaller relative error. For example, suppose that two instruments measure a dimension whose true value is 0.250". Instrument A may read 0.248", while instrument B may read 0.259". The relative error of instrument A is $(0.250 - 0.248)/0.250 = 0.8\%$; the relative error of instrument B is $(0.259 - 0.250)/0.250 = 3.6\%$. Thus, instrument A is said to be more accurate than instrument B.

Precision, or *repeatability*, is defined as the closeness of agreement between randomly selected individual measurements or results. Precision, therefore, relates to the variance of repeated measurements. A measuring instrument with a low variance is more precise than another having a higher variance. Low precision is due to random variation that is built into the instrument, such as friction among its parts. This random variation may be the result of a poor design or lack of maintenance.

A measurement system may be precise but not necessarily accurate at the same time. In the preceding example, suppose that each instrument measures a dimension three times. Instrument A records values of 0.248, 0.246, and 0.251; instrument B records values of 0.259, 0.258, and 0.259. Instrument B is more precise than instrument A since its values are clustered closer together. The relationships between accuracy and precision are summarized in Figure 14.5. The figure illustrates four possible frequency distributions of ten repeated measurements of some quality characteristic. In Figure 14.5(a), the average measurement is not close to the true value. Moreover, a wide range of values fall around the average. In this case, the measurement is neither accurate nor precise. In Figure 14.5(b), even though the average measurement is not close to the true value, the range of variation is small. Thus, the measurement is precise but not accurate. In Figures 14.5(c) and (d), the average value is close to the true value—that is, the measurement is accurate—but in 14.5(c) the distribution is widely dispersed and therefore not precise, while the measurement in 14.5(d) is both accurate *and* precise. Thus, Figure 14.5 demonstrates the vital nature of properly calibrating and maintaining all instruments used for quality measurements.

Reproducibility is the variation in the same measuring instrument when it is used by different individuals to measure the same parts. Causes of poor reproducibility include poor training of the operators in the use of the instrument or unclear calibrations on the gauge dial.

The quality of a product depends on the use of accurate, precise, and reproducible measurement and test equipment. One of the most important functions of metrology is **calibration.** Calibration is the comparison of a measurement device or system having a known relationship to national standards to another device or system whose relationship to national standards is unknown. Measurements made with uncalibrated or inadequately calibrated equipment can lead to erroneous and costly decisions. For example, suppose that an inspector has a micrometer that is reading 0.002" too low. When measurements are made close to the upper limit, parts that are as much as 0.002" over the maximum tolerance limit will be accepted as good, while

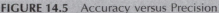

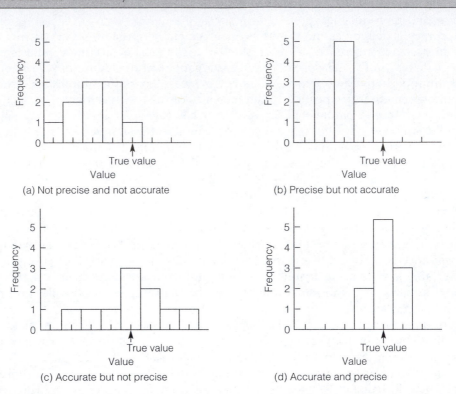

FIGURE 14.5 Accuracy versus Precision

those at the lower tolerance limit or that are as much as 0.002" above the limit will be rejected as nonconforming.

National standards are maintained and monitored by the National Institute of Standards and Technology (NIST). NIST works with various metrology laboratories in industry and government to assure that measurements made by different people in different places yield the same results. Thus, the measurement of "voltage" or "resistance" in an electrical component has a precise and universal meaning. This process is accomplished in a hierarchical fashion. NIST calibrates the reference-level standards of those organizations requiring the highest level of accuracy. These organizations calibrate their own working-level standards and those of other metrology laboratories. These working-level standards are used to calibrate the measuring instruments used in the field. The usual recommendation is that equipment be calibrated against working-level standards that are 10 times as accurate as the equipment. When possible, at least a four-to-one accuracy ratio between the reference and working-level standards is desired; that is, the reference standards should be at least four times as accurate as the working-level standards.

The ability to quantify a laboratory's measurement uncertainty in relationship to national standards is called **traceability.** Traceability is based on analyses of measurement error along each step of the calibration process, from the NIST standards, to the measurement laboratory, and finally to the measurement of the item itself. Such traceability is usually required in government contracts.

A typical calibration system involves the following activities:

■ Evaluation of equipment to determine its capability

■ Identification of calibration requirements

■ Selection of standards to perform calibration

■ Selection of methods and procedures to perform the calibration

■ Establishment of calibration frequency and rules for adjusting this frequency

■ Establishment of a system to ensure that instruments are calibrated according to schedule

■ Implementation of a documentation and reporting system

■ Evaluation of the calibration system through an established auditing process

■ Repeatability and Reproducibility Studies

The accuracy, repeatability, and reproducibility of any measurement system must be quantified and evaluated. Accuracy can be measured by comparing the observed average of a set of measurements to the true value of a reference standard. Repeatability and reproducibility require a study of variation and can be addressed through statistical analysis. A repeatability and reproducibility study is conducted in the following manner.[12]

1. Select m operators and n parts. Typically at least two operators and 10 parts are chosen. Number the parts so that the numbers are not visible to the operators.

2. Calibrate the measuring instrument.

3. Let each operator measure each part in a random order and record the results. Repeat this for a total of r trials. At least two trials must be used. Let M_{ijk} represent the kth measurement of operator i on part j.

4. Compute the average measurement for each operator:

$$\bar{x}_i = \left(\sum_j \sum_k M_{ijk} \right) / nr$$

The difference between the largest and smallest average is

$$\bar{x}_D = \max_i \{\bar{x}_i\} - \min_i \{\bar{x}_i)$$

5. Compute the range for each part and each operator:

$$R_{ij} = \max_k \{M_{ijk}\} - \min_k \{M_{ijk}\}$$

These values show the variability of repeated measurements of the same part by the same operator. Next, compute the average range for each operator:

$$\bar{R}_i = \left(\sum_j R_{ij} \right) / n$$

The overall average range is then computed as

$$\bar{\bar{R}} = \left(\sum_i \bar{R}_i \right) / m$$

TABLE 14.1   Values of K_1 and K_2

Number of Trials	2	3	4	5
K_1	4.56	3.05	2.50	2.21
Number of Operators	2	3	4	5
K_2	3.65	2.70	2.30	2.08

6. Calculate a "control limit" on the individual ranges R_{ij}:

$$\text{control limit} = D_4 \overline{\overline{R}}$$

where D_4 is a constant that depends on the sample size (number of trials, r) and can be found in Appendix B at the end of this book. Any range value beyond this limit might result from some assignable cause, not random error. Possible causes should be investigated and, if found, corrected. The operator should repeat these measurements using the same part. If no assignable cause is found, these values should be discarded and all statistics in step 5 as well as the control limit should be recalculated.

Once these basic calculations are made, an analysis of repeatability and reproducibility can be performed. The repeatability, or equipment variation (EV) is computed as

$$EV = K_1 \overline{\overline{R}}$$

Reproducibility, or operator variation (OV) is computed as

$$OV = \sqrt{(K_2 \overline{x}_D)^2 - (EV^2/nr)}$$

The constants K_1 and K_2 depend on the number of trials and number of operators, respectively. Some values of these constants are given in Table 14.1. These constants provide a 99 percent confidence interval on these statistics.

An overall measure of repeatability and reproducibility (RR) is given by

$$RR = \sqrt{(EV)^2 + (OV)^2}$$

Repeatability and reproducibility are often expressed as a percent of the tolerance of the quality characteristic being measured. The American Society for Quality Control suggests the following guidelines for evaluating repeatability and reproducibility:

■ *Under 10% error:* This rate is acceptable.

■ *10 to 30% error:* This rate may be acceptable based on the importance of the application, cost of the instrument, cost of repair, and so on.

■ *Over 30% error:* Generally, this rate is not acceptable. Every effort should be made to identify the problem and correct it.

EXAMPLE 2   A Gauge Repeatability and Reproducibility Study.   The gauge used to measure the thickness of a gasket having a specification of 0.50 to 1.0 mm is to be evaluated. Ten parts have been selected for measurement by three operators. Each part is measured twice with the results as shown in Table 14.2.

TABLE 14.2   Gasket Thickness Measurements

Part Number/Trial	OPERATOR 1		OPERATOR 2		OPERATOR 3	
	1	2	1	2	1	2
1	0.63	0.59	0.56	0.56	0.51	0.54
2	1.00	1.00	1.04	0.96	1.05	1.01
3	0.83	0.77	0.80	0.76	0.81	0.81
4	0.86	0.94	0.82	0.78	0.81	0.81
5	0.59	0.51	0.43	0.43	0.46	0.49
6	0.98	0.98	1.00	1.04	1.04	1.00
7	0.96	0.96	0.94	0.90	0.95	0.95
8	0.86	0.83	0.72	0.74	0.81	0.81
9	0.97	0.97	0.98	0.94	1.03	1.03
10	0.64	0.72	0.56	0.52	0.84	0.81

The average measurement for each operator, $\bar{x}_i$, is

$$\bar{x}_1 = 0.8295 \qquad \bar{x}_2 = 0.7740 \qquad \bar{x}_3 = 0.8285$$

Thus, $\bar{x}_D = 0.8295 - 0.7740 = 0.0555$. The range for each operator, R_{ij}, is shown in Table 14.3.

The average range for each operator is

$$\bar{R}_1 = 0.037 \qquad \bar{R}_2 = 0.034 \qquad \bar{R}_3 = 0.017$$

The overall average range is $\bar{\bar{R}} = (0.037 + 0.034 + 0.017)/3 = 0.029$. From Appendix B at the end of the book, $D_4 = 3.267$ since two trials were conducted. Hence the control limit is $(3.267)(0.029) = 0.095$. Because all range values fall below this limit, no assignable causes of variation are suspected. Compute the repeatability and reproducibility measures:

$$EV = (4.56)(0.029) = 0.132$$

$$OV = \sqrt{[(0.0555)(2.70)]^2 - (0.132)^2/(10)(2)} = 0.147$$

$$RR = \sqrt{(0.132)^2 + (0.147)^2} = 0.198$$

TABLE 14.3   Gasket Thickness Ranges

Part Number	OPERATOR 1			OPERATOR 2			OPERATOR 3		
	1	2	Range	1	2	Range	1	2	Range
1	0.63	0.59	0.04	0.56	0.56	0.00	0.51	0.54	0.03
2	1.00	1.00	0.00	1.04	0.96	0.08	1.05	1.01	0.04
3	0.83	0.77	0.06	0.80	0.76	0.04	0.81	0.81	0.00
4	0.86	0.94	0.08	0.82	0.78	0.04	0.81	0.81	0.00
5	0.59	0.51	0.08	0.43	0.43	0.00	0.46	0.49	0.03
6	0.98	0.98	0.00	1.00	1.04	0.04	1.04	1.00	0.04
7	0.96	0.96	0.00	0.94	0.90	0.04	0.95	0.95	0.00
8	0.86	0.83	0.03	0.72	0.74	0.02	0.81	0.81	0.00
9	0.97	0.97	0.00	0.98	0.94	0.04	1.03	1.03	0.00
10	0.64	0.72	0.08	0.56	0.52	0.04	0.84	0.81	0.03

Since the tolerance of the gasket is $1.00 - 0.50 = 0.50$, these measures expressed as a percent of tolerance are:

Equipment variation $= 100(0.132)/0.50 = 26.4\%$

Operator variation $= 100(0.147)/0.50 = 29.4\%$

Total R and R variation $= 100(0.198)/0.50 = 39.6\%$

While individually, the equipment and operator variation may be acceptable, their combined effect is not. Efforts should be made to reduce the variation to an acceptable level.

PROCESS CAPABILITY

Process capability is the range over which the natural variation of a process occurs as determined by the system of common causes. It is the ability of the combination of people, machines, methods, materials, and measurements to produce a product or service that will consistently meet design specifications. Process capability is measured by the proportion of output that can be produced within design specifications; in other words, it is a measure of the uniformity of the process. Process capability can be measured only if all special causes of variation have been eliminated and the process is in a state of statistical control. For general purposes in subsequent discussions, assume that the process is in control.

Process capability is important to both product designers and manufacturing engineers. Process capability studies allow one to predict, quantitatively, how well a process will meet specifications and to specify the level of control necessary as well as equipment requirements. For example, if a design specification requires a length of metal tubing to be cut within one-tenth of an inch, a process consisting of a worker using a ruler and hacksaw will probably result in a large percentage of nonconforming product. In such a case, the process is not capable of meeting the design specifications. Management then faces three possible decisions: (1) measure each piece and either recut or scrap nonconforming parts, (2) develop a better process by investing in new technology, or (3) change the design specifications.

Such decisions are usually based on economics. Scrap and rework are poor strategies, since labor and materials have already been invested in a bad product. Also, inspection errors will probably allow some nonconforming products to leave the production facility. New technology might require substantial investment the firm cannot afford. Changes in design may sacrifice fitness-for-use requirements and result in a lower quality product. Thus, these factors demonstrate the need to consider process capability in product design and acceptance of new contracts. Many firms now require process capability data from their suppliers.

Unfortunately, product design often takes place in isolation, with inexperienced designers applying tolerances to parts or products while having little awareness of the capabilities of the production process to meet these design requirements. Even experienced designers may be hard pressed to remain up-to-date on the capabilities of processes that involve constant equipment changes, shifting technology, and difficult-to-measure variations in methods at scores of plants located hundreds or thousands of miles away from a centralized product design department. Process capability should be carefully considered in determining design specifications.

Process capability information can also be used by production personnel to compare the natural variability to specifications and predict the amount of yield of conforming product in situations in which investing in new technology or changing the design specifications is impractical. Knowledge of existing process capability aids in planning production schedules and inspection strategies.

Process capability has three important components: (1) the design specifications, (2) the centering of the natural variation, and (3) the range, or spread, of variation. Figure 14.6 illustrates four possible outcomes that can arise when natural process variability is compared with design specifications. In Figure 14.6(a), the specifications are looser than the natural variation; one would expect that the process will always produce conforming products as long as it remains in control. It may even be possible to reduce costs by investing in a cheaper technology that allows for a larger variation in the process output. In Figure 14.6(b), the natural variation and specifications are the same. A small percentage of nonconforming products might be produced; thus, the process should be closely monitored.

In Figure 14.6(c), the range of natural variability is larger than the specification; thus, the current process could not meet specifications even when it is in control. This situation often results from a lack of adequate communication between the design department and manufacturing. If the process is in control but cannot produce according to the design specifications, the question should be raised whether the specifications have been correctly applied or if they may be relaxed without adversely affecting the assembly or use of the product. If the specifications are realistic, an effort must be made to improve the process to the point where it is capable of producing consistently within specifications.

Finally, in Figure 14.6(d), the variability is the same, but the process average is off-center. A faulty machine setting or poorly calibrated inspection equipment frequently is the cause of the variation in this situation. In such cases, adjustment is required to move the process back within specification. If no action is taken, a substantial portion of output will fall outside the specification limit even though the process may appear to be in control.

Product specifications and process capability form an unbreakable link between design, manufacturing, and quality. If product specifications of parts and components are good (that is, not too tight and not too loose), manufacturing units will use the capability of their processes and equipment to produce good,

FIGURE 14.6 Natural Variability versus Specifications for Process Capability

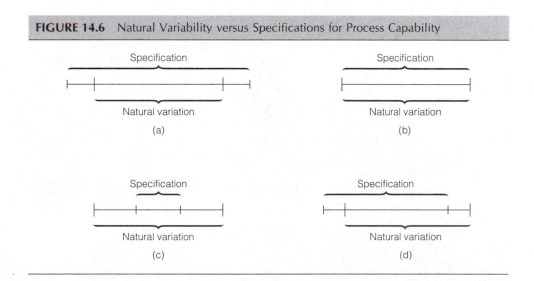

standard high-quality parts and assemblies, although a small percentage may be nonconforming. However, if product specifications are too tight, the product will be seen as excessively difficult to make by manufacturing units, and a large proportion of nonconforming products may result. Close tolerances often are hard to achieve, hard to hold, and hard to measure and, of course, can be very costly. Although customers using such products often appreciate the apparent high quality, the products are often difficult to maintain.

On the other hand, one must be cautious about product specifications that are too loose. In this case, process capability and assembly of the product will be easy to achieve, but fitness for use may be negatively affected, resulting in frequent breakdowns and repairs. Designers and manufacturing engineers both must consider these issues carefully in determining product specifications and processes to achieve the quality objectives of the firm.

■ Statistical Analysis of Process Variation

A **process capability study** is a carefully planned study designed to yield specific information about the performance of a process under specified operating conditions. Typical questions that are asked in a process capability study are

- Where is the process centered?
- How much variability exists in the process?
- Is the performance acceptable?
- Is the process stable?
- What factors contribute to variability?

Many reasons exist for conducting a capability study. Manufacturing may wish to determine a performance baseline for a process, to prioritize projects for quality improvement, or to provide statistical evidence of quality for customers. Purchasing might conduct a study at a supplier plant to evaluate a new piece of equipment or to compare different suppliers. Engineering might conduct a study to determine the adequacy of R&D pilot facilities or to evaluate new processes.

Three types of studies are often conducted. A *peak performance study* determines how a process performs under ideal conditions. A *process characterization study* is designed to determine how a process performs under actual operating conditions. A *component variability study* assesses the relative contribution of different sources of total variation. The methods by which each study is conducted vary. A peak performance study is conducted under carefully controlled conditions over a short time interval to ensure that no special causes can affect variation. A process characterization study is performed over a longer time interval under actual operating conditions to capture the variations in materials and operators. A component variability study uses a designed experiment to control the sources of variability. Although this section considers a process characterization study, the general approach applies to a peak performance study with appropriate modifications.

The six steps in a process capability study are similar to any systematic study and include the following:

1. Choose a representative machine or segment of the process.
2. Define the process conditions.
3. Select a representative operator.

4. Provide materials that are of standard grade, with sufficient materials for uninterrupted study.

5. Specify the gauging or measurement method to be used.

6. Provide for a method of recording measurements and conditions, in order, on the units produced.

Two statistical techniques are commonly used to establish process capability. One is the frequency distribution histogram, the other is the control chart. The use of histograms is covered in this section, but the discussion of control charts is deferred to a later chapter.

EXAMPLE 3 Process Capability Analysis. To illustrate the use of histograms for process capability, consider the data in Table 14.4 (p. 594) for Consolidated Auto Supply Company. The company is a primary supplier of U-bolts for one of the major auto manufacturers. Table 14.4 shows a large sample of 120 measurements of the inside distance (a critical dimension in auto assembly) between ends of a U-bolt (illustrated in Figure 14.7, p. 594) and are accurate to 0.05 centimeter. For the purpose of process capability estimates, assume that these 120 measurements are representative of the population from which they were drawn, that is, the process is in statistical control.

Figure 14.8 shows a histogram of the data presented in Table 14.4 in which the dimensions are spread out between 10.50 and 10.90 centimeters, with a high proportion of values toward the center of the distribution. Descriptive measures for this data can be computed using either Table 14.4 directly or the histogram in Figure 14.8. A frequency distribution of these data is given here:

Midpoint, x	Frequency, f
10.50	2
10.55	2
10.60	13
10.65	25
10.70	22
10.75	24
10.80	16
10.85	14
10.90	2
	120

Estimating the mean and standard deviation using this frequency distribution yields:

$$\bar{x} = \frac{1}{n}\sum fx = 10.7171 \qquad s = \sqrt{\frac{\sum fx^2 - (\sum fx)^2/n}{n-1}} = 0.0868$$

Hence, the mean is $\bar{x} = 10.7171$, and the sample standard deviation is $s = 0.0868$. Oftentimes, frequency distributions of the output from a production process follow some common probability distribution. The most common distribution that models many production processes or is assumed in many applications is the normal distribution.

The histogram in Figure 14.8 appears to be close to a normal distribution. If this is true, calculations using the normal distribution can be used to predict the yield of conforming product for various manufacturing specifications. Testing

TABLE 14.4	Measurements of U-Bolts				
Sample	Observations				
1	10.65	10.70	10.65	10.65	10.85
2	10.75	10.85	10.75	10.85	10.65
3	10.75	10.80	10.80	10.70	10.75
4	10.60	10.70	10.70	10.75	10.65
5	10.70	10.75	10.65	10.85	10.80
6	10.60	10.75	10.75	10.85	10.70
7	10.60	10.80	10.70	10.75	10.75
8	10.75	10.80	10.65	10.75	10.70
9	10.65	10.80	10.85	10.85	10.75
10	10.60	10.70	10.60	10.80	10.65
11	10.80	10.75	10.90	10.50	10.85
12	10.85	10.75	10.85	10.65	10.70
13	10.70	10.70	10.75	10.75	10.70
14	10.65	10.70	10.85	10.75	10.60
15	10.75	10.80	10.75	10.80	10.65
16	10.90	10.80	10.80	10.75	10.85
17	10.75	10.70	10.85	10.70	10.80
18	10.75	10.70	10.60	10.70	10.60
19	10.65	10.65	10.85	10.65	10.70
20	10.60	10.60	10.65	10.55	10.65
21	10.50	10.55	10.65	10.80	10.80
22	10.80	10.65	10.75	10.65	10.65
23	10.65	10.60	10.65	10.60	10.70
24	10.65	10.70	10.70	10.60	10.65

for normality can be done in several ways. The simplest and most practical method is to use normal probability paper. Normal probability paper is a special type of graph paper scaled so that the plot of a cumulative normal distribution will be a straight line. Usually the "straightness" of the line can be determined by visual inspection, and one can reach valid conclusions most of the time. Many computer packages have the ability to draw normal probability plots.

To test whether a frequency distribution is normal, first convert the data to a cumulative frequency distribution, that is, the number of observations less than or equal to a specified value. These cumulative frequencies are next converted

FIGURE 14.7   U-Bolt Produced by Consolidated Auto Supply Company

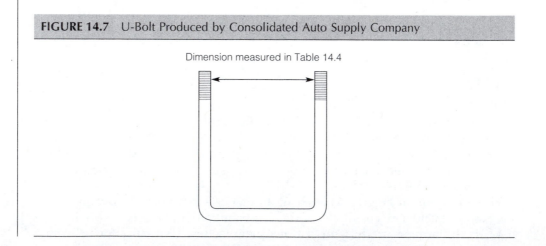

Dimension measured in Table 14.4

FIGURE 14.8   Histogram of U-Bolt Dimensions

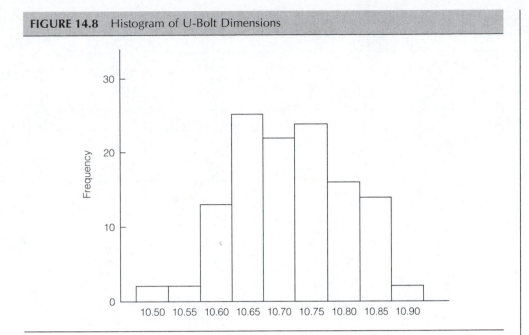

to relative frequencies or probabilities by dividing the cumulative frequencies by the number of observations (120). From Figure 14.8 relative frequencies are as follows:

Dimensional Value	Frequency	Cumulative Frequency	Cumulative Relative Frequency
10.50	2	2	0.017
10.55	2	4	0.033
10.60	13	17	0.142
10.65	25	42	0.350
10.70	22	64	0.533
10.75	24	88	0.733
10.80	16	104	0.867
10.85	14	118	0.983
10.90	2	120	1.000

A plot of the cumulative relative frequencies on normal probability paper is shown in Figure 14.9 (p. 596). Since this results in approximately a straight line, one can reasonably conclude that the process output follows a normal distribution.[13]

One of the properties of a normal distribution is that 99.73 percent of the observations will fall within three standard deviations from the mean. Thus, a process that is in control can be expected to produce a large percentage of output between $\mu - 3\sigma$ and $\mu + 3\sigma$, where μ is the process average. Therefore, the *natural tolerance limits* of the process are $\mu \pm 3\sigma$. A six standard deviation spread is used as a measure of process capability.

For the Consolidated example, use the sample statistics $\bar{x} = 10.7171$ and $s = 0.0868$ as estimates of the population parameters μ and σ. Nearly all of the U-bolt dimensions are expected to fall between $10.7171 - 3(0.0868) = 10.4566$ and $10.7171 + 3(0.0868) = 10.9766$. These calculations tell the production manager

FIGURE 14.9   Normal Probability Plot

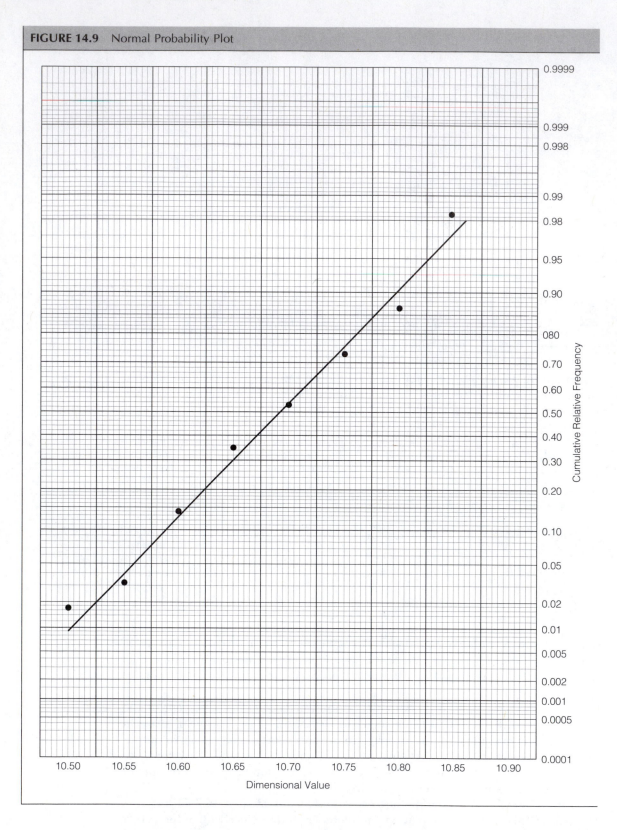

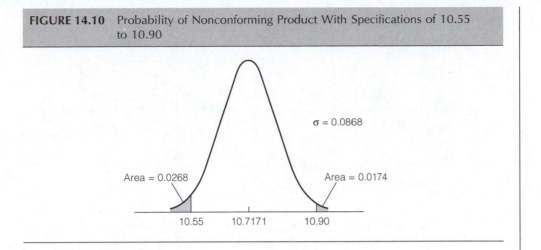

FIGURE 14.10   Probability of Nonconforming Product With Specifications of 10.55 to 10.90

$\sigma = 0.0868$

Area = 0.0268

Area = 0.0174

10.55   10.7171   10.90

that if the design specifications are between 10.45 and 11.00, for instance, the process will be capable of producing nearly 100 percent conforming product. Suppose, however, that design specifications are such that the dimension must lie between 10.55 and 10.90. Calculate the expected percentage of nonconforming U-bolts by computing the area under a normal distribution having a mean of 10.7171 and standard deviation 0.0868 to the left and right of these specifications, as illustrated in Figure 14.10.

Converting 10.55 to a standard normal value yields $z = (10.55 - 10.7171)/0.0868 = -1.93$. Appendix A at the end of the book gives a value for the area to the *left* of $z = -1.93$ as $0.5000 - 0.4732 = 0.0268$. Similarly, the z value corresponding to 10.90 is $z = (10.90 - 10.7171)/0.0868 = 2.11$. The area to the *right* of $z = 2.11$ is $0.5000 - 0.4826 = 0.0174$. Therefore, the probability that a part will not meet specifications is $0.0268 + 0.0174 = 0.0442$ or, expressed as a percentage, is 4.42 percent. Similar computations can be used to estimate the percentage of nonconforming parts for other tolerances. This information can be used to help management determine scrap and rework policies, new equipment justification, and so on.

As this example showed, examining the distribution of output from a process can provide evidence of whether the actual characteristics of the products being produced are within, outside, or overlapping the desired tolerances. One need not attempt to fit the distribution to a normal curve, however, but can work directly with the histogram. Figure 14.11 shows some typical examples of process variations that might be detected by the use of frequency distribution plots. Figure 14.11(a) shows an ideal situation in which the natural variation is well within the specified tolerance limits. In 14.11(b), the variation is approximately the same as the tolerance limits. The graph in 14.11(c) shows a distribution with a natural variation greater than the specification limits; in this case, the process is not capable of meeting specifications, resulting in some nonconforming output.

The graphs in Figures 14.11(d), (e), and (f) correspond to those in Figures 14.11(a), (b), and (c), except that the process is off-center from the specified tolerance limits. In 14.11(g), the bimodal shape suggests that perhaps the data were drawn from two different machines or that two different materials or products were involved. The small distribution to the right in 14.11(h) may be the result

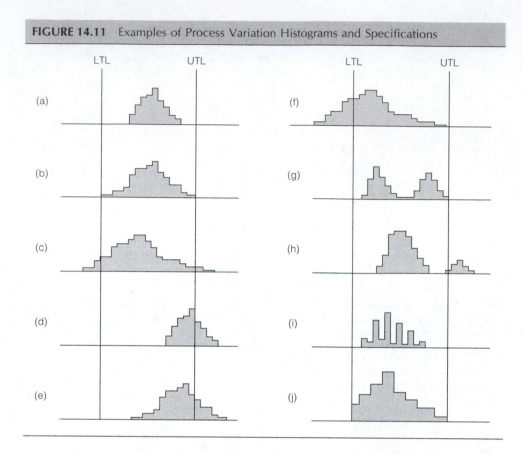

FIGURE 14.11 Examples of Process Variation Histograms and Specifications

of including pieces from a trial setup run while the machine was being adjusted. The graph in 14.11(i) might be the result of inadequate gauging or rounding values during inspection. Finally, the truncated distribution in 14.11(j) is often the result of sorting nonconforming parts.

Not all of the conditions shown in Figure 14.11 are due to a lack of process capability, however. Some may simply occur because a process that is in control drifts out. Others may be indicators of various types of process capability problems, technical mistakes, or system problems that should be corrected to improve long-term quality of the products. Thus, a good control system is a necessity, since a histogram alone will not provide complete information.

An important issue that is often ignored in process capability studies is the error resulting from using the sample standard deviation, s, rather than the true standard deviation, σ. A simple table can be constructed to find confidence intervals on the true value for σ for a given sample size. Such a table is shown in Table 14.5 and is easily explained by an example. For a given sample size, σ will be less than or equal to s times the factor in that row with probability p, where p is the column heading. Thus, for a sample of size 30, $\sigma \leq 0.744s$ with probability 0.005; $\sigma \leq 1.280s$ occurs 95 percent of the time; and so on. A 90 percent confidence interval for σ can be found by using the factors in the columns corresponding to $p = 0.050$ and $p = 0.950$. Thus, for a sample size of 30, a 95 percent confidence interval would be $(0.825s, 1.280s)$. The interpretation of process capability information should be tempered by such an analysis.

TABLE 14.5   Ratio of Population to Sample Standard Deviation

NUMBER OF SAMPLES	FRACTION OF POPULATION LESS THAN OR EQUAL TO VALUE IN TABLE							
	0.005	0.010	0.025	0.050	0.100	0.950	0.975	0.995
2	0.356	0.388	0.446	0.510	0.608	15.952	31.911	159.516
3	0.434	0.466	0.521	0.578	0.659	4.407	6.287	14.142
4	0.483	0.514	0.567	0.620	0.693	2.919	3.727	6.468
5	0.519	0.549	0.599	0.649	0.717	2.372	2.875	4.396
6	0.546	0.576	0.624	0.672	0.736	2.090	2.453	3.484
7	0.569	0.597	0.644	0.690	0.751	1.918	2.202	2.979
8	0.588	0.616	0.661	0.705	0.763	1.797	2.035	2.660
9	0.604	0.631	0.675	0.718	0.774	1.711	1.916	2.440
10	0.618	0.645	0.688	0.729	0.783	1.645	1.826	2.278
11	0.630	0.656	0.699	0.739	0.791	1.593	1.755	2.154
12	0.641	0.667	0.708	0.748	0.798	1.551	1.698	2.056
13	0.651	0.677	0.717	0.755	0.804	1.515	1.651	1.976
14	0.660	0.685	0.725	0.762	0.810	1.485	1.611	1.910
15	0.669	0.693	0.732	0.769	0.815	1.460	1.577	1.854
16	0.676	0.700	0.739	0.775	0.820	1.437	1.548	1.806
17	0.683	0.707	0.745	0.780	0.824	1.418	1.522	1.764
18	0.690	0.713	0.750	0.785	0.828	1.400	1.499	1.727
19	0.696	0.719	0.756	0.790	0.832	1.385	1.479	1.695
20	0.702	0.725	0.760	0.794	0.836	1.370	1.461	1.666
21	0.707	0.730	0.765	0.798	0.839	1.358	1.444	1.640
22	0.712	0.734	0.769	0.802	0.842	1.346	1.429	1.617
23	0.717	0.739	0.773	0.805	0.845	1.335	1.415	1.595
24	0.722	0.743	0.777	0.809	0.848	1.325	1.403	1.576
25	0.726	0.747	0.781	0.812	0.850	1.316	1.391	1.558
26	0.730	0.751	0.784	0.815	0.853	1.308	1.380	1.542
27	0.734	0.755	0.788	0.818	0.855	1.300	1.370	1.526
28	0.737	0.758	0.791	0.820	0.857	1.293	1.361	1.512
29	0.741	0.762	0.794	0.823	0.859	1.286	1.352	1.499
30	0.744	0.765	0.796	0.825	0.861	1.280	1.344	1.487
31	0.748	0.768	0.799	0.828	0.863	1.274	1.337	1.475
36	0.762	0.781	0.811	0.838	0.872	1.248	1.304	1.427
41	0.774	0.792	0.821	0.847	0.879	1.228	1.280	1.390
46	0.784	0.802	0.829	0.854	0.885	1.212	1.260	1.361
51	0.793	0.810	0.837	0.861	0.890	1.199	1.243	1.337
61	0.808	0.824	0.849	0.871	0.898	1.179	1.217	1.299
71	0.820	0.835	0.858	0.879	0.905	1.163	1.198	1.272
81	0.829	0.844	0.866	0.886	0.910	1.151	1.183	1.250
91	0.838	0.852	0.873	0.892	0.915	1.141	1.171	1.233
101	0.845	0.858	0.879	0.897	0.919	1.133	1.161	1.219

SOURCE: Thomas D. Hall, "How Close Is *s* to σ? *Quality* (December 1991), 45. Note: The table published in this article was incorrect. An error notice was published in a subsequent issue and the correct table was made available by *Quality* magazine.

■ Process Capability Index

The importance of process capability is in assessing the relationship between the natural variation of a process and the design specifications. This relationship is often quantified by a measure known as the **process capability index.** The process capability index, C_p, is defined as the ratio of the specification width to the natural tolerance of the process. C_p relates the natural variation of the process with the design specifications in a single, quantitative measure.

In numerical terms, the formula is

$$C_p = \frac{UTL - LTL}{6\sigma}$$

where

UTL = upper tolerance limit

LTL = lower tolerance limit

σ = standard deviation of the process

Managers often use C_p in objective setting and in discussions of contracts with suppliers.

To illustrate the computation and interpretation of C_p, suppose that the design specifications of a dimension have a tolerance spread (UTL − LTL) of 6 units and that the standard deviation of the process is 1.00. The process capability is therefore $6\sigma = 6(1.00) = 6.00$. Therefore

$$C_p = (UTL - LTL)/6\sigma = 6/6(1) = 1.00$$

If $\sigma = 2$, then

$$C_p = 6/6(2) = 0.50$$

Finally, if $\sigma = 0.50$, then

$$C_p = 6/6(.5) = 2.00$$

Figure 14.12 illustrates these three cases. Note that a C_p value of 1.0 occurs when the natural variation equals the design tolerance spread. A value less than one indicates that the process is not capable of meeting specifications; a value greater than one corresponds to a process that is highly capable of meeting specifications.

The process capability index can be used for setting objectives and improving processes. Suppose that a quality manager in a firm has a process with a standard deviation of one and a tolerance spread of 8. The value of C_p for this situation is 1.33. The manager realizes that the natural spread is within specifications at this time, but new contracts call for increasing the value of the capability index. Targets are set for increasing the index to 1.66 within three months, to 2.00 within six months, and to 3.00 within a year. Given that the tolerance spread (UTL − LTL) is held at the previous level of 8, the following table shows the required process standard deviation for each phase of the project.

C_p	UTL − LTL	6σ	σ
1.33	8	6	1
1.66	8	4.8	0.8
2.00	8	4	0.67
3.00	8	2.67	0.44

Operationally, this task involves reducing the variability in the process from a standard deviation of 1.000 to 0.444, which results in the desired increase of C_p from the current level of 1.33 to the final level of 3.00, which can be accomplished using process improvement and minor equipment upgrades.

FIGURE 14.12   Illustrations of Process Capability Indexes

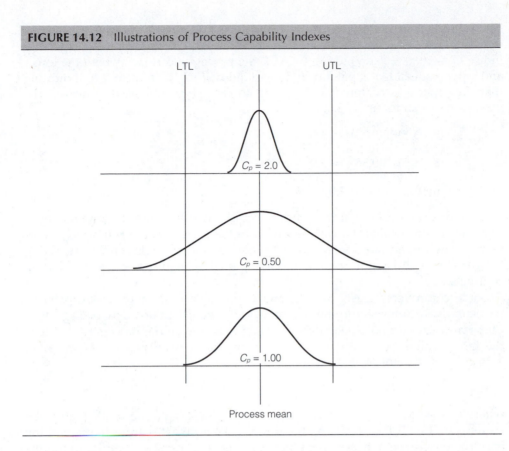

Two important facts about the C_p index should be pointed out. One relates to process conditions and the other relates to interpretation of the values that have been calculated. First, the calculation of the C_p has no meaning if the process is not under statistical control. The natural spread (6σ) should be calculated using a sufficiently large sample to get a meaningful estimate of the population standard deviation (σ). Second, a C_p of 1.00 would require that the process be perfectly centered on the mean of the tolerance spread to prevent some units from being produced outside the limits. The goal of all units being produced within specifications with a C_p of 1.33 is much easier to achieve, and still easier with a C_p of 2.00. Based on the experience of a number of practitioners, they have suggested a "safe" lower limit C_p of 1.5. A value above this level will practically guarantee that all units produced by a controlled process will be within specifications. Many firms require C_p values of 2 or greater from their suppliers.

The previous discussion assumed that the process was centered; clearly the value of C_p does not depend on the mean of the process. To include information on process centering, one-sided indexes are often used. One-sided process capability indexes are as follows:

$$C_{pu} = \frac{\text{UTL} - \mu}{3\sigma} \text{ (upper one-sided index)}$$

$$C_{pl} = \frac{\mu - \text{LTL}}{3\sigma} \text{ (lower one-sided index)}$$

$$C_{pk} = \min(C_{pl}, C_{pu})$$

For example, consider a process having a lower tolerance limit of 5.0, an upper tolerance limit of 9.0, and a standard deviation of 0.33. The process capability index, $C_p = (9.0 - 5.0)/6(0.33) = 2.0$. If the process mean is 7.0, both the lower and upper one-sided capability indexes (and also C_{pk}) are also 2.0, indicating that the process is centered with respect to the specifications. If, however, the process mean shifts up to 8.0, then

$$C_{pu} = (9 - 8)/3(0.33) = 1.0$$

$$C_{pl} = (8 - 5)/3(0.33) = 3.0$$

$$C_{pk} = \min(3.0, 1.0) = 1.0$$

These indexes indicate that the process would have difficulty meeting its upper tolerance limit but that it would easily meet the lower tolerance limit. C_{pk} summarizes the upper and lower capability indexes into a single number reflecting the worst case; it is often used in specifying quality requirements in purchasing contracts.

Some controversy exists over C_p and C_{pk} as measures of process capability, particularly with respect to the economic loss function philosophy of Taguchi.[14] These measures do not adequately account for how well the process can achieve the target value. Several alternative measures have been proposed. One is to adjust C_p by a factor $(1 - k)$ as follows:

$$C_{pk} = C_p(1 - k)$$

where $k = 2|\text{mean} - \text{target}|/\text{tolerance}$. When the sample mean is equal to the target, $k = 0$ and $C_{pk} = C_p$. As the sample mean deviates from the target, the absolute difference between them increases and k increases. Specification limits are used only to determine the tolerance; thus the focus of this measure is on the target value rather than on acceptable specification limits. Another index that has been proposed is

$$C_{pm} = C_p/\sqrt{1 + (\text{mean} - \text{target})^2/\sigma^2}$$

This measure also accounts for deviations from the target value.

■ Six Sigma Quality

One might think that having the natural tolerance equal to design tolerance would be good quality. After all, if the distribution is normal, only 0.27 percent of the output would be expected to fall outside the design tolerance range. Consider what such a level of quality really means:

■ at least 20,000 wrong drug prescriptions each year

■ more than 15,000 babies accidentally dropped each year by nurses and obstetricians

■ no electricity, water, or heat for about nine hours each year

■ 500 incorrect surgical operations each week

■ 2000 lost pieces of mail each hour

Are you satisfied with such quality? Neither was Motorola, one of the first recipients of the Malcolm Baldrige National Quality Award, which set the following goal in 1987:

Improve product and services quality ten times by 1989, and at least one hundred fold by 1991. Achieve six sigma capability by 1992. With a deep sense of urgency, spread dedication to quality to every facet of the corporation, and achieve a culture of continual improvement to assure total customer satisfaction. There is only one ultimate goal: zero defects—in everything we do.

The concept of *six sigma quality*—shrinking the process variation to half of the design tolerance ($C_p = 2.0$) while allowing the mean to shift as much as 1.5σ from the target—is explained by Figure 14.13. The area under the shifted curves *beyond* the six sigma ranges (the tolerance limits) is only 0.0000034, or 3.4 parts per million. If the process mean can be controlled to within 1.5 standard deviations of the target, a maximum of 3.4 defects per million can be expected. If it is held *exactly* on target (the shaded distribution in Figure 14.13), only 2.0 defects per *billion* would be expected.

You might wonder why one would allow a process shift of 1.5 standard deviations. As discussed in the next chapter, many common statistical process control plans are based on sample sizes that only allow detection of shifts of about two standard deviations. Thus, it would not be unusual for a process to drift this much and not be noticed.

A quality level of 3.4 defects per million can be achieved in several ways, for instance;

- with 0.5 sigma off-centering and five sigma quality
- with 1.0 sigma off-centering and 5.5 sigma quality
- with 1.5 sigma off-centering and 6 sigma quality[15]

These combinations are found in Table 14.6, which shows the number of non-conformances per million for different levels of quality and different levels of off-centering. In many cases, controlling the process to the target is less expensive than reducing the process variability. This table can help assess these tradeoffs.

At Motorola, six sigma became part of the common language of all employees. To them, it means near perfection, even if they do not understand the statistical details. (Some tell their co-workers, "Have a six-sigma weekend!") Since stating its goal, Motorola has made great strides in meeting this goal, achieving six

---

FIGURE 14.13   Six Sigma Quality

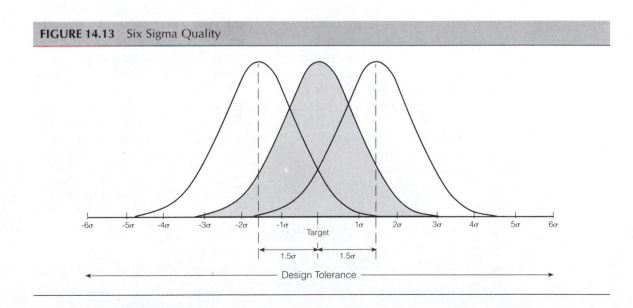

TABLE 14.6   The Number of Defectives (Parts per Million) for Specified Off-Centering of the Process and Quality Levels

Off-Centering	QUALITY LEVEL						
	3 sigma	3.5 sigma	4 sigma	4.5 sigma	5 sigma	5.5 sigma	6 sigma
0	2,700	465	63	6.8	0.57	0.034	0.002
0.25 sigma	3,577	666	99	12.8	1.02	0.1056	0.0063
0.5 sigma	6,440	1,382	236	32	3.4	0.71	0.019
0.75 sigma	12,288	3,011	665	88.5	11	1.02	0.1
1 sigma	22,832	6,433	1,350	233	32	3.4	0.39
1.25 sigma	40,111	12,201	3,000	577	88.5	10.7	1
1.5 sigma	66,803	22,800	6,200	1,350	233	32	3.4
1.75 sigma	105,601	40,100	12,200	3,000	577	88.4	11
2 sigma	158,700	66,800	22,800	6,200	1,300	233	32

sigma capability in many processes and four or five sigma levels in most others. Even in those departments that have reached the goal, Motorola employees continue their improvement efforts in order to reach the ultimate goal of zero defects. Many other companies have adopted this standard to challenge their own improvement efforts.

QUALITY CONTROL IN SERVICES

The most common quality characteristics in services, time (waiting time, service time, delivery time) and number of nonconformances, can be measured rather easily. Insurance companies, for example, measure the time to complete different transactions such as new issues, claim payments, and cash surrenders. Hospitals measure the percentage of nosocomial infections and the percentage of unplanned re-admissions to the emergency room, intensive care, or operating room within, say, 48 hours. Other quality characteristics are observable. These include the types of errors (wrong kind, wrong quantity, wrong delivery date, etc.) and behavior (courtesy, promptness, competency, and so on). Hospitals might monitor the completeness of medical charts and the quality of radiology readings, measured by a double-reading process.

Internal measurements of service quality are commonly performed with some type of data sheet or checklist. Time is easily measured by taking two observations: starting time and finishing time. Many observed data assume only "yes" or "no" values. For example, a survey of pharmaceutical operations in a hospital might include the following questions:

■ Are drug storage and preparation areas within the pharmacy under the supervision of a pharmacist?

■ Are drugs requiring special storage conditions properly stored?

■ Are drug emergency boxes inspected on a monthly basis?

■ Is the drug emergency box record book filled out completely?

Simple checksheets can be designed to record the types of errors that occur.

Even though human behavior is easily observable; describing and classifying the observations are far more difficult. The major obstacle is developing operational definitions of behavioral characteristics. For example, how does one define courteous versus discourteous, or understanding versus indifferent? Defining such distinctions is best done by comparing behavior against understandable standards. For instance, a standard for "courtesy" might be to address the customer as "Mr." or "Ms." Failure to do so is an instance of an error. "Promptness" might be defined as greeting a customer within five seconds of entering the store, or answering letters within two days of receipt. These behaviors can easily be recorded and counted. Figure 14.14 shows some behavioral questions used in a patient survey by a group of Southern California hospitals.[16]

The approach used by the Ritz-Carlton Hotel Company to capture and use customer satisfaction and quality-related data is proactive because of their intensive personalized service environment.[17] Systems for collecting and using customer reaction and satisfaction are widely deployed and used extensively throughout the organization. Their efforts are centered on various customer segments and product lines.

The Ritz-Carlton uses systems that allow every employee to collect and utilize quality-related data on a daily basis. These systems provide critical, responsive data, such as

1. On-line guest preference information
2. Quantity of error-free products and services

FIGURE 14.14 Sample Hospital Staff Behavior Questions

Admissions
11. Altogether, how long did you have to wait to be admitted?
    More than 1 hour: _____ (1)   1 hour: _____ (2)   30 min.: _____ (3)   15 min.: _____ (4)
12. If you had to wait 30 minutes or longer before someone met with you, were you told why?
    YES: _____ (1)   NO: _____ (2)   Did not wait 30 minutes: _____ (3)

Nursing Staff
21. Did a nurse talk to you about the procedures for the day?
    Never: _____ (1)   Sometimes: _____ (2)   Often: _____ (3)   Always: _____ (4)
22. Were you on IV fluids?
    YES: _____ (1)   NO: _____ (2)
    A. If YES, did the IV fluids ever run out?
       YES: _____ (1)   NO: _____ (2)

Medical Staff
28. Did the doctor do what he/she told you he was going to do?
    Never: _____ (1)   Sometimes: _____ (2)   Often: _____ (3)   Always: _____ (4)

Housekeeping
36. Did the housekeeper come into your room at least once a day?
    YES: _____ (1)   NO: _____ (2)
39. Was the bathroom adequately supplied?
    Always: _____ (1)   Often: _____ (2)   Sometimes: _____ (3)   Never: _____ (4)

X-Ray
When you received services from the x-ray technician, were the procedures explained to you?
    Always: _____ (1)   Often: _____ (2)   Sometimes: _____ (3)   Never: _____ (4)

Food
34. Generally, were your meals served at the same time each day?
    Always: _____ (1)   Often: _____ (2)   Sometimes: _____ (3)   Never: _____ (4)

3. Opportunities for quality improvement

An automated property management system gives employees on-line access to guest preference information at the individual customer level. All employees collect and input this data and then use the data as part of their service delivery with individual guests. The quality production reporting system is a method of aggregating hotel-level data from nearly two dozen sources into a summary format. It serves as an early warning system and facilitates analysis. The processes employees use to identify quality opportunities for improvement are standardized in a textbook, which is available throughout the organization. Individuals and teams have access to eight improvement mechanisms. Team improvement methods are functional (within a work area) while others are cross-functional (within a hotel). Some improvement opportunities receive the attention of national cross-functional teams (across hotels).

Employee performance data collected and utilized within the system are also used extensively to assess the capabilities of a prospective employee to meet specific job requirements. (Characteristic behaviors displayed by successful employees form the basis of a structured, empirical interview and selection process.)

Today, the goal of The Ritz-Carlton's business management system is to become more integrated, more proactive, and more preventive. Efforts are underway to check work continuously and evaluate whether employees are providing what the customer wants most: on time, every time. These test measures are then statistically charted to help teams determine when and where to act. The quality, marketing, and financial results of each hotel are aggregated and integrated to determine what quality factors are driving the financial outcome. These systems enable leaders and teams to better determine goals and justify expenditures.

◼ Sampling Techniques in Service Quality Control

Suppose that you worked in a 1000-bed hospital and wanted to determine the attitude of a certain group of patients toward the quality of care they received while in the hospital. Several factors should be considered before making this study:

1. What is the objective of the study?
2. What type of sample should be used?
3. What possible error might result from sampling?
4. What will the study cost?

One approach to tackling this problem would be to take a complete census—a survey of every person in the entire population. However, the objective of the study will dictate which method should be used to perform the study in the most effective and efficient manner. This decision requires sensitivity to the needs of the user and an understanding of the strengths and weaknesses of the specific techniques being used. Would sampling work just as well? If the user needs the results next week to make a decision involving the expenditure of $1000, the study will require a much different design from one in which the results influence a decision that will be made in six months and has a $1,000,000 expenditure. Sampling provides a distinct advantage over a complete census in that much less time and cost are required to gather the data. In many cases, such as inspection, sampling may be more accurate than 100 percent inspection because of reduction of inspection errors. However, sampling is frequently subject to a *higher degree* of error.

The second issue relates to different methods of sampling. The following are some of the most common:

■ *Simple random sampling:* Every item in the population has an equal probability of being selected.

■ *Stratified sampling:* The population is partitioned into groups, or strata, and a sample is selected from each stratum.

■ *Systematic sampling:* Every nth (4th, 5th, etc.) item is selected.

■ *Cluster sampling:* A typical group (division of the company, for example) is selected, and a random sample is taken from within the group.

■ *Judgment sampling:* Expert opinion is used to determine the location and characteristics of a definable sample group.

In choosing the appropriate type of sampling method, an analyst must consider what the sample is designed to do. A sampling study has a goal of selecting a sample at the lowest cost that will provide the best possible representation of the population, consistent with the objectives of precision and reliability that have been determined for the study.

Suppose that your objective is to provide a report to top management of the hospital to help them decide whether to expand the use of quality control measures within the hospital. Some issues that would have to be considered before choosing a sample would be the time frame for completing the study, the size and cost limitations of the sample, the accessibility of the population of patients, and the desired accuracy.

Assume that you have six weeks to complete the study, a limited operating budget of $1500, and a population of 800 maternity patients (the category in which you are interested) who could be involved in the quality study. Further assume that the accuracy of your study requires a sample of at least 400 patients and that the cost of each response would vary from $2 to $4, depending on how the survey is administered. Obviously, you would have to select a sample, since a complete census of all patients would not be feasible because of the budget limitation. Time limitations would make travel to conduct face-to-face interviews virtually impossible. Thus, the only feasible alternatives would be mailed questionnaires, telephone interviews, or a combination of the two.

Given this information, what type of sample should be chosen? Each type has advantages and disadvantages. A simple random sample would be easy to select but might not include sufficient representation by floor or ward. If a list of the patients, perhaps in alphabetical order, was available, a systematic sample of every fourth name could be easily selected. It would have the same disadvantages as the random sample, however. On the other hand, a cluster sample or judgment sample could be selected to include more representatives from floors or wards. However, cluster and judgment samples frequently take more time to identify and select appropriate sampling units. Also, because more subjective judgment is involved, a biased, nonrepresentative sampling plan is more likely to be developed.

The third issue in sampling relates to error. Errors in sampling generally stem from two causes: sampling error and systematic (often called nonsampling) error. Sampling error occurs naturally and results from the fact that a sample may not always be representative of the population, no matter how carefully it is selected. The only way to reduce sampling error is to take a *larger* sample from the population. Systematic errors, however, can be reduced or eliminated by design.

Sources of systematic error include the following:

■ *Bias:* the tendency to see problems and solutions from one's own viewpoint.

■ *Noncomparable data:* data that come from two populations but are erroneously considered to have come from one.

■ *Uncritical projection of trends:* the assumption that what has happened in the past will continue into the future.

■ *Causation:* the assumption that because two variables are related, one must be the cause of changes in the other.

■ *Improper sampling:* the use of an erroneous method for gathering data, thus biasing results (for example, using electronic mail surveys to get opinions from a population having few individuals with electronic mail services).

Sources of error can be overcome through careful planning of the sampling study. *Bias* can be reduced by frequent interaction with end-users of the study as well as cross-checking of research designs with knowledgeable analysts. *Noncomparable data* can be avoided by a sensitivity to conditions that could contribute to development of dissimilar population segments. In the hospital example, data gathered from different floors, wards, or shifts could prove to be noncomparable. In production firms, different shifts, machines, or products may define different populations, even though the characteristics being measured are the same for each. *Uncritical projection of trends* can be avoided by analysis of the underlying causes of trends and a constant questioning of the assumption that tomorrow's population will be the same as yesterday's. *Reasons for causation* must be investigated. Relationships between variables alone is not sufficient to conclude that causality exists. Causation can often be tested by holding one variable constant while changing the other to determine effects of the change. Finally, *improper sampling* can be avoided by a thorough understanding of sampling techniques and a determination of whether the method being used is capable of reaching any unit in the population in an unbiased fashion. This section concludes with some examples of sampling applications in quality control.

SIMPLE RANDOM SAMPLING

A **simple random sample** is a small sample of size n drawn from a large population of size N in such a way that every possible sample of size n has an equal chance of being selected. For example, if a box of 1000 plastic components for electrical connectors is thoroughly mixed and 25 parts are selected randomly without replacement, the random aspect of this definition has been satisfied. Simple random sampling forms the basis for most scientific statistical surveys, such as auditing, and is a useful tool for quality assurance studies. Many statistical procedures depend on taking random samples. If random samples are not used, bias may be introduced. For instance, if the items are rolled in coils, sampling only from the exposed end of the coil (a *convenience sample*) can easily result in bias if the production process that produced the coils varies over time.

Simple random samples can be selected by using a table of random numbers (see Appendix C). A unique number is assigned to each element of the population by using serial numbers, by placing the items in racks or trays with unique row and column numbering, or by associating with each item a physical distance (such as depth in a card file). Numbers are then chosen from the table in a systematic fashion. A sample is formed by selecting the items that correspond to the chosen random numbers. The selection may begin at any point in the table and move in any direction, using any set of digits that serves the sampler's purpose. An illustration of the use of the random number table for simple random sampling follows.

EXAMPLE 3   Sampling Medical Patient Records.   A particular nursing unit has 30 patients. Five patient records are to be sampled to verify the correctness of a medical procedure. To determine which patients to select, assign numbers 1 through 30 to the 30 patients. Select, for example, the first row in Appendix C and examine consecutive two-digit integers until five different numbers between 01 and 30 are found. (Any two-digit number greater than 30 is rejected since it does not correspond to an item in our population.) Thus, the following sequence of random numbers and decisions occurs.

Number	Decision
63	reject
27	select
15	select
99	reject
86	reject
71	reject
74	reject
45	reject
11	select
02	select
15	duplicate
14	select

Based on the preceding sequence, 2, 11, 14, 15, and 27 are selected.

Simple random sampling is generally used to estimate population parameters such as means, proportions, and variances. When using $\bar{x}$ to estimate a population mean, for example, one also needs to know how close the estimate is to the true population mean. The error due to sampling variability is given by the standard error of the mean, which is used to construct a confidence interval on the true population mean. The amount of error is determined by the sample size and is a crucial issue in sampling.

First, consider the sample size when using $\bar{x}$ to provide a point estimate of the population mean for variables data. A $100(1 - \alpha)$ percent confidence interval on $\bar{x}$ is given by

$$\bar{x} \pm z_{\alpha/2}\sigma/\sqrt{n}$$

Thus, a $1 - \alpha$ probability exists that the value of the sample mean will provide a sampling error of $z_{\alpha/2}\sigma/\sqrt{n}$ or less. This sampling error is denoted by E. Solving the equation

$$E = z_{\alpha/2}\sigma/\sqrt{n}$$

for n,

$$n = (z_{\alpha/2})^2\sigma^2/E^2$$

Thus, a sample size n will provide a point estimate having a sampling error of E or less at a confidence level of $100(1 - \alpha)$ percent.

To use this formula, specify the confidence level (from which $z_{\alpha/2}$ is obtained); the maximum sampling error E: and the standard deviation σ. If σ is unknown, at least a preliminary value is needed in order to compute n. A preliminary sample or a good guess based on prior data or similar studies can be used to estimate σ.

EXAMPLE 4   Sample Size Determination for Variables Data.   A firm conducting a process capability study on a critical quality dimension wishes to determine the sample size required to estimate the process mean with a sampling error of at most 0.1 at a 95 percent confidence level. From control chart data, an estimate of the standard deviation of the process was found to be 0.47. To find the appropriate sample size, the following calculations are used.

$$n = (z_{\alpha/2})^2\sigma^2/E^2$$

$$= (1.96)^2(0.47)^2/(0.1)^2$$

$$= 84.86 \text{ or } 85 \text{ units}$$

The next task is to determine the sample size for estimating a population proportion for attributes data. A point estimate of the population proportion, p, is given by the sample proportion $\bar{p}$. The standard error of the proportion is

$$\sigma_{\bar{p}} = \sqrt{p(1 - p)/n}$$

Thus, a $100(1 - \alpha)$ percent confidence interval for the population proportion is

$$\bar{p} \pm z_{\alpha/2}\sqrt{p(1 - p)/n}$$

The sampling error is given by $E = z_{\alpha/2}\sqrt{p(1 - p)/n}$. Solving this equation for n provides the following formula for the sample size:

$$n = (z_{\alpha/2})^2p(1 - p)/E^2$$

To apply this formula, a prior estimate of p is needed. If a good estimate is not known, use $p = 0.5$ since this value provides the largest sample size recommendation that guarantees the required level of precision.

EXAMPLE 5   Sample Size Determination for Attributes Data.   Suppose a sample from a large finished goods inventory is needed to determine the proportion of nonconforming product. Historically, about 0.5 percent level of nonconformance has been observed. A 90 percent confidence level with an allowable error of 0.25 percent is desired. Thus, $E = 0.0025$, $p = 0.005$, $z_{0.05} = 1.645$. The required sample size is

$$n = (1.96)^20.005(1 - 0.005)/(0.0025)^2 = 3058$$

In some situations, certain activities are so critical that only a small number of nonconformances is tolerable. A typical example is in health care; compliance with rigorous procedures must be adhered to 100 percent of the time. A nursing manager, for instance, will need to determine a sample size necessary to reveal at least one error in the sample if the population occurrence rate is equal to or greater than a specified critical rate of occurrence.

A technique used in such situations is called *discovery sampling.* Discovery sampling is a statistical sampling plan used for attributes in which the expected rate of occurrence in most cases is zero, and the maximum tolerable rate of occurrence is critical and thus very small. Discovery sampling tables have been published for selecting the appropriate sample size.[18] An example is shown in Table 14.7. One must know the population size and critical rate of occurrence and must specify the desired confidence level. The table gives the probability of finding at least one occurrence in the sample.

EXAMPLE 6 An Application of Discovery Sampling. Suppose that a nursing manager wants to be 95 percent confident of finding at least one incident in which nursing personnel have failed to comply with a critical procedure. If 1000 patient charts were prepared during the period under consideration and the critical rate of occurrence is 2 percent, Table 14.7 shows that 200 charts must be examined. If one occurrence is found in this random sample, the manager can conclude with 98.9 percent confidence that the quality of patient care in this area is unacceptable.

TABLE 14.7 Discovery Sampling Table

	CRITICAL OCCURRENCE RATE						
	0.05%	0.1%	0.5%	1%	2%	5%	10%
Sample Size	*Probability of Finding at Least One Occurrence*						
				Population Size: 1000			
10		1.0%	4.9%	9.6%	18.4%	40.3%	65.3%
25		2.5	11.9	22.5	40.0	72.7	93.1
50		5.0	22.7	40.3	64.5	92.8	99.6
100		10.0	41.0	65.3	88.1	99.6	100.0
200		20.0	67.3	89.4	98.9	100.0	100.0
400		40.0	92.3	99.4	100.0	100.0	100.0
				Population Size: 2000			
10	0.5%	1.0%	4.9%	9.6%	18.3%	40.2%	65.2%
50	2.5	4.9	22.4	39.9	64.0	92.6	99.5
100	5.0	9.8	40.2	64.3	87.4	99.5	100.0
200	10.0	19.0	65.2	88.0	98.6	100.0	100.0
400	20.0	36.0	89.3	98.9	100.0	100.0	100.0
600	30.0	51.0	97.2	99.9	100.0	100.0	100.0

SOURCE: Adapted from H. P. Hill, J. L. Roth and H. Arkin, *Sampling in Auditing: A Simplified Guide and Statistical Tables,* (New York: Ronald Press, 1962).

OTHER TYPES OF SAMPLING PROCEDURES

Alternatives to simple random sampling are available and are discussed briefly here. These methods have distinct advantages over simple random sampling in many situations.

■ **Stratified Random Sampling** A **stratified random sample** is one obtained by separating the population into nonoverlapping groups, and then selecting a simple random sample from each group. The groups might be different machines, wards in a hospital, departments, and so on. For example, suppose a population of 28,000 items is produced on three different machines:

Machine	Group Size
1	20,000
2	5,000
3	3,000

Assume that a specific confidence level requires a sample of 525 units in this case. One could draw these units randomly from the entire population. Under stratified random sampling, a simple random sample of 250 units from machine 1, 150 units from machine 2, and 125 units from machine 3 might be taken. Formulas are available for combining the results of individual samples into an overall estimate of the population parameter of interest. This technique will demonstrate quality differences that may exist between machines.

Stratified random sampling will provide results similar to simple random sampling but with a smaller total sample size. It produces a smaller bound on the error of the estimation that would be produced by a simple random sample of the same size. These statements are particularly true if measurements within each group are homogeneous, that is, if the units within strata are alike.

■ **Systematic Sampling** In some situations, particularly with large populations, selecting a simple random sample using random number tables and searching through the population for the corresponding element is impractical. With systematic sampling, the population size is divided by the sample size required, yielding a value for n. The first item is chosen at random from among the first n items. Thereafter, every nth item is selected. For example, suppose that a population has 4000 units and a sample of size 50 is required. Select the first unit randomly from among the first 80 units. Every 80th (4000/50) item after that would be selected.

Systematic sampling is based on the assumption that since the first element is chosen at random, the entire sample will have the properties of a simple random sample. This method should be used with caution since quality characteristics may vary in some periodic fashion with the length of the sampling interval and thus bias the results.

■ **Cluster Sampling** In **cluster sampling,** the population is first partitioned into groups of elements called clusters. A simple random sample of the clusters is selected. The elements within the clusters selected constitute the sample. For example, suppose that products are boxed in groups of 50. Each box can be regarded as a cluster. We would draw a sample of boxes and inspect all units in the boxes selected.

Cluster sampling tends to provide good results when the elements within the clusters are not alike (heterogeneous). In this case, each cluster would be representative of the entire population.

■ **Judgment Sampling** With **judgment sampling,** an arbitrary sample of pertinent data is examined and the percentage of nonconformances is calculated.

Since judgment sampling is not random, the risks associated with making an incorrect conclusion cannot be quantified. Thus, it is not a preferred method of sampling.

J. Boutaris & Sons, S.A., is a major wine producer in Greece with annual sales of about $40 million. The company operates two major wineries and three smaller local wineries, producing 20 different wines and the traditional Greek ouzo. Thirty percent are exported around the world. As international competition increased in the early 1990s, Boutaris decided to become more systematic about quality by shaping a more specific quality policy and designing quality control procedures for incoming materials, for its products, and for its bottling and packaging processes.

A pilot study began with an analysis of the entire production process of two representative wines, from gathering grapes to storing the final products. Activities were grouped into four categories: operations, inspections, transportation, and storage. This analysis resulted in two detailed process flowcharts. Next, the study team identified quality characteristics of the final products and the key quality factors at intermediate steps of the production process, which were classified in a four-level hierarchy. At the first level, they defined three categories: content (wine), bottling (materials and processes), and packaging. At the second level, they classified quality characteristics of the final product according to the three categories of the first level. At the third level, materials supplied by external suppliers and production processes were considered. Finally, at the fourth level, all quality factors for every material and production process of the previous level, as well as the inspection points on the flowchart at which every quality factor may be controlled was recorded. Their efforts resulted in the two tree diagrams shown in Figure 14.15. Figure 14.15(a) shows the first and second levels for one product; Figure 14.15(b) shows the third and fourth levels for a single quality characteristic (hermeticity - the tightness of the seal). The second diagram shows the controllable quality factors in materials and processes that affect the product quality characteristic. For each of the two pilot products, more than 200 factors were identified.

After these quality characteristics were identified, the team established quantitative or qualitative specifications based on current company practice, quality goals, international standards, legislation of the European Economic Community, supplier and internal process capabilities, and accuracy of inspection and measurement methods.

The large number of quality factors made it too difficult to develop detailed quality control schemes for all of them. As an alternative, they classified quality factors into two categories: procedural and statistical. The first category included all those factors for which deviations from specifications arose from failure to follow established procedures, rather than from random causes—about 20–30 factors for the two products. Most of these factors related to the wine-making process, such as the duration of aging and the correspondence between label and actual content. Procedures were written and incorporated into the company's quality manual.

The second category contained the remaining factors that were attributable to common and special causes. The team evaluated the relative importance of these factors along two dimensions: frequency and economic consequence of nonconformance. They used Pareto analysis to identify the most important factors along these dimensions. As a result, they identified approximately 45 critical factors for control using statistical quality control methods.

The team performed repeated measurements to establish the accuracy of measuring methods, especially for quality factors during the wine-making process, such as total acidity. Random samples from lots of incoming materials were drawn, and all critical quality factors were measured and recorded. Finally, they monitored critical processes, such as filling, closely under controlled conditions for several weeks to measure the process capabilities. The analysis of the data indicated that in some cases, specifications were too tight for the process capabilities. After reexamination, some were found to be unnecessarily strict and were relaxed. In some critical cases, specifications were revised to give

FIGURE 14.15   Hierarchy of Quality Characteristics

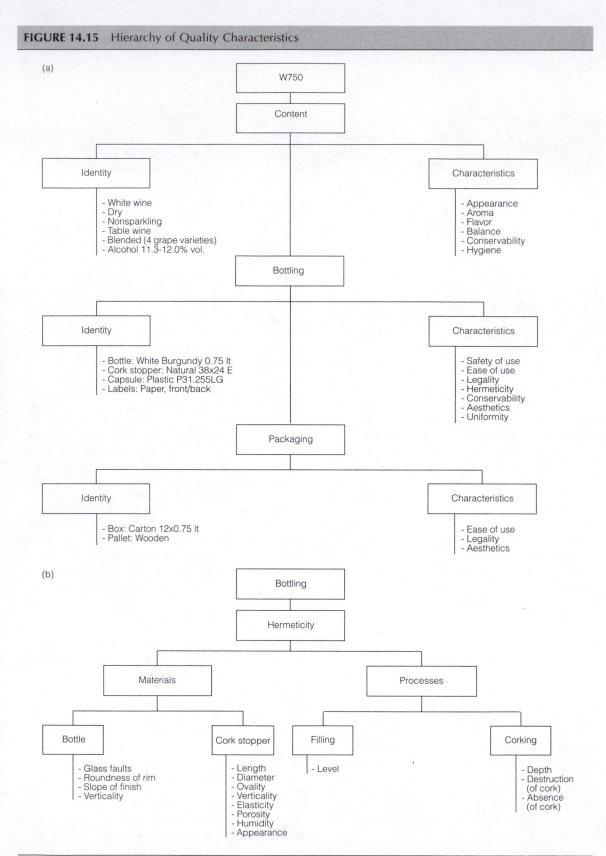

suppliers the time to improve their quality, with the understanding that they would be gradually tightened to promote continuous improvement.

For critical supplier quality factors, acceptance sampling plans were designed, and control charts were developed for process control characteristics. These procedures were implemented in actual production and receiving processes for a trial period to uncover any problems that might result. Training at all levels of managers and operators was an important part of the implementation process. The company revised nearly all job descriptions to reflect the new roles of employees in quality control and improvement. Employees reacted positively to these efforts, mainly because of the personal approach to their quality training and involvement in the project from the early stages.

Before it implemented this quality assurance system, Boutaris's lack of proper analysis of inspection results often led it to make poor decisions. The formal statistical methods allowed the company to make a reliable quantitative evaluation of each lot of incoming materials and each internal process, helping suppliers and process managers understand their weaknesses and improve quality. One example of the success of the program was improved her-

meticity. Hermeticity is expressed as the pressure required for air to penetrate the bottle and is the most important factor in the longevity of wine. Bottle characteristics such as roundness of rim and cork length, diameter, and porosity influence this characteristic. In 18 months, the percent nonconforming fell from 15 percent to less than 5 percent. The positioning of labels, which affects the aesthetics of the final product, was improved through statistical process control from a 10 percent nonconforming level to less than 2 percent. The introduction of these new procedures helped Boutaris achieve ISO 9002 certification a few years later.

Key Issues for Discussion

1. Explain the use of flowcharts and tree diagrams for identifying critical quality characteristics. How might this approach be used to develop quality assurance procedures for pizza preparation (or some other product with which you are familiar)?

2. Explain the importance of understanding process capability in setting standards and specifications. How can lessons learned from this case be generalized?

A PROCESS CAPABILITY STUDY[20]

The Hydraulic Lift Company (HLC) manufactures freight elevators and automotive lifts used in garages and service stations. Figure 14.16 shows a sim-

plified diagram of a hydraulic lift. The check valve is an important component in the system. Its purpose is to control the flow of hydraulic oil from the

---

FIGURE 14.16   Simplified Diagram of a Hydraulic Lift

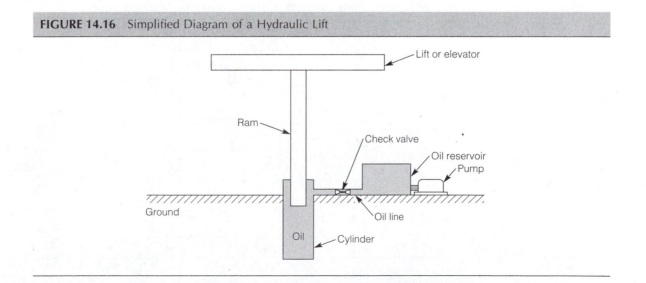

FIGURE 14.17   Average Scrap Cost per Month

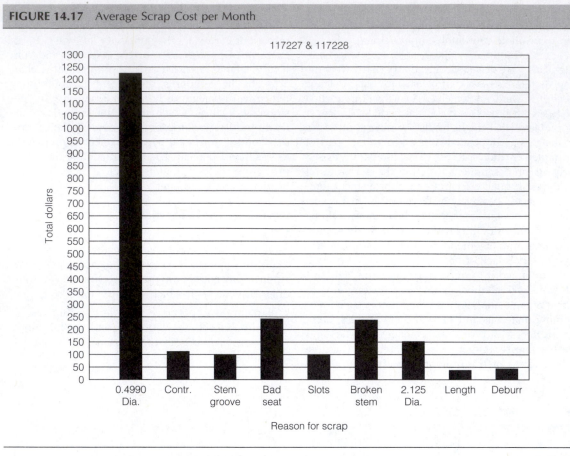

FIGURE 14.18   Part No. 117227 Check Valve Piston

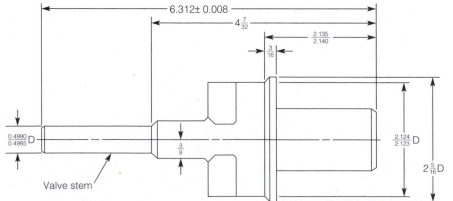

oil reservoir to the cylinder when the elevator is rising. As the elevator descends, the rate at which oil flows from the cylinder back to the reservoir is also controlled by the check valve.

One of the most important parts of the check valve is the piston, which moves within the valve body as the valve is opened or closed. The quality manager at HLC noticed that scrap rates on the piston had been very high over the past three years. Two models (part numbers 117227 and 117228) of check valve pistons are being manufactured. Because of extremely critical tolerances, these parts are among the most difficult ones produced in the machine shop.

A study to determine the magnitude of the problem revealed that approximately $2200 per month worth of parts had been scrapped over the past three years (see Figure 14.17). This amount translates to about 14 percent of total production of the parts, a scrap rate that is considered unacceptable. About half of the defective items were scrapped due to inability of the process to hold a 0.4990/0.4985 inch tolerance on the valve stem (see Figure 14.18). The machining operation used to shape the valve stem

FIGURE 14.19   Process Capability Data for the Hydraulic Lift Company

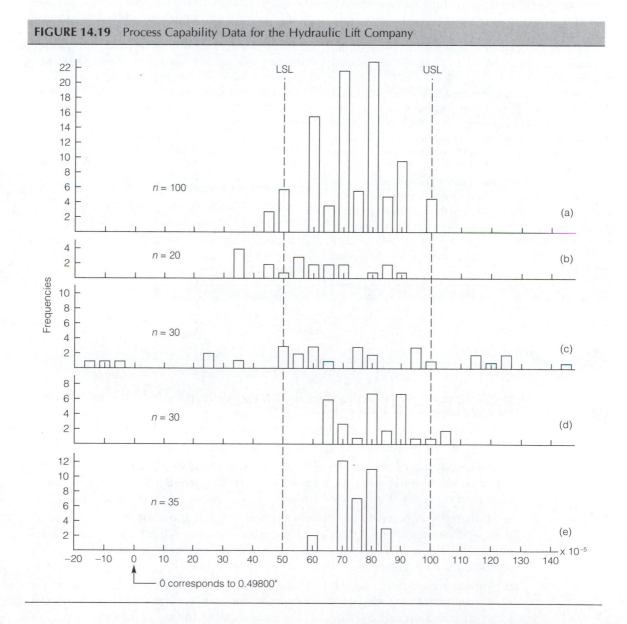

is performed on a grinding machine, which should have the capability of holding a tolerance within 0.0001–0.0002 inch under standard operating conditions. Manufacturing engineers and the quality manager decided to do a process capability study on one part (no. 117227) to gather statistical data on the stem problem and make a recommendation for improvements.

For the first step, an operator ran 100 parts using the standard production methods. Results of the study [see the histogram in Figure 14.19(a)] revealed that a machine problem existed. The data showed that a few parts were being produced outside the specifications. In addition, the strange shape of the histogram for dimensions within the specification limits prompted an investigation into the possibility of instability of the process. The study team observed that the operator was constantly adjusting the machine setting to try to hold to the specified tolerance.

As a check on machine capability, the team asked the operator to run 20 parts without adjusting the machine, which resulted in scrapping six of 20 parts, a 30 percent scrap rate [see Figure 14.19(b)]. This test verified that the machine needed some major adjustments.

The machine manufacturer was contacted and a technician was dispatched to the plant. A run of 30 parts was made to show how the machine operated. Twelve of the thirty pieces were defective, with the stem dimension out of tolerance [see Figure 14.19(c)]. The technician made the following adjustments:

- Installed new gaskets.
- Cleaned machine, adding oil and coolant.
- Loaded hand wheel bearing for more positive control.
- Reset retard pressure on grind wheel.
- Adjusted stone dresser mechanism.
- Reset dwell time (time the grindstone stays on the work piece after reaching final diameter).

The results of these adjustments were significant. Another 30 parts were run, with only two falling outside the tolerance limits [Figure 14.19(d)]. The team still did not consider the process to be fully satisfactory. The manufacturer's technician said that the grinder "ways" (channels on which the machine head travels) would have to be reground and that some parts in the machine would have to be replaced. This recommendation was made to management, who agreed to have the machine overhauled as required.

After the work was completed, a run of 35 parts was made. The results, shown in Figure 14.19(e), showed that all parts were well within tolerance limits. As a final step, operators and maintenance personnel were instructed on the proper use and care of the machine.

Key Issues for Discussion

1. Using the histograms in Figure 14.19, estimate the process capability indexes for each situation.

2. Discuss the approach used in this case in terms of the general program-solving process presented in Chapter 9.

SUMMARY OF KEY POINTS

- Traditional inspection practices involve heavy inspection of incoming materials and final product, with a focus on separating the good from the bad. These practices are inefficient and ineffective. Inspection should be used as an auditing tool to control processes and identify opportunities for improvement.
- Various types of gauges, measuring instruments, and automated technology are used in manufacturing to measure quality characteristics. In services, measurement typically is conducted by surveys and other forms of observation.
- Statistics is concerned with the collection, organization, analysis, interpretation, and presentation of data and has extensive applications in quality assurance. The three basic components of statistical methodology are descriptive statistics, statistical inference, and predictive statistics.
- Sample statistics are used to obtain estimates of population parameters. To make probability statements about sample statistics, we need to know the sampling distribution and its standard deviation, called the standard error.

■ Statistical methods are useful in metrology to assess the accuracy, precision, and reproducibility of measurement instruments.

■ Process capability is the range over which the natural variation of a process occurs as determined by the system of common causes. It is determined through statistical analysis of variation in a production process and measured relative to specifications by process capability indexes.

■ *Six sigma* is a term coined by Motorola to designate at most 3.4 defects per million opportunities and has become a stretch standard for many world-class companies. Formally, the six sigma concept refers to acceptable variation that is one-half the tolerance, allowing for a drift in the mean of 1.5 standard deviations in either direction.

■ Many service quality characteristics are measurable; others are observable. In either case, they may be controlled in a manner similar to the control of manufacturing characteristics. Statistical sampling is used extensively in services to collect data for analysis and control.

REVIEW QUESTIONS

1. List the reasons why inspection will always be around to some extent, despite the total quality management philosophy.

2. Briefly describe the different types and applications of fixed and variable gauges.

3. Describe some of the uses of automated technology in inspection and measurement.

4. Discuss the differences between the three major components of statistical methodology (descriptive statistics, statistical inference, and predictive statistics). Why might this distinction be important to a manager?

5. Define a population and a sample. What are their major characteristics?

6. State the meaning of the central limit theorem in your own terms. How important is it to the development and use of statistical quality control techniques?

7. What is the standard error of the mean? How does it differ from the standard deviation?

8. Contrast traditional and modern inspection practices in receiving and manufacturing. How do modern practices support the quality philosophies of Deming and others?

9. What is an *acceptance sampling plan*?

10. Why is acceptance sampling no longer a preferred method for quality control?

11. What factors should determine which quality characteristics to inspect in manufacturing?

12. Describe approaches used to locate inspection activities in manufacturing.

13. Explain the economic tradeoffs in determining whether to inspect all or nothing.

14. What are the challenges of visual inspection? How can human-factor impediments to visual inspection be reduced?

15. What is the difference between accuracy, precision, and reproducibility?

16. What is calibration and why is it important to managing data?

17. Explain the term *process capability*.

18. Explain how a process can be in control but simultaneously outside design specifications. Relate this occurrence to process capability and to product design specifications.

19. Discuss the methodology of conducting a process capability study.

20. Define the process capability index, C_p, and explain how it may be used to establish or improve quality policies in operating areas or with suppliers.

21. Explain the concept of *six sigma*.

22. Discuss service quality measurements that would be applicable to the following:

    a. local and intercity buses

    b. sightseeing tours

    c. department stores

    d. electric power company

    e. hotel and motels.

23. What two factors influence sampling procedures?

24. Discuss the basic questions that must be addressed in a sampling study.

25. Describe the different methods of sample selection and provide an example in which each would be most appropriate.

26. What are the sources of systematic error in sampling? How can systematic error be overcome?

PROBLEMS

1. A radio manufacturer using 100 percent inspection was finding an average of two nonconforming items out of lots of 10,000 purchased electronic components. The estimated cost of inspecting the component is $0.25, while the cost of replacing a nonconforming component after it has been assembled is about $25. What is the best economic inspection decision? How much is the manufacturer saving or losing per radio under the current inspection practice if each radio contains 60 of these components?

2. The cost to inspect a credit card statement in a bank is 25 cents, while correction of a mistake later amounts to $500. What is the break-even point in errors per thousand transactions for which 100 percent inspection is no more economical than no inspection?

3. Ten parts are measured using two different instruments. The nominal specification for the part is 0.05. Which instrument is more accurate? More precise? Which one is the better instrument?

Instrument A					Instrument B				
0.06	0.07	0.06	0.05	0.06	0.05	0.07	0.07	0.06	0.04
0.05	0.06	0.06	0.07	0.06	0.05	0.04	0.07	0.04	0.05

4. A gauge repeatability and reproducibility study collected the following data. Analyze these data. The part specification is 1.0 ± 0.06.

Part/Trial	OPERATOR 1			OPERATOR 2		
	1	2	3	1	2	3
1	0.97	0.99	0.99	0.96	0.99	1.00
2	0.94	0.96	0.97	0.95	1.00	1.00
3	1.00	1.00	0.99	1.02	1.03	1.00
4	0.97	1.00	0.99	0.96	0.98	0.98
5	0.99	1.00	1.00	1.01	1.01	1.03
6	1.02	1.04	1.03	0.99	1.02	1.02
7	0.96	1.01	0.98	0.97	0.97	0.99
8	1.00	1.02	0.97	1.07	1.02	1.00
9	1.03	1.01	1.00	1.04	1.02	0.98
10	0.96	0.98	0.95	0.99	0.95	0.95

(Except as indicated, all of the following problems assume that the quality characteristics are normally distributed.)

5. Jamaican Punch is sold in 11-ounce cans. The mean number of ounces placed in a can is 10.75 with a standard deviation of 0.1 ounce. Assuming a normal distribution, what is the probability that the filling machine will cause an overflow in a can, that is, the probability that more than 11 ounces will be placed in the can?

6. The standard deviation of the weight of filled containers is 0.7 ounce. If 3 percent of the containers contain less than 20 ounces, what is the mean filling weight of the containers?

7. In filling bottles of cola, the average amount of overfilling should be kept as low as possible. If the mean fill volume is 16.05 ounces and the standard deviation is 0.03 ounce, what percentage of bottles will have less than 16 ounces? More than 16.10 ounces (assuming no overflow)?

8. The data and histogram show the weight of castings (in kilograms) being made in a foundry. Based on this sample of 100 castings, find the mean and standard deviation of the sample.

Class	Midpoint	Frequency
1	37.5	1
2	37.8	4
3	38.1	9
4	38.4	29
5	38.7	30
6	39.0	15
7	39.3	7
8	39.6	3
9	39.9	2

9. Plot the data from Problem 8 on normal probability paper to determine if the distribution of the data is approximately normal.

10. Referring again to Problem 8, if the upper tolerance limit (UTL) of the process is 40.5 and the lower tolerance limit (LTL) is 36.9, calculate the process capability index. Is it within satisfactory limits? How much reduction in the *sample* standard deviation would be required to bring the process capability index up to 2.00?

11. Sets of precision weights are being manufactured for use with pharmaceutical scales. One of the set is a 100-gram weight with a tolerance of ±0.05 gram. Two production lines manufacture the weights. The following values (obtained by subtracting 100 from the measured values and then multiplying by 100) were observed when a sample of 60 weights was taken from each line.

Line 1						Line 2					
4	5	3	2	1	3	−4	−1	−1	−4	−3	1
4	−1	4	3	1	3	3	−1	−1	1	−2	−2
−1	2	1	0	1	2	2	−5	0	0	−6	3
2	2	3	3	2	3	−3	1	2	−1	2	−1
2	3	5	0	0	1	0	0	−4	−2	0	−1
5	0	2	3	0	3	−1	1	0	−3	−1	−2
0	−1	4	2	−1	4	1	0	−3	0	−6	1
7	1	4	1	2	1	−2	0	0	−3	−2	−2
4	1	3	5	4	5	−4	2	−5	0	2	0
6	3	2	−2	4	3	−3	1	−1	−1	−2	1

a. Construct histograms for each line and for the two lines combined.

b. Check the relationships of the distributions to the tolerance limits using the histograms and calculated means and standard deviations.

c. Interpret your results.

12. A machining process has a required dimension on a part of 0.575 ± 0.007". Five samples of five parts each were measured as given below. What is its capability for producing within acceptable limits?

		SAMPLE		
1	2	3	4	5
0.557	0.574	0.573	0.575	0.576
0.566	0.587	0.578	0.565	0.577
0.576	0.578	0.577	0.582	0.576
0.564	0.573	0.579	0.573	0.572
0.580	0.584	0.580	0.578	0.574

13. Adjustments were made in the process discussed in Problem 12 and five more samples of five parts each were measured. The results are given below. What can you observe about the process now? What is its capability for producing within acceptable limits now?

		SAMPLE		
1	2	3	4	5
0.571	0.575	0.573	0.576	0.576
0.578	0.575	0.574	0.571	0.574
0.576	0.573	0.571	0.577	0.575
0.579	0.577	0.575	0.570	0.575
0.574	0.576	0.579	0.575	0.576

14. Samples for three parts were taken as shown below. Data set 1 is for part 1, data set 2 is for part 2, and data set 3 is for part 3.

Data set 1				
1.74831	1.7574	1.75134	1.73316	1.75134
1.71498	1.75437	1.73619	1.73922	1.73619
1.74528	1.74831	1.76346	1.74528	1.76952
1.70892	1.75134	1.71195	1.74831	1.77861
1.7574	1.73619	1.74225	1.74528	1.73922
Data set 2				
2.01144	2.00448	2.01492	2.00448	2.00448
2.001	2.00796	2.001	1.98708	1.99752
1.99752	2.001	1.99404	2.00796	2.00448
2.00448	2.001	1.99752	2.001	2.001
1.98708	1.99404	1.98708	1.9836	2.001
Data set 3				
1.25426	1.24775	1.24558	1.24992	1.23907
1.2586	1.25643	1.25209	1.25426	1.24341
1.25643	1.24775	1.24341	1.24558	1.23907
1.24124	1.24558	1.24992	1.25209	1.24992
1.24992	1.24558	1.24992	1.24775	1.24775

a. Calculate the mean and standard deviations for each part and compare them to the specification limits given below:

Part	Nominal	Tolerance
1	1.750	±0.045
2	2.000	±0.060
3	1.250	±0.030

b. Will the production process permit an acceptable fit of all parts into a slot with a specification of 5 ± 0.081 at least 99.73 percent of the time?

15. A utility requires service operators to answer telephone calls from customers in an average time of 0.1 minute, with a tolerance of +0.04 and −0.06 minute. A sample of 50 actual operator times was drawn, and the results are given in the following table. In addition, operators are expected to ascertain customer needs and either respond to them or refer the customer to the proper department within 0.5 minute with a tolerance of +0.20 and −0.30 minute. Another sample of 50 times was taken for this activity and is also given in the table. If these variables can be considered to be independent, how often can the total time be expected to vary from 0.6 minute, with a tolerance of +0.24 and −0.36 minute?

Component	Mean Time	Standard Deviation
Answer	0.1023	0.0183
Service	0.5044	0.0902

16. For the following data, construct a histogram and estimate the process capability. If the specifications are 24 ± 0.03, estimate the percentage of parts that will be nonconforming. Finally, compute C_p, C_{pu}, and C_{pl}.

24.029	24.003	24.020	23.991	24.008
23.996	23.991	24.000	24.005	24.011
23.989	24.023	24.020	24.004	24.004
24.002	23.998	23.993	24.016	24.010
23.991	24.008	24.015	23.990	24.013
24.010	23.995	23.997	23.988	23.996
23.995	24.004	23.994	24.001	24.006
23.986	24.001	23.995	24.013	23.990
24.008	23.996	24.010	24.002	24.005
23.999	24.000	23.991	24.007	23.992
23.994	23.997	23.995	23.994	24.001
24.000	24.001	24.007	23.995	24.000
23.984	24.001	23.996	24.013	23.999
23.984	24.000	23.994	23.971	24.008
24.011	24.015	23.998	23.997	24.009
23.995	23.999	24.005	23.985	24.002
23.994	24.010	23.988	24.003	24.009
24.005	24.009	24.018	24.003	23.998
23.983	24.001	24.003	24.006	23.996
24.000	24.013	24.009	24.019	24.007

17. An agricultural fertilizer is packed in 100-pound bags. The weights of 15 randomly selected bags are given at the top of the next page. Using normal probability paper, determine whether or not the data are normal and estimate the process capability.

94.75	97.05	97.70	97.75	98.60
99.60	99.65	99.75	100.50	100.75
101.00	101.75	101.80	102.00	102.50

18. Suppose that a process with a normally distributed output has a mean of 50.25 and a variance of 2.25.

   a. If the specifications are 50.25 ± 4.00, compute C_p and the one-sided process capability indexes and interpret their meaning.

   b. Suppose the mean shifts of 50.00. Recompute and interpret the process capability indexes.

   c. If the variance can be reduced to 81 percent of its original value, how do the process capability indexes change (using the original mean of 50.25)?

19. A process has upper and lower tolerance limits of 5.60 and 5.20, respectively. If the customer requires a demonstrated C_p of 2.0, what must the process capability be? If both C_{pu} and C_{pl} must also be 2.0, determine the mean and standard deviation of the process, assuming a normal distribution of output.

20. Ten samples of five items each were taken on a drilled hole dimension in an engine block, as given below. What is the estimated population process capability (6-sigma spread) based on these samples?

1	2	3	4	5	6	7	8	9	10
0.207	0.211	0.206	0.207	0.210	0.205	0.206	0.210	0.206	0.208
0.209	0.207	0.208	0.209	0.210	0.207	0.210	0.208	0.208	0.209
0.207	0.208	0.210	0.208	0.205	0.211	0.211	0.206	0.206	0.209
0.206	0.207	0.203	0.209	0.207	0.208	0.212	0.207	0.208	0.207
0.211	0.207	0.231	0.209	0.213	0.211	0.204	0.206	0.210	0.209

21. Prepare a frequency distribution histogram for the data in Problem 20. Show the mean and standard deviation and the estimated 6-sigma spread for the process.

22. If the required tolerance in Problem 20 is 0.210 ± 0.005, calculate and interpret the process capability indexes C_p and C_{pk}.

23. You wish to obtain a simple random sample from your class in order to conduct a survey. Describe how to use the random numbers in Appendix C to obtain a sample of 50 percent of your class. Draw the sample and compare it to the class profile (male/female, academic major, etc.).

24. Using Table 14.7, suppose that the population consists of 2,000 units. The critical rate of occurrence is 1 percent, and you wish to be 99 percent confident of finding at least one nonconformity. What sample size should you select?

25. Determine the appropriate sample size to estimate the proportion of sorting errors at a post office at a 95 percent confidence level. Historically, the error rate is 0.022 percent, and you wish to have an allowable error of 0.01.

CASE

Acme Parts Ltd.

Acme Parts Ltd. (APL) is a small manufacturing company that produces various parts for tool manufacturers. One of APL's production processes in-

volves producing a metal spacer plate that has a tolerance of 0.05 to 0.100 cm in thickness. On the recommendation of the quality assurance (QA) department and over objections of the plant manager, APL had just purchased some new equipment to make these parts. Recently, the production manager was receiving complaints from customers about high levels of nonconforming parts. He suspected the new equipment, but neither QA nor plant management would listen.

The manager discussed the issue with one of his production supervisors who mentioned that she had just collected some process data for a study that the quality assurance department was undertaking. The manager decided that he would prove his point by showing that the new equipment was not capable of meeting the specifications. Table 14.8 shows data provided by the supervisor.

Assignment

Perform the process capability study on these data and interpret your results. [Hint: *The Quality Management Analyst* software provided with the Instructor's Manual may be used to make these calculations.]

When the production manager shared these results with QA, one of the quality assurance engineers laughingly noted that the data were actually collected as part of a gauge verification study. The data in columns 1 and 2 actually were two observations by the same operator using his assigned gauge, and with no knowledge of the measurements that he had made earlier of the same part. Likewise, the data in columns 3 and 4 were observations on *exactly* the same parts, by a second operator, using her different, assigned gauge. Thus, data were from two operators, two gauges, and 15 parts that were measured twice, independently by the two operators.

Assignment

What questions should the production manager now raise to ensure that he has the "right" data on which to make a decision and recommendation about the process?

The engineer pointed out that variations in the data could be traced to three causes: repeatability

TABLE 14.8   Original Data Set

Sample	Observations			
1	.0650	.0600	.0650	.0550
2	.100	.105	.1050	.0950
3	.085	.080	.0820	.0750
4	.085	.095	.0820	.0940
5	.055	.058	.0485	.0525
6	.0875	.0915	.0945	.0925
7	.0920	.0880	.0990	.0900
8	.0850	.0800	.0750	.0700
9	.8900	.9800	.9200	.0990
10	.0600	.0700	.0550	.0640
11	.0680	.0750	.0670	.0720
12	.0545	.0500	.0525	.0495
13	.0800	.0910	.0870	.0820
14	.0700	.0805	.0865	.0830
15	.0750	.0650	.0650	.0680

problems (equipment variation or EV), reproducibility variations (operator variation or OV), and process variation (part variation or PV). Thus, total variation (TV) could be seen as made up of repeatability and reproducibility (RR) variation and PV. Team members had heard about EV, OV, and RR in a training class on measurement, but realized that the last item was an obvious, but important point that they had not previously considered. They were given the following formulas for computation of the PV and TV:

$$PV = R_p \times K_3$$

and

$$TV = \sqrt{(RR)^2 + (PV)^2}$$

The R_p value is obtained by calculating the range of the sample averages in a gauge study. The K_3 value depends on the number of parts measured in the study. Some of these values are found in Table 14.9.

Assignment

Calculate the RR, process and total variation for the data.[21] Using the TV as the divisor, calculate the percentage of *total variation* that the EV, OV, RR, and

TABLE 14.9   Numbers of Parts versus K_3 Factors

NUMBER OF PARTS IN THE STUDY										
5	6	7	8	9	10	11	12	13	14	15
2.08	1.93	1.82	1.74	1.67	1.62	1.57	1.54	1.51	1.48	1.45

PV encompass. (Note: these variations are not directly related to one another, so the percentages will not total to 100 percent.) What conclusions can you draw about the variations that were observed?

Based on your analysis, what recommendations could you make on how the measurement system could be improved? What would *you* tell the production manager?

NOTES

1. Stuart F. Brown, "Building Cars with Machines that See," *Popular Science* (October 1985).
2. *Fortune*, 27 June, 1994, 131.
3. J. M. Juran and Frank M. Gryna, Jr., *Quality Planning and Analysis*, 2d ed. (New York: McGraw-Hill, 1980), 35.
4. Frank H. Squires, "The Triumph of Statistics," *Quality*, February 1982, 75.
5. Adapted from G. J. Hahn and W. Q. Meeker, "Assumptions for Statistical Inference," *The American Statistician* 47 (1993), 1–11.
6. Dan K. Fitzsimmons, "Gaining Acceptance for Accpetance Sampling," *Quality Progress* (April 1989), 46–48.
7. Douglas C. Montgomery, *Introduction to Statistical Quality Control* (New York: John Wiley & Sons, 1991).
8. Texas Instruments Defense Systems & Electronics Group, *Malcolm Baldrige Application Summary* (1992).
9. Thomas Pyzdek, *Pyzdek's Guide to SPC, Volume Two—Applications and Special Topics* (Milwaukee, WI: ASQC Quality Press, 1992).
10. Ed Pena, "Motorola's Secret to Total Quality Control," *Quality Progress* (October 1990), 43–45.
11. Douglas H. Harris and Frederick B. Chaney, *Human Factors in Quality Assurance* (New York: John Wiley, 1969).
12. *ASQC Automotive Division Statistical Process Control Manual* (Milwaukee, WI: American Society for Quality Control, 1986).
13. The point (10.90,1.000) is not plotted, since the normal curve extends to infinity and no finite value has a cumulative probability of 1.0.
14. Paul F. McCoy, "Using Performance Indexes to Monitor Production Processes," *Quality Progress* 24, no. 2 (February 1991), 49–55; see also Fred A. Spring, "The Cpm Index," *Quality Progress* 24, no. 2 (February 1991), 57–61.
15. Pandu R. Tadikamalla, "The Confusion over Six-Sigma Quality," *Quality Progress* 27, no. 11 (November 1994), 83–85. Reprinted with permission of Pandu R. Tadikamalla and *Quality Progress*.
16. Adapted from K. M. Casarreal, J. I. Mills, and M. A. Plant, "Improving Service through Patient Surveys in a Multihospital Organization," *Hospital & Health Services Administration*, Health Administration Press, Ann Arbor, MI (March/April 1986), 41–52. © 1986, Foundation of the American College of Health Care Executives.
17. Adapted from the Ritz-Carlton Hotel Company Application Summary for the 1992 Malcolm Baldrige National Quality Award.
18. H. P. Hill, J. L. Roth, and H. Arkin, *Sampling in Auditing: A Simplified Guide and Statistical Tables* (New York: Copyright © Ronald Press 1962). Reprinted by permission of John Wiley & Sons, Inc.
19. Reprinted by permission of George Tagaras, Patroklos Georgiadis, and Dimitris Psoinos, "Development of a Quality-Assurance System for a Wine Producer in Greece," *Interfaces* 24, no. 6 (November–December 1994), 1–13. Copyright 1994, the Institute for Operations Research and the Management Sciences, 290 Westminster Street, Providence, Rhode Island 02903 USA.
20. This example has been adapted from an actual study in an organization within which one of the authors worked.
21. Note: Readers who have need for professional software for performing extensive R&R studies or keeping track of gauge records and calibration may wish to look at R&Rpack® and GAGEpack® software developed and distributed by PQ Systems, Inc., P.O. Box 10, Dayton, OH 45475–0010.

BIBLIOGRAPHY

American National Standard: Guide to Inspection Planning, ANSI/ASQC E-2-1984. American Society for Quality Control, 310 W. Wisconsin Ave., Milwaukee, WI 53203.
Boser, Robert B., and Cheryl L. Christ. "Whys, Whens, and Hows of Conducting a Process Capability Study." Presentation at the ASQC/ASA 35th Annual Fall Technical Conference, Lexington, Kentucky, 1991.
Case, Kenneth E. and Lynn L. Jones. *Profit through Quality: Quality Assurance Programs for Manufacturers*. Norcross, GA: American Institute of Industrial Engineers, 1978.
Chatfield, Christopher. *Statistics for Technology: A Course in Applied Statistics*. New York: Halstead Press, Div. of John Wiley & Sons, 1978.
Duncan, Acheson J. *Quality Control and Industrial Statistics*, 5th ed. Homewood, IL: Richard D. Irwin, 1986.
Ferdeber, Charles J. "Measuring Quality and Productivity in a Service Environment." *Industrial Engineering* (July 1981), 193–201.
Griffith, Gary. *Quality Technician's Handbook*. New York: John Wiley, 1986.
Gunter, Bert. "Process Capability Studies Part I: What Is a Process Capability Study?" *Quality Progress* 24, no. 2 (February 1991), 97–99.
Holm, Richard A. "Fulfilling the New Role of Inspection." *Manufacturing Engineering* (May 1988), 43–46.

Lapin, Lawrence L. *Statistics for Modern Business Decisions*, 4th ed. San Diego: Harcourt Brace Jovanovich, Inc., 1987.

MIL-HDBK-53-1A, *Military Handbook, Guide for Attribute Lot Sampling Inspection and MIL-STD-105*. Washington, D.C.: Department of Defense, 30 June, 1965.

Puma, Maurice. "Quality Technology in Manufacturing," *Quality Progress* 13, no. 8 (August 1980), 16–19.

Rice, George O. "Metrology." In *Quality Management Handbook*, Loren Walsh, Ralph Wurster, and Raymond J. Kimber (eds.). New York: Marcel Dekker (1986), 517–530.

Robbins, C. L., and W. A. Robbins. "What Nurse Managers Should Know about Sampling Techniques." *Nursing Management* 20, no. 6 (June 1989), 46–48.

Sherman, William H. "Inspection: Do We Need It?" *Manufacturing Engineering* (May 1988), 39–42.

Tomas, Sam. "Six Sigma: Motorola's Quest for Zero Defects." *APICS, The Performance Advantage* (July 1991), 36–41.

_____ . "What Is Motorola's Six Sigma Product Quality?" *American Production and Inventory Control Society 1990 Conference Proceedings*. Falls Church, VA: APICS, 27–31.

Troxell, Joseph R. "Service Time Quality Standards." *Quality Progress* 14, no. 9, (September 1981), 35–37.

_____ . "Standards for Quality Control in Service Industries." *Quality Progress* 12, no. 1 (January 1979), 32–34.

Tedaldi, Michael, Fred Seaglione, and VIncent Russotti. *A Beginner's Guide to Quality in Manufacturing*. Milwaukee, WI: ASQC Quality Press, 1992.

Zubairi, Mazhar M. "Statistical Process Control Management Issues." *1985 IIE Fall Conference Proceedings*. Reprinted in Sepehri, Mehran, ed. *Quest for Quality: Managing the Total System*. Norcross, GA: Industrial Engineering & Management Press, 1987.

Chapter 14 Appendix
IMPORTANT PROBABILITY DISTRIBUTIONS

Certain discrete distributions describe many natural phenomena and have broad applications in statistical process control. Two of them are the binomial distribution and the Poisson distribution, discussed next. Later, some important continuous probability distributions are introduced.

BINOMIAL DISTRIBUTION

The **binomial distribution** describes the probability of obtaining exactly x "successes" in a sequence of n identical experiments, called trials. A *success* can be any one of two possible outcomes of each experiment. In some situations, it might represent a defective item, in others, a good item. The probability of success in each trial is a constant value p. The binomial probability function is given by the following formula:

$$f(x) = \binom{n}{x} p^x (1 - p)^{n-x}$$

$$= \frac{n!}{x!(n - x)!} p^x (1 - p)^{n-x} \qquad x = 0, 1, 2, \ldots, n$$

where p is the probability of a success, n is the number of items in the sample, and x is the number of items for which the probability is desired $(0, 1, 2, \ldots, n)$. The expected value, variance, and standard deviation of the binomial distribution are

$$E(p) = \mu = np$$

$$\sigma^2 = np(1 - p)$$

$$\sigma = \sqrt{np(1 - p)}$$

Binomial probabilities for selected values of p and n have been tabulated in Appendix D. Naturally, computer programs are also available to make binomial computations easier.

EXAMPLE 1   Silicon Chip Defectives.   To illustrate the use of the binomial distribution, suppose that a new process for producing silicon chips is averaging 40 percent defective items. If a quality supervisor takes a sample of five items to test for defectives, what is the probability of finding 0, 1, 2, 3, 4, or 5 defectives in the sample, and what is the expected number of defectives? For this problem, $n = 5$ and $p = 0.4$. Therefore, the binomial distribution for this experiment is

$$f(x) = \binom{5}{x} (0.4)^x (1 - 0.4)^{5-x}$$

$$= \frac{5!}{x!(5 - x)!} (0.4)^x (0.6)^{5-x}$$

TABLE 14A.1 Binomial Probability Values

x	$\dfrac{5!}{x!(5-x)!}$	$(0.4)^x(0.6)^{5-x}$	$f(x)$
0	1	0.07776	0.0778
1	5	0.05184	0.2592
2	10	0.03456	0.3456
3	10	0.02304	0.2304
4	5	0.01536	0.0768
5	1	0.01024	0.0102
			1.0000

Table 14A.1 shows the detailed calculations required to compute individual probabilities. (You may wish to check the binomial probability table in Appendix D to verify these answers.)

Thus, the probability of finding exactly zero defectives in the sample of five is 0.0778, the probability of finding one defective is 0.2592, and so on. The expected number of defectives and the variance are given by

$$\mu = np = 5(0.4) = 2.0$$

$$\sigma^2 = np(1 - p) = 2.0(0.6) = 1.2$$

Figure 14A.1 shows a graph of this probability distribution.

FIGURE 14A.1 Binomial Probability Distribution

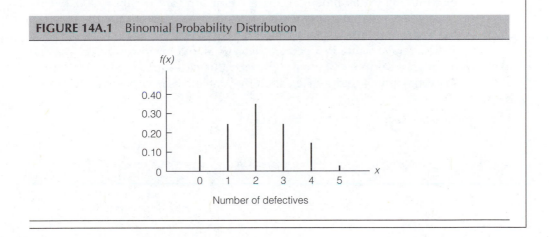

POISSON DISTRIBUTION

The second discrete distribution often used in quality control is the **Poisson distribution.** The Poisson probability distribution is given by

$$f(x) = \frac{e^{-\mu}\mu^x}{x!}$$

where μ = expected value or average number of occurrences, $x = 0, 1, 2, 3,$ . . . , and $e \approx 2.71828$, a constant.

The Poisson distribution is closely related to the binomial distribution. It is derived by allowing the sample size (n) to become very large (approaching infinity) and the probability of success or failure (p) to become very small (approaching zero) while the expected value (np) remains constant. Thus, when n is large relative to p, the Poisson distribution can be used as an approximation to the binomial. A common rule of thumb is if $p \leq 0.05$ and $n \geq 20$, the Poisson will be a good approximation with $\mu = np$. It is also used to calculate the number of occurrences of an event over a specified interval of time or space, such as the number of scratches per square inch on a polished surface.

EXAMPLE 2   Using the Poisson Distribution.   Example 1 can be extended to show how the Poisson distribution can be used in quality control problems. Suppose that improvements are made in the production process that bring the average level of defects down to 5 percent from the previous level of 40 percent. The quality supervisor now decides to use a sample size of 30 parts to detect changes in the quality level of the process with a much longer time period between samples. What is the probability of finding five or fewer defective items in any randomly selected sample of 30 parts?

Since the task requires finding discrete probabilities of 0, 1, 2, 3, 4, or 5 defectives, calculate each probability and add the results:

$$P(x \leq 5) = P(x = 0) + P(x = 1) + P(x = 2)$$
$$+ P(x = 3) + P(x = 4) + P(x = 5)$$

As an approximation to the binomial, the relationship to $\mu = np = 30(0.05) = 1.5$ can be used. This relationship then becomes the parameter μ for the Poisson distribution. The computations are given in Table 14A.2.

Thus, if the average value is 5 percent defectives, five or fewer defectives are likely to occur in a sample of 30 parts. In fact, this case carries a 0.99552 probability. The probability of finding *more* than five defectives is very small. It would be only

$$1 - P(x \leq 5) = 1 - 0.99552 = 0.00448$$

TABLE 14A.2   Poisson Probability Values

x	$e^{-1.5}$	$\dfrac{(1.5)^x}{x!}$	$f(x) = \dfrac{e^{-1.5}(1.5)^x}{x!}$
0	0.22313	1.00000	0.22313
1	0.22313	1.50000	0.33467
2	0.22313	1.12500	0.25102
3	0.22313	0.56250	0.12551
4	0.22313	0.21094	0.04707
5	0.22313	0.06328	0.01412
			0.99552

Note that the previously stated conditions under which the Poisson distribution is a good approximation of the binomial have been met; that is, $n \geq 20$ and $p \leq 0.05$. Table 14A.3 compares these probability values to the true values using the binomial distribution. The results show that the Poisson distribution does

TABLE 14A.3 Binomial versus Poisson Probability Values

x	Binomial Probability	Poisson Probability
0	0.21464	0.22313
1	0.33890	0.33467
2	0.25864	0.25102
3	0.12705	0.12551
4	0.04514	0.04707
5	0.01235	0.01412
	0.99672	0.99552

provide a good approximation to the binomial probabilities when the specified conditions are met. If the conditions for the Poisson approximation cannot be met, a normal approximation to the binomial, discussed in the next section, may be of use.

Two of the most frequently used continuous probability distributions are the normal distribution and the exponential distribution. They form the basis for many of the statistical analyses performed in quality assurance today.

NORMAL DISTRIBUTION

The probability density function of the **normal distribution** is represented graphically by the familiar bell-shaped curve. However, not every symmetric, unimodal curve is a normal distribution, nor can all data from a sample or population be assumed to fit a normal distribution. However, data are often assumed to be normally distributed to simplify certain calculations. In most cases, this assumption makes little difference in the results but is important from a theoretical perspective.

The probability density function for the normal distribution is as follows:

$$f(x) = \frac{1}{\sqrt{2\pi\sigma^2}} e^{-(x-\mu)^2/2\sigma^2} \quad -\infty < x < \infty$$

where μ = the mean of the random variable x

σ^2 = the variance of x

e = 2.71828 . . .

π = 3.14159 . . .

If a normal random variable has a mean $\mu = 0$ and a standard deviation $\sigma = 1$, it is called a **standard normal distribution.** The letter z is usually used to represent this particular random variable. By using the constants 0 and 1 for the mean and standard deviation, respectively, the probability density function for the normal distribution can be simplified as

$$f(z) = \frac{1}{\sqrt{2\pi}} e^{-z^2/2}$$

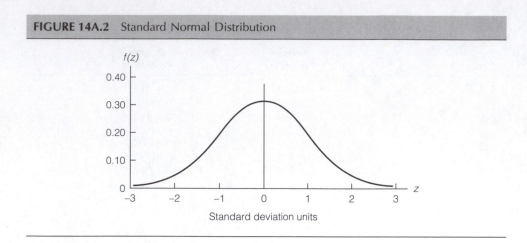

FIGURE 14A.2   Standard Normal Distribution

This standard normal distribution function is shown in Figure 14A.2. Since $\sigma = 1$, the scale on the z axis is given in units of standard deviations. Special tables of areas under the normal curve have been developed as an aid in computing probabilities. Such a table is given in Appendix A.

Fortunately, *any* normal distribution involving a random variable x with a known (or estimated) mean and standard deviation is easily transformed into a standard normal distribution using the following formula:

$$z = \frac{x - \mu}{\sigma}$$

This formula takes the value of the variable of interest (x), subtracts the mean value (μ), and divides by the standard deviation (σ). This calculation yields a random variable z, which has a standard normal distribution. Probabilities for this variable can then be found in the table in Appendix A.

EXAMPLE 3   Normal Probability Calculations.   Randomly selected temperatures from a drying oven in an enamel wire manufacturing process exhibit a normal distribution with $\mu = 49$ and $\sigma = 7$. Given this information, calculate three probabilities [shown in Figures 14A.3(a), (b), and (c), respectively]: (1) that a sample value x will fall between 42 and 49, (2) that it will be less than 42, and (3) that it will fall between 50 and 57.

Referring to Figure 14A.3(a), to compute the probability that the random variable x will fall between 42 and 49, convert these values to standard normal deviates (z values):

$$z_1 = \frac{x - \mu}{\sigma} = \frac{42 - 49}{7} = -1.0 \text{ and } z_2 = \frac{49 - 49}{7} = 0$$

Since this case is bounded on the right by the mean of the distribution, simply read the normal table for the z_1 value and obtain the probability without further calculations. The table indicates that the area under the curve between -1.0 and 0 is 0.3413. This number means 34.13 percent of the values taken from this population would be expected to fall in the specified interval, and that a 34.13 per-

FIGURE 14A.3(a) Calculation of Probabilities from the Standard Normal Distribution

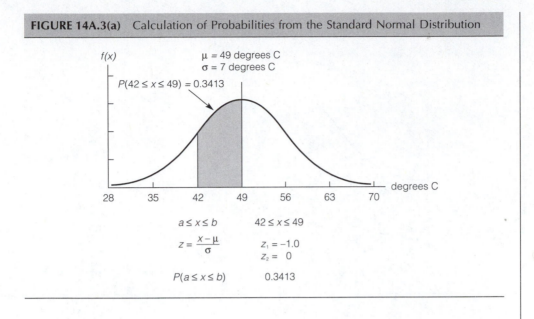

cent probability of obtaining a value within that interval exists, given a random observation of the oven temperature.

To compute the probability that x is less than 42 for the second case, find the area under the normal curve from minus infinity to:

$$z_2 = \frac{42 - 49}{7} = -1.0$$

This value is 0.5 minus the area from -1.0 to 0, which is 0.3413 as found in Appendix A. Thus, the probability of obtaining a temperature reading of less than 42 degrees C is $0.5 - 0.3413 = 0.1587$. This result is shown in Figure 14A.3(b).

FIGURE 14A.3(b) Calculation of Probabilities from the Standard Normal Distribution

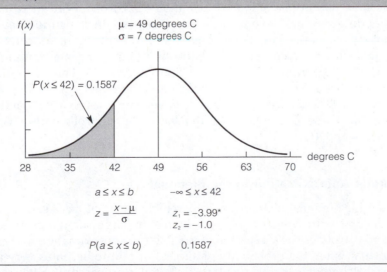

*Note: The left (lower most) limit of the distribution using the standard normal table in Appendix A is a z value of -3.99. Actually, the lower limit of the distribution extends to $-\infty$.

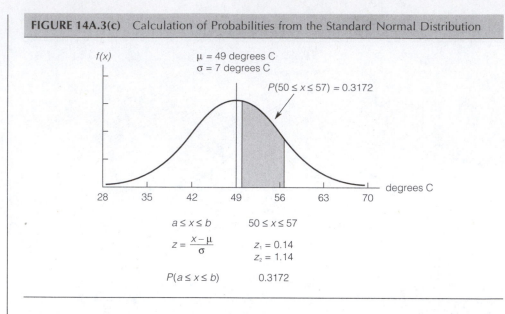

FIGURE 14A.3(c) Calculation of Probabilities from the Standard Normal Distribution

Finally, for the third case, transform $x = 50$ and $x = 57$ to standard normal values and obtain:

$$z_1 = \frac{x - \mu}{\sigma} = \frac{50 - 49}{7} = 0.14 \text{ and } z_2 = \frac{57 - 49}{7} = 1.14$$

The area from 0 to $z_2 = 1.14$ can be read from the table as 0.3729. The area from 0 to $z_1 = 0.14$ is 0.0557. Then subtract the smaller area from the larger to obtain $0.3729 - 0.0557 = 0.3172$, the area of interest. Thus, a probability of 0.3172 exists for observing an oven temperature between 50 and 57 degrees C. These calculations are summarized in Figure 14A.3(c).

The area under the curve that corresponds to one standard deviation from the mean is 0.3413; therefore, the probability that the value of a normal random variable falls within one standard deviation ($\pm 1\sigma$) of the mean is 0.6826. The corresponding x-values are often called *1-sigma limits* in statistical quality control terminology. Two standard deviations on one side of the mean corresponds to 0.4772 area under the curve, so the probability that a normal random variable falls within a *2-sigma limit* is twice that figure, or 0.9544. Three standard deviations encompasses 0.4986 area under the curve on either side of the mean, or a total area of 0.9972. Hence, the *3-sigma limit* encompasses nearly all of the normal distribution. These concepts form the basis for control charts discussed in Chapters 15 and 16.

■ Normal Approximation to the Binomial

Although the binomial distribution is extremely useful, it has a serious limitation when dealing with either small probabilities or large sample sizes—it is very tedious to calculate. The discussion of the Poisson approximation to the binomial showed that when the probability of success or failure becomes very small, the Poisson distribution permits calculation of similar probability values more easily than the binomial. Also, as the same size gets very large (approaches infinity), the binomial distribution approaches the normal distribution as a limit. Hence, for large sample sizes, good approximations of probabilities that would have been calculated using the binomial distribution can be obtained by using the normal distribution. The normal approximation holds well when $np \geq 5$ and $n(1 - p) \geq 5$.

EXAMPLE 4   Normal Approximation.   To illustrate, two changes in assumptions are made in the silicon chip example. Suppose, instead of using a small sample size, the sample size is 50. The probability of finding a defective item is still 0.40. To determine the probability of finding between 15 and 20 defective items in the sample, use the binomial distribution to calculate the probabilities.

$$f(x) = \binom{50}{x}(0.4)^x(1 - 0.4)^{50-x}$$

$$= \frac{50!}{x!(50 - x)!}(0.4)^x(0.6)^{50-x}$$

This equation would have to be evaluated for $x = 15, 16, 17, 18\ 19$ and 20, since

$$P(15 \leq x \leq 20) = P(x = 15) + P(x = 16) + P(x = 17) + P(x = 18)$$
$$+ P(x = 19) + P(x = 20)$$

These calculations would be difficult and time-consuming, even with a good electronic calculator!

By using the normal approximation, a reasonably accurate estimate of the probability is obtained. The calculations are as follows:

$$\mu = np = 50(0.40) = 20$$

$$\sigma_p^2 = np(1 - p) = 20(0.60) = 12$$

$$\sigma_p = \sqrt{12} = 3.46$$

$$z_1 = \frac{x - \mu}{\sigma_p} = \frac{15 - 20}{3.46} = -1.45 \quad z_2 = \frac{20 - 20}{3.46} = 0$$

Using the table in Appendix A, the value for $P(-1.45 \leq z \leq 0) = 0.4265$. Thus, the probability of obtaining between 15 and 20 defectives in a sample of 50 parts is 0.4265. This result is shown in Figure 14A.4.

FIGURE 14A.4   Normal Approximation to the Binomial

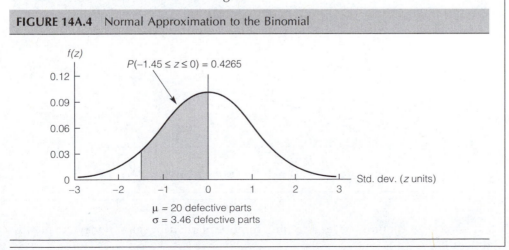

EXPONENTIAL DISTRIBUTION

Another continuous distribution commonly used in quality assurance is the **exponential distribution.** The exponential distribution is used extensively in reliability estimation, discussed in Chapter 17. The probability density function for the exponential distribution is much simpler than the one for the normal distribution. Therefore, direct evaluation is easier, although tabulated values for the exponential distribution are also readily available (see Appendix F). The formula for the exponential probability density function is

$$f(x) = \frac{1}{\mu}e^{-x/\mu}, \quad x \geqslant 0$$

where μ = mean value for the distribution

x = time or distance over which the variable extends

e = 2.71828 . . .

Integrating this function between 0 and x results in the cumulative distribution function

$$F(x) = 1 - e^{-x/\mu}$$

EXAMPLE 5   Distribution of Light Bulb Failure Times.   To illustrate an application of the exponential distribution, suppose that the maintenance manager of an office building is trying to schedule the maintenance crew that changes floodlights used to illuminate the exterior of the building. The manager is told by the light bulb supplier that the mean time between failure for the bulbs being used is 1,000 hours. What is the probability that the *actual* time between any two successive failures will be 750 hours or less? For this example, μ = 1000 and x = 750. Thus,

$$F(x) = 1 - e^{-x/\mu} = 1 - e^{-0.75} = 1 - 0.4724 = 0.5276$$

Therefore, the probability is 0.5276 that the time between two successive failures will be 750 hours or less. The problem is shown graphically in Figure 14A.5.

FIGURE 14A.5   Exponential Distribution of Time between Failures

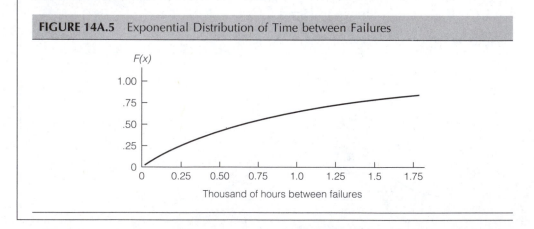

Figure 14A.6 summarizes the four important distributions reviewed in this appendix.

FIGURE 14A.6 Summary of Common Probability Distributions Used in Quality Assurance

Distribution	Form	Probability Function	Comments on Application
Normal		$y = \dfrac{1}{\sigma\sqrt{2\pi}} e^{-\frac{(x-\mu)^2}{2\sigma^2}}$ μ = Mean σ = Standard deviation	Applicable when a concentration of observations falls about the average and when observations are equally likely to occur above and below the average. Variation in observations is usually the result of many small causes.
Exponential		$y = \dfrac{1}{\mu} e^{-\frac{x}{\mu}}$	Applicable when more observations are likely to occur below the average than above.
Poisson		$y = \dfrac{e^{-\mu}\mu^x}{x!}$ n = Number of trials p = Probability of occurrence x = Number of occurrences $\mu = np$	Same as binomial but particularly applicable when many opportunities for occurrence of an event are possible but have a low probability (less than 0.10) on each trial.
Binomial		$y = \dfrac{n!}{x!(n-x)!}\, p^x q^{n-x}$ n = Number of trials x = Number of occurrences p = Probability of occurrence $q = 1 - p$	Applicable in defining the probability of x occurrences in n trials of an event that has a constant probability of occurrence on each independent trial.

SOURCE: Adapted from J. M. Juran and F. M. Gryna, Jr., instructor's manual to accompany *Quality Planning and Analysis* (New York: McGraw-Hill, 1980), 125. Copyright © 1980 by McGraw-Hill, Inc., used with permission.

CHAPTER 15

Fundamentals of Statistical Process Control

Chapter 3 introduced the concepts of common causes and special causes of variation as well as the idea of statistical control. To recall, a process is in statistical control if the variation in the process is due to common causes alone. When special causes are present, the process is deemed to be out of control. Process improvement is based on reducing common cause variation; process control is the approach for identifying and eliminating special causes of variation. Process capability cannot be determined unless the process is in statistical control.

Control charts were introduced in Chapter 9 as one of the seven fundamental tools of quality. **Statistical process control,** or **SPC,** is a methodology in which operators, supervisors, and managers use control charts to monitor the output from a process to identify and to eliminate special causes of variation. SPC is a proven technique for reducing scrap and rework, thus, increasing productivity. It also provides the basis for determining process capability and predicting the yield from a process. In many industries, suppliers are *required* to provide evidence of statistical process control to their customers. SPC provides the means by which a firm may demonstrate its quality capability, an activity necessary for survival in today's highly competitive markets. This chapter provides the details of how control charts are developed and used.

THE NEED FOR SPC

Firms use SPC for two basic reasons: First, through SPC, a firm can determine *when to take action* to adjust a process that has fallen out of control. Second, SPC tells a firm when to *leave a process alone*. Knowing when to take action on a process is an important step in defect prevention and eliminates inspection and sorting of product after a large batch has been made. Knowing when to leave a process alone is equally important in keeping variation at a minimum. Many production workers struggle with this concept because they do not understand the nature of variation and the difference between common and special causes of variation. Often, they believe that whenever process output is off-target, some adjustment must be made. Such overadjustment will actually *increase* the variation in the process output, as shown in the following simulation.

Suppose that in a specific process, 60 percent of the output falls exactly on the process mean; the remaining 40 percent of the time, however, it is off in either direction by 0.1. If the process mean is 5.0, for example, then out of ten parts, on the average, six will have a value of 5.0, two will have a value of 4.9, and two will have a value of 5.1. Under these assumptions, all of the output will fall between 4.9 and 5.1 if the process is left alone.

Assume that the operator can make adjustments in the process mean, but cannot determine its true value; he or she can only measure the output, which may differ from the mean because of the natural variation of the process. Suppose that the operator inspects and measures each part and decides to make an adjustment to the process mean if the measurement is off-target. If the value is above the target, the operator will adjust the process setting downward by the difference; if the value is below the target, an adjustment upward will be made.

Assume the process mean is equal to a target value of 5.0. What would happen if the process variation results in the following sequence of deviations away from the process mean?

Mean	5.0	5.0	5.0	5.0	5.0	5.0	5.0	5.0	5.0	5.0
Deviation	−0.1	+0.1	0	0	−0.1	0	0	0	+0.1	0
Output	4.9	5.1	5.0	5.0	4.9	5.0	5.0	5.0	5.1	5.0

Notice that the distribution of process output follows the assumptions if the process mean is left alone.

Now suppose the same sequence of deviations occurs, but the process is adjusted up or down after each part is produced according to the rule stated earlier. Assume that the initial mean is 5.0. Since the first measurement is 4.9, the operator would adjust the process setting up by 0.1. This action actually changes the process mean to 5.1, but the operator really thinks that he or she is adjusting it "back" to 5.0. Applying this rule for all ten parts provides the following sequence:

Mean	5.0	5.1	4.9	5.0	5.0	5.1	5.0	5.0	5.0	4.9
Deviation	−0.1	+0.1	0	0	−0.1	0	0	0	+0.1	0
Output	4.9	5.2	4.9	5.0	4.9	5.1	5.0	5.0	5.1	4.9

Only three of the ten parts now meet the target; four have a value of 4.9; two have a value of 5.1; and one has a value of 5.2. Clearly, the variation in the process output actually has increased.

The second use of SPC is that of knowing when it is necessary to adjust a process. Table 15.1 shows 150 measurements of a quality characteristic from a manufacturing process. Each row corresponds to a sample size 5 taken every 15 minutes. The mean of each sample is also given in Table 15.1. A histogram of these data is shown in Figure 15.1. The data form a relatively symmetric distribution around the overall mean of 10.7616. From the histogram alone, what can you conclude about the state of control for this process? Very little, because histograms do not allow you to distinguish between common and special causes of variation. In a histogram, the dimension of *time* is not considered. This factor is critical since special causes occur sporadically over time. For example, tools

TABLE 15.1   Sample Observations

Sample	Observations					Mean
1	10.682	10.689	10.776	10.798	10.714	10.7318
2	10.787	10.860	10.601	10.746	10.779	10.7546
3	10.780	10.667	10.838	10.785	10.723	10.7586
4	10.591	10.727	10.812	10.775	10.730	10.7270
5	10.693	10.708	10.790	10.758	10.671	10.7240
6	10.749	10.714	10.738	10.719	10.606	10.7052
7	10.791	10.713	10.689	10.877	10.603	10.7346
8	10.744	10.779	10.660	10.737	10.822	10.7484
9	10.769	10.773	10.641	10.644	10.725	10.7104
10	10.718	10.671	10.708	10.850	10.712	10.7318
11	10.787	10.821	10.764	10.658	10.708	10.7476
12	10.622	10.802	10.818	10.872	10.727	10.7682
13	10.657	10.822	10.893	10.544	10.750	10.7332
14	10.806	10.749	10.859	10.801	10.701	10.7832
15	10.660	10.681	10.644	10.747	10.728	10.6920
16	10.816	10.817	10.768	10.716	10.649	10.7532
17	10.826	10.777	10.721	10.770	10.809	10.7806
18	10.828	10.829	10.865	10.778	10.872	10.8344
19	10.805	10.719	10.612	10.938	10.807	10.7762
20	10.802	10.756	10.786	10.815	10.801	10.7920
21	10.876	10.803	10.701	10.789	10.672	10.7682
22	10.855	10.783	10.722	10.856	10.751	10.7934
23	10.762	10.705	10.804	10.805	10.809	10.7770
24	10.703	10.837	10.759	10.975	10.732	10.8012
25	10.737	10.723	10.776	10.748	10.732	10.7432
26	10.748	10.686	10.856	10.811	10.838	10.7878
27	10.826	10.803	10.764	10.823	10.886	10.8204
28	10.728	10.721	10.820	10.772	10.639	10.7360
29	10.803	10.892	10.741	10.816	10.770	10.8044
30	10.774	10.837	10.872	10.849	10.818	10.8300

FIGURE 15.1 Histogram of Quality Measurements

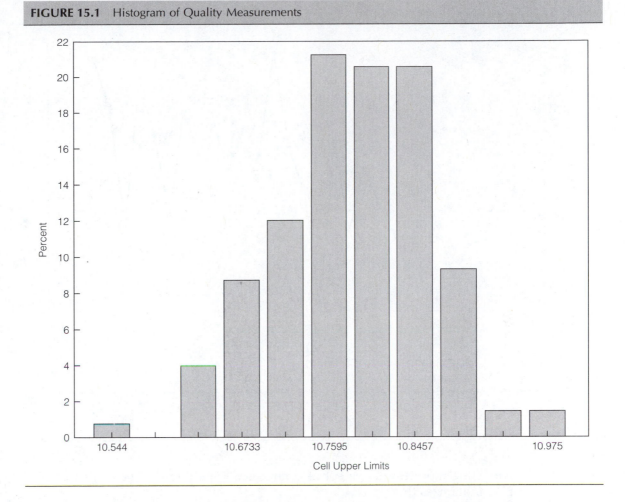

Cell Upper Limits

wear out after a period of use, materials from different shipments may vary, or a substitute operator may run a process when the regular operator is absent.

To include the time factor, the mean of each sample is plotted against the time at which the sample was taken. Since the time increments between samples are equal, the sample number is an appropriate surrogate for time, as shown in Figure 15.2. Clearly, Table 15.1 shows that the mean has shifted up at about sample 17. Some special cause has probably caused this shift and some adjustment is necessary to bring the process back on target, an aspect that is not indicated by the histogram.

SPC, as summarized in Table 15.2, can be viewed as making a test of a hypothesis:

H_0: the process is in control

versus

H_1: the process is out of control

The correct decisions are to adjust the process when it is out of control and to leave the process alone when it is in control. Of course, incorrect decisions may be made due to sampling error or errors in interpreting the data. The risk of unnecessarily adjusting a process in control is equivalent to a Type I error; not

FIGURE 15.2   Graph of Sample Means Versus Time

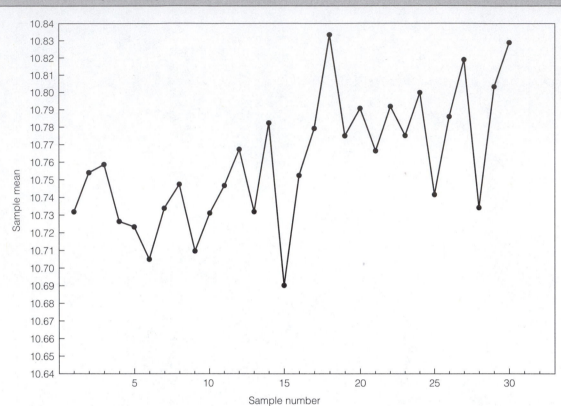

correcting a process that is out of control is a Type II error. The correct use of SPC minimizes these risks.

CONTROL CHARTS FOR VARIABLES DATA

Variables data are those that are measured along a continuous scale. Examples of variables data are length, weight, and distance. The charts most commonly used for variables data are the $\bar{x}$-chart ("x-bar" chart), and the R-chart (range chart). The $\bar{x}$-chart is used to monitor the centering of the process, and the R-chart is used to monitor the variation in the process. These charts are used together for the analysis of variables data. The range is used as a measure of

TABLE 15.2   Decisions and Risks in Process Control

	PROCESS STATE	
DECISION	**In Control**	**Out of Control**
Adjust process	Type I error	Correct decision
Leave alone	Correct decision	Type II error

variation simply for convenience, particularly when workers on the factory floor perform control chart calculations by hand. For large samples and when data are analyzed by computer programs, the standard deviation is a better measure of variability (discussed in the next chapter). In this section the construction, interpretation, and use of variables control charts are discussed. Control charts have three basic applications: (1) to establish a state of statistical control, (2) to monitor a process and signal when the process goes out of control, and (3) to determine process capability.

■ Constructing Variables Control Charts and Establishing Statistical Control

The first step in developing $\bar{x}$- and R-charts is to gather data. Usually, about 25 to 30 samples are collected. Samples between size 3 and 10 are generally used, with 5 being the most common. The number of samples is indicated by k, and n denotes the sample size. For each sample i, the mean (denoted $\bar{x}_i$) and the range (R_i) are computed. These values are then plotted on their respective control charts. Next, the *overall mean* and *average range* calculations are made. These values specify the center lines for the $\bar{x}$- and R-charts, respectively. The overall mean is the average of the sample means $\bar{x}_i$:

$$\bar{\bar{x}} = \frac{\sum_{i=1}^{k} \bar{x}_i}{k}$$

The average range is similarly computed, using the formula

$$\bar{R} = \frac{\sum_{i=1}^{k} R_i}{k}$$

The average range and average mean are used to compute control limits for the R- and $\bar{x}$-charts. Control limits are easily calculated using the following formulas:

$$\text{UCL}_R = D_4\bar{R} \qquad \text{UCL}_{\bar{x}} = \bar{\bar{x}} + A_2\bar{R}$$

$$\text{LCL}_R = D_3\bar{R} \qquad \text{LCL}_{\bar{x}} = \bar{\bar{x}} - A_2\bar{R}$$

where the constants D_3, D_4, and A_2 depend on the sample size and can be found in Appendix B at the end of the book.

The control limits represent the range between which all points are expected to fall if the process is in statistical control. If any points fall outside of the control limits or if any unusual patterns are observed, then some special cause has probably affected the process. The process should be studied to determine the cause. If special causes are present, then they are *not* representative of the true state of statistical control, and the calculations of the center line and control limits will be biased. The corresponding data points should be eliminated, and new values for $\bar{\bar{x}}$, $\bar{R}$, and the control limits should be computed.

In determining whether a process is in statistical control, the R-chart is always analyzed first. Since the control limits in the $\bar{x}$-chart depend on the average range, special causes in the R-chart may produce unusual patterns in the $\bar{x}$-chart, even when the centering of the process is in control. (An example of this is given later in this chapter.) Once statistical control is established for the R-chart, attention may turn to the $\bar{x}$-chart.

Figure 15.3 ASQC Control Chart Data Sheet

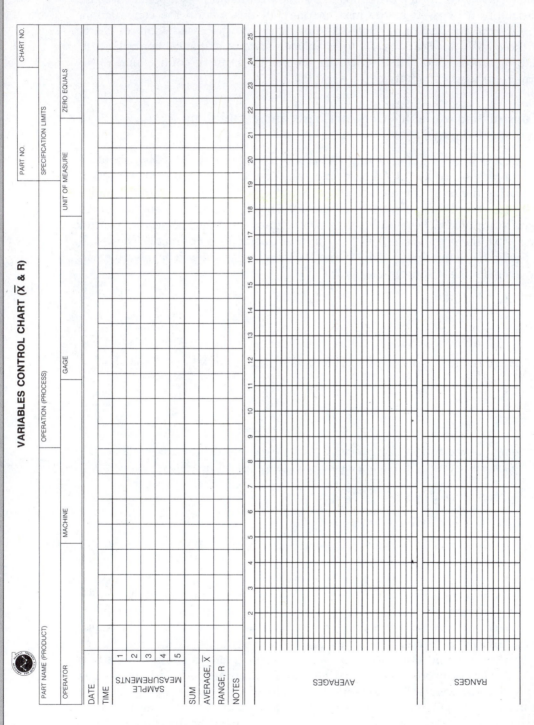

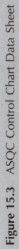

FIGURE 15.4 ASQC Control Chart Calculation Work Sheet

CALCULATION WORK SHEET

CONTROL LIMITS

SUBGROUPS INCLUDED ________ ________

$\bar{R} = \frac{\Sigma R}{k}$ = ____ = ____ =

$\bar{\bar{X}} = \frac{\Sigma \bar{X}}{k}$ = ____ = ____ =

OR

$\bar{X}'$ (MIDSPEC. OR STD.) = =

$A_2\bar{R}$ = x = ____ x = ____

$UCL_{\bar{X}} = \bar{\bar{X}} + A_2\bar{R}$ = =

$LCL_{\bar{X}} = \bar{\bar{X}} - A_2\bar{R}$ = =

$UCL_R = D_4\bar{R}$ = x = x =

LIMITS FOR INDIVIDUALS

COMPARE WITH SPECIFICATION OR TOLERANCE LIMITS

$\bar{\bar{X}}$ =

$\frac{3}{d_2}\bar{R}$ = x = ____

$UL_x = \bar{\bar{X}} + \frac{3}{d_2}\bar{R}$ =

$LL_x = \bar{\bar{X}} - \frac{3}{d_2}\bar{R}$ =

US =

LS = ____

US − LS =

$6\sigma = \frac{6}{d_2}\bar{R}$ =

MODIFIED CONTROL LIMITS FOR AVERAGES

BASED ON SPECIFICATION LIMITS AND PROCESS CAPABILITY.
APPLICABLE ONLY IF: $US - LS > 6\sigma$.

US = LS =

$A_M\bar{R}$ = x = ____ $A_M\bar{R}$ = ____

$URL_{\bar{X}} = US - A_M\bar{R}$ = $LRL_{\bar{X}} = LS + A_M\bar{R}$ =

FACTORS FOR CONTROL LIMITS

n	A_2	D_4	d_2	$\frac{3}{d_2}$	A_M
2	1.880	3.268	1.128	2.659	0.779
3	1.023	2.574	1.693	1.772	0.749
4	0.729	2.282	2.059	1.457	0.728
5	0.577	2.114	2.326	1.290	0.713
6	0.483	2.004	2.534	1.184	0.701

SOURCE: Reprinted with permission of ASQC.

Figure 15.3 shows a typical data sheet used for recording data and drawing control charts, which is available from the American Society for Quality Control (ASQC). This form provides space for descriptive information about the process, recording of sample observations and computed statistics, and drawing the control charts. On the back of this form (Figure 15.4), is a work sheet for computing control limits and process capability information. The construction and analysis of control charts is best seen by example. The ASQC chart is used in the following example.

EXAMPLE 1 Control Charts for Silicon Wafer Production. The thickness of silicon wafers used in the production of semiconductors must be carefully controlled. The tolerance of one such product is specified as ±0.0050 inches. In one production facility, three wafers were selected each hour and the thickness measured carefully to within one ten-thousandth of an inch. Figure 15.5 shows the results obtained for 25 samples. For example, the mean of the first sample is

$$\bar{x}_1 = \frac{41 + 70 + 22}{3} = \frac{113}{3} = 44$$

The range of sample 1 is 70 − 22 = 48. (Note: calculations are rounded to the nearest integer for simplicity.)

The calculations of the average range, overall mean, and control limits are shown in Figure 15.6. The average range is the sum of the sample ranges (676) divided by the number of samples (25); the overall mean is the sum of the sample averages (1221) divided by the number of samples (25). Since the sample size is 3, the factors used in computing the control limits are $A_2 = 1.023$ and

FIGURE 15.5. Silicon Wafer Thickness Data

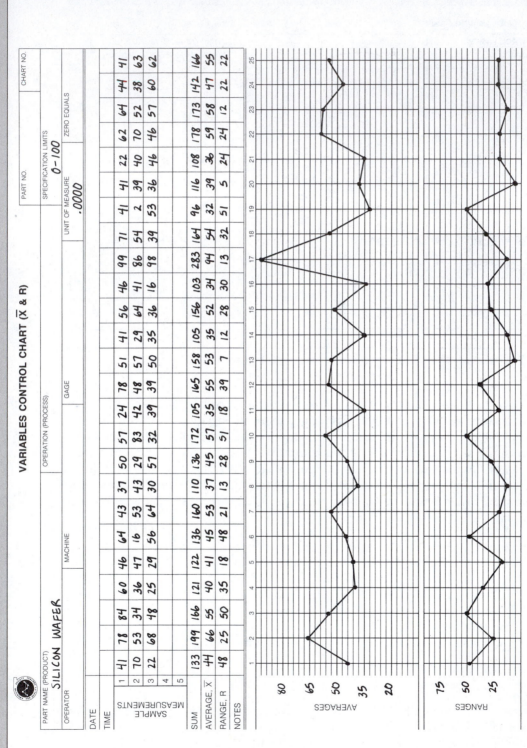

FIGURE 15.6   Control Limit Calculations

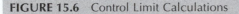

CALCULATION WORK SHEET

CONTROL LIMITS		**LIMITS FOR INDIVIDUALS**

SUBGROUPS INCLUDED _ALL_ _____   _____

COMPARE WITH SPECIFICATION OR TOLERANCE LIMITS

$\bar{R} = \dfrac{\Sigma R}{k} = \dfrac{676}{25}$ = 27   _____   =

$\bar{\bar{x}} = \dfrac{\Sigma \bar{x}}{k} = \dfrac{1221}{25}$ = 48.8   _____   =

OR

$\bar{X}'$ (MIDSPEC. OR STD.)   = 50   =

$A_2\bar{R} = 1.023 \times 27$ = 27.6   ×   = _____

$UCL_{\bar{x}} = \bar{\bar{x}} + A_2\bar{R}$ = 76.4   =

$LCL_{\bar{x}} = \bar{\bar{x}} - A_2\bar{R}$ = 21.2   =

$UCL_R = D_4\bar{R} = 2.574 \times 27$ = 69.5   ×   =

$\bar{\bar{x}}$ =

$\dfrac{3}{d_2}\bar{R}$ =   ×   =

$UL_x = \bar{\bar{x}} + \dfrac{3}{d_2}\bar{R}$ =

$LL_x = \bar{\bar{x}} - \dfrac{3}{d_2}\bar{R}$ =

US   =

LS   =

US − LS   = _____

$6\sigma = \dfrac{6}{d_2}\bar{R}$ =

MODIFIED CONTROL LIMITS FOR AVERAGES

BASED ON SPECIFICATION LIMITS AND PROCESS CAPABILITY. APPLICABLE ONLY IF: US − LS > 6σ.

US   =   LS   =

$A_M\bar{R} =$ ×   = _____ $A_M\bar{R}$ = _____

$URL_{\bar{x}} = US - A_M\bar{R}$ = $LRL_{\bar{x}} = LS + A_M\bar{R}$ =

FACTORS FOR CONTROL LIMITS

n	A_2	D_4	d_2	$\dfrac{3}{d_2}$	A_M
2	1.880	3.268	1.128	2.659	0.779
3	1.023	2.574	1.693	1.772	0.749
4	0.729	2.282	2.059	1.457	0.728
5	0.577	2.114	2.326	1.290	0.713
6	0.483	2.004	2.534	1.184	0.701

$D_4 = 2.574$. (For sample sizes of 6 or less, factor $D_3 = 0$; therefore, the lower control limit on the range chart is zero.) The center lines and control limits are drawn on the chart in Figure 15.7 (p. 648).

Examining the range chart first, it appears that the process is in control. All points lie within the control limits and no unusual patterns exist. In the $\bar{x}$-chart, however, sample 17 lies above the upper control limit. On investigation, some defective material was actually used. These data should be eliminated from the control chart calculations. Figure 15.8 (p. 649) shows the calculations after sample 17 was removed. The revised center lines and control limits are shown in Figure 15.9 (p. 650). Customarily, out-of-control points are noted on the chart. The resulting chart appears to be in control.

■ Interpreting Patterns in Control Charts

When a process is in statistical control, the points on a control chart fluctuate randomly between the control limits with no recognizable pattern. The following checklist provides a set of general rules for examining a process to determine if it is in control:

1. No points are outside control limits.
2. The number of points above and below the center line is about the same.
3. The points seem to fall randomly above and below the center line.
4. Most points, but not all, are near the center line, and only a few are close to the control limits.

The underlying assumption behind these rules is that the distribution of sample means is normal. This assumption follows from the central limit theorem of

FIGURE 15.7   Initial Control Chart

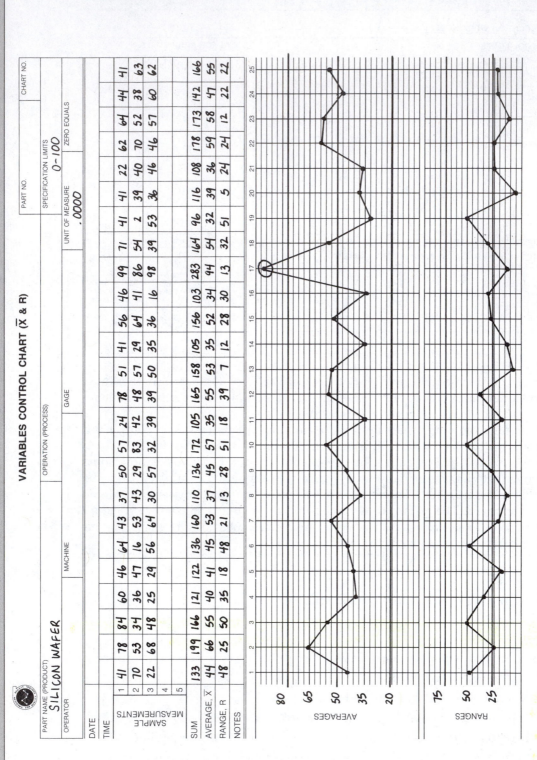

VARIABLES CONTROL CHART (X̄ & R)

PART NAME (PRODUCT): SILICON WAFER
OPERATION (PROCESS):
PART NO:
CHART NO:
SPECIFICATION LIMITS: 0–100
OPERATOR:
MACHINE:
GAGE:
UNIT OF MEASURE: .0000
ZERO EQUALS:

	1	2	3	4	5	6	7	8	9	10	11	12	13	14	15	16	17	18	19	20	21	22	23	24	25
SAMPLE MEASUREMENTS 1	41	78	84	60	46	64	43	37	50	57	24	78	51	41	56	46	99	71	41	41	22	62	64	44	41
2	70	53	34	36	47	16	53	43	29	83	42	48	57	29	64	41	86	54	2	39	40	70	52	38	63
3	22	68	48	25	29	56	64	30	57	32	39	39	50	35	36	16	98	39	53	36	46	46	57	60	62
4																									
5																									
SUM	133	199	166	121	122	136	160	110	136	172	105	165	158	105	156	103	283	164	96	116	108	178	173	142	166
AVERAGE, X̄	44	66	55	40	41	45	53	37	45	57	35	55	53	35	52	34	94	54	32	39	36	59	58	47	55
RANGE, R	48	25	50	35	18	48	21	13	28	51	18	39	7	12	28	30	13	32	51	5	24	24	12	22	22
NOTES																									

DATE
TIME

AVERAGES: 80 65 50 35 20

RANGES: 75 50 25

FIGURE 15.8   Revised Control Chart Calculations

CALCULATION WORK SHEET

CONTROL LIMITS		LIMITS FOR INDIVIDUALS

CONTROL LIMITS

SUBGROUPS INCLUDED __ALL__   __#17 REMOVED__

$\bar{R} = \dfrac{\Sigma R}{k} = \dfrac{676}{25}$ = 27 $\dfrac{663}{24}$ = 27.6

$\bar{\bar{X}} = \dfrac{\Sigma \bar{X}}{k} = \dfrac{1221}{25}$ = 48.8 $\dfrac{1127}{24}$ = 47.0

OR

$\bar{X}'$ (MIDSPEC. OR STD.) = 50   = 50

$A_2\bar{R} = 1.023 \times 27$ = 27.6 $1.023 \times 27.6 =$ 28.2

$UCL_{\bar{X}} = \bar{\bar{X}} + A_2\bar{R}$ = 76.4   = 75.2

$LCL_{\bar{X}} = \bar{\bar{X}} - A_2\bar{R}$ = 21.2   = 18.8

$UCL_R = D_4\bar{R} = 2.574 \times 27$ = 69.5 $2.574 \times 27.6 =$ 71.0

LIMITS FOR INDIVIDUALS

COMPARE WITH SPECIFICATION OR TOLERANCE LIMITS

$\bar{\bar{X}}$ =

$\dfrac{3}{d_2}\bar{R}$ =   x   = _____

$UL_x = \bar{\bar{X}} + \dfrac{3}{d_2}\bar{R}$ =

$LL_x = \bar{\bar{X}} - \dfrac{3}{d_2}\bar{R}$ =

US =

LS =   = _____

US – LS =

$6\sigma = \dfrac{6}{d_2}\bar{R}$ =

MODIFIED CONTROL LIMITS FOR AVERAGES

BASED ON SPECIFICATION LIMITS AND PROCESS CAPABILITY. APPLICABLE ONLY IF: US – LS > 6σ.

US   =   LS   =

$A_M\bar{R}$ =   x   = _____ $A_M\bar{R}$ =   = _____

$URL_{\bar{X}} = US - A_M\bar{R}$ = $LRL_{\bar{X}} = LS + A_M\bar{R}$ =

FACTORS FOR CONTROL LIMITS

n	A_2	D_4	d_2	$\dfrac{3}{d_2}$	A_M
2	1.880	3.268	1.128	2.659	0.779
3	1.023	2.574	1.693	1.772	0.749
4	0.729	2.282	2.059	1.457	0.728
5	0.577	2.114	2.326	1.290	0.713
6	0.483	2.004	2.534	1.184	0.701

statistics, which states that the distribution of sample means approaches a normal distribution as the sample size increases regardless of the original distribution. Of course, for small sample sizes, the distribution of the original data must be reasonably normal for this assumption to hold. The upper and lower control limits are computed to be three standard deviations from the overall mean. Thus, the probability that any sample mean falls outside of the control limits is very small. This probability is the origin of rule 1.

Since the normal distribution is symmetric, about the same number of points fall above as below the center line. Also, since the mean of the normal distribution is the median, about half the points fall on either side of the center line. Finally, about 68 percent of a normal distribution falls within one standard deviation of the mean; thus, most—but not all—points should be close to the center line. These characteristics will hold provided that the mean and variance of the original data have not changed during the time the data were collected; that is, the process is *stable*.

Several types of unusual patterns arise in control charts, which are reviewed here along with an indication of the typical causes of such patterns.[1]

ONE POINT OUTSIDE CONTROL LIMITS

A single point outside the control limits (see Figure 15.10) is usually produced by a special cause. Often, the R-chart provides a similar indication. Once in a while, however, they are a normal part of the process and occur simply by chance.

A common reason for a point falling outside a control limit is an error in the calculation of $\bar{x}$ or R for the sample. You should always check your calculations whenever this occurs. Other possible causes are a sudden power surge, a broken tool, measurement error, or an incomplete or omitted operation in the process.

FIGURE 15.9   Revised Control Chart

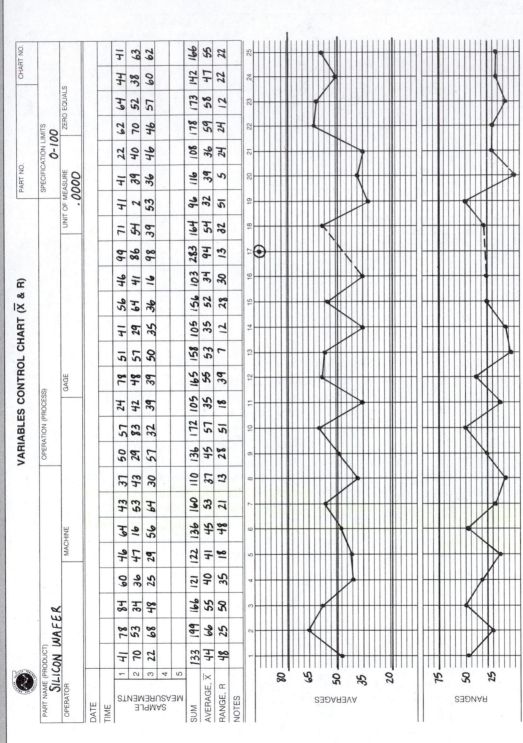

FIGURE 15.10   Single Point Outside Control Limits

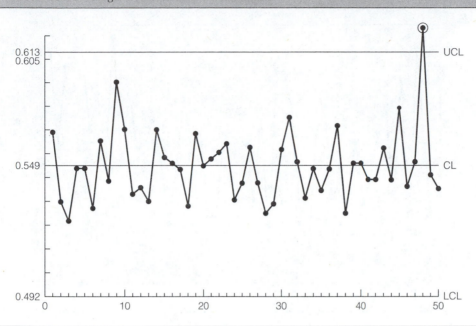

SUDDEN SHIFT IN THE PROCESS AVERAGE

An unusual number of consecutive points falling on one side of the center line (see Figure 15.11) is usually an indication that the process average has suddenly shifted. Typically, this occurrence is the result of an external influence that has affected the process, which would be considered a special cause. In both the $\bar{x}$- and R-charts, possible causes might be a new operator, a new inspector, a new machine setting, or a change in the setup or method.

If the shift is up in the R-chart, the process has become less uniform. Typical causes are carelessness of operators, poor or inadequate maintenance, or possibly a fixture in need of repair. If the shift is down in the R-chart, the uniformity of the process has improved. This might be the result of improved workmanship or better machines or materials. As mentioned, every effort should be made to determine the reason for the improvement and to maintain it.

Three rules of thumb are used for early detection of process shifts. A simple rule is that if eight consecutive points fall on one side of the center line, one could conclude that the mean has shifted. Second, divide the region between the center line and each control limit into three equal parts. Then if (1) two of three consecutive points fall in the outer one-third region between the center line and one of the control limits or (2) four of five consecutive points fall within the outer two-thirds region, one would also conclude that the process has gone out of control. Examples are illustrated in Figure 15.12.

CYCLES

Cycles are short, repeated patterns in the chart, having alternative high peaks and low valleys (see Figure 15.13). These patterns are the result of causes that come and go on a regular basis. In the $\bar{x}$-chart, cycles may be the result of operator rotation or fatigue at the end of a shift, different gauges used by different inspectors, seasonal effects such as temperature or humidity, or differences

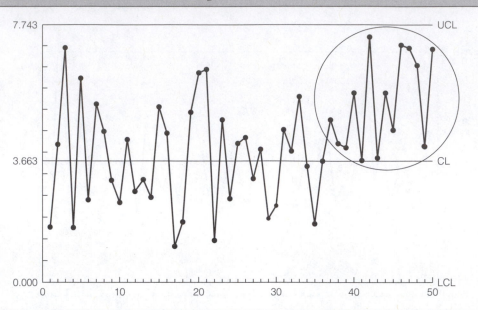

FIGURE 15.11   Shift in Process Average

between day and night shifts. In the R-chart, cycles can occur from maintenance schedules, rotation of fixtures or gauges, differences between shifts, or operator fatigue.

TRENDS

A trend is the result of some cause that gradually affects the quality characteristics of the product and causes the points on a control chart to gradually move up or down from the center line (see Figure 15.14). As a new group of operators gains experience on the job, for example, or as maintenance of equipment improves over time, a trend may occur. In the $\bar{x}$-chart, trends may be the result of improving operator skills, dirt or chip buildup in fixtures, tool wear, changes in temperature or humidity, or aging of equipment. In the R-chart, an increasing trend may be due to a gradual decline in material quality, operator fatigue, gradual loosening of a fixture or a tool, or dulling of a tool. A decreasing trend often is the result of improved operator skill, improved work methods, better purchased materials, or improved or more frequent maintenance.

HUGGING THE CENTER LINE

Hugging the center line occurs when nearly all the points fall close to the center line (see Figure 15.15). In the control chart, it appears that the control limits are too wide. A common cause of hugging the center line occurs when the sample includes one item systematically taken from each of several machines, spindles, operators, and so on. A simple example will serve to illustrate this pattern. Suppose that one machine produces parts whose diameters average 7.508 with variation of only a few thousandths; a second machine produces parts whose diameters average 7.502, again with only a small variation. Taken together, parts from both machines would yield a range of variation that would probably be between 7.500 and 7.510, and average about 7.505. Now suppose that one part

FIGURE 15.12 Examples of Out-of-Control Processes

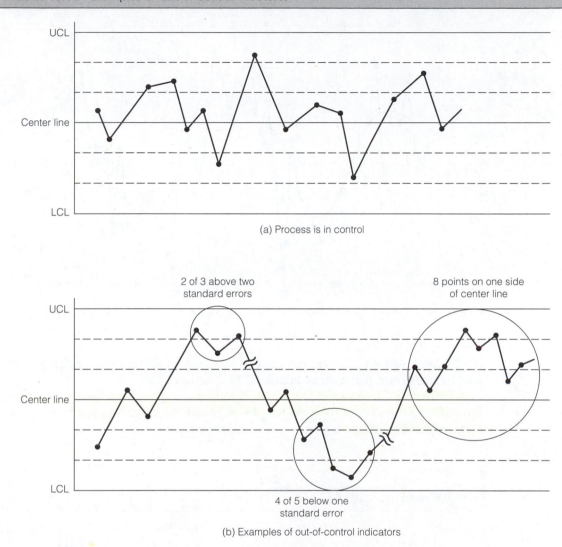

(a) Process is in control

(b) Examples of out-of-control indicators

from *each* machine is sampled, and a sample average computed to plot on an $\bar{x}$-chart. The sample averages will consistently be around 7.505, since one will always be high and the second will always be low. Even though a large variation will occur in the parts taken as a whole, the sample averages will not reflect this variation. In such a case, a control chart should be constructed for *each* machine, spindle, operator, and so on.

An often overlooked cause for this pattern is miscalculation of the control limits, perhaps by using the wrong factor from the table, or misplacing the decimal point in the computations.

HUGGING THE CONTROL LIMITS

This pattern shows up when many points are near the control limits with very few in between (see Figure 15.16). It is often called a mixture and is actually a

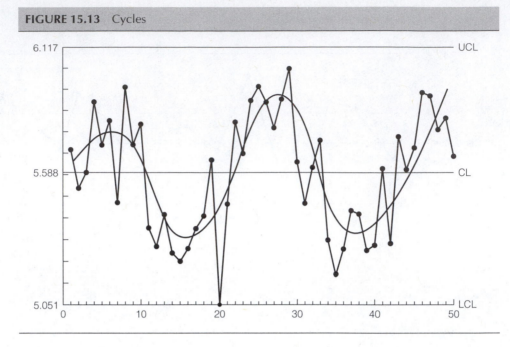

FIGURE 15.13 Cycles

combination of two different patterns on the same chart. A mixture can be split into two separate patterns, as Figure 15.17 illustrates.

A mixture pattern can result when different lots of material are used in one process, or when parts are produced by different machines but fed into a common inspection group.

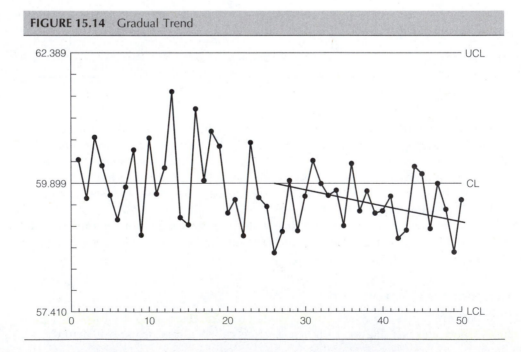

FIGURE 15.14 Gradual Trend

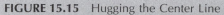

FIGURE 15.15 Hugging the Center Line

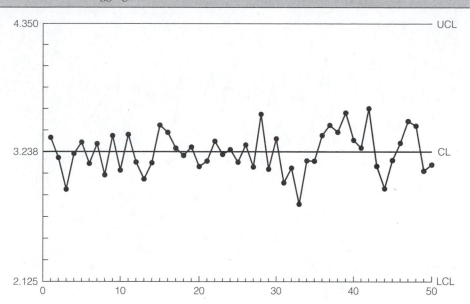

INSTABILITY

Instability is characterized by unnatural and erratic fluctuations on both sides of the chart over a period of time (see Figure 15.18). Points will often lie outside of both the upper and lower control limits without a consistent pattern. Assignable causes may be more difficult to identify in this case than when specific patterns are present. A frequent cause of instability is overadjustment of a machine, or the same reasons that cause hugging the control limits.

FIGURE 15.16 Hugging Control Limits

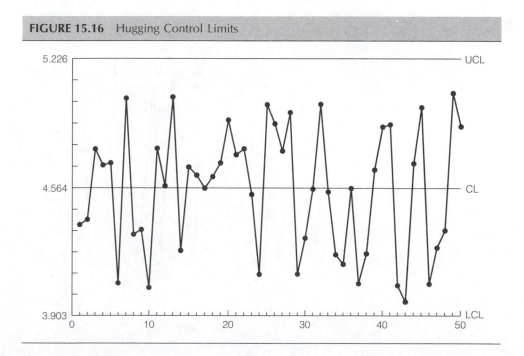

FIGURE 15.17 Illustration of Mixture

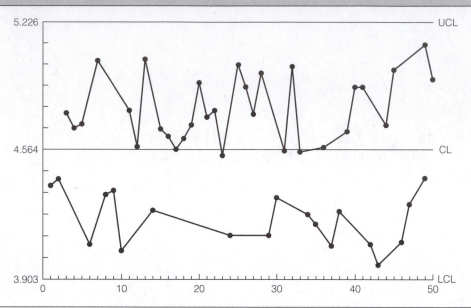

As suggested earlier, the ==R-chart should be analyzed before the $\bar{x}$-chart,== because some out-of-control conditions in the R-chart may *cause* out-of-control conditions in the $\bar{x}$-chart. Figure 15.19 gives an example of this situation. The range shows a drastic trend downward. If you examine the $\bar{x}$-chart, you will notice that the last several points seem to be hugging the center line. As the variability in the process decreases, all the sample observations will be closer to the true

FIGURE 15.18 Instability

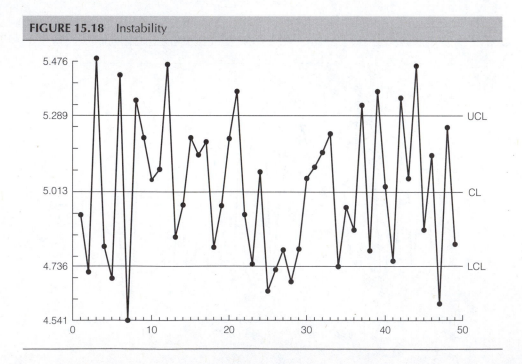

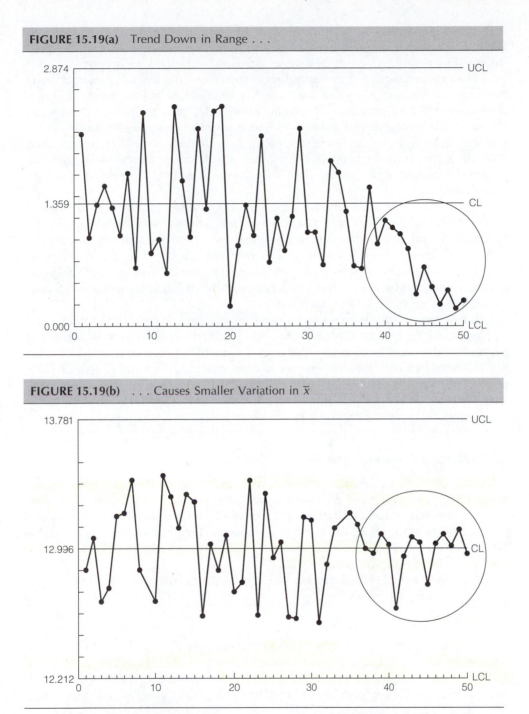

FIGURE 15.19(a) Trend Down in Range . . .

FIGURE 15.19(b) . . . Causes Smaller Variation in $\bar{x}$

population mean, and therefore their average, $\bar{x}$, will not vary much from sample to sample. If this reduction in the variation can be identified and controlled, then new control limits should be computed for both charts.

Process Monitoring and Control

After a process is determined to be in control, the charts should be used on a daily basis to monitor production, identify any special causes that might arise, and make corrections as necessary. More importantly, the chart tells when to leave the process alone. Unnecessary adjustments to a process result in nonproductive labor, reduced production, and increased variability of output.

It is more productive if the operators themselves take the samples and chart the data. In this way, they can react quickly to changes in the process and immediately make adjustments. To do this effectively, training of the operators is essential. Many companies conduct in-house training programs to teach operators and supervisors the elementary methods of statistical quality control. Not only does this training provide the mathematical and technical skills that are required, but it also gives the shop-floor personnel increased quality-consciousness.

Improvements in conformance typically follow the introduction of control charts on the shop floor, particularly when the process is labor intensive. Apparently, management involvement in operators' work often produces positive behavioral modifications (as first demonstrated in the famous Hawthorne studies). Under such circumstances, and as good practice, management and operators should revise the control limits periodically and determine a new process capability as improvements take place.

Control charts are designed to be used by production operators rather than by inspectors or quality control personnel. Under the philosophy of statistical process control, the burden of quality rests with the operators themselves. The use of control charts allows operators to react quickly to special causes of variation. The range is used in place of the standard deviation for the very reason that it allows shop floor personnel to easily make the necessary computations to plot points on a control chart. Only simple calculations are required.

◼ Estimating Process Capability

After a process has been brought to a state of statistical control by eliminating special causes of variation, the data may be used to estimate process capability. This approach is not as accurate as that described in Chapter 14 since it uses the average range rather than the estimated standard deviation of the original data. Nevertheless, it is a quick and useful method, provided that the distribution of the original data is reasonably normal.

Under the normality assumption, the standard deviation of the original data can be estimated as follows:

$$\sigma = \overline{R}/d_2$$

where d_2 is a constant that depends on the sample size and is also given in Appendix B. Process capability is therefore given by 6σ. The natural variation of individual measurements is given by $\overline{\overline{x}} + 3\sigma$. The back of the ASQC control chart form provides a work sheet for determining this. The following example illustrates these calculations.

EXAMPLE 2   Estimating Process Capability for the Silicon Wafer Thickness. Figure 15.20 shows the calculations for the silicon wafer example discussed earlier in the "Limits for Individuals" section of the form. For a sample of size 3, $d_2 = 1.693$. In Figure 15.20, UL_x and LL_x represent the upper and lower limit on individual observations, based on 3σ limits. Thus, the scaled thickness is expected to vary between -1.9 and 95.9. The zero point of the data is the lower specification, meaning that the thickness is expected to vary from 0.0019 below

FIGURE 15.20 Process Capability Calculations

CALCULATION WORK SHEET

CONTROL LIMITS

SUBGROUPS
INCLUDED _ALL_   _# 17 REMOVED_

$\bar{R} = \dfrac{\Sigma R}{k} = \dfrac{676}{25} = 27$ $\dfrac{663}{24} = 27.6$

$\bar{\bar{X}} = \dfrac{\Sigma \bar{X}}{k} = \dfrac{1221}{25} = 48.8$ $\dfrac{1127}{24} = 47.0$

OR

$\bar{X}'$ (MIDSPEC. OR STD.) $= 50$ $= 50$

$A_2\bar{R} = 1.023 \times 27 = 27.6$ $1.023 \times 27.6 = 28.2$

$UCL_{\bar{x}} = \bar{\bar{X}} + A_2\bar{R} = 76.4$ $= 75.2$

$LCL_{\bar{x}} = \bar{\bar{X}} - A_2\bar{R} = 21.2$ $= 18.8$

$UCL_R = D_4\bar{R} = 2.574 \times 27 = 69.5$ $2.574 \times 27.6 = 71.0$

LIMITS FOR INDIVIDUALS

COMPARE WITH SPECIFICATION OR
TOLERANCE LIMITS

$\bar{X} = 47.0$

$\dfrac{3}{d_2}\bar{R} = 1.772 \times 27.6 = 48.9$

$UL_x = \bar{X} + \dfrac{3}{d_2}\bar{R} = 95.9$

$LL_x = \bar{X} - \dfrac{3}{d_2}\bar{R} = -1.9$

$US = 100$

$LS = 0$

$US - LS = 100$

$6\sigma = \dfrac{6}{d_2}\bar{R} = 97.8$

MODIFIED CONTROL LIMITS FOR AVERAGES

BASED ON SPECIFICATION LIMITS AND PROCESS CAPABILITY.
APPLICABLE ONLY IF: $US - LS > 6\sigma$.

$US = $ $LS = $

$A_M\bar{R} = $ $x = $ _____ $A_M\bar{R} = $ _____

$URL_{\bar{x}} = US - A_M\bar{R} = $ $LRL_{\bar{x}} = LS + A_M\bar{R} = $

FACTORS FOR CONTROL LIMITS

n	A_2	D_4	d_2	$\dfrac{3}{d_2}$	A_M
2	1.880	3.268	1.128	2.659	0.779
3	1.023	2.574	1.693	1.772	0.749
4	0.729	2.282	2.059	1.457	0.728
5	0.577	2.114	2.326	1.290	0.713
6	0.483	2.004	2.534	1.184	0.701

the lower specification to 0.0959 above the lower specification. The process capability index (see Chapter 14) is

$$C_p = 100/97.8 = 1.02$$

However, the lower and upper capability indexes are

$$C_{pl} = (47 - 0)/48.9 = 0.96$$

$$C_{pu} = (100 - 47)/48.9 = 1.08$$

This analysis suggests that both the centering and the variation must be improved.

If the individual observations are normally distributed, then the probability of being out of specification can be computed. In the example above, assume that the data are normal. The mean is 47 and the standard deviation is $97.8/6 = 16.3$. Figure 15.21 shows the calculations for specification limits of 0 and 100. In Appendix A, the area between 0 and the mean (47) is 0.4980. Thus 0.2 percent of the output would be expected to fall below the lower specification. The area to the right of 100 is approximately zero. Therefore all the output can be expected to meet the upper specification.

A word of caution deserves emphasis here. Control limits are often confused with specification limits. Specification dimensions are usually stated in relation to individual parts for "hard" goods, such as automotive hardware. However, in other applications, such as in chemical processes, specifications are stated in terms of average characteristics. Thus, control charts might mislead one into thinking that if all sample averages fall within the control limits, all output will be conforming. This assumption is not true. Control limits relate to *averages,*

FIGURE 15.21　Process Capability Probability Computations

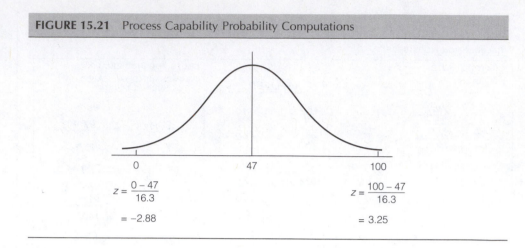

$$z = \frac{0 - 47}{16.3}$$

$$= -2.88$$

$$z = \frac{100 - 47}{16.3}$$

$$= 3.25$$

while specification limits relate to individual measurements. A sample average may fall within the upper and lower control limits even though some of the individual observations are out of specification. Since $\sigma_{\bar{x}} = \sigma/\sqrt{n}$, control limits are narrower than the natural variation in the process and do not represent process capability.

■ Modified Control Limits

The calculation work sheet on the back of the ASQC control chart form has one additional section entitled "Modified Control Limits for Averages." Modified control limits often are used when process capability is good. For example, suppose that the process capability is 60 percent of tolerance ($C_p = 1.67$) and that the mean can be controlled by a simple adjustment. A company may quickly discover the impracticality of investigating every isolated point that falls outside of the usual control limits because the output is probably well within specifications. In such cases, the usual control limits may be replaced with the following:

$$URL_x = US - A_m \bar{R}$$

$$LRL_x = LS + A_m \bar{R}$$

where URL_x is the upper reject level, LRL_x is the lower reject level, and US and LS are the upper and lower specifications, respectively. Factors for A_m are found on the work sheet. These modified control limits allow for more variation than the ordinary control limits and still provide high confidence that the product produced is within specifications. While the ASQC chart states that these modified limits apply only if the tolerance is greater than 6σ, many suggest that process capability should be at least 60 to 75 percent of tolerance. If the mean must be controlled closely, a conventional $\bar{x}$-chart should be used even if the process capability is good. Also, if the standard deviation of the process is likely to shift, then modified control limits are not appropriate.

EXAMPLE 3　Computing Modified Control Limits for the Silicon Wafer Case.
Figure 15.22 shows the completed work sheet for the silicon wafer thickness example illustrated in this chapter. Since the sample size is 3, $A_m = 0.749$. Therefore, the modified limits are

FIGURE 15.22 Modified Control Limit Calculations

CALCULATION WORK SHEET

CONTROL LIMITS		**LIMITS FOR INDIVIDUALS**

SUBGROUPS INCLUDED __ALL__   __#17 REMOVED__

COMPARE WITH SPECIFICATION OR TOLERANCE LIMITS

$\bar{R} = \frac{\Sigma R}{k} = \frac{676}{25}$ = 27 $\frac{663}{24}$ = 27.6

$\bar{\bar{X}} = \frac{\Sigma \bar{X}}{k} = \frac{1221}{25}$ = 48.8 $\frac{1127}{24}$ = 47.0

OR

$\bar{X}'$ (MIDSPEC. OR STD.) = 50   = 50

$A_2\bar{R} = 1.023 \times 27$ = 27.6 $1.023 \times 27.6 = 28.2$

$UCL_{\bar{x}} = \bar{\bar{X}} + A_2\bar{R}$ = 76.4   = 75.2

$LCL_{\bar{x}} = \bar{\bar{X}} - A_2\bar{R}$ = 21.2   = 18.8

$UCL_R = D_4\bar{R} = 2.574 \times 27$ $= 69.5$ $2.574 \times 27.6 = 71.0$

$\bar{X}$ = 47.0

$\frac{3}{d_2}\bar{R} = 1.772 \times 27.6 =$ 48.9

$UL_x = \bar{\bar{X}} + \frac{3}{d_2}\bar{R}$ = 95.9

$LL_x = \bar{\bar{X}} - \frac{3}{d_2}\bar{R}$ = -1.9

US = 100

LS = 0

US − LS = 100

$6\sigma = \frac{6}{d_2}\bar{R}$ = 97.8

MODIFIED CONTROL LIMITS FOR AVERAGES

BASED ON SPECIFICATION LIMITS AND PROCESS CAPABILITY.
APPLICABLE ONLY IF: US − LS > 6σ.

US = 100   LS = 0

$A_M\bar{R} = .749 \times 27.6 =$ 20.7 $A_M\bar{R}$ = 20.7

$URL_{\bar{x}} = US - A_M\bar{R}$ = 79.3 $LRL_{\bar{x}} = LS + A_M\bar{R} =$ 20.7

FACTORS FOR CONTROL LIMITS

n	A_2	D_4	d_2	$\frac{3}{d_2}$	A_M
2	1.880	3.268	1.128	2.659	0.779
3	1.023	2.574	1.693	1.772	0.749
4	0.729	2.282	2.059	1.457	0.728
5	0.577	2.114	2.326	1.290	0.713
6	0.483	2.004	2.534	1.184	0.701

$$URL_x = US - A_m\bar{R} = 100 - 0.749(27.6) = 79.3$$

$$LRL_x = LS + A_m\bar{R} = 0 + 0.749(27.6) = 20.7$$

Observe that if the process is centered on the nominal, these control limits are looser than the ordinary control limits. In this example, the centering would first have to be corrected from its current estimated value of 47.0.

CONTROL CHARTS FOR ATTRIBUTES

Attributes data assume only two values—good or bad, pass or fail, and so on. Attributes usually cannot be measured, but they can be observed and counted and are useful in many practical situations. For instance, in printing packages for consumer products, color quality can be rated as acceptable or not acceptable, or a sheet of cardboard either is damaged or is not. Usually, attributes data are easy to collect, often by visual inspection. Many accounting records, such as percent scrapped, are readily available. However, one drawback in using attributes data is that large samples are necessary to obtain valid statistical results.

Several different types of control charts are used for attributes data. One of the most common is the *p*-chart (introduced in this section). Other types of attributes charts are presented in the next chapter. One distinction that we must make is between the terms *defects* and *defectives*. A **defect** is a single nonconforming quality characteristic of an item. An item may have several defects. The term **defective** refers to items having one or more defects. Since certain attributes charts are used for defectives while others are used for defects, one must understand the difference. As pointed out in Chapter 14, the term *nonconforming* is often used instead of defective.

A **p-chart** monitors the proportion of nonconforming items produced in a lot. Often it is also called a **fraction nonconforming** or **fraction defective** chart. As with variables data, a p-chart is constructed by first gathering 25 to 30 samples of the attribute being measured. The size of each sample should be large enough to have several nonconforming items. If the probability of finding a nonconforming item is small, a large sample size is usually necessary. Samples are chosen over time periods so that any special causes that are identified can be investigated.

Let us suppose that k samples, each of size n, are selected. If y represents the number nonconforming in a particular sample, the proportion nonconforming is y/n. Let p_i be the fraction nonconforming in the ith sample; the average fraction nonconforming for the group of k samples then is

$$\bar{p} = \frac{p_1 + p_2 + \ldots + p_k}{k}$$

This statistic reflects the capability of the process. One would expect a high percentage of samples to have a fraction nonconforming within three standard deviations of $\bar{p}$. An estimate of the standard deviation is given by

$$s_{\bar{p}} = \sqrt{\frac{\bar{p}(1 - \bar{p})}{n}}$$

Therefore, upper and lower control limits are given by

$$\text{UCL}_p = \bar{p} + 3s_{\bar{p}}$$

$$\text{LCL}_p = \bar{p} - 3s_{\bar{p}}$$

If LCL_p is less than zero, a value of zero is used.

Analysis of a p-chart is similar to that of an $\bar{x}$- or R-chart. Points outside the control limits signify an out-of-control situation. Patterns and trends should also be sought to identify special causes. However, a point on a p-chart below the lower control limit or the development of a trend below the center line indicates that the process might have improved, since the ideal is zero defectives. Caution is advised before such conclusions are drawn, because errors may have been made in computation. An example of a p-chart is presented next.

EXAMPLE 4   Constructing an Attribute Chart.   The operators of automated sorting machines in a post office must read the ZIP code on a letter and divert the letter to the proper carrier route. Over one month's time, 25 samples of 100 letters were chosen, and the number of errors was recorded. This information is summarized in Table 15.3. The fraction nonconforming is found by dividing the number of errors by 100. The average fraction nonconforming, $\bar{p}$, is determined to be

$$\bar{p} = \frac{0.03 + 0.01 + \ldots + 0.01}{25} = 0.022$$

The standard deviation is computed as

$$s_{\bar{p}} = \sqrt{\frac{0.022(1 - 0.022)}{100}} = 0.01467$$

TABLE 15.3	Sorting Errors at a Post Office													
Sample	**1**	**2**	**3**	**4**	**5**	**6**	**7**	**8**	**9**	**10**	**11**	**12**	**13**	**14**	**15**
Errors	3	1	0	0	2	5	3	6	1	4	0	2	1	3	4
Sample	**16**	**17**	**18**	**19**	**20**	**21**	**22**	**23**	**24**	**25**					
Errors	1	1	2	5	2	3	4	1	0	1					

Thus, the upper control limit, UCL_p, is $0.022 + 3(0.01467) = 0.066$, and the lower control limit, LCL_p, is $0.022 - 3(0.01467) = -0.022$. Since this later figure is negative, zero is used. The control chart for this example is shown in Figure 15.23. The sorting process appears to be in control. Any values found above the upper control limit or evidence of an upward trend might indicate the need for more experience or training of the operators.

FIGURE 15.23 p-Chart for Post Office

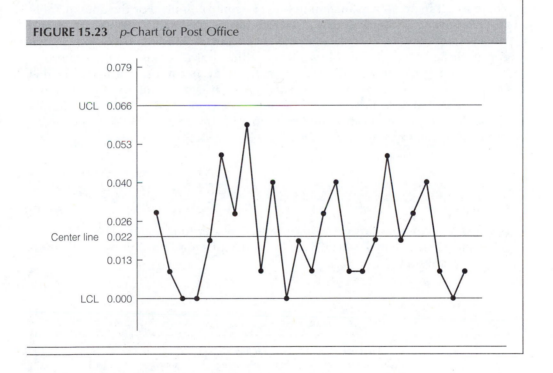

■ Variable Sample Size

Often 100 percent inspection is performed on process output during fixed sampling periods; however, the number of units produced in each sampling period may vary. In this case, the p-chart would have a variable sample size. One way of handling this is to compute a standard deviation for each individual sample. Thus, if the number of observations in the ith sample is n_i, control limits are given by

$$\bar{p} \pm 3 \sqrt{\frac{\bar{p}(1 - \bar{p})}{n_i}}$$

$$\text{where } \bar{p} = \frac{\sum \text{ number nonconforming}}{\sum n_i}$$

To illustrate this, suppose that data were recorded over 10 shifts as given in Table 15.4. Upper and lower control limits are also shown in the table. Figure 15.24 illustrates the resulting control chart.

Another approach is to use the average sample size, $\bar{n}$, to compute approximate control limits. Using the average sample size, the control limits are computed as

$$\text{UCL}_p = \bar{p} + 3 \sqrt{\frac{\bar{p}(1 - \bar{p})}{\bar{n}}}$$

and

$$\text{LCL}_p = \bar{p} - 3 \sqrt{\frac{\bar{p}(1 - \bar{p})}{\bar{n}}}$$

These result in an approximation to the true control limits. For the data in Table 15.4, the average sample size is $\bar{n} = 50.5$. Using this value, the upper control limit is calculated to be 0.1627, and the lower control limit is zero. However, this approach has several disadvantages. Since the control limits are only approximate, points that are actually out of control may not appear to be so on this chart. Second, runs or nonrandom patterns are difficult to interpret because the standard deviation differs between samples as a result of the variable sample sizes. Hence, this approach should be used with caution; a constant sample size is recommended whenever possible.

DESIGNING CONTROL CHARTS

Designers of control chart procedures must consider four issues: (1) the basis for sampling, (2) the sample size, (3) the frequency of sampling, and (4) the location of the control limits.

TABLE 15.4 Data for Variable Sample Sizes

Shift	n_i	Number Nonconforming	Fraction Nonconforming	3-sigma	UCL	LCL
1	40	2	0.050	0.114	0.175	0
2	55	3	0.055	0.097	0.158	0
3	45	3	0.067	0.107	0.168	0
4	40	4	0.100	0.114	0.175	0
5	65	3	0.046	0.089	0.150	0
6	60	3	0.050	0.093	0.154	0
7	35	2	0.057	0.122	0.183	0
8	70	3	0.043	0.086	0.147	0
9	50	4	0.080	0.102	0.163	0
10	45	4	0.089	0.107	0.168	0
	505	31				

$$\bar{p} = 31/505 = 0.0614$$

FIGURE 15.24   Control Chart for Variable Sample Size

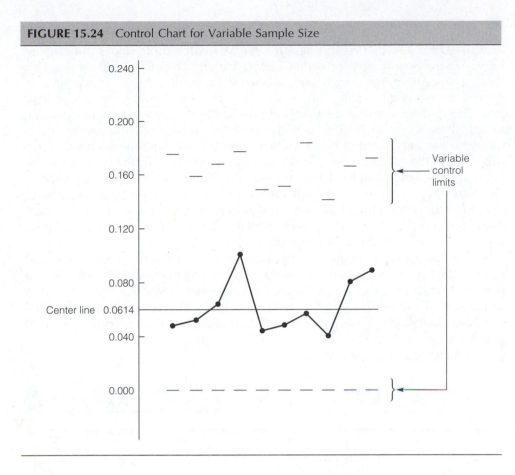

Basis for Sampling

Samples should be chosen to be as homogeneous as possible so that each sample reflects the system of common causes or assignable causes that may be present at that point in time. That is, if assignable causes are present, the chance of observing differences between samples should be high, while the chance of observing differences within a sample should be low. Samples that satisfy these criteria are called **rational subgroups.**

One approach to constructing rational subgroups is to use consecutive measurements from a machine over a short period of time. Consecutive measurements minimize the chance of variability within the sample while allowing variation between samples to be detected. This approach is useful when control charts are used to detect shifts in process level. A second approach is to take a random sample of all units produced since the last sample was taken, which would allow one to make a decision on the acceptance of all units produced since the last sample was taken. However, care must be taken when interpreting the *R*-chart using this method, since a shift in the process level would cause points on the *R*-chart to be out of control, even if no change in the variability of the process actually occurred. One must also be careful not to overlap production shifts, different batches of material, and so on, when selecting the basis for sampling. Thus, the method of selecting samples should be carefully chosen so as not to bias the results.

■ Sample Size

Sample size is a second critical design issue. A small sample size is desirable to minimize the opportunity for within-sample variation due to special causes. This issue is important, since each sample should be representative of the state of control at one point in time. In addition, the cost of sampling should be kept low. The time an operator spends taking the sample measurements and plotting a control chart represents nonproductive time (in a strict accounting sense only!). On the other hand, control limits are based on the assumption of a normal distribution of the sample means. If the process is not normal, this assumption is valid only for large samples. Large samples also allow smaller changes in process characteristics to be detected with higher probability. In practice, samples of about five have been found to work well in detecting process shifts of two standard deviations or larger. To detect smaller shifts in the process mean, larger sample sizes of 15 to 25 must be used.

Figure 15.25 shows the probability of detecting a shift in the mean in the next sample (that is, the probability of seeing the next point outside the 3-sigma control limit when the process has shifted some number of standard deviations) as a function of the sample size for an $\bar{x}$-chart. Thus, if a process has shifted 1.5 standard deviations, a sample size of 5 provides only a 64 percent chance of detection. For a 90 percent chance of detecting this particular process shift, a sample of at least eight is needed.

FIGURE 15.25   Probability of Detecting a Shift in Mean

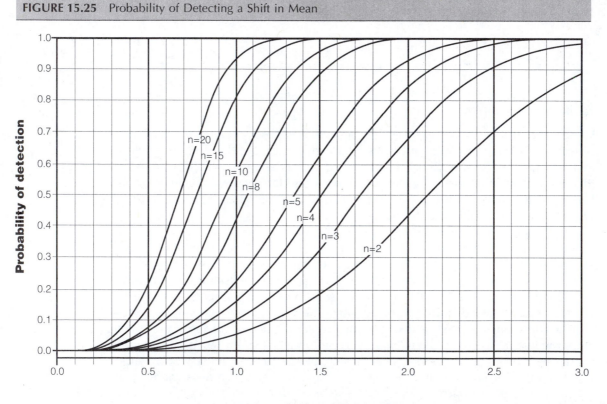

SOURCE: Adapted from Lyle Dockendorf, "Choosing Appropriate Sample Subgroup Sizes for Control Charts," *Quality Progress* 25, no. 10 (October 1992), 160.

For attributes data, too small a sample size can make a p-chart meaningless. Even though many guidelines such as "use at least 100 observations" have been suggested, the proper sample size should be determined statistically, particularly when the true portion of nonconformances is small. If p is small, n should be large enough to have a high probability of detecting at least one nonconformance. For example, if $p = .01$, then to have at least a 95 percent chance of finding at least one nonconformance, the sample size must be at least 300. Other approaches for determining attribute data sample sizes include choosing n large enough to provide a 50 percent chance of detecting a process shift of some specified amount, or choosing n so that the control chart will have a positive lower control limit. The reader is referred to the book by Montgomery in the bibliography for details on these calculations.

Sampling Frequency

The third design issue is the sampling frequency. Taking large samples on a frequent basis is desirable but clearly not economical. No hard and fast rules exist for the frequency of sampling. Samples should be close enough to provide an opportunity to detect changes in process characteristics as soon as possible and reduce the chances of producing a large amount of nonconforming output. However, they should not be so close that the cost of sampling outweighs the benefits that can be realized. This decision depends on the individual application and production volume.

Location of Control Limits

The location of control limits is closely related to the risk involved in making an incorrect assessment about the state of control. A Type I error occurs when an incorrect conclusion is reached that a *special cause is present when in fact one does not exist*. This error results in the cost of trying to find a nonexistent problem. A Type II error occurs when *special causes are present but are not signaled in the control chart* because points fall within the control limits by chance. Since nonconforming products have a greater chance to be produced, a cost will eventually be incurred as a result. The size of a Type I error depends only on the control limits that are used; the wider the limits, the less chance of a point falling outside the limits, and consequently the smaller is the chance of making a Type I error. A Type II error, however, depends on the width of the control limits, the degree to which the process is out of control, and the sample size. For a fixed sample size, wider control limits increase the risk of making a Type II error.

The traditional approach of using three-sigma limits implicitly assumes that the cost of a Type I error is large relative to that of a Type II error; that is, a Type I error is essentially minimized. This situation will not always be the case, however. Much research has been performed on economic design of control charts.[2] Cost models attempt to find the best combination of design parameters (center line, control limits, sample size, and sampling interval) that minimize expected cost or maximize expected profit.

Certain costs are associated with making both Type I and Type II errors. A Type I error results in unnecessary investigation for an assignable cause, including costs of lost production time and special testing. A Type II error can be more significant. If an out-of-control process is not recognized, defectives that are produced may result in higher costs of scrap and rework in later stages of production or after the finished good reaches the customer. Unfortunately, the cost of a Type II error is nearly impossible to estimate, since it depends on the amount of nonconforming products—a quantity that is unknown.

The costs associated with Type I and Type II errors conflict as control limits change. The tighter the control limits, the greater is the probability that a sample will indicate that the process is out of control. Hence, the cost of a Type I error increases as control limits are reduced. On the other hand, tighter control limits will reduce the cost of a Type II error, since out-of-control states will be more easily identified and the amount of defective output will be reduced.

The costs associated with sampling and testing may include lost productive time when the operator takes sample measurements, performs calculations, and plots the points on the control chart. If testing is destructive, the value of lost products would also be included. Thus, larger sample sizes and more frequent sampling result in higher costs.

The sample size and frequency also affect the costs of Type I and Type II errors. As the sample size or frequency is increased, both Type I and Type II errors are reduced, since better information is provided for decision making. Table 15.5 summarizes this discussion of the three-way interaction of costs. In the economic design of control charts, we must consider these simultaneously. Most models for such decisions can become quite complex and are beyond the scope of this text.

As a practical matter, one often uses judgment about the nature of operations and the costs involved in making these decisions. Mayer suggests the following guidelines:

1. If the cost of investigating an operation to identify the cause of an apparent out-of-control condition is high, a Type I error becomes important, and wider control limits should be adopted. Conversely, if that cost is low, narrower limits should be selected.

2. If the cost of the defective output generated by an operation is substantial, a Type II error is serious, and narrower control limits should be used. Otherwise, wider limits should be selected.

3. If the cost of a Type I error and the cost of a Type II error for a given activity are both significant, wide control limits should be chosen, and consideration should be given to reducing the risk of a Type II error by increasing the sample size. Also, more frequent samples should be taken to reduce the duration of any out-of-control condition that might occur.

4. If past experience with an operation indicates that an out-of-control condition arises quite frequently, narrower control limits should be favored because of the large number of opportunities for making a Type II error. In the event that the probability of an out-of-control condition is small, wider limits are preferred.[3]

TABLE 15.5 Economic Decisions for Control Chart Construction

Source of Cost	Sample Size	Sampling Frequency	Control Limits
Type I error	large	high	wide
Type II error	large	high	narrow
Sampling and testing	small	low	—

SPC FOR SHORT PRODUCTION RUNS

Control charts were developed for high-volume manufacturing situations in which production runs lasted for weeks or months. In some industries, particularly as the pressures for increased manufacturing flexibility increase, short production runs, perhaps for only a few hours, are common. In such situations enough samples to compute control limits may be impossible to collect. Even if it is possible, by the time the data are collected and the chart is constructed, the production run might be over, thus defeating the purpose of the chart.

Fortunately, classical SPC methods can often be modified to apply to short production runs. Three approaches can be used for variables data. First, tables of special control chart constants for control limits compensate for the fact that a limited number of samples are available.[4] As more data become available, this approach updates control limits until no further updates are needed and standard control chart factors can be used. A second approach is to "code" the data by subtracting the nominal value from the actual measurements. For example, consider a drill press in which each run requires varying depths of cut. Instead of measuring values of the actual depth of cut for a particular part, one can measure the deviation of depth from the target. In this way, differences between products and production runs are removed. In effect, this approach monitors *process* characteristics rather than *product* characteristics. Finally, the data can be transformed so that they are independent of the unit of measure; such charts are called **stabilized control charts.** The idea is similar to the familiar statistical concept of transforming normally distributed random variables to a normal random variable with mean 0 and variance 1 by subtracting the mean and dividing by the standard deviation. Common transformations are $(\bar{x} - \bar{\bar{x}})/\bar{R}$ and $R/\bar{R}$. For the $\bar{x}$-chart, control limits on the transformation $(\bar{x} - \bar{\bar{x}})/\bar{R}$ are UCL $= A_2$ and LCL $= -A_2$. Control limits for the R-chart based on the transformation $R/\bar{R}$ are UCL $= D_4$ and LCL $= D_3$.

Stabilized charts can be developed for any type of attribute chart by using the transformation

$z = $ (sample statistic $-$ process average)/standard deviation

For example, to develop a stabilized p-chart, use

$z = (p - \bar{p})/s_p$

Readers are encouraged to consult Pyzdek's book cited in the notes for further information.

IMPLEMENTING STATISTICAL PROCESS CONTROL

Control charts, like the other basic tools for quality improvement, are relatively simple to use. The following is a summary of the methodology for developing and using control charts:

1. Preparation
   a. Choose the variable or attribute to be measured.
   b. Determine the basis, size, and frequency of sampling.
   c. Set up the control chart.

2. Data collection
   a. Record the data.
   b. Calculate relevant statistics: averages, ranges, proportions, and so on.
   c. Plot the statistics on the chart.

3. Determination of trial control limits
   a. Calculate the average mean and range for $\bar{x}$- and R-charts or the average proportion for p-charts.
   b. Draw the center line on the chart.
   c. Compute the upper and lower control limits.

4. Analysis and interpretation
   a. Investigate the chart for lack of control.
   b. Eliminate out-of-control points.
   c. Recompute control limits if necessary.
   d. Determine process capability.

5. Use as a problem-solving tool
   a. Continue data collection and plotting.
   b. Identify out-of-control situations and take corrective action.

Control charts can provide significant benefits to a company. For example, Edgewood Tool and Manufacturing Company in Taylor, Michigan, had a problem with misformed parts on hood hinges for Ford trucks.[5] One critical dimension, the distance from the edge of a pierced hole to the edge of the part, was monitored with a control chart. They found that the variation increased whenever the operator loaded a new coil onto the machine. The solution was an inexpensive gauging block, which made loading and positioning the coil a more precise operation.

A number of reasons explain why control charts sometimes fail in organizations. Operators might not trust a new tool. Old methods, such as correcting a process only if production is out of specification or adjusting the machine after every batch, are difficult habits to break. Perhaps operators did not receive enough training or practice or do not fully understand the benefits. Another reason is the lack of a corrective action plan. The concept of control requires that assignable causes be identified and corrected. Failure to act on control chart signals increases variability, reduces the importance of the chart, and undermines the entire quality program.

One must also be careful to use the appropriate chart. Attributes charts are easier to use. However, using an attributes chart when a variables chart is more appropriate leads to loss of sensitivity, loss of information for corrective action, and interpretation of quality in terms of defects rather than uniformity to a target.

Management has the responsibility to show commitment, not simply give lip service. Their commitment will become evident in cases in which the use of control charts means that corrective action will delay a shipment. If not supported by management, operators will quickly see that they are wasting their time and stop using SPC. In addition, management must accept the fact that control charts require maintenance. Control limits must be periodically updated as elements of the process change and as assignable causes are eliminated—an outdated chart is useless. Upper management must commit financial resources for measurement instruments, calculators, or computers and software, as well as training for workers to learn the mechanics of SPC. Management must demonstrate that SPC is not a fad that will disappear in a few months, but is an ongoing commitment to improve quality. Integrating SPC into daily work will disrupt production to some extent, and managers must recognize and prepare for this cost of improvement.

Second, successful SPC projects need a champion, that is, some individual in the company who has both the responsibility and the authority to make it work. Any kind of new business venture invariably fails without a champion to promote it and ensure its success.

Third, only one problem should be addressed at a time. If a company has never used SPC before, it makes little sense to try to introduce it throughout an entire plant or even an entire department at once. Mistakes will be made at the beginning from which the company will learn. In choosing an initial project, managers should select one that stands to benefit the most from SPC and that will have high visibility both to top management and other workers. One good success story will lead others to try SPC; therefore, they need to be well publicized within the company. Pareto diagrams and cause-and-effect diagrams are useful tools for choosing projects to tackle.

Fourth, education and training of all employees is absolutely necessary. Everyone needs to understand why SPC is being used and what it can do to improve quality and help the worker do a better job. Workers must understand that SPC will benefit them and is not a scheme set up by management to place blame on them.

Finally, the gauging and measurement system must first be evaluated for accuracy, repeatability, and reproducibility before implementing SPC. These features must be evaluated statistically, not on the basis of intuition or "experience."

Numerous implementation problems can arise because of poor planning. A case in point is the Uniroyal Goodrich Tire Plant in Fort Wayne, Indiana.[6] The plant began its process of implementing SPC by sending managers to an SPC seminar sponsored by an automobile manufacturer. In-house training began in 1982 and several tracking charts (not true control charts) had been established by 1983 to monitor various quality characteristics. With some positive results, SPC appeared to be working, and indications were that the initial success would multiply. In 1984, a full-time coordinator was assigned to implement SPC. A basic course was developed for first-line supervisors. Next, one or two hours of training in basic control charting were given to small groups of hourly employees. By 1985, the number of charts used in production increased. Soon afterward however, management realized that insufficient resources existed to follow up on the information being collected. Some employees began to question the value of keeping the charts. Obviously, something had gone wrong.

In 1985, the plant manager took a different direction. He established a seven-member steering committee consisting of two production managers, the SPC coordinator, an SPC instructor, the QA manager, and two department facilitators. In reviewing the history to that point, the committee reached several conclusions:

1. The charts being developed were tracking documents, not control charts, and had limited value.

2. The SPC process was primarily an educational exercise. Much of the training had not been put to practical use.

3. SPC was not made a part of daily business.

4. Employees did not understand the factors that led to successful implementation of SPC.

One of their first tasks was to visit a local company that had an established SPC program and an excellent reputation for quality. As a result they developed a six-step implementation process that involved a project group approach instead of traditional classroom training, with heavy emphasis on employee participation. This process involved the following steps:

1. *Define the process:* What are the important parts of an operation? Flowcharts provide a useful visual means of characterizing a process. This step is not a trivial exercise. Conflicting opinions often abound, and these must be resolved. Bringing people together in this task produces a sharing of perceptions and insights and can be an enlightening experience for all participants. A focus on customer satisfaction—and identification of the customer—helps to clarify the process and break down barriers to communication.

2. *Identify characteristics to study:* What are the important quality parameters? Most processes have many characteristics; all of them cannot be monitored. Pareto analysis is one method for prioritizing these characteristics. Are they machine-controllable or operator-controllable? For operator-controllable parameters, the operators must monitor themselves. A good management–employee relationship is necessary.

3. *Determine the ability to measure the characteristic:* A shortcoming of many SPC programs is the failure to assess the measurement tools. If the measurement system is unsatisfactory, all subsequent SPC activities may be useless. Many employees often resist the idea of performing such studies. SPC groups should be trained in the methods and importance of gauge studies (see Chapter 14).

4. *Perform capability studies:* Both Chapter 14 and this chapter discuss this topic. One of the fundamental purposes of SPC is to establish a state of statistical control so that process capability can be determined. Knowing process capability is the first step toward resolving chronic problems and reducing common causes of variation. Workers must be taught the concept of variation, the use of control charts, and their role in capability studies. Process capability studies can become quite popular with employees since they show the variation that is management-controllable and for which the workers cannot be blamed.

5. *Study process performance.* This step is an extension of capability studies to determine what actual variation is present. Using control charts to monitor performance and identify special causes leads to identification of various sources of variation and, eventually, to their elimination.

6. *Implement process control:* Most companies start their SPC programs with this step after formal training is provided, which is the reason why many programs are not successful. Starting with steps 1 through 5 provides a foundation of training, employee involvement, and problem solving. By the time an SPC group reaches this step, they are thoroughly familiar with using control charts, and little training, if any, is needed to make the transition to real-time control using SPC. Because of the extensive employee participation in the previous steps, implementation is usually quite easy.

Control charts themselves need to be controlled.[7] As part of an ongoing process, managers should look for signs that indicate operators are just going through the motions. Control limits need periodic review and possible revision if the process has changed. Records should be kept showing the data and the calculations used. Control charts should provide information about the process. Managers who review actions taken as a result of control chart indicators can determine how effective the control charts are for improving processes.

■ SPC Computer Software

Many different sortware packages exist for implementing SPC on computers. *Quality Progress*, a publication of the American Society for Quality Control, publishes a quality-related software directory in its March issue. In 1995, the directory listed more than 120 companies that offered SPC software products. These commercial packages are highly sophisticated. To illustrate the capability of current SPC software, this section briefly discusses *SQCpack/PLUS®*, a product developed by PQ Systems, Inc., headquartered in Dayton, Ohio. PQ Systems is a full-service firm offering a comprehensive array of products and services designed to improve quality and productivity.

SQCpack/PLUS includes the following capabilities:

■ *X-bar and range charts:* The user can select multiple sets of control limits to show process improvement, compute accurate statistics even with incomplete subgroup data, perform out-of-control tests, and show raw data on reports.

■ *Multichart:* This feature combines histograms, capability indexes, and control charts on one page in a user-customized layout.

■ *Pearson curve fitting:* With this feature, the user can perform non-normal data analysis and goodness-of-fit tests for non-normal data.

■ *Scatter diagram:* As discussed in Chapter 9, a scatter diagram shows correlations among key variables.

■ *Attributes charts:* These include *p-* *np-* *c,-* and *u*-charts (see the next chapter), along with out-of-control tests.

■ *Cause-and-effect diagrams:* These diagrams allow the user to enter an unlimited number of branches with multiple levels of subbranches, printing on multiple pages for large displays, and zoom-in capability on small parts of the diagram.

■ *Pareto diagrams:* Pareto data can be drawn directly from attributes files, and multiple charts can be displayed.

■ *SQCreport™:* This feature presents customized reports that summarize SPC analysis.

■ *SQC Quality Advisor™:* This feature provides on-line, real-time SPC assistance and advice, such as what type of chart to use and how to interpret the information.

Figure 15.26 shows a summary file of 25 samples for the groove depth of an O-ring. The charts, shown in Figure 15.27, indicate two out-of-control points. The software allows the user to obtain summary statistics on individual data points as well as a histogram as shown in Figure 15.28. Such user-friendly software packages make SPC easy to use for front-line operators in monitoring and analyzing data for quality improvement. Development in SPC software continues. For example, PQ Systems, Inc., recently released a Windows™ version: *SQCpack®* for Windows™.

FIGURE 15.26   *SQC pack/PLUS* Sample Summary File

File: O-RING   Date: 11-03-1994

Characteristic...Groove depth of an O-ring
Company..........University of Cincinnati
Plant............   Part name........
Department.......Carole   Part number......
Machine.........shaft   Sample frequency.30 min.
Operation........TQT data p.4   Units............001"

#	ID	X-bar	Range	Median	Sigma	Cause	Observations				
1	7:00	44.80	1.1	45.00	0.44		45.3	45.0	44.2	45.0	44.5
2	7:30	45.06	0.5	45.00	0.19		45.2	44.8	45.0	45.3	45.0
3	8:00	45.80	1.5	46.00	0.67		46.0	46.3	46.5	45.2	45.0
4	8:30	44.88	0.7	45.00	0.28		45.0	45.2	44.5	44.7	45.0
5	9:00	45.36	1.0	45.30	0.42		45.0	45.3	45.5	45.0	46.0
6	9:30	45.72	1.2	45.80	0.46		46.0	46.2	45.0	45.8	45.6
7	10:00	45.46	1.0	45.50	0.46		45.0	45.0	45.5	46.0	45.8
8	10:30	45.04	1.5	45.00	0.62		46.0	44.5	44.5	45.0	45.2
9	11:00	45.26	0.5	45.30	0.25		45.0	45.3	45.5	45.5	45.0
10	11:30	45.80	2.0	46.00	0.77		44.5	46.2	46.5	46.0	45.8
11	12:00	44.92	1.0	45.00	0.37		44.3	45.0	45.0	45.3	45.0
12	12:30	44.82	0.7	45.00	0.30		45.0	44.3	45.0	44.8	45.0
13	1:00	46.06	1.7	46.00	0.70	TC	47.0	45.5	45.3	46.5	46.0
14	1:30	44.80	2.0	44.50	0.80		44.3	44.5	44.0	46.0	45.2
15	2:00	45.00	1.0	45.00	0.38		45.2	45.0	45.5	44.8	44.5
16	2:30	45.32	1.0	45.50	0.41		45.5	45.8	45.5	44.8	45.0
17	3:00	46.20	1.8	46.30	0.67	ETW	46.9	46.3	46.5	45.1	46.2
18	3:30	45.26	0.5	45.30	0.25		45.5	45.3	45.0	45.5	45.0
19	4:00	45.52	1.0	45.50	0.40		45.0	45.5	45.3	46.0	45.8
20	4:30	45.00	1.0	45.00	0.38		45.5	45.2	44.5	44.8	45.0
21	5:00	45.40	0.7	45.50	0.29		45.7	45.5	45.2	45.0	45.6
22	5:30	45.16	1.3	45.00	0.53		45.0	45.9	44.8	45.5	44.6
23	6:00	45.38	0.7	45.50	0.28		45.5	45.2	45.7	45.5	45.0
24	6:30	45.34	1.5	45.50	0.59		46.0	44.5	45.0	45.7	45.5
25	7:00	45.70	0.7	45.70	0.31		46.0	45.7	46.0	45.3	45.5

TC=Tool Change   ETW=Excessive Tool Wear

SOURCE: Chart produced by *SQCpack/PLUS*® 2.0 from PQ Systems, Inc.

SPC IN SERVICE ORGANIZATIONS

Earlier chapters observed that service organizations all share common features that differ from manufacturing. These features include direct contact with the customer, large volumes of transactions and processing, and often large amounts of paperwork. One can easily see that the sources of error are considerable in recording transactions and in processing. Newspaper reports of large errors in

FIGURE 15.27 *SQC pack/PLUS* Charts

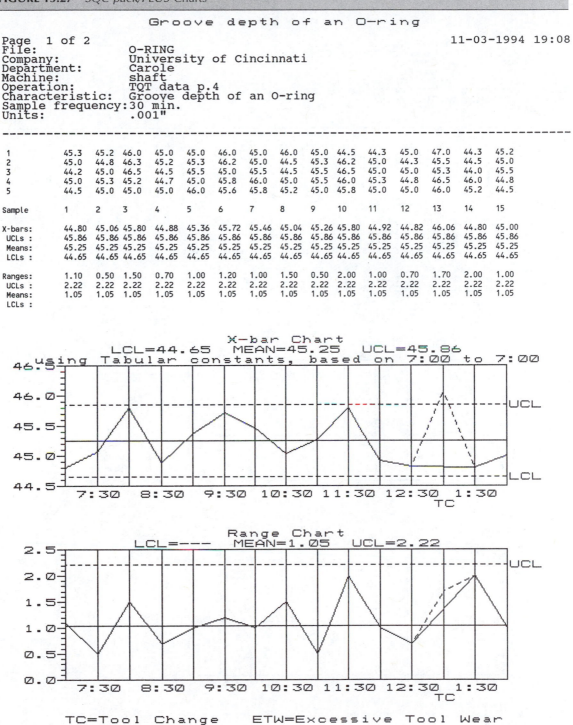

```
                 Groove depth of an O-ring

Page  1 of 2                              11-03-1994 19:08
File:              O-RING
Company:           University of Cincinnati
Department:        Carole
Machine:           shaft
Operation:         TQT data p.4
Characteristic:    Groove depth of an O-ring
Sample frequency:30 min.
Units:             .001"
-----------------------------------------------------------

1      45.3  45.2  46.0  45.0  45.0  46.0  45.0  46.0  45.0  44.5  44.3  45.0  47.0  44.3  45.2
2      45.0  44.8  46.3  45.2  45.3  46.2  45.0  44.5  45.3  46.2  45.0  44.3  45.5  45.0
3      44.2  45.0  46.5  44.5  45.5  45.0  45.5  44.5  45.5  46.5  45.0  45.0  45.3  44.0  45.5
4      45.0  45.3  45.2  44.7  45.0  45.8  46.0  45.0  45.5  46.0  45.3  44.8  46.5  46.0  44.8
5      44.5  45.0  45.0  45.0  46.0  45.6  45.8  45.2  45.0  45.8  45.0  45.0  46.0  45.2  44.5

Sample  1     2     3     4     5     6     7     8     9    10    11    12    13    14    15

X-bars: 44.80 45.06 45.80 44.88 45.36 45.72 45.46 45.04 45.26 45.80 44.92 44.82 46.06 44.80 45.00
UCLs :  45.86 45.86 45.86 45.86 45.86 45.86 45.86 45.86 45.86 45.86 45.86 45.86 45.86 45.86 45.86
Means:  45.25 45.25 45.25 45.25 45.25 45.25 45.25 45.25 45.25 45.25 45.25 45.25 45.25 45.25 45.25
LCLs :  44.65 44.65 44.65 44.65 44.65 44.65 44.65 44.65 44.65 44.65 44.65 44.65 44.65 44.65 44.65

Ranges: 1.10  0.50  1.50  1.00  1.00  1.20  1.00  1.50  0.50  2.00  1.00  0.70  1.70  2.00  1.00
UCLs :  2.22  2.22  2.22  2.22  2.22  2.22  2.22  2.22  2.22  2.22  2.22  2.22  2.22  2.22  2.22
Means:  1.05  1.05  1.05  1.05  1.05  1.05  1.05  1.05  1.05  1.05  1.05  1.05  1.05  1.05  1.05
LCLs :
```

X-bar Chart

LCL=44.65 MEAN=45.25 UCL=45.86

using Tabular constants, based on 7:00 to 7:00

Range Chart

LCL=--- MEAN=1.05 UCL=2.22

TC=Tool Change   ETW=Excessive Tool Wear

Continued

FIGURE 15.27   *SQC pack/PLUS* Charts—*Continued*

```
                  Groove  depth  of  an  O-ring
Page  2 of 2                                              11-03-1994 19:08
File:                O-RING
Company:             University of Cincinnati
Department:          Carole
Machine:             shaft
Operation:           TQT data p.4
Characteristic:      Groove depth of an O-ring
Sample frequency:30 min.
Units:               .001"
```

1	45.2	45.5	46.9	45.5	45.0	45.5	45.7	45.0	45.5	46.0	46.0
2	45.0	45.8	46.3	45.3	45.5	45.2	45.5	45.9	45.2	44.5	45.7
3	45.5	45.5	46.5	45.0	45.3	44.5	45.2	44.8	45.7	45.0	46.0
4	44.8	44.8	45.1	45.5	46.0	44.8	45.0	45.5	45.5	45.7	45.3
5	44.5	45.0	46.2	45.0	45.8	45.0	45.6	44.6	45.0	45.5	45.5

Sample	15	16	17	18	19	20	21	22	23	24	25

X-bars:	45.00	45.32	46.20	45.26	45.52	45.00	45.40	45.16	45.38	45.34	45.70
UCLs :	45.86	45.86	45.86	45.86	45.86	45.86	45.86	45.86	45.86	45.86	45.86
Means:	45.25	45.25	45.25	45.25	45.25	45.25	45.25	45.25	45.25	45.25	45.25
LCLs :	44.65	44.65	44.65	44.65	44.65	44.65	44.65	44.65	44.65	44.65	44.65

Ranges:	1.00	1.00	1.80	0.50	1.00	1.00	0.70	1.30	0.70	1.50	0.70
UCLs :	2.22	2.22	2.22	2.22	2.22	2.22	2.22	2.22	2.22	2.22	2.22
Means:	1.05	1.05	1.05	1.05	1.05	1.05	1.05	1.05	1.05	1.05	1.05
LCLs :											

```
                         X-bar  Chart
          LCL=44.65    MEAN=45.25    UCL=45.86
        using Tabular constants, based on 7:00 to 7:00
  46.5
  46.0  - - - - - - - - - - - - - - - - - - - - - - - UCL
  45.5
  45.0
  44.5  - - - - - - - - - - - - - - - - - - - - - - - LCL
         2:30    3:30    4:30    5:30    6:30
         ETW
```

```
                         Range  Chart
          LCL=---       MEAN=1.05    UCL=2.22
  2.5
  2.0  - - - - - - - - - - - - - - - - - - - - - - - UCL
  1.5
  1.0
  0.5
  0.0
         2:30    3:30    4:30    5:30    6:30
         ETW

  TC=Tool Change    ETW=Excessive Tool Wear
```

FIGURE 15.28   *SQC pack/PLUS* Histogram

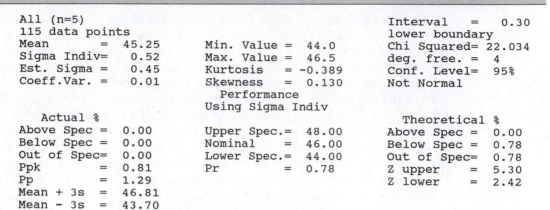

```
All (n=5)                                              Interval    =   0.30
115 data points                                        lower boundary
Mean         =   45.25    Min. Value =   44.0          Chi Squared=  22.034
Sigma Indiv=     0.52     Max. Value =   46.5          deg. free. =  4
Est. Sigma =     0.45     Kurtosis   =  -0.389         Conf. Level=  95%
Coeff.Var. =     0.01     Skewness   =   0.130         Not Normal
                             Performance
                          Using Sigma Indiv
       Actual %                                           Theoretical %
Above Spec =    0.00      Upper Spec.=  48.00          Above Spec =   0.00
Below Spec =    0.00      Nominal    =  46.00          Below Spec =   0.78
Out of Spec=    0.00      Lower Spec.=  44.00          Out of Spec=   0.78
Ppk        =    0.81      Pr         =   0.78          Z upper    =   5.30
Pp         =    1.29                                   Z lower    =   2.42
Mean + 3s  =   46.81
Mean - 3s  =   43.70
```

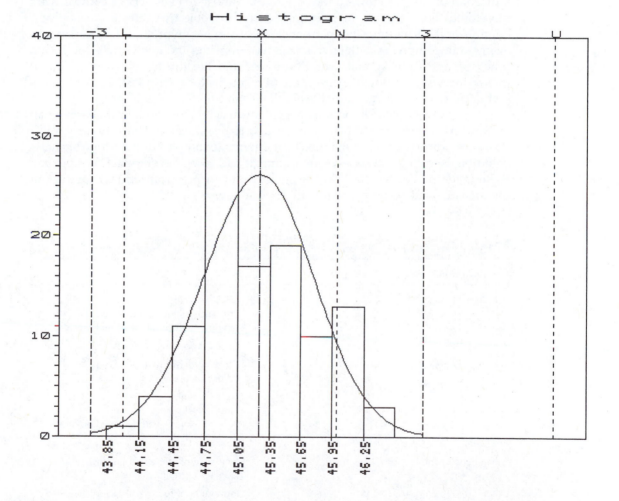

SOURCE: Chart produced by *SQC pack/PLUS*® 2.0 from PQ Systems, Inc.

billing that amounts to thousands or hundreds of thousands of dollars are not uncommon.

Although control charts were first developed and used in a manufacturing context, they are easily applied to service organizations. The major difference is the quality characteristic that is controlled. Many of the standards used in service industries form the basis for quality control charts. Table 15.6 lists just a few of the many potential applications of control charts for services.

IBM's Kingston, New York, facility provides a good example of the application of SPC in service organizations.[8] IBM Kingston tests and ships mainframe computers in addition to developing hardware and software products. Meeting customer requirements and reducing costs are principal goals that extend to the purchasing, security, administration, maintenance, and personnel departments. Each department identifies objectives for its business and user customers, and then develops a set of measurements to provide senior management with a quarterly indication of progress toward the objectives. Almost 200 key service processes are monitored. For example, in personnel safety, the objectives are to develop and administer the Kingston site's personnel safety and health programs, to assist management in complying with government requirements and good safety and health practices, and to make and keep IBM a safe and healthy place to work without interfering with employee's jobs. Measurements include days lost, worker's compensation cases, OSHA recordable accidents, and first-aid cases.

When the IBM site services management decided to try control charts as an aid toward improvement, managers needed to be educated. Unfortunately, most texts treated the subject in manufacturing terms. Examples of how control charts could be used in a site services environment had to be developed. Concepts had to be taken out of the statistical realm and put in practical terms. Examples of the areas in which control charts are used follow.

TABLE 15.6 Control Chart Applications in Service Organizations

Organization	Quality Measure
Hospital	Lab test accuracy
	Insurance claim accuracy
	On-time delivery of meals and medication
Bank	Check-processing accuracy
Insurance company	Claims-processing response time
	Billing accuracy
Post office	Sorting accuracy
	Time of delivery
	Percent express mail delivered on time
Ambulance	Response time
Police department	Incidence of crime in a precinct
	Number of traffic citations
Hotel	Proportion of rooms satisfactorily cleaned
	Checkout time
	Number of complaints received
Transportation	Proportion of freight cars correctly routed
	Dollar amount of damage per claim
Auto service	Percent of time work completed as promised
	Number of parts out of stock

SPEAK-UP!

The Speak-Up! program is an employee communications channel. It provides a way for employees to pass along a grievance, an idea, a comment, or a thank you to management. An employee forwards an informal letter to the Speak-Up! administrator. The administrator has the letter typed, deleting the employee's name to ensure confidentiality. The letter is routed to the appropriate functional manager who investigates and drafts a reply for the signature of a senior manager. The administrator mails the signed response to the employee.

Response time is critical to the program. Those assigned to answer the letters must meet a number of requirements. Responses must admit when mistakes have occurred, describe any change that will be implemented, avoid defensive tone, answer all questions raised, be short, and be written in a style used by the senior manager. A deficiency in any of these areas can cause a delay because the response will have to be revised. In looking at historical data, management noticed that in certain functional areas replies took longer than in other areas. Control charts were used to track response time by functional area. A workshop was also set up to assure that people writing answers knew how to do so.

Control charts used samples of five letters per week for 20 weeks. The average was found to be below the previous average, showing the impact of the tracking and the workshop. As the use of the chart continued, two consecutive weeks with sample averages beyond two standard errors were noted. The cause was vacation coverage—the answers were written by people who had not attended the workshop.

PREEMPLOYMENT MEDICAL EXAMS

Preemployment medical exams took too long and taxed the medical staff assigned to conduct them. Examinations were vital to assure that employees could do the job without excess stress and posed no clinical threat to other employees. The challenge IBM faced was to maintain the quality of the exam while reducing the time required for it. They did so by identifying and eliminating waiting periods between various parts of the exam.

Preliminary control charts revealed that the average time required for the physical was 74 minutes; the range, however, varied greatly. New equipment and additional training of the medical staff were suggested as a means of shortening the time. Initial charts were out of control, but continued monitoring and process improvements lowered the average time to 40 minutes, and both the average and range charts were brought into statistical control.

PURCHASE ORDERS

The steps involved in processing purchase orders were fairly routine. The person requesting an item or service filled out a requisition and forwarded it to a buyer who translated it into an order. The buyer selected a supplier, usually after a number of bids.

Time and money were being lost through human error. Both requesters and buyers were contributing to the situation. The purchasing organization was concerned with nonconforming documents originating from the purchasing department iteslf. The department started to count them. Data on weekly purchase orders and orders in error were monitored, and a *p*-chart was constructed that showed an average error rate of 5.9 percent. After the buyers reviewed the data, they found that the process had actually changed during the data collection period, resulting in a shift in the mean to 3.7 percent. The use of the chart also showed out-of-control conditions resulting from vacations. Substitute buyers created a high percentage of rework because of the workload and their unfamiliarity with particular aspects of the process. Preventive measures were created for peak vacation periods to provide sufficient coverage and to ensure that temporary replacements understood the process better.

These examples show how control charts can be used to improve both quality and productivity. The key is in defining the appropriate quality measures to monitor. Once these definitions are articulated and agreed on by management, the use of control charts becomes routine. Most service processes can be improved through the appropriate application of control charts.

QUALITY IN PRACTICE

USING SQC FOR PROCESS IMPROVEMENT AT DOW CHEMICAL COMPANY[9]

The magnesium department of the Dow Chemical Company in Freeport, Texas, has produced magnesium, a silvery light metal, for over 70 years. This department was the first major group in Texas Operations to train all its technical people and managers in the use of statistical quality control (SQC) techniques, following the example set by the automobile industry.

Some of the earliest successful applications of SQC were in chemical process areas. Figures 15.29 and 15.30 show the improvement in the drier analysis after SQC and retraining were implemented. In addition to the fact that the process control required significant improvement, differences between operators were found. The blackened circles in Figure 15.29 represent one operator in question; the open circles represent the other operators. On examination, management discovered that the operator had

not been properly trained in the use of SQC even though he had been performing this analysis for two years. An immediate improvement in the consistency of the analysis between the operators occurred after retraining.

The use of control charts in the control room made the operators realize that their attempts to fine tune the process introduced a great deal of unwanted variation. A comparison of the before and after range charts shows the improvement (see Figure 15.30).

As with many chemical and manufacturing operations, when the variability of the feedstock to one operation is reduced, the variability of the basic operation can be reduced as well. With tighter control over the concentration of magnesium hydroxide from the filter plant, Dow was able to exert much tighter control of the subsequent neutralization op-

FIGURE 15.29 Before and After x-Bar Charts on Drier Analysis

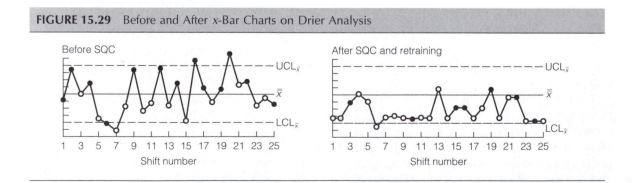

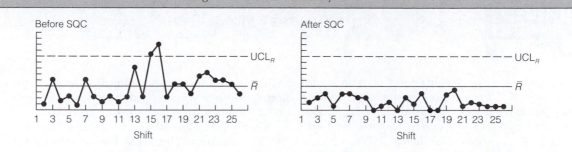

FIGURE 15.30 Before and After Range Charts on Drier Analysis

eration. As seen in Figure 15.31, the differences are substantial. The upper control limit on the second range chart is about where the center line is on the first range chart. A similar situation exists on the $\bar{x}$-charts. These improvements resulted without any additional instrumentation or operators.

Another application involved the casting operation. On primary magnesium, for example, Dow calculated a process capability index, C_{pk}, of meeting a minimum magnesium content of 99.8 percent purity and found it to be over 10, based on more than 10,000 samples. Thus the comfortable level of compliance in this operation resulted in little incentive to use control charts. However, ingots are also graded according to their surface quality. Using control charts, Dow found that the process was in control but that the number of rejects was much higher than desired. After several months of analysis and modifications, this process was improved.

Dow Chemical Company experienced success everywhere that SQC was implemented in the magnesium process. Documented savings of several hundred thousand dollars per year were realized, with new applications continually being discovered.

Key Issues for Discussion

1. What conclusions are indicated by the control charts in Figures 15.29, 15.30, and 15.31?

2. For primary magnesium, the high C_{pk} value suggested that control charts were not needed. How might the company maintain control of the process at this level without them?

FIGURE 15.31 *x*-Bar and *R*-Charts on Neutralizer Excess Alkalinity Before and After SQC

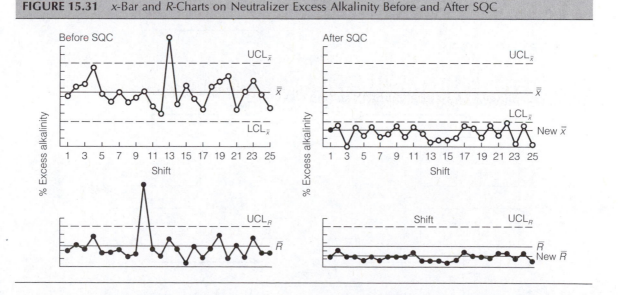

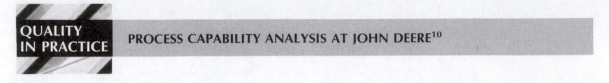

QUALITY IN PRACTICE

PROCESS CAPABILITY ANALYSIS AT JOHN DEERE[10]

John Deere, a major manufacturer of farm equipment, uses SPC to assess the capability of machine tools that it purchases. At Deere Harvester Works, almost all machine tool purchases have been subjected to SPC analysis since the late 1970s.

When Deere decided to acquire a vertical column bandsaw that could make angle as well as straight cuts, a Marvel 81A PC bandsaw produced by

Armstrong-Blum Manufacturing Company was selected. Before it was shipped, however, Deere studied its ability to meet performance criteria.

Figure 15.32 shows the basic analysis. Process capability is measured by testing the machine with the materials and tooling that will be used in its intended application. The natural variation must be less than two-thirds of the tolerance to be acceptable.

FIGURE 15.32   Quality Control at John Deere

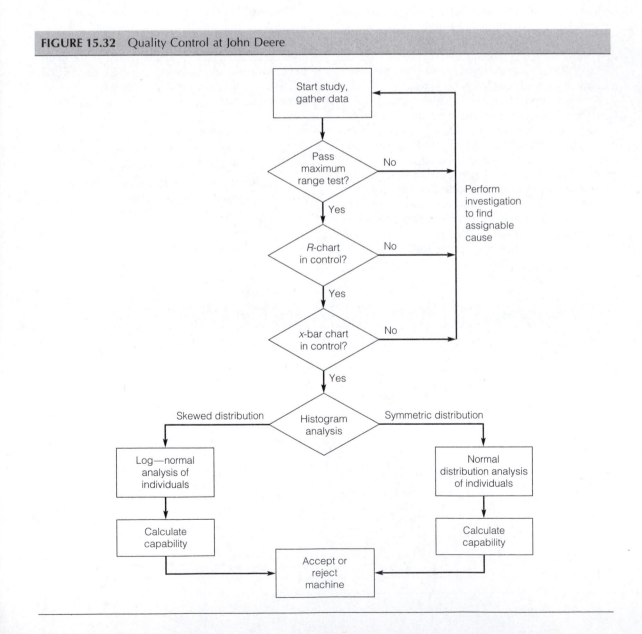

Deere engineers begin testing at the supplier's plant if possible. The Deere quality or engineering staff observes the test and records the data for analysis. They prefer to send the operator who will use the machine at their plant to perform the tests. In addition to testing for process capability, reliability is demonstrated by operating the machine for eight hours continuously without a failure.

Deere's capability study sets up specific guidelines. The key elements are:

■ No change in operators during the test.

■ No change in raw material batches.

■ No change in measuring devices. The devices must be calibrated at the beginning and end of the test and may also be checked periodically during the test. Repeatability is also verified.

■ No change in inspectors.

■ No change in temperature of equipment, material, or coolant.

■ No change in coolant level.

Deere has also developed a patented software package for collecting, storing, and analyzing the data collected. This system, called CAIR (Computer-Aided Inspection and Reporting System), generates reports to analyze variability and control. Control charts from tests on the Marvel saw to check cut length on an 875-mm rectangular steel tube are shown in Figure 15.33. Figure 15.34 shows the results of the process capability analysis.

One of Deere's managers noticed that suppliers often learn additional details about their machine's capabilities during the testing. In one case, a CNC punch press supplier's chief engineer discovered that the machine's capability deteriorated as steel shafts of heavier weight were used. By reprogramming the machine control, the vendor was able to improve the machine's capability on heavy sheets. The tests also showed that the flatness of the sheet was crucial and could be correlated with process capability.

While this process consumes time, Deere believes that the long-term benefits far outweigh the costs. As one manager stated, "Usually we end up with a better supplier and a better machine than we would have gotten otherwise."

Key Issues for Discussion

1. From the control chart data in Figure 15.32, verify the control limits and estimate of the standard deviation using the formulas in this chapter.

FIGURE 15.33 CAIR System Control Analysis

Default select range used: 1 to 15

Number of pieces per sample: 3

Upper limit on x-bar: 875.400208	Upper limit on R: 0.312424
Average of x-bars: 875.275800	Average of R's: 0.121330
Lower limit on x-bar: 875.151917	Lower limit on R: 0.000000
R-bar/D2 estimate: 0.071666	

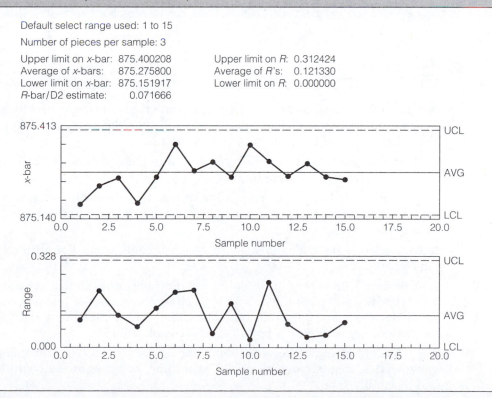

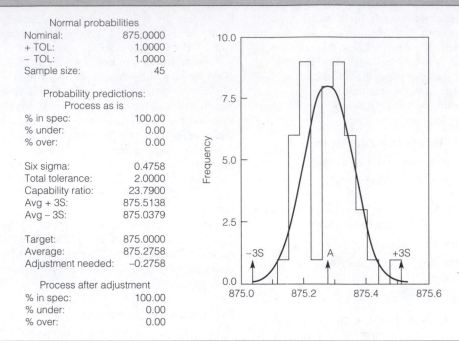

FIGURE 15.34 CAIR System Capability Analysis

Normal probabilities
Nominal: 875.0000
+ TOL: 1.0000
− TOL: 1.0000
Sample size: 45

Probability predictions:
Process as is
% in spec: 100.00
% under: 0.00
% over: 0.00

Six sigma: 0.4758
Total tolerance: 2.0000
Capability ratio: 23.7900
Avg + 3S: 875.5138
Avg − 3S: 875.0379

Target: 875.0000
Average: 875.2758
Adjustment needed: −0.2758

Process after adjustment
% in spec: 100.00
% under: 0.00
% over: 0.00

2. Discuss the data found in Figure 15.33. What is the process capability index? What conclusions do the charts indicate about the machine tool?

3. Discuss the guidelines set for Deere's capability test. Why does Deere require strict adherence to these guidelines?

SUMMARY OF KEY POINTS

■ Statistical process control (SPC) helps workers determine when to adjust a process and when to leave it alone, thereby reducing the incidence of Type I and Type II errors resulting from incorrect decisions.

■ Overadjustment of a process actually increases the variation; production workers must understand this important fact.

■ Control charts have three basic applications: (1) establishing a state of statistical control, (2) monitoring a process to identify special causes, and (3) determining process capability.

■ For variables data, $\bar{x}$- and R-charts are commonly used. For attributes data, the p-chart is used.

■ A process is in control if no points are outside control limits, the number of points above and below the center line is about the same; the points seem to fall randomly above and below the center line; and most points (but not all) are near the center line, with only a few close to the control limits.

■ Typical out-of-control conditions are represented by sudden shifts in the mean value, cycles, trends, hugging of the center line, hugging of the control limits, and instability.

■ Modified control limits can be used when the process capability is known to be good. These wider limits reduce the amount of investigation of isolated points that would fall outside the usual control limits.

■ In designing control charts, one must be concerned with how the sample data are taken, the sample size, the sampling frequency, and the location of the control limits.

■ SPC can be adapted to short production runs by using special factors for control limits, coding the data, or using stabilized control charts.

■ Successful implementation of SPC requires top management commitment, a project champion, an initial workable project, employee education and training, and an accurate measurement system.

■ Service organizations can benefit from the use of control charts. The difficult steps are identifying the appropriate variables or attributes measurements to track and helping users understand the nature of control charts outside of a manufacturing context.

REVIEW QUESTIONS

1. Describe statistical process control and its advantages.

2. Discuss the two basic reasons for using SPC.

3. Why is consistent quality important in a production process?

4. What does the term *in statistical control* mean?

5. Explain the decisions and risks facing managers in process control decisions.

6. What are the disadvantages of simply using histograms to study process capability?

7. Discuss the three primary applications of control charts.

8. Describe the difference between variables and attributes data. What types of control charts are used for each?

9. Briefly describe the methodology of constructing $\bar{x}$- and R-charts and establishing statistical control.

10. What does one look for in interpreting control charts? Explain the possible causes of different out-of-control indicators.

11. How should control charts be used by shop floor pesonnel?

12. What are modified control limits? Under what conditions should they be used?

13. How are control charts used to determine process capability?

14. Describe the difference between control limits and specification limits.

15. What risks and costs are involved in using control charts? Discuss guidelines for setting control limits that consider such risks and costs.

16. Explain the difference between defects and defectives.

17. Briefly describe the process of constructing a p-chart.

18. Discuss the concept of rational subgroups.

19. What tradeoffs are involved in selecting the sample size for a control chart?

20. Discuss the implications of control limit location in terms of Type I and Type II errors.

21. Explain the economic tradeoffs to consider when designing a control chart.

22. Describe approaches for applying SPC to short production runs.

23. What factors are necessary for successful implementation of SPC? Why?

24. Discuss applications of control charts in service organizations.

25. Discuss the lessons learned by Uniroyal in implementing SPC.

26. List 10 applications of control charts in service organizations not already discussed in this chapter.

PROBLEMS

1. Thirty samples of size 3 listed in the following table were taken from a machining process over a 15-hour period.

Sample	Observations		
1	3.55	3.64	4.37
2	3.61	3.42	4.07
3	3.61	3.36	4.34
4	4.13	3.50	3.61
5	4.06	3.28	3.07
6	4.48	4.32	3.71
7	3.25	3.58	3.51
8	4.25	3.38	3.00
9	4.35	3.64	3.20
10	3.62	3.61	3.43
11	3.09	3.28	3.12
12	3.38	3.15	3.09
13	2.85	3.44	4.06
14	3.59	3.61	3.34
15	3.60	2.83	2.84
16	2.69	3.57	3.28
17	3.07	3.18	3.11
18	2.86	3.69	3.05
19	3.68	3.59	3.93
20	2.90	3.41	3.37
21	3.57	3.63	2.72
22	2.82	3.55	3.56
23	3.82	2.91	3.80
24	3.14	3.83	3.80
25	3.97	3.34	3.65
26	3.77	3.60	3.81
27	4.12	3.38	3.37
28	3.92	3.60	3.54
29	3.50	4.08	4.09
30	4.23	3.62	3.00

   a. Compute the mean and standard deviation of the data and plot a histogram.

   b. Compute the mean and range of each sample and plot them on control charts. Does the process appear to be in statistical control? Why or why not?

2. Thirty samples of size 6 yielded $\bar{\bar{x}} = 480$ and $\bar{R} = 34$. Compute control limits for $\bar{x}$- and R-charts and estimate the standard deviation of the process.

3. Twenty-five samples of size 5 resulted in $\bar{\bar{x}} = 5.42$ and $\bar{R} = 2.0$. Compute control limits for $\bar{x}$- and R-charts and estimate the standard deviation of the process.

4. Use the following sample data and construct $\bar{x}$- and R-charts. The sample size used is $n = 4$.

Sample	$\bar{x}$	R	Sample	$\bar{x}$	R
1	95.72	1.0	11	95.80	0.6
2	95.24	0.9	12	95.22	0.2
3	95.18	0.8	13	95.56	1.3
4	95.44	0.4	14	95.22	0.5
5	95.46	0.5	15	95.04	0.8
6	95.32	1.1	16	95.72	1.1
7	95.40	0.9	17	94.82	0.6
8	95.44	0.3	18	95.46	0.5
9	95.08	0.2	19	95.60	0.4
10	95.50	0.6	20	95.74	0.6

5. In testing the resistance of a component used in a microcomputer, the following data were obtained:

Sample	Observations		
1	414	388	402
2	408	382	406
3	396	402	392
4	390	398	362
5	398	442	436
6	400	400	414
7	444	390	410
8	430	372	362
9	376	398	382
10	342	400	402
11	400	402	384
12	408	414	388
13	382	430	400
14	402	409	400
15	399	424	413
16	460	375	445
17	404	420	437
18	375	380	410
19	391	392	414
20	394	399	380
21	396	416	400
22	370	411	403
23	418	450	451
24	398	398	415
25	428	406	390

Construct $\bar{x}$- and R-charts for these data. Determine if the process is in control. If not, eliminate any assignable causes and compute revised limits.

6. Construct $\bar{x}$- and R-charts for the following data. What conclusions do you reach?

Sample	Observations				
1	1.45	−0.15	−0.93	−1.55	−2.96
2	0.79	−1.02	−2.61	−0.85	−1.89
3	1.08	−0.54	−1.34	−2.03	−1.48
4	0.32	−0.41	−0.52	−1.87	−1.70
5	0.21	0.41	−1.09	−1.44	−2.34
6	−0.12	0.00	−1.56	−2.40	−1.19

Continued

Continued

Sample	Observations				
7	1.66	−0.50	−1.62	−2.25	−2.87
8	−1.28	0.44	−2.29	−1.20	−1.75
9	−0.23	−1.41	−0.15	0.33	−2.61
10	0.65	−1.21	−0.54	−1.74	−1.59
11	0.55	−0.77	−2.08	−1.99	−1.72
12	−0.61	−0.40	−0.81	−2.07	−0.99
13	0.01	−0.50	−1.10	−0.71	−3.24
14	−0.46	−0.82	−1.28	−1.37	−2.05
15	0.80	−0.52	−1.77	−1.16	−2.09
16	0.84	−0.39	−0.16	−1.50	−2.47
17	0.41	−0.91	−2.04	−2.60	−1.26
18	−0.30	0.01	0.09	−1.12	−2.54
19	−0.16	0.44	−0.64	−1.94	−3.81
20	−0.83	0.59	−1.68	−2.73	−1.19
21	−0.02	−0.83	−0.68	−1.52	−1.58
22	−0.02	0.81	−1.42	−1.62	−2.97
23	1.26	−0.64	−0.44	−0.73	−1.80
24	0.00	1.13	−1.09	−2.04	−1.89
25	−0.13	−0.27	−1.41	−1.40	−3.55
26	−0.66	−0.97	−0.75	−2.13	−1.73
27	1.21	−0.28	0.33	−2.38	−1.61
28	−0.98	0.40	−1.85	−2.40	−2.89
29	0.39	−0.12	−1.55	−3.99	−2.49
30	−0.45	0.63	−1.57	−2.36	−3.26

7. General Hydraulics, Inc., is a manufacturer of hydraulic machine tools. It has had a history of leakage trouble resulting from a certain critical fitting. Twenty-five samples of machined parts were selected, one per shift, and the diameter of the fitting was measured. The results are given in the following table:

	Diameter Measurement (cm)			
	Observations			
Sample	1	2	3	4
1	10.94	10.64	10.88	10.70
2	10.66	10.66	10.68	10.68
3	10.68	10.68	10.62	10.68
4	10.03	10.42	10.48	11.06
5	10.70	10.46	10.76	10.80
6	10.38	10.74	10.62	10.54
7	10.46	10.90	10.52	10.74
8	10.66	10.04	10.58	11.04
9	10.50	10.44	10.74	10.66
10	10.58	10.64	10.60	10.26
11	10.80	10.36	10.60	10.22
12	10.42	10.36	10.72	10.68
13	10.52	10.70	10.62	10.58
14	11.04	10.58	10.42	10.36
15	10.52	10.40	10.60	10.40
16	10.38	10.02	10.60	10.60
17	10.56	10.68	10.78	10.34
18	10.58	10.50	10.48	10.60
19	10.42	10.74	10.64	10.50
20	10.48	10.44	10.32	10.70
21	10.56	10.78	10.46	10.42

Continued

Continued

	Diameter Measurement (cm) Observations			
Sample	1	2	3	4
22	10.82	10.64	11.00	10.01
23	10.28	10.46	10.82	10.84
24	10.64	10.56	10.92	10.54
25	10.84	10.68	10.44	10.68

a. Construct control charts for these data.

b. If the regular machine operator was absent when samples 4, 8, 14, and 22 were taken, how will the results in part (a) be affected?

c. The following table represents measurements taken during the next 10 shifts. What information does this table provide to the quality control manager?

Addition Sample	Observations			
	1	2	3	4
1	10.40	10.76	10.54	10.64
2	10.60	10.28	10.74	10.86
3	10.56	10.58	10.64	10.70
4	10.70	10.60	10.74	10.52
5	11.02	10.36	10.90	11.02
6	10.68	10.38	10.22	10.32
7	10.64	10.56	10.82	10.80
8	10.28	10.62	10.40	10.70
9	10.50	10.88	10.58	10.54
10	10.36	10.44	10.40	10.66

8. Discuss the interpretation of each of the following control charts:

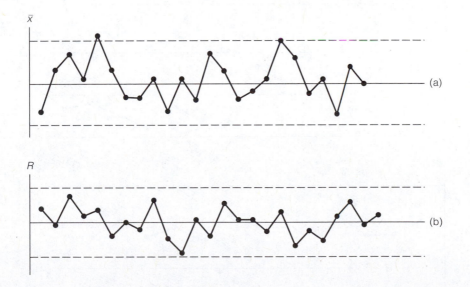

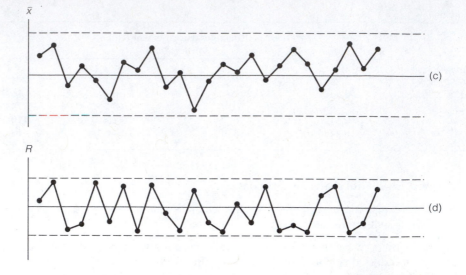

(c)

(d)

9. For each of the following control charts, assume that the process has been operating in statistical control for some time. What conclusions should the operators reach at this point?

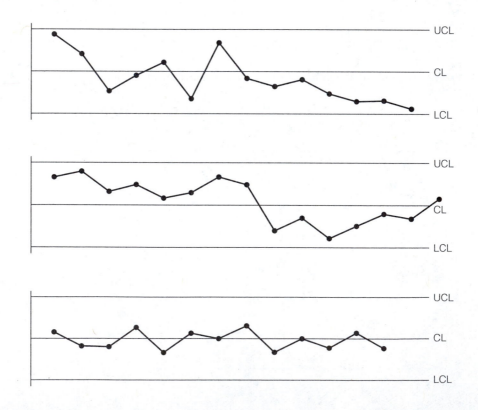

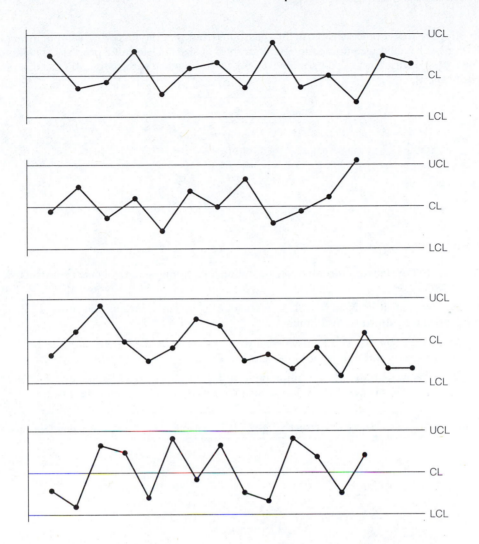

10. Consider the following 10 samples of size 5. Compute control limits for $\bar{x}$- and R-charts using the statistic $\bar{R}/d_2$ as an estimate of the standard deviation. Then construct the chart and plot the data, interpreting the results.

Sample	Observations				
1	0.077	0.080	0.078	0.072	0.078
2	0.076	0.079	0.073	0.074	0.073
3	0.076	0.077	0.072	0.076	0.074
4	0.074	0.078	0.075	0.077	0.077
5	0.080	0.073	0.075	0.076	0.074
6	0.078	0.081	0.079	0.076	0.076
7	0.075	0.077	0.075	0.076	0.077
8	0.079	0.075	0.078	0.077	0.076
9	0.076	0.075	0.074	0.075	0.075
10	0.071	0.073	0.071	0.070	0.073

11. For problem 10, estimate the process capability by using both the sample standard deviation and $\bar{R}/d_2$. Why are they different?

12. Suppose that a process is normally distributed and that the following sample means and ranges have been computed for eight samples of size 5. Determine process capability limits. If specifications are determined to be 46 ± 5, what percentage will be out of specification?

Sample	$\bar{x}$	R
1	51.6	5.2
2	40.1	7.1
3	42.3	5.4
4	48.9	5.0
5	36.5	6.3
6	53.1	3.9
7	47.3	4.8
8	49.6	5.9

13. Estimate the standard deviation of the individuals from the control chart constructed in Problem 5.

14. Suppose that in Problem 5, USL = 500 and LSL = 300. Compute the process capability and the modified control limits.

15. Twenty-five samples of 100 items each were inspected, and 68 were found to be defective. Compute control limits for a p-chart.

16. The fraction defective for an automotive piston is given here for 20 samples. Two hundred units are inspected each day. Construct a p-chart and interpret the results.

Sample	Fraction Defective	Sample	Fraction Defective
1	0.11	11	0.16
2	0.16	12	0.23
3	0.12	13	0.15
4	0.10	14	0.12
5	0.09	15	0.11
6	0.12	16	0.11
7	0.12	17	0.14
8	0.15	18	0.16
9	0.09	19	0.10
10	0.13	20	0.13

17. One hundred insurance claim forms are inspected daily over 25 working days, and the number of forms with errors have been recorded in the following table. Construct a p-chart. If any points occur outside the control limits, assume that assignable causes have been determined. Then construct a revised chart.

Day	Number Defective	Day	Number Defective
1	3	14	4
2	3	15	1
3	3	16	2
4	2	17	4
5	0	18	0
6	3	19	1
7	0	20	1
8	1	21	0
9	7	22	2

Continued

Continued

Day	Number Defective	Day	Number Defective
10	3	23	8
11	2	24	2
12	0	25	1
13	0		

18. Samples of size 100 have been randomly selected during each shift of 25 shifts in a production process. The data are given in the following table. Construct a p-chart and determine if the process is in control. If not, eliminate any data points that appear to be due to assignable causes and construct a new chart.

Sample	Number of Defectives	Sample	Number of Defectives
1	10	14	16
2	14	15	13
3	22	16	18
4	17	.17	20
5	27	18	23
6	42	19	27
7	49	20	59
8	36	21	52
9	17	22	25
10	20	23	16
11	35	24	45
12	39	25	68
13	12		

19 A hospital surveys all outgoing patients by means of a patient satisfaction questionnaire. The number of patients surveyed each month varies. Control charts that monitor the proportion of unsatisfied patients for key questions are constructed and studied. Construct a p-chart for the following data, which represent responses to a question on satisfaction with hospital meals.

Month	Number of Patients	Number Unsatisfied
1	256	10
2	202	11
3	234	8
4	307	10
5	280	7
6	298	15
7	231	22
8	201	9
9	314	12
10	223	6
11	300	13
12	245	14
13	224	9
14	278	16
15	215	10
16	287	16
17	234	11
18	310	17
19	285	26
20	251	8

FIGURE 15.35 End Cap Control Chart

VARIABLES CONTROL CHART ($\bar{X}$ & R)

PART NAME (PRODUCT)	OPERATION (PROCESS)	PART NO.	CHART NO.
END CAP	BORE	21819	
		SPECIFICATION LIMITS	
		3.9375-3.9380	

OPERATOR	MACHINE	GAGE	UNIT OF MEASURE	ZERO EQUALS
		BORE GAUGE	.0000	

	1	2	3	4	5	6	7	8	9	10	11	12	13	14	15	16	17	18	19	20	21	22	23	24	25
DATE																									
TIME			12	19						12	20					12	15								
SAMPLE MEASUREMENTS 1	75	77	76	76	70	73	77	75	78	76	70	81	79	74	76	80	75	80							
2	76	80	76	78	76	72	78	76	79	77	78	77	76	84	82	81	84	75							
3	77	79	82	70	77	82	79	79	80	81	75	78	78	79	74	75	78	75							
4	79	83	74	73	78	75	77	70	76	81	76	76	70	84	81	78	80	76							
5	75	80	75	76	74	74	75	75	71	75	80	80	70	75	75	76	74	70							
SUM																									
AVERAGE, $\bar{X}$																									
RANGE, R																									
NOTES																									

AVERAGES

RANGES

TABLE 15.7 Bottle Diameter Samples

Sample	Head 1 x_1	Head 2 x_2	Head 3 x_3	Head 4 x_4
1	.01	.08	.08	.04
2	−.03	.03	.09	.10
3	.03	.09	.08	.07
4	−.04	.06	.07	.11
5	−.06	.02	.06	.11
6	.01	.03	.07	.11
7	.00	.04	.09	.06
8	.01	.08	.09	.09
9	.01	.00	.02	.07
10	.01	−.04	.08	.11
11	−.01	−.01	.09	.10
12	−.02	.02	.03	.08
13	−.01	−.02	.05	.04
14	.01	.05	.07	.08
15	.00	.05	.06	.06
16	.00	.00	.08	.14
17	.01	.00	.05	.15
18	.03	.09	.11	.12
19	−.01	.10	.09	.09
20	.01	.01	.01	.11

20. The Bell Vader Company, which produces heavy-duty electrical motors, machines a part called an end cap. To meet competitive pressures, the company began to apply statistical quality control to its processes. Because each motor produced by the company uses two end caps that could cost as much as $200 each, the company sees the importance of bringing the process under control. Figure 15.35 shows data collected to construct a control chart.

   a. Compute control limits and construct and analyze the $\bar{x}$- and R-charts for this process. What conclusions can you reach about the state of statistical control?

   b. Using the control chart, estimate the process capability. Determine what percentage of end caps would be expected to fall outside specifications. What conclusions and recommendations can you make?

21. An injection molding machine for plastic bottles has four molding heads. The outside diameter of the bottle is an important measure of process performance. Table 15.7 shows the results of 20 samples in which the data are coded by subtracting the actual value from the nominal dimension. Construct $\bar{x}$- and R-charts and discuss the results.

CASE

Dean Door Corporation

The Dean Door Corporation (DDC) manufactures steel and aluminum exterior doors for commercial and residential applications. DDC landed a major contract as a supplier to Walker Homes, a builder of residential communities in several major cities throughout the Upper Midwest. Because of the large volume of demand, DDC had to expand its manufacturing operations to three shifts and hire additional workers.

Not long after DDC began shipping doors to Walker Homes, it began receiving some complaints about excessive gaps between the door and frame.

This problem was somewhat alarming to DDC, because its reputation as a high-quality manufacturer was the principal reason that it was selected as a supplier to Walker Homes. DDC placed a great deal of confidence in its manufacturing capability because of its well-trained and dedicated employees, and it never felt the need to consider formal process control approaches. In view of the recent complaints, Jim Dean, the company president, suspected that the expansion to a three-shift operation and the pressures to produce higher volumes and meet just-in-time delivery requests was causing a breakdown in their quality.

On the recommendation of the plant manager, DDC hired a quality consultant to train the shift supervisors and selected line workers in statistical process control methods. As a trial project, the plant manager wants to evaluate the capability of a critical cutting operation that he suspects might be the source of the gap problem. The nominal specification for this cutting operation is 30.000" with a tolerance of 0.125"; therefore, the upper and lower specifications are LSL = 29.875" and USL = 30.125". The consultant suggested inspecting five consecutive door panels in the middle of each shift over a ten-day period and recording the dimension of the cut. Table 15.8 shows 10 days' data collected for each shift.

Assignment

1. Interpret the data in Table 15.8, establish a state of statistical control, and evaluate the capability of the process to meet specifications. Consider the following questions: What do the initial control charts tell you? Do any out-of-control conditions exist? If the process is not in control, what might be the likely

TABLE 15.8 Production Data

Shift	Operator	Sample	Observation 1	2	3	4	5
1	Terry	1	30.046	29.978	30.026	29.986	29.961
2	Jordan	2	29.972	29.966	29.964	29.942	30.025
3	Dana	3	30.046	30.004	30.028	29.986	30.027
1	Terry	4	29.997	29.997	29.980	30.000	30.034
2	Jordan	5	30.018	29.922	29.992	30.008	30.053
3	Dana	6	29.973	29.990	29.985	29.991	30.004
1	Terry	7	29.989	29.952	29.941	30.012	29.984
2	Jordan	8	29.969	30.000	29.968	29.976	29.973
3	Cameron	9	29.852	29.978	29.964	29.896	29.876
1	Terry	10	29.987	29.976	30.021	29.957	30.042
2	Jordan	11	30.028	29.999	30.022	29.942	29.998
3	Dana	12	29.955	29.984	29.977	30.008	30.033
1	Terry	13	30.040	29.965	30.001	29.975	29.970
2	Jordan	14	30.007	30.024	29.987	29.951	29.994
3	Dana	15	29.979	30.007	30.000	30.042	30.000
1	Terry	16	30.073	29.998	30.027	29.986	30.011
2	Jordan	17	29.995	29.966	29.996	30.039	29.976
3	Dana	18	29.994	29.982	29.998	30.040	30.017
1	Terry	19	29.977	30.013	30.042	30.001	29.962
2	Jordan	20	30.021	30.048	30.037	29.985	30.005
3	Cameron	21	29.879	29.882	29.990	29.971	29.953
1	Terry	22	30.043	30.021	29.963	29.993	30.006
2	Jordan	23	30.065	30.012	30.021	30.024	30.037
3	Cameron	24	29.899	29.875	29.980	29.878	29.877
1	Terry	25	30.029	30.011	30.017	30.000	30.000
2	Jordan	26	30.046	30.006	30.039	29.991	29.970
3	Dana	27	29.993	29.991	29.984	30.022	30.010
1	Terry	28	30.057	30.032	29.979	30.027	30.033
2	Jordan	29	30.004	30.049	29.980	30.000	29.986
3	Dana	30	29.995	30.000	29.922	29.984	29.968

TABLE 15.9   Additional Production Data

Shift	Operator	Sample	Observation				
			1	2	3	4	5
1	Terry	31	29.970	30.017	29.898	29.937	29.992
2	Jordan	32	29.947	30.013	29.993	29.997	30.079
3	Dana	33	30.050	30.031	29.999	29.963	30.045
1	Terry	34	30.064	30.061	30.016	30.041	30.006
2	Jordan	35	29.948	30.009	29.962	29.990	29.979
3	Dana	36	30.016	29.989	29.939	29.981	30.017
1	Terry	37	29.946	30.057	29.992	29.973	29.955
2	Jordan	38	29.981	30.023	29.992	29.992	29.941
3	Dana	39	30.043	29.985	30.014	29.986	30.000
1	Terry	40	30.013	30.046	30.096	29.975	30.019
2	Jordan	41	30.043	30.003	30.062	30.025	30.023
3	Dana	42	29.994	30.056	30.033	30.011	29.948
1	Terry	43	29.995	30.014	30.018	29.966	30.000
2	Jordan	44	30.018	29.982	30.028	30.029	30.044
3	Dana	45	30.018	29.994	29.995	30.029	30.034
1	Terry	46	30.025	29.951	30.038	30.009	30.003
2	Jordan	47	30.048	30.046	29.995	30.053	30.043
3	Dana	48	30.030	30.054	29.997	29.993	30.010
1	Terry	49	29.991	30.001	30.041	30.036	29.992
2	Jordan	50	30.022	30.021	30.022	30.008	30.019

causes, based on the information that is available? What is the process capability? What do the process capability indexes tell the company? Is DDC facing a serious problem that it needs to address? How might the company ensure that the problems that Walker Homes found be eliminated?

2. The plant manager implemented the recommendations that resulted from the initial study. Because of the success in using control charts, DDC made a decision to continue using them on the cutting operation. After establishing control, additional samples were taken over the next 20 shifts, shown in Table 15.9. Evaluate whether the process remains in control, and suggest any actions that should be taken. Consider the following issues: Does any evidence suggest that the process has changed relative to the established control limits? If any out-of-control patterns are suspected, what might be the cause? What should the company investigate?

▮ NOTES

1. This discussion is adapted from James R. Evans, *Statistical Process Control for Quality Improvement: A Training Guide to Learning SPC* (Englewood Cliffs, NJ: Prentice-Hall, © 1991). Reprinted with permission of Prentice-Hall, Englewood Cliffs, NJ.

2. D. C. Montgomery, "The Economic Design of Control Charts: A Review and Literature Survey," *Journal of Quality Technology* 12, no. 2 (1980), 75–87.

3. Raymond R. Mayer, "Selecting Control Limits," *Quality Progress* 16, no. 9, 24–26.

4. See Thomas Pyzdek, *Pyzdek's Guide to SPC, Volume Two—Applications and Special Topics* (Milwaukee, WI: ASQC Quality Press, 1992).

5. Jerry Houston, "Start Small for Successful SPC," *Quality* (August 1985), Q12.

6. Frank X. Cantello, John E. Chalmers, and James E. Evans, "Evolution to an Effective and Enduring SPC System," *Quality Progress* 23, no. 2 (February 1990), 60–64.

7. Michael J. Boccacino, "Get Control of Your Control Charts," *Quality Progress* 26, no. 10 (October 1993), 99–102.

8. Adapted from W. J. McCabe, Manager of Quality Programs, IBM Corp., "Improving Quality and Cutting Costs in a Service Organization," *Quality Progress* 18, no. 6 (June 1985), 85–89.

9. Adapted from Clifford B. Wilson, "SQC + Mg. A Positive Reaction," *Quality Progress* 20, no. 4 (April 1988), 47–49.

10. Adapted from Jean V. Owen, "Picking a Marvel at Deere," *Manufacturing Engineering Magazine* (January 1989), 74–77.

■ BIBLIOGRAPHY

American National Standard, Definitions, Symbols, Formulas, and Tables for Control Charts. ANSI/ASQC A1-1987. American Society for Quality Control, 310 W. Wisconsin Ave., Milwaukee, WI 53203.

Brown, Bradford S. "Control Charts: The Promise and the Performance." Presentation at the ASQC/ASA 35th Annual Fall Technical Conference, Lexington, Kentucky, 1991.

Mayer, Raymond R. "Selecting Control Chart Limits." *Quality Progress* 16, no. 9 (September 1983), 24–26.

Montgomery, D. C. *Introduction to Statistical Quality Control,* 2d ed. New York: John Wiley & Sons, 1991.

Rosander, A. C. *Applications of Quality Control in the Service Industries.* New York: Marcel Dekker and ASQC Quality Press, 1985.

Squires, Frank H. "What Do Quality Control Charts Control?" *Quality* (November 1982), 63.

Vance, Lonnie C. "A Bibliography of Statistical Quality Control Chart Techniques, 1970–1980," *Journal of Quality Technology* 15, no. 12 (April 1983).

Additional Topics in Statistical Process Control

The previous chapter introduced the fundamental concepts of statistical process control. It showed how control charts can be used to track process variation over time and signal the need for corrective action by identifying special causes. For variables data, $\bar{x}$- and R-charts were introduced; for attributes data, the p-chart was discussed. This chapter presents several other types of control charts for both variables and attributes data, as well as alternatives to the traditional $\bar{x}$- and R-charts. For readers interested in the theory behind control charts, statistical foundations for many of the charts and the rules used to interpret the charts are also discussed.

SPECIAL CONTROL CHARTS FOR VARIABLES DATA

Several alternatives to the popular $\bar{x}$- and R-charts for process control of variables measurements are available. This section discusses some of these alternatives.

■ $\bar{x}$- and s-Charts

An alternative to using the R-chart along with the $\bar{x}$-chart is to compute and plot the standard deviation s of each sample. Although the range has traditionally been used, since it involves less computational effort and is easier to understand by shop floor personnel, using s rather than R has its advantages. The sample standard deviation is a more sensitive and better indicator of process variability, especially for larger sample sizes. Thus, when tight control of variability is required, s should be used. With the use of modern calculators and microcomputers, the computational burden of computing s is reduced or eliminated and has thus become a viable alternative to R.

The sample standard deviation is computed as

$$s = \sqrt{\frac{\sum_{i=1}^{n}(x_i - \bar{x})^2}{n - 1}}$$

To construct an s-chart, compute the standard deviation for each sample. Next, compute the average standard deviation $\bar{s}$ by averaging the sample standard deviations over all samples. (Notice that this computation is analogous to computing $\bar{R}$). Control limits for the s-chart are given by

$$\text{UCL}_s = B_4\bar{s}$$

$$\text{LCL}_s = B_3\bar{s}$$

where B_3 and B_4 are constants found in Appendix B.

For the associated $\bar{x}$-chart, the control limits derived from the overall standard deviation are

$$\text{UCL}_{\bar{x}} = \bar{\bar{x}} + A_3\bar{s}$$

$$\text{LCL}_{\bar{x}} = \bar{\bar{x}} - A_3\bar{s}$$

where A_3 is a constant found in Appendix B.

Observe that the formulas for the control limits are equivalent to those for $\bar{x}$- and R-charts except that the constants differ.

EXAMPLE 1   Constructing $\bar{x}$- and s-Charts.   To illustrate the use of the $\bar{x}$- and s-charts, consider the data given in Table 16.1. These data represent measurements of deviations from a nominal specification for some machined part. Samples of size 10 are used; for each sample, the mean and standard deviation have been computed.

The average (overall) mean is computed to be $\bar{\bar{x}} = 0.108$, and the average standard deviation is $\bar{s} = 1.791$. Since the sample size is 10, $B_3 = 0.284$, $B_4 = 1.716$, and $A_3 = 0.975$. Control limits for the s-chart are

TABLE 16.1   Data for $\bar{x}$- and s-Chart Example

Data Row	1	2	3	4	5	6	7	8	9	10	11	12	13	14
1	1	9	0	1	-3	-6	-3	0	2	0	-3	-12	-6	-3
2	8	4	8	1	-1	2	-1	-2	0	0	-2	2	-3	-5
3	6	0	0	0	0	0	0	-3	-1	-2	2	0	0	5
4	9	3	0	2	-4	0	-2	-1	-1	-1	-1	-4	0	0
5	7	0	3	1	0	2	-1	-2	-3	-1	1	-1	-8	-5
6	9	0	1	1	1	-1	-1	1	0	0	-2	4	-4	1
7	2	3	2	2	0	2	-3	-3	-1	-1	-2	2	-6	5
8	7	4	0	0	-2	0	0	0	-3	-2	1	-3	-1	-4
9	9	8	2	0	0	-3	-2	-3	-1	-2	1	-4	-1	-1
10	7	3	3	1	-2	0	-2	-2	0	0	1	0	-2	-5
Mean	6.5	3.4	1.9	0.9	-1.1	-0.4	-1.5	-1.5	-0.6	-0.9	-0.6	-1.6	-3.1	-1.2
Standard deviation	2.83823	3.13404	2.46981	0.73786	1.59513	2.50333	1.08012	1.43372	1.57762	0.87559	1.71269	4.52646	2.80673	3.91010

	15	16	17	18	19	20	21	22	23	24	25
	-1	-1	-2	0	0	1	1	-1	0	1	2
	-1	-2	2	4	3	2	2	0	0	0	2
	-1	-2	-1	0	-3	1	2	2	-1	0	1
	-2	0	0	0	3	1	2	-1	0	1	2
	-1	-4	-1	0	3	-3	2	2	1	-1	-1
	0	0	-1	3	1	2	1	2	0	2	2
	-2	-2	2	0	0	1	1	-1	0	0	2
	-1	-4	-1	0	1	-2	2	0	0	0	1
	0	-1	1	1	2	3	1	0	-1	-1	-1
	-1	0	-2	0	-2	0	2	-1	0	0	2
Mean	-1	-1.6	-0.3	0.8	0.8	0.6	1.5	0.2	-0.1	0.4	1.2
Standard Deviation	0.66666	1.50554	1.49443	1.47572	2.09761	1.83787	0.52704	1.31656	0.56764	0.84327	1.22927

$$LCL_s = 0.284(1.791) = 0.509$$

$$UCL_s = 1.716(1.791) = 3.063$$

For the $\bar{x}$-chart, the control limits are

$$LCL_{\bar{x}} = 0.108 - 0.975(1.791) = -1.638$$

$$UCL_{\bar{x}} = 0.108 + 0.975(1.791) = 1.854$$

The $\bar{x}$- and s-charts are shown in Figures 16.1 and 16.2, respectively. This evidence shows that this process is not in control, and an investigation as to the reasons for the variation, particularly in the $\bar{x}$-chart, is warranted.

■ Charts for Individuals

With the development of automated inspection for many processes, manufacturers can now easily inspect and measure quality characteristics on every item produced. Hence, the sample size for process control is $n = 1$, and a control chart for *individual measurements*—also called an *x-chart*—can be used. Other examples in which x-charts are useful include accounting data such as shipments, orders, absences, and accidents; production records of temperature, humidity, voltage, or pressure; and the results of physical or chemical analyses.

With individual measurements, the process standard deviation can be estimated and three-sigma control limits used. As in Chapter 15, $\bar{R}/d_2$ provides an estimate of the process standard deviation. Thus, an x-chart for individual measurements would have three-sigma control limits defined by

FIGURE 16.1 $\bar{x}$-Chart

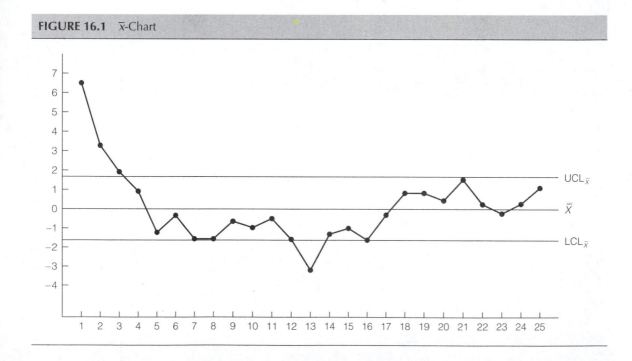

FIGURE 16.2 *s*-Chart

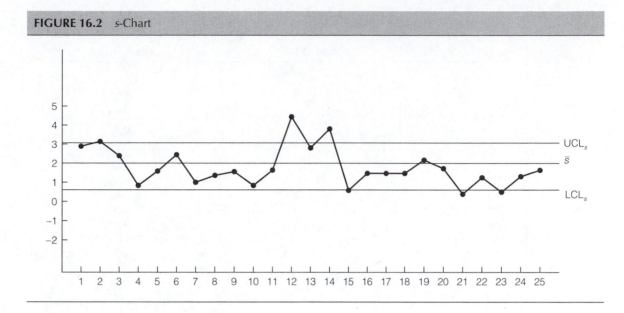

$$UCL_x = \bar{x} + 3\bar{R}/d_2$$

$$LCL_x = \bar{x} - 3\bar{R}/d_2$$

Samples of size 1, however, do not furnish enough information for process variability measurement. However, process variability can be determined by using a moving average of ranges, or a **moving range,** of n successive observations. For example, a moving range for $n = 2$ is computed by finding the absolute difference between two successive observations. The number of observations used in the moving range determines the constant d_2; hence, for $n = 2$, from Appendix B, $d_2 = 1.128$. In a similar fashion, larger values of n can be used to compute moving ranges. The moving range chart has control limits defined by

$$UCL_R = D_4\bar{R}$$

$$LCL_R = D_3\bar{R}$$

which is comparable to the ordinary range chart.

EXAMPLE 2 Constructing an *x*-Chart with Moving Ranges. To illustrate; consider a set of observations measuring the percent cobalt in a chemical process as given in Table 16.2. The moving range is computed as shown by taking absolute values of successive ranges and using the constants in Appendix B.

$$LCL_R = 0$$
$$UCL_R = (3.267)(0.377) = 1.232$$

The moving range chart, shown in Figure 16.3 indicates that the process is in control.

Next, the *x*-chart is constructed for the individual measurements:

$$LCL_x = 3.517 - 3(0.377)/1.128 = 2.514$$

$$UCL_x = 3.517 + 3(0.377)/1.128 = 4.520$$

TABLE 16.2 Individual Observations and Moving Ranges

Sample	Percent Cobalt	Moving Range	
1	3.75		
2	3.80	0.05 = |3.80 − 3.75|	
3	3.70	0.10 = |3.70 − 3.80|	
4	3.20	0.50	.
5	3.50	0.30	.
6	3.05	0.45	.
7	3.50	0.45	etc.
8	3.25	0.25	
9	3.60	0.35	
10	3.10	0.50	
11	4.00	0.90	
12	4.00	0.00	
13	3.50	0.50	
14	3.00	0.50	
15	3.80	0.80	
	$\bar{x}$ = 3.517	$\bar{R}$ = 0.377	

This x-chart is shown in Figure 16.4 (p. 705); this process also appears to be in control.

FIGURE 16.3 Moving Range Chart

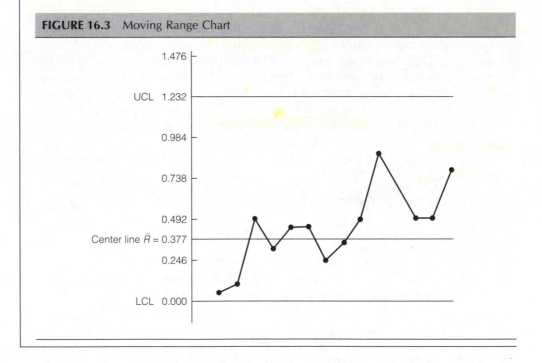

Some caution is necessary when interpreting patterns on the moving range chart. Points beyond control limits are signs of assignable causes. Successive ranges, however, are correlated, and they may cause patterns or trends in the chart that are not indicative of out-of-control situations. On the x-chart, individual observations are assumed to be uncorrelated; hence, patterns and trends should be investigated.

FIGURE 16.4 *x*-Chart for Individuals

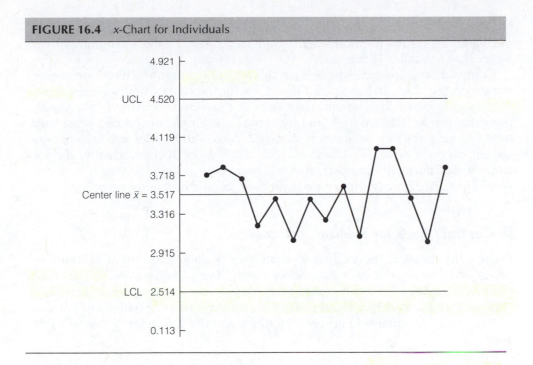

Moving averages of individual observations can also be computed and plotted like moving ranges. This practice is common in the chemical industry when batches of chemical are produced. Control limits are computed as for $\bar{x}$-charts. For example, using $n = 2$ in Table 16.2, the moving average is computed as shown in Table 16.3. For $n = 2$, Appendix B provides $A_2 = 1.880$. Therefore, the control limits for the moving average chart are

$$UCL_{\bar{x}} = 3.498 + 1.880(0.377) = 4.207$$

$$LCL_{\bar{x}} = 3.498 - 1.880(0.377) = 2.789$$

TABLE 16.3 Two-Sample Moving Average

Sample	Percent Cobalt	Moving Average
1	3.75	
2	3.80	3.775
3	3.70	3.75
4	3.20	3.45
5	3.50	3.35
6	3.05	3.275
7	3.50	3.275
8	3.25	3.375
9	3.60	3.425
10	3.10	3.35
11	4.00	3.55
12	4.00	4.00
13	3.50	3.75
14	3.00	3.25
15	3.80	3.40
		$\bar{\bar{x}} = 3.498$

Note that these limits are tighter than those computed for individual measurements, which results from considering samples of size 2, whose sampling distribution has a smaller variance.

Control charts for individuals have the advantage that specifications can be drawn on the chart and compared directly with the control limits. Some disadvantages also exist. Individuals' charts are less sensitive to many of the conditions that can be detected by $\bar{x}$- and R-charts; for example, the process must vary a lot before a shift in the mean is detected. Also, short cycles and trends may appear on an individual's chart and not on an $\bar{x}$- or R-chart. Finally, the assumption of normality of observations is more critical than for $\bar{x}$- and R-charts; when the normality assumption does not hold, greater chance for error is present.

■ Control Charts for Medians

Besides the mean, $\bar{x}$, the median, $\tilde{x}$, is another popular measure of central tendency and can be used as a statistic for controlling variables data. The median chart is often used for small sample sizes and is easier to use on the shop floor because it requires only a visual scan of the observations (for odd sample sizes). The formulas for control limits are as follows and use the factors given in Table 16.4:

$$\text{UCL}_{\tilde{x}} = \tilde{\tilde{x}} + A_5 \tilde{R}$$

$$\text{LCL}_{\tilde{x}} = \tilde{\tilde{x}} - A_5 \tilde{R}$$

where $\tilde{\tilde{x}}$ is the grand median (median of the medians) and $\tilde{R}$ is the median range. The mean of the medians, $\bar{\tilde{x}}$, can be substituted for $\tilde{\tilde{x}}$.

The range chart can be constructed using the median range $\tilde{R}$ instead of the average range $\bar{R}$. The control limits are

$$\text{LCL}_R = D_5 \tilde{R}$$

$$\text{UCL}_R = D_6 \tilde{R}$$

The range for each sample is plotted just as on the ordinary range chart.

The median chart is not as efficient from a statistical point of view as the $\bar{x}$-chart. Nelson noted that roughly the same amount of statistical information

TABLE 16.4 Factors for Computing 3σ Control Limits for Median and Range Charts from the Median Range

Subgroup Size	A_5	D_5	D_6	d_3
2	2.224	0	3.865	0.954
3	1.265	0	2.745	1.588
4	0.829	0	2.375	1.978
5	0.712	0	2.179	2.257
6	0.562	0	2.055	2.472
7	0.520	0.078	1.967	2.645
8	0.441	0.139	1.901	2.791
9	0.419	0.187	1.850	2.916
10	0.369	0.227	1.809	3.024

SOURCE: P. C. Clifford, "Control Charts Without Calculations," *Industrial Quality Control* 15, no. 6 (May 1959), 44.

can be obtained from two-thirds as large a sample if the mean is used instead of the median.[1] He stressed that he median is nevertheless better than no statistic at all. Thus, in some situations, the median chart can be a useful tool.

EXAMPLE 3   Constructing a Median Chart.   Median charts can be illustrated using the silicon wafer data of Chapter 15 (Figure 15.5, p. 646). The median for each sample is:

Sample	Median	Sample	Median
1	41	14	35
2	68	15	56
3	48	16	41
4	36	17	98
5	46	18	54
6	56	19	41
7	53	20	39
8	37	21	40
9	50	22	62
10	57	23	57
11	39	24	44
12	48	25	62
13	51		

The grand median is $\tilde{\tilde{x}} = 48$, and the median range is $\tilde{R} = 24$. For a sample size of three, $A_5 = 1.265$, $D_5 = 0$, and $D_6 = 2.745$. The control limits on the R-chart are

$$LCL_R = 0$$

$$UCL_R = 2.745(24) = 65.88$$

For the $\tilde{x}$-chart, we have

$$LCL_{\tilde{x}} = 48 - 1.265(24) = 17.64$$

$$UCL_{\tilde{x}} = 48 + 1.265(24) = 78.36$$

FIGURE 16.5 $\tilde{x}$-Chart

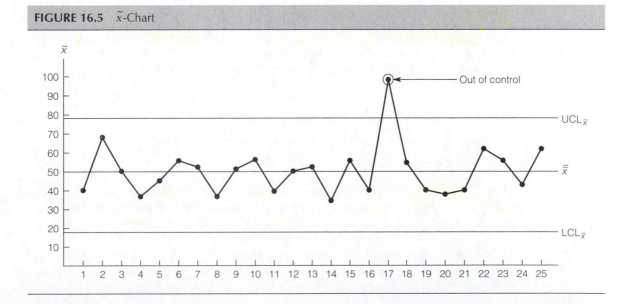

FIGURE 16.6 *R*-Chart

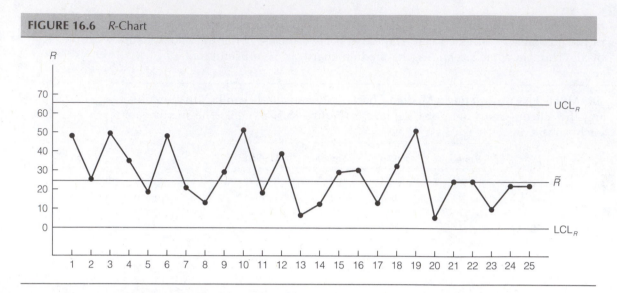

Figures 16.5 and 16.6 display the $\tilde{x}$- and *R*-charts for this example. The charts provide the same conclusions as the $\bar{x}$- and *R*-charts in Figure 15.7 (p. 648).

SPECIAL CONTROL CHARTS FOR ATTRIBUTES DATA

The *p*-chart, or fraction nonconforming chart, was discussed in Chapter 15 for process control of attributes measurements. Recall that the *p*-chart measures the proportion of nonconforming items produced in a lot. The fraction nonconforming of the *i*th sample is given by

$$p_i = y_i / n$$

where y_i is the number found nonconforming and n is the sample size. Many situations exist in which use of the *p*-chart is neither desirable nor proper. This section introduces variations of the *p*-chart used in such situations.

■ *np*-Charts for Number Nonconforming

Multiplying both sides of the equation $p_i = y_i/n$ by n, yields

$$y_i = np_i$$

That is, the number nonconforming is equal to the sample size times the proportion nonconforming. Instead of using a chart for the fraction nonconforming, an equivalent alternative—a chart for the *number* of nonconforming items—is useful. Such a control chart is called a *np*-chart.

The *np*-chart is a control chart for the number of nonconforming items in a sample. To use the *np*-chart, the size of each sample must be constant. Suppose that two samples of sizes 10 and 15 each have four nonconforming items. Clearly, the fraction nonconforming in each sample is different, which would be reflected in a *p*-chart. An *np*-chart, however, would indicate no difference between samples. Thus, equal sample sizes are necessary to have a common base for measurement. Equal sample sizes are not required for *p*-charts, since the fraction nonconforming is invariant to the sample size. Recall, though, that a *p*-chart with variable sample size will have variable control limits as explained in Chapter 15. Therefore, constant samples are much preferred.

The *np*-chart is a useful alternative to the *p*-chart because it is often easier to understand for production personnel—the number of nonconforming items is more meaningful than a fraction. Also, since it requires only a count, the computations are simpler.

The control limits for the *np*-chart, like the *p*-chart, are based on the binomial probability distribution. The center line is the average number of nonconforming items per sample as denoted by $n\bar{p}$, which is calculated by taking M samples of size n, summing the number of nonconforming items y_i in each sample, and dividing by M. That is,

$$n\bar{p} = \frac{y_1 + y_2 + \ldots + y_M}{M}$$

An estimate of the standard deviation is

$$s_{n\bar{p}} = \sqrt{n\bar{p}(1 - \bar{p})}$$

where $\bar{p} = (n\bar{p})/n$. Using three-sigma limits as before, the control limits are specified by

$$\text{UCL}_{n\bar{p}} = n\bar{p} + 3\sqrt{n\bar{p}(1 - \bar{p})}$$

$$\text{LCL}_{n\bar{p}} = n\bar{p} - 3\sqrt{n\bar{p}(1 - \bar{p})}$$

EXAMPLE 4   An *np*-Chart for a Post Office.   The post office example discussed in Chapter 15 illustrates the *np*-chart. Table 15.3 (p. 663) showed the number of errors found in 25 samples of 100 letters over a month's period.

$$n\bar{p} = \frac{3 + 1 + \ldots + 0 + 1}{25} = 2.2$$

$$\bar{p} = \frac{2.2}{100} = 0.022$$

$$s_{n\bar{p}} = \sqrt{2.2(1 - .022)}$$

$$= \sqrt{2.2(0.978)}$$

$$= \sqrt{2.1516} = 1.4668$$

The control limits are then computed as

$$\text{UCL}_{n\bar{p}} = 2.2 + 3(1.4668) = 6.6$$

$$\text{LCL}_{n\bar{p}} = 2.2 - 3(1.4668) = -2.20$$

Since the lower control limit is less than zero, a value of 0 is used. The control chart for this example is given in Figure 16.7.

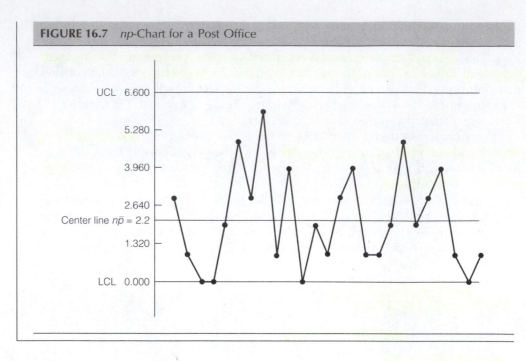

FIGURE 16.7   *np*-Chart for a Post Office

Charts for Defects

Chapter 15 made an important distinction between a *defect* and a *defective*. Recall that a defect is a single nonconforming characteristic of an item, while a defective refers to an item that has one or more defects. In some situations, quality assurance personnel may be interested not only in whether an item is defective but also in how many defects it has. For example, in complex assemblies such as electronics, the number of defects is just as important as whether the product is defective. Two charts can be applied in such situations. The *c*-chart is used to control the total number of defects per unit when subgroup size is constant. If subgroup sizes are variable, a *u*-chart is used to control the average number of defects per unit.

The *c*-chart is based on the Poisson probability distribution. To construct a *c*-chart, first estimate the average number of defects per unit, $\bar{c}$, by taking at least 25 samples of equal size, counting the number of defects per sample, and finding the average. The standard deviation of the Poisson distribution is the square root of the mean and yields

$$s_c = \sqrt{\bar{c}}$$

Thus, three-sigma control limits are given by

$$\text{UCL}_c = \bar{c} + 3\sqrt{\bar{c}}$$

$$\text{LCL}_c = \bar{c} - 3\sqrt{\bar{c}}$$

EXAMPLE 5   Constructing a *c*-Chart.   Table 16.5 shows the number of machine failures over a 25-day period. The total number of failures is 45; therefore, the average number of failures per day is

$$c = 45/25 = 1.8$$

TABLE 16.5   Daily Machine Failure Data

Day	Number of Failures	Day	Number of Failures
1	2	14	2
2	3	15	4
3	0	16	1
4	1	17	2
5	3	18	0
6	5	19	3
7	3	20	2
8	1	21	1
9	2	22	4
10	2	23	0
11	0	24	0
12	1	25	3
13	0		
		Total	45

Control limits for a c-chart are therefore given by

$$\text{UCL}_c = 1.8 + 3\sqrt{1.8} = 5.82$$

$$\text{LCL}_c = 1.8 - 3\sqrt{1.8} = -2.22 \text{ or zero}$$

The chart is shown in Figure 16.8 and appears to be in control. Such a chart can be used for continued control or for monitoring the effectiveness of a quality improvement program.

FIGURE 16.8   A c-Chart for Machine Failures Per Day

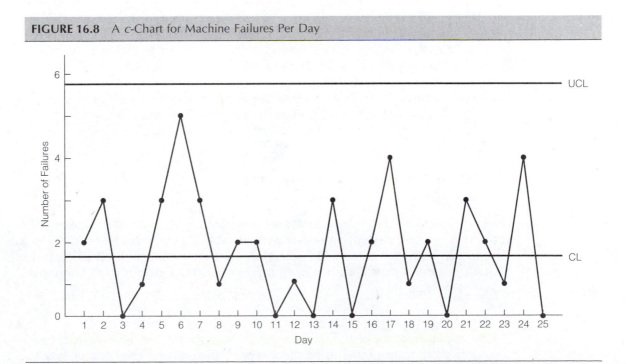

As long as the subgroup size is constant, a *c*-chart is appropriate. In many cases, however, the subgroup size is not constant or the nature of the production process does not yield discrete, measurable units. For example, suppose that in an auto assembly plant, several different models are produced that vary in surface area. The number of defects will not then be a valid comparison among different models. Other applications, such as the production of textiles, photographic film, or paper, have no convenient set of items to measure. In such cases, a standard unit of measurement is used, such as defects per square foot or defects per square inch. The control chart used in these situations is called a *u*-chart.

The variable *u* represents the average number of defects per unit of measurement, that is $u = c/n$, where *n* is the size of the subgroup (such as square feet). The center line $\bar{u}$ for *M* samples each of size n_i is computed as follows:

$$\bar{u} = \frac{c_1 + c_2 + \ldots + c_M}{n_1 + n_2 + \ldots + n_M}$$

The standard deviation of the *i*th sample is estimated by

$$s_u = \sqrt{\bar{u}/n_i}$$

The control limits, based on three standard deviations for the *i*th sample, are then

$$UCL_u = \bar{u} + 3\sqrt{\bar{u}/n_i}$$

$$LCL_u = \bar{u} - 3\sqrt{\bar{u}/n_i}$$

Note that if the size of the subgroups varies, so will the control limits. This result is similar to the *p*-chart with variable sample sizes. In general, whenever the sample size *n* varies, the control limits will also vary.

EXAMPLE 6   Constructing a *u*-Chart.   A catalog distributor ships a variety of orders each day. The packing slips often contain errors such as wrong purchase order numbers, wrong quantities, or incorrect sizes. Table 16.6 shows the error data collected during August. Since the sample size varies each day, a *u*-chart is appropriate.

To construct the chart, first compute the number of errors per slip as shown in column 3. The average number of errors per slip, $\bar{u}$, is found by dividing the total number of errors (213) by the total number of packing slips (2565):

$$\bar{u} = 213/2565 = .083$$

The standard deviation for a particular sample size n_i is therefore

$$s_u = \sqrt{.083/n_i}$$

Using this statistic, the control limits are computed in the last two columns of Table 16.6 (p. 713). As with a *p*-chart with variable sample sizes, substitute the sample size in the formula for the standard deviation to find individual control limits. The control chart is shown in Figure 16.9 (p. 714). One point (#2) appears to be out of control.

One application of *c*-charts and *u*-charts is in a quality rating system. When some defects are considered to be more serious than others, they can be rated, or categorized, into different classes. For instance,

TABLE 16.6 Packing Slip Error Data

Day	Packing Slips	Number of Errors	Errors/Slip	LCL	UCL
1	92	8	0.087	0.000	0.173
2	69	13	0.188	0.000	0.187
3	86	6	0.070	0.000	0.176
4	85	13	0.153	0.000	0.177
5	101	5	0.050	0.000	0.169
6	87	5	0.057	0.000	0.176
7	71	3	0.042	0.000	0.186
8	83	8	0.096	0.000	0.178
9	103	4	0.039	0.000	0.168
10	82	6	0.073	0.000	0.179
11	90	7	0.078	0.000	0.174
12	80	4	0.050	0.000	0.180
13	70	4	0.057	0.000	0.186
14	73	11	0.151	0.000	0.184
15	89	13	0.146	0.000	0.175
16	91	6	0.066	0.000	0.174
17	78	6	0.077	0.000	0.181
18	88	6	0.068	0.000	0.175
19	76	8	0.105	0.000	0.182
20	101	9	0.089	0.000	0.169
21	92	8	0.087	0.000	0.173
22	70	2	0.029	0.000	0.186
23	72	11	0.153	0.000	0.185
24	83	5	0.060	0.000	0.178
25	69	6	0.087	0.000	0.187
26	79	3	0.038	0.000	0.180
27	79	8	0.101	0.000	0.180
28	76	6	0.079	0.000	0.182
29	92	7	0.076	0.000	0.173
30	80	4	0.050	0.000	0.180
31	78	8	0.103	0.000	0.181
Total	2565	213			

■ A - very serious

■ B - serious

■ C - moderately serious

■ D - not serious

Each category can be weighted using a point scale, such as 100 for A, 50 for B, 10 for C, and 1 for D.[2] These points, or demerits, can be used as the basis for a c- or u-chart that would measure total demerits or demerits per unit, respectively. Such charts are often used for internal quality control and as a means of rating suppliers.

■ Choosing Between c- and u-Charts

Confusion often exists over which chart is appropriate for a specific application, since the c- and u-charts apply to situations in which the quality characteristics inspected do not necessarily come from discrete units. The key issue to consider is *whether the sampling unit is constant*. For example, suppose that an electronics manufacturer produces circuit boards. The boards may contain various defects,

FIGURE 16.9 A *u*-Chart for Packing Slip Errors

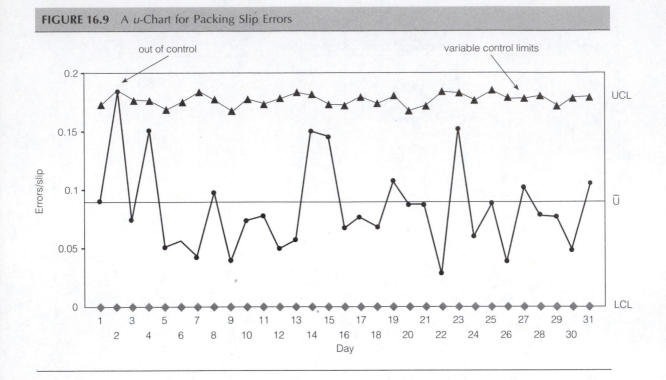

such as faulty components and missing connections. Because the sampling unit—the circuit board—is constant (assuming that all boards are the same), a *c*-chart is appropriate. If the process produces boards of varying sizes with different numbers of components and connections, then a *u*-chart would apply.

As another example, consider a telemarketing firm that wants to track the number of calls needed to make one sale. In this case, the firm has no physical sampling unit. However, an analogy can be made with the circuit boards. The sale corresponds to the circuit board, and the number of calls to the number of defects. In both examples, the number of occurrences in relationship to a constant entity is being measured. Thus, a *c*-chart is appropriate.

SUMMARY OF CONTROL CHART CONSTRUCTION

Table 16.7 summarizes the formulas used for constructing the different types of control charts discussed thus far. Figure 16.10 provides a summary of guidelines for chart selection.

OTHER SPECIAL CONTROL CHARTS

Chapter 15 and this chapter have discussed a variety of control charts: $\bar{x}$ and $\bar{R}$, $\bar{x}$ and s, p, np, c, u, and charts for individuals and medians. Several other types of control charts are used in industry. This section briefly reviews three of them: exponentially weighted moving average charts, cumulative sum control charts, and zone

TABLE 16.7   Summary of Control Chart Formulas

Type of Chart	LCL	CL	UCL
$\bar{x}$ (with R)	$\bar{\bar{x}} - A_2\bar{R}$	$\bar{\bar{x}}$	$\bar{\bar{x}} + A_2\bar{R}$
R	$D_3\bar{R}$	$\bar{R}$	$D_4\bar{R}$
p	$\bar{p} - 3\sqrt{\bar{p}(1-\bar{p})/n}$	$\bar{p}$	$\bar{p} + 3\sqrt{\bar{p}(1-\bar{p})/n}$
$\bar{x}$ (with s)	$\bar{\bar{x}} - A_3\bar{s}$	$\bar{\bar{x}}$	$\bar{\bar{x}} + A_3\bar{s}$
s	$B_3\bar{s}$	$\bar{s}$	$B_4\bar{s}$
x	$\bar{\bar{x}} - 3\bar{R}/d_2$	$\bar{\bar{x}}$	$\bar{\bar{x}} + 3\bar{R}/d_2$
np	$n\bar{p} - 3\sqrt{n\bar{p}(1-\bar{p})}$	$n\bar{p}$	$n\bar{p} + 3\sqrt{n\bar{p}(1-\bar{p})}$
c	$\bar{c} - 3\sqrt{\bar{c}}$	$\bar{c}$	$\bar{c} - 3\sqrt{\bar{c}}$
u	$\bar{u} - 3\sqrt{\bar{u}/n}$	$\bar{u}$	$\bar{u} + 3\sqrt{\bar{u}/n}$
$\tilde{x}$	$\tilde{\tilde{x}} - A_5\tilde{R}$	$\tilde{\tilde{x}}$	$\tilde{\tilde{x}} + A_5\tilde{R}$
R (with $\tilde{x}$)	$D_5\tilde{R}$	$\tilde{R}$	$D_6\tilde{R}$

FIGURE 16.10   Control Chart Selection

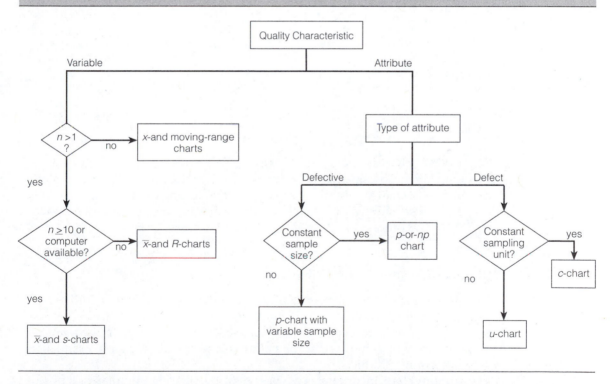

control charts. The reader is encouraged to study more advanced books on statistical quality control for further details on these and other types of control charts.

◼ EWMA Charts

The exponentially weighted moving average (EWMA) chart was introduced for applications in chemical and process industries in which only one observation per time period may be available. These measurement applications are the same situations in which charts for individuals are used, except that the EWMA chart incorporates information on all the past data, not simply the last observation. The term *exponentially weighted* refers to the fact that the data are weighted, with more weight being given to the most recent data. (You may have studied exponential smoothing as a forecasting technique; the same principle applies.)

The statistic that is plotted on the chart is

$$z_t = \alpha \bar{x}_t + (1 - \alpha)z_{t-1}$$

Here, z_t is the exponentially weighted moving average after observation t is taken; $\bar{x}_t$ is the value of observation t; z_{t-1} is the previous exponentially weighted moving average; and α is a weighting factor between 0 and 1. This formula can be written in an alternate fashion:

$$z_t = z_{t-1} + \alpha(\bar{x}_t - z_{t-1})$$

which states that the current value of the statistic is equal to the previous value plus some fraction of the difference between the current observation and its last estimate. Note that when $\alpha = 1$, the formula reduces to the ordinary $\bar{x}$-chart.

The standard error of the exponentially weighted moving average is

$$\sigma z_t = \sigma_{\bar{x}}\sqrt{\frac{\alpha}{2-\alpha}} = \frac{\sigma_x}{\sqrt{n}}\sqrt{\frac{\alpha}{2-\alpha}}$$

Therefore the control limits are given by

$$UCL_z = \bar{\bar{x}} + 3\frac{\sigma_x}{\sqrt{n}}\sqrt{\frac{\alpha}{2-\alpha}}$$

$$LCL_z = \bar{\bar{x}} - 3\frac{\sigma_x}{\sqrt{n}}\sqrt{\frac{\alpha}{2-\alpha}}$$

The EWMA chart is more sensitive to small process level shifts than $\bar{x}$- or individual charts. The smaller the value of α, the more easily are smaller shifts detectable. This chart is useful when the acceptable process limits are narrow. However, this sensitivity can lead to an excessive number of unnecessary adjustments to the process and, consequently, unnecessary costs.

Cumulative Sum Control Charts

The cumulative sum control chart (CuSum chart) was designed to identify small but sustained shifts in a process level much faster than ordinary $\bar{x}$-charts. Because it gives an early indication of process changes, it is consistent with the management philosophy of doing it right the first time and not allowing the production of nonconforming products.

The CuSum chart incorporates all past data by plotting cumulative sums of the deviations of sample values from a target value; that is,

$$S_t = \sum_{i=1}^{t}(\bar{x}_i - \bar{x}_0)$$

where $\bar{x}_i$ is the average of the ith subgroup, $\bar{x}_0$ is the standard or reference value, and S_t is the cumulative sum when the ith observation is taken. Note that when $n = 1$, $\bar{x}_i$ is the value of the ith observation.

The CuSum chart looks different from ordinary $\bar{x}$- and R-charts. In place of a center line and horizontal control limits, a "mask" is constructed that consists of a location pointer and two angled control limits as illustrated in Figure 16.11. The mask is located on the chart so that the point P lies on the last point plotted. The distance d and the angle θ are the design parameters of the mask. [This text does not discuss how these are computed. Readers are referred to Chapter 10 of Grant and Leavenworth or Chapter 7 of Montgomery (cited in the bibliography at the end of the chapter) for details.]

If no previous points lie outside the control limits, the process is assumed to be in control. If, for example, a shift in the process mean raises it above the reference value, each new value added to the cumulative sum will cause S_t to increase and result in an upward trend in the chart. Eventually a point will fall outside the upper control limit, indicating that the process has fallen out of control (illustrated in Figure 16.12). The opposite will occur if the mean shifts downward.

■ Zone Control Charts

A new type of control chart, called a *zone control chart*, has been proposed recently as a simpler alternative to the $\bar{x}$- and R-charts.[3] The $\bar{x}$- or R-chart is divided into eight zones as shown in Figure 16.13. As initially developed, scores are assigned to data points falling in each zone as follows:

Zone	Score
A	1
B	2
C	4
D	8

For the first data point, the score corresponding to the initial observed value is placed in a circle near the point. As new observations are plotted on the chart,

---

FIGURE 16.11 CuSum Chart for Sample Averages

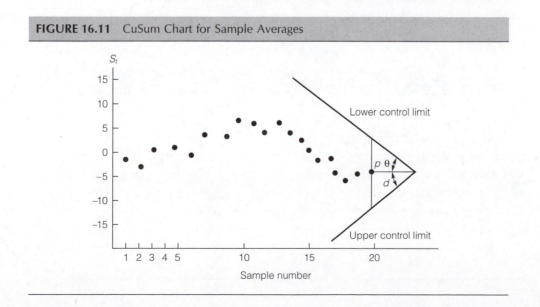

Part 3 Technical Issues in Quality

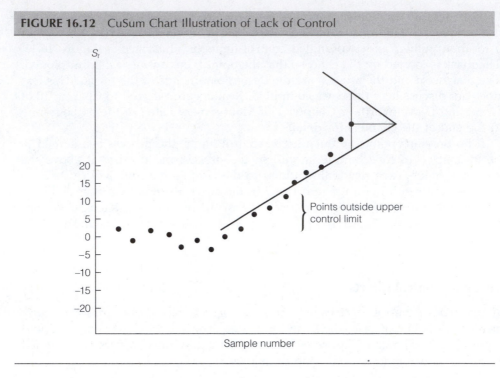

FIGURE 16.12 CuSum Chart Illustration of Lack of Control

the scores are added to the previous point *until* an observation falls on the other side of the center line. At this point, the score is reinitialized to that of the last observation. If the score for any point reaches or exceeds 8, it signals that the process has gone out of control. Since the cumulative score determines when a signal is produced, no study of patterns or counts of points is necessary by personnel monitoring the chart. Thus, it is much simpler to analyze than traditional $\bar{x}$- and R-charts.

The concept behind the zone control chart is to allow for automatic signaling of the following out-of-control indicators in the Shewart chart:

1. A point falls outside the 3σ limits.

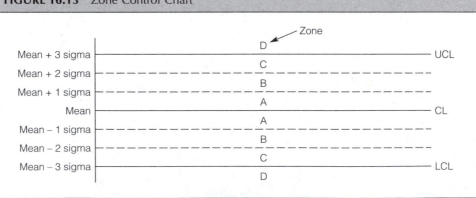

FIGURE 16.13 Zone Control Chart

2. Two of three successive points fall outside the 2σ limits on the same side of the center line.

3. Four of five successive points fall outside the 1σ limits on one side of the center line.

4. Eight consecutive points fall on the same side of the center line.

A study of the performance of the chart has shown that it is only slightly better than using ordinary control chart interpretation rules.[4] In particular, the false alarm rate (Type I error) is high, even though it detects shifts in the mean quickly. However, a simple modification in which a score of 0 is assigned to points within one standard deviation of the center line greatly improves the performance of the chart, and actually outperforms charts analyzed using the standard interpretation rules. Thus, the following scoring system is recommended:

Zone	Score
A	0
B	2
C	4
D	8

Zone control charts provide several important benefits. They are easy to understand and use; the process of tediously seeking where to plot points is eliminated; when to take action is automatically decided by the control charting procedure; changes in targets and control limits can be made easily without the need to rescale a new chart; and one standard blank form for the zone control chart usually meets all needs. Operators' acceptance of the zone control chart has been exceptional. The chart has been successfully used in production operations at Consolidated Papers, Inc. in Wisconsin, Lake Superior Paper Industries in Duluth, Minnesota, and other companies.

EXAMPLE 7 Analyzing a Zone Control Chart. This illustration of the modified zone control chart using the $\bar{x}$-chart is based on the silicon wafer example in Chapter 15. Figure 15.6 (p. 647) indicates that the range between the center line and the control limits is 27.6. Thus, the zones are partitioned as follows:

Zone	Range
D	>76.4
C	67.2–76.4
B	58–67.2
A	39.6–58 (center line = 48.8)
B	30.4–39.6
C	21.2–30.4
D	<21.2

The first point, 44, falls in zone A and therefore is assigned a score of 0. The second point, 66, falls in zone B. However, it is on the other side of the center line, so the process starts anew with its score of 2. The third point, 55, is in zone A; thus the cumulative score for this point is 2. Figure 16.14, p. 720, shows the complete results. An out-of-control condition is signaled at point 17.

FIGURE 16.14 Zone Control Chart for Silicon Wafer Example

VARIABLES CONTROL CHART ($\overline{X}$ & R)

PART NAME (PRODUCT): SILICON WAFER
OPERATOR

PART NO.
CHART NO.

SPECIFICATION LIMITS 0–100
ZERO EQUALS

UNIT OF MEASURE .0000

SAMPLE MEASUREMENTS	1	2	3	4	5	6	7	8	9	10	11	12	13	14	15	16	17	18	19	20	21	22	23	24	25
1	41	78	84	60	46	64	43	37	50	57	24	78	51	41	56	46	99	71	41	41	22	62	64	44	41
2	70	53	34	36	47	16	53	43	29	83	42	48	57	29	64	41	86	54	2	39	40	70	52	38	63
3	22	68	48	25	29	56	64	30	57	32	39	39	50	35	36	16	98	39	53	36	46	46	57	60	62
4																									
5																									
SUM	133	199	166	121	122	136	160	110	136	172	105	165	158	105	156	103	283	164	96	116	108	178	173	142	166
AVERAGE, $\overline{X}$	44	66	55	40	41	45	53	37	45	57	35	55	53	35	52	34	94	54	32	39	36	59	58	47	55
RANGE, R	48	25	50	35	18	48	21	13	28	51	18	39	7	12	28	30	13	32	51	5	24	12	22	22	22
NOTES																									

DATE
TIME
OPERATION (PROCESS)
MACHINE
GAGE

ZONE
D C B A A B C D — AVERAGES

RANGES

80 65 50 35 20
75 50 25

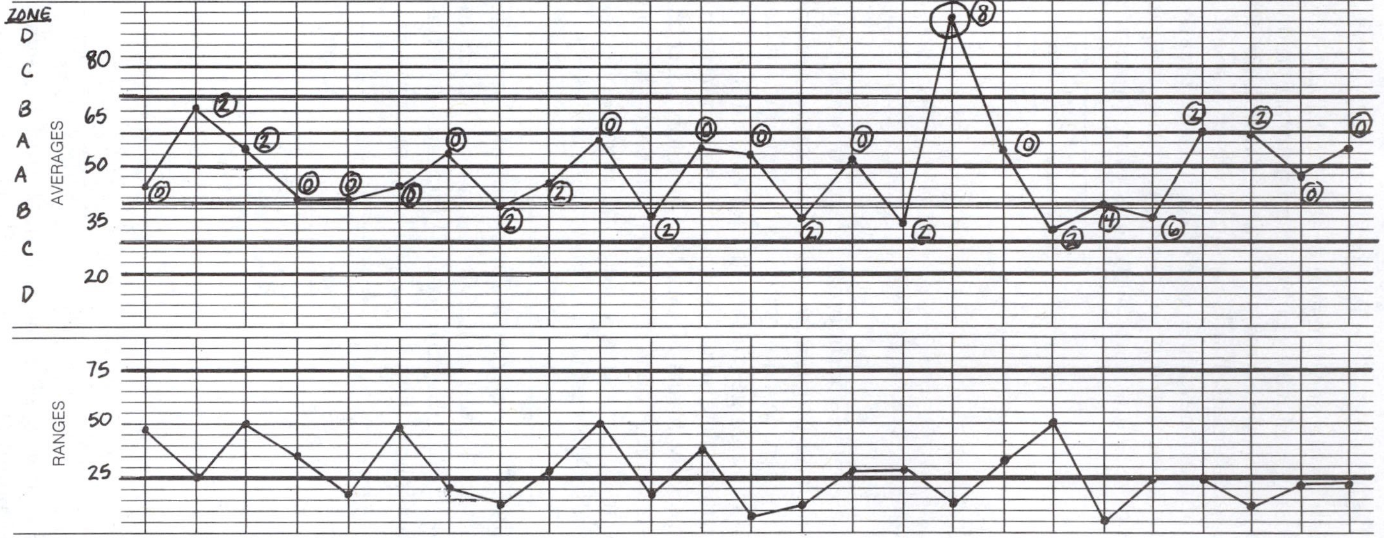

■ Pre-Control[5]

Pre-control is an alternative to $\bar{x}$- and R-charts that is useful for short manufacturing runs and in other applications in which operators do not have time to record, calculate, and plot data. A major advantage of pre-control is its direct relationship to specifications, which requires no recording, calculating, or plotting of data.

The idea behind pre-control is to divide the tolerance range into zones by setting two *pre-control lines* halfway between the center of the specification and the tolerance limits (see Figure 16.15). The center zone, called the *green zone*, comprises one-half of the total tolerance. Between the pre-control lines and the tolerance limits are the *yellow zones*. Outside the tolerance limits are the *red zones*.

Pre-control is applied as follows. As a manufacturing run is initiated, five consecutive parts must fall within the green zone. If not, the production setup must be reevaluated before the full production run can be started. Once regular operations commence, two parts are sampled; if the first falls within the green zone, production continues, which eliminates the need to measure the second part. If the first part falls in a yellow zone, the second part is inspected. If the second part falls in the green zone, production can continue; if not, production should stop and a special cause should be investigated. If any part falls in a red zone, then action should be taken.

The rationale behind pre-control can be explained using basic statistical arguments. Suppose that the process capability is equal to the tolerance spread (see Figure 16.16). The area of each yellow zone is approximately 0.07, while that of the red zone is less than 0.01. The probability of two consecutive parts falling in a yellow zone is $(0.07)(0.07) = 0.0049$ if the process mean has not shifted. If $C_p > 1$, this probability is even less. Such an outcome would more than likely indicate a special cause. If both parts fall in the same yellow zone, you would conclude that the mean has shifted; if in different yellow zones, you would conclude that the variation has increased.

The frequency of sampling is often determined by dividing the time period between two successive out-of-control signals by six. Thus, if the process deteriorates, sampling frequency is increased; if it improves; the frequency is decreased.

FIGURE 16.15   Pre-Control Ranges

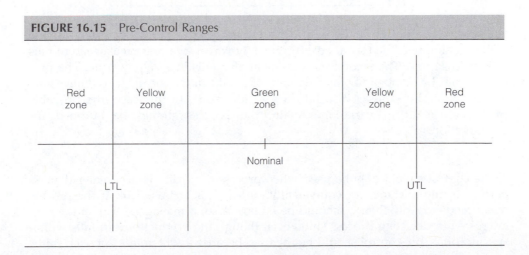

Red zone	Yellow zone	Green zone	Yellow zone	Red zone

Nominal

LTL

UTL

FIGURE 16.16   Basis for Pre-Control Rules

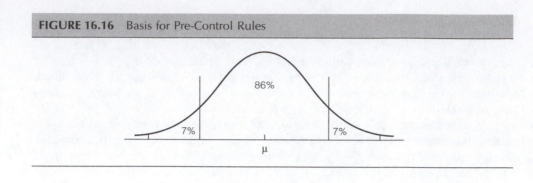

EXAMPLE 8   An Example of Pre-Control.   The force necessary to break a wire used in electrical circuitry has a specification of 3 gm–7 gm. Thus, the pre-control zones are

Range	Zone
<3	Red
3–4	Yellow
4–6	Green
6–7	Yellow
>7	Red

The following samples were collected:

Sample	First Measurement	Second Measurement
1	4.7	
2	4.5	
3	4.4	
4	4.2	
5	4.2	
6	4.0	
7	4.0	
8	3.7	3.6
9	6.5	3.5

For samples 1 through 7, the first measurement falls in the green zone; thus no further action need be taken. For sample 8, however, the first measurement falls in a yellow zone. The second measurement also falls in a yellow zone. The process should be stopped for investigation of a shift in the mean. At the next time of inspection, both pieces also fall in a yellow zone. In this case, the probable cause is a shift in variation. Again, the process should be stopped for investigation.

Pre-control should only be used when process capability is no greater than 88 percent of the tolerance, or equivalently, when C_p is at least 1.14. If the process mean tends to drift, then C_p should be higher. Also, if managers or operators are interested in detecting process shifts even though the product output falls within specifications, pre-control should not be used because it will not detect such shifts.

STATISTICAL FOUNDATIONS OF CONTROL CHARTS

Control charts are defined by the center line, upper control limit, and lower control limit. These values are related to the expected value and variance of the statistics plotted on the charts. In Chapter 15, the upper and lower control limits were specified through the use of certain constants given in Appendix B. This section shows how these factors are developed and discusses the statistical basis for the rules used to interpret control charts.

■ Variables Control Charts

When a process is in control, the distribution of *individual measurements* for variables data is assumed to have a mean μ and a variance σ_x^2. If a sample of size n is chosen, the sampling distribution of $\bar{x}$ will also have a mean μ but will have a variance $\sigma_{\bar{x}}^2 = \sigma_x^2/n$. If the original distribution of individuals is normal, the sampling distribution of averages will also be normal. If not, the central limit theorem states that the sampling distribution of averages will be approximately normal for large sample sizes. Since control chart samples are usually small ($n = 4$ or 5), the central limit theorem does not always apply. However, normality is usually assumed in developing variables control charts.

Under this assumption, $100(1 - \alpha)$ percent of the sample means fall between $\mu - z_{\alpha/2}\sigma_{\bar{x}}$ and $\mu + z_{\alpha/2}\sigma_{\bar{x}}$; these values become the lower and upper control limits. A value of $z_{\alpha/2} = 3$ gives a six-standard deviation range with $\alpha/2 = 0.0014$. Thus, only about 0.3% of the sample observations will be expected to fall outside these limits. If the process is in control, the likelihood that a sample will fall outside the control limits is extremely small. On the other hand, if the true mean has shifted, this probability will be much larger. This reasoning is the theoretical basis for assigning three-sigma control limits.

The value of $z_{\alpha/2}$ can, of course, be chosen arbitrarily. In the United States, the value of 3 is commonly accepted. In England, however, $z_{\alpha/2}$ is selected by first setting the probability of a Type I error—usually chosen as $\alpha/2 = 0.001$. Thus, $z_{0.001} = 3.09$ is commonly used to establish control limits. Such limits are called **probability limits.**

R-Chart

The range is used as a substitute for the standard deviation primarily because of its simplicity. As noted in Chapter 15, the factor d_2 in Appendix B is used to relate the range to the actual process standard deviation. The factor d_2 is determined as follows. Consider an experiment in which samples of size n are drawn from a normal distribution having a known standard deviation σ_x. If the range R of each sample is computed, the distribution of the statistic R/σ_x can be determined. The expected value of this statistic is the factor d_2, that is

$$E(R/\sigma_x) = d_2$$

or, since R is a random variable and σ_x is known,

$$E(R)/\sigma_x = d_2$$

This experiment can be performed for each n, and corresponding values of d_2 can be computed.

The hypothesis tested in the R-chart is $H_0: R = E(R)$. The expected value of R is estimated by the sample range $\overline{R}$. Thus $\overline{R}/d_2$ is an estimate of the process standard deviation σ_x. To establish control limits for an R-chart, an estimate of the standard deviation of the random variable R, namely σ_R, is needed. From the distribution of the statistic R/σ_x, the ratio σ_R/σ_x can be computed for each n, resulting in another constant d_3.

$$\sigma_R = d_3\sigma_x$$

When $\overline{R}/d_2$ is substituted into the equation as an estimate for σ_x, $d_3\overline{R}/d_2$ then becomes the estimate for σ_R. The control limits for the R-chart are based on three standard deviations about the estimate of the mean. Thus,

$$\text{UCL}_R = \overline{R} + 3d_3\overline{R}/d_2 = (1 + 3d_3/d_2)\overline{R} = D_4\overline{R}$$

$$\text{LCL}_R = \overline{R} - 3d_3\overline{R}/d_2 = (1 - 3d_3/d_2)\overline{R} = D_3\overline{R}$$

For convenience, the constants $1 + 3d_3/d_2$ and $1 - 3d_3/d_2$ are computed as D_4 and D_3, respectively. The control limits for the R-chart are therefore based on the distribution of the process standard deviation, adjusted to correspond to the range.

$\overline{\text{X}}$-Chart

The statistic $\overline{\overline{x}}$ is an estimate of the population mean μ. Since $\overline{R}/d_2$ is an estimate of σ_x, an estimate of the sample standard deviation is

$$\sigma_{\overline{x}} = \frac{\overline{R}}{d_2\sqrt{n}}$$

Three-sigma limits on $\overline{x}$ are then given by

$$\overline{\overline{x}} \pm \frac{3\overline{R}}{d_2\sqrt{n}}$$

Letting $A_2 = 3/d_2\sqrt{n}$ provides the control limits presented in Chapter 15:

$$\text{UCL}_x = \overline{\overline{x}} + A_2\overline{R}$$

$$\text{LCL}_x = \overline{\overline{x}} - A_2\overline{R}$$

■ Fraction Nonconforming Control Charts

The theory underlying the p-chart is based on the binomial distribution, since attributes data assume only one of two values: conforming or nonconforming. If p represents the probability of producing a nonconforming item and a sample of n items is selected, the binomial distribution

$$f(x) = \binom{n}{x}p^x(1 - p)^{n-x} \quad x = 0, 1, 2, \ldots, n$$

gives the probability of finding x nonconforming items in the sample.

The sample statistic $\overline{p}$ is an estimate of the population parameter p. An estimate of the standard deviation σ_p is given by

$$\sigma_p = \sqrt{\overline{p}(1 - \overline{p})/n}$$

Three-sigma limits on the parameter p are therefore given by

$$\text{UCL}_p = \bar{p} + 3\sqrt{\bar{p}(1 - \bar{p})/n}$$

$$\text{LCL}_p = \bar{p} - 3\sqrt{\bar{p}(1 - \bar{p})/n}$$

The critical assumptions in using a p-chart are the constant probability of a defective and independence of the trials. If these assumptions cannot be assured, the p-chart is not appropriate. (A previous section contained examples of other attributes charts that are based on different assumptions.)

▪ Basis for Control Chart Interpretation Rules

The use of a control chart represents a statistical test of hypothesis each time a sample is taken and plotted on the chart. In general, the null hypothesis, H_0, is that the process is in control, and the alternate hypothesis, H_1, is that the process is out of control. Specifically, a control chart tests the hypothesis that the sample statistic used in the chart—$\bar{x}$, R, or p—drawn from a population having specified parameters. For example, in an $\bar{x}$-chart, to determine whether the process mean has shifted, the hypothesis

$$H_0: \mu = \mu_0$$

is tested against the alternative hypothesis

$$H_1: \mu \neq \mu_0$$

where μ is the population mean and μ_0 is a specified value. Other hypotheses—for example, that the distribution is normal or the pattern above and below the center line is random—can also be tested.

Chapter 15 presented several rules based on such hypotheses for analyzing and interpreting control charts. For example, a point outside the control limits indicates the possibility that the process is out of control. Under the normality assumption, a 0.9973 probability exists that any sample value will fall within three-sigma limits. Thus, under H_0, a sample value has only a $1 - 0.9973 = 0.0027$ probability of exceeding these limits. Unless the process mean, range, or fraction nonconforming has shifted, a point is highly unlikely to fall outside the control limits. The chance remains, however remote, that the process is still under control even though a sample point falls outside the control limits. A person would typically conclude that the process is out of control. This situation represents the probability of a Type I error.

A second rule for interpreting control charts discussed in Chapter 15 was that about two-thirds of the points should fall within the middle one-third of the region between the control limits. This rule follows from the normality assumption that about 68 percent of a normal distribution falls within one standard deviation on either side of the mean (see Figure 16.17). Therefore, if the process is in control and all samples are chosen from a common population, this assumption should be true. If, however, the value of the population parameter has shifted, the distribution of sample statistics will also change. In such a case, an assignable cause needs to be found.

Another significant indication of an out-of-control situation is the presence of patterns in the control chart over time. If the process is in control, the distribution of sample values should be randomly distributed above and below the center line. A disproportionate number of points either above or below the center line should be suspect. For example, the probability that a point will fall either above

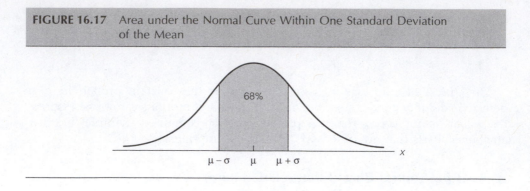

FIGURE 16.17   Area under the Normal Curve Within One Standard Deviation of the Mean

or below the center line is 0.5. The probability of obtaining k successive points on one side of the center line is $(0.5)^k$. Thus, the probability that eight consecutive points will fall on one side of the center line is only $(0.5)^8 = 0.0039$. The probability that 10 of 11 consecutive points will fall on one side of the center line can be computed using the binomial formula:

$$f(10) = \binom{11}{10}(0.5)^{10}(0.5)^1 = 0.00537$$

If the process is in control, either of these events is highly unlikely.

The rules of thumb presented in Chapter 15 are based on statistical theories of randomness. Sample data collected over time are not random if a dependency exists between successive values. Statistical tests for randomness can be performed that verify whether the observations obtained are similar to what might be expected from a truly random sequence. One such test is a nonparametric procedure called the **number-of-runs test.**

The number-of-runs test is used when sample data can be separated into two mutually exclusive categories. Let a denote the event that the sample belongs to the first category and b the event that it belongs to the second. A **run** is a string of consecutive a's or b's. Thus the sequence

aababbbaabbbbabaaabaabbb

consists of 12 runs, six runs of a's and six runs of b's.

The test for randomness is based on the number of runs. If there are n_a a's and n_b b's, one can show that if n_a and n_b are greater than or equal to 10, the sampling distribution of the random variable T, the total number of runs, is approximately normal with mean

$$\mu = E(T) = \frac{2n_a n_b}{n_a + n_b} + 1$$

and variance

$$\sigma^2 = \text{var}(T) = \frac{2n_a n_b (2n_a n_b - n_a - n_b)}{(n_a + n_b)^2 (n_a + n_b - 1)}$$

The standardized variable $z = (T - \mu)/\sigma$ can be used in a two-tailed test of the hypothesis:

H_0: the sequence is random
H_1: the sequence is not random

FIGURE 16.18   A Run of Seven Consecutive Observations Up

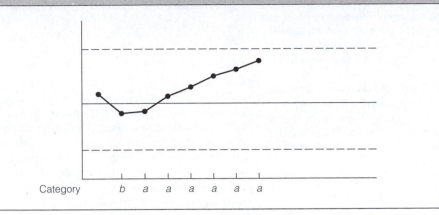

where T is the observed number of runs. If z falls above or below the critical values of the normal distribution for a specified Type I error, the hypothesis is rejected.

In a control chart, category a can represent sample points that fall *above* the previous point, and category b can represent sample points that fall *below* the previous point. The number-of-runs test can be applied directly to the number of runs up and down that are observed. To illustrate, use this test (as an approximate test of the hypothesis) to determine if the pattern in Figure 16.18 appears to be random. The figure shows a run of seven consecutive points up and, according to the given heuristics, indicates a lack of control. The second point is below the first, so it is assigned to category b; the remaining points are above the previous ones, so each is assigned to category a. Therefore, $n_a = 6$ and $n_b = 1$. Using the preceding formulas, $E(T) = 2.714$ and $var(T) = 0.204$. Since the pattern contains two runs, $T = 2$ and $z = (2 - 2.714)/(0.204) = -3.5$. For a level significance of 0.05, this value of z falls well beyond the critical value of $z_{0.025} = 1.96$; therefore, the null hypothesis of randomness is rejected.

Although this discussion has not examined every rule that was presented in Chapter 15, these examples have shown how some of the interpretive rules of thumb in common practice are derived through fundamental principles of statistics.

QUALITY IN PRACTICE   **USING A u-CHART IN A RECEIVING PROCESS[6]**

Cincinnati Belting and Transmission is a distributor of electrical and power transmission products. The company began to implement a Total Quality Management process in early 1990. One manager was eager to collect data about the organization's receiving process because of a decrease in the organization's on-time deliveries. The manager suspected that the data entry person in the purchasing department was not entering data in the computer in a timely fashion; consequently, packages could not be properly processed for subsequent shipping to the customer. A preliminary analysis indicated that the manager's notion was inaccurate. In fact, the manager was able to see that the data entry person was doing an excellent job. The analysis showed that the handling of packages that were destined for a branch operation in the same fashion as other packages created significant delays. A simple process change of placing a branch designation letter in front of the purchase order number communicated to the receiving clerk to place those packages on a separate skid for delivery to where they should be received.

However, this analysis revealed a variety of other problems. Generally, anywhere from 65 to 110 packing slips are processed each day. These were found to contain many other errors in addition to the wrong destination designation that contributed to the delays. Errors included

- wrong purchase order
- wrong quantity
- purchase order not on the system
- original order not on the system

- parts do not match
- purchase order was entered incorrectly
- double shipment
- wrong parts
- no purchase order

Many packing slips contained multiple errors. Table 16.8 shows the number of packing slips and total errors during early 1992. A u-chart was constructed for each day to track the number of packing slip errors—defects—found. A u-chart was used because the sample size varied each day. Thus, the statistic monitored was the number of errors per packing slip. Figure 16.19 shows the u-chart that was constructed for this period. (The change in the branch designation described above took place on January 24, resulting in significant improvement, as shown on the chart.)

TABLE 16.8   Cincinnati Belting and Transmission Packing Slip Error Counts

Date	Packing Slips	Errors	Date	Packing Slips	Errors
21 Jan	87	15	4 Mar	92	8
22 Jan	79	13	5 Mar	69	13
23 Jan	92	23	6 Mar	86	6
24 Jan	84	3	9 Mar	85	13
27 Jan	73	7	10 Mar	101	5
28 Jan	67	11	11 Mar	87	5
29 Jan	73	8	12 Mar	71	3
30 Jan	91	8	13 Mar	83	8
31 Jan	94	11	16 Mar	103	4
3 Feb	83	12	17 Mar	82	6
4 Feb	89	12	18 Mar	90	7
5 Feb	88	6	19 Mar	80	4
6 Feb	69	11	20 Mar	70	4
7 Feb	74	8	23 Mar	73	11
10 Feb	67	4	24 Mar	89	13
11 Feb	83	10	25 Mar	91	6
12 Feb	79	8	26 Mar	78	6
13 Feb	75	8	27 Mar	88	6
14 Feb	69	3	30 Mar	76	8
17 Feb	87	8	31 Mar	101	9
18 Feb	99	13	1 Apr	92	8
19 Feb	101	13	2 Apr	70	2
20 Feb	76	7	3 Apr	72	11
21 Feb	90	4	6 Apr	83	5
24 Feb	92	7	7 Apr	69	6
25 Feb	80	4	8 Apr	79	3
26 Feb	81	5	9 Apr	79	8
27 Feb	105	8	10 Apr	76	6
28 Feb	80	8	13 Par	92	7
2 Mar	82	5	14 Apr	80	4
3 Mar	75	3	15 Apr	78	8

FIGURE 16.19 *u*-Chart for Cincinnati Belting and Transmission Packing Slip Errors

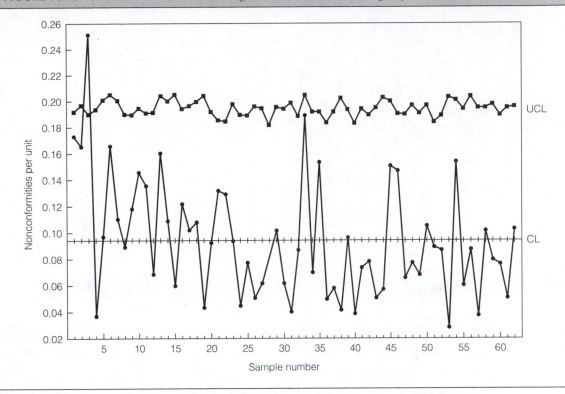

Although the chart shows that the process is in control (since the branch designation change), the average error rate of over 9 percent still was not considered acceptable. After consolidating the types of errors into five categories, a Pareto analysis was performed. This analysis showed the following:

Category	Percentage
Purchase order error	35
Quantity error	22
No purchase order on system	17
Original order not on system	16
Parts error	10

The analysis is illustrated in Figure 16.20.

The first two categories accounted for over half of the errors. The remedy for these problems was to develop a training module on proper purchasing methods to ensure that vendors knew the correct information needed on the purchase orders. The third category—no purchase order on the computer system—caused receiving personnel to stage the orders until an investigation could find the necessary information. Because of this problem the company realized it needed to revamp the original order-writing process. Specifically, the order-writing and purchase order activities needed to be improved.

An analysis of the control chart in Figure 16.19 shows that the average error rate has gradually improved. To a large extent, this was due to the recognition of the problems and improved communication among the constituents. While the full training program has not been implemented at the time this case was written, the company believes that a significant reduction in the error rate will result once the training is completed.

Key Issues for Discussion

1. Verify the computation of the center line and control limits in Figure 16.19.

2. What information might a separate chart for each error category provide? Would you recommend spending the time and effort to do this?

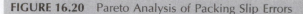

FIGURE 16.20	Pareto Analysis of Packing Slip Errors

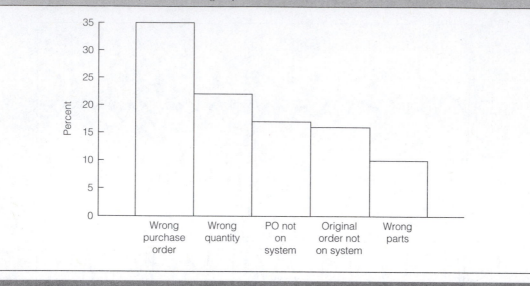

SUMMARY OF KEY POINTS

■ $\bar{x}$- and s-charts are alternatives to $\bar{x}$- and R-charts for larger sample sizes. The sample standard deviation provides a better indication of process variability than the range.

■ Individuals charts are useful when every item can be inspected and when a long lead time exists for producing an item. Moving ranges are used to measure the variability in individuals charts.

■ Charts for medians are often used for small sample sizes and are easier to implement on the factory floor.

■ The np-chart is an alternative to the p-chart, and controls the number nonconforming for attributes data.

■ Charts for defects include the c-chart and u-chart. The c-chart is used for constant sample size while the u-chart is used for variable sample size.

■ Additional charts used in special situations include exponentially weighted moving average charts, cumulative sum control charts, and zone control charts.

■ Pre-control is useful for short manufacturing runs and in applications in which operators do not have the time to construct conventional control charts.

■ Rules for control chart interpretation that were presented in Chapter 15 are based on simple arguments from probability and statistics.

REVIEW QUESTIONS

1. Why is the s-chart sometimes used in place of the R-chart?

2. Describe some situations in which a chart for individual measurements would be used.

3. Explain the concept of a moving range. Why is a moving range chart difficult to interpret?

4. Why is a median chart easier to use on a factory floor than an $\bar{x}$-chart?

5. Does an np-chart provide any different information than a p-chart? Why would an np-chart be used?

6. Explain the difference between a c-chart and a u-chart.

7. Discuss how to use charts for defects in a quality rating system.

8. Explain the concept behind zone control charts. Why might it be preferred to the usual $\bar{x}$-chart?

9. Describe the use of pre-control. Why is pre-control not appropriate when process capability is poor?

10. Explain why three-sigma control limits are used in control charts.

11. What are probability limits and how are they used in control chart construction?

12. List the null and alternate hypotheses corresponding to the rules used in interpreting control charts.

13. Explain how the number-of-runs test is used in developing decision rules for determining out-of-control conditions in a control chart.

PROBLEMS

1. Suppose that the following sample means and standard deviations are observed for samples of size 5:

$\bar{x}$	s	$\bar{x}$	s
2.15	0.14	2.10	0.17
2.07	0.10	2.19	0.13
2.10	0.11	2.14	0.07
2.14	0.12	2.13	0.11
2.18	0.12	2.14	0.11
2.11	0.12	2.12	0.14
2.10	0.14	2.08	0.07
2.11	0.10	2.18	0.10
2.06	0.09	2.06	0.06
2.15	0.08	2.13	0.14

Construct $\bar{x}$- and s-charts for these data.

2. Construct an s-chart for the data given in Table 15.1

3. Construct an $\bar{x}$- and s-chart for the data in Problem 1 of Chapter 15.

4. Construct an $\bar{x}$- and s-chart for the data in Problem 6 of Chapter 15.

5. Construct charts for individuals using both two-period and three-period moving ranges for the following observations:

9.0, 9.5, 8.4, 11.5, 10.3, 12.1, 11.4, 11.4, 10.0, 11.0, 12.7, 11.3, 17.2, 12.6, 12.5, 13.0, 12.0, 11.2, 11.1, 11.5, 12.5, 12.1

6. Assume that the data in Problem 10 of Chapter 15 represent individual measurements instead of samples. Construct an x-chart and R-chart using a five-sample moving range.

7. Construct a median chart for the data in Problem 1 of Chapter 15.

8. Construct a median chart for the data in Problem 5 of Chapter 15.

9. Construct an *np*-chart for the data in Problem 17 of Chapter 15.

10. Construct an *np*-chart for the data in Problem 18 of Chapter 15.

11. Construct both a *c*-chart and a *u*-chart for a situation involving 25 samples of size 9 and having a total of 400 defects.

12. Consider the following data:

Sample	Number of Defects
1	4
2	15
3	13
4	20
5	17
6	22
7	26
8	17
9	20
10	22

Construct a *c*-chart for these data.

13. Find three-sigma control limits for a *c*-chart with an average number of defects equal to 9.

14. Find three-sigma control limits for a *u*-chart with $c = 9$ and $n = 4$.

15. Develop and analyze a zone control chart for Problem 1 of Chapter 15.

16. Develop and analyze a zone control chart for Problem 5 of Chapter 15.

17. Suppose that the specification limits for Problem 5 in this chapter are 9.0 to 12.0. Illustrate how pre-control would operate in this situation.

18. If control limits are based on 2.75 standard deviations, what percentage of observations will be expected to fall beyond the limits?

19. What are the probability limits corresponding to a Type I error of $\alpha = 0.04$?

20. Write a computer program to sample three observations from a normal distribution with mean 0 and variance 1. Use this simulation to estimate the value of d_2 in Appendix B and compare your result.

21. What is the probability of observing 11 consecutive points on one side of the center line if the process is in control? 10 of 11 points? 9 of 11 points? How many points out of 11 on one side of the center line would indicate lack of control?

CASE

Murphy Trucking, Inc.[7]

Murphy Trucking, Inc. (MTI) supplies contract transportation services to many different manufacturing firms. One of its principal customers, Crawford Consumer Products (CCP), is actively improving quality by using the Malcolm Baldrige National Quality Award criteria. In an effort to improve supplier quality, Crawford Consumer Products has mandated that all suppliers provide factual evidence of quality improvement efforts that lead to highly capable processes.

As part of its supplier development program, CCP held a seminar for all its suppliers to outline this initiative and provide initial assistance. The executive officers of MTI participated in this seminar and recognized that MTI was seriously lacking in its quality improvement efforts. More importantly, Jeff Blaine, the purchasing manager at CCP, told them privately that many errors had been found in MTI's shipping documents. CCP would not continue to tolerate this high number of errors; and if no improvements were made, they would seek transportation services elsewhere. Rick Murphy, president and CEO of MTI, was very concerned.

In an off-site meeting, Mr. Murphy and other MTI executives developed a comprehensive blueprint to help MTI develop a total quality focus. One of the key objectives was to establish an SPC effort to gain control of key customer-focused processes and establish priorities for improvement.

The Billing Study—Part I

Responding to CCP's feedback, MTI turned their attention to biller input errors. To gain some understanding of the situation, MTI conducted an initial study by sampling 20 bills of lading over a 20-day period. Table 16.9 shows the results of this study. The study revealed that field employees were correcting the errors as they found them, but this re-

TABLE 16.9 MTI Defective Billing Data

Day	Number of Defective Bills
1	10
2	9
3	13
4	10
5	15
6	10
7	14
8	13
9	14
10	14
11	12
12	13
13	14
14	13
15	12
16	12
17	14
18	16
19	14
20	10

TABLE 16.10 Distribution of Billing Errors

Day	Number of Bills	ERROR CATEGORY							
		1	2	3	4	5	6	7	8
1	54	4	6	3	3	2	6	2	10
2	76	5	8	2	6	4	4	3	10
3	67	7	8	3	5	4	6	2	7
4	89	5	20	2	9	5	7	3	14
5	76	7	13	2	7	2	5	2	10
6	84	6	11	3	7	3	8	2	9
7	61	4	11	2	6	2	3	2	6
8	73	7	10	2	7	4	4	3	10
9	90	7	14	3	7	4	9	2	15
10	98	9	10	3	6	5	6	4	8
11	82	8	13	3	5	2	7	3	13
12	64	4	13	1	4	3	6	1	10
13	72	4	10	1	6	3	7	2	6
14	88	5	11	3	8	4	5	4	11
15	86	8	12	3	9	3	5	4	8
16	93	9	18	4	5	5	9	2	16
17	81	5	14	2	5	3	9	2	11
18	88	9	16	2	7	3	6	2	14
19	66	7	10	3	4	3	4	1	10
20	92	10	16	2	6	5	8	4	15
21	57	3	7	2	5	2	4	2	9
22	68	4	14	3	4	3	4	3	8
23	85	5	15	3	5	3	8	2	9
24	79	7	7	1	6	5	6	3	9
25	96	10	13	4	5	5	5	3	16

work was costing the company almost $2 per error—a clear economic incentive to improve quality. Furthermore, field employees did not always catch the errors, which lead to field service and other problems.

Assignment

At this point, MTI is unsure of how to interpret these results. You have been hired as a consultant by the executive committee to analyze this data and provide additional recommendations for integrating SPC concepts into MTI's quality system. Using the results in Table 16.9, determine the performance, that is, the process capability of the billing input. What is the average rate of defective bills? Is the process in control? What error rates might the company expect in the future? What general conclusions do you reach?

The Billing Study—Part II

The revelations from the initial study were startling. Mr. Murphy personally led a group problem-solving session to address the root causes of the high error rate. During this session, the group members constructed a cause-and-effect diagram to help determine the causes of incorrect bills of lading. Eight categories of causes were identified:

1. Incomplete shipper name or address
2. Incomplete consignee name or address
3. Missing container type
4. Incomplete description of freight
5. Weight not shown on bill of lading
6. Improper destination code
7. Incomplete driver's signature information
8. Inaccurate piece count

Assignment

Using Deming's plan-do-study-act process, the group designed a plan to examine all bills of lading over a 25-day period and count the number of errors in each of these categories. Table 16.10 shows the data. Analyze the data to determine whether the system is in control by constructing the appropriate control chart. Develop a Pareto diagram to gain additional insight into the problem, and suggest recommendations to reduce billing errors.

◼ NOTES

1. Lloyd S. Nelson, "Control Chart for Medians," *Journal of Quality Technology* 14, no. 4 (October 1982), 226–227.
2. H. F. Dodge and M. N. Torrey, "A Check Inspection and Demerit Weighting Plan," *Industrial Quality Control* 13, no. 1 (July 1956), 5–12.
3. A. H. Jaehn, "Improving QC Efficiency with Zone Control Charts," *ASQC Chemical and Process Industries Division News* 4, 1–2; "Zone Control Charts: SPC Made Easy," *Quality* (October 1987), 51–53; and A. H. Jaehn, "The Zone Control Chart," *Quality Progress* 22, no. 7 (July 1991), 65–68.
4. Robert B. Davis, Anthony Homer, and William H. Woodall, "Performance of the Zone Control Chart,"

Communications in Statistics: Theory and Methods 19, no. 5 (1990), 1581–1587.
5. Robert W. Traver, "Pre-Control: A Good Alternative to $\overline{X}$-R Charts," *Quality Progress*, September 1985.
6. We are grateful to Mr. Rick Casey for supplying this application.
7. The scenario was inspired by Cort Dondero, "SPC Hits the Road," *Quality Progress* 22, no. 1 (January 1991), 43–44. The case background and most of the data are fictitious.

◼ BIBLIOGRAPHY

American National Standard, Definitions, Symbols, Formulas, and Tables for Control Charts. ANSI/ASQC A1-1987. American Society for Quality Control, 310 W. Wisconsin Ave., Milwaukee, WI 53203.

Grant, Eugene, L., and Richard S. Leavenworth. *Statistical Quality Control,* 6th ed. New York: McGraw-Hill, 1988.

Montgomery, Douglas C. *Introduction to Statistical Quality Control.* New York: John Wiley, 1985.

Nelson, Lloyd S. "Control Charts for Individual Measurements." *Journal of Quality Technology* 14, no. 3 (July 1982), 172–173.

Wadsworth, Harrison M.; Kenneth S. Stephens; and A. Blanton Godfrey. *Modern Methods for Quality Control and Improvement.* New York: John Wiley, 1986.

Reliability

Reliability—the ability of a product to perform as expected over time—is one of the principal dimensions of quality discussed in Chapter 1. Reliability is an essential aspect of both product and process design. Sophisticated equipment used today in such areas as transportation, communications, and medicine require high reliability. For example, high reliability is absolutely necessary for safety in space and air travel and for medical products such as pacemakers and artificial organs. High reliability can also provide a competitive advantage for many consumer goods. Japanese automobiles gained large market shares in the 1970s primarily due to high reliability. As the overall quality of products continues to improve, consumers expect higher reliability with each purchase; they simply are not satisfied with products that fail unexpectedly. However, the increased complexity of modern products makes high reliability more difficult to achieve. Likewise in manufacturing, the increased use of automation, complexity of machines, low profit margins, and time-based competitiveness make reliability in production processes a critical issue for survival of the business.

The subject of reliability became a serious concern during World War II. Sixty percent of the aircraft destined for the Far East proved unserviceable; 50 percent of electronic devices failed while still in storage; the service life of electronic devices used in bombers was only 20 hours; and 70 percent of naval electronics devices failed.[1] The Department of Defense established an ad hoc group in 1950 to study reliability of electronic equipment and components for the armed forces. The official report, released in 1952, led to the development of the Advisory Group on Reliability of Electronic Equipment (AGREE) to further study issues involving reliability, testing, military contracts, packaging, and storage. Military specifications—coded MIL-R for military-reliability—became a mandatory part of military contracts to ensure procurement of equipment and components that met reliability requirements. Because of this military research, which spread rapidly throughout various industries, reliability engineering became a distinct area of expertise.

The American Society for Quality Control (ASQC) provides a certification program for reliability engineering. ASQC defines a certified reliability engineer as

> a professional who can understand and apply the principles of performance evaluation and prediction to improve product/systems safety, reliability and maintainability. This body of knowledge and applied technologies include but are not limited to design review and control; prediction, estimation and apportionment methodology; failure mode; the planning, operation and analysis of reliability testing and field failures, including mathematical modeling; understanding of human factors in reliability; the knowledge and ability to develop and administer reliability information systems for failure analysis, design and performance improvement, and reliability program management over the entire product life cycle.

This chapter formally defines reliability, presents various techniques for measuring and computing reliability, and discusses methods of reliability engineering and management.

BASIC CONCEPTS AND DEFINITIONS

Like quality, reliability is often defined in a similar "transcendent" manner as a sense of trust in a product's ability to perform satisfactorily or resist failure. However, reliability is an issue that requires a more objective, quantitative treatment. Formally, reliability is defined as *the probability that a product, piece of equipment, or system performs its intended function for a stated period of time under specified operating conditions.* This definition has four important elements: probability, time, performance, and operating conditions.

First, reliability is defined as a *probability,* that is, a value between 0 and 1. Thus, it is a numerical measure with a precise meaning. Expressing reliability in this way provides a valid basis for comparison of different designs for products and systems. For example, a reliability of 0.97 indicates that, on average, 97 of 100 items will perform their function for a given period of time and under certain operating conditions. Often reliability is expressed as a percentage simply for descriptive purposes.

The second element of the definition is *time.* Clearly a device having a reliability of 0.97 for 1,000 hours of operation is inferior to one having the same reliability for 5,000 hours of operation, assuming that the mission of the device is long life.

Performance is the third element and refers to the objective for which the product or system was made. The term *failure* is used when expectations of performance of the intended function are not met. Two types of failures can occur: *functional failure* at the start of product life due to manufacturing or material defects such as a missing connection or a faulty component, and **reliability failure** after some period of use. Examples of reliability failures include the following: a device does not work at all (car will not start); the operation of a device is unstable (car idles rough); or the performance of a device deteriorates (shifting becomes difficult). Since the nature of failure in each of these cases is different, the failure must be clearly defined.

The final component of the reliability definition is *operating conditions,* which involves the type and amount of usage and the environment in which the product is used. For example, Texas Instruments once manufactured electronic digital and analog watches (they have since eliminated these products as part of their strategic business plan). The typical operating conditions and environments for a watch are summarized in Table 17.1. Notice that reliability must include extreme environments and conditions as well as the typical on-the-arm use.

By defining a product's intended environment, performance characteristics, and lifetime, a manufacturer can design and conduct tests to measure the probability of product survival (or failure). The analysis of such tests enable better prediction of reliability and improved product and process designs.

Reliability engineers distinguish between **inherent reliability,** which is the predicted reliability determined by the design of the product or process, and the **achieved reliability,** which is the actual reliability observed during use. Actual reliability can be less than the inherent reliability due to the effects of the manufacturing process and the conditions of use.

The field of reliability has evolved through three distinct phases, much like the evolution of quality assurance. Initial efforts were directed at the measure-

---

TABLE 17.1 Some Typical Watch Environments

Environment	Condition	Quantifiable Characteristics	Exposure Time
Typical use	On-the-arm	31°C (88°F)	16 hours/day
Transportation	In packing box	Vibration and shock ($-20°C$ to $+80°C$)	Specifications for truck/rail/air shipping
Handling accident	Drop to hard floor	1200 g, 2 milliseconds	1 drop/year
Extreme temperature	Hot, closed automobile	85°C (185°F)	4–6 hours 5 times/year
Humidity and chemicals	Perspiration, salt, soaps	35°C (95°F) with 90% pH, rain	500 hours/year
Altitude	Pike's Peak	15,000 feet, $-40°C$	1 time

SOURCE: Adapted from William R. Taylor, "Quality Assured in New Products Via Comprehensive Systems Approach," *Industrial Engineering* 13, no. 3 (March 1981), 28–32.

ment and prediction of reliability through statistical studies. The major focus was on the determination of failure rates of individual components such as transistors and resistors. Knowledge of component failure rates helps to predict the reliability of complex systems of these components. As knowledge about reliability grew, new methods of analysis were developed to increase the reliability built into products and processes. A new discipline called **reliability engineering** was established. Like total quality management, reliability must become an integrated part of all organizational functions: marketing, design, purchasing, manufacturing, and field service. The total process of establishing, achieving, and maintaining reliability objectives is called **reliability management.**

RELIABILITY MEASUREMENT

In practice, reliability is determined by the number of failures per unit time during the duration under consideration (called the **failure rate**). The reciprocal of the failure rate is used as an alternative measure. Some products must be scrapped and replaced upon failure; others can be repaired. For items that must be replaced when a failure occurs, the reciprocal of the failure rate (having dimensions of time units per failure) is called the **mean time to failure (MTTF).** For repairable items, the **mean time between failures (MTBF)** is used.

■ Failure Rate and Product Life Characteristics Curve

In considering the failure rate of a product, suppose that a large group of items is tested or used until all fail, and that the time of failure is recorded for each item. Plotting the cumulative percent of failures against time results in a curve such as the one shown in Figure 17.1. The slope of the curve at any point (that is, the slope of the straight line tangent to the curve) gives the instantaneous

FIGURE 17.1   Cumulative Failure Curve over Time

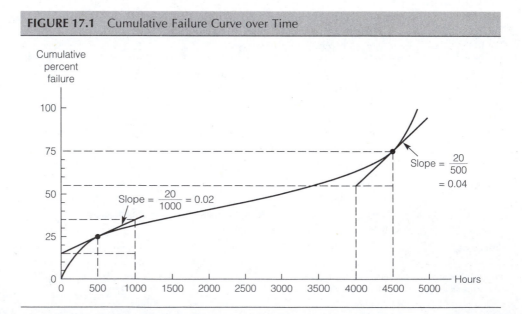

failure rate (failures per unit time) at any point in time. Figure 17.2 shows the failure rate curve, generally called a **product life characteristics curve,** corresponding to the cumulative failure curve in Figure 17.1. This curve was obtained by plotting the slope of the curve at every point. Notice that the slope of the curve and thus the failure rate may change over time. Thus, in Figure 17.2, the failure rate at 500 hours is 0.2 failures per hour while the failure rate at 4500 hours is 0.4 failures per hour. The **average failure rate** over any interval of time is the slope of the line between the two endpoints of the interval on the curve. As shown in Figure 17.3, the average failure rate over the entire 5000 hour time period is 0.02 failures per hour. Many research institutes and large manufacturers conduct extensive statistical studies to identify distinct patterns of failure over time.

Gathering enough data about failures to generate as smooth a curve as shown in Figure 17.3 is not always possible. If limited data are available, the failure rate is computed using the following formula:

$$\text{failure rate} = \lambda = \frac{\text{number of failures}}{\text{total unit operating hours}}$$

or alternatively,

$$\lambda = \frac{\text{number of failures}}{(\text{units tested}) \times (\text{number of hours tested})}$$

A fundamental assumption in this definition allows for different interpretations. Since the total unit operating hours equal the number of units tested times the number of hours tested, no difference occurs in total unit operating hours between testing 10 units for 100 hours or one unit for 1000 hours. However, the difference in Figure 17.2 is clear since the failure rate varies over time. For example, if useful life began at 10 hours and the wearout period began at 200 hours, a failure would almost certainly occur before 1000 hours, whereas a failure would not likely occur in 100-hour tests. During a product's useful life, however, the failure rate is assumed to be constant, and different test lengths during this period of time should show little difference. This assumption is the reason that time is an important element of the definition of reliability.

FIGURE 17.2   Failure Rate Curve

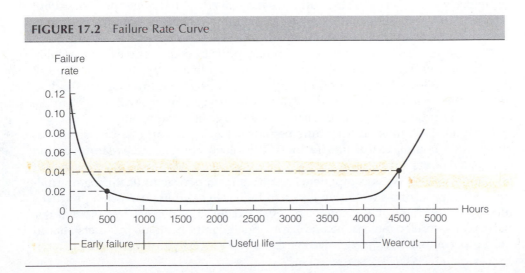

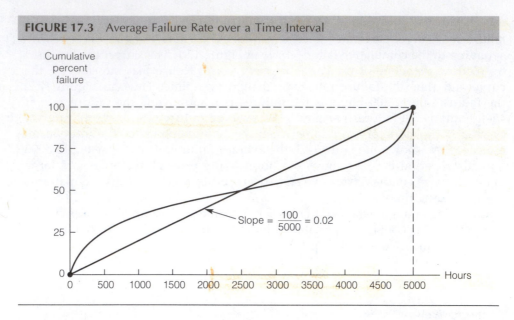

FIGURE 17.3 Average Failure Rate over a Time Interval

To illustrate the computation of λ, suppose that 10 units are tested over a 100-hour period. Four units failed with one unit each failing after 6, 35, 65, and 70 hours; the remaining six units performed satisfactorily until the end of the test. The total unit operating hours are

$$
\begin{aligned}
1 \times 6 &= 6 \\
1 \times 35 &= 35 \\
1 \times 65 &= 65 \\
1 \times 70 &= 70 \\
6 \times 100 &= \underline{600} \\
& 776
\end{aligned}
$$

Therefore, λ = (4 failures)/(776 unit operating hours) = 0.00515 failures per hour. In other words, in a one-hour period, about 0.5 percent of the units would be expected to fail. On the other hand, over a 100-hour period, about $(0.00515)(100)$ = 0.515 or 51.5 percent of the units would be expected to fail. In the actual test, only 40 percent failed.

An electronic component such as a semiconductor commonly exhibits a high, but decreasing, failure rate early in its life (as evidenced by the steep slope of the curve), followed by a period of a relatively constant failure rate, and ending with an increasing failure rate. The failure rate curve in Figure 17.2 is an example of a typical product life characteristics curve for such components.

In Figure 17.2, three distinct time periods are evident: early failure (from 0 to about 1000 hours), useful life (from 1000 to 4000 hours), and wearout period (after 4000 hours). The first is the early failure period, sometimes called the **infant mortality period.** Weak components resulting from poor manufacturing or quality control procedures will often lead to a high rate of failure early in a product's life. This high rate usually cannot be detected through normal test procedures, particularly in electronic semiconductors. Such components or products should not be permitted to enter the marketplace. The second phase of the life characteristics curve describes the normal pattern of random failures during a product's useful life. This period usually has a low, relatively constant failure rate caused by uncontrollable factors, such as sudden and unexpected stresses due to complex interactions in materials or the environment. These factors are usually impossible to predict on an individual basis. However, the collective behavior of such failures can be modeled statistically, as shown later in the chapter. Finally, as age takes over, the wearout period begins, and the failure rate increases, a common experience with automobile components or other consumer products.

Knowing the product life characteristics curve for a particular product helps engineers predict behavior and make decisions accordingly. For instance, if a manufacturer knows that the early failure period for a microprocessor is 600 hours, it can test the chip for 600 hours (or more) under actual or simulated operating conditions before releasing the chip to the market.

Knowledge of a product's reliability is also useful in developing warranties. As an illustration, consider a tire manufacturer who must determine a mileage warranty policy for a new line of tires. From engineering test data, the reliability curve shown in Figure 17.4 was constructed. This graph shows the probability of tread separation within a certain number of miles. Half the tires will fail by 36,500 miles, 87 percent will wear out by 42,000 miles, and only 14 percent will wear out by 31,000 miles. Thus, if a 31,000-mile warranty is established, management can compute the expected cost of replacing 14 percent of the tires. On the other hand, these data may indicate a poor design in relation to similar products of competitors. Design changes might be necessary to improve reliability. Note that in this example time is not measured chronologically, but in terms of product usage.

FIGURE 17.4   Cumulative Probability Distribution for Tire Mileage

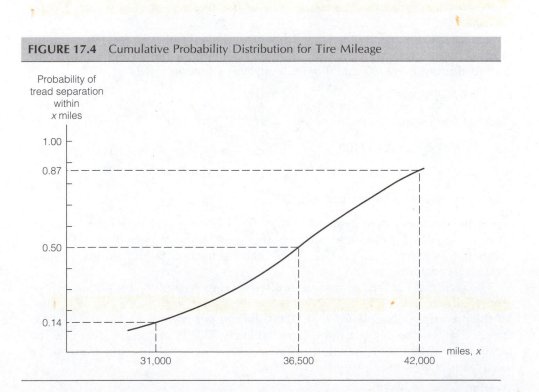

▪ Reliability Function

Reliability was defined earlier as the probability that an item will *not* fail over a given period of time. However, the probability distribution of failures is usually a more convenient figure to use in reliability computations. Recall that during the useful life of a product the failure rate is assumed to be constant. Thus, the fraction of good items that fails during any time period is constant. One can assume then that the probability of failure over time can be modeled mathematically by an exponential probability distribution. Not only is this model mathematically justified, but it has been empirically validated for many observable phenomena, such as failures of light bulbs, electronic components, and repairable systems such as automobiles, computers, and industrial machinery.

If λ is the failure rate, the probability density function representing failures is given by the exponential density

$$f(t) = \lambda e^{-\lambda t} \qquad t \geq 0$$

The probability of failing during a time interval (t_1, t_2) can be shown to be

$$e^{-\lambda(t_2 - t_1)}$$

Specifically, the probability of failure in the interval $(0, T)$ is given by the cumulative distribution function

$$F(T) = 1 - e^{-\lambda T}$$

Since reliability is the probability of *survival*, the **reliability function** is calculated as

$$R(T) = 1 - F(T) = e^{-\lambda T}$$

This function represents the probability that the item will not fail within T units of time.

Consider, for example, an item having a reliability of 0.97 for 100 hours of normal use. Determine the failure rate λ by solving the equation $R = e^{-\lambda T}$ for λ. Substituting $R = 0.97$ and $T = 100$ into this equation yields

$$0.97 = e^{-\lambda(100)}$$

$$\ln 0.97 = -100\lambda$$

$$\lambda = -(\ln 0.97)/100$$

$$= 0.0304/100$$

$$\approx 0.0003 \text{ failure per hour}$$

Thus, the reliability function is $R(T) = e^{-.0003T}$. The cumulative fraction of items that are expected to fail and survive after each 10-hour period may then be tabulated as given in Table 17.2. Note that the fraction failing in any 10-hour period is constant.

The reciprocal of the failure rate is often used in reliability computations. For nonrepairable items, $\theta = 1/\lambda$ is defined as the *mean time to failure (MTTF)*. Thus, in the preceding example for $\lambda = 0.0003$ failure per hour, $\theta = 1/.0003 = 3333$ hours. That is, one failure can be expected every 3333 hours on the average. The probability distribution function of failures and the reliability function can be equivalently expressed using the MTTF as

$$F(T) = 1 - e^{-T/\theta}$$

TABLE 17.2 Cumulative Fraction Failing and Surviving

Time, T	Failures, $F(T)$	Survivors, $R(T)$
10	0.003	0.997
20	0.006	0.994
30	0.009	0.991
40	0.012	0.988
50	0.015	0.985
60	0.018	0.982
70	0.021	0.979
80	0.024	0.976
90	0.027	0.973
100	0.030	0.970

and

$$R(T) = e^{-T/\theta}$$

Suppose, for example, that an electronic component has a failure rate of $\lambda = 0.0001$ failure per hour. The MTTF is $\theta = 1/0.0001 = 10{,}000$ hours. The probability that the component will not fail in 15,000 hours is

$$R(15{,}000) = e^{-15000/10000}$$

$$= e^{-1.5}$$

$$= 0.223$$

For repairable items, θ is usually called the *mean time between failures (MTBF).* For example, suppose that a machine is operated for 10,000 hours and experiences four failures that are immediately repaired. The mean time between failures is

$$\text{MTBF} = 10{,}000/4 = 2500 \text{ hours}$$

and the failure rate is

$$\lambda = 1/2500 = 0.0004 \text{ failure per hour}$$

MTBF is a useful statistic in many management decisions. Consider a company such as Xerox, which leases copying equipment and maintains a service staff throughout the United States. The MTBF can be used to predict the volume of service calls expected, determine labor requirements for service and geographical assignments, and plan the purchase or manufacture of spare parts. In fact, Xerox actually has used an analytical model to determine service staff size. One of the parameters in the model is the average rate at which machines need service.[2]

The failure distribution can also be used to establish preventive maintenance policies for repairable systems.

EXAMPLE 1 Determining a Preventive Maintenance Policy. A part of a bathroom tissue production system is a saw/wrapper machine, which cuts long rolls into smaller pieces and wraps them into packages before they are placed into cartons. Historical data on the time between failures are presented in Table 17.3. From this information, calculate MTBF by adding together the expected values—

TABLE 17.3 Historical Data on Time between Failures

Hours between Failures	Probability
25–30	0.2
30–35	0.4
35–40	0.3
40–45	0.1
	Total 1.0

that is, the midpoint of each time interval—multiplied by their associated probability:

$$\text{MTBF} = 27.5(0.2) + 32.5(0.4) + 37.5(0.3) + 42.5(0.1)$$

$$= 34 \text{ hours}$$

At present, the machine is repaired only when it fails, at an average cost of $50. The company is considering a preventive maintenance program that will cost $30 for each inspection and adjustment.

To determine whether this program is economically justified, compute and compare average annual costs. Consider, for instance, the current policy. Assuming 260 working days per year and one shift per day, the machine has 2080 hours of available time. If the mean time between failures is 34 hours, 2080/34 = 61.2 breakdowns per year can be expected. Hence, the annual cost will be 61.2 × $50 = $3060. Now suppose that the machine is inspected every 25 hours and adjusted. If the time until the next failure after adjustment follows the distribution in Table 17.3, the probability of a failure under this policy is zero. However, inspection every 25 hours will occur 2080/25 = 83.2 times per year, resulting in a cost of 83.2 × $30 = $2496. Next, suppose the machine receives inspection every 30 hours. From Table 17.3, the probability of a failure occurring before the next inspection is 0.20. Thus, the total expected annual cost will be the cost of inspection, $30 × 2080/30 = $2080, plus the expected cost of emergency repair, $50 × 2080/30 × 0.20 = $693. The total cost is therefore $2773. Table 17.4 summarizes similar calculations for other maintenance intervals and reveals that a maintenance interval of 25 hours results in a minimal cost policy.

TABLE 17.4 Cost Computation for Preventive Maintenance

Time between Inspection	Number of Inspections Per Year	Probabilty of Failure before Next Inspection	Inspection Cost	Failure Cost	Total Cost
25	83.2	0.0	$2,496	$ 0	$2,496
30	69.3	0.2	$2,080	$ 693	$2,773
35	59.4	0.6	$1,782	$1,782	$3,564
40	52	0.9	$1,560	$2,340	$3,900

Other probability distributions are often used for modeling reliability. One of the most common is the Weibull distribution, whose probability density function is

$$f(t) = \alpha\beta t^{\beta-1} e^{-\alpha t^{\beta}} \qquad t > 0$$

The constants α and β are called the **scale** and **shape** parameters, respectively. By varying these constants, the Weibull distribution assumes a variety of shapes as illustrated in Figure 17.5. Thus, it is a flexible modeling tool for fitting empirical failure data to a theoretical distribution. The Weibull distribution is often used in modeling failure data for memory components and structural elements in automobiles and airplanes. The reliability function based on the Weibull distribution is

$$R(T) = e^{-\alpha T^{\beta}}$$

To illustrate the use of the Weibull distribution, suppose that a particular electric component has a Weibull failure distribution with $\alpha = 0.02$ and $\beta = 0.5$. (Determining α and β is an exercise in curve fitting.) Then

$$R(T) = e^{-0.02\sqrt{T}}$$

The fraction of components expected to survive 400 hours is thus

$$R(400) = e^{-0.02\sqrt{400}} = e^{-0.4} = 0.67$$

The following table presents some values of $R(T)$ for selected values of T:

T	R(T)
100	0.82
200	0.75
300	0.71
400	0.67
500	0.64
1000	0.53
5000	0.24
10000	0.14

For example, only 24 percent of the components will be expected to survive 5000 hours or more.

FIGURE 17.5   Weibull Distribution for $\alpha = 1$ and $\beta = 0.5, 1, 2,$ and 4

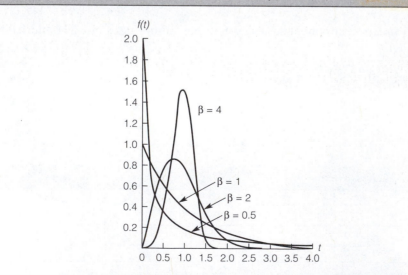

RELIABILITY PREDICTION

Random failures during useful life are uncontrollable, but they can be described by probability distributions. Many systems are composed of individual components with known reliabilities. The reliability data of individual components can be used to predict the reliability of the system. Systems of components may be configured in *series*, in *parallel*, or in some mixed combination. This section presents formulas and techniques for determining system reliability for each of these situations.

Series Systems

A **series system** is illustrated in Figure 17.6. In such a system, all components must function or the system will fail. If the reliability of component i is R_i the reliability of the system is the product of the individual reliabilities, that is

$$R_S = R_1 R_2 \ldots R_n$$

This equation is based on the multiplicative law of probability. For example, suppose that a personal computer system is composed of the processing unit, modem, and printer with reliabilities of 0.997, 0.980, and 0.975, respectively. The reliability of the system is therefore given by

$$R_S = (0.997)(0.980)(0.975) = 0.953$$

Note that since reliabilities are less than one, system reliability decreases as additional components are added in series. Thus, the more complex a series system is, the greater the chance of failure.

If the reliability function is exponential, i.e., $R_i = e^{-\lambda_i T}$, then

$$R_S = e^{-\lambda_1 T} e^{-\lambda_2 T} \cdots e^{-\lambda_n T}$$

$$= e^{-\lambda_1 T - \lambda_2 T \cdots - \lambda_n T}$$

$$= e^{-\left(\sum_{i=1}^{n} \lambda_i\right) T}$$

Suppose that a two-component series system has failure rates of 0.004 and 0.001 per hour. Then

$$R_S(T) = e^{-(0.004 + 0.001)T}$$

$$= e^{-0.005T}$$

FIGURE 17.6 Series System

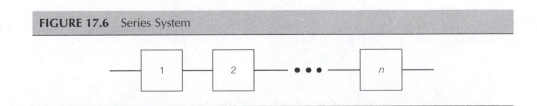

The probability of survival for 100 hours would be

$$R_S(100) = e^{-0.005(100)}$$

$$= e^{-0.5}$$

$$= 0.6065$$

◼ Parallel Systems

A **parallel system** is illustrated in Figure 17.7. In such a system, failure of an individual component is less critical than in series systems; the system will successfully operate as long as one component functions. Hence, the additional components are *redundant*. Redundancy is often built into systems to improve their reliability. However, as mentioned earlier, tradeoffs in cost, size, weight, and so on must be taken into account.

The reliability of the parallel system in Figure 17.7 is derived as follows. If $R_1, R_2, \ldots, R_n$ are the reliabilities of the individual components, the probabilities of failure are $1 - R_1, 1 - R_2, \ldots, 1 - R_n$, respectively. Since the system fails only if each component fails, the probability of system failure is

$$(1 - R_1)(1 - R_2) \ldots (1 - R_n)$$

Hence, the system reliability is computed as

$$R_S = 1 - (1 - R_1)(1 - R_2) \ldots (1 - R_n)$$

If all components have identical reliabilities R, then

$$R_S = 1 - (1 - R)^n$$

The computers on the space shuttle were designed with built-in redundancy in case of failure. Five computers were designed in parallel. Thus, for example, if the reliability of each is 0.99, the system reliability is

$$R_S = 1 - (1 - 0.99)^5 = 0.9999999999$$

FIGURE 17.7 Parallel System

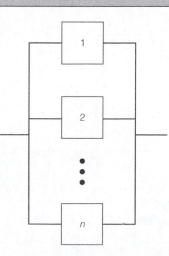

■ Series–Parallel Systems

Most systems are composed of combinations of series and parallel systems. Consider the system shown in Figure 17.8(a). To determine the reliability of such a system, first compute the reliability of the parallel subsystem B:

$$R_B = 1 - (1 - 0.9)^3 = 0.999$$

This level of reliability is equivalent to replacing the three parallel components B with a single component B having a reliability of 0.999 in series with A, C, and D [Figure 17.8(b)]. Next, compute the reliability of the equivalent series system:

$$R_S = (0.99)(0.999)(0.96)(0.98) = 0.93$$

A second type of series–parallel arrangement is shown in Figure 17.9(a). System reliability is determined by first computing the reliability of the series systems ABC and DE:

$$R_{ABC} = (0.95)(0.98)(0.99) = 0.92169$$

$$R_{DE} = (0.99)(0.97) = 0.9603$$

The result is an equivalent parallel system shown in Figure 17.9(b). The system reliability is then computed as

$$R_S = 1 - (1 - 0.92169)(1 - 0.9603) = 0.9969$$

By appropriately decomposing complex systems into series and/or parallel components as shown in these examples, the system reliability can be easily computed. Reliability requirements are determined during the product design phase. The designer may use these techniques to determine the effects of adding redundancy, substituting different components, or reconfiguring the design.

FIGURE 17.8   Series–Parallel System and Equivalent Series System

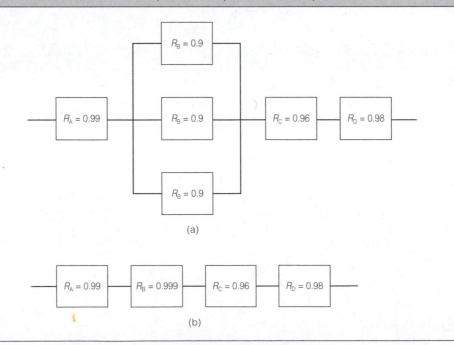

FIGURE 17.9   Series–Parallel System and Equivalent Series System

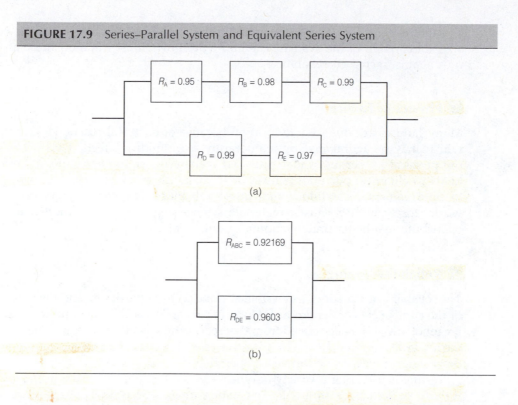

(a)

(b)

RELIABILITY ENGINEERING

Reliability engineering is a relatively new discipline concerned with the design, manufacture, and assurance of products having high reliability. Many techniques of reliability engineering have been developed. This section provides a review of some of the common methods of reliability engineering.

■ Standardization

One method of ensuring high reliability is to use components with proven track records of reliability over years of actual use. If failure rates of components can be established, then standard components can be selected and used in the design process. The use of standardized components not only achieves higher reliability, but also reduces costs since standardized components are used in many different products.

■ Redundancy

Redundancy is providing backup components that can be used when the failure of any one component in a system can cause a failure of the entire system. The previous section provided examples of how redundant components can increase reliability dramatically. Redundant components are designed either in a standby configuration or a parallel configuration. In a *standby system*, the standby unit is switched in when the operating unit fails; in the *parallel configuration*, both units operate normally but only one is required for proper functioning. Redundancy is crucial to systems in which failures can be extremely costly, such as aircraft or satellite communications systems. Redundancy, however, increases the cost, size, and weight of the system. Therefore, designers must trade off these attributes against increased reliability.

Physics of Failure

Many failures are due to deterioration because of chemical reactions over time, which may be aggravated by temperature or humidity effects. Understanding the physical properties of materials and their response to environmental effects helps to eliminate potential failures or to make the product robust with respect to environmental conditions that affect reliability. Reliability engineers must work closely with chemists, materials science engineers, and others who can contribute to a better understanding of failure mechanisms.

Reliability Testing

The reliability of a product is determined principally by the design and the reliability of the components of the product. However, reliability is such a complex issue that it cannot always be determined from theoretical analysis of the design alone. Hence, formal testing is necessary, which involves simulating environmental conditions to determine a product's performance, operating time, and mode of failure.

Testing is useful for a variety of other reasons. Test data are often necessary for liability protection, as means for evaluating designs or vendor reliability, and in process planning and selection. Often, reliability test data are required in military contracts. Testing is necessary to evaluate warranties and to avoid high costs related to early field failure. Good testing leads to good reliability and hence good quality.

Product testing is performed by various methods. The purpose of *life testing*, that is, running devices until they fail, is to measure the distribution of failures to better understand and eliminate their causes. However, such testing can be expensive and time-consuming. For devices that have long natural lives, life testing is not practical. *Accelerated life testing* involves overstressing components to reduce the time to failure and find weaknesses. This form of testing might involve running a motor faster than typically found in normal operating conditions. However, failure rates must correlate well to actual operating conditions if accelerated life testing is to be useful.

Other testing studies the robustness of products. For example, Tandy Corporation performs a variety of tests on its computers.[3] Products are disassembled and destructive testing is performed on the electromechanical, mechanical, and physical properties of components. *Environmental testing* consists of varying the temperature from −40 degrees (the temperature inside trucks in the northern United States and Canada) to 165 degrees (the temperature inside trucks in the southwest United States) to shock the product to see if it can withstand extremes. Since old wiring exhibits a wide range of variation, AC power is varied from 105 to 135 volts. *Vibration and shock testing* are used to simulate trucks driving from the East to the West Coast to determine the product's ability to withstand rough handling and accidents.

Burn-in

Semiconductors are the basic building blocks of numerous modern products such as videocasette recorders, automotive ignition systems, computers, and military weapons systems. Semiconductors have a small proportion of defects, called *latent defects*, that can cause them to fail during the first 1000 hours of normal operation. After that, the failure rate stabilizes, perhaps for as long as 25 years, before beginning to rise again as components wear out. These infant mortalities can be as high as 10 percent in a new technology or as low as 0.01 percent in proven technologies. The sooner a faulty component is detected, the cheaper is its replacement or repair. A correction on an integrated circuit fabrication line costs about 50 cents; at the board level it might cost $5; at the system level about $50; and in the field, $500. If a printed circuit board contains 100 semiconductors, a failure rate of 0.01 percent would cause a board failure rate of 1 percent.

Burn-in, or component stress testing, involves exposing integrated circuits to elevated temperatures in order to force latent defects to occur. For example, a device that might normally fail after 300 hours at 25°C might fail in less than 20 hours at 150°C. Survivors are likely to have long, trouble-free operating lives.

Studies and experience have demonstrated the economic advantages of burn-in. For example, a recent large-scale study of the effect of burn-in on enhancing reliability of dynamic MOS memories was conducted in Europe. The failure rate without burn-in conditioning and testing to eliminate infant mortality was 0.24 percent per thousand hours, while burn-in and testing reduced the rate to 0.02 percent per thousand hours. When considering the cost of field service and warranty work, for instance, reduction of semiconductor failure rates in a large system by an order of magnitude translates roughly into an average of one repair call per year versus one repair call per month.

Since burn-in requires considerable time—48 to 96 hours is common—designers attempt to produce equipment that can perform some functional tests during the burn-in cycle rather than after. Modern systems exist to test and burn-in integrated circuits. One system has the capacity of 18,000 64K DRAMs (dynamic random access memory) per load and is flexible in its burn-in and test procedures to accommodate future types without modification of the hardware. The system can accumulate and display information on the devices under test, both for real-time evaluation and for lot documentation.

■ Failure Mode and Effects Analysis

The purpose of failure mode and effects analysis (FMEA) is to identify all the ways in which a failure can occur, to estimate the effect and seriousness of the failure, and to recommend corrective design actions. An FMEA usually consists of specifying the following information for each critical component:

- Failure mode (i.e., how the component can fail)
- Cause of failure
- Effect on the product or system within which it operates (safety, downtime, repair requirements, tools required)
- Corrective action (design changes, better user instructions)
- Comments

Figure 17.10 gives an (incomplete) example of a typical FMEA for an ordinary household light socket.

FIGURE 17.10   FMEA on Common Household Lamp

Failure Mode and Effects Analysis
Analyst *J.A. White*

Product *2C Lamp*   Date *10 Jan. 1995*

Component Name	Failure Mode	Cause of Failure	Effect of Failure on System	Correction of Problem	Comments
Plug part no. P-3	Loose wiring	Use vibration, handling	Will not conduct current; may generate heat	Molded plug and wire	Uncorrected, could cause fire
	Not a failure of plug per se	User contacts prongs when plugging or unplugging	May cause severe shock or death	Enlarged safety tip on molded plug	Children
Metal base and stem	Bent or nicked	Dropping, bumping, shipping	Degrades looks	Distress finish, improved packaging.	Cosmetic
Lamp socket	Cracked	Excessive heat, bumping, forcing	May cause shock if contacts metal base and stem; may cause shock upon bulb replacement	Improve material used for socket.	Dangerous
Wiring	Broken, frayed, from lamp to plug	Fatigue, heat, carelessness, childbite	Will not conduct current; may generate heat, blow breakers, or cause shock	Use of wire suitable for long life in extreme environment anticipated	Dangerous; warning on instructions
	Internal short circuit	Heat, brittle insulation	May cause electrical shock or render lamp useless	Use of wire suitable for long life in extreme environment anticipated.	
	Internal wire broken	Socket slipping and twisting wires	May cause electrical shock or render lamp useless	Use of indent or notch to prevent socket from turning	

SOURCE: K. E. Case, and L. L. Jones, *Profit Through Quality: Quality Assurance Programs for Manufacturers,* QC & RE Monograph Series No. 2 (New York: Institute of Industrial Engineers, 1978).

Fault Tree Analysis

Fault tree analysis (FTA) is a logical procedure that begins with a list of potential hazards or undesired states and works backward to develop a list of causes and origins of failure. Its purpose is to show logical relationships between failures and causes. In this fashion, ways to avoid potential dangers can be uncovered.

An example of an FTA is given in Figure 17.11 for an industrial brake that is assumed to operate similar to a regular drum type of automobile brake. The fault tree is composed of branches connected to two different types of nodes: AND nodes, denoted by the symbol

and OR nodes, depicted by

If a set of events are connected below an AND node, then *all* events must occur for the event above the node to occur. Below an OR node, *at least one* of the events must occur. Thus, in Figure 17.11 the event "brake doesn't release" can occur if any of the following conditions hold:

 broken springs
OR fluid pressure not free to release
OR oversize shoe for drum (width)
OR weak springs
 AND
 no grease on shoe lands at facing contact.

FIGURE 17.11   Fault Tree Analysis

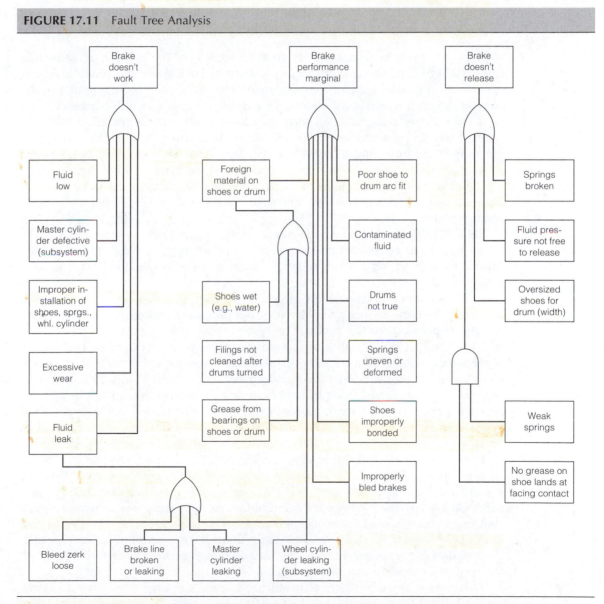

SOURCE: K. E. Case, and L. L. Jones, *Profit Through Quality: Quality Assurance Programs for Manufacturers*, QC & RE Monograph Series No. 2 (New York: Institute of Industrial Engineers, 1978).

RELIABILITY MANAGEMENT

Effective reliability management should include the following steps:

■ Define customer performance requirements.

■ Determine important economic factors and assess their relationship with reliability requirements.

■ Define the environment and conditions in which the product will be used.

■ Select components, designs, and vendors that meet reliability as well as cost criteria.

■ Determine reliability requirements for machines and equipment as well as their impacts on product reliability during manufacturing.

■ Analyze field reliability data as a method for quality improvement.

High reliability results in lower costs to society in the context of Taguchi's loss function. Consumers would like products to be 100 percent reliable, which is certainly a worthy goal for manufacturers. However, the production of a product having perfect reliability under all conditions is impractical. To achieve high reliability, better materials and more precise manufacturing processes must be used. These improvements will increase manufacturing costs to the point that consumers are unwilling to pay the price. Thus, management must balance the economic factors and seek to minimize total cost, keeping in mind that too low a reliability may damage the firm's reputation and result in lost sales or product liability suits. Such decisions must be addressed strategically by upper management.

Reliability is a concern in many areas of the production system and should be an important consideration in design, manufacturing, storage, and transportation, as well as supporting functions such as purchasing, field service, and maintenance.

As a fundamental dimension of quality, reliability must be *designed* into a product. The performance characteristics, operating conditions, and performance duration specified for the product or system drive the technical design. Variations in product performance arise because of the way it is used or because of environmental conditions. Changes take place over time because of chemical changes in components, vibration and stress, or expansion and contraction of materials due to fluctuations in temperature or humidity, for example. Sooner or later, products fail. Creating products that will not fail is nearly impossible. The question is not whether a product will fail, but when. Designers must decide to what extent failure is acceptable and establish specifications for reliability.

Many consumers will not always use a product correctly or follow suggested maintenance procedures. Designers must account for operating errors that will result in failure, and they must maintain safety when failure does occur. Fail-safe designs provide safety in the event of failure. An example is a railway signal that turns red when a failure occurs. Foolproof designs prevent operation in the event of an operating error, thus avoiding failure. An example is a temperature control that prevents overheating by not allowing a heating switch to be closed without prior closure of a fan switch.

Whatever is done in the manufacturing process can and does have an effect on the reliability of the final product sold to customers. To manufacture reliable products from good designs, companies must use good materials, well-maintained machines, and trained workers. The greater the capability of a process to conform to design specifications and targets, the more likely it is that the product will have high reliability. Preventive maintenance in manufacturing is crucial to equipment reliability. Manufacturing, marketing, and financial managers must work together to ensure adequate time, schedules, and budgets for preventive maintenance activities. Operations control strategies such as just-in-time, the use of inspection, and statistical process control all contribute to the achievement of reliability objectives.

Packaging and transportation cannot be neglected. Poor protection and handling can adversely affect the reliability of the product when it reaches the customer. Denton relates a situation in which Tandy Corporation accidentally packed a half-full load of computers in a 40-foot truck.[4] The boxes dropped from 12 feet high and tumbled around inside the truck from South Carolina to Boston. The cartons were demolished and all the computers were believed to be destroyed. However, not one computer was damaged because of the careful attention to and testing of packaging.

As noted elsewhere in this book, purchasing plays an active role in the final quality of a product. Purchasing must understand the reliability requirements of purchased parts and components and clearly communicate these to suppliers. Field service personnel must understand the nature of failures for preventive maintenance and maintain an adequate supply of spare and replacement parts. Feedback on failures completes the never-ending cycle of product improvement, leading to improved market knowledge and better designs.

RELIABILITY IN COMPUTER SOFTWARE

Many consumer goods are becoming more and more dependent on computers (strictly speaking, microprocessors), which in turn depend on the accompanying software. Reliability failures in computer software are unacceptable departures from requirements. The average software product in the United States contains an estimated 8 to 10 errors per thousand lines of code.

Software reliability problems can cause considerable inconvenience or harm. One January 15, 1990, a software flaw in one programming statement controlling some AT&T switching systems caused a nine-hour nationwide saturation in their telephone network because the switches abnormally shut down.[5]

A more serious problem involved a radiation therapy machine problem that resulted in the deaths of several patients.[6] The accidents were caused by software controlling the machine. If the operator entered an unusual but nonetheless possible sequence of commands, the computer control would place the machine into an erroneous and hazardous state, subjecting the patient to a massive overdose. Unfortunately, at that time, the Food and Drug Administration had no requirements regarding software development practices or software quality in medical devices. Only after these incidents occurred did the FDA announce that it would begin reviewing software in medical devices.

Software with high quality and reliability is essential for global competitiveness. While the United States has been the leader in the software and related services market, worldwide competition is growing. According to *Business Week*,

> Quality could be the Achilles' heel of the U.S. software industry—and industry executives know it. "In the U.S., we have a history of shipping the product and getting the details right later," concedes David Reed, chief scientist at Lotus. "The Japanese seem to focus on getting every detail right."[7]

Techniques used in quality control of manufacturing can be applied to software as well. Countries from Japan to India to a $400 million European consortium called the Eureka Software Factory are racing to find ways to design software quickly, while improving quality and reducing costs. Most of these approaches revolve around ways to use pretested blocks of code as building blocks for the final software product.

Estimating and predicting software reliability is not easy. Software failures result from inherent design flaws that only reveal themselves under appropriate operational circumstances. These software "bugs" arise from flaws in design specifications, routine coding errors, testing errors, or a variety of incompatibilities with hardware or other support software.

Computer software bears more similarity to services than to manufactured goods. With software, simply inspecting the end product is not practical. Once the program is completed and stored on magnetic media, any bugs have already been included in the product. Hence, particular care must be taken in the design phase. Unfortunately, many software producers are under great pressure to ship products before they are fully tested, which often results in expensive after-market support, not to mention damage to the company's reputation.

The environment in which software is produced has certain characteristics that negatively affect software quality.[8]

- Programmers of widely varying levels of skill
- Small project staffs (often one person)
- Software-naive customers who are usually interested only in software output
- Poorly defined but often highly complex customer objectives
- High turnover rate for programmers
- Externally or internally generated constraints such as cost and time
- Hardware complexities that occasionally force the applications programmer to operate as a systems programmer, rather than working directly toward the actual goals outlined by the customer
- Poor quality of existing programs that were produced without the benefit of modern support tools

Building quality and reliability into software begins with good planning. A software quality assurance system must be integrated into existing practices and procedures. When software quality assurance is isolated from the software design system, such procedures can be easily ignored or forgotten. All functional groups involved must participate under the guidance of quality assurance personnel. Since quality assurance programs are usually new to software design groups, behavioral and motivational techniques for gaining acceptance are often necessary.

Several techniques have been developed to guide the software development process and to ensure quality and reliability. These techniques include configuration management, reviews and audits, and a variety of testing methods. Each of these activities is based on objective measurement and feedback to the project manager or development team members.

Configuration management has been used extensively for hardware projects in the aerospace and defense industries and has been adapted to software projects. It is an essential requirement in government contracts. Configuration management is a process for designing and maintaining software by tightly controlling the set of software components that make up a complex system. It provides an effective means of incorporating changes during development and use. The process consists of three activities:

1. Establishing approved baseline configurations (designs) for computer programs (configuration definition). These baselines support systematic evaluation, coordination, and disposition of all proposed changes.

2. Maintaining control over all changes in the baseline programs (change control). Many software problems arise due to frequent changes. A rigorous system for monitoring change is an important quality control function.

3. Providing traceability of baselines and changes (configuration accounting). Maintaining a paper trail of configurations and modifications is essential for ensuring that specifications are being met and for determining sources of errors and means of correction.

Through independent reviews, problems or potential problems can be discovered and reported. Software quality assurance groups are responsible for maintaining control over specifications, documentation, and code to assure that performance and design requirements are being met. They also review software designs prior to coding, audit development activities, review and approve testing plans, and monitor actual requirements testing.

A variety of methods for software verification are used. These methods include inspection for requirements that cannot be verified through operational testing such as examination of flow diagrams and program listings; comparing the execution of a program with a standard program with known results; analysis of program outputs to validate complex equations whose results are not directly related to inputs; and conducting tests with known inputs that should generate known outputs.

Achieving reliable software is expensive. One of the most ambitious projects was the software for the space shuttle. NASA paid $1000 for each line of code; a total of $500 million. However, the space shuttle software has been found to contain only 0.1 errors per thousand lines.[9] Correcting software defects is often so expensive that completely rewriting the code is usually cheaper than attempting to modify it. Errors not removed until the maintenance phase of a product's life cycle can cost up to 10 times more to correct than if discovered earlier. Today, more than 50 percent of a data processing department's budget goes to maintenance of software.

In some cases, reliable software is seemingly not even possible. President Reagan's Strategic Defense Initiative had been criticized by many computer scientists because the software required for space-based weapons is supposedly too complex to be developed reliably using current technology. Clearly, further research into better methods for achieving quality and reliability in software is necessary as the twenty-first century approaches.

MAINTAINABILITY AND AVAILABILITY

Failures will eventually occur, resulting in equipment shutdown and downtime. The amount of downtime is affected by the diagnosis effort required to determine the cause of failure, the ease of access to components, repair procedures, and the availability of spare parts. **Maintainability** is the totality of design factors that allows maintenance to be accomplished easily. Maintenance is usually of two types: preventive or corrective. *Preventive maintenance* such as oiling equipment, can reduce the risks of failure—even though it requires a certain amount of downtime—and is usually economically justified. *Corrective maintenance* is the response to failures and is a function of the reliability. Good maintenance adds to reliability, since it increases the probability that the equipment will operate satisfactorily over a period of time. However, a tradeoff between reliability and maintainability is inevitable. Higher reliability will usually result in less frequent maintenance but higher design and production costs. Designing for frequent repair or replacement may be a more economical option.

Several design issues are related to maintainability.

■ *Access of parts for repair:* One of the biggest consumer complaints about today's automobiles over those before the early 1970s is the difficulty of accessing many parts without special tools. While automotive reliability has increased, the complexity of today's engines makes maintenance difficult for a nonprofessional. For good maintainability, components must be easily accessible to maintenance personnel.

■ *Modular construction and standardization:* Electronic equipment, such as televisions, is now designed with easily replaceable modular components. This group-type standardization makes diagnosis much easier, since problems can be isolated at the board level rather than for individual components. Of course, it also increases the cost of replacement parts. Greater design effort also is necessary. Hence, these tradeoffs must be considered on an economic basis. Standardization results in interchangeability of components between products, a reduction in inventory requirements for spare parts, and the increased possibility that parts may not be available when needed.

■ *Diagnostic repair procedures:* During the design process, provisions must be made for diagnosis and repair. Clear instructions need to be written. For complex equipment, diagnosis can be time-consuming. Modern information technology and artificial intelligence techniques, known as *expert systems*, are being developed to assist personnel in diagnosis of equipment.

Availability is the probability that equipment is not down due to failure. The two principal definitions of availability include *operational availability,* which is defined as

$$A_o = \frac{MTBM}{MTBM + MDT}$$

where MTBM = mean time between maintenance, including both corrective and preventive maintenance, and MDT = mean downtime. MDT is the amount of time needed for corrective and preventive maintenance and waiting time. This definition of availability is useful to operations managers in planning equipment utilization but is difficult to employ in design. Instead, designers use *inherent availability*, defined as

$$A_t = \frac{MTBF}{MTBF + MTTR}$$

where MTBF and MTTR represent mean time between failures and mean time to repair, respectively, as previously defined. This equation assumes no preventive maintenance downtime, waiting time, etc., since these variables cannot be determined in a design environment. Inherent availability assumes ideal conditions and can be used to establish tradeoffs between reliability (as measured by MTBF) and maintainability (as measured by MTTR). To illustrate, suppose that availability is specified as 0.99:

$$0.99 = \frac{MTBF}{MTBF + MTTR}$$

or

$$MTBF = 99 \ MTTR$$

Thus, if MTTR = 2 hours, MTBF must be equal to 198 hours. The designer can use such information to evaluate a proposed design and make appropriate modifications. On the other hand, this information can also be used to reduce MTTR through maintainability improvements given a specified reliability.

QUALITY IN PRACTICE   **TESTING AUDIO COMPONENTS AT SHURE BROS., INC.**[10]

The philosophy at Shure Bros., Inc., is reliability oriented. Microphones and phonograph cartridges are tested for reliability well beyond the warranty period, with the goal of providing the customer long-term service and satisfaction. Audio transducers, for example, are sensitive and rather fragile devices. Stylus shanks for some cartridges are formed from 0.0005-inch beryllium foil. A precisely cut and polished diamond weighing only 20 micrograms is attached to the shank. Dynamic microphone coils are wound with fine wire only one-fifth the diameter of a human hair. Although their sensitivity ranks them among the finest of laboratory instruments, they must be able to perform under conditions much less than ideal in locations all over the world.

These types of audio components have four major classes of end-use environments:

1. *The home:* The potential for damage—ranging from accidental dropping of the cartridge onto the turntable or scraping the stylus across the record to cleaning the cartridge with various agents—is significant. Here, the cartridges also experience the extremes of temperature and humidity.

2. *Public address systems:* Microphones are found in environments as diverse as churches, schools, bars, stores, and the outdoors. All these places represent potential challenges to the integrity of the microphone, which can be damaged by handling, mishandling, or long-term abuse. Random drops from a height of several feet are not uncommon.

3. *Mobile applications:* In vehicles, extremes of heat and cold, vibration, shock, and repeated switch actuation and cable flexing must be considered. Sand and dust are likely to be present. Reliability is critical since backup is not usually available in an emergency on the road.

4. *Professional recording and sound reinforcement:* Sound professionals require reliability and cannot tolerate a dead or noisy microphone in the middle of a live performance or recording session. Yet, repeated setups and teardowns during concert tours pose many problems.

Many standardized destructive tests developed by the military, the Electronic Industry Association, and the American Society for Testing and Materials are employed to gain knowledge of product failure. In addition, the following specialized environmental tests are conducted:

■ *Cartridge drop test:* This test simulates the accidental dropping of the tone arm and cartridge onto a moving record. The vertical tracking force is set to the maximum recommended for the unit under test, and the minimum required number of drops is 100. This test simulates and exceeds the normal type of abuse accidentally given to a stylus.

■ *Cartridge scrape test:* This test consists of moving the cartridge mounted in a tone arm across a moving record 100 times. The tone arm is pushed down hard enough to bottom out the cartridge.

■ *Microphone drop test:* This unpackaged test consists of a random free fall onto the floor. The test height is six feet, designed to simulate a fall from a tall shelf or an accidental drop by a tall person at shoulder height. Ten drops must be sustained without significant loss of performance.

■ *Barrel tumble:* A specially constructed barrel is used to tumble small microphones without packaging. This test exceeds the roughest treatment expected in handling or transporting microphones loose in a case.

■ *Stair tumble test.* A shipping carton is packed with a dozen units, sealed with tape, and tumbled down 17 steel stairs onto a concrete floor. Ten tumbles must be sustained without loss of function or severe loss of appearance of the packaging. This test allows for evaluation of possible damage during shipping.

■ *Outside weathering test:* This test actually exposes test units to outside weather. It aids in evaluating finishes and the performance of products that might actually be used outside such as microphones and sound reinforcement equipment.

The preceding are some examples of in-house reliability testing designed to simulate actual operating conditions. They help meet the company's goal of marketing products with a long life of useful service.

Key Issues for Discussion

1. Which tests can be used to study the reliability of the product in each of the four end-use environments?

QUALITY IN PRACTICE — SOFTWARE QUALITY ASSURANCE AT LOS ALAMOS NATIONAL LABORATORY[11]

A quality assurance program was created at Los Alamos National Laboratory to develop software that contained fewer defects and was more maintainable and flexible while also speeding program development. During management planning sessions, objectives were defined that would help produce a quality product, including developing methods for optimizing software maintainability, flexibility, and reliability; facilitating the creation of an environment whereby these goals can be accomplished; and monitoring improvement over time. The software features selected for optimization were the ones causing the most problems and therefore representing the greatest opportunity for payoff.

To assure true quality, the quality assurance program was fully integrated into the development process. The program included a structure for project planning, peer reviews of software products, availability of current sets of standards and guidelines, cost-effective testing procedures, accurate measurements of actual effort, and reliable project estimating tools.

Effective product reviews were the most significant element of the quality assurance process. Peer reviews, commonly called walkthroughs, consisted of the developer's presentation of the product to a small group of peers to discover errors or potential defects. The results and actions taken during a

walkthrough were formally recorded and sent to the developers after the review. Further walkthroughs were scheduled until no defects could be found.

Management decided that the standards to be used had to be current and easily accessible. Before development of the quality assurance program, standards manuals sat unopened and gathering dust, mostly because the methods in the manuals rarely conformed with the way business was normally conducted. The effort involved in writing, editing, and printing such a manual almost guaranteed that a significant portion of the contents would be obsolete before publication. The solution was to enter and update all guidelines and standards using computerized word-processing equipment, with read-only access to all software development personnel.

Traditional software quality assurance programs typically emphasize testing the operation of software in an actual computing environment, which is commonly called machine testing. Machine testing uncovers symptoms of problems, not the causes. Unlike the walkthrough process, no amount of machine testing can provide a cure for poorly designed and written computer programs. Dynamic testing is not 100 percent effective for uncovering all possible symptoms of problems, since all possible paths through a program are never exercised in testing. Thus, many problems occur when the program is actually used.

The plan developed at Los Alamos called for taking machine testing out of the hands of developers by creating a separate testing group and rewarding the members on the basis of the number of programs they could break. Testing teams were made responsible for creating test beds as well as for testing programs using live data. Performance evaluations were geared to finding the best new methodologies for testing.

During preliminary management discussions of the plan, management recognized that when projects are estimated accurately from the beginning, quality assurance can be built into the development schedule, allowing a more maintainable, flexible, and reliable product to be delivered. This ability also addressed the problem of budget and schedule slips, which contributed to quality assurance deterioration. An automated estimating system would generate accurate estimates from historical data.

True quality assurance at Los Alamos is achieved by developing reliable methods to detect and remove defects early in the development process and by measuring the actual quality of finished products. By integrating the program into the development process, the entire staff is responsible for producing a quality product, and the program can be accepted by the software organization as a whole.

Key Issues for Discussion

1. Describe the approach used by Los Alamos National Laboratory to assure the quality and reliability of their software.

2. Does the use of the separate testing group conflict with TQM principles? Why or why not?

SUMMARY OF KEY POINTS

■ Reliability is the probability that a product, piece of equipment, or system performs its intended function for a stated period of time under specified operating conditions.

■ Failures in products include functional failure at the start of product life and reliability failure after some period of use.

■ Inherent reliability is the predicted reliability determined by the design of the product or process, and achieved reliability is the actual reliability observed during use.

■ Reliability is measured by the number of failures per unit time, called the failure rate. The reciprocal of the failure rate is the mean time to failure, or for repairable items, the mean time between failures.

■ The product life characteristics curve shows the instantaneous failure rate at any point in time. These curves are used to determine design and testing policies as well as for developing warranties.

■ The probability of survival as a function of time is called the reliability function, and typically is modeled using an exponential distribution. Reliability functions of individual components can be used to predict reliability for complex systems of series, parallel, or series–parallel configurations.

■ Reliability engineering involves techniques such as standardization, redundancy, failure physics, various testing methods, failure mode and effects analysis, and fault tree analysis.

■ Reliability management should include the consideration of customer performance requirements, economic factors, environmental conditions, cost, and analysis of field data.

■ Reliability in computer software is a difficult, but important issue. Many techniques have been developed to help ensure reliability in software.

REVIEW QUESTIONS

1. What is the importance of reliability and why has it become such a prominent area within the quality disciplines?

2. Define reliability. Explain the definition thoroughly.

3. What is the difference between a functional failure and a reliability failure?

4. What is the definition of failure rate? How is it measured?

5. Explain the differences and relationships between the cumulative failure rate curve and the failure rate curve. How is the average failure rate over a time interval computed?

6. Explain the product life characteristics curve and how it can be used.

7. What is a reliability function? Discuss different ways of expressing this function.

8. Explain how to compute the reliability of series, parallel, and series–parallel systems.

9. What is reliability engineering? Briefly discuss some of the major techniques of reliability engineering.

10. Describe different forms of product testing.

11. What does the term *latent defect* mean?

12. Explain the purpose of failure mode and effects analysis and fault tree analysis.

13. What should be included in an effective reliability management program?

14. Discuss the importance of reliability in computer software. Why is it difficult to achieve?

15. What is configuration management? How is it used in quality assurance for software?

16. What is maintainability? Discuss the principal design issues related to it.

17. Discuss the two definitions of availability. What are the differences between them?

PROBLEMS

1. Given the cumulative failure curve in Figure 17.12, sketch the failure rate curve.

2. Compute the average failure rate during the intervals 0 to 50, 50 to 100, and 0 to 100, based on the information in Figure 17.12.

3. The life of a battery is normally distributed with a mean of 1200 days and standard deviation of 60 days.

    a. What fraction of batteries is expected to survive beyond 1300 days?

    b. What fraction will survive less than 900 days?

    c. Sketch the reliability function.

    e. What length of warranty is needed so that no more than 10 percent of the batteries will be expected to fail during the warranty period?

4. Compute the failure rate for five transformers that were tested for 500 hours each, two of which failed after 40 and 220 hours.

5. A test of 10 items is conducted for 200 hours. Three items fail at 8, 54, and 162 hours. What is the failure rate?

6. Assuming an exponential distribution, a particular light bulb has a failure rate of 0.001 unit per hour. What is the probability of failure within 800 hours? What is the reliability function?

FIGURE 17.12   Cumulative Failure Curve

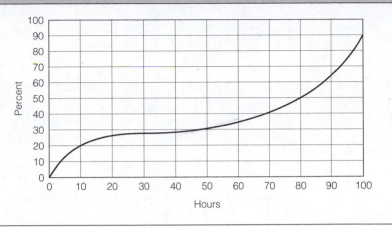

7. An electrical component has a reliability of 0.90 over 500 hours of normal use. What is the failure rate? What fraction will survive after 100, 200, and 500 hours?

8. Find the mean time to failure for the data in Problems 4 and 5.

9. A piece of equipment operated for 4500 hours and experienced two failures. What is the MTTF?

10. The MTBF of a circuit is 1000 hours. Calculate the failure rate.

11. The MTBF for a computer's central processing unit is normally distributed with a mean of 14 days and a standard deviation of 3 days. Each failure costs the company $500 in lost computing time and repair costs. A shutdown for preventive maintenance can be scheduled during nonpeak times and will cost only $100. As the manager in charge of computer operations, you are to determine if a preventive maintenance program is worthwhile. What is your recommendation? Assume 260 operating days per year.

12. Refer to the failure data for the equipment maintenance example in Table 17.3. What preventive maintenance period would you recommend if the preventive maintenance cost were $50 and the average cost for an equipment failure were $30? How many breakdowns a year should you expect under your preventive maintenance program?

13. For a particular piece of equipment, the probability of failure during a given week is as follows:

Week of Operation	Probability of Failure
1	0.20
2	0.10
3	0.10
4	0.15
5	0.20
6	0.25

Management is considering a preventive maintenance program that would be implemented at the end of a given week of production. The production loss and downtime costs associated with an equipment failure are estimated to be $1500 per failure. If it costs $100 to perform the preventive maintenance, when should the firm implement the preventive maintenance program? What is the total maintenance and failure cost associated with your recommendation, and how many failures can be expected each year? Assume 52 weeks of operation per year.

14. An electronic missile guidance system consists of the following components:

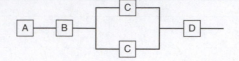

Components A, B, C, and D have reliabilities of 0.95, 0.98, 0.90, and 0.99, respectively. What is the reliability of the entire system?

15. A manufacturer of portable radios purchases major electronic components as modules. The reliabilities of components differ by supplier. Suppose that the configuration of the major components is given by

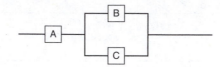

The components can be purchased from three different suppliers. The reliabilities of the components are as follows:

		SUPPLIER	
Component	1	2	3
A	.95	.92	.94
B	.80	.86	.90
C	.90	.93	.85

Transportation and purchasing considerations require that only one supplier be chosen. Which one should be selected if the radio is to have the highest possible reliability?

16. In a complex manufacturing process, three operations are performed in series. Because of the nature of the process, machines frequently fall out of adjustment and must be repaired. To keep the system going, two identical machines are used at each stage; thus, if one fails, the other can be used while the first is repaired (see accompanying figure). The reliabilities of the machines are as follows:

Machine	Reliability
A	.60
B	.75
C	.70

a. Analyze the system reliability, assuming only *one* machine at each stage.

b. How much is the reliability improved by having two machines at each stage?

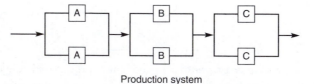

Production system

17. An automated production system consists of three operations: turning, milling, and grinding. Individual parts are transferred from one operation to the next by a robot. Hence, if one machine or the robot fails, the process stops.

a. If the reliabilities of the robot, turning center, milling machine, and grinder are 0.99, 0.98, 0.99, and 0.96, respectively, what is the reliability of the system?

b. Suppose that two grinders are available and the system does not stop if one fails. What is the reliability of the system?

18. Military radar and missile detection systems are designed to warn a country of enemy attacks. A system reliability question deals with the ability of the detection system to identify the attack and perform the warning correctly. Assume that a particular detection system has a 0.90 probability of detecting a missile attack.

a. What is the reliability of the system?

b. Assume that two detection systems are installed in the same area and that the system operates satisfactorily if at least one of the two detection systems performs correctly. Assume that the probability of detecting an attack is 0.90 for each system. What is the reliability of the two systems?

C A S E

Automotive Air Bag Reliability[12]

Automotive air bags are designed to protect passengers from frontal or near-frontal crashes of about 12 to 14 mph. Sensors are placed on a structural member in the front of the vehicle or in the passenger compartment. The sensor sends a signal to inflate the air bag (which takes about 1/30 second). The bag then quickly deflates. Air bags have significantly improved automotive safety. The Insurance Institute for Highway Safety noted that during 1985–1992, air bags helped reduce deaths by 24 percent. By 1994, air bags were deployed approximately 200,000 times.

One important design question is the reliability of air bags. Two manufacturers set a reliability goal of at least 0.9999. An air bag system has three essential elements: a sensor, an actuating mechanism, and an inflating air bag. Three types of sensors—mechanical, electromechanical, and electronic—are in use. The all-mechanical sensor (AMS) is the simplest. The basic mechanism is shown in Figure 17.13. A steel ball in a tube or cylinder detects the deceleration of a crash. As the ball moves forward in the tube, it is resisted by a bar on a pivot. The other end of the bar is loaded by a bias spring. As the bar moves, it rotates two shafts that move off the edge of spring-loaded firing pins. The pins stab dual primers, igniting a charge of boron potassium nitrate, which in turn ignites a compound of sodium azide, which then releases nitrogen gas. The gas is filtered and cooled, inflating the bag. The cover (e.g., on the steering wheel) splits open to allow the bag to inflate without damage. Figure 17.14 shows a block diagram of the system with reliability values

of the individual components over a 10-year operating life.

Electromechanical sensor systems (EMS) also use a ball-in-tube or ball/cylinder mechanism. The ball is held in place by a magnet instead of a spring. When deceleration occurs, the ball overcomes the magnetic retention forces and travels forward until it touches two electrical contacts, closing a switch that sends current from the battery (or a large capacitor if the battery fails) to heat a bridgewire in a pyrotechnic squib, which then ignites a mixture contained in the squib cavity. The heat ignites a charge of sodium azide, producing nitrogen gas to inflate the bag. This system also has an arming sensor that

FIGURE 17.13 AMS Air Bag Sensor

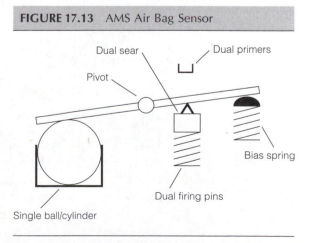

FIGURE 17.14   AMS Sensor Block Diagram

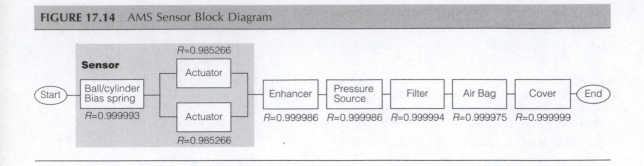

FIGURE 17.15   EMS Sensor Reliability Diagram

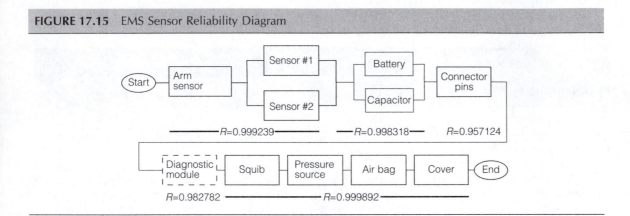

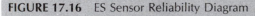

FIGURE 17.16   ES Sensor Reliability Diagram

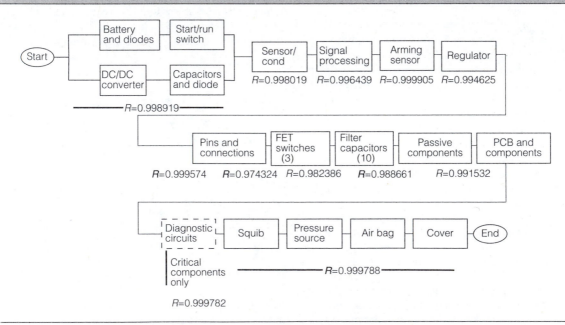

prevents unwanted deployment. The electrical portion of the system is monitored by a diagnostic module to pinpoint an electrical failure if it occurs. Figure 17.15 shows this system and some engineering estimates of the reliability of various system components.

The third type of design is an electronic sensor system (ES). Without delving into the details of its operation, which are somewhat more complex than the others, Figure 17.16 shows the system diagram and reliability values.

Discussion Questions

1. What is the role of the dual actuators in the mechanical air bag system? Describe the effect of having only one.

2. Compute the reliabilities of each system. What conclusions do the data suggest?

3. The table below lists some engineering calculations of system reliabilities for each type of system over time when repairability is taken into account. Plot these data on a graph. What do the data suggest?

System	Year			
	5	10	15	17
AMS	0.999844	0.999716	0.999588	0.999537
EMS	0.999870	0.999759	0.999648	0.999604
ES	0.999190	0.998494	0.997799	0.997521

NOTES

1. *Reliablity Guidebook,* The Japanese Standards Association (Tokyo: Asian Productivity Organization, 1972), 4.
2. W. H. Blevel, "Management Science's Impact on Service Strategy," *Interfaces* 6, no. 1, pt. 2 (November 1974), 4–12.
3. Keith Denton, "Reducing DOAs (and other Q.C. Problems)," *P&IM Review with APICS News* (December 1989), 35–36.
4. Denton, see note 3.
5. Peter G. Neumann, "Some Reflections on a Telephone Switching Problem," *Communications of the ACM* 33, no. 7 (1990), 154.
6. Jonathan Jacky, "Risks in Medical Electronics," *Communications of the ACM* 33, no. 12 (1990), 138.
7. Richard Brandt, with Evan I. Schwartz and Neil Gross, "Can the U.S. Stay Ahead in Software?" *Business Week,* 11 March, 1991, 98–105.
8. G. G. Gustafson, and R. J. Kerr, "Some Practical Experience with a Software Quality Assurance Program," *Communications of the ACM* 25, no. 1 (January 1982), 4–12. Copyright 1982, Association for Computing Machinery, Inc.
9. Edward J. Joyce, "Is Error-Free Software Achievable?" *Datamation,* 15 February, 1989, 53, 56.
10. Adapted from Roger Franz, "Audio Component Reliability," *Quality* (June 1983), 50–51. Reprinted with permission from Hitchcock Publishing, a Capital Cities/ABC Inc., Company.
11. Adapted from John Connell and Linda Brice, "Practical Quality Assurance," *Datamation,* 1 March, 1985, 106–114. Copyright © 1985 by Cahners Publ. Co.
12. Adapted from Howard Frank, "Automotive Air Bag Reliability," Source: *Reliability Review* ISSN 0277–9633, 14, no. 3 (September 1994), 11–22. Published for Reliability Division, ASQC by Williams Enterprises.

BIBLIOGRAPHY

Bernstein, Amy. "Putting Software to the Test." *Business Computer Systems* (December 1984), 48–51.
Buck, Carl N. "Improving Reliability." *Quality* (February 1990), 58–60.
Chowdhury, A. R. "Reliability as It Relates to QA/QC." *Quality Progress* 18, no. 12 (December 1985), 27–30.
Halpern, S. *The Assurance Sciences, an Introduction to Quality Control and Reliability.* Englewood Cliffs, NJ: Prentice-Hall, 1978.
Juran, J. M., and F. M. Gryna. *Quality Planning and Analysis,* 2nd ed. New York: McGraw-Hill, 1980.
Lawrence Joseph D., Jr. "Semiconductor Quality Considerations," *Quality* (December 1983), 39–41.
Posedel, Rhea J. "Burn-in: The Way to Reliability." *Quality* (August 1982), 22–23.
Singh, B. P. "Reliability, Availability, and Maintainability Program in a Metal Processing Facility." *Proceedings, AIIE 1978 Spring Annual Conference.* Norcross, GA: American Institute of Industrial Eingineers, 1978.
Smith, Charles O. *Introduction to Reliability in Design.* New York: McGraw-Hill, 1976.

Appendixes

APPENDIX A

Areas for the Standard Normal Distribution

Entries in the table give the area under the curve between the mean and z standard deviations above the mean. For example, for $z = 1.25$ the area under the curve between the mean and z is 0.3944.

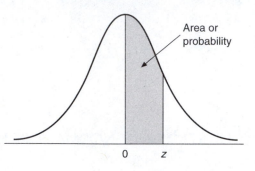

z	0.00	0.01	0.02	0.03	0.04	0.05	0.06	0.07	0.08	0.09
0.0	0.0000	0.0040	0.0080	0.0120	0.0160	0.0199	0.0239	0.0279	0.0319	0.0359
0.1	0.0398	0.0438	0.0478	0.0517	0.0557	0.0596	0.0636	0.0675	0.0714	0.0753
0.2	0.0793	0.0832	0.0871	0.0910	0.0948	0.0987	0.1026	0.1064	0.1103	0.1141
0.3	0.1179	0.1217	0.1255	0.1293	0.1331	0.1368	0.1406	0.1443	0.1480	0.1517
0.4	0.1554	0.1591	0.1628	0.1664	0.1700	0.1736	0.1772	0.1808	0.1844	0.1879
0.5	0.1915	0.1950	0.1985	0.2019	0.2054	0.2088	0.2123	0.2157	0.2190	0.2224
0.6	0.2257	0.2291	0.2324	0.2357	0.2389	0.2422	0.2454	0.2486	0.2518	0.2549
0.7	0.2580	0.2612	0.2642	0.2673	0.2704	0.2734	0.2764	0.2794	0.2823	0.2852
0.8	0.2881	0.2910	0.2939	0.2967	0.2995	0.3023	0.3051	0.3078	0.3106	0.3133
0.9	0.3159	0.3186	0.3212	0.3238	0.3264	0.3289	0.3315	0.3340	0.3365	0.3389
1.0	0.3413	0.3438	0.3461	0.3485	0.3508	0.3531	0.3554	0.3577	0.3599	0.3621
1.1	0.3643	0.3665	0.3686	0.3708	0.3729	0.3749	0.3770	0.3790	0.3810	0.3830
1.2	0.3849	0.3869	0.3888	0.3907	0.3925	0.3944	0.3962	0.3980	0.3997	0.4015
1.3	0.4032	0.4049	0.4066	0.4082	0.4099	0.4115	0.4131	0.4147	0.4162	0.4177
1.4	0.4192	0.4207	0.4222	0.4236	0.4251	0.4265	0.4279	0.4292	0.4306	0.4319
1.5	0.4332	0.4345	0.4357	0.4370	0.4382	0.4394	0.4406	0.4418	0.4429	0.4441
1.6	0.4452	0.4463	0.4474	0.4484	0.4495	0.4505	0.4515	0.4525	0.4535	0.4545
1.7	0.4554	0.4564	0.4573	0.4582	0.4591	0.4599	0.4608	0.4616	0.4625	0.4633
1.8	0.4641	0.4649	0.4656	0.4664	0.4671	0.4578	0.4686	0.4693	0.4699	0.4706
1.9	0.4713	0.4719	0.4726	0.4732	0.4738	0.4744	0.4750	0.4756	0.4761	0.4767
2.0	0.4772	0.4778	0.4783	0.4788	0.4793	0.4798	0.4803	0.4808	0.4812	0.4817
2.1	0.4821	0.4826	0.4830	0.4834	0.4838	0.4842	0.4846	0.4850	0.4854	0.4857
2.2	0.4861	0.4864	0.4868	0.4871	0.4875	0.4878	0.4881	0.4884	0.4887	0.4890
2.3	0.4893	0.4896	0.4898	0.4901	0.4094	0.4906	0.4909	0.4911	0.4913	0.4916
2.4	0.4918	0.4920	0.4922	0.4925	0.4927	0.4929	0.4931	0.4932	0.4934	0.4936
2.5	0.4938	0.4940	0.4941	0.4943	0.4945	0.4946	0.4948	0.4949	0.4951	0.4952
2.6	0.4953	0.4955	0.4956	0.4957	0.4959	0.4960	0.4961	0.4962	0.4963	0.4964
2.7	0.4965	0.4966	0.4967	0.4968	0.4969	0.4970	0.4971	0.4972	0.4973	0.4974
2.8	0.4974	0.4975	0.4976	0.4977	0.4977	0.4978	0.4979	0.4979	0.4980	0.4981
2.9	0.4981	0.4982	0.4982	0.4983	0.4984	0.4984	0.4985	0.4985	0.4986	0.4986
3.0	0.4986	0.4987	0.4987	0.4988	0.4988	0.4989	0.4989	0.4989	0.4990	0.4990

APPENDIX B

Factors for Control Charts

n	x̄-charts				s-Charts				R-charts					
	A	A_2	A_3	c_4	B_3	B_4	B_5	B_6	d_2	d_3	D_1	D_2	D_3	D_4
2	2.121	1.880	2.659	0.7979	0	3.267	0	2.606	1.128	0.853	0	3.686	0	3.267
3	1.732	1.023	1.954	0.8862	0	2.568	0	2.276	1.693	0.888	0	4.358	0	2.574
4	1.500	0.729	1.628	0.9213	0	2.266	0	2.088	2.059	0.880	0	4.698	0	2.282
5	1.342	0.577	1.427	0.9400	0	2.089	0	1.964	2.326	0.864	0	4.918	0	2.114
6	1.225	0.483	1.287	0.9515	0.030	1.970	0.029	1.874	2.534	0.848	0	5.078	0	2.004
7	1.134	0.419	1.182	0.9594	0.118	1.882	0.113	1.806	2.704	0.833	0.204	5.204	0.076	1.924
8	1.061	0.373	1.099	0.9650	0.185	1.815	0.179	1.751	2.847	0.820	0.388	5.306	0.136	1.864
9	1.000	0.337	1.032	0.9693	0.239	1.761	0.232	1.707	2.970	0.808	0.547	5.393	0.184	1.816
10	0.949	0.308	0.975	0.9727	0.284	1.716	0.276	1.669	3.078	0.797	0.687	5.469	0.223	1.777
11	0.905	0.285	0.927	0.9754	0.321	1.679	0.313	1.637	3.173	0.787	0.811	5.535	0.256	1.744
12	0.866	0.266	0.886	0.9776	0.354	1.646	0.346	1.610	3.258	0.778	0.922	5.594	0.283	1.717
13	0.832	0.249	0.850	0.9794	0.382	1.618	0.374	1.585	3.336	0.770	1.025	5.647	0.307	1.693
14	0.802	0.235	0.817	0.9810	0.406	1.594	0.399	1.563	3.407	0.763	1.118	5.696	0.328	1.672
15	0.775	0.223	0.789	0.9823	0.428	1.572	0.421	1.544	3.472	0.756	1.203	5.741	0.347	1.653
16	0.750	0.212	0.763	0.9835	0.448	1.552	0.440	1.526	3.532	0.750	1.282	5.782	0.363	1.637
17	0.728	0.203	0.739	0.9845	0.466	1.534	0.458	1.511	3.588	0.744	1.356	5.820	0.378	1.622
18	0.707	0.194	0.718	0.9854	0.482	1.518	0.475	1.496	3.640	0.739	1.424	5.856	0.391	1.608
19	0.688	0.187	0.698	0.9862	0.497	1.503	0.490	1.483	3.689	0.734	1.487	5.891	0.403	1.597
20	0.671	0.180	0.680	0.9869	0.510	1.490	0.504	1.470	3.735	0.729	1.549	5.921	0.415	1.585
21	0.655	0.173	0.663	0.9876	0.523	1.477	0.516	1.459	3.778	0.724	1.605	5.951	0.425	1.575
22	0.640	0.167	0.647	0.9882	0.534	1.466	0.528	1.448	3.819	0.720	1.659	5.979	0.434	1.566
23	0.626	0.162	0.633	0.9887	0.545	1.455	0.539	1.438	3.858	0.716	1.710	6.006	0.443	1.557
24	0.612	0.157	0.619	0.9892	0.555	1.445	0.549	1.429	3.895	0.712	1.759	6.031	0.451	1.548
25	0.600	0.153	0.606	0.9896	0.565	1.435	0.559	1.420	3.931	0.708	1.806	6.056	0.459	1.541

SOURCE: Adapted from Table 27 of ASTM STP 15D *ASTM Manual on Presentation of Data and Control Chart Analysis.* Copyright 1976 American Society for Testing and Materials, Philadelphia, PA.

APPENDIX C

Random Digits

63271	59986	71744	51102	15141	80714	58683	93108	13554	79945
88547	09896	95436	79115	08303	01041	20030	63754	08459	28364
55957	57243	83865	09911	19761	66535	40102	26646	60147	15702
46276	87453	44790	67122	45573	84358	21625	16999	13385	22782
55363	07449	34835	15290	76616	67191	12777	21861	68689	03263
69393	92785	49902	58447	42048	30378	87618	26933	40640	16281
13186	29431	88190	04588	38733	81290	89541	70290	40113	08243
17726	28652	56836	78351	47327	18518	92222	55201	27340	10493
36520	64465	05550	30157	82242	29520	69753	72602	23756	54935
81628	36100	39254	56835	37636	02421	98063	89641	64953	99337
84649	48968	75215	75498	49539	74240	03466	49292	36401	45525
63291	11618	12613	75055	43915	26488	41116	64531	56827	30825
70502	53225	03655	05915	37140	57051	48393	91322	25653	06543
06426	24771	59935	49801	11082	66762	94477	02494	88215	27191
20711	55609	29430	70165	45406	78484	31639	52009	18873	96927
41990	70538	77191	25860	55204	73417	83920	69468	74972	38712
72452	36618	76298	26678	89334	33938	95567	29380	75906	91807
37042	40318	57099	10528	09925	89773	41335	96244	29002	46453
53766	52875	15987	46962	67342	77592	57651	95508	80033	69828
90585	58955	53122	16025	84299	53310	67380	84249	25348	04332
32001	96293	37203	64516	51530	37069	40261	61374	05815	06714
62606	64324	46354	72157	67248	20135	49804	09226	64419	29457
10078	28073	85389	50324	14500	15562	64165	06125	71353	77669
91561	46145	24177	15294	10061	98124	75732	00815	83452	97355
13091	98112	53959	79607	52244	63303	10413	63839	74762	50289
73864	83014	72457	22682	03033	61714	88173	90835	00634	85169
66668	25467	48894	51043	02365	91726	09365	63167	95264	45643
84745	41042	29493	01836	09044	51926	43630	63470	76508	14194
48068	26805	94595	47907	13357	38412	33318	26098	82782	42851
54310	96175	97594	88616	42035	38093	36745	56702	40644	83514
14877	33095	10924	58013	61439	21882	42059	24177	58739	60170
78295	23179	02771	43464	59061	71411	05697	67194	30495	21157
67524	02865	39593	54278	04237	92441	26602	63835	38032	94770
58268	57219	68124	73455	83236	08710	04284	55005	84171	42596
97158	28672	50685	01181	24262	19427	52106	34308	73685	74246
04230	16831	69085	30802	65559	09205	71829	06489	85650	38707
94879	56606	30401	02602	57658	70091	54986	41394	60437	03195
71446	15232	66715	26385	91518	70566	02888	79941	39684	54315
32886	05644	79316	09819	00813	88407	17461	73925	53037	91904
62048	33711	25290	21526	02223	75947	66466	06232	10913	75336

APPENDIX D

Binomial Probabilities

Entries in the table give the probability of x successes in n trials of a binomial experiment, where p is the probability of a success on one trial. For example, with six trials and $p = 0.40$, the probability of two successes is 0.3110.

n	x	0.05	0.10	0.15	0.20	0.25	0.30	0.35	0.40	0.45	0.50
							p				
1	0	0.9500	0.9000	0.8500	0.8000	0.7500	0.7000	0.6500	0.6000	0.5500	0.5000
	1	0.0500	0.1000	0.1500	0.2000	0.2500	0.3000	0.3500	0.4000	0.4500	0.5000
2	0	0.9025	0.8100	0.7225	0.6400	0.5625	0.4900	0.4225	0.3600	0.3025	0.2500
	1	0.0950	0.1800	0.2550	0.3200	0.3750	0.4200	0.4550	0.4800	0.4950	0.5000
	2	0.0025	0.0100	0.0225	0.0400	0.0625	0.0900	0.1225	0.1600	0.2025	0.2500
3	0	0.8574	0.7290	0.6141	0.5120	0.4219	0.3430	0.2746	0.2160	0.1664	0.1250
	1	0.1354	0.2430	0.3251	0.3840	0.4219	0.4410	0.4436	0.4320	0.4084	0.3750
	2	0.0071	0.0270	0.0574	0.0960	0.1406	0.1890	0.2389	0.2880	0.3341	0.3750
	3	0.0001	0.0010	0.0034	0.0080	0.0156	0.0270	0.0429	0.0640	0.0911	0.1250
4	0	0.8145	0.6561	0.5220	0.4096	0.3164	0.2401	0.1785	0.1296	0.0915	0.0625
	1	0.1715	0.2916	0.3685	0.4096	0.4219	0.4116	0.3845	0.3456	0.2995	0.2500
	2	0.0135	0.0486	0.0975	0.1536	0.2109	0.2646	0.3105	0.3456	0.3675	0.3750
	3	0.0005	0.0036	0.0115	0.0256	0.0469	0.0756	0.1115	0.1536	0.2005	0.2500
	4	0.0000	0.0001	0.0005	0.0016	0.0039	0.0081	0.0150	0.0256	0.0410	0.0625
5	0	0.7738	0.5905	0.4437	0.3277	0.2373	0.1681	0.1160	0.0778	0.0503	0.0312
	1	0.2036	0.3280	0.3915	0.4096	0.3955	0.3602	0.3124	0.2592	0.2059	0.1562
	2	0.0214	0.0729	0.1382	0.2048	0.2637	0.3087	0.3364	0.3456	0.3369	0.3125
	3	0.0011	0.0081	0.0244	0.0512	0.0879	0.1323	0.1811	0.2304	0.2757	0.3125
	4	0.0000	0.0004	0.0022	0.0064	0.0146	0.0284	0.0488	0.0768	0.1128	0.1562
	5	0.0000	0.0000	0.0001	0.0003	0.0010	0.0024	0.0053	0.0102	0.0185	0.0312
6	0	0.7351	0.5314	0.3771	0.2621	0.1780	0.1176	0.0754	0.0467	0.0277	0.0156
	1	0.2321	0.3543	0.3993	0.3932	0.3560	0.3025	0.2437	0.1866	0.1359	0.0938
	2	0.0305	0.0984	0.1762	0.2458	0.2966	0.3241	0.3280	0.3110	0.2780	0.2344
	3	0.0021	0.0146	0.0415	0.0819	0.1318	0.1852	0.2355	0.2765	0.3032	0.3125
	4	0.0001	0.0012	0.0055	0.0154	0.0330	0.0595	0.0951	0.1382	0.1861	0.2344
	5	0.0000	0.0001	0.0004	0.0015	0.0044	0.0102	0.0205	0.0369	0.0609	0.0938
	6	0.0000	0.0000	0.0000	0.0001	0.0002	0.0007	0.0018	0.0041	0.0083	0.0156
7	0	0.6983	0.4783	0.3206	0.2097	0.1335	0.0824	0.0490	0.0280	0.0152	0.0078
	1	0.2573	0.3720	0.3960	0.3670	0.3115	0.2471	0.1848	0.1306	0.0872	0.0547
	2	0.0406	0.1240	0.2097	0.2753	0.3115	0.3177	0.2985	0.2613	0.2140	0.1641
	3	0.0036	0.0230	0.0617	0.1147	0.1730	0.2269	0.2679	0.2903	0.2918	0.2734
	4	0.0002	0.0026	0.0109	0.0287	0.0577	0.0972	0.1442	0.1935	0.2388	0.2734
	5	0.0000	0.0002	0.0012	0.0043	0.0115	0.0250	0.0466	0.0774	0.1172	0.1641
	6	0.0000	0.0000	0.0001	0.0004	0.0013	0.0036	0.0084	0.0172	0.0320	0.0547
	7	0.0000	0.0000	0.0000	0.0000	0.0001	0.0002	0.0006	0.0016	0.0037	0.0078
8	0	0.6634	0.4305	0.2725	0.1678	0.1001	0.0576	0.0319	0.0168	0.0084	0.0039
	1	0.2793	0.3826	0.3847	0.3355	0.2670	0.1977	0.1373	0.0896	0.0548	0.0312
	2	0.0515	0.1488	0.2376	0.2936	0.3115	0.2965	0.2587	0.2090	0.1569	0.1094
	3	0.0054	0.0331	0.0839	0.1468	0.2076	0.2541	0.2786	0.2787	0.2568	0.2188
	4	0.0004	0.0046	0.0185	0.0459	0.0865	0.1361	0.1875	0.2322	0.2627	0.2734
	5	0.0000	0.0004	0.0026	0.0092	0.0231	0.0467	0.0808	0.1239	0.1719	0.2188
	6	0.0000	0.0000	0.0002	0.0011	0.0038	0.0100	0.0217	0.0413	0.0703	0.1094
	7	0.0000	0.0000	0.0000	0.0001	0.0004	0.0012	0.0033	0.0079	0.0164	0.0312
	8	0.0000	0.0000	0.0000	0.0000	0.0000	0.0001	0.0002	0.0007	0.0017	0.0039

		p									
n	x	0.05	0.10	0.15	0.20	0.25	0.30	0.35	0.40	0.45	0.50
9	0	0.6302	0.3874	0.2316	0.1342	0.0751	0.0404	0.0207	0.0101	0.0046	0.0020
	1	0.2985	0.3874	0.3679	0.3020	0.2253	0.1556	0.1004	0.0605	0.0339	0.0176
	2	0.0629	0.1722	0.2597	0.3020	0.3003	0.2668	0.2162	0.1612	0.1110	0.0703
	3	0.0077	0.0446	0.1069	0.1762	0.2336	0.2668	0.2716	0.2508	0.2119	0.1641
	4	0.0006	0.0074	0.0283	0.0661	0.1168	0.1715	0.2194	0.2508	0.2600	0.2461
	5	0.0000	0.0008	0.0050	0.0165	0.0389	0.0735	0.1181	0.1672	0.2128	0.2461
	6	0.0000	0.0001	0.0006	0.0028	0.0087	0.0210	0.0424	0.0743	0.1160	0.1641
	7	0.0000	0.0000	0.0000	0.0003	0.0012	0.0039	0.0098	0.0212	0.0407	0.0703
	8	0.0000	0.0000	0.0000	0.0000	0.0001	0.0004	0.0013	0.0035	0.0083	0.0176
	9	0.0000	0.0000	0.0000	0.0000	0.0000	0.0000	0.0001	0.0003	0.0008	0.0020
10	0	0.5987	0.3487	0.1969	0.1074	0.0563	0.0282	0.0135	0.0060	0.0025	0.0010
	1	0.3151	0.3874	0.3474	0.2684	0.1877	0.1211	0.0725	0.0403	0.0207	0.0098
	2	0.0746	0.1937	0.2759	0.3020	0.2816	0.2335	0.1757	0.1209	0.0763	0.0439
	3	0.0105	0.0574	0.1298	0.2013	0.2503	0.2668	0.2522	0.2150	0.1665	0.1172
	4	0.0010	0.0112	0.0401	0.0881	0.1460	0.2001	0.2377	0.2508	0.2384	0.2051
	5	0.0001	0.0015	0.0085	0.0264	0.0584	0.1029	0.1536	0.2007	0.2340	0.2461
	6	0.0000	0.0001	0.0012	0.0055	0.0162	0.0368	0.0689	0.1115	0.1596	0.2051
	7	0.0000	0.0000	0.0001	0.0008	0.0031	0.0090	0.0212	0.0425	0.0746	0.1172
	8	0.0000	0.0000	0.0000	0.0001	0.0004	0.0014	0.0043	0.0106	0.0229	0.0439
	9	0.0000	0.0000	0.0000	0.0000	0.0000	0.0001	0.0005	0.0016	0.0042	0.0098
	10	0.0000	0.0000	0.0000	0.0000	0.0000	0.0000	0.0000	0.0001	0.0003	0.0010
11	0	0.5688	0.3138	0.1673	0.0859	0.0422	0.0198	0.0088	0.0036	0.0014	0.0005
	1	0.3293	0.3835	0.3248	0.2362	0.1549	0.0932	0.0518	0.0266	0.0125	0.0054
	2	0.0867	0.2131	0.2866	0.2953	0.2581	0.1998	0.1395	0.0887	0.0513	0.0269
	3	0.0137	0.0710	0.1517	0.2215	0.2581	0.2568	0.2254	0.1774	0.1259	0.0806
	4	0.0014	0.0158	0.0536	0.1107	0.1721	0.2201	0.2428	0.2365	0.2060	0.1611
	5	0.0001	0.0025	0.0132	0.0388	0.0803	0.1321	0.1830	0.2207	0.2360	0.2256
	6	0.0000	0.0003	0.0023	0.0097	0.0268	0.0566	0.0985	0.1471	0.1931	0.2256
	7	0.0000	0.0000	0.0003	0.0017	0.0064	0.0173	0.0379	0.0701	0.1128	0.1611
	8	0.0000	0.0000	0.0000	0.0002	0.0011	0.0037	0.0102	0.0234	0.0462	0.0806
	9	0.0000	0.0000	0.0000	0.0000	0.0001	0.0005	0.0018	0.0052	0.0126	0.0269
	10	0.0000	0.0000	0.0000	0.0000	0.0000	0.0000	0.0002	0.0007	0.0021	0.0054
	11	0.0000	0.0000	0.0000	0.0000	0.0000	0.0000	0.0000	0.0000	0.0002	0.0005
12	0	0.5404	0.2824	0.1422	0.0687	0.0317	0.0138	0.0057	0.0022	0.0008	0.0002
	1	0.3413	0.3766	0.3012	0.2062	0.1267	0.0712	0.0368	0.0174	0.0075	0.0029
	2	0.0988	0.2301	0.2924	0.2835	0.2323	0.1678	0.1088	0.0639	0.0339	0.0161
	3	0.0173	0.0853	0.1720	0.2362	0.2581	0.2397	0.1954	0.1419	0.0923	0.0537
	4	0.0021	0.0213	0.0683	0.1329	0.1936	0.2311	0.2367	0.2128	0.1700	0.1208
	5	0.0002	0.0038	0.0193	0.0532	0.1032	0.1585	0.2039	0.2270	0.2225	0.1934
	6	0.0000	0.0005	0.0040	0.0155	0.0401	0.0792	0.1281	0.1766	0.2124	0.2256
	7	0.0000	0.0000	0.0006	0.0033	0.0115	0.0291	0.0591	0.1009	0.1489	0.1934
	8	0.0000	0.0000	0.0001	0.0005	0.0024	0.0078	0.0199	0.0420	0.0762	0.1208
	9	0.0000	0.0000	0.0000	0.0001	0.0004	0.0015	0.0048	0.0125	0.0277	0.0537
	10	0.0000	0.0000	0.0000	0.0000	0.0000	0.0002	0.0008	0.0025	0.0068	0.0161
	11	0.0000	0.0000	0.0000	0.0000	0.0000	0.0000	0.0001	0.0003	0.0010	0.0029
	12	0.0000	0.0000	0.0000	0.0000	0.0000	0.0000	0.0000	0.0000	0.0001	0.0002
13	0	0.5133	0.2542	0.1209	0.0550	0.0238	0.0097	0.0037	0.0013	0.0004	0.0001
	1	0.3512	0.3672	0.2774	0.1787	0.1029	0.0540	0.0259	0.0113	0.0045	0.0016
	2	0.1109	0.2448	0.2937	0.2680	0.2059	0.1388	0.0836	0.0453	0.0220	0.0095
	3	0.0214	0.0997	0.1900	0.2457	0.2517	0.2181	0.1651	0.1107	0.0660	0.0349
	4	0.0028	0.0277	0.0838	0.1535	0.2097	0.2337	0.2222	0.1845	0.1350	0.0873
	5	0.0003	0.0055	0.0266	0.0691	0.1258	0.1803	0.2154	0.2214	0.1989	0.1571
	6	0.0000	0.0008	0.0063	0.0230	0.0559	0.1030	0.1546	0.1968	0.2169	0.2095
	7	0.0000	0.0001	0.0011	0.0058	0.0186	0.0442	0.0833	0.1312	0.1775	0.2095

n	x	p 0.05	0.10	0.15	0.20	0.25	0.30	0.35	0.40	0.45	0.50
	8	0.0000	0.0000	0.0001	0.0011	0.0047	0.0142	0.0336	0.0656	0.1089	0.1571
	9	0.0000	0.0000	0.0000	0.0001	0.0009	0.0034	0.0101	0.0243	0.0495	0.0873
	10	0.0000	0.0000	0.0000	0.0000	0.0001	0.0006	0.0022	0.0065	0.0162	0.0349
	11	0.0000	0.0000	0.0000	0.0000	0.0000	0.0001	0.0003	0.0012	0.0036	0.0095
	12	0.0000	0.0000	0.0000	0.0000	0.0000	0.0000	0.0000	0.0001	0.0005	0.0016
	13	0.0000	0.0000	0.0000	0.0000	0.0000	0.0000	0.0000	0.0000	0.0000	0.0001
14	0	0.4877	0.2288	0.1028	0.0440	0.0178	0.0068	0.0024	0.0008	0.0002	0.0001
	1	0.3593	0.3559	0.2539	0.1539	0.0832	0.0407	0.0181	0.0073	0.0027	0.0009
	2	0.1229	0.2570	0.2912	0.2501	0.1802	0.1134	0.0634	0.0317	0.0141	0.0056
	3	0.0259	0.1142	0.2056	0.2501	0.2402	0.1943	0.1366	0.0845	0.0462	0.0222
	4	0.0037	0.0349	0.0998	0.1720	0.2202	0.2290	0.2022	0.1549	0.1040	0.0611
	5	0.0004	0.0078	0.0352	0.0860	0.1468	0.1963	0.2178	0.2066	0.1701	0.1222
	6	0.0000	0.0013	0.0093	0.0322	0.0734	0.1262	0.1759	0.2066	0.2088	0.1833
	7	0.0000	0.0002	0.0019	0.0092	0.0280	0.0618	0.1082	0.1574	0.1952	0.2095
	8	0.0000	0.0000	0.0003	0.0020	0.0082	0.0232	0.0510	0.0918	0.1398	0.1833
	9	0.0000	0.0000	0.0000	0.0003	0.0018	0.0066	0.0183	0.0408	0.0762	0.1222
	10	0.0000	0.0000	0.0000	0.0000	0.0003	0.0014	0.0049	0.0136	0.0312	0.0611
	11	0.0000	0.0000	0.0000	0.0000	0.0000	0.0002	0.0010	0.0033	0.0093	0.0222
	12	0.0000	0.0000	0.0000	0.0000	0.0000	0.0000	0.0001	0.0005	0.0019	0.0056
	13	0.0000	0.0000	0.0000	0.0000	0.0000	0.0000	0.0000	0.0001	0.0002	0.0009
	14	0.0000	0.0000	0.0000	0.0000	0.0000	0.0000	0.0000	0.0000	0.0000	0.0001
15	0	0.4633	0.2059	0.0874	0.0352	0.0134	0.0047	0.0016	0.0005	0.0001	0.0000
	1	0.3658	0.3432	0.2312	0.1319	0.0668	0.0305	0.0126	0.0047	0.0016	0.0005
	2	0.1348	0.2669	0.2856	0.2309	0.1559	0.0916	0.0476	0.0219	0.0090	0.0032
	3	0.0307	0.1285	0.2184	0.2501	0.2252	0.1700	0.1110	0.0634	0.0318	0.0139
	4	0.0049	0.0428	0.1156	0.1876	0.2252	0.2186	0.1792	0.1268	0.0780	0.0417
	5	0.0006	0.0105	0.0449	0.1032	0.1651	0.2061	0.2123	0.1859	0.1404	0.0916
	6	0.0000	0.0019	0.0132	0.0430	0.0917	0.1472	0.1906	0.2066	0.1914	0.1527
	7	0.0000	0.0003	0.0030	0.0138	0.0393	0.0811	0.1319	0.1711	0.2013	0.1964
	8	0.0000	0.0000	0.0005	0.0035	0.0131	0.0348	0.0710	0.1181	0.1647	0.1964
	9	0.0000	0.0000	0.0001	0.0007	0.0034	0.0116	0.0298	0.0612	0.1048	0.1527
	10	0.0000	0.0000	0.0000	0.0001	0.0007	0.0030	0.0096	0.0245	0.0515	0.0916
	11	0.0000	0.0000	0.0000	0.0000	0.0001	0.0006	0.0024	0.0074	0.0191	0.0417
	12	0.0000	0.0000	0.0000	0.0000	0.0000	0.0001	0.0004	0.0016	0.0052	0.0139
	13	0.0000	0.0000	0.0000	0.0000	0.0000	0.0000	0.0001	0.0003	0.0010	0.0032
	14	0.0000	0.0000	0.0000	0.0000	0.0000	0.0000	0.0000	0.0000	0.0001	0.0005
	15	0.0000	0.0000	0.0000	0.0000	0.0000	0.0000	0.0000	0.0000	0.0000	0.0000
16	0	0.4401	0.1853	0.0743	0.0281	0.0100	0.0033	0.0010	0.0003	0.0001	0.0000
	1	0.3706	0.3294	0.2097	0.1126	0.0535	0.0228	0.0087	0.0030	0.0009	0.0002
	2	0.1463	0.2745	0.2775	0.2111	0.1336	0.0732	0.0353	0.0150	0.0056	0.0018
	3	0.0359	0.1423	0.2285	0.2463	0.2079	0.1465	0.0888	0.0468	0.0215	0.0085
	4	0.0061	0.0514	0.1311	0.2001	0.2252	0.2040	0.1553	0.1014	0.0572	0.0278
	5	0.0008	0.0137	0.0555	0.1201	0.1802	0.2099	0.2008	0.1623	0.1123	0.0667
	6	0.0001	0.0028	0.0180	0.0550	0.1101	0.1649	0.1982	0.1983	0.1684	0.1222
	7	0.0000	0.0004	0.0045	0.0197	0.0524	0.1010	0.1524	0.1889	0.1969	0.1746
	8	0.0000	0.0001	0.0009	0.0055	0.0197	0.0487	0.0923	0.1417	0.1812	0.1964
	9	0.0000	0.0000	0.0001	0.0012	0.0058	0.0185	0.0442	0.0840	0.1318	0.1746
	10	0.0000	0.0000	0.0000	0.0002	0.0014	0.0056	0.0167	0.0392	0.0755	0.1222
	11	0.0000	0.0000	0.0000	0.0000	0.0002	0.0013	0.0049	0.0142	0.0337	0.0667
	12	0.0000	0.0000	0.0000	0.0000	0.0000	0.0002	0.0011	0.0040	0.0115	0.0278
	13	0.0000	0.0000	0.0000	0.0000	0.0000	0.0000	0.0002	0.0008	0.0029	0.0085
	14	0.0000	0.0000	0.0000	0.0000	0.0000	0.0000	0.0000	0.0001	0.0005	0.0018
	15	0.0000	0.0000	0.0000	0.0000	0.0000	0.0000	0.0000	0.0000	0.0001	0.0002
	16	0.0000	0.0000	0.0000	0.0000	0.0000	0.0000	0.0000	0.0000	0.0000	0.0000

						p					
n	x	0.05	0.10	0.15	0.20	0.25	0.30	0.35	0.40	0.45	0.50
17	0	0.4181	0.1668	0.0631	0.0225	0.0075	0.0023	0.0007	0.0002	0.0000	0.0000
	1	0.3741	0.3150	0.1893	0.0957	0.0426	0.0169	0.0060	0.0019	0.0005	0.0001
	2	0.1575	0.2800	0.2673	0.1914	0.1136	0.0581	0.0260	0.0102	0.0035	0.0010
	3	0.0415	0.1556	0.2359	0.2393	0.1893	0.1245	0.0701	0.0341	0.0144	0.0052
	4	0.0076	0.0605	0.1457	0.2093	0.2209	0.1868	0.1320	0.0796	0.0411	0.0182
	5	0.0010	0.0175	0.0668	0.1361	0.1914	0.2081	0.1849	0.1379	0.0875	0.0472
	6	0.0001	0.0039	0.0236	0.0680	0.1276	0.1784	0.1991	0.1839	0.1432	0.0944
	7	0.0000	0.0007	0.0065	0.0267	0.0668	0.1201	0.1685	0.1927	0.1841	0.1484
	8	0.0000	0.0001	0.0014	0.0084	0.0279	0.0644	0.1134	0.1606	0.1883	0.1855
	9	0.0000	0.0000	0.0003	0.0021	0.0093	0.0276	0.0611	0.1070	0.1540	0.1855
	10	0.0000	0.0000	0.0000	0.0004	0.0025	0.0095	0.0263	0.0571	0.1008	0.1484
	11	0.0000	0.0000	0.0000	0.0001	0.0005	0.0026	0.0090	0.0242	0.0525	0.0944
	12	0.0000	0.0000	0.0000	0.0000	0.0001	0.0006	0.0024	0.0081	0.0215	0.0472
	13	0.0000	0.0000	0.0000	0.0000	0.0000	0.0001	0.0005	0.0021	0.0068	0.0182
	14	0.0000	0.0000	0.0000	0.0000	0.0000	0.0000	0.0001	0.0004	0.0016	0.0052
	15	0.0000	0.0000	0.0000	0.0000	0.0000	0.0000	0.0000	0.0001	0.0003	0.0010
	16	0.0000	0.0000	0.0000	0.0000	0.0000	0.0000	0.0000	0.0000	0.0000	0.0001
	17	0.0000	0.0000	0.0000	0.0000	0.0000	0.0000	0.0000	0.0000	0.0000	0.0000
18	0	0.3972	0.1501	0.0536	0.0180	0.0056	0.0016	0.0004	0.0001	0.0000	0.0000
	1	0.3763	0.3002	0.1704	0.0811	0.0338	0.0126	0.0042	0.0012	0.0003	0.0001
	2	0.1683	0.2835	0.2556	0.1723	0.0958	0.0458	0.0190	0.0069	0.0022	0.0006
	3	0.0473	0.1680	0.2406	0.2297	0.1704	0.1046	0.0547	0.0246	0.0095	0.0031
	4	0.0093	0.0700	0.1592	0.2153	0.2130	0.1681	0.1104	0.0614	0.0291	0.0117
	5	0.0014	0.0218	0.0787	0.1507	0.1988	0.2017	0.1664	0.1146	0.0666	0.0327
	6	0.0002	0.0052	0.0301	0.0816	0.1436	0.1873	0.1941	0.1655	0.1181	0.0708
	7	0.0000	0.0010	0.0091	0.0350	0.0820	0.1376	0.1792	0.1892	0.1657	0.1214
	8	0.0000	0.0002	0.0022	0.0120	0.0376	0.0811	0.1327	0.1734	0.1864	0.1669
	9	0.0000	0.0000	0.0004	0.0033	0.0139	0.0386	0.0794	0.1284	0.1694	0.1855
	10	0.0000	0.0000	0.0001	0.0008	0.0042	0.0149	0.0385	0.0771	0.1248	0.1669
	11	0.0000	0.0000	0.0000	0.0001	0.0010	0.0046	0.0151	0.0374	0.0742	0.1214
	12	0.0000	0.0000	0.0000	0.0000	0.0002	0.0012	0.0047	0.0145	0.0354	0.0708
	13	0.0000	0.0000	0.0000	0.0000	0.0000	0.0002	0.0012	0.0045	0.0134	0.0327
	14	0.0000	0.0000	0.0000	0.0000	0.0000	0.0000	0.0002	0.0011	0.0039	0.0117
	15	0.0000	0.0000	0.0000	0.0000	0.0000	0.0000	0.0000	0.0002	0.0009	0.0031
	16	0.0000	0.0000	0.0000	0.0000	0.0000	0.0000	0.0000	0.0000	0.0001	0.0006
	17	0.0000	0.0000	0.0000	0.0000	0.0000	0.0000	0.0000	0.0000	0.0000	0.0001
	18	0.0000	0.0000	0.0000	0.0000	0.0000	0.0000	0.0000	0.0000	0.0000	0.0000
19	0	0.3774	0.1351	0.0456	0.0144	0.0042	0.0011	0.0003	0.0001	0.0002	0.0000
	1	0.3774	0.2852	0.1529	0.0685	0.0268	0.0093	0.0029	0.0008	0.0002	0.0000
	2	0.1787	0.2852	0.2428	0.1540	0.0803	0.0358	0.0138	0.0046	0.0013	0.0003
	3	0.0533	0.1796	0.2428	0.2182	0.1517	0.0869	0.0422	0.0175	0.0062	0.0018
	4	0.0112	0.0798	0.1714	0.2182	0.2023	0.1491	0.0909	0.0467	0.0203	0.0074
	5	0.0018	0.0266	0.0907	0.1636	0.2023	0.1916	0.1468	0.0933	0.0497	0.0222
	6	0.0002	0.0069	0.0374	0.0955	0.1574	0.1916	0.1844	0.1451	0.0949	0.0518
	7	0.0000	0.0014	0.0122	0.0443	0.0974	0.1525	0.1844	0.1797	0.1443	0.0961
	8	0.0000	0.0002	0.0032	0.0166	0.0487	0.0981	0.1489	0.1797	0.1771	0.1442
	9	0.0000	0.0000	0.0007	0.0051	0.0198	0.0514	0.0980	0.1464	0.1771	0.1762
	10	0.0000	0.0000	0.0001	0.0013	0.0066	0.0220	0.0528	0.0976	0.1449	0.1762
	11	0.0000	0.0000	0.0000	0.0003	0.0018	0.0077	0.0233	0.0532	0.0970	0.1442
	12	0.0000	0.0000	0.0000	0.0000	0.0004	0.0022	0.0083	0.0237	0.0529	0.0961
	13	0.0000	0.0000	0.0000	0.0000	0.0001	0.0005	0.0024	0.0085	0.0233	0.0518
	14	0.0000	0.0000	0.0000	0.0000	0.0000	0.0001	0.0006	0.0024	0.0082	0.0222
	15	0.0000	0.0000	0.0000	0.0000	0.0000	0.0000	0.0001	0.0005	0.0022	0.0074
	16	0.0000	0.0000	0.0000	0.0000	0.0000	0.0000	0.0000	0.0001	0.0005	0.0018

n	x	0.05	0.10	0.15	0.20	p 0.25	0.30	0.35	0.40	0.45	0.50
	17	0.0000	0.0000	0.0000	0.0000	0.0000	0.0000	0.0000	0.0000	0.0001	0.0003
	18	0.0000	0.0000	0.0000	0.0000	0.0000	0.0000	0.0000	0.0000	0.0000	0.0000
	19	0.0000	0.0000	0.0000	0.0000	0.0000	0.0000	0.0000	0.0000	0.0000	0.0000
20	0	0.3585	0.1216	0.0388	0.0115	0.0032	0.0008	0.0002	0.0000	0.0000	0.0000
	1	0.3774	0.2702	0.1368	0.0576	0.0211	0.0068	0.0020	0.0005	0.0001	0.0000
	2	0.1887	0.2852	0.2293	0.1369	0.0669	0.0278	0.0100	0.0031	0.0008	0.0002
	3	0.0596	0.1901	0.2428	0.2054	0.1339	0.0716	0.0323	0.0123	0.0040	0.0011
	4	0.0133	0.0898	0.1821	0.2182	0.1897	0.1304	0.0738	0.0350	0.0139	0.0046
	5	0.0022	0.0319	0.1028	0.1746	0.2023	0.1789	0.1272	0.0746	0.0365	0.0148
	6	0.0003	0.0089	0.0454	0.1091	0.1686	0.1916	0.1712	0.1244	0.0746	0.0370
	7	0.0000	0.0020	0.0160	0.0545	0.1124	0.1643	0.1844	0.1659	0.1221	0.0739
	8	0.0000	0.0004	0.0046	0.0222	0.0609	0.1144	0.1614	0.1797	0.1623	0.1201
	9	0.0000	0.0001	0.0011	0.0074	0.0271	0.0654	0.1158	0.1597	0.1771	0.1602
	10	0.0000	0.0000	0.0002	0.0020	0.0099	0.0308	0.0686	0.1171	0.1593	0.1762
	11	0.0000	0.0000	0.0000	0.0005	0.0030	0.0120	0.0336	0.0710	0.1185	0.1602
	12	0.0000	0.0000	0.0000	0.0001	0.0008	0.0039	0.0136	0.0355	0.0727	0.1201
	13	0.0000	0.0000	0.0000	0.0000	0.0002	0.0010	0.0045	0.0146	0.0366	0.0739
	14	0.0000	0.0000	0.0000	0.0000	0.0000	0.0002	0.0012	0.0049	0.0150	0.0370
	15	0.0000	0.0000	0.0000	0.0000	0.0000	0.0000	0.0003	0.0013	0.0049	0.0148
	16	0.0000	0.0000	0.0000	0.0000	0.0000	0.0000	0.0000	0.0003	0.0013	0.0046
	17	0.0000	0.0000	0.0000	0.0000	0.0000	0.0000	0.0000	0.0000	0.0002	0.0011
	18	0.0000	0.0000	0.0000	0.0000	0.0000	0.0000	0.0000	0.0000	0.0000	0.0002
	19	0.0000	0.0000	0.0000	0.0000	0.0000	0.0000	0.0000	0.0000	0.0000	0.0000
	20	0.0000	0.0000	0.0000	0.0000	0.0000	0.0000	0.0000	0.0000	0.0000	0.0000

APPENDIX E

Poisson Probabilities

Entries in the table give the probability of x occurrences for a Poisson process with a mean μ. For example, when $\mu = 2.5$, the probability of four occurrences is 0.1336.

					μ					
x	0.1	0.2	0.3	0.4	0.5	0.6	0.7	0.8	0.9	1.0
0	0.9048	0.8187	0.7408	0.6703	0.6065	0.5488	0.4966	0.4493	0.4066	0.3679
1	0.0905	0.1637	0.2222	0.2681	0.3033	0.3293	0.3476	0.3595	0.3659	0.3679
2	0.0045	0.0164	0.0333	0.0536	0.0758	0.0988	0.1217	0.1438	0.1647	0.1839
3	0.0002	0.0011	0.0033	0.0072	0.0126	0.0198	0.0284	0.0383	0.0494	0.0613
4	0.0000	0.0001	0.0002	0.0007	0.0016	0.0030	0.0050	0.0077	0.0111	0.0153
5	0.0000	0.0000	0.0000	0.0001	0.0002	0.0004	0.0007	0.0012	0.0020	0.0031
6	0.0000	0.0000	0.0000	0.0000	0.0000	0.0000	0.0001	0.0002	0.0003	0.0005
7	0.0000	0.0000	0.0000	0.0000	0.0000	0.0000	0.0000	0.0000	0.0000	0.0001

					μ					
x	1.1	1.2	1.3	1.4	1.5	1.6	1.7	1.8	1.9	2.0
0	0.3329	0.3012	0.2725	0.2466	0.2231	0.2019	0.1827	0.1653	0.1496	0.1353
1	0.3662	0.3614	0.3543	0.3452	0.3347	0.3230	0.3106	0.2975	0.2842	0.2707
2	0.2014	0.2169	0.2303	0.2417	0.2510	0.2584	0.2640	0.2678	0.2700	0.2707
3	0.0738	0.0867	0.0998	0.1128	0.1255	0.1378	0.1496	0.1607	0.1710	0.1804
4	0.0203	0.0260	0.0324	0.0395	0.0471	0.0551	0.0636	0.0723	0.0812	0.0902
5	0.0045	0.0062	0.0084	0.0111	0.0141	0.0176	0.0216	0.0260	0.0309	0.0361
6	0.0008	0.0012	0.0018	0.0026	0.0035	0.0047	0.0061	0.0078	0.0098	0.0120
7	0.0001	0.0002	0.0003	0.0005	0.0008	0.0011	0.0015	0.0020	0.0027	0.0034
8	0.0000	0.0000	0.0001	0.0001	0.0001	0.0002	0.0003	0.0005	0.0006	0.0009
9	0.0000	0.0000	0.0000	0.0000	0.0000	0.0000	0.0001	0.0001	0.0001	0.0002

					μ					
x	2.1	2.2	2.3	2.4	2.5	2.6	2.7	2.8	2.9	3.0
0	0.1225	0.1108	0.1003	0.0907	0.0821	0.0743	0.0672	0.0608	0.0550	0.0498
1	0.2572	0.2438	0.2306	0.2177	0.2052	0.1931	0.1815	0.1703	0.1596	0.1494
2	0.2700	0.2681	0.2652	0.2613	0.2565	0.2510	0.2450	0.2384	0.2314	0.2240
3	0.1890	0.1966	0.2033	0.2090	0.2138	0.2176	0.2205	0.2225	0.2237	0.2240
4	0.0992	0.1082	0.1169	0.1254	0.1336	0.1414	0.1488	0.1557	0.1622	0.1680
5	0.0417	0.0476	0.0538	0.0602	0.0668	0.0735	0.0804	0.0872	0.0940	0.1008
6	0.0146	0.0174	0.0206	0.0241	0.0278	0.0319	0.0362	0.0407	0.0455	0.0540
7	0.0044	0.0055	0.0068	0.0083	0.0099	0.0118	0.0139	0.0163	0.0188	0.0216
8	0.0011	0.0015	0.0019	0.0025	0.0031	0.0038	0.0047	0.0057	0.0068	0.0081
9	0.0003	0.0004	0.0005	0.0007	0.0009	0.0011	0.0014	0.0018	0.0022	0.0027
10	0.0001	0.0001	0.0001	0.0002	0.0002	0.0003	0.0004	0.0005	0.0006	0.0008
11	0.0000	0.0000	0.0000	0.0000	0.0000	0.0001	0.0001	0.0001	0.0002	0.0002
12	0.0000	0.0000	0.0000	0.0000	0.0000	0.0000	0.0000	0.0000	0.0000	0.0001

					μ					
x	3.1	3.2	3.3	3.4	3.5	3.6	3.7	3.8	3.9	4.0
0	0.0450	0.0408	0.0369	0.0344	0.0302	0.0273	0.0247	0.0224	0.0202	0.0183
1	0.1397	0.1304	0.1217	0.1135	0.1057	0.0984	0.0915	0.0850	0.0789	0.0733
2	0.2165	0.2087	0.2008	0.1929	0.1850	0.1771	0.1692	0.1615	0.1539	0.1465
3	0.2237	0.2226	0.2209	0.2186	0.2158	0.2125	0.2087	0.2046	0.2001	0.1954
4	0.1734	0.1781	0.1823	0.1858	0.1888	0.1912	0.1931	0.1944	0.1951	0.1954

x	μ 3.1	3.2	3.3	3.4	3.5	3.6	3.7	3.8	3.9	4.0
5	0.1075	0.1140	0.1203	0.1264	0.1322	0.1377	0.1429	0.1477	0.1522	0.1563
6	0.0555	0.0608	0.0662	0.0716	0.0771	0.0826	0.0881	0.0936	0.0989	0.1042
7	0.0246	0.0278	0.0312	0.0348	0.0385	0.0425	0.0466	0.0508	0.0551	0.0595
8	0.0095	0.0111	0.0129	0.0148	0.0169	0.0191	0.0215	0.0241	0.0269	0.0298
9	0.0093	0.0040	0.0047	0.0056	0.0066	0.0076	0.0089	0.0102	0.0116	0.0132
10	0.0010	0.0013	0.0016	0.0019	0.0023	0.0028	0.0033	0.0039	0.0045	0.0053
11	0.0003	0.0004	0.0005	0.0006	0.0007	0.0009	0.0011	0.0013	0.0016	0.0019
12	0.0001	0.0001	0.0001	0.0002	0.0002	0.0003	0.0003	0.0004	0.0005	0.0006
13	0.0000	0.0000	0.0000	0.0000	0.0001	0.0001	0.0001	0.0001	0.0002	0.0002
14	0.0000	0.0000	0.0000	0.0000	0.0000	0.0000	0.0000	0.0000	0.0000	0.0001

x	μ 4.1	4.2	4.3	4.4	4.5	4.6	4.7	4.8	4.9	5.0
0	0.0166	0.0150	0.0136	0.0123	0.0111	0.0101	0.0091	0.0082	0.0074	0.0067
1	0.0679	0.0630	0.0583	0.0540	0.0500	0.0462	0.0427	0.0395	0.0365	0.0337
2	0.1393	0.1323	0.1254	0.1188	0.1125	0.1063	0.1005	0.0948	0.0894	0.0842
3	0.1904	0.1852	0.1798	0.1743	0.1687	0.1631	0.1574	0.1517	0.1460	0.1404
4	0.1951	0.1944	0.1933	0.1917	0.1898	0.1875	0.1849	0.1820	0.1789	0.1755
5	0.1600	0.1633	0.1662	0.1687	0.1708	0.1725	0.1738	0.1747	0.1753	0.1755
6	0.1093	0.1143	0.1191	0.1237	0.1281	0.1323	0.1362	0.1398	0.1432	0.1462
7	0.0640	0.0686	0.0732	0.0778	0.0824	0.0869	0.0914	0.0959	0.1002	0.1044
8	0.0328	0.0360	0.0393	0.0428	0.0463	0.0500	0.0537	0.0575	0.0614	0.0653
9	0.0150	0.0163	0.0188	0.0209	0.0232	0.0255	0.0280	0.0307	0.0334	0.0363
10	0.0061	0.0071	0.0081	0.0092	0.0104	0.0118	0.0132	0.0147	0.0164	0.0181
11	0.0023	0.0027	0.0032	0.0037	0.0043	0.0049	0.0056	0.0064	0.0073	0.0082
12	0.0008	0.0009	0.0011	0.0014	0.0016	0.0019	0.0022	0.0026	0.0030	0.0034
13	0.0002	0.0003	0.0004	0.0005	0.0006	0.0007	0.0008	0.0009	0.0011	0.0013
14	0.0001	0.0001	0.0001	0.0001	0.0002	0.0002	0.0003	0.0003	0.0004	0.0005
15	0.0000	0.0000	0.0000	0.0000	0.0001	0.0001	0.0001	0.0001	0.0001	0.0002

x	μ 5.1	5.2	5.3	5.4	5.5	5.6	5.7	5.8	5.9	6.0
0	0.0061	0.0055	0.0050	0.0045	0.0041	0.0037	0.0033	0.0030	0.0027	0.0025
1	0.0311	0.0287	0.0265	0.0244	0.0225	0.0207	0.0191	0.0176	0.0162	0.0149
2	0.0793	0.0746	0.0701	0.0659	0.0618	0.0580	0.0544	0.0509	0.0477	0.0446
3	0.1348	0.1293	0.1239	0.1185	0.1133	0.1082	0.1033	0.0985	0.0938	0.0892
4	0.1719	0.1681	0.1641	0.1600	0.1558	0.1515	0.1472	0.1428	0.1383	0.1339
5	0.1753	0.1748	0.1740	0.1728	0.1714	0.1697	0.1678	0.1656	0.1632	0.1606
6	0.1490	0.1515	0.1537	0.1555	0.1571	0.1584	0.1594	0.1601	0.1605	0.1606
7	0.1086	0.1125	0.1163	0.1200	0.1234	0.1267	0.1298	0.1326	0.1353	0.1377
8	0.0692	0.0731	0.0771	0.0810	0.0849	0.0887	0.0925	0.0962	0.0998	0.1033
9	0.0392	0.0423	0.0454	0.0486	0.0519	0.0552	0.0586	0.0620	0.0654	0.0688
10	0.0200	0.0220	0.0241	0.0262	0.0285	0.0309	0.0334	0.0359	0.0386	0.0413
11	0.0093	0.0104	0.0116	0.0129	0.0143	0.0157	0.0173	0.0190	0.0207	0.0225
12	0.0039	0.0045	0.0051	0.0058	0.0065	0.0073	0.0082	0.0092	0.0102	0.0113
13	0.0015	0.0018	0.0021	0.0024	0.0028	0.0032	0.0036	0.0041	0.0046	0.0052
14	0.0006	0.0007	0.0008	0.0009	0.0011	0.0013	0.0015	0.0017	0.0019	0.0022
15	0.0002	0.0002	0.0003	0.0003	0.0004	0.0005	0.0006	0.0007	0.0008	0.0009
16	0.0001	0.0001	0.0001	0.0001	0.0001	0.0002	0.0002	0.0002	0.0003	0.0003
17	0.0000	0.0000	0.0000	0.0000	0.0000	0.0001	0.0001	0.0001	0.0001	0.0001

	μ									
x	6.1	6.2	6.3	6.4	6.5	6.6	6.7	6.8	6.9	7.0
0	0.0022	0.0020	0.0018	0.0017	0.0015	0.0014	0.0012	0.0011	0.0010	0.0009
1	0.0137	0.0126	0.0116	0.0106	0.0098	0.0090	0.0082	0.0076	0.0070	0.0064
2	0.0417	0.0390	0.0364	0.0340	0.0318	0.0296	0.0276	0.0258	0.0240	0.0223
3	0.0848	0.0806	0.0765	0.0726	0.0688	0.0652	0.0617	0.0584	0.0552	0.0521
4	0.1294	0.1249	0.1205	0.1162	0.1118	0.1076	0.1034	0.0992	0.0952	0.0912
5	0.1579	0.1549	0.1519	0.1487	0.1454	0.1420	0.1385	0.1349	0.1314	0.1277
6	0.1605	0.1601	0.1595	0.1586	0.1575	0.1562	0.1546	0.1529	0.1511	0.1490
7	0.1399	0.1418	0.1435	0.1450	0.1462	0.1472	0.1480	0.1486	0.1489	0.1490
8	0.1066	0.1099	0.1130	0.1160	0.1188	0.1215	0.1240	0.1263	0.1284	0.1304
9	0.0723	0.0757	0.0791	0.0825	0.0858	0.0891	0.0923	0.0954	0.0985	0.1014
10	0.0441	0.0469	0.0498	0.0528	0.0558	0.0588	0.0618	0.0649	0.0679	0.0710
11	0.0245	0.0265	0.0285	0.0307	0.0330	0.0353	0.0377	0.0401	0.0426	0.0452
12	0.0124	0.0137	0.0150	0.0164	0.0179	0.0194	0.0210	0.0227	0.0245	0.0264
13	0.0058	0.0065	0.0073	0.0081	0.0089	0.0098	0.0108	0.0119	0.0130	0.0142
14	0.0025	0.0029	0.0033	0.0037	0.0041	0.0046	0.0052	0.0058	0.0064	0.0071
15	0.0010	0.0012	0.0014	0.0016	0.0018	0.0020	0.0023	0.0026	0.0029	0.0033
16	0.0004	0.0005	0.0005	0.0006	0.0007	0.0008	0.0010	0.0011	0.0013	0.0014
17	0.0001	0.0002	0.0002	0.0002	0.0003	0.0003	0.0004	0.0004	0.0005	0.0006
18	0.0000	0.0001	0.0001	0.0001	0.0001	0.0001	0.0001	0.0002	0.0002	0.0002
19	0.0000	0.0000	0.0000	0.0000	0.0000	0.0000	0.0000	0.0001	0.0001	0.0001

	μ									
x	7.1	7.2	7.3	7.4	7.5	7.6	7.7	7.8	7.9	8.0
0	0.0008	0.0007	0.0007	0.0006	0.0006	0.0005	0.0005	0.0004	0.0004	0.0003
1	0.0059	0.0054	0.0049	0.0045	0.0041	0.0038	0.0035	0.0032	0.0029	0.0027
2	0.0208	0.0194	0.0180	0.0167	0.0156	0.0145	0.0134	0.0125	0.0116	0.0107
3	0.0492	0.0464	0.0438	0.0413	0.0389	0.0366	0.0345	0.0324	0.0305	0.0286
4	0.0874	0.0836	0.0799	0.0764	0.0729	0.0696	0.0663	0.0632	0.0602	0.0573
5	0.1241	0.1204	0.1167	0.1130	0.1094	0.1057	0.1021	0.0986	0.0951	0.0916
6	0.1468	0.1445	0.1420	0.1394	0.1367	0.1339	0.1311	0.1282	0.1252	0.1221
7	0.1489	0.1486	0.1481	0.1474	0.1465	0.1454	0.1442	0.1428	0.1413	0.1396
8	0.1321	0.1337	0.1351	0.1363	0.1373	0.1382	0.1388	0.1392	0.1395	0.1396
9	0.1042	0.1070	0.1096	0.1121	0.1144	0.1167	0.1187	0.1207	0.1224	0.1241
10	0.0740	0.0770	0.0800	0.0829	0.0858	0.0887	0.0914	0.0941	0.0967	0.0993
11	0.0478	0.0504	0.0531	0.0558	0.0585	0.0613	0.0640	0.0667	0.0695	0.0722
12	0.0283	0.0303	0.0323	0.0344	0.0366	0.0388	0.0411	0.0434	0.0457	0.0481
13	0.0154	0.0168	0.0181	0.0196	0.0211	0.0227	0.0243	0.0260	0.0278	0.0296
14	0.0078	0.0086	0.0095	0.0104	0.0113	0.0123	0.0134	0.0145	0.0157	0.0169
15	0.0037	0.0041	0.0046	0.0051	0.0057	0.0062	0.0069	0.0075	0.0083	0.0090
16	0.0016	0.0019	0.0021	0.0024	0.0026	0.0030	0.0033	0.0037	0.0041	0.0045
17	0.0007	0.0008	0.0009	0.0010	0.0012	0.0013	0.0015	0.0017	0.0019	0.0021
18	0.0003	0.0003	0.0004	0.0004	0.0005	0.0006	0.0006	0.0007	0.0008	0.0009
19	0.0001	0.0001	0.0001	0.0002	0.0002	0.0002	0.0003	0.0003	0.0003	0.0004
20	0.0000	0.0000	0.0001	0.0001	0.0001	0.0001	0.0001	0.0001	0.0001	0.0002
21	0.0000	0.0000	0.0000	0.0000	0.0000	0.0000	0.0000	0.0000	0.0001	0.0001

	μ									
x	8.1	8.2	8.3	8.4	8.5	8.6	8.7	8.8	8.9	9.0
0	0.0003	0.0003	0.0002	0.0002	0.0002	0.0002	0.0002	0.0002	0.0001	0.0001
1	0.0025	0.0023	0.0021	0.0019	0.0017	0.0016	0.0014	0.0013	0.0012	0.0011
2	0.0100	0.0092	0.0086	0.0079	0.0074	0.0068	0.0063	0.0058	0.0054	0.0050
3	0.0269	0.0252	0.0237	0.0222	0.0208	0.0195	0.0183	0.0171	0.1060	0.0150
4	0.0544	0.0517	0.0491	0.0466	0.0443	0.0420	0.0398	0.0377	0.0357	0.0337

					μ					
x	8.1	8.2	8.3	8.4	8.5	8.6	8.7	8.8	8.9	9.0
5	0.0882	0.0849	0.0816	0.0784	0.0752	0.0722	0.0692	0.0663	0.0635	0.0607
6	0.1191	0.1160	0.1128	0.1097	0.1066	0.1034	0.1003	0.0972	0.0941	0.0911
7	0.1378	0.1358	0.1338	0.1317	0.1294	0.1271	0.1247	0.1222	0.1197	0.1171
8	0.1395	0.1392	0.1388	0.1382	0.1375	0.1366	0.1356	0.1344	0.1332	0.1318
9	0.1256	0.1269	0.1280	0.1290	0.1299	0.1306	0.1311	0.1315	0.1317	0.1318
10	0.1017	0.1040	0.1063	0.1084	0.1104	0.1123	0.1140	0.1157	0.1172	0.1186
11	0.0749	0.0776	0.0802	0.0828	0.0853	0.0878	0.0902	0.0925	0.0948	0.0970
12	0.0505	0.0530	0.0555	0.0579	0.0604	0.0629	0.0654	0.0679	0.0703	0.0728
13	0.0315	0.0334	0.0354	0.0374	0.0395	0.0416	0.0438	0.0459	0.0481	0.0504
14	0.0182	0.0196	0.0210	0.0225	0.0240	0.0256	0.0272	0.0289	0.0306	0.0324
15	0.0098	0.0107	0.0116	0.0126	0.0136	0.0147	0.0158	0.0169	0.0182	0.0194
16	0.0050	0.0055	0.0060	0.0066	0.0072	0.0079	0.0086	0.0093	0.0101	0.0109
17	0.0024	0.0026	0.0029	0.0033	0.0036	0.0040	0.0044	0.0048	0.0053	0.0058
18	0.0011	0.0012	0.0014	0.0015	0.0017	0.0019	0.0021	0.0024	0.0026	0.0029
19	0.0005	0.0005	0.0006	0.0007	0.0008	0.0009	0.0010	0.0011	0.0012	0.0014
20	0.0002	0.0002	0.0002	0.0003	0.0003	0.0004	0.0004	0.0005	0.0005	0.0006
21	0.0001	0.0001	0.0001	0.0001	0.0001	0.0002	0.0002	0.0002	0.0002	0.0003
22	0.0000	0.0000	0.0000	0.0000	0.0001	0.0001	0.0001	0.0001	0.0001	0.0001

					μ					
x	9.1	9.2	9.3	9.4	9.5	9.6	9.7	9.8	9.9	10
0	0.0001	0.0001	0.0001	0.0001	0.0001	0.0001	0.0001	0.0001	0.0001	0.0000
1	0.0010	0.0009	0.0009	0.0008	0.0007	0.0007	0.0006	0.0005	0.0005	0.0005
2	0.0046	0.0043	0.0040	0.0037	0.0034	0.0031	0.0029	0.0027	0.0025	0.0023
3	0.0140	0.0131	0.0123	0.0115	0.0107	0.0100	0.0093	0.0087	0.0081	0.0076
4	0.0319	0.0302	0.0285	0.0269	0.0254	0.0240	0.0226	0.0213	0.0201	0.0189
5	0.0581	0.0555	0.0530	0.0506	0.0483	0.0460	0.0439	0.0418	0.0398	0.0378
6	0.0881	0.0851	0.0822	0.0793	0.0764	0.0736	0.0709	0.0682	0.0656	0.0631
7	0.1145	0.1118	0.1091	0.1064	0.1037	0.1010	0.0982	0.0955	0.0928	0.0901
8	0.1302	0.1286	0.1269	0.1251	0.1232	0.1212	0.1191	0.1170	0.1148	0.1126
9	0.1317	0.1315	0.1311	0.1306	0.1300	0.1293	0.1284	0.1274	0.1263	0.1251
10	0.1198	0.1210	0.1219	0.1228	0.1235	0.1241	0.1245	0.1249	0.1250	0.1251
11	0.0991	0.1012	0.1031	0.1049	0.1067	0.1083	0.1098	0.1112	0.1125	0.1137
12	0.0752	0.0776	0.0799	0.0822	0.0844	0.0866	0.0888	0.0908	0.0928	0.0948
13	0.0526	0.0549	0.0572	0.0594	0.0617	0.0640	0.0662	0.0685	0.0707	0.0729
14	0.0342	0.0361	0.0380	0.0399	0.0419	0.0439	0.0459	0.0479	0.0500	0.0521
15	0.0208	0.0221	0.0235	0.0250	0.0265	0.0281	0.0297	0.0313	0.0330	0.0347
16	0.0118	0.0127	0.0137	0.0147	0.0157	0.0168	0.0180	0.0192	0.0204	0.0217
17	0.0063	0.0069	0.0075	0.0081	0.0088	0.0095	0.0103	0.0111	0.0119	0.0128
18	0.0032	0.0035	0.0039	0.0042	0.0046	0.0051	0.0055	0.0060	0.0065	0.0071
19	0.0015	0.0017	0.0019	0.0021	0.0023	0.0026	0.0028	0.0031	0.0034	0.0037
20	0.0007	0.0008	0.0009	0.0010	0.0011	0.0012	0.0014	0.0015	0.0017	0.0019
21	0.0003	0.0003	0.0004	0.0004	0.0005	0.0006	0.0006	0.0007	0.0008	0.0009
22	0.0001	0.0001	0.0002	0.0002	0.0002	0.0002	0.0003	0.0003	0.0004	0.0004
23	0.0000	0.0001	0.0001	0.0001	0.0001	0.0001	0.0001	0.0001	0.0002	0.0002
24	0.0000	0.0000	0.0000	0.0000	0.0000	0.0000	0.0000	0.0001	0.0001	0.0001

x	μ 11	12	13	14	15	16	17	18	19	20
0	0.0000	0.0000	0.0000	0.0000	0.0000	0.0000	0.0000	0.0000	0.0000	0.0000
1	0.0002	0.0001	0.0000	0.0000	0.0000	0.0000	0.0000	0.0000	0.0000	0.0000
2	0.0010	0.0004	0.0002	0.0001	0.0000	0.0000	0.0000	0.0000	0.0000	0.0000
3	0.0037	0.0018	0.0008	0.0004	0.0002	0.0001	0.0000	0.0000	0.0000	0.0000
4	0.0102	0.0053	0.0027	0.0013	0.0006	0.0003	0.0001	0.0001	0.0000	0.0000
5	0.0224	0.0127	0.0070	0.0037	0.0019	0.0010	0.0005	0.0002	0.0001	0.0001
6	0.0411	0.0255	0.0152	0.0087	0.0048	0.0026	0.0014	0.0007	0.0004	0.0002
7	0.0646	0.0437	0.0281	0.0174	0.0104	0.0060	0.0034	0.0018	0.0010	0.0005
8	0.0888	0.0655	0.0457	0.0304	0.0194	0.0120	0.0072	0.0042	0.0024	0.0013
9	0.1085	0.0874	0.0661	0.0473	0.0324	0.0213	0.0135	0.0083	0.0050	0.0029
10	0.1194	0.1048	0.0859	0.0663	0.0486	0.0341	0.0230	0.0150	0.0095	0.0058
11	0.1194	0.1144	0.1015	0.0844	0.0663	0.0496	0.0355	0.0245	0.0164	0.0106
12	0.1094	0.1144	0.1099	0.0984	0.0829	0.0661	0.0504	0.0368	0.0259	0.0176
13	0.0926	0.1056	0.1099	0.1060	0.0956	0.0814	0.0658	0.0509	0.0378	0.0271
14	0.0728	0.0905	0.1021	0.1060	0.1024	0.0930	0.0800	0.0655	0.0514	0.0387
15	0.0534	0.0724	0.0885	0.0989	0.1024	0.0992	0.0906	0.0786	0.0650	0.0516
16	0.0367	0.0543	0.0719	0.0866	0.0960	0.0992	0.0963	0.0884	0.0772	0.0646
17	0.0237	0.0383	0.0550	0.0713	0.0847	0.0934	0.0963	0.0936	0.0863	0.0760
18	0.0145	0.0256	0.0397	0.0554	0.0706	0.0830	0.0909	0.0936	0.0911	0.0844
19	0.0084	0.0161	0.0272	0.0409	0.0557	0.0699	0.0814	0.0887	0.0911	0.0888
20	0.0046	0.0097	0.0177	0.0286	0.0418	0.0559	0.0692	0.0798	0.0866	0.0888
21	0.0024	0.0055	0.0109	0.0191	0.0299	0.0426	0.0560	0.0684	0.0783	0.0846
22	0.0012	0.0030	0.0065	0.0121	0.0204	0.0310	0.0433	0.0560	0.0676	0.0769
23	0.0006	0.0016	0.0037	0.0074	0.0133	0.0216	0.0320	0.0438	0.0559	0.0669
24	0.0003	0.0008	0.0020	0.0043	0.0083	0.0144	0.0226	0.0328	0.0442	0.0557
25	0.0001	0.0004	0.0010	0.0024	0.0050	0.0092	0.0154	0.0237	0.0336	0.0446
26	0.0000	0.0002	0.0005	0.0013	0.0029	0.0057	0.0101	0.0164	0.0246	0.0343
27	0.0000	0.0001	0.0002	0.0007	0.0016	0.0034	0.0063	0.0109	0.0173	0.0254
28	0.0000	0.0000	0.0001	0.0003	0.0009	0.0019	0.0038	0.0070	0.0117	0.0181
29	0.0000	0.0000	0.0001	0.0002	0.0004	0.0011	0.0023	0.0044	0.0077	0.0125
30	0.0000	0.0000	0.0000	0.0001	0.0002	0.0006	0.0013	0.0026	0.0049	0.0083
31	0.0000	0.0000	0.0000	0.0000	0.0001	0.0003	0.0007	0.0015	0.0030	0.0054
32	0.0000	0.0000	0.0000	0.0000	0.0001	0.0001	0.0004	0.0009	0.0018	0.0034
33	0.0000	0.0000	0.0000	0.0000	0.0000	0.0001	0.0002	0.0005	0.0010	0.0020
34	0.0000	0.0000	0.0000	0.0000	0.0000	0.0000	0.0001	0.0002	0.0006	0.0012
35	0.0000	0.0000	0.0000	0.0000	0.0000	0.0000	0.0000	0.0001	0.0003	0.0007
36	0.0000	0.0000	0.0000	0.0000	0.0000	0.0000	0.0000	0.0001	0.0002	0.0004
37	0.0000	0.0000	0.0000	0.0000	0.0000	0.0000	0.0000	0.0000	0.0001	0.0002
38	0.0000	0.0000	0.0000	0.0000	0.0000	0.0000	0.0000	0.0000	0.0000	0.0001
39	0.0000	0.0000	0.0000	0.0000	0.0000	0.0000	0.0000	0.0000	0.0000	0.0001

SOURCE: Reprinted from *Handbook of Probability and Statistics with Tables*, 2nd Ed., by R. S. Burington and D. C. May. New York: McGraw-Hill Book Company, Inc., 1970, by permission of the authors' trustees.

APPENDIX F

Values of e^{-iN}

To find $e^{-1.5}$, choose $N = 15$ and $i = .10$.

N	.01	.02	.03	.04	.05	.06	.07	.08	.09	.10	.11	.12
						i						
1	0.990	0.980	0.970	0.961	0.951	0.942	0.932	0.923	0.914	0.905	0.896	0.887
2	0.980	0.961	0.942	0.923	0.905	0.887	0.869	0.852	0.835	0.819	0.803	0.787
3	0.970	0.942	0.914	0.887	0.861	0.835	0.811	0.787	0.763	0.741	0.719	0.698
4	0.961	0.923	0.887	0.852	0.819	0.787	0.756	0.726	0.698	0.670	0.644	0.619
5	0.951	0.905	0.861	0.819	0.779	0.741	0.705	0.670	0.638	0.607	0.577	0.549
6	0.942	0.887	0.835	0.787	0.741	0.698	0.657	0.619	0.583	0.549	0.517	0.487
7	0.932	0.869	0.811	0.756	0.705	0.657	0.613	0.571	0.533	0.497	0.463	0.432
8	0.923	0.852	0.787	0.726	0.670	0.619	0.571	0.527	0.487	0.449	0.415	0.383
9	0.914	0.835	0.763	0.698	0.638	0.583	0.533	0.487	0.445	0.407	0.372	0.340
10	0.905	0.819	0.741	0.670	0.607	0.549	0.497	0.449	0.407	0.368	0.333	0.301
11	0.896	0.803	0.719	0.644	0.577	0.517	0.463	0.415	0.372	0.333	0.298	0.267
12	0.887	0.787	0.698	0.619	0.549	0.487	0.432	0.383	0.340	0.301	0.267	0.237
13	0.878	0.771	0.677	0.595	0.522	0.458	0.403	0.353	0.310	0.273	0.239	0.210
14	0.869	0.756	0.657	0.571	0.497	0.432	0.375	0.326	0.284	0.247	0.214	0.186
15	0.861	0.741	0.638	0.549	0.472	0.407	0.350	0.301	0.259	0.223	0.192	0.165
16	0.852	0.726	0.619	0.527	0.449	0.383	0.326	0.278	0.237	0.202	0.172	0.147
17	0.844	0.712	0.600	0.507	0.427	0.361	0.304	0.257	0.217	0.183	0.154	0.130
18	0.835	0.698	0.583	0.487	0.407	0.340	0.284	0.237	0.198	0.165	0.138	0.115
19	0.827	0.684	0.566	0.468	0.387	0.320	0.264	0.219	0.181	0.150	0.124	0.102
20	0.819	0.670	0.549	0.449	0.368	0.301	0.247	0.202	0.165	0.135	0.111	0.091
21	0.811	0.657	0.533	0.432	0.350	0.284	0.230	0.186	0.151	0.122	0.099	0.080
22	0.803	0.644	0.517	0.415	0.333	0.267	0.214	0.172	0.138	0.111	0.089	0.071
23	0.795	0.631	0.502	0.399	0.317	0.252	0.200	0.159	0.126	0.100	0.080	0.063
24	0.787	0.619	0.487	0.383	0.301	0.237	0.186	0.147	0.115	0.091	0.071	0.056
25	0.779	0.607	0.472	0.368	0.287	0.223	0.174	0.135	0.105	0.082	0.064	0.050
26	0.771	0.595	0.458	0.353	0.273	0.210	0.162	0.125	0.096	0.074	0.057	0.044
27	0.763	0.583	0.445	0.340	0.259	0.198	0.151	0.115	0.088	0.067	0.051	0.039
28	0.756	0.571	0.432	0.326	0.247	0.186	0.141	0.106	0.080	0.061	0.046	0.035
29	0.748	0.560	0.419	0.313	0.235	0.176	0.131	0.098	0.074	0.055	0.041	0.031
30	0.741	0.549	0.407	0.301	0.223	0.165	0.122	0.091	0.067	0.050	0.037	0.027

N	.13	.14	.15	.16	.17	.18	.19	.20	.21	.22	.23	.24
1	0.878	0.869	0.861	0.852	0.844	0.835	0.827	0.819	0.811	0.803	0.795	0.787
2	0.771	0.756	0.741	0.726	0.712	0.698	0.684	0.670	0.657	0.644	0.631	0.619
3	0.677	0.657	0.638	0.619	0.600	0.583	0.566	0.549	0.533	0.517	0.502	0.487
4	0.595	0.571	0.549	0.527	0.507	0.487	0.468	0.499	0.432	0.415	0.399	0.383
5	0.522	0.497	0.472	0.449	0.427	0.407	0.387	0.368	0.350	0.333	0.317	0.301
6	0.458	0.432	0.407	0.383	0.361	0.340	0.320	0.301	0.284	0.267	0.252	0.237
7	0.403	0.375	0.350	0.326	0.304	0.284	0.264	0.247	0.230	0.214	0.200	0.186
8	0.353	0.326	0.301	0.278	0.257	0.237	0.219	0.202	0.186	0.172	0.159	0.147
9	0.310	0.284	0.259	0.237	0.217	0.198	0.181	0.165	0.151	0.138	0.126	0.115
10	0.273	0.247	0.223	0.202	0.183	0.165	0.150	0.135	0.122	0.111	0.100	0.091
11	0.239	0.214	0.192	0.172	0.154	0.138	0.124	0.111	0.099	0.089	0.080	0.071
12	0.210	0.186	0.165	0.147	0.130	0.115	0.102	0.091	0.080	0.071	0.063	0.056
13	0.185	0.162	0.142	0.125	0.110	0.096	0.085	0.074	0.065	0.057	0.050	0.044
14	0.162	0.141	0.122	0.106	0.093	0.080	0.070	0.061	0.053	0.046	0.040	0.035
15	0.142	0.122	0.105	0.091	0.078	0.067	0.058	0.050	0.043	0.037	0.032	0.027
16	0.125	0.106	0.091	0.077	0.066	0.056	0.048	0.041	0.035	0.030	0.025	0.021
17	0.110	0.093	0.078	0.066	0.056	0.047	0.040	0.033	0.028	0.024	0.020	0.017
18	0.096	0.080	0.067	0.056	0.047	0.039	0.033	0.027	0.023	0.019	0.016	0.013
19	0.085	0.070	0.058	0.048	0.040	0.033	0.027	0.022	0.018	0.015	0.013	0.010
20	0.074	0.061	0.050	0.041	0.033	0.027	0.022	0.018	0.015	0.012	0.010	0.008
21	0.065	0.053	0.043	0.035	0.028	0.023	0.018	0.015	0.012	0.010	0.008	0.006
22	0.057	0.046	0.037	0.030	0.024	0.019	0.015	0.012	0.010	0.008	0.006	0.005
23	0.050	0.040	0.032	0.025	0.020	0.016	0.013	0.010	0.008	0.006	0.005	0.004
24	0.044	0.035	0.027	0.021	0.017	0.013	0.010	0.008	0.006	0.005	0.004	0.003
25	0.039	0.030	0.024	0.018	0.014	0.011	0.009	0.007	0.005	0.004	0.003	0.002
26	0.034	0.026	0.020	0.016	0.012	0.009	0.007	0.006	0.004	0.003	0.003	0.002
27	0.030	0.023	0.017	0.013	0.010	0.008	0.006	0.005	0.003	0.003	0.002	0.002
28	0.026	0.020	0.015	0.011	0.009	0.006	0.005	0.004	0.003	0.002	0.002	0.001
29	0.023	0.017	0.013	0.010	0.007	0.005	0.004	0.003	0.002	0.002	0.001	0.001
30	0.020	0.015	0.011	0.008	0.006	0.005	0.003	0.002	0.002	0.001	0.001	0.001

Solutions to Even-Numbered Problems

■ Chapter 7

2. For a specification of 75 ± 5 mv:

   a. $L(x) = k(x - T)^2$
     $\$300 = k(5)^2$
     $k = 12$

   b. $EL(x) = k(\sigma^2 + D^2) = 12(2^2 + 0^2) = \$48$

4. This problem requires the use of concepts of calculus.

   $I = [p - C(q) - m]D(q)$

   Therefore: $dI/dq = [p - C(q) - m]D'(q) - D(q)C'(q) = 0$

For the firm to remain in business, $p - C(q) - m$ must be greater than 0. Given this, at the point where $DI/dq = 0$, $C'(q) > 0$ in order for a solution to exist. This point may be called q^*. The value of q, called q_0 that minimizes $c(q)$ must satisfy $C'(q_0) = 0$. Therefore, $q_0 < q^*$.

6. The best way to prioritize the voice of the customer would be to have a focus group of typical customers, such as craftspeople, "do-it-yourselfers," and hobbyists to provide input on how they use the screwdriver and what their priorities are.

8. a. The information in the scoreboard that applies to QFD, the customer attributes, are listed as row headings: (1) Competitive Rates, through (5) Courteous, knowledgeable personnel. The equivalent to technical characteristics would be the bases for scoring, such as "Based on number of institutional representatives that customers had to deal with," listed at the bottom of the table, below the "weighted score" line.

   b. To develop a House of Quality, the available information would give a good start; however, more information would be needed about the relationships between attributes and counterpart characteristics and the interrelationships between those characteristics. Also, the relative priorities of customers and the selling points would have to be determined.

   c. In attempting to develop a competing mortgage loan service, current or prospective companies could look at the strengths of the strongest product (National Mortgage) and attempt to meet or exceed the excellence of the customer attributes there. They could also look at the attributes that aren't well covered by any product, such as (4) Single point of contact, and try to develop a product that would fill the gap, if customers consider the attribute(s) to be very important to this product.

■ Chapter 8

2. The composite index for quality costs shows that total quality cost has been stable at $.07/total \$ of sales. Internal failure rates have been reduced substantially, from $\$168.20$ in the first quarter to $\$66.40$ in the fourth quarter. External failure rates have shown improvement in the fourth quarter, dropping from $\$42.80$ in the third quarter to $\$28.60$ in the fourth. Increases in prevention and appraisal expenditures have apparently led to improvements in failure costs. The overall index has fallen slightly. Management should maintain or increase the level of prevention and appraisal in an effort to reduce quality costs, especially failure costs.

4. The largest costs are internal failure (56.6%) and appraisal (27.1%). It appears that more can and must be done in the area of quality training, a component of prevention (currently 7.8%), if failure, appraisal, and overall quality costs are to be brought under control. External failure costs only represent 8.6% of quality costs, so it appears that screening methods are working fairly well. Note that the above proportions are fractions of the total quality costs of $247,450.

■ Chapter 9

2. From a histogram (such as available from the Quality Management Analyst software, or a spreadsheet), graphical analysis shows that the machine running time until failure is fairly evenly distributed, with frequencies rising to a peak in the 10.14–14.95 hour category and then falling off from there.

Minimum value:	4.20000
Maximum value:	27.50000
First quartile:	8.90000
Median:	12.40000
Third quartile:	15.40000
Average:	12.54500
Variance:	31.39313
Standard Deviation:	5.60296
Range:	23.30000
No. of observations:	20

HISTOGRAM

Cell	Upper Limit	Frequency	
1	0.54	0	
2	5.34	2	**
3	10.14	5	*****
4	14.95	7	*******
5	19.75	4	****
6	24.55	1	*
7	infinity	1	*

4. The following scatter diagram (really, a regression plot from the Quality Management Analyst software) shows an interesting, and perhaps counterintuitive result. As the production rate increases, the defect rate decreases. This relationship could be the result of the "learning curve" effect; as operators become more skilled and familiar with the process and production runs are longer, the defect rate is improved.

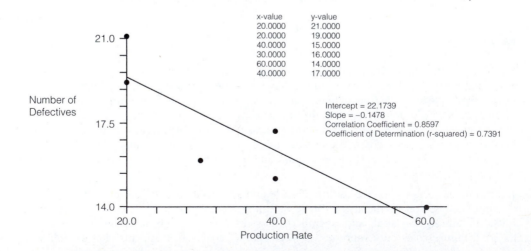

x-value	y-value
20.0000	21.0000
20.0000	19.0000
40.0000	15.0000
30.0000	16.0000
60.0000	14.0000
40.0000	17.0000

Intercept = 22.1739
Slope = –0.1478
Correlation Coefficient = 0.8597
Coefficient of Determination (r-squared) = 0.7391

Chapter 14

2. For $C_1 = \$0.25$ and $C_2 = \$500.00$

$$p = \frac{C_1}{C_2} = \frac{0.25}{500} = 0.0005, \text{ or } 0.5 \text{ errors}/1000 \text{ transactions}$$

4. $\bar{x}_1 = 0.9907;\ \bar{R}_1 = 0.028$
$\bar{x}_2 = 0.9967;\ \bar{R}_2 = 0.038$
$\bar{x}_D = 0.0060;\ \bar{\bar{R}} = 0.033$
$D_4 = 2.574;\ \text{UCL}_R = 0.0849,$ all ranges below
$K_1 = 3.05;\ K_2 = 3.65$ (from Table)
$\text{EV} = 0.10065;\ \text{OV} = 0.0119;\ \text{RR} = 0.1014$

Equipment variation = 83.88%, Operator variation = 9.92%, and R&R variation = 84.50%.

$\therefore$ Concentrate on reducing equipment variation.

6. $z = -1.88;\ \therefore\ \mu = 21.316$

8. $\bar{x} = 38.649;\ s = 0.443$

10. $c_p = 1.35;$ not satisfactory
New $\sigma = 0.3$ for $c_p = 2.0$, instead of the current $\sigma = 0.443$

12. $\bar{x} = 0.5750;\ \sigma = 0.0065$
$c_p = 0.359;$ not satisfactory

14. a. Data set 1: $\bar{x} = 1.7446;\ s = 0.0163;\ 3s = 0.0489$
Data set 2: $\bar{x} = 1.9999;\ s = 0.0078;\ 3s = 0.0234$
Data set 3: $\bar{x} = 1.2485;\ s = 0.0052;\ 3s = 0.0156$

Part 1 will not consistently meet tolerance limits, but Parts 2 and 3 will.

b. $\bar{x}_T = 4.9930;\ \sigma_{\text{Process}} = 0.0188$
Process limits: $4.9930 \pm 3(0.0188)$ *or*
4.9366 to 5.0494 vs. specification limits of 4.919 or 5.081 for a confidence level of 0.9973.

16. $\bar{x} = 24.0014;\ s = 0.0097$
$c_p = 1.031;$ within limits
$c_{pu} = 0.983;$ out of limits
$c_{pl} = 1.079;$ within limits

18. $\bar{x} = 50.25;\ \sigma = 1.5$

a. $c_p = 0.889$
$c_{pl} = 0.889$
$c_{pu} = 0.889$ Conclusion: the process does not have adequate capability.

b. $c_p = 0.889$
$c_{pl} = 0.944$
$c_{pu} = 0.833$ Conclusion: the process *still* does not have adequate capability.

c. $\sigma_{\text{new}} = 1.35$
$c_p = 0.988$
$c_{pl} = 0.988$
$c_{pu} = 0.988$

Conclusion: the process *still* does not have adequate capability, although all of the capability indices are close to minimum acceptable level of 1.0.

20. $\bar{\bar{x}} = 0.2085;\ s = 0.0039;\ \bar{\bar{x}} \pm 3s = 0.1968$ to 0.2202

22. $c_p = 0.427$
$c_{pu} = 0.556$
$c_{pl} = 0.299$

The MIN $(c_{pu}, c_{pl}) = 0.299$. Conclusion: the process does not have adequate capability.

24. For a population of 2,000, table 14.7 shows that the sample size required for a critical 1% rate, with a 99% confidence level is *approximately* 400 (use 98.9% confidence, critical rate of 1%).

■ Chapter 15

2. For $\bar{\bar{x}} = 480$; $\bar{R} = 34$

$\text{UCL}_{\bar{x}} = 496.422$; $\text{LCL}_{\bar{x}} = 463.578$
$\text{UCL}_R = 68.136$; $\text{LCL}_R = 0$

Estimated $\sigma = 13.418$

4. $\bar{\bar{x}} = 95.398$; $\bar{R} = 0.665$

$\text{UCL}_{\bar{x}} = 95.883$; $\text{LCL}_{\bar{x}} = 94.913$
$\text{UCL}_R = 1.518$; $\text{LCL}_R = 0$

6. $\bar{\bar{x}} = -1.0349$; $\bar{R} = 3.0337$

$\text{UCL}_{\bar{x}} = 0.7155$; $\text{LCL}_{\bar{x}} = -2.7854$
$\text{UCL}_R = 6.4132$; $\text{LCL}_R = 0$

Conclusion: the process appears to be out of control; points are "hugging" the center line.

8. a. Two points outside upper control limit.
b. Process is in control.
c. Mean shifts upward in second half of control chart.
d. Points hugging upper and lower control limits.

10. $\bar{\bar{x}} = 0.0756$; $\bar{R} = 0.0046$

$\text{UCL}_{\bar{x}} = 0.0783$; $\text{LCL}_{\bar{x}} = 0.0729$
$\text{UCL}_R = 0.0097$; $\text{LCL}_R = 0$

Estimated $\sigma = 0.0020$

Limits on individual values $= \bar{\bar{x}} \pm 3\sigma_{est} = 0.0816$ to 0.0696

12. $\bar{\bar{x}} = 46.175$; $\bar{R} = 5.45$

$\text{UCL}_{\bar{x}} = 49.320$; $\text{LCL}_{\bar{x}} = 43.030$
$\text{UCL}_R = 11.521$; $\text{LCL}_R = 0$

Estimated $\sigma = 2.343$

Limits on individual values $= \bar{\bar{x}} \pm 3\sigma_{est} = 53.2$ to 39.5

% below LSL $= 1.36\%$
% above USL $= 1.97\%$
Total % outside $= 3.33\%$ However, note that the process is *out of control*.

14. With data from Problem 5 and USL $= 500$, LSL $= 300$:

a. $c_p = 1.772$
   $c_{pl} = 1.778$
   $c_{pu} = 1.767$
   $c_{pk} = 1.767$

% outside $= 0\%$, indicating that the process is well within specification limits.

b. $\text{URL}_x = 476.813$
   $\text{LRL}_x = 323.187$

16. Initially, $\bar{p} = 0.13$, $s_p = 0.0238$

Revised $\bar{p} = 0.1247$ (after sample 12 was removed), $s_p = 0.0234$

$\text{UCL}_p = 0.1948$
$\text{LCL}_p = 0.0546$

18. Initially, $\bar{p} = 0.2888$, $s_p = 0.0453$

Throw out all 39 and over, revise, throw out all over 30, revise again.

Revised $\bar{p} = 0.1856$, $s_p = 0.0389$

$\text{UCL}_p = 0.3023$
$\text{LCL}_p = 0.0690$

20. Using data from Figure 15.35:

a. $\text{CL}_{\bar{x}} : \bar{\bar{x}} = 3.9376$; $\text{CL}_{\bar{R}} : \bar{R} = 0.00077$

For the $\bar{x}$-chart:

$\text{UCL}_{\bar{x}} = \bar{\bar{x}} + A_2\bar{R} = 3.9380$

$\text{LCL}_{\bar{x}} = \bar{\bar{x}} - A_2\bar{R} = 3.9372$

For the R-chart: $\text{UCL}_R = D_4\bar{R} = 0.0016$

$$\text{LCL}_R = D_3\bar{R} = 0$$

The control chart establishes that the process is *in control*.

b. The limits above apply to *sample groups* of five items each.
% outside calculations are based on specification limits for *individual* items.

Estimated $\sigma = \bar{R}/d_2 = 0.00033$

$\therefore c_p = 0.253$; very poor capability.

% outside specification limits (3.9375 to 3.9380) = 49.52%.

Obviously, the problem is that the process is not capable of producing good end caps that consistently fall within specification limits. Bell Vader Company needs to investigate current materials, equipment, machining methods, etc., to improve the process.

■ Chapter 16

2. The data obtained by comparing the range chart from Chapter 15 and the s-chart from Chapter 16 show the following:

$\bar{R} = 0.1680$; $\text{UCL}_R = 0.3552$; $\text{LCL}_R = 0$

$\bar{s} = 0.0717$; $\text{UCL}_s = 0.1498$; $\text{LCL}_s = 0$

The patterns of both charts appear to be similar, but the s-chart shows tighter limits.

4. The data from Chapter 15, Problem 6 on the $\bar{x}$–s chart shows:

$\text{CL}_{\bar{x}} = \bar{\bar{x}} = -1.0349$

$\text{CL}_{\bar{s}} = \bar{s} = 1.2409$

$\text{UCL}_{\bar{x}} = 0.7359$

$\text{LCL}_{\bar{x}} = -2.8057$

*$\text{UCL}_{\bar{s}} = 2.5922$

$\text{LCL}_{\bar{s}} = 0(1.2409) = 0$

*The process is probably *not* under control, since points appear to be "hugging" the center line on the x-bar *and* s-charts.

6. Using data from Chapter 15, Problem 10, as individual measures, with five sample moving ranges, the $\bar{x}$–R chart shows:

$\bar{R} = 0.0048$; $\text{UCL}_R = 0.0010$; $\text{LCL}_R = 0$

$\bar{\bar{x}} = 0.0756$; $\text{UCL}_{\bar{x}} = 0.0818$; $\text{LCL}_{\bar{x}} = 0.0694$

All points appear to be in control.

8. Using data from Chapter 15, Problem 5 the median chart shows:

$\tilde{\bar{x}} = 400; \tilde{R} = 26$

$UCL_{\tilde{x}} = 432.89; LCL_{\tilde{x}} = 367.11$

$UCL_R = 71.37; LCL_R = 0$

Point 23 on the $\tilde{x}$-chart is out of control.
Point 16 on the R-chart is out of control.
These findings are identical to those of Problem 15–5.

10. For the np-chart control limits: $28.88 \pm 3\sqrt{28.88(0.7122)} = 28.88 \pm 13.6 = 15.28$ to 42.48

After identifying and correcting the assignable causes, outside the range ± 13.6, the revised range is:

$18.56 \pm 3\sqrt{18.56(0.8144)} = 18.56 \pm 11.67 = 6.89$ to 30.23

12. For the c-chart: number defective = 176, number of samples = 10

$\bar{c} = 176/10 = 17.6$

$\bar{c} + 3\sqrt{c} = 17.6 \pm 3\sqrt{17.6} = 17.6 \pm 12.59 = 5.01$ to 30.19

14. For the u-chart conditions: four total samples, with a total of nine defective items

$\bar{u} = 9/4 = 2.25$

$\bar{u} \pm 3\sqrt{\bar{u}/n} = 2.25 \pm 3\sqrt{2.25/4} = 2.25 \pm 2.25 = 0$ to 4.50

16. Using data from Chapter 15, Problem 5, the zone control chart shows:

Zone		
D	>	431.958 [UCL]
C		421.402 − 431.958
B		410.846 − 421.402
A		389.734 − 410.846 (center line = 400.290)
B		379.178 − 389.734
C		368.621 − 379.174
D	<	368.621 [LCL]

All points are in control.

18. For $z = \pm 2.75$, $P(z > 2.75) = P(z < -2.75)$
% outside = $2(0.003) = 0.006$ or 0.6%.

20. This problem is an exercise for an advanced, computer-literate student.

▮ Chapter 17

2. From 0–50, slope = 0.6.
From 50–100, slope = 1.2.
From 0–100, slope = 0.9.

4. $\lambda = \dfrac{2}{1760}$

6. $\lambda = 0.001$; $P(x < 800) = 0.55$

8. For $\theta = \dfrac{1760}{2} = 880$ hours; for $\theta = \dfrac{1624}{3} = 541.3$ hours.

10. $\lambda = \dfrac{1}{1000}$

12. For no preventive maintenance, MTBF = 34 hours. Expect 61.2 failures per year.
Cost = \$1836, therefore, do no maintenance.

14. $R_{cc} = 0.99$
    System $R = 0.912$

16. **a.** 0.315
    b. 0.717—an increase of 0.402

18. **a.** 0.90
    b. 0.99 for parallel systems

■ Index

0–314–06215–7

90000

9 780314 062154